International Commercial Litigation

This carefully structured, practice-orientated textbook provides everything the law student needs to know about international commercial litigation.

The strong comparative component provides a thought-provoking international perspective, while at the same time allowing readers to gain unique insights into litigation in English courts. Three important themes of the book analyse how the international element may call into question the power of the court to hear the case, whether it should exercise this power, whether foreign law applies, and whether the court should take into account any foreign judgment.

Hartley provides the reader with extracts from leading cases and relevant legislation, together with an extensive reference library of further reading for those who wish to explore the topic in more detail, making this a valuable, single-source textbook.

International commercial litigation is an area where the law changes fast. To keep the book up to date, new material will be posted on the book's website, www.cambridge.org/thartley/. This will cover both cases and legislation.

Trevor C. Hartley is Professor of Law Emeritus at the London School of Economics, where he specializes in private international law and European Community law.

International Commercial Litigation

Text, Cases and Materials on Private International Law

Trevor C. Hartley

CAMBRIDGE
UNIVERSITY PRESS

CAMBRIDGE UNIVERSITY PRESS
Cambridge, New York, Melbourne, Madrid, Cape Town, Singapore, São Paulo, Delhi

Cambridge University Press
The Edinburgh Building, Cambridge CB2 8RU, UK

Published in the United States of America by Cambridge University Press, New York

www.cambridge.org
Information on this title: www.cambridge.org/9780521687485

First published 2009

Printed in the United Kingdom at the University Press, Cambridge

A catalogue record for this publication is available from the British Library

ISBN 978-0-521-86807-5 hardback
ISBN 978-0-521-68748-5 paperback

Law is made for man, not man for the law.

I have taken this epigraph as the motto of my book. It is not clear
where it comes from: a Google search suggests various possibilities,
including Jesus and St Paul. No matter who said it first, it expresses
better than anything else the approach I take. The same idea was
advanced, less pithily and more mundanely, by the Supreme Court
of Canada in 2006, in *Pro Swing* v. *Elta Golf*, when Deschamps J said,
'The law and the justice system are servants of society, not the
reverse.' That is what I believe too.

Contents

Table of panels

Figures

Preface

This is a book about international commercial transactions and the litigation that results from them. It focuses on litigation in national courts, not international ones. The international element may affect the proceedings in three main ways:

1. the international element may call into question the power of the court to hear the case (its jurisdiction) and raise the issue of whether it should exercise that power, even if it has it;
2. the court may have to consider the application of foreign law (choice of law); and
3. the court may have to take account of a foreign judgment.

These three issues form the main themes of the book, but we will also look at other aspects of international civil procedure – for example, international freezing injunctions and the procedures for obtaining evidence from abroad – as well as questions that verge on public international law, such as extraterritoriality.

The reference in the subtitle to 'Private International Law' links up with the more traditional subject that deals with these matters. However, this is not a traditional book. First, it is practice-oriented, not theory-oriented: extensive analysis of abstruse concepts will not be found. Secondly, it adopts a functional approach. Law should serve economic and social objectives: it is not an end in itself, based on supposedly self-justifying principles. This does not mean that logic has no place: it has a function, that of promoting certainty. But legal logic fulfils that function only to the extent that it makes the answer clear to the ordinary person, or at least the ordinary lawyer. Legal logic has no place if it goes beyond this. The convoluted reasoning of some cases in the past that has extended legal logic beyond the wildest imaginings of any reasonable lawyer has no place in a modern system of private international law.

A third characteristic of the book is that it gives jurisdiction and other aspects of international civil procedure more attention than choice of law, the main topic of more traditional books. This is because they are more important. The book also focuses on *commercial* litigation. Although there is discussion of personal-injury litigation and other topics in which the relevant legal principles are the same as those applied to commercial cases, there is no discussion of family law or succession.

The book includes a comparative element. Although focused primarily on English law, and the law of Commonwealth countries like Canada and Australia that follow the English tradition, it pays attention to the wider world. The United Kingdom is part of the European Community, and a significant part of the subject-matter of the book has been taken over by the EC. Here, Community law *is* UK law. It is the law of the land and we have to know it. In addition, the book contains material on US law. The United States is so important today, especially in international business, that any book on international transactions and litigation has to take account of its law. A lawyer who lacks at least a basic grasp of some of its concepts and procedures cannot be regarded as qualified to practise in the area.

One final point: this is an area of law that changes rapidly. If the book simply presented a snapshot of the law as it existed at a given moment, it would be of only limited use. Within five years things would have changed. Of course, it is not possible to predict what will happen in the future. However, if we study the past, we can understand the forces that shape the present. These forces will continue to operate in the future. So, if we look at the past development of the law, we can get some idea of how it may change. Solutions that were rejected in the past are unlikely to prove any more successful in the future. For this reason, cases that have been superseded are sometimes set out in the text. They may no longer be good law, but they are still worth knowing about.

International commercial litigation is an area where the law changes fast. To keep the book up to date, new material will be posted on the book's website, www.cambridge.org/thartley. This will cover both cases and legislation.

Acknowledgments

I would like to thank the following for kindly granting me permission to reproduce extracts from cases for which they hold the copyright:

- the High Court of Australia;
- the Incorporated Council of Law Reporting for England and Wales;
- Lloyd's Reports; and
- the Scottish Council of Law Reporting.

I am grateful for their generosity. I am also grateful that cases from certain other jurisdictions may be reproduced free of charge without the need to obtain permission. Books of this kind are possible only if authors are able to reproduce extracts from judicial decisions without having to make excessive payments.

The discussion in Chapter 10 of *Owusu* v. *Jackson*, *Turner* v. *Grovit* and *Gasser* v. *MISRAT* is based on my analysis of these cases in the *International and Comparative Law Quarterly* for October 2005;[1] and some of the material on the Rome II Regulation in Chapter 23 has been used as the basis for an article entitled 'Choice of Law for Non-Contractual Liability: Selected Problems under the "Rome II" Regulation', published in (2008) 57 *International and Comparative Law Quarterly* 899. In both cases, I am grateful for being able to reuse the material here.

In 2006, I gave the General Course on Private International Law at the Hague Academy of International Law, under the title 'The Modern Approach to Private International Law: International Litigation and Transactions from a Common-Law Perspective'.[2] Much material from those lectures has been incorporated into this book. In addition, the discussion of some cases in Part V of this book is based on a previous set of lectures given at the Hague Academy on 'Mandatory Rules in International Contracts: The Common Law Approach'.[3] In both cases, I am grateful that I can reuse the material here.

The discussion of the Brussels Convention/Regulation in various chapters draws on work first published in 'Introduction to the Brussels Jurisdiction and Judgments Convention' (1994) V-1 *Collected Courses of the Academy of European Law* 223. I am grateful that I can reuse this material here.

I would like to thank Mr Peter Ringsted, attorney in Odense, Denmark, for telling me about the Danish case of *F ApS* v. *J (UK) Ltd*.

1 'The European Union and the Systematic Dismantling of the Common Law of Conflict of Laws' (2005) 54 ICLQ 813.
2 *Recueil des Cours*, Volume 319 (2006).
3 *Recueil des Cours*, Volume 266 (1997).

I have learnt a great deal over the years from my students, especially those in the International Business Transactions courses at the London School of Economics. I also owe a debt of gratitude to my own teachers of conflict of laws, Professor D. V. Cowan at the University of Cape Town in 1961 and Professor Otto Kahn-Freund at the London School of Economics in 1963/4. Both had the rare ability to awaken an interest in the subject in their students. In my case, the interest was abiding.

My greatest debt is to my wife, Sandra, my life-long companion and friend, who has helped me in many ways in the writing of this book.

Terminology

When the Civil Procedure Rules came into force in 1999, they made important changes to legal terminology in England. Some of these changes are as follows:

- 'Claim form' replaces 'writ'
- 'Claimant' replaces 'plaintiff'
- 'Disclosure' replaces 'discovery'
- 'Freezing injunction' replaces 'Mareva injunction'
- 'Interim injunction' replaces 'interlocutory injunction'
- 'Interim remedy' replaces 'interlocutory relief'
- 'Search order' replaces 'Anton Piller order'
- 'Statement of case' replaces 'pleadings'

This is now the accepted terminology in England. These changes do not apply in the Commonwealth and the United States. In these countries, words such as 'writ' and 'plaintiff' remain correct usage.

Table of Latin phrases

Action/judgment *in personam*	action/judgment against a person
Action/judgment *in rem*	action/judgment against (regarding) a thing (property)
Forum conveniens	appropriate court for hearing the action
Forum non conveniens	inappropriate court for hearing the action
Lex contractus	law governing a contract
Lex loci actus	law of the country where a transaction was concluded
Lex loci contractus	law of the country where a contract was concluded
Lex situs	law of the country in which property is situated
Lis pendens or *lis alibi pendens*	case pending elsewhere
Qui facit per alium facit per se	he who acts through another acts himself

Abbreviations

AJIL	*American Journal of International Law*
BYIL	*British Year Book of International Law*
CLC	*Commercial Law Cases* (a series of law reports published in England)
CLJ	*Cambridge Law Journal*
CLP	*Current Legal Problems*
CPR	Civil Procedure Rules (England)
ECHR	European Convention on Human Rights
ECtHR	European Court of Human Rights
EHRR	*European Human Rights Reports*
ICLQ	*International and Comparative Law Quarterly*
ILPr	*International Litigation Procedure* (a series of law reports published in England)
LQR	*Law Quarterly Review*
Ont.	Ontario (Canada)
R or r	Rule (rule)
RSC	Rules of the Supreme Court
USC	United States Code (not a code in the civil-law sense, but a compilation of statutes)

Table of cases

Table of cases (European Court of Justice, numerical order)

or more, he is presumed to have a substantial connection with the area in question unless the contrary is proved. This means that, for example, a student who has resided in England for three months will be presumed to be domiciled there, unless he can prove that he does not have a substantial connection with England.

§6.4 Domicile of legal persons (corporations)

These rules do not apply to corporations. Instead of applying Member State law to determine where a company is domiciled, Article 60 of the Regulation (Panel 3.7) lays down a Community rule on the subject. It states that a company or other legal person or association of natural or legal persons is domiciled at the place where it has:

(a)   its statutory seat, or

(b)   its central administration, or

(c)   its principal place of business.

> **Panel 3.7 Domicile of companies**
> **Brussels I Regulation (Regulation 44/2001), Article 60**
>
> **Article 60**
> 1. For the purposes of this Regulation, a company or other legal person or association of natural or legal persons is domiciled at the place where it has its:
>   (a) statutory seat, or
>   (b) central administration, or
>   (c) principal place of business.
> 2. For the purposes of the United Kingdom and Ireland 'statutory seat' means the registered office or, where there is no such office anywhere, the place of incorporation or, where there is no such place anywhere, the place under the law of which the formation took place.
> 3. In order to determine whether a trust is domiciled in the Member State whose courts are seised of the matter, the court shall apply its rules of private international law.

The desirability of having a Community-wide rule of domicile is obvious.[21] However, the reason these particular tests were selected needs some explanation.

In the common law, the law of the place of incorporation is traditionally regarded as important for deciding issues relating to the internal affairs of the company. It is the legal system that gives birth to it and endows it with legal personality.[22] The registered office of the company will be in the country of incorporation, and the company will be subject to the jurisdiction of the courts of that country.

For jurisdictional purposes, however, the principal place of business and the place of its central management are also important. The latter is the administrative centre of the company, the place where the most important decisions are taken. The principal place of business is the centre of its economic activities. Though normally in the same place, these two could be different. For example, a mining company with its headquarters in London (central administration) might carry on its mining activity in Namibia (principal place of business).

Although some civil-law systems also look to the law of the place of incorporation as the personal law of the company,[23] the dominant view favours the law of the 'corporate seat' (in French, the *siège social*). The place of the corporate seat is also regarded as the domicile of the company. However, there are two views

---

21 Article 60 was actually one of the innovations of the Brussels I Regulation. Under the Brussels Convention (Article 53), each State applied its own law to determine the domicile of a company.
22 See Chapter 22, § 2.3.2, below.
23 For example, the Netherlands.

as to how the corporate seat is to be determined. According to the first view, one looks to the legal document under which the company was constituted (the *statut* of the company). This will state where the corporate seat is. The corporate seat thus determined is called the *siège statutaire*, usually translated into English as 'statutory seat'.[24]

The *siège statutaire* may not, however, be the actual corporate headquarters. The second view is that one should look to the place where the company in fact has its central administration, sometimes called the *siège réel* (real seat). This corresponds to the common-law concept of the central administration.

To cover all points of view, the Regulation provides that a company is domiciled where it has its 'statutory seat', *and* where it has its central administration, *and* where it has its principal place of business. It further provides that, for the purposes of the United Kingdom and Ireland, 'statutory seat' means the registered office.[25] This means that, in the common-law Member States, a company has a domicile in the country in which it was incorporated.

As a result, a company could have three domiciles at the same time. In practice, however, the State where it has its central administration will usually be that in which it has its principal place of business. On the other hand, it is not uncommon for a company to be incorporated in one State – for example, Panama or Liechtenstein – and to have its central administration and principal place of business in another. Thus, a company may well have two domiciles, even if it is unlikely to have three.

§ 6.5   *The role of domicile*

When a court of a Member State is faced with an action covered by the Regulation, its first step must always be to determine the domicile of the defendant. If the defendant is domiciled within its own territory, it has general jurisdiction.[26] This follows from Article 2 (first paragraph) of the Regulation (Panel 3.4, set out at the beginning of § 6, above). In such a case, the court does not have to consider whether the defendant might also be domiciled in another Member State. As we have seen, it is possible that the defendant may be domiciled in two or more Member States. However, this does not matter: if the defendant is domiciled in the territory of the forum, the court has general jurisdiction, even if he also has a domicile in another Member State.

If, on the other hand, the court finds that the defendant is not domiciled within its territory, it must consider whether he is domiciled in another Member State.[27] This is necessary in order to determine whether the jurisdictional rules

---

24 This term is misleading in English because it does not refer to the company's seat as laid down by some statute (legislation) but as laid down by the *statut*, the document containing the constitution of the company – for example, the articles of association.

25 Article 60(2). This provision goes on to state that, where there is no registered office anywhere, 'statutory seat' means the place of incorporation or, where there is no such place anywhere, the place under the law of which the formation took place.

26 General jurisdiction is jurisdiction that applies irrespective of where the cause of action arose.

27 In the case of a natural person (individual), the court should in theory consider the law of domicile of each Member State to decide whether the defendant is, according to that law, domiciled in that State. In

of the Regulation apply (Article 3 of the Regulation, set out in Panel 4.1, Chapter 4, § 1, below).[28] If they do not, the court will apply its own rules of jurisdiction. In the case of an English court, these will be the rules described in Chapter 5.

§ 7   Jurisdiction irrespective of domicile

Although domicile is the fundamental principle of the Regulation, there are some special situations in which the Regulation applies irrespective of domicile. The most important are:

- where a court in an EC or Lugano State has exclusive jurisdiction over the subject-matter of the proceedings – for example, where the case concerns rights *in rem* in land in such a State;[29]
- where there is a choice-of-court agreement in favour of a court in an EC or Lugano State;[30] or
- where a court in another EC or Lugano State was seised first of proceedings involving the same cause of action between the same parties.[31]

These will be considered in later chapters. It should also be noted that the provisions on the recognition and enforcement of judgments apply irrespective of the domicile of the defendant. The important thing here is the court that gave the judgment.

§ 8   Which instrument applies?

Since the Lugano States are not bound by the Brussels I Regulation (or by the Brussels Convention), a court in such a State will apply only the Lugano Convention. The position is more complicated with regard to a court in a Community State. This section explains which instrument must be applied by such a court.

The relevant provision (at present) is Article 54B of the 1988 Convention (Panel 3.8).[32] The basic rule is that the Brussels I Regulation applies where the

practice, this will not normally be necessary, since the facts of the case will make clear whether there is any possibility of the defendant's being domiciled in a given Member State.

28 Although the general rule is that the jurisdictional provisions of the Regulation are applicable only if the defendant is domiciled in a Member State, there are a number of exceptions. These are set out in § 7, below.

29 Article 22 of the Regulation.

30 The position here is more complicated. A choice-of-court agreement can have two aspects: it grants jurisdiction to the court chosen and, if it is exclusive, it precludes all other courts from hearing the case. Under the Regulation, the provision granting jurisdiction to the chosen court applies only if one of the parties – not necessarily the defendant – is domiciled in a Member State: Article 23(1). However, the rule that, in the case of an exclusive choice-of-court agreement, other courts are precluded from hearing the case, even if they would otherwise have had jurisdiction under the Regulation, applies irrespective of domicile: Article 23(3).

31 See Articles 27–30 of the Regulation. These provisions do not expressly say that they apply irrespective of domicile, but see *Overseas Union Insurance* v. *New Hampshire Insurance*, Case C-351/89, [1991] ECR I-3317.

32 This is the text in force at the time of writing (February 2009); the 2007 revision, which has not yet been adopted by the Council, is not available.

Panel 3.8 Which instrument applies? Lugano Convention, Article 54B (as set out in Schedule 1 to the Civil Jurisdiction and Judgments Act 1991)

Article 54B

1. This Convention shall not prejudice the application by the Member States of the European Communities of the Convention on Jurisdiction and the Enforcement of Judgments in Civil and Commercial Matters, signed at Brussels on 27 September 1968 and of the Protocol on interpretation of that Convention by the Court of Justice, signed at Luxembourg on 3 June 1971, as amended by the Conventions of Accession to the said Convention and the said Protocol by the States acceding to the European Communities, all of these Conventions and the Protocol being hereinafter referred to as the 'Brussels Convention'.

2. However, this Convention shall in any event be applied:
   (a) in matters of jurisdiction, where the defendant is domiciled in the territory of a Contracting State which is not a member of the European Communities, or where Article 16 or 17 of this Convention confers a jurisdiction on the courts of such a Contracting State;
   (b) in relation to a *lis pendens* or to related actions as provided for in Articles 21 and 22, when proceedings are instituted in a Contracting State which is not a member of the European Communities and in a Contracting State which is a member of the European Communities;
   (c) in matters of recognition and enforcement, where either the State of origin or the State addressed is not a member of the European Communities.

3. In addition to the grounds provided for in Title III recognition or enforcement may be refused if the ground of jurisdiction on which the judgment has been based differs from that resulting from this Convention and recognition or enforcement is sought against a party who is domiciled in a Contracting State which is not a member of the European Communities, unless the judgment may otherwise be recognised or enforced under any rule of law in the State addressed.

---

defendant is domiciled in a State to which the Regulation applies,[33] and the Lugano Convention applies when the defendant is domiciled in a Lugano State.[34] However, the Lugano Convention will also apply where it is applicable irrespective of the domicile of the defendant. This will occur in situations analogous to those outlined in § 7, above. Thus, for example, an English court would apply the Lugano Convention if the proceedings concerned a right *in rem* in land in a Lugano State, even if the defendant was domiciled in England.

Where neither instrument applies, national law will govern.

§ 9   Subject-matter scope

Under Article 1 (Panel 3.9), the scope of the Regulation is limited to civil and commercial matters, though it applies whatever the nature of the court or tribunal hearing the case.[35] It is, however, provided by the second paragraph of Article 1 that the Regulation does not apply to certain specified matters, even though some of them are clearly

---

Panel 3.9 Subject-matter scope
Brussels I Regulation (Regulation 44/2001), Article 1

Article 1

1. This Regulation shall apply in civil and commercial matters whatever the nature of the court or tribunal. It shall not extend, in particular, to revenue, customs or administrative matters.

2. The Regulation shall not apply to:
   (a) the status or legal capacity of natural persons, rights in property arising out of a matrimonial relationship, wills and succession;
   (b) bankruptcy, proceedings relating to the winding-up of insolvent companies or other legal persons, judicial arrangements, compositions and analogous proceedings;
   (c) social security;
   (d) arbitration.

---

33 In principle, these are the Member States of the EC. For exceptions, see note 2, above.
34 The meaning of 'Lugano State' is explained in § 3, above.
35 As a result, a civil case would not be excluded merely because it was heard by an administrative court; on the other hand, an administrative case would not be brought within the scope of the Convention merely because it was heard by a civil court.

civil or commercial.[36] Arbitration was excluded because it was already covered by the New York Convention. Bankruptcy was intended to be covered by a separate instrument.[37] Status, matrimonial property, wills and succession were excluded because of the important differences between the laws of the Member States in these areas and the fact that they were of little relevance for international business.[38]

If a case falls within one of the excluded areas, the court hearing it is not bound by the jurisdictional rules laid down in the Regulation. An English court would apply the traditional English rules. On the other hand, other Member States are not required by the Regulation to recognize the resulting judgment. Whether they do so or not would depend on their own law.

§ 9.1   What law decides?

How is a court to decide whether a case concerns a matter that falls within the scope of the Regulation? Should it apply its own law or that of another Member State? This question came before the European Court in our first case. At the time, the Brussels Convention was the relevant instrument, but Article 1 of the Convention was identical to Article 1 of the Regulation.

European Community
LTU v. Eurocontrol
Court of Justice of the European Communities
Case 29/76, [1976] ECR 1541

Background

Eurocontrol, an international air-traffic-control organization with its seat in Brussels, sued LTU, a German airline, for charges payable for the use of Eurocontrol's services. The action was brought in a commercial court in Brussels, and LTU challenged the court's jurisdiction on the ground that the case was not a commercial action. The court, however, held that, under Belgian law, it was commercial. Judgment was given against LTU. When Eurocontrol tried to enforce the judgment in Germany, LTU raised the same argument again: it claimed that the proceedings were of a public-law nature and were consequently outside the scope of the Brussels Convention.

Eurocontrol argued that the classification of the proceedings should be based on the law of the State that granted the original judgment. Since the Belgian court had already determined that the proceedings were commercial, this would have meant that the case fell within the scope of the Convention. Advocate

---

36 In addition to these matters, the European Court has held that proceedings in a Member State to recognize a judgment from a non-member State are outside the scope of the Regulation: *Owens Bank Ltd* v. *Fulvio Bracco and Bracco Industria Chimica SpA*, Case C-129/92, [1994] ECR I-117, set out in Chapter 16, §1, below.
37 See now Regulation 1346/2000, OJ 2000, L 160, p. 1, a provision which took more than thirty years to adopt.
38 The intention was to cover these areas in separate instruments. One such instrument, the Brussels II Regulation (Regulation 2201/2003, OJ 2003, L 338, p. 1), has already been adopted.

General Reischl took the same view. LTU, however, argued that the law of the State asked to recognize the judgment should apply, and it seems possible that under German law the action might have been regarded as public.

Judgment

3. . . . As Article 1 serves to indicate the area of application of the Convention it is necessary, in order to ensure, as far as possible, that the rights and obligations which derive from it for the Contracting States and the persons to whom it applies are equal and uniform, that the terms of that provision should not be interpreted as a mere reference to the internal law of one or other of the States concerned.

By providing that the Convention shall apply 'whatever the nature of the court or tribunal' Article 1 shows that the concept 'civil and commercial matters' cannot be interpreted solely in the light of the division of jurisdiction between the various types of courts existing in certain States.

The concept in question must therefore be regarded as independent and must be interpreted by reference, first, to the objectives and scheme of the Convention and, secondly, to the general principles which stem from the corpus of the national legal systems.

4. If the interpretation of the concept is approached in this way, in particular for the purpose of applying the provisions of Title III[1] of the Convention, certain types of judicial decision must be regarded as excluded from the area of application of the Convention, either by reason of the legal relationships between the parties to the action or of the subject-matter of the action.

Although certain judgments given in actions between a public authority and a person governed by private law may fall within the area of application of the Convention, this is not so where the public authority acts in the exercise of its powers.

Such is the case in a dispute which, like that between the parties to the main action, concerns the recovery of charges payable by a person governed by private law to a national or international body governed by public law for the use of equipment and services provided by such body, in particular where such use is obligatory and exclusive.

This applies in particular where the rate of charges, the methods of calculation and the procedures for collection are fixed unilaterally in relation to the users, as is the position in the present case where the body in question unilaterally fixed the place of performance of the obligation at its registered office and selected the national courts with jurisdiction to adjudicate upon the performance of the obligation.

The answer to be given to the question referred must therefore be that in the interpretation of the concept 'civil and commercial matters' for the purposes of the application of the Convention and in particular of Title III thereof, reference must

---

1 *Editor's note*: Title III is the part of the Convention dealing with the recognition and enforcement of judgments. In the Regulation, it is called 'Chapter' III.

not be made to the law of one of the States concerned but, first, to the objectives and scheme of the Convention and, secondly, to the general principles which stem from the corpus of the national legal systems.

On the basis of these criteria, a judgment given in an action between a public authority and a person governed by private law, in which the public authority has acted in the exercise of its powers, is excluded from the area of application of the Convention.

QUESTIONS

1 What precise features of Eurocontrol's claim were decisive, in the court's view, for determining that it was public?
2 Can you imagine a similar claim that might be characterized differently?

The fact that a judgment is outside the scope of the Regulation does not mean that it cannot be recognized on some other basis. In a later case based on almost identical facts, *Bavaria Fluggesellschaft Schwabe* v. *Eurocontrol*,[39] the European Court ruled that the Convention did not preclude the enforcement of a judgment such as that in the *LTU* case under a bilateral convention between Belgium and Germany which existed before the Brussels Convention came into force.[40]

The use of European rules to determine the scope of the Regulation has both advantages and disadvantages. Its chief disadvantage is that it produces uncertainty. Since no European definition of any of the concepts exists until the European Court rules on the matter, the scope of the Regulation cannot be determined without a reference for such a ruling. This can take several years.

Its advantage is that it provides uniformity: if the rules of either the State of origin or the State asked to recognize the judgment were applied, a situation could arise in which State A would be obliged to recognize a judgment granted by State B, while State B would not be obliged to recognize a similar judgment granted by State A. This would have been the situation in the *Eurocontrol* case if German law had considered the proceedings to be of a public-law nature. If the test of the State of origin were applied, Germany would have been required to recognize the Belgian judgment, while a similar judgment granted by a German court would not have had to be recognized in Belgium.

So far, the European Court has always given a Community interpretation to the concepts relevant to the scope of the Convention/Regulation;[41] it has also

---

39 Cases 9 and 10/77, [1977] ECR 1517.
40 Such conventions, which were of the traditional kind, existed between many of the Contracting States. Under Article 55 of the Brussels Convention, they were superseded by the latter, but they continued to apply to matters outside the scope of the Brussels Convention: Article 56 of the Brussels Convention. Most of them applied only to civil and commercial matters, but, if that concept is defined differently, there could be issues that fall within their scope but outside that of the Brussels Convention. The position is the same under the Regulation: see Articles 69 and 70 of the Regulation.
41 See, for example, *De Cavel* v. *De Cavel*, Case 143/78, [1979] ECR 1055; *De Cavel* v. *De Cavel*, Case 120/79, [1980] ECR 731; *Gourdain* v. *Nadler*, Case 133/78, [1979] ECR 733; *Netherlands* v. *Rüffer*, Case 814/79, [1980] ECR 3807;

given such an interpretation to most – but not all – of the other concepts used in the Convention/Regulation.[42]

§ 9.2   Applying the test

As the European Court held in the *LTU* case, proceedings do not cease to be civil or commercial just because one party is a public authority. The crucial question is whether that authority is basing its claim on the exercise of governmental powers. In other words, if the claim arose out of a transaction in which the public authority was doing something that any ordinary citizen could do – concluding a private-law contract, for example – the proceedings would be civil or commercial. If, on the other hand, it was exercising governmental powers – imposing a tax, for example – the proceedings would be public.

This test, which is derived from French law, seems clear enough at first sight. However, it is not always easy to apply in practice. Our next two cases illustrate some of these difficulties.

> **European Community**
> ***Netherlands* v. *Rüffer***
> **Court of Justice of the European Communities**
> **Case 814/79, [1980] ECR 3807**

Background

The defendant, Rüffer, was domiciled in Germany. He owned a ship, the *Otrate*, which sank in the Bight of Watum, a waterway at the mouth of the River Ems, in an area claimed by both Germany and the Netherlands as part of their territory. Under a treaty between the two States, the Ems–Dollard Treaty, the Netherlands was given 'river-police' functions on the waterway. Since the wreck was a danger to other ships, the Dutch Government raised it and disposed of it. They claimed the costs of this operation from Rüffer in proceedings brought before a Dutch court. The question before the European Court, to which the matter had been referred by the Dutch court, was whether the proceedings came within the scope of the Brussels Convention, the relevant instrument at the time.

Under Dutch law, the person responsible for a waterway has the right to reclaim the cost of removing a wreck from the owner of the wrecked vessel. The action is based on the ordinary private law of tort. In the past, privately operated waterways existed, and the operator had the same rights. In Dutch law, therefore, the claim was a civil matter. In the other Member States, however, the raising of wrecks and the recovery of the costs is regarded as a public function. A similar claim in those States would be regarded as a public matter. For this

---

Footnote 41 (*cont.*)
Marc Rich and Co. v. *Società Italiana Impianti*, Case C-190/89, [1991] ECR I-3855; *Sonntag* v. *Waidmann*, Case C-172/91, [1993] ECR I-1963.
42 See, for example, *Peters* v. *Zuid Nederlandse Aannemers Vereniging*, Case 34/82, [1983] ECR 987; *Arcado* v. *Haviland*, Case 9/87, [1988] ECR 1539; *Handte* v. *TMCS*, Case C-26/91, [1992] ECR I-3967. For exceptions, see *Tessili* v. *Dunlop*, Case 12/76, [1976] ECR 1473; *Zelger* v. *Salinitri (No. 2)*, Case 129/83, [1984] ECR 2397.

reason, Advocate General Warner considered that the claim before the Dutch court should be regarded as public in nature and, therefore, outside the scope of the Convention.

Judgment

7. It is apparent from the case-law of the Court . . . that the concept 'civil and commercial matters' used in Article 1 of the Brussels Convention must be regarded as an independent concept which must be construed with reference first to the objectives and scheme of the Convention and secondly to the general principles which stem from the corpus of the national legal systems.

8. In the light of those considerations the Court has specifically held in that same case-law that whilst certain judgments given in an action between a public authority and a person governed by private law may come within the area of application of the Convention that is not the case if the public authority is acting in the exercise of its public authority powers.

9. Such a case is an action for the recovery of the costs involved in the removal of a wreck in a public waterway, administered by the State responsible in performance of an international obligation and on the basis of provisions of national law which, in the administration of that waterway confer on it the status of public authority in regard to private persons.

10. It is common ground that in this case the Netherlands State had the wreck of the *Otrate* removed in performance of an obligation which was assumed under . . . the Ems-Dollard Treaty within the framework of the river-police functions conferred on it in that waterway by the said Treaty and that consequently it acted in this case as the body invested with public authority.

11. The granting of such status to the agent responsible for policing public waterways, for the purpose of removing wrecks located in those waterways, is furthermore in keeping with the general principles which stem from the corpus of the national legal systems of the Member States whose provisions on the administration of public waterways precisely show that the agent administering those waterways does so, when removing wrecks, in the exercise of public authority.

12. In view of those factors the action brought by the Netherlands State before the national court must be regarded as being outside the ambit of the Brussels Convention, as defined by the concept of 'civil and commercial matters' within the meaning of the first paragraph of Article 1 of that Convention, since it is established that the Netherlands State acted in the instant case in the exercise of public authority.

13. The fact that in this case the action pending before the national court does not concern the actual removal of the wreck but the costs involved in that removal and that the Netherlands State is seeking to recover those costs by means of a claim for redress and not by administrative process as provided for by the national law of other Member States cannot be sufficient to bring the matter in dispute within the ambit of the Brussels Convention.

14. As the Court has stated in the authorities cited above the Brussels Convention must be applied in such a way as to ensure, as far as possible, that the rights and obligations which derive from it for the Contracting States and the persons to whom it applies are equal and uniform. By that same case-law such a requirement rules out the possibility of the Convention's being interpreted solely in the light of the division of jurisdiction between the various types of courts existing in certain States: on the contrary it implies that the area of application of the Convention is essentially determined either by reason of the legal relationships between the parties to the action or of the subject-matter of the action.

15. The fact that in recovering those costs the administering agent acts pursuant to a debt which arises from an act of public authority is sufficient for its action, whatever the nature of the proceedings afforded by national law for that purpose, to be treated as being outside the ambit of the Brussels Convention.

The judgment in this case has been criticized on the ground that it could have a detrimental effect on environmental law.[43] If a company from one Member State caused pollution in another Member State, proceedings brought in the latter State by the relevant public authority to recover the costs of an environmental clean-up might be outside the scope of the Regulation; consequently, the costs might be more difficult to recover in another Member State.

In Canada, the courts have taken a different approach. In *United States of America* v. *Ivey*,[44] the Ontario courts enforced the judgment of a court in the United States under which the relevant US authority was granted recovery of the costs of cleaning up pollution caused by a Canadian company operating at the time in the United States. The enforcement of the judgment was based on the common law, which also has a rule that a judgment based on public law cannot be enforced, but the Canadian courts held that the proceedings in question were not of a public-law nature for this purpose.

Our next case shows a different context in which the question can arise.

European Community
Baten
Court of Justice of the European Communities
Case C-271/00, [2002] ECR I-10489

Background

There is a rule in many legal systems that, if a public authority gives social assistance (welfare) to a person in need, it can reclaim the money from another person who was responsible for the support of the needy person. In *Baten*, Mr Baten and Mrs Kil were married and subsequently divorced in Belgium. It was agreed that

---

43 Betlem and Bernasconi, 'European Private International Law, the Environment and Obstacles for Public Authorities' (2006) 122 LQR 124 at pp. 132–7.
44 (1996) 130 DLR (4th) 674 (Ontario High Court, Canada); affirmed (1998) 139 DLR (4th) 570 (Ontario Court of Appeal).

Mr Baten would not pay any maintenance to Mrs Kil, though he agreed to make monthly payments towards the maintenance of their daughter. Mrs Kil and the daughter then moved to the Netherlands where they both received social assistance from the relevant public authority. That authority then sought to recover the money from Mr Baten. When he failed to pay, the authority obtained a judgment in a Dutch court, which it then sought to enforce in Belgium. Mr Baten claimed that the Dutch judgment was inconsistent with the terms of the divorce. The question then arose whether it was within the scope of the Brussels Convention.

Judgement

[After referring to the previous cases, the court continued:]

30. Thus the Court has held that, although certain judgments in actions between a public authority and a person governed by private law may come within the scope of the Brussels Convention, it is otherwise where the public authority is acting in the exercise of its public powers (*LTU*, cited above, paragraph 4, and *Rüffer*, paragraph 8).

31. In order to determine whether that is so in a case such as that in point in the main proceedings, in which a public body seeks from a person governed by private law recovery of sums paid by it by way of social assistance to the former spouse and the child of that person, it is necessary to examine the basis and the detailed rules governing the bringing of that action.

32. In that regard, it appears from Article 93 of the ABW [the Dutch law on social assistance] that the costs of social assistance are recoverable up to the limit of the maintenance obligation under Book I of the Netherlands Civil Code. Thus it is the rules of the civil law which determine the cases in which the public body may bring an action under a right of recourse, namely where there is a person under a statutory obligation to pay maintenance. It is on the basis of those same rules that the person against whom the public body may proceed, namely the person under a statutory obligation to pay maintenance, is identified, and that the limits to the amounts recoverable by that body are determined, those limits being coterminous with those of the statutory maintenance obligation itself.

33. As regards the detailed rules governing the bringing of an action under a right of recourse, Article 103 of the ABW states that that action must be brought before the civil courts and [that it is] governed by the rules of civil procedure.

34. Accordingly, as the Advocate General stated at paragraph 36 of his Opinion, the legal situation of the public body *vis-à-vis* the person liable for maintenance is comparable to that of an individual who, having paid on whatever ground another's debt, is subrogated to the rights of the original creditor, or is comparable to the situation of a person who, having suffered loss as a result of an act or omission imputable to a third party, seeks reparation from that party.

35. However, that finding calls for some qualification by reason of Article 94 of the ABW under which an agreement between spouses or former spouses for the purpose of precluding or limiting their maintenance obligations after their divorce does not preclude recovery from one of the parties and is without prejudice to determination of the amounts to be recovered.

36. To the extent to which that provision allows the public body, in a proper case, to disregard an agreement lawfully entered into between spouses or former spouses, producing binding effects between them and enforceable against third parties, it places the public body in a legal situation which derogates from the ordinary law. That is all the more so inasmuch as that provision allows the public body to disregard an agreement approved by a judicial decision and covered by the force of *res judicata* attaching to that decision. In those circumstances, the public body is no longer acting under rules of the civil law but under a prerogative of its own, specifically conferred on it by the legislature.

37. In light of the foregoing considerations, the reply to the first question must be that the first paragraph of Article 1 of the Brussels Convention must be interpreted as meaning that the concept of 'civil matters' encompasses an action under a right of recourse whereby a public body seeks from a person governed by private law recovery of sums paid by it by way of social assistance to the divorced spouse and the child of that person, provided that the basis and the detailed rules relating to the bringing of that action are governed by the rules of the ordinary law in regard to maintenance obligations. Where the action under a right of recourse is founded on provisions by which the legislature conferred on the public body a prerogative of its own, that action cannot be regarded as being brought in 'civil matters'.

Note

In a subsequent part of the judgment, the European Court ruled that proceedings of the kind in issue were not excluded from the scope of the Convention on the basis that they fell under the heading 'social security' in what is now Article 1(2)(c) of the Regulation.

QUESTION

Is the reasoning of this case inconsistent with that in *Rüffer*?

Further reading

Kruger (Thalia), *Civil Jurisdiction Rules of the EU and their Impact on Third States* (Oxford University Press, Oxford, 2007)

Betlem and Bernasconi, 'European Private International Law, the Environment and Obstacles for Public Authorities' (2006) 122 LQR 124

General works on the Brussels Convention, the Brussels Regulation and the Lugano Convention

Bogdan (Michael), *Concise Introduction to EU Private International Law* (Europa Law Publishing, Groningen, the Netherlands, 2006), Chapter 3

Bogdan (Michael) and Maunsbach (Ulf), *EU Private International Law: An EC Court Casebook* (Europa Law Publishing, Groningen, the Netherlands, 2006)

Briggs (Adrian), *Civil Jurisdiction and Judgments* (LLP, London, 4th edn, 2005)

Gaudemet-Tallon (Hélène), *Compétence et exécution des jugements en Europe* (LGDJ, Paris, 3rd edn, 2002)

Jenard, 'Report on the Convention of 27 September 1968 on Jurisdiction and the Enforcement of Judgments in Civil and Commercial Matters', OJ 1979 C 59, p. 1

Jenard and Möller, 'Report on the Lugano Convention' (original text), OJ 1990 C 189, p. 57

Layton (Alexander) and Mercer (Hugh) (eds.), *European Civil Practice* (Sweet & Maxwell, London, 2nd edn, 2004)

Schlosser, 'Report on the Convention of 9 October 1968' (Denmark, Ireland and UK Accessions), OJ 1979 C 59, p. 71

CHAPTER 4

EC law: special jurisdiction

§ 1   Article 5

The only rule of jurisdiction we considered in Chapter 3 was the rule that the Member State in which the defendant is domiciled has general jurisdiction. We also saw that, if the defendant is not domiciled in any Member State, the jurisdictional rules of the Regulation do not (in general) apply at all. Now the time has come to consider the special rules that apply if the defendant is not domiciled in the State of the forum, but is domiciled in another Member State. If the forum does not have jurisdiction under these rules, it cannot hear the case at all. This is made clear by Article 3, which is set out in Panel 4.1.

The rules of jurisdiction applicable to defendants domiciled in another Member State are those in Sections 2 to 7 of Chapter II of the Regulation. These are Articles 5–24. In addition to rules of a general nature (in Section 2), these Articles contain rules on insurance (Section 3), consumer contracts (Section 4), individual contracts of employment (Section 5), exclusive jurisdiction (Section 6) and choice-of-court agreements (Section 7).[1]

We shall first consider the rules in Article 5 of the Regulation. As the heading of Section 2 indicates, these confer only special jurisdiction ('specific' in US terminology): they apply only when there is an appropriate connection between the cause of action and the State of the forum. We shall examine only those rules that are of importance in commercial cases.

Panel 4.1 Persons domiciled in another Member State
Brussels I Regulation (Regulation 44/2001), Article 3

Article 3

1. Persons domiciled in a Member State may be sued in the courts of another Member State only by virtue of the rules set out in Sections 2 to 7 of this Chapter.
2. In particular the rules of national jurisdiction set out in Annex I shall not be applicable as against them.

[*Editor's note*: Annex I contains a list of particular rules of national law that are regarded as especially objectionable.]

---

§ 1.1   Contracts

Actions relating to a contract are dealt with in Article 5(1). This is a provision where the Regulation differs from the Convention. As originally drafted, the Convention contained a simple provision: Article 5(1) provided that, in matters

---

[1] As mentioned above, the rules in Section 6 and Section 7 can apply even if the defendant is not domiciled in any Member State.

relating to a contract, a person domiciled in one Member State could, in another Member State, be sued in the courts for 'the place of performance of the obligation in question'. This provision gave rise to a number of problems, and it has been amended twice, first in one of the revisions of the Brussels Convention,[2] and then in the Regulation. The first amendment introduced a special rule for employment contracts;[3] the second introduced a special rule for contracts for the sale of goods or the provision of services. The current version of Article 5(1) is set out in Panel 4.2, § 1.1.4, below, where the effect of the change is considered. First, however, we must discuss some preliminary matters.

§ 1.1.1 When does a claim relate to contract? Since Article 5(1) applies only 'in matters relating to a contract', it is necessary to answer this question in order to discover the scope of Article 5(1). One might have thought that this would depend on how the claimant framed his claim and on the provisions of national law. The European Court, however, has decided that a Community solution must apply.[4] In other words, a rule of Community law – created, in each case, by the European Court – decides whether a claim, however formulated, relates to contract or not. This is only for purposes of jurisdiction: once the jurisdictional issues have been settled, the matter proceeds on the basis of the classification under national law.

The European Court's method of dealing with these matters can best be illustrated by taking its decision in *Handte* v. *TMCS*[5] as an example.

European Community
Handte* v. *TMCS
Court of Justice of the European Communities
Case C-26/91, [1992] ECR I-3967

Background

A German company, Handte Germany, manufactured goods and sold them to a French company, Handte France. The latter resold them to a second French company, TMCS. The goods were allegedly defective and the question arose whether the sub-purchaser (TMCS) could bring an action in the French courts directly against the German manufacturer, Handte Germany.

The question whether a sub-purchaser can bring an action against the manufacturer is subject to different solutions in different legal systems. In many legal systems, the position is that, in the absence of special circumstances, no action can be brought in contract against the manufacturer. In the common law, this is said to be due to the combined effect of the doctrines of privity and consideration. On the other hand, if the defective goods cause injury to a person or damage to property, an action in tort may exist. However, in the *Handte* case, there was

---

2 The 1989 Accession Convention (Article 4).
3 Now contained in Articles 18–21 of the Regulation.
4 *Arcado* v. *Haviland*, Case 9/87, [1988] ECR 1539.
5 For earlier decisions on the matter, see *Arcado* v. *Haviland*, Case 9/87, [1988] ECR 1539; and *Peters* v. *Zuid Nederlandse Aannemers Vereniging*, Case 34/82, [1983] ECR 987.

no such injury. In these circumstances, many legal systems would give no direct remedy against the manufacturer.

According to the Advocate General, French law adopted a different analysis. At the time in question, it took the view that an action in contract could be brought by the sub-purchaser against the manufacturer. It seems that this was based on a theory of implied assignment, by the original purchaser to the sub-purchaser, of his contractual rights against the manufacturer. Consequently, French law granted a remedy in contract in circumstances in which the law of most of the other Member States would grant a remedy, if at all, only in tort.[6]

The facts of the case are not entirely clear, but it seems that the claimant framed his claim in contract. This required the French court to consider what the 'obligation in question' was. Clearly, it was the delivery of goods in sound condition, but was it the obligation of the manufacturer towards the original purchaser (Handte France) or that of the latter towards the sub-purchaser (TMCS)? Since the place of delivery was almost certainly different in the two cases, and may possibly have been outside France in the former, this was a vital question.[7] The French court referred it to the European Court. The latter, however, did not answer it. Instead, it considered whether the action should be regarded as being covered by Article 5(1) of the Convention at all. Should TMCS's claim be regarded as a matter 'relating to a contract'?

Judgment

[After stating that a major objective of the Convention was to achieve certainty, the court said:]

13. The Convention achieves that objective by laying down a number of jurisdictional rules which determine the cases, exhaustively listed in Sections 2 to 6 of Title II of the Convention, in which a defendant domiciled or established in a Contracting State may, under a rule of special jurisdiction, or must, under a rule of exclusive jurisdiction or prorogation of jurisdiction, be sued before a court of another Contracting State.

14. The rules on special and exclusive jurisdiction and those relating to prorogation of jurisdiction thus derogate from the general principle, set out in the first paragraph of Article 2 of the Convention, that the courts of the Contracting State in which the defendant is domiciled are to have jurisdiction. That jurisdictional rule is a general principle because it makes it easier, in principle, for a defendant to defend himself. Consequently, the jurisdictional rules which derogate from that general principle must not lead to an interpretation going beyond the situations envisaged by the Convention.

15. It follows that the phrase 'matters relating to a contract', as used in Article 5(1) of the Convention, is not to be understood as covering a situation in which there is no obligation freely assumed by one party towards another.

---

6 According to the Advocate General, the only other Contracting States to adopt the French approach were Belgium and Luxembourg.
7 If the French theory was based on an implied assignment by the manufacturer to the original purchaser, it should be the place of delivery under the contract between these two parties.

16. Where a sub-buyer of goods purchased from an intermediate seller brings an action against the manufacturer for damages on the ground that the goods are not in conformity, it must be observed that there is no contractual relationship between the sub-buyer and the manufacturer because the latter has not undertaken any contractual obligation towards the former.

17. Furthermore, particularly where there is a chain of international contracts, the parties' contractual obligations may vary from contract to contract, so that the contractual rights which the sub-buyer can enforce against his immediate seller will not necessarily be the same as those which the manufacturer will have accepted in his relationship with the first buyer.

18. The objective of strengthening legal protection of persons established in the Community, which is one of the objectives which the Convention is designed to achieve, also requires that the jurisdictional rules which derogate from the general principle of the Convention should be interpreted in such a way as to enable a normally well-informed defendant reasonably to predict before which courts, other than those of the State in which he is domiciled, he may be sued.

19. However, in a situation such as that with which the main proceedings are concerned, the application of the special jurisdictional rule laid down by Article 5(1) of the Convention to an action brought by a sub-buyer of goods against the manufacturer is not foreseeable by the latter and is therefore incompatible with the principle of legal certainty.

20. Apart from the fact that the manufacturer has no contractual relationship with the sub-buyer and undertakes no contractual obligation towards that buyer, whose identity and domicile may, quite reasonably, be unknown to him, it appears that in the great majority of Contracting States the liability of a manufacturer towards a sub-buyer for defects in the goods sold is not regarded as being of a contractual nature.

21. It follows that the answer to the question submitted by the national court must be that Article 5(1) of the Convention is to be understood as meaning that it does not apply to an action between a sub-buyer of goods and the manufacturer, who is not the seller, relating to defects in those goods or to their unsuitability for their intended purpose.

QUESTIONS

1 In paragraph 19, the court said that an action by a sub-purchaser against a manufacturer is not foreseeable by the latter 'and is therefore incompatible with the principle of legal certainty'. Is this really true in a normal business situation?

2 Was it likely to have been true in the *Handte* case, given that the original purchaser (Handte France) was probably a subsidiary of the manufacturer?

3 If the defective product had caused injury to one of TMCS's employees, the latter could have sued Handte Germany in tort in the courts for the place where the damage (injury) occurred (*Bier* case, § 1.2, below). Would this have been any more foreseeable?

4 Would foreseeability have been any less important if the action had been in tort?

The rule laid down by the European Court in paragraph 15 (that there must be an obligation freely assumed by one party towards another) cannot be accepted at face value, since it ignores the possibility of assignment, express or implied. There are in fact many situations in modern law in which one person may bring a claim in contract against another, even though there is no direct agreement between them. The holder of a cheque, for example, may sue the maker, even if there is no direct agreement between them. In at least some legal systems, such an action is in contract. The same applies to claims by the holder of a bill of lading against the shipowner. In this latter case, the European Court itself seems to have recognized that the claim is in contract.[8]

A slightly different example is a claim by a company against a shareholder under a provision in the constitutive document (articles of association, etc.) of the company. In *Powell Duffryn* v. *Petereit*,[9] it was argued that such a claim cannot be in contract because the shareholder in question might not have consented to the provision: it might have been adopted, after he became a shareholder, by an amendment to the *statut* that he voted against. In spite of this, the European Court held such a claim to be contractual. This cannot be reconciled with the reasoning in *Handte*.

The result of the judgment in *Handte* was that the French courts could not take jurisdiction under Article 5(1). However, in an earlier case, *Kalfelis* v. *Schröder*,[10] the European Court held that all actions which seek to establish the liability of a defendant and which are not related to 'contract' within the meaning of Article 5(1) are to be regarded as falling under Article 5(3), which deals with claims in tort. So it would seem that the French court might have had jurisdiction under this latter provision (discussed in § 1.2, below).[11] Thus, the claim would have to be regarded as being in tort for jurisdictional purposes, even if it was framed by the claimant in contract and might be so regarded by the applicable law. Once it was decided that the French courts had jurisdiction (if it were so decided), they would then decide the substance of the matter on the basis that the claim was in contract: the characterization of the claim as relating to a tort would apply only to jurisdictional issues.[12]

---

8 *Tilly Russ* v. *Nova*, Case 71/83, [1984] ECR 2417.

9 Case C-214/89, [1992] ECR I-1745. See also *Peters* v. *Zuid Nederlandse Aannemers Vereniging*, Case 34/82, [1983] ECR 987.

10 Case 189/87, [1988] ECR 5565.

11 This would depend on where the 'harmful event' occurred, something not altogether easy to determine. The sensible solution would be to say that, in the absence of injury to a person or damage to property, this was where the goods were delivered under the contract between the manufacturer and the original purchaser.

12 For a fuller discussion, see Hartley, 'Unnecessary Europeanization under the Brussels Jurisdiction and Judgments Convention: The Case of the Dissatisfied Sub-Purchaser' (1993) 18 *European Law Review* 506, especially at pp. 510–16.

§ 1.1.2 **The place of performance.** The next question is how the place of performance of the obligation is to be determined. This will normally be clear from the terms of the contract, but, if it is not, it may be necessary to apply a legal presumption. Such a presumption may be different in different systems of law. Take the example of a contract that requires a sum of money to be paid, but does not specify the place of payment. Under English law, the presumption is that the debtor must seek out his creditor and pay the debt at the latter's place of residence.[13] Many Continental systems adopt the opposite presumption. So what law is to be applied for the purpose of the Brussels Convention? The rule here was laid down in our next case.[14]

European Community
Tessili* v. *Dunlop
Court of Justice of the European Communities
Case 12/76, [1976] ECR 1473

Background

In this case, a firm domiciled in Italy (Tessili) agreed to sell a consignment of ski suits to a firm domiciled in Germany (Dunlop). Dunlop claimed that the suits were defective, and sued Tessili in Germany, relying on Article 5(1) of the Convention (original version). It claimed that the place of performance was Germany. Tessili objected. It said the place of performance was Italy. A reference was made to the European Court. As this was the first case decided by the court under the Convention, it introduced its judgment with some background material.

Judgment
The interpretation of the Convention in general

9.   Article 220 of the EEC Treaty provides that Member States shall, so far as necessary, enter into negotiations with each other with a view to securing for the benefit of their nationals the establishment of rules intended to facilitate the achievement of the common market in the various spheres listed in that provision. The Convention was established to implement Article 220 and was intended according to the express terms of its preamble to implement the provisions of that article on the simplification of formalities governing the reciprocal recognition and enforcement of judgments of courts or tribunals and to strengthen in the Community the legal protection of persons therein established. In order to eliminate obstacles to legal relations and to settle disputes within the sphere of intra-Community relations in civil and commercial matters the Convention contains, *inter alia*, rules enabling the jurisdiction in these matters of courts of Member States to be determined and facilitating the recognition and execution of courts' judgments. Accordingly, the Convention must be

---

13 *The Eider* [1893] P 119 (CA); *Robey* v. *Snaefell Mining Co.* (1887) 20 QBD 152; *Bremer Oeltransport GmbH* v. *Drewry* [1933] 1 KB 753 (CA).
14 See also *Custom Made Commercial* v. *Stawa Metallbau*, Case C-288/92, [1994] ECR I-2913; *GIE Groupe Concorde* v. *Master of the Vessel Suhadiwarno Panjan*, Case C-440/97, [1999] ECR I-6307.

interpreted having regard both to its principles and objectives and to its relationship with the Treaty.

10. The Convention frequently uses words and legal concepts drawn from civil, commercial and procedural law and capable of a different meaning from one Member State to another. The question therefore arises whether these words and concepts must be regarded as having their own independent meaning and as being thus common to all the Member States or as referring to substantive rules of the law applicable in each case under the rules of conflict of laws of the court before which the matter is first brought.

11. Neither of these two options rules out the other since the appropriate choice can only be made in respect of each of the provisions of the Convention to ensure that it is fully effective having regard to the objectives of Article 220 of the Treaty. In any event it should be stressed that the interpretation of the said words and concepts for the purpose of the Convention does not prejudge the question of the substantive rule applicable to the particular case.

The question raised by the national court

12. Article 5 of the Convention provides: 'A person domiciled in a Contracting State may, in another Contracting State, be sued: (1) in matters relating to a contract, in the courts for the place of performance of the obligation in question'. This provision must be interpreted within the framework of the system of conferment of jurisdiction under Title II of the Convention. In accordance with Article 2 the basis of this system is the general conferment of jurisdiction on the court of the defendant's domicile. Article 5 however provides for a number of cases of special jurisdiction at the option of the plaintiff.

13. This freedom of choice was introduced in view of the existence in certain well-defined cases of a particularly close relationship between a dispute and the court which may be most conveniently called upon to take cognizance of the matter. Thus in the case of an action relating to contractual obligations Article 5 (1) allows a plaintiff to bring the matter before the court for the place 'of performance' of the obligation in question. It is for the court before which the matter is brought to establish under the Convention whether the place of performance is situate within its territorial jurisdiction. For this purpose it must determine in accordance with its own rules of conflict of laws what is the law applicable to the legal relationship in question and define in accordance with that law the place of performance of the contractual obligation in question.

14. Having regard to the differences obtaining between national laws of contract and to the absence at this stage of legal development of any unification in the substantive law applicable, it does not appear possible to give any more substantial guide to the interpretation of the reference made by Article 5 (1) to the 'place of performance' of contractual obligations. This

> is all the more true since the determination of the place of performance of obligations depends on the contractual context to which these obligations belong.
>
> 15. In these circumstances the reference in the Convention to the place of performance of contractual obligations cannot be understood otherwise than by reference to the substantive law applicable under the rules of conflict of laws of the court before which the matter is brought.

Comment

This is one of the small number of cases in which the European Court did not adopt an autonomous (European) solution to determine the meaning of a concept used in the Convention.

§ 1.1.3 The obligation in question. In its original form, Article 5(1) gave jurisdiction to the courts 'for the place of performance of the obligation in question'. Article 5(1)(a) is still drafted in these terms, though there is now an exception in sub-paragraph (b). So, to determine the scope of Article 5(1), we must ascertain what the 'obligation in question' is.

According to the European Court, it is the obligation the breach of which gives rise to the claim.[15] However, this is not entirely clear. Assume that a Danish company agrees to perform a service for an English company in England. Payment is to be made in Denmark. The Danish company performs the service, but the English company claims that it is defective. As a result, it refuses to pay. If the Danish company sues for payment, what is the 'obligation in question'? Is it the obligation to pay (in which case the Danish courts would have jurisdiction) or is it the obligation to perform the service (in which case only the English courts would have jurisdiction)?[16] If one takes a formalistic approach, it is the former, since the actual claim before the court is for payment. However, on this approach, jurisdiction would be entirely dependent on procedural manoeuvring: if the English company had sued for rescission of the contract, the obligation in question would have been the obligation to perform the service. The English courts would then have had jurisdiction.

It was to avoid these problems that Article 5(1) was amended by inserting two further paragraphs. The amended version of Article 5(1) (set out in Panel 4.2) makes clear that, for the two most important kinds of contract – contracts for the sale of goods and contracts for the provision of services – the courts having jurisdiction under Article 5(1) are those for the place of delivery of the goods or the performance of the service, even if the actual claim concerns payment. In other contracts, the problem remains unresolved. Today, therefore, the answer to the question in the previous paragraph would be that the Danish company must

---

15 *De Bloos* v. *Bouyer*, Case 14/76, [1976] ECR 1497; *Shenavai* v. *Kreischer*, Case 266/85, [1987] ECR 239. The French text of Article 5(1) of the Convention was modified to make this clear. After modification, it read, 'l'obligation qui sert de base à la demande' ('the obligation which constitutes the basis of the claim').
16 These facts are taken from *F ApS* v. *J (UK) Ltd*, [1993] *Ugeskrift for Retsvæsen* 802 (*Østre Landsret* (Eastern High Court), Denmark, 24 June 1993). The Danish courts held they had no jurisdiction.

sue the English company in England: Article 5(1) would not give jurisdiction to the Danish courts.

§ 1.1.4 The revised version of Article 5(1). As already mentioned, the Brussels I Regulation (Regulation 44/2001) brought in a new version of Article 5(1) (set out in Panel 4.2).[17] This retains the old rule for contracts in general, but lays down exceptions for the two most important kinds of contract, contracts of sale and contracts for the provision of services. As Article 5(1) makes clear, these new rules are *exceptions*: where they do not apply, the old rule continues to operate even for these two kinds of contract. There are two circumstances in which this might occur:

- where sub-paragraph (b) does not apply (for example, because the goods are to be delivered in a non-member State); or
- where the parties have agreed otherwise.

The 'unless otherwise agreed' clause gives the parties the power to agree that sub-paragraph (b) will not apply to their contract. This can probably be done without having to satisfy the requirements of form laid down for choice-of-court agreements (Article 23); if this were not the case, the clause would have no point. However, the parties cannot choose a court other than that which would have had jurisdiction under sub-paragraph (a).

Our next case is the only one so far decided by the European Court on the new version of Article 5(1).[18]

European Community
Color Drack* v. *LEXX International
Court of Justice of the European Communities
Case C-386/05, [2007] ECR I-3699

Background

Color Drack was an Austrian firm with its registered office in Schwarzach, Austria, and LEXX International was a German firm with its registered office in Nuremberg, Germany. Color Drack ordered a consignment of sunglasses from LEXX. Payment accompanied the order. It was agreed that the sunglasses would

---

17 For an analysis of these provisions, see Takahashi, 'Jurisdiction in Matters Relating to Contract: Article 5(1) of the Brussels Convention and Regulation' (2002) 27 *European Law Review* 530.
18 But see *Rehder*, Case C-204/08 (not yet decided). This case concerned the second indent of Article 5(1)(b) (the provision of services): if the claimant buys an air ticket on a flight from a place in Germany to a place in Lithuania, and wishes to sue the airline, where is the service provided – in the place of departure, in the place of arrival or in both?

be delivered directly to customers in various parts of Austria. The sunglasses were delivered, but, when Color Drack returned unsold glasses for a refund, no refund was made. Color Drack then sued LEXX in the district court of St Johann im Pongau, the place in Austria where Color Drack had its headquarters.

It should be explained that, unlike England, Austria has no first-instance court with jurisdiction over the whole country; each district has its own court, even for proceedings involving large claims.[19] The phrase 'local jurisdiction' or 'territorial jurisdiction' is used to refer to the question which district court in Austria should hear the case; the phrase 'international jurisdiction' refers to the question whether *any* court in Austria can hear it. It is generally assumed that, while some provisions of the Brussels I Regulation (for example, Article 1(2))[20] are concerned only with international jurisdiction, others (for example, Article 5(1))[21] apply to both.

The court of first instance (the district court of St Johann im Pongau) held that it had territorial and international jurisdiction. On appeal, the appeal court for Salzburg said that, as delivery was to be made in various parts of Austria, Article 5(1)(b) could not apply and that, under Article 5(1)(a), the court with jurisdiction was the court for the place where repayment should have been made. It held that this was Nuremberg, the place where LEXX had its registered office. A further appeal was made to the Supreme Court of Austria, which referred the matter to the European Court. There, LEXX International, Germany and Italy argued that, where, in the case of a contract for the sale of goods, the goods are to be delivered in more than one place (even within the same Member State), sub-paragraph (b) cannot apply: they maintained that the applicable provision in the case was sub-paragraph (a).

Judgment

15. By its question, the national court is essentially asking whether the first indent of Article 5(1)(b) of Regulation No. 44/2001 applies in the case of a sale of goods involving several places of delivery within a single Member State and, if so, whether, where the claim relates to all those deliveries, the plaintiff may sue the defendant in the court for the place of delivery of its choice.

16. As a preliminary point, it must be stated that the considerations that follow apply solely to the case where there are several places of delivery within a single Member State and are without prejudice to the answer to be given where there are several places of delivery in a number of Member States.

[After considering the general scheme and policy of the Regulation, the court continued:]

25. Pursuant to the first indent of Article 5(1)(b) of that regulation, the place of performance of the obligation in question is the place in a Member State where, under the contract, the goods were delivered or should have been delivered.

19 This is normally the case in Continental countries.
20 This is because it refers to domicile in a *Member State*.
21 This is because it refers to the courts for *the place* of performance.

26. In the context of Regulation No. 44/2001, contrary to Lexx's submissions, that rule of special jurisdiction in matters relating to a contract establishes the place of delivery as the autonomous linking factor to apply to all claims founded on one and the same contract for the sale of goods rather than merely to the claims founded on the obligation of delivery itself.

27. It is in the light of those considerations that it must be determined whether, where there are several places of delivery in a single Member State, the first indent of Article 5(1)(b) of Regulation No. 44/2001 applies and, if so, whether, where the claim relates to all the deliveries, the plaintiff may sue the defendant in the courts for the place of delivery of its choice.

28. First of all, the first indent of Article 5(1)(b) of the regulation must be regarded as applying whether there is one place of delivery or several.

29. By providing for a single court to have jurisdiction and a single linking factor, the Community legislature did not intend generally to exclude cases where a number of courts may have jurisdiction nor those where the existence of that linking factor can be established in different places.

30. The first indent of Article 5(1)(b) of Regulation No. 44/2001, determining both international and local jurisdiction,[1] seeks to unify the rules of conflict of jurisdiction[2] and, accordingly, to designate the court having jurisdiction directly, without reference to the domestic rules of the Member States.

31. In that regard, an answer in the affirmative to the question whether the provision under consideration applies where there are several places of delivery within a single Member State does not call into question the objectives of the rules on the international jurisdiction of the courts of the Member States set out in that regulation.

32. Firstly, the applicability of the first indent of Article 5(1)(b) of Regulation No. 44/2001 where there are several places of delivery within a single Member State complies with the regulation's objective of predictability.

33. In that case, the parties to the contract can easily and reasonably foresee before which Member State's courts they can bring their dispute.

34. Secondly, the applicability of the first indent of Article 5(1)(b) of Regulation No. 44/2001 where there are several places of delivery within a single Member State also complies with the objective of proximity underlying the rules of special jurisdiction in matters relating to a contract.

35. Where there are several places of delivery within a single Member State, that objective of proximity is met since, in application of the provision under consideration, it will in any event be the courts of that Member State which will have jurisdiction to hear the case.

---

1 *Editor's note:* the meaning of these terms was explained above.
2 *Editor's note:* this phrase is a direct translation of the standard French term, *conflits de juridictions*. Its meaning is explained in Chapter 1, § 2, above.

36. Consequently, the first indent of Article 5(1)(b) of Regulation No. 44/2001 is applicable where there are several places of delivery within a single Member State.

37. However, it cannot be inferred from the applicability of the first indent of Article 5(1)(b) of Regulation No. 44/2001 in circumstances such as those of the main proceedings that that provision necessarily confers concurrent jurisdiction on a court for any place where goods were or should have been delivered.

38. With regard, secondly, to the question whether, where there are several places of delivery within a single Member State and the claim relates to all those deliveries, the plaintiff may sue the defendant in the court for the place of delivery of its choice on the basis of the first indent of Article 5(1)(b) of Regulation No. 44/2001, it is necessary to point out that one court must have jurisdiction to hear all the claims arising out of the contract.

39. In that regard, it is appropriate to take into consideration the origins of the provision under consideration. By that provision, the Community legislature intended, in respect of sales contracts, expressly to break with the earlier solution under which the place of performance was determined, for each of the obligations in question, in accordance with the private international rules of the court seised of the dispute. By designating autonomously as 'the place of performance' the place where the obligation which characterises the contract is to be performed, the Community legislature sought to centralise at its place of performance jurisdiction over disputes concerning all the contractual obligations and to determine sole jurisdiction for all claims arising out of the contract.

40. In that regard it is necessary to take account of the fact that the special jurisdiction under the first indent of Article 5(1)(b) of Regulation No. 44/2001 is warranted, in principle, by the existence of a particularly close linking factor between the contract and the court called upon to hear the litigation, with a view to the efficient organisation of the proceedings. It follows that, where there are several places of delivery of the goods, 'place of delivery' must be understood, for the purposes of application of the provision under consideration, as the place with the closest linking factor between the contract and the court having jurisdiction. In such a case, the point of closest linking factor will, as a general rule, be at the place of the principal delivery, which must be determined on the basis of economic criteria.

41. To that end, it is for the national court seised to determine whether it has jurisdiction in the light of the evidence submitted to it.

42. If it is not possible to determine the principal place of delivery, each of the places of delivery has a sufficiently close link of proximity to the material elements of the dispute and, accordingly, a significant link as regards jurisdiction. In such a case, the plaintiff may sue the defendant in the court for the place of delivery of its choice on the basis of the first indent of Article 5(1)(b) of Regulation No. 44/2001.

43. Giving the plaintiff such a choice enables it easily to identify the courts in which it may sue and the defendant reasonably to foresee in which courts it may be sued.

44. That conclusion cannot be called into question by the fact that the defendant cannot foresee the particular court of that Member State in which it may be sued; it is sufficiently protected since it can only be sued, in application of the provision under consideration, where there are several places of performance in a single Member State, in the courts of that Member State for the place where a delivery has been made.

45. In the light of all the foregoing considerations, the answer to the question referred must be that the first indent of Article 5(1)(b) of Regulation No. 44/2001 applies where there are several places of delivery within a single Member State. In such a case, the court having jurisdiction to hear all the claims based on the contract for the sale of goods is that for the principal place of delivery, which must be determined on the basis of economic criteria. In the absence of determining factors for establishing the principal place of delivery, the applicant may sue the plaintiff in the court for the place of delivery of its choice.

Comment

As stated in paragraph 16 of the judgment, this decision leaves open the question whether sub-paragraph (b) applies where delivery is to take place in two or more Member States, or partly in a Member State and partly in a non-member State.

§ 1.1.5 Contracts not covered by Article 5(1). There are three kinds of contracts to which Article 5(1) does not apply: matters relating to insurance (dealt with in Section 3 of the Regulation); consumer contracts (dealt with in Section 4); and individual contracts of employment (dealt with in Section 5). Special rules apply in these cases: see § 4.1, below.

§ 1.2   Tort

As was mentioned previously, the question whether, for jurisdictional purposes, a claim is to be regarded as being in tort is determined according to a Community rule. The rule is that all actions which seek to establish the liability of a defendant and which are not related to a 'contract' within the meaning of Article 5(1) are to be regarded as falling under Article 5(3).[22] It thus covers restitution and unjust enrichment, as well as tort.

The rule laid down in Article 5(3) is that the courts having jurisdiction are those for the place where the 'harmful event' occurred (Panel 4.3). This phrase is deliberately vague and the European

Panel 4.3 Matters relating to a tort
Brussels I Regulation (Regulation 44/2001), Article 5(3)

Article 5(3)

A person domiciled in a Member State may, in another Member State, be sued:

. . .

3. in matters relating to tort, delict or quasi-delict, in the courts for the place where the harmful event occurred or may occur . . .

22 *Kalfelis* v. *Schröder*, Case 189/87, [1988] ECR 5565.

Court has had to explain what it means. Our next case is the first in which it did this.

European Community
Bier* v. *Mines de Potasse d'Alsace
Court of Justice of the European Communities
Case 21/76, [1976] ECR 1735

Background

In this case, a Dutch nurseryman sued a French mining company in the Netherlands. The latter had poured waste matter into the Rhine in France and this polluted the river to such an extent that, when the claimant drew water from the river downstream in the Netherlands in order to water his flower beds, it would have killed the plants if it had not been subject to a special purification process. The proceedings were brought to recover the cost of purification.

The alleged wrongful act of the defendant, the pouring of the pollutant into the river, took place in France. The harm suffered by the claimant occurred in the Netherlands. The claimant argued that the 'harmful event' was the loss suffered by him, while the defendant claimed that it was the alleged wrongful act. If it was the former, the Dutch courts would have jurisdiction under Article 5(3) of the Convention; if it was the latter, they would not.

Judgment

[After discussing the basic scheme of the Convention, the court continued:]

12. Thus in matters of tort, delict or quasi-delict Article 5 (3) allows the plaintiff to bring his case before the courts for 'the place where the harmful event occurred'.
13. In the context of the Convention, the meaning of that expression is unclear when the place of the event which is at the origin of the damage is situated in a State other than the one in which the place where the damage occurred is situated, as is the case *inter alia* with atmospheric or water pollution beyond the frontiers of a State.
14. The form of words 'place where the harmful event occurred', used in all the language versions of the Convention, leaves open the question whether, in the situation described, it is necessary, in determining jurisdiction, to choose as the connecting factor the place of the event giving rise to the damage, or the place where the damage occurred, or to accept that the plaintiff has an option between the one and the other of those two connecting factors.
15. As regards this, it is well to point out that the place of the event giving rise to the damage no less than the place where the damage occurred can, depending on the case, constitute a significant connecting factor from the point of view of jurisdiction.
16. Liability in tort, delict or quasi-delict can only arise provided that a causal connexion can be established between the damage and the event in which that damage originates.

17. Taking into account the close connexion between the component parts of every sort of liability, it does not appear appropriate to opt for one of the two connecting factors mentioned to the exclusion of the other, since each of them can, depending on the circumstances, be particularly helpful from the point of view of the evidence and of the conduct of the proceedings.

18. To exclude one option appears all the more undesirable in that, by its comprehensive form of words, Article 5 (3) of the Convention covers a wide diversity of kinds of liability.

19. Thus the meaning of the expression 'place where the harmful event occurred' in Article 5 (3) must be established in such a way as to acknowledge that the plaintiff has an option to commence proceedings either at the place where the damage occurred or the place of the event giving rise to it.

20. This conclusion is supported by the consideration, first, that to decide in favour only of the place of the event giving rise to the damage would, in an appreciable number of cases, cause confusion between the heads of jurisdiction laid down by Articles 2 and 5 (3) of the Convention, so that the latter provision would, to that extent, lose its effectiveness.

21. Secondly, a decision in favour only of the place where the damage occurred would, in cases where the place of the event giving rise to the damage does not coincide with the domicile of the person liable, have the effect of excluding a helpful connecting factor with the jurisdiction of a court particularly near to the cause of the damage.

22. Moreover, it appears from a comparison of the national legislative provisions and national case law on the distribution of jurisdiction – both as regards internal relationships, as between courts for different areas, and in international relationships – that, albeit by differing legal techniques, a place is found for both of the two connecting factors here considered and that in several States they are accepted concurrently.

23. In these circumstances, the interpretation stated above has the advantage of avoiding any upheaval in the solutions worked out in the various national systems of law, since it looks to unification, in conformity with Article 5 (3) of the Convention, by way of a systematization of solutions which, as to their principle, have already been established in most of the States concerned.

24. Thus it should be answered that where the place of the happening of the event which may give rise to liability in tort, delict or quasi-delict and the place where that event results in damage are not identical, the expression 'place where the harmful event occurred', in Article 5(3) of the Convention, must be understood as being intended to cover both the place where the damage occurred and the place of the event giving rise to it.

25. The result is that the defendant may be sued, at the option of the plaintiff, either in the courts for the place where the damage occurred or in the courts for the place of the event which gives rise to and is at the origin of that damage.

Comment

This generous rule should be particularly valuable to claimants in products-liability actions, since it would make clear that a person injured by a defective product could bring his action where the injury took place.

In a later case, *Dumez* v. *Hessische Landesbank*,[23] the European Court imposed a limitation on the rule. A German bank had allegedly caused harm to the German subsidiary of a French company. As a result, the subsidiary became bankrupt and the parent suffered loss. The parent sued the bank in France and claimed that the French courts had jurisdiction under Article 5(3). It argued that its loss (the diminution in value of its shares in its subsidiary) was felt in France. The European Court, however, held that the rule laid down in *Bier* v. *Mines de Potasse* applies only to harm directly suffered as a result of the wrongful act. The direct harm in the *Dumez* case had of course been suffered in Germany by the subsidiary: that suffered by the parent was indirect; consequently, the French courts had no jurisdiction under Article 5(3).

Our next case develops this principle further.

European Community
Marinari* v. *Lloyds Bank
Court of Justice of the European Communities
Case C-364/93, [1995] ECR I-2719

Background

This case arose when an Italian, Mr Marinari, walked into the Manchester branch of Lloyds Bank and presented the bank with promissory notes to the value of US$752 million made by a provincial government in the Philippines in favour of a Beirut company. Not surprisingly, the bank called the police. They arrested Mr Marinari, though he was later released. It seems that the police kept the promissory notes.

Mr Marinari returned to Italy where he sued Lloyds Bank. His claims included damages for loss of the promissory notes, for his arrest and for harm to his reputation. He argued that the damage took place in Italy where his reputation and his bank account were situated. The Italian *Corte Suprema di Cassazione* (Supreme Court of Cassation) made a reference to the European Court, asking it whether the rule in the *Bier* case was limited to physical harm to the person or to property or whether it also covered economic loss.

Judgment

[After referring to the *Bier* case and the *Shevill* case (discussed in Chapter 11, § 2.2, below), the court continued:]

12. In those two judgments, the Court considered that the place of the event giving rise to the damage no less than the place where the damage occurred could constitute a significant connecting factor from the point of view of jurisdiction. It added that to decide in favour only of the place of the event giving rise to the damage would, in an appreciable number of cases,

---

23 Case C-220/88, [1990] ECR I-49.

cause confusion between the heads of jurisdiction laid down by Articles 2 and 5(3) of the Convention, so that the latter provision would, to that extent, lose its effectiveness.

13.   The choice thus available to the plaintiff cannot however be extended beyond the particular circumstances which justify it. Such extension would negate the general principle laid down in the first paragraph of Article 2 of the Convention that the courts of the Contracting State where the defendant is domiciled are to have jurisdiction. It would lead, in cases other than those expressly provided for, to recognition of the jurisdiction of the courts of the plaintiff's domicile, a solution which the Convention does not favour since, in the second paragraph of Article 3, it excludes application of national provisions which make such jurisdiction available for proceedings against defendants domiciled in the territory of a Contracting State.

14.   While it has thus been recognized that the term 'place where the harmful event occurred' within the meaning of Article 5(3) of the Convention may cover both the place where the damage occurred and the place of the event giving rise to it, that term cannot be construed so extensively as to encompass any place where the adverse consequences can be felt of an event which has already caused damage actually arising elsewhere.

[After rejecting certain arguments put forward by the German Government, the court concluded:]

21.   The answer to the national court's question should therefore be that the term 'place where the harmful event occurred' in Article 5(3) of the [Brussels] Convention does not, on a proper interpretation, cover the place where the victim claims to have suffered financial damage following upon initial damage arising and suffered by him in another Contracting State.

QUESTIONS

1 A German driver goes to France on holiday. He there injures a British tourist. The latter returns to England, where he suffers pain, incurs medical expenses and financial losses (he is self-employed and cannot work because of the accident) and is permanently disabled. Can he sue the driver in England under Article 5(3)?[24]

2 A British company manufactures a machine, which it sells to a retailer in England. A Spanish businessman buys it from the retailer and takes it back to Spain, where he uses it. He is injured owing to a defect in the machine. Can he sue the British manufacturer in tort in Spain?

3 Do arguments based on foreseeability justify different results in these two cases?

---

[24] For the position in Canadian law, see *Muscutt* v. *Courcelles* (2002) 213 DLR (4th) 577 (Ontario CA), set out in Chapter 6, § 3, below.

§ 1.3 Branches, agencies and other establishments

Article 5(5) is concerned with the situation in which a person or company domiciled in one Contracting State has a branch, agency or other establishment (all three concepts are hereinafter referred to as a 'subordinate establishment') in another Contracting State. Article 5(5) grants jurisdiction, in a dispute arising out of the operations of the subordinate establishment, to the courts for the place in which it is situated (Panel 4.4). Article 5(5) applies where the action is against the parent, not the subordinate establishment. If the subordinate establishment has separate legal personality and the action is brought against it, Article 5(5) would be inapplicable. However, since the subordinate establishment would normally be domiciled within the territory of the forum, it would be unnecessary to resort to Article 5.

> **Panel 4.4 Branch, agency or other establishment**
> **Brussels I Regulation (Regulation 44/2001), Article 5(5)**
>
> **Article 5(5)**
>
> A person domiciled in a Member State may, in another Member State, be sued:
>
> ...
> 5. as regards a dispute arising out of the operations of a branch, agency or other establishment, in the courts for the place in which the branch, agency or other establishment is situated . . .

§ 1.3.1 What constitutes a branch, agency or other establishment? According to the European Court, the branch must be subject to the control of the head office,[25] and it must hold itself out as an extension of the latter. In a later case, it said the following:[26]

> The concept of branch, agency or other establishment implies a place of business which has the appearance of permanency, such as the extension of a parent body, has a management and is materially equipped to negotiate business with third parties so that the latter, although knowing that there will if necessary be a legal link with the parent body, the head office of which is abroad, do not have to deal directly with such parent body but may transact business at the place of business constituting the extension.

This means that normally there must be an office.

In *Blanckaert and Willems* v. *Trost*,[27] the European Court had to decide whether an independent representative is to be regarded as an agent for the purpose of Article 5(5). In this case, a Belgian company appointed a sales representative in Germany to sell its product. The German representative was not an employee of the parent company and was able to organize the main aspects of his work without being subject to instructions from the head office. He was free to represent competitors and he had no effective say in the conduct of the business: he merely passed orders back to the head office, which was responsible for filling them. On these facts, the European Court held that the representative

---

25 *De Bloos* v. *Bouyer*, Case 14/76, [1976] ECR 1497. See, however, *SAR Schotte* v. *Parfums Rothschild*, Case 218/86, [1987] ECR 4905, in which the European Court held that a parent company can constitute a branch, agent or other establishment of its subsidiary if it holds itself out to third parties as acting on behalf of the subsidiary.
26 *Somafer* v. *Saar-Ferngas*, Case 33/78, [1978] ECR 2183, paragraph 2 of the ruling.
27 Case 139/80, [1981] ECR 819.

was not an agent of the company for the purpose of Article 5(5). This decision is in line with the English cases on the point, discussed in Chapter 5, § 3.3, below.[28]

§ 1.3.2 What disputes are covered? Article 5(5) applies only to disputes arising out of the activities of the branch, agency or other establishment. In the first case in which it considered the matter, *Somafer* v. *Saar-Ferngas*,[29] the European Court did not define what disputes are covered, but merely gave examples:[30]

> The concept of 'operations' comprises:
>
> – actions relating to rights and contractual or non-contractual obligations concerning the management properly so-called of the agency, branch or other establishment itself such as those concerning the situation of the building where such entity is established or the local engagement of staff to work there;
> – actions relating to undertakings which have been entered into at the above-mentioned place of business in the name of the parent body and which must be performed in the Contracting State where the place of business is established and also actions concerning non-contractual obligations arising from the activities in which the branch, agency or other establishment within the above defined meaning, has engaged at the place in which it is established on behalf of the parent body.

What is remarkable about these examples is that the courts for the place where the local office is situated will almost always have jurisdiction on other grounds as well. An employment contract with local staff would, at the time of the case, have been covered by Article 5(1);[31] an agreement to rent or buy office space would be covered by Article 22(1);[32] contracts entered into by the local office and to be performed in the State in question would be covered by Article 5(1); and torts resulting from activities by the local entity would be covered by Article 5(3). In all these situations, Article 5(5) would add almost nothing to the other provisions of the Convention. In view of this, it is hardly surprising that the European Court has since gone further.

European Community
Lloyd's Register of Shipping* v. *Campenon Bernard
Court of Justice of the European Communities
Case C-439/93, [1995] ECR I-961

Background

In this case, the French branch of Lloyd's Register, an English charity, agreed with a French company that Lloyd's Register (acting through its Spanish branch) would inspect goods in Spain and report on whether they met a certain technical

---

28 *Saccharin Corporation* v. *Chemische Fabrik von Heyden* [1911] 2 KB 516 (CA); *Okura* v. *Forsbacka Jernverks* [1914] 1 KB 715 (CA).
29 Case 33/78, [1978] ECR 2183.
30 Paragraph 3 of the ruling.
31 Today, it would usually come under Articles 19 and 20 of the Regulation.
32 Article 22(1) of the Regulation is equivalent to Article 16(1) of the Convention.

standard. The Spanish branch carried out the tests and certified that the goods complied with the standard. It subsequently turned out that they did not. The French company wanted to sue Lloyd's Register for damages. It brought proceedings in the French courts on the basis of Article 5(5). The French *Cour de Cassation* made a reference to the European Court to ask whether this was possible.

Judgment

12. Lloyd's Register contends that in its judgment in Case 33/78 *Somafer v. Saar Ferngas* [1978] ECR 2183, at paragraph 13, the Court held that the rule set out in Article 5(5) applies to actions relating to undertakings which have been entered into by that establishment in the name of the parent body, provided that they are to be performed in the Contracting State of the ancillary establishment.

13. According to Lloyd's Register, such a requirement as to place is in accordance with the interests of the proper administration of justice which underlie the provision. It is aimed at enabling an action that has its origin in the actual activities of a branch to be heard by the courts for the place in which it is situated on practical and evidential grounds.

14. Moreover, it states, since an ancillary establishment may not confine itself to transmitting orders to its parent body but must also take part in their performance, and in that connection the range of activity of an ancillary establishment is naturally confined to the territory of the Contracting State in which it has been set up, jurisdiction under Article 5(5) is justified only where the undertakings in question entered into by the ancillary establishment in the name of its parent body are to be performed on the territory of the Contracting State in which it is situated.

15. That argument cannot be accepted.

16. First, the actual wording of Article 5(5) of the Convention in no way requires that the undertakings negotiated by a branch should be performed in the Contracting State in which it is established in order for them to form part of its operations.

17. Secondly, the interpretation put forward by the appellant in the main proceedings would render Article 5(5) almost wholly redundant. Since Article 5(1) already allows the plaintiff to bring an action in contract in the courts for the place of performance of the obligation in question, Article 5(5) would duplicate that provision if it applied solely to undertakings entered into by a branch which were to be performed in the Contracting State in which the branch was established. At the very most it would create a second head of special jurisdiction where, within the Contracting State of the branch, the place of performance of the obligation in question was situated in a judicial area other than that of the branch.

18. Thirdly, it should be noted that an ancillary establishment is a place of business which has the appearance of permanency such as the extension of a parent body, has a management and is equipped to negotiate business with third parties so that the latter, although knowing that there will if necessary be a legal link with the parent body, whose seat is in another

19. Contracting State, do not have to deal directly with such parent body (see *Somafer*, cited above, at paragraph 12).

19. A branch, agency or other ancillary establishment within the meaning of Article 5(5) is therefore an entity capable of being the principal, or even exclusive, interlocutor for third parties in the negotiation of contracts.

20. There does not necessarily have to be a close link between the entity with which a customer conducts negotiations and places an order and the place where the order will be performed. Accordingly, undertakings may form part of the operations of an ancillary establishment within the meaning of Article 5(5) of the Convention even though they are to be performed outside the Contracting State where it is situated, possibly by another ancillary establishment.

21. That interpretation is, moreover, in conformity with the objective of the special rules of jurisdiction. As the Jenard Report (OJ 1979 C 59, at p. 22) makes clear, those rules allow the plaintiff to sue the defendant in courts other than those of his domicile because there is a specially close connecting factor between the dispute and the court with jurisdiction to resolve it.

22. In the light of the foregoing considerations, the answer to the question referred by the Cour de Cassation must be that the expression 'dispute arising out of the operations of a branch, agency or other establishment' in Article 5(5) of the Convention does not presuppose that the undertakings in question entered into by the branch in the name of its parent body are to be performed in the Contracting State in which the branch is established.

Subsequently, the English courts went even further still.

England
Anton Durbeck* v. *Den Norske Bank
Court of Appeal
[2003] 2 WLR 1296

Background

The defendant in this case was a Norwegian bank. Acting through its London branch, it had entered into a loan agreement with the owners of a ship, the loan being secured by a charge on the ship. The owners defaulted, and the bank, acting through its London branch, took steps to arrest the ship to enforce the charge. The arrest took place in Panama. The ship had a cargo of bananas, which perished as a result of the arrest. The bananas belonged to the claimants, who claimed that the bank was responsible for the loss. Could they sue the bank in tort in England under Article 5(5)?

Since the defendant was domiciled in Norway, the Lugano Convention was the relevant instrument. References to the European Court are not possible in such cases; however, previous decisions of the European Court on the Brussels

Convention or the Brussels I Regulation are always followed unless there is a difference in the wording of the Lugano Convention.

Lord Phillips of Worth Maltravers MR

[After referring to the decisions of the European Court mentioned above, Lord Phillips continued:]

40. In my judgment, the decision in the *Lloyd's Register* case . . . robs the geographical limit in the *Somafer* case . . . of such authority as it might otherwise have had, bearing in mind that it was an *obiter dictum* on a matter not referred to the court and in respect of which no submissions had been made to it. This must be true of claims in tort as well as claims in contract. What the *Lloyd's Register* case . . . demonstrates is that there must be such nexus between the branch and the dispute as to render it natural to describe the dispute as one which has arisen out of the activities of the branch. Where the claim is in contract, that nexus can be derived from the negotiations between the claimant and the branch which gave rise to the contractual obligation, the alleged breach of which is the subject of the dispute. Where the claim is in tort or delict, there will be no such nexus.

41. The events which give rise to liability in tort can vary widely – compare the liability of the publishers of a defamatory book with the vicarious liability of a company for the negligent driving of an employee in the course of his employment. In these circumstances, I do not think it desirable to attempt to formulate any test to determine whether a dispute has arisen out of the activities of a branch. The answer to that question must depend on the facts of the individual case. I would, however, venture some general observations.

42. As Laws LJ observed in the course of argument, paragraph 5 of article 5 differs from the other paragraphs of that article. The other paragraphs address different specific causes of action. Paragraph 5 is of general application. It would seem designed to cover situations where the connection of the claim with the activities of the branch, agency or other establishment is such as to make it appropriate in the interests of the due administration of justice to permit suit to be brought in the state where the branch, agency or other establishment is situated.

43. I would endorse the conclusions of the Advocate General in the *Lloyd's Register* case . . . that one purpose of article 5(5) is to approximate the place where a branch carries on business with third parties to the point of departure of the first paragraph of article 2. Article 5(5) provides a quasi-defendant's domicile basis for jurisdiction. Once the existence of an entity which qualifies as a 'branch, agency or other establishment' of the defendant is established in a state, it accords with the due administration of justice from the view point of the defendant, the claimant and the court to permit suit to be brought in that state in relation to disputes which arise out of the activities of the branch, agency or establishment, regardless of where those activities take effect.

44. I have set out positive reasons for giving article 5(5) a meaning which is not subject to the geographical limitation suggested by the court in the *Somafer* case . . . There are, however, powerful negative reasons which point in the same direction. In the *Lloyd's Register* case . . . which was a case involving contract, the court observed that the *Somafer* interpretation would render article 5(5) almost wholly redundant having regard to the provisions of article 5(1). Advocate General Elmer made a similar observation in relation to matters relating to tort, delict or quasi-delict, having regard to the provisions of article 5(3). The only such claim that Mr Parsons could suggest in respect of which, on his interpretation, article 5(5) would make a difference was a claim in restitution.

45. In considering the application of article 5(5), the judge considered it pertinent to compare the connection between the dispute and London with the connection between the dispute and Panama. Mr Meeson suggested that this was not a helpful comparison. Rather, the judge should have compared the connection between the dispute and London with the connection between the dispute and Norway. Had he done so, he would have reached the conclusion that this was a case in which it could properly be said that the dispute arose out of the activities of the defendants' London branch.

46. I think that Mr Meeson is correct. The actions giving rise to the dispute arose out of London banking business, conducted by the defendants' London branch. The loan in respect of which the security over the vessel was taken was negotiated in London. The decision to enforce the security was taken in London. The London branch gave instructions to enforce the security and the power of attorney to enable it to be done. Giving the words of article 5(5) their natural meaning, the dispute in this case has arisen out of the activities of the London branch. It is true that in this case these factors do not point to London as the most convenient forum. If the jurisdiction to stay is soundly based, the action will be fought in Panama and not here. It seems to me, however, that if considerations of, or akin to, domicile are to govern the available forum, it makes good sense and accords with the due administration of justice that London should be available to the parties as an alternative to Norway.

Therefore, the English courts had jurisdiction under Article 5(5).[33]

§ 2 Multiple parties

Article 6(1) contains an important rule that applies where there are several defendants. Under it, a group of defendants domiciled in two or more of the

---

33 In the end the claimant lost: see *Anton Durbeck* v. *Den Norske Bank* [2005] EWHC 2497 (Comm); [2005] All ER (D) 158 (QBD).

Member States may all be sued in the courts of the Member State in which any one of them is domiciled (Panel 4.5).[34] This is to avoid having to split the proceedings. However, it can have strange consequences: if four Englishmen and a Spaniard commit a joint tort against an Englishman in England, they may all be sued in Spain. This sounds like a forum-shopper's charter. Nevertheless, England has a similar provision.[35] In the United States, on the other hand, such a rule would be unconstitutional: as we shall see in Chapter 7, in the United States the 'minimum contacts' doctrine must be satisfied separately with regard to *each* defendant.

Article 6(1) is concerned with the situation where the claimant wishes to sue two or more joint defendants. Article 6(2) is concerned with the case where the claimant sues one defendant and the latter wishes to bring in another defendant as a third party. This might occur where the first defendant considers that, if he is liable to the claimant, the second defendant should indemnify him. Article 6(2) provides that a defendant domiciled in a Member State may be sued in another Member State in third-party proceedings in the court seised of the original proceedings, 'unless these were instituted solely with the object of removing him from the jurisdiction of the court which would be competent in his case' (see Panel 4.5, above). Under Article 6(2), it is not necessary that the original defendant should be sued in the courts of his domicile: any ground of jurisdiction would be sufficient.[36] This form of jurisdiction would also be unconstitutional in the United States. Nevertheless, if it did not exist, the first defendant could be put in a difficult situation: if he was held liable, he would have to go to another court to claim indemnification, and that other court might not accept the ruling of the first court that he was liable.

The European Court has read the proviso to Article 6(2) ('unless these were instituted . . .') into Article 6(1). Our next case illustrates this, but is also important for another reason.

Panel 4.5 Multiple parties
Brussels I Regulation (Regulation 44/2001), Article 6

Article 6

A person domiciled in a Member State may also be sued:

1. where he is one of a number of defendants, in the courts for the place where any one of them is domiciled, provided the claims are so closely connected that it is expedient to hear and determine them together to avoid the risk of irreconcilable judgments resulting from separate proceedings;

2. as a third party in an action on a warranty or guarantee or in any other third party proceedings, in the court seised of the original proceedings, unless these were instituted solely with the object of removing him from the jurisdiction of the court which would be competent in his case . . .

---

34 The claims against all of them must be so closely connected that it is expedient to determine them together to avoid the risk of irreconcilable judgments resulting from separate proceedings: Article 6(1). See, further, *Kalfelis* v. *Schröder*, Case 189/87, [1988] ECR 5565.

35 CPR 6.36 and Practice Direction 6 B, paragraph 3.1(3). This goes further in one respect. It is not necessary that any of the defendants should be domiciled in England: all that is needed is that the English courts should have jurisdiction over one of them on some ground other than paragraph 3.1(3). Once this is established, paragraph 3.1(3) can be used to obtain jurisdiction over any other defendant who is a 'necessary or proper party' to the claim.

36 This might even include jurisdiction under national law: Hélène Gaudemet-Tallon, *Compétence et exécution des jugements en Europe* (LGDJ, Paris, 3rd edn 2002), paragraph 250, n. 11. Such an interpretation would be desirable on policy grounds. The purpose of the rule is to help the defendant: there is no reason why defendants domiciled outside the EC and Lugano States should suffer discrimination in this regard.

European Community
Reisch Montage v. *Kiesel Baumaschinen*
Court of Justice of the European Communities
Case C-103/05, [2006] ECR I-6827

Background

The claimant, Reisch Montage, was a company domiciled in Liechtenstein. It brought proceedings before an Austrian court against a man called Gisinger, who was domiciled in Austria. Kiesel, a company domiciled in Germany, was joined as co-defendant. The claim was for a debt, which was owed by Gisinger to Reisch Montage. Kiesel had guaranteed the debt. The problem was that, some six months earlier, bankruptcy proceedings had been commenced against Gisinger. Under Austrian law, this meant that proceedings against him to enforce a claim against his assets were barred. So the claim against him was struck out (declared inadmissible) by the Austrian court. This raised the question whether the court still had jurisdiction over Kiesel.

Judgment

26. As regards the special jurisdiction provided for in Article 6(1) of Regulation No. 44/2001, a defendant may be sued, where he is one of a number of defendants, in the courts for the place where any one of them is domiciled, provided 'the claims are so closely connected that it is expedient to hear and determine them together to avoid the risk of irreconcilable judgments resulting from separate proceedings'.

27. In that regard, it must be found, first, that that provision does not include any express reference to the application of domestic rules or any requirement that an action brought against a number of defendants should be admissible, by the time it is brought, in relation to each of those defendants under national law.

28. Second, independently of that first finding, the question referred seeks to determine whether a national rule introducing an objection of lack of jurisdiction may stand in the way of the application of Article 6(1) of Regulation No. 44/2001.

29. It is settled case law that the provisions of the regulation must be interpreted independently, by reference to its scheme and purpose . . .

30. Consequently, since it is not one of the provisions, such as Article 59 of Regulation No. 44/2001, for example, which provide expressly for the application of domestic rules and thus serve as a legal basis therefore, Article 6(1) of the Regulation cannot be interpreted in such a way as to make its application dependent on the effects of domestic rules.

31. In those circumstances, Article 6(1) of Regulation No. 44/2001 may be relied on in the context of an action brought in a Member State against a defendant domiciled in that State and a co-defendant domiciled in another Member State even when that action is regarded under a national provision as inadmissible from the time it is brought in relation to the first defendant.

32.   However, the special rule on jurisdiction provided for in Article 6(1) of
       Regulation No. 44/2001 cannot be interpreted in such a way as to allow
       a plaintiff to make a claim against a number of defendants for the sole
       purpose of removing one of them from the jurisdiction of the courts of the
       Member State in which that defendant is domiciled . . . However, this does
       not seem to be the case in the main proceedings.[37]
33.   In the light of all of the above considerations, the answer to the question
       referred must be that Article 6(1) of Regulation No. 44/2001 must be
       interpreted as meaning that, in a situation such as that in the main
       proceedings, that provision may be relied on in the context of an action
       brought in a Member State against a defendant domiciled in that State and
       a co-defendant domiciled in another Member State even when that action
       is regarded under a national provision as inadmissible from the time it is
       brought in relation to the first defendant.

Comment

The only justification for the ground of jurisdiction laid down in Article 6(1) is to
avoid splitting proceedings that ought to be decided together. This is why Article
6(1) says that there must be a risk of irreconcilable judgments if there are separate
proceedings. Since the claim against Gisinger had been struck out, there was no
such risk in the case before the court.[38] However, the court's statement in paragraph 32 of the judgment will go some of the way towards preventing abuse.

§ 3   Counterclaims

Article 6(3) permits a counterclaim to be brought in the court in which the
original claim is pending, provided it is based on the same contract or facts as
the original claim (Panel 4.6). A counterclaim is a new claim that is linked to a
claim already pending. It is similar to set-off in that it is based on another claim,
but it is different in that it is brought as an independent claim. A counterclaim
can result in a judgment for damages in favour of the party making it. Set-off,
on the other hand, is merely a defence: it can never result in such a judgment.
Since set-off is not a separate claim,
the question of jurisdiction does not
arise: the court hearing the proceedings in which it is raised always has
jurisdiction to hear a defence based on
set-off; however, the question whether
the defendant may raise the defence
depends on national law.[39]

Panel 4.6 Counterclaims
Brussels I Regulation (Regulation 44/2001), Article 6(3)

Article 6(3)
A person domiciled in a Member State may also be sued:
. . .
3.   on a counter-claim arising from the same contract or facts on
      which the original claim was based, in the court in which the
      original claim is pending . . .

---

37 *Editor's note:* it is not clear why the court thought that this was not the case. Perhaps the claimant did
not know, when it brought the proceedings, that Gisinger was bankrupt. In any event, as this is a question of
fact, it would be for the Austrian court to decide it.
38 This point was made by the German Government, but the court ignored it.
39 *Danværn Production* v. *Schuhfabriken Otterbeck*, Case C-341/93, [1995] ECR I-2053.

§ 4   Weak parties

It has already been mentioned that the Regulation gives special protection to parties regarded as economically weak. This is contained in the Sections on insurance,[40] consumer contracts[41] and individual contracts of employment.[42] We shall consider only the last of these. The other two are based on similar principles.

§ 4.1   Employment contracts

Most European legal systems take the view that employees, being in a weak bargaining position, need protection. Many countries have special tribunals for hearing employment cases and the normal rule is that jurisdiction is given to the tribunal for the place where the employee works. Usually this cannot be changed by means of a choice-of-court agreement.

Although the Brussels Convention has always had special rules to protect insured persons and consumers, it originally contained no such rules on employees. When the Brussels Convention was being drafted, it was intended to have special rules on employees, but these rules were dropped from the final version. The reason was that the Rome Convention (which dealt with choice of law in contractual matters) was being drafted at the same time and it had special rules on choice of law in employment contracts. It was thought desirable that jurisdiction should follow choice of law; consequently, it was decided to defer the adoption of jurisdictional rules on employees until the corresponding choice-of-law rules in the Rome Convention were finalized.

Thus, when the Brussels Convention was first adopted, it contained no special provisions on employment contracts: the normal rules applied. Moreover, a choice-of-court clause in the employment contract could give exclusive jurisdiction to the courts of any Contracting State, even one in which the employee had never worked.[43] Although the European Court never took any action on the latter point, it did create a special judge-made rule on the application of Article 5(1) to employment contracts. It held that, regardless of what the claim was, the 'obligation in question' in an employment contract was always to be regarded as the obligation of the employee to carry out his work. So the courts for the place of work always had jurisdiction under Article 5(1).[44] Thus, for example, if a German company employed someone to work in France, and the latter wished to sue his employer for unpaid wages, the courts of France would have jurisdiction, even if the wages were payable in Germany.[45]

This rule of judge-made law was subsequently adopted by the Contracting

---

40 Articles 8–14.
41 Articles 15–17.
42 Articles 18–21.
43 See *Sanicentral* v. *Collin*, Case 25/79, [1979] ECR 3423.
44 *Ivenel* v. *Schwab*, Case 133/81, [1982] ECR 1891.
45 *Ibid.*

States in an amendment to the Convention, where it constituted an exception to Article 5(1).[46] This provided that, in matters relating to individual contracts of employment, the place of performance was to be regarded as being the place where the employee habitually carried out his work. If the employee did not habitually carry out his work in any one country, the employer could be sued in the courts of the place where the business which engaged the employee 'was or is now situated'. These rules could not be changed by a choice-of-court agreement, unless it was entered into after the dispute had arisen or it was invoked by the employee, not the employer.[47]

This new provision was taken over (with a few modifications) by the Regulation, where it has been moved out of Article 5 and, as we have seen, put into a special section on individual contracts of employment (Section 5), where it consists of Articles 18–21 (Panel 4.7). Article 5(1) no longer applies to such contracts.[48]

The new provision has different rules depending on whether the employer is suing the employee or the employee is suing the employer. The latter are wider, in keeping with the policy of favouring the employee.

Panel 4.7 Individual contracts of employment
Brussels I Regulation (Regulation 44/2001), Articles 18–21

Article 18

1. In matters relating to individual contracts of employment, jurisdiction shall be determined by this Section, without prejudice to Article 4 and point 5 of Article 5.
2. Where an employee enters into an individual contract of employment with an employer who is not domiciled in a Member State but has a branch, agency or other establishment in one of the Member States, the employer shall, in disputes arising out of the operations of the branch, agency or establishment, be deemed to be domiciled in that Member State.

Article 19

An employer domiciled in a Member State may be sued:
  1. in the courts of the Member State where he is domiciled; or
  2. in another Member State:
    (a) in the courts for the place where the employee habitually carries out his work or in the courts for the last place where he did so, or
    (b) if the employee does not or did not habitually carry out his work in any one country, in the courts for the place where the business which engaged the employee is or was situated.

Article 20

1. An employer may bring proceedings only in the courts of the Member State in which the employee is domiciled.
2. The provisions of this Section shall not affect the right to bring a counter-claim in the court in which, in accordance with this Section, the original claim is pending.

Article 21

The provisions of this Section may be departed from only by an agreement on jurisdiction:
  1. which is entered into after the dispute has arisen; or
  2. which allows the employee to bring proceedings in courts other than those indicated in this Section.

---

46 See Article 4 of the 1989 Accession Convention.
47 Article 17, last paragraph, as amended by Article 7 of the 1989 Accession Convention.
48 Article 4 and Article 5(5) (disputes arising out of the operations of a branch, agency or other establishment of a person domiciled in another Member State) still apply to individual contracts of employment.

If the employer sues the employee, he may do so only in the courts of the Member State in which the employee is domiciled.[49] On the other hand, if the employee sues the employer, he has two options. Under Article 19(1), he may sue the employer in the courts of the Member State in which the employer is domiciled.[50] Alternatively, under Article 19(2), he may sue the employer:

- in the courts for the place where the he habitually carries out his work, or in the courts for the last place where he did so; or
- if he does not (or did not) habitually carry out his work in any one country, in the courts for the place where the business which engaged him is or was situated.

This provision, it will be seen, has two prongs. Under the first, jurisdiction is given to the courts for the place in which the employee habitually carries out his work. As the word 'habitually' makes clear, it is not necessary that all the work should be performed in one place. As long as the employee *habitually* works within the country concerned, it is irrelevant that the claim arose while he was temporarily employed elsewhere.[51]

If the first prong does not apply, the second comes into play. This allows the employee to sue the employer in the courts for the place where the business through which he was employed was situated. If the location of that business has been changed, the employee may sue where it was situated when the contract of employment was made or where it is situated at the time when the action is brought.[52]

The new provisions on employment contracts have not yet come before the European Court for scrutiny. There is, however, a case which, though it was decided under the Brussels Convention before it was amended, is of relevance to the new provisions, since it was based on the judge-made rule that was subsequently given statutory form in the Brussels I Regulation.

European Community
Mulox* v. *Geels
Court of Justice of the European Communities
Case C-125/92, [1993] ECR I-4075

Background

In this case, the employer was an English company and the employee, though domiciled in the Netherlands, was resident in France. The employee acted as a sales representative for the employer in Germany, Denmark and a number of other Continental countries. Originally, his sales territory did not include France, but, a few months before the dispute arose, it was changed to cover

---

49 Article 20(1).
50 Under Article 18(2), the employer who is not domiciled in any Member State but has a branch, agency or other establishment in one of the Member States is deemed to be domiciled in that Member State where the employment dispute arises out of the operations of that branch, agency or other establishment.
51 If he no longer habitually works anywhere, it is the place where he last did so.
52 This is the meaning of the words 'is or was situated'.

France only. At all times, he used his French residence as his office and that was his base for his selling activities. It was from there that he went out on sales trips, and it was to that base that customers were invited to send correspondence.

He was eventually dismissed and he brought an action against the employer in the French courts. Did Article 5(1) of the Brussels Convention give them jurisdiction? Though the Convention did not at the time have anything equivalent to Article 19 of the Regulation, the judge-made rule mentioned above[53] was applicable. Consequently, the issue was the same as it would be under Article 19: where did the employee work? The answer could depend on what one regarded as his real work: if visiting customers was what really mattered and the office activities were mere backup, one would not regard France as being the place of work until France became his sales territory. If, on the other hand, one looked at his activities as a whole, one might feel that, since they were centred in France, his real place of work was France – even before France became his sales territory.

Judgment

21. Where, as in this case, the work is performed in more than one Contracting State, it is important to interpret the Convention so as to avoid any multiplication of courts having jurisdiction, thereby precluding the risk of irreconcilable decisions and facilitating the recognition and enforcement of judgments in States other than those in which they were delivered . . .

22. In that connection, the Court has held that, where various obligations derive from the same contract and form the basis of the plaintiff's action, it is the principal obligation which must be relied on in order to determine jurisdiction . . .

23. It follows that Article 5(1) of the Convention cannot be interpreted as conferring concurrent jurisdiction on the courts of each Contracting State in whose territory the employee performs part of his work.[1]

24. Where the work entrusted to the employee is performed in the territory of more than one Contracting State, it is important to define the place of performance of the contractual obligation, within the meaning of Article 5(1) of the Convention, as being the place where or from which the employee principally discharges his obligations towards his employer.

25. In order to determine the place of performance, which is a matter for the national court, it is necessary to take account of the fact that, in this case, the work entrusted to the employee was carried out from an office in a Contracting State, where the employee had established his residence, from which he performed his work and to which he returned after each business trip. Furthermore, it is open to the national court to take account of the fact that, when the dispute before it arose, the employee was carrying out his work solely in the territory of that Contracting State. In the absence of other determining factors, that place must be deemed, for the purposes of Article

1 *Editor's note:* the reference to Article 5(1) of the Convention in this and the following paragraphs should now be read as a reference to Article 19(2) of the Regulation.

53 The rule in *Ivenel* v. *Schwab*.

> 5(1) of the Convention, to be the place of performance of the obligation on which a claim relating to a contract of employment is based.
>
> 26. It follows from all the foregoing considerations that Article 5(1) of the Convention must be interpreted as meaning that, in the case of a contract of employment in pursuance of which the employee performs his work in more than one Contracting State, the place of performance of the obligation characterizing the contract, within the meaning of that provision, is the place where or from which the employee principally discharges his obligations towards his employer.

Note

It is of interest that the Advocate General briefly considered the amended version of Article 5(1) and said that, in applying it, one should make a 'determined effort' to identify a principal or habitual place of employment in order to bring the case under the first prong of the exception, rather than allowing it to be decided by the second, which he regarded as unsatisfactory since it could lead to the application of a system of law having little connection with the dispute.[54] The same argument could apply with regard to Article 19(2) of the Regulation.

§ 5   Exclusive jurisdiction

Section 6 of Part II of the Regulation (Article 22) deals with exclusive jurisdiction (Panel 4.8). The particular feature of this provision is that it does two things: it grants jurisdiction to the courts specified in it, and it denies jurisdiction to all other courts, even the courts of the State in which the defendant is domiciled. Article 22 is in fact entirely independent of domicile: it applies just the same if the defendant is not domiciled in *any* Member State. It, therefore, constitutes an exception to the principle that the jurisdictional rules of the Regulation apply only if the defendant is domiciled in a Member State.

§ 5.1   Scope

The scope of Article 22 is quite limited. It covers proceedings concerning:

- rights *in rem* in, and tenancies of, immovable property;[55]
- the incorporation of companies and certain other aspects of company law;
- the validity of entries in public registers;
- the registration or validity of registered intellectual property rights;[56] and
- the enforcement of judgments.

---

54 *Per* Advocate General Jacobs, [1993] ECR at p. I-4097.
55 Under Article 6(4), contractual claims that may be combined with claims relating to rights *in rem* in immovable property may be brought in the appropriate court of the Member State in which the property is situated.
56 On this, see Chapter 12, § 1, below.

> **Panel 4.8 Exclusive jurisdiction**
> **Brussels I Regulation (Regulation 44/2001), Article 22**
>
> **Article 22**
> The following courts shall have exclusive jurisdiction, regardless of domicile:
> 1. in proceedings which have as their object rights *in rem* in immovable property or tenancies of immovable property, the courts of the Member State in which the property is situated.
>   However, in proceedings which have as their object tenancies of immovable property concluded for temporary private use for a maximum period of six consecutive months, the courts of the Member State in which the defendant is domiciled shall also have jurisdiction, provided that the tenant is a natural person and that the landlord and the tenant are domiciled in the same Member State;
> 2. in proceedings which have as their object the validity of the constitution, the nullity or the dissolution of companies or other legal persons or associations of natural or legal persons, or of the validity of the decisions of their organs, the courts of the Member State in which the company, legal person or association has its seat. In order to determine that seat, the court shall apply its rules of private international law;
> 3. in proceedings which have as their object the validity of entries in public registers, the courts of the Member State in which the register is kept;
> 4. in proceedings concerned with the registration or validity of patents, trade marks, designs, or other similar rights required to be deposited or registered, the courts of the Member State in which the deposit or registration has been applied for, has taken place or is under the terms of a Community instrument or an international convention deemed to have taken place.
>   Without prejudice to the jurisdiction of the European Patent Office under the Convention on the Grant of European Patents, signed at Munich on 5 October 1973, the courts of each Member State shall have exclusive jurisdiction, regardless of domicile, in proceedings concerned with the registration or validity of any European patent granted for that State;
> 5. in proceedings concerned with the enforcement of judgments, the courts of the Member State in which the judgment has been or is to be enforced.

The European Court generally interprets these concepts narrowly. Thus, a contract for the sale of a retail business would not be covered, even if the purchaser agreed to pay the rent of the premises in which the business operated.[57]

In our next case, the European Court had to decide whether proceedings concerning equitable rights in land are covered.

European Community
Webb v. *Webb*
Court of Justice of the European Communities
Case C-294/92, [1994] ECR I-1733; [1994] 3 WLR 801

Background

This case concerned a dispute between father and son. The father bought a flat in the south of France in 1971, when exchange control was still in force in the United Kingdom. Exchange-control permission was obtained in the name of the son. The father paid for the property, but it was registered in the son's name. Subsequently, the father and son fell out, and the father brought proceedings against the son in England for a declaration that the latter held the property on trust for the father. The father also sought an order that the son should do whatever was necessary under French law to have the property registered in the father's name. At the time the case was decided, the Brussels Convention was in

---

57 *Sanders* v. *Van der Putte*, Case 73/77, [1977] ECR 2383.

force. The equivalent provision in the Convention was Article 16(1), which was worded identically to Article 22(1) of the Regulation.

Judgment

15.   The aim of the proceedings before the national court is to obtain a declaration that the son holds the flat for the exclusive benefit of the father and that in that capacity he is under a duty to execute the documents necessary to convey ownership of the flat to the father. The father does not claim that he already enjoys rights directly relating to the property which are enforceable against the whole world, but seeks only to assert rights as against the son. Consequently, his action is not an action *in rem* within the meaning of Article 16(1) of the Convention but an action *in personam*.

16.   Nor are considerations relating to the proper administration of justice underlying Article 16(1) of the Convention applicable in this case.

17.   As the Court has held, the conferring of exclusive jurisdiction in the matter of rights *in rem* in immovable property on the courts of the State in which the property is situated is justified because actions concerning rights *in rem* in immovable property often involve disputes frequently necessitating checks, inquiries and expert assessments which must be carried out on the spot (see the judgment in Case 73/77 *Sanders v. Van der Putte* [1977] ECR 2383, at paragraph 13).

18.   As the father and the United Kingdom rightly point out, the immovable nature of the property held in trust and its location are irrelevant to the issues to be determined in the main proceedings which would have been the same if the dispute had concerned a flat situated in the United Kingdom or a yacht.

19.   The answer to be given to the question submitted to the Court must therefore be that an action for a declaration that a person holds immovable property as trustee and for an order requiring that person to execute such documents as should be required to vest the legal ownership in the plaintiff does not constitute an action *in rem* within the meaning of Article 16(1) of the Convention.

Comment

A different ruling would have required the French courts to grapple with difficult legal concepts to decide a controversy that really had nothing to do with France.

§ 5.2   Non-member States

The purpose of Article 22 is not to protect the interests of the defendant, but to protect the interests of the State which has exclusive jurisdiction.[58] This explains

---

[58] This is shown by the fact that a defendant cannot give a court jurisdiction if it is precluded from hearing the case under Article 22. Thus, Article 24 (discussed in § 6, below) does not apply where another court has exclusive jurisdiction under Article 22; moreover, a choice-of-court agreement is invalid if it conflicts with Article 22: Article 23(5).

why Article 22 applies irrespective of domicile. However, the Regulation is not interested in protecting the interests of non-member (or non-Lugano) States. Consequently, Article 22 applies only when the court with exclusive jurisdiction is situated in an EC (or Lugano) State.

It is not clear what happens when the courts of a State other than an EC or Lugano State would have had jurisdiction if Article 22 had applied to them. Assume that the defendant is domiciled in England and the case is concerned with rights *in rem* in land in Australia. Is the English court required to give up jurisdiction in favour of the Australian courts?[59] Is it even *permitted* to do so? The answer is unclear. In *Owusu* v. *Jackson*,[60] the English Court of Appeal asked the European Court these questions, but the latter did not answer them.[61]

§ 6   Procedure

Articles 24–26 of the Regulation contain provisions of a procedural nature. Article 24 (Panel 4.9) provides that, unless he entered it to contest jurisdiction, the entry of an appearance by a defendant itself gives the court jurisdiction.[62] The purpose of this rule is to force the defendant to contest jurisdiction as soon as he is able to do so.[63] He cannot fight the case on the merits and then, if he loses, claim that the court never had jurisdiction.[64]

Article 25 (Panel 4.10) provides that, when a court is seised of a case principally concerning a matter over which the court of another Member State has exclusive jurisdiction under Article 22, it must of its own motion declare that it has no jurisdiction. This rule follows from the fact that the primary purpose of Article 22 is to protect the interests

> **Panel 4.9 Submission**
> **Brussels I Regulation (Regulation 44/2001), Article 24**
>
> **Article 24**
>
> Apart from jurisdiction derived from other provisions of this Regulation, a court of a Member State before which a defendant enters an appearance shall have jurisdiction. This rule shall not apply where appearance was entered to contest the jurisdiction, or where another court has exclusive jurisdiction by virtue of Article 22.

---

59 For the traditional English rules on this point, see Chapter 5, § 7, below.
60 Case C-281/02, [2005] ECR I-1383.
61 See, further, Chapter 10, § 2, below.
62 This rule does not apply if another court has exclusive jurisdiction under Article 22. It does, however, apply if another court has exclusive jurisdiction under a choice-of-court agreement: *Elefanten Schuh* v. *Jacqmain*, Case 150/80, [1981] ECR 1671 (paragraph 1 of the ruling).
63 Despite the use of the word 'solely' in the English text of Article 18 of the Brussels Convention (the equivalent provision to Article 24 of the Regulation), the European Court has held that entering an appearance and pleading to the merits does not confer jurisdiction if *at the same time* the defendant contests jurisdiction: *Elefanten Schuh* v. *Jacqmain*, Case 150/80, [1981] ECR 1671 (paragraph 2 of the ruling). It seems that, in some Member States, a defendant who contests the jurisdiction of the court, without at the same time pleading to the substance, loses the right to defend the case on the merits if the jurisdictional point goes against him. It was for this reason, and also because the French text omitted the word 'solely', that the European Court gave the ruling it did.
64 The most important consequence of this rule is that it prevents the defendant from raising the jurisdictional point for the first time on appeal. The rule would not often apply in enforcement proceedings, since, once the enforcement stage is reached, it is not normally possible to challenge the jurisdiction of the court of origin. There are, however, exceptions. One such exception is where a court other than the court of origin had exclusive jurisdiction under Article 22. However, Article 24 does not apply in such a case. The rules on insurance and consumer contracts are also exceptions and in these cases Article 24 *does* apply. Consequently, an insured person or a consumer, who fails to challenge the jurisdiction of the court of origin when first able to do so, will not be able to challenge it when enforcement proceedings are brought.

Panel 4.10 Examination as to jurisdiction
Article 22: Brussels I Regulation (Regulation 44/2001),
Article 25

Article 25

Where a court of a Member State is seised of a claim which is
principally concerned with a matter over which the courts of another
Member State have exclusive jurisdiction by virtue of Article 22, it shall
declare of its own motion that it has no jurisdiction.

Panel 4.11 Examination as to jurisdiction: service
Brussels I Regulation (Regulation 44/2001), Article 26

Article 26

1. Where a defendant domiciled in one Member State is sued in a
   court of another Member State and does not enter an appearance,
   the court shall declare of its own motion that it has no jurisdiction
   unless its jurisdiction is derived from the provisions of this
   Regulation.
2. The court shall stay the proceedings so long as it is not shown that
   the defendant has been able to receive the document instituting the
   proceedings or an equivalent document in sufficient time to enable
   him to arrange for his defence, or that all necessary steps have been
   taken to this end.
3. Article 19 of Council Regulation (EC) No 1348/2000 of 29 May 2000
   on the service in the Member States of judicial and extrajudicial
   documents in civil or commercial matters (10) shall apply instead
   of the provisions of paragraph 2 if the document instituting the
   proceedings or an equivalent document had to be transmitted from
   one Member State to another pursuant to this Regulation.
4. Where the provisions of Regulation (EC) No 1348/2000 are not
   applicable, Article 15 of the Hague Convention of 15 November
   1965 on the Service Abroad of Judicial and Extrajudicial Documents
   in Civil or Commercial Matters shall apply if the document instituting
   the proceedings or an equivalent document had to be transmitted
   pursuant to that Convention.

of the State with exclusive jurisdiction, not to protect the interests of the defendant. It will be remembered that a defendant cannot confer jurisdiction on a court in such a case by means of a choice-of-court agreement[65] or by entering an appearance without challenging the jurisdiction of the court.[66]

Article 26, on the other hand, *is* intended to protect the interests of the defendant (Panel 4.11). The first paragraph provides that, where a defendant domiciled in another Member State does not enter an appearance, the court must of its own motion declare that it has no jurisdiction, unless its jurisdiction is derived from the provisions of the Regulation. If the defendant is not before the court and therefore unable to speak up for himself, the court must itself ensure that it has jurisdiction over him.

The remaining paragraphs of Article 26 are concerned with service of the claim form. In the Community, the mechanism for doing this is provided by another regulation, Regulation 1348/2000,[67] sometimes known as the Service Regulation, which operates when a claim form or other document has to be transmitted from one Member State[68] to another for service in the latter. Service is carried out through official channels: the claim form is delivered to a 'transmitting agency' in the State of origin, which sends it to a 'receiving agency' in the State in which service is to be effected. The latter has it served, and provides a certificate establishing that this has been done.

Although the Service Regulation is the normal means of serving a claim form in another Member State, service may also (in at least some cases)[69] be

---

65 Article 23(5).
66 Article 24.
67 OJ 2000 L 160, p. 37. It was largely based on an EC convention of 1997, which never came into force: OJ 1997 C 261, p. 1. For the Report on the latter (helpful for understanding the Service Regulation), see OJ 1997 C 261, p. 26.
68 It does not apply to Denmark.
69 The Regulation does not authorize service to be effected in a way that is contrary to the law of the State in which it takes place: see (with regard to the EC Service Convention of 1997) OJ 1997 C 261, p. 26 (commentary on Article 15).

effected through diplomatic or consular agents,[70] by post,[71] or 'directly through the judicial officers, officials or other competent persons of the Member State addressed'.[72] Where this is the case, the Service Regulation will not apply. It will also be inapplicable where the address of the recipient is unknown,[73] or if service has to be effected outside the Community. However, a similar system is laid down by the Hague Service Convention,[74] which was adopted in 1965, many years before the Service Regulation.[75] The Hague Convention, which is in force in many countries throughout the world, served as a model for the Service Regulation.

Under the second paragraph of Article 26 of the Brussels I Regulation (Panel 4.11, above), a court hearing a case must stay the proceedings unless and until it is shown that the defendant has received the claim form, or that all necessary steps have been taken to this end. However, the third and fourth paragraphs provide that, where the Service Regulation or the Hague Service Convention applies, the provisions of the latter instruments apply instead. These lay down similar requirements, though they are more complex. The relevant provisions (Article 19 of the Regulation and Articles 15 and 16 of the Convention) are identical in substance.[76] Article 19 of the Regulation is set out in Panel 4.12.

Panel 4.12 Examination as to jurisdiction: service
Service Regulation (Regulation 1348/2000), Article 19

Article 19 Defendant not entering an appearance

1. Where a writ of summons or an equivalent document has had to be transmitted to another Member State for the purpose of service, under the provisions of this Regulation, and the defendant has not appeared, judgment shall not be given until it is established that:
   (a) the document was served by a method prescribed by the internal law of the Member State addressed for the service of documents in domestic actions upon persons who are within its territory; or
   (b) the document was actually delivered to the defendant or to his residence by another method provided for by this Regulation;
   and that in either of these cases the service or the delivery was effected in sufficient time to enable the defendant to defend.
2. Each Member State shall be free to make it known, in accordance with Article 23(1), that the judge, notwithstanding the provisions of paragraph 1, may give judgment even if no certificate of service or delivery has been received, if all the following conditions are fulfilled:
   (a) the document was transmitted by one of the methods provided for in this Regulation;
   (b) a period of time of not less than six months, considered adequate by the judge in the particular case, has elapsed since the date of the transmission of the document;

---

70 Article 13(1) of Regulation 1348/2000. Article 13(2), however, provides that a Member State may make it known that it is opposed to such service within its territory, unless the document is to be served on a national of the Member State in which the document originates.
71 Article 14(1) of Regulation 1348/2000. Article 14(2), however, provides that a Member State may specify the conditions under which it will accept service by post.
72 Article 15(1) of Regulation 1348/2000. Article 15(2), however, provides that a Member State may make it known that it is opposed to such service within its territory.
73 Article 1(1) of Regulation 1348/2000.
74 Hague Convention on the Service Abroad of Judicial and Extrajudicial Documents in Civil or Commercial Matters of 15 November 1965, available on the website of the Hague Conference on Private International Law, www.hcch.net.
75 Article 20(1) of the Service Regulation provides that it prevails over the Hague Service Convention; so, where service is made within the Community (except Denmark), the applicable instrument will be the Regulation.
76 Article 19 of the Regulation was copied directly from the Convention. The only changes are of a purely formal nature – for example 'this Convention' is changed to 'this Regulation'.

> **Panel 4.12** *(cont.)*
>
> (c) no certificate of any kind has been received, even though every reasonable effort has been made to obtain it through the competent authorities or bodies of the Member State addressed.
>
> 3. Notwithstanding paragraphs 1 and 2, the judge may order, in case of urgency, any provisional or protective measures.
>
> 4. When a writ of summons or an equivalent document has had to be transmitted to another Member State for the purpose of service, under the provisions of this Regulation, and a judgment has been entered against a defendant who has not appeared, the judge shall have the power to relieve the defendant from the effects of the expiration of the time for appeal from the judgment if the following conditions are fulfilled:
>
>   (a) the defendant, without any fault on his part, did not have knowledge of the document in sufficient time to defend, or knowledge of the judgment in sufficient time to appeal; and
>
>   (b) the defendant has disclosed a *prima facie* defence to the action on the merits.
>
>   An application for relief may be filed only within a reasonable time after the defendant has knowledge of the judgment.
>
>   Each Member State may make it known, in accordance with Article 23(1), that such application will not be entertained if it is filed after the expiration of a time to be stated by it in that communication, but which shall in no case be less than one year following the date of the judgment.
>
> 5. Paragraph 4 shall not apply to judgments concerning status or capacity of persons.

§ 7   Conclusions

There is no doubt that the European instruments (the Brussels Convention, the Lugano Convention and the Brussels I Regulation) are a major intellectual achievement. It is doubtful whether there is anything comparable anywhere in the world. They have been carefully elaborated over a period of many years with the intention that their provisions should fit together to form a coherent whole in the tradition of the great Continental codes. Their interpretation has been clarified in the European Court in some 150 cases. However, they have defects. The policy of discriminating against litigants domiciled outside Europe has already been criticized. Further defects will be pointed out in Chapter 10. Despite this, however, the instruments have gone a long way towards finding the right balance between the interests of claimants and defendants in international litigation, as well as that between Member States and private parties.

Further reading

For general works, see the 'Further reading' section of Chapter 3

Bigos, 'Jurisdiction over Cross-Border Wrongs on the Internet' (2005) 54 ICLQ 585

Hartley, 'Unnecessary Europeanization under the Brussels Jurisdiction and Judgments Convention: The Case of the Dissatisfied Sub-Purchaser' (1993) 18 *European Law Review* 506

Øren, 'International Jurisdiction over Consumer Contracts in e-Europe' (2003) 52 ICLQ 665

Takahashi, 'Jurisdiction in Matters Relating to Contract: Article 5(1) of the Brussels Convention and Regulation' (2002) 27 *European Law Review* 530

Tang, 'Multiple Defendants in the European Jurisdiction Regulation' (2009) 34 *European Law Review* 80

CHAPTER 5

The traditional English rules

§ 1   Introduction

In this chapter, we consider the basic common-law rules of jurisdiction as they developed in England over the centuries. Originally, these rules constituted a complete statement of the law of jurisdiction applied in actions *in personam* in England. As we have seen, however, they have now been replaced by European Community law where the defendant is domiciled in the United Kingdom or in another European State that is a member of the European Community or a party to the Lugano Convention.[1] As a result, the traditional rules of English law now apply only with regard to defendants domiciled in other countries, such as the United States, Canada, Australia, Japan, China, Russia, India, Brazil, etc.[2] However, since these latter countries make up by far the greater part of the world, the traditional rules are still of considerable importance; in many ways, they are more important than the EC rules we considered in the last two chapters. Moreover, they still constitute the foundation of the law in common-law countries like Australia, Canada and the United States.

§ 2   Service of the claim form

The original attitude of the common law might strike some people as strange: jurisdiction was regarded as entirely a matter of procedure. An action in the common law was (and is) begun with the service (delivery) on the defendant of a claim form – originally, a writ of summons (writ)[3] – a document issued in the king's (or queen's) name, ordering (summoning) the defendant to attend court at a specified time and place. If the claim form was not served, the case could not proceed. So jurisdiction was regarded as being dependent – and wholly dependent – on the service of the claim form. If the claim form was properly served, the court had jurisdiction.[4] If it was not, it did not.

Though the issuing of a claim form is an official act performed by a court

---

1 As we saw in Chapter 3, § 7, and Chapter 4, § 5, above, they also apply in certain situations even if the defendant is not domiciled in any EC or Lugano State.
2 This is subject to the exceptions mentioned in the previous footnote.
3 The term 'claim form' replaced 'writ' in England as a result of the adoption of the CPR in 1999. 'Writ' is still the correct term in the Commonwealth and the United States.
4 There were (and are) exceptions. For example, the court will not have jurisdiction to decide questions of rights *in rem* in foreign immovables: *British South Africa Co.* v. *Companhia de Moçambique* [1893] AC 602 (HL). See § 7, below.

official, the *service* of a claim form was traditionally carried out by the party himself or by someone on his behalf.[5] Traditionally, the claim form had to be given (or shown)[6] personally to the defendant.[7] If he could not be found, it could not be served. Subsequently, provision was made for service by an alternative method: with prior permission of the court, the claim form could be served by other means.[8] Today, in England, it is also possible for a claim form to be served without prior permission by various other methods specified in the Civil Procedure Rules – for example, by post or fax.[9] However, these are all later developments: originally, personal service was required.

Since the claim form was issued in the name of the king, it could be served only within his dominions (the territory he ruled). However, since the claim form was actually issued by a court, service had to take place within that part of the king's dominions over which the court had jurisdiction. Thus, a claim form issued by an English court could be served only in England, not in Scotland or a British colony.[10]

Thus, the traditional rule was that an English court had jurisdiction (in the international sense) if, but only if, the claim form was served on the defendant in England. This meant that the jurisdiction of the English courts depended on the presence – even if temporary – of the defendant within the territory of the court, coupled with the service of the claim form on him.

This complies with the principle of a link between the defendant and the territory of the court, but it does so only to a limited extent. Many people would consider temporary presence too weak a link to found general jurisdiction in civil matters. However, two points should be borne in mind. The first is that, weak though it is, presence is still a link between the defendant and the territory of the court. Entering a country is a voluntary act,[11] an act that the defendant might reasonably be expected to regard as subjecting him, in some sense at least, to the jurisdiction of that country. It is, therefore, less objectionable than rules such as that found in Article 14 of the French Civil Code[12] that give a court jurisdiction on the basis of a link between the *claimant* and the territory of the forum.

The second point is that the excessive nature of this rule is mitigated by the doctrine of *forum non conveniens*, a doctrine that allows the court to refuse to exercise jurisdiction if it considers that another court is in a better position to do justice in the case. This will be considered in Chapter 9. Here, it is enough to say that, in recent times,[13] a common-law court has always had to consider two questions when an action is brought before it:

---

5 Today, a court will serve a claim form: CPR 6.4.

6 The original might be shown to him, and a copy given to him.

7 Today, it is left with the defendant: CPR 6.5(3)(a).

8 See now CPR 6.15.

9 CPR 6.3(1).

10 Except for proceedings involving small sums of money, England is not divided into different judicial districts: there is a single court of unlimited civil jurisdiction for the whole of England and Wales – the High Court. Under the Civil Procedure Rules, 'jurisdiction' is defined as meaning England and Wales: CPR 2.3.

11 If the defendant was enticed or tricked into entering the country – still less, if he were kidnapped by the claimant and brought within it by force – service of a claim form on him would not give the court jurisdiction: see *Stein* v. *Valkenhuysen* (1858) EB & E 65; *Watkins* v. *North American Lands Co.* (1904) 20 TLR 534 (HL).

12 See Chapter 3, § 5, n. 14, above.

13 The doctrine of *forum non conveniens* was developed during the twentieth century.

- Does it have jurisdiction?
- If it does, should it exercise that jurisdiction?

These two questions are different. The first is based on fairly clear-cut rules; the second is based on an assessment of all relevant considerations.

However, though the doctrine of *forum non conveniens* mitigates the excessive nature of the rule, it does not entirely cure it. A foreign resident might feel that the uncertainty inherent in *forum non conveniens* means that he does not get full protection. For this reason, it might be better if (in the absence of special circumstances) the common-law rule were restricted to proceedings arising out of the defendant's activities during his visit to England.

Our first case illustrates the basic rule that service of a claim form on the defendant in England gives the English courts jurisdiction in an action *in personam*, even if the defendant's presence in England is only temporary (unless he was tricked into coming to England).

England
Colt Industries Inc.* v. *Sarlie
High Court (Queen's Bench Division)
[1966] 1 WLR 440

Background

While the defendant, who was not resident in England, was staying for a few days at a hotel in London for reasons unconnected with the litigation, the claimants issued a claim form and served it on him.[14] The defendant challenged the jurisdiction of the court.

Lyell J

[Counsel for the defendant] claims that where a defendant is not a resident in this country and has not otherwise submitted to the jurisdiction, the court has no jurisdiction to adjudicate upon a claim merely because the writ is issued and served while he is temporarily staying – and I use the neutral term – in this country; what he says is, that as the defendant was merely a visitor for a few days, the court has no power to implead him to answer the claim of the plaintiffs; he further says that this is a point which has never been the subject of direct decision.

The first authority to which I was referred was Dicey's *Conflict of Laws*, 7th ed. (1958) p. 175, r. 25, which reads as follows:

'When the defendant in an action *in personam* is, at the time for the service of the writ, in England, the court has jurisdiction in respect of any cause of action, in whatever country such cause of action arises.'

---

14 The English action was actually brought to enforce an American judgment. Under the common law, a judgment given by a foreign court which had jurisdiction under the rules of English law creates a new cause of action (claim) which may be sued upon in England. In such proceedings, the defendant cannot challenge the substance of the foreign judgment, but may raise only a limited number of defences – for example, that the proceedings were contrary to natural justice. The fact that the action in *Colt Industries v. Sarlie* was brought on a foreign judgment was, however, irrelevant to the jurisdictional issue. This would have been exactly the same if the proceedings had been brought on an original cause of action.

> . . .
>
> That rule, so far as my own experience goes, has always been acted upon by practitioners, but nevertheless, in view of the argument put forward by [counsel for the defendant], it is my duty to examine its foundation.

Lyell J then considered *Carrick* v. *Hancock*,[15] a case in which it had to be decided whether a Swedish court had jurisdiction over an English defendant under the principles of English law, a question which arose in the context of proceedings to enforce the judgment of the Swedish court in England. The defendant in that case was resident in England and the claim form had been served on him in Sweden during a short visit there. Counsel for the plaintiff in *Carrick* v. *Hancock* referred to *Calvin's Case*,[16] and founded his argument on the statement 'when an alien in amity cometh into England, because so long as he is within England he is within the King's protection; therefore so long as he is here he oweth unto the King a local obedience or ligeance, for the one (as it hath been said), draweth the other'. After explaining this, Lyell J continued:

> The argument, therefore, was that as he had protection and owed allegiance, he was impleadable in any matter before the courts. The judgment of Lord Russell of Killowen CJ is only shortly reported, and after reviewing the facts, he went on to observe[17] 'that the jurisdiction of a court was based upon the principle of territorial dominion, and that all persons within any territorial dominion owe their allegiance to its sovereign power and obedience to all its laws and to the lawful jurisdiction of its courts.' In his opinion, that duty of allegiance was correlative to the protection given by a State to any person within its territory, this relationship and its inherent rights depended upon the fact of the person being within its territory, and it seemed to him that the question of the time the person was actually in the territory was wholly immaterial.

Lyell J then turned to *Watkins* v. *North American Land and Timber Co. Ltd.*[18] and continued:

> In my judgment it is implicit in that decision that in the absence of fraud inducing the defendant to come into the country so that he . . . is tricked to come within the jurisdiction for the sole purpose of serving him with a writ, the House of Lords was implicitly holding that jurisdiction was well founded by serving a writ upon a foreigner who was here merely casually, and that accords entirely with the rule as stated in Dicey now for over forty years.
>
> In this case there is no question but that the defendant came here, not on any invitation of the plaintiffs, but entirely for his own purposes, and in those circumstances the refusal of the master to set aside the writ and service was entirely right and proper. The defendant's appeal is, therefore, dismissed.

The defendant sought leave to appeal on two grounds, one of which was that the mere transitory presence of the defendant in the United Kingdom did not confer jurisdiction on the English courts since neither of the parties was

---

15 (1895) 12 TLR 59 (Div. Ct).
16 (1608) 7 Co Rep 1a.
17 12 TLR 59 at p. 60.
18 (1904) 20 TLR 534 (HL).

domiciled, resident or carried on business in the United Kingdom or was a British subject or had any business connection with the United Kingdom. The Court of Appeal (Sellers, Davies and Salmon LJJ) heard the defendant's applications on 17 January 1964.

> **Sellers LJ**
>
> This court is unanimously of opinion that we should refuse the defendant leave to appeal against the decision of Lyell J. We are content to leave the judgment of Lyell J as it stands on both the points which have been argued. We extend the time for appealing, but we do not give the defendant leave to appeal.

QUESTION

Are you convinced by the argument based on temporary allegiance?[19]

Our next case is not so much concerned with the question whether service of a claim form on a non-resident defendant during a visit to England confers jurisdiction on the court, but rather with the question whether it is right for the court to exercise its jurisdiction in such circumstances (under the principle now known as *forum non conveniens*). At the time of the case, the principle of *forum non conveniens* had not been fully developed and the question depended simply on whether or not the proceedings were vexatious or oppressive.[20] If they were, the court would stay (suspend) the proceedings. The most authoritative statement of this principle was in *St Pierre* v. *South American Stores*,[21] where Scott LJ said:

> In order to justify a stay two conditions must be satisfied, one positive and the other negative: (a) the defendant must satisfy the court that the continuance of the action would work an injustice because it would be oppressive or vexatious to him or would be an abuse of the process of the court in some other way; and (b) the stay must not cause an injustice to the plaintiff. On both the burden of proof is on the defendant.

It was the application of this rule that was in issue in our next case.

England
Maharanee of Baroda* v. *Wildenstein
Court of Appeal
[1972] 2 QB 283; [1972] 2 WLR 1077; [1972] 2 All ER 689

Background

The claimant, the Maharanee of Baroda, was an Indian princess, resident in France. The defendant, Mr Wildenstein, was an art dealer, also resident in France. The case concerned a painting bought by the Maharanee from Wildenstein in

---

19 For further arguments on this point, see the judgment of the US Supreme Court in *Burnham* v. *Superior Court of California*, 495 US 604; 110 S Ct 2105; 109 L Ed 2d 631 (1990), set out in Chapter 7, below.
20 Today, proceedings will be stayed under the doctrine of *forum non conveniens* (discussed in Chapter 9, below) in a wider range of situations. However, the mere fact that the claim form was served on the defendant during a temporary visit to England is not in itself a ground for staying the proceedings.
21 [1936] 1 KB 382 at p. 398 (HL).

France. Wildenstein certified that the picture was by the famous French artist, Boucher. However, the English firm of art dealers, Christie's, said it was not. So the Maharanee sued Wildenstein to obtain rescission of the contract: she wanted her money back. She decided to bring the proceedings in an English court, rather than a court in France. The claim form was served on the defendant while he was at the horse races during a temporary visit to England. The defendant challenged the jurisdiction of the court, and the court of first instance set service aside. The Maharanee appealed to the Court of Appeal.

Lord Denning MR

In this case the writ has been properly served on the defendant in this country. This makes the case very different from those in which the defendant is in a foreign country and the plaintiff has to seek leave to serve him out of the jurisdiction. It is also different from those cases in which the plaintiff has already started an action in another country, and the question is whether he should be allowed to start another action in this country on the same subject-matter. In this case the plaintiff has validly invoked the jurisdiction of our courts in this, the one and only action she has brought.

[Lord Denning then referred to the statement in *St Pierre* v. *South American Stores* set out above and certain other cases, and continued:]

A similar case was put by Sir Gorell Barnes P in *Logan* v. *Bank of Scotland (No 2):*[1]

> 'If, for instance, as was put in argument, a dispute of a complicated character had arisen between two foreigners in a foreign country, and one of them were made defendant in an action in this country by serving him with a writ while he happened to be here for a few days' visit, I apprehend that, although there would be jurisdiction in the court to entertain the suit, it would have little hesitation in treating the action as vexatious and staying it.'

The judge seems to have taken that instance given by Sir Gorell Barnes P and founded on it a presumption which he stated in these words: 'But a presumption arises that the proceedings are oppressive if the defendant is served when he appears to be here on a visit . . .' I cannot agree with that statement. There is no such presumption. If a defendant is properly served with a writ while he is in this country, albeit on a short visit, the plaintiff is *prima facie* entitled to continue the proceedings to the end. He has validly invoked the jurisdiction of the Queen's courts; and he is entitled to require those courts to proceed to adjudicate upon his claim. The courts should not strike it out unless it comes within one of the acknowledged grounds, such as that it is vexatious or oppressive, or otherwise an abuse of the process of the court . . . It does not become within those grounds simply because the writ is served on the defendant while he is on a visit to this country . . .

[Counsel for the defendant] likened this case to a road accident in Rome, when two Italian citizens were in collision. Suppose that one of them was served with

---

1 [1906] 1 KB 141 at p. 152.

an English writ while on a short holiday in England. I would agree that such an action would be stayed. The issue would be solely Italian. But, here the main issue is whether this painting was a genuine Boucher or not. That issue is one of fact which is crucial to the case in French law as well as in English law. It is not solely a French issue. The art world is so international in character today that this issue has itself something of an international character. The parties on either side are citizens of the world. The Maharanee has associations, not only with France, but also with India, England and Ireland. Mr Wildenstein himself has, of course, close associations with France, but also with America, England and Ireland. He was for years the principal director of the English company of Daniel Wildenstein Ltd, and was so at the beginning of this action. He has now ceased to be a director, but he is still a shareholder. If anybody could be said to have an international reputation, it is he . . .

[T]he burden is on Mr Wildenstein to show that it would be an injustice to him to have the case tried here. I do not think he has discharged that burden. The judge was, I think, in error, in raising the presumption that he did. We can review his discretion. On so doing, I think the case should continue in England. I would allow the appeal, accordingly.

Appeal allowed.

§ 3 Service on a company

§ 3.1 Introduction

As we have seen,[22] the jurisdiction of an English court over companies domiciled in England depends on EC law. EC law also governs the jurisdiction of an English court over companies domiciled in other EC or Lugano States. So the traditional English rules now apply in England only with regard to companies not domiciled in any of these States. In this chapter, we are concerned only with such defendants. Again, they constitute a large proportion of the foreign businesses operating in the United Kingdom. Here too, jurisdiction depends on service of the claim form.

How do you serve a claim form on a company? When is a company present in the jurisdiction so that service may take place on it? The traditional answer has always been that a company was present in the jurisdiction for this purpose if it was incorporated in England[23] or if it had a place of business there. However, the traditional English rule no longer applies when the company is incorporated in England (and has its registered office there), when its central administration is in England or when it has its principal place of business there: in all these cases, it will be domiciled in England.[24] In these cases, the English courts will have jurisdiction by virtue of Community law, not English law. So the traditional rule will

---

22 Chapter 3, § 6.4, below.
23 If the company is incorporated in England, it must have a registered office within the country. The claim form may be served on it there: the Companies Act 1985, section 725. This provision re-enacts earlier provisions to the same effect.
24 See Chapter 3, § 6.4, above.

apply only when the company is incorporated in a foreign country (not being an EC or Lugano State) and has a place of business in England that is not its central administration or its principal place or business. Service of the claim form on the company at that place will then give the court jurisdiction over it.[25]

To come within this rule, the place of business must be at a fixed location. A representative who visits England and travels about from place to place doing business would not be enough.[26] Even if the president of the company came to England and the claim form was served on him there, that would not give the court jurisdiction over the company. This was made clear in *The Theodohos*,[27] a case brought against a Panamanian company. The company had no place of business in England and the claim form was served on the president of the company while he was in England. The court held that, if there was no place of business in England, there could be no jurisdiction over the company.

To understand what is meant by a place of business, we must distinguish between the situation where the company has an office (or equivalent establishment) in its own name, staffed by its own employees, and the situation where it carries on business through an agent or representative. We will consider these two situations separately.

§ 3.2   Company's own office

We first consider the situation where the company's operations in England are directly controlled by it through its own officers or employees, not through an agent or representative.

Our next case throws light on what is meant by a place of business in this situation.

> **England**
> ***Dunlop Pneumatic Tyre Co. Ltd** v. **A. G. Cudell & Co.***
> **Court of Appeal**
> **[1902] 1 KB 342**

Background

The defendants, a German company, hired a stand at a cycle show at the Crystal Palace in London to exhibit their products and to take orders. The stand was manned by their employees. The show lasted nine days. Apart from the stand, they had no other place of business in England. The action was brought by a British company for patent infringement, and the claim form was served on one of the persons manning the stand. The defendants claimed that this did not give the court jurisdiction. The judge at first instance refused to set aside service and the defendants appealed.

---

25 CPR 6.3(2) and the table in CPR 6.9(2). This is subject to the exceptions already mentioned.
26 See *Littauer Glove Corporation* v. *Millington Ltd* (1928) 44 TLR 746, a case in which the principle was applied to a foreign judgment.
27 [1977] 2 Lloyd's Rep 428.

Collins MR

[After saying that the method of service was proper, assuming that the defendants could be served with a claim form at all, he continued:]

In order to see whether they were liable to be so served, it is necessary to consider whether, upon the facts, they can be said to have been resident in England when the service was effected. It has been held in a number of cases . . . that the true test in such cases is whether the foreign corporation is conducting its own business at some fixed place within the jurisdiction, that being the only way in which a corporation can reside in this country. It can only so reside through its agent,[1] not being a concrete entity itself; but, if it so resides by its agent, it must be considered for this purpose as itself residing within the jurisdiction. In several of the cases decided on this subject the difficulty has been to determine whether the business carried on by an agent at a certain place within the jurisdiction was the business of the company itself carried on by that agent as representing them, or was really the business of the agent. With regard to that point very nice questions of fact have in some cases arisen. But in the present case we are relieved from any such difficulty. The defendants did not resort, for the purposes of their business, to some person who was himself carrying on an independent business of his own at some place in this country; and therefore we are not called on in this case to consider the question whether a foreign corporation, making use, for their purposes, of a person carrying on a business of his own, can under the circumstances be regarded as themselves carrying on their own business within the jurisdiction . . . [2] Here the defendants hired premises for their own exclusive use, and did not resort for their purposes to some person who was carrying on an independent business, but employed their own servant to conduct the business. The only difficulty in this case arises from the fact that the time during which the defendants can be said to have carried on business in this country is limited to that of the duration of the show at the Crystal Palace, namely, nine days. It was argued by the counsel for the defendants that, in determining the question of residence or no residence, length of time is an essential element. I agree that it is an element to be considered; but it was, as I understood, admitted that, if a foreign corporation were to announce their intention of carrying on their own business, and were to carry it on, at a certain place in this country for a limited period, the mere fact that they so carried it on only for a limited period would not prevent the company from being considered as resident within the jurisdiction for that period. The period of nine days is not necessarily a negligible quantity; it may in many cases be a very substantial period. In the case of an exhibition, such as the show in the present case, which is largely resorted to by manufacturers for the purpose of exhibiting a particular class of goods, and by customers desirous of purchasing such goods, as much business in the kind of goods exhibited might probably be done in nine days as in as many months in an ordinary town. I do not think that, where a foreign company carries on business in this country so as in all other respects to

---

1 *Editor's note*: the court is here using 'agent' in a general sense to mean any person acting for a company, including an employee of the company.
2 This is the situation considered in § 3.3, below.

fulfil the conditions necessary to constitute residence within the jurisdiction, they can be said not to have so resided, merely because that residence was confined to a period such as nine days. In the present case I think we have in other respects all the elements necessary to constitute for this purpose residence by the defendants. It appears to be suggested that the defendants cannot be said to have carried on business in this country, because they did not carry on the whole of their business here. It was said that their business was that of manufacturers of motor-cars, and that manufacture was carried on abroad, and not at the Crystal Palace. It seems to me that it is only necessary to state that point in plain terms in order to confute it. It is clearly not necessary that a company should carry on the whole of its business in this country. A substantial part of the defendants' business was the selling of their manufactures, and that was during the show carried on here. Customers had during that period an opportunity of inspecting the defendants' wares, and prices were quoted, and orders accepted for them by the defendants. Nothing more could have been done with regard to the sale of the defendants' wares at their place of business abroad. For these reasons I think the appeal must be dismissed.

Romer and Mathew LJJ agreed.

Appeal dismissed.

QUESTIONS

1 Do you think that nine days is long enough?
2 It is not clear whether the claim in this case arose out of the activities of the company in England. If it did not, would it still be right to take jurisdiction?[28]

If the company has a fixed place of business at a specific location, it must carry on business there. Our next case is concerned with what constitutes carrying on business.

England
South India Shipping* v. *Bank of Korea
Court of Appeal
[1985] 1 WLR 585; [1985] 2 All ER 219; [1985] 1 Lloyd's Rep 413

Background

In this case, the defendant, a Korean bank, opened an office in London, which was rented in its name and staffed by its employees. The function of the office was to gather information and make contacts; it concluded no financial transactions. The bank had previously registered the office under the Companies Act 1948, but had subsequently cancelled this registration on the ground that no business transactions were concluded through it. The claimant was an Indian

---

28 Compare the 'systematic and continuous' doctrine applied by American courts, discussed in Chapter 7, § 2, below.

shipping company. It had had a ship built in Korea and the Bank of Korea had issued two letters of guarantee in connection with the contract. The claim (for US$13 million) was under the letters of guarantee: it had no connection with the activities of the office in England. The claim form was served on the office in England.

On the bank's application, the judge at first instance declared that the bank had not been duly served because the office was not a place of business. The claimant appealed.

Ackner LJ

[After considering the authorities, continued:]

In my judgment the facts in this appeal are clear. The defendant bank is an import-export bank, not a high street bank. It has both premises and staff within the jurisdiction. It conducts external relations with other banks and financial institutions. It carries out preliminary work in relation to granting or obtaining loans. It seeks to give publicity to the foreign bank and encourage trade between Korea and the United Kingdom, and it consults with other banks and financial institutions on the usual operating matters. It has therefore established a place of business within Great Britain and it matters not that it does not conclude within the jurisdiction any banking transactions or have banking dealings with the general public as opposed to other banks or financial institutions . . . I would accordingly allow this appeal.

Browne-Wilkinson LJ and Sir George Waller agreed.

Appeal allowed.

Comment

This case shows that a foreign company can still be doing business in England even though it does not conclude any contracts.

§ 3.3 *Acting through an agent*

Where the company does not open an office of its own but acts through an agent, it must be shown that the agent does the company's business, rather than his own. Two cases may be contrasted, both decided by the Court of Appeal in the early years of the twentieth century. In the first, *Saccharin Corporation* v. *Chemische Fabrik von Heyden*,[29] a German company appointed a representative in England. The representative was paid by commission, rented his office in his own name and was free to represent other companies. However, he had the power to accept orders in the name of the company without referring them back to it, and even had a stock of the company's goods under his control, which he could deliver to customers. The court held that his office was a place of business of the company so that jurisdiction over it could be obtained by serving a claim form on it there.

---

29 [1911] 2 KB 516 (CA).

In *Okura* v. *Forsbacka Jernverks*,[30] on the other hand, a Swedish company with a similar arrangement was held not to be doing business within the jurisdiction. The difference was that, in this case, the representative had no power to accept orders himself without first obtaining the consent of the company.

More recently, it has been established that this distinction, though important, is not necessarily decisive.

England
Adams* v. *Cape Industries
Court of Appeal
[1990] 2 WLR 657

Background

The issue in this case was whether an American judgment should be recognized in England. This depended on whether the American court that gave the judgment had jurisdiction under English law.[31] So the decision on the jurisdiction of the American courts also constitutes an authority on the jurisdiction of the English courts. It is not necessary to consider the facts. The following extract lays down the general principles that the court considered applicable in this situation.

Slade LJ

General principles derived from the authorities relating to the 'presence' issue

. . . In relation to trading corporations, we derive the three following propositions from consideration of the many authorities cited to us relating to the 'presence' of an overseas corporation.

(1) The English courts will be likely to treat a trading corporation incorporated under the law of one country ('an overseas corporation') as present within the jurisdiction of the courts of another country only if either (i) it has established and maintained at its own expense (whether as owner or lessee) a fixed place of business of its own in the other country and for more than a minimal period of time has carried on its own business at or from such premises by its servants or agents (a 'branch office' case),[1] or (ii) a representative of the overseas corporation has for more than a minimal period of time been carrying on *the overseas corporation's* business in the other country at or from some fixed place of business.[2]

(2) In either of these two cases presence can only be established if it can fairly be said that the *overseas corporation's* business (whether or not together with the representative's own business) has been transacted at or from the fixed place of business. In the first case, this condition is likely to present few problems. In the second, the question whether the representative has been carrying on the

1 *Editor's note*: this is the 'own office' situation discussed in § 3.2, above.
2 *Editor's note*: this is the 'acting through an agent' situation.

30 [1914] 1 KB 715 (CA).
31 As we shall see in Chapter 15, English courts sometimes apply more restrictive rules for the purpose of recognizing foreign judgments than for deciding whether they themselves have jurisdiction; however, this was not the case here.

overseas corporation's business or has been doing no more than carry on his own business will necessitate an investigation of the functions which he has been performing and all aspects of the relationship between him and the overseas corporation.

(3) In particular, but without prejudice to the generality of the foregoing, the following questions are likely to be relevant on such investigation: (a) whether or not the fixed place of business from which the representative operates was originally acquired for the purpose of enabling him to act on behalf of the overseas corporation; (b) whether the overseas corporation has directly reimbursed him for (i) the cost of his accommodation at the fixed place of business; (ii) the cost of his staff; (c) what other contributions, if any, the overseas corporation makes to the financing of the business carried on by the representative; (d) whether the representative is remunerated by reference to transactions, e.g. by commission, or by fixed regular payments or in some other way; (e) what degree of control the overseas corporation exercises over the running of the business conducted by the representative; (f) whether the representative reserves (i) part of his accommodation, (ii) part of his staff for conducting business related to the overseas corporation; (g) whether the representative displays the overseas corporation's name at his premises or on his stationery, and, if so, whether he does so in such a way as to indicate that he is a representative of the overseas corporation; (h) what business, if any, the representative transacts as principal exclusively on his own behalf; (i) whether the representative makes contracts with customers or other third parties in the name of the overseas corporation, or otherwise in such manner as to bind it; (j) if so, whether the representative requires specific authority in advance before binding the overseas corporation to contractual obligations.

This list of questions is not exhaustive, and the answer to none of them is necessarily conclusive. If the judge [against whose decision this case was an appeal] was intending to say that in any case, other than a branch office case, the presence of the overseas company can *never* be established unless the representative has authority to contract on behalf of and bind the principal, we would regard this proposition as too widely stated. We accept [counsel for the plaintiffs'] submission to this effect. Every case of this character is likely to involve 'a nice examination of all the facts, and inferences must be drawn from a number of facts adjusted together and contrasted:' *La Bourgogne* [1899] P 1, 18, *per* Collins LJ. Nevertheless, we agree with the general principle stated thus by Pearson J in *Jabbour* v. *Custodian of Israeli Absentee Property* [1954] 1 WLR 139, 146:

> 'A corporation resides in a country if it carries on business there at a fixed place of business, and, in the case of an agency, the principal test to be applied in determining whether the corporation is carrying on business at the agency is to ascertain whether the agent has authority to enter into contracts on behalf of the corporation without submitting them to the corporation for approval . . .'

On the authorities, the presence or absence of such authority is clearly regarded as being of great importance one way or the other. *A fortiori*, the fact that a representative, whether with or without prior approval, never makes contracts

> in the name of the overseas corporation or otherwise in such manner as to bind it must be a powerful factor pointing against the presence of the overseas corporation.

This case shows that establishing jurisdiction over a foreign company is much more difficult when it operates through an agent than when it opens its own office. In *South India Shipping* v. *Bank of Korea* (an 'own office' case), for example, the local office could not conclude contracts on behalf of the bank; nevertheless, it was still considered to be a place of business. Service on the office gave the court jurisdiction. It is unlikely that the court would have reached the same conclusion if the office had been that of an independent agent.

§ 3.4   *A short-lived anomaly*

We must now consider an anomaly that entered English law in 1992 and was removed when the CPR came into force in 1999. Since it is no longer of importance, it is not necessary to go into all the details.

Until the CPR came into force, the Companies Act 1985 (and earlier legislation which it replaced) provided the exclusive means of serving a claim form on a company in England.[32] As it existed before 1992, section 691(1)(b)(ii) of the Companies Act 1985[33] provided that, when a company incorporated outside Great Britain[34] established a place of business in Great Britain, it had to deliver to the Registrar of Companies within one month the names and addresses of one or more persons resident in Great Britain authorized to accept service on behalf of the company. It was further provided by section 695(1)[35] that service on the company could be effected by serving the claim form on one of the persons whose name and address had thus been registered. Section 695(2)[36] then provided that, if the company failed to deliver the name and address of anyone authorized to accept service, or if the person concerned was dead or had ceased to reside there or for some other reason could not be served, the claim form could be served on any place of business established by the company in Great Britain.[37]

In 1992, however, the Companies Act was amended by the Oversea Companies and Credit and Financial Institutions (Branch Disclosure) Regulations 1992,[38] which were intended to implement certain EC directives that had nothing to do with jurisdiction.[39] However, the Regulations also amended the jurisdictional provisions of the Companies Act in a way that made the law both complicated and anomalous.

---

32 *Boocock* v. *Hilton International Co.* [1993] 1 WLR 1065, approving *The Theodohos* [1977] 2 Lloyd's Rep 428, *per* Brandon J at p. 431.
33 The amended version of this is set out in Panel 5.2, below.
34 Great Britain is England and Wales (one unit for legal purposes) together with Scotland.
35 The amended version of this is set out in Panel 5.2, below.
36 The amended version of this is set out in Panel 5.2, below.
37 It was under an earlier version of this provision, section 412 of the Companies Act 1948, that the claim form was served on the Bank of Korea in the case set out above.
38 SI 1992 No. 3179. The Regulations came into force on 1 January 1993.
39 They were adopted to give effect to the Eleventh EC Company Law Directive, Directive 89/666, OJ 1989 L 395, pp. 36–9, and the Bank Branches Directive, Directive 89/117, OJ 1989 L 44, pp. 40–2.

The Regulations introduced a distinction (that had not previously existed in English law) between a branch and a place of business other than a branch.[40] In the case of a place of business other than a branch, the relevant provision was section 695 of the Companies Act (Panel 5.2). Under this, the law remains as it was. In the case of a branch, however, a new provision became applicable. This was section 694A (Panel 5.1). Under this, service of a claim form gives jurisdiction only if the claim arises out of the activities of the branch. As we saw in Chapter 4, this is the rule in EC law. However, the changes apply in all cases, even when the company is not domiciled in any EC or Lugano State. No one seems to know why this was done. However, the relevant provisions of the CPR[41] (Panel 5.3) put things back the way they were before the 1992 Regulations came into force. Our next case explains matters.

Panel 5.1 Branch in England Companies Act 1985, as amended by the Oversea Companies and Credit and Financial Institutions (Branch Disclosure) Regulations 1992 (SI 1992 No. 3179), sections 690A and 694A

Section 690A

(1)   This section applies to any limited company which—
    (a) is incorporated outside the United Kingdom and Gibraltar, and
    (b) has a branch in Great Britain.

Section 694A

(1)   This section applies to any company to which section 690A applies.
(2)   Any process or notice required to be served on a company to which this section applies in respect of the carrying on of the business of a branch registered by it under paragraph 1 of Schedule 21A is sufficiently served if—
    (a) addressed to any person whose name has, in respect of the branch, been delivered to the registrar as a person falling within paragraph 3(e) of that Schedule, and
    (b) left at or sent by post to the address for that person which has been so delivered.
(3)   Where—
    (a) a company to which this section applies makes default, in respect of a branch, in delivering to the registrar the particulars mentioned in paragraph 3(e) of Schedule 21A, or
    (b) all the persons whose names have, in respect of a branch, been delivered to the registrar as persons falling within paragraph 3(e) of that Schedule are dead or have ceased to reside in Great Britain, or refuse to accept service on the company's behalf, or for any reason cannot be served,
    a document may be served on the company in respect of the carrying on of the business of the branch by leaving it at, or sending it by post to, any place of business established by the company in Great Britain.

Panel 5.2 Place of business other than a branch Companies Act 1985, as amended by the Oversea Companies and Credit and Financial Institutions (Branch Disclosure) Regulations 1992 (SI 1992 No. 3179), sections 690B, 691 and 695

Section 690B

Sections 691 . . . shall not apply to any limited company which—
    (a) is incorporated outside the United Kingdom and Gibraltar, and
    (b) has a branch in the United Kingdom.

Section 691

(1)   When a company incorporated outside Great Britain establishes a place of business in Great Britain, it shall within one month of doing so deliver to the registrar of companies for registration—

---

40 Under the Regulations, 'branch' has the meaning given in the Eleventh EC Company Law Directive, Directive 89/666, OJ 1989 L 395, pp. 36–9.
41 The CPR came into force on 26 April 1999.

Panel 5.2 *(cont.)*

(a) ...
(b) a return in the prescribed form containing—
  (i) ...
  (ii) a list of the names and addresses of some one or more persons resident in Great Britain authorised to accept on the company's behalf service of process and any notices required to be served on it,

Section 695

(1) Any process or notice required to be served on an oversea company to which section 691 applies is sufficiently served if addressed to any person whose name has been delivered to the registrar under preceding sections in this Part and left at or sent by post to the address which has been so delivered.

(2) However—
  (a) where such a company makes default in delivering to the registrar the name and address of a person resident in Great Britain who is authorised to accept on behalf of the company service of process or notices, or
  (b) if at any time all the persons whose names and addresses have been so delivered are dead or have ceased so to reside, or refuse to accept service on the company's behalf, or for any reason cannot be served,

a document may be served on the company by leaving it at, or sending it by post to, any place of business established by the company in Great Britain.

Panel 5.3 Service on a company under the Civil Procedure Rules, Rules 6.3 and 6.9

Methods of service

Rule 6.3

(2) A company may be served
  (a) by any method permitted under this Part; or
  (b) by any of the methods of service set out in the Companies Act 1985 or the Companies Act 2006

Service of the claim form where the defendant does not give an address at which the defendant may be served

Rule 6.9

...

(2) Subject to paragraphs (3) to (6), the claim form must be served on the defendant at the place shown in the following table.

6. Company registered in England and Wales	• Principal office of the company: or
	• Any place of business of the company within the jurisdiction which has a real connection with the claim.
7. Any other company or corporation	• Any place within the jurisdiction where the corporation carries on its activities; or
	• Any place of business of the company within the jurisdiction

England
Saab v. *Saudi American Bank*
Court of Appeal
[1999] 1 WLR 1861

Background

The claimants were two Lebanese businessmen who had concluded a contract with the Saudi American Bank, a Saudi Arabian bank with its head office in Riyadh. Under the contract, the bank agreed to market shares throughout most of the world, including the United Kingdom. The claimants subsequently sued the bank in England for breach of that contract. The bank had a branch in England, and the claim form was served on the branch under section 694A of the Companies Act (Panel 5.1, above). As explained above, this provision allows a claim form to be served on a branch only with respect to business carried on by the branch.

The bank argued that the court did not have jurisdiction because the claim did not arise out of business carried on by the branch in England. This argument was rejected by the trial judge and an appeal was taken to the Court of Appeal. The Court of Appeal held that the claim *did* relate, in part, to business carried on by the branch in England, since the shares were to be marketed in England as well as in other countries. It held that this was sufficient to satisfy the requirements of section 694A. It also rejected the argument that the proceedings should be stayed on the ground of *forum non conveniens*. This was sufficient to dispose of the appeal, but the court also considered the effect of the 1992 Regulations. This part of the judgment is set out below.

Clarke LJ

7. . . . [R]ule 6.2(2) [now 6.3(2)] . . . CPR . . . provides that a company may be served by any method permitted by Part 6 of the CPR as an alternative to the methods of service set out in sections 725, 695 and 694A of the Companies Act 1985. By CPR rule 6.5(6) [now 6.9(2)] a document, which includes a claim form, may be served on a company incorporated outside England and Wales at any place of business of the company within the jurisdiction . . . The importance of the new rule is of course that it appears that the position has now reverted to what it was before section 694A was enacted, namely that process can be served on a foreign company with a place of business in, say, London without the necessity for establishing any link between the process and the business being conducted in London.

    . . .

11. . . . [I]t is I think helpful to put section 694A into its statutory and historical context. A number of sections including sections 690A, 690B and 694A, were inserted into the Companies Act 1985 by the Oversea Companies Credit and Financial Institutions (Branch Disclosure) Regulations 1992,[1] which were introduced to give effect as from 1 January 1993 to the Eleventh Council Directive (89/666 EEC) of 21 December 1989. Some of the changes introduced, including those made by section 694A, are very curious.

12. Before they were introduced the position was and had for many years been the same as it is (or would appear to be) now under CPR, rule 6.2(2) [now 6.3(2)] and 6.5(6) [now 6.9(2)]. By section 695 of the 1985 Act an oversea company could be served with process either at an address notified to the Registrar or in the absence of such notification at any place of business established by the company in Great Britain. It was not necessary to allege or prove any link between the subject-matter of the proceedings and the business being carried on in Great Britain. A plaintiff was entitled to serve the company in that way and to proceed with the action unless or until the company sought and obtained a stay on the ground of *forum non conveniens* . . . The interests of the oversea company were thus protected in that way.

13. The Directive is principally concerned with disclosure of information . . .

14. There is nothing in the Directive which explains why section 694A(2) was drafted in the way it was. The effect of the change introduced by the new

---

1 *Editor's note*: the correct title of the Regulations is actually 'The Oversea Companies *and* Credit and Financial Institutions (Branch Disclosure) Regulations 1992'.

sections was that for companies incorporated outside the United Kingdom and Gibraltar, as from 1 January 1993, a different regime existed between those companies with a branch in Great Britain and those companies without a branch but with only a place of business in Great Britain. In the latter case the position remained the same as before, namely that such companies could be served with process without any need for the plaintiff to show a link between the process and the place of business. On the other hand, in the former case, by the express terms of section 694A(2), process could only be served on the branch 'in respect of the carrying on of the business' of the branch. Moreover section 690B made it clear that these two regimes were not complementary (as appears now to be the case under the Civil Procedure Rules) but mutually exclusive because it expressly provided that sections 691 and 692 did not apply to any company which was incorporated outside the United Kingdom and Gibraltar and had a branch in the United Kingdom. It followed that the service provisions in section 695 did not apply to such a company because it only applied to companies to which section 691 applied.

15. It is I think common ground that a branch is a more permanent establishment than a mere place of business. The effect of these provisions thus created this anomalous result. In order to serve a branch it was necessary to satisfy the link between the process and the business of the branch required by section 694A(2), namely that it must be in respect of the carrying on of the business of the branch, whereas in a case where the company did not have a branch, in order to serve a place of business it was not necessary to establish any link at all. Despite considerable research neither party has been able to explain the reason for this anomaly and no one was able to think of a reason for it during the argument. It may be that it is because it has now been appreciated how anomalous the position is that new rules substantially restoring the position as it was for many years before 1993 have now been introduced in the Civil Procedure Rules.

The present situation, therefore, is that, although the 1992 Regulations are still in force, their effect has been largely nullified by the CPR, since a claim form may be served under the CPR on a place of business, including a branch, in England, even if the claim has no connection with the activities of that place of business. For this reason, the provisions of the Companies Act are of little importance. There is, however, one exception. In cases decided before the 1992 Regulations came into force, it was held that, where the claim form is served on a person whose name and address have been registered as someone who can receive service on behalf of the company, it is not necessary that the company should still be doing business in England when the claim form is served.[42] Since this form of service is possible only under the Companies Act, the anomalies introduced by the 1992 Regulations would appear still to apply. Where, on the other hand, the claim form is served on a place of business (including a branch) either under

---

42 *Sabatier* v. *Trading Company* [1927] 1 Ch 495; *Rome* v. *Punjab National Bank (No. 2)* [1989] 1 WLR 1211 (CA).

the Companies Act[43] or, it would seem, under the CPR, the company must *still* be doing business there.

§ 3.5 Subsidiaries

A subsidiary is a separate company in which the 'parent' company owns a controlling shareholding. In law, it is a separate legal person from the parent. It is, therefore, different from a branch or other place of business, which is not a separate legal person. If the subsidiary is incorporated in England, it will be domiciled there and the English courts will have (general) jurisdiction over it under Community law. If the claim is against the subsidiary, there is, therefore, no problem.

What if the claim is against the parent? Since the subsidiary is a separate legal person, it is not (normally) liable for the obligations of the parent. Moreover, establishing a subsidiary in England is not the same thing as establishing a branch there. The latter operates in the name of the head office and holds itself out as an extension of the latter. This is not, in general, true of a subsidiary. Thus, if a foreign company incorporates a subsidiary in England, that does not automatically give jurisdiction to the English courts over the parent in the way that the opening of a branch does. However, it is possible for the subsidiary to act as agent for the parent and to transact business in the name of the parent. If it does this, the rules on agents explained above in § 3.3 will be applicable.[44]

§ 3.6 Conclusions

It will be seen from what has been said that the traditional rules for jurisdiction over a foreign company in England are similar to those under Article 5(5) of the Brussels I Regulation (and under the Brussels and Lugano Conventions). The decisions on what constitutes a 'branch, agency or other establishment' under the European instruments would almost all be good law in England. The extract from *Adams* v. *Cape Industries* set out above suggests that *Blanckaert and Willems* v. *Trost*,[45] (discussed in Chapter 4, § 1.3.1, above) would have been decided the same way under English law.

There is, however, one important difference. Under EC law, the presence of a place of business gives the court jurisdiction only with regard to claims arising out of the activities of that place of business. In English law, on the other hand, it gives rise to *general* jurisdiction. This is made clear by cases such as *South India Shipping* v. *Bank of Korea*, where there was no connection between the claim (which arose under letters of guarantee issued in Korea in favour of an Indian company) and the activities of the bank in England.

English lawyers argue that the doctrine of *forum non conveniens* ensures that this does not produce hardship for the defendant. Continental lawyers, however,

---

43 *Deverall* v. *Grant Advertising Inc.* [1954] 3 WLR 688 (CA).
44 Cf. *The Theodohos* [1977] 2 Lloyd's Rep 428.
45 Case 139/80, [1981] ECR 819.

feel that the flexible and uncertain nature of *forum non conveniens* (discussed below in Chapter 9) puts potential defendants in a difficult position, since, without embarking on an expensive lawsuit, they cannot be sure whether or not they will be subject to the jurisdiction of the English courts.

§ 4   Service outside the jurisdiction

§ 4.1   Introduction

Under the original common law, service of the claim form on the defendant within England was the only means of establishing jurisdiction. In the nineteenth century, however, the legislature intervened to make it possible to serve a claim form outside England and thus to obtain jurisdiction over persons outside the country. This power, first granted by the Common Law Procedure Act 1852, was for many years exercised under Order 11 of the Rules of the Supreme Court (RSC), the forerunner of the CPR. Under this, a claim form could be served in a wide range of situations in which a connection existed either between the defendant and England or between the claim and England. The Rules of the Supreme Court have now been replaced by the CPR, and similar provisions are contained in Rule 6.36 and Practice Direction 6 B, paragraph 3.1. A notable feature of all these provisions is that the claimant must obtain the permission of the court before serving the claim form. This requirement does not apply under the European instruments or where the claim form is served within the jurisdiction.

An application for permission is made without notice to the defendant, and is usually heard on affidavit[46] evidence.[47] The onus is on the claimant to show both that the case comes within one of the jurisdictional rules contained in the CPR and that it is appropriate for it to be heard in England (*forum non conveniens*). It is not necessary for him to give full proof of the facts necessary to establish these matters, but he must show that a good arguable case exists. As regards the merits (substance) of his claim, he must show that there is a serious question to be tried – a substantial question of law or fact (or both) that he *bona fide* desires to be tried.[48] All these rules are based on the supposition that service of a claim form in a foreign country is a serious matter that should not be lightly undertaken. For this reason, the court will refuse permission if the case comes within the letter, but not the spirit, of the relevant provision. It will also resolve doubtful points of interpretation of the jurisdictional rules of the CPR against the claimant.

Since the defendant is not at this point present to put his side of the matter, the claimant must make a full and fair disclosure of the facts. In other words, he must put all relevant facts before the court, even those that are against his

---

46 An affidavit is a written statement made under oath.
47 A good explanation of the procedure is to be found in Dicey, Morris and Collins, pp. 363–7, as amended by the Second Supplement, where authority will be found for the statements made in this and the following paragraphs.
48 *Seaconsar Ltd* v. *Bank Markazi* [1994] 1 AC 438; [1993] 3 WLR 756 (HL).

interest. Failure to do so could be a ground for setting aside service at a later stage.

If permission is given, the claimant must then ensure that the claim form is served.[49] There are various ways in which this may be done, including the procedure under the EC Service Regulation and the Hague Service Convention (both discussed in Chapter 4, § 6, above).[50] However, the claim form must not be served in a way that is against the law of the foreign country.[51] In this regard, there is a difference of view between the common-law countries and some civil-law countries. Common-law countries do not consider the service of a foreign claim form in their territories to be an infringement of their sovereignty. If a foreign lawyer wants to come to England and serve a claim form there, he is perfectly entitled to do so. He could, if he wants, come personally to England, take a taxi to the defendant's home, and deliver the claim form to him. Some countries take a different view. They regard the service of a claim form as an official act that would infringe their sovereignty unless permission was first obtained. In Switzerland, the service of a foreign claim form without such permission is even a criminal offence. If an English claim form is served in such a country, the claimant must ensure that it is done in a way approved by the foreign State.

When the claim form has been served on the defendant, he can then come back to court and argue that permission should not have been given. In other words, he can reopen the issues set out above.[52] The same rules regarding onus of proof and standards of proof will be applied. If the defendant fails to avail himself of this opportunity (or if he avails himself of it but is unsuccessful) the jurisdiction of the court cannot thereafter be challenged. Thus, if the court takes jurisdiction on the ground that a tort was committed in England and it is eventually established that there was no tort, the court will give judgment for the defendant on the merits (substance): it will not rule that it has no jurisdiction.

We will now consider the circumstances in which service outside the jurisdiction may be permitted. We will consider only the most important rules.

§ 4.2 *Contracts*

The provisions of CPR 6.36 and Practice Direction 6 B dealing with claims in contract are set out in Panel 5.4. There are six separate grounds of jurisdiction.

§ 4.2.1 Contract made within the jurisdiction.[53] This ground of jurisdiction has no equivalent in the Brussels I Regulation. It could be objected that it constitutes a rather tenuous link, especially when the parties are not negotiating face to face. In such a case, there is no objective way of determining where

---

49 The claim form must normally be served personally on the defendant; however, where there is a special reason, it is possible, with the permission of the court, to serve it by an alternative method. In such a case, it may even be served in England. See CPR 6.15.
50 See CPR 6.40 *et seq.*
51 CPR 6.40(4).
52 CPR 11.
53 Practice Direction 6 B, paragraph 3.1(6)(a).

Panel 5.4 Contracts
Civil Procedure Rules, Rule 6.36 and Practice Direction 6 B

6.36 Service of the claim form where the permission of the court is required

In any proceedings to which rule 6.32 or 6.33 does not apply, the claimant may serve a claim form out of the jurisdiction with the permission of the court if any of the grounds set out in paragraph 3.1 of Practice Direction B supplementing this Part apply.

. . .

Practice Direction 6 B

Service out of the jurisdiction

3.1   The claimant may serve a claim form out of the jurisdiction with the permission of the court under rule 6.36 where—

. . .

Claims in relation to contracts

(6)   A claim is made in respect of a contract where the contract—
  (a) was made within the jurisdiction;
  (b) was made by or through an agent trading or residing within the jurisdiction;
  (c) is governed by English law; or
  (d) contains a term to the effect that the court shall have jurisdiction to determine any claim in respect of the contract.

(7)   A claim is made in respect of a breach of contract committed within the jurisdiction.

(8)   A claim is made for a declaration that no contract exists where, if the contract was found to exist, it would comply with the conditions set out in paragraph (6).

the contract is made. Artificial rules have to be applied and these rules are different in different countries. The English rule is that, where the parties communicate by instantaneous (or near-instantaneous) means of communication (for example, telephone, fax or e-mail), the contract is made where the offeror receives the acceptance. Where, on the other hand, it is by non-instantaneous means of communication (for example, by post), it is where the letter of acceptance is mailed.[54] Different rules apply in other countries.[55]

§ 4.2.2 Made by or through an agent trading or residing within the jurisdiction.[56] This head of jurisdiction has two limbs: contracts made 'by' an agent and contracts made 'through' an agent. In *National Mortgage and Agency Company of New Zealand* v. *Gosselin*,[57] it

was held that 'by' an agent covers the case where the agent has the power to bind the principal, and 'through' an agent applies where he has to refer orders back to the head office. A claim form may be served in both cases.

This rule appears to have something in common with the rule considered in § 3.3, above (company acting through an agent). However, the two rules are actually very different. The rule considered in § 3.3 is concerned with determining when a foreign company can be regarded as doing business in England so that it is present in the jurisdiction. If it is present, a claim form may be served on it. The rule we are considering here is not concerned with establishing whether the company is present in England. It assumes that it is not, and permits service on it abroad.

The second difference is that the rule considered here is wider than that discussed in § 3.3. It also covers cases in which the 'agent' had no authority to conclude contracts on behalf of his principal and had to refer all orders back to the head office. None of the other factors referred to in *Adams* v. *Cape Industries* (§ 3.3, above) is relevant.

The third difference is that the rule being considered here permits jurisdiction to be assumed only if the claim is made in respect of a contract made by

---

54 *Entores* v. *Miles Far Eastern Corporation* [1955] 2 QB 327 (CA).
55 An English court will always apply the English rules on this matter: there is no room for choice of law.
56 Practice Direction 6 B, paragraph 3.1(6)(b).
57 (1922) 18 TLR 832 (CA).

or through the agent. In this regard, it is similar to Article 5(5) of the Brussels I Regulation. The rule discussed in § 3.3, above, on the other hand, gives the court *general* jurisdiction: the claim need not relate to the activities of the company in England.

§ 4.2.3 Governed by English law.[58]

This ground of jurisdiction has no counterpart under the Brussels I Regulation. Foreign businessmen often insert into their contracts a choice-of-law clause specifying English law, and a choice-of-court clause giving jurisdiction to the courts of England. In this situation, the English courts would take jurisdiction under the choice-of-court clause and the ground of jurisdiction considered here would be unnecessary. It only comes into play, therefore, where the contract is governed by English law – either because there is a choice-of-law clause in favour of English law or on other grounds – but there is no choice-of-court clause.

§ 4.2.4 Choice-of-court clause.[59]

Choice-of-court agreements will be considered in detail in Chapter 8.

§ 4.2.5 Breach committed within the jurisdiction.[60]

This rule has a great deal in common with that laid down in Article 5(1) of the Brussels I Regulation, at least where the 'obligation in question' is regarded as being the obligation the breach of which gives rise to the claim.

§ 4.2.6 Declaration that no contract exists.[61]

This is a useful rule. If there would have been jurisdiction on some other ground if there had been a contract, there should be jurisdiction to obtain a declaration that no contract exists.

This same problem could arise with regard to Article 5(1) of the Brussels I Regulation. It is probable that the European Court would interpret it along the same lines as the English rule.

§ 4.3   Tort

The provisions of Practice Direction 6 B (read with CPR 6.36) dealing with claims in tort are set out in Panel 5.5. They are more or less identical to those contained in Article 5(3) of the Brussels I Regulation, as the latter has been interpreted by the European Court (see the discussion in Chapter 4, § 1.2, above). One question which the

---

Panel 5.5 Tort
Practice Direction 6 B

Service out of the jurisdiction

3.1 The claimant may serve a claim form out of the jurisdiction with the permission of the court under rule 6.36 where—

. . .

Claims in tort
(9) A claim is made in tort where
    (a) damage was sustained within the jurisdiction; or
    (b) the damage sustained resulted from an act committed within the jurisdiction.

---

58 Practice Direction 6 B, paragraph 3.1(6)(c).
59 Practice Direction 6 B, paragraph 3.1(6)(d).
60 Practice Direction 6 B, paragraph 3.1(7).
61 Practice Direction 6 B, paragraph 3.1(8).

European Court has not yet had to decide is whether the entire wrongful act must take place within the territory of the forum and whether the whole of the damage must occur there. This issue arose in England in our next case.

England
Metall und Rohstoff* v. *Donaldson Lufkin & Jenrette
Court of Appeal
[1990] 1 QB 391; [1989] 3 WLR 563

Background

This was an action by a Swiss company against two American companies in which the Swiss company claimed that the American companies had, in New York, induced a third party to break, in England, his contract with the claimant. The English court had to decide whether it had jurisdiction under Order 11, Rule 1(1)(f), of the Rules of the Supreme Court, the forerunner of Practice Direction 6 B, paragraph 3.1(9). The following is a short extract from the judgment.

Slade LJ (giving the judgment of the court)

Until 1987 leave could be given only if the action begun by the writ was 'founded on a tort committed within the jurisdiction' and most of the decided cases turn on that wording. The rule was changed to give effect to the Brussels Convention . . . and the decision of the European Court of Justice in [*Bier* v. *Mines de Potasse*].

As the rule now stands it is plain that jurisdiction may be assumed only where (a) the claim is founded on a tort and either (b) the damage was sustained within the jurisdiction or (c) the damage resulted from an act committed within the jurisdiction. Condition (a) poses a question which we consider below: what law is to be applied in resolving whether the claim is 'founded on a tort?' Condition (b) raises the question: what damage is referred to? It was argued for ACLI [one of the defendants] that since the draftsman had used the definite article and not simply referred to 'damage', it is necessary that all the damage should have been sustained within the jurisdiction. No authority was cited to support the suggestion that this is the correct construction of the Convention to which the rule gives effect[1] and it could lead to an absurd result if there were no one place in which all the plaintiff's damage had been suffered. The judge rejected this argument and so do we. It is enough if some significant damage has been sustained in England. Condition (c) prompts the inquiry: what if damage has resulted from acts committed partly within and partly without the jurisdiction? This will often be the case where a series of acts, regarded by English law as tortious, are committed in an international context. It would not, we think, make sense to require all the acts to have been committed within the jurisdiction, because again there might be no single jurisdiction where that would be so. But it would certainly contravene the spirit, and also we think the letter, of the rule if jurisdiction were assumed on the strength of some relatively minor or insignificant act having been committed here, perhaps fortuitously. In our view condition (c) requires the court to look at the tort alleged in a common sense way and ask whether damage has resulted from substantial and efficacious acts

1 *Editor's note*: this was the Brussels Convention.

committed within the jurisdiction (whether or not other substantial and efficacious acts have been committed elsewhere): if the answer is yes, leave may (but of course need not) be given. But the defendants are, we think, right to insist that the acts to be considered must be those of the putative defendant, because the question at issue is whether the links between him and the English forum are such as to justify his being brought here to answer the plaintiffs' claim.

It is probable that the European Court would interpret Article 5(3) of the Brussels I Regulation in the same way. It is also likely that the English courts would apply the *Marinari* decision of the European Court (set out in Chapter 4, § 1.2, above) when interpreting Practice Direction 6 B, paragraph 3.1(9).[62]

§ 4.4 Multiple parties

Under Practice Direction 6 B, paragraph 3.1(3) (Panel 5.6), the court has jurisdiction over a defendant if he is a 'necessary or proper' party to proceedings against another party and the court has jurisdiction over that other party on some other ground. This is similar to Article 6(1) and (2) of the Brussels I Regulation (discussed in Chapter 4, § 2, above), but it is wider. It is wider than the rule in Article 6(1) (claimant suing two defendants) because it is not limited to the case in which the 'anchor' defendant is sued in the court of his domicile. Thus, under the English rule, the 'anchor' defendant may be served while on a short visit to England.

> **Panel 5.6 Multiple parties**
> **Practice Direction 6 B, paragraph 3.1(3)**
>
> **Service out of the jurisdiction where permission is required**
>
> 3.1 The claimant may serve a claim form out of the jurisdiction with the permission of the court under rule 6.36 where—
> . . .
> (3) A claim is made against a person ('the defendant') on whom the claim form has been or will be served (otherwise than in reliance on this paragraph) and—
> (a) there is between the claimant and the defendant a real issue which it is reasonable for the court to try; and
> (b) the claimant wishes to serve the claim form on another person who is a necessary or proper party to that claim.

The second difference is that, under Article 6(1), the claims must be so closely connected that it is expedient to hear and determine them together to avoid the risk of irreconcilable judgments resulting from separate proceedings. There is no similar limitation on the English rule, though the requirement that the second defendant must be a necessary or proper party goes some of the way in the same direction.[63]

The policy arguments concerning this ground of jurisdiction were discussed in Chapter 4, § 2, above.

§ 4.5 Weak parties

The traditional English rules contain no special provisions on parties regarded as being in a weak bargaining position – for example, consumers or employees.

---

62 For developments in Canada in this area, see Chapter 6, § 3, below.
63 It is said that the English courts must exercise special care when deciding whether to permit service out of the jurisdiction on this ground: Dicey, Morris and Collins, p. 371, paragraph 11-166. In particular, service should not be permitted simply in order to avoid two sets of proceedings: *ibid*. These requirements probably cover the same ground as the requirement in EC law that the proceedings must not have been instituted solely with the object of removing the defendant from the jurisdiction of the court which would otherwise be competent in his case.

§ 5   Jurisdiction by consent

In addition to jurisdiction based on the service of the claim form, jurisdiction may also be obtained through the consent of the defendant. It is traditionally regarded that there are three ways in which this may be given: the defendant may agree expressly that the court will have jurisdiction (choice-of-court agreement); he may plead to the merits without challenging the jurisdiction of the court (submission); or he may himself invoke the jurisdiction of the court, in which case he is regarded as consenting to its jurisdiction to make an order against him (for example, as regards costs) and with regard to a counterclaim.

Choice-of-court agreements will be considered in Chapter 8. All that need be said here is that, even though the jurisdiction of the court is not dependent on the service of the claim form, it must nevertheless be served for procedural reasons. As we saw above, this may be done under Practice Direction 6 B, paragraph 3.1(6)(d) (Panel 5.4, above).

Whenever a claim form is served on a potential defendant, he always has the opportunity to contest jurisdiction before pleading to the merits. This does not constitute submission. However, if he fails to do this (or if he does it, but is unsuccessful) any attempt thereafter to defend the case on the merits will constitute submission. Article 24 of the Brussels I Regulation contains a similar rule (see Chapter 4, § 6, above). It prevents a defendant from contesting a case on the merits and then, if he loses, claiming that the court had no jurisdiction over him.

It is obvious that, if a claimant invokes the jurisdiction of a court, he must be taken as accepting its jurisdiction to decide the case against him. This includes an order to pay costs. A counterclaim is different. Under the Brussels I Regulation, a court before which proceedings are brought has jurisdiction to decide a counterclaim against the claimant, but only if it arises from the same contract or facts as those on which the original claim was based (see Chapter 4, § 3, above). English law does not have this limitation, though an English court would not allow a counterclaim to be made unless this was desirable in the interests of justice.[64] Where it was not desirable, the claim would have to be brought in separate proceedings, in which case there would have to be an independent ground of jurisdiction.

§ 6   Exclusive jurisdiction

Like EC law, English law recognizes the concept of exclusive jurisdiction. If a foreign court has exclusive jurisdiction, the English courts will not be able to hear the case, even if the claim form is served in England (or if it is served outside England under the provisions of the CPR). The most important example (as under

---

[64] Dicey, Morris and Collins, pp. 356–7 (paragraph 11-131).

EC law) concerns land in a foreign country.[65] Under a rule originally laid down by the House of Lords in the nineteenth century in *British South Africa Company* v. *Companhia de Moçambique*,[66] English courts have no jurisdiction to hear proceedings for determination of title to, or the right to possession of, immovable property situated outside England. This rule, which is subject to certain exceptions,[67] was originally wider in scope and also precluded English courts from hearing actions in tort for trespass to foreign land and (probably) for other torts affecting foreign land. However, it was provided by the Civil Jurisdiction and Judgments Act 1982, section 30 (set out in Panel 5.7), that the court was not barred from hearing such actions unless the case was principally concerned with title to, or the right to possession of, the property.[68] Except in these latter cases, the normal rules of jurisdiction apply.

Where the immovable property is situated in a State to which the Brussels I Regulation or the Lugano Convention applies, the English courts will have no jurisdiction where these instruments give exclusive jurisdiction to the courts of the State in which the property is situated.[69]

What is the position where the immovable property is situated in a State to which the European instruments do not apply? If the defendant is not domiciled in a State to which the European instruments apply (and there is no other ground on which they

> **Panel 5.7 Foreign land**
> **Civil Jurisdiction and Judgments Act 1982 (as amended), section 30**
>
> **30 Proceedings in England and Wales or Northern Ireland for torts to immovable property**
>
> (1) The jurisdiction of any court in England and Wales or Northern Ireland to entertain proceedings for trespass to, or any other tort affecting, immovable property shall extend to cases in which the property in question is situated outside that part of the United Kingdom unless the proceedings are principally concerned with a question of the title to, or the right to possession of, that property.
>
> (2) Subsection (1) has effect subject to the 1968 Convention and the Lugano Convention and the Regulation[1] and to the provisions set out in Schedule 4.
>
> 1 Editor's note: this is the Brussels I Regulation.

are applicable), the English rule will apply. The answer is not clear, however, where the English courts have jurisdiction under the European instruments – for example, because the defendant is domiciled in England (see Chapter 4, § 5, above). The English courts *ought* to be permitted to stay the proceedings in such cases,[70] but one cannot be certain that the European Court will accept this.

§ 7 Conclusions

The traditional English rules of jurisdiction have been developed over many years through the traditional common-law method of a slow accretion of precedents. In view of the highly international nature of the British economy, especially the

---

65 See Dicey, Morris and Collins, pp. 1142 *et seq*., especially pp. 1148–54 (paragraphs 23-034 to 23-052).
66 [1893] AC 602.
67 These exceptions apply where there is a contract or equity between the parties, or where the issue has to be decided for the purpose of the administration of an estate or trust and the property consists of movables or immovables in England as well as immovables outside England.
68 Civil Jurisdiction and Judgments Act 1982, section 30.
69 See Chapter 4, § 5, above.
70 Dicey, Morris and Collins, pp. 1145–6 (paragraph 23-027).

financial-services industry centred on London, these rules place great emphasis on meeting the needs of international business. They are considerably more flexible than comparable rules in the legal systems of Continental Europe. In contrast to Continental judges, for whom the judiciary is almost always a career in itself rather than the culmination of a career in legal practice, the English judges have been able to draw on their experience as practising lawyers to ensure that their decisions reflect practical needs and concerns. In their hands, the wide discretion given to judges by the common law has been exercised in the interests of litigants and of the sound administration of justice, rather than to advance objectives of a theoretical nature. It is this difference of approach that is the hallmark of the common law system.

Further reading

Bell, 'The Negative Declaration in Transnational Litigation' (1995) 111 LQR 674

Bigos, 'Jurisdiction over Cross-Border Wrongs on the Internet' (2005) 54 ICLQ 585

Dicey, Morris and Collins, *The Conflict of Laws* (Sweet and Maxwell, London, 14th edn, 2006), pp. 346–96

Enonchong, 'Service of Process in England on Overseas Companies and Article 5(5) of the Brussels Convention' (1999) 48 ICLQ 921

Fawcett, 'A New Approach to Jurisdiction over Companies in Private International Law' (1988) 37 ICLQ 645

   'Jurisdiction and Subsidiaries' [1985] *Journal of Business Law* 16

Stein, 'Personal Jurisdiction and the Internet' (2004) 98 *Northwestern University Law Review* 411

CHAPTER 6

Developments in Canada

For many years, Canadian law was more or less the same as English law. More recently, however, Canada has begun to establish a distinctive approach of its own. In this chapter, we will look at developments in the area of jurisdiction. We take tort as an example.

§ 1   Introduction

Canada is a federation consisting of a number of provinces, together with certain territories. Each province has its own government and legislature. Under the Canadian Constitution, legislative jurisdiction is divided between the federation (Canada) and the provinces. Most matters of private (civil) law – for example, the law of contract, tort and property – fall within provincial jurisdiction. All the provinces except Quebec base their legal system on the common law of England. Quebec has a civil-law system, originally based on that of France.

Each province has its own court system. However, superior-court[1] judges in the provinces are appointed and paid by the federal authorities,[2] and appeals from all the provinces go to the Supreme Court of Canada, in the federal capital of Ottawa. Unlike the Supreme Court of the United States, the Supreme Court of Canada can hear appeals on provincial law as well as on federal law. The judges on the Supreme Court of Canada represent both the common-law and the civil-law traditions. At the federal level, English and French have equal status.

For the purpose of conflict of laws, each province normally constitutes a separate jurisdiction. Most cases concern inter-provincial, rather than international, conflicts. Thus the issue will be whether the courts of Ontario, rather than those of Quebec, have jurisdiction; whether the law of Nova Scotia or that of New Brunswick should be applied; or whether a judgment from Alberta should be recognized in Manitoba. At least in the past, the same rules were applied to decide inter-provincial conflicts as were applied to decide international conflicts. Thus, for example, the same rules were applied to decide whether a judgment from California should be recognized in Saskatchewan as were applied to decide whether a judgment from British Columbia should be recognized there.

In the 1990s, all this began to change.

---

1 Superior courts are courts with full jurisdiction, as distinct from tribunals with limited jurisdiction. The superior courts are the courts which hear civil actions other than those involving small sums of money.
2 In this respect, Canada is different from the United States, where state-court judges are appointed by the states – they are usually elected – and paid out of state funds.

§ 2   Ontario

Most of the cases in this chapter concern the province of Ontario, a common-law province. In general, its jurisdictional system is similar to that of England. Jurisdiction is based on service of a writ (as a claim form is still called) within the province, service of a writ outside the province under the Rules of Civil Procedure (the Ontario equivalent to the CPR) and submission. Rule 17 of the Rules of Civil Procedure provides for service outside the province (for extracts, see Panel 6.1, below). It lays down a number of specific grounds of jurisdiction, which are similar to those in CPR 6.36 and Practice Direction 6 B. For example, in the case of proceedings in respect of a contract (Rule 17.02(f)), the grounds of jurisdiction are virtually identical to those applicable in England under Practice Direction 6 B, paragraph 3.1(6), (7) and (8) (see Chapter 5, Panel 5.4, above).

There is, however, one important difference: under the Ontario system, a writ may be served *without leave* if the claim falls within the terms of Rule 17.[3] Moreover, even if it does not fall within any of the specific grounds of jurisdiction set out in Rule 17, the writ may *still* be served; however, in such a case leave of court is required.[4]

In an application for leave, the plaintiff (as a claimant is still called) must convince the court that Ontario is an appropriate forum. Once the defendant has been served (whether or not leave was obtained), he can appear before the court and ask it to set aside service.[5] If the writ was wrongly served without leave (because the claim did not come within any of the grounds specified in Rule 17), but the court considers that it would have been appropriate to grant leave if an application had been made, it may make an order validating service.[6]

§ 3   Service out of the jurisdiction in tort cases

The grounds of jurisdiction regarding actions in tort are set out in Panel 6.1. Our next case explains how they operate.

Panel 6.1 Rules of Civil Procedure (Ontario) (RPO 1990), Regulation 194

Service outside Ontario without leave

17.02 A party to a proceeding may, without a court order, be served outside Ontario with an originating process or notice of a reference where the proceeding against the party consists of a claim or claims . . .

Tort committed in Ontario

 (g) in respect of a tort committed in Ontario;

Damage sustained in Ontario

 (h) in respect of damage sustained in Ontario arising from a tort, breach of contract, breach of fiduciary duty or breach of confidence, wherever committed . . .

---

3 Rule 17.02, Panel 6.1.
4 Rule 17.03, Panel 6.1.
5 Rule 17.06, Panel 6.1.
6 Rule 17.06(3), Panel 6.1.

Panel 6.1 *(cont.)*

Service outside Ontario with leave

17.03 (1) In any case to which rule 17.02 does not apply, the court may grant leave to serve an originating process or notice of a reference outside Ontario.

Motion to set aside service outside Ontario

17.06 (1) A party who has been served with an originating process outside Ontario may move, before delivering a defence, notice of intent to defend or notice of appearance,

(a) for an order setting aside the service and any order that authorized the service; or

(b) for an order staying the proceeding.

2 The court may make an order under subrule (1) or such other order as is just where it is satisfied that,

(a) service outside Ontario is not authorized by these rules;

(b) an order granting leave to serve outside Ontario should be set aside; or

(c) Ontario is not a convenient forum for the hearing of the proceeding.

3 Where on a motion under subrule (1) the court concludes that service outside Ontario is not authorized by these rules, but the case is one in which it would have been appropriate to grant leave to serve outside Ontario under rule 17.03, the court may make an order validating the service.

4 The making of a motion under subrule (1) is not in itself a submission to the jurisdiction of the court over the moving party.

> **Ontario**
> *Muscutt* v. *Courcelles*
> **Ontario Court of Appeal**
> **(2002) 60 OR (3d) 20; (2002) 213 DLR (4th) 577**

Background

The plaintiff in the case was Muscutt. He had been resident in Ontario, but moved to the province of Alberta on a contract for his Ontario-based employer. He then accepted his employer's offer to work at a new Alberta office and was planning to move his residence to Alberta. At this point, however, he was involved in a serious motor accident in Alberta. He was badly injured and, on being released from hospital in Alberta, returned to Ontario to live with his mother. He needed extensive ongoing medical care in Ontario. He brought legal proceedings in Ontario against the driver of the car in which he was travelling, the driver of the other vehicle and various other people. All the defendants were resident in Alberta at the time of the accident, though one of them subsequently moved to Ontario. The question before the Ontario Court of Appeal was whether the courts of Ontario had jurisdiction. The extract given below is interesting both for the light it sheds on English law and for the ways in which Canadian law has now developed independently.

Sharpe JA (giving the judgment of the court)

[12.] The jurisdictional issues that arise on this appeal emerge from a rapidly evolving area of law. Until the early 1990s, this area was governed by a set of rigid common law rules developed in England in the nineteenth century. These rules, discussed below, were shaped by the sovereignty concerns of a dominant nineteenth century world power anxious to safeguard its territorial sovereignty and jealous of any attempt by foreign states to intrude.

[13.] Towards the end of the twentieth century, it became increasingly apparent that these rules were out of keeping with the reality of modern interprovincial and international commerce and the frequent and rapid movement of people, goods and services across borders. The rules were especially ill-suited for resolving issues of jurisdiction, enforcement and choice of law between the interdependent sister provinces of Canada.

[14.] In four seminal decisions between 1990 and 1994, the Supreme Court of Canada radically changed the entire area of law. The decisions recognized that a new approach was necessary for a modern federal state with integrated national markets and a justice system that featured closely shared values, a common appointment process for judges and a single final court of appeal for all courts.

[15.] *Morguard*[1] and *Hunt*[2] rewrote the law of jurisdiction and enforcement. For the first time, jurisdiction and enforcement were recognized as being governed by common values. The Supreme Court held that the principles of 'order and fairness' require limits on the reach of provincial jurisdiction against out-of-province defendants and that jurisdiction can only be asserted against an out-of-province defendant on the basis of a 'real and substantial connection'. However, the Court also held that the courts of a province must give 'full faith and credit' to the judgments of the courts of a sister province where the real and substantial connection test is satisfied.[3]

. . .

(a) The development of assumed jurisdiction

[19.] There are three ways in which jurisdiction may be asserted against an out-of-province defendant: (1) presence-based jurisdiction; (2) consent-based jurisdiction; and (3) assumed jurisdiction. Presence-based jurisdiction permits jurisdiction over an extraprovincial defendant who is physically present within the territory of the court. Consent-based jurisdiction permits jurisdiction over an extraprovincial defendant who consents, whether by voluntary submission, attornment[4] by appearance and defence, or prior agreement to submit disputes to the jurisdiction of the domestic court. Both bases of jurisdiction also provide bases for the recognition and enforcement of extraprovincial judgments.

[20.] This appeal raises the issue of assumed jurisdiction. Assumed jurisdiction is initiated by service of the court's process out of the jurisdiction pursuant to rule 17.02. Unlike presence-based jurisdiction and consent-based jurisdiction, prior to *Morguard* and *Hunt*, assumed jurisdiction did not provide a basis for recognition and enforcement.

---

1 *Morguard Investments Ltd* v. *De Savoye* (1990) 76 DLR (4th) 256; [1990] 3 SCR 1077 (set out in Chapter 17, § 1, below).
2 *Hunt* v. *T&N plc* [1993] 4 SCR 289; 109 DLR (4th) 16.
3 *Editor's note*: developments in Canada on the recognition of foreign judgments will be considered in Chapter 17, below.
4 *Editor's note*: 'attornment' means 'submission'.

[21.] Service of process out of the jurisdiction (service *ex juris*) was originally introduced by statute in mid-nineteenth century England and was gradually but cautiously introduced in Canada by rules of court. The traditional approach was concerned with a state's interference with the territorial sovereignty of another state . . .

[22.] Concern over territorial sovereignty and foreign sensibilities was reflected in the text and interpretation of service *ex juris* rules. Until 1975 in Ontario, the plaintiff was required to obtain leave of the court by *ex parte* motion[5] before serving process outside the jurisdiction. Further, an established body of case law mandated a cautious approach that narrowly interpreted the rules and resolved any doubt in favour of the foreign defendant . . .

[23.] Courts also had an overriding discretion to refuse leave even where the plaintiff satisfied the black letter of the rules . . . In addition, courts had a discretion to decline jurisdiction on the basis of *forum non conveniens*, which applies where jurisdiction is inconvenient in light of all of the circumstances. This traditional approach to service out of the jurisdiction was protective of foreign defendants and made it relatively difficult for domestic plaintiffs to sue foreign defendants in domestic courts.

[24.] However, by the mid-1970s, this approach came to be perceived as out of keeping with modern patterns of commerce, travel and trade and with modern values of comity between cooperating interdependent states. In *Jannock Corporation* v. *RT Tamblyn & Partners Ltd.* (1975) 8 OR (2d) 622 at 632; 58 DLR (3d) 678 (CA) . . . this court held that it was 'quite unrealistic to treat as a foreigner one who lives in a Province of this country and does business in his own and other Provinces'. Concern for the rights of domestic plaintiffs who sought justice in the courts of their home province began to prevail over concern for the sovereignty of other states.

[25.] The first significant step in judicial law reform came in *Moran* v. *Pyle* [set out in Chapter 11, § 1.2, below] . . .

[26.] In 1975, the rules governing service out of the jurisdiction were amended and many of the traditional constraints were removed. In *Singh* v. *Howden Petroleum Ltd.* (1979) 24 OR (2d) 769; 100 DLR (3d) 121 (CA), this court reviewed the nature, purpose and effect of these changes. Arnup JA held that as a result of the changes, if the case fell within an enumerated category, plaintiffs were no longer required to seek leave of the court before serving an out-of-province defendant. A subsequent change (now rule 17.03) allowed plaintiffs to obtain leave to serve an out-of-province defendant in cases not specifically mentioned in the rule. In other provinces, the changes were even more dramatic. Nova Scotia and Prince Edward Island allow a plaintiff to serve an out-of-province defendant in any case anywhere in Canada or the United States.

---

5 *Editor's note*: an *ex parte* motion is one made without notice to the other party.

[27.] Rule 17.02(h) was enacted in 1975. As mentioned above, this rule allows for service out of the jurisdiction in respect of a claim for damage sustained in Ontario arising from a tort committed elsewhere. This 'damage sustained' rule represented a legislative response to the type of problem confronted by the Supreme Court of Canada in *Moran v. Pyle*.

[28.] Courts have given the 'damage sustained' rule a generous and liberal interpretation. The rule has been applied to a plaintiff who undergoes medical treatment and endures pain and suffering in Ontario as a result of a tort committed elsewhere. In *Vile* v. *Von Wendt* (1979) 26 OR (2d) 513 at 517; 103 DLR (3d) 356 (Div. Ct), the court held that the rule was intended 'to enable the people of Ontario to use their own Courts more easily' and to overcome decisions under the old rule, which had required Ontario residents to pursue foreign tortfeasors elsewhere . . .

[29.] As will be explained below, the 'damage sustained' rule is now subject to the principles articulated in *Morguard* regarding the need for a real and substantial connection and the need for order, fairness and jurisdictional restraint.

The court then considered subsequent developments in the Supreme Court of Canada, which were partly based on constitutional law.[7] The first step was taken in the *Morguard*[8] case. This case, which concerned the recognition in one province of a judgment given in another province, is set out in Chapter 17, § 1, below. In it, the Supreme Court of Canada laid down a rule that a judgment from a sister province must be recognized and enforced if there is a 'real and substantial' connection with the court of origin, a test derived from the more general principles of order and fairness. This test was not originally regarded as constitutionally mandated, but, in *Hunt*,[9] the Supreme Court of Canada held that it had constitutional force.[10]

These developments had an impact on the law of 'assumed jurisdiction' (jurisdiction based on the service of the writ outside the province). The test of a real and substantial connection came to be applicable in the court of origin as well: before a court could take jurisdiction, it had to ensure that the test was satisfied.[11] Since the test was intended to be flexible, the question arises of how it differs from *forum non conveniens*. The court answered this by saying that the 'real and substantial connection' test decides when a court is entitled to hear a case while the doctrine of *forum non conveniens* assumes that two or more courts are entitled to hear it, and lays down a discretionary test as to when a court should decline jurisdiction in favour of another court.[12] Where proceedings are

---

7 This and the following three paragraphs are a summary of paragraphs 30–53 of the judgment.

8 *Morguard Investments Ltd v. De Savoye* (1990) 76 DLR (4th) 256; [1990] 3 SCR 1077.

9 *Hunt* v. *T&N plc* [1993] 4 SCR 289; 109 DLR (4th) 16.

10 *Editor's note*: it is now the Canadian equivalent of the 'Full Faith and Credit' Clause of the US Constitution.

11 *Editor's note*: the test of a real and substantial connection now seems to fulfil the same function in Canada as the 'minimum contacts' test in the United States (see Chapter 7, § 2, below). For the difference between the two tests, see paragraphs 57–74 of the judgment in *Muscutt*.

12 *Editor's note*: in practice, the tests for determining whether there is a real and substantial connection cover much the same ground as those applicable for deciding whether to grant a stay on the ground of *forum non conveniens*.

brought in Ontario, therefore, the court must consider whether there is a real and substantial connection with Ontario. If there is not, the court has no jurisdiction. If there is, but if the courts of another province (or foreign country) also have jurisdiction, the Ontario court may decide to stay the proceedings under the doctrine of *forum non conveniens*.

The Ontario Court of Appeal next considered[13] whether Rule 17.02(h) (set out in Panel 6.1, above) was constitutionally valid. This was the rule invoked by the plaintiff. It was argued by the defendants that the rule was invalid because it did not incorporate the 'real and substantial connection' test. The court rejected this challenge. It held that Rule 17.02(h) was purely procedural and did not itself confer jurisdiction. It was concerned merely with service. Jurisdiction depended on the 'real and substantial connection' test, which now had to be regarded as constitutionally binding. However, the Ontario rules were not unconstitutional because they gave defendants ample opportunity to raise the issue when service of the writ was challenged under Rule 17.06 (Panel 6.1, above). Thus, the court concluded that Rule 17.02(h) must now be read as being subject to the 'real and substantial connection' test: it is not sufficient for a plaintiff to show that the case comes within the terms of the Rule; he must establish that there is a real and substantial connection with Ontario.[14]

The court's next task was to decide whether the 'real and substantial connection' test was satisfied in the case before it.

Issue 2: Did the motions court judge err in finding that the Ontario Superior Court could assume jurisdiction against the out-of-province defendants?

[54.] The appellants urge us to adopt an interpretation of the real and substantial connection test that focuses on the nature and extent of the defendant's contacts with the jurisdiction. The appellants submit that a court can only assume jurisdiction against an extra-provincial defendant where it is reasonable to infer that the defendant has voluntarily submitted to Ontario's jurisdiction or where it was reasonably within the defendant's contemplation that his or her conduct could cause an injury in Ontario and give rise to a claim in Ontario courts.

[55.] The respondents contend that an approach that focuses solely upon the nature and extent of the defendant's contacts with the jurisdiction would be unduly restrictive and would fail to pay adequate heed to the interests of the injured plaintiff. They submit that the connection between the forum and the subject matter of the action and the connection between the forum and the damages suffered by the plaintiff are equally relevant in determining whether there is a real and substantial connection.

[56.] The Supreme Court of Canada has insisted that the real and substantial connection test must be flexible. The Court has not attempted to define

---

13 Paragraphs 46–53.
14 On this point, contrast *Spar Aerospace Ltd* v. *American Mobile Satellite Corporation* [2002] 4 SCR 205; 2002 SCC 7 (Supreme Court of Canada), set out below.

the precise nature of the connection to the jurisdiction that is required, and the Court's language is ambiguous. While certain passages in *Morguard* suggest that the connection must be with the defendant, others suggest that the connection must be with the subject matter of the action or with the damages suffered by the plaintiff.

[57.] In his comment on *Morguard*, (1991) 70 Can. Bar Rev. 733 at 741, Professor Joost Blom observes that the Court's language lends itself to two possible approaches: the 'personal subjection' approach, and the 'administration of justice' approach. Under the personal subjection approach, jurisdiction is legitimate if the defendant regularly lived or carried on business in the province, or if the defendant voluntarily did something that related to the province so as to make it reasonable to contemplate that he or she might be sued in the province. By contrast, under the administration of justice approach, the basis for assuming jurisdiction is broader than personal subjection. The forum need only meet a minimum standard of suitability, under which it must be fair for the case to be heard in the province because the province is a 'reasonable place for the action to take place'.

[58.] These two approaches provide a useful way of analyzing the case law. In the discussion that follows, I outline the cases that have emphasized personal subjection as a basis for assumed jurisdiction as well as the cases that have followed a broader approach. I then explain why I consider the broader approach to be supportable and outline several factors relevant to assumed jurisdiction under this broader approach.

(a) The personal subjection approach

[59.] The personal subjection approach has been followed in the United States and in several Canadian decisions at the trial level.

[The court then considered the American 'minimum contacts' doctrine (explained below in Chapter 7) and continued:]

[62.] Although Canadian decisions do not use the term 'minimum contacts', several trial level decisions have adopted a similar personal subjection approach, under which a significant degree of contact between the defendant and the forum is a pre-requisite for the assumption of jurisdiction. For example, in *Long* v. *Citi Club*, [1995] OJ No. 1411 at para. 7 (Gen. Div.), Binks J held:

> The plaintiff must do more than allege that he has suffered damage in the forum province (Ontario). In order for Ontario to assume jurisdiction over this defendant, there must exist a substantial connection *between Ontario and the defendant*, such that it makes it reasonable to infer that *the defendant has voluntarily submitted himself or herself to the risk of litigation in the courts of the forum province*. [Emphasis added]

[Further citations omitted.]

(b) An approach broader than personal subjection

[63.] The weight of post-*Morguard* appellate authority holds that a real and substantial connection may be found on a broader basis than personal subjection. One of the leading authorities is the Nova Scotia Court of Appeal's decision in *Oakley* v. *Barry* (1998) 158 DLR (4th) 679. The plaintiff, at the time a resident of New Brunswick, received treatment from the defendant physicians and hospital in New Brunswick. The defendant physicians performed a liver biopsy and told the plaintiff that she suffered from infectious hepatitis 'B'. The plaintiff then moved to Nova Scotia, where physicians advised her that she did not suffer from that illness. The plaintiff was in poor health, lacked financial resources and was unable to travel. She brought her action against the New Brunswick defendants in Nova Scotia.

[64.] Pugsley JA dismissed the defendants' appeal from an order refusing to stay the action. Acknowledging the ambiguity in *Morguard*'s articulation of the real and substantial connection test, Pugsley JA held at p. 691 that there was 'a real and substantial connection between the *subject matter of the action* and the Province of Nova Scotia, as well as a real and substantial connection between the *damages* caused by the alleged negligence of the appellant physicians, and the defendant hospital, and the Province of Nova Scotia'. [Emphasis added]. In support of this finding, he noted that the plaintiff's cause of action did not accrue until she was advised in Nova Scotia of the problems with the diagnosis she had been given in New Brunswick and that, since the plaintiff was being treated in Nova Scotia, that province had a significant financial interest in her well-being.

[The court then analysed a fairly substantial number of decisions supporting the broader approach.]

(c) The preferability of a broader approach

[72.] In 'Constitutional Limits on Service *Ex Juris*: Unanswered Questions from *Morguard*', [(2000), 23 Adv. Q 167] Watson and Au argue that Canadian courts should not adopt a personal subjection approach that requires 'minimum contacts' between the defendant and the forum. At pp. 198–211, they outline several objections to the adoption of this American approach:

- In the United States, the Constitution's due process guarantee explicitly protects property rights, and due process jurisprudence focuses on the defendant's liberty interest. By contrast, s. 7 of the *Canadian Charter of Rights and Freedoms* does not protect property rights, and the Canadian approach to jurisdiction does not rest on constitutionally-entrenched individual rights but on the territorial concerns of a federal state.
- Insisting on a substantial connection between the defendant and the forum may result in multiple actions and inconsistent judgments in complex litigation involving several defendants in different jurisdictions.
- In the United States, the personal subjection approach to jurisdiction has led to practical uncertainty and frequent preliminary challenges to jurisdiction, which are often used strategically to prolong litigation. Watson and Au argue that 'courts should exercise care in interpreting rules and developing legal principles so as not

to encourage unnecessary motions'. To this end, they suggest that Canadian courts should show greater deference to the policy underlying provincial service *ex juris* rules than American courts do.

- A narrow focus on the defendant's connection with the forum could lead to decisions that are contrary to 'common sense and practicability'. Watson and Au argue that 'cases should be allowed to be heard in a forum which, having regard to *all relevant circumstances*, is one appropriate to hear the dispute. The defendant's interest should be *among* the factors to be weighed, and should not itself be determinative of the choice of forum'. [Emphasis in original]

- Deciding jurisdictional questions primarily on the basis of the defendant's connection with the forum may pay insufficient attention to the fairness component of the *forum non conveniens* analysis. The threshold of the jurisdiction test should be sufficiently low as to allow for the more detailed weighing of factors that occurs under the *forum non conveniens* test.

[73.] On the basis of these objections, Watson and Au conclude that the real and substantial connection test should be interpreted as requiring a connection either between the forum and the defendant or between the forum and the subject matter of the action. In their view, the defendant's connection with the forum should not determine the choice of forum. Rather, the defendant's connection should simply be a relevant factor to be weighed together with other factors.

[74.] I find these arguments to be persuasive. While the defendant's contact with the jurisdiction is an *important* factor, it is not a *necessary* factor. In my view, to hold otherwise would be contrary to the Supreme Court of Canada's direction that the real and substantial connection test is flexible. It would also be contrary to the weight of Canadian appellate authority outlined above.

(d) The relevant factors under the broader approach

[75.] It is apparent from *Morguard*, *Hunt* and subsequent case law that it is not possible to reduce the real and substantial connection test to a fixed formula. A considerable measure of judgment is required in assessing whether the real and substantial connection test has been met on the facts of a given case. Flexibility is therefore important.

[76.] But clarity and certainty are also important. As such, it is useful to identify the factors emerging from the case law that are relevant in assessing whether a court should assume jurisdiction against an out-of-province defendant on the basis of damage sustained in Ontario as a result of a tort committed elsewhere. No factor is determinative. Rather, all relevant factors should be considered and weighed together. In my view, a weighing of the factors in the present case favours the assumption of jurisdiction against the out-of-province defendants in this case.

1) The connection between the forum and the plaintiff's claim

[77.] The forum has an interest in protecting the legal rights of its residents and affording injured plaintiffs generous access for litigating claims against tortfeasors . . .

. . .

[81.] In the present case, the plaintiff has required extensive medical attention in Ontario. His claim is, *inter alia*, for pain and suffering in Ontario. These damages represent a significant connection with Ontario.

2) The connection between the forum and the defendant

[82.] If the defendant has done anything within the jurisdiction that bears upon the claim advanced by the plaintiff, the case for assuming jurisdiction is strengthened.

[83.] *Moran* v. *Pyle* holds that conduct outside the territory may render the defendant subject to the jurisdiction of the forum where it was reasonably foreseeable that the defendant's conduct would result in harm within the jurisdiction. This foreseeability should be distinguished from a situation in which the wrongful act and injury occur outside the jurisdiction and the plaintiff returns and suffers consequential damage. It seems to me that in the latter situation, the fact that it was foreseeable that the plaintiff would return home does not bring the case within the *Moran* principle.

[84.] In this case, the defendants did not have any connection with Ontario that would justify the assumption of jurisdiction. Although the defendants were engaged in an activity that carried with it an inherent risk of an accident with an out-of-province party, their conduct fell well short of what might constitute personal subjection or submission to the jurisdiction of the Ontario courts.

[85.] While conduct of the defendant amounting to personal subjection provides a strong basis for assumed jurisdiction, such conduct is not necessary in all cases. Even if there is no act or conduct by the defendant that amounts to personal subjection or makes litigation in the forum a foreseeable risk, it is still necessary to consider other factors to determine whether or not the real and substantial connection test has been met.

3) Unfairness to the defendant in assuming jurisdiction

[86.] The consideration of the defendant's position should not end with an inquiry as to acts or conduct that would render the defendant subject to the jurisdiction. The principles of order and fairness require further consideration, because acts or conduct that are insufficient to render the defendant subject to the jurisdiction may still have a bearing on the fairness of assumed jurisdiction. Some activities, by their very nature, involve a sufficient risk of harm to extra-provincial parties that any unfairness in assuming jurisdiction is mitigated or eliminated.

[87.] In my view, in the present case, the assumption of jurisdiction would not result in any significant unfairness to the defendants. The defendants were engaged in an activity that involves an inherent risk of harm to extra-provincial parties. Mandatory motor vehicle insurance requirements across Canada reflect the reciprocal risk of harm caused and faced by all motorists. There was evidence that the defendants are insured and that the terms of their insurance clearly contemplate and provide coverage for suits in other Canadian provinces, which would include a suit involving an accident with an out-of-province defendant. The standard form Power of Attorney and Undertaking requires motor vehicle insurers to appear and defend claims brought in any Canadian province or territory. These insurance arrangements reflect the reasonable expectations of the motoring public. The burden of defending the suit will fall on the defendants' insurer and not on the defendants themselves. I would give no weight to the argument that the assumption of jurisdiction would be unfair to the defendants.

4) Unfairness to the plaintiff in not assuming jurisdiction

[88.] The principles of order and fairness should be considered in relation to the plaintiff as well as the defendant . . .

. . .

[90.] In this case, if jurisdiction were refused, the plaintiff would be compelled to litigate in Alberta. This would undoubtedly be inconvenient to the plaintiff, especially given the injuries he has sustained. Further, unlike the defendant, the plaintiff does not have the benefit of an insurer to cover the cost of litigation. While the unfairness to the plaintiff of having to litigate in Alberta may not be as strong as it was in *Oakely* v. *Barry*, on balance, a consideration of unfairness favours the plaintiff.

5) The involvement of other parties to the suit

. . .

[92.] In this case, the involvement of other parties to the suit is not a significant factor.

6) The court's willingness to recognize and enforce an extra-provincial judgment rendered on the same jurisdictional basis

[93.] In considering whether to assume jurisdiction against an extra-provincial defendant, the court must consider whether it would recognize and enforce an extra-provincial judgment against a domestic defendant rendered on the same jurisdictional basis, whether pursuant to common law principles or any applicable legislation. Every time a court assumes jurisdiction in favour of a domestic plaintiff, the court establishes a standard that will be used to force domestic defendants who are sued elsewhere to attorn to the jurisdiction of the foreign court or face enforcement of a default judgment against them. This principle is fundamental to the approach in *Morguard* and *Hunt* and may be seen as a self-imposed constraint inherent in the real and substantial connection test. It follows that where a court would not be willing to recognize and enforce an extra-provincial judgment rendered on the same jurisdictional basis, the court cannot assume jurisdiction, because the real and substantial connection test has not been met.

[94.] In my view, it is appropriate for Ontario courts to recognize and enforce judgments from the courts of sister provinces rendered on the same jurisdictional basis as in the case at bar. *Morguard* and *Hunt* recognize the modern reality of rapid and frequent movement by Canadian citizens across provincial borders. Further, the risk of accidents with and injury to the residents of another province is inherent in motor vehicle travel, and insurance arrangements reflecting this risk are common across Canada. The spirit of *Morguard* and *Hunt* favours recognition and enforcement of the judgments of the courts of sister provinces where jurisdiction has been assumed on the basis that serious damages have been suffered within the province as a result of a motor vehicle accident in another province.

7) Whether the case is interprovincial or international in nature

[95.] The decisions in *Morguard, Tolofson* and *Hunt* suggest that the assumption of jurisdiction is more easily justified in interprovincial cases than in international cases. The jurisdictional standards developed in *Morguard* and *Hunt* were strongly influenced by the need to adapt the rules of private international law to the demands of the Canadian federation.

[96.] In *Morguard* at pp. 1098 and 1101, La Forest J held that the 'considerations underlying the rules of comity apply with much greater force between the units of a federal state', that a federation 'implies a fuller and more generous acceptance of the judgments of the courts of other constituent units of the federation', and that 'the rules of comity or private international law as they apply between the provinces must be shaped to conform to the federal structure of the Constitution'. At pp. 1099–1100, La Forest J mentioned several features that foster consistency and uniformity between provinces and thereby minimize the risk of unfairness within Canada:

> The Canadian judicial structure is so arranged that any concerns about differential quality of justice among the provinces can have no real foundation. All superior court judges – who also have superintending control over other provincial courts and tribunals – are appointed and paid by the federal authorities. And all are subject to final review by the Supreme Court of Canada, which can determine when the courts of one province have appropriately exercised jurisdiction in an action and the circumstances under which the courts of another province should recognize such judgments. Any danger resulting from unfair procedure is further avoided by sub-constitutional factors, such as for example the fact that Canadian lawyers adhere to the same code of ethics throughout Canada.

Further, while La Forest J held at p. 1103 that 'fairness to the defendant requires that the judgment be issued by a court acting through fair process and with properly restrained jurisdiction', he also held that 'fair process is not an issue within the Canadian federation'.

. . .

[100.] The fact that this is an interprovincial case clearly weighs in favour of assuming jurisdiction.

8) *Comity and the standards of jurisdiction, recognition and enforcement prevailing elsewhere*

[101.] In *Morguard* at p. 1096, La Forest J adopted the following formulation of comity expressed in *Hilton* v. *Guyot* 159 US 113 at 163–64 (1895):

> [T]he recognition which one nation allows within its territory to the legislative, executive or judicial acts of another nation, having due regard both to international duty and convenience, and to the rights of its own citizens or of other persons who are under the protection of its laws . . .

[102.] One aspect of comity is that in fashioning jurisdictional rules, courts should consider the standards of jurisdiction, recognition and enforcement that prevail elsewhere. In interprovincial cases, this consideration is unnecessary, since the same standard necessarily applies to assumed jurisdiction, recognition and enforcement within Canada. However, in international cases, it may be helpful to consider international standards, particularly the rules governing assumed jurisdiction and the recognition and enforcement of judgments in the location in which the defendant is situated.

[The court then discussed equivalent jurisdictional rules in other countries and under international instruments. It referred to Article 5(3) of the Brussels Convention and to the decision of the European Court in *Bier* v. *Mines de Potasse*, but not to *Marinari*, even though the latter was decided some seven years previously. It concluded:]

[108.] However, there are indications that these provisions, like the *Moran* test, are aimed at situating jurisdiction in the place in which the injury actually occurs. The provisions refer to 'injury' rather than 'damage', and the background papers prepared in connection with the draft support this interpretation.

[109.] In my view, in cases involving international defendants, international standards and the standards applied in the defendant's jurisdiction are helpful in determining whether the real and substantial connection test has been met on the basis of damage sustained within the jurisdiction.

[110] As this is an interprovincial case, this factor is not applicable.

(e) Conclusion

[111.] In my view, a fair weighing of the factors I have outlined clearly favours assumed jurisdiction in the present case. Accordingly, I would affirm the finding of the motions court judge that the real and substantial connection test has been met.

[112.] Since the motions court judge did not err in finding that the Ontario Superior Court could assume jurisdiction against the out-of-province defendants, the only issue that remains is whether he erred in refusing to exercise his discretion to decline jurisdiction on the ground that Ontario is not the *forum conveniens*.

The court then considered the issue of *forum non conveniens* and concluded that there were no grounds for overruling the decision of the trial judge refusing a stay. The appeal was dismissed.

QUESTION

It is unlikely that an English court would have reached the same conclusion, whether it was acting under the CPR or under the Brussels I Regulation. Was the decision of the Ontario Court of Appeal justified by the inter-provincial nature of the case?

Muscutt v. *Courcelles* was one of a group of cases with similar facts decided at the same time by the Ontario Court of Appeal.[15] There was one importance difference, however: in all the other cases, the accident occurred outside Canada and some or all of the defendants resided outside Canada. Our next case is one of that group.

Ontario
Gajraj* v. *DeBernardo
Ontario Court of Appeal
(2002) 60 OR (3d) 68; (2002) 213 DLR (4th) 651; (2002) 160 OAC 60

Background

The three plaintiffs were Ontario residents. While on a visit to New York, their car was involved in a motor accident in which the two other cars were driven by the two defendants, DeBernardo and Manusami.[16] The latter were both New York residents. The plaintiffs returned to Ontario where they received medical treatment. They brought the action in an Ontario court. The defendants challenged the jurisdiction of the court. The trial court held that that there was no jurisdiction. The plaintiffs appealed.

Sharpe JA (delivering the judgment of the court)

Issue 1: Did the motions court judge err in finding that the Ontario Superior Court could not assume jurisdiction against the out-of-province defendants?

[13.] In *Muscutt*, I identified eight factors to be considered when determining whether the real and substantial connection test and the principles of order and fairness . . . have been satisfied. In my view, the application of those factors to the facts of this case indicates that Ontario courts cannot assume jurisdiction against the out-of-province defendants DeBernardo and Manusami.

---

15 The other cases in the group were *Sinclair* v. *Cracker Barrel Old Country Store Inc.* (2002) 60 OR (3d) 76; (2002) 213 DLR (4th) 643; (2002) 160 OAC 54; *Leufkens* v. *Alba Tours International Inc.* (2002) 60 OR (3d) 84; (2002) 213 DLR (4th) 614; (2002) 160 OAC 43; *Gajraj* v. *DeBernardo* (below); and *Lemmex* v. *Sunflight Holidays Inc.* (below). In all these cases, the Ontario Court of Appeal held that the Ontario courts had no jurisdiction.
16 An insurance company was also involved, but this part of the judgment is omitted.

1) The connection between the forum and the plaintiff's claim

[14.]   The plaintiff Daneshwar Gajraj is a resident of Ontario. In the affidavit he filed on DeBernardo's motion to stay the action for lack of jurisdiction, he deposed that he has undergone extensive treatment in Ontario from several medical practitioners as well as other health care and vocational advisers. He states that he has suffered on-going pain as a result of the accident and that he has been unable to return to work. Gajraj's allegations represent a significant connection with Ontario. However, this is only one of the relevant factors to consider.

2) The connection between the forum and the defendant

[15.]   Neither the defendant DeBernardo nor the defendant Manusami has any contact or connection with Ontario. There is nothing in their conduct that could amount to subjection or submission to the jurisdiction of Ontario courts. As motorists, these defendants might well have foreseen that negligence on their part could cause an injury to an out-of-state motorist who would return home and assert a claim for damages. However, as explained in *Muscutt*, the fact that it was foreseeable that the plaintiff would return home after sustaining an injury does not bring the case within the principle enunciated in *Moran* v. *Pyle* . . .

3) Unfairness to the defendant in assuming jurisdiction

[16.]   In my view, there would be an element of unfairness to DeBernardo and Manusami if jurisdiction were assumed in this case. In this regard, I would distinguish this case from *Muscutt*, in which the accident occurred in another Canadian province. I agree with the motions court judge that since the accident occurred in New York and the defendants had no connection with Ontario, the parties' reasonable expectations would be that the action would be tried in New York.

[17.]   I note that there is no evidence of the nature or existence of the defendants' insurance arrangements or of any applicable Power of Attorney and Undertaking obliging the insurer to attorn to Ontario jurisdiction. Nor is there evidence regarding standard terms of motor vehicle insurance coverage in the United States. I have no reason to doubt the submission of counsel for DeBernardo that the nature and terms of insurance vary widely from state to state.

4) Unfairness to the plaintiff in not assuming jurisdiction

[18.]   If the order of the motions court judge refusing jurisdiction is affirmed, the plaintiff will be compelled to litigate in New York. This would undoubtedly be inconvenient to the plaintiff. However . . . I am not persuaded that forcing the plaintiff to litigate this claim in New York would cause any significant degree of unfairness. The reasonable expectations of the parties are relevant to some degree, and I agree with the finding of the motions court judge that where a party travels to another country and is involved in a motor vehicle accident there, it is reasonable to expect that a dispute with a local driver will be litigated in the foreign jurisdiction.

. . .

6) The court's willingness to recognize and enforce an extra-provincial judgment rendered on the same jurisdictional basis

[22.] To assume jurisdiction in the present case would create a rule requiring Ontario courts to recognize and enforce judgments of foreign courts for damages arising from Ontario motor vehicle accidents. In my view, Ontario courts should hesitate to adopt a jurisdictional rule requiring Ontario motorists to defend themselves in foreign courts against suits for damages arising from accidents in Ontario or face enforcement of a default judgment against them. I do not think that by engaging in the everyday act of driving a motor vehicle in Ontario, a driver should be taken to have assumed the risk of defending his or her conduct in a foreign court. As explained below, I would distinguish this case from *Muscutt*, which involved a motor vehicle accident in another Canadian province.

7) Whether the case is interprovincial or international in nature

[23.] This is an international case. In my view, foreign motor vehicle accidents should be distinguished from accidents that occur in one Canadian province and result in consequential damage in another province. For the reasons given in *Muscutt*, it seems to me entirely appropriate for the Canadian legal system to provide motor vehicle accident victims ready access to the courts of their home province. However, the problems created by foreign accidents are more complex, since the issue cannot be governed entirely by Canadian jurisdictional standards. Consideration must be given to the norms that prevail elsewhere, a factor to which I now turn.

8) Comity and the standards of jurisdiction, recognition and enforcement prevailing elsewhere

[24.] As explained in *Muscutt*, under international standards, it is only in certain limited circumstances that damages sustained within the jurisdiction are accepted as a basis for assumed jurisdiction. The minimum contacts doctrine[1] that governs jurisdiction in the United States is particularly relevant to this appeal. Under the minimum contacts doctrine, the assumption of jurisdiction requires an act or conduct by the defendant that amounts to personal subjection to the jurisdiction. It is virtually certain that New York courts would not recognize or enforce an Ontario judgment against a New York defendant for damages sustained in Ontario as a result of a motor vehicle accident in New York unless the defendant voluntarily attorned to Ontario's jurisdiction: *World-Wide Volkswagen Corporation v. Woodson* [set out in Chapter 7, § 2.1, below]. Further, the generally prevailing international standards explained in *Muscutt* also militate against

---

1 *Editor's note*: this is discussed in Chapter 7, § 2, below.

assuming jurisdiction in this case. Since assumed jurisdiction would accord neither with the law of the foreign jurisdiction implicated nor with international standards, this factor weighs against assuming jurisdiction.

Conclusion

[25.] In my view, a fair consideration of the factors I have outlined does not favour assuming jurisdiction in the present case. While the fact that the plaintiff has sustained significant damages in Ontario weighs in favour of assumed jurisdiction, the other factors are either neutral or weigh against assumed jurisdiction. This leads me to conclude that the real and substantial connection test has not been satisfied and that assuming jurisdiction against the out-of-province defendants would violate the principles of order and fairness. Accordingly, the motions court judge did not err in finding that the Ontario Superior Court could not assume jurisdiction against DeBernardo and Manusami.

QUESTION

Are you convinced by the court's reasoning?

Ontario
Lemmex v. Sunflight Holidays Inc.
Ontario Court of Appeal
(2002) 60 OR (3d) 54; (2002) 213 DLR (4th) 627; (2002) 160 OAC 31

Background

This was another case in the same group as the last two. The plaintiffs, Mr and Mrs Lemmex, were resident in Ontario. They booked a package holiday with a Canadian tour company, Sunflight Holidays. The package included their flights and a cruise in the Caribbean. The cruise was on a liner operated by a Florida company, Premier Cruises. On board ship, the Lemmexes received pamphlets indicating that they could go on various shore trips. They chose one on Grenada, and booked it on board the cruise liner through Premier Cruises, who acted as agents for the company responsible for the trip. The latter was a Grenadian company, Huggins Ltd. When the liner reached Grenada, the Lemmexes went on the trip. They travelled in a minibus driven by a man called George Bernard. In the course of the trip, Mr Lemmex suffered from carbon monoxide poisoning, which left him with permanent injuries. He received medical treatment when he arrived back home in Ontario.

The Lemmexes sued Sunflight and Premier Cruises in Ontario. Sunflight and Premier Cruises then brought a third-party action against Huggins Ltd and Bernard. Subsequently, the Lemmexes also brought proceedings against the two Grenadians. The actions were consolidated. Neither Sunflight nor Premier Cruises challenged the jurisdiction of the court. However, the two Grenadian defendants, Huggins Ltd and Bernard, did challenge it. The court of first instance (motions judge) held that the courts of Ontario had jurisdiction over the two Grenadians, and this was upheld (by a majority) by the Divisional Court. The case then came before the Ontario Court of Appeal.

Sharpe JA delivered the judgment of the court

[He first referred to *Muscutt* v. *Courcelles*, and then applied the same criteria as before. The following are extracts from the judgment:]

3) Unfairness to the defendant in assuming jurisdiction

[35.] In my view, there would be an element of unfairness to Huggins Ltd and Bernard if the Ontario Superior Court were to assume jurisdiction in this case. Both Huggins Ltd and Bernard have confined their activities to the Island of Grenada. Although they offer a service aimed specifically at tourists, it would be unduly onerous to require them to defend actions in the home jurisdictions of each of their customers.

. . .

4) Unfairness to the plaintiff in not assuming jurisdiction

[37.] If this court holds that Ontario courts cannot assume jurisdiction against Huggins Ltd and Bernard, the plaintiffs will be required to bring their action against these defendants in Grenada. Such a holding would inconvenience the plaintiffs, particularly given the injuries that Richard Lemmex alleges to have sustained. However, such a holding would not, in my view, result in significant unfairness to the plaintiffs . . .

[38.] On this point, I would adopt the following passage from the reasons of Aitken J . . . granting leave to appeal to the Divisional Court:

> International travel has become financially feasible for many residents of Ontario. Some reasons for travel include to learn about other countries and cultures, to experience new adventures, and to find more favourable climates. These goals take Ontario residents to the far corners of the world, often to countries economically less developed than Canada, many of whose citizens are financially very significantly disadvantaged in comparison with Canadians. Many individuals in those countries, who may provide goods or services to Ontario tourists during their stay, have never travelled outside of the boundaries of their region or country, for social, cultural or financial reasons.

> Lemmex, his wife and his daughter chose to leave Ontario and travel to Grenada for a vacation. They chose to take a tour on Grenada offered by a Grenadian company. They were aware that injuries could be sustained in Grenada, just like they could be anywhere else one goes. Was it reasonable for them to expect that if one of them was injured through the negligence of a Grenadian, an action would be heard in Ontario, the law of Grenada would have to be proven in the Ontario court, and Grenadian witnesses might have to travel to Ontario to give their evidence?

> Do Ontario courts foster order and fairness by assuming jurisdiction in the first action where Huggins and Bernard are defendants? Is it fair to expect Bernard, a local taxi driver in Grenada, to come to Ontario to defend this action?

[39.] In the circumstances of this case, I respectfully disagree with the majority of the Divisional Court that the parties could reasonably have expected that the Lemmexes would be able to sue the Grenadian company and Grenadian driver in Ontario courts if they were injured in Grenada.

[40.] With respect to Premier's third party claim, refusing to assume jurisdiction against Huggins Ltd and Bernard will compel Premier to pursue its claim against the Grenadian defendants in Grenada. There is an element of unfairness to Premier in dividing the proceedings in this manner. On the other hand, Premier had a direct contractual relationship with Huggins Ltd and could have insisted that Huggins Ltd agree to attorn to foreign jurisdiction in the event of a suit such as the present one.

5) The involvement of other parties to the suit

[41.] The plaintiffs brought two actions, which have been consolidated. Premier has brought a third party claim. The Ontario courts have jurisdiction over the Canadian defendant Sunflight, and the American defendant Premier has attorned to Ontario's jurisdiction. Refusing to assume jurisdiction over Huggins Ltd and Bernard could result in more than one proceeding, with the possibility of inconsistent outcomes in the proceedings.

[42.] However, the core of this action lies in Grenada. The alleged injury occurred entirely in Grenada and the action centers around a claim in negligence for harm inflicted in Grenada by Grenadian defendants.

Thus, the courts of Ontario had no jurisdiction over the two Grenadian defendants.

Comment

If this case had come before an English court applying the traditional English rules, it would have found the question of jurisdiction absolutely clear cut. Since the court had jurisdiction over Sunflight and Premier Cruises, and since the two Grenadian defendants were necessary or proper parties, it would have had jurisdiction over them as well (see Chapter 5, § 4.4, above). The only problematic issue would have been *forum non conveniens*, but an English court would probably have rejected a challenge on this ground in view of the desirability of not splitting closely linked proceedings.[17]

Under the Brussels I Regulation, there could be no question of *forum non conveniens*, since this is not part of EC law. If all the defendants had been domiciled in Member States, the third-party action would have come under Article 6(2) and there could have been no argument about jurisdiction. The action by the Lemmexes would have come under Article 6(1). Provided one of the 'anchor' defendants was domiciled in the territory of the forum, jurisdiction would have existed here as well.[18] Once this requirement was satisfied, the court would have

---

17 However, it might have stayed *all* the actions (including those against the local defendants): see the decision of the judge at first instance in *Owusu* v. *Jackson*, referred to in the judgment of the English Court of Appeal, [2002] ILPr 45 at paragraph 20 of the judgment.

18 It is not clear in the Canadian case whether Sunflight was domiciled in Ontario or in another province.

given no thought to the question whether taking jurisdiction was fair to the other defendants.

---

§4   Tort cases in Quebec

In a case decided at the same time as *Muscutt* v. *Courcelles* and the other cases,[19] the Supreme Court of Canada took a rather different approach, as our next case demonstrates.

Canada
Spar Aerospace Ltd* v. *American Mobile Satellite Corporation
Supreme Court of Canada
[2002] 4 SCR 205; 2002 SCC 7

Background

One of the defendants in this case, an American company called American Mobile Satellite Corporation (referred to in the judgment as 'Motient'), had entered into a contract with another American company, Hughes Aircraft, under which the latter would construct a satellite. Hughes Aircraft concluded a subcontract with Spar Aerospace, an Ontario company, under which Spar would build the communications payload. The work was carried out in Spar's plant in Ste-Anne-de-Bellevue, in the province of Quebec. The communications payload was tested and found to be satisfactory. The satellite was accepted by Motient. The latter then engaged various other American companies to conduct further tests. These resulted in serious damage to the satellite; so Hughes Aircraft refused to give Spar certain performance-incentive payments.

Spar considered that the American companies responsible for the tests that caused the damage had been negligent. It brought proceedings against them in Quebec, claiming a little over $800,000 for the loss of incentive payments, $50,000 for loss of future profits caused by loss of reputation and $50,000 for expenses incurred in investigating the damages to the satellite.

---

19 Because they were decided at the same time, neither judgment refers to the other.

Under the common law of tort as applied in most common-law jurisdictions, it is not possible to sue in tort for pure economic loss (economic loss not caused by injury to the defendant or damage to his property). In Quebec, on the other hand, damages for such loss can be obtained. Since there was no damage to the property of the plaintiffs in this case – the satellite no longer belonged to them when the damage occurred – this difference in the substantive law made Quebec an attractive forum.

Under Article 3148(3) of the Quebec Civil Code (CCQ) (Panel 6.2), the Quebec courts had jurisdiction when damage was suffered in Quebec. Spar claimed that this provision was applicable to the proceedings. The defendants objected. All of them were American, and the damage to the satellite had occurred in America. The plaintiff had its head office in Ontario. The only link with Quebec was that the factory where the satellite had been manufactured was located in Quebec.[20] For this reason, one would have thought that there were insufficient contacts with Quebec to justify jurisdiction. Nevertheless, the Quebec courts held that they had jurisdiction.[21] An appeal was taken to the Supreme Court of Canada.

> **Panel 6.2 Jurisdiction of Quebec courts**
> **Quebec Civil Code, Article 3148**
>
> **Article 3148**
> In personal actions of a patrimonial nature, a Québec authority has jurisdiction where
> . . .
> (3) a fault was committed in Québec, damage was suffered in Québec, an injurious act occurred in Québec or one of the obligations arising from a contract was to be performed in Québec . . .

> **LeBel J delivered the judgment of the court**
>
> [It was argued by the defendants that the 'real and substantial connection' test had to be satisfied in addition to showing that the case was covered by the Quebec jurisdictional rule. LeBel J dealt with this argument as follows:]
>
> 50.   Turning to the substantive arguments, I cannot accept the appellants' arguments that the 'real and substantial connection' requirement set out in *Morguard* and *Hunt* is an additional criterion that must be satisfied in determining the jurisdiction of the Quebec courts in this case. My conclusion with respect to this issue is based on two considerations: (i) the context of the 'real and substantial connection' and its relationship with the principles of comity, order and fairness; and (ii) the nature of the private international law scheme set out in Book Ten of the *CCQ*.
>
> **(i) The context of the 'real and substantial connection' and its relationship with the principle of comity**
>
> 51.   I agree with the appellants that *Morguard* and *Hunt* establish that it is a constitutional imperative that Canadian courts can assume jurisdiction only where a 'real and substantial connection' exists: see La Forest J in *Hunt, supra*, at p. 328: 'courts are required, *by constitutional restraints*, to

---

20 This was subsequently sold by Spar.
21 The motions judge held that jurisdiction existed because the damage had been suffered in Quebec; the Quebec Court of Appeal held that it existed because an 'injurious act' had occurred in Quebec.

assume jurisdiction only where there are real and substantial connections to that place' (emphasis added). However, it is important to emphasize that *Morguard* and *Hunt* were decided in the context of interprovincial jurisdictional disputes. In my opinion, the specific findings of these decisions cannot easily be extended beyond this context . . .

(ii) The private international law scheme of Book Ten of the CCQ

55. As mentioned above, Book Ten of the *CCQ* sets out the private international law rules for the Province of Quebec and must be read as a coherent whole and in light of the principles of comity, order and fairness. In my view, it is apparent from the explicit wording of art. 3148, as well as the other provisions of Book Ten, that the system of private international law is designed to ensure that there is a 'real and substantial connection' between the action and the province of Quebec and to guard against the improper assertion of jurisdiction.

56. Looking at the wording of art. 3148 itself, it is arguable that the notion of a 'real and substantial connection' is already subsumed under the provisions of art. 3148(3), given that each of the grounds listed (fault, injurious act, damage, contract) seems to be an example of a 'real and substantial connection' between the province of Quebec and the action. Indeed, I am doubtful that a plaintiff who succeeds in proving one of the four grounds for jurisdiction would not be considered to have satisfied the 'real and substantial connection' criterion, at least for the purposes of jurisdiction *simpliciter*.

57. Next, from my examination of the system of rules found in Book Ten, it seems that the 'real and substantial connection' criterion is captured in other provisions, to safeguard against the improper assumption of jurisdiction. In particular, it is my opinion that the doctrine of *forum non conveniens*, as codified at art. 3135, serves as an important counterweight to the broad basis for jurisdiction set out in art. 3148. In this way, it is open to the appellants to demonstrate, pursuant to art. 3135, that although there is a link to the Quebec authorities, another forum is, in the interests of justice, better suited to take jurisdiction.

. . .

61. I note that STS argues that the criterion of damage in art. 3148(3) should be read narrowly and refers to cases decided by the European Court of Justice under the . . .'*Brussels Convention*'. In my view, it is important to note that, unlike the *CCQ*, the *Brussels Convention* does not provide the same safeguard against the inappropriate exercise of jurisdiction, namely, the power to stay actions on the basis of *forum non conveniens* or otherwise . . . It is perhaps understandable, then, that the European Court of Justice would seek to interpret the jurisdictional ground of the *Brussels Convention* in a narrower fashion than would a court who enjoys a further discretionary power to decline jurisdiction.

. . .

> 63.   In the case at bar, it seems reasonable to conclude that the requirement
>   for a 'real and substantial connection' between the action and the authority
>   asserting jurisdiction is reflected in the overall scheme established by
>   Book Ten. In my view, the appellants have not provided, nor does there
>   seem to be, given the context of this case, any basis for the courts to apply
>   the *Morguard* constitutional principle in order to safeguard against this
>   action being heard in a forum with which it has no real and substantial
>   connection.
> 64.   At this point, assuming for the sake of argument that this appeal would fall
>   to be decided under a pure 'real and substantial connection test', without
>   any reference to the provisions of the code, it is interesting to note that the
>   result would not change . . .

The appeal was dismissed.

Comment

The most important way in which this judgment differs from that in *Muscutt* v.
Courcelles is with regard to the 'real and substantial connection' test. In *Muscutt*,
the Ontario Court of Appeal held that, for constitutional reasons, this had to be
applied directly by courts: it was not enough to show that the case came within
one of the specific grounds set out in the Rules of Civil Procedure. This contention was rejected in *Spar*. The reason, however, is far from clear. The following,
either alone or in combination, are possibilities:

- the 'real and substantial connection' test is directly applicable only in an
  inter-provincial context, not in an international context;
- the jurisdictional provisions of the Quebec Civil Code were based on it;
  therefore, it did not have to be applied independently;
- the doctrine of *forum non conveniens* provided a sufficient safeguard.

With regard to the first possibility, it is interesting that the Ontario Court of
Appeal considered that the grounds of jurisdiction should be *narrower* in an
international context, because it is more difficult for a defendant to fight a case
in a foreign country than in another part of the same federal State. This is clear
from *Gajraj* v. *DeBarnardo Spar*, on the other hand, suggests the opposite.

With regard to the third possibility, the Supreme Court's reasoning seems to
imply that *forum non conveniens* covers much the same ground as the 'real and
substantial connection' test. However, the fact that the former contains a large
element of discretion indicates that any possible constitutional limitations on
jurisdiction are of a limited nature.

All in all, this case contrasts strongly with the cases decided by the Ontario
Court of Appeal. The latter exhibit a much more internationalist attitude.
Indeed, it seems impossible to reconcile *Spar* with cases like *Gajraj* and *Lemmex*.
As we shall see in the next chapter, an American court would almost certainly be
prohibited on constitutional grounds from taking jurisdiction over a Canadian
defendant if the facts of *Spar* were reversed. It seems unfortunate, therefore,

that the Supreme Court of Canada was not prepared to take a more restrained approach. Subsequent cases seem to have followed *Muscutt* and *Gajraj*, rather than *Spar*. For this reason, it might be possible to say that the former more truly represent Canadian law, at least in the common-law provinces.[22]

QUESTIONS

1 In *Gajraj* (and the other cases), the Ontario Court of Appeal said that the grounds of jurisdiction should be narrower in an international context than in an inter-provincial context. We saw in Chapter 3, however, that, in the European Community, courts generally apply wider grounds of jurisdiction when the defendant is from outside the EC than they are permitted to apply when he is domiciled in another Member State. We shall see in the next chapter that, in the United States, the same rules of jurisdiction are generally applied in both situations. Which approach do you prefer?

2 Was the Supreme Court of Canada right in saying that a narrower interpretation of 'damage' is needed in cases under the Brussels Convention because the Convention contains no provision for *forum non conveniens*?

3 The law and procedure applicable to the plaintiff's claim in *Muscutt* was probably no different in Ontario and Alberta, nor was there any reason to think that the Ontario court would have been more sympathetic to the plaintiff than the Alberta court. The position was different in *Spar*: the substantive provisions of Quebec law were more favourable to the plaintiff than those of the common-law jurisdictions of Canada. Could one accuse the plaintiff of forum-shopping? If so, was this a relevant consideration?

§ 5 Uniform law

The Uniform Law Conference of Canada has proposed a uniform law on jurisdiction.[23] Extracts are set out in Panel 6.3. So far, this has been adopted in British Columbia,[24] Nova Scotia[25] and Saskatchewan.[26] Under the uniform legislation, jurisdiction no longer depends on service of the writ. Jurisdiction based on consent (in its three traditional forms) remains as before.[27] Ordinary residence

---

22 Pitel and Dusten, 'Lost in Transition: Answering the Questions Raised by the Supreme Court of Canada's New Approach to Jurisdiction' (2006) 85 *Canadian Bar Review* 61 at pp. 77 *et seq.*
23 See www.ulcc.ca/en/home/.
24 Court Jurisdiction and Proceedings Transfer Act 2003 (British Columbia).
25 Court Jurisdiction and Proceedings Transfer Act, SNS 2003 (2d Sess.), c. 2.
26 Court Jurisdiction and Proceedings Transfer Act, SS 1997, c. C-41.1.
27 Section 3(a), (b) and (c).

Panel 6.3 Uniform Court Jurisdiction and Proceedings Transfer Act (Uniform Law Conference of Canada), sections 3 and 10 (extracts)

Proceedings in personam

3 A court has territorial competence in a proceeding that is brought against a person only if:

   (a) that person is the plaintiff in another proceeding in the court to which the proceeding in question is a counterclaim;

   (b) during the course of the proceeding that person submits to the court's jurisdiction;

   (c) there is an agreement between the plaintiff and that person to the effect that the court has jurisdiction in the proceeding;

   (d) that person is ordinarily resident in [enacting province or territory] at the time of the commencement of the proceeding; or

   (e) there is a real and substantial connection between [enacting province or territory] and the facts on which the proceeding against that person is based.

Real and substantial connection

10 Without limiting the right of the plaintiff to prove other circumstances that constitute a real and substantial connection between [enacting province or territory] and the facts on which a proceeding is based, a real and substantial connection between [enacting province or territory] and those facts is presumed to exist if the proceeding:

   . . .

   (e) concerns contractual obligations, and:

   (i) the contractual obligations, to a substantial extent, were to be performed in [enacting province or territory];

   (ii) by its express terms, the contract is governed by the law of [enacting province or territory]; or

   (iii) the contract:

   (A) is for the purchase of property, services or both, for use other than in the course of the purchaser's trade or profession; and

   (B) resulted from a solicitation of business in [enacting province or territory] by or on behalf of the seller;

   (f) concerns restitutionary obligations that, to a substantial extent, arose in [enacting province or territory];

   (g) concerns a tort committed in [enacting province or territory];

   (h) concerns a business carried on in [enacting province or territory];

---

of the defendant within the territory of the forum replaces service within the jurisdiction,[28] and the 'real and substantial connection' test replaces the rules for service out of the jurisdiction.[29] The specific grounds of jurisdiction are brought in as mere presumptions.[30] The end result is something not very different from the system laid down in *Muscutt*. It has the merit of providing a degree of certainty, while respecting the 'real and substantial connection' test.

§ 6 Conclusions

These Canadian cases (more will be considered in later chapters) show that the Canadian courts have been going back to basics in order to create a new foundation for conflict of laws. They employ a more sophisticated and multifaceted analysis than that found in the judgments of the European Court or even the

---

28 Section 3(d).

29 Section 3(e).

30 Section 10. These are somewhat different from those previously applicable – for example, the 'necessary or proper party' rule has been abolished: additional parties can be joined only if the 'real and substantial connection' test is directly satisfied with regard to them.

English courts, and the reasoning is more carefully tailored to the individual circumstances of the case. In the next chapter, we will study some of the basic principles of US law. We will then see that many of the ideas expressed by the Canadian courts in the new wave of cases are inspired by US thinking, though the Canadian courts do not always reach the same conclusions.[31] In both the US and Canada, more concern is shown towards the interests of foreign litigants and foreign countries than has been traditional in Europe outside the EC context. Europeans have much to learn from these developments.

Further reading

Blom, 'Private International Law in a Globalizing Age: The Quiet Canadian Revolution' (2002) 4 *Yearbook of Private International Law* 83

Pitel and Dusten, 'Lost in Transition: Answering the Questions Raised by the Supreme Court of Canada's New Approach to Jurisdiction' (2006) 85 *Canadian Bar Review* 61

---

31 See, for example, paragraphs 54–74 of the judgment in *Muscutt* v. *Courcelles.*

CHAPTER 7

US law: an outline

§ 1   The US legal system

In this chapter, we consider the basic rules of jurisdiction in the United States. First, however, we must take a look at the US legal system.

As in the case of Canada, the relevant unit – even for the purpose of international jurisdiction – is normally a particular state,[1] not the United States as a whole. For this reason, it is essential to understand the relationship between the United States and the individual states, which is more complicated than in the case of Canada.

As in the case of Canada, governmental authority is divided between the federation (the United States) and the states. Each has its own system of government, made up of legislative, executive and judicial branches. There are state legislatures enacting state laws and the federal legislature (Congress) enacting federal laws. Certain areas of law are largely governed by federal statutes (for example, patents) but many general areas, including contract, tort and property, are largely controlled by state law, though federal legislation may impinge in particular cases.

Each state has a complete court system. Typically, there will be a trial level, an intermediate appeal level and a state supreme court. In addition, there is a complete federal judicial system. The trial courts are called federal district courts.[2] The United States is divided into a number of federal judicial districts, each with its own federal district court. Federal judicial districts may consist of a whole state or part of a state. Each state, therefore, has at least one federal district court, as well as the state courts. Above the district courts are the United States courts of appeals for the various circuits (each circuit being made up of the federal judicial districts in a number of states) and at the very top there is the Supreme Court of the United States. Thus, for example, the *Bremen* case (discussed in Chapter 8, below) began in a federal district court in Florida, went on appeal to the United States Court of Appeals for the Fifth Circuit and then came before the United States Supreme Court on certiorari.[3]

---

1 It should be remembered that in this book the word 'state' with a lower-case 's' refers to a unit of a federal State, while 'State' with a capital 'S' refers to a State in the international sense.
2 In Canada, there are also federal courts at the trial level, but their jurisdiction is limited to certain specific subject areas – for example, immigration.
3 The appellate jurisdiction of the Supreme Court falls into two main categories, appeals in the strict sense (which are available in only a limited range of situations) and certiorari (which is available in a much wider, though still limited, range of cases): see 28 USC §§ 1252–1254. Appeals in the strict sense are (in theory) mandatory; certiorari, on the other hand, is discretionary: the party wishing to appeal must petition the court for certiorari and the court decides whether or not to grant it, i.e. whether to hear the appeal. Certiorari is denied in the great majority of cases.

The federal court system and the court systems in each of the states are intended to be complete in themselves: a case will usually run its full course in either the one or the other. However, the US Supreme Court can review the decisions of the highest court in any state where a question of federal law is involved.[4] The first four cases discussed below all fall into this category: they are appeals from the supreme courts of Washington, Oklahoma, Texas and California. In each case, the issue was whether the assertion of jurisdiction by the courts of the state in question was compatible with the United States Constitution.

Unlike the position in Canada, there is no appeal from a state court to the US Supreme Court where no question of federal law is involved: on questions of state law, the state supreme court is the final authority. Since the common law is, in general, state law,[5] this means that the common law can develop along different lines in different states. In effect, there is a separate common law in each state. In this respect, Canada is significantly different.

§ 1.1 Federal jurisdiction

Since there are two separate court systems, the question must be asked: when will a case come before a state court and when will it come before a federal court? The answer to this question involves jurisdiction in a different sense from that considered in previous chapters (and in the remainder of this chapter): it is not concerned with international (or inter-state) jurisdiction but with what is sometimes called 'subject-matter' jurisdiction.[6] In other words, we are not considering whether the case can be brought in a particular state, or indeed in the United States at all. The question is: assuming that the case can be brought in a particular state (international or inter-state jurisdiction), must it be brought in the federal courts in that state or in the state courts? This is what is meant by 'federal jurisdiction'. For reasons that will become clear as we proceed, we must discuss this question before we can consider the question of international jurisdiction.

The law in this area is complicated and still not entirely settled, but one can begin by saying that, as a general principle, the state courts will always have jurisdiction unless some particular rule deprives them of it; federal courts, on the other hand, have no jurisdiction unless the case comes within the terms of some specific rule giving them jurisdiction.[7]

The most important heads of federal jurisdiction are federal-question jurisdiction and diversity jurisdiction. Under the former,[8] the federal district courts have jurisdiction in all civil actions involving federal law (i.e. the US Constitution, federal statutes, treaties between the United States and a foreign

---

4 See 28 USC § 1257. The distinction between appeal and certiorari applies here too.
5 In certain special cases, it is possible to have federal common law.
6 This term is not entirely satisfactory since the subject-matter of the case will not necessarily be determinative; moreover, the term is sometimes used to mean something quite different: see *per* Hoffmann J in *MacKinnon v. Donaldson, Lufkin & Jenrette Securities Corporation*, set out in Chapter 20, § 2.1, below.
7 The basic provision is Article III, § 2, of the US Constitution; there are also a number of statutes enacted by Congress under this provision: see, in particular, 28 USC §§ 1331–1361.
8 See 28 USC § 1331.

country, and – in a few special cases – federal common law).[9] Under the latter, they have jurisdiction in any civil action between:

- citizens of different states;
- citizens of a state and citizens or subjects of a foreign State;
- citizens of different states in which citizens or subjects of a foreign State are additional parties;
- a foreign State as plaintiff and citizens of a state or different states.[10]

This means that the federal courts will have diversity jurisdiction if a citizen of California sues a citizen of Texas, or if a British citizen sues (or is sued by) a citizen of California.[11] They will not have jurisdiction on this ground if a British citizen sues a German citizen: such an action must be brought in the state courts.

To be a citizen of a state, an individual must be a United States citizen (or an alien admitted for permanent residence) and he must be domiciled[12] in the state in question.[13] A corporation is a citizen of the state in which it is incorporated and of the state in which it has its principal place of business.[14]

There is also a rule that federal courts do not have subject-matter jurisdiction on diversity grounds unless there is *complete* diversity. This means that there is no diversity if *any* party on the one side is a citizen of the same state as *any* party on the other side. This is important in major commercial cases, in which there are often many parties on each side. If a single party on one side has the citizenship of a state of which a party on the other side is a citizen, there will be no diversity.

Federal-question jurisdiction and diversity jurisdiction are not the only heads of federal-court jurisdiction, but they are by far the most important. Others depend on the subject-matter of the action. For example, the federal courts have jurisdiction in Admiralty actions.[15]

In most cases in which the federal courts have jurisdiction, the state courts have concurrent jurisdiction. The plaintiff can then choose where he wants to bring the action. If the plaintiff chooses the state courts, the defendant may wish to have the case removed to the federal courts. This is normally possible if there is concurrent jurisdiction, but in diversity cases (or any case not involving federal-question jurisdiction) removal is not permitted if any of the defendants is a citizen of the state where the action is brought.[16] This means that, if an English plaintiff sues a Californian defendant in a state court in Texas, the defendant can have the case removed to a federal court; but, if the plaintiff brings the action in a state court in California, removal will not be possible unless the case is based on federal law.

---

9 Under US law, self-executing treaties are part of the law of the land and are applied directly by courts.
10 28 USC § 1332. In addition to the above requirements, the matter in controversy must exceed a specified sum of money, at present US$75,000.
11 It is not necessary for either party to be a citizen of the state in which the action is brought: citizenship of any American state is sufficient.
12 For this purpose, domicile is really the same as residence.
13 A US citizen domiciled outside the United States would not be a citizen of any state.
14 28 USC § 1332(c).
15 28 USC § 1333.
16 The justification usually given for diversity jurisdiction is that a state court may be biased against a party from another state; but, if the plaintiff has chosen a state court, and if the defendant is a citizen of the state concerned, there can be no justification for removing the case to a federal court.

The 'complete diversity' rule becomes especially important in this context. Assume that the plaintiff wants the case to be heard by the state courts. To ensure this, he must not only bring it there; he must also prevent the defendant from removing it to a federal court. If diversity is the only possible ground of federal jurisdiction, the plaintiff must try to defeat it. In a multi-party case, he can do this by ensuring that one party on his side is a citizen of the same state of at least one party on the other side.

It should finally be mentioned that the great majority of cases are heard in state courts. However, federal courts decide many important cases, including many of those involving international business transactions.

§1.2 Applicable law

This question must be considered separately for state courts and federal courts.

§1.2.1 State courts. A state court always applies state law as regards procedure. As far as substantive law is concerned, it will also apply state law unless some provision of federal law is relevant. Where federal law *is* relevant, it must be applied. In the event of a conflict, it overrides state law.[17]

§1.2.2 Federal courts. If the case comes before a federal court, federal law governs matters of procedure.[18] As regards matters of substance, the general principle, which was laid down by the Supreme Court in the celebrated case of *Erie Railroad Company* v. *Thompkins*,[19] is that, in the absence of a relevant provision in the US Constitution, a federal statute or a treaty, a federal court must apply state law. The *Erie* case held, in particular, that there is in general no federal common law: if common law applies, it is the common law of the state in which the federal district court is sitting.[20] This means that a federal court must follow the precedents laid down by the state courts. Where choice of law is a matter of common law (as it normally is), a federal court must apply the choice-of-law rules of the state in which it is sitting.

These principles might suggest that it would make little difference whether a case was brought in a state or federal court. However, foreign businessmen usually prefer to litigate in the federal courts, where the judges have life tenure, rather than in the state courts, where they are usually elected by the people of the state and have to face re-election at frequent intervals.[21] Foreign businessmen are afraid that state judges might be too influenced by popular feeling.

---

17 This is made clear by the Supremacy Clause, Article VI, § 2, of the US Constitution.
18 Procedure in federal courts is determined by the Federal Rules of Civil Procedure, which are enacted by the Supreme Court under a power delegated to it by Congress.
19 58 S Ct 817; 304 US 674; 82 L Ed 1188 (1938).
20 In has since been established that, in certain exceptional cases, federal law *can* exist.
21 Unlike the position in Canada, where all superior-court judges (provincial and federal) are appointed and paid by the federal authorities, the appointment and remuneration of state judges is governed by state law.

§ 2   International jurisdiction

Having examined the US legal system, we are now in a position to consider the US rules of international jurisdiction. We start with state law.

§ 2.1   State courts

In many ways, the state rules of jurisdiction are similar to those in England. Originally, jurisdiction could be obtained only by service of the writ in the territory of the state in question. In the twentieth century, states started extending their jurisdiction by legislation. Companies from another state or a foreign country doing business in the state in question were required (as in England) to appoint an agent on whom process could be served; or provision might be made (again as in England) for service to be made at the company's place of business in the state. Later legislation provided for service outside the state, along similar lines to the provisions now found in the English Civil Procedure Rules. These state statutes, which of course differ from state to state, are collectively known as 'long-arm statutes', because they extend the arm of the law, permitting it to reach out and compel people outside the state to appear before the courts of the state. It should be emphasized that all these rules were developed primarily in the context of inter-state litigation. However, they are applied equally to international jurisdiction. In the United States, foreigners are generally in the same position as Americans from another state when it comes to jurisdiction.

The Full Faith and Credit Clause of the US Constitution[22] requires states to grant automatic recognition to judgments from sister states; however, there is no provision in the Constitution explicitly limiting the grounds on which the courts of a state may take jurisdiction over citizens of another state. This caused no problems in the past, when states based their jurisdiction on the common-law rule of service of the writ within the state, but the position changed when they began expanding their jurisdiction by passing long-arm statutes.

§ 2.1.1 The 'minimum contacts' doctrine. To solve the problem the United States Supreme Court turned to the Due Process Clause of the Fourteenth Amendment to the US Constitution (Panel 7.1).

> **United States**
> ***International Shoe Co. v. State of Washington***
> **US Supreme Court**
> **326 US 310; 66 S Ct 154; 90 L Ed 2d 95 (1945)**

Background

International Shoe was a Missouri-based company (incorporated in Delaware) that had a number of salesmen in the state of Washington selling its product

---

22 Article IV, § 1.

there under the control of a manager in Missouri. The salesmen resided in Washington and worked on a commission basis. The orders they obtained were transmitted to Missouri for

acceptance or rejection and the goods were shipped directly to customers in Washington. The question before the court was whether the company was subject to the jurisdiction of the Washington courts in an action for payment of contributions to the state unemployment compensation fund. Service was made on a salesman in Washington and a copy mailed to the company in Missouri. The state courts in Washington held that they had jurisdiction. An appeal was taken from the Supreme Court of Washington to the Supreme Court of the United States.

Mr Chief Justice Stone delivered the opinion of the court

Historically, the jurisdiction of courts to render judgment *in personam* is grounded on their *de facto* power over the defendant's person. Hence, his presence within the territorial jurisdiction of a court was prerequisite to its rendition of a judgment personally binding him . . . But now . . . due process requires only that, in order to subject a defendant to a judgment *in personam*, if he be not present within the territory of the forum, he have certain minimum contacts with it such that the maintenance of the suit does not offend 'traditional notions of fair play and substantial justice.'

Since the corporate personality is a fiction, although a fiction intended to be acted upon as though it were a fact . . . it is clear that, unlike an individual, its 'presence' without, as well as within, the state of its origin can be manifested only by activities carried on in its behalf by those who are authorized to act for it. To say that the corporation is so far 'present' there as to satisfy due process requirements, for purposes of taxation or the maintenance of suits against it in the courts of the state, is to beg the question to be decided. For the terms 'present' or 'presence' are used merely to symbolize those activities of the corporation's agent within the state which courts will deem to be sufficient to satisfy the demands of due process . . . Those demands may be met by such contacts of the corporation with the state of the forum as make it reasonable, in the context of our federal system of government, to require the corporation to defend the particular suit which is brought there. An 'estimate of the inconveniences' which would result to the corporation from a trial away from its 'home' or principal place of business is relevant in this connection . . .

. . .

It is evident that the criteria by which we mark the boundary line between those activities which justify the subjection of a corporation to suit and those which do not cannot be simply mechanical or quantitative . . . Whether due process is satisfied must depend, rather, upon the quality and nature of the activity in relation to the fair and orderly administration of the laws which it was the purpose of the due process clause to insure. That clause does not contemplate that a state may make binding a judgment *in personam* against an individual or corporate defendant with which the state has no contacts, ties, or relations . . .

But, to the extent that a corporation exercises the privilege of conducting activities within a state, it enjoys the benefits and protection of the laws of that state. The exercise of that privilege may give rise to obligations, and, so far as those obligations arise out of or are connected with the activities within the state, a procedure which requires the corporation to respond to a suit brought to enforce them can, in most instances, hardly be said to be undue . . .

Applying these standards, the activities carried on in behalf of appellant in the State of Washington were neither irregular nor casual. They were systematic and continuous throughout the years in question. They resulted in a large volume of interstate business, in the course of which appellant received the benefits and protection of the laws of the state, including the right to resort to the courts for the enforcement of its rights. The obligation which is here sued upon arose out of those very activities. It is evident that these operations establish sufficient contacts or ties with the state of the forum to make it reasonable and just, according to our traditional conception of fair play and substantial justice, to permit the state to enforce the obligations which appellant has incurred there. Hence, we cannot say that the maintenance of the present suit in the State of Washington involves an unreasonable or undue procedure.

. . .

Result: The courts of Washington were constitutionally entitled to exercise jurisdiction. The judgment of the Supreme Court of Washington was affirmed.

Comment

The case thus upheld the extension of jurisdiction that had already begun in some states.[23] Its most important feature, however, is that it made clear that the 'minimum contacts' doctrine is the test for due process. This provides the outer limit for state-court jurisdiction: anything beyond that is unconstitutional.

The minimum contacts test was not intended to constitute a jurisdictional rule: it did not *confer* jurisdiction on the courts of a state; it merely imposed limits on the jurisdiction that the states could confer on their courts. However, some states soon contrived to turn it into a jurisdictional rule by adopting long-arm statutes that stated simply that courts could assume jurisdiction in any case not inconsistent with the US Constitution.[24] In these states, the minimum-contacts test thus became a jurisdictional rule by the back door.

§ 2.1.2 Specific jurisdiction. Further cases show how the test has been developed. We consider first the situation where the claim arises out of the defendant's contacts with the forum.

---

23 After the case was decided, long-arm statutes became widespread.
24 California is an example. It enacted such a statute in 1970: see West's Ann. Cal. Code Civ. Proc., § 410.10.

United States
World-Wide Volkswagen Corporation* v. *Woodson
US Supreme Court
444 US 286; 62 L Ed 2d 490; 100 S Ct 559 (1980)

Background

The respondents (plaintiffs), Harry and Kay Robinson, bought an Audi car from a dealer in New York. Later they left for a new home in Arizona. While passing through Oklahoma, the Audi was struck in the rear by another car. The result was a fire, which severely burned Kay Robinson and the two children. The Robinsons brought a products-liability action in a state court in Oklahoma, claiming that the fire was caused by the defective design of the fuel tank. The defendants were:

1. the manufacturer (Audi NSU);
2. the importer (Volkswagen of America);
3. the regional distributor (World-Wide Volkswagen); and
4. the retail dealer (Seaway).

World-Wide Volkswagen and Seaway challenged the jurisdiction of the Oklahoma courts. World-Wide Volkswagen was an independent corporation, not owned by Audi or by Volkswagen of America. It was incorporated in New York and distributed Volkswagen products to dealers in New York, New Jersey and Connecticut. Seaway, also an independent company, was one of those dealers, doing business in New York. There was no evidence that either World-Wide Volkswagen or Seaway had any contacts with Oklahoma, or that any car they had sold had ever gone there – with the single exception of the Robinson's vehicle.

The Supreme Court of Oklahoma held that the Oklahoma courts were entitled to take jurisdiction. It said that a car is by its very design and purpose so mobile that the defendants could have foreseen that the car sold to the Robinsons might be used in Oklahoma.

Mr Justice White delivered the opinion of the Court

II

The Due Process Clause of the Fourteenth Amendment limits the power of a state court to render a valid personal judgment against a nonresident defendant . . . A judgment rendered in violation of due process is void in the rendering State and is not entitled to full faith and credit elsewhere . . . Due process requires that the defendant be given adequate notice of the suit . . . and be subject to the personal jurisdiction of the court [*International Shoe*]. In the present case, it is not contended that notice was inadequate; the only question is whether these particular petitioners were subject to the jurisdiction of the Oklahoma courts.

As has long been settled, and as we reaffirm today, a state court may exercise personal jurisdiction over a nonresident defendant only so long as there exist 'minimum contacts' between the defendant and the forum . . . The concept of minimum contacts, in turn, can be seen to perform two related, but distinguishable, functions. It protects the defendant against the burdens of litigating in a distant or inconvenient forum. And it acts to ensure that the States, through their courts, do not reach out beyond the limits imposed on them by their status as coequal sovereigns in a federal system.

The protection against inconvenient litigation is typically described in terms of 'reasonableness' or 'fairness.' We have said that the defendant's contacts with the forum State must be such that maintenance of the suit 'does not offend "traditional notions of fair play and substantial justice."' The relationship between the defendant and the forum must be such that it is 'reasonable . . . to require the corporation to defend the particular suit which is brought there.' Implicit in this emphasis on reasonableness is the understanding that the burden on the defendant, while always a primary concern, will in an appropriate case be considered in light of other relevant factors, including the forum State's interest in adjudicating the dispute . . . the plaintiff's interest in obtaining convenient and effective relief . . . at least when that interest is not adequately protected by the plaintiff's power to choose the forum . . . the interstate judicial system's interest in obtaining the most efficient resolution of controversies; and the shared interest of the several States in furthering fundamental substantive social policies . . .

The limits imposed on state jurisdiction by the Due Process Clause, in its role as a guarantor against inconvenient litigation, have been substantially relaxed over the years . . .

. . .

Nevertheless, we have never accepted the proposition that state lines are irrelevant for jurisdictional purposes, nor could we, and remain faithful to the principles of interstate federalism embodied in the Constitution. The economic interdependence of the States was foreseen and desired by the Framers. In the Commerce Clause, they provided that the Nation was to be a common market, a 'free trade unit' in which the States are debarred from acting as separable economic entities . . . But the Framers also intended that the States retain many essential attributes of sovereignty, including, in particular, the sovereign power to try causes in their courts. The sovereignty of each State, in turn, implied a limitation on the sovereignty of all of its sister States – a limitation express or implicit in both the original scheme of the Constitution and the Fourteenth Amendment.

. . .

Thus, the Due Process Clause 'does not contemplate that a state may make binding a judgment *in personam* against an individual or corporate defendant with which the state has no contacts, ties, or relations.' [*International Shoe*]. Even if the defendant would suffer minimal or no inconvenience from being forced to litigate before the tribunals of another State; even if the forum State has a strong interest in applying its law to the controversy; even if the forum State is the most convenient location for litigation, the Due Process Clause, acting as an instrument of interstate federalism, may sometimes act to divest the State of its power to render a valid judgment . . .

III

Applying these principles to the case at hand, we find in the record before us a total absence of those affiliating circumstances that are a necessary predicate to any exercise of state-court jurisdiction. Petitioners carry on no activity whatsoever in Oklahoma. They close no sales and perform no services there. They avail themselves of none of the privileges and benefits of Oklahoma law. They solicit no business there either through salespersons or through advertising reasonably calculated to reach the State. Nor does the record show that they regularly sell cars at wholesale or retail to Oklahoma customers or residents or that they indirectly, through others, serve or seek to serve the Oklahoma market. In short, respondents seek to base jurisdiction on one, isolated occurrence and whatever inferences can be drawn therefrom: the fortuitous circumstance that a single Audi automobile, sold in New York to New York residents, happened to suffer an accident while passing through Oklahoma.

It is argued, however, that because an automobile is mobile by its very design and purpose it was 'foreseeable' that the Robinsons' Audi would cause injury in Oklahoma. Yet 'foreseeability' alone has never been a sufficient benchmark for personal jurisdiction under the Due Process Clause . . .

. . .

This is not to say, of course, that foreseeability is wholly irrelevant. But the foreseeability that is critical to due process analysis is not the mere likelihood that a product will find its way into the forum State. Rather, it is that the defendant's conduct and connection with the forum State are such that he should reasonably anticipate being haled into court there . . . The Due Process Clause, by ensuring the 'orderly administration of the laws', [*International Shoe*] gives a degree of predictability to the legal system that allows potential defendants to structure their primary conduct with some minimum assurance as to where that conduct will and will not render them liable to suit.

When a corporation 'purposefully avails itself of the privilege of conducting activities within the forum State', it has clear notice that it is subject to suit there, and can act to alleviate the risk of burdensome litigation by procuring insurance, passing the expected costs on to customers, or, if the risks are too great, severing its connection with the State. Hence if the sale of a product of a manufacturer or distributor such as Audi or Volkswagen is not simply an isolated occurrence, but arises from the efforts of the manufacturer or distributor to serve, directly or indirectly, the market for its product in other States, it is not unreasonable to subject it to suit in one of those States if its allegedly defective merchandise has there been the source of injury to its owner or to others. The forum State does not exceed its powers under the Due Process Clause if it asserts personal jurisdiction over a corporation that delivers its products into the stream of commerce with the expectation that they will be purchased by consumers in the forum State . . .

But there is no such or similar basis for Oklahoma jurisdiction over World-Wide or Seaway in this case. Seaway's sales are made in Massena [New York]. World-Wide's market, although substantially larger, is limited to dealers in New York,

New Jersey, and Connecticut. There is no evidence of record that any automobiles distributed by World-Wide are sold to retail customers outside this tristate area. It is foreseeable that the purchasers of automobiles sold by World-Wide and Seaway may take them to Oklahoma. But the mere 'unilateral activity of those who claim some relationship with a nonresident defendant cannot satisfy the requirement of contact with the forum State.'

. . .

Because we find that petitioners have no 'contacts, ties, or relations' with the State of Oklahoma . . . the judgment of the Supreme Court of Oklahoma is

Reversed.

Result: The Oklahoma courts have no jurisdiction.

An important distinction, which was implicit in this case, and explicit in our next case, is that between general jurisdiction and specific jurisdiction.[25] As was explained in Chapter 2, § 5, above, general jurisdiction is jurisdiction that applies in general to any cause of action; specific jurisdiction, on the other hand, is limited to claims related to, or arising out of, the defendant's activities in the state in question. General jurisdiction requires closer contacts with the state of the forum than specific jurisdiction. To provide sufficient contacts for general jurisdiction, the defendant's activities in that state must be continuous and systematic.

§ 2.1.3 General jurisdiction. The rules regarding general jurisdiction are illustrated by the decision of the US Supreme Court in our next case.

> **United States**
> ***Helicopteros Nacionales de Colombia* v. *Hall* ('Helicol' case)**
> **US Supreme Court**
> **466 US 408; 104 S Ct 1868; 80 L Ed 2d 404 (1984)**

Background

WSH, a joint venture of three American companies, had its headquarters in Texas. It wished to contract with a Peruvian oil company to build a pipeline in Peru. It established a Peruvian consortium, Consorcio, which the US Supreme Court said was its *alter ego*. Helicol (Helicopteros Nacionales de Colombia) was a Colombian company providing transport by helicopter for oil companies and construction companies in South America. Consorcio/WSH contracted with Helicol to provide transport for their personnel in Peru. A helicopter, which was owned by Helicol, crashed in Peru while operating under this contract. Among those killed were four Americans who were employees of Consorcio. Their relatives brought wrongful-death actions in a state court in Texas against Consorcio/WSH, Helicol and Bell Helicopter Company, the Texas manufacturer of the helicopter. Helicol claimed the Texas courts had no jurisdiction over it, a contention rejected by the Supreme Court of Texas. The case went to the US

---

25 See footnotes 8 and 9 in the opinion of the court in the *Helicol* case (not set out below).

Supreme Court on certiorari. The plaintiffs conceded that their claims did not arise out of, and were not related to, Helicol's activities in Texas.[26] So they had to establish that the Texas courts had general jurisdiction. Helicol's only contacts with Texas were:

- 1. it had sent its chief executive to Houston, Texas, for a contract-negotiation session;
- 2. it had paid cheques (from Consorcio/WSH) drawn on a Houston bank into its New York banking account;
- 3. it had purchased helicopters, equipment and training services from Bell Helicopter in Texas; and
- 4. it had sent personnel to Fort Worth (Bell's Texas headquarters) for training.

Justice Blackmun delivered the opinion of the Court

II

The Due Process Clause of the Fourteenth Amendment operates to limit the power of a State to assert *in personam* jurisdiction over a nonresident defendant ... Due process requirements are satisfied when *in personam* jurisdiction is asserted over a nonresident corporate defendant that has 'certain minimum contacts with [the forum] such that the maintenance of the suit does not offend "traditional notions of fair play and substantial justice."' When a controversy is related to or 'arises out of' a defendant's contacts with the forum, the Court has said that a 'relationship among the defendant, the forum, and the litigation' is the essential foundation of *in personam* jurisdiction ...

Even when the cause of action does not arise out of or relate to the foreign corporation's activities in the forum State, due process is not offended by a State's subjecting the corporation to its *in personam* jurisdiction when there are sufficient contacts between the State and the foreign corporation ...

All parties to the present case concede that respondents' claims against Helicol did not 'arise out of', and are not related to, Helicol's activities within Texas. We thus must explore the nature of Helicol's contacts with the State of Texas to determine whether they constitute the kind of continuous and systematic general business contacts the Court found to exist in *Perkins*.[1] We hold that they do not.

It is undisputed that Helicol does not have a place of business in Texas and never has been licensed to do business in the State. Basically, Helicol's contacts with Texas consisted of sending its chief executive officer to Houston for a contract-negotiation session; accepting into its New York bank account checks drawn on a Houston bank; purchasing helicopters, equipment, and training services from Bell Helicopter for substantial sums; and sending personnel to Bell's facilities in Fort Worth for training.

1 *Editor's note*: this is *Perkins v. Benguet Consolidated Mining Co.*, 342 US 437; 72 S Ct 413; 96 L Ed 485 (1952).

---

26 It is possible that this concession was a mistake.

> The one trip to Houston by Helicol's chief executive officer for the purpose of negotiating the transportation-services contract with Consorcio/WSH cannot be described or regarded as a contact of a 'continuous and systematic' nature . . . and thus cannot support an assertion of *in personam* jurisdiction over Helicol by a Texas court. Similarly, Helicol's acceptance from Consorcio/WSH of checks drawn on a Texas bank is of negligible significance for purposes of determining whether Helicol had sufficient contacts in Texas. There is no indication that Helicol ever requested that the checks be drawn on a Texas bank or that there was any negotiation between Helicol and Consorcio/WSH with respect to the location or identity of the bank on which checks would be drawn. Common sense and everyday experience suggest that, absent unusual circumstances, the bank on which a check is drawn is generally of little consequence to the payee and is a matter left to the discretion of the drawer. Such unilateral activity of another party or a third person is not an appropriate consideration when determining whether a defendant has sufficient contacts with a forum State to justify an assertion of jurisdiction . . .
>
> . . .
>
> **III**
>
> We hold that Helicol's contacts with the State of Texas were insufficient to satisfy the requirements of the Due Process Clause of the Fourteenth Amendment. Accordingly, we reverse the judgment of the Supreme Court of Texas.
>
> [Dissenting opinion of Justice Brennan is omitted.]

Result: the Texas courts had no jurisdiction over Helicl.

Comment

This case shows how a foreign company that is not resident or domiciled in the United States can benefit from the protection of the 'minimum contacts' doctrine. In Europe, the result would have been different. First of all, a Colombian company would not be entitled to benefit from the protection of the Brussels I Regulation. Moreover, even if it had been entitled to benefit, it would still have been subject to the jurisdiction of the court. If Texas had been England, for example, the English court could have taken jurisdiction over Consorcio/WSH and Bell on the basis of their domicile in England; jurisdiction over Helicol could then have been taken under the 'necessary or proper party' rule in CPR 6.36 and Practice Direction 6 B, paragraph 3.1(3) (Chapter 5, § 4.4 and Panel 5.6, above). If Helicol had been domiciled in another EC State, the result would have been the same: Article 6(1) of the Brussels I Regulation (Chapter 4, § 2 and Panel 4.5, above). In the United States, there is no equivalent to these rules: minimum contacts must be established with regard to each defendant independently. If Texas had been France, the French courts could have taken jurisdiction over Helicol simply on the basis of the French nationality of the plaintiffs. This shows that jurisdiction can, in some instances, be more restrained in the United States than in Europe.

§ 2.1.4 Transient jurisdiction. The next question is whether 'tag jurisdiction', also called 'transient jurisdiction' (jurisdiction based on service of the writ on the defendant during a temporary visit to the forum state) satisfies the constitutional test. If we look back to the *International Shoe* case, the first of the cases discussed above, we can find support for the view that the minimum-contacts test applies only if the defendant is not present within the territory of the forum. That case refers to 'traditional notions of fair play and substantial justice', a phrase that might also be regarded as implicit approval for the traditional means of obtaining jurisdiction under the common law. However, there had been various developments since that case. In particular, the Supreme Court had said in *Schaffer* v. *Heitner* that 'all assertions of state-court jurisdiction must be evaluated according to the [*International Shoe*] standards'.[27] In our next case, the US Supreme Court had to confront the issue.

> **United States**
> ***Burnham* v. *Superior Court of California***
> **US Supreme Court**
> **495 US 604; 110 S Ct 2105; 109 L Ed 2d 631 (1990)**

Background

It is not necessary to give the facts of the case. The issue was simply whether the courts of California could obtain jurisdiction over an out-of-state defendant on the ground that he was served with a writ while on a temporary visit. The petitioner argued that, in the absence of continuous and systematic contacts with the forum, a non-resident defendant can be subjected to the jurisdiction of a state court only with regard to matters that arise out of, or relate to, his contacts with the state of the forum. In other words, he claimed that the service of a writ cannot confer general jurisdiction on a temporary visitor. The US Supreme Court rejected that view. Unfortunately, different judges gave different reasons.

Justice Scalia announced the judgment of the Court and delivered an opinion in which the Chief Justice and Justice Kennedy join, and in which Justice White joins with respect to Parts I, II-A, II-B, and II-C.

The question presented is whether the Due Process Clause of the Fourteenth Amendment denies California courts jurisdiction over a nonresident, who was personally served with process while temporarily in that State, in a suit unrelated to his activities in the State.

. . .

II–B

Among the most firmly established principles of personal jurisdiction in American tradition is that the courts of a State have jurisdiction over nonresidents who are physically present in the State. The view developed early that each State had

---

27 433 US 186 at 212; 97 S Ct 2569 at 2584 (1977).

the power to hale before its courts any individual who could be found within its borders, and that once having acquired jurisdiction over such a person by properly serving him with process, the State could retain jurisdiction to enter judgment against him, no matter how fleeting his visit . . . That view had antecedents in English common-law practice . . . Justice Story believed the principle, which he traced to Roman origins, to be firmly grounded in English tradition: '[B]y the common law[,] personal actions, being transitory, may be brought in any place, where the party defendant may be found', for 'every nation may . . . rightfully exercise jurisdiction over all persons within its domains.' J. Story, *Commentaries on the Conflict of Laws* §§ 554, 543 (1846) . . .

Recent scholarship has suggested that English tradition was not as clear as Story thought . . . Accurate or not, however, judging by the evidence of contemporaneous or near-contemporaneous decisions, one must conclude that Story's understanding was shared by American courts at the crucial time for present purposes: 1868, when the Fourteenth Amendment was adopted. The following passage in a decision of the Supreme Court of Georgia, in an action on a debt having no apparent relation to the defendant's temporary presence in the State, is representative:

> 'Can a citizen of Alabama be sued in this State, as he passes through it? Undoubtedly he can . . .' *Murphy* v. *J. S. Winter & Co.*, 18 Ga. 690, 691–692 (1855) . . .

Decisions in the courts of many States in the 19th and early 20th centuries held that personal service upon a physically present defendant sufficed to confer jurisdiction, without regard to whether the defendant was only briefly in the State or whether the cause of action was related to his activities there . . . Although research has not revealed a case deciding the issue in every State's courts, that appears to be because the issue was so well settled that it went unlitigated . . . Most States, moreover, had statutes or common-law rules that exempted from service of process individuals who were brought into the forum by force or fraud . . . or who were there as a party or witness in unrelated judicial proceedings . . . These exceptions obviously rested upon the premise that service of process conferred jurisdiction . . . Particularly striking is the fact that, as far as we have been able to determine, *not one* American case from the period (or, for that matter, not one American case until 1978) held, or even suggested, that in-state personal service on an individual was insufficient to confer personal jurisdiction . . .

This American jurisdictional practice is, moreover, not merely old; it is continuing. It remains the practice of, not only a substantial number of the States, but as far as we are aware all the States and the Federal Government – if one disregards (as one must for this purpose) the few opinions since 1978 that have erroneously said, on grounds similar to those that petitioner presses here, that this Court's due process decisions render the practice unconstitutional . . . We do not know of a single state or federal statute, or a single judicial decision resting upon state law, that has abandoned in-state service as a basis of jurisdiction. Many recent cases reaffirm it . . .

C

Despite this formidable body of precedent, petitioner contends, in reliance on our decisions applying the *International Shoe* standard, that in the absence of 'continuous and systematic' contacts with the forum . . . a nonresident defendant can be subjected to judgment only as to matters that arise out of or relate to his contacts with the forum. This argument rests on a thorough misunderstanding of our cases.

[Justice Scalia then pointed out that originally it was thought that a court could obtain jurisdiction *only* on the basis of service within the territory of the state. Subsequently states began to adopt long-arm statutes, though these were initially based on the fiction that service had somehow been effected within the state. He then continued:]

Our opinion in *International Shoe* cast those fictions aside and made explicit the underlying basis of these decisions: due process does not necessarily *require* the States to adhere to the unbending territorial limits on jurisdiction set forth in *Pennoyer*.[1] The validity of assertion of jurisdiction over a nonconsenting defendant who is not present in the forum depends upon whether 'the quality and nature of [his] activity' in relation to the forum . . . renders such jurisdiction consistent with 'traditional notions of fair play and substantial justice.'

Nothing in *International Shoe* or the cases that have followed it, however, offers support for the very different proposition petitioner seeks to establish today: that a defendant's presence in the forum is not only unnecessary to validate novel, nontraditional assertions of jurisdiction, but is itself no longer sufficient to establish jurisdiction. That proposition is unfaithful to both elementary logic and the foundations of our due process jurisprudence . . .

The short of the matter is that jurisdiction based on physical presence alone constitutes due process because it is one of the continuing traditions of our legal system that define the due process standard of 'traditional notions of fair play and substantial justice.' That standard was developed by *analogy* to 'physical presence', and it would be perverse to say it could now be turned against that touchstone of jurisdiction.

D

Petitioner's strongest argument, though we ultimately reject it, relies upon our decision in *Shaffer* v. *Heitner* . . .

[Justice Scalia then considered the passage in *Shaffer* v. *Heitner* quoted above that 'all assertions of state-court jurisdiction must be evaluated according to the [*International Shoe*] standards' and concluded that the petitioner took it out of context. It was intended, he said, to apply only to *quasi in rem* jurisdiction.[2] It

1 *Editor's note*: *Pennoyer v. Neff*, 95 US 714; 24 L Ed 565 (1878), a case which laid down the rule – usually thought to have been based on the Due Process Clause of the Fourteenth Amendment, though actually decided before the Fourteenth Amendment was adopted – that jurisdiction may be exercised only on the basis of service within the territory of the forum or on the basis of consent.
2 This is a kind of jurisdiction *in rem* (jurisdiction based on the presence of property of the defendant within the territory of the forum): see Chapter 2, § 3, above.

was not intended to apply where the defendant was personally served within the territory of the forum.]

It is fair to say, however, that while our holding today does not contradict *Shaffer*, our basic approach to the due process question is different. We have conducted no independent inquiry into the desirability or fairness of the prevailing in-state service rule, leaving that judgment to the legislatures that are free to amend it; for our purposes, its validation is its pedigree, as the phrase *'traditional notions of fair play and substantial justice'* makes clear. *Shaffer* did conduct such an independent inquiry, asserting that '"traditional notions of fair play and substantial justice" can be as readily offended by the perpetuation of ancient forms that are no longer justified as by the adoption of new procedures that are inconsistent with the basic values of our constitutional heritage.' Perhaps that assertion can be sustained when the 'perpetuation of ancient forms' is engaged in by only a very small minority of the States. Where, however, as in the present case, a jurisdictional principle is both firmly approved by tradition and still favored, it is impossible to imagine what standard we could appeal to for the judgment that it is 'no longer justified.' While in no way receding from or casting doubt upon the holding of *Shaffer* or any other case, we reaffirm today our time-honored approach ... For new procedures, hitherto unknown, the Due Process Clause requires analysis to determine whether 'traditional notions of fair play and substantial justice' have been offended ... But a doctrine of personal jurisdiction that dates back to the adoption of the Fourteenth Amendment and is still generally observed unquestionably meets that standard.

. . .

Because the Due Process Clause does not prohibit the California courts from exercising jurisdiction over petitioner based on the fact of in-state service of process, the judgment is

Affirmed.

[Judgment of Justice White (concurring in the result) omitted.]

Justice Brennan, with whom Justice Marshall, Justice Blackmun, and Justice O'Connor join, concurring in the judgment.

I agree with Justice Scalia that the Due Process Clause of the Fourteenth Amendment generally permits a state court to exercise jurisdiction over a defendant if he is served with process while voluntarily present in the forum State. I do not perceive the need, however, to decide that a jurisdictional rule that 'has been immemorially the actual law of the land' automatically comports with due process simply by virtue of its 'pedigree.' Although I agree that history is an important factor in establishing whether a jurisdictional rule satisfies due process requirements, I cannot agree that it is the *only* factor such that all traditional rules of jurisdiction are, *ipso facto*, forever constitutional. Unlike Justice Scalia, I would undertake an 'independent inquiry into the . . . fairness of the prevailing in-state service rule.' I therefore concur only in the judgment.

[After stating that the approach adopted by Justice Scalia – reliance solely on tradition – was contrary to *International Shoe* and *Shaffer* v. *Heitner*, Justice Brennan continued:]

II

Tradition, though alone not dispositive, is of course *relevant* to the question whether the rule of transient jurisdiction is consistent with due process. Tradition is salient not in the sense that practices of the past are automatically reasonable today; indeed, under such a standard, the legitimacy of transient jurisdiction would be called into question because the rule's historical 'pedigree' is a matter of intense debate. The rule was a stranger to the common law and was rather weakly implanted in American jurisprudence 'at the crucial time for present purposes: 1868, when the Fourteenth Amendment was adopted.' For much of the 19th century, American courts did not uniformly recognize the concept of transient jurisdiction, and it appears that the transient rule did not receive wide currency until well after our decision in *Pennoyer* v. *Neff* . . .

Rather, I find the historical background relevant because, however murky the jurisprudential origins of transient jurisdiction, the fact that American courts have announced the rule for perhaps a century (first in dicta, more recently in holdings) provides a defendant voluntarily present in a particular State today 'clear notice that [he] is subject to suit' in the forum [*World-Wide Volkswagen*] . . . Regardless of whether Justice Story's account of the rule's genesis is mythical, our common understanding *now*, fortified by a century of judicial practice, is that jurisdiction is often a function of geography. The transient rule is consistent with reasonable expectations and is entitled to a strong presumption that it comports with due process. 'If I visit another State . . . I knowingly assume some risk that the State will exercise its power over my property or my person while there. My contact with the State, though minimal, gives rise to predictable risks.'

By visiting the forum State, a transient defendant actually 'avail[s]' himself, [*Burger King*] of significant benefits provided by the State. His health and safety are guaranteed by the State's police, fire, and emergency medical services; he is free to travel on the State's roads and waterways; he likely enjoys the fruits of the State's economy as well. Moreover, the Privileges and Immunities Clause of Article IV [of the US Constitution] prevents a state government from discriminating against a transient defendant by denying him the protections of its law or the right of access to its courts . . . Subject only to the doctrine of *forum non conveniens*, an out-of-state plaintiff may use state courts in all circumstances in which those courts would be available to state citizens. Without transient jurisdiction, an asymmetry would arise: A transient would have the full benefit of the power of the forum State's courts as a plaintiff while retaining immunity from their authority as a defendant . . .

The potential burdens on a transient defendant are slight. '[M]odern transportation and communications have made it much less burdensome for a party sued to defend himself' in a State outside his place of residence. [*Burger King*] . . . That the defendant has already journeyed at least once before to the forum – as evidenced by the fact that he was served with process there – is an indication that suit in the

> forum likely would not be prohibitively inconvenient. Finally, any burdens that do arise can be ameliorated by a variety of procedural devices. For these reasons, as a rule the exercise of personal jurisdiction over a defendant based on his voluntary presence in the forum will satisfy the requirements of due process.
>
> In this case, it is undisputed that petitioner was served with process while voluntarily and knowingly in the State of California. I therefore concur in the judgment.
>
> [Judgment of Justice Stevens (concurring in the result) omitted.]

Result: the appeal was dismissed: the California courts have jurisdiction.

Comment

This judgment illustrates the tension between the historical approach to the interpretation of the Due Process Clause and the analytical approach. Transient jurisdiction was established as a ground of jurisdiction when the Fourteenth Amendment was adopted in 1868.[28] Historically speaking, it is hard to argue that the Amendment was intended to outlaw it. This provides the main justification of the approach of Scalia J. However, there is a widely held view that the Constitution must be interpreted on the basis of contemporary ideas. This explains the judgment of Brennan J. With regard to this particular issue, both strands of thought lead to the same conclusion: in practice, it is extremely unlikely that transient jurisdiction would ever be regarded as unconstitutional, even where the cause of action was unrelated to the activities of the defendant in the forum state.[29]

QUESTION

Do you agree that service of a writ on a transient defendant is a satisfactory basis of jurisdiction if the claim is unrelated to the activities of the defendant within the state concerned?

---

§ 2.2 Federal courts. Except in certain specific instances, federal law does not provide for the international or inter-state jurisdiction of federal courts. In the absence of a federal jurisdictional rule applicable in the case before it, a federal court will apply the jurisdictional rules of the state in which it is sitting.[30] State long-arm statutes may, therefore, be used to bring a defendant into the federal courts as well as into the state courts.

Panel 7.2 Due Process Clause of the Fifth Amendment (US Constitution) (1791)

No person shall . . . be deprived of life, liberty or property, without due process of law . . .

---

28 As was pointed out by Brennan J, however, it was not quite so well established as is generally thought.
29 There would almost certainly be an exception, however, where the defendant was forcibly brought within the state of the forum; there might also be an exception where he was fraudulently enticed within the state.
30 See the Federal Rules of Civil Procedure, Rule 4(k)(1)(A).

The Fourteenth Amendment (adopted in 1868) applies only to the states. However, the Due Process Clause of the Fifth Amendment (adopted in 1791) (Panel 7.2) imposes the same requirements on the United States. So the minimum-contacts doctrine applies also to actions in a federal court.

> **Panel 7.3 Federal Rules of Civil Procedure, Rule 4(k)(2) (1993)**
>
> **Rule 4(k)(2)**
> If the exercise of jurisdiction is consistent with the Constitution and laws of the United States, serving a summons or filing a waiver of service is also effective, with respect to claims arising under federal law, to establish personal jurisdiction over the person of any defendant who is not subject to the jurisdiction of the courts of general jurisdiction of any state.

In most ways, therefore, the rules of international and inter-state jurisdiction are the same in federal courts as in state courts. However, if the action is brought in a state court, the minimum contacts must be with the *state* in question. If jurisdiction is based on state law, this is also the position in the federal courts.[31] However, where no state jurisdictional rule covers the case, a federal court may, under Rule 4(k)(2) (Panel 7.3), an amendment to the Federal Rules of Civil Procedure adopted in 1993,[32] obtain jurisdiction on the basis of a nationwide minimum-contacts test.[33] Under this provision, the defendant's contacts with the whole of the United States may be taken into account, provided all the following conditions are satisfied:

- the action must be brought in a federal court;
- it must be brought under federal law (not under state law or under the law of a foreign country);[34]
- the defendant must not be subject to the jurisdiction[35] of the courts of general jurisdiction of any state.

Our next case explains how it works.

United States (Massachusetts)
United States of America v. *Swiss American Bank*
US Court of Appeals for the First Circuit
191 F 3d 30 (1999)

Background

In this case, the US Government was suing a number of foreign banks to obtain funds deposited with the banks by an individual who had been convicted in the United States of various criminal offences. The proceedings were brought in a federal district court in Massachusetts. That court held that it lacked jurisdiction. The government appealed.

---

31 *United Electrical, Radio and Machine Workers of America* v. *163 Pleasant St Corporation*, 960 F 2d 1080 (1st Cir. 1992). See further *Omni Capital International* v. *Wolff*, 484 US 97; 18 S Ct 404; 98 L Ed 2d 415 (US Supreme Court, 1987).
32 For a discussion of this provision, see Born and Vollmer, 'The Effect of the Revised Federal Rules of Civil Procedure on Personal Jurisdiction, Service and Discovery in International Cases', 150 *Federal Rules Decisions* 221 (1993).
33 This is another situation in which the minimum-contacts test is not merely a limit on jurisdiction, but actually constitutes the jurisdictional rule.
34 It would not, therefore, apply when the court is sitting in diversity.
35 This means personal (international or inter-state) jurisdiction, not subject-matter jurisdiction: see the *Swiss American Bank* case, below.

Selya, Circuit Judge

After discussing the constitutional requirements and saying that in order to be able to hear a case a court must possess statutory authorization to exercise specific personal jurisdiction over defendants of the type that the plaintiff targets, the court continued:]

This authorization may derive from a federal statute, *see, e.g.*, 15 USC § 22 (providing for worldwide service of process on certain corporate antitrust defendants), or from a state statute of general application, *see, e.g.*, Mass. Gen. Laws ch. 223A, § 3 (providing 'long-arm' jurisdiction). A state long-arm statute furnishes a mechanism for obtaining personal jurisdiction in federal as well as state courts. *See* Fed. R Civ. P 4(k)(1)(A).

In limited circumstances, the requisite authorization can be provided by Rule 4(k)(2) . . . which functions as a sort of federal long-arm statute. When a plaintiff depends upon this recently adopted rule to serve as the necessary statutory authorization for the exercise of specific personal jurisdiction, the constitutional requirements are the same as those limned[1] above, but the analytic exercises are performed with reference to the United States as a whole, rather than with reference to a particular state. The defendant's national contacts take center stage because the rule applies only to situations in which federal courts draw jurisdictional authority from the federal sovereign (unreinforced by 'borrowed' state statutes), and, thus, the applicable constitutional requirements devolve from the Fifth rather than the Fourteenth Amendment . . .

[After considering the Massachusetts long-arm statute and deciding that it was not applicable, the court continued:]

C. Jurisdiction under Rule 4(k)(2).

The government claims, in the alternative, that the district court possessed *in personam* jurisdiction under Rule 4(k)(2). The rule, first enacted in December 1993, provides . . .

[See Panel 7.3, above.]

The rule's fabric contains three strands: (1) the plaintiff's claim must be one arising under federal law; (2) the putative defendant must be beyond the jurisdictional reach of any state court of general jurisdiction; and (3) the federal courts' exercise of personal jurisdiction over the defendant must not offend the Constitution or other federal law . . .

1.   *The Negation Requirement.* By its terms, Rule 4(k)(2) requires that the putative defendant not be subject to jurisdiction in any state court of general jurisdiction. The government argues that this requirement encompasses both subject matter and personal jurisdiction, and that, therefore, it can satisfy the negation requirement simply by showing that the state courts have no subject matter jurisdiction over a particular cause of action . . .

---

1 *Editor's note*: 'limned' means depicted or sketched.

We find this reasoning unconvincing . . . [W]e . . . consider it pellucid that Rule 4(k)(2)'s reference to defendants who are 'not subject to the jurisdiction . . .' refers to the absence of *personal* jurisdiction. We explain briefly.

[After discussing the case law on the matter, the court continued:]

The advisory committee's explanation of the rationale behind the adoption of Rule 4(k)(2) cinches matters. The drafters created this proviso to deal with a gap in personal jurisdiction noted by the Supreme Court in *Omni Capital Int'l Ltd* v. *Rudolf Wolff & Co.* 484 US 97, 111 (1987). Before Rule 4(k)(2) was conceived, federal courts 'borrowed' from state law when a federal statute did not otherwise provide a mechanism for service of process (regardless of the state courts' subject matter jurisdiction). Accordingly, foreign defendants who lacked single-state contacts sufficient to bring them within the reach of a given state's long-arm statute (whether by reason of the paucity of the contacts or of limitations built into the statute itself), but who had enough contacts with the United States as a whole to make personal jurisdiction over them in a United States court constitutional, could evade responsibility for civil violations of federal laws that did not provide specifically for service of process . . .

To close this loophole, the drafters designed the new Rule 4(k)(2) to function as a species of federal long-arm statute. *See* Fed. R Civ. P 4 advisory committee note. The rule's final clause, restricting its application to those cases in which the putative defendant 'is not subject to the jurisdiction of the courts of general jurisdiction of any state' works to cabin the rule's sweep and ensure its application only in the relatively narrow range of cases identified by the *Omni* court (in which the states' personal jurisdiction rules prove impuissant[2]). The government's self-serving interpretation of the term 'jurisdiction', as used here, would extend the rule's scope well beyond its intended purpose and, in the bargain, would allow plaintiffs with claims falling within exclusive federal jurisdiction statutes complete discretion to forum-shop without any regard for concentrated contacts. Apart from a linguistic fortuity – the word 'jurisdiction' is protean and has a wide variety of meanings, depending on the context in which it is used – there is nothing to endorse so expansive a construction of Rule 4(k)(2). We hold, therefore, that the absence of state court subject matter jurisdiction does not enter into the negation equation.

The government's better argument is that its case falls within the limits of Rule 4(k)(2) even when the rule is interpreted – as it must be – to require negation of personal jurisdiction over the defendant in any state court. The defendants' rejoinder is that, while the government alleged in its complaint that Rule 4(k)(2) supplied the necessary means for obtaining personal jurisdiction, it failed to plead or prove facts demonstrating the absence of personal jurisdiction over the defendants throughout the fifty states. This thrust and parry raises an issue of first impression concerning the order and allocation of proof in respect to Rule 4(k)(2)'s negation requirement, for no appellate court has offered a clear resolution of that problem. In a world of exponential growth in international transactions, the practical importance of this issue looms large.

2 *Editor's note*: 'impuissant' means impotent or powerless.

The defendants (and the district court) certainly are correct in their insistence that a plaintiff ordinarily must shoulder the burden of proving personal jurisdiction over the defendant . . . Some district courts, relying on this shibboleth, have assigned outright to plaintiffs the burden of proving the Rule 4(k)(2) negation requirement . . . This paradigm in effect requires a plaintiff to prove a negative fifty times over – an epistemological quandary which is compounded by the fact that the defendant typically controls much of the information needed to determine the existence and/or magnitude of its contacts with any given jurisdiction. There is a corresponding problem with assigning the burden of proof on the Rule 4(k)(2) negation requirement to defendants: doing so threatens to place a defendant in a 'Catch-22' situation, forcing it to choose between conceding its potential amenability to suit in federal court (by denying that any state court has jurisdiction over it) or conceding its potential amenability to suit in some identified state court . . .

Faced with such dilemmas, courts historically have tailored special burden-of-proof regimes for specific classes of cases in order to strike an equitable balance . . . We believe that Rule 4(k)(2) is fertile territory for such an innovation. The architects of the rule – and Congress, by adopting it – clearly intended to close the gap identified by the *Omni* court and to ensure that persons whose contacts with this country exceeded the constitutional minimum could not easily evade civil liability in the American justice system. At the same time, however, the drafters also wrote the rule to preserve the established modalities for obtaining personal jurisdiction previously available under Rule 4(k)(1)(A) as the primary avenue to service on foreign defendants. The desire to achieve this secondary purpose led the authors of the rule to restrict its reach to those defendants with sufficient nationwide contacts to subject them to federal jurisdiction, but whose contacts were too exiguous to permit any state court to exercise personal jurisdiction over them. Viewed in this light, the application of traditional burden-of-proof principles to Rule 4(k)(2) cases not only would be inequitable, but also would shield foreign defendants who were constitutionally within the reach of federal courts from the exercise of personal jurisdiction, and, thus, thwart the core purpose that underlies the rule.

In our view, this core purpose can be achieved much more salubriously by crafting a special burden-shifting framework. To accomplish the desired end without placing the judicial thumb too heavily on the scale, we will not assign the burden of proof on the negation issue to either party in a monolithic fashion. We prefer instead to draw upon the burden-shifting arrangement devised by the court to cope with somewhat analogous problems of proof in the discrimination context . . . We etch the contours of this proposed standard in detail below.

We hold that a plaintiff who seeks to invoke Rule 4(k)(2) must make a prima facie case for the applicability of the rule. This includes a tripartite showing (1) that the claim asserted arises under federal law, (2) that personal jurisdiction is not available under any situation-specific federal statute, and (3) that the putative defendant's contacts with the nation as a whole suffice to satisfy the applicable constitutional requirements. The plaintiff, moreover, must certify that, based on the information that is readily available to the plaintiff and his counsel, the defendant is not subject to suit in the courts of general jurisdiction of any state. If the plaintiff makes out his prima facie case, the burden shifts to the defendant to produce evidence which, if credited, would show either that one or more specific states exist in which it would be subject to suit or that its contacts with the United States are constitutionally insufficient . . . Should the defendant default on its burden of production, the trier[36] may infer that personal jurisdiction over the defendant is not available in any state court of general jurisdiction. If, however, the defendant satisfies its second-stage burden of production, then the aforementioned inference drops from the case.

What happens next depends on how the defendant satisfies its burden. If the defendant produces evidence indicating that it is subject to jurisdiction in a particular state, the plaintiff has three choices: he may move for a transfer to a district within that state, or he may discontinue his action (preliminary, perhaps, to the initiation of a suit in the courts of the identified state), or he may contest the defendant's proffer. If the plaintiff elects the last-mentioned course, the defendant will be deemed to have waived any claim that it is subject to personal jurisdiction in the courts of general jurisdiction of any state other than the state or states which it has identified, and the plaintiff, to fulfill the negation requirement, must prove that the defendant is not subject to suit in the identified forum(s).

Of course, the defendant may satisfy its burden of production by maintaining that it cannot constitutionally be subjected to jurisdiction in any state court. In that event, the defendant will be deemed to have conceded the negation issue, and the plaintiff, to succeed in his Rule 4(k)(2) initiative, need only prove that his claim arises under federal law and that the defendant has contacts with the United States as a whole sufficient to permit a federal court constitutionally to exercise personal jurisdiction over it . . .

QUESTION

Since a resident of the United States will always be subject to the jurisdiction of the state courts of the state in which he resides, this provision can apply only to persons resident outside the US. Is it fair to treat foreigners differently in this way?

§3 Venue

In addition to establishing jurisdiction, the plaintiff must also comply with the rules regarding venue. These rules are different for state and federal courts (and also different in each state). The federal venue rules are intended to decide in which federal judicial district the action should be brought; in other words, they

---

36 *Editor's note*: 'trier' means judge.

point to a federal judicial district, rather than to a state. Therefore, if the plaintiff establishes that the courts of California have jurisdiction *in personam*, and that the federal courts have subject-matter jurisdiction, he will look to the rules regarding venue to decide in which federal district court in California the action should be brought. The federal venue rules, which are contained in 28 USC §§ 1391–1392, are in fact fairly easy to satisfy. Generally speaking, the action may be brought either in the judicial district in which the defendant resides or in that in which the claim arose. If neither of these is possible, it may be brought in any judicial district in which the defendant is subject to *in personam* (international or inter-state) jurisdiction.

§ 4   The United States and Europe compared

It is often thought (at least by Europeans) that American courts exercise wider jurisdiction than their European counterparts. The time has come to consider whether this is true.

The most obvious point is one that has already been mentioned. The constitutional limitations fashioned by the US Supreme Court from the Due Process Clause are applied to foreigners in the same way as they are applied to Americans. In Europe, on the other hand, the protective provisions of the Brussels I Regulation are solely for the benefit of defendants domiciled in the Community.[37] This means that, in Europe, Americans and other non-Europeans are systematically discriminated against; in the United States, on the other hand, there is no discrimination against Europeans and other foreigners.[38]

In this section, we shall give examples of cases in which European jurisdiction is more extensive than American, as well as cases in which American jurisdiction is more extensive than European. In the case of Europe, we shall consider the position of defendants from other European States as well as defendants from outside Europe.[39]

§ 4.1   Cases where European jurisdiction is more extensive

For our first example, let us take *World-Wide Volkswagen Corporation* v. *Woodson*.[40] In that case, it will be remembered, a New York resident bought an imported car from a dealer in New York. He later moved to Arizona and, on the way, had an accident in Oklahoma. He sued the regional distributor and the dealer in the

---

37 Under the Lugano Convention, they are extended to persons domiciled in Iceland, Norway and Switzerland.
38 Rule 4(k)(2), discussed in § 2.2, above, is a small exception.
39 In the paragraphs that follow, France is often used as an example when discussing national rules of jurisdiction in Europe. This is done as a matter of convenience: it is not suggested that French law is necessarily more extensive than the law of other Member States. For a list of jurisdictional rules of EC Member States that are regarded as exorbitant, see Annex 1 to the Brussels I Regulation (as amended): these rules may not be used against defendants domiciled in a Member State of the EC; they may, however, be used against defendants not so domiciled. For a discussion of these rules, see Alexander Layton and Hugh Mercer (eds.), *European Civil Practice* (Sweet & Maxwell, London, 2nd edn, 2004).
40 444 US 286; 62 L Ed 2d 490; 100 S Ct 559 (US Supreme Court, 1980).

courts of Oklahoma, but the Supreme Court of the United States ruled that the courts of Oklahoma had no jurisdiction over them. Even though it might have been foreseeable that the car would be involved in an accident in Oklahoma, the distributor and dealer had not purposefully availed themselves of the privilege of conducting activities there.

If this case were transposed to Europe, what would the result be? Assume that a German buys an imported Japanese car in Germany. He takes it to Belgium and has an accident there. He brings proceedings in a Belgian court against the regional distributor, whose territory covers three German *Länder*, including the *Land* where the car was purchased. Would the court have jurisdiction? The action would come under Article 5(3) of the Brussels I Regulation.[41] The Belgian court would, therefore, have jurisdiction over the defendant, even though he had no contacts whatsoever with Belgium. He would not even be able to plead *forum non conveniens*, since that doctrine is (as we shall see) outlawed in the Community. In this example, jurisdiction in Europe (even against a Community-domiciled defendant) would be more extensive than jurisdiction under US law.

Our second example is *Helicopteros Nacionales de Colombia* v. *Hall* (the 'Helicol' case).[42] In this case, the families of the American victims of a helicopter crash in Peru brought wrongful-death proceedings in Texas against Helicol (the Colombian operator of the helicopter), Bell Helicopter Company (the manufacturer of the helicopter) and WSH (the employer of the victims). Bell Helicopter and WSH were both domiciled in Texas. The Supreme Court of the United States held that the Texas courts had no jurisdiction over Helicol because it did not have sufficient contacts with Texas. The fact that it was one of a group of defendants, the others of which were domiciled in Texas, made no difference.

If we transpose this case to Europe, we could get the following. A French company has a contract to build a pipeline in Peru. It contracts with a Colombian helicopter-transport company, Helicol, to provide transport for its personnel in Peru. Helicol uses helicopters manufactured by a second French company. One of the helicopters crashes in Peru, killing some French employees of the first French company. Their families bring proceedings in the French courts against the first French company (the employer), the second French company (the helicopter manufacturer) and Helicol.

Would the French courts have jurisdiction against Helicol? Clearly, they would. Since the plaintiffs are French citizens, they can resort to Article 14 of the French Civil Code. That gives the French courts jurisdiction on the basis of the French nationality of the plaintiff.[43] As Helicol is domiciled outside the European Community, it cannot invoke the protective rules of the Regulation.

What would the position be if Helicol had been domiciled in the European Community? Assume that it had domiciled in Spain. Here, the plaintiffs

---

41 *Handte* v. *TMCS*, Case C-26/91, [1992] ECR I-3967.
42 466 US 408; 104 S Ct 1868; 80 L Ed 2d 404 (1984).
43 Although the specific terms of Article 14 limit it to contracts, the French courts have interpreted it as covering other obligations as well.

would no longer be able to use Article 14 of the French Civil Code. However, Helicol would be one of a number of defendants. The others would be domiciled in France. The claims between the parties would be so closely connected that it would be expedient to hear and determine them together to avoid the risk of irreconcilable judgments.[44] So Article 6(1) of the Brussels I Regulation would give the French courts jurisdiction over Helicol.

§ 4.2 Cases where American jurisdiction is more extensive

The most important situation in which American jurisdiction is wider, at least when compared to the Regulation, is where the defendant has sufficient contacts with the state of the forum to justify the assertion of general jurisdiction. We shall consider individuals and companies separately.

§ 4.2.1 Individuals. As we saw in § 2.1.4, above, the US Supreme Court has held that a court can constitutionally obtain general jurisdiction by the service of a writ on an individual while he is temporarily present within the territory of the forum.[45] Similar rules are found in the common-law Member States of the Community, but not in the civil-law Member States. Thus a Frenchman visiting California and served with a writ there might find himself subject to the jurisdiction of the California courts with regard to a matter that had no connection with California. An American in France could not be subjected to French jurisdiction in the same way.

However, if the Frenchman were sued in California, the California courts would almost certainly dismiss the proceedings under the doctrine of *forum non conveniens*, unless the plaintiff was Californian or the claim arose out of the defendant's activities in California. On the other hand, if the American were sued in France, the French courts would have jurisdiction under Article 14 of the French Civil Code if the plaintiff was French or was domiciled in France.[46] Since the French rule would apply even if the American never set foot in France, it might be regarded (at least by common lawyers) as even more objectionable than the American rule.

Where the defendant is from another Community (or Lugano) State, there is nothing equivalent to 'tag jurisdiction' in Europe. Thus, for example, a Portuguese domiciliary temporarily present in England cannot be subjected to the jurisdiction of the English courts by the service of a writ on him. Here, the European rules are more restrained.

---

44 If the action against the helicopter manufacturer was heard in France, the court might decide that the cause of the accident was faulty maintenance of the helicopter or pilot error. If the action against Helicol was heard in Spain, the court might decide that the cause of the accident was a design fault. These judgments would be irreconcilable. For Article 6(1) to apply, it does not have to be impossible to enforce both judgments: Hélène Gaudemet-Tallon, *Compétence et exécution des jugements en Europe* (LGDJ, Paris, 3rd edn 2002), p. 201; Hartley, 'Jurisdictional Issues under Articles 5(1), 5(3) and 6(1)' (1989) 14 *European Law Review* 172. Indeed, if the judgments were against different parties, as they must be in the context of Article 6(1), it would *never* be impossible to enforce both of them.

45 *Burnham* v. *Superior Court of California*, 495 US 604; 110 S Ct 2105; 109 L Ed 2d 631 (1990).

46 The extension of Article 14 to cover persons domiciled in France, even if not of French nationality, results from Article 4(2) of the Brussels I Regulation, which goes out of its way to make the most objectionable rules of national law available to foreigners domiciled in the State of the forum – provided, of course, that the defendant is not domiciled in a Member State.

§ 4.2.2 Companies. From the commercial point of view, jurisdiction over companies is more important than jurisdiction over individuals. In the United States, general jurisdiction over a foreign company is constitutional if the company has contacts with the state of the forum[47] that are continuous and systematic. This means that (as in England) opening a branch would normally give general jurisdiction over the company.

Assume, for example, that an aircraft owned by a French airline crashes in France on a flight to Mexico. The passengers are German. Their families bring proceedings against the airline in New York, where it has an office which sells tickets. A trial in New York, probably with a jury, would almost certainly result in higher damages than a trial in France. Assuming that the activities of the airline in New York are continuous and systematic – which they almost certainly would be – the New York courts could constitutionally take jurisdiction.[48] Since none of the passengers is American, however, the New York courts would probably dismiss the proceedings on the ground of *forum non conveniens*.[49]

This example shows a situation in which the American courts have wider jurisdiction than the equivalent in the civil-law countries of Europe. However, in the reverse situation, French plaintiffs could sue an American airline in France under Article 14 of the French Civil Code, even if the airline had no office there. The resulting judgment could be enforced in other EC or Lugano States if the airline had no assets in France.[50]

§ 4.3   Assessment

Taken together, these examples suggest that, in personal injury and wrongful-death cases, American law is not generally more extensive than French law. It may even be more restrained.

The reason Europeans feel strongly about forum-shopping in America is not (it is suggested) because of the extensive nature of American jurisdiction in itself, but because of the *combined effect* of the jurisdictional rules *and* other features of American law that put plaintiffs in a strong position in wrongful-death and personal-injury cases. These other features include:

- the contingent-fee system, which allows a plaintiff with a strong case (and the prospect of winning large damages) to obtain the services of a top-quality lawyer even if he has no money;[51]

---

47 As we saw in § 2.2, above, there are certain limited situations in which a nationwide minimum-contacts test is applicable.
48 We assume, as in all the examples concerning American jurisdiction, that the relevant state law confers jurisdiction.
49 However, a few lingering doubts on this score might induce the airline to increase its settlement offer.
50 The reverse would also be true: a judgment by a New York court could, if constitutional, be enforced in any other American state.
51 In European countries, impecunious litigants may be entitled to public funds to pay their lawyer, or lawyers may be expected to take the case without fee (*pro bono publico* or *pro deo*). However, it is often difficult in practice to obtain representation on this basis (at least, if the litigant is not extremely indigent) and the quality of the legal representation thus obtained is not always of the best. Under the US system, on the other hand, a litigant who stands to win a large award is an attractive proposition for a lawyer. It is not necessary to appeal to his sense of public duty to get him to take the case.

- the American rule on costs, under which the plaintiff does not normally have to pay the defendant's attorney fees if he loses;
- wide-ranging pre-trial discovery (disclosure), which makes it easier to obtain the necessary evidence; and
- jury trials, which usually result in much higher damages in personal-injury and wrongful-death cases.

Put together, these rules, which are of a procedural nature and not subject to choice of law, give the plaintiff a formidable advantage in an American court. As Lord Denning once said:[52]

> As a moth is drawn to the light, so is a litigant drawn to the United States. If he can only get his case into their courts, he stands to win a fortune. At no cost to himself, and at no risk of having to pay anything to the other side. The lawyers there will conduct the case 'on spec' as we say, or on a 'contingency fee' as they say.[53] The lawyers will charge the litigant nothing for their services but instead they will take 40 per cent of the damages,[54] if they win the case in court, or out of court on a settlement. If they lose, the litigant will have nothing to pay to the other side.[55] The courts in the United States have no such costs deterrent as we have. There is also in the United States a right to trial by jury. These are prone to award fabulous damages. They are notoriously sympathetic and know that the lawyers will take their 40 per cent before the plaintiff gets anything.[56] All this means that the defendant can be readily forced into a settlement. The plaintiff holds all the cards.

What upsets Europeans is that a plaintiff can obtain these procedural advantages in cases that have only tenuous links with the United States. However, a Third-World airline might feel equally aggrieved if it was sued in France or England[57] in a similar situation. To someone from the Third World, French or English damages might seem just as 'fabulous' as US damages would to a Frenchman or Englishman.

Assume, for example, that a French citizen boards a Bolivian aircraft for a flight from Bolivia to Peru. The plane crashes shortly after take-off. The Frenchman is killed, and his family sues in France, using their French citizenship to obtain jurisdiction. A French trial would undoubtedly be more advantageous to the plaintiff than a trial in Bolivia. Like the French airline sued in New York, the Bolivian airline might feel that the plaintiff should not be entitled to obtain those advantages when the case has no real connection with France.

If the defendant were from another Community State, the position would be different. Under the Brussels I Regulation, the presence of an office (branch) does not confer jurisdiction on the courts for the place where it is situated unless the

---

52 *Smith Kline & French* v. *Bloch* [1983] 2 All ER 72 at p. 74 (Court of Appeal, England).

53 Today, English law permits conditional fees. However, most of the other advantages mentioned by Lord Denning do not apply in England.

54 The contingent fee will not necessarily be 40 per cent, though it might amount to this in some cases.

55 The losing litigant might have to pay certain court fees, though he would not normally have to pay the other side's attorney fees.

56 What Lord Denning meant by this is that the jury would increase the size of the award to take account of the lawyer's fee.

57 Under English law, the airline would have to have an office in England for the English courts to take jurisdiction.

claim arose out of the activities of the branch in that State. So, unless the victim bought his ticket from the branch office, the courts of that State would have no jurisdiction. Here, European jurisdiction is more limited – though only if the defendant is European.

§ 5 Conclusions

This survey suggests that there is no ground for saying that American jurisdiction over European defendants is in general more extensive than European jurisdiction over Americans – though it may be in certain cases.[58] The real ground for European resentment is the combination of jurisdictional rules that are fairly extensive – though not necessarily more extensive than comparable European ones – with procedural rules that are significantly more favourable to the plaintiff. From a purely jurisdictional point of view, American law is no more extensive than the law of many European countries.[59]

The American constitutional rules (though not the state long-arm statutes) are, however, based on a different theoretical approach. In Europe, unless the defendant consents, jurisdiction is based on one or other of two principles. The first is that there must be a link between the defendant and the territory of the forum; the second is that there must be a link between the claim and the territory of the forum. It will be seen from the cases set out previously in this chapter, that the minimum-contacts doctrine in the United States does not apply the second principle. Under this doctrine, there must be a link between the defendant and the state of the forum in every case.[60] However, the nature of that link is different. It is not necessary that the defendant should be domiciled or resident in the state of the forum; nevertheless, there must be some deliberate, voluntary act on his part that is aimed at that state. The act must be of such a nature as to make it reasonable for that state to assert jurisdiction over him. This is true in the case of both general jurisdiction and specific jurisdiction – though, in the latter case, the link does not need to be so strong.

In Europe, there must also be a link between the defendant and the State of the forum in cases of general jurisdiction, though it is a link of a stronger kind. Under the Brussels I Regulation, it is domicile. However, there does not have to be any such link in the case of specific jurisdiction. There, it is enough if there is a link between the *claim* and the State of the forum.

This difference has two consequences. The first is that American courts may constitutionally claim general jurisdiction in cases in which, at least under the Regulation, it could not be claimed in Europe. On the other hand, European

---

58 The position is different if one compares it with European jurisdiction over defendants from another Member State of the European Community – but that is not a fair comparison.
59 For details of European jurisdictional rules, see Annex 1 to the Brussels I Regulation (as amended); Alexander Layton and Hugh Mercer (eds.), *European Civil Practice* (Sweet & Maxwell, London, 2nd edn, 2004).
60 See the discussion in *Muscutt* v. *Courcelles* in Chapter 6, § 3, above, where the court contrasts the 'personal subjection' approach (that followed in the US) with the 'administration of justice' approach (that followed in Europe): see paragraphs 54–74 of the judgment. It will be remembered that the court adopted the latter approach.

courts (even under the Regulation) may claim specific jurisdiction in situations in which this would not be constitutionally possible in the United States. In Europe, it is possible – even under the Regulation – for a person to be subject to the jurisdiction of a State with which he has never had the slightest contact and towards which he has never directed any activity. Articles 5(3) and 6(1) of the Regulation are examples. There is thus a clear difference of philosophy between American and European law. Americans are concerned that a person should not be subject to the jurisdiction of a state unless he has done something which he knew, or should have known, would expose him to that risk. Europeans have no similar concern, or, if they do, they consider that other objectives can override it.

Further reading

Born and Vollmer, 'The Effect of the Revised Federal Rules of Civil Procedure on Personal Jurisdiction, Service, and Discovery in International Cases', 150 *Federal Rules Decisions* 221

Morse, 'International Shoe v. Brussels and Lugano: Principles and Pitfalls in the Law of Personal Jurisdiction', (1995) 28 *UC Davis Law Review* 999

Von Mehren and Trautman, 'Jurisdiction to Adjudicate: A Suggested Analysis' (1966) 79 *Harvard Law Review* 1121

Recent US textbooks and casebooks

Born, Garry B., and Rutledge, Peter R., *International Civil Litigation in United States Courts* (Aspen Publishers, New York, 4th edn, 2006)

Lowenfeld, Andreas F., *Conflict of Laws: Federal, State and International Perspectives* (LexisNexis, Newark, NJ, and San Francisco, CA, 2nd edn, 1998)

Symeonides, Symeon C., Perdue, Wendy Collins, and von Mehren, Arthur Taylor, *Cases and Materials on Conflict of Laws: American, Comparative and International* (West, St Paul, MN, 2nd edn, 2003)

CHAPTER 8

Choice-of-court agreements

§ 1   Introduction

Choice-of-court agreements (also called 'jurisdiction agreements'[1] or 'forum-selection agreements'[2]) are agreements as to where litigation will take place. They are one of the most important jurisdictional devices of modern times. If the courts respect them, they enable the parties to know in advance where the case will be brought. This in turn makes it possible to plan ahead and to ensure that the terms of the contract, and the activities that take place under it, will not be regarded as unlawful by the court hearing the case.

§ 1.1   Court specified

Choice-of-court agreements usually confer jurisdiction on a particular court (for example, the Federal District Court for the Southern District of New York) or the courts of a particular country (for example, the courts of England). It is, however, possible to specify two or more courts – for example, 'either the Tokyo District Court or the Kobe District Court' – in which case, the claimant may bring proceedings in either. It is even possible to make the choice of court depend on which party is bringing the action – for example, 'X may bring proceedings in the courts of England; Y may bring them in the courts of Belgium'.[3]

§ 1.2   Exclusive jurisdiction

In addition to conferring jurisdiction on the court chosen, a choice-of-court agreement may deprive other courts of jurisdiction, thus making the jurisdiction exclusive. Unless this is done, the choice-of-court agreement will not provide the predictability that is so important. Where it is done, a choice-of-court agreement has two functions: a jurisdiction-conferring function and a jurisdiction-depriving function. These two functions are not treated the same by the courts. Most courts are willing to accept jurisdiction if it is conferred on them, but they may not be so happy when it comes to giving up jurisdiction that they would otherwise have.

---

1 Mainly British usage.
2 Mainly US usage.
3 See *Meeth* v. *Glacetal*, Case 23/78, [1978] ECR 2133.

§ 1.3   Asymmetric choice-of-court agreements

An asymmetric choice-of-court agreement is a choice-of-court agreement that is more favourable to one party than to the other. They are much loved by banks. International loan agreements often provide that proceedings by the lender against the borrower may be brought in the court chosen or in any other court having jurisdiction under its law, while proceedings by the borrower against the lender may be brought only in the court chosen. Such an agreement is exclusive as regards proceedings against the lender, but non-exclusive as regards proceedings against the borrower: he can be sued wherever the lender can find him.

§ 1.4   Proceedings covered

Since choice-of-court agreements are *agreements*, there must be a contract between the parties. Normally, the choice-of-court agreement will relate to that contract – for example, 'All proceedings under this contract shall be brought exclusively in the courts of England.' However, it is perfectly possible for the choice-of-court agreement to cover other proceedings as well. For example, an agreement reading 'All proceedings under, or relating to, this contract shall be brought exclusively in the courts of England' would probably be interpreted as covering tort actions relating to the subject of the agreement.[4]

A choice-of-court agreement may cover claims that have already arisen, as well as future claims, or it may be limited to one or other of these. The former is rare, though it might occur if the parties are unable to settle the dispute, but can agree on the most suitable court to hear it. Most choice-of-court agreements relate to future disputes concerning a particular contract or business relationship. They are usually found in conjunction with a choice-of-law agreement.

Having discussed choice-of-court agreements in general, we are now in a position to consider particular legal systems. We start with the law of the European Community.

§ 2   The European Community

§ 2.1   Introduction

The treatment given to choice-of-court agreements by EC law appears, at first sight, wholly admirable.[5] It deals with what the US Supreme Court calls 'overweening bargaining power' by having special provisions for three categories of persons regarded as especially vulnerable: consumers, employees and insured persons. The problem of being taken to have consented to a choice-of-court agreement without realizing what you are doing is solved by special formal requirements. Subject to this, EC law makes choice-of-court agreements absolutely

---

4 See, for example, *Continental Bank* v. *Aeakos Compania Naviera* [1994] 1 WLR 588; [1994] 1 Lloyd's Rep 505 (Court of Appeal, England).
5 But see Chapter 10, § 4, below.

**Panel 8.1 Choice-of-court agreements:
Brussels I Regulation (Regulation 44/2001), Article 23**

Section 7 Prorogation of jurisdiction

Article 23

1. If the parties, one or more of whom is domiciled in a Member State, have agreed that a court or the courts of a Member State are to have jurisdiction to settle any disputes which have arisen or which may arise in connection with a particular legal relationship, that court or those courts shall have jurisdiction. Such jurisdiction shall be exclusive unless the parties have agreed otherwise. Such an agreement conferring jurisdiction shall be either:
   (a) in writing or evidenced in writing; or
   (b) in a form which accords with practices which the parties have established between themselves; or
   (c) in international trade or commerce, in a form which accords with a usage of which the parties are or ought to have been aware and which in such trade or commerce is widely known to, and regularly observed by, parties to contracts of the type involved in the particular trade or commerce concerned.
2. Any communication by electronic means which provides a durable record of the agreement shall be equivalent to 'writing'.
3. Where such an agreement is concluded by parties, none of whom is domiciled in a Member State, the courts of other Member States shall have no jurisdiction over their disputes unless the court or courts chosen have declined jurisdiction.
4. The court or courts of a Member State on which a trust instrument has conferred jurisdiction shall have exclusive jurisdiction in any proceedings brought against a settlor, trustee or beneficiary, if relations between these persons or their rights or obligations under the trust are involved.
5. Agreements or provisions of a trust instrument conferring jurisdiction shall have no legal force if they are contrary to Articles 13, 17 or 21, or if the courts whose jurisdiction they purport to exclude have exclusive jurisdiction by virtue of Article 22.

binding – provided the chosen court is in the Community. In keeping with general EC policy on these matters, there is no discretion.

The relevant provision was originally Article 17 of the Brussels Convention. It is now Article 23 of the Brussels I Regulation, which is set out in Panel 8.1. Its salient features are as follows:

- It applies both where the choice-of-court agreement specifies a particular court and where it specifies the courts (in general) of a State.
- It applies only if the court chosen is in a Member State of the European Community (or a Lugano State).
- It applies both to disputes that have arisen and to those that may arise in the future in connection with a particular legal relationship.
- It applies to both exclusive and (where appropriate) non-exclusive choice-of-court agreements.[6]
- Choice-of-court agreements are presumed to be exclusive unless the parties have agreed otherwise.[7]

6 This was not clear until the change in the text discussed in the following footnote.
7 This provision was not found in the Brussels Convention. Before the adoption of the Brussels I Regulation, non-exclusive choice-of-court agreements caused much controversy. This was because Article 17 of the Brussels Convention stated simply that choice-of-court agreements that were formally valid conferred exclusive jurisdiction on the court or courts chosen. This ignored the possibility that the agreement might expressly state that it was non-exclusive. What would happen in such a case? Did the agreement nevertheless confer exclusive jurisdiction? Was it void? Different writers expressed different views: compare Fentiman, 'Jurisdiction – When Non-Exclusive Means Exclusive' [1992] *Cambridge Law Journal* 234, with the argument for the defendant in the English case of *Kurz* v. *Stella Musical GmbH* [1992] Ch 196. The new wording of Article 23 now makes clear that neither of these views is correct. Choice-of-court agreements are presumed to be exclusive, but, if they say that they are not exclusive, they will be given effect according to their terms. They will confer jurisdiction on the court chosen (provided they are formally valid and provided

- In so far as the choice-of-court agreement confers jurisdiction, Article 23 applies only if at least one of the parties (not necessarily the defendant) is domiciled in a Member State.
- If none of the parties is so domiciled, Article 23 does not cover the jurisdiction-conferring aspect of a choice-of-court agreement;[8] nevertheless, if the agreement is exclusive, it deprives the courts of all other Member States of jurisdiction unless the court or courts chosen have declined jurisdiction.
- It requires persons bound by a choice-of-court agreement to have consented to it.
- It lays down rules on the form of choice-of-court agreements.
- It provides that choice-of-court agreements have no legal force if they are contrary to the provisions in the Brussels I Regulation on insurance,[9] consumer[10] or employment contracts,[11] or if the courts whose jurisdiction they purport to exclude have exclusive jurisdiction by virtue of Article 22 of the Regulation.[12]

Some of these features require further discussion.

§ 2.2   Consent and form

Under Article 23 (as in all legal systems), the parties must have consented to the choice-of-court agreement. Although simple at first sight, consent is actually a complicated matter. The purpose of formal requirements in contract law is usually to ensure that the parties really did consent by requiring them to do things that are likely to bring to their attention what they are agreeing to. This is also the case with the formal requirements under Article 23. However, consent is more than this, since it concerns a question of substance: did the person concerned actually know what he was agreeing to or should he be regarded as bound even if he did not? Consent also involves questions like fraud and duress.

Although Article 23 makes clear that there must be agreement between the parties, it does not deal expressly with the problem of consent. It does, however, contain some fairly complex requirements of form, and most of the case law has been concerned with these. Originally, these requirements were fairly simple: the agreement had to be in writing or evidenced in writing. Subsequently, this has been expanded. Article 23(1) now provides that the choice-of-court agreement must be either:

Footnote 7 (*cont.*)

that at least one of the parties is domiciled in a Member State) but they will not deprive other courts of jurisdiction.

8 Here, the law of the Member State in which the court chosen is situated will decide whether the choice-of-court agreement confers jurisdiction.

9 Article 13.

10 Article 17.

11 Article 21.

12 This latter provision (on Article 22) will no doubt apply even if the choice-of-court agreement is non-exclusive and does not, therefore, exclude the jurisdiction of the court specified by Article 22, but *in addition* confers jurisdiction on another court.

(a)   in writing or evidenced in writing; or

(b)   in a form which accords with practices which the parties have established between themselves; or

(c)   in international trade or commerce, in a form which accords with a usage of which the parties are or ought to have been aware and which in such trade or commerce is widely known to, and regularly observed by, parties to contracts of the type involved in the particular trade or commerce concerned.

Sub-paragraph (a) contains the original provision. The thinking behind sub-paragraph (b) is that, if the parties have established certain practices between themselves as to the form of choice-of-court agreements – if such agreements have been in a particular form in the past and both parties have accepted them – a party is unlikely to be misled if that same form is used again. The thinking behind sub-paragraph (c) is that parties in international trade or commerce are likely to be reasonably sophisticated and should be aware of the form that choice-of-court agreements usually take in the trade or commerce in question.

§ 2.2.1 **Sub-paragraph (a).** There are a significant number of cases interpreting what is now sub-paragraph (a). In *Colzani* v. *RÜWA*,[13] the European Court considered the following question. A contract is made on the business notepaper of one of the parties. It is entirely contained on the front of the sheet; the back of the sheet contains the party's standard terms and conditions, one of which is a choice-of-court agreement. There is no reference in the body of the contract or on the front of the sheet to the terms and conditions on the other side.

Is the choice-of-court agreement binding? This is as much a question of consent as of form: did the other party consent to what was written on the back of the sheet of paper? The European Court could have referred this to national law. However, it did not do so: it laid down a uniform rule that such a clause does not comply with the requirements now contained in sub-paragraph (a), unless there is an express reference in the body of the contract to the provisions on the back of the sheet.

In *Segoura* v. *Bonakdarian*,[14] the European Court considered the following. The parties enter into an oral contract for the sale of goods. No mention of a choice-of-court agreement is made. When the goods are delivered, the seller hands the buyer a document which states on the front that the sale and delivery take place subject to the conditions on the reverse. On the back of the document a number of conditions are printed, one of which is a choice-of-court agreement.

The European Court held that this again does not satisfy the requirements of sub-paragraph (a), unless the buyer expressly assents to the document by signing it or agreeing in writing. Moreover, the court made clear that the position would be the same if the seller stated in the original oral contract that he wished to rely on his general conditions of sale.

These two cases show that, at the time in question, the European Court had

---

13 Case 24/76, [1976] ECR 1831.
14 Case 25/76, [1976] ECR 1851.

a policy of interpreting the formal requirements of Article 23 in a strict way. However, even in its original form, Article 23 did not insist that a choice-of-court agreement had to be in writing: it was also possible for it to be *evidenced* in writing. The meaning of this requirement was considered by the European Court in our next case.

European Community
Berghoefer v. *ASA*
Court of Justice of the European Communities
Case 221/84, [1985] ECR 2699

Background

The facts in this case were somewhat similar to those in *Segoura* v. *Bonakdarian* (above), but there was a vital difference. In *Berghoefer*, there was a contract between a German company, Berghoefer, and a French company, ASA. The contract had a choice-of-court clause in favour of a French court. Subsequently, the parties agreed orally that, in exchange for the German company being responsible for certain costs, the chosen court would be in Germany. The claimant then wrote to the defendant confirming that this had been agreed. The defendant received the letter but never replied. A reference was made by the German Supreme Court (*Bundesgerichtshof*) to determine whether the choice-of-court agreement was valid. One of the issues was whether the confirmation of the oral agreement could be made by the party for whose benefit it was concluded, in this case the German party, Berghoefer.[15]

Judgment

14. It must be pointed out that, unlike the provisions concerning persons domiciled in Luxembourg contained in the second paragraph of Article 1 of the protocol Annexed to the Convention, Article 17 of the Convention does not expressly require that the written confirmation of an oral argument should be given by the party who is to be affected by the agreement. Moreover, as the various observations submitted to the court have rightly emphasized, it is sometimes difficult to determine the party for whose benefit a jurisdiction agreement has been concluded before proceedings have actually been instituted.

15. If it is actually established that jurisdiction has been conferred by express oral agreement and if confirmation of that oral agreement by one of the parties has been received by the other and the latter has raised no objection to it within a reasonable time thereafter, the aforesaid literal interpretation of Article 17 will also, as the court has already decided in another context . . . be in accordance with the purpose of that Article, which is to ensure that the parties have actually consented to the clause. It would therefore be a breach of good faith for a party who did not raise any objection subsequently to contest the application of the oral agreement. It

15 One of the lower German courts had held that the confirmation had to be made by the party who stood to lose from it.

is not necessary in this case to decide the question of whether and to what extent objections raised by the other party to the written confirmation of an oral agreement could, in an appropriate case, be taken into consideration.

16. The reply to the question referred to the court must therefore be that the first paragraph of Article 17 of the Convention of 27 September 1968 on Jurisdiction and the Enforcement of Judgments in Civil and Commercial Matters must be interpreted as meaning that the formal requirements therein laid down are satisfied if it is established that jurisdiction was conferred by express oral agreement, that written confirmation of that agreement by one of the parties was received by the other and that the latter raised no objection.

Comment

This case may be distinguished from *Segoura* v. *Bonakdarian* since in the *Segoura* case the parties may have agreed that the seller's general conditions would apply but, though these conditions did in fact contain a choice-of-court agreement, there was no express agreement between the parties on this point. Consequently, when the written confirmation was delivered to the seller, this was not sufficient to comply with the requirements of Article 23: there may have been confirmation in writing, but there was no prior oral agreement. In the *Berghoefer* case, on the other hand, there was an express oral agreement regarding jurisdiction. In such a situation, all that was needed was for one party to put it into writing and communicate it to the other.

§ 2.2.2 Sub-paragraph (b). Sub-paragraph (b) appears to have been derived from a statement by the European Court in *Segoura* v. *Bonakdarian*,[16] in which the court said that, if an oral agreement regarding jurisdiction forms part of a continuing trading relationship between the parties and if it were established that the dealings as a whole between the parties were governed by general conditions containing a choice-of-court agreement, that clause would be binding on the parties, since it would be contrary to good faith for either of them to deny that he had agreed to it.

§ 2.2.3 Sub-paragraph (c). Our next case deals with the meaning of sub-paragraph (c).

European Community
Mainschiffahrts-Genossenschaft eG v. Les Gravières Rhénanes
Court of Justice of the European Communities
Case C-106/95, [1997] ECR I-911

Background

The claimant, Mainschiffahrts-Genossenschaft eG (MSG), was domiciled in Germany. It chartered an inland-waterway vessel to the defendant, a French company, Les Gravières Rhénanes, by oral agreement. This agreement contained no

---

16 Case 25/76, [1976] ECR 1851, paragraph 11 of the judgment.

choice-of-court clause. Subsequently, however, MSG sent a letter of confirmation which stated that the courts of Würzburg would have exclusive jurisdiction over any dispute relating to the contract. The invoices it sent, and which were paid by Les Gravières Rhénanes, contained a similar statement.

On the basis of the court's previous case law, one might have thought that the choice-of-court agreement was invalid. However, after these cases were decided, the Brussels Convention was first amended (by the 1978 Accession Convention[17] and subsequently by the 1989 Accession Convention[18]) and then replaced by the Brussels I Regulation. The *MSG* case was decided on the basis of the amendments in the 1978 Accession Convention;[19] however, its reasoning applies equally to the present version.

Judgment

14.   It should be observed in this regard that, according to the Court's case-law, the requirements laid down by Article 17 of the Convention must be strictly interpreted in so far as that article excludes both jurisdiction as determined by the general principle of the defendant's courts laid down in Article 2 and the special jurisdictions provided for in Articles 5 and 6 . . .

15.   The Court has further held with regard to the initial version of Article 17 that, by making the validity of a jurisdiction clause subject to the existence of an 'agreement' between the parties, Article 17 imposes on the court before which the matter is brought the duty of examining, first, whether the clause conferring jurisdiction upon it was in fact the subject of consensus between the parties, which must be clearly and precisely demonstrated, and that the purpose of the requirements as to form imposed by Article 17 is to ensure that consensus between the parties is in fact established . . .

16.   However, in order to take account of the specific practices and requirements of international trade, the aforementioned Accession Convention of 9 October 1978 added to the second sentence of the first paragraph of Article 17 of the Convention a third hypothesis providing that, in international trade or commerce, a jurisdiction clause may be validly concluded in a form which accords with practices in that trade or commerce of which the parties are or ought to have been aware.

17.   Yet that relaxation incorporated in Article 17 by the 1978 Accession Convention does not mean that there is not necessarily any need for consensus between the parties on a jurisdiction clause, since it is still one of the aims of that provision to ensure that there is real consent on the part of the persons concerned. The weaker party to the contract should be protected by avoiding jurisdiction clauses incorporated in a contract by one party alone going unnoticed.

---

17 Accession of Denmark, Ireland and the United Kingdom.
18 Accession of Spain and Portugal.
19 As amended by the 1978 Convention, Article 17 stated that a choice-of-court agreement must be 'in writing or evidenced in writing or, in international trade or commerce, in a form which accords with practices in that trade or commerce of which the parties are or ought to have been aware'.

18. To take the view, however, that the relaxation thus introduced relates solely to the requirements as to form laid down by Article 17 by merely eliminating the need for a written form of consent would be tantamount to disregarding the requirements of non-formalism, simplicity and speed in international trade or commerce and to depriving that provision of a major part of its effectiveness.

19. Thus, in the light of the amendment made to Article 17 by the 1978 Accession Convention, consensus on the part of the contracting parties as to a jurisdiction clause is presumed to exist where commercial practices in the relevant branch of international trade or commerce exist in this regard of which the parties are or ought to have been aware.

20. It must therefore be considered that the fact that one of the parties to the contract did not react or remained silent in the face of a commercial letter of confirmation from the other party containing a pre-printed reference to the courts having jurisdiction and that one of the parties repeatedly paid without objection invoices issued by the other party containing a similar reference may be deemed to constitute consent to the jurisdiction clause in issue, provided that such conduct is consistent with a practice in force in the area of international trade or commerce in which the parties in question are operating and the parties are or ought to have been aware of that practice.

21. Whilst it is for the national court to determine whether the contract in question comes under the head of international trade or commerce and to find whether there was a practice in the branch of international trade or commerce in which the parties are operating and whether they were aware or are presumed to have been aware of that practice, the Court should nevertheless indicate the objective evidence which is needed in order to make such a determination.

22. It should first be considered that a contract concluded between two companies established in different Contracting States in a field such as navigation on the Rhine comes under the head of international trade or commerce.

23. Next, whether a practice exists must not be determined by reference to the law of one of the Contracting Parties. Furthermore, whether such a practice exists should not be determined in relation to international trade or commerce in general, but to the branch of trade or commerce in which the parties to the contract are operating. There is a practice in the branch of trade or commerce in question in particular where a particular course of conduct is generally and regularly followed by operators in that branch when concluding contracts of a particular type.

24. Lastly, actual or presumptive awareness of such practice on the part of the parties to a contract is made out where, in particular, they had previously had commercial or trade relations between themselves or with other parties operating in the sector in question or where, in that

sector, a particular course of conduct is sufficiently well known because it is generally and regularly followed when a particular type of contract is concluded, with the result that it may be regarded as being a consolidated practice.

25. The answer to the second question must therefore be that the third hypothesis in the second sentence of the first paragraph of Article 17 of the Convention, as amended by the Accession Convention of 9 October 1978, must be interpreted as meaning that, under a contract concluded orally in international trade or commerce, an agreement conferring jurisdiction will be deemed to have been validly concluded under that provision by virtue of the fact that one party to the contract did not react to a commercial letter of confirmation sent to it by the other party to the contract or repeatedly paid invoices without objection where those documents contained a pre-printed reference to the courts having jurisdiction, provided that such conduct is consistent with a practice in force in the field of international trade or commerce in which the parties in question operate and the latter are aware or ought to have been aware of the practice in question. It is for the national court to determine whether such a practice exists and whether the parties to the contract were aware of it. A practice exists in a branch of international trade or commerce in particular where a particular course of conduct is generally followed by contracting parties operating in that branch when they conclude contracts of a particular type. The fact that the contracting parties were aware of that practice is made out in particular where they had previously had trade or commercial relations between themselves or with other parties operating in the branch of trade or commerce in question or where, in that branch, a particular course of conduct is generally and regularly followed when concluding a certain type of contract, with the result that it may be regarded as being a consolidated practice.

Comment

This approach was confirmed by the court's decision in *Trasporti Castelletti* v. *Hugo Trumpy*,[20] in which it made clear that sub-paragraph (c) does not itself impose any particular form: it is the relevant usage that determines the form. It is not even necessary that the agreement should be in a written document.

§ 2.2.4 Electronic communications. Paragraph 2 of Article 23 makes clear that communication by electronic means which provides a durable record of the agreement is equivalent to writing for the purpose of Article 23. This would cover fax and e-mail.

§ 2.2.5 Relationship with Article 5(1). Since Article 5(1) gives jurisdiction to the courts for the place of performance of the relevant obligation, a contractual clause designating the place of performance could be regarded as having the

---

20 Case C-159/97, [1999] ECR I-1597.

same effect as a choice-of-court agreement. Does this mean that it must comply with the formal requirements of Article 23? This question arose in *Zelger* v. *Salinitri (No. 1)*,[21] which concerned payment of a debt under a contract between an Italian and a German. In the absence of agreement as to the place of payment, the debt would, under both Italian and German law, have been payable in Italy. The German, however, claimed that there was an oral agreement requiring payment to be made in Germany. He brought suit in Germany, claiming that the German courts had jurisdiction under Article 5(1). The Italian argued that the oral agreement could not operate to confer jurisdiction on the German courts unless it complied with the formal requirements laid down by Community law (then, Article 17 of the Brussels Convention); otherwise, he said, the policy of that provision could be frustrated.

The European Court rejected this argument. An agreement as to the place of performance fulfils only one of the functions of a choice-of-court agreement: although it operates to confer jurisdiction on the courts for the place where performance is to occur, it does not deprive other courts of jurisdiction. In view of this distinction, the European Court was right in rejecting the defendant's argument.

In *MSG* v. *Les Gravières Rhénanes*,[22] however, the European Court held that this rule applies only to a *genuine* place-of-performance clause. If the parties insert a false place-of-performance clause simply in order to give jurisdiction to the courts for that place, it will have no jurisdictional effect unless it complies with the requirements for a choice-of-court agreement.

§ 2.3   *Choice-of-court agreement in the constitution of a company*

Article 23 applies only where the parties 'have agreed' that a particular court, or the courts of a particular Member State, are to have jurisdiction. This means that the choice-of-court agreement must be contractual. In *Powell Duffryn* v. *Petereit*,[23] the European Court held that a choice-of-court agreement in the constitution of a company (articles of association, etc.) is to be regarded as contractual. This is the case in the law of most Member States but not, it seems, in all. It was argued in the *Powell Duffryn* case that the question should be decided according to the relevant national law. The European Court, however, rejected this in favour of a 'European' solution: irrespective of the relevant national law, a choice-of-court agreement in the constitution of a company is to be regarded as contractual for the purpose of Article 23.

§ 2.4   *Validity*

What law determines whether a choice-of-court agreement is valid? This question came before the European Court in our next case.

21 Case 76/79, [1980] ECR 89.
22 Case C-106/95, [1997] ECR I-911.
23 Case C-214/89, [1992] ECR I-1745.

European Community
Elefanten Schuh v. *Jacqmain*
Court of Justice of the European Communities
Case 150/80, [1981] ECR 1671

Background

This case concerned an employment contract, written in German, between a German employer and a Belgian employee. The contract contained a choice-of-court agreement conferring jurisdiction on a German court. Today, choice-of-court agreements in employment contracts are subject to special rules, but at the time in question the normal rules applied. The employee brought proceedings before a Belgian court and argued that the whole contract, including the choice-of-court agreement, was void under Belgian law since there was a mandatory requirement in Belgian law that all employment contracts had to be in the official language of the part of Belgium where the work was to be performed. As the work was to be performed in the Dutch-speaking part of Belgium, the contract should have been in Dutch.

Judgment

24. According to the Report on the Convention submitted to the Governments of the Contracting States at the same time as the draft Convention those formal requirements were inserted out of the concern not to impede commercial practice, yet at the same time to cancel out the effects of clauses in contracts which might go unread, such as clauses in printed forms for business correspondence or in invoices, if they were not agreed to by the party against whom they operate. For those reasons jurisdiction clauses should be taken into consideration only if they are the subject of a written agreement, and that implies the consent of all the parties. Furthermore, the draftsmen of Article 17 were of the opinion that, in order to ensure legal certainty, the formal requirements applicable to agreements conferring jurisdiction should be expressly prescribed.

25. Article 17 is thus intended to lay down itself the formal requirements which agreements conferring jurisdiction must meet; the purpose is to ensure legal certainty and that the parties have given their consent.

26. Consequently Contracting States are not free to lay down formal requirements other than those contained in the Convention. That is confirmed by the fact that the second paragraph of Article 1 of the Protocol annexed to the Convention expressly prescribes special requirements of form with regard to persons domiciled in Luxembourg.

27. When those rules are applied to provisions concerning the language to be used in an agreement conferring jurisdiction they imply that the legislation of a Contracting State may not allow the validity of such an agreement to be called in question solely on the ground that the language used is not that prescribed by that legislation.

28. Moreover, any different interpretation would run counter to Article 17 of the Convention the very purpose of which is to enable a court of a Contracting

> State to be chosen by agreement where that court, if not so chosen, would not normally have jurisdiction. That choice must therefore be respected by the courts of all the Contracting States.
>
> 29. Consequently, the answer to Question 3 must be that Article 17 of the Convention must be interpreted as meaning that the legislation of a Contracting State may not allow the validity of an agreement conferring jurisdiction to be called in question solely on the ground that the language used is not that prescribed by that legislation.

Note

In the end, the Belgian court was allowed to hear the claim, since the German defendant had not raised the jurisdictional issue until after it had pleaded to the merits of the case. The Belgian court therefore had jurisdiction under Article 18 of the Convention (now Article 24 of the Regulation, discussed in Chapter 4, § 6, above).

The *Elefanten Schuh* case left open the question of substantive validity. In a later case, *Coreck Maritime* v. *Handelsveem*,[24] the European Court held that the validity of a choice-of-court agreement conferring jurisdiction on the courts of a *non-contracting* State is determined by the forum's choice-of-law rules.[25] It is not entirely clear whether the same rule would apply to determine the substantive validity of a choice-of-court agreement conferring jurisdiction on the courts of a Contracting State, today a Member State. The other possible solution would be to apply the law of the court chosen in the choice-of-court agreement (possibly including its choice-of-law rules).[26] This is the solution adopted by the 2005 Hague Convention on Choice of Court Agreements.[27]

§ 2.5 Effect on third parties

In principle, a choice-of-court agreement can bind only those who have agreed to it. However, if a person who did not agree to the choice-of-court agreement brings proceedings on the basis that he has stepped into the shoes of someone who did, and is therefore entitled to the rights of that person under the contract, he should be regarded as bound by the choice-of-court agreement. He cannot take the benefits of the contract without also being subject to the obligations under it.[28]

One situation in which this question can arise is where goods are shipped under a bill of lading. The original contract of carriage is between the shipper

---

24 Case C-387/98, [2000] ECR I-9337.
25 Paragraph 19 of the judgment, following paragraph 176 of the Schlosser Report (Schlosser, 'Report on the Convention of 9 October 1968' (Denmark, Ireland and UK Accessions), OJ 1979 C 59, p. 71). In the case of England, these would be the common-law rules, since the Rome Convention does not apply to choice-of-court agreements: Article 1(2)(d).
26 See *per* Advocate General Slynn in the *Elefanten Schuh* case, [1981] ECR 1671 at pp. 1697–9.
27 Articles 5(1), 6(a) and 9(a).
28 *Coreck Maritime* v. *Handelsveem*, Case C-387/98, [2000] ECR I-9337, paragraphs 22 *et seq.*

and the shipowner. The contract is evidenced by, or contained in, the bill of lading, a copy of which is given by the shipowner to the shipper. In many legal systems, the bill of lading serves as a document entitling the holder to obtain possession of the goods when they arrive at their destination. The shipper usually gives a copy[29] to the person to whom the goods are to be delivered (the consignee) and the latter can use it to obtain possession of the goods.

In addition to transferring to the consignee the right to possession of the goods, the transfer of the bill of lading has, in many legal systems, the effect of assigning to the consignee the rights and obligations of the shipper under the contract of carriage. If the consignee uses the bill of lading to obtain possession of the goods, he becomes subject to obligations under the contract and can benefit from rights under it. If the goods are damaged in transit, for example, he can sue the carrier under the contract of carriage. In a situation such as this, it is only right that he should be subject to a choice-of-court agreement contained in the bill of lading. Consequently, in *Tilly Russ* v. *Nova*,[30] the European Court held that, if a choice-of-court agreement in the bill of lading meets the requirements of Community law as between the original parties to it, and if, under the relevant law, the consignee is regarded as having succeeded to the shipper's rights and obligations under the contract of carriage, the choice-of-court agreement will be binding on the consignee.

§ 2.6   *Insurance contracts, consumer contracts and employment contracts*

The Brussels I Regulation contains special rules dealing with three kinds of contracts in which there is generally an imbalance of bargaining power (Panel 8.2).[31] These are insurance contracts, consumer contracts and employment contracts (see Chapter 4, § 4, above). In each of these cases, choice-of-court agreements are prohibited except in situations where they would not conflict with the policy of protecting the weaker party – for example, where the choice-of-court agreement is concluded after the dispute has arisen (in which case, the inequality of bargaining power would no longer apply) or where it is wholly beneficial to the weaker party by allowing him, in addition, to bring proceedings in courts other than those specified by the Regulation.

§ 2.7   *The Community and the outside world*

Although the Brussels Convention, and now the Brussels I Regulation, have been in operation for many years, some of the most important questions under them remain unanswered. These concern their scope. This is limited because they were

---

29 Endorsed, if necessary.
30 Case 71/83, [1984] ECR 2417; [1984] 3 CMLR 499; [1985] 3 WLR 179.
31 These rules apply only if the defendant is domiciled in a Member State (or is deemed to be so domiciled under Articles 9(2), 15(2) or 18(2)). See Articles 3(1) and 4(1).

Panel 8.2 Protection of weak parties
Brussels I Regulation (Regulation 44/2001), Articles 8, 13, 15, 17, 18 and 21

Section 3 Jurisdiction in matters relating to insurance

Article 8

In matters relating to insurance, jurisdiction shall be determined by this Section, without prejudice to Article 4 and point 5 of Article 5.

Article 13

The provisions of this Section may be departed from only by an agreement:
1. which is entered into after the dispute has arisen, or
2. which allows the policyholder, the insured or a beneficiary to bring proceedings in courts other than those indicated in this Section, or
3. which is concluded between a policyholder and an insurer, both of whom are at the time of conclusion of the contract domiciled or habitually resident in the same Member State, and which has the effect of conferring jurisdiction on the courts of that State even if the harmful event were to occur abroad, provided that such an agreement is not contrary to the law of that State, or
4. which is concluded with a policyholder who is not domiciled in a Member State, except in so far as the insurance is compulsory or relates to immovable property in a Member State, or
5. which relates to a contract of insurance in so far as it covers one or more of the risks set out in Article 14.

Section 4 Jurisdiction over consumer contracts

Article 15

1. In matters relating to a contract concluded by a person, the consumer, for a purpose which can be regarded as being outside his trade or profession, jurisdiction shall be determined by this Section, without prejudice to Article 4 and point 5 of Article 5, if . . .

Article 17

The provisions of this Section may be departed from only by an agreement:
1. which is entered into after the dispute has arisen; or
2. which allows the consumer to bring proceedings in courts other than those indicated in this Section; or
3. which is entered into by the consumer and the other party to the contract, both of whom are at the time of conclusion of the contract domiciled or habitually resident in the same Member State, and which confers jurisdiction on the courts of that Member State, provided that such an agreement is not contrary to the law of that Member State.

Section 5 Jurisdiction over individual contracts of employment

Article 18

1. In matters relating to individual contracts of employment, jurisdiction shall be determined by this Section, without prejudice to Article 4 and point 5 of Article 5.

Article 21

The provisions of this Section may be departed from only by an agreement on jurisdiction:
1. which is entered into after the dispute has arisen; or
2. which allows the employee to bring proceedings in courts other than those indicated in this Section.

---

drafted almost entirely on the basis of relations among the Member States:[32] relations with the outside world were largely ignored.[33]

---

[32] The Brussels I Regulation does not, as such, apply to Denmark. However, the same provisions are made applicable to it by virtue of a Convention between Denmark and the Community, signed in Brussels on 19 October 2005, OJ 2005 L 299/62.

[33] The only exception is the Lugano Convention, which has the effect of extending the provisions of the Regulation to certain non-member States in Europe. The provisions of the Lugano Convention concerning choice-of-court agreements are intended to be the same as those applicable in the Community. (At the

To understand these limitations, we must look separately at the jurisdiction-conferring and jurisdiction-depriving aspects of Article 23. In so far as it *confers* jurisdiction on the court chosen, it applies only if that court is in a Member State. This could not be otherwise, since EC law cannot confer jurisdiction on a court outside the EC. It has no power to do so. In addition, however, it applies to confer jurisdiction on the court chosen only if at least one of the parties is domiciled in a Member State. Its jurisdiction-conferring scope is, therefore, limited in these two ways.

If the choice-of-court agreement is exclusive (which it is presumed to be unless the parties have agreed otherwise), it also has a jurisdiction-depriving aspect. It precludes courts other than that chosen from hearing the case. Its jurisdiction-depriving scope is also limited, though in different ways. First, it is addressed only to courts in the Community: it *precludes* courts from hearing the case only if those courts are in the EC. Again, this must necessarily be so: the Community cannot preclude courts of non-member States from hearing a case. However, EC courts are precluded from hearing a case only if the *court chosen* is in a Member State: if the court chosen is in a non-member State, Article 23 does not apply to preclude courts in EC States from hearing the case.

In considering the consequences of these limitations, we shall take England as an example, but what is said applies equally to other Member States. It will be assumed in the discussion that follows that the choice-of-court agreement is exclusive.

§ 2.7.1 Choice-of-court agreement in favour of the English courts.

If neither party is domiciled in a Member State, English law decides whether or not the English courts will take jurisdiction. Even if the requirements of the Brussels I Regulation are met, the English courts will not be obliged to take jurisdiction (but the courts of other Member States will not be permitted to do so unless and until the English courts have decided not to hear the case). If the requirements of the Brussels I Regulation are not met, the English courts will not be precluded from taking jurisdiction (unless some other provision of the Regulation prohibits them from doing so);[34] in this case, however, courts in other Member States will not be prevented from taking jurisdiction.

If the defendant is domiciled in a Member State, the English courts will be obliged to hear the case if the requirements of the Brussels I Regulation are met, and will be precluded from doing so if they are not met.[35] If the requirements

---

Footnote 33 (*cont.*)
time of writing, the Lugano Convention is still based on the Brussels Convention and the changes brought about by the Regulation have not yet been incorporated.) For the sake of simplicity, the Lugano Convention will be ignored in the discussion that follows. To get the full picture, however, any reference to a Member State should be read as including the parties to the Lugano Convention. Thus, a reference to domicile in a Member State should be read as including domicile in one of those States, and a reference to a court in a Member State should be read as including a court in such a State.

34 Examples are Article 22 (exclusive jurisdiction of the courts of another Member State); Article 23 (exclusive choice-of-court agreement in favour of a court in another Member State) or Article 27 (court of another Member State seised first). Articles 22, 23 (in so far as it deprives a court of jurisdiction) and 27 all apply irrespective of the domicile of the parties.

35 Unless they have jurisdiction under some other provision of the Regulation.

of the Regulation are met, the courts of other Member States will be precluded from hearing the case.

If the claimant (but not the defendant) is domiciled in a Member State, the English courts will be obliged to take jurisdiction if the requirements of the Brussels I Regulation are met; the courts of other Member States will be precluded from hearing the case. If the requirements of the Regulation are not met, the English courts will still be permitted to take jurisdiction (under English law)[36] unless some other provision of the Regulation prevents them from doing so;[37] however, the courts of other Member States will not be precluded from hearing the case.

§ 2.7.2 Choice-of-court agreement in favour of the courts of a non-member State.

In this situation, it would seem that the English courts would never be obliged to decline jurisdiction. Whether they would be *permitted* to do so might depend on whether they had jurisdiction under the Brussels I Regulation or only under English law.[38] There seems to be no reason why they should not decline jurisdiction in the latter situation on the basis of English law (irrespective of whether or not the other requirements of the Brussels I Regulation are met), but in the former situation the position is controversial.

The Schlosser Report,[39] published in 1979, takes the view that such agreements are, in principle, capable of depriving the courts of a Member State of jurisdiction conferred on them by the Convention/Regulation. The Report says that, if the choice-of-court agreement confers jurisdiction on the courts of a non-member State and proceedings are nevertheless brought in the courts of a Member State, the latter must apply their own law (including their rules of choice of law) to determine whether the choice-of-court agreement is valid. If it is, they are permitted – Schlosser suggests that they may be *obliged* – to decline jurisdiction. This view finds support in the decision of the European Court in *Coreck Maritime* v. *Handelsveem*,[40] discussed above (§ 2.4).

The *Coreck* case was decided by a three-judge chamber of the European Court in 2000. However, there is a passage in the judgment of the Full Court in the *Lugano* case,[41] decided in 2006, which could be taken as suggesting that a court of a Member State that has jurisdiction under the Regulation is *not* permitted to decline jurisdiction on the ground that the courts of a non-member State have exclusive jurisdiction under a choice-of-court agreement. So the matter remains in doubt.

---

36 Article 4(1) of the Regulation provides that, if the defendant is not domiciled in a Member State, the jurisdiction of each Member State shall, subject to Articles 22 and 23, be determined by the law of that Member State.
37 As before, Articles 22, 23 and 27 are examples.
38 English law would apply if the defendant was not domiciled in a Member State (and if Articles 22 and 23 did not apply): Article 4(1).
39 Paragraph 176.
40 Case C-387/98, [2000] ECR I-9337.
41 Opinion 1/03, [2006] ECR I-1145, paragraph 153.

§ 2.8   Arbitration agreements

This is a good moment to say something about arbitration agreements. In many ways, arbitration agreements and choice-of-court agreements have a great deal in common and are sometimes considered together. However, their position under the Brussels I Regulation is very different. While the Regulation contains detailed provisions on choice-of-court agreements, it contains nothing on arbitration agreements. Indeed, they are expressly excluded from its scope.[42] The effects of this will be considered below.[43] The problem to be considered here is what happens if the parties conclude an arbitration agreement and then, in contravention of that agreement, one of them sues the other in a court of a Member State that has jurisdiction under the Regulation. Is that court either permitted or required to decline jurisdiction?

The answer to this question is to be found in Article 71(1) of the Regulation, which provides that the Regulation 'shall not affect any conventions to which the Member States are parties and which, in relation to particular matters, govern jurisdiction or the recognition or enforcement of judgments'. All the Member States are parties to the United Nations Convention on the Recognition and Enforcement of Foreign Arbitral Awards (New York, 10 June 1958), Article II(3) of which (Panel 8.3) requires the court of a Contracting State, when seised of an action in a matter in respect of which the parties have made an arbitration agreement, to refer the parties to arbitration. This requires the court to decline jurisdiction, or to stay the proceedings before it, so that the arbitration can proceed. Since the Regulation does not affect this obligation, the Regulation cannot require the court to hear the case. However, the Regulation does not oblige the court to give effect to the arbitration agreement; it merely *permits* it to do so. It is the New York Convention, which is not part of Community law,[44] that obliges it to do so; consequently, the European Court will not enforce the Convention. On the other hand, it makes no difference whether the arbitration is to take place in a Member State or a non-member State.

Panel 8.3 New York Arbitration Convention 1958, Article II(3)

Article II(3)

The court of a Contracting State, when seized of an action in a matter in respect of which the parties have made an agreement within the meaning of this article, shall, at the request of one of the parties, refer the parties to arbitration, unless it finds that the said agreement is null and void, inoperative or incapable of being performed.

---

§ 3   England

For many years, English courts were unwilling to accept that a choice-of-court agreement in favour of a foreign court could deprive them of jurisdiction. Their view was that the jurisdiction of a court depended on the law, and that a private agreement

---

42 Article 1(2)(d).
43 See Chapter 10, § 5, and Chapter 14, § 7, below.
44 The Community is not itself a party to the New York Convention.

could not affect it. In theory, this is still the official view under the common law, since a court has discretion not to give effect to such an agreement. In practice, however, there has been a major change of policy. The change began in our next case.

England
The Fehmarn
Court of Appeal
[1958] 1 WLR 159; [1958] 1 All ER 333; [1957] Lloyd's Rep 551

Background

In this case, a German ship, the *Fehmarn*, had agreed to carry a cargo of turpentine from a Baltic port to a port in England. The shippers were from the Soviet Union (as it then was), and the bills of lading contained an exclusive choice-of-court agreement in favour of the Soviet Union. The English buyers became holders of the bills of lading. They claimed that contamination and short delivery had occurred, and sued the shipowners in England. The latter pleaded the choice-of-court agreement. The trial court rejected that plea. An appeal was taken to the Court of Appeal.

Lord Denning

Then, the next question is whether the action ought to be stayed because of the provision in the bill of lading that all disputes are to be judged by the Russian Courts. I do not regard this provision as equal to an arbitration clause, but I do say that the English Courts are in charge of their own proceedings; and one of the rules which they apply is that a stipulation that all disputes should be judged by the tribunals of a particular country is not absolutely binding. It is a matter to which the Courts of this country will pay much regard and to which they will normally give effect, but it is subject to the overriding principle that no one, by his private stipulation, can oust these Courts of their jurisdiction in a matter that properly belongs to them.

I would ask myself therefore: Is this dispute a matter which properly belongs to the Courts of this country? Here are English importers who, when they take delivery of the goods in England, find them contaminated. The goods are surveyed by surveyors on both sides, with the result that the English importers make a claim against the German shipowners. The vessel is a frequent visitor to this country. In order to be sure that their claim, if substantiated, is paid by the shipowners, the English importers are entitled, by the procedure of our Courts of Admiralty, to arrest the ship whenever she comes here in order to have security for their claim. There seems to me to be no doubt that such a dispute is one that properly belongs for its determination to the Courts of this country. But still the question remains: Ought these Courts, in their discretion, to stay this action?

It has been said by Mr. Roche [counsel for the shipowners] that this contract is governed by Russian law and should be judged by the Russian Courts, who know that law. And the dispute may involve evidence from witnesses in Russia about the condition of the goods on shipment. Then why, says Mr. Roche, should it not be judged in Russia as the condition says?

I do not regard the choice of law in the contract as decisive. I prefer to look to see with what country is the dispute most closely concerned. Here the Russian element in the dispute seems to me to be comparatively small. The dispute is between the German owners of the ship and the English importers. It depends on evidence here as to the condition of the goods when they arrived here in London and on evidence of the ship, which is a frequent visitor to London. The correspondence leaves in my mind, just as it did in the learned Judge's mind,[45] the impression that the German owners did not object to the dispute being decided in this country but wished to avoid the giving of security.

I think the dispute is more closely connected with England than Russia, and I agree with the Judge that sufficient reason has been shown why the proceedings should continue in these Courts and should not be stayed. I would therefore dismiss the appeal.

[Hodson and Morris LJJ gave judgments to the same effect.]

Comment

One might have thought that the factors in favour of the two jurisdictions were fairly evenly balanced. It is possible, however, that the court's ruling was influenced by political factors, since the case was decided in 1958 at the height of the Cold War.

A later case, *The Eleftheria*,[46] decided in 1969, applied the same test, but with a different outcome.

England
The Eleftheria
High Court
**[1970] P 94; [1969] 2 WLR 1073; [1969] 2 All ER 641; [1969] 1 Lloyd's
    Rep 237**

Background

This was also a shipping case. It concerned the carriage of goods from Romania to England aboard a Greek ship. The bills of lading contained an exclusive choice-of-court agreement (jurisdiction clause) in favour of Greece and a choice-of-law clause in favour of Greek law. The goods should have been discharged in Hull, but the shipowners said that this was impossible because of a labour dispute there. So they discharged them in Rotterdam instead. The owners of the goods brought proceedings in England. The shipowners asked the court to stay the proceedings in view of the choice-of-court clause.

Brandon J

The principles established by the authorities can, I think, be summarized as follows: (1) Where plaintiffs sue in England in breach of an agreement to refer disputes to a foreign Court, and the defendants apply for a stay, the English

---

45 *Editor's note*: this was the judge who decided the case at first instance.
46 [1970] P 94; [1969] 2 WLR 1073; [1969] 2 All ER 641; [1969] 1 Lloyd's Rep 237 (England).

Court, assuming the claim to be otherwise within the jurisdiction, is not bound to grant a stay but has a discretion whether to do so or not. (2) The discretion should be exercised by granting a stay unless strong cause for not doing so is shown. (3) The burden of proving such strong cause is on the plaintiffs. (4) In exercising its discretion the Court should take into account all the circumstances of the particular case. (5) In particular, but without prejudice to (4), the following matters, where they arise, may be properly regarded: (a) In what country the evidence on the issues of fact is situated, or more readily available, and the effect of that on the relative convenience and expense of trial as between the English and foreign Courts. (b) Whether the law of the foreign Court applies and, if so. whether it differs from English law in any material respects. (c) With what country either party is connected, and how closely. (d) Whether the defendants genuinely desire trial in the foreign country, or are only seeking procedural advantages. (e) Whether the plaintiffs would be prejudiced by having to sue in the foreign Court because they would (i) be deprived of security for that claim; (ii) be unable to enforce any judgment obtained; (iii) be faced with a time-bar not applicable in England; or (iv) for political, racial, religious or other reasons be unlikely to get a fair trial.

[Brandon J then said that there was no suggestion that the claimants would not get a fair trial in Greece; there was no question of a time bar; and the defendants agreed that the security obtained by the claimants should be available in the Greek proceedings. After setting out the arguments of both sides, he continued:]

First, as to the *prima facie* case for a stay arising from the Greek jurisdiction clause. I think that it is essential that the Court should give full weight to the *prima facie* desirability of holding the plaintiffs to their agreement. In this connection I think that the Court must be careful not just to pay lip service to the principle involved, and then fail to give effect to it because of a mere balance of convenience.

[He then considered two earlier decisions and concluded that the governing factor in them was the principle that a party should be bound by a jurisdiction clause to which he has agreed, unless there is strong reason to the contrary.]

Second, as to the factors tending to rebut the *prima facie* case for a stay. I think there is much force in the main point taken by Counsel for the plaintiffs, that the bulk of the factual evidence is in England. While it may be that some of the facts with regard to labour disputes, etc., can be agreed or proved by documents, I accept the plaintiffs' case that they will probably wish to call a substantial number of witnesses on this topic, and that, if they have to take them to Greece, it will cause them substantial inconvenience and expense. The evidence of such witnesses would, moreover, have to be interpreted, with the difficulties and further expense involved in that process. Against all that it must be borne in mind that, if the dispute is tried in England, the reverse situation will arise as regards at least one, and perhaps two witnesses of fact for the defendants, certainly in relation to inconvenience and expense, and possibly, though not necessarily, also in relation to interpretation.

These considerations about evidence must, however, be viewed in perspective. Many commercial and Admiralty disputes are tried or arbitrated in England every year, in which most or all of the evidence comes from abroad. In these cases the parties are often content to have their disputes decided here, even though it causes inconvenience and expense with regard to bringing witnesses to England and examining them through interpreters. Bearing in mind these matters, I cannot regard the inconvenience and expense which the plaintiffs would suffer through having to take witnesses to Greece as being in any way overwhelming or insuperable.

Third, as to factors tending to reinforce the *prima facie* case for a stay. Of these I regard as carrying some weight the very real connection of the defendants with Greece and their willingness to protect the plaintiffs in relation to security for their claim. I further regard of substantial importance the circumstances that Greek law governs, and is, in respects which may well be material, different from English law.

I recognize that an English Court can, and often does, decide questions of foreign law on the basis of expert evidence from foreign lawyers. Nor do I regard such legal concepts as contractual good faith and morality as being so strange as to be beyond the capacity of an English Court to grasp and apply. It seems to be clear, however, that, in general, and other things being equal, it is more satisfactory for the law of a foreign country to be decided by the Courts of that country . . .

Apart from the general advantage which a foreign Court has in determining and applying its own law, there is a significant difference in the position with regard to appeal. A question of foreign law decided by a Court of the foreign country concerned is appealable as such to the appropriate Appellate Court of that country. But a question of foreign law decided by an English Court on expert evidence is treated as a question of fact for the purposes of appeal, with the limitations in the scope of an appeal inherent in that categorization.[1] This consideration seems to me to afford an added reason for saying that, in general and other things being equal, it is more satisfactory for the law of a foreign country to be decided by the Courts of that country. Moreover, by more satisfactory I mean more satisfactory from the point of view of ensuring that justice is done.

Fourth, as to my conclusion. I have started by giving full weight to the *prima facie* case for a stay, and I have gone on to weigh on the one hand the factors tending to rebut that *prima facie* case, and on the other hand the factors tending to reinforce it. With regard to these, it appears to me that there are considerations of substantial weight on either side, which more or less balance each other out, leaving the *prima facie* case for a stay largely, if not entirely, intact. On this basis I have reached the clear conclusion that the plaintiffs, on whom the burden lies, have not, on the whole of the matter, established good cause why they should not be held to their agreement. The question whether to grant a stay or not, and if so on what terms, is one for the discretion of the Court. Having arrived at the clear conclusion which I have stated, I shall exercise my discretion by granting a stay, subject to appropriate terms as regards security.

1 *Editor's note*: see Chapter 22, § 5, below.

Of all the factors mentioned by Brandon J, the most controversial is whether the defendant will receive a fair trial in the chosen court. While everyone agrees that effect should not be given to a choice-of-court agreement if this would deprive the claimant of a fair trial, courts are generally reluctant to hold that another court would be prejudiced – for example, on political, racial or religious grounds. They are equally reluctant (perhaps even more reluctant) to hold that another court might be corrupt. Unfortunately, bias and corruption are facts of life in some parts of the world. To ignore them would be to ignore reality. However, they are hard to prove.

Our next case is one in which the question arose.

England
Carvalho* v. *Hull Blyth Ltd
Court of Appeal
[1979] 1 WLR 1228; [1979] 3 All ER 280; [1980] 1 Lloyd's Rep 172

Background

The claimant, Carvalho, was Portuguese; the defendant, Hull Blyth, was an English-registered company, which did all its business in Angola. Hull Blyth had a number of subsidiaries in Angola, each of which was 51 per cent owned by it and 49 per cent owned by Carvalho. In 1973, they signed a contract under which Hull Blyth would buy out Carvalho. Payment was to take place in four instalments. Three were paid, but not the fourth.[47] Carvalho sued in England for this sum.

Clause 14 of the contract contained an exclusive choice-of-court agreement specifying the District Court of Luanda, Angola. When the contract was made, Angola was an overseas province (in effect, a colony) of Portugal. After a period of protracted guerrilla war, it gained independence in 1979. This was after the first three instalments had been paid, but before payment of the fourth. Carvalho fled from Angola, fearing for his life. All his property there was confiscated.

Hull Blyth asked the court for a stay. The trial judge refused to grant it. This refusal was based on two grounds. The first was that the court now called the 'District Court of Luanda' was not, in view of the constitutional changes in Angola, the same as the court of that name that existed when the contract was concluded. From this it followed that it was no longer possible to give effect to the choice-of-court agreement. The judge also refused a stay as a matter of discretion, though his grounds for doing so were not clearly expressed.[48] Hull Blyth appealed.

Browne LJ

[After saying that counsel for Carvalho submitted that the District Court of Luanda was now a different court while counsel for Hull Blyth submitted that it was not, Browne LJ continued:]

It is clear from the affidavits filed on behalf of the plaintiff, and it is not disputed by the defendants, that, when the contract was made in December 1973, Angola

---

47 Hull Blyth claimed that it was unable to pay the fourth because of Angolan exchange controls.
48 One assumes that he thought that Carvalho would not get a fair trial in Angola, though he did not expressly say so.

was a province of Portugal. The law applied was Portuguese law and the legal system then in force was procedurally and substantively Portuguese. The judicial organization of Portuguese Angola was part of the judicial system of Portuguese Europe and was in every respect identical with it. The qualification of judges was the same as in Portugal . . . Angola clearly then had no separate legal system and there was no such thing as Angolan law except, perhaps, in some native customary courts. Now Angola is an independent sovereign state with a new constitution. It is true that it seems, from the affidavits filed on behalf of the defendants, that, in general, Portuguese law is still applied and that the previous structure of the courts still exists, except for the abolition of the right of appeal to the Supreme Court in Lisbon. But it seems to me plain from the constitution that this situation can be changed at any moment . . . It seems . . . that, without any formal change, the previous law will not be applied if it does 'conflict with the spirit of this law and the Angolan revolutionary process.'

It is also clear from the defendants' evidence that the system for the appointment of judges has completely changed. According to the evidence filed on behalf of the defendants, the District Court of Luanda still exists under the same name but, in my judgment, the judge was right in holding that it is a different court from the court in contemplation when the contract was made. It was then a Portuguese court in all the respects to which I have already referred. It is now an Angolan court operating within the framework of the Angolan constitution and legal system and applying Angolan law.

One can perhaps test it in this way. If the parties had known in December 1973 what the situation would be in Angola now, would they have agreed to include clause 14[1] in the contract? I think it is impossible to say that the answer must be 'Yes.' There is a complete conflict in the affidavit evidence about the present situation as to the administration of justice in Angola. This court cannot resolve this conflict but, in my view, it is unnecessary to do so to arrive at the conclusion that the present District Court of Luanda is a different court from that contemplated by the contract.

[Browne LJ then considered whether there were grounds for interfering with the exercise of the trial judge's discretion (the other ground on which the stay was refused). He decided there were not.]

Geoffrey Lane LJ also gave reasons for dismissing the appeal.

Appeal dismissed.

1 *Editor's note*: this was the clause containing the choice-of-court agreement.

Comment

Though undoubtedly correct in principle, the first ground gives rise to the question how much the court chosen must have changed before it will become a 'different court'.[49] The answer seems to be that one must consider whether the

49 The changes mentioned in the case usually apply when a territory gains independence. The Republic of Ireland is an example. It used to be part of the United Kingdom, but then gained independence. After independence, there was no longer any appeal to London, the courts were no longer part of the United

parties would have concluded the choice-of-court agreement in the same terms if they had known what was going to happen. This is not an easy test to apply.[50]

Though there are strong arguments for giving effect to choice-of-court agreements, several difficulties exist. The question whether the defendant will receive a fair trial is one of them. Another is that a choice-of-court agreement could be used to evade mandatory rules of the country that would otherwise have had jurisdiction. Countries often have rules of law that cannot be rendered inapplicable by a contractual provision. Thus, in a purely domestic (non-international) context, a rule making it illegal to sell drugs or to discriminate in employment on grounds of sex or race cannot be rendered non-applicable by a provision in a contract. A contract to sell illegal drugs is void even if it contains a provision that it will not be subject to the legislation making drug dealing illegal. Likewise, a discriminatory provision in a contract of employment is invalid, even if the victim expressly agrees that he or she may be discriminated against. Rules of law that cannot be rendered inapplicable in this way are often called 'mandatory rules'.

What if the parties agree that their contract is to be governed by foreign law? A choice-of-law clause of this kind is generally upheld, but (as we shall see in Chapter 25, below) this does not prevent the application of the mandatory rules of the forum.[51] Thus, a party cannot use a choice-of-law clause to evade the mandatory rules of the forum. But, what if a choice-of-law clause is coupled with a choice-of-court clause? If effect is given to the choice-of-court clause, and if the court chosen is in the country whose law is chosen, the mandatory rules of the first country might not be applied.

This problem came before the English courts in *The Hollandia (Morviken)*.[52] Like the first two cases considered, this also concerned carriage of goods by sea. When goods are shipped, the shipowner gives the shipper a document called a bill of lading, which contains the terms of the contract. Since these are written by the shipowner, they are usually rather one-sided. In the past, they would often totally exempt the shipowner from liability for loss of the goods. Shippers usually had no option but to accept these terms. If they went to another shipping company, the terms would usually be the same.

To solve this problem, and to try to bring some uniformity to international shipping law, a conference was held in The Hague in 1921, attended by representatives of the various interests. They drew up a set of rules, commonly called the Hague Rules, which were adopted by the International Convention for the Unification of Certain Rules of Law relating to Bills of Lading, signed in Brussels in 1924. One provision of this Convention stated that the bill of lading could not exempt the carrier, below a specified minimum sum, from liability for damage

---

Kingdom legal system, and the common law, though it continued to apply, did so only to the extent that it was compatible with the Constitution.

50 For example, would a choice-of-court agreement in favour of a court in the former German Democratic Republic be upheld by an English court after the reunification of Germany?

51 In most cases, this applies only if the rule in question is (under the law of the forum) mandatory irrespective of the applicable law (internationally mandatory).

52 [1983] AC 565; [1983] 1 Lloyd's Rep 1 (HL).

to, or loss of, the goods. Since this liability could not be avoided by contract, it constituted a mandatory rule in the sense explained above. The Hague Rules were enacted by the United Kingdom under the Carriage of Goods by Sea Act 1924. The Act stated that the Rules applied to any shipment from any port in the United Kingdom. The minimum-liability rule was, therefore, mandatory whenever the goods were shipped from a port in the United Kingdom.

Some years later, another conference was held in Visby, Sweden, and this resulted in a series of amendments, adopted by the Brussels Protocol 1968. The minimum level of liability was also raised. The amended rules, usually known as the 'Hague–Visby Rules' or the 'New Hague Rules', were enacted by the United Kingdom in the Carriage of Goods by Sea Act 1971.

Shortly after the 1971 Act came into force, some machinery was shipped from Leith, Scotland, to Bonaire in the Netherlands Antilles. The carriers were Dutch. They issued a bill of lading for shipment to Bonaire via Amsterdam. On the first leg of the journey, the machinery was carried in a Dutch vessel called the *Haico Holwerde*. On the second leg, it was carried by a Norwegian vessel, the *Morviken*, of which the carriers were the charterers. The bills of lading provided that the governing law was the law of the Netherlands. There was a choice-of-court agreement in favour of a Dutch court. The machinery was damaged and the shippers brought proceedings *in rem* in England against a sister ship of the *Haico Holwerde*, the *Hollandia*. The shipowners asked for a stay by reason of the choice-of-court agreement.

At the time in question, the Hague–Visby Rules were in force in the United Kingdom, but not in the Netherlands. Under the old Hague Rules, as applied in the Netherlands, the minimum liability of the shipowner was approximately £250 per package; under the Hague–Visby Rules it was over £11,000. Since the bills of lading contained a provision limiting the liability of the shipowner to this former sum, and since they contained a choice-of-law clause in favour of Dutch law, a Dutch court would have held the shipowners liable for no more than £250 per package.[53] An English court, on the other hand, would hold them liable for over £11,000 per package (if the shippers could prove their case).

The House of Lords held that the proceedings should not be stayed. The United Kingdom statute provided that the Hague–Visby Rules were to have the force of law in the United Kingdom. The Rules provided that any clause in a contract of carriage lessening the liability of the carrier (otherwise than as provided in the Rules) would be null and void. The House of Lords held that, since the choice-of-court agreement would have the practical effect of lessening the liability of the carrier, it was null and void in the United Kingdom. Any other ruling would have meant that mandatory British law could be made non-applicable by the simple expedient of a choice-of-law agreement coupled with a choice-of-court agreement.[54]

---

53 The Netherlands has since adopted the Hague–Visby Rules.

54 It might be argued that, just because a rule of law cannot be rendered inapplicable by contract in a domestic case, it should not necessarily be regarded as mandatory in an international case. However, the rule at issue in *The Hollandia* had been adopted by an international convention precisely for application in international cases. It was intended to be internationally mandatory.

This case was decided before the Brussels Convention/Regulation came into force. Would the result be the same today?

There are two lines of argument in favour of the view that it would. If the substantive validity of a choice-of-court agreement is governed by the choice-of-law rules of the forum, the choice-of-court agreement would, in a situation such as that in *The Hollandia (Morviken)*, be invalid under English conflict of laws as being contrary to a mandatory rule of the forum.[55]

The second line of argument is that the Hague–Visby Rules, being an international convention, would prevail over the Brussels I Regulation by virtue of Article 71 of the latter. This states that the Regulation does not affect any conventions to which the Member States are parties and which, in relation to particular matters, govern jurisdiction or the recognition or enforcement of judgments. Since the Hague–Visby Rules invalidate choice-of-court agreements that have the consequence of lessening the carrier's liability in a way not permitted by the Rules, they could be regarded as governing jurisdiction in this particular situation. In this situation, therefore, they prevail over the Brussels I Regulation.

In three of the four cases discussed above, the English courts refused to give effect to a choice-of-court agreement. It should not, however, be thought that this is the usual outcome. English courts routinely enforce them; the cases where they do not are exceptional.

§ 4 The United States

The story in the US is similar. Originally, choice-of-court agreements in favour of foreign courts were given little effect. They were simply one factor in a *forum-non-conveniens* analysis. Then there was a change of policy. This occurred in our next case.

United States
M/S Bremen v. Zapata Off-Shore Company
US Supreme Court
407 US 1; 32 L Ed 2d 513; 92 S Ct 1907 (1972)

Background

In this case, a German company, Unterweser Reederei, contracted with a Texas company, Zapata Offshore, to tow Zapata's oil rig, the Chaparral, from Louisiana to a point off Ravenna, Italy. The towage was to be carried out by Unterweser's tug, the Bremen. The contract of towage contained a choice-of-court clause in favour of the English courts.[56] It also contained two clauses exculpating Unterweser from liability for damage to the oil rig. Shortly after the tow began, a severe storm arose in the Gulf of Mexico. The Chaparral was seriously damaged,

---

55 It must be remembered that the Rome I Regulation does not apply to choice-of-court agreements: Article 1(2)(e). However, the result would be the same under it: see Article 9(2).
56 They were intended to be a neutral forum.

and Zapata instructed the Bremen to go to the nearest port of refuge, which was Tampa, Florida. There, Zapata brought suit in Admiralty in a Federal District Court for damages for negligent towage against Unterweser *in personam* and the *Bremen in rem*. Unterweser asked for a stay in favour of the English courts.

Meanwhile, Unterweser brought proceedings against Zapata before the English courts. The latter applied the rule laid down in the cases considered above, namely, that choice-of-court agreements are not absolutely binding, but that effect will be given to them unless there is a good reason to the contrary. The trial court considered that no such reason existed; this was upheld by the Court of Appeal.[57]

In Florida, the District Court rejected Unterweser's motion to stay. The court held that choice-of-court agreements concluded prior to the dispute were contrary to public policy and should not be enforced. Instead, it conducted a *forum-non-conveniens* analysis and concluded that the arguments in favour of the English courts were not sufficiently strong to justify a stay. At Zapata's request, it granted an antisuit injunction precluding Unterweser from proceeding further with the action in England.

The District Court's decision was upheld by the Court of Appeals (though six of the fourteen judges in the *en banc* rehearing dissented) and the case then came before the US Supreme Court.

Mr Chief Justice Burger delivered the opinion of the Court

. . .

For at least two decades we have witnessed an expansion of overseas commercial activities by business enterprises based in the United States. The barrier of distance that once tended to confine a business concern to a modest territory no longer does so. Here we see an American company with special expertise contracting with a foreign company to tow a complex machine thousands of miles across seas and oceans. The expansion of American business and industry will hardly be encouraged if, notwithstanding solemn contracts, we insist on a parochial concept that all disputes must be resolved under our laws and in our courts. Absent a contract forum, the considerations relied on by the Court of Appeals would be persuasive reasons for holding an American forum convenient in the traditional sense, but in an era of expanding world trade and commerce, the absolute aspects of the doctrine of the *Carbon Black*[1] case have little place and would be a heavy hand indeed on the future development of international commercial dealings by Americans. We cannot have trade and commerce in world markets and international waters exclusively on our terms, governed by our laws, and resolved in our courts.

Forum-selection clauses have historically not been favored by American courts. Many courts, federal and state, have declined to enforce such clauses on the ground that they were 'contrary to public policy', or that their effect was to 'oust the jurisdiction' of the court. Although this view apparently still has considerable

1 *Editor's note*: this is a reference to *Carbon Black Export Inc.* v. *Monrosa*, 254 F 2d 297 (5th Cir. 1958), the case on which the District Court relied.

57 *Unterweser Reederei* v. *Zapata Off-Shore Company (The 'Chaparral')* [1968] 2 Lloyd's Rep 158 (CA).

acceptance, other courts are tending to adopt a more hospitable attitude toward forum-selection clauses. This view, advanced in the well-reasoned dissenting opinion in the instant case, is that such clauses are *prima facie* valid and should be enforced unless enforcement is shown by the resisting party to be 'unreasonable' under the circumstances. We believe this is the correct doctrine to be followed by federal district courts sitting in Admiralty . . .

This approach is substantially that followed in other common-law countries including England. It is the view advanced by noted scholars and that adopted by the Restatement of the Conflict of Laws. It accords with ancient concepts of freedom of contract and reflects an appreciation of the expanding horizons of American contractors who seek business in all parts of the world. Not surprisingly, foreign businessmen prefer, as do we, to have disputes resolved in their own courts, but if that choice is not available, then in a neutral forum with expertise in the subject matter. Plainly, the courts of England meet the standards of neutrality and long experience in Admiralty litigation. The choice of that forum was made in an arm's-length negotiation by experienced and sophisticated businessmen, and absent some compelling and countervailing reason it should be honored by the parties and enforced by the courts.

The argument that such clauses are improper because they tend to 'oust' a court of jurisdiction is hardly more than a vestigial legal fiction. It appears to rest at core on historical judicial resistance to any attempt to reduce the power and business of a particular court and has little place in an era when all courts are overloaded and when businesses once essentially local now operate in world markets. It reflects something of a provincial attitude regarding the fairness of other tribunals. No one seriously contends in this case that the forum-selection clause 'ousted' the District Court of jurisdiction over Zapata's action. The threshold question is whether that court should have exercised its jurisdiction to do more than give effect to the legitimate expectations of the parties, manifested in their freely negotiated agreement, by specifically enforcing the forum clause.

There are compelling reasons why a freely negotiated private international agreement, unaffected by fraud, undue influence, or overweening bargaining power, such as that involved here, should be given full effect. In this case, for example, we are concerned with a far from routine transaction between companies of two different nations contemplating the tow of an extremely costly piece of equipment from Louisiana across the Gulf of Mexico and the Atlantic Ocean, through the Mediterranean Sea to its final destination in the Adriatic Sea. In the course of its voyage, it was to traverse the waters of many jurisdictions. The Chaparral could have been damaged at any point along the route, and there were countless possible ports of refuge. That the accident occurred in the Gulf of Mexico and the barge was towed to Tampa in an emergency were mere fortuities. It cannot be doubted for a moment that the parties sought to provide for a neutral forum for the resolution of any disputes arising during the tow. Manifestly much uncertainty and possibly great inconvenience to both parties could arise if a suit could be maintained in any jurisdiction in which an accident might occur or if jurisdiction were left to any place where the Bremen or Unterweser might happen to be found. The elimination of all such uncertainties by agreeing in advance on a forum acceptable to both parties is an indispensable element in international trade, commerce, and contracting. There is strong evidence that the forum clause was a vital part of the agreement, and it would be unrealistic to think that the parties did not conduct their negotiations, including fixing the monetary terms, with the consequences of the forum clause figuring prominently in their calculations. Under these circumstances, as Justice Karminski reasoned in sustaining jurisdiction over Zapata in the High Court of Justice, '(t)he force of an agreement for litigation in this country, freely entered into between two competent parties, seems to me to be very powerful.'[2]

Thus, in the light of present-day commercial realities and expanding international trade we conclude that the forum clause should control absent a strong showing that it should be set aside. Although their opinions are not altogether explicit, it seems reasonably clear that the District Court and the Court of Appeals placed the burden on Unterweser to show that London would be a more convenient forum than Tampa, although the contract expressly resolved that issue. The correct approach would have been to enforce the forum clause specifically unless Zapata could clearly show that enforcement would be unreasonable and unjust, or that the clause was invalid for such reasons as fraud or overreaching. Accordingly, the case must be remanded for reconsideration.

We note, however, that there is nothing in the record presently before us that would support a refusal to enforce the forum clause. The Court of Appeals suggested that enforcement would be contrary to the public policy of the forum under *Bisso* v. *Inland Waterways Corporation*, 349 US 85, 75 S Ct 629, 99 L Ed. 911 (1955), because of the prospect that the English courts would enforce the clauses of the towage contract purporting to exculpate Unterweser from liability for damages to the Chaparral. A contractual choice-of-forum clause should be held unenforceable if enforcement would contravene a strong public policy of the forum in which suit is brought, whether declared by statute or by judicial decision . . . It is clear, however, that whatever the proper scope of the policy expressed in *Bisso*, it does not reach this case. *Bisso* rested on considerations with respect to the towage business strictly in American waters, and those considerations are not controlling in an international commercial agreement . . .

Courts have also suggested that a forum clause, even though it is freely bargained for and contravenes no important public policy of the forum, may nevertheless be 'unreasonable' and unenforceable if the chosen forum is seriously inconvenient for the trial of the action. Of course, where it can be said with reasonable assurance that at the time they entered the contract, the parties to a freely negotiated private international commercial agreement contemplated the claimed inconvenience, it is difficult to see why any such claim of inconvenience should be heard to render the forum clause unenforceable.

We are not here dealing with an agreement between two Americans to resolve their essentially local disputes in a remote alien forum. In such a case, the serious

---

2 *Editor's note*: this was in the English proceedings.

inconvenience of the contractual forum to one or both of the parties might carry greater weight in determining the reasonableness of the forum clause. The remoteness of the forum might suggest that the agreement was an adhesive one, or that the parties did not have the particular controversy in mind when they made their agreement; yet even there the party claiming should bear a heavy burden of proof. Similarly, selection of a remote forum to apply differing foreign law to an essentially American controversy might contravene an important public policy of the forum. For example, so long as *Bisso* governs American courts with respect to the towage business in American waters, it would quite arguably be improper to permit an American tower to avoid that policy by providing a foreign forum for resolution of his disputes with an American towee.

This case, however, involves a freely negotiated international commercial transaction between a German and an American corporation for towage of a vessel from the Gulf of Mexico to the Adriatic Sea. As noted, selection of a London forum was clearly a reasonable effort to bring vital certainty to this international transaction and to provide a neutral forum experienced and capable in the resolution of Admiralty litigation. Whatever 'inconvenience' Zapata would suffer by being forced to litigate in the contractual forum as it agreed to do was clearly foreseeable at the time of contracting. In such circumstances it should be incumbent on the party seeking to escape his contract to show that trial in the contractual forum will be so gravely difficult and inconvenient that he will for all practical purposes be deprived of his day in court. Absent that, there is no basis for concluding that it would be unfair, unjust, or unreasonable to hold that party to his bargain.

In the course of its ruling on Unterweser's second motion to stay the proceedings in Tampa, the District Court did make a conclusory finding that the balance of convenience was 'strongly' in favor of litigation in Tampa. However, as previously noted, in making that finding the court erroneously placed the burden of proof on Unterweser to show that the balance of convenience was strongly in its favor. Moreover, the finding falls far short of a conclusion that Zapata would be effectively deprived of its day in court should it be forced to litigate in London. Indeed, it cannot even be assumed that it would be placed to the expense of transporting its witnesses to London. It is not unusual for important issues in international Admiralty cases to be dealt with by deposition. Both the District Court and the Court of Appeals majority appeared satisfied that Unterweser could receive a fair hearing in Tampa by using deposition testimony of its witnesses from distant places, and there is no reason to conclude that Zapata could not use deposition testimony to equal advantage if forced to litigate in London as it bound itself to do. Nevertheless, to allow Zapata opportunity to carry its heavy burden of showing not only that the balance of convenience is strongly in favor of trial in Tampa (that is, that it will be far more inconvenient for Zapata to litigate in London than it will be for Unterweser to litigate in Tampa), but also that a London trial will be so manifestly and gravely inconvenient to Zapata that it will be effectively deprived of a meaningful day in court, we remand for further proceedings.

. . .

The judgment of the Court of Appeals is vacated and the case is remanded for further proceedings consistent with this opinion.

Vacated and remanded.

Separate opinions were given by White J (concurring) and Douglas J (dissenting).

In *Zapata*, the Supreme Court emphasized that the contract was negotiated between two experienced businessmen. In our next case, however, it adopted the same policy in a consumer contract.

United States
Carnival Cruise Lines* v. *Shute
US Supreme Court
499 US 585; 111 S Ct 1522; 113 L Ed 2d 622 (1991)

Background

Mr and Mrs Shute bought tickets in the state of Washington for a sea cruise on a liner operated by Carnival Cruise. The tickets contained an exclusive choice-of-court agreement in favour of the courts of Florida, about as far away from the state of Washington as it is possible to get in the continental United States. However, this was not done to inconvenience passengers: Carnival Cruise's headquarters were in Florida. The voyage began in Los Angeles. When the vessel was off the coast of Mexico, Mrs Shute fell and injured herself. The Shutes brought proceedings against Carnival Cruise in Washington state.

Justice Blackmun delivered the opinion of the Court

We begin by noting the boundaries of our inquiry. First, this is a case in Admiralty, and federal law governs the enforceability of the forum-selection clause we scrutinize . . . Second, we do not address the question whether respondents had sufficient notice of the forum clause before entering the contract for passage. Respondents essentially have conceded that they had notice of the forum-selection provision . . .

Within this context, respondents urge that the forum clause should not be enforced because, contrary to this Court's teachings in *The Bremen*, the clause was not the product of negotiation, and enforcement effectively would deprive respondents of their day in court . . .

IV

A

Both petitioner and respondents argue vigorously that the Court's opinion in *The Bremen* governs this case, and each side purports to find ample support for its position in that opinion's broad-ranging language. This seeming paradox derives in large part from key factual differences between this case and *The Bremen*, differences that preclude an automatic and simple application of *The Bremen*'s general principles to the facts here.

In *The Bremen*, this Court addressed the enforceability of a forum-selection clause in a contract between two business corporations . . . The Court did not define precisely the circumstances that would make it unreasonable for a court to enforce a forum clause. Instead, the Court discussed a number of factors that made it reasonable to enforce the clause at issue in *The Bremen* and that, presumably, would be pertinent in any determination whether to enforce a similar clause.

In this respect, the Court noted that there was 'strong evidence that the forum clause was a vital part of the agreement, and [that] it would be unrealistic to think that the parties did not conduct their negotiations, including fixing the monetary terms, with the consequences of the forum clause figuring prominently in their calculations.' Further, the Court observed that it was not 'dealing with an agreement between two Americans to resolve their essentially local disputes in a remote alien forum', and that in such a case, 'the serious inconvenience of the contractual forum to one or both of the parties might carry greater weight in determining the reasonableness of the forum clause.' The Court stated that even where the forum clause establishes a remote forum for resolution of conflicts, 'the party claiming [unfairness] should bear a heavy burden of proof.' Ibid.

In applying *The Bremen*, the Court of Appeals in the present litigation took note of the foregoing 'reasonableness' factors and rather automatically decided that the forum-selection clause was unenforceable because, unlike the parties in *The Bremen*, respondents are not business persons and did not negotiate the terms of the clause with petitioner. Alternatively, the Court of Appeals ruled that the clause should not be enforced because enforcement effectively would deprive respondents of an opportunity to litigate their claim against petitioner.

The Bremen concerned a 'far from routine transaction between companies of two different nations contemplating the tow of an extremely costly piece of equipment from Louisiana across the Gulf of Mexico and the Atlantic Ocean, through the Mediterranean Sea to its final destination in the Adriatic Sea.' These facts suggest that, even apart from the evidence of negotiation regarding the forum clause, it was entirely reasonable for the Court in *The Bremen* to have expected Unterweser and Zapata to have negotiated with care in selecting a forum for the resolution of disputes arising from their special towing contract.

In contrast, respondents' passage contract was purely routine and doubtless nearly identical to every commercial passage contract issued by petitioner and most other cruise lines . . . In this context, it would be entirely unreasonable for us to assume that respondents – or any other cruise passenger – would negotiate with petitioner the terms of a forum-selection clause in an ordinary commercial cruise ticket. Common sense dictates that a ticket of this kind will be a form contract the terms of which are not subject to negotiation, and that an individual purchasing the ticket will not have bargaining parity with the cruise line. But by ignoring the crucial differences in the business contexts in which the respective contracts were executed, the Court of Appeals' analysis seems to us to have distorted somewhat this Court's holding in *The Bremen*.

In evaluating the reasonableness of the forum clause at issue in this case, we must refine the analysis of *The Bremen* to account for the realities of form passage contracts. As an initial matter, we do not adopt the Court of Appeals' determination that a nonnegotiated forum-selection clause in a form ticket contract is never enforceable simply because it is not the subject of bargaining. Including a reasonable forum clause in a form contract of this kind well may be permissible for several reasons: First, a cruise line has a special interest in limiting the fora in which it potentially could be subject to suit. Because a cruise ship typically carries passengers from many locales, it is not unlikely that a mishap on a cruise could subject the cruise line to litigation in several different fora . . . Additionally, a clause establishing ex ante the forum for dispute resolution has the salutary effect of dispelling any confusion about where suits arising from the contract must be brought and defended, sparing litigants the time and expense of pretrial motions to determine the correct forum and conserving judicial resources that otherwise would be devoted to deciding those motions . . . Finally, it stands to reason that passengers who purchase tickets containing a forum clause like that at issue in this case benefit in the form of reduced fares reflecting the savings that the cruise line enjoys by limiting the fora in which it may be sued . . .

We also do not accept the Court of Appeals' 'independent justification' for its conclusion that *The Bremen* dictates that the clause should not be enforced because '[t]here is evidence in the record to indicate that the Shutes are physically and financially incapable of pursuing this litigation in Florida.' We do not defer to the Court of Appeals' findings of fact. In dismissing the case for lack of personal jurisdiction over petitioner, the District Court made no finding regarding the physical and financial impediments to the Shutes' pursuing their case in Florida. The Court of Appeals' conclusory reference to the record provides no basis for this Court to validate the finding of inconvenience. Furthermore, the Court of Appeals did not place in proper context this Court's statement in *The Bremen* that 'the serious inconvenience of the contractual forum to one or both of the parties might carry greater weight in determining the reasonableness of the forum Clause.' The Court made this statement in evaluating a hypothetical 'agreement between two Americans to resolve their essentially local disputes in a remote alien forum.' In the present case, Florida is not a 'remote alien forum', nor – given the fact that Mrs. Shute's accident occurred off the coast of Mexico – is this dispute an essentially local one inherently more suited to resolution in the State of Washington than in Florida. In light of these distinctions, and because respondents do not claim lack of notice of the forum clause, we conclude that they have not satisfied the 'heavy burden of proof', required to set aside the clause on grounds of inconvenience.

It bears emphasis that forum-selection clauses contained in form passage contracts are subject to judicial scrutiny for fundamental fairness. In this case, there is no indication that petitioner set Florida as the forum in which disputes were to be resolved as a means of discouraging cruise passengers from pursuing legitimate claims. Any suggestion of such a bad-faith motive is belied by two facts: Petitioner has its principal place of business in Florida, and many of its cruises depart from and return to Florida ports. Similarly, there is no evidence that petitioner obtained respondents' accession to the forum clause by fraud or overreaching. Finally, respondents have conceded that they were given notice of the forum provision and, therefore, presumably retained the option of rejecting the contract with impunity. In the case before us, therefore, we conclude that the Court of Appeals erred in refusing to enforce the forum-selection clause.

...

The judgment of the Court of Appeals is reversed.

Justice Stevens, with whom Justice Marshall joined, dissented.

QUESTIONS

1 Is this decision consistent with that in *The Bremen*?
2 Would the result be the same under the Brussels I Regulation?
3 Was the result fair?

Both *Zapata* and *Carnival Cruise* were Admiralty cases.[58] As such, they were within the subject-matter jurisdiction of the federal courts and were governed by federal law.[59] Neither involved carriage of goods by sea. Like the United Kingdom, the United States became a party to the (old) Hague Rules, and effect was given to them by the Carriage of Goods by Sea Act 1936 (COGSA). In *Zapata*, the Supreme Court said that choice-of-court agreements might not be upheld in COGSA cases.[60] For this reason, it was held that an earlier case, *Indussa Corporation* v. *SS Ranborg*,[61] was not applicable. In the *Indussa* case, it was held that choice-of-court agreements in favour of a foreign court necessarily constituted a lessening of the shipowner's liability, and were, therefore, contrary to the Hague Rules. The reasons were, first, that the foreign court might not apply the Hague Rules; secondly, that, if it did, it might interpret them differently; and, thirdly, that, even if it did not, the difficulty, inconvenience and expense of having to sue in a foreign court would make it harder for cargo-owners to sue shipowners and would thus itself constitute a lessening of the latter's liability. For some years after it was decided, therefore, the *Zapata* decision was not applied by American courts in COGSA cases.[62]

This policy came to an end in our next case.

---

58 In both cases, the Supreme Court expressly limited its holding to cases in federal courts sitting in Admiralty.
59 US Constitution, Article III, § 2; 28 USC § 1333.
60 See note 11 in the original judgment (not reproduced above).
61 377 F 2d 200 (2nd Cir. 1967) (*en banc*).
62 See, for example, *Union Insurance* v. *SS Elikon*, 642 F 2d 721 (4th Cir. 1981).

United States
Vimar Seguros v. *M/V Sky Reefer*
US Supreme Court
515 US 528; 115 S Ct 2322; 132 L Ed 2d 462 (1995)

Background

This case concerned carriage of goods to an American port. The bills of lading contained a clause providing for arbitration in Japan. The Supreme Court, however, expressly said that its ruling applied equally to choice-of-court agreements.

Justice Kennedy delivered the opinion of the Court

. . . We consider the two arguments made by petitioner. The first is that a foreign arbitration clause lessens COGSA liability by increasing the transaction costs of obtaining relief. The second is that there is a risk foreign arbitrators will not apply COGSA.

A

The leading case for invalidation of a foreign forum selection clause is the opinion of the Court of Appeals for the Second Circuit in *Indussa Corporation* v. *S.S. Ranborg*, 377 F 2d 200 (1967) (en banc). The court there found that COGSA invalidated a clause designating a foreign judicial forum because it 'puts "a high hurdle" in the way of enforcing liability, and thus is an effective means for carriers to secure settlements lower than if cargo [owners] could sue in a convenient forum.' The court observed 'there could be no assurance that [the foreign court] would apply [COGSA] in the same way as would an American tribunal subject to the uniform control of the Supreme Court.' Following *Indussa*, the Courts of Appeals without exception have invalidated foreign forum selection clauses under § 3(8) . . . As foreign arbitration clauses are but a subset of foreign forum selection clauses in general . . . the *Indussa* holding has been extended to foreign arbitration clauses as well . . . The logic of that extension would be quite defensible, but we cannot endorse the reasoning or the conclusion of the *Indussa* rule itself.

The determinative provision in COGSA, examined with care, does not support the arguments advanced first in *Indussa* and now by petitioner. Section 3(8) of COGSA provides as follows:

> 'Any clause, covenant, or agreement in a contract of carriage relieving the carrier or the ship from liability for loss or damage to or in connection with the goods, arising from negligence, fault, or failure in the duties and obligations provided in this section, or lessening such liability otherwise than as provided in this chapter, shall be null and void and of no effect.'

The liability that may not be lessened is 'liability for loss or damage . . . arising from negligence, fault, or failure in the duties and obligations provided in this section.' The statute thus addresses the lessening of the specific liability imposed by the Act, without addressing the separate question of the means and costs of enforcing that liability. The difference is that between explicit statutory guarantees and the procedure for enforcing them, between applicable liability principles and the forum in which they are to be vindicated.

The liability imposed on carriers under COGSA § 3 is defined by explicit standards of conduct, and it is designed to correct specific abuses by carriers. In the 19th century it was a prevalent practice for common carriers to insert clauses in bills of lading exempting themselves from liability for damage or loss, limiting the period in which plaintiffs had to present their notice of claim or bring suit, and capping any damages awards per package . . . Thus, § 3, entitled 'Responsibilities and liabilities of carrier and ship', requires that the carrier 'exercise due diligence to . . . [m]ake the ship seaworthy' and '[p]roperly man, equip, and supply the ship' before and at the beginning of the voyage, § 3(1), 'properly and carefully load, handle, stow, carry, keep, care for, and discharge the goods carried', § 3(2), and issue a bill of lading with specified contents, § 3(3) . . . Section 3(6) allows the cargo owner to provide notice of loss or damage within three days and to bring suit within one year. These are the substantive obligations and particular procedures that § 3(8) prohibits a carrier from altering to its advantage in a bill of lading. Nothing in this section, however, suggests that the statute prevents the parties from agreeing to enforce these obligations in a particular forum. By its terms, it establishes certain duties and obligations, separate and apart from the mechanisms for their enforcement.

Petitioner's contrary reading of § 3(8) is undermined by the Court's construction of a similar statutory provision in *Carnival* Cruise . . .

If the question whether a provision lessens liability were answered by reference to the costs and inconvenience to the cargo owner, there would be no principled basis for distinguishing national from foreign arbitration clauses. Even if it were reasonable to read § 3(8) to make a distinction based on travel time, airfare, and hotels bills, these factors are not susceptible of a simple and enforceable distinction between domestic and foreign forums. Requiring a Seattle cargo owner to arbitrate in New York likely imposes more costs and burdens than a foreign arbitration clause requiring it to arbitrate in Vancouver. It would be unwieldy and unsupported by the terms or policy of the statute to require courts to proceed case by case to tally the costs and burdens to particular plaintiffs in light of their means, the size of their claims, and the relative burden on the carrier.

Our reading of 'lessening such liability' to exclude increases in the transaction costs of litigation also finds support in the goals of the Brussels Convention for the Unification of Certain Rules Relating to Bills of Lading . . . (Hague Rules),[1] on which COGSA is modeled. Sixty-six countries, including the United States and Japan, are now parties to the Convention . . . and it appears that none has interpreted its enactment of § 3(8) of the Hague Rules to prohibit foreign forum selection clauses . . . The English courts long ago rejected the reasoning later adopted by the *Indussa* court . . . And other countries that do not recognize foreign forum selection clauses rely on specific provisions to that effect in their domestic versions of the Hague Rules . . . In light of the fact that COGSA is the culmination of a multilateral effort 'to establish uniform ocean bills of lading to govern the rights and liabilities of carriers and shippers inter se in international trade' we decline to interpret our version of the Hague Rules in a manner contrary to every other nation to have addressed this issue . . .

1 *Editor's note*: these are the old Hague Rules.

It would also be out of keeping with the objects of the Convention for the courts of this country to interpret COGSA to disparage the authority or competence of international forums for dispute resolution. Petitioner's skepticism over the ability of foreign arbitrators to apply COGSA or the Hague Rules, and its reliance on this aspect of *Indussa* . . . must give way to contemporary principles of international comity and commercial practice . . .

B

Petitioner's second argument against enforcement of the Japanese arbitration clause is that there is no guarantee foreign arbitrators will apply COGSA. This objection raises a concern of substance. The central guarantee of § 3(8) is that the terms of a bill of landing may not relieve the carrier of the obligations or diminish the legal duties specified by the Act. The relevant question, therefore, is whether the substantive law to be applied will reduce the carrier's obligations to the cargo owner below what COGSA guarantees . . .

Petitioner argues that the arbitrators will follow the Japanese Hague Rules, which, petitioner contends, lessen respondents' liability in at least one significant respect. The Japanese version of the Hague Rules, it is said, provides the carrier with a defense based on the acts or omissions of the stevedores hired by the shipper . . . while COGSA, according to petitioner, makes nondelegable the carrier's obligation to 'properly and carefully . . . stow . . . the goods carried', COGSA § 3(2) . . .

Whatever the merits of petitioner's comparative reading of COGSA and its Japanese counterpart, its claim is premature. At this interlocutory stage it is not established what law the arbitrators will apply to petitioner's claims or that petitioner will receive diminished protection as a result. The arbitrators may conclude that COGSA applies of its own force or that Japanese law does not apply so that, under another clause of the bill of lading, COGSA controls. Respondents seek only to enforce the arbitration agreement. The District Court has retained jurisdiction over the case and 'will have the opportunity at the award-enforcement stage to ensure that the legitimate interest in the enforcement of the . . . laws has been addressed.' cf. 1 Restatement (Third) of Foreign Relations Law of the United States § 482(2)(d) (1986) ('A court in the United States need not recognize a judgment of the court of a foreign state if . . . the judgment itself, is repugnant to the public policy of the United States'). Were there no subsequent opportunity for review and were we persuaded that 'the choice-of-forum and choice-of-law clauses operated in tandem as a prospective waiver of a party's right to pursue statutory remedies . . . we would have little hesitation in condemning the agreement as against public policy.' *Mitsubishi Motors* . . . Cf . . . *The Hollandia*, [1983] AC 565, 574–575 (HL1982) (noting choice-of-forum clause 'does not ex facie offend against article III, paragraph 8', but holding clause unenforceable where 'the foreign court chosen as the exclusive forum would apply a domestic substantive law which would result in limiting the carrier's liability to the sum lower than that to which he would be entitled if [English COGSA] applied'). Under the circumstances of this case, however, the First Circuit was correct to reserve judgment on the choice-of-law question . . . as it must be decided in the first instance by the arbitrator

... As the District Court has retained jurisdiction, mere speculation that the foreign arbitrators might apply Japanese law which, depending on the proper construction of COGSA, might reduce respondents' legal obligations, does not in and of itself lessen liability under COGSA § 3(8).

... The judgment of the Court of Appeals is affirmed, and the case is remanded for further proceedings consistent with this opinion.

It is so ordered.

O'Connor J concurred and Stevens J dissented.

QUESTION

Is this decision consistent with that of the House of Lords in *The Hollandia*?[63]

Although there have been no Supreme Court decisions on international choice-of-court agreements outside the Admiralty field,[64] federal courts seem willing to give general effect to choice-of-court agreements in cases before them.[65] In state courts, the position is less clear. Many state courts take the same view as the federal courts,[66] but some may not.

§ 5   The Hague Choice-of-Court Convention

On 30 June 2005, more than forty States, meeting in The Hague, adopted the Convention on Choice of Court Agreements.[67] Although not yet in force, it will probably be widely ratified. All the world's major economic powers took part: the United States, the European Community, China, Japan, Russia, Canada, Australia, Brazil and many others. For this reason, it is worth considering some of its features.

It was inspired by the Brussels I Regulation and follows its general lines. Like the Regulation, it lays down requirements for the form of choice-of-court agreements. These are less complex than those of the Regulation: they state simply that the agreement must be concluded or documented in writing. There is the same provision as regards electronic communications.[68] The problem of inequality of bargaining power is solved by excluding consumer and employment contracts

---

63 See § 3, above.
64 For a case in a purely US context, see *Stewart Organization Inc.* v. *Ricoh Corporation*, 487 US 22; 108 S Ct 2239; 101 L Ed 2d 22 (US Supreme Court, 1988).
65 In diversity cases, this could be supported on the ground that the effect of a choice-of-court agreement is a matter of procedure and thus governed by federal law when it arises in a federal court.
66 See, for example, *Minorplanet Systems USA Ltd* v. *American Aire Inc.*, 368 SC 146; 628 SE 2d 43 (Supreme Court of South Carolina, 2006).
67 The text of the Convention may be found on the website of the Hague Conference on Private International Law, www.hcch.nl.
68 The wording of both instruments was inspired by Article 6(1) of the UNCITRAL Model Law on Electronic Commerce 1996.

altogether from the scope of the Convention, which is intended to apply largely to business-to-business relationships. Insurance is covered, unless taken out by a consumer.[69] Carriage of goods (and passengers) by sea (and by other means) is excluded,[70] but most other areas of shipping law are covered.[71]

The salient features of the Convention are as follows (italics indicating where it differs from the Regulation):

- It applies both where the choice-of-court agreement specifies a particular court and where it specifies the courts (in general) of a State.
- It applies only if the court chosen is in a *State Party to the Convention.*[72]
- It applies both to disputes that have arisen and to those that may arise in the future in connection with a particular legal relationship.
- *It applies only to exclusive choice-of-court agreements, but a special opt-in clause extends its provisions to the recognition and enforcement of judgments given under non-exclusive agreements.*[73]
- Choice-of-court agreements are presumed to be exclusive unless the parties have *expressly* agreed otherwise.
- *It applies only to choice-of-court agreements in international cases.*[74]
- It requires persons bound by a choice-of-court agreement to have consented to it.

The formal validity of choice-of-court agreements is determined exclusively by the Convention. As is the case with the Regulation, Contracting States cannot lay down additional rules of a formal nature. Substantive validity is determined by the law of the chosen court.[75] Article 6 provides that a court in a Contracting State other than that of the chosen court must suspend or dismiss proceedings to which an exclusive choice-of-court agreement applies. There are, however, five exceptions (set out in paragraphs (a) to (e) of Article 6). The first, set out in paragraph (a), is that the choice-of-court agreement is null and void under the law of the chosen court. Of the other four, the most important is probably that in paragraph (c), which applies where giving effect to the agreement would lead

---

69 It is covered even if the contract of insurance relates to a matter excluded from the scope of the Convention – for example, carriage of goods.

70 Article 2(2)(f).

71 However, Article 2(2)(g) excludes marine pollution, limitation of liability for maritime claims, general average, and emergency towage and salvage.

72 Under the Brussels I Regulation, the equivalent provisions apply only if the chosen court is in an EC Member State.

73 Article 22.

74 It defines 'international' in paragraphs 2 and 3 of Article 1. Paragraph 2 states that, for jurisdictional purposes, a case is international unless the parties are resident in the same Contracting State and all relevant elements other than the location of the chosen court are connected only with that State. In other words, if a case is otherwise wholly domestic, the choice of a foreign court does not make it international. A different definition applies for the purpose of recognition and enforcement (paragraph 3). Here, it is enough that the judgment was given by a foreign court. This means that a case that was non-international when the original judgment was given may become international if proceedings are brought to enforce the judgment in another State. According to the Schlosser Report (Schlosser, 'Report on the Convention of 9 October 1968' (Denmark, Ireland and UK Accessions), OJ 1979 C 59, p. 71 at paragraph 174), the provisions in the Brussels I Regulation on choice-of-court agreements apply only in an international situation. The Schlosser Report states that a case is not international merely because the parties choose the courts of another State. It is unclear whether this is so and, if it is, what exactly would make the case international.

75 Article 5(1).

to a manifest injustice or would be manifestly contrary to the public policy of the State of the court seised.[76] It is important to appreciate the difference in approach between these two provisions. Under paragraph (a), the court before which proceedings are brought must apply the law of the State of the chosen court (including its rules of conflict of laws); under paragraph (c), on the other hand, it applies its own concepts of justice and public policy.

Article 8(1) provides for the recognition and enforcement of judgments under choice-of-court agreements.[77] Again, there are exceptions, most of which are set out in Article 9.[78] Some mirror those in Article 6 – for example, the exception applicable where the choice-of-court agreement is null and void under the law of the State of the chosen court.[79] Recognition or enforcement may also be refused where this would be manifestly incompatible with the public policy of the requested State.[80] Further exceptions concern the service of the writ,[81] and fraud in connection with a matter of procedure.[82]

Article 26 provides what happens when the Convention conflicts with another convention. The rules are too complicated to discuss here; however, it might be of value to summarize their application with regard to the Brussels I Regulation. As far as jurisdiction is concerned, the Brussels I Regulation will prevail over the Convention where none of the parties is resident in a Contracting State to the Hague Convention that is not an EC Member State. Where at least one of the parties is resident in such a State, the Convention will prevail.[83] Thus, for example, if an American company and a German company choose the Rotterdam district court, the Convention will prevail; if, on the other hand, a Belgian company and a German company choose the Rotterdam court, the Brussels I Regulation will prevail.

With regard to the recognition and enforcement of judgments, the Brussels I Regulation will prevail where the court that granted the judgment and the court in which recognition is sought are both located in the European Community. This means that the generally more limited grounds for non-recognition laid down in Article 34 of the Brussels I Regulation will apply in place of the wider grounds in Article 9 of the Convention.

---

[76] The other exceptions are: (b) a party lacked capacity to conclude the agreement under the law of the State of the court seised; (d) for exceptional reasons beyond the control of the parties, the agreement cannot reasonably be performed; and (e) the chosen court has decided not to hear the case. These provisions are a more developed version of the provisions in Article II(3) of the United Nations Convention on the Recognition and Enforcement of Foreign Arbitral Awards (New York, 10 June 1958).

[77] 'Recognition', as understood by the Convention, means accepting the determination of the rights and obligations made by the court of origin. 'Enforcement' means ensuring that the judgment-debtor obeys the order of the court of origin.

[78] For another possible exception, see Article 20.

[79] Article 6(a) is reflected in Article 9(a); Article 6(b) is reflected in Article 9(b); and Article 6(c) is reflected in Article 9(e), though the latter only partly coincides with the former.

[80] Article 9(e).

[81] Article 9(c).

[82] Article 9(d).

[83] Article 4(2) of the Convention provides that a corporation is resident in each and all of the following: the State where it has its statutory seat; the State under whose law it was incorporated or formed; the State where it has its central administration; and the State where it has its principal place of business. It follows from this that a company could in theory be resident in four States. If any one of these is a party to the Hague Convention but not a Member State of the EC, the Hague Convention will prevail over the Brussels I Regulation as far as jurisdiction is concerned.

§ 6   Conclusions

It will have been noticed that decisions from courts in the two common-law countries considered tend to focus on broad questions of policy, while those from the European Court are much more technical, often hinging on whether the complex formalities of Community law have been satisfied. This is the inevitable consequence of the policy of having detailed rules, something that was regarded as necessary in order to ensure that all the Member States took the same approach.

Further reading

Bell (Andrew), *Forum Shopping and Venue in Transnational Litigation* (Oxford University Press, Oxford, 2003) (Chapter 5)

Briggs (Adrian), *Agreements on Jurisdiction and Choice of Law* (Oxford University Press, Oxford, 2008)

Fentiman, (2005) 42 *Common Market Law Review* 241 (comment on *Gasser* case)

Hartley, 'The Validity of Forum-Selection Agreements', in White and Smythe (eds.), *Current Issues in International and European Law: Essays in Memory of Frank Dowrick* (Sweet & Maxwell, London, 1990)

'The Hague Choice-of-Court Convention' (2006) 31 *European Law Review* 414

Joseph (David), *Jurisdiction and Arbitration Agreements and their Enforcement* (Sweet & Maxwell, London, 2005)

Kahn-Freund, 'Jurisdiction Agreements: Some Reflections' (1977) 26 ICLQ 825

Merrett, 'Enforcement of Jurisdiction Agreements within the Brussels Regime' (2006) 55 ICLQ 315

Morse, 'Forum-Selection Clauses – EEC Style' (1989) 1 *African Journal of International and Comparative Law* 551

Park, 'Illusion and Reality in International Forum Selection' (1995) 30 *Texas International Law Journal* 135

Pryles, 'Comparative Aspects of Prorogation and Arbitration Agreements' (1976) 25 ICLQ 543

Schulz, 'The Hague Convention of 30 June 2005 on Choice of Court Agreements' (2006) 2 *Journal of Private International Law* 243

Takahashi, 'Damages for Breach of a Choice-of-Court Agreement' (2008) 10 *Yearbook of Private International Law* 57

CHAPTER 9

Forum non conveniens and antisuit injunctions

§ 1 Introduction

The discussion so far has focused on the court before which proceedings have been brought. Now, we must broaden the scope of our investigation and look at the wider picture. It will be clear from what has been said that it can often happen that more than one court has jurisdiction in a case, something that can lead to potential or actual conflicts of jurisdiction. How are these resolved?

Here the common law and the civil law have radically different solutions. The civil law does nothing until there is an actual conflict, until the same case comes before two different courts. Then it applies the doctrine of *lis pendens* (more fully, *lis alibi pendens*).[1] Under this, a court cannot hear proceedings if the same action is already pending before a court in another country. In other words, the court seised second must give the case up in favour of the court seised first. This approach has the advantage of simplicity. It is also fairly objective: though there is sometimes room for dispute as to exactly when a case is pending before a court, both courts will normally agree on which of them was seised first. Its disadvantage is that it makes no attempt to determine which court is more appropriate. Thus, a court that is ill placed to decide the case might get to hear it instead of one that is well placed. Getting your claim form in first is more important than suing in the right court, something that gives an advantage to litigants who know how to work the system.

The common law adopts a different theory, that of *forum non conveniens*. This attempts to determine which court is more appropriate to hear the case. It is of little importance which was seised first. The advantage of this approach is that it tries to find a rational solution. Its disadvantage is that there is a large measure of subjectivity involved, which means that the two courts may reach different conclusions even if they apply the same criteria.

The doctrine of *forum non conveniens* is different in another way: it does not wait until a *lis pendens* situation has actually arisen. It operates not only when the case is pending before the courts of another country, but also when it *could have been* brought before them. It applies even if there is no conflict of courts. Its purpose is wider: it is concerned not only with resolving a conflict of courts – an essentially public-law purpose – but with doing justice to the parties by ensuring that the most appropriate court hears the case. The latter is the main objective. It

---

1 *Lis alibi pendens* is Latin for 'case pending elsewhere'.

constitutes another example of the common law giving greater weight to private interests than to public interests.

Thus, the common law and the civil law are, to some extent, working at cross-purposes. The civil law is concerned with avoiding an unseemly battle between two courts. The common law wants to ensure that the most appropriate court decides the case. In the common-law world, one would expect there to be fewer instances where the same litigation was brought before two courts. This is because the court first seised will (if so requested by the defendant) consider whether the courts of another country have jurisdiction and, if they do, decide whether they are better suited to hearing the case. If they are, it will stay the proceedings. In the civil-law world, on the other hand, it is generally accepted that a court with jurisdiction *must* hear any proceedings brought before it: it has no discretion to decline jurisdiction in favour of the courts of another country.

On the other hand, where proceedings *are* brought before the courts of two countries, the conflict is more likely to be resolved in the civil-law world. The two sets of courts are more likely to agree which should hear the case. In the common-law world, it is more likely that both sets of courts will want to hear it. This could mean that the case will continue in both, though when judgment is given in one set of proceedings this may constitute *res judicata* in the other.

What happens when one action is in a common-law country and the other in a civil-law country? If the common-law court was seised first, there is unlikely to be a problem. It would (if so requested by the defendant) decide whether it or the other court was the more appropriate. If it considered that the other court was more appropriate, it would stay the proceedings and invite the claimant to bring the action in the other court. The civil-law court would then hear the case. If, on the other hand, it considered that *it* was more appropriate, it would reject the motion to stay. If a second action was then brought before the civil-law court, the latter would apply the *lis pendens* doctrine and decline jurisdiction.

The position would be different where the civil-law court was seised first. It would not listen to any argument based on *forum non conveniens*. It would hear the case irrespective of appropriateness. If proceedings were subsequently brought before the common-law court, that court would not be deterred by the fact that it was seised second. It would carry out a *forum-non-conveniens* analysis and, if it concluded that it was more appropriate, it would allow the proceedings to continue.

This latter situation is the one which is the most controversial. Civil lawyers say it would be wrong for the court seised second to hold on to the case, since this would constitute an affront to the court seised first. Common lawyers, however, feel that the interests of the litigants should come before the dignity of the court. If the common-law court is more appropriate, it should not deny justice to the party who invoked its jurisdiction.

Having two sets of proceedings is of course against the interests of the parties, as well as being an affront to the courts involved. Here the common law comes up with its most controversial remedy: the antisuit injunction. This is an order directed to the party who is claimant in the foreign action to discontinue that action (or not to continue it).[2] Failure to comply could put him in contempt of court. The penalties include not being permitted to continue with the action in the court granting the injunction (if he is the claimant there) or not being permitted to defend it (if he is the defendant). In addition, his property could be seized, he could be fined or (in theory) sent to prison. Civil lawyers regard antisuit injunctions as a particularly serious affront to the dignity of the foreign court, even though the injunction is directed at the litigant, not the court. Common lawyers say that it is contrary to justice for a person to be sued in an inappropriate court when the action is being heard by an appropriate one. Again, this reveals a clash of values: what is more important – the interests of the court or the interests of the litigant?

In this chapter, we will consider how the common law developed, a study that will be concerned with *forum non conveniens* and antisuit injunctions. In the next chapter, we will see what happened when the United Kingdom joined the civil-law world through membership of the European Union; we will also examine something that is little discussed in the academic context, but which is a serious problem in the real world: the bad-faith litigant.

§ 2   England

§ 2.1   *Forum non conveniens*

The doctrine of *forum non conveniens* was invented in Scotland (a mixed civil-law/common-law country) in the nineteenth century,[3] and for many years the English were reluctant to accept it. In two special situations, however, they applied a similar doctrine, though the phrase *forum non conveniens* was not used. These situations were applications for permission to serve a claim form outside the jurisdiction and applications to stay proceedings on the ground of a choice-of-court agreement in favour of a foreign court.

Choice-of-court agreements were discussed in the last chapter. It will be remembered that, when they would otherwise have jurisdiction, the English courts will not accord absolute effect to a choice-of-court agreement in favour of a foreign court; nevertheless, they will stay the proceedings before them, if so requested by the defendant, unless the claimant can establish a good reason why this should not be done. He must show that England is clearly more appropriate than the foreign country for the resolution of the dispute. The factors to be taken

---

2 Most antisuit injunctions are ancillary to substantive proceedings: their purpose is to protect the jurisdiction of the court hearing the substantive proceedings and to ensure that any order it gives will be effective. In such a situation, jurisdiction to hear the substantive proceedings automatically confers jurisdiction to grant the antisuit injunction: *Masri v. Consolidated Contractors International* [2008] EWCA Civ 625 (CA). However, if the injunction is not ancillary to other proceedings, some specific ground of jurisdiction for granting the injunction will have to be found. The most usual ground would be the domicile of the defendant in England, which gives the court general jurisdiction (jurisdiction that is not dependent on the existence of a link between the claim and the territory of the forum) under Article 2(1) of the Brussels I Regulation.
3 *Sim v. Robinow* (1892) 19 R 665.

into account were set out in *The Eleftheria*,[4] discussed in Chapter 8, § 3, above. This is similar to a *forum-non-conveniens* analysis.

It will be remembered from Chapter 5 that, under the common law, jurisdiction depends on the service of a claim form. Originally, this had to be done within England. At a later date, service outside the jurisdiction was permitted. Since this was regarded as less firmly based in international law, it was necessary to obtain permission (leave) before service could take place. To obtain permission, the claimant had to establish two things: first, that the case came within the terms of the relevant legislation (originally the Rules of the Supreme Court, now the Civil Procedure Rules) and, secondly, that, in all the circumstances, it was appropriate to assume jurisdiction. The second requirement in effect entailed a *forum-non-conveniens* analysis. This took place before the claim form was served, and thus before the court was seised of the case.[5] The assumption of jurisdiction was, therefore, conditional on the English court's being a *forum conveniens*. For this reason, one could say that *forum non conveniens* was built into the jurisdictional rule.

These principles still apply today, though convincing a court that it should refuse a stay when there is a choice-of-court agreement in favour of a foreign court is considerably more difficult than convincing it that it should allow service outside the jurisdiction. In both cases, however, the onus of proof is on the claimant.

Outside these special situations, the English courts originally had no power to stay proceedings on the ground that the courts of another country were more appropriate. This was true even if the foreign courts were seised first.[6] There was, however, a power to stay proceedings if they were vexatious and oppressive. Legal procedures are created for a purpose, that of ensuring that justice is done. If a claimant abuses the law by bringing them simply in order to vex (annoy or hurt) or oppress the defendant, he is guilty of an abuse of process and the proceedings will be stayed or struck out. The concept of vexation and oppression is generally regarded as incorporating an element of moral blameworthiness, 'a desire on the plaintiff's part to harass the defendant by putting him to unnecessary trouble or expense, rather than to improve the plaintiff's own prospects of success or enhance what he stands to gain from the litigation'.[7] Thus, if a wealthy person brings proceedings that he knows are baseless against a defendant who may have difficulty defending them (perhaps for lack of funds), he will be guilty of vexation and oppression. The proceedings will be struck out.

This usually has nothing to do with conflict of laws. The doctrine was developed in a domestic context and was based on the desire to prevent abuse of process. However, it is possible for vexation and oppression to occur in an international

---

4 [1970] P 94; [1969] 2 WLR 1073; [1969] 2 All ER 641; [1969] 1 Lloyd's Rep 237 (England).
5 The proceedings to obtain permission were *ex parte*. After the claim form was served, the defendant could apply to have service set aside on the ground either that the case did not come within the terms of the relevant legislation, or that England was not an appropriate forum. The same issues were, therefore, subject to reconsideration after service.
6 *St Pierre* v. *South American Stores* [1936] 1 KB 382 (CA).
7 *MacShannon* v. *Rockware Glass* [1978] AC 795 at p. 810, *per* Lord Diplock.

context. This happened in *Logan* v. *Bank of Scotland (No. 2)*,[8] which involved a claim against a Scottish bank for a comparatively small sum of money.[9] The claimant was Scottish and all the evidence (both witnesses and documents) was in Scotland.[10] However, the action was brought in London.[11] According to the defendants, the claimant hoped that the inconvenience of defending the action in London would induce them to settle the case. Instead, they applied for a stay. This was granted by the Court of Appeal on the ground that the proceedings were vexatious and oppressive. In his judgment, Sir Gorell Barnes, President, put the matter as follows:[12]

> [I]t is difficult to conceive anything more harassing to the defendant bank than to have their officials dragged up to London for a lengthy trial, when the Court of Session [the Scottish court] is, so to speak, across the way in Edinburgh, and when together with their officials they would have to bring up here, and keep away from their business, numerous other witnesses with a mass of books, papers and documents, if they can get them at all, which there seems to be some difficulty about without orders from the Court of Session as to some of them.

In a case decided in 1935, *St Pierre* v. *South American Stores*, in which the Court of Appeal refused a stay, even though the courts of Chile had been seised first[13] and were clearly more convenient, Scott LJ said:[14]

> In order to justify a stay two conditions must be satisfied, one positive and the other negative: (a) the defendant must satisfy the court that the continuance of the action would work an injustice because it would be oppressive or vexatious to him or would be an abuse of the process of the court in some other way; and (b) the stay must not cause an injustice to the plaintiff. On both the burden of proof is on the defendant.

This much-cited passage was accepted as a correct statement of the law until 1978, when the House of Lords decided *MacShannon* v. *Rockware Glass*. This case concerned a man who was injured at work.[15] The injury took place in Scotland at the defendant's factory there. The injured man was Scottish. However, the action was brought in England where the defendant had its headquarters. This was not done in order to make life difficult for the defendant. The claimant was a member of a trade union and the union had undertaken the conduct of the action, something it did for its members. The union was organized on

---

8 [1906] 1 KB 141 (CA).
9 The claim was for £50, worth more then than now, but still not a great deal of money.
10 In addition to the bank, there were also a number of individual defendants, one of whom was resident in England. However, he was an undischarged bankrupt.
11 The bank had a branch in London and was, therefore, subject to English jurisdiction, even though the claim did not arise out of the activities of the London branch.
12 [1906] 1 KB 141 at p. 153 (CA).
13 According to Scott LJ, there was some dispute about this, but he said that it would make no difference even if they were seised first. In the case, the claimant in England was the defendant in Chile; it might have been different if the same party had been claimant in both.
14 [1936] 1 KB 382 at p. 398 (CA). As late as 1973, this statement of the law was affirmed by the House of Lords in *The Atlantic Star* [1974] AC 436. In that case, their lordships were invited to discard Scott LJ's statement and substitute the Scottish doctrine of *forum non conveniens*. They declined to do so. However, they did interpret 'vexation and oppression' in a more flexible way, in which the connotation of moral blameworthiness was lessened or even entirely removed.
15 There were actually a number of cases, in which the facts were similar, heard together. *MacShannon* was just one of them.

an all-British basis and its headquarters happened to be in London. It had an arrangement with an English firm of solicitors to handle personal-injury actions on its behalf. The solicitors felt it would be more convenient to proceed in the English courts. They said that there were important advantages to suing in England: the level of damages would be higher; the proceedings would be quicker; the costs would be lower; and, if successful, the claimant's costs would be paid by the other side on a higher scale.

The defendant applied for a stay. It said the action should have been brought in Scotland. Under the doctrine of vexation and oppression, a stay would not have been justified, since the claimant had not sued in England in order to harm the defendant. He genuinely believed that it was to his advantage to do so. The House of Lords, however, adopted a new principle. This was stated by Lord Diplock in the following words:[16]

> In order to justify a stay two conditions must be satisfied, one positive and the other negative:
>
> (a) the defendant must satisfy the court that there is another forum to whose jurisdiction he is amenable in which justice can be done between the parties at substantially less inconvenience or expense, and
>
> (b) the stay must not deprive the plaintiff of a legitimate personal or juridical advantage which would be available to him if he invoked the jurisdiction of the English court.

This formula is generally known as the '*MacShannon* test'. It was regarded as coming close to the Scottish doctrine of *forum non conveniens*; nevertheless, the phrase *forum non conveniens* was not used.

If one applies the new test to the facts of the case, it is fairly clear that the defendant could satisfy the first prong: it was amenable to the jurisdiction of the Scottish courts, and justice could be done there at substantially less inconvenience and expense.[17] What about the second prong? The claimant said that there were significant advantages to bringing proceedings in England (higher damages, etc.). The House of Lords, however, said that, in applying this test, one must consider the actual, objective situation, not the subjective beliefs of the claimant, however honestly held. This was an important development of the test laid down by Scott LJ in *St Pierre* v. *South American Stores*.[18] Since the House of Lords hears appeals in civil cases from Scotland as well as from England, and could indeed be considered as much a Scottish court as an English one, their lordships were in a unique position to assess the relative merits of the two systems. They said that, in fact, there were no advantages to proceeding in England. So the stay was granted.

It should be mentioned at this point that there was a significant political element in the background. It seems that it was common for industrial-injury

---

16 [1978] AC 795 at p. 812.

17 The claimant lived in Scotland, the injury took place there; the witnesses lived there; the claimant was treated for his injuries there; medical and other expert witnesses lived there.

18 According to Lord Diplock in *MacShannon*, the change actually took place five years earlier in *The Atlantic Star* [1974] AC 436 (HL).

cases originating in Scotland to be heard in England, simply because there was normally one trade union for the whole United Kingdom.[19] The Scottish legal profession might, however, have felt that these cases were rightfully theirs, and that the English legal profession was 'poaching' work from them. Although not mentioned in the judgment, these factors must have weighed with the House of Lords, some of whose members were Scotsmen. It would certainly have been undiplomatic for the House of Lords to say that the English system was better than the Scottish.

Though the *MacShannon* judgment represented a significant development of the test, it nevertheless did not constitute a full-blown *forum-non-conveniens* doctrine. Even if the foreign court was substantially more convenient, the claimant could still resist a stay if he showed that he could obtain a legitimate advantage by suing in England. Higher damages, speedier proceedings, easier means of obtaining evidence and better ways of enforcing the judgment could all constitute such an advantage.

In 1984, the law was further developed in *The Abidin Daver*,[20] another decision of the House of Lords. A Turkish ship and a Cuban ship had collided in Turkish waters. The Turks immediately brought proceedings against the Cubans before a Turkish court. Some time later, the Cubans arrested a sister ship of the Turkish vessel in England to found jurisdiction there. The House of Lords upheld the decision of the trial judge to stay the proceedings. Lord Diplock put the matter as follows:[21]

> Where a suit about a particular subject-matter between a plaintiff and a defendant is already pending in a foreign court which is a natural and appropriate forum for the resolution of the dispute between them, and the defendant in the foreign suit seeks to institute as plaintiff an action in England about the same matter to which the person who is plaintiff in the foreign suit is made defendant, then the additional inconvenience and expense which must result from allowing two sets of legal proceedings to be pursued concurrently in two different countries where the same facts will be in issue and the testimony of the same witnesses required, can only be justified if the would-be plaintiff can establish objectively by cogent evidence that there is some personal or juridical advantage that would be available to him only in the English action that is of such importance that it would cause injustice to him to deprive him of it.

Thus, in a *lis pendens* situation at least, it was no longer sufficient for the claimant in England to establish that he would be deprived of a legitimate juridical advantage: he had to show that the advantage would be of such importance that it would be unjust to deprive him of it.

It was also in this case that Lord Diplock made his famous statement that English judges should no longer assume that the quality of justice obtainable in England was better than that in foreign countries: 'judicial chauvinism', he said, 'has been replaced by judicial comity.'[22] He accepted that the English

---

19 According to Lord Diplock in *MacShannon*, there had been forty-four such cases in the three years prior to *MacShannon*.
20 [1984] AC 398.
21 [1984] AC 398 at pp. 411–12.
22 *Ibid.*, p. 411.

test was now indistinguishable from the Scottish legal doctrine of *forum non conveniens*.

The final step was taken in 1986 in our next case.

England
Spiliada Maritime Corporation v. Cansulex
House of Lords
[1987] AC 460; [1986] 3 WLR 972; [1986] 3 All ER 843

Background

This case concerned a shipment of sulphur from Vancouver, British Columbia, to ports in India. The contract of carriage contained an English choice-of-law clause. The ship was registered in Liberia and the shipowner, Spiliada, was a Liberian-registered corporation. The ship was managed partly in Greece and partly in England. It was chartered to an Indian company. Spiliada claimed that the sulphur was wet when loaded and had corroded the ship's hold. It claimed that this was the fault of the shipper, Cansulex, a Canadian company. It brought pro-ceedings against Cansulex in England. It obtained permission to serve the claim form outside the jurisdiction on the ground that the contract of carriage was governed by English law. Cansulex applied to have the permission set aside.

Lord Goff of Chieveley

. . .

(5) The fundamental principle

In cases where jurisdiction has been founded as of right, i.e. where in this country the defendant has been served with proceedings within the jurisdiction, the defendant may now apply to the court to exercise its discretion to stay the proceedings on the ground which is usually called *forum non conveniens*. That principle has for long been recognised in Scots law; but it has only been recognised comparatively recently in this country. In *The Abidin Daver* . . . Lord Diplock stated that, on this point, English law and Scots law may now be regarded as indistinguishable. It is proper therefore to regard the classic statement of Lord Kinnear in *Sim* v. *Robinow* (1892) 19 R 665 as expressing the principle now applicable in both jurisdictions. He said . . .

> 'the plea can never be sustained unless the court is satisfied that there is some other tribunal, having competent jurisdiction, in which the case may be tried more suitably for the interests of all the parties and for the ends of justice.'

I feel bound to say that I doubt whether the Latin tag *forum non conveniens* is apt to describe this principle. For the question is not one of convenience, but of the suitability or appropriateness of the relevant jurisdiction. However the Latin tag (sometimes expressed as *forum non conveniens* and sometimes as *forum conveniens*) is so widely used to describe the principle, not only in England and Scotland, but in other Commonwealth jurisdictions and in the United States, that it is probably sensible to retain it. But it is most important not to allow it to mislead us into thinking that the question at issue is one of 'mere practical convenience.' Such a suggestion was emphatically rejected by Lord Kinnear in *Sim* v. *Robinow* . . . and by Lord Dunedin, Lord Shaw of Dunfermline and Lord Sumner in the *Société du Gaz*[1] case . . . Lord Dunedin, with reference to the expressions *forum non competens* and *forum non conveniens*, said.[2] . . .

> 'In my view, "competent" is just as bad a translation for *"competens"* as "convenient" is for *"conveniens."* The proper translation for these Latin words, so far as this plea is concerned, is "appropriate."'

Lord Sumner referred to a phrase used by Lord Cowan in *Clements* v. *Macaulay*.[3] . . . viz. 'more convenient and preferable for securing the ends of justice', and said . . .

> 'one cannot think of convenience apart from the convenience of the pursuer[4] or the defender[5] or the court, and the convenience of all these three, as the cases show, is of little, if any, importance. If you read it as "more convenient, that is to say, preferable, for securing the ends of justice", I think the true meaning of the doctrine is arrived at. The object, under the words *"forum non conveniens"* is to find that *forum* which is the more suitable for the ends of justice, and is preferable because pursuit of the litigation in that *forum* is more likely to secure those ends.'

In the light of these authoritative statements of the Scottish doctrine, I cannot help thinking that it is wiser to avoid use of the word 'convenience' and to refer rather, as Lord Dunedin did, to the *appropriate* forum.

(6) How the principle is applied in cases of stay of proceedings

When the principle was first recognised in England, as it was (after a breakthrough in *The Atlantic Star* . . .) in *MacShannon* v. *Rockware Glass Ltd* . . . it cannot be said that the members of the Judicial Committee of this House spoke with one voice. This is not surprising; because the law on this topic was then in an early stage of a still continuing development. The leading speech was delivered by Lord Diplock.

[Lord Goff then quoted the 'MacShannon test', set out above, and continued:]

This passage has been quoted on a number of occasions in later cases in your Lordships' House. Even so, I do not think that Lord Diplock himself would have regarded this passage as constituting an immutable statement of the law, but rather as a tentative statement at an early stage of a period of development . . .

In my opinion, having regard to the authorities (including in particular the Scottish authorities), the law can at present be summarised as follows.

(a)   The basic principle is that a stay will only be granted on the ground of *forum non conveniens* where the court is satisfied that there is some other available forum, having competent jurisdiction, which is the appropriate

---

1 *Société du Gaz de Paris* v. *Société Anonyme de Navigation Les Armateurs Français*, 1926 SC 13 (HL, Scotland).
2 *Ibid.*, p. 18.
3 (1866) 4 Macph 583 at p. 594.
4 *Editor's note*: 'pursuer' is Scottish terminology for 'claimant/plaintiff'.
5 *Editor's note*: 'defender' is Scottish terminology for 'defendant'.

forum for the trial of the action, i.e. in which the case may be tried more suitably for the interests of all the parties and the ends of justice.

(b) As Lord Kinnear's formulation of the principle indicates, in general the burden of proof rests on the defendant to persuade the court to exercise its discretion to grant a stay . . . It is however of importance to remember that each party will seek to establish the existence of certain matters which will assist him in persuading the court to exercise its discretion in his favour, and that in respect of any such matter the evidential burden will rest on the party who asserts its existence. Furthermore, if the court is satisfied that there is another available forum which is *prima facie* the appropriate forum for the trial of the action, the burden will then shift to the plaintiff to show that there are special circumstances by reason of which justice requires that the trial should nevertheless take place in this country (see (f), below).

(c) The question being whether there is some other forum which is the appropriate forum for the trial of the action, it is pertinent to ask whether the fact that the plaintiff has, *ex hypothesi*, founded jurisdiction as of right in accordance with the law of this country, of itself gives the plaintiff an advantage in the sense that the English court will not lightly disturb jurisdiction so established. Such indeed appears to be the law in the United States, where 'the court hesitates to disturb the plaintiff's choice of forum and will not do so unless the balance of factors is strongly in favor of the defendant',: see Scoles and Hay, *Conflict of Laws* (1982), p. 366, and cases there cited; and also in Canada, where it has been stated (see *Castel, Conflict of Laws* (1974), p. 282) that 'unless the balance is strongly in favor of the defendant, the plaintiff's choice of forum should rarely be disturbed.' This is strong language. However, the United States and Canada are both federal states; and, where the choice is between competing jurisdictions within a federal state, it is readily understandable that a strong preference should be given to the forum chosen by the plaintiff upon which jurisdiction has been conferred by the constitution of the country which includes both alternative jurisdictions.

A more neutral position was adopted by Lord Sumner in the *Société du Gaz*[6] case . . . where he said:

> 'All that has been arrived at so far is that the burden of proof is upon the defender to maintain that plea. I cannot see that there is any presumption in favour of the pursuer.'

However, I think it right to comment that that observation was made in the context of a case where jurisdiction had been founded by the pursuer by invoking the Scottish principle that, in actions *in personam*, exceptionally jurisdiction may be founded by arrest of the defender's goods within the Scottish jurisdiction. Furthermore, there are cases where no particular forum can be described as the natural forum for the trial of the action. Such cases are particularly likely to occur in commercial disputes, where there can be pointers to a number of

---

6 1926 SC 13 at p. 21 (HL).

different jurisdictions . . . or in Admiralty, in the case of collisions on the high seas. I can see no reason why the English court should not refuse to grant a stay in such a case, where jurisdiction has been founded as of right. It is significant that, in all the leading English cases where a stay has been granted, there has been another clearly more appropriate forum . . . In my opinion, the burden resting on the defendant is not just to show that England is not the natural or appropriate forum for the trial, but to establish that there is another available forum which is clearly or distinctly more appropriate than the English forum. In this way, proper regard is paid to the fact that jurisdiction has been founded in England as of right . . . and there is the further advantage that, on a subject where comity is of importance, it appears that there will be a broad consensus among major common law jurisdictions. I may add that if, in any case, the connection of the defendant with the English forum is a fragile one (for example, if he is served with proceedings during a short visit to this country), it should be all the easier for him to prove that there is another clearly more appropriate forum for the trial overseas.

(d) Since the question is whether there exists some other forum which is clearly more appropriate for the trial of the action, the court will look first to see what factors there are which point in the direction of another forum . . . Having regard to the anxiety expressed . . . concerning the use of the word 'convenience' in this context, I respectfully consider that it may be more desirable, now that the English and Scottish principles are regarded as being the same, to adopt the expression used by my noble and learned friend, Lord Keith of Kinkel, in *The Abidin Daver* . . . when he referred to the 'natural forum' as being 'that with which the action had the most real and substantial connection.' So it is for connecting factors in this sense that the court must first look; and these will include not only factors affecting convenience or expense (such as availability of witnesses), but also other factors such as the law governing the relevant transaction . . . and the places where the parties respectively reside or carry on business.

(e) If the court concludes at that stage that there is no other available forum which is clearly more appropriate for the trial of the action, it will ordinarily refuse a stay . . . It is difficult to imagine circumstances when, in such a case, a stay may be granted.

(f) If however the court concludes at that stage that there is some other available forum which *prima facie* is clearly more appropriate for the trial of the action, it will ordinarily grant a stay unless there are circumstances by reason of which justice requires that a stay should nevertheless not be granted. In this inquiry, the court will consider all the circumstances of the case, including circumstances which go beyond those taken into account when considering connecting factors with other jurisdictions. One such factor can be the fact, if established objectively by cogent evidence, that the plaintiff will not obtain justice in the foreign jurisdiction; see *The Abidin Daver* . . . *per* Lord Diplock, a passage which now makes plain that, on this inquiry, the burden of proof shifts to the plaintiff.

How far other advantages to the plaintiff in proceeding in this country may be relevant in this connection, I shall have to consider at a later stage.

(7) How the principle is applied in cases where the court exercises its discretionary power under RSC, Ord. 11

[Lord Goff then considered how the principle would be applied when the court exercises its discretionary power to allow service outside the jurisdiction under what are now the CPR. He concluded:]

The effect is, not merely that the burden of proof rests on the plaintiff to persuade the court that England is the appropriate forum for the trial of the action, but that he has to show that this is clearly so. In other words, the burden is, quite simply, the obverse of that applicable where a stay is sought of proceedings started in this country as of right . . .

(8) Treatment of 'a legitimate personal or juridical advantage'

Clearly, the mere fact that the plaintiff has such an advantage in proceedings in England cannot be decisive. As Lord Sumner said of the parties in the *Société du Gaz*[7] case . . .

> 'I do not see how one can guide oneself profitably by endeavouring to conciliate and promote the interests of both these antagonists, except in that ironical sense, in which one says that it is in the interests of both that the case should be tried in the best way and in the best tribunal, and that the best man should win.'

Indeed, as Oliver LJ . . . pointed out in his judgment in the present case an advantage to the plaintiff will ordinarily give rise to a comparable disadvantage to the defendant; and simply to give the plaintiff his advantage at the expense of the defendant is not consistent with the objective approach inherent in Lord Kinnear's statement of principle in *Sim* v. *Robinow* . . .

The key to the solution of this problem lies, in my judgment, in the underlying fundamental principle. We have to consider where the case may be tried 'suitably for the interests of all the parties and for the ends of justice.' Let me consider the application of that principle in relation to advantages which the plaintiff may derive from invoking the English jurisdiction. Typical examples are: damages awarded on a higher scale; a more complete procedure of discovery; a power to award interest; a more generous limitation period. Now, as a general rule, I do not think that the court should be deterred from granting a stay of proceedings, or from exercising its discretion against granting leave [to serve the claim form outside the jurisdiction], simply because the plaintiff will be deprived of such an advantage, provided that the court is satisfied that substantial justice will be done in the available appropriate forum. Take, for example, discovery. We know that there is a spectrum of systems of discovery applicable in various jurisdictions, ranging from the limited discovery available in civil law countries on the continent of Europe to the very generous pre-trial oral discovery procedure applicable in the United States of America. Our procedure lies somewhere in the middle of this

---

7 *Ibid.*, p. 22 (HL).

spectrum. No doubt each of these systems has its virtues and vices; but, generally speaking, I cannot see that, objectively, injustice can be said to have been done if a party is, in effect, compelled to accept one of these well-recognised systems applicable in the appropriate forum overseas. In this, I recognise that we appear to be differing from the approach presently prevailing in the United States: see, e.g., the recent opinion of Judge Keenan in *Re Union Carbide Corporation* 634 F Supp. 842 (1986) in the District Court for the Southern District of New York, where a stay of proceedings in New York, commenced on behalf of Indian plaintiffs against Union Carbide arising out of the tragic disaster in Bhopal, was stayed subject to, *inter alia*, the condition that Union Carbide was subject to discovery under the model of the United States Federal Rules of Civil Procedure after appropriate demand by the plaintiff. But in the *Trendtex* case . . . this House thought it right that a stay of proceedings in this country should be granted where the appropriate forum was Switzerland, even though the plaintiffs were thereby deprived of the advantage of the more extensive English procedure of discovery of documents in a case of fraud. Then take the scale on which damages are awarded. Suppose that two parties have been involved in a road accident in a foreign country, where both were resident, and where damages are awarded on a scale substantially lower than those awarded in this country. I do not think that an English court would, in ordinary circumstances, hesitate to stay proceedings brought by one of them against the other in this country merely because he would be deprived of a higher award of damages here.

But the underlying principle requires that regard must be had to the interests of all the parties and the ends of justice; and these considerations may lead to a different conclusion in other cases. For example, it would not, I think, normally be wrong to allow a plaintiff to keep the benefit of security obtained by commencing proceedings here, while at the same time granting a stay of proceedings in this country to enable the action to proceed in the appropriate forum . . . Again, take the example of cases concerned with time bars. Let me consider how the principle of *forum non conveniens* should be applied in a case in which the plaintiff has started proceedings in England where his claim was not time barred, but there is some other jurisdiction which, in the opinion of the court, is clearly more appropriate for the trial of the action, but where the plaintiff has not commenced proceedings and where his claim is now time barred. Now, to take some extreme examples, suppose that the plaintiff allowed the limitation period to elapse in the appropriate jurisdiction, and came here simply because he wanted to take advantage of a more generous time bar applicable in this country; or suppose that it was obvious that the plaintiff should have commenced proceedings in the appropriate jurisdiction, and yet he did not trouble to issue a protective writ [8] there; in cases such as these, I cannot see that the court should hesitate to stay the proceedings in this country, even though the effect would be that the plaintiff's claim would inevitably be defeated by a plea of the time bar in the appropriate

---

8 *Editor's note*: a protective writ is a writ (claim form) served in a jurisdiction in which the claimant would prefer *not* to bring proceedings; it is served before the expiry of the time limit there, so that, if it turns out in the end that he cannot proceed in his preferred forum, he will not find that his claim in the alternative forum is time barred.

jurisdiction. Indeed a strong theoretical argument can be advanced for the proposition that, if there is another clearly more appropriate forum for the trial of the action, a stay should generally be granted even though the plaintiff's action would be time barred there. But, in my opinion, this is a case where practical justice should be done and practical justice demands that, if the court considers that the plaintiff acted reasonably in commencing proceedings in this country, and that, although it appears that (putting on one side the time bar point) the appropriate forum for the trial of the action is elsewhere than England, the plaintiff did not act unreasonably in failing to commence proceedings (for example, by issuing a protective writ) in that jurisdiction within the limitation period applicable there, it would not, I think, be just to deprive the plaintiff of the benefit of having started proceedings within the limitation period applicable in this country . . . It is not to be forgotten that, by making its jurisdiction available to the plaintiff – even the discretionary jurisdiction [to allow service outside the jurisdiction] – the courts of this country have provided the plaintiff with an opportunity to start proceedings here; accordingly, if justice demands, the court should not deprive the plaintiff of the benefit of having complied with the time bar in this country. Furthermore, as the applicable principles become more clearly established and better known, it will, I suspect, become increasingly difficult for plaintiffs to prove lack of negligence in this respect. The fact that the court has been asked to exercise its discretion [to allow service out of the jurisdiction], rather than that the plaintiff has served proceedings upon the defendant in this country as of right, is, I consider, only relevant to consideration of the plaintiff's conduct in failing to save the time bar in the other relevant alternative jurisdiction. The appropriate order, where the application of the time bar in the foreign jurisdiction is dependent upon its invocation by the defendant, may well be to make it a condition of the grant of a stay, or the exercise of discretion against giving leave to serve out of the jurisdiction, that the defendant should waive the time bar in the foreign jurisdiction; this is apparently the practice in the United States of America.

Lord Goff then applied these principles to the facts of the case. One might have thought that a stay would have been granted. The case had its most real and substantial connection with British Columbia. One of the parties was resident there and that was the place of loading. The other party was Liberian, not English. The main connection with England was that English law applied. Normally, this would not have been enough. However, there was another case pending before the English courts in which the facts were substantially similar. It also concerned Cansulex. It also concerned the loading of sulphur, allegedly wet, in British Columbia. However, in that case, *The Cambridgeshire*,[23] the ship-owners were English. Cansulex had also asked the court to set aside permission to serve the claim form outside England, but this had been refused. Cansulex had not appealed against that decision, and the case had proceeded to trial. Since the essential facts were almost exactly the same in both cases, and since the teams of lawyers and expert witnesses were the same, the result of the action

---

[23] 6 October 1982, unreported.

in *The Cambridgeshire* would almost certainly have been determinative in the *Spiliada* case if the latter were decided in England.[24] For this reason, the trial judge in *Spiliada* decided that no stay should be granted. The House of Lords held that there were no grounds for interfering with this decision. The action could proceed in England.

QUESTIONS

1 What is the difference between the situation in which the claim form is served in England and that in which it is served outside England under the CPR?

2 What is the 'natural forum' and how is it determined?

3 Do you agree with the result: was it right to make the outcome depend on the chance fact that another case involving Cansulex had been brought in England?

Note

In a later case before the House of Lords, *Société Nationale Industrielle Aérospatiale* v. *Lee Kui Jak* (set out in § 2.2, below), Lord Goff explained more fully the significance of the 'Cambridgeshire factor' in *Spiliada*:[25]

In *Spiliada's* case the question at issue was the effect of wet sulphur upon the holds of ships. This question was of profound importance, not only to the shipping industry, but to the whole sulphur exporting industry in British Columbia. The first case in which the question was investigated in depth was concerned with a ship called the *Cambridgeshire*, and was plainly recognised as in the nature of a test case. Armies of lawyers and experts were engaged. An enormous amount of preparatory work was undertaken; the documentation was voluminous in the extreme. The scientific investigation was of a most fundamental kind, and indeed approached the limits of scientific knowledge. The trial of the *Cambridgeshire* action was begun and had proceeded for about a month when the application was made for a stay of proceedings in *Spiliada's* case, a parallel case raising the same profound scientific questions as those which had arisen in the *Cambridgeshire*. The application came on for hearing before Staughton J, the trial judge in the *Cambridgeshire* action. In these somewhat unusual circumstances, it is scarcely surprising that he regarded the building up of expertise and understanding among the teams of lawyers and experts in England as being a relevant factor to be taken into account when deciding whether or not to order a stay of the English proceedings in *Spiliada's* case; this view was shared by the House of Lords, where it was pointed out that, in addition, the parties in both

---

24 *The Cambridgeshire* was in fact settled before the House of Lords decided *Spiliada*. What was really in issue in *Spiliada* was, therefore, whether the proceedings in *Spiliada* should be settled on the basis that the trial would take place in England or whether it should be settled on the basis that the trial would take place in Canada. It seems that the latter would have been more favourable to Cansulex.
25 [1987] AC 871 at p. 898.

actions were substantially the same – Cansulex Ltd being defendants in both actions, and the plaintiff shipowners in both actions being insured by the same P and I club[1] who were financing and controlling both sets of proceedings, and instructing the same lawyers in both.

1 The P & I club was the shipowner's insurer.

Comment

As Lord Goff made clear in *Spiliada*, the test in England 'is not just to show that England is not the natural or appropriate forum for the trial, but to establish that there is another available forum which is clearly or distinctly more appropriate than the English forum'. Under Australian law, on the other hand, the defendant must prove that Australia is a clearly inappropriate forum.[26] This is different from proving that the foreign forum is clearly more appropriate: if Australia is not clearly inappropriate, a stay will not be granted, even if a foreign country is clearly more appropriate.[27]

Whatever the exact test, the existence of an alternative forum is an indispensable requirement for a stay or dismissal of proceedings in both England and the Commonwealth. This is generally thought to be true in the United States as well.[28] However, the principle was not applied in *Islamic Republic of Iran* v. *Pahlavi*.[29] After the Iranian Revolution, the former Shah and his family fled to America and took up residence in New York, where the Shah was receiving medical treatment. The Government of Iran served him with a writ there, claiming the return of billions of dollars which he and his family had allegedly embezzled when he ruled Iran. The New York courts dismissed the proceedings on the ground of *forum non conveniens*, though they admitted that there was no alternative forum.[30] This was an abuse of the doctrine: for political reasons, the courts were determined to shield the Shah, and *forum non conveniens* was the tool they chose.

Spiliada remains the leading case in England today and the test laid down in it remains the applicable test. We can, therefore, assess the doctrine of *forum non conveniens*, at least as far as England is concerned, on the basis of this test. The main objection to *forum non conveniens* is that it produces uncertainty: a claimant should know with confidence, it is said, where he can bring proceedings. It is generally not too difficult, however, to weigh up the normal connecting factors: what can cause uncertainty is deciding the effect to be given to special circumstances.

We have already seen that, in *Spiliada*, it was the existence of parallel proceedings that tipped the balance. In *Du Pont* v. *Agnew*[31] it was the fact that English public policy was involved. In this case, an American company had

26 *Voth* v. *Manildra Flour Mills Pty Ltd* (1990) 171 CLR 538; (1990) 65 ALJR 83; (1990) 97 ALR 124 (High Court of Australia); *CSR Ltd* v. *Cigna Insurance Australia Ltd* (1997) 189 CLR 345 and 405 (High Court of Australia).
27 Both may be appropriate, but the foreign forum may be clearly more appropriate.
28 See *Gulf Oil* v. *Gilbert*, 330 US 501, at pp. 506–7, *per* Justice Jackson (US Supreme Court, 1947).
29 62 NY 2d 474; 467 NE 2d 245; 478 NYS 2d 597; 57 ALR 4th 955 (New York Court of Appeals, 1984).
30 If the Iranian courts had given judgment against the Shah, that judgment would not have been recognized in the United States: see *Bank Melli Iran* v. *Pahlavi*, 58 F 3d 1406 (9th Cir. 1995).
31 [1987] 2 Lloyd's Rep 585 (CA).

taken out insurance from an English insurer to indemnify it against liability for its products. Subsequently, it was sued in Illinois by someone who had used one of its products and suffered injury as a result. It was held liable, both compensatory and punitive damages being awarded. It then claimed against the insurer. The latter was unwilling to indemnify it for the punitive damages. It claimed that insurance for punitive damages was against public policy in Illinois: the idea was that, as punitive damages were meant to punish the person concerned for wrongful conduct, it would defeat their object if he could insure against them. Whether this was also the law in England was uncertain. The American company sued the insurer in England to obtain indemnification; shortly afterwards, the insurer brought proceedings against the company in Illinois for a declaration that it was not liable. Thus the English party wanted the case to be decided in America, and the American party wanted it to be decided in England.

The insurer applied to have the English action stayed on the ground of *forum non conveniens*. The Court of Appeal held, however, that the applicable law was that of England and that an English court was best situated to decide questions of English law and English public policy. 'If English public policy is to be held to deny the right to indemnity in these circumstances', said Bingham LJ, 'then this court and no other must so hold. I do not regard this as a question capable of fair resolution in any foreign court, however distinguished and well instructed.'[32] He therefore held that England was clearly the more appropriate forum. The stay was refused.

However, the Illinois court would have applied Illinois public policy: from its point of view, English public policy was irrelevant;[33] so there was actually no question of a foreign court deciding questions of English public policy. In view of this, the real issue seems to have been whether English public policy or Illinois public policy should be applied. It was on this ground that the English court refused a stay.

Roneleigh Ltd v. *MII Exports Inc.*[34] concerned the difference between American and English law on the payment of lawyers' fees. In England, as in most European countries, the unsuccessful party normally has to pay the successful party's costs, and these include the fee he has to pay to his lawyer. In the United States, on the other hand, costs do not normally include attorney fees: each party pays his lawyer himself.[35]

In the *Roneleigh* case, an English company had bought steel from a New Jersey company. The steel was delivered in New York. The English company claimed that it was not in accordance with the contract, and obtained permission in England to serve a claim form outside the jurisdiction (on the ground that the contract was made in England). The American company asked for the permission

---

32 *Ibid.*, p. 594. This was because English public policy on the issue had not yet been formulated.
33 See the later decision of the English Court of Appeal in the *Du Pont* case, reported at [1988] 2 Lloyd's Rep 240, *per* Dillon LJ at p. 242.
34 [1989] 1 WLR 619 (CA).
35 If the claimant concluded a contingent-fee agreement with his attorney, he would pay nothing if he lost the case and would pay a percentage of the award if he won.

to be set aside. The English court accepted that New Jersey was the more appropriate forum, but refused to set the permission aside on the ground that it would be unjust to the claimant to have to sue in the United States because, if it won, it would not recover its lawyer's fee.

The disadvantage to the claimant was, however, balanced by an equivalent advantage to the defendant. Moreover, if the claimant lost – something that the court thought unlikely, but which nevertheless could have happened – the claimant would have benefited. The judgment was based on the second prong of the *Spiliada* test, but it is hard to see why the American rule was so unjust that it required a stay to be refused.[36] Since American courts almost always apply their rule, this case would suggest that proceedings should never be stayed when the alternative forum is in the United States, something that cannot be correct.

Perhaps both cases depended on their own special facts. Nevertheless, they show that *forum non conveniens* involves a significant degree of subjectivity. This is probably inevitable if one tries to reach a just result, instead of applying an arbitrary rule. Perhaps the second prong of the *Spiliada* test should be regarded as the jurisdictional equivalent of the public-policy test in choice of law. As we shall see in Chapter 22, § 2.4.3, below, the rules of choice of law are always subject to an exception of a subjective nature based on public policy. Since a similar exception applies to the recognition of foreign judgments,[37] it is hardly surprising that it also applies to jurisdiction.

§ 2.2   Antisuit injunctions

Antisuit injunctions have a long history in English law. Their development may be traced back to the common injunction, which was used in the fifteenth century in a purely domestic context as part of the long struggle between the courts of equity and the courts of common law. Unlike the common-law writ of prohibition, the equitable injunction was not directed against the other court, but against the claimant in that court. Once the court of Chancery had established its power to issue injunctions to preclude proceedings in other English courts, it was only a small step to start issuing them with regard to proceedings outside England. This was first done in the case of proceedings in Scottish, Irish and colonial courts; then they were issued with regard to proceedings in foreign countries.[38]

The leading case today in England is actually a decision of the Privy Council on appeal from Brunei. In the past, the Privy Council – to a large extent, the House of Lords under a different name – heard appeals from Commonwealth countries, though today most of them have abolished this right.

---

36 In many situations, American courts award higher damages, partly to take account of the American rule on attorney fees.
37 See, for example, Chapter 14, § 5, and Chapter 16, § 2, below.
38 See, for example, *Hope* v. *Carnegie* (1866) 1 Ch App 320.

Brunei
Société Nationale Industrielle Aérospatiale v. *Lee Kui Jak*
Privy Council
[1987] AC 871; [1987] 3 WLR 59; [1987] 3 All ER 510

Background

The case arose out of a helicopter crash in Brunei in which a Brunei businessman was killed. The helicopter was made by a French company, Aérospatiale; it was owned by an English company and operated by a Malaysian company under contract to a Sarawak company. Claims by the widow against these latter defendants had already been settled for US$430,000. She then brought proceedings against Aérospatiale in a state court in Texas: at the time, Texas law did not recognize *forum non conveniens* in wrongful-death cases.[39] Since Aérospatiale could not get the proceedings stayed or dismissed in Texas, its only chance was to apply to the courts of Brunei for an antisuit injunction against the widow. The Brunei courts refused to grant it, and Aérospatiale appealed to the Privy Council in London.

Lord Goff of Chieveley

The law relating to injunctions restraining a party from commencing or pursuing legal proceedings in a foreign jurisdiction has a long history, stretching back at least as far as the early nineteenth century. From an early stage, certain basic principles emerged which are now beyond dispute. First, the jurisdiction is to be exercised when the 'ends of justice' require it . . . This fundamental principle has been reasserted in recent years . . . Second, where the court decides to grant an injunction restraining proceedings in a foreign court, its order is directed not against the foreign court but against the parties so proceeding or threatening to proceed. As Sir John Leach V-C said in *Bushby* v. *Munday* 5 Madd. 297, 307:

> 'If a defendant who is ordered by this court to discontinue a proceeding which he has commenced against the plaintiff, in some other Court of Justice, either in this country or abroad, thinks fit to disobey that order, and to prosecute such proceeding, this court does not pretend to any interference with the other court; it acts upon the defendant by punishment for his contempt in his disobedience to the order of the court . . .'

There are, of course, many other statements in the cases to the same effect. Third, it follows that an injunction will only be issued restraining a party who is amenable to the jurisdiction of the court against whom an injunction will be an effective remedy . . . Fourth, it has been emphasised on many occasions that, since such an order indirectly affects the foreign court, the jurisdiction is one which must be exercised with caution . . . All of this is, their Lordships think, uncontroversial; but it has to be recognised that it does not provide very much guidance to judges at first instance who have to decide whether or not to exercise the jurisdiction in any particular case.

The decided cases, stretching back over a hundred years and more, provide however a useful source of experience from which guidance may be drawn. They

---

39 The Texas courts had jurisdiction because Aérospatiale sold its aircraft there; it thus had sufficient contacts to establish general jurisdiction over it.

show, moreover, judges seeking to apply the fundamental principles in certain categories of case, while at the same time never asserting that the jurisdiction is to be confined to those categories. Their Lordships were helpfully taken through many of the authorities by counsel in the present case. One such category of case arises where an estate is being administered in this country, or a petition in bankruptcy has been presented in this country, or winding up proceedings have been commenced here, and an injunction is granted to restrain a person from seeking, by foreign proceedings, to obtain the sole benefit of certain foreign assets. In such cases, it may be said that the purpose of the injunction is to protect the jurisdiction of the English court. Indeed, one of their Lordships has been inclined to think that such an idea generally underlies the jurisdiction to grant injunctions restraining the pursuit of foreign proceedings . . . but their Lordships are persuaded that this is too narrow a view. Another important category of case in which injunctions may be granted is where the plaintiff has commenced proceedings against the defendant in respect of the same subject matter both in this country and overseas, and the defendant has asked the English court to compel the plaintiff to elect in which country he shall alone proceed. In such cases, there is authority that the court will only restrain the plaintiff from pursuing the foreign proceedings if the pursuit of such proceedings is regarded as vexatious or oppressive . . . Since in these cases the court has been presented with a choice whether to restrain the foreign proceedings or to stay the English proceedings, we find in them the germ of the idea that the same test (i.e. whether the relevant proceedings are vexatious or oppressive) is applicable in both classes of case, an idea which was to bear fruit in the statement of principle by Scott LJ in *St Pierre* v. *South American Stores* . . . [1936] 1 KB 382, 398 in relation to staying proceedings in this country, a statement of principle now overlaid by the adoption in such cases of the Scottish principle of *forum non conveniens*, which has been gratefully incorporated into English law.

The old principle that an injunction may be granted to restrain the pursuit of foreign proceedings on the grounds of vexation or oppression, though it should not be regarded as the only ground upon which the jurisdiction may be exercised, is of such importance, and of such apparent relevance in the present case, that it is desirable to examine it in a little detail. As with the basic principle of justice underlying the whole of this jurisdiction, it has been emphasised that the notions of vexation and oppression should not be restricted by definition. As Bowen LJ said in *McHenry* v. *Lewis* 22 Ch D 397, 407–408:

> 'I agree that it would be most unwise, unless one was actually driven to do so for the purpose of deciding this case, to lay down any definition of what is vexatious or oppressive, or to draw a circle, so to speak, round this court unnecessarily, and to say that it will not move outside it. I would much rather rest on the general principle that the court can and will interfere whenever there is vexation and oppression to prevent the administration of justice being perverted for an unjust end. I would rather do that than attempt to define what vexation and oppression mean; they must vary with the circumstances of each case.'

In *Peruvian Guano Co.* v. *Bockwoldt* (1883) 23 Ch D 225, 230, Jessel MR gave two examples of vexatious proceedings. One, which he called pure vexation, occurs when the proceedings are so utterly absurd that they cannot possibly succeed. Another occurs when the plaintiff, not intending to annoy or harass the defendant, but thinking he could get some fanciful advantage, sues him in two courts at the same time under the same jurisdiction. He went on to say that similar, although not perhaps the same, considerations apply in a case where the actions are brought, one in a foreign country and one in this country. Referring to *McHenry* v. *Lewis* [above], he summed up the position as follows: that it is not vexatious to bring an action in each country where there are substantial reasons of benefit to the plaintiff. Now, it is easy to see why in many cases this is so, as indeed the 19th century cases show. For example, there may be assets available for execution in a foreign country, or another party may only be amenable to the jurisdiction of the courts of the foreign country. Indeed, it has been stressed that there is no presumption that a multiplicity of proceedings is vexatious . . . and that proceedings are not to be regarded as vexatious merely because they are brought in an inconvenient place . . . But their Lordships, bearing in mind the words of caution expressed by Bowen LJ in *McHenry* v. *Lewis* . . . quoted above, think it wise to remember the breadth of the jurisdiction. In particular, the possibility must be borne in mind that foreign proceedings may be restrained not only where they are vexatious, in the sense of being frivolous or useless, but also where they are oppressive; and also that, as Bowen LJ observed, everything depends on the circumstances of the particular case, and new circumstances have emerged which were not, perhaps, foreseen by our Victorian predecessors. Their Lordships refer, in particular, to the fact that litigants may now be encouraged to proceed in foreign jurisdictions, having no connection with the subject matter of the dispute, which exercise an exceptionally broad jurisdiction and which offer such great inducements, in particular greatly enhanced, even punitive, damages, that they may tempt litigants to pursue their remedies there. In normal circumstances, application of the now very widely recognised principle of *forum non conveniens* should ensure that the foreign court will itself, where appropriate, decline to exercise its own jurisdiction, especially as the existence of any particular advantage to the plaintiff in that jurisdiction (e.g. availability of assets for execution within the jurisdiction) can usually be protected, if thought appropriate, by granting a stay upon terms. But a stay may not be granted; and if, in particular, the English court concludes that it is the natural forum for the adjudication of the relevant dispute, and that by proceeding in the foreign court the plaintiff is acting oppressively, the English court may, in the interests of justice, grant an injunction restraining the plaintiff from pursuing the proceedings in the foreign court. As Bowen LJ said in *Peruvian Guano Co.* v. *Bockwoldt* 23 Ch D 225, 233, the court will interfere when a party is acting under colour of asking for justice 'in a way which necessarily involves injustice' to others.

[Lord Goff then considered the view that the test applied to decide whether to stay English proceedings on the ground of *forum non conveniens* should also be used to determine whether an antisuit injunction should be granted. This would mean that the English courts would grant an antisuit injunction whenever they considered the English courts to be the natural forum, unless justice required that the claimant should be allowed to continue the proceedings in the foreign jurisdiction. He rejected this approach on the ground that it would be inconsistent with comity and with the fundamental requirement that an injunction will only be granted where the ends of justice so require. He then continued:]

In the opinion of their Lordships, in a case such as the present where a remedy for a particular wrong is available both in the English (or, as here, the Brunei) court and in a foreign court, the English or Brunei court will, generally speaking, only restrain the plaintiff from pursuing proceedings in the foreign court if such pursuit would be vexatious or oppressive. This presupposes that, as a general rule, the English or Brunei court must conclude that it provides the natural forum for the trial of the action; and further, since the court is concerned with the ends of justice, that account must be taken not only of injustice to the defendant if the plaintiff is allowed to pursue the foreign proceedings, but also of injustice to the plaintiff if he is not allowed to do so. So the court will not grant an injunction if, by doing so, it will deprive the plaintiff of advantages in the foreign forum of which it would be unjust to deprive him. Fortunately, however, as the present case shows, that problem can often be overcome by appropriate undertakings given by the defendant, or by granting an injunction upon appropriate terms; just as, in cases of stay of proceedings, the parallel problem of advantages to the plaintiff in the domestic forum which is, *prima facie*, inappropriate, can likewise often be solved by granting a stay upon terms.

Lord Goff then applied the law he had laid down to the facts of the case. He first said that Brunei was the natural forum. The fact that extensive pre-trial discovery had already taken place in Texas did not alter this fact. As regards the requirement of injustice to the defendant, it could not be argued that the application of Texas law on strict liability, punitive damages or jury trial would be unjust to the defendant, since the claimant had undertaken to waive these rights. However, it seemed that the cause of the crash might have been faulty maintenance by the operators of the helicopter. Thus, if Aérospatiale were found liable, it would want to claim a contribution from the operators. They were probably not subject to Texas jurisdiction – the issue was being contested before the Texas courts at the time – and, if they were not, Aérospatiale would have to bring separate proceedings against them in Brunei. The problem with this was that it was uncertain whether Aérospatiale could rely on the Texas judgment against the operator to establish that they were liable to the widow. Consequently, they might have to pay the widow, without being able to recover from the operator. According to Lord Goff, it was this fact that made the Texas proceedings unjust. As far as injustice to the claimant was concerned, Aérospatiale was willing to give various undertakings to ensure that this did not occur. The injunction was, therefore, made subject to a number of conditions: Aérospatiale had to provide security to ensure that any judgment given against it would be satisfied; it had to provide various documents; the Texas proceedings were to continue until pre-trial discovery was complete; the costs of the Texas proceedings were to be treated as costs in the Brunei proceedings; Aérospatiale was to co-operate in the temporary admission to the Brunei bar of the Texas attorneys; and it was to do everything possible to ensure that the documents obtained in the Texas proceedings were admitted in the Brunei proceedings. Thus, the appeal was allowed and an injunction granted.

It will be seen from this case that subjective factors – what justice requires – play an even greater role with regard to antisuit injunctions. This is probably inevitable. However, since an antisuit injunction could be regarded as interfering with the other court, it is important that it should be used only in exceptional cases. Opinions may differ as to whether the facts in the *Aérospatiale* case were sufficiently exceptional. However, many cases exist in which the grant of an antisuit injunction is clearly right. *Fakih Brothers* v. *A. P. Moller*[40] is an example. In some ways, this was a fairly standard case. It is only a decision at first instance: the judgment was so clearly right that no appeal was taken. Moller was a Danish shipowner (Maersk Lines). One of their ships delivered a cargo to Sierra Leone in Africa. The recipients were Fakih Brothers, a firm domiciled in Sierra Leone. They claimed short delivery. Moller said the claim was fraudulent. Fakih Brothers subsequently threatened to arrest one of Moller's vessels in England.[41] To prevent this, Moller agreed to accept the jurisdiction of the English courts and put up security to cover the claim. In return, Fakih Brothers agreed not to arrest any of Moller's vessels anywhere in the world in respect of the claim. Proceedings began in England, but shortly afterwards Fakih Brothers arrested one of Moller's ships in Sierra Leone and began proceedings there on the claim. At Moller's request, the English court granted an antisuit injunction. Since Fakih Brothers appeared to have had assets in England, this could be enforced. It is in cases such as this that the value of antisuit injunctions becomes apparent.

As was said in the *Aérospatiale* case, an antisuit injunction should not be granted just because the court asked to grant it thinks that it is the natural forum. *Du Pont* v. *Agnew*, discussed above, is a good example. It will be recalled that, in the *Du Pont* case, there was a contract of insurance between an English insurer and an American company. The question was whether the insurer had to indemnify the company for punitive damages. Under the law of Illinois, the state where the liability had been incurred, this was against public policy. Under English law, the position was uncertain. The English court considered that English law and English public policy should be applied; the Illinois court considered that Illinois law and Illinois public policy should be applied. In view of this difference, the American company wanted the case decided in England, and brought proceedings there. The insurer sued in Illinois for a declaration of non-liability. The American court thought that it was the appropriate forum and refused the application for a stay on *forum-non-conveniens* grounds made by the American company. The English court thought that *it* was the appropriate forum and refused the application for a stay made by the insurer.

In subsequent proceedings in England,[42] the American company asked the English court for an antisuit injunction to preclude the insurer from continuing

---

40 [1994] 1 Lloyd's Rep 103.
41 This was unnecessary since the bills of lading contained a choice-of-court clause giving jurisdiction to the English courts. Any judgment given against Moller could have been enforced in Denmark under the Brussels Convention.
42 *Du Pont* v. *Agnew (No. 2)* [1988] 2 Lloyd's Rep 240 (CA).

the American proceedings. The English court refused this. The American court had previously refused to grant an injunction to preclude the American company from continuing the English proceedings. Each court thought that it was the appropriate forum, but neither granted an injunction.[43]

Though it is not enough for the English court to believe that it is the natural forum, it will not normally grant an injunction if it does not believe this. This is illustrated by the decision of the House of Lords in *Airbus Industrie* v. *Patel*,[44] a case that arose out of a crash of an Airbus aircraft in India. The families of the victims had claimed compensation in India from the airline and the airport authority, but they had been able to obtain only a small sum. They then sued the manufacturers in Texas. Patel and some of the other claimants were resident in England; so the manufacturers asked the English courts to grant an antisuit injunction.[45] The situation was similar to that in the *Aérospatiale* case, but there was one vital difference: in *Aérospatiale*, the crash had taken place in Brunei, and Brunei was the natural forum; in *Airbus*, on the other hand, the crash had occurred in a third country, India, and the English courts were not the natural forum. For this reason, the House of Lords refused to grant the injunction: according to Lord Goff, who gave the leading judgment, the English courts should not 'take it on themselves to act as policeman of the world'.[46]

§ 2.3   Conclusions

The final result is best summed up in the words of Lord Goff in *Airbus*:[47]

> This part of the law is concerned with the resolution of clashes between jurisdictions. Two different approaches to the problem have emerged in the world today, one associated with the civil law jurisdictions of continental Europe, and the other with the common law world. Each is the fruit of a distinctive legal history, and also reflects to some extent cultural differences which are beyond the scope of an opinion such as this. On the continent of Europe, in the early days of the European Community, the essential need was seen to be to avoid any such clash between Member States of the same community. A system, developed by distinguished scholars, was embodied in the Brussels Convention on Jurisdiction and the Enforcement of Judgments in Civil and Commercial Matters (1968) (Schedule 1 to the Civil Jurisdiction and Judgments Act 1982), under which

---

43 What normally happens in a situation such as this is that the judgment given first is conclusive in the other proceedings, either as *res judicata* or on the basis of issue estoppel. (Under *res judicata*, also known as 'estoppel *per rem judicatam*', the final ruling or order would be binding in the other proceedings, provided the parties were the same and the issue was the same; under issue estoppel, known in the United States as 'issue preclusion' or 'collateral estoppel', a ruling on a preliminary issue can also be binding.) In the English proceedings, the American company tried to obtain an injunction precluding the insurer from relying on the American judgment in the English proceedings. This was also refused, as was an application for a declaration that it could not rely on the American judgment. It is not known what happened in the end, though as the American court was likely to give judgment first, the insurer appears to have been in the stronger position.
44 [1999] 1 AC 119; [1998] 2 WLR 686; [1998] 2 All ER 257 (HL).
45 The Indian courts had already granted an antisuit injunction, but, as the defendants were not subject to Indian jurisdiction, this could not be enforced.
46 [1999] 1 AC 119 at p. 121.
47 *Ibid.*, pp. 131–3.

jurisdiction is allocated on the basis of well-defined rules. This system achieves its purpose, but at a price. The price is rigidity, and rigidity can be productive of injustice. The judges of this country, who loyally enforce this system, not only between United Kingdom jurisdictions and the jurisdictions of other Member States, but also as between the three jurisdictions within the United Kingdom itself, have to accept the fact that the practical results are from time to time unwelcome. This is essentially because the primary purpose of the Convention is to ensure that there shall be no clash between the jurisdictions of Member States of the Community.

In the common law world, the situation is precisely the opposite. There is, so to speak, a jungle of separate, broadly based, jurisdictions all over the world. In England, for example, jurisdiction is founded on the presence of the defendant within the jurisdiction, and in certain specified (but widely drawn) circumstances on a power to serve the defendant with process outside the jurisdiction. But the potential excesses of common law jurisdictions are generally curtailed by the adoption of the principle of *forum non conveniens* – a self-denying ordinance under which the court will stay (or dismiss) proceedings in favour of another clearly more appropriate forum ... The principle is directed against cases being brought in inappropriate jurisdictions and so tends to ensure that, as between common law jurisdictions, cases will only be brought in a jurisdiction which is appropriate for their resolution. The purpose of the principle is therefore different from that which underlies the Brussels Convention. It cannot, and does not aim to, avoid all clashes between jurisdictions; indeed parallel proceedings in different jurisdictions are not of themselves regarded as unacceptable. In that sense the principle may be regarded as an imperfect weapon; but it is both flexible and practical and, where it is effective, it produces a result which is conducive to practical justice. It is however dependent on the voluntary adoption of the principle by the state in question; and, as the present case shows, if one state does not adopt the principle,[1] the delicate balance which the universal adoption of the principle could achieve will to that extent break down.

1 *Editor's note*: at the time of the *Airbus* case, Texas did not apply *forum non conveniens* in wrongful-death actions.

§ 3   The United States

§ 3.1   *Forum non conveniens*

The United States adopted the doctrine of *forum non conveniens* before England did, partly as a way of relieving congestion in the court system. The first Supreme Court decision was *Gulf Oil* v. *Gilbert*,[48] decided in 1947. Jackson J gave the judgment of the court. He divided the factors to be considered into two categories, private-interest factors and public-interest factors. With regard to the former, he said:[49]

48 330 US 501; 67 S Ct 839; 91 L Ed 1055 (1947).
49 At p. 508.

Important considerations are the relative ease of access to sources of proof; availability of compulsory process for attendance of unwilling, and the cost of obtaining attendance of willing, witnesses; possibility of view of premises, if view would be appropriate to the action; and all other practical problems that make trial of a case easy, expeditious and inexpensive. There may also be questions as to the enforceability of a judgment if one is obtained. The court will weigh relative advantages and obstacles to fair trial. It is often said that the plaintiff may not, by choice of an inconvenient forum, 'vex', 'harass', or 'oppress' the defendant by inflicting upon him expense or trouble not necessary to his own right to pursue his remedy. But unless the balance is strongly in favor of the defendant, the plaintiff's choice of forum should rarely be disturbed.

With regard to the latter, he said:[50]

Factors of public interest also have place in applying the doctrine. Administrative difficulties follow for courts when litigation is piled up in congested centers instead of being handled at its origin. Jury duty[51] is a burden that ought not to be imposed upon the people of a community which has no relation to the litigation. In cases which touch the affairs of many persons, there is reason for holding the trial in their view and reach rather than in remote parts of the country where they can learn of it by report only. There is a local interest in having localized controversies decided at home. There is an appropriateness, too, in having the trial of a diversity case[52] in a forum that is at home with the state law that must govern the case, rather than having a court in some other forum untangle problems in conflict of laws, and in law foreign to itself.

This shows a significant difference compared with England: English courts normally consider only the private interests of the parties.

The *Gulf Oil* case concerned a conflict of jurisdiction between two American states. The way the doctrine applies in international cases is illustrated by our next case.

United States
Piper Aircraft* v. *Reyno
US Supreme Court
454 US 235; 102 S Ct 252; 70 L Ed 2d 419 (1981)

Background

A light aircraft made by an American company, Piper Aircraft, crashed in Scotland. A British company owned the aircraft, and all the victims were British. A British Government investigation found no evidence that the aircraft was defective. Nevertheless, proceedings on behalf of the passengers were brought in a federal court in the United States against the manufacturers of the aircraft (Piper) and of the propeller (Hartzell).[53] The trial court dismissed[54] the case: it considered that Scotland was the appropriate forum. The Court of Appeals

---

50 At pp. 508–9.
51 *Editor's note*: in the United States, jury trials are common in civil actions.
52 A diversity case is a case brought in a federal court on the ground that the parties are citizens of different states. The applicable law is state law.
53 Proceedings against the owners and operators of the aircraft, and against the pilot's estate, were brought in Scotland.
54 American courts usually dismiss the case where *forum non conveniens* is established; English courts normally stay (suspend) the proceedings. In practice, there is no great difference.

reversed on the ground that proceedings in the Scottish court would be less favourable to the plaintiffs.

Justice Marshall delivered the opinion of the Court

II

The Court of Appeals erred in holding that plaintiffs may defeat a motion to dismiss on the ground of *forum non conveniens* merely by showing that the substantive law that would be applied in the alternative forum is less favorable to the plaintiffs than that of the present forum. The possibility of a change in substantive law should ordinarily not be given conclusive or even substantial weight in the *forum non conveniens* inquiry . . .

The Court of Appeals' decision is inconsistent with this Court's earlier *forum non conveniens* decisions in another respect. Those decisions have repeatedly emphasized the need to retain flexibility. In [*Gulf Oil Corporation v.*] *Gilbert*, the Court refused to identify specific circumstances 'which will justify or require either grant or denial of remedy . . .' And in *Williams* v. *Green Bay & Western R Co.*, 326 US 459, 557; 90 L Ed. 311; 66 S Ct 284 (1946) we stated that we would not lay down a rigid rule to govern discretion, and that '[e]ach case turns on its facts.' If central emphasis were placed on any one factor, the *forum non conveniens* doctrine would lose much of the very flexibility that makes it so valuable.

In fact, if conclusive or substantial weight were given to the possibility of a change in law, the *forum non conveniens* doctrine would become virtually useless. Jurisdiction and venue requirements are often easily satisfied. As a result, many plaintiffs are able to choose from among several forums. Ordinarily, these plaintiffs will select that forum whose choice-of-law rules are most advantageous. Thus, if the possibility of an unfavorable change in substantive law is given substantial weight in the *forum non conveniens* inquiry, dismissal would rarely be proper.

Except for the court below, every Federal Court of Appeals that has considered this question after *Gilbert* has held that dismissal on grounds of *forum non conveniens* may be granted even though the law applicable in the alternative forum is less favorable to the plaintiff's chance of recovery . . .

The Court of Appeals' approach is not only inconsistent with the purpose of the *forum non conveniens* doctrine, but also poses substantial practical problems. If the possibility of a change in law were given substantial weight, deciding motions to dismiss on the ground of *forum non conveniens* would become quite difficult. Choice-of-law analysis would become extremely important, and the courts would frequently be required to interpret the law of foreign jurisdictions. First, the trial court would have to determine what law would apply if the case were tried in the chosen forum, and what law would apply if the case were tried in the alternative forum. It would then have to compare the rights, remedies, and procedures available under the law that would be applied in each forum. Dismissal would be appropriate only if the court concluded that the law applied by the alternative forum is as favorable to the plaintiff as that of the chosen forum. The doctrine of *forum non conveniens*, however, is designed in part to help courts avoid conducting complex exercises in comparative law . . .

Upholding the decision of the Court of Appeals would result in other practical problems. At least where the foreign plaintiff named an American manufacturer as defendant, a court could not dismiss the case on grounds of *forum non conveniens* where dismissal might lead to an unfavorable change in law. The American courts, which are already extremely attractive to foreign plaintiffs, would become even more attractive. The flow of litigation into the United States would increase and further congest already crowded courts . . .

III

The Court of Appeals also erred in rejecting the District Court's *Gilbert* analysis . . .

A

The District Court acknowledged that there is ordinarily a strong presumption in favor of the plaintiff's choice of forum, which may be overcome only when the private and public interest factors clearly point towards trial in the alternative forum. It held, however, that the presumption applies with less force when the plaintiff or real parties in interest are foreign.[1]

The District Court's distinction between resident or citizen plaintiffs and foreign plaintiffs is fully justified. In *Koster* [*v. Lumbermens Mut. Cas. Co.*], the Court indicated that a plaintiff's choice of forum is entitled to greater deference when the plaintiff has chosen the home forum. 330 US, at 524; 91 L Ed. 2d 1067; 67 S Ct 828. When the home forum has been chosen, it is reasonable to assume that this choice is convenient. When the plaintiff is foreign, however, this assumption is much less reasonable. Because the central purpose of any *forum non conveniens* inquiry is to ensure that the trial is convenient, a foreign plaintiff's choice deserves less deference.

B

The *forum non conveniens* determination is committed to the sound discretion of the trial court. It may be reversed only when there has been a clear abuse of discretion; where the court has considered all relevant public and private interest factors, and where its balancing of these factors is reasonable, its decision deserves substantial deference . . . Here, the Court of Appeals expressly acknowledged that the standard of review was one of abuse of discretion. In examining the District Court's analysis of the public and private interests, however, the Court of Appeals seems to have lost sight of this rule, and substituted its own judgment for that of the District Court.

(1)

In analyzing the private interest factors, the District Court stated that the connections with Scotland are 'overwhelming . . .' This characterization may be somewhat exaggerated. Particularly with respect to the question of relative ease of access to sources of proof, the private interests point in both directions.

---

1 *Editor's note*: the nominal plaintiff, Reyno, was an American appointed by a California probate court as administratrix of the estates of the five passengers. She did not know any of them; she was a legal secretary to the attorney who filed the lawsuit.

As respondent emphasizes, records concerning the design, manufacture, and testing of the propeller and plane are located in the United States. She would have greater access to sources of proof relevant to her strict liability and negligence theories if trial were held here. However, the District Court did not act unreasonably in concluding that fewer evidentiary problems would be posed if the trial were held in Scotland. A large proportion of the relevant evidence is located in Great Britain . . .

The District Court correctly concluded that the problems posed by the inability to implead potential third-party defendants clearly supported holding the trial in Scotland . . . If Piper and Hartzell can show that the accident was caused not by a design defect, but rather by the negligence of the pilot, the plane's owners, or the charter company, they will be relieved of all liability. It is true, of course, that if Hartzell and Piper were found liable after a trial in the United States, they could institute an action for indemnity or contribution against these parties in Scotland. It would be far more convenient, however, to resolve all claims in one trial. The Court of Appeals rejected this argument. Forcing petitioners to rely on actions for indemnity or contributions would be 'burdensome' but not 'unfair . . .' Finding that trial in the plaintiff's chosen forum would be burdensome, however, is sufficient to support dismissal on grounds of *forum non conveniens* . . .

(2)

The District Court's review of the factors relating to the public interest was also reasonable. On the basis of its choice-of-law analysis, it concluded that if the case were tried in the Middle District of Pennsylvania, Pennsylvania law would apply to Piper and Scottish law to Hartzell. It stated that a trial involving two sets of laws would be confusing to the jury. It also noted its own lack of familiarity with Scottish law. Consideration of these problems was clearly appropriate under *Gilbert*; in that case we explicitly held that the need to apply foreign law pointed towards dismissal. The Court of Appeals found that the District Court's choice-of-law analysis was incorrect, and that American law would apply to both Hartzell and Piper. Thus, lack of familiarity with foreign law would not be a problem. Even if the Court of Appeals' conclusion is correct, however, all other public interest factors favored trial in Scotland.

Scotland has a very strong interest in this litigation. The accident occurred in its airspace. All of the decedents were Scottish. Apart from Piper and Hartzell, all potential plaintiffs and defendants are either Scottish or English. As we stated in *Gilbert*, there is 'a local interest in having localized controversies decided at home . . .' Respondent argues that American citizens have an interest in ensuring that American manufacturers are deterred from producing defective products, and that additional deterrence might be obtained if Piper and Hartzell were tried in the United States, where they could be sued on the basis of both negligence and strict liability. However, the incremental deterrence that would be gained if this trial were held in an American court is likely to be insignificant. The American interest in this accident is simply not sufficient to justify the enormous commitment of judicial time and resources that would inevitably be required if the case were to be tried here.

IV

The Court of Appeals erred in holding that the possibility of an unfavorable change in law bars dismissal on the ground of *forum non conveniens*. It also erred in rejecting the District Court's *Gilbert* analysis. The District Court properly decided that the presumption in favor of the respondent's forum choice applied with less than maximum force because the real parties in interest are foreign. It did not act unreasonably in deciding that the private interests pointed towards trial in Scotland. Nor did it act unreasonably in deciding that the public interests favored trial in Scotland. Thus, the judgment of the Court of Appeals is

Reversed.

Comment

This shows an approach similar to that of the English courts in cases like *Spiliada*. All the factors were considered without undue predominance being given to any one of them. However, the policy of favouring local plaintiffs does not seem to apply in England. Nor, as we shall see, do English courts take public-interest factors into account: they consider only the interests of the parties and of justice.[55]

In *Piper Aircraft*, the real plaintiffs were foreign, and the defendants were American. Where the plaintiff is American and the defendants foreign, American courts seem to be significantly more reluctant to dismiss the proceedings. *Rudetsky* v. *O'Dowd*[56] is an example. In many ways, this was a run-of-the-mill case and there appears to have been no appeal from the decision of the trial judge. Its only distinguishing feature was that the defendant, O'Dowd, was a well-known English pop singer, whose stage name was 'Boy George'. Michael Rudetsky, an American, had contracted with O'Dowd and his agents in New York to work in London. O'Dowd was to provide Rudetsky with accommodation. Two days later, while working with O'Dowd in London, Rudetsky ingested heroin. When it appeared that he was not well, O'Dowd put him to bed. The next morning, he died of morphine intoxication. Michael's mother, Mrs Rudetsky, held O'Dowd to blame for not providing proper medical care. She sued him in New York.[57] O'Dowd asked to have the case dismissed on *forum-non-conveniens* grounds.

The case was clearly more closely connected with England. Michael's death took place there; the evidence was there; and English law was applicable. The only significant factor in favour of New York was that Mrs Rudetsky said she would have difficulty in bringing proceedings in England. She was not poor enough to obtain the (government-funded) legal aid then available to litigants, but was not rich enough to afford to pay an English lawyer. If she lost the case, she would have to pay both her own lawyer and her opponent's lawyer.[58] In New

---

55 See the judgment of Lord Hope in *Lubbe* v. *Cape plc*, set out in Chapter 12, § 2.3, below.
56 660 F Supp 341 (Eastern District of New York, 1987).
57 It is not clear on what ground the New York courts had jurisdiction, but it was probably because the employment contract with Rudetsky was concluded in New York. In any event, O'Dowd did not contest the issue.
58 At the time, conditional-fee agreements (the English equivalent of US contingent-fee agreements) were not available in England.

York, on the other hand, she could obtain an attorney on a contingent-fee basis: if she lost, she would have to pay nothing; if she won, she would give him a percentage of her winnings. She would not have to pay her opponent's attorney even if she lost.

In some ways, this argument was the reverse of that put before the English court in the *Roneleigh* case. The American court regarded it as important, though not decisive. It weighed all the factors up and decided to let the case continue. It emphasized that the plaintiff's choice of forum is entitled to even greater deference than usual when she has chosen her home court.

§ 3.2   Antisuit injunctions

The American law on antisuit injunctions is much the same as that in England. Although some decisions suggest that they will be granted only in very limited circumstances,[59] other cases show that this is not so.[60] Ironically, most international antisuit cases seem to involve English courts granting injunctions with regard to proceedings in American courts or *vice versa*.

§ 4   Conclusions

This survey shows that common-law judges make a strenuous effort to ensure that the case is decided in the most suitable court. This necessarily involves a subjective factor, which produces uncertainty. If they are to be criticized, however, it is probably because they do not stay or dismiss proceedings often enough, rather than because they deprive the claimant of his rightful forum.

Further reading

Bell (Andrew), *Forum Shopping and Venue in Transnational Litigation* (Oxford University Press, Oxford, 2003)
  'The Negative Declaration in Transnational Litigation' (1995) 111 LQR 674
Briggs, 'The Impact of Recent Judgments of the European Court on English Procedural Law and Practice' (2005) 124 II *Zeitschrift für Schweizerisches Recht* 231
Fawcett (James J.) (ed.), *Declining Jurisdiction in Private International Law: Reports to the XIVth Congress of the International Academy of Comparative Law, Athens, August 1994* (Clarendon Press, Oxford, 1995)
Fentiman, 'Civil Jurisdiction and Third States: *Owusu* and After' (2006) 43 *Common Market Law Review* 705
Garnett, 'Stay of Proceedings in Australia: A "Clearly Inappropriate" Test?' (1999) 23 *Melbourne University Law Review* 30
Harris, 'Stay of Proceedings and the Brussels Convention' (2005) 54 ICLQ 933

---

59 See, for example, *Laker Airways* v. *Sabena*, 731 F 2d 909 (DC Cir. 1984).
60 See, for example, *Seattle Totems Hockey Club* v. *National Hockey League*, 652 F 2d 852 (9th Cir. 1981); cert. denied, 457 US 1105 (1982).

Hartley, 'Comity and the Use of Antisuit Injunctions in International Litigation' (1987) 35 *American Journal of Comparative Law* 487

Merrett, 'Uncertainties in the First Limb of the *Spiliada* Test' (2005) 54 ICLQ 211

O'Brien, 'Transnational Injunction' (1989) 12 *Adelaide Law Review* 201

Prince, 'Bhopal, Bougainville and Ok Tedi: Why Australia's Forum Non Conveniens Approach Is Better' (1998) 47 ICLQ 573

Pryles, 'Judicial Darkness on the Oceanic Sun' (1988) 62 *Australian Law Journal* 774

Robertson, 'Forum Non Conveniens in England and America: A Rather Fantastic Fiction' (1987) 103 LQR 398

Slater, 'Forum Non Conveniens: A View from the Shop Floor' (1988) 104 LQR 554

Takahashi, 'Forum Non-Conveniens Discretion in Third Party Proceedings' (2002) 51 ICLQ 127

Westbrook, 'International Judicial Negotiation' (2003) 38 *Texas International Law Journal* 567

CHAPTER 10

Overlapping jurisdiction in EC law

Since EC law is – in practice, if not in theory – based on the civil law, it is hardly surprising that the doctrine of *forum non conveniens* finds no place in the scheme established by the Brussels I Regulation. Instead, the doctrine of *lis pendens* is laid down in Article 27.

§ 1 Lis pendens

Article 27 of the Regulation[1] (set out in Panel 10.1) provides that, where proceedings involving the same cause of action and between the same parties are brought in the courts of different Member States, any court other than the court first seised must of its own motion stay its proceedings until such time as the jurisdiction of the court first seised is established. Once this occurs, it must decline jurisdiction in favour of that court.

Panel 10.1 Lis pendens: related actions
Brussels I Regulation (Regulation 44/2001), Articles 27–30

Article 27

1. Where proceedings involving the same cause of action and between the same parties are brought in the courts of different Member States, any court other than the court first seised shall of its own motion stay its proceedings until such time as the jurisdiction of the court first seised is established.
2. Where the jurisdiction of the court first seised is established, any court other than the court first seised shall decline jurisdiction in favour of that court.

Article 28

1. Where related actions are pending in the courts of different Member States, any court other than the court first seised may stay its proceedings.
2. Where these actions are pending at first instance, any court other than the court first seised may also, on the application of one of the parties, decline jurisdiction if the court first seised has jurisdiction over the actions in question and its law permits the consolidation thereof.
3. For the purposes of this Article, actions are deemed to be related where they are so closely connected that it is expedient to hear and determine them together to avoid the risk of irreconcilable judgments resulting from separate proceedings.

Article 29

Where actions come within the exclusive jurisdiction of several courts, any court other than the court first seised shall decline jurisdiction in favour of that court.

---

1 The equivalent provision in the Convention is Article 21.

Article 30

For the purposes of this Section, a court shall be deemed to be seised:

1. at the time when the document instituting the proceedings or an equivalent document is lodged with the court, provided that the plaintiff has not subsequently failed to take the steps he was required to take to have service effected on the defendant, or
2. if the document has to be served before being lodged with the court, at the time when it is received by the authority responsible for service, provided that the plaintiff has not subsequently failed to take the steps he was required to take to have the document lodged with the court.

Under the Brussels Convention, there was considerable dispute as to when a court was seised for the purpose of the *lis pendens* rule;[2] the Regulation therefore lays down a uniform rule. This is in Article 30, which contains two paragraphs. Under the first paragraph, a court is deemed to be seised when the claim form (or equivalent document) is lodged with the court, provided the claimant subsequently takes the necessary steps to ensure that service is effected. The second paragraph deals with the situation where the claim form is served before being lodged with the court: it provides that the court is seised when the claim form is received by the authority responsible for service.

English procedure comes under the first paragraph. Proceedings are commenced when the court issues a claim form at the request of the claimant. The date of issue is entered on the form by the court. This is the date on which the court is seised for the purpose of Article 30. The claim form is then served by the claimant or by the court on his behalf. When the claim form is issued, a copy is deposited in the records of the court and this would constitute lodging with the court.

In spite of this clarification, two problems remain: the meaning of 'the same cause of action' and the meaning of 'between the same parties'.

§ 1.1   *The same cause of action*

This problem came before the European Court in our next case.

European Community
Gubisch Maschinenfabrik* v. *Palumbo
Court of Justice of the European Communities
Case 144/86, [1987] ECR 4861

Background

This case concerned a contract for the sale of goods between a German seller and an Italian buyer. The seller sued the buyer in Germany for the price of the goods; the buyer subsequently sued the seller in Italy for rescission of the contract. It was argued in the Italian proceedings that the *lis pendens* rule applied and

---

2 In *Zelger* v. *Salinitri No. 2*, Case 128/83, [1984] ECR 2397, the European Court held that, in order to determine at what moment in the procedure a court is seised of a case, one must apply the *lex fori* of that court. Thus, if the contest is between a German court and an Italian court, German law decides when the German court is seised and Italian law decides when the Italian court is seised.

that the Italian court should decline jurisdiction. This depended upon whether the two sets of proceedings were to be regarded as involving the same cause of action.

Judgment

[After stating that Community law must decide what constitutes the same cause of action, the court said:]

14. It must be observed first of all that according to its wording Article 21 applies where two actions are between the same parties and involve the same cause of action and the same subject-matter; it does not lay down any further conditions. Even though the German version of Article 21 does not expressly distinguish between the terms 'subject-matter' and 'cause of action', it must be construed in the same manner as the other language versions, all of which make that distinction.

15. In the procedural situation which has given rise to the question submitted for a preliminary ruling the same parties are engaged in two legal proceedings in different Contracting States which are based on the same 'cause of action', that is to say the same contractual relationship. The problem which arises, therefore, is whether those two actions have the same 'subject-matter' when the first seeks to enforce the contract and the second seeks its rescission or discharge.

16. In particular, in a case such as this, involving the international sale of tangible moveable property, it is apparent that the action to enforce the contract is aimed at giving effect to it, and that the action for its rescission or discharge is aimed precisely at depriving it of any effect. The question whether the contract is binding therefore lies at the heart of the two actions. If it is the action for rescission or discharge of the contract that is brought subsequently, it may even be regarded as simply a defence against the first action, brought in the form of independent proceedings before a court in another Contracting State.

17. In those procedural circumstances it must be held that the two actions have the same subject-matter, for that concept cannot be restricted so as to mean two claims which are entirely identical.

18. If, in circumstances such as those of this case, the questions at issue concerning a single international sales contract were not decided solely by the court before which the action to enforce the contract is pending and which was seised first, there would be a danger for the party seeking enforcement that under Article 27 (3) a judgment given in his favour might not be recognized, even though any defence put forward by the defendant alleging that the contract was not binding had not been accepted. There can be no doubt that a judgment given in a Contracting State requiring performance of the contract would not be recognized in the State in which recognition was sought if a court in that State had given a judgment rescinding or discharging the contract. Such a result, restricting the effects of each judgment to the territory of the State concerned, would run counter to the objectives of the Convention, which is intended to strengthen legal

> protection throughout the territory of the Community and to facilitate recognition in each Contracting State of judgments given in any other Contracting State.
>
> 19.   The answer to the question submitted by the national court must therefore be that the concept of *lis pendens* pursuant to Article 21 of the [Brussels Convention] covers a case where a party brings an action before a court in a Contracting State for the rescission or discharge of an international sales contract whilst an action by the other party to enforce the same contract is pending before a court in another Contracting State.

Comment

This case shows that the European Court gives a fairly wide meaning to the idea of the same cause of action. It seems that, if the orders sought in the two sets of proceedings could contradict one another, the proceedings will be held to be the same.

§ 1.2   The same parties

What is the position where some, but not all, of the parties are the same? Assume, for example, that A and B sue C and D in State X, while A and E subsequently sue D and F in State Y? The European Court considered this question in *The Maciej Rataj (The Tatry)*,[3] an Admiralty case referred to it by a court in England: it held that, where some but not all of the parties to the second action are the same as the parties to the first action, the *lis pendens* rule applies only to the extent to which the parties *are* the same;[4] consequently, in the example given above, the court in State Y, being the court seised second, would be required to stay the proceedings (or decline jurisdiction) with regard to A's claim against D, but could otherwise let the case continue.[5]

§ 1.3   Related proceedings

Article 28 of the Regulation[6] (set out in Panel 10.1, above) is as near as Community law gets to recognizing the doctrine of *forum non conveniens*, though it must be admitted that it does not really get very near. What Article 28 does is to provide that, where two sets of proceedings pending in courts of different Member States are related, the court seised second *may* stay the proceedings before it.[7] It therefore has a discretion – it is not obliged to stay them – and to this extent it resembles the common law doctrine. However, it applies only when both actions

---

3 Case C-406/92, [1994] ECR I-5439.
4 It held, however, that the application of the *lis pendens* rule is not affected by the fact that one set of proceedings might be *in personam* and the other *in rem*.
5 The court in State Y would be permitted (but not required) to stay the latter proceedings under Article 22 of the Convention (Article 28 of the Regulation), discussed below.
6 The equivalent provision in the Convention is Article 22.
7 Article 28 goes on to provide that, where the two actions are pending at first instance, the court seised second may, on the application of one of the parties, dismiss the proceedings before it, if the court first seised has jurisdiction over them and if its law permits the two actions to be consolidated.

have actually been commenced and it applies only to the court seised second: the court seised first is not permitted to stay its proceedings.

Article 28 will not apply if Article 27 applies; however, it is not easy to know exactly when a case will fall under the one and when it will fall under the other. If the parties are different, there is no problem: the case cannot fall under Article 27. The difficulty concerns the distinction between the 'same cause of action' under Article 27 and a related cause of action under Article 28. Article 28(3) defines 'related' by saying that two actions are deemed to be related 'where they are so closely connected that it is expedient to hear and determine them together to avoid the risk of irreconcilable judgments resulting from separate proceedings'. The problem with this definition is that the risk of irreconcilable judgments seems to have been a key element in the reasoning of the European Court in the *Gubisch* case (above) when it considered whether the two actions in that case involved the same cause of action.[8] No doubt, further judgments will be required before the matter is clarified.

§ 1.4 Conclusions

The *lis pendens* theory, as applied in Community law, attains its objective of ensuring that conflicts of jurisdiction are largely avoided. However, as Lord Goff said in *Airbus* (quoted in Chapter 9, § 2.3, above), it does this at a price – a price paid by the individual litigant, who may find that the proceedings go ahead in an inappropriate court. This is because the *lis pendens* doctrine is not intended primarily to benefit the individual litigant: it is intended to serve the public purpose of avoiding a dispute between two courts as to which should hear the case.

Articles 27 and 28 apply only if the other court is in a Member State. (The Lugano Convention applies equivalent provisions to cases where the other court is in a Lugano State.) Community law contains no rule on the position where the other court is in any other State. What happens in such a case is subject to acute controversy. One possibility is that Articles 27 and 28 are applied by analogy; another is that national law applies; the third possibility is that the foreign proceedings must be ignored. At the present time, it is impossible to tell which of these is correct.[9]

§ 2 Forum non conveniens

It is recognized in England, as much as anywhere else, that *forum non conveniens* has no place under the Regulation. The question is: when does a case fall under the Regulation for this purpose? In the past, the English courts took the view that the purpose of the Convention/Regulation was to regulate relations among the courts of the EC States; consequently, they considered that, if the

---

8 Paragraph 18 of the judgment.
9 In *Owusu* (below), the European Court was asked to rule on this, but it declined to do so.

more appropriate forum was outside the Community (and outside the Lugano States), the Convention or Regulation was inapplicable and the common law could apply.

The leading case was *Re Harrods (Buenos Aires) Ltd*.[10] Harrods (Buenos Aires) Ltd was a company incorporated in England which did all its business outside England. It had no connection with the well-known London department store of the same name, but ran a store in Buenos Aires, Argentina. The shares in the company were owned by two Swiss companies. The minority shareholder claimed that the company was operated in a way that was unfairly prejudicial to it. It presented a petition to the English court for an order that the majority shareholder should purchase its shares, or alternatively that the company should be wound up. The majority shareholder argued that leave to serve the petition should be set aside on the ground of *forum non conveniens*. At the time in question, the Brussels Convention was in force, and two previous decisions of the English courts at first instance had held that, where an English court has jurisdiction under the Convention – in this case the English court had jurisdiction under Article 2 because the company, which was also a party, was domiciled in England – the Convention precluded the operation of the doctrine.[11] The Court of Appeal, however, overruled the decisions, and held that, where the alternative forum is in a non-contracting State (here, Argentina), the Convention does not exclude *forum non conveniens*. In a subsequent hearing,[12] the Court of Appeal held by a majority that Argentina was indeed a more convenient forum, and stayed the proceedings. The case went on appeal to the House of Lords, which made a reference to the European Court. However, the case was settled and the reference withdrawn. The European Court, therefore, had no opportunity to rule on the matter.

The foundation of the Court of Appeal's judgment in *Re Harrods* was the contention that the Convention should apply only if there is some Community interest in the case. If there is none, it was thought that the rules of English law should operate in the normal way. One could regard this as a sort of rule of reason. The purpose of the *lis pendens* doctrine is to regulate relations among the courts of the different Contracting States.[13] Where these are not involved, English courts should be allowed to apply *forum non conveniens*.

The position is actually a little more complicated than this, since regulating the relations among courts of the different Contracting States might not be the only purpose of the ban on *forum non conveniens*. Another purpose might be to protect the claimant by ensuring that he can always find a forum in a Contracting State, where the Convention so provides.[14] However, this objective

---

10 [1992] Ch 72; [1991] 3 WLR 397; [1991] 4 All ER 334 (CA).
11 *S&W Berisford plc* v. *New Hampshire Insurance Co.* [1990] 2 QB 631; *Arkwright Mutual Insurance Co.* v. *Bryanston Insurance Co. Ltd* [1990] 2 QB 649. For a critical comment on these cases, which was cited in the *Harrods* case, see Collins, (1990) 106 LQR 535.
12 [1991] 3 WLR 397 at p. 423.
13 The *lis pendens* rule does not apply if the court seised first is in a non-contracting State: see Article 21 of the Convention (Article 27 of the Regulation).
14 This argument is supported by the terms of Article 4 (second paragraph) of the Convention (and Regulation), which states that a person domiciled in a Contracting State must be given the same rights as

would be relevant only if the claimant was domiciled in a Contracting State other than that of the forum. It is only to such persons that the Convention should extend its concern. If the claimant is domiciled in a non-contracting State (as was the case in *Re Harrods*[15]) or in the State of the forum, the Community has no interest in his protection.

In our next case, the correctness of this analysis arose for decision before the European Court.

European Community
Owusu* v. *Jackson
Court of Justice of the European Communities
Case C-281/02, [2005] ECR I-1383; [2005] QB 801; [2005] 2 WLR 942;
   [2005] 2 All ER (Comm) 577[16]

Background

Mr Owusu was domiciled in England. He made a contract with Mr Jackson, who was also domiciled in England, under which the latter rented him a holiday villa in Jamaica. The contract contained a provision that Owusu would have access to a private beach nearby. He maintained that this included an implied term that the beach would be safe for bathing. He went on the holiday and swam from the beach. Unfortunately, he struck a hidden obstacle and seriously injured himself.

In addition to suing Jackson, he also brought proceedings against a number of Jamaican companies, including the company that owned the beach and the company that was responsible for its management and upkeep. All the Jamaican defendants were sued in tort. The court had jurisdiction against Jackson under the Convention, since Jackson was domiciled in England. The other defendants were not domiciled in any Contracting State; so jurisdiction over them depended on the traditional rules of English law. Owusu claimed that the court had jurisdiction over them as necessary or proper parties, under CPR 6.20(3), now Practice Direction 6 B, paragraph 3.1(3).[17]

The defendants claimed that Jamaica was a more appropriate forum and asked the English court to stay the proceedings. The accident had occurred in Jamaica, and almost all the evidence was there.[18] It would certainly have been easier for the defendants to defend the case in Jamaica, since the court would have been able to view the beach and see whether a reasonable person would

---

nationals of that State to bring proceedings against persons not domiciled in any Contracting State. The main purpose of this is to extend to persons domiciled in France who are not French citizens the same rights as are given to French citizens by Article 14 of the French Civil Code. This provision provides that anyone in the world can be sued in France for obligations contracted anywhere in the world, provided the claimant is a French citizen. This rule cannot be used against a defendant domiciled in another Contracting State, but the Convention and Regulation extend it to non-citizens domiciled in France.

15 The claimant was domiciled in Switzerland. At the relevant time, the Lugano Convention was not in force.

16 Also available on www.curia.eu.int/en/.

17 The Court of Appeal reserved judgment on the correctness of this claim until it had obtained a ruling from the European Court on the question of *forum non conveniens*.

18 It also seems that Jackson's insurance would cover a judgment given by a Jamaican court but not by an English one.

have known that he should take care. Moreover, a judgment by an English court against the Jamaican companies would probably not be enforced in Jamaica, unless they voluntarily submitted to the jurisdiction of the English court. One might say that this was Owusu's problem; however, if Jackson were held liable to Owusu but was entitled to an indemnity from the Jamaican defendants, he would have to bring new proceedings in Jamaica, with the possibility of a different outcome, in order to enforce the indemnity. If the proceedings were stayed in favour of Jamaica, on the other hand, all the claims could be disposed of in one set of proceedings.[19]

The trial judge decided that Jamaica was the more appropriate forum. However, he considered that an earlier decision of the European Court[20] precluded him from staying the proceedings against Jackson. Since he could not send the whole case to Jamaica, he decided not to stay the proceedings against any of the defendants. The latter appealed, and the Court of Appeal made a reference to the European Court, asking whether a stay was permissible against Jackson.[21]

Judgment

[After referring to various preliminary matters, the court said:]

22. [T]he [English] Court of Appeal decided to stay its proceedings and to refer the following questions to the Court for a preliminary ruling:

'1. Is it inconsistent with the Brussels Convention . . . where a claimant contends that jurisdiction is founded on Article 2, for a court of a Contracting State to exercise a discretionary power, available under its national law, to decline to hear proceedings brought against a person domiciled in that State in favour of the courts of a non-Contracting State:

(a) if the jurisdiction of no other Contracting State under the 1968 Convention is in issue;
(b) if the proceedings have no connecting factors to any other Contracting State?

2. If the answer to question 1(a) or (b) is yes, is it inconsistent in all circumstances or only in some and if so which?'

On the questions referred

The first question

23. In order to reply to the first question it must first be determined whether Article 2 of the Brussels Convention is applicable in circumstances such as those in the main proceedings, that is to say, where the claimant and one of the defendants are domiciled in the same Contracting State and the case between them before the courts of that State has certain connecting factors with a non-Contracting State, but not with another Contracting State. Only if

---

19 If necessary, the English court could grant Jackson's application for a stay on condition that he submitted to the jurisdiction of the Jamaican courts, thus ensuring that the resulting judgment would be recognized and enforced in England.
20 *Group Josi Reinsurance Company* v. *Universal General Insurance Company*, Case C-412/98, [2000] ECR I-5925.
21 *Owusu* v. *Jackson* [2002] EWCA Civ 877; [2003] 1 CLC 246; [2002] ILPr 45 (CA).

it is will the question arise whether, in the circumstances of the case in the main proceedings, the Brussels Convention precludes the application by a court of a Contracting State of the *forum non conveniens* doctrine where Article 2 of that convention would permit that court to claim jurisdiction because the defendant is domiciled in that State.

The applicability of Article 2 of the Brussels Convention

24. Nothing in the wording of Article 2 of the Brussels Convention suggests that the application of the general rule of jurisdiction laid down by that article solely on the basis of the defendant's domicile in a Contracting State is subject to the condition that there should be a legal relationship involving a number of Contracting States.

25. Of course, as is clear from the Jenard report on the Convention . . . for the jurisdiction rules of the Brussels Convention to apply at all the existence of an international element is required.

26. However, the international nature of the legal relationship at issue need not necessarily derive, for the purposes of the application of Article 2 of the Brussels Convention, from the involvement, either because of the subject-matter of the proceedings or the respective domiciles of the parties, of a number of Contracting States. The involvement of a Contracting State and a non-Contracting State, for example because the claimant and one defendant are domiciled in the first State and the events at issue occurred in the second, would also make the legal relationship at issue international in nature. That situation is such as to raise questions in the Contracting State, as it does in the main proceedings, relating to the determination of international jurisdiction, which is precisely one of the objectives of the Brussels Convention, according to the third recital in its preamble.

27. Thus the Court has already interpreted the rules of jurisdiction laid down by the Brussels Convention in cases where the claimant was domiciled or had its seat in a non-Contracting State while the defendant was domiciled in a Contracting State . . .

28. Moreover, the rules of the Brussels Convention on exclusive jurisdiction or express prorogation of jurisdiction are also likely to be applicable to legal relationships involving only one Contracting State and one or more non-Contracting States. That is so, under Article 16 of the Brussels Convention, in the case of proceedings which have as their object rights *in rem* in immovable property or tenancies of immovable property between persons domiciled in a non-Contracting State and relating to an asset in a Contracting State, or, under Article 17 of the Brussels Convention, where an agreement conferring jurisdiction binding at least one party domiciled in a non-Contracting State opts for a court in a Contracting State.

29. Similarly, as the Advocate General pointed out . . . whilst it is clear from their wording that the Brussels Convention rules on *lis pendens* and related actions or recognition and enforcement of judgments apply to relationships between different Contracting States, provided that they

concern proceedings pending before courts of different Contracting States or judgments delivered by courts of a Contracting State with a view to recognition and enforcement thereof in another Contracting State, the fact nevertheless remains that the disputes with which the proceedings or decisions in question are concerned may be international, involving a Contracting State and a non-Contracting State, and allow recourse, on that ground, to the general rule of jurisdiction laid down by Article 2 of the Brussels Convention.

30. To counter the argument that Article 2 applies to a legal situation involving a single Contracting State and one or more non-Contracting States, the defendants in the main proceedings and the United Kingdom Government cited the principle of the relative effect of treaties, which means that the Brussels Convention cannot impose any obligation on States which have not agreed to be bound by it.

31. In that regard, suffice it to note that the designation of the court of a Contracting State as the court having jurisdiction on the ground of the defendant's domicile in that State, even in proceedings which are, at least in part, connected, because of their subject-matter or the claimant's domicile, with a non-Contracting State, is not such as to impose an obligation on that State.

32. Mr Jackson and the United Kingdom Government also emphasised, in support of the argument that Article 2 of the Brussels Convention applied only to disputes with connections to a number of Contracting States, the fundamental objective pursued by the Convention which was to ensure the free movement of judgments between Contracting States.

33. The purpose of the fourth indent of Article 220 of the EC Treaty (now the fourth indent of Article 293 EC), on the basis of which the Member States concluded the Brussels Convention, is to facilitate the working of the common market through the adoption of rules of jurisdiction for disputes relating thereto and through the elimination, as far as is possible, of difficulties concerning the recognition and enforcement of judgments in the territory of the Contracting States . . . In fact it is not disputed that the Brussels Convention helps to ensure the smooth working of the internal market.

34. However, the uniform rules of jurisdiction contained in the Brussels Convention are not intended to apply only to situations in which there is a real and sufficient link with the working of the internal market, by definition involving a number of Member States. Suffice it to observe in that regard that the consolidation as such of the rules on conflict of jurisdiction and on the recognition and enforcement of judgments, effected by the Brussels Convention in respect of cases with an international element, is without doubt intended to eliminate obstacles to the functioning of the internal market which may derive from disparities between national legislations on the subject (see, by analogy, as regards harmonisation directives based on

Article 95 EC intended to improve the conditions for the establishment and working of the internal market . . .)

35. It follows from the foregoing that Article 2 of the Brussels Convention applies to circumstances such as those in the main proceedings, involving relationships between the courts of a single Contracting State and those of a non-Contracting State rather than relationships between the courts of a number of Contracting States.

36. It must therefore be considered whether, in such circumstances, the Brussels Convention precludes a court of a Contracting State from applying the *forum non conveniens* doctrine and declining to exercise the jurisdiction conferred on it by Article 2 of that Convention.

The compatibility of the forum non conveniens doctrine with the Brussels Convention

37. It must be observed, first, that Article 2 of the Brussels Convention is mandatory in nature and that, according to its terms, there can be no derogation from the principle it lays down except in the cases expressly provided for by the Convention [references to *Gasser* and *Turner*, both set out below]. It is common ground that no exception on the basis of the *forum non conveniens* doctrine was provided for by the authors of the Convention, although the question was discussed when the Convention of 9 October 1978 on the Accession of Denmark, Ireland and the United Kingdom was drawn up, as is apparent from the report on that Convention by Professor Schlosser . . .

38. Respect for the principle of legal certainty, which is one of the objectives of the Brussels Convention . . . would not be fully guaranteed if the court having jurisdiction under the Convention had to be allowed to apply the *forum non conveniens* doctrine.[1]

39. According to its preamble, the Brussels Convention is intended to strengthen in the Community the legal protection of persons established therein, by laying down common rules on jurisdiction to guarantee certainty as to the allocation of jurisdiction among the various national courts before which proceedings in a particular case may be brought . . .

40. The Court has thus held that the principle of legal certainty requires, in particular, that the jurisdictional rules which derogate from the general rule laid down in Article 2 of the Brussels Convention should be interpreted in such a way as to enable a normally well-informed defendant reasonably to foresee before which courts, other than those of the State in which he is domiciled, he may be sued . . .

41. Application of the *forum non conveniens* doctrine, which allows the court seised a wide discretion as regards the question whether a foreign court would be a more appropriate forum for the trial of an action, is liable to undermine

---

1 *Editor's note*: the court's English is incorrect here. What it meant to say was 'if the court having jurisdiction under the Convention *were* allowed to apply the *forum non conveniens* doctrine'.

the predictability of the rules of jurisdiction laid down by the Brussels Convention, in particular that of Article 2, and consequently to undermine the principle of legal certainty, which is the basis of the Convention.

42. The legal protection of persons established in the Community would also be undermined. First, a defendant, who is generally better placed to conduct his defence before the courts of his domicile, would not be able, in circumstances such as those of the main proceedings, reasonably to foresee before which other court he may be sued. Second, where a plea is raised on the basis that a foreign court is a more appropriate forum to try the action, it is for the claimant to establish that he will not be able to obtain justice before that foreign court or, if the court seised decides to allow the plea, that the foreign court has in fact no jurisdiction to try the action or that the claimant does not, in practice, have access to effective justice before that court, irrespective of the cost entailed by the bringing of a fresh action before a court of another State and the prolongation of the procedural time-limits.

43. Moreover, allowing *forum non conveniens* in the context of the Brussels Convention would be likely to affect the uniform application of the rules of jurisdiction contained therein in so far as that doctrine is recognised only in a limited number of Contracting States, whereas the objective of the Brussels Convention is precisely to lay down common rules to the exclusion of derogating national rules.

44. The defendants in the main proceedings emphasise the negative consequences which would result in practice from the obligation the English courts would then be under to try this case, *inter alia* as regards the expense of the proceedings, the possibility of recovering their costs in England if the claimant's action is dismissed, the logistical difficulties resulting from the geographical distance, the need to assess the merits of the case according to Jamaican standards, the enforceability in Jamaica of a default judgment and the impossibility of enforcing cross-claims against the other defendants.

45. In that regard, genuine as those difficulties may be, suffice it to observe that such considerations, which are precisely those which may be taken into account when *forum non conveniens* is considered, are not such as to call into question the mandatory nature of the fundamental rule of jurisdiction contained in Article 2 of the Brussels Convention, for the reasons set out above.

46. In the light of all the foregoing considerations, the answer to the first question must be that the Brussels Convention precludes a court of a Contracting State from declining the jurisdiction conferred on it by Article 2 of that convention on the ground that a court of a non-Contracting State would be a more appropriate forum for the trial of the action even if the jurisdiction of no other Contracting State is in issue or the proceedings have no connecting factors to any other Contracting State.

[The court then turned to the second question asked by the English court. This was whether it would be permissible to stay proceedings if (a) the same, or related, proceedings were pending before a court of a non-contracting State; (b) where a choice-of-court agreement gives exclusive jurisdiction to such a court; or (c) where such a court would have exclusive jurisdiction under the principles of Article 16 of the Brussels Convention (Article 22 of the Regulation). The court said that as none of these situations had arisen in the case before it, it was not necessary to answer this question. It then concluded:]

On those grounds, the Court (Grand Chamber) rules as follows:

The [Brussels] Convention . . . precludes a court of a Contracting State from declining the jurisdiction conferred on it by Article 2 of that convention on the ground that a court of a non-Contracting State would be a more appropriate forum for the trial of the action even if the jurisdiction of no other Contracting State is in issue or the proceedings have no connecting factors to any other Contracting State.

Comment

The case was heard by a Grand Chamber of the European Court, a panel composed of nine judges. None of them was from a common-law country. Since the common law was, in some sense, itself on trial, one might have thought that at least one common-law judge – from Ireland, if not from England – could have been found.

The court said that respect for the principle of legal certainty would not be fully guaranteed if a court having jurisdiction under the Convention could apply the *forum non conveniens* doctrine. No attempt was made to consider for whose benefit this principle of legal certainty was intended to operate. The only attempt to set out any specific objections to *forum non conveniens* was made in paragraphs 42 and 43 of the judgment. The first argument was that a defendant (who is generally better placed to conduct his defence before the courts of his domicile) would not, under the doctrine of *forum non conveniens*, be able to foresee in which other courts he might be sued. This suggests that the purpose of the ban on *forum non conveniens* is to protect the defendant. The glaring fallacy of this argument is that it is the defendant who applies for a stay: if he wants to be sued in his own courts, all he has to do is not to apply for a stay.[22] Moreover, since the defendant is by definition a domiciliary of the State of the forum, it is hard to see what interest the Community would have in protecting him from his own law.

The second argument put forward by the court was that, in objecting to an application for a stay, the onus is on the claimant to establish that he will not obtain justice in the foreign court, or that the foreign court does not have jurisdiction, or that he does not in practice have effective access to justice in that court. These arguments are all based on the idea that the Convention is intended

---

22 The only exception might be if there were several defendants and some of them wanted a stay and others did not. This was not, however, the case in *Owusu*, where it was Jackson himself who applied for the stay.

to protect the claimant. However, if the claimant is domiciled in the Contracting State of the forum (or in a non-contracting State), it is hard to see what interest the Community has in his protection.

The final argument was that, since most EC States do not have the doctrine of *forum non conveniens*, allowing those that do to apply it would affect the uniform application of the rules of jurisdiction in the Convention. No attempt was made to explain why this was a bad thing.

The various difficulties that would ensue in the *Owusu* case if the English court were not allowed to stay the proceedings were dismissed on the ground that they were 'not such as to call into question the mandatory nature of the fundamental rule of jurisdiction contained in Article 2 of the Brussels Convention',[23] a statement that displays a startling lack of concern for the interests of the parties.

This case establishes that *forum non conveniens* has no role to play where the court's jurisdiction is based on the domicile of the defendant in the State of the forum. It seems highly likely that the position would be the same where he was domiciled in another Member State, since the forum's jurisdiction would again depend on the Regulation.

It seems, therefore, that the doctrine of *forum non conveniens* can now apply in England only where the defendant is not domiciled in any Community or Lugano State, and the court's jurisdiction is based purely on English law – for example, where a defendant not domiciled in Europe is served with a claim form outside England under the rules contained in the CPR.

§ 3   Antisuit injunctions

Antisuit injunctions are not mentioned in the Regulation. One might have thought, therefore, that they were unaffected by it. Out next case shows that this is not so.

European Community
Turner* v. *Grovit
Court of Justice of the European Communities
Case C-159/02, [2004] ECR I-3565[24]

Background

Paul Turner was a young solicitor who worked for Harada Ltd, a company that came under the control of a certain Mr Grovit. Turner's contract of employment as group solicitor stated that he would be based in London or 'as you may be directed'. In 1997, he was moved to Madrid, where he worked at the office of a Spanish company called Changepoint SA. It was the Spanish member of the same group of companies as Harada Ltd. The move was intended to be merely tempo-

---

23 Paragraph 45 of the judgment.
24 Also available on www.curia.eu.int/en/. For a comment, see Briggs, (2004) 120 LQR 529.

rary: he was still employed by Harada Ltd, which continued to pay his salary. The Spanish company paid Harada Ltd for his services.

A few months after arriving in Madrid, Turner found that the whole group of companies was involved in a tax fraud. Money deducted for tax from the salaries of employees was being used to pay creditors. Turner was expected to justify and defend this. Since he could not do so, he resigned and returned home. He brought proceedings against Harada Ltd before an English employment tribunal. The tribunal held that it had jurisdiction under the Convention,[25] and found for Turner on the merits: it ruled that he had been unfairly and wrongfully dismissed.

Grovit responded to this by bringing proceedings against Turner in Spain in the name of the Spanish company where Turner had worked (Changepoint SA). Damages were claimed against Turner for his 'unjustified departure' from the company's Madrid office and for bringing a 'baseless' claim in England. This was an attempt to re-litigate the issues already decided by the employment tribunal in England. Moreover, the sum claimed, some 85 million pesetas (almost £500,000), was ridiculously large. Since Turner was a man of limited means, there was a real danger that he would run out of money and be unable to retain Spanish lawyers to defend the claim. He would then be forced to settle on Grovit's terms. This, no doubt, was what Grovit hoped.

Turner brought proceedings before the English courts for an antisuit injunction. The Court of Appeal found that the Spanish proceedings had been brought in bad faith. Their sole purpose was to vex and oppress Turner. It therefore granted the injunction.[26] Grovit appealed to the House of Lords.[27] At this point, Turner ran out of funds, and was unable to defend the case, but the House of Lords appointed an *amicus curiae* to ensure that his case did not go by default. A reference was made to the European Court. Again, the case was heard by a Full Court; again, there was not a single common lawyer among the eleven judges hearing the case.

Judgment

[After stating that a major objective of the Convention was to achieve certainty, the court said:]

24. At the outset, it must be borne in mind that the Convention is necessarily based on the trust which the Contracting States accord to one another's legal systems and judicial institutions. It is that mutual trust which has enabled a compulsory system of jurisdiction to be established, which all the

---

25 The employment tribunal found that no less than three provisions of the Convention gave it jurisdiction. The first was Article 2, which confers jurisdiction on the courts of the defendant's domicile: although Harada Ltd was incorporated in Ireland, its central management and control were in England and it was therefore domiciled there: Civil Jurisdiction and Judgments Act 1982, section 42(1) and (3)(b). The second was Article 5(1), which provides that, in employment cases, the courts of the State in which the employee habitually carries out his work have jurisdiction. Turner habitually worked in England: his employment in Spain was only temporary. The third provision was Article 5(5), which provides that a dispute arising out of the operations of a branch, agency or other establishment of the defendant is subject to the jurisdiction of the courts of the place in which the branch, agency or establishment is located.
26 *Turner* v. *Grovit* [1999] 3 WLR 794 (CA). The defendants were Grovit, Harada Ltd and Changepoint SA.
27 Leave to appeal was granted on special terms: if the appeal was successful, Turner would not be liable for his opponents' costs; if the appeal failed, Turner could recover his costs.

courts within the purview of the Convention are required to respect, and as a corollary the waiver by those States of the right to apply their internal rules on recognition and enforcement of foreign judgments in favour of a simplified mechanism for the recognition and enforcement of judgments [reference to *Gasser* (below), paragraph 72].

25. It is inherent in that principle of mutual trust that, within the scope of the Convention, the rules on jurisdiction that it lays down, which are common to all the courts of the Contracting States, may be interpreted and applied with the same authority by each of them . . .

26. Similarly, otherwise than in a small number of exceptional cases listed in the first paragraph of Article 28 of the Convention, which are limited to the stage of recognition or enforcement and relate only to certain rules of special or exclusive jurisdiction that are not relevant here, the Convention does not permit the jurisdiction of a court to be reviewed by a court in another Contracting State . . .

27. However, a prohibition imposed by a court, backed by a penalty, restraining a party from commencing or continuing proceedings before a foreign court undermines the latter court's jurisdiction to determine the dispute. Any injunction prohibiting a claimant from bringing such an action must be seen as constituting interference with the jurisdiction of the foreign court which, as such, is incompatible with the system of the Convention.

28. Notwithstanding the explanations given by the referring court and contrary to the view put forward by Mr Turner and the United Kingdom Government, such interference cannot be justified by the fact that it is only indirect and is intended to prevent an abuse of process by the defendant in the proceedings in the forum State. In so far as the conduct for which the defendant is criticised consists in recourse to the jurisdiction of the court of another Member State, the judgment made as to the abusive nature of that conduct implies an assessment of the appropriateness of bringing proceedings before a court of another Member State. Such an assessment runs counter to the principle of mutual trust which, as pointed out in paragraphs 24 to 26 of this judgment, underpins the Convention and prohibits a court, except in special circumstances which are not applicable in this case, from reviewing the jurisdiction of the court of another Member State.

29. Even if it were assumed, as has been contended, that an injunction could be regarded as a measure of a procedural nature intended to safeguard the integrity of the proceedings pending before the court which issues it, and therefore as being a matter of national law alone, it need merely be borne in mind that the application of national procedural rules may not impair the effectiveness of the Convention . . . However, that result would follow from the grant of an injunction of the kind at issue which, as has been established in paragraph 27 of this judgment, has the effect of limiting the application of the rules on jurisdiction laid down by the Convention.

30. The argument that the grant of injunctions may contribute to attainment of the objective of the Convention, which is to minimise the risk of conflicting decisions and to avoid a multiplicity of proceedings, cannot be accepted. First, recourse to such measures renders ineffective the specific mechanisms provided for by the Convention for cases of *lis alibi pendens* and of related actions. Second, it is liable to give rise to situations involving conflicts for which the Convention contains no rules. The possibility cannot be excluded that, even if an injunction had been issued in one Contracting State, a decision might nevertheless be given by a court of another Contracting state. Similarly, the possibility cannot be excluded that the courts of two Contracting States that allowed such measures might issue contradictory injunctions.

31. Consequently, the answer to be given to the national court must be that the Convention is to be interpreted as precluding the grant of an injunction whereby a court of a Contracting State prohibits a party to proceedings pending before it from commencing or continuing legal proceedings before a court of another Contracting State, even where that party is acting in bad faith with a view to frustrating the existing proceedings.

Comment

Again, protecting the interests of States prevails over doing justice to individuals. Thanks to the European Court, bad-faith litigants can now go about their business without fear of antisuit injunctions, at least if they do not stray beyond the confines of the European Union.

As an example of the value of antisuit injunctions in the Community context, it is worth considering an earlier case, *Continental Bank* v. *Aeakos SA*.[28] In that case, the Athens branch of an American bank lent a large sum of money to a group of Greek-owned companies. The loan agreement, which was guaranteed by a number of Greek individuals, contained an English choice-of-law clause and an English choice-of-court clause. The borrowers defaulted and the bank accelerated the loan. The Greeks responded by bringing proceedings in a Greek court, claiming that the manner in which the bank had exercised its rights under the loan agreement was contrary to business morality, and therefore a tort under Greek law.[29] Damages were claimed in the sum of US$63 million, approximately twice what was owed under the loan agreement. The action also had a contractual aspect, and the Greek court was asked to make a declaration that the guarantors had been released. It is not entirely clear what the bank was supposed to have done, but it seems that the essence of its wrongdoing was that it had demanded its money back according to the terms of the contract, even though it was inconvenient for the borrowers to repay it. The bank went to the Greek court and invoked the choice-of-court agreement. However, the court seemed disinclined to stay the proceedings.

The bank then brought proceedings in England for an antisuit injunction.

---

28 [1994] 1 WLR 588 (CA).
29 Article 919 of the Greek Civil Code states: 'Whoever intentionally, in a manner which violates the commands of morality, causes damages to another is bound to make reparation to the other for any damage this caused.'

The Court of Appeal held that the choice-of-court clause (which was governed by English law) was wide enough to cover proceedings in tort arising out of the loan. It also held that it was exclusive. Counsel for the Greeks asked the court to trust the Greek court. It pointedly refused to do so. An antisuit injunction was granted. We now know that this was wrong: the Greeks should have been allowed to continue their proceedings in Greece for as long as the Greek courts were willing to entertain them. If damages had eventually been awarded against the bank, English courts would have been required to enforce them. Under the Convention, the fact that a judgment was given in breach of a choice-of-court agreement is not a reason for refusing to enforce it.[30]

The result of this case is that English courts are no longer able to grant antisuit injunctions to restrain proceedings in the courts of other Member States or, no doubt, Lugano States. This applies even if those proceedings are brought in bad faith.

§ 4   Choice-of-court agreements and the 'Italian torpedo'

Because the *lis pendens* rule makes no attempt to determine which court is appropriate to hear the case, it encourages well-advised, but unscrupulous, parties to win the race to the courthouse by commencing proceedings at the first hint of a dispute, often choosing a court precisely because it is *inappropriate*, though inappropriate in a way that advantages them. For example, if a party fears that it will lose in the end but wants to put off the evil day as long as possible, it might bring proceedings (perhaps for a declaration of non-liability) in a country where the courts are slow-moving. It could then invoke the *lis pendens* rule to block proceedings in any other Contracting State.

There are a number of countries, in both Europe and beyond, in which legal proceedings move extremely slowly. In the European Union, the most notorious example is Italy. The case of *Trasporti Castelletti* v. *Hugo Trumpy*[31] provides an example. In this case, a Danish shipping company delivered bills of lading to an Argentinean shipper for a voyage from Argentina to Italy. The bills of lading contained a choice-of-court clause in favour of England. There was nothing at all unusual about the terms of this clause: it was exactly the same as similar clauses contained in hundreds of other bills of lading issued every day in different countries around the world. Nevertheless, when the receiver of the cargo brought proceedings in Italy, it took ten years for it to be decided that the Italian courts had no jurisdiction. Admittedly, two years of this were taken up by a reference to the European Court, itself not renowned for speediness; nevertheless, for the Italian courts to take eight years to decide such a simple issue was grossly excessive.

This raises the question of human rights. Article 6(1) of the European Convention on Human Rights grants everyone the right to a fair hearing within

---

30 There are only a limited number of grounds for non-recognition, and this is not one of them: see Articles 27 and 28 of the Convention (Articles 34 and 35 of the Regulation).
31 Case C-159/97, [1999] ECR I-1597.

a reasonable period of time to determine his civil rights and obligations. The Italian court system has been held in massive breach of this requirement. The (old) European Commission on Human Rights condemned Italy in over 1,400 reports on this count, and by 1999 the European Court of Human Rights had given more than sixty-five judgments against it.[32] Since then, proceedings against Italy have continued apace: in 2000, more judgments were given against Italy on this one question than the combined total of all other judgments against all other Contracting States on all questions. It is indisputable, therefore, that the Italian court system is woefully slow-moving.

In 1997, an Italian *avvocato*, Mario Franzosi, indicated how litigants could turn this to their advantage: persons facing possible patent-infringement actions in other EU States could protect themselves by bringing proceedings in Italy for a declaration of non-liability.[33] Even if they lost in the end, they could keep the proceedings going for many years, thus blocking infringement actions in other Member States.[34] Franzosi called this device the 'Italian torpedo'.[35] The *Trasporti Castelletti* case shows that it would work even if the Italian courts lacked jurisdiction, since it would take many years to obtain a definitive ruling to this effect.[36] Franzosi's advice to patent-holders was to sue first and write letters afterwards.

The effectiveness of the 'Italian torpedo' came before the European Court of Justice in our next case. This was not an intellectual property case, but a case involving a choice-of-court agreement. These were discussed in Chapter 8, § 2, above, where it was pointed out that the system laid down in the Brussels Regulation appears, at first sight, to be excellent. But what happens if the agreement is the target of a 'torpedo'? This occurred in the *Gasser* case. It was also considered by a Full Court, consisting of thirteen judges.

European Community
Gasser v. *MISRAT*
Court of Justice of the European Communities
Case C-116/02, [2003] ECR I-14693[37]

Background

Gasser was an Austrian firm that entered into a contract with MISRAT, an Italian company, under which Gasser sold children's clothing to MISRAT. The original contract contained no choice-of-court agreement, but a provision granting

---

32 See the judgment of the European Court of Human Rights in *Ferrari* v. *Italy*, 28 July 1999, available on www.echr.coe.int/hudoc/. According to the European Court of Human Rights, such breaches 'reflect a continuing situation that has not yet been remedied': *ibid.*, p. 5 (paragraph 21).
33 Franzosi, 'Worldwide Patent Litigation and the Italian Torpedo' (1997) 7 *European Intellectual Property Review* 382.
34 He said the Italian proceedings would take an 'outrageous' period of time.
35 Franzosi stressed that he was not inviting litigants to launch 'torpedoes' to block justified infringement actions, only *unjustified* ones – though he did not explain why defendants would want to launch 'torpedoes' if the claims were unjustified.
36 The grounds on which the Italian courts might assume jurisdiction are discussed by Franzosi, 'Worldwide Patent Litigation and the Italian Torpedo' [1997] 7 *European Intellectual Property Review* 382 at pp. 383–4.
37 Also available on www.curia.eu.int/en/. For a comment, see Mance, (2004) 120 LQR 357.

jurisdiction to a specified Austrian court appeared in all the invoices sent by Gasser to MISRAT. The latter paid the invoices without protest. This probably constituted a valid and exclusive choice-of-court agreement under Article 17 of the Brussels Convention, as it stood at the relevant time.[38] When a dispute arose, however, MISRAT brought proceedings before a court in Italy, claiming that the contract had been terminated and that it was not guilty of breaching it.[39] After the Italian court was seised, Gasser brought proceedings before the Austrian court specified in the choice-of-court agreement. MISRAT claimed that these proceedings were barred by its prior action in Italy: the 'torpedo' had been launched.

The case eventually found its way to the European Court on a reference from an appeal court in Austria, the *Oberlandesgericht* Innsbruck. One of the questions asked by the latter was whether the *lis pendens* rule applies even when proceedings in the court first seised take an unreasonably long period of time. It also asked whether the court seised second is entitled to consider whether the court seised first actually had jurisdiction under the Convention. In the case, if the choice-of-court agreement was valid, the Italian court clearly did not have jurisdiction.

The United Kingdom intervened in these proceedings (as it was entitled to do) to put submissions before the European Court. It argued that, where there is a choice-of-court agreement giving exclusive jurisdiction to the court seised second, that court should be entitled to determine the validity of the agreement, and, if it holds it valid and applicable to the case, it should be allowed to continue with the proceedings. It argued that, otherwise, dishonest parties would be encouraged to start proceedings before courts other than that chosen, simply as a delaying tactic.

Judgment

41. It must be borne in mind at the outset that Article 21 of the Brussels Convention, together with Article 22 on related actions, is contained in Section 8 of Title II of the Convention, which is intended, in the interests of the proper administration of justice within the Community, to prevent parallel proceedings before the courts of different Contracting States and to avoid conflicts between decisions which might result therefrom. Those rules are therefore designed to preclude, so far as possible and from the outset, the possibility of a situation arising such as that referred to in Article 27(3) of the Convention, that is to say the non-recognition of a judgment on account of its irreconcilability with a judgment given in proceedings between the same parties in the State in which recognition is sought (see *Gubisch Maschinenfabrik* . . . paragraph 8). It follows that, in order to achieve those aims, Article 21 must be interpreted broadly so as to cover, in principle, all situations of *lis pendens* before courts in Contracting States, irrespective of the parties' domicile (*Overseas Union Insurance* . . . [Case C-351/89, [1991] ECR I-3317], paragraph 16).

---

38 The Austrian appeal court, the *Oberlandesgericht* Innsbruck, took the view that it was valid under subparagraph (c) of Article 17.
39 For good measure, it also asked for damages against Gasser for failure to fulfil the obligations of fairness, diligence and good faith.

42. From the clear terms of Article 21 it is apparent that, in a situation of *lis pendens*, the court second seised must stay proceedings of its own motion until the jurisdiction of the court first seised has been established and, where it is so established, must decline jurisdiction in favour of the latter.

43. In that regard, as the Court also observed in paragraph 13 of *Overseas Union Insurance*, Article 21 does not draw any distinction between the various heads of jurisdiction provided for in the Brussels Convention.

44. It is true that, in paragraph 26 of *Overseas Union Insurance*, before holding that Article 21 of the Brussels Convention must be interpreted as meaning that, where the jurisdiction of the court first seised is contested, the court second seised may, if it does not decline jurisdiction, only stay proceedings and may not itself examine the jurisdiction of the court first seised, the Court stated that its ruling was without prejudice to the case where the court second seised has exclusive jurisdiction under the Convention and in particular under Article 16 thereof.

45. However, it is clear from paragraph 20 of the same judgment that, in the absence of any claim that the court second seised had exclusive jurisdiction in the main proceedings, the Court of Justice simply declined to prejudge the interpretation of Article 21 of the Convention in the hypothetical situation which it specifically excluded from its judgment.

46. In this case, it is claimed that the court second seised has jurisdiction under Article 17 of the Convention.

47. However, that fact is not such as to call in question the application of the procedural rule contained in Article 21 of the Convention, which is based clearly and solely on the chronological order in which the courts involved are seised.

48. Moreover, the court second seised is never in a better position than the court first seised to determine whether the latter has jurisdiction. That jurisdiction is determined directly by the rules of the Brussels Convention, which are common to both courts and may be interpreted and applied with the same authority by each of them (see, to that effect, *Overseas Union Insurance*, paragraph 23).

49. Thus, where there is an agreement conferring jurisdiction within the meaning of Article 17 of the Brussels Convention, not only, as observed by the Commission, do the parties always have the option of declining to invoke it and, in particular, the defendant has the option of entering an appearance before the court first seised without alleging that it lacks jurisdiction on the basis of a choice-of-court clause, in accordance with Article 18 of the Convention, but, moreover, in circumstances other than those just described, it is incumbent on the court first seised to verify the existence of the agreement and to decline jurisdiction if it is established, in accordance with Article 17, that the parties actually agreed to designate the court second seised as having exclusive jurisdiction.

50.   The fact nevertheless remains that, despite the reference to usage in international trade or commerce contained in Article 17 of the Brussels Convention, real consent by the parties is always one of the objectives of that provision, justified by the concern to protect the weaker contracting party by ensuring that jurisdiction clauses incorporated in a contract by one party alone do not go unnoticed . . .

51.   In those circumstances, in view of the disputes which could arise as to the very existence of a genuine agreement between the parties, expressed in accordance with the strict formal conditions laid down in Article 17 of the Brussels Convention, it is conducive to the legal certainty sought by the Convention that, in cases of *lis pendens*, it should be determined clearly and precisely which of the two national courts is to establish whether it has jurisdiction under the rules of the Convention. It is clear from the wording of Article 21 of the Convention that it is for the court first seised to pronounce as to its jurisdiction, in this case in the light of a jurisdiction clause relied on before it, which must be regarded as an independent concept to be appraised solely in relation to the requirements of Article 17 . . .

52.   Moreover, the interpretation of Article 21 of the Brussels Convention flowing from the foregoing considerations is confirmed by Article 19 of the Convention which requires a court of a Contracting State to declare of its own motion that it has no jurisdiction only where it is 'seised of a claim which is principally concerned with a matter over which the courts of another Contracting State have exclusive jurisdiction by virtue of Article 16.' Article 17 of the Brussels Convention is not affected by Article 19.

53.   Finally, the difficulties of the kind referred to by the United Kingdom Government, stemming from delaying tactics by parties who, with the intention of delaying settlement of the substantive dispute, commence proceedings before a court which they know to lack jurisdiction by reason of the existence of a jurisdiction clause are not such as to call in question the interpretation of any provision of the Brussels Convention, as deduced from its wording and its purpose.

54.   In view of the foregoing, the answer to the second question must be that Article 21 of the Brussels Convention must be interpreted as meaning that a court second seised whose jurisdiction has been claimed under an agreement conferring jurisdiction must nevertheless stay proceedings until the court first seised has declared that it has no jurisdiction.

Comment

This judgment constitutes a blank refusal, despite the abundant evidence to the contrary, to contemplate that the Italian legal system might be anything other than perfect. Contracting States must trust one another.

The judgment shows again that the European Court puts the desirability of maintaining good relations among the Contracting States above that of doing justice to the parties. It also shows the court's disdain for practical considerations.

This case gives the green light to 'Italian torpedoes'.[40] Franzosi's ideas have been vindicated. While Italian lawyers (and litigants) will be jubilant, honest businessmen in other countries will be dismayed. Thanks to the European Court, a litigant can now bring proceedings in bad faith in Italy simply to prevent himself from being sued elsewhere.[41]

§ 5 Arbitration: a 'torpedo-free' zone

We have seen that an 'Italian torpedo' can sink a choice-of-court agreement. We must now consider what it does to an arbitration agreement. Arbitration agreements were discussed above (Chapter 8, § 2.8).[42] It will be remembered that they are in a different position from choice-of-court agreements because arbitration is excluded from the scope of the Regulation by Article 1(2)(d). The effect of this on 'torpedoes' came before the European Court in our next case, a case decided more than ten years prior to *Gasser*.

> **European Community**
> ***Marc Rich and Co.* v. *Società Italiana Impianti***
> **Court of Justice of the European Communities**
> **Case C-190/89, [1991] ECR I-3855**

Background

Marc Rich was a Swiss company, and Impianti was Italian. They concluded a contract for the purchase of crude oil. The contract was subject to an English choice-of-law clause and a clause providing for arbitration in England. Subsequently, a dispute arose: Marc Rich (the buyer) claimed that the oil was contaminated. Impianti then launched an 'Italian torpedo': he brought proceedings in an Italian court for a declaration that he was not liable. He claimed that the arbitration agreement was invalid under Italian law. Marc Rich invoked the arbitration clause, which required each party to appoint one arbitrator and for those two arbitrators to appoint the third. Impianti refused to co-operate by appointing his arbitrator. In such a situation, English law provides a remedy: the other party can go to court and ask it to appoint an arbitrator on behalf of the defaulting party. Marc Rich did this, but Impianti objected. He said that the Brussels Convention (in force at the time) prevented the English court from acting. He said the Italian

---

40 See, for example, the article by Pierre Véron, 'ECJ Restores Torpedo Power' (2004) 35 *International Review of Industrial Property and Copyright Law* 638.

41 The European Court's judgment could give rise to a clash between the Brussels Convention and the European Convention on Human Rights. If the Italian proceedings were to drag on so long that Article 6 ECHR was infringed, Gasser could arguably bring proceedings against Austria (as well as Italy) before the European Court of Human Rights. It could be argued, therefore, that, by staying the proceedings out of deference to Article 21 of the Brussels Convention, the Austrian courts might be violating Article 6 ECHR. For a discussion of the legal issues involved in such a clash, see Hartley, 'International Law and the Law of the European Union – A Reassessment' (2001) 72 BYIL 1 at pp. 22–35.

42 See also Chapter 14, § 10, below

court was seised first and that proceedings in England were blocked by the *lis pendens* rule. Marc Rich argued that the proceedings were outside the scope of the Convention because they concerned arbitration, which was excluded by Article 1(4) of the Convention, the equivalent of Article 1(2)(d) of the Regulation. The Court of Appeal referred the matter to the European Court.

Judgment

11.   The first question submitted by the national court seeks, in substance, to determine whether Article 1(4) of the Convention must be interpreted in such a manner that the exclusion provided for therein extends to proceedings pending before a national court concerning the appointment of an arbitrator and, if so, whether that exclusion also applies where in those proceedings a preliminary issue is raised as to whether an arbitration agreement exists or is valid. These two points will be considered successively.

         . . .

Exclusion of proceedings for the appointment of an arbitrator from the scope of the Convention

13.   Impianti considers that the exclusion in Article 1(4) of the Convention does not apply to proceedings before national courts or to decisions given by them. It contends that 'arbitration' in the strict sense concerns proceedings before private individuals on whom the parties have conferred the authority to settle the dispute between them. Impianti bases that view essentially on the purpose of Article 220 of the Treaty[1] which, it argues, is to establish a complete system for the free movement of decisions determining a dispute. Consequently, it is legitimate to interpret Article 1(4) of the Convention in such a way as to avoid lacunae in the legal system for ensuring the free movement of decisions terminating a dispute.

14.   Marc Rich and the governments which have submitted observations support a wide interpretation of the concept of arbitration, which would exclude completely from the scope of the Convention any disputes relating to the appointment of an arbitrator.

15.   The purpose of the Convention, according to the preamble thereto, is to implement the provisions of Article 220 of the EEC Treaty concerning the reciprocal recognition and enforcement of judgments of courts or tribunals. Pursuant to the fourth paragraph of Article 220, the Member States shall, so far as is necessary, enter into negotiations with each other with a view to securing for the benefit of their nationals the simplification of formalities governing the reciprocal recognition and enforcement of judgments of courts or tribunals and of arbitration awards.

16.   In referring to decisions of courts and tribunals and to arbitration awards, Article 220 of the Treaty thus relates both to proceedings brought before national courts and tribunals which culminate in a judicial decision and to

1 *Editor's note*: Article 220 is now numbered 293.

those commenced before private arbitrators which culminate in arbitral awards. However, it does not follow that the Convention, whose purpose is in particular the reciprocal recognition and enforcement of judicial decisions, must necessarily have attributed to it a wide field of application. In so far as the Member States are called upon, by virtue of Article 220, to enter into negotiations 'so far as necessary', it is incumbent on them to determine the scope of any agreement concluded between them.

17. With respect to the exclusion of arbitration from the scope of the Convention, the report by the group of experts set up in connection with the drafting of the Convention (Official Journal 1979 C 59, p. 1) explains that

> There are already many international agreements on arbitration. Arbitration is, of course, referred to in Article 220 of the Treaty of Rome. Moreover, the Council of Europe has prepared a European Convention providing a uniform law on arbitration, and this will probably be accompanied by a Protocol which will facilitate the recognition and enforcement of arbitral awards to an even greater extent than the New York Convention. This is why it seemed preferable to exclude arbitration.

18. The international agreements, and in particular the abovementioned New York Convention on the recognition and enforcement of foreign arbitral awards (New York, 10 June 1958, *United Nations Treaty Series*, Vol. 330, p. 3), lay down rules which must be respected not by the arbitrators themselves but by the courts of the Contracting States. Those rules relate, for example, to agreements whereby parties refer a dispute to arbitration and the recognition and enforcement of arbitral awards. It follows that, by excluding arbitration from the scope of the Convention on the ground that it was already covered by international conventions, the Contracting Parties intended to exclude arbitration in its entirety, including proceedings brought before national courts.

19. More particularly, it must be pointed out that the appointment of an arbitrator by a national court is a measure adopted by the State as part of the process of setting arbitration proceedings in motion. Such a measure therefore comes within the sphere of arbitration and is thus covered by the exclusion contained in Article 1(4) of the Convention.

20. That interpretation is not affected by the fact that the international agreements in question have not been signed by all the Member States and do not cover all aspects of arbitration, in particular the procedure for the appointment of arbitrators.

21. That conclusion is also corroborated by the opinion expressed by the experts in the report drawn up by them at the time of the accession of Denmark, Ireland and the United Kingdom to the Convention, according to which the Convention does not apply to court proceedings which are ancillary to arbitration proceedings, for example the appointment or dismissal of arbitrators (Official Journal 1979 C 59, p. 93). Similarly, in the report drawn up at the time of the accession of the Hellenic Republic to the

Convention, the experts considered that cases where a court is instrumental in setting up the arbitration body are not covered by the Convention (Official Journal 1986 C 298, p. 1).

Whether a preliminary issue concerning the existence or validity of an arbitration agreement affects the application of the Convention to the dispute in question

22. Impianti contends that the exclusion in Article 1(4) of the Convention does not extend to disputes or judicial decisions concerning the existence or validity of an arbitration agreement. In its view, that exclusion likewise does not apply where arbitration is not the principal issue in the proceedings but is merely a subsidiary or incidental issue.

23. Impianti argues that, if that were not so, a party could avoid the application of the Convention merely by alleging the existence of an arbitration agreement.

24. Impianti contends that, in any event, the exception in Article 1(4) of the Convention does not apply where the existence or validity of an arbitration agreement is being disputed before different courts to which the Convention applies, regardless of whether that issue has been raised as a main issue or as a preliminary issue.

25. The Commission shares Impianti' s opinion in so far as the question of the existence or validity of an arbitration agreement is raised as a preliminary issue.

26. Those interpretations cannot be accepted. In order to determine whether a dispute falls within the scope of the Convention, reference must be made solely to the subject-matter of the dispute. If, by virtue of its subject-matter, such as the appointment of an arbitrator, a dispute falls outside the scope of the Convention, the existence of a preliminary issue which the court must resolve in order to determine the dispute cannot, whatever that issue may be, justify application of the Convention.

27. It would also be contrary to the principle of legal certainty, which is one of the objectives pursued by the Convention . . . for the applicability of the exclusion laid down in Article 1(4) of the Convention to vary according to the existence or otherwise of a preliminary issue, which might be raised at any time by the parties.

28. It follows that, in the case before the Court, the fact that a preliminary issue relates to the existence or validity of the arbitration agreement does not affect the exclusion from the scope of the Convention of a dispute concerning the appointment of an arbitrator.

29. Consequently, the reply must be that Article 1(4) of the Convention must be interpreted as meaning that the exclusion provided for therein extends to litigation pending before a national court concerning the appointment of an arbitrator, even if the existence or validity of an arbitration agreement is a preliminary issue in that litigation.

Comment

This case establishes that an 'Italian torpedo' does not work against an arbitration agreement. This is because proceedings ancillary to an arbitration, such as the appointment or dismissal of an arbitrator,[43] or for the enforcement or setting aside of an award, as well as the arbitration proceedings themselves, are outside the scope of the Regulation. As a result, the *lis pendens* rule does not apply to them. So the arbitration cannot be blocked by bringing proceedings in the courts of another Member State. This means that arbitration agreements are more effective than choice-of-court agreements within Europe.

§ 6 Conclusions

The decisions of the European Court in *Gasser*, *Turner* and *Owusu* caused something of a crisis of confidence among English lawyers. The view began to gain ground that the European Court could not be trusted in private-law cases: it seemed unwilling to take practical considerations into account and to consider the needs of litigants. This is a serious development.

Appendix

The following table shows the careers of the members of the European Court who were involved in the *Gasser*, *Turner* and *Owusu* decisions. It will be seen that, with few exceptions, they have been mainly involved in public law, public administration, diplomacy and politics. Only a few have had any apparent experience in private-law litigation, or indeed commercial-law activities of any kind. This might explain their judgments in these cases.

Judge	*Gasser* (2003)	*Turner* (2004)	*Owusu* (2005)	Career highlights
Skouris	P	P		Professor of Public Law; Minister of Internal Affairs; President of Greek Economic and Social Council
Jann	•	R	P[46]	Austrian judge; Ministry of Justice; member of Austrian Constitutional Court
Timmermans	•	•	•	Legal Secretary at ECJ; official at European Commission; Professor of European Law; Deputy Director-General of the Legal Service of the European Commission
Gulmann	•	•	•	Professor of Public International Law; Member of Administrative Appeal Tribunal (Denmark)
Cunha Rodrigues	•	•	•	Various government positions in Portugal; Portuguese Attorney General

43 According to the Schlosser Report (Schlosser, 'Report on the Convention of 9 October 1968' (Denmark, Ireland and UK Accessions), OJ 1979 C 59, p. 71 at p. 93, paragraph 64), the exclusion also covers proceedings for the fixing of the place of the arbitration, the extension of the time limit for making awards and the obtaining of preliminary rulings on points of law. In addition, it covers rulings on the validity of an arbitration agreement and orders not to go to arbitration (if the agreement is invalid).
46 Acting for the President.

Judge	*Gasser* (2003)	*Turner* (2004)	*Owusu* (2005)	Career highlights
Rosas	•	•	•	Professor; various positions concerning international law, human rights law and constitutional law; represented Finland in various international bodies; Legal Service of the European Commission
Edward	•			Advocate (practising lawyer) in Scotland; Professor of European Institutions
La Pergola	•	•		Professor of Public Law; President of Italian Constitutional Court; Minister for Community Policy; Member of European Parliament
Puissochet	•	•	•	Counsellor of State (France); Director-General of Legal Service of EC Council; OECD; French Ministry of Foreign Affairs
Schintgen	R	•	R	Ministry of Labour; President of Economic and Social Council; various public posts
Macken	•			Irish barrister (practising lawyer); Legal Advisor, Patents and Trade Marks Agents; Irish judge
Colneric	•	•	•	German employment tribunal judge; Professor of Labour Law
Von Bahr	•	•	•	Swedish Cabinet Office; judge in Supreme Administrative Court (Sweden); various positions concerning finance and tax
Léger	AG		AG	French Ministry of Justice; various civil service posts, especially in Ministry of Justice; French judge
Colomer		AG		Spanish judge, various courts including Supreme Court

P = President; R = Rapporteur (drafting judge); AG = Advocate General. Source: ECJ website (www.curia.eu.int).

Further reading

Bomhoff, *Judicial Discretion in European Law on Conflicts of Jurisdiction* (SDU Uitgevers (Publishers), The Hague, 2005, ISBN 90-5409-492-3) (Allen & Overy Research Series)

Fawcett (James J.) (ed.), *Declining Jurisdiction in Private International Law: Reports to the XIVth Congress of the International Academy of Comparative Law, Athens, August 1994* (Clarendon Press, Oxford, 1995)

Fentiman, 'Jurisdiction, Discretion and the Brussels Convention' (1993) 26 *Cornell International Law Journal* 59

'Ousting Jurisdiction and the European Conventions' (2000) *Cambridge Yearbook of European Legal Studies* 109

Kennett, 'Forum Non Conveniens in Europe' [1995] CLJ 552

CHAPTER 11

Special topics – I

In this chapter, we consider the jurisdictional aspects of two special topics. We consider two more in the next chapter.

§ 1   Products liability

Our first topic is products liability. Assume that a product is manufactured in country X and marketed in country Y. It causes injury. Where can the victim sue the manufacturer? Can he sue in country Y, or must he go to country X?

In the past, he often had to go to the country where the product was manufactured. If the manufacturer had no presence in the country in which the product was marketed, and could not be served there, the right of the victim to sue in his own country depended on the rules for service out of the jurisdiction. In the earlier part of the twentieth century, the rule in most common-law countries was that the tort had to have been committed in the territory of the forum, or the cause of action had to have arisen there. Originally, courts tended to say that the tort was committed (and the cause of action arose) in the country of manufacture.[1]

This was unfair to the victim, who would have found it difficult to travel to the manufacturer's country to bring the action; so courts began to look for a way of allowing suit to be brought in the country in which the product was marketed, even if the manufacturer had no place of business there.

§ 1.1   England

We now consider how the law developed in England. Our first case is actually from Australia, but, as it was decided by the Privy Council, it is also an authority on English law.

---

1 See, for example, *George Monro Ltd* v. *American Cyanamid and Chemical Corporation* [1944] KB 432; *Abbott-Smith* v. *Governors of University of Toronto* (1964) 49 MPR 329; 45 DLR (2d) 672 (Nova Scotia CA, Canada); *Anderson* v. *Nobels Explosive Co.* (1906) 12 OLR 644 (Ontario CA, Canada).

Australia
Distillers Co. v. Thompson
Privy Council
[1971] AC 458; [1971] 2 WLR 441; [1971] 1 All ER 694

Background

Distillers was an English pharmaceutical company that had no place of business in Australia. Some of its products contained thalidomide, a substance now known to cause severe birth defects if taken by the mother during pregnancy. Distillers marketed products containing thalidomide in Australia through its Australian subsidiary. One such product was a sedative called 'Distival'. The tablets were sold in a box with a leaflet describing their use. The tablets, box and leaflet were manufactured as a unit by Distillers and were sold to the Australian company in the form in which they were intended to reach the ultimate consumer. The claimant's mother was prescribed the tablets by her doctor. The mother bought them in New South Wales, Australia, and took them. As a result, the claimant, a baby girl, was born badly deformed: she had no arms. The question before the Privy Council was whether the courts of New South Wales had jurisdiction over Distillers. The relevant legislation was the Common Law Procedure Act of New South Wales 1899 as amended, section 18(4)(a) of which allowed service of a claim form out of the jurisdiction if the cause of action arose within the jurisdiction. The Australian courts held that they had jurisdiction under this provision. Distillers appealed to the Privy Council.

Lord Pearson

...

Next to be considered is the question of principle – what is required in order to show, for the purpose of section 18(4)(a) of the Act of 1899, 'that there is a cause of action which arose within the jurisdiction.' There seem to be three possible theories: (i) that the 'cause of action' must be the whole cause of action, so that every part of it, every ingredient of it, must have occurred within the jurisdiction; (ii) that it is necessary and sufficient that the last ingredient of the cause of action, the event which completes a cause of action and brings it into being, has occurred within the jurisdiction; and (iii) that the act on the part of the defendant which gives the plaintiff his cause of complaint must have occurred within the jurisdiction.

[After discussing English case law under sections 18 and 19 of the English Common Law Procedure Act 1852, Lord Pearson concluded that the first theory was contrary to authority. He then continued:]

That rules out no. (i) of the three possible theories set out above – the theory that 'cause of action' means the whole cause of action and the courts of a country do not have jurisdiction unless all the ingredients of the cause of action occurred within the country (unless the defendant happens to be present in the country). In any case that theory is too restrictive for the needs of modern times. The defendant has no major grievance if he is sued in the country where most of the ingredients of the cause of action against him took place. In such a case, if the theory no. (i) were accepted, the plaintiff, if lacking time and money for following the defendant to the defendant's country and suing him there, would be deprived of any remedy.

No. (ii) of the three possible theories – viz., that it is necessary and sufficient that the last ingredient of the cause of action, the event which completes it and brings it into being, has occurred within the jurisdiction – seems to their Lordships to be wrong as a theory. The last event might happen in a particular case to be the determining factor on its own merits, by reason of its inherent importance, but not because it is the last event. Decisions under statutes of limitation are not applicable. The question in that context being when did the cause of action accrue so that the plaintiff became able to sue, the answer is that the cause of action accrued when it became complete, as the plaintiff could not sue before then. But when the question is which country's courts should have jurisdiction to try the action, the approach should be different: the search is for the most appropriate court to try the action, and the degree of connection between the cause of action and the country concerned should be the determining factor . . . In a negligence case the happening of damage to the plaintiff is a necessary ingredient in the cause of action, and it is the last event completing the cause of action. But the place where it happens may be quite fortuitous and should not by itself be the sole determinant of jurisdiction. One example would be this: suppose that a defendant carries on business in New South Wales and there he manufactures and distributes Distival and sells a packet of it to the plaintiff's mother without warning of the danger: the defendant very soon afterwards gives up his business and retires to live in another country or state: the plaintiff's mother after purchasing the packet goes on holiday to any country in the world, say South Africa, and there consumes the Distival whereby (it is assumed) the damage to the plaintiff is caused: the plaintiff's mother returns to her home in New South Wales. On those facts, if the theory were right, the courts of New South Wales would have no jurisdiction and the courts of South Africa (if there was a South African statute containing provisions similar to section 18 (4) (a) of the Act of 1899) would have jurisdiction to entertain the action, though perhaps in the exercise of their discretion they might decline to entertain it. That is the result of the theory in such a case, and it is not a sensible result: the jurisdiction is wrongly allocated. It is manifestly just and reasonable that a defendant should have to answer for his wrongdoing in the country where he did the wrong. It is at any rate not manifestly just or reasonable that the defendant should have to answer for his wrongdoing in any country in the world to which the plaintiff (or the plaintiff's mother in a case such as this) may have happened to go before the damage occurred. It is not the right approach to say that, because there was no complete tort until the damage occurred, therefore the cause of action arose wherever the damage happened to occur. The right approach is, when the tort is complete, to look back over the series of events constituting it and ask the question, where in substance did this cause of action arise?

Theory no. (iii) is that the cause of action arose within the jurisdiction if the act on the part of the defendant, which gives the plaintiff his cause of complaint has occurred within the jurisdiction. That is the rule laid down in *Jackson* v. *Spittall*

(1870) LR 5 CP 542, which is an authoritative case, and the rule is inherently reasonable, as the defendant is called upon to answer for his wrong in the courts of the country where he did the wrong. The rule does not, however, provide a simple answer for all cases. In *Jackson* v. *Spittall* . . . the wrongdoing was a breach of contract and there was no difficulty in determining where it occurred. The court did not have to consider where the wrongful act should be considered to have taken place in an action for negligence. The defendant does not merely by behaving negligently give the plaintiff any cause for complaint in law. The plaintiff has such a cause for complaint if the defendant's negligence has caused damage to the plaintiff. In the great majority of cases the place where the defendant is negligent is the same as the place where the negligence causes damage to the plaintiff. For instance the defendant while driving his car negligently runs into and injures the plaintiff. But in some cases, particularly those in which the principle of *Donoghue* v. *Stevenson* [1932] AC 562 is relied upon, there may be a separation in time and place between the negligent behaviour of the defendant and the resulting damage to the plaintiff . . . On the one hand X is the country where the defendant was negligent and on the other hand Y is the country in which the defendant's negligence caused the plaintiff to be hurt. The problem is a difficult one and there is no need to express any opinion on it in the present case.

In the present case on the assumptions made for the purpose of testing jurisdiction there was negligence by the English company in New South Wales causing injury to the plaintiff in New South Wales. So far as appears, the goods were not defective or incorrectly manufactured. The negligence was in failure to give a warning that the goods would be dangerous if taken by an expectant mother in the first three months of pregnancy. That warning might have been given by putting a warning notice on each package as it was made up in England. It could also have been given by communication to persons in New South Wales – the medical practitioners, the wholesale and retail chemists, patients and purchasers. The plaintiff is entitled to complain of the lack of such communication in New South Wales as negligence by the defendant in New South Wales causing injury to the plaintiff there. That is the act (which must include omission) on the part of the English company which has given the plaintiff a cause of complaint in law. The cause of action arose within the jurisdiction.

For the reasons which have been given their Lordships are of opinion that the decision of [the Australian courts] was right and should be affirmed. Their Lordships will humbly advise Her Majesty that the appeal should be dismissed. The appellants must pay the costs of the appeal.

Comment

By saying that the defendant's wrongdoing was its failure to warn (and that that failure took place in New South Wales), the Privy Council was able to side-step the problem, raised by Lord Pearson but which was unnecessary to decide, in which the defendant acts negligently in country X and thus causes harm to the claimant in country Y. Later cases have taken the sentence, 'The right approach is, when the tort is complete, to look back over the series of events constituting it and ask the question, where in substance did this cause of action arise?', and treated this as the key for finding a solution to this problem. Our next case is an example.

England
Castree* v. *Squibb Ltd
Court of Appeal
[1980] 1 WLR 1248; [1980] 2 All ER 589

Background

This case concerned a machine called a centrifuge. Squibb had bought it from the manufacturer, a German company. Ms Castree was an employee of Squibb. She had used it in the course of her work, and had been injured when it disintegrated. She sued Squibb, and Squibb wanted to join the German manufacturer in third-party proceedings. The German company had no place of business in England, and had marketed the machine there through its agent. The German company claimed that the English courts had no jurisdiction over it. It said that, if it was negligent, that negligence took place in Germany where the machine was manufactured. As the action was brought before the Brussels Convention came into force in the United Kingdom, the traditional rules of English law were applicable.

Ackner LJ

[After discussing the authorities, including the *Distillers* case]

[The] question seems to me to be clearly this: that which gave, or gives, the plaintiff her cause of complaint is not the mere manufacture of the defective machinery, which of course took place in Germany; the mere manufacture of the defective machinery is not in my judgment even the beginning of tort. That manufacture might have been manufacture for experimental purposes, or it might have been for the development of some part of the machinery. The substantial wrongdoing in this case alleged to have been committed by the appellants is putting on the English market a defective machine with no warning as to its defects. That being, in my judgment, the position, and applying the test which is accepted on all sides to be the appropriate test, namely, to look back over the series of events constituting the tort and to ask the question where in substance this cause of action arose, I would conclude that it arose in this country.

Accordingly I would dismiss this appeal.

Oliver and Buckley LJJ agreed.

The appeal was dismissed: the English courts have jurisdiction.

Comment

Here the court achieved the desired result by saying that the essence of the tort was not the manufacture of a defective product, but the marketing of that product.

These two cases show that, by the 1980s, the English courts had found a fairly satisfactory solution. This allowed the victim to sue in the country in which the product was marketed, even if it was not marketed directly by the manufacturer. This solution, which (as we shall see) still applies in the United States, requires the court to decide whether the manufacturer intended (or foresaw) that the product would be marketed in the territory of the forum. This requires some concept of 'targeting' or deliberate conduct ('purposeful availment' in American terminology), something that is not always easy to define.

Subsequently, many countries, both in Europe and beyond, went further by permitting jurisdiction *either* if the defendant acted within the territory of the forum *or* if the claimant suffered harm there. The judgment of the European Court in *Bier* v. *Mines de Potasse d'Alsace*, discussed in Chapter 4, § 1.2, above, to some extent paved the way for this development. This rule applies in England under the Brussels I Regulation. A similar rule now applies under the CPR: see Chapter 5, § 4.3, above. As applied to a products-liability case, this would allow the victim to sue either where the defendant acted (possibly by marketing the product) or where he (the claimant) suffered harm.

However, by getting away from the idea of 'targeting', this approach could lead to exorbitant jurisdiction. Take the example posed by Lord Pearson in the *Distillers* case: the producer manufactures and markets the product in New South Wales, Australia. The claimant's mother buys it there and takes it to South Africa. She consumes it in South Africa and the claimant is born there. Since the harm is suffered by the victim in South Africa, the new rule would allow suit to be brought there. If the product was never marketed there, this would be unfair to the manufacturer, especially if it was a small-scale producer that might have confined its marketing activities to its home state of New South Wales. Common-law jurisdictions (not governed by EC law) might solve this problem through *forum non conveniens*, but it is hard to see how it could be solved within the context of the Brussels I Regulation.[2]

§ 1.2   *Canada*

Our next case, though fairly old, is still the leading case in Canada.

Canada (Saskatchewan)
Moran* v. *Pyle National (Canada) Ltd
Supreme Court of Canada
[1975] 1 SCR 393; (1973) 43 DLR (3d) 239; [1974] 2 WWR 586

Background

Moran, an electrician, was fatally injured in the province of Saskatchewan while removing a spent light bulb manufactured by Pyle National (Canada) Ltd. The plaintiffs-appellants, who were the widow and children of the deceased, claimed

---

2 The *Marinari* case (discussed in Chapter 4, § 1.2, above) does not solve the problem, since, in the example given, the direct harm would have been suffered in South Africa.

that Pyle had been negligent in the manufacture and construction of the bulb and negligent in failing to provide an adequate system of safety checks to prevent faulty products leaving its plant. Pyle did not carry on business in Saskatchewan; all of its manufacturing and assembly operations were in Ontario. It sold its products to distributors, but none directly to consumers. It had no salesmen or agents within Saskatchewan.

Dickson J

[After referring to the *Distillers* case]

As I understand it, their Lordships rejected any mechanical application of the 'last event' theory in favour of a more flexible, qualitative and quantitative test . . .

Generally speaking, in determining where a tort has been committed, it is unnecessary, and unwise, to have resort to any arbitrary set of rules. The place of acting and the place of harm theories are too arbitrary and inflexible to be recognized in contemporary jurisprudence. In the *Distillers'* case . . . a real and substantial connection test was hinted at. Cheshire, [*Private International Law*] 8th ed., p. 281, has suggested a test very similar to this; the author says that it would not be inappropriate to regard a tort as having occurred in any country substantially affected by the defendant's activities or its consequences and the law of which is likely to have been in the reasonable contemplation of the parties. Applying this test to a case of careless manufacture, the following rule can be formulated: where a foreign defendant carelessly manufactures a product in a foreign jurisdiction which enters into the normal channels of trade and he knows or ought to know both that as a result of his carelessness a consumer may well be injured and it is reasonably foreseeable that the product would be used or consumed where the plaintiff used or consumed it, then the forum in which the plaintiff suffered damage is entitled to exercise judicial jurisdiction over that foreign defendant. This rule recognizes the important interest a state has in injuries suffered by persons within its territory. It recognizes that the purpose of negligence as a tort is to protect against carelessly inflicted injury and thus that the predominating element is damage suffered. By tendering his products in the market place directly or through normal distributive channels, a manufacturer ought to assume the burden of defending those products wherever they cause harm as long as the forum into which the manufacturer is taken is one that he reasonably ought to have had in his contemplation when he so tendered his goods. This is particularly true of dangerously defective goods placed in the interprovincial flow of commerce.

In the result, I am of the opinion that the courts of the Province of Saskatchewan have jurisdiction to entertain the action herein . . .

I would allow the appeal with costs here and in the Court of Appeal for Saskatchewan.

Comment

This case (together with the 'real and substantial connection' test generally applied in at least the common-law provinces) indicates that Canadian courts will probably not claim excessive jurisdiction in products-liability actions.

§ 1.3   The United States

Our next case shows the approach in the United States.

United States
Asahi Metal Industry* v. *Superior Court of California
US Supreme Court
480 US 102; 107 S Ct 1026; 94 L Ed 2d 92 (1987)

Background

The original plaintiff in this case, Gary Zurcher, crashed his Honda motorcycle on a California highway. His wife was killed and he was severely injured. He claimed the accident was caused by a blow-out in the rear tyre and sued (among others) the manufacturer of the tyre, Cheng Shin, a Taiwanese company. Cheng Shin then filed a cross-complaint seeking indemnification from the manufacturer of the valve, a Japanese company called Asahi. Zurcher's action against Cheng Shin and the other original defendants was eventually settled, leaving only Cheng Shin's indemnity action against Asahi.

Asahi made its valves in Japan and sold them to tyre manufacturers, including Cheng Shin. In 1981, sales to Cheng Shin accounted for less than 2 per cent of Asahi's income. The sales to Cheng Shin took place in Taiwan and the goods were shipped from Japan to Taiwan.

The action was brought in a state court in California. The Supreme Court of California held that the courts of California had jurisdiction. Although it noted that Asahi had no offices, property or agents in California, made no direct sales there and did not control the distribution system in California, it nevertheless held that the Due Process Clause was satisfied because Asahi knew that some of its valves would be incorporated into tyres sold in California, and that it benefited indirectly from those sales. It considered that Asahi's intentional act of placing its components into the stream of commerce – that is, by delivering them to Cheng Shin – coupled with Asahi's awareness that some of the components would find their way to California, was sufficient to satisfy the constitutional requirement.

The United States Supreme Court reversed this judgment. It held that, in determining whether the exercise of jurisdiction is reasonable, several factors must be taken into account. These include the burden on the defendant, the interests of the forum state, and the plaintiff's interest in obtaining relief. The inter-state judicial system's interest in obtaining the most efficient resolution of controversies must also be considered. Since, in the case before the court, the American party had dropped out, neither the plaintiff (Cheng Shin) nor the state of California had a sufficiently great interest in having the proceedings brought in California to outweigh the considerable burden that would be placed on the defendant if it had to defend the action there.

This rationale was applicable only because of the rather unusual situation. The court, however, also considered the wider picture: what would have happened if Zurcher had still been a party. Here they were divided. Four judges,[3] led by O'Connor J, took one position; four,[4] led by Brennan J, took another; and the ninth judge, Stevens J,[5] took an intermediate position, thus leaving no majority view.

We consider only this latter question.

Justice O'Connor (minority opinion of four judges out of nine):

II

A

The Due Process Clause of the Fourteenth Amendment limits the power of a state court to exert personal jurisdiction over a nonresident defendant. '[T]he constitutional touchstone' of the determination whether an exercise of personal jurisdiction comports with due process 'remains whether the defendant purposefully established "minimum contacts" in the forum State.' Most recently we have reaffirmed the oft-quoted reasoning of *Hanson* v. *Denckla*, 357 US 235, 253; 78 S Ct 1228, 1239; 2 L Ed. 2d 1283 (1958), that minimum contacts must have a basis in 'some act by which the defendant purposefully avails itself of the privilege of conducting activities within the forum State, thus invoking the benefits and protections of its laws.' Jurisdiction is proper . . . where the contacts proximately result from actions by the defendant *himself* that create a 'substantial connection' with the forum State.' Ibid . . .

[O'Connor J then considered the *World-Wide Volkswagen* case. She continued:]

The Supreme Court of California held that, because the stream of commerce eventually brought some valves Asahi sold Cheng Shin into California, Asahi's awareness that its valves would be sold in California was sufficient to permit California to exercise jurisdiction over Asahi consistent with the requirements of the Due Process Clause. The Supreme Court of California's position was consistent with those courts that have held that mere foreseeability or awareness was a constitutionally sufficient basis for personal jurisdiction if the defendant's product made its way into the forum State while still in the stream of commerce . . .

Other courts, however, have understood the Due Process Clause to require something more than that the defendant was aware of its product's entry into the forum State through the stream of commerce in order for the State to exert jurisdiction over the defendant. In the present case, for example, the State Court of Appeal did not read the Due Process Clause, as interpreted by *World-Wide Volkswagen*, to allow 'mere foreseeability that the product will enter the forum state [to] be enough by itself to establish jurisdiction over the distributor and retailer.'

We now find this latter position to be consonant with the requirements of due process. The 'substantial connection' between the defendant and the forum State necessary for a finding of minimum contacts must come about by *an action of*

---

3 O'Connor, Rehnquist, Powell and Scalia JJ.
4 Brennan, White, Marshall and Blackmun JJ.
5 Supported by White and Blackmun JJ.

the defendant purposefully directed toward the forum State . . . The placement of a product into the stream of commerce, without more, is not an act of the defendant purposefully directed toward the forum State. Additional conduct of the defendant may indicate an intent or purpose to serve the market in the forum State, for example, designing the product for the market in the forum State, advertising in the forum State, establishing channels for providing regular advice to customers in the forum State, or marketing the product through a distributor who has agreed to serve as the sales agent in the forum State. But a defendant's awareness that the stream of commerce may or will sweep the product into the forum State does not convert the mere act of placing the product into the stream into an act purposefully directed toward the forum State.

Assuming, *arguendo*, that respondents have established Asahi's awareness that some of the valves sold to Cheng Shin would be incorporated into tire tubes sold in California, respondents have not demonstrated any action by Asahi to purposefully avail itself of the California market. Asahi does not do business in California. It has no office, agents, employees, or property in California. It does not advertise or otherwise solicit business in California. It did not create, control, or employ the distribution system that brought its valves to California . . . There is no evidence that Asahi designed its product in anticipation of sales in California . . . On the basis of these facts, the exertion of personal jurisdiction over Asahi by the Superior Court of California exceeds the limits of Due Process.

Justice Brennan (minority opinion of four judges out of nine)

The plurality states that 'a defendant's awareness that the stream of commerce may or will sweep the product into the forum State does not convert the mere act of placing the product into the stream into an act purposefully directed toward the forum State.'The plurality would therefore require a plaintiff to show '[a]dditional conduct' directed toward the forum before finding the exercise of jurisdiction over the defendant to be consistent with the Due Process Clause . . . I see no need for such a showing, however. The stream of commerce refers not to unpredictable currents or eddies, but to the regular and anticipated flow of products from manufacture to distribution to retail sale. As long as a participant in this process is aware that the final product is being marketed in the forum State, the possibility of a lawsuit there cannot come as a surprise. Nor will the litigation present a burden for which there is no corresponding benefit. A defendant who has placed goods in the stream of commerce benefits economically from the retail sale of the final product in the forum State, and indirectly benefits from the State's laws that regulate and facilitate commercial activity. These benefits accrue regardless of whether that participant directly conducts business in the forum State, or engages in additional conduct directed toward that State. Accordingly, most courts and commentators have found that jurisdiction premised on the placement of a product into the stream of commerce is consistent with the Due Process Clause, and have not required a showing of additional conduct.

The plurality's endorsement of what appears to be the minority view among Federal Courts of Appeals represents a marked retreat from its analysis in *World-*

Wide Volkswagen v. *Woodson* . . . In that case, 'respondents [sought] to base jurisdiction on one, isolated occurrence and whatever inferences can be drawn therefrom: the fortuitous circumstance that a single Audi automobile, sold in New York to New York residents, happened to suffer an accident while passing through Oklahoma.'The Court held that the possibility of an accident in Oklahoma, while to some extent foreseeable in light of the inherent mobility of the automobile, was not enough to establish minimum contacts between the forum State and the retailer or distributor . . . The Court then carefully explained:

> '[T]his is not to say, of course, that foreseeability is wholly irrelevant. But the foreseeability that is critical to due process analysis is not the mere likelihood that a product will find its way into the forum State. Rather, it is that the defendant's conduct and connection with the forum State are such that he should reasonably anticipate being haled into Court there.'

The Court reasoned that when a corporation may reasonably anticipate litigation in a particular forum, it cannot claim that such litigation is unjust or unfair, because it 'can act to alleviate the risk of burdensome litigation by procuring insurance, passing the expected costs on to consumers, or, if the risks are too great, severing its connection with the State.'

To illustrate the point, the Court contrasted the foreseeability of litigation in a State to which a consumer fortuitously transports a defendant's product (insufficient contacts) with the foreseeability of litigation in a State where the defendant's product was regularly *sold* (sufficient contacts). The Court stated:

> 'Hence if the *sale* of a product of a manufacturer or distributor such as Audi or Volkswagen is not simply an isolated occurrence, but arises from the efforts of the manufacturer or distributor to serve, *directly or indirectly*, the market for its product in other States, it is not unreasonable to subject it to suit in one of those States if its allegedly defective merchandise has there been the source of injury to its owner or to others. The forum State does not exceed its powers under the Due Process Clause if it asserts personal jurisdiction over a corporation that delivers its products into the stream of commerce *with the expectation that they will be purchased by consumers* in the forum State.'

The Court in *World-Wide Volkswagen* thus took great care to distinguish 'between a case involving goods which reach a distant State through a chain of distribution and a case involving goods which reach the same State because a consumer . . . took them there.'(Brennan, J, dissenting). The California Supreme Court took note of this distinction, and correctly concluded that our holding in *World-Wide Volkswagen* preserved the stream-of-commerce theory . . .

In this case, the facts found by the California Supreme Court support its finding of minimum contacts. The court found that '[a]lthough Asahi did not design or control the system of distribution that carried its valve assemblies into California, Asahi was aware of the distribution system's operation, and it knew that it would benefit economically from the sale in California of products incorporating its components.'Accordingly, I cannot join the plurality's determination that Asahi's regular and extensive sales of component parts to a manufacturer it knew was making regular sales of the final product in California is insufficient to establish minimum contacts with California.

Justice Stevens (minority opinion)

[After stating that it was unnecessary to consider whether minimum contacts had been established – even if they had, the constitutional requirement still would not have been satisfied, given that Zurcher had dropped out – continued:]

Second, even assuming that the test ought to be formulated here, Part II-A misapplies it to the facts of this case. The plurality seems to assume that an unwavering line can be drawn between 'mere awareness' that a component will find its way into the forum State and 'purposeful availment' of the forum's market . . . Over the course of its dealings with Cheng Shin, Asahi has arguably engaged in a higher quantum of conduct than '[t]he placement of a product into the stream of commerce, without more . . .' Ibid. Whether or not this conduct rises to the level of purposeful availment requires a constitutional determination that is affected by the volume, the value, and the hazardous character of the components. In most circumstances I would be inclined to conclude that a regular course of dealing that results in deliveries of over 100,000 units annually over a period of several years would constitute 'purposeful availment' even though the item delivered to the forum State was a standard product marketed throughout the world.

Comment

This fundamental difference of view as to what is required in a products-liability case has still not been finally resolved at the Supreme Court level.[6]

QUESTIONS

1 Which approach do you prefer in this case: that of O'Connor, Brennan or Stevens?
2 Generally, which approach do you prefer: that of the European, Canadian or US courts?

§ 1.4   Conclusions

In products-liability cases, the EC claims wider jurisdiction than either the United States or Canada, since the mere fact that the claimant has suffered damage within the territory of the forum will confer jurisdiction, irrespective (it seems) of foreseeability. This is not the case in the US or Canada. This is another situation where US jurisdictional rules are more restrained than those of Europe. (England has the same jurisdictional rule as the EU, but, when the traditional rules apply, it is tempered by *forum non conveniens*; so it would be more restrained in practice.) The test in Canada – at least, if one takes *Moran* v. *Pyle* as a guide – seems similar to that put forward by Brennan J in the *Asahi* case. The test advanced by O'Connor J is the most restricted of all.

---

6 Some lower courts have followed the one view and some have followed the other. For a full analysis, see Born and Rutledge, *International Civil Litigation in United States Courts*, (2007), pp. 146 *et seq*.

In jurisdictions (outside the US) that operate a 'necessary or proper party' rule, the court would have jurisdiction in the *Asahi* case on that basis, since the claim against Asahi was brought by the original defendant, Cheng Shin. There is something to be said for this rule: if the California courts would have had jurisdiction if Zurcher had still been a party, and if Cheng Shin had had to negotiate a settlement with Zurcher on this basis, it would seem only fair that its indemnity action should be settled or decided on the same basis.

§ 2 Defamation

§ 2.1 Introduction

London is said to be the libel capital of the world.[7] The rich and the famous from every continent flock to London to bring libel actions against newspapers, periodicals, broadcasters and persons who put material on the Internet. This applies not only to English publishers, but also – one might almost say 'in particular' – to foreign publishers. Thus, a Russian businessman who claims to have been libelled by an American business magazine might choose London in preference to either Moscow or New York;[8] and a boxing promoter resident in the United States who claims to have been libelled by material put on the Internet by another US resident might again prefer London.[9] To paraphrase the words of Lord Denning, said with reference to the United States,[10] 'As a moth is drawn to the light, so is a [libel] litigant drawn to [England].'[11]

The reason for this extraordinary attraction is that English substantive law is extremely favourable to claimants in libel actions. Damages are high.[12] There is no need to prove special damage (financial loss actually suffered): it is sufficient if the statement is defamatory in the abstract. Nor need the claimant prove that the defendant intended to do him harm. The claimant need not prove that the offending statement is false, though it is a good defence for the defendant if he can prove it true. In this one area, therefore, England is a more attractive forum than the United States, where free speech and freedom of the press enjoy special protection under the First Amendment to the US Constitution, a protection that makes libel actions more difficult.

On the other hand, English law gives extremely limited remedies for invasion of privacy, much more limited than those available under the law of, for example, France or Germany. If the news story is true, the claimant will be better off suing in another country. Thus, a French starlet who wishes to sue an English newspaper for publishing a photograph of her sunbathing topless in her back

---

7 Morse, 'Rights Relating to Personality, Freedom of the Press and Private International Law: Some Common Law Comments' (2005) 58 *Current Legal Problems* 133 at p. 134, n. 5.
8 *Berezovsky* v. *Michaels* [2000] 1 WLR 1004; [2000] 2 All ER 986 (HL).
9 *King* v. *Lewis*, § 2.3, below.
10 Quoted in Chapter 7, § 4.2.2, above.
11 *Smith Kline & French* v. *Bloch* [1983] 2 All ER 72 at p. 74 (CA).
12 Today, the courts are making a conscious effort to reduce them; nevertheless, they remain generous by international standards.

garden should sue in France; while a German politician seeking a remedy against an English newspaper for asserting (correctly) that he dyes his hair should confine his litigation to Germany. In either case, the resulting judgment will be enforceable in England under the Brussels I Regulation.

As we shall see in Chapter 23, § 7, below, choice of law for defamation and invasion of privacy is not covered by the EC's Rome II Regulation. If the proceedings are brought in England, the common-law choice-of-law rules will apply.[13] Under these, English substantive law will apply whenever the tort is committed in England.

Another feature of English law is the rule in *Duke of Brunswick* v. *Harmer*,[14] a rule under which every publication is a separate tort. A 'publication' occurs whenever the offending material comes to the attention of another person. Each time a newspaper vendor sells a newspaper to a commuter rushing to catch his train home in the evening, and every time a viewer tunes into a TV broadcast and hears a news item, there is another publication.[15] Under English law, the 'place of publication' is every place where this occurs: it is not limited to the place where the newspaper or TV company has its main place of business.[16] This means that a tort is committed in England whenever a single copy of a foreign newspaper is sold in England or a foreign radio or TV broadcast is received in England.

In the United States, the law is different. Under the 'single publication' rule (followed by the great majority of states), only one action can be brought. However, in that action, damages may be claimed for every occasion on which there is a 'publication' in the sense in which that word is understood by English law.[17]

§ 2.2   EC law

Under the Brussels I Regulation, the claimant can sue the publisher where the latter is domiciled (under Article 2(1) of the Regulation), or he may sue it under Article 5(3) in the place where the 'harmful event' (tort) occurred. Our next case concerns the latter possibility.

> **European Community**
> ***Shevill* v. *Presse Alliance SA***
> **Court of Justice of the European Communities**
> **Case C-68/93, [1995] ECR I-415; [1995] 2 AC 18; [1995] 2 WLR 499;**
> **[1995] All ER (EC) 289**

Background

This case concerned a person domiciled in England who was working in France for a French company.[18] A French newspaper, *France Soir*, alleged that she and

---

13 The Private International Law (Miscellaneous Provisions) Act 1995 does not apply to defamation.
14 (1849) 14 QB 185.
15 A claimant can nevertheless sue for all (or some) of them in a single action.
16 This terminology sometimes causes confusion to lawyers from civil-law countries.
17 For further discussion of this rule, see American Law Institute, *Restatement of the Law Second, Torts* (American Law Institute Publishers, St Paul, MN, 1977), Volume 3, § 577A.
18 This company was part of the same group of companies (controlled by Mr Grovit) as was involved in the *Turner* case, discussed in Chapter 10, § 3, above.

her employer were involved in laundering drug money in Paris. She and the employer sued the newspaper in England for libel. Its circulation in France was approximately 200,000; in England it was something in the region of 250, and there was no evidence that anyone who had read the article knew the claimant. Nevertheless, the English courts held that they had jurisdiction under Article 5(3).[19]

Judgment

[After referring to Article 5(3) of the Convention, the court continued:]

19. It is settled case-law . . . that that rule of special jurisdiction, the choice of which is a matter for the plaintiff, is based on the existence of a particularly close connecting factor between the dispute and courts other than those of the State of the defendant's domicile which justifies the attribution of jurisdiction to those courts for reasons relating to the sound administration of justice and the efficacious conduct of proceedings.

20. It must also be emphasized that in *Mines de Potasse d' Alsace*[1] the Court held (at paragraphs 24 and 25) that, where the place of the happening of the event which may give rise to liability in tort, delict or quasi-delict and the place where that event results in damage are not identical, the expression 'place where the harmful event occurred' in Article 5(3) of the Convention must be understood as being intended to cover both the place where the damage occurred and the place of the event giving rise to it, so that the defendant may be sued, at the option of the plaintiff, either in the courts for the place where the damage occurred or in the courts for the place of the event which gives rise to and is at the origin of that damage.

21. In that judgment, the Court stated (at paragraphs 15 and 17) that the place of the event giving rise to the damage no less than the place where the damage occurred could constitute a significant connecting factor from the point of view of jurisdiction, since each of them could, depending on the circumstances, be particularly helpful in relation to the evidence and the conduct of the proceedings.

22. The Court added (at paragraph 20) that to decide in favour only of the place of the event giving rise to the damage would, in an appreciable number of cases, cause confusion between the heads of jurisdiction laid down by Articles 2 and 5(3) of the Convention, so that the latter provision would, to that extent, lose its effectiveness.

23. Those observations, made in relation to physical or pecuniary loss or damage, must equally apply, for the same reasons, in the case of loss or damage other than physical or pecuniary, in particular injury to the reputation and good name of a natural or legal person due to a defamatory publication.

24. In the case of a libel by a newspaper article distributed in several Contracting States, the place of the event giving rise to the damage, within the meaning of those judgments, can only be the place where the publisher of the newspaper

---

1 *Editor's note*: this is the *Bier* case, set out in Chapter 4, § 1.2, above.

19 The claimants limited their claim to damages for publication in England.

in question is established, since that is the place where the harmful event originated and from which the libel was issued and put into circulation.

25. The court of the place where the publisher of the defamatory publication is established must therefore have jurisdiction to hear the action for damages for all the harm caused by the unlawful act.

26. However, that forum will generally coincide with the head of jurisdiction set out in the first paragraph of Article 2 of the Convention.

27. As the Court held in *Mines de Potasse d' Alsace*, the plaintiff must consequently have the option to bring proceedings also in the place where the damage occurred, since otherwise Article 5(3) of the Convention would be rendered meaningless.

28. The place where the damage occurred is the place where the event giving rise to the damage, entailing tortious, delictual or quasi-delictual liability, produced its harmful effects upon the victim.

29. In the case of an international libel through the press, the injury caused by a defamatory publication to the honour, reputation and good name of a natural or legal person occurs in the places where the publication is distributed, when the victim is known in those places.

30. It follows that the courts of each Contracting State in which the defamatory publication was distributed and in which the victim claims to have suffered injury to his reputation have jurisdiction to rule on the injury caused in that State to the victim' s reputation.

31. In accordance with the requirement of the sound administration of justice, the basis of the rule of special jurisdiction in Article 5(3), the courts of each Contracting State in which the defamatory publication was distributed and in which the victim claims to have suffered injury to his reputation are territorially the best placed to assess the libel committed in that State and to determine the extent of the corresponding damage.

32. Although there are admittedly disadvantages to having different courts ruling on various aspects of the same dispute, the plaintiff always has the option of bringing his entire claim before the courts either of the defendant' s domicile or of the place where the publisher of the defamatory publication is established.

33. In light of the foregoing, the answer to the first, second, third and sixth questions referred by the House of Lords must be that, on a proper construction of the expression 'place where the harmful event occurred' in Article 5(3) of the Convention, the victim of a libel by a newspaper article distributed in several Contracting States may bring an action for damages against the publisher either before the courts of the Contracting State of the place where the publisher of the defamatory publication is established, which have jurisdiction to award damages for all the harm caused by the defamation, or before the courts of each Contracting State in which the publication was distributed and where the victim claims to have suffered

> injury to his reputation, which have jurisdiction to rule solely in respect of the harm caused in the State of the court seised.

Comment

In this case, the European Court said there were two alternative grounds of jurisdiction in a libel case: the place where the material is distributed and the place where the publisher is 'established'. The statement in paragraph 26 of the judgment that this latter forum will 'generally coincide' with that set out in Article 2(1) makes clear, however, that 'establishment' is not necessarily the same as domicile. Thus, the jurisdiction of *both* the courts of the place of distribution *and* the courts of the place of establishment are derived from Article 5(3). Suit in the place of the defendant's domicile is, therefore, a third possibility.

This analysis makes sense only if the publisher sells all the copies of the paper to independent distributors in Paris (or wherever else its headquarters happen to be), and the copies distributed in England find their way there independently of the intention of the publisher. However, this is not the way newspapers are normally distributed. One would expect the publisher itself to arrange for most of the copies to reach their intended destination in England. In such a case, it makes more sense to say that the publisher acted in England.[20] The publisher can still be sued at its principal place of business,[21] but this would be under Article 2(1), not Article 5(3).

Another objection to the concept of 'establishment' is that it is far from clear what it means. Does it refer to the editorial centre, or the printing centre? These may be in different places. Moreover, some English and American newspapers are printed in more than one country. The editorial headquarters may be in London or New York and the paper may be printed there, but the European edition may be printed in, for example, Belgium and distributed from there. Similar problems can arise with radio, TV and Internet publications.

Under the court's analysis, as well as under the alternative analysis suggested above, a claim brought in the place of distribution (not being the country of establishment/domicile) must be limited to damage flowing from the copies of the publication distributed there. As we shall see below, the rule in English law is the same. In the United States, on the other hand, a plaintiff can sue in any state in which the material was distributed and claim damages for publication *throughout* the United States.[22] This follows from the 'single publication' rule, discussed above.

The leading case is *Keeton* v. *Hustler Magazine*,[23] in which the plaintiff sued the publisher in New Hampshire, a small state in which sales were limited. The plaintiff lived in New York and had no particular connection with New

---

20 The acts of the publisher's agents in England must count as acts of the publisher itself: *qui facit per alium facit per se*, a principle known equally to the civil and the common law.
21 Under Article 60(1)(c) of the Brussels I Regulation, it would be domiciled there.
22 It is not clear whether this also covers publication outside the US.
23 465 US 770; 104 S Ct 1473; 79 L Ed 2d 790 (1984).

Hampshire.[24] The reason she chose that state was that the limitation period had expired in all other states.[25] The Supreme Court held that she could sue in New Hampshire and that she could claim damages for publication nationwide. It was not necessary that she should have any special contacts with New Hampshire.

§ 2.3 English law

The position under the traditional rules of English jurisdiction is similar to that under EC law. If proceedings are brought against a foreign defendant (not domiciled in an EC or Lugano State) and jurisdiction depends on service of the claim form outside England on the basis that the tort was committed in England,[26] the English court will have jurisdiction only with regard to material published (distributed) in England. If the claimant has no reputation in England or if publication in England is so minimal that damage to the claimant's reputation is insignificant, the court will normally stay the proceedings on *forum-non-conveniens* grounds[27] or strike out the claim as an abuse of process.[28]

Internet libel raises special problems. Our next case is the leading English decision on the subject.

England
King* v. *Lewis
Court of Appeal
[2004] EWCA Civ 1329

Background

Don King was a boxing promoter. He was an American citizen, resident in Florida. He had promoted a number of fights in Britain and was well known in English boxing circles. He had earned a great deal of money from his business activities in England. Lennox Lewis, a former world heavyweight champion, was a British citizen, resident mainly in New York. He was one of three defendants. The claim was based on an alleged libel of King on a California-based website, www.fightnews.com: it was said that he was anti-Semitic. King sued in England, apparently because it would have been difficult for him to win under US law. The defendant argued that England was not a *forum conveniens*, but the trial court allowed the action to go ahead. The defendants appealed.

---

24 The defendant was an Ohio corporation.
25 In New Hampshire (as in many states), statutes of limitation are considered procedural and therefore governed by the law of the forum: see footnote 10 in the judgment. The Supreme Court recognized that this rule might be open to criticism, but said that it was a matter to be decided once the jurisdiction of the New Hampshire court was established.
26 CPR 6.36 and Practice Direction 6 B, paragraph 3.1(9), set out in Panel 5.5 and discussed in Chapter 5, § 4.3, above.
27 *Kroch* v. *Rossell et Cie* [1937] All ER 725, discussed in Morse, 'Rights Relating to Personality, Freedom of the Press and Private International Law: Some Common Law Comments' (2005) 58 *Current Legal Problems* 133 at pp. 146–7. See, further, *Berezovsky* v. *Michaels* [2000] 1 WLR 1004; [2000] 2 All ER 986 (HL).
28 *Jameel (Yousef)* v. *Dow Jones & Co. Inc.* [2005] QB 946; [2005] 2 WLR 1614 (CA). This latter remedy would probably be applicable even if the English court had jurisdiction under EC law, since it is not based on jurisdictional considerations.

Judgment

[After saying that there were four strands of learning relevant to the case, the court continued:]

24. The first of these strands is that there exists an initial presumption that the natural or appropriate forum for trial of the dispute will be the courts of the place where the tort is committed . . .

27. Thus the starting-point for the ascertainment of what is clearly the most appropriate forum is to identify the place where the tort has been committed. That will, of course, by definition be England in a defamation case where leave to serve out has been obtained on the basis of publication here. But – and here is our second proposition from the cases – the more tenuous the claimant's connection with this jurisdiction (and the more substantial any publication abroad), the weaker this consideration becomes.

28. The third strand in the learning to which we would draw attention was initially prompted by what Lord Steyn in *Berezovsky*[1] called 'trans-national' libels, thus including libels perpetrated on the internet. The present case is of course an example . . . [I]n *Berezovsky*[2] Lord Steyn said this:

> 'counsel put forward the global theory on a reformulated basis. He said that when the court, having been satisfied that it has jurisdiction, has to decide under Order 11[3] whether England is the most appropriate forum "the correct approach is to treat the entire publication – whether by international newspaper circulation, trans-border or satellite broadcast or Internet posting – *as if* it gives rise to one cause of action and to ask whether it has been clearly proved that *this action* is best tried in England." If counsel was submitting that in respect of trans-national libels the court exercising its discretion must consider the global picture, his proposition would be uncontroversial. Counsel was, however, advancing a more ambitious proposition. He submitted that in respect of trans-national libels the principles enunciated by the House in the *Spiliada* case . . . should be recast to proceed on assumption that there is in truth one cause of action. The result of such a principle, if adopted, will usually be to favour a trial in the home courts of the foreign publisher because the bulk of the publication will have taken place there.'

This 'more ambitious' proposition was rejected by Lord Steyn. But we consider with respect that his reference to the court's need, in the case of trans-national libels, to 'consider the global picture' is something more than a passing aside. What is 'the global picture'? Where there is publication, say in two jurisdictions only, it remains relatively confined, and [the rule that the starting point is to identify the place where the tort is committed] may remain very meaningful. But in relation to Internet libel, bearing in mind the rule in *Duke of Brunswick* v. *Harmer* that each publication constitutes a separate tort, a defendant who publishes on the Web may at least in theory find himself vulnerable to multiple actions in different jurisdictions. The place where the tort is committed ceases to be a potent limiting factor.

---

1 *Editor's note*: this is *Berezovsky* v. *Michaels* [2000] 1 WLR 1004 (HL).
2 At p. 1012.
3 *Editor's note*: Order 11 was the forerunner of the provisions of the CPR on service of a claim form outside the jurisdiction.

29. In *Gutnick* v. *Dow Jones*[4] the High Court of Australia firmly rejected a
     challenge, in the context of Internet libel, to the applicability of such
     established principles as that vouchsafed in *Duke of Brunswick*. In doing so
     the court made certain observations about internet publication which with
     respect, we think we may usefully bear in mind:[5]

> '39. It was suggested that the World Wide Web was different from radio and
> television because the radio or television broadcaster could decide how far
> the signal was to be broadcast. It must be recognised, however, that satellite
> broadcasting now permits very wide dissemination of radio and television and
> it may, therefore, be doubted that it is right to say that the World Wide Web has
> a uniquely broad reach. It is no more or less ubiquitous than some television
> services. In the end, pointing to the breadth or depth of reach of particular forms
> of communication may tend to obscure one basic fact. However broad may be the
> reach of any particular means of communication, those who post information on
> the World Wide Web do so knowing that the information they make available is
> available to all and sundry without any geographic restriction.'

> '181. A publisher, particularly one carrying on the business of publishing, does not
> act to put matter on the Internet in order for it to reach a small target. It is its ubiquity
> which is one of the main attractions to users of it. And any person who gains
> access to the Internet does so by taking an initiative to gain access to it in a manner
> analogous to the purchase or other acquisition of a newspaper, in order to read it.'

> '192. . . . Comparisons can, as I have already exemplified, readily be made. If a
> publisher publishes in a multiplicity of jurisdictions it should understand, and must
> accept, that it runs the risk of liability in those jurisdictions in which the publication
> is not lawful and inflicts damage.'

30. So far, then, the *Duke of Brunswick* has well survived the Internet, certainly
     in the High Court of Australia. And the court's vindication of traditional
     principles relating to publication and jurisdiction in defamation cases
     marches with Lord Steyn's rejection, in *Berezovsky*, of counsel's 'more
     ambitious proposition . . . in respect of trans-national libels'.

31. We do not suggest, nor did [counsel for the respondents], that *Gutnick* is a
     gateway for the introduction of a new rule in the law of England relating to
     Internet publications. It established no new rule in Australia. But the court's
     rejection of sweeping submissions that would have done away with *Duke
     of Brunswick* in favour of the 'single publication rule' known in many States
     of the USA, alongside the *dicta* in *Gutnick* which emphasise the Internet
     publisher's very choice of a ubiquitous medium, at least suggests a robust
     approach to the question of forum: a global publisher should not be too
     fastidious as to the part of the globe where he is made a libel defendant.
     We by no means propose a free-for-all for claimants libelled on the Internet.
     The court must still ascertain the most appropriate forum; the parties'
     connections with this or that jurisdiction will still have to be considered;
     there will be cases (like the present) where only two jurisdictions are really
     in contention. We apprehend this third strand in the learning demonstrates

4 *Dow Jones & Co. Inc.* v. *Gutnick* (2003) 210 CLR 575; 77 ALJR 255; 194 ALR 433 (High Court of Australia).
5 *Editor's note*: the paragraph numbering in the quotations that follow are those in the judgment of the
Australian court.

no more than this, that in an internet case the court's discretion will tend to be more open-textured than otherwise; for that is the means by which the court may give effect to the publisher's choice of a global medium. But as always, every case will depend upon its own circumstances ...

33.   Before we come to the fourth and last strand, which concerns 'juridical advantage', we have two further observations at this stage. The first is to notice [counsel for the appellants'] submission that in deciding, in an Internet case, what is the most appropriate forum the court should be more ready to stay proceedings 'where defendants did not target their publications towards the jurisdiction in which they have been sued. That is, it might be argued that for the purposes of *forum non conveniens* enquiries involving material published via the Internet, the intention of the defendant should be taken into account.'[29]

34.   We would reject this submission out of hand. As the Lord Chief Justice pointed out in the course of argument, it makes little sense to distinguish between one jurisdiction and another in order to decide which the defendant has 'targeted', when in truth he has 'targeted' every jurisdiction where his text may be downloaded. Further, if the exercise required the ascertainment of what it was the defendant subjectively intended to 'target', it would in our judgment be liable to manipulation and uncertainty, and much more likely to diminish than enhance the interests of justice.

Result: the Court of Appeal held that the trial judge had not abused his discretion. It dismissed the appeal and allowed the action to go ahead in England.

Comment

American courts tend to take a different view. They are often unwilling to accept that proceedings may be brought in any jurisdiction in which the material can be downloaded; instead, they say that the forum must be specifically 'targeted'.[30] The objections to this approach were set out in *King* v. *Lewis*, above. The English courts prefer to use *forum non conveniens* and other devices to limit forum-shopping and ensure that proceedings are brought only in appropriate courts.

Our last case in this section, *Jeyaretnam* v. *Mahmood*,[31] concerns a problem that was touched on in previous chapters – the problem that the claimant may not get a fair trial in the alternative forum, perhaps for reasons of racial, religious or political bias. The judgment in this case was given in chambers (not in open court) and appears to have been reported only in *The Times*. The claimant was a Singaporean citizen, who alleged that an article about him in a local newspaper was libellous. Instead of suing in Singapore, however, he sued in England.[32] He

---

29 Collins, *The Law of Defamation and the Internet* (Oxford University Press, Oxford, 1st edn, 2001), Chapter 24, paragraph 24.52. (There is now a second edition of this book, published in 2005.)
30 See, for example, *Young* v. *New Haven Advocate*, 315 F 3d 256 (4th Cir. 2002); *Revell* v. *Lidov*, 317 F 3d 467 (5th Cir. 2002).
31 *The Times*, 21 May 1992 (QBD).
32 Some copies of the newspaper must have been published in England so as to provide a ground for service of the claim form outside the jurisdiction.

claimed that he would not get a fair trial in Singapore.[33] It seems he thought the judges there would be biased against him for political reasons.

In *The Abidin Daver*,[34] a case in which proceedings were already pending before a foreign court when the action was brought in England, Lord Diplock said:[35]

> But where there is already a *lis alibi pendens* in a foreign jurisdiction which constitutes a natural and appropriate forum for the resolution of the dispute, a plaintiff in an English action, if he wishes to resist a stay upon the ground that even-handed justice may not be done to him in that particular foreign jurisdiction, must assert this candidly and support his allegations with positive and cogent evidence.

Jeyaretnam was willing to produce positive and cogent evidence. The court, however, would have none of it. It refused to listen to his claim that the Singaporean courts would be biased against him. The judge said that he was precluded from doing so by considerations of judicial restraint. He ruled that Lord Diplock's statement applied only to situations in which a citizen of one country claims that the courts of another country might be biased against him. He said that a court should not entertain such a plea by a claimant against the courts of his own country.

While one can understand the court's reluctance to get involved in the matter, a blanket refusal to consider the possibility of bias would seem to run counter to Article 6 of the European Convention on Human Rights, which guarantees a litigant a fair trial in civil and criminal cases. If a court that admittedly has jurisdiction refuses to hear a case on the ground that a court of another country is more appropriate, but it refuses to consider whether the claimant would receive a fair trial in that country, it would seem to be denying the litigant his rights under Article 6.

The application of Article 6 in *forum-non-conveniens* cases was considered many years later in *Lubbe* v. *Cape plc*[36] (a case set out in Chapter 12, § 2.3, below). There, the issue was whether the claimant would receive a fair trial in the alternative forum (South Africa) in view of the fact that he lacked the funding to obtain legal representation. Lord Bingham said:

> The plaintiffs submitted that to stay these proceedings in favour of the South African forum would violate the plaintiff's rights guaranteed by article 6 of the European Convention for the Protection of Human Rights and Fundamental Freedoms (1953) . . . since it would, because of the lack of funding and legal representation in South Africa, deny them a fair trial on terms of litigious equality with the defendant. For reasons already given, I have concluded that a stay would lead to a denial of justice to the plaintiffs. Since, as the *Spiliada* case . . . makes clear, a stay will not be granted where it is established by cogent evidence that the plaintiff will not obtain justice in the foreign forum, I cannot conceive that the court would grant a stay in any case where adequate funding and legal representation of the plaintiff were judged to be necessary to the doing of justice and these were clearly shown to be unavailable in the foreign

---

33 Under normal circumstances, England would not have been regarded as a *forum conveniens* in view of the fact that the defendant had no substantial reputation in England.
34 [1984] AC 398.
35 At p. 411.
36 [2000] 1 WLR 1545 (HL).

forum although available here. I do not think article 6 supports any conclusion which is not already reached on application of *Spiliada* principles. I cannot, however, accept the view of the second Court of Appeal that it would be right to decline jurisdiction in favour of South Africa even if legal representation were not available there.

Since the House of Lords had decided to refuse a stay on the basis of the principles in *Spiliada*, it was unnecessary to consider the human-rights point in detail. However, if the issue in *Jeyaretnam* v. *Mahmood* came before the courts again, it would surely be extremely relevant.

Further reading

Fawcett, 'The Impact of Article 6(1) of the ECHR on Private International Law' (2007) 56 ICLQ 1 (especially at pp. 9–11)

Morse, 'Rights Relating to Personality, Freedom of the Press and Private International Law: Some Common Law Comments' (2005) 58 CLP 133

CHAPTER 12

Special topics – II

In this chapter, we consider two more topics.

§ 1   Intellectual property

Intellectual-property rights are a key element in modern business. They come in a variety of forms. Some – such as patents, copyright and trade marks – are well established; others are of recent origin. Depending on the legal system involved, they may have to be registered in order to be valid – this is true, for example, in the case of patents – or they may not have to be registered – this is usually the case with copyright.

The essence of an intellectual-property right is that it grants a monopoly: the holder can do something that others may not do. If another person infringes that monopoly, the holder of the right may sue the infringer in tort. In such an action, the defendant can normally defend himself in two ways: he can claim that what he is doing does not constitute an infringement (because it is outside the scope of the monopoly); or he can argue that the intellectual-property right is invalid.

There are various ways in which the latter option may be pursued. The validity of the intellectual-property right may be raised as a defence in the infringement action, in which case it will have to be decided before judgment can be given. In some legal systems, the court hearing the infringement action may decide it as a preliminary issue; in others, it may have to be decided in separate proceedings – in the case of a patent, for example, proceedings may have to be brought before the national patent office. Where the validity of the right is decided in separate proceedings, the infringement proceedings will have to be stayed (suspended) to await their outcome.

Another possibility is that the defendant may challenge the validity of the intellectual-property right by means of a counterclaim to the infringement action; alternatively, he may bring separate proceedings, possibly even before the commencement of the infringement action. Again, the infringement proceedings may have to be stayed.

An interesting aspect of this procedure is that, if the defendant seeks to establish that what he did was not an infringement, he will want to interpret the scope of the intellectual-property right as narrowly as possible (in order to show that what he is doing falls outside its ambit), while the right-holder will want to interpret it as broadly as possible (to show that the defendant's act is within the scope of the right). However, if the validity of the right is in issue, the opposite will be the case: the defendant will seek to interpret its scope as broadly as possible (because it will then be easier to attack), while the right-holder will interpret it as narrowly as possible (to make it easier to defend). If the defendant pursues both options and if they are both decided by the same court, that court will usually be in a position to ensure that neither party acts inconsistently with regard to the two pleas. However, this will be more difficult when they are decided by different courts.

In this section, we consider some of the jurisdictional issues that arise in international intellectual-property litigation.

§ 1.1   EC law

Intellectual property is within the subject-matter scope of the Brussels I Regulation: it falls under the heading 'civil and commercial matters' in Article 1(1) of the Regulation and is not excluded by any provision in Article 1(2). In principle, therefore, all the grounds of jurisdiction laid down in the Regulation apply in intellectual-property actions. However, as we saw in Chapter 4, § 5, above, there is an express provision in Article 22(4) concerning the registration or validity of registered intellectual-property rights. This grants exclusive juris-diction (regardless of domicile) to the courts of the Member State of registration (for the exact words, see Panel 12.1). This means that only the courts (or patent office) of the Member State of registration may decide questions of validity.

Three points should, however, be noted: Article 22(4) applies only to intel-lectual-property rights that have to be deposited or registered; it applies only where deposit or registration occurs in a Member State; and it applies only to proceedings 'concerned' with registra-tion or validity. It does not, therefore, apply to copyright and other intellec-tual-property rights that do not have to be registered or deposited; it does not apply where registration occurs in a non-member State; and it does not apply where the proceedings are not 'con-cerned' with registration or validity.

> **Panel 12.1 Intellectual property**
> **Brussels I Regulation (Regulation 44/2001), Article 22**
>
> **Exclusive jurisdiction**
>
> **Article 22**
> The following courts shall have exclusive jurisdiction, regardless of domicile:
>
> . . .
>
> 4. in proceedings concerned with the registration or validity of patents, trade marks, designs, or other similar rights required to be deposited or registered, the courts of the Member State in which the deposit or registration has been applied for, has taken place or is under the terms of a Community instrument or an international convention deemed to have taken place.
>
>   Without prejudice to the jurisdiction of the European Patent Office under the Convention on the Grant of European Patents, signed at Munich on 5 October 1973, the courts of each Member State shall have exclusive jurisdiction, regardless of domicile, in proceedings concerned with the registration or validity of any European patent granted for that State . . .

In our next case, the European Court had to consider when proceedings are 'concerned' with these matters.

European Community
Duijnstee v. *Goderbauer*
Court of Justice of the European Communities
Case 288/82, [1983] ECR 3663; [1985] 1 CMLR 220

Background

Duijnstee was the liquidator of a bankrupt Dutch company. Goderbauer was the former manager of the company. He had registered various patents in his own name in a number of different countries. Duijnstee claimed that, as the inventions had been made in the course of his employment, Goderbauer should have registered them in the name of the company. He therefore brought proceedings against Goderbauer before the Dutch courts for an order requiring him to transfer the patents to the company. The question then arose whether, in so far as the patents were registered in other Contracting States to the Brussels Convention (the instrument in force at the time), the Dutch courts were deprived of jurisdiction under Article 16(4) of the Convention, the equivalent of Article 22(4) of the Regulation. The Dutch Supreme Court (*Hoge Raad*) referred the question to the European Court.

Judgment

[The European Court first considered whether a national court faced with a jurisdictional issue under the Convention must decide that issue of its own motion if it is not raised by either of the parties.[1] It ruled that it must, even if this means overriding national procedural law. It also held that the concept of 'proceedings concerned with the registration or validity of patents' must be interpreted according to Community law, not national law.[2] It then continued:]

21. In order to reply to the third question, reference must again be made to the objectives and scheme of the Convention.

22. In that regard, it must be noted that the exclusive jurisdiction in proceedings concerned with the registration or validity of patents conferred upon the courts of the Contracting State in which the deposit or registration has been applied for is justified by the fact that those courts are best placed to adjudicate upon cases in which the dispute itself concerns the validity of the patent or the existence of the deposit or registration.

23. On the other hand, as is expressly stated in the report on the Convention (Official Journal 1979, C 59, p. 1, at p. 36), 'other actions, including those for infringement of patents, are governed by the general rules of the Convention'. That statement confirms the restrictive nature of the provision contained in Article 16 (4).

24. It follows that proceedings 'concerned with the registration or validity of patents' must be regarded as proceedings in which the conferring of exclusive jurisdiction on the courts of the place in which the patent was granted is justified in the light of the factors mentioned above, such as

1 Under Dutch law, an appeal court was limited to the grounds of appeal raised by the parties.
2 For other judgments along similar lines, see Chapter 3, § 9.1, above.

proceedings relating to the validity, existence or lapse of a patent or an alleged right of priority by reason of an earlier deposit.

25. If, on the other hand, the dispute does not itself concern the validity of the patent or the existence of the deposit or registration, there is no special reason to confer exclusive jurisdiction on the courts of the Contracting State in which the patent was applied for or granted and consequently such a dispute is not covered by Article 16 (4).

26. In a case such as the present, neither the validity of the patents nor the legality of their registration in the various countries is disputed by the parties to the main action. The outcome of the case in fact depends exclusively on the question whether Mr Goderbauer or the insolvent company . . . is entitled to the patent, which must be determined on the basis of the legal relationship which existed between the parties concerned. Therefore the special jurisdiction rule contained in Article 16 (4) should not be applied.

Comment

The proceedings before the Dutch courts were not concerned with the question whether Mr Goderbauer or the company *was* the owner of the patents; they were concerned with the question whether the company was *entitled to become* the owner. If the Dutch courts had granted the order, Mr Goderbauer would then have been obliged to go to the State of registration to take the steps required by the law of that State to transfer the patents to the company. In this respect, therefore, the case is similar to that of *Webb* v. *Webb* (discussed in Chapter 4, § 5.1, above), in which the question arose whether an English court had jurisdiction to grant an order requiring the defendant to transfer immovable property in France to the claimant. That too was not covered by Article 16.

Our next case concerns the effect of Article 16(4) on patent-infringement actions.

European Community
Gesellschaft für Antriebstechnik mbH & Co. KG (GAT)* v. *Lamellen und Kupplungsbau Beteiligungs KG (LuK)
Court of Justice of the European Communities (First Chamber)
Case C-4/03, [2006] ECR I-6509

Background

The claimant, GAT, and the defendant, LuK, were both German companies. GAT was hoping to win a contract to supply a component to a third German company. LuK claimed that what GAT was proposing would constitute a violation of its (LuK's) French patents. GAT, therefore, brought proceedings against LuK before a German court seeking a declaration that the French patents were invalid and that, in any event, what it was proposing would not constitute an infringement.

This created the classic situation described above, in which an alleged infringer claims that he is not liable for infringement because the intellectual-property right he is alleged to have infringed is invalid. The only difference was that the alleged infringer had struck first by asking for a declaration of non-liability. The issue, however, was the same: whether Article 16(4) applies where the issue of validity arises as an incidental question in proceedings in which the main issue is infringement.

In a situation such as this, there are three possible approaches. The first is to say that, as soon as the defendant raises the issue of validity, the court hearing the infringement action (or the action for a declaration of non-infringement) is automatically deprived of jurisdiction. The argument in favour of this view, which has been supported by the English courts,[1] is that the validity of the patent then becomes the central issue in the proceedings.

The second possibility is that the court seised can decide the question of validity, but only as a preliminary issue. Under this solution, its ruling on validity will not be binding on the holder in any other proceedings – for example, if he subsequently brings an infringement action against another person.

The third possibility is that the court before which the infringement action is brought can hear it, but cannot decide the question of validity. Once that question is raised, the court must suspend the proceedings to allow the court (or patent office) of the State of registration to decide it. Once it has been decided, the infringement action can continue.

Each of these solutions has its advantages and disadvantages. The first solution might be regarded as unduly restrictive. It would mean that, in practice, the question of infringement could never be decided by a court other than that of registration, since the defendant would almost invariably raise the question of validity.

The third solution is extremely cumbersome, since it requires two actions. First, the infringement action must be brought in a court with jurisdiction over the alleged infringer. Then, when he raises the issue of validity, a second action must be brought, presumably by the defendant, in the State of registration. If this results in a ruling that the intellectual-property right is valid, the infringement action can then proceed.

The second solution allows all issues to be decided by the same court, though it does not fully respect the exclusive jurisdiction of the courts of the Member State of registration. Although the ruling on validity applies only in the proceedings in which it is given, those proceedings may in fact be the most important in which it is ever likely to arise.

These were the policy issues raised by the parties before the European Court.[2]

Judgment

[After referring to its judgment in *Duijnstee*, the court continued:]

24.   In relation to the position of Article 16 within the scheme of the Convention, it should be pointed out that the rules of jurisdiction provided

---

1 *Coin Controls v. Suzo International* [1998] 3 WLR 420; [1997] 3 All ER 45; approved in *Fort Dodge Animal Health Ltd v. Akzo Nobel NV* [1998] FSR 222 (CA).

2 Although they were considered by the court in only a rather superficial way, they were dealt with in detail by the Advocate General, whose preferred solution was eventually adopted by the court.

for in that article are of an exclusive and mandatory nature, the application of which is specifically binding on both litigants and courts. Parties may not derogate from them by an agreement conferring jurisdiction (fourth paragraph of Article 17 of the Convention) or by the defendant's voluntary appearance (Article 18 of the Convention). Where a court of a Contracting State is seised of a claim which is principally concerned with a matter over which the courts of another Contracting State have jurisdiction by virtue of Article 16, it must declare of its own motion that it has no jurisdiction (Article 19 of the Convention). A judgment given which falls foul of the provisions of Article 16 does not benefit from the system of recognition and enforcement under the Convention (first paragraph of Article 28 and second paragraph of Article 34 thereof).

25. In the light of the position of Article 16(4) within the scheme of the Convention and the objective pursued, the view must be taken that the exclusive jurisdiction provided for by that provision should apply whatever the form of proceedings in which the issue of a patent's validity is raised, be it by way of an action or a plea in objection, at the time the case is brought or at a later stage in the proceedings.

26. First, to allow a court seised of an action for infringement or for a declaration that there has been no infringement to establish, indirectly, the invalidity of the patent at issue would undermine the binding nature of the rule of jurisdiction laid down in Article 16(4) of the Convention.

27. While the parties cannot rely on Article 16(4) of the Convention, the claimant would be able, simply by the way it formulates its claims,[1] to circumvent the mandatory nature of the rule of jurisdiction laid down in that article.

28. Second, the possibility which this offers of circumventing Article 16(4) of the Convention would have the effect of multiplying the heads of jurisdiction and would be liable to undermine the predictability of the rules of jurisdiction laid down by the Convention, and consequently to undermine the principle of legal certainty, which is the basis of the Convention . . .

29. Third, to allow, within the scheme of the Convention, decisions in which courts other than those of a State in which a particular patent is issued to rule indirectly on the validity of that patent would also multiply the risk of conflicting decisions which the Convention seeks specifically to avoid . . .

30. The argument, advanced by LuK and the German Government, that under German law the effects of a judgment indirectly ruling on the validity of a patent are limited to the parties to the proceedings, is not an appropriate response to that risk. The effects flowing from such a decision are in fact determined by national law. In several Contracting States, however,

1 *Editor's note*: in this paragraph, the court's English is not very good. It should have said either '*If* the parties cannot rely on Article 16(4) of the Convention, the claimant *will* be able, simply by the way it formulates its claims . . .' or (preferably) '*If* the parties *could not* rely on Article 16(4) of the Convention, the claimant would be able, simply by the way it *formulated* its claims . . .'.

a decision to annul a patent has *erga omnes* effect. In order to avoid the risk of contradictory decisions, it is therefore necessary to limit the jurisdiction of the courts of a State other than that in which the patent is issued to rule indirectly on the validity of a foreign patent to only those cases in which, under the applicable national law, the effects of the decision to be given are limited to the parties to the proceedings. Such a limitation would, however, lead to distortions, thereby undermining the equality and uniformity of rights and obligations arising from the Convention for the Contracting States and the persons concerned (*Duijnstee*, paragraph 13).

31. In the light of the foregoing, the answer to the question referred must be that Article 16(4) of the Convention is to be interpreted as meaning that the rule of exclusive jurisdiction laid down therein concerns all proceedings relating to the registration or validity of a patent, irrespective of whether the issue is raised by way of an action or a plea in objection.

Comment

The solution adopted by the court is the safest of the three outlined above. It does more than the other possibilities to preserve the system of the Regulation, though it does so at the cost of judicial efficiency. As we shall see below, it was rejected by the Hague Conference on Private International Law when it drew up the Convention on Choice of Court Agreements, but in that Convention the issue arises only in a rather special situation.

Our last case on EC law is concerned with multi-party proceedings. To understand the issues, it is necessary to know something about the development of national and international patent law in Europe. For many years, patents were territorial. They were granted by the State and applied only within the territory of the State that granted them.[3] In other words, the monopoly given to the patent-holder applied only within that territory. If an inventor wished to patent his invention throughout the European Union, he had to obtain a separate patent in each Member State. Each patent was registered in the State in question and was governed by national law, which might differ in some respects from the law of other States. The rights of the patent-holder might, therefore, be different in different States.

Valuable inventions – for example, in the pharmaceutical industry – are usually patented in each Member State in the Community; indeed, they are often patented in each State in the world. In practice, it is common for multinational companies to register the national patent for a particular State in the name of the subsidiary operating in that State. These 'parallel' patents (patents for the same invention registered in different States) would, therefore, be held by different companies, but the companies would normally be part of the same group and ultimately controlled by the parent company.

---

3 In most federal States – for example, Canada and the United States – patent law falls within federal jurisdiction. The relevant unit is, therefore, Canada or the United States, not a particular province or state. In the United Kingdom, patent law is governed by United Kingdom law, not by English, Scots or Northern Irish law.

The result is that, when an issue arises on the validity or scope of a patent right, that issue cannot be determined once and for all for the entire Community. Although the invention – for example, a pharmaceutical product – may be the same for the entire Community, the patent rights will be different in each Member State and they will often be held by different legal persons. Litigation would therefore have to take place in each Member State with possibly conflicting results. These in turn could have undesirable commercial consequences, since the sale of a given product might be legal in one Member State but illegal in another.[4]

The Munich Convention of 1973 was the first attempt to solve these problems in Europe; however, it did so only to a limited extent. Under it, it is possible for an inventor to patent his product in all Contracting States through a single application, thus making it much easier to obtain protection throughout Europe. However, the Convention does not establish a single European patent: what the inventor gets is a bundle of national patents. He is thus in the same position as he would have been if he had registered his patent separately in each Contracting State. His rights are governed by national law in each State and the national law of that State applies to infringements in that State. The European Community is now moving ahead with a Community patent system that will establish a single patent for the EC; at the time of writing, however, this has not yet come into effect.

In this situation, Article 6(1) of the Regulation/Convention (discussed in Chapter 4, § 2, above) is potentially important. Would it be possible to use this provision to bring a single set of proceedings against all the European patent-holders in the courts of the Member State in which one of them is domiciled? We now know that, under the *GAT* case, questions of *validity* would have to be determined separately for each national patent; however, other questions that arise in an infringement action – in particular, the scope of the patent – could be decided in a single set of proceedings. This idea found particular favour in the Netherlands, where it was argued that, at least if the forum is in the State in which the group as a whole is centred, it should be possible to use Article 6(1) for this purpose. The correctness of this view was put to the test in our next case.[5]

European Community
Roche Nederland* v. *Primus and Goldenberg
Court of Justice of the European Communities
Case C-539/03, [2006] ECR I-6535 (First Chamber)

Background

The defendants in this case were a Dutch company, Roche Nederland and eight other companies in the Roche group domiciled (respectively) in the United States, Switzerland and various Member States (Belgium, Germany, France, the

---

4 It is to avoid these problems that patents are a federal matter in most federal states.
5 Judgment in this case was given on the same day as that in the *GAT* case. Moreover, both cases were decided by the First Chamber of the European Court. The reporting judge, Judge Jann, was the same in both cases, though the composition of the Chamber was otherwise largely different. It is clear from the reference to *GAT* in paragraph 40 of *Roche Nederland* that the two judgments were co-ordinated.

United Kingdom, etc.). The claimants were two Americans who held a European patent for a medical product. As mentioned above, European patents were established by the Munich Convention, which provided that a European patent would confer on the proprietor, in each Contracting State in respect of which it was granted, the same rights as would be conferred by a national patent granted by that State.[6] Infringement proceedings would be governed by national law.[7] The claimants claimed that each of the defendants had infringed their patent by marketing a particular product in the countries in which they were established. In other words, they claimed that the Dutch company had infringed it in the Netherlands, the French company in France and the United Kingdom company in the United Kingdom.

The question before the court was whether all the EC defendants could be sued in the Netherlands under Article 6(1) in view of the fact that one of them, Roche Nederland, was domiciled there. In favour of this view, it was argued that they were all members of the same commercial group and that they were acting pursuant to a common policy. Moreover, the acts that were alleged to constitute the infringement (the marketing of the product) were all the same or virtually the same. The argument on the other side was that the effect of the Munich Convention was that what the holder of a European Patent obtained was in effect a bundle of national patents. This meant that the claim against the Dutch company was that its actions in the Netherlands constituted an infringement of the rights granted to the claimants under Dutch law; the claim against the French company was that its actions in France constituted an infringement of the rights granted to the claimants under French law; etc. In view of this, it was said, the claims against each defendant were different; consequently, there could be no question of irreconcilable judgments if each claim was heard by a different court: the question whether the Dutch company had violated Dutch law was a different one from the question whether the French company had violated French law.

Judgment

20. In the judgment in Case 189/87 *Kalfelis* [1988] ECR 5565, paragraph 12, the Court held that for Article 6(1) of the Brussels Convention to apply there must exist, between the various actions brought by the same plaintiff against different defendants, a connection of such a kind that it is expedient to determine the actions together in order to avoid the risk of irreconcilable judgments resulting from separate proceedings.

21. The requirement of a connection does not derive from the wording of Article 6(1) of the Brussels Convention.[1] It has been inferred from that provision by the Court in order to prevent the exception to the principle that jurisdiction is vested in the courts of the State of the defendant's domicile laid down in Article 6(1) from calling into question the very existence of

1 *Editor's note*: this requirement did not exist in the Brussels Convention. It was inserted into the text of Article 6(1) when the Brussels I Regulation was adopted.

6 Munich Convention, Article 64(1).
7 Munich Convention, Article 64(2).

that principle . . . That requirement . . . was expressly enshrined in the drafting of Article 6(1) of [the Brussels I Regulation].

[The court then considered whether a broad or a narrow interpretation should be given to the concept of an 'irreconcilable' judgment. It continued:]

25.   However, it does not appear necessary in this case to decide that issue. It is sufficient to observe that, even assuming that the concept of 'irreconcilable' judgments for the purposes of the application of Article 6(1) of the Brussels Convention must be understood in the broad sense of contradictory decisions, there is no risk of such decisions being given in European patent infringement proceedings brought in different Contracting States involving a number of defendants domiciled in those States in respect of acts committed in their territory.

26.   As the Advocate General observed, in point 113 of his Opinion, in order that decisions may be regarded as contradictory it is not sufficient that there be a divergence in the outcome of the dispute, but that divergence must also arise in the context of the same situation of law and fact.

27.   However, in the situation referred to by the national court in its first question referred for a preliminary ruling, that is in the case of European patent infringement proceedings involving a number of companies established in various Contracting States in respect of acts committed in one or more of those States, the existence of the same situation of fact cannot be inferred, since the defendants are different and the infringements they are accused of, committed in different Contracting States, are not the same.

28.   Possible divergences between decisions given by the courts concerned would not arise in the context of the same factual situation.

29.   Furthermore, although the Munich Convention lays down common rules on the grant of European patents, it is clear from Articles 2(2) and 64(1) of that convention that such a patent continues to be governed by the national law of each of the Contracting States for which it has been granted.

30.   In particular, it is apparent from Article 64(3) of the Munich Convention that any action for infringement of a European patent must be examined in the light of the relevant national law in force in each of the States for which it has been granted.

31.   It follows that, where infringement proceedings are brought before a number of courts in different Contracting States in respect of a European patent granted in each of those States, against defendants domiciled in those States in respect of acts allegedly committed in their territory, any divergences between the decisions given by the courts concerned would not arise in the context of the same legal situation.

32.   Any diverging decisions could not, therefore, be treated as contradictory.

33.   In those circumstances, even if the broadest interpretation of 'irreconcilable' judgments, in the sense of contradictory, were accepted as the criterion

for the existence of the connection required for the application of Article 6(1) of the Brussels Convention, it is clear that such a connection could not be established between actions for infringement of the same European patent where each action was brought against a company established in a different Contracting State in respect of acts which it had committed in that State.

34. That finding is not called into question even in the situation referred to by the national court in its second question, that is where defendant companies, which belong to the same group, have acted in an identical or similar manner in accordance with a common policy elaborated by one of them, so that the factual situation would be the same.

35. The fact remains that the legal situation would not be the same (see paragraphs 29 and 30 of this judgment) and therefore there would be no risk, even in such a situation, of contradictory decisions.

36. Furthermore, although at first sight considerations of procedural economy may appear to militate in favour of consolidating such actions before one court, it is clear that the advantages for the sound administration of justice represented by such consolidation would be limited and would constitute a source of further risks.

37. Jurisdiction based solely on the factual criteria set out by the national court would lead to a multiplication of the potential heads of jurisdiction and would therefore be liable to undermine the predictability of the rules of jurisdiction laid down by the Convention, and consequently to undermine the principle of legal certainty, which is the basis of the Convention . . .

38. The damage would be even more serious if the application of the criteria in question gave the defendant a wide choice, thereby encouraging the practice of forum shopping which the Convention seeks to avoid and which the Court, in its judgment in *Kalfelis*, specifically sought to prevent (see *Kalfelis*, paragraph 9).

39. It must be observed that the determination as to whether the criteria concerned are satisfied, which is for the applicant to prove, would require the court seised to adjudicate on the substance of the case before it could establish its jurisdiction. Such a preliminary examination could give rise to additional costs and could prolong procedural time-limits where that court, being unable to establish the existence of the same factual situation and, therefore, a sufficient connection between the actions, would have to decline jurisdiction and where a fresh action would have to be brought before a court of another State.

40. Finally, even assuming that the court seised by the defendant were able to accept jurisdiction on the basis of the criteria laid down by the national court, the consolidation of the patent infringement actions before that court could not prevent at least a partial fragmentation of the patent proceedings, since, as is frequently the case in practice and as is the case in the main proceedings, the validity of the patent would

be raised indirectly. That issue, whether it is raised by way of an action or a plea in objection, is a matter of exclusive jurisdiction laid down in Article 16(4) of the Brussels Convention in favour of the courts of the Contracting State in which the deposit or registration has taken place or is deemed to have taken place (*GAT*, paragraph 31). That exclusive jurisdiction of the courts of the granting State has been confirmed, as regards European patents, by Article V(d) of the Protocol annexed to the Brussels Convention.

41. Having regard to all of the foregoing considerations, the answer to the questions referred must be that Article 6(1) of the Brussels Convention must be interpreted as meaning that it does not apply in European patent infringement proceedings involving a number of companies established in various Contracting States in respect of acts committed in one or more of those States even where those companies, which belong to the same group, may have acted in an identical or similar manner in accordance with a common policy elaborated by one of them.

Comment

In the particular circumstances of the case, it would probably have done no harm if all the actions had been decided together by the Dutch courts. Indeed, it would have simplified matters. However, the precedent laid down could have had unfortunate consequences in other circumstances, since it would have opened the way for forum-shopping by an unscrupulous claimant. Assume that a dishonest operator wants to find a way of marketing a product in the European Union that infringes the patent rights of a group of companies. If Article 6(1) had been held applicable in the circumstances under consideration, he could select any EC country in which the patent was registered and bring proceedings there for a declaration of non-liability against all the companies in the group. The country chosen might be one in which there is a high level of corruption among the judiciary; it might be a country in which criminal elements are able to carry out assassinations with seeming impunity.[8] It would not be desirable that the courts of such a country should be able to determine the scope of a patent right for the whole EC.

In addition, such a ruling would greatly increase the potency of the 'Italian torpedo'. The 'torpedo' was first put forward as a weapon for use in intellectual-property infringement proceedings.[9] The idea was that a would-be infringer could bring proceedings in Italy for a declaration of non-liability. The Italian member of the group would constitute the 'anchor' defendant. Since he would

---

8 Such countries exist in the EC: see, for example, the Commission reports on corruption in Bulgaria and Romania issued in June 2007: *Report from the Commission to the European Parliament and the Council on Bulgaria's Progress on Accompanying Measures Following Accession*, COM (2007) 377 final (Brussels, 27 June 2007), section 3, 'Judicial Reform and the Fight Against Corruption and Organized Crime', pp. 5 *et seq.*; *Report from the Commission to the European Parliament and the Council on Romania's Progress on Accompanying Measures Following Accession*, COM (2007) 378 final (Brussels, 27 June 2007), section 3, 'Judicial Reform and the Fight Against Corruption', pp. 4 *et seq.* These reports are summarized in *The Independent*, 28 June 2007, p. 30.
9 See Franzosi, 'Worldwide Patent Litigation and the Italian Torpedo' (1997) 7 *European Intellectual Property Review* 382, discussed in Chapter 10, § 4, above.

be sued in the Member State of his domicile, Article 6(1), if it applied to such proceedings, would permit all the other members of the group to be joined as co-defendants. The *lis pendens* rule in Articles 27–30 of the Regulation would then thwart infringement actions by the group in any Member State for many years to come. As a result, the infringer could, it was said, enjoy trouble-free infringement.[10]

In view of these dangers, it is fortunate that the European Court gave the ruling it did.

§ 1.2   English law

We saw in Chapter 5, § 6, above, that, under a rule laid down in *British South Africa Company* v. *Companhia de Moçambique*,[11] English courts have no jurisdiction to hear proceedings for determination of title to, or the right to possession of, immovable property situated outside England. Originally, this rule also pre-cluded English courts from hearing actions in tort for trespass to foreign land and (probably) for other torts affecting foreign land, but this part of the rule was abolished by section 30 of the Civil Jurisdiction and Judgments Act 1982 (which stated that actions in tort could be heard, provided the case was not principally concerned with title to, or the right to possession of, the property).

Subsequently, a similar rule was held to apply to foreign intellectual-property rights;[12] however, since such rights were not immovable property – they were merely treated *as if* they were immovable property – section 30 of the Civil Jurisdiction and Judgments Act 1982 did not apply to them. The result is that the exclusionary rule for intellectual property covers *both* validity *and* infringement. It also applies to *all* intellectual-property rights, not only to registered ones.[13] It is, therefore, significantly wider than the corresponding rule under EC law.

The following extract explains some of the policy reasons behind the rule.

England
Coin Controls* v. *Suzo International (UK)
High Court (Chancery Division)
[1998] 3 WLR 420

Laddie J

The principles which applied to land in the *Moçambique* case apply equally well to attempts to litigate foreign intellectual property rights in English courts. Those rights give rise to monopolies or quasi-monopolies which are strictly territorial in nature. In the case of patents, historically their purpose was to encourage and protect local industry. So courts following the common law tradition have declined

---

10 Whether this would actually have happened is not certain. The patent-holders could probably obtain temporary injunctions against the infringer in other countries under Article 31 of the Brussels I Regulation. These would not be subject to the *lis pendens* rule. See Chapter 19, § 8, below.
11 [1893] AC 602.
12 *Potter* v. *Broken Hill Pty Ltd* (1906) 3 CLR 479 (High Court of Australia); *Tyburn Productions Ltd* v. *Conan Doyle* [1991] Ch 75; *Coin Controls* v. *Suzo International* [1998] 3 WLR 420; [1997] 3 All ER 45.
13 The *Tyburn Productions* case (above) concerned copyright.

to entertain actions concerned with the enforcement of foreign intellectual property rights; see *Potter* v. *Broken Hill Pty Ltd* (1906) 3 CLR 479 and *Tyburn Productions Ltd* v. *Conan Doyle* [1991] Ch 75. In *Plastus Kreativ AB* v. *Minnesota Mining and Manufacturing Co.* [1995] RPC 438, 447, Aldous J explained some of the reasons why he was not attracted to the task of adjudicating here on foreign intellectual property, and particularly patent, rights:

> For myself I would not welcome the task of having to decide whether a person had infringed a foreign patent. Although patent actions appear on their face to be disputes between two parties, in reality they also concern the public. A finding of infringement is a finding that a monopoly granted by the state is to be enforced. The result is invariably that the public have to pay higher prices than if the monopoly did not exist. If that be the proper result, then that result should, I believe, come about from a decision of a court situated in the state where the public have to pay the higher prices. One only has to imagine a decision of this court that the German public should pay to a British company substantial sums of money to realise the difficulties that might arise. I believe that, if the local courts are responsible for enforcing and deciding questions of validity and infringement, the conclusions reached are likely to command the respect of the public. Also a conclusion that a patent is infringed or not infringed involves in this country a decision on validity as in this country no man can infringe an invalid patent. In the present case the plaintiffs admit the validity of the patent and therefore there is no dispute upon the matter. However, it will be implicit in the judgment of this court that there has been infringement, and that, between the parties, the patent is valid. Thus, I believe it is at least convenient that infringement, like validity, is decided in the state in which it arises.

Comment

The reason for the rule put forward in this extract is just as applicable in proceedings concerned simply with the scope of the patent as in proceedings on validity. It therefore suggests that there is some justification for the English approach of excluding infringement actions, even if they do not involve validity.

When does the English rule apply? If the State of registration is an EC or Lugano State, the EC/Lugano rule applies: the criterion for application is the location of the court having exclusive jurisdiction, not the domicile of the defendant. What is the position where the intellectual-property right arises under the law of a State other than an EC/Lugano State? Here the answer may depend on the ground on which the English court is alleged to have jurisdiction. If it is a ground laid down by the Brussels I Regulation – for example, the domicile of the defendant – the position is unclear.[14] If, on the other hand, the jurisdiction of the English court is based on one of the traditional rules of English law, there is no reason why the exclusionary rule we are considering should not apply. If, for example, the defendant is a Japanese company doing business in England, and the claimant sues it for a declaration that what it (the claimant) is doing in Japan is not an infringement of the Japanese company's Japanese patent, the jurisdiction of the English court would be excluded on the basis of the English

---

14 See the discussion in Chapter 5, § 6, above.

rule. This would be so, even if the claimant did not contest the validity of the Japanese patent.

§ 1.3   The Hague Convention on Choice of Court Agreements

A general outline of this Convention was given in Chapter 8, § 5, above. Its application to contracts concerning intellectual property is explained in the following extract from the official Report on the Convention.[15]

Convention of 30 June 2005 on Choice of Court Agreements, Explanatory Report by Trevor Hartley and Masato Dogauchi[1]

Part II: Overview

33. *Intellectual property*. The application of the Convention to intellectual property was subject to intense negotiation. The outcome was to make a distinction between copyright and related rights, on the one hand, and other intellectual property rights (such as patents, trade marks and designs), on the other hand. We shall treat these two classes of rights separately.

34. *Copyright and related rights*. Copyright and related rights (neighbouring rights) are fully covered by the Convention. This is the case even with regard to disputes as to validity. However, since a judgment is enforceable under the Convention only as against persons bound by the choice of court agreement, a judgment on validity can never have *in rem*[2] effect under the Convention; consequently, a judgment that a copyright is invalid is not, under the Convention, binding on third parties.

35. *Intellectual property rights other than copyright and related rights*. Article 2(2) n) excludes the validity of intellectual property rights other than copyright and related rights from the scope of the Convention. Thus, proceedings for revocation or for a declaration of invalidity are not covered.

36. *Licensing agreements*. The Convention applies to licensing agreements and other contracts concerning intellectual property. If the agreement contains a choice of court clause, a judgment by the chosen court ordering payment of royalties will be enforceable under the Convention.

37. *Challenging validity as a defence*. If the licensor sues the licensee for payment of royalties, the latter may respond by claiming that the intellectual property right is invalid. This might constitute a defence to the claim, unless the licensing agreement contains a clause that royalties are due regardless of any challenge to the validity of the intellectual property right (assuming such a clause is legal). If the obligation to pay royalties exists only if the right is valid, the court hearing the claim for payment of

1 Published by the Permanent Bureau of the Conference, Scheveningseweg 6, 2517 KT, The Hague, Netherlands; available on the website of the Conference, www.hcch.net.
2 *In rem* effect is sometimes also called *erga omnes* effect.

15 Some of the footnotes have been deleted. The remainder have been renumbered.

royalties will have to decide the validity issue. This does not mean that the claim for payment of royalties ceases to be covered by the Convention. However, the preliminary ruling on validity is not entitled to recognition under the Convention.

38. *Enforcement of a judgment based on a preliminary ruling.* If proceedings are brought to enforce the judgment for payment of royalties, and if that judgment was based on a preliminary ruling on the validity of the intellectual property right, the court addressed may refuse to enforce the judgment if the preliminary ruling is inconsistent with a judgment[3] on the validity of the intellectual property right given by the appropriate court in the State under the law of which the intellectual property right arose (usually the State of registration). Moreover, if proceedings on the validity of the right are pending in that State, the court addressed may suspend the enforcement proceedings to await the outcome of the proceedings on the validity. If it is not possible for it to suspend the proceedings, it may dismiss them, provided that new proceedings may be brought once the question of validity has been settled.

39. *Infringement proceedings.* Article 2(2) o) excludes from the Convention proceedings for the infringement of intellectual property rights other than copyright and related rights. This, however, is subject to an important exception. Infringement proceedings that are brought, or could have been brought, for breach of a contract between the parties are not excluded from the scope of the Convention. This applies to proceedings following an alleged breach of a licensing agreement, though it is not limited to such agreements. If the licensing agreement permits the licensee to use the right in certain ways but not others, he will have committed a breach of contract if he uses the right in a way that is forbidden. However, since he would no longer be protected by the licence, he might also be guilty of infringement of the intellectual property right. The exception to Article 2(2) o) provides that such an action is covered by the Convention. This applies even if it is brought in tort, rather than in contract: infringement actions are covered, even if brought in tort, provided they could have been brought in contract.

3 This includes the decision of a patent office or other competent authority.

§ 2   Multinationals and the Third World

§ 2.1   *Introduction*

In this section, we consider the jurisdictional aspects of a major world problem: how to prevent multinational companies harming people in the Third World. Multinational companies, especially those exploiting mineral resources, often carry on their activities in Third World countries. Sometimes they cause major environmental pollution; sometimes they cause serious health problems, and even death, to large numbers of people; sometimes they do both. If they had been acting in a developed country, such as the United Kingdom or the United

States, the law would provide a remedy; indeed, they would probably not have done what they did. In Third World countries, however, the position is different. The governments of many such countries are so weak and short of resources that they cannot stand up to big companies. For example, the *Texaco* case, set out below, concerned the activities of Texaco (now owned by Chevron) in Ecuador. In 2005, Chevron earned nearly £97 billion, more than six times Ecuador's gross domestic product.[16] Even if the whole of Ecuador united against the company, it would still be puny in comparison.

In situations such as this, the victims have two options. They can sue in their own country, or they can sue in the multinational's home country. The first option often has serious drawbacks. These include the following:

- Litigants without funds may be unable to gain access to good-quality legal representation.
- Even if they are willing to take on the case, local law firms may lack the resources to prepare it: in a big case, thousands of hours of work will be required to interview victims and witnesses.[17]
- The local court system may be clogged up with cases and unable to process the claim within a reasonable time.
- Local judges may lack the expertise to understand the scientific and medical evidence needed to prove the claim.
- Local judges may be corrupt, and may be bought off by the company.
- Local politicians and officials may be bought off by the company, and they may put obstacles in the way of the claimants.

For these reasons, the victims often prefer to sue in the company's home country.[18] Here, however, the doctrine of *forum non conveniens* can block the action, at least if the home country applies the common law. To counter this, a number of Latin American countries have enacted 'anti-*forum-non-conveniens*' laws.[19] Typically, these provide that, if a citizen (or resident) of the enacting State brings proceedings in a foreign country, this automatically deprives the local courts of any jurisdiction they might otherwise have had. The idea is that, if there is no alternative forum, the American courts will be forced to hear the case. In general, this tactic has not worked.

§ 2.2   The United States

Most multinationals have their home in the United States, the world's leading economy. In many ways, the US provides enormous advantages to plaintiffs in personal-injury and environmental-damage cases.

The contingent-fee system allows plaintiffs with no money to obtain the services of a top-quality legal team. The victims pay nothing up front. If they lose in

---

16 See the article by Trudie Styler, *Daily Mail*, 2 July 2007, available on www.chevrontoxico.com.
17 In the *Texaco* case, for example, there were some 30,000 claimants, each of whom had to be interviewed.
18 If, as is often the case, the actual harm is done by a local subsidiary, this will mean suing the parent company.
19 See Article 40 of the Statute of Private International Law (Venezuela); *Decreto Numero* 34-97 (1997) (Guatemala); *Ley* 55 (Ecuador); and *Ley de Defensa de Derechos Procesales de Nacionales y Residentes* (Law in Defence of the Procedural Rights of Nationals and Residents) (Honduras).

the end, they owe their lawyers nothing, nor do they have to pay the other side's lawyers.[20] If they win, their lawyers get a cut of the winnings. If the potential winnings are large – in the *Texaco* case, the claim was for billions of dollars – leading law firms will be lining up to take on the work.

Another advantage of US law is that it allows class actions, a form of procedure invented in the US. Under this system, a claim may (with the approval of the court) be brought on behalf of a defined class of litigants – for example, all persons living in a specified locality who suffered health problems as a result of emissions from a specified chemical plant during a specified period. It is not necessary to list all the plaintiffs by name.

Technical and scientific expertise is readily available in the US, and judges are usually qualified to understand scientific evidence. The US court system is not corrupt, and cases move with reasonable speed. It is generally easier to hold a parent company responsible for the wrongs of its subsidiaries than in most other legal systems. The US system of pre-trial discovery is the most effective in the world in enabling litigants to gain the evidence they need to prove their case. Damages are the highest in the world. It is small wonder that foreign litigants will do all they can to get the case heard in the United States. On the other hand, the company will fight tooth and nail to keep it out. Various arguments are put forward. We shall concentrate on *forum non conveniens*.

In the past, some states – for example, Texas – did not apply *forum non conveniens* in personal-injury and wrongful-death cases. This made Texas a favoured location for suits by foreign litigants. Some notable victories were won. The following is an example.

Texas
Dow Chemical Company* v. *Castro Alfaro
Supreme Court of Texas
786 SW 2d 674 (1990)

Background

Dow and Shell (co-defendants) produced an insecticide containing a chemical called DBCP, a substance banned in the US. Dow and Shell, however, exported several thousand gallons of the insecticide to Costa Rica for use by a company called Standard Fruit. As a result, the plaintiffs (workers employed by Standard Fruit, who were exposed to the chemical) claimed to have suffered severe medical problems, including sterility. They sued Dow and Shell in a state court in Texas. The defendants sought to have the case dismissed on the ground of *forum non conveniens*, but a majority in the Supreme Court of Texas held that Texas legislation had the effect of abolishing the doctrine in personal-injury and wrongful-death cases. Not all the judges agreed. We give brief excerpts from two of the dissents.

---

20 In the US, the losing party may have to pay the winning party's costs, but 'costs' do not include attorney fees. Subject to very limited exceptions, each party pays their own attorney fees, win or lose.

Gonzalez, Justice, dissenting

Under the guise of statutory construction, the court today abolishes the doctrine of *forum non conveniens* in suits brought pursuant to section 71.031 of the Civil Practice and Remedies Code. This decision makes us one of the few states in the Union without such a procedural tool, and if the legislature fails to reinstate this doctrine, Texas will become an irresistible forum for all mass disaster lawsuits ...'Bhopal'-type litigation, with little or no connection to Texas will add to our already crowded dockets, forcing our residents to wait in the corridors of our courthouses while foreign causes of action are tried ...

Cook, Justice, dissenting

Like turn-of-the-century wildcatters,[1] the plaintiffs in this case searched all across the nation for a place to make their claims. Through three courts they moved, filing their lawsuits on one coast and then on the other. By each of those courts the plaintiffs were rejected, and so they continued their search for a more willing forum. Their efforts are finally rewarded. Today they hit pay dirt in Texas ...

1 *Editor's note:* 'wildcatters' were persons who drilled speculatively for oil, in areas not generally known to be productive, in the hope of a lucky strike.

Comment

Unfortunately, such a callous attitude towards people whose lives have been ruined by poisonous chemicals is not unknown among American judges. An American company had caused them harm: was it unreasonable for them to seek a remedy in America?

Although the Costa Ricans succeeded in getting their claims heard in Texas, the dissenting voices won the day on the question of principle. After a battle that pitted the Texas trial bar against big business, the Texas legislature changed the law to make *forum non conveniens* applicable in cases such as this.[21] So, future litigants will no longer 'hit pay dirt' in Texas.

Today, actions of the kind we are considering are almost always dismissed on *forum-non-conveniens* grounds in the United States. Our next case is an example.

United States (New York)
Aguinda* v. *Texaco Inc.
US Court of Appeals for the Second Circuit
303 F 3d 470 (2002)

Background

This was a class action brought in a federal court in New York by a group of persons living mainly in Ecuador. They claimed that Texaco, while extracting oil from the Amazonian basin from 1967 to 1992,[22] had polluted a large area of rain

21 Texas Civil Practice and Remedies Code Annotated § 71.051(i).
22 Texaco's activities in Ecuador were carried on by its subsidiary, TexPet, a company incorporated in Delaware. TexPet extracted the oil on behalf of a consortium ('the Consortium') in which Texaco had a financial interest through TexPet. The Government of Ecuador also had an interest in the Consortium.

forest in Eastern Ecuador. According to the plaintiffs, it had dumped 18 billion gallons of toxic waste water into the rainforest, and had abandoned more than a thousand pits filled with sludge. The resulting pollution caused severe health problems for the indigenous people in the area.

Texaco fought to get the action out of the American courts. It agreed to submit to the jurisdiction of the courts of Ecuador, which, it said, were well suited to try the action. The plaintiffs argued that they were corrupt and inefficient. They said that class actions were unknown in Ecuador and that tort actions were rare. There was restricted pre-trial discovery. Ecuador also had an 'anti-*forum-non-conveniens*' statute (*Ley* (Law) 55) that deprived the Ecuadorian courts of jurisdiction.

Texaco challenged these claims. It also pointed out that the 'anti-*forum-non-conveniens*' statute had been adopted after the proceedings had begun, and it was doubtful whether it was retroactive. It said that the action was more closely connected with Ecuador: the plaintiffs lived there; the alleged damage took place there; and on-site inspections would be possible if the proceedings were held there. Most of the witnesses spoke only Spanish or one of the indigenous languages, which would cause translation problems if the case were heard in New York.

The case had a complicated procedural history, but the showdown came in 2001 when the federal district court dismissed it on grounds of *forum non conveniens*. The plaintiffs appealed to the Second Circuit.

Leval, Circuit Judge

Plaintiffs contend that the district court abused its discretion in determining that Ecuador was an adequate alternative forum and that the balance of private and public interest factors tilted in favor of dismissal . . . Finding no abuse of discretion, we affirm with modification . . .

A. Does an Adequate Alternative Forum Exist?

. . . Plaintiffs raise several objections to the availability and adequacy of an Ecuadorian forum.

Plaintiffs contend first that Ecuador does not offer an alternative forum because Law 55 precludes them from proceeding in Ecuadorian courts. Law 55 provides, '[S]hould the lawsuit be filed outside Ecuadorian territory, this will definitely terminate national competency as well as any jurisdiction of Ecuadorian judges over the matter.' Plaintiffs argue that Law 55 deprives Ecuadorian courts of competency to assert jurisdiction because both suits were first filed in the United States. They contend that dismissal for *forum non conveniens* would leave them without a forum in which to proceed. We agree with the district court's skepticism as to the law's retroactivity, as well as its application to cases dismissed for *forum non conveniens*. We note furthermore that following oral argument the parties submitted to us an April 30, 2002 decision of the Ecuadorian Constitutional Court declaring Law 55 unconstitutional. We need not determine the scope of Law 55, as the district court qualified its dismissal specifying that, in the event the

In 1992, the Ecuadorian state-owned oil company, PetroEcuador, took over the operation. Texaco tried to blame it for much of the pollution. In 2001, Chevron acquired Texaco.

cases were dismissed in Ecuador under Law 55 and this result were affirmed by Ecuador's highest court, it would be open to reconsider the question . . .

We find no merit in plaintiffs' further argument that Ecuadorian courts are unreceptive to tort claims . . .

Plaintiffs' third objection is that Ecuadorian courts do not recognize class actions. On the other hand, Ecuador permits litigants with similar causes of action arising out of the same facts to join together in a single lawsuit. While the need for thousands of individual plaintiffs to authorize the action in their names is more burdensome than having them represented by a representative in a class action, it is not so burdensome as to deprive the plaintiffs of an effective alternative forum . . .

Plaintiffs point further to several respects in which Ecuadorian procedure is less efficient than US procedure. While Ecuador's judicial procedures may be less streamlined than ours, that does not make Ecuador's procedures ineffective or render Ecuador inadequate as an alternative forum . . .

Plaintiffs contend that Ecuadorian courts are subject to corrupt influences and are incapable of acting impartially. After ordering supplemental briefing on this question, Judge Rakoff[1] made detailed findings. He found: 1) no evidence of impropriety by Texaco or any past member of the Consortium in any prior judicial proceeding in Ecuador; 2) there are presently pending in Ecuador's courts numerous cases against multinational corporations without any evidence of corruption; 3) Ecuador has recently taken significant steps to further the independence of its judiciary; 4) the State Department's general description of Ecuador's judiciary as politicized applies primarily to cases of confrontations between the police and political protestors; 5) numerous US courts have found Ecuador adequate for the resolution of civil disputes involving US companies; and 6) because these cases will be the subject of close public and political scrutiny, as confirmed by the Republic's involvement in the litigation, there is little chance of undue influence being applied . . .

Finally, plaintiffs challenge the district court's allowance of only 60 days for the assertion of plaintiffs' claims in Ecuador exempt from claims of preclusion. We agree with this objection. In the district court, timely claims were brought on behalf of nearly 55,000 plaintiffs. In Ecuador, because class action procedures are not recognized, signed authorizations would need to be obtained for each individual plaintiff. This presents a formidable administrative task for which we believe 60 days is inadequate time. We therefore direct the district court to modify its ruling to make dismissal conditioned on Texaco's agreeing to waive any defense based on a statute of limitations for limitation periods expiring between the date of filing these United States actions and one year (rather than 60 days) following the dismissal of these actions.

B. Balancing Private and Public Interest Factors

[The court then examined the way in which the district court had balanced the private and public interest factors. It noted that Texaco had agreed that evidence already obtained in the discovery process in the United States could be used in proceedings in Ecuador (a common condition of dismissal in cases of this kind); it furthermore noted that Texaco's counsel had agreed in oral argument that Texaco

---

1 *Editor's note*: Judge Rakoff was the judge in the district court.

would not oppose further discovery in Ecuador that would otherwise be available in the US. The court concluded:]

We conclude that the district court was within its discretion in dismissing the actions on the basis of *forum non conveniens*.

Conclusion

The district court's judgment dismissing for *forum non conveniens* is AFFIRMED, subject to the modification that the judgment be conditioned on Texaco's agreement to waive defenses based on statutes of limitation for limitation periods expiring between the institution of these actions and a date one year subsequent to the final judgment of dismissal.

The case then began anew in Ecuador. In 2008 – fifteen years after the claim was first filed in New York – the claimants came significantly closer to victory when a court-appointed expert recommended that the defendants should be held liable and that damages should be assessed at between US$7 billion and US$16 billion. Chevron's response was characteristic: according to *Newsweek*, it immediately began to lobby the US Government to impose sanctions on Ecuador.[23] Contrary to what it said in the New York proceedings, it now claimed that the Ecuadorian court system was corrupt. Chevron said that, if it lost the case, a dangerous precedent could be set for other multinationals. 'The ultimate issue here is Ecuador has mistreated a US company', said a Chevron lobbyist, who asked *Newsweek* not to identify him. 'We can't let little countries screw around with big companies like this – companies that have made big investments around the world.'[24]

If they obtain an award, and if Texaco refuses to pay up, the judgment may have to be enforced in the United States. The enforcement of foreign judgments is a topic dealt with in the next Part of this book. If enforcement proceedings are brought, it would be difficult for Texaco to argue that the Ecuadorian courts lacked jurisdiction, since it expressly accepted their jurisdiction as part of the price it had to pay for getting the proceedings dismissed in the US. It would probably claim that it did not get a fair trial because the Ecuadorian courts were biased and corrupt. Whether it would be estopped from denying its earlier assertion that the Ecuadorian courts would give a fair hearing to the claim is not known. No doubt, it will come up with other reasons for not paying.

Even if all goes well for the Ecuadorians, the fact will still remain that, in general, the victims of corporate wrongdoing are better off in the United States. In the *Texaco* case, a great deal was gained by proceeding first in the US:

- Texaco agreed to accept the jurisdiction of the courts of Ecuador.[25]
- Texaco accepted that the courts of Ecuador were a fair and just forum for the trial.

---

23 Michael Isikoff, 'A $16 Billion Problem', *Newsweek*, 26 July 2008.
24 *Ibid*. For future developments, see the website established by campaigners for the victims, www. chevrontoxico.com.
25 The Ecuadorian courts might anyway have had jurisdiction under Ecuadorian law, but this might not necessarily have been recognized by the American courts in judgment-enforcement proceedings.

- The Ecuadorians were able to obtain pre-trial discovery against Texaco under US law.[26]

These added up to significant advantages.

§ 2.3   England

Although English law does not give claimants all the advantages found in the US, they are nevertheless significantly better off than in many other countries. In the past, legal aid was available in civil proceedings, provided the claimant was so lacking in funds that he could not pay the lawyer himself. Under this system, which was open to foreign litigants bringing proceedings in English courts, the claimant could obtain the services of a lawyer in private practice, and the lawyer's fee, payable at the rate applicable in the case of a private client, would be paid out of public funds.

This system had great advantages for indigent claimants; unfortunately, it put too great a burden on the public purse. It was replaced by a system of conditional fees. Under this system, the client pays his lawyer only in the event of success, in which case the lawyer charges a fee based on an hourly rate that is higher than normal. This will be paid by the defendant.[27] The claimant takes out insurance to cover the risk of having to pay his opponent's costs (including lawyers' fee) in event that the action fails. Though this may not have all the advantages of an American contingent fee, it nevertheless provides a satisfactory alternative in many situations.

The English court system provides efficient, skilled, impartial judges. Cases move fairly quickly. English judges are well qualified to understand scientific evidence. In appropriate cases, parent companies are liable for the wrongs of their subsidiaries. Group actions are available and, though they may lack some of the advantages of American class actions, they have nevertheless proved effective in mass litigation. Pre-trial disclosure is much more limited than in the US, but wider than on the continent of Europe. Damages are lower than in the US, but significantly higher than in the Third World. For these reasons, an English forum can be attractive to litigants from the Third World.

The first case to consider is *Connelly* v. *RTZ (No. 2)*.[28] Connelly was a Scotsman. He emigrated to South Africa in 1971. From 1977 to 1982, he worked in a uranium mine in Namibia owned by Rossing Uranium, a subsidiary of the English mining company, RTZ. In 1983, he returned to Scotland, and, in 1986, he was diagnosed as suffering from cancer of the throat. He then underwent an operation and has since breathed through a tube in his throat. He claimed the cancer was caused by uranium dust in the mine. He tried to get compensation in Namibia, but failed. He then obtained legal aid and sued RTZ in England, claiming that they controlled Rossing's health policy. RTZ applied for a stay on *forum-non-conveniens* grounds.

---

26 This probably provided valuable evidence.
27 Under the English system, the lawyers' fees are part of the 'costs' of the action.
28 [1998] AC 854; [1997] 3 WLR 373; [1997] 4 All ER 335 (HL).

Connelly accepted that Namibia was *prima facie* the appropriate forum. However, there was no legal aid there and, as he had no money, he could not obtain legal representation. This made it impossible for him to sue in Namibia. Despite this, the Court of Appeal granted a stay: they said that the non-availability of legal aid in Namibia was not a relevant factor. Connelly's solicitors then agreed to take the case on a conditional-fee basis, conditional fees having been recently introduced in England. In a second decision, the Court of Appeal lifted the stay: they said that the availability of conditional fees in England but not in Namibia *was* a relevant factor. Both sides appealed: Connelly appealed against the first decision and RTZ appealed against the second.

The House of Lords allowed Connelly's appeal and dismissed RTZ's appeal. On the legal-aid point, they said that the absence of legal aid (or a conditional-fee system) in the alternative forum is not an automatic bar to a stay; nevertheless, in exceptional cases, where this made it impossible to sue in the foreign forum, it could be a factor.[29] After this decision, business interests in England tried to get the government to introduce legislation to change the law; but they were unsuccessful.

This provides the context for our next case.

England
Lubbe* v. *Cape plc
House of Lords
[2000] 1 WLR 1545; [2000] 4 All ER 268

Background

Cape was an English company. Through its subsidiaries, it carried on activities in South Africa concerned with asbestos, exposure to which causes a slow-acting but incurable disease, asbestosis. The claimants were mainly black South Africans. They were extremely poor. They had contracted asbestosis either as a result of working for one of Cape's South African subsidiaries, or because they lived in the neighbourhood of one of its plants. In 1997, Mrs Lubbe and four other claimants brought proceedings against Cape in England. Subsequently, Mrs Lubbe died and her claim was continued by her husband as her personal representative. The claimants maintained that Cape knew the dangers of asbestos and failed to take the appropriate steps to protect their workers and the persons who lived near their plants. On this basis, they claimed that Cape was liable.

Cape asked for a stay on the ground of *forum non conveniens*. This was granted by the trial judge. The Court of Appeal reversed this decision and, when leave to appeal to the House of Lords was refused, some 3,000 other claimants joined in the proceedings, which were consolidated into a group action. With this new development, Cape renewed its application for a stay. This was granted by the trial judge and upheld by the Court of Appeal. Leave to appeal was granted by the House of Lords.

---

29 The complexity of the case and the necessity for substantial scientific and medical evidence meant that a trial would be impossible in Namibia for a man in Connelly's situation.

There was no doubt that South Africa was the natural forum. However, the claimants argued that a stay should be refused under the second prong of the *Spiliada* test. They said that justice could not be done in South Africa because of the difficulty of getting a firm of attorneys to take on the case. (The claimants' English solicitors were doing the work under a conditional-fee agreement.)

Lord Bingham of Cornhill

The applicable principles

Where a plaintiff sues a defendant as of right in the English court and the defendant applies to stay the proceedings on grounds of *forum non conveniens*, the principles to be applied by the English court in deciding that application in any case not governed by article 2 of the Brussels Convention are not in doubt . . .

[Lord Bingham summarized the principles laid down in *Spiliada*. He outlined the first prong of the test (determining the natural forum) and continued:]

If the court concludes at that stage that there is no other available forum which is clearly more appropriate for the trial of the action, that is likely to be the end of the matter. But if the court concludes at that stage that there is some other available forum which *prima facie* is more appropriate for the trial of the action it will ordinarily grant a stay unless the plaintiff can show that there are circumstances by reason of which justice requires that a stay should nevertheless not be granted. In this second stage the court will concentrate its attention not only on factors connecting the proceedings with the foreign or the English forum . . . but on whether the plaintiff will obtain justice in the foreign jurisdiction. The plaintiff will not ordinarily discharge the burden lying upon him by showing that he will enjoy procedural advantages, or a higher scale of damages or more generous rules of limitation if he sues in England; generally speaking, the plaintiff must take a foreign forum as he finds it, even if it is in some respects less advantageous to him than the English forum . . . It is only if the plaintiff can establish that substantial justice will not be done in the appropriate forum that a stay will be refused . . .

This is not an easy condition for a plaintiff to satisfy, and it is not necessarily enough to show that legal aid is available in this country but not in the more appropriate foreign forum. Lord Goff of Chieveley said in the *Connelly* case . . .

'I therefore start from the position that, at least as a general rule, the court will not refuse to grant a stay simply because the plaintiff has shown that no financial assistance, for example in the form of legal aid, will be available to him in the appropriate forum, whereas such financial assistance will be available to him in England. Many smaller jurisdictions cannot afford a system of legal aid. Suppose that the plaintiff has been injured in a motor accident in such a country, and succeeds in establishing English jurisdiction on the defendant by service on him in this country where the plaintiff is eligible for legal aid, I cannot think that the absence of legal aid in the appropriate jurisdiction would of itself justify the refusal of a stay on the ground of *forum non conveniens*. In this connection it should not be forgotten that financial assistance for litigation is not necessarily regarded as essential, even in sophisticated legal systems. It was not widely available in this country until 1949; and even since that date it has been only available for persons with limited means. People above that limit may well lack the means to litigate, which provides one reason for the recent legalization of conditional fee agreements. Even so, the availability of financial assistance in this country, coupled with its non-availability in the appropriate forum, may exceptionally be a relevant factor in this context. The question, however, remains whether the plaintiff can establish that substantial justice will not in the particular circumstances of the case be done if the plaintiff has to proceed in the appropriate forum where no financial assistance is available.'

In the *Connelly* case a majority of the House held that the case before it was such an exceptional case. The nature and complexity of the case were such that it could not be tried at all without the benefit of legal representation and expert scientific assistance, available in this country but not in the more appropriate forum, Namibia. That being so, the majority of the House concluded that the Namibian forum was not one in which the case could be tried more suitably for the interests of all the parties and for the ends of justice.

The present cases

The issues in the present cases fall into two segments. The first segment concerns the responsibility of the defendant as a parent company for ensuring the observance of proper standards of health and safety by its overseas subsidiaries. Resolution of this issue will be likely to involve an inquiry into what part the defendant played in controlling the operations of the group, what its directors and employees knew or ought to have known, what action was taken and not taken, whether the defendant owed a duty of care to employees of group companies overseas and whether, if so, that duty was broken. Much of the evidence material to this inquiry would, in the ordinary way, be documentary and much of it would be found in the offices of the parent company, including minutes of meetings, reports by directors and employees on visits overseas and correspondence.

The second segment of the cases involves the personal injury issues relevant to each individual: diagnosis, prognosis, causation (including the contribution made to a plaintiff's condition by any sources of contamination for which the defendant was not responsible) and special damage. Investigation of these issues would necessarily involve the evidence and medical examination of each plaintiff and an inquiry into the conditions in which that plaintiff worked or lived and the period for which he did so. Where the claim is made on behalf of a deceased person the inquiry would be essentially the same, although probably more difficult.

[After discussing the rulings of the lower courts, Lord Bingham continued:]

The emergence of over 3,000 new plaintiffs following the decision of the first Court of Appeal had an obvious and significant effect on the balance of the proceedings. While the parent company responsibility issue remained very much what it had always been, the personal injury issues assumed very much greater significance. To investigate, prepare and resolve these issues, in relation to each of the plaintiffs, would plainly involve a careful, detailed and cumbersome factual inquiry and, at least potentially, a very large body of expert evidence. In this changed situation Buckley J, applying the first stage of the *Spiliada* test, regarded South Africa as clearly the more appropriate forum for trial of the group action and the second Court of Appeal agreed. Both courts were in my view plainly correct. The enhanced significance of the personal injury issues tipped the balance very clearly in favour of South Africa at the first stage of the *Spiliada* exercise, and no effective criticism has been made of that conclusion. The brunt of the plaintiff's argument on these appeals to the House has been directed not against the decisions of Buckley J[1] and the second Court of Appeal on the first stage of the Spiliada test but against their conclusion that the plaintiffs had not shown that substantial justice would not be done in the more appropriate South African forum.

Funding

The plaintiffs submitted that legal aid in South Africa had been withdrawn for personal injury claims, that there was no reasonable likelihood of any lawyer or group of lawyers being able or willing to fund proceedings of this weight and complexity under the contingency fee arrangements permitted in South Africa since April 1999 and that there was no other available source of funding open to the plaintiffs. These were, they argued, proceedings which could not be effectively prosecuted without legal representation and adequate funding. To stay proceedings in England, where legal representation and adequate funding are available, in favour of the South African forum where they are not would accordingly deny the plaintiffs any realistic prospect of pursuing their claims to trial.

[The defendant challenged these assertions, but the House of Lords found them proved. Extensive expert evidence of a scientific nature would be required. The expert witnesses would need to be remunerated. It was illegal in South Africa for the fee payable to an expert witness to be conditional on the plaintiff's winning the case; so the attorneys acting for the claimants would have to pay these fees themselves. If, in the end, the claimants lost, the financial blow might be too great for a small firm of attorneys. Only a large firm could take the risk. Such firms did not exist in South Africa.]

The clear, strong and unchallenged view of the attorneys who provided statements to the plaintiffs was that no firm of South African attorneys with expertise in this field had the means or would undertake the risk of conducting these proceedings on a contingency fee basis . . .

If these proceedings were stayed in favour of the more appropriate forum in South Africa the probability is that the plaintiffs would have no means of obtaining the professional representation and the expert evidence which would be essential if these claims were to be justly decided. This would amount to a denial of justice. In the special and unusual circumstances of these proceedings, lack of the means, in South Africa, to prosecute these claims to a conclusion provides a compelling ground, at the second stage of the *Spiliada* test, for refusing to stay the proceedings here.

. . .

Conclusion

I would dismiss the defendant's appeal against the decision of the first Court of Appeal. I would allow the plaintiff's appeal against the decision of the second

---

1 *Editor's note*: Buckley J was the judge who heard the second application for a stay at first instance (after the 3,000 additional claimants were joined).

Court of Appeal and remove the stay which that court upheld. The defendant must bear the costs of both appeals, and also the costs of the proceedings before Buckley J and the second Court of Appeal.

[One of the arguments put forward by both sides was that their respective positions were supported by public-interest factors. Lord Bingham rejected the view that these factors should be considered. On this point, he agreed with Lord Hope of Craighead. The following extract from Lord Hope's judgment deals with this issue.]

Lord Hope of Craighead

Public interest

In my opinion the principles on which the doctrine of *forum non conveniens* rest leave no room for considerations of public interest or public policy which cannot be related to the private interests of any of the parties or the ends of justice in the case which is before the court.

[After considering the authorities, he continued:]

The proper approach therefore is to start from the proposition that a claimant who is able to establish jurisdiction against the defendant as of right in this country is entitled to call upon the courts of this country to exercise that jurisdiction. So, if the plea of *forum non conveniens* cannot be sustained on the ground that the case may be tried more suitably in the other forum . . .'for the interests of all the parties and for the ends of justice', the jurisdiction must be exercised – however desirable it may be on grounds of public interest or public policy that the litigation should be conducted elsewhere and not in the English courts. On the other hand, if the interests of all parties and the ends of justice require that the action in this country should be stayed, a stay ought to be granted however desirable it may be on grounds of public interest or public policy that the action should be tried here.

I would therefore decline to follow those judges in the United States who would decide issues as to where a case ought to be tried on broad grounds of public policy . . . [2] the court is not equipped to conduct the kind of inquiry and assessment of the international as well as the domestic implications that would be needed if it were to follow that approach. However tempting it may be to give effect to concerns about the expense and inconvenience to the administration of justice of litigating actions such as these in this country on the one hand or in South Africa on the other, the argument must be resolved upon an examination of their effect upon the interests of the parties who are before the court and securing the ends of justice in their case. I would hold that considerations of policy which cannot be dealt with in this way should be left out of account in the application to the case of the *Spiliada* principles.

2 *Editor's note*: this is a reference to the public-interest factors that are a basic part of an American-style *forum-non-conveniens* analysis.

Result: the action can go ahead in England.[30]

30 After losing on the jurisdictional issue, Cape agreed to settle.

In the *Lubbe* case, the defendant was sued in the courts of its domicile, England. The question whether Community law precluded a stay in these circumstances was considered but not decided. Subsequently, the *Owusu* case (set out in Chapter 10, § 2, above) made clear that, where the English court has jurisdiction on the ground of the defendant's domicile (or on some other ground laid down in the Brussels I Regulation), a stay is not permitted, even if the alternative forum is outside the EC. In future, therefore, the *Spiliada* test will not be applicable in cases of this kind. A stay will be automatically refused.

§ 2.4   Conclusions

Common-law countries – especially the US, but also England – give significant advantages to claimants. In the US, these are cancelled out by the doctrine of *forum non conveniens*. Today, English courts are obliged to apply the civil-law ban on *forum non conveniens*, but they retain many of the advantages that the common law gives to claimants. This combination will make England the forum of choice for Third-World claimants who have suffered at the hands of English companies.

Further reading

Intellectual property

Drexl (Joseph) and Kur (Annette), *Intellectual Property and Private International Law* (Hart Publishing, Oxford, 2005)

Fawcett (James J.) and Torremans (Paul), *Intellectual Property and Private International Law* (Oxford University Press, Oxford, 1998)

Fentiman, 'Justiciability, Discretion and Foreign Rights', in Nuyts (Arnaud) (ed.), *International Litigation in Intellectual Property and Information Technology* (Wolters Kluwer, Austin, Boston, Chicago, New York and the Netherlands, 2008)

Pertegás Sender (Marta), *Cross-Border Enforcement of Patent Rights: An Analysis of the Interface between Intellectual Property and Private International Law* (Oxford University Press, Oxford, 2002)

Multinationals

Fawcett, 'The Impact of Article 6(1) of the ECHR on Private International Law' (2007) 56 ICLQ 1 (especially at pp. 9–11)

Muchlinski (Peter T.), *Multinational Enterprises and the Law* (Oxford University Press, Oxford, 2nd edn, 2007)

'Corporations in International Litigation: Problems of Jurisdiction and the United Kingdom Asbestos Cases' (2001) 50 ICLQ 1

PART III
FOREIGN JUDGMENTS

CHAPTER 13

Introduction to Part III

§ 1   Principles

The principle of *res judicata* requires that, unless the proceedings were flawed in some way, the successful party should not have to fight the case again. Once it is decided, that should be the end of the matter.

In the international context, this means that, unless there is a legitimate objection to the proceedings, a litigant should be able to rely on a judgment obtained in another country. If the judgment is for the defendant, the claimant should not be able to sue him again. If the judgment is for the claimant, he should be able to enforce it. In neither case should the matter be reopened.

However, this applies only if the foreign proceedings were just and fair. This raises, first and foremost, the question whether it was reasonable for the foreign court to hear the case. Was it reasonable for it to take jurisdiction? This raises the same issues as were considered above, though in a different situation. Now it is another court deciding whether the first court should have assumed jurisdiction.

Procedural questions, usually subsumed under the terms 'natural justice' or 'due process of law', are another issue. Other matters might also be relevant, but if the court asked to recognize the judgment goes much further than this it will come close to reopening the case. This would defeat the object of the exercise.

§ 2   Recognition and enforcement

A distinction is generally drawn between the recognition of a foreign judgment and its enforcement. 'Recognition' means accepting the determination of the rights and obligations made by the court of origin; 'enforcement' means ensuring that the judgment-debtor obeys the order of the court of origin. Since enforcement of a foreign judgment would be unjustified if the court enforcing it did not accept the determination of the rights and obligations of the parties made by the court of origin, enforcement must be preceded by recognition.

§ 3   Theories

There are two basic theories as to why one should recognize and enforce foreign judgments. The first is that it is done out of respect for the foreign State. This is usually known as the 'comity theory'. This theory is often regarded as requiring the application of reciprocity. It may also be regarded as requiring a treaty between the two States. The second theory is that judgments are recognized in order to do justice to the parties. The idea is that, if the proceedings were fair and if the foreign court had jurisdiction, a judgment in favour of the claimant creates an obligation (or debt) in the same way as a contract. For this reason, it is called the 'obligation theory'. This is the theory applied in England.

§ 4   Giving effect to a judgment

There are three ways in which effect may be given to a foreign judgment. The first, and most obvious, is that it may be enforced. This means that the court addressed (the court asked to give effect to the foreign judgment) must ensure – by force, if necessary – that the judgment-debtor obeys the judgment. The second way in which effect may be given to it is that it may be recognized as a defence to a claim. Thus, if the foreign court decides that the claim is unfounded, recognition of the judgment means that the claimant cannot sue again on the same cause of action.[1] The third way in which effect may be given to a foreign judgment is that it may operate as a transfer of property: if the foreign judgment declares that the claimant is the owner of an item of property, recognition of the judgment means that the court addressed accepts that the claimant does indeed own it. If the court addressed would otherwise have considered that someone else owned it, this means that the judgment had the effect of transferring title from that other person to the claimant.

§ 5   Res judicata and estoppel

When a foreign judgment is recognized, what exactly is it that is recognized? Here there seems to be a difference between the common law and the civil law. In the civil law, it seems that the final ruling or order (in German, the *Tenor* or *Spruch*; in French, the *dispositif*) is all that is recognized. In the common-law world, however, the doctrine known variously as issue estoppel,[2] collateral estoppel or issue preclusion[3] requires a court in certain circumstances to recognize rulings by the court of origin on preliminary issues.[4]

---

1 If the foreign judgment is in favour of the claimant, recognition may also mean that the claimant cannot sue again on the same cause of action, but must instead enforce the judgment. In England, in the past, this was the case only if the judgment had been satisfied; otherwise, the claimant could choose whether to enforce the judgment or sue again on the original cause of action. Today, the claimant no longer has this option: enforcement is his only remedy. See the Civil Jurisdiction and Judgments Act 1982, section 34.
2 British and Commonwealth terminology.
3 These latter two expressions are both United States terminology.
4 This raises the question which law should decide whether issue estoppel applies: should it be the law of the State of origin or that of the State of recognition? The former is supported by the argument that a judgment cannot have greater effect in the State of recognition than in the State of origin. However, issue estoppel is not based on the idea of recognizing the effect of a foreign judgment, but rather that of fairness

Estoppel is a doctrine peculiar to the common law. It is too complex to sum up in a few words, but the underlying idea may be explained by saying that a person should not be allowed to say one thing at one time and another thing at another time, depending on what suits him. In essence, it is a rule of evidence: the person concerned is estopped (prevented) from denying the truth of the earlier statement.

The creation of an estoppel through a judgment (whether local or foreign) is an extension of the basic idea. It is known as estoppel *per rem judicatam*. It originally applied to local judgments, but it is now recognized that it applies also to foreign judgments. Common-law courts often use the language of estoppel when they are recognizing a foreign judgment but not enforcing it, even if it is the final ruling that they are recognizing.[5] This is known as cause-of-action estoppel. Thus, estoppel based on a judgment (estoppel *per rem judicatam*) may be regarded as having two sub-categories: cause-of-action estoppel and issue estoppel.[6] The former would apply to the final ruling by the foreign court, the latter to a ruling on a preliminary issue.

In this Part, we shall consider the recognition and enforcement of foreign judgments under both the civil-law system of the Brussels I Regulation and under the common law. In England, the Regulation applies when the judgment is from another EC State and, if it is from a Lugano State, the similar system under the Lugano Convention applies. Judgments from Scotland and Northern Ireland are recognized and enforced in England under a modified version of the Regulation system laid down by the Civil Jurisdiction and Judgments Act 1982. Judgments from other countries come under the common-law system.

Further reading

Von Mehren, 'Recognition and Enforcement of Sister State Judgments: Reflections on General Theory and Current Practice in the EEC and the US' (1981) 81 *Columbia Law Review* 1044

---

between the parties. The original form of estoppel (estoppel by representation) was not even based on a judgment, but on a mere statement or other representation by a person. In England, it has been said that the law of the State of recognition should apply, since issue estoppel is a rule of evidence: Cheshire, North and Fawcett, p. 548. See also the Canadian decision of *Jacobs* v. *Beaver* (1908) 17 OLR 496 (Ontario Court of Appeal), where there is a *dictum* by Garrow JA that supports the application of the law of the State of recognition. For a discussion of the American case law (which is inconclusive), see Casad, 'Issue Preclusion and Foreign Country Judgments: Whose Law?' (1984) 70 *Iowa Law Review* 53.

5 This may be because the 'obligation' theory does not provide such a good explanation of why a foreign judgment should be recognized – for example, as a defence to a new action on the original claim – without being enforced.

6 Cheshire, North and Fawcett, pp. 544–50.

CHAPTER 14

EC law

§ 1 Introduction

The rules on the recognition of judgments contained in the Brussels I Regulation apply only to judgments from other EC States.[1] Similar rules in the Lugano Convention extend the system to the Lugano States. The recognition of judgments not covered by either of these two instruments depends on Member State law. We shall consider the English rules in the next chapter. In this chapter, therefore, we are considering only the recognition and enforcement of judgments from EC and Lugano States. The discussion that follows will be framed in terms of the Brussels I Regulation and the Member States of the European Community; however, it should be understood that, in almost all cases, these provisions apply also to the Lugano States.

Since the Brussels I Regulation lays down a system of detailed jurisdictional rules which is generally quite restrained, it might seem reasonable for it to provide that judgments from other Member States must be recognized without any further jurisdictional test. There is, however, a problem. As we saw in Chapter 3, the EC rules on jurisdiction apply, in general, only where the defendant is domiciled in another EC State. Where the defendant is not so domiciled, each Member State is entitled to apply its own rules of jurisdiction. Some of these rules are exorbitant in the extreme. In spite of this, the principle of recognition without a jurisdictional test applies to these judgments as well. In other words, while the rules in the Regulation on the taking of jurisdiction apply only when the defendant is domiciled in a Member State, the rules on recognition and enforcement apply to *all* judgments from other Member States, even when the defendant is not domiciled in a Member State. This means, for example, that a French citizen can bring proceedings in France under Article 14 of the French Civil Code[2] against anyone in the world (provided the defendant is not domiciled in another Member State), and he can then 'export' that judgment to

---

1 The Regulation does not, as such, apply to judgments from Denmark. These are governed by the Agreement of 19 October 2005 between the Community and Denmark on jurisdiction and the recognition and enforcement of judgments in civil and commercial matters, OJ 2005 L 299, p. 62. The agreement, however, makes the provisions of the Regulation applicable to Denmark under international law, rather than under Community law. Provision is also made for references to the European Court. The result is that everything in the text concerning the Regulation applies also to Denmark, though on a different basis.
2 This provision, it will be remembered, gives the French courts jurisdiction in proceedings against non-French citizens on the basis of the nationality of the *claimant*. Its use against persons domiciled in a Member State is prohibited by Article 3(2) of and Annex I to the Regulation; nevertheless, it can be, and is, used against persons not so domiciled.

all other Member States. It is hardly surprising that other countries regard this as outrageous.

We shall now consider the principles laid down in the Regulation, bearing in mind that the original judgment may have been on jurisdictionally exorbitant grounds.

§ 2   Principles

The basic principle of the Regulation, laid down in Article 33, is that all judgments granted by a court in a Member State that are within the subject-matter scope of the Regulation will be recognized and enforced in all other Member States (Panel 14.1). Having established that principle, the Regulation then lays down certain exceptions. These will be discussed below. Before we do so, however, it should be mentioned that the Regulation expressly states in Article 32 that 'judgment' means 'any judgment given by a court or tribunal of a Member State, whatever the judgment may be called'. This covers any 'decree, order, decision or writ of execution, as well as the determination of costs or expenses by an officer of the court'. There is no provision that limits the judgments that may be enforced to money judgments; so injunctions and orders for specific performance are also covered.

There is no rule in the Regulation that a judgment must be final before it can be enforced. It is, however, stated in Article 37 (Panel 14.2) that the court asked to recognize the judgment may stay the proceedings if an 'ordinary' appeal against it has been lodged.[3] In the case of a judgment from the United Kingdom and Ireland, this rule applies if enforcement is suspended in the State of origin by reason of an appeal.

Panel 14.1 Recognition and enforcement
Brussels I Regulation (Regulation 44/2001), Articles 33 and 38

Recognition

Article 33

1. A judgment given in a Member State shall be recognised in the other Member States without any special procedure being required.
2. Any interested party who raises the recognition of a judgment as the principal issue in a dispute may, in accordance with the procedures provided for in Sections 2 and 3 of this Chapter, apply for a decision that the judgment be recognised.
3. If the outcome of proceedings in a court of a Member State depends on the determination of an incidental question of recognition that court shall have jurisdiction over that question.

Enforcement

Article 38

1. A judgment given in a Member State and enforceable in that State shall be enforced in another Member State when, on the application of any interested party, it has been declared enforceable there.
2. However, in the United Kingdom, such a judgment shall be enforced in England and Wales, in Scotland, or in Northern Ireland when, on the application of any interested party, it has been registered for enforcement in that part of the United Kingdom.

Panel 14.2 Appeal in the court of origin
Brussels I Regulation (Regulation 44/2001), Article 37

Article 37

1. A court of a Member State in which recognition is sought of a judgment given in another Member State may stay the proceedings if an ordinary appeal against the judgment has been lodged.
2. A court of a Member State in which recognition is sought of a judgment given in Ireland or the United Kingdom may stay the proceedings if enforcement is suspended in the State of origin, by reason of an appeal.

---

3 As to the meaning of this, see *Industrial Diamond Supplies* v. *Riva*, Case 43/77, [1977] ECR 2175.

§ 3   Jurisdiction

As we have explained, the Brussels Regulation does not in general allow the court addressed to ascertain whether the court of origin had jurisdiction. This is laid down by Article 35(3) of the Regulation, which states that the jurisdiction of the State that granted the judgment may not be reviewed.

There are, however, four exceptional cases where a jurisdictional test may be applied.[4] These concern insurance,[5] consumer contracts,[6] exclusive jurisdiction[7] and the provisions of Article 72.[8] The first three exceptions are similar in nature and may be considered together. In cases involving insurance, consumer contracts or exclusive jurisdiction, the Regulation allows the court addressed to decide for itself whether the court of origin really did have jurisdiction according to the terms of the Regulation. If it did not, the judgment will not be recognized. Precisely why these three items should be singled out for special treatment is unclear. It is hard to see why the defendant requires greater protection in these cases than in other cases – for example, actions in tort. Presumably, this was the result of a political compromise.

Article 72 (Panel 14.3) raises different issues. This provision is based on Article 59 of the Brussels Convention, a provision that was intended to offset, to some extent, the policy adopted by the Convention, and now followed by the Regulation, under which protection against exorbitant jurisdiction is denied to defendants not domiciled in a Member State. What Article 59 did was to allow any Contracting State to enter into a convention with a non-contracting State under which the two States in question would recognize each other's judgments; it then provided that such a convention could go further and require the EC State not to recognize judgments granted by another EC State against persons domiciled or habitually resident in the non-member State in cases in which the court of origin took jurisdiction on one of the grounds specifically outlawed (with regard to defendants domiciled in a Member State) under the second paragraph of Article 3 of the Convention. The Convention then gave the EC State the power to determine whether the court that granted the judgment did in fact take jurisdiction on one of the prohibited grounds. Since Article 59 was concerned with cases in which

**Panel 14.3 Conventions with third countries
Brussels I Regulation (Regulation 44/2001), Article 72**

Article 72

This Regulation shall not affect agreements by which Member States undertook, prior to the entry into force of this Regulation pursuant to Article 59 of the Brussels Convention, not to recognise judgments given, in particular in other Contracting States to that Convention, against defendants domiciled or habitually resident in a third country where, in cases provided for in Article 4 of that Convention, the judgment could only be founded on a ground of jurisdiction specified in the second paragraph of Article 3 of that Convention.

---

4 Even in these four exceptional cases, however, the court addressed is bound by the findings of fact on which the court of origin based its jurisdiction: Article 35(2).
5 Section 3 of Chapter II of the Regulation (Articles 8–14).
6 Section 4 of Chapter II of the Regulation (Articles 15–17).
7 Section 6 of Chapter II of the Regulation (Article 22).
8 Strangely, Section 5 of Chapter II of the Regulation (Articles 18–21), which covers individual contracts of employment, is not covered. It seems that the framers of the Regulation thought that protecting the rights of employees was less important than protecting the rights of consumers and insured persons.

the defendant was not domiciled in a Member State, the court which granted the judgment would not have looked to the Convention for its jurisdiction; so there could have been no question of trusting that court.

When the Regulation was adopted, the power to enter into such conventions with non-member States was abolished; however, conventions already concluded were respected.[9] Thus, Article 72 of the Regulation permits the court addressed to ascertain whether the judgment is covered by such a convention, and, if it is, not to recognize or enforce it if the court of origin took jurisdiction on one of the grounds specified in the second paragraph of Article 3 of the Brussels Convention.

It should also be mentioned that Article 22, the provision relating to exclusive jurisdiction, applies only where the court having exclusive jurisdiction is a court of a Member State. The best-known example of exclusive jurisdiction is actions relating to rights *in rem* in land. Only a court of the country where the land is situated may hear such actions. Thus, if a French court gives a judgment concerning ownership of land in Germany, an English court is not only permitted, but is obliged, to refuse recognition to it. Moreover, Article 35(1) permits the English court to decide for itself whether an infringement of Article 22 actually took place. However, if the French court had given judgment concerning ownership of land in California, the English court would not, it seems, be permitted to refuse recognition. This is another example of the unfortunate chauvinism exhibited by the Regulation.

§ 4 Judgments outside the scope of the Regulation

The court asked to recognize the judgment must decide for itself whether the judgment is within the subject-matter scope of the Regulation. It is not bound by any ruling of the court of origin on this point. This is made clear by the decision of the European Court in *LTU* v. *Eurocontrol*,[10] a case discussed in Chapter 3, § 9.1, above.

§ 5 Public policy

Article 34(1) (Panel 14.4) provides that a judgment may be refused recognition if recognition would be manifestly contrary to the public policy of the State in which recognition is sought. However, it is expressly laid down in Article 35(3) (also in Panel 14.4) that the public-policy clause may

---

Panel 14.4 Public policy
Brussels I Regulation (Regulation 44/2001), Articles 34 and 35

Article 34

A judgment shall not be recognised:
1. if such recognition is manifestly contrary to public policy in the Member State in which recognition is sought . . .

Article 35

3. . . . The test of public policy referred to in point 1 of Article 34 may not be applied to the rules relating to jurisdiction.

---

9 The only such conventions in existence appear to be two concluded by the United Kingdom, one with Canada and one with Australia.
10 Case 29/76, [1976] ECR 1541.

not be used as an indirect way of ensuring that the court that granted the judgment had jurisdiction.

Our next case is an illustration of these principles.

European Community
Krombach v. *Bamberski*
Court of Justice of the European Communities
Case C-7/98, [2000] ECR I-1935

Background

This unusual case concerned two men, Krombach (a German) and Bamberski (a Frenchman). Bamberski had been married and had had two children, one of whom was a daughter. He and his wife divorced. She then married Krombach and went to live with him in Germany. One day, when the two children were visiting their mother and Krombach in Germany, the daughter, who had spent the day windsurfing, complained of feeling tired. Krombach, who was a doctor, gave her an injection intended to treat anaemia. The next day, she was found dead. The German authorities instituted a criminal investigation, but it was eventually discontinued on the ground that there was no evidence that a crime had been committed.

This was not the end of the matter, however. The French authorities then interested themselves in the case and, as a result, a criminal prosecution was brought against Krombach in France. The French court assumed jurisdiction on the ground that the daughter was a French citizen. It was not possible to extradite Krombach because Germany had a rule that German citizens could not be extradited to stand trial in a foreign country.[11] Krombach was summoned to appear in France and, when he failed to do so, it was decided to try him in his absence.

Under French law, if a crime also constitutes a civil wrong, the wronged party may bring a civil claim in the course of the criminal proceedings. Provision is made for this under the Brussels Convention (in force at the time) and the Brussels Regulation. Article 5(4) of both the Convention and the Regulation (Panel 14.5) provides that, with regard to a civil claim based on an act giving rise to criminal proceedings, the court hearing the criminal proceedings has jurisdiction to hear the civil claim if it has such jurisdiction under its own law. Bamberski availed himself of this possibility and instituted civil proceedings against Krombach that were joined to the criminal trial.

Krombach wanted to defend himself in these proceedings, but did not want to go to France. If he had done so, he would have been arrested. So he briefed lawyers to defend the case in

---

Panel 14.5 Civil claim in criminal proceedings
Brussels I Regulation (Regulation 44/2001), Article 5

Article 5

A person domiciled in a Member State may, in another Member State, be sued:

. . .

4. as regards a civil claim for damages or restitution which is based on an act giving rise to criminal proceedings, in the court seised of those proceedings, to the extent that that court has jurisdiction under its own law to entertain civil proceedings;

---

11 At the time in question, there was no EC provision on extradition.

his absence. The lawyers duly appeared, but the French court refused to hear them. This was based on a rule of French law under which a fugitive from justice is not allowed to defend himself in legal proceedings unless he appears in person. This rule seems to be based on the idea that a person should not be entitled to avail himself of legal remedies if at the same time he is trying to thwart justice by absconding. (A similar rule applies in the United States.)

The French court found Krombach guilty of manslaughter and sentenced him to fifteen years in prison. The court also awarded Bamberski civil damages. The criminal sentence could not be carried out while Krombach remained in Germany. However, Bamberski brought proceedings in Germany to enforce the civil award. Krombach resisted these on the ground that, as he had not been allowed to defend himself in the French proceedings, it would be contrary to German public policy to enforce the judgment. At the time of the case, the Brussels Convention was in force and the public-policy clause was contained in Article 27(1). Its wording was identical to Article 34(1) of the Regulation.

The lower German courts held that the French judgment must be enforced. Krombach appealed to the Federal Supreme Court (*Bundesgerichtshof*), which made a reference to the European Court, asking it two questions.

In the first question, it asked whether the public-policy clause may be used to deny recognition to a judgment from another Contracting State for civil damages in a criminal case if the State of origin took jurisdiction on the ground that the victim was one of its citizens. The point about this question is that Article 3 of the Convention expressly forbade France from assuming jurisdiction on the basis of Article 14 of the French Civil Code with regard to a defendant domiciled in another Contracting State.[12] Article 14 is the provision that allows French courts to take jurisdiction on the ground that the claimant is a French citizen. However, if a French court took jurisdiction in a criminal case on the ground that the victim was a French citizen, and if a civil claim was joined to the criminal proceedings, the end result would be that the French courts *could* take jurisdiction over a defendant domiciled in another Contracting State on the ground of the victim's (or claimant's) French nationality. In other words, Article 5(4) could provide a means of circumventing the ban on this ground of jurisdiction. The German Federal Supreme Court wanted to know, therefore, whether the public-policy clause could be used to prevent this.

The second question was whether the public-policy clause could be invoked on the ground that the defendant had been denied the right to defend himself.

Two further points should be made. The first is that, under Article II of the Protocol annexed to the Convention, a provision now found in Article 61 of the Regulation (Panel 14.6), a person domiciled in one Contracting State who is prosecuted in another Contracting State (of which he is not a national) is entitled to be legally represented even if he does not appear in person. If he is denied this right, any civil judgment does not have to be recognized in other Contracting States. However, this provision, which seems to have been intended to apply

---

12 A similar provision is laid down in Article 3(1) of and Annex I to the Regulation.

Panel 14.6 The right to defend oneself
Brussels I Regulation (Regulation 44/2001), Article 61

Article 61

Without prejudice to any more favourable provisions of national laws, persons domiciled in a Member State who are being prosecuted in the criminal courts of another Member State of which they are not nationals for an offence which was not intentionally committed may be defended by persons qualified to do so, even if they do not appear in person. However, the court seised of the matter may order appearance in person; in the case of failure to appear, a judgment given in the civil action without the person concerned having had the opportunity to arrange for his defence need not be recognised or enforced in the other Member States.

mainly with regard to traffic accidents, applies only to non-intentional offences. This made it inapplicable to the proceedings against Krombach. Could it be argued that this meant that, in the case of an intentional offence, the denial of the right to defend oneself could not be used as a reason for applying the public policy exception?

The second point is that the European Court of Human Rights has consistently held that it is contrary to Article 6 of the European Convention on Human Rights[13] to deny a civil litigant or criminal defendant the right to legal representation on the ground that he is a fugitive from justice.[14] Indeed, Krombach himself subsequently brought successful proceedings against France on this very ground.[15] Did this mean that this *could* be a ground for invoking the public-policy clause?

Judgment

21. So far as Article 27 of the Convention is concerned, the Court has held that this provision must be interpreted strictly inasmuch as it constitutes an obstacle to the attainment of one of the fundamental objectives of the Convention . . . With regard, more specifically, to recourse to the public-policy clause in Article 27, point 1, of the Convention, the Court has made it clear that such recourse is to be had only in exceptional cases . . .

22. It follows that, while the Contracting States in principle remain free, by virtue of the proviso in Article 27, point 1, of the Convention, to determine, according to their own conceptions, what public policy requires, the limits of that concept are a matter for interpretation of the Convention.

23. Consequently, while it is not for the Court to define the content of the public policy of a Contracting State, it is none the less required to review the limits within which the courts of a Contracting State may have recourse to that concept for the purpose of refusing recognition to a judgment emanating from a court in another Contracting State.

24. It should be noted in this regard that, since the Convention was concluded on the basis of Article 220 of the Treaty and within the framework which it defines, its provisions are linked to the Treaty . . .

---

13 This is the provision that guarantees the right to a fair trial in civil and criminal proceedings.
14 *Poitrimol* v. *France*, judgment of 23 November 1993, (1994) 18 EHRR 130. See also *Pelladoah* v. *Netherlands*, judgment of 22 September 1994; *Van Geyseghem* v. *Netherlands*, judgment of 21 January 1999; *Lala* v. *Netherlands*, judgment of 22 September 1999; *Khalfaoui* v. *France*, judgment of 14 December 1999 (all available on www.echr.coe.int).
15 *Krombach* v. *France*, judgment of 13 February 2001. See also *Papon* v. *France*, judgment of 25 July 2002 (both cases available on www.echr.coe.int).

25.   The Court has consistently held that fundamental rights form an integral part of the general principles of law whose observance the Court ensures ... For that purpose, the Court draws inspiration from the constitutional traditions common to the Member States and from the guidelines supplied by international treaties for the protection of human rights on which the Member States have collaborated or of which they are signatories. In that regard, the European Convention for the Protection of Human Rights and Fundamental Freedoms (hereinafter the ECHR) has particular significance ...

26.   The Court has thus expressly recognised the general principle of Community law that everyone is entitled to fair legal process, which is inspired by those fundamental rights ...

27.   Article F(2) of the Treaty on European Union (now, after amendment, Article 6(2) EU) embodies that case-law. It provides:

> The Union shall respect fundamental rights, as guaranteed by the European Convention for the Protection of Human Rights and Fundamental Freedoms signed in Rome on 4 November 1950 and as they result from the constitutional traditions common to the Member States, as general principles of Community law.

28.   It is in the light of those considerations that the questions submitted for a preliminary ruling fall to be answered.

The first question

29.   By this question, the national court is essentially asking whether, regard being had to the public-policy clause contained in Article 27, point 1, of the Convention, the court of the State in which enforcement is sought can, with respect to a defendant domiciled in that State, take into account the fact that the court of the State of origin based its jurisdiction on the nationality of the victim of an offence.

30.   It should be noted at the outset that it follows from the specific terms of the first paragraph of Article 1 of the Convention that the Convention applies to decisions given in civil matters by a criminal court ...

31.   Under the system of the Convention, with the exception of certain cases exhaustively listed in the first paragraph of Article 28, none of which corresponds to the facts of the case in the main proceedings, the court before which enforcement is sought cannot review the jurisdiction of the court of the State of origin. This fundamental principle, which is set out in the first phrase[1] of the third paragraph of Article 28 of the Convention, is reinforced by the specific statement, in the second phrase[2] of the same paragraph, that the test of public policy referred to in point 1 of Article 27 may not be applied to the rules relating to jurisdiction.

---

1 *Editor's note*: in this paragraph, 'phrase' would have been more accurately translated by 'sentence'.
2 *Editor's note*: see previous footnote.

32. It follows that the public policy of the State in which enforcement is sought cannot be raised as a bar to recognition or enforcement of a judgment given in another Contracting State solely on the ground that the court of origin failed to comply with the rules of the Convention which relate to jurisdiction.

33. Having regard to the generality of the wording of the third paragraph of Article 28 of the Convention, that statement of the law must be regarded as being, in principle, applicable even where the court of the State of origin wrongly founded its jurisdiction, in regard to a defendant domiciled in the territory of the State in which enforcement is sought, on a rule which has recourse to a criterion of nationality.

34. The answer to the first question must therefore be that the court of the State in which enforcement is sought cannot, with respect to a defendant domiciled in that State, take account, for the purposes of the public-policy clause in Article 27, point 1, of the Convention, of the fact, without more, that the court of the State of origin based its jurisdiction on the nationality of the victim of an offence.

The second question

35. By this question, the national court is essentially asking whether, in relation to the public-policy clause in Article 27, point 1, of the Convention, the court of the State in which enforcement is sought can, with respect to a defendant domiciled in its territory and charged with an intentional offence, take into account the fact that the court of the State of origin refused to allow that defendant to have his defence presented unless he appeared in person.

36. By disallowing any review of a foreign judgment as to its substance, Article 29 and the third paragraph of Article 34 of the Convention prohibit the court of the State in which enforcement is sought from refusing to recognise or enforce that judgment solely on the ground that there is a discrepancy between the legal rule applied by the court of the State of origin and that which would have been applied by the court of the State in which enforcement is sought had it been seised of the dispute. Similarly, the court of the State in which enforcement is sought cannot review the accuracy of the findings of law or fact made by the court of the State of origin.

37. Recourse to the public-policy clause in Article 27, point 1, of the Convention can be envisaged only where recognition or enforcement of the judgment delivered in another Contracting State would be at variance to an unacceptable degree with the legal order of the State in which enforcement is sought inasmuch as it infringes a fundamental principle. In order for the prohibition of any review of the foreign judgment as to its substance to be observed, the infringement would have to constitute a manifest breach of a rule of law regarded as essential in the legal order of the State in which enforcement is

sought or of a right recognised as being fundamental within that legal order.

38. With regard to the right to be defended, to which the question submitted to the Court refers, this occupies a prominent position in the organisation and conduct of a fair trial and is one of the fundamental rights deriving from the constitutional traditions common to the Member States.

39. More specifically still, the European Court of Human Rights has on several occasions ruled in cases relating to criminal proceedings that, although not absolute, the right of every person charged with an offence to be effectively defended by a lawyer, if need be one appointed by the court, is one of the fundamental elements in a fair trial and an accused person does not forfeit entitlement to such a right simply because he is not present at the hearing . . .

40. It follows from that case-law that a national court of a Contracting State is entitled to hold that a refusal to hear the defence of an accused person who is not present at the hearing constitutes a manifest breach of a fundamental right.

41. The national court is, however, unsure as to whether the court of the State in which enforcement is sought can take account, in relation to Article 27, point 1, of the Convention, of a breach of this nature having regard to the wording of Article II of the Protocol. That provision, which involves extending the scope of the Convention to the criminal field because of the consequences which a judgment of a criminal court may entail in civil and commercial matters . . . recognises the right to be defended without appearing in person before the criminal courts of a Contracting State for persons who are not nationals of that State and who are domiciled in another Contracting State only in so far as they are being prosecuted for an offence committed unintentionally. This restriction has been construed as meaning that the Convention clearly seeks to deny the right to be defended without appearing in person to persons who are being prosecuted for offences which are sufficiently serious to justify this . . .

42. However, it follows from a line of case-law developed by the Court on the basis of the principles referred to in paragraphs 25 and 26 of the present judgment that observance of the right to a fair hearing is, in all proceedings initiated against a person which are liable to culminate in a measure adversely affecting that person, a fundamental principle of Community law which must be guaranteed even in the absence of any rules governing the proceedings in question . . .

43. The Court has also held that, even though the Convention is intended to secure the simplification of formalities governing the reciprocal recognition and enforcement of judgments of courts or tribunals, it is not permissible to achieve that aim by undermining the right to a fair hearing . . .

44. It follows from the foregoing developments in the case-law that recourse to the public-policy clause must be regarded as being possible in exceptional cases where the guarantees laid down in the legislation of the State of origin and in the Convention itself have been insufficient to protect the defendant from a manifest breach of his right to defend himself before the court of origin, as recognised by the ECHR. Consequently, Article II of the Protocol cannot be construed as precluding the court of the State in which enforcement is sought from being entitled to take account, in relation to public policy, as referred to in Article 27, point 1, of the Convention, of the fact that, in an action for damages based on an offence, the court of the State of origin refused to hear the defence of the accused person, who was being prosecuted for an intentional offence, solely on the ground that that person was not present at the hearing.

45. The answer to the second question must therefore be that the court of the State in which enforcement is sought can, with respect to a defendant domiciled in that State and prosecuted for an intentional offence, take account, in relation to the public-policy clause in Article 27, point 1, of the Convention, of the fact that the court of the State of origin refused to allow that person to have his defence presented unless he appeared in person.

Comment

This judgment makes clear that, if a court of a Member State takes jurisdiction over a defendant domiciled in another Member State on grounds prohibited by the Regulation, there is nothing that other Member States can do about it. They cannot use the public-policy clause to block enforcement. This is expressly stated in paragraph 32 of the judgment.[16]

§ 6   Conflicting judgments

Panel 14.7 Conflicting judgments
Brussels I Regulation (Regulation 44/2001), Article 34

Article 34

A judgment shall not be recognised:

. . .

3. if it is irreconcilable with a judgment given in a dispute between the same parties in the Member State in which recognition is sought;

4. if it is irreconcilable with an earlier judgment given in another Member State or in a third State involving the same cause of action and between the same parties, provided that the earlier judgment fulfils the conditions necessary for its recognition in the Member State addressed.

The Regulation gives separate treatment to the case where the judgment sought to be recognized conflicts with a judgment from the State in which recognition is sought and where it conflicts with a judgment from another State. The relevant provisions are Article 34(3) and (4) (Panel 14.7).

---

16 After the European Court's ruling, the case went back to the German Federal Supreme Court, which held that the judgment would not be recognized in Germany: *Krombach v. Bamberski* [2002] ILPr 4.

§ 6.1 Judgments from the State of recognition

Article 34(3) provides that a judgment will not be recognized if it is irreconcilable[17] with a judgment given in a dispute between the same parties in the Member State in which recognition is sought. It does not matter whether the local judgment was given before or after the judgment for which recognition is sought.

§ 6.2 Judgments from another State

Article 34(4) of the Regulation provides that a judgment will not be recognized if it is irreconcilable[18] with an *earlier* judgment given in another Member State or in a third State involving the same cause of action and between the same parties, provided that the earlier judgment fulfils the conditions necessary for its recognition in the Member State addressed. The inclusion of judgments from non-member States in this provision constitutes a rare acknowledgment that the rest of the world actually exists. This stands in stark contrast to provisions such as Article 22 (exclusive jurisdiction), Article 23 (choice-of-court agreements) and Article 27 (*lis pendens*), all of which seem to ignore this possibility.

§ 6.3 Judgments outside the scope of the Regulation

What happens if the conflicting judgment (the judgment that conflicts with the judgment sought to be recognized) is outside the scope of the Regulation? One's first reaction is to say that a judgment outside the scope of the Regulation cannot be taken into account. However, our next case shows that this is not so.

European Community
Hoffmann* v. *Krieg
Court of Justice of the European Communities
Case 145/86, [1988] ECR 645

Background

A husband and wife were both German. They married in Germany and established their matrimonial home there. After some years, the husband left the wife and went to live in the Netherlands. The wife obtained a maintenance order from a German court. The husband then obtained a divorce from a Dutch court. The husband claimed that the continued enforcement of the maintenance order after the divorce became final would be incompatible with the divorce, since under Dutch law maintenance is not payable once the marriage is terminated. The Dutch court asked to enforce the German maintenance order made a reference to the European Court.

The complication in this case is that maintenance orders were covered by the

---

17 On the meaning of 'irreconcilable', see paragraphs 22 *et seq.* of the judgment in *Hoffmann* v. *Krieg* (set out in § 6.3, below).
18 See previous note.

Brussels Convention (in force at the time) but divorce was not. (The position is the same under the Brussels I Regulation, but there is now a separate instrument dealing with divorce.) For this reason, the German court was not obliged to recognize the Dutch divorce under the Convention, and had not done so. As far as it was concerned, the couple were still married. In the eyes of the Dutch court, on the other hand, they were not. Both positions were legitimate under Community law.

Judgment

12. In the circumstances of the main proceedings, as disclosed by the documents before the court, the national court's second question seeks, in essence, to establish whether a foreign judgment whose enforcement has been ordered in a Contracting State pursuant to Article 31 of the Convention must continue to be enforced in all cases in which it would still be enforceable in the State in which it was given even when, under the law of the State in which enforcement is sought, the judgment ceases to be enforceable for reasons which lie outside the scope of the Convention.

13. In this instance, the judgment whose enforcement is at issue is one which orders a husband to make maintenance payments to his spouse by virtue of his obligations, arising out of the marriage, to support her. Such a judgment necessarily presupposes the existence of the matrimonial relationship.

14. Consideration should therefore be given to whether the dissolution of that matrimonial relationship by a decree of divorce granted by a court of the State in which the enforcement is sought can terminate the enforcement of the foreign judgment even when that judgment remains enforceable in the State in which it was given, the decree of divorce not having been recognized there.

15. In that connection it must be observed that indent (1) of the second paragraph of Article 1 of the Convention provides that the Convention does not apply inter alia to the status or legal capacity of natural persons. Moreover, it contains no rule requiring the court of the State in which enforcement is sought to make the effects of a national decree of divorce conditional on recognition of that decree in the State in which the foreign maintenance order is made.

16. That is confirmed by Article 27 (4) of the Convention, which excludes in principle the recognition of any foreign judgment involving a conflict with a rule – concerning inter alia the status of natural persons – of the private international law of the State in which the recognition is sought. That provision demonstrates that, as far as the status of natural persons is concerned, it is not the aim of the Convention to derogate from the rules which apply under the domestic law of the court before which the action has been brought.

17. It follows that the Convention does not preclude the court of the State in which enforcement is sought from drawing the necessary inferences from a national decree of divorce when considering the enforcement of the foreign maintenance order.

18. Thus the answer to be given to the national court is that a foreign judgment whose enforcement has been ordered in a Contracting State pursuant to Article 31 of the Convention and which remains enforceable in the State in which it was given must not continue to be enforced in the State where enforcement is sought when, under the law of the latter State, it ceases to be enforceable for reasons which lie outside the scope of the Convention.

19. The national court' s third question seeks, in essence, to establish whether a foreign judgment ordering a person to make maintenance payments to his spouse by virtue of his conjugal obligations to support her is irreconcilable within the meaning of Article 27 (3) of the Convention with a national judgment pronouncing the divorce of the spouses or, alternatively, whether such a foreign judgment is contrary to public policy in the State in which recognition is sought within the meaning of Article 27 (1).

20. The provisions to be interpreted set out the grounds for not recognizing foreign judgments. Under the second paragraph of Article 34, an enforcement order may be refused for those same reasons.

21. As far as the second part of the third question is concerned, it should be noted that, according to the scheme of the Convention, use of the public-policy clause, which 'ought to operate only in exceptional cases' (Jenard Report . . . at p. 44) is in any event precluded when, as here, the issue is whether a foreign judgment is compatible with a national judgment; the issue must be resolved on the basis of the specific provision under Article 27 (3), which envisages cases in which the foreign judgment is irreconcilable with a judgment given in a dispute between the same parties in the State in which enforcement is sought.

22. In order to ascertain whether the two judgments are irreconcilable within the meaning of Article 27 (3), it should be examined whether they entail legal consequences that are mutually exclusive.

23. It is apparent from the documents before the court that, in the present case, the order for enforcement of the foreign maintenance order was issued at a time when the national decree of divorce had already been granted and had acquired the force of *res judicata*, and that the main proceedings are concerned with the period following the divorce.

24. That being so, the judgments at issue have legal consequences which are mutually exclusive. The foreign judgment, which necessarily presupposes the existence of the matrimonial relationship, would have to be enforced although that relationship has been dissolved by a judgment given in a dispute between the same parties in the State in which enforcement is sought.

25 The answer to be given to the third question submitted by the national court is therefore that a foreign judgment ordering a person to make maintenance payments to his spouse by virtue of his conjugal obligations

> to support her is irreconcilable within the meaning of Article 27 (3) of the Convention with a national judgment pronouncing the divorce of the spouses.

Comment

In paragraph 16 of the judgment, there is a reference to Article 27(4) of the Convention (Panel 14.8), a provision omitted from the Regulation. However, paragraph 16 says merely that the conclusion already reached is 'confirmed' by Article 27(4). This suggests that the fact that the provisions of Article 27(4) no longer apply does not affect the ruling in the case, which seems to lay down a general rule that the conflicting judgment need not be within the scope of the Convention or Regulation.[19]

Panel 14.8 Brussels Convention, Article 27(4)

Article 27

A judgment shall not be recognized:

. . .

4. if the court of the State of origin, in order to arrive at its judgment, has decided a preliminary question concerning the status or legal capacity of natural persons, rights in property arising out of a matrimonial relationship, wills or succession in a way that conflicts with a rule of the private international law of the State in which the recognition is sought, unless the same result would have been reached by the application of the rules of private international law of that State . . .

The judgment in *Hoffmann* v. *Krieg* is in fact consistent with the policy underlying the rule in Article 34(3) and (4), which is to avoid inconsistencies and contradictions in the legal system of a Member State. The undesirability of such inconsistencies does not depend on whether or not the two judgments in conflict are within the scope of the Regulation.

§ 7   Conflicts with an arbitration award

What happens if a judgment of another Member State conflicts with an arbitration award? We have seen that arbitration is excluded from the scope of the Regulation,[20] but that does not solve the problem. The answer is found in Article 71(1) of the Regulation, which provides that the Regulation 'shall not affect any conventions to which the Member States are parties and which in relation to particular matters, govern jurisdiction or the recognition or enforcement of judgments'. Since all the Member States are parties to the United Nations Convention on the Recognition and Enforcement of Foreign Arbitral Awards (New York, 10 June 1958), and since Article III of that Convention requires Contracting States to recognize and enforce arbitral awards, the Regulation cannot prevent a Member State from recognizing an award, even if it conflicts with a judgment from another Member State. Thus the obligation to recognize awards prevails over the obligation to recognize judgments. So a judgment would not be recognized if it was irreconcilable with an award that was enforceable under the New York Convention.

---

19 See Gaudemet-Tallon, *Compétence et exécution des jugements en Europe* (LGDJ, Paris, 3rd edn 2002), paragraph 420. The rule should also apply to judgments from another Member State or from a non-member State, provided (in both cases) that the requirements of Article 34(4) are satisfied.
20 Chapter 10, § 5, above.

§ 8   Provisional measures

Article 31 of the Regulation allows a court to grant provisional, including protective, measures even if it does not have jurisdiction over the substance of the case. In *Van Uden* v. *Deco-Line*[21] (see Chapter 19, § 8.2, below), the European Court held that this could include provisional payment of part, or even all, of the sum claimed by the claimant. In such a case, however, the order must relate only to specific assets of the defendant located, or to be located, within the confines of the territorial jurisdiction of the court that makes the order. In *Mietz* v. *Intership Yachting Sneek*[22] (see Chapter 19, § 8.2, below), the European Court held that, if proceedings are brought for the recognition and enforcement of such a judgment under the Convention (now the Regulation), the court addressed is entitled to inquire whether the court of origin took jurisdiction under what is now Article 31 of the Regulation. If it did, the judgment will not be enforced.

§ 9   Choice-of-court agreements

Unlike the position under English, Canadian or American law, there is no provision in the Regulation permitting a court to refuse recognition and enforcement to a judgment on the ground that the court of origin heard the case contrary to a choice-of-court agreement.

As we have seen, a court may refuse to recognize a judgment if it is irreconcilable with a judgment given in the State of the court addressed, or if it is irreconcilable with an earlier judgment given in another State. So, if the judgment under the choice-of-court agreement is given first, the other judgment will not be recognized. However, this is unlikely to be of much comfort to a party wishing to enforce a choice-of-court agreement, since the European Court has held that, if the other court is seised first, the court specified in the choice-of-court agreement cannot entertain the proceedings until the other court has declined jurisdiction.[23] If the other court gives judgment despite the choice-of-court agreement, that judgment must be recognized and enforced in all Member States, including that of the chosen court. There is nothing any other State can do about it.

§ 10   Arbitration agreements

We have seen that arbitration is excluded from the scope of the Regulation.[24] Since the decision in *Marc Rich and Co.* v. *Società Italiana Impianti*[25] (set out in Chapter 10, § 5, above), it has been accepted that, for the purposes of the Brussels

---

21 Case C-391/95, [1998] ECR I-7091.
22 Case C-99/96, [1999] ECR I-2277.
23 *Gasser* v. *MISRAT*, Case C-116/02, [2003] ECR I-14693.
24 See Chapter 10, § 5, above.
25 Case C-190/89, [1991] ECR I-3855.

I Regulation, 'arbitration' covers proceedings before a court directly relating to arbitration, such as proceedings for the appointment or dismissal of an arbitrator, or for the enforcement or setting aside of an award.[26] However, it is a matter of controversy whether the exclusion of arbitration allows a court of a Member State to refuse recognition to a judgment from another Member State on the ground that the court of origin took jurisdiction contrary to an arbitration agreement. The United Kingdom considers that it does, but this is not accepted by most of the other Member States.[27] If the other Member States are right, it may not be possible to refuse recognition to a judgment from another Member State just because it was given in contravention of an arbitration agreement.[28]

§ 11   Fraud

There is no rule providing for non-recognition on grounds of fraud. Moreover, Article 36 states that in no circumstances may a foreign judgment be reviewed as to its substance. In view of this, fraud by a party cannot in itself constitute a ground of non-recognition, though there may be situations in which a court would regard it as being contrary to its public policy to recognize a judgment obtained by fraud. In England, it has been held that the public-policy clause in Article 34(1) does cover fraud by a party, but that it applies only if there is no remedy in the country where the judgment was obtained.[29] Since it is probably possible to set aside a judgment on grounds of fraud in all Member States, it is unlikely that an English court would ever refuse to recognize a judgment on this ground.[30]

Fraud by the court of origin is a different issue. Bias (in particular, against foreigners) and corruption are not unknown in the courts of Member States. Corruption in public life, including corruption in the judiciary, was often mentioned in Commission reports on States applying for membership of the Community.[31] It is hard to believe that these habits were miraculously cured

---

26 See Schlosser, 'Report on the Convention of 9 October 1968' (Denmark, Ireland and UK Accessions), OJ 1979 C 59, p. 71 at pp. 92–3.

27 *Ibid.*

28 The position where the award has been given (and it conflicts with the judgment) was discussed in § 7 above.

29 *Interdesco* v. *Nullifire* [1992] 1 Lloyd's Rep 180; *Société d'Informatique Service Réalisation Organisation (SISRO)* v. *Ampersand Software* [1994] ILPr 55; (1993) 90(35) LSG 36; (1993) 137 SJLB 189; *The Times*, 29 July 1993 (Court of Appeal, 15 July 1993).

30 For a discussion of what happens if there is a conflict between the ECHR and the EC Treaties, see Hartley, 'International Law and the Law of the European Union – A Reassessment' [2001] BYIL 1 at pp. 22–35.

31 See, for example, the comprehensive report and the country-by-country reports of the Commission in 2003 on the States then applying for membership of the Community: www.europa.eu.int/comm/enlargement/report_2003/index.htm#comprehensive. In the *Comprehensive Monitoring Report on Poland's Preparation for Membership*, it is stated, at p. 14: 'In general the level of public trust in the efficiency and fairness of the judicial system remains low and the perception of corruption by the public is high.' In the *Comprehensive Monitoring Report on Lithuania's Preparation for Membership*, it is stated, at p. 13: 'As acknowledged by the Lithuanian authorities, corruption remains a source of concern, in particular in the customs, public procurement, traffic police and health sectors as well as in the judiciary.' In the *Comprehensive Monitoring Report on Slovakia's Preparations for Membership*, it is said, at p. 12: 'The level of public trust in the efficiency and fairness of the judicial system remains low.' At p. 13, it is said: 'There is a continuously high public and professional perception of widespread corruption in Slovakia . . . The most affected areas appear to be the health care sector, education, the police and the judiciary.' These comments were first brought to public

once the country concerned joined the Community; nor is there any reason to believe that courts in the older Member States are immune from these failings. These matters are notoriously difficult to prove, but, if it were proved that the foreign court was guilty of bias or corruption, recognition of the judgment would be contrary to Article 6 of the European Convention on Human Rights, which guarantees the right to a fair hearing by an independent and impartial tribunal.[32] This could allow non-recognition, either under the public-policy clause in Article 34(1)[33] or under Article 71 of the Regulation.[34] If neither of these provisions was held to be applicable, some Member State courts might decide that the European Convention on Human Rights overrode EC law.

§ 12   Natural justice

For practical purposes, the most important ground of non-recognition is that contained in Article 34(2), which is intended to ensure that the rules of natural justice are, to a certain extent at least, applied by the court of origin.

Article 34(2) operates only if the judgment was given in default of appearance, though it has been held by the European Court that a default judgment does not cease to be such merely because the defendant tries unsuccessfully to have it set aside.[35]

Article 34(2) states that the judgment will not be enforced if the defendant was not served with the document which instituted the proceedings (or with an equivalent document) in sufficient time and in such a way as to enable him to arrange for his defence, unless the defendant failed to commence proceedings to challenge the judgment when it was possible for him to do so.

This provision replaces Article 27(2) of the Brussels Convention. The latter was, however, in slightly different terms. It provided that the defendant must have been 'duly served' with the document which instituted the proceedings (or with an equivalent document) in 'sufficient time to enable him to arrange for his defence'. The European Court held that this laid down two separate requirements: first, the claim form (writ) must be duly served;[36] and, secondly, it must be served in sufficient time.[37] The problem with the first requirement was that it could involve the recognizing court in deciding questions of procedural law that should really have been settled by the court of origin.

The revised provision abolishes the first requirement. The court of origin must decide whether the claim form was properly served: the recognizing court

attention, at least in Britain, by Andrew Dickinson in his article 'A Charter for Tactical Litigation in Europe?' [2004] LMCLQ 273 at pp. 279–80.

32 Cf. *Pellegrini* v. *Italy*, judgment of 20 July 2001 (ECtHR) (available on www.echr.coe.int).

33 *Krombach* v. *Bamberski*, § 5, above.

34 Article 71 provides that the Regulation will not affect any Conventions to which the Member States are parties and which, in relation to particular matters, govern the recognition or enforcement of judgments. In so far as the ECHR prohibits the recognition of judgments resulting from an unfair trial, it is such a convention.

35 *Klomps* v. *Michel*, Case 166/80, [1981] ECR 1593.

36 On this, see *Pendy Plastic Products* v. *Pluspunkt*, Case 228/81, [1982] ECR 2723.

37 *Klomps* v. *Michel*, Case 166/80, [1981] ECR 1593.

cannot reconsider this question. Under the new provision, therefore, there is now a purely factual test: was the claim form served in sufficient time and in such a way as to enable the defendant to arrange for his defence? The 'sufficient time' requirement is based on the assumption that the defendant will need time to find a lawyer, and that the lawyer will need time to gather evidence and research the law. How much time is needed will depend on the facts: more time will be needed to prepare a defence to a complex claim than to a simple one. The 'such a way' requirement is intended to ensure that the defendant is actually aware of service.

So far, there have been no cases under the revised provision. However, cases on the 'sufficient time' requirement of the Brussels Convention throw light on the issues that arise. According to the European Court, what constitutes sufficient time is a question of fact.[38] The court addressed is not bound by the finding of the court of origin on this point.[39] Article 26 of the Regulation states that, where the defendant is domiciled in a Member State other than that in which the proceedings take place, a court may not grant a default judgment unless it has been shown that the defendant was able to receive the document instituting the proceedings, or an equivalent document, in sufficient time to enable him to arrange for his defence, or that all necessary steps have been taken to this end. It follows that, in default-judgment cases, the court of origin will have made a finding that the claim form was served on the defendant in sufficient time. However, the court addressed is not bound by such a ruling.[40]

Under the Convention, there was considerable debate as to when time began to run. Did it run from the moment when the claim form was duly served at the appropriate address or from the moment when it reached the defendant personally? In favour of the latter alternative it was argued that, until the claim form comes to the knowledge of the defendant, he is unable to take *any* steps to arrange for his defence and therefore, from a practical point of view, it is irrelevant that the claim form might have been served prior to this. On the other hand, however, the claimant cannot usually tell when the claim form came to the notice of the defendant: all he knows is when it was served.

In *Klomps* v. *Michel*,[41] the European Court adopted a compromise solution. It held that it does not have to be proved that the claim form reached the defendant personally: in normal cases, time begins to run from the moment of service. However, in exceptional cases, the court addressed can decide that time does not begin to run until the claim form actually comes to the notice of the defendant. In deciding whether a case is exceptional for this purpose, the court addressed has to consider the means adopted for service, the relationship between the parties and the steps necessary to avoid a default judgment. The European Court also said that, if the dispute concerns commercial relations, service at a place of business will normally be acceptable even if the defendant is away, especially

38 *Ibid.*
39 *Ibid.*
40 *Ibid.*
41 *Ibid.*

if a representative of the defendant could take the steps necessary to avoid a default judgment.

The problem arose again in *Debaecker* v. *Bouwman*,[42] which concerned a lease of the premises in which the lessee had established his residence. The premises were in Antwerp, Belgium. The lessee left the premises without notice and initially without providing the landlord with a forwarding address. It seems that he was in default over his rent.

The lessee left the premises on 21 September. The landlord served the claim form on 24 September. The claim form was served on the local police station for the area in which the premises were situated. It appears that this constituted due service under Belgian law. On 28 September, the landlord received a letter from the lessee giving the latter's new address, which was in another part of Belgium. The landlord, however, made no attempt to inform the lessee that the action was pending. The hearing took place on 1 October and resulted in a default judgment. The default judgment was then served on the lessee in the same way as before, namely, by delivering it to the same police station. Again, no attempt was made to inform the defendant. He therefore remained ignorant of the proceedings.

Subsequently, the defendant moved to the Netherlands and the claimant took steps to enforce the judgment there. The Dutch court had to consider whether the claim form had been served in sufficient time. As the defendant did not hear of the action until some time after the proceedings had taken place, he clearly had insufficient time – if time was regarded as running from the date of his actual knowledge. If, on the other hand, time was regarded as running from the date on which the claim form was served, it could be argued that it *had* been served in sufficient time. The case therefore hinged on the question whether the circumstances were sufficient to bring it into the 'exceptional' category.

The European Court held that the requirement of sufficient time applies even if the defendant is domiciled at the time of the judgment in the same country as that in which the hearing takes place and that service complies with the law of that country. It then considered whether the circumstances were exceptional and ruled that this is a matter for the court addressed to decide. In doing so, it can take into account facts arising after service, for example that the claimant subsequently learned of the defendant's new address. It must, however, also take into account whether the defendant was himself to some extent to blame for the fact that the claim form did not reach him. These two elements must be balanced.

These cases show the kind of problems that arise under this provision. It would be unduly optimistic to think that they will not continue to cause difficulties under the Regulation, but the new wording may perhaps make them a little easier to solve.

---

42 Case 49/84, [1985] ECR 1779.

§ 13   Conclusions

It will be seen from the above discussion that the judgment-recognition provisions of the Brussels I Regulation are far from perfect. Most of the defects stem from the unwillingness of those responsible for its drafting to give fair consideration to the interests of States outside Europe or of persons resident or doing business there. A second problem is the failure to face up to the fact that the legal systems of Member States are defective in some ways.

Appendix: principal grounds on which recognition may be refused

A judgment from another Member State may be refused recognition and enforcement on the grounds specified below. In all cases, the court addressed may decide for itself (subject to a reference to the European Court) whether the grounds in question exist. The grounds are:

1. The judgment is outside the subject-matter scope of the Regulation.[43]
2. The judgment concerns insurance (Articles 8–14), consumer protection (Articles 15–17) or exclusive jurisdiction (Article 22) and the court of origin lacked jurisdiction.[44]
3. The defendant is domiciled or habitually resident in a non-member State with which the State of the court addressed has concluded a convention to which Article 72 applies, and the court of origin took jurisdiction on one of the grounds specified in the second paragraph of Article 3 of the Brussels Convention.[45]
4. The judgment concerns provisional, including protective, measures and the court of origin took jurisdiction under Article 31.[46]
5. Recognition of the judgment would be manifestly contrary to the public policy of the Member State in which recognition is sought.[47]
6. The judgment was given in default of appearance, and the defendant was not served with the document which instituted the proceedings (or with an equivalent document) in sufficient time and in such a way as to enable him to arrange for his defence, unless the defendant failed to commence proceedings to challenge the judgment when it was possible for him to do so.[48]
7. The judgment is irreconcilable with a judgment given in a dispute between the same parties in the Member State in which recognition is sought.[49]

---

43 Article 1.
44 Article 35.
45 *Ibid.*
46 *Mietz* v. *Intership Yachting Sneek*, Case C-99/96, [1999] ECR I-2277.
47 Article 34(1).
48 Article 34(2).
49 Article 34(3).

8.   The judgment is irreconcilable with an earlier judgment given in another Member State or in a third State, involving the same cause of action and between the same parties, provided that the earlier judgment fulfils the conditions necessary for its recognition in the Member State addressed.[50]

9.   The judgment is irreconcilable with an arbitration award that qualifies for recognition under an international convention binding on the State of the court addressed.[51]

Further reading

The relevant parts of the following general works:

Briggs (Adrian), *Civil Jurisdiction and Judgments* (LLP, London, 4th edn 2005)

Cuniberti, 'The Recognition of Foreign Judgments Lacking Reasons in Europe: Access to Justice, Foreign Court Avoidance, and Efficiency' (2008) 57 ICLQ 25

Gaudemet-Tallon (Hélène), *Compétence et exécution des jugements en Europe* (LGDJ, Paris, 3rd edn 2002)

Jenard, 'Report on the Convention of 27 September 1968 on Jurisdiction and the Enforcement of Judgments in Civil and Commercial Matters', OJ 1979 C 59, p. 1

Jenard and Möller, Report on the Lugano Convention (original text), OJ 1990 C 189, p. 57

Kennett, 'Reviewing Service: Double Check or Double Fault?' (1992) *Civil Justice Quarterly* 115

   The Enforcement of Judgments in Europe (Oxford University Press, Oxford, 2000)

Schlosser, 'Report on the Convention of 9 October 1968' (Denmark, Ireland and UK Accessions), OJ 1979 C 59, p. 71

---

50 Article 34(4).
51 Article 71(1).

CHAPTER 15

English law: jurisdiction

The rules discussed in the previous chapter apply only to judgments from EC or Lugano States. Judgments from all other States are subject to the traditional rules of English law. In this chapter, after considering certain introductory matters, we discuss the traditional English rules in so far as they concern the jurisdiction of foreign courts. In the next chapter, we discuss various defences open to the defendant.

In England, the recognition and enforcement of foreign judgments originally depended solely on the common law. Today, there are various legislative provisions; nevertheless, the common law is still of great importance. We shall first consider the common law and then look at the legislation.

§ 1   Theoretical basis for recognition and enforcement

English common law does not apply the comity theory (explained in Chapter 13, § 3, above).[1] Reciprocity has never been required; nor is it necessary for there to be a treaty with the State of origin, though such treaties do exist. This fits in with the general tendency of the common law to give greater emphasis to the rights of the parties than to State interests – though the latter are not ignored.

English common law adopts the obligation theory. This was established in a series of cases in the nineteenth century. For example, in *Williams* v. *Jones*,[2] Parke B said:[3]

> Where a court of competent jurisdiction has adjudicated a certain sum to be due from one person to another, a legal obligation arises to pay that sum, on which an action of debt to enforce the judgment may be maintained. It is in this way that the judgments of foreign and colonial courts are supported and enforced.

This is the basic idea behind the obligation theory.

Though the foreign judgment is regarded as creating an obligation, it is not enforced by a procedure equivalent to the *exequatur* of the civil law. The claimant must bring a new action.[4] However, this action is not on the original obligation,

---

1 Some very early cases – for example, *Geyer* v. *Aguilar* (1798) 7 Term Rep 681 at p. 697 – suggest the contrary, but they have not been followed in later cases.
2 (1845) 13 M & W 628, quoted by Blackburn J in *Godard* v. *Gray* (1870) LR 6 QB 139 at pp. 148–9 and again by the Court of Appeal in *Adams* v. *Cape Industries* [1990] Ch 433 (CA) at p. 513.
3 At p. 633.
4 CPR 6.36 and Practice Direction 6 B, paragraph 3.1(10), provides for the service of the claim form outside the jurisdiction in such cases.

but on the new obligation created by the foreign judgment. All the claimant has to prove is that the foreign judgment exists, that it is in his favour and against the other party and that the foreign court had jurisdiction. Then, unless the other party can establish certain limited defences, the English court will grant a judgment in his favour for the sum awarded by the foreign court. *Procedurally*, therefore, a new action is brought; in *substance*, however, the foreign judgment is recognized and enforced.

Two rules of English law that may be regarded as consequences of the obligation theory are, first, that the foreign judgment must be final and conclusive; and, secondly, that it can be enforced only if it is for a sum of money. The first rule means that the judgment must not be subject to revision in the court that gave it.[5] Provisional awards cannot be enforced. However, it does not matter if the judgment is subject to appeal,[6] though, if the appeal is successful, the enforcement will be set aside. Under the second rule, a judgment will not be enforced (though it may be recognized) if it is not for a fixed and definite sum of money;[7] thus, injunctions and decrees of specific performance will not be enforced.[8] This is still the position in England, though (as we shall see in Chapter 17, § 2, below), the Canadian courts are now willing in principle to enforce such judgments.

§ 2 Legislation

Today, the common law has been modified by legislation. This legislation falls into three categories. The first concerns the recognition and enforcement of judgments between the different parts of the United Kingdom (England and Wales, Scotland, and Northern Ireland).[9] It will not be considered. The second concerns the recognition and enforcement of judgments from Member States of the European Community and from Lugano States. This was considered in the last chapter. The third category concerns judgments from certain other countries. Two statutes are relevant: the Administration of Justice Act 1920 (Part II) and the Foreign Judgments (Reciprocal Enforcement) Act 1933.

Both these Acts are based on the principle of reciprocity, though a formal

---

5 *Nouvion* v. *Freeman* (1889) 15 App Cas 1 (HL). This rule applies under the two statutes discussed below, the Administration of Justice Act 1920 and the Foreign Judgments (Reciprocal Enforcement) Act 1933. For the 1933 Act, see section 1(2)(a) (as amended). There is no express provision to this effect in the 1920 Act, but, since that Act does not apply if an appeal is pending, or if the judgment-debtor is entitled and intends to appeal (section 9(2)(e)), it is hard to believe that it would not apply if the award could be revised by the court which granted it.
6 This is not the case under the Administration of Justice Act 1920 Act (discussed below): see section 9(2)(e).
7 The 'fixed and definite' requirement means that an English court will not enforce a judgment that simply requires the defendant to compensate the claimant for loss suffered, unless it assesses that loss in monetary terms. However, the English court is willing to undertake a simple arithmetical calculation. Thus, a judgment for £1,000 plus interest at 10 per cent per annum from a given day will be enforced.
8 For the 1920 Act, see section 12(1) (definition of 'judgment'); for the 1933 Act, see section 11(1) (definition of 'judgment') and section 1(2)(b) (as amended).
9 See section 18 of the Civil Jurisdiction and Judgments Act 1982 (together with Schedules 6 and 7), which provides for virtually automatic recognition and enforcement of judgments within the United Kingdom.

treaty is not necessary: they apply only to those countries with regard to which the United Kingdom Government considers that reciprocity exists. These are listed in Orders in Council.[10] The 1920 Act applies only to Commonwealth countries, but the 1933 Act can apply to both Commonwealth and non-Commonwealth countries, though only a small number of countries are involved.[11] Many of the most important countries – for example, the United States, Japan, China and Russia – are not covered by any legislation. The common law applies to them.

The Acts of 1920 and 1933 were not intended to change to any significant extent the substantive principles on which foreign judgments are recognized and enforced.[12] They were merely intended to provide a simpler procedure. Where they apply, the judgment-creditor does not have to bring a new action; instead, he simply registers the judgment. The judgment-debtor is informed and has a specified period to apply to set the registration aside. If he fails to do this, or if he makes an application but it is unsuccessful, the foreign judgment may be enforced as if it were an English judgment.

The grounds on which registration may be set aside were based on those on which a judgment would be refused recognition under the common law. The 1920 Act does not specify them in detail and it has been read as incorporating the common law, except where it provides otherwise. The 1933 Act, on the other hand, attempted to codify the common law. It has subsequently appeared that it did not perfectly reflect the common law; consequently, there are minor differences of substance between it (and, to a lesser extent, the 1920 Act) and the common law.

Where the judgment comes from a country to which the 1920 Act applies, the judgment-creditor has a choice: he can either enforce it under the Act or he can bring an action under the common law, though in the latter case he may be penalized as regards costs.[13] On the other hand, where the judgment is granted by a court in a country covered by the 1933 Act, the judgment-creditor *must* proceed under that Act.[14]

The discussion that follows will be based on the common law, but differences of substance between it and the Acts will be mentioned as they arise.

§ 3 Jurisdiction

As stated previously, the most important requirement for the recognition of a foreign judgment is that the foreign court had jurisdiction. This is determined by English law, not by the law of the State of origin. Moreover, the rules applied by English law to decide whether a foreign court has jurisdiction for this purpose are not necessarily the same as those applied to decide whether an English court has

---

10 See section 14 of the 1920 Act and section 1 of the 1933 Act.
11 They include Australia, Canada, India and Israel.
12 For the 1933 Act, see the Report of the Foreign Judgments (Reciprocal Enforcement) Committee, Cmd 4213 (1932), paragraphs 2, 16, 18 and Annex V, paragraph 7.
13 Administration of Justice Act 1920, section 9(5).
14 Foreign Judgments (Reciprocal Enforcement) Act 1933, section 6.

jurisdiction. English courts thus apply a double standard in some cases: they claim wider jurisdiction for themselves than they are willing to accord to foreign courts.

It was said in Chapter 2, § 5, above, that there are three main principles underlying the law of jurisdiction *in personam*. The first is that a court is entitled to hear the action if there is an appropriate connection between the defendant and the forum. The second is that it is entitled to hear the action if there is an appropriate connection between the claim and the forum. The third is that it is entitled to hear the action if the defendant consented to its jurisdiction. It was explained in Chapter 5 how the jurisdiction of English courts under the traditional rules is based on these principles. We shall now consider how they are applied to the jurisdiction of foreign courts.

§ 3.1 'Home-court' jurisdiction

First, we consider jurisdiction based on a connection between the defendant and the forum.

§ 3.1.1 Individuals. Under the first principle, the English courts take jurisdiction over individual (non-corporate) defendants if they are served with a claim form while physically present within the territory of the forum. Until the decision of the Court of Appeal in *Adams* v. *Cape Industries*,[15] it was thought that this principle did not apply to foreign courts: mere temporary presence was regarded as too weak a link. This view revealed a double standard: temporary presence was accepted for English courts – partly because it was tempered by the doctrine of *forum non conveniens* – but not for foreign courts. Instead, it was considered that the appropriate test was residence. The *Adams* case, however, changed all this.

England
Adams* v. *Cape Industries
Court of Appeal
[1990] Ch 433; [1990] 2 WLR 657

Background

The facts are irrelevant, since the case concerned a company; so everything said about individuals was actually *obiter*. However, the case has been generally regarded as changing the law, and the following extract is accepted as an accurate statement of the current position.

Judgment

[After discussing the authorities on the jurisdiction of foreign courts over individuals, the court extracted the following principles:]

First, in determining the jurisdiction of the foreign court in such cases, our court is directing its mind to the competence or otherwise of the foreign court 'to summon the defendant before it and to decide such matters as it has decided:'

---

15 [1990] Ch 433 (CA).

see *Pemberton* v. *Hughes* [1899] 1 Ch 781, 790, *per* Lindley MR. Secondly, in the absence of any form of submission to the foreign court, such competence depends on the physical presence of the defendant in the country concerned at the time of suit. (We leave open the question whether residence without presence will suffice.) From the last sentence of the dictum of Lord Parmoor cited above, and from a dictum of Collins MR in *Dunlop Pneumatic Tyre Co. Ltd* v. *Actiengesellschaft für Motor und Motorfahrzeugbau vorm. Cudell & Co.* [1902] 1 KB 342, 346, it would appear that the date of service of process rather than the date of issue of proceedings is to be treated as 'the time of suit' for these purposes. But nothing turns on this point in the present case and we express no final view on it. Thirdly, we accept the submission of [counsel] . . . that the temporary presence of a defendant in the foreign country will suffice provided at least that it is voluntary (i.e. not induced by compulsion, fraud or duress) . . .

The decision in *Carrick* v. *Hancock*,[1] 12 TLR 59, has been the subject of criticism in *Cheshire & North's Private International Law*, 11th ed. (1987), p. 342, and in *Dicey & Morris*, 11th ed., vol. 1, where it is said, at pp. 439–440:

> 'It may be doubted, however, whether casual presence, as distinct from residence, is a desirable basis of jurisdiction if the parties are strangers and the cause of action arose outside the country concerned. For the court is not likely to be the *forum conveniens*, in the sense of the appropriate court most adequately equipped to deal with the facts or the law. Moreover, the English case referred to above is open to the comment that the jurisdiction of the foreign court might just as well have been based on the defendant's submission as on his presence.'

Our own courts regard the temporary presence of a foreigner in England at the time of service of process as justifying the assumption of jurisdiction over him . . . However, *Cheshire & North*, 11th ed., comment, at p. 342:

> 'any analogy based on the jurisdiction of the English courts is not particularly convincing, since the rules on jurisdiction are operated in conjunction with a discretion to stay the proceedings, and the exercise of the discretion is likely to be an issue when jurisdiction is founded on mere presence.'

We see the force of these points. They highlight the possible desirability of a further extension of reciprocal arrangements for the enforcement (or non-enforcement) of foreign judgments by convention. Nevertheless, while the use of the particular phrase 'temporary allegiance' may be a misleading one in this context, we would, on the basis of the authorities referred to above, regard the source of the territorial jurisdiction of the court of a foreign country to summon a defendant to appear before it as being his obligation for the time being to abide by its laws and accept the jurisdiction of its courts while present in its territory. So long as he remains physically present in that country, he has the benefit of its laws, and must take the rough with the smooth, by accepting his amenability to the process of its courts. In the absence of authority compelling a contrary conclusion, we would conclude that the voluntary presence of an individual in a foreign country, whether permanent or temporary and whether or not

---

1 *Editor's note*: this case was the main authority for the principle that mere presence coupled with service of the claim form was sufficient to confer jurisdiction on a foreign court.

accompanied by residence, is sufficient to give the courts of that country territorial jurisdiction over him under our rules of private international law.

This decision puts English law in the same position as American and Canadian law (both of which are discussed in later chapters). It is interesting that a recent decision of South Africa's highest court establishes that South Africa, a civil-law country with strong common-law influence, adopts the same rule.

South Africa
Richman* v. *Ben-Tovim
Supreme Court of Appeal
[2006] SCA 148; 2007 (2) South African Law Reports [SA] 283

Background

The defendant in this case was an individual (not a company). He had been served in England with a claim form issued by an English court while on a temporary visit there. He was neither resident not domiciled in England. He did not defend the action and a default judgment was obtained. The claimant brought proceedings in South Africa to enforce the English judgment. The trial court held for the defendant on the ground that the English court lacked international jurisdiction. The claimant appealed.

Zulman JA

[After establishing that the English court had jurisdiction under English law, Zulman JA continued:]

[7] The fact that the English court had jurisdiction according to English law is not enough. The matter must also be decided according to the principles recognised by South African domestic law. Van Dijkhorst J put the matter as follows in *Reiss Engineering Co Ltd v Isamcor (Pty) Ltd*:[1]

> The fact that the English Court may have had jurisdiction in terms of its own law does not entitle its judgment to be recognised and enforced in South Africa. It must have had jurisdiction according to the principles recognised by our law with reference to the jurisdiction of foreign courts.
> The South African conflict of law rules relevant to the present action are clear. I quote from Pollak, *The South African Law of Jurisdiction* (1937) at 219:
>
>> A foreign court has jurisdiction to entertain an action for a judgment sounding in money against a defendant who is a natural person in the following cases:
>> 1. If at the time of the commencement of the action the defendant is physically present within the state to which the court belongs;
>> 2. If at the time of the commencement of the action the defendant, although not physically present within such state, is either (a) domiciled, or (b) resident within such state;
>> 3. If the defendant has submitted to the jurisdiction of the court.
>
> There are no other grounds for jurisdiction.

1 1983 (1) SA 1033 (W) at 1037G–H.

[The court then considered other authorities and concluded that the view expressed by Pollak should be followed.]

Result: the appeal was allowed (judgment enforced).[16]

Thus, the 'home-court' jurisdiction of a foreign court is based on the service of a claim form on the defendant while he is present in the territory of the foreign forum. What the Americans call 'tag' jurisdiction, or transient jurisdiction, is now regarded in England as an acceptable basis for foreign-court jurisdiction.[17] So, in this respect, the same rules apply to foreign courts as apply to English courts: there is no double standard here.

The position is different under the statutes. They provide that the defendant must have been resident in the foreign country.[18] It seems that temporary physical presence, even if coupled with service, is not enough. Under the 1920 Act, this is not important, since the claimant can simply enforce the judgment under the common law. This is not possible under the 1933 Act. So, by extending the 1933 Act to a country, the Government is actually making it *less* easy, in at least one respect, to enforce judgments from that country.

It is not clear to what extent doing business in a country, without being resident or present there, is a ground of jurisdiction over an individual (as distinct from a corporation). In *Blohn* v. *Desser*,[19] it was held that an individual resident in England who did business in Austria through a partnership registered there could be subject to the jurisdiction of the Austrian courts for claims arising out of the activities of the partnership. This was based on a theory of implied consent, a theory that has been doubted in a subsequent case[20] and is probably incorrect.[21] However, the result seems reasonable. Under the 1920 Act, carrying on business within the foreign country is a ground of jurisdiction in addition to residence.[22] Under the 1933 Act, a foreign court has jurisdiction if the defendant had an office or place of business in the foreign country, but only if the claim concerned a transaction effected through or at that office or place.[23] The same is true under Article 5(5) of the Brussels I Regulation. There is nothing in any of these provisions that limits them to corporations. It would be strange if the common law was more restrictive.

§ 3.1.2 Corporations. As far as corporations are concerned, the rules of 'home-court' jurisdiction seem to be largely, if not entirely, the same as those applicable

---

16 For a comment on this case, see Oppong, 'Mere Presence and International Competence in Private International Law' (2007) 3 *Journal of Private International Law* 321.
17 For further arguments in favour of this form of jurisdiction, see *Burnham* v. *Superior Court of California*, set out in Chapter 7, § 2.1, above.
18 For the 1920 Act, see section 9(2)(b), which requires that the defendant was 'ordinarily resident' in the country of origin; for the 1933 Act, see section 4(2)(a)(iv), which requires that the defendant was resident there when the proceedings were instituted.
19 [1962] 2 QB 116; [1961] 3 WLR 719; [1961] 3 All ER 1.
20 *Vogel* v. *Kohnstamm* [1973] 1 QB 133. The judgment is set out below, but not the part rejecting the theory of implied consent.
21 See, further, Dicey, Morris and Collins, pp. 498–9, and the authorities cited there.
22 Section 9(2)(b).
23 Section 4(2)(a)(v).

to English courts.[24] These were discussed in Chapter 5, § 3, above. The leading case today is *Adams* v. *Cape Industries*,[25] the relevant parts of which are set out in Chapter 5, § 3.3, above (though a case on the recognition of a foreign judgment, it is also regarded as an authority on the jurisdiction of English courts). Here, we illustrate the point with an earlier case.

England
Vogel v. Kohnstamm Ltd
High Court
[1973] 1 QB 133; [1971] 3 WLR 537; [1971] 2 All ER 1428

Background

Kohnstamm Ltd was an English company. It appointed a certain Mr Kornbluth as its representative in Israel. His job was to obtain orders for Kohnstamm Ltd, but he had no authority to conclude contracts on its behalf. All orders had to be referred back to London for acceptance and dispatch. Two orders obtained by Kornbluth were with Vogel. Kohnstamm Ltd accepted them and the goods were shipped to Israel. Vogel claimed that the goods were defective and sued Kohnstamm Ltd in Israel. The Israeli claim form was served on Kornbluth. Kohnstamm Ltd did not defend the action and a default judgment was entered against it. Vogel then sought to enforce this in England. Kohnstamm Ltd claimed that the Israeli courts had no jurisdiction.

Ashworth J

[After considering various other matters, said:]

I find it more convenient to consider the question whether the defendants [Kohnstamm Ltd] can be said to have been at the material time resident[1] in the State of Israel. As has been said in many cases, residence is a question of fact and when one is dealing with human beings one can normally approach the matter on the footing that residence involves physical residence by the person in question. I keep open the possibility that even in regard to such a person he may be constructively resident in another country although his physical presence is elsewhere. But in the case of a corporation there is broadly speaking no question of physical residence. A corporation or company, if resident in another country, is resident there by way of agents.

[Ashworth J then considered the authorities and continued:]

Dealing still only with residence I now have to examine in what sense can it be said that the defendants were resident in Israel. They had no office of their own there. All the material correspondence was conducted with them in England and

1 *Editor's note*: since the *Adams* case, it would be more correct to ask whether the defendant was *present*, rather than *resident*, in the foreign country. In the case of a company, however, the test remains largely the same.

24 See *Littauer Glove Company* v. *Millington Ltd* (1928) 44 TLR 746; [1973] 1 QB 133; [1971] 3 WLR 537; [1971] 2 All ER 1428.
25 [1990] Ch 433 (CA).

their connection with the State of Israel was limited, in my view, to their dealings through Mr. Kornbluth.

In examining how far the presence of a representative or agent will, so to speak, impinge on the absent company so as to render that absent company subject to the relevant jurisdiction, I find help to be obtained from cases in which the converse situation has been considered: namely, where the English courts have been invited to allow process to issue to foreign companies on the footing that such foreign companies are 'here.'

Much the most useful authority which has been cited to me is *Okura and Co. Lid*. v. *Forsbacka Jernverks Akeiebolag* [1914] 1 KB 715. It is worth reading the headnote:

> 'The defendants were a foreign corporation carrying on business in Sweden as manufacturers. They employed as their sole agents in the United Kingdom a firm in London who also acted as agents for other firms and carried on business as merchants on their account. The agents had no general authority to enter into contracts on behalf of the defendants, but they obtained orders and submitted them to the defendants for their approval. On being notified by the defendants that they accepted the orders the agents signed contracts with the purchasers as agents for the defendants. The goods were shipped direct from the defendants in Sweden to the purchasers. The agents in some cases received payment in London from the purchasers and remitted the amount to the defendants less their agreed commission: – *Held*, that the defendants were not carrying on their business at the agents' office in London so as to be resident at a place within the jurisdiction, and that service of a writ on the agents at their office was, therefore, not a good service on the defendants.'

As [counsel for Kohnstamm Ltd] said, having read to me the headnote, if that was the view of the court in that case how much stronger in his favour is the present, because on the face of it there are details in the facts of that case which might have led the court to think that the corporation in question was indeed 'here', whereas such features are absent in the present case. There is force in that, but the matter for which I am citing the authority is the passage from Buckley LJ's judgment where he said, at pp. 718–719:

> 'In one sense, of course, the corporation cannot be "here." The question really is whether this corporation can be said to be "here" by a person who represents it in a sense relevant to the question which we have to decide. The point to be considered is, do the facts show that this corporation is carrying on its business in this country? In determining that question, three matters have to be considered. First, the acts relied on as showing that the corporation is carrying on business in this country must have continued for a sufficiently substantial period of time. That is the case here. Next, it is essential that these acts should have been done at some fixed place of business. If the acts relied on in this case amount to a carrying on of a business, there is no doubt that those acts were done at a fixed place of business. The third essential, and one which it is always more difficult to satisfy, is that the corporation must be "here" by a person who carries on business for the corporation in this country. It is not enough to show that the corporation has an agent here; he must be an agent who does the corporation's business for the corporation in this country.'

> Then he goes on to refer to authorities, all of them relevant and all of them in a sense interesting as showing the line of distinction which the courts have drawn in the past between the situations which were, on the face of it, somewhat similar.
>
> At the end of the day there is a test which the courts have used as part of the material on which to reach a conclusion, namely, is the person in question doing his business or doing the absent corporation's business? Conversely, are they doing business through him or by him?
>
> I confess I find these aphorisms, if that is what they are, apt to lead one astray; one can find the choice phrase and then fit the facts to it and so on. But they are useful and I have asked myself anxiously in this case whether in any real sense of the word the defendants can be said to have been there in Israel; and all that emerges from this case is that there was a man called Kornbluth who sought customers for them, transmitted correspondence to them and received it from them, had no authority whatever to bind the defendants in any shape or form. I have come to the conclusion really without any hesitation that the defendants were not resident in Israel at any material time.

Note

It was also argued that, by appointing Kornbluth as their representative, Kohnstamm Ltd had impliedly consented to the jurisdiction of the Israeli courts, but this was rejected by the court. The result was that the Israeli judgment was not recognized.

The effect of these cases is that a foreign court will be regarded as having jurisdiction over a company if the company has established its own place of business there, or if it did business there through an agent in circumstances that would give jurisdiction to an English court if the facts were reversed.[26]

Under the 1920 Act, jurisdiction exists over a company if it carries on business in the foreign country.[27] This imports the common-law test.[28] Under the 1933 Act, the company must have had its *principal* place of business in the foreign country; alternatively, as in the case of an individual defendant, there will be jurisdiction if it had an office or place of business in the foreign country and the claim concerned a transaction effected through or at that office or place.[29]

Although the law is not entirely clear in all respects, it seems that, as regards 'home-court' jurisdiction, the rules applied to foreign courts are largely, if not entirely, the same as those applied to English courts.

§ 3.2 'Cause-of-action' jurisdiction

This was discussed, in relation to English courts, in Chapter 5, § 4, above. It will be remembered that jurisdiction based on a connection between the cause of

---

26 There does not seem to be any authority as to whether the country of incorporation has jurisdiction over a company. In principle, it should. It is expressly mentioned in the US Uniform Act (discussed in Chapter 18, § 2, below): see § 5(a)(4) of the Act.
27 Section 9(2)(b).
28 *Sfeir & Co.* v. *National Insurance Company of New Zealand* [1964] 1 Lloyd's Rep 330.
29 Section 4(2)(a)(v).

action and the territory of the forum was not recognized by the common law. It was introduced by legislation and is now contained in the Civil Procedure Rules (CPR). It is perhaps for this reason that the common law does not recognize any jurisdiction based on this principle with regard to foreign courts. Thus, the fact that the contract was breached in the foreign country or that the tort was committed there does not suffice to confer jurisdiction on the foreign court. Here, there is a double standard of major proportions. This is equally true under the two statutes.

§ 3.3   Submission

A foreign court is regarded as having jurisdiction over a person if he submitted to it. For this purpose, submission may take three forms. First, where the parties have concluded a choice-of-court agreement in favour of the foreign court, they are deemed to have submitted to its jurisdiction. Secondly, if a claimant brings proceedings in a foreign court, he is deemed to have submitted to the jurisdiction of that court with regard to any counterclaim on a related matter.[30] Thirdly, if the defendant defends the case on the merits (substance), he is deemed to have submitted to the jurisdiction of the court with regard to any judgment in that case. Unlike the position in some legal systems, this is true even if he (unsuccessfully) challenged the jurisdiction of the court.

This last rule is of particular importance. It means that, if a person is sued in a foreign country, he can challenge the jurisdiction of the court. If the challenge is successful, that is the end of the matter. If it fails, however, he is faced with a difficult choice. He can either take no further part in the proceedings, in which case a default judgment will be given against him. This will be enforceable in the foreign country, and possibly in third countries, but it will not be enforceable in England unless the court had jurisdiction on one of the recognized grounds. On the other hand, he can fight the case on the merits. If he wins, well and good; but, if he loses, the judgment will be enforceable in England, even if the foreign court would not otherwise have had jurisdiction in English eyes. The idea behind this rule is that a defendant ought not to gain the benefits of the foreign proceedings if he wins, but be able to repudiate them if he loses. The consequence of this rule is that the other rules on jurisdiction are of importance only in the case of default judgments.

The rules on submission are the same under the statutes as under the common law.[31]

Determining exactly what constitutes submission has caused problems. In a Canadian case,[32] decided in the days when the common-law provinces of Canada applied the English principles, a British Columbia company was sued in Germany. The German court had no jurisdiction under the common-law rules. However, the Canadian company wrote an informal letter to the German court explaining why it thought that it was not liable. The German court considered

---

30 This also applies to an order for costs.
31 For the 1920 Act, see section 9(2)(b); for the 1933 Act, see section 4(2)(a)(i), (ii) and (iii).
32 *Re Brand and Overseas Food Importers and Distributors* (1981) 27 BCLR 31 (British Columbia Court of Appeal).

that this did not constitute a formal entering of an appearance; so it granted a default judgment to the claimant. When the claimant took enforcement proceedings in Canada, however, the Canadian court held that the judgment was enforceable because the defendant had submitted to the jurisdiction of the German court. This seems wrong: if the German court was not willing to consider the defendant's arguments, there was no submission.

In an English case, *Henry* v. *Geoprosco*,[33] proceedings had been brought before a court in Alberta. The defendant applied for a stay on the ground of *forum non conveniens*. When this was refused, it withdrew from the case. A default judgment was given against it. Enforcement proceedings were brought in England. It argued that the Alberta court had no jurisdiction. The English court held, however, that the defendant had submitted: by asking for a stay, it was impliedly accepting that the Alberta court had jurisdiction. This seems unreasonable, and it is now laid down by section 33 of the Civil Jurisdiction and Judgments Act 1982 (Panel 15.1) that a defendant is not deemed to submit just because he argues that the court ought not to hear the case on the ground of *forum non conveniens*, or because of an arbitration agreement or choice-of-court agreement in favour of another court.

Panel 15.1 Submission: Civil Jurisdiction and Judgments Act 1982 (as amended), section 33

Section 33 Certain steps not to amount to submission to jurisdiction of overseas court

(1) For the purposes of determining whether a judgment given by a court of an overseas country should be recognised or enforced in England and Wales or Northern Ireland, the person against whom the judgment was given shall not be regarded as having submitted to the jurisdiction of the court by reason only of the fact that he appeared (conditionally or otherwise) in the proceedings for all or any one or more of the following purposes, namely—

(a) to contest the jurisdiction of the court;

(b) to ask the court to dismiss or stay the proceedings on the ground that the dispute in question should be submitted to arbitration or to the determination of the courts of another country;

(c) to protect, or obtain the release of, property seized or threatened with seizure in the proceedings.

(2) Nothing in this section shall affect the recognition or enforcement in England and Wales or Northern Ireland of a judgment which is required to be recognised or enforced there under the 1968 Convention or the Lugano Convention [or the Regulation].

---

§ 3.4 Exceptions

All the above rules of jurisdiction are subject to certain exceptions:

- Under section 32 of the Civil Jurisdiction and Judgments Act 1982 (Panel 15.2), the judgment will not be recognized if the foreign court took jurisdiction contrary to a choice-of-court agreement or arbitration agreement (unless the defendant submitted).[34]

- Under section 31 of the Civil Jurisdiction and Judgments Act 1982 (Panel 15.3), it will not be recognized if the assumption of jurisdiction by the foreign court was contrary to the rules of State (sovereign) immunity as recognized in the United Kingdom.[35]

---

33 [1976] QB 726 (CA).
34 This exception does not apply where the defendant submitted.
35 Civil Jurisdiction and Judgments Act 1982, section 31; see also section 4(3)(c) of the 1933 Act.

Panel 15.2 Choice-of-court and arbitration agreements
Civil Jurisdiction and Judgments Act 1982 (as amended), section 32

Section 32 Overseas judgments given in proceedings brought in breach of agreement for settlement of disputes

(1)   Subject to the following provisions of this section, a judgment given by a court of an overseas country in any proceedings shall not be recognised or enforced in the United Kingdom if—

(a) the bringing of those proceedings in that court was contrary to an agreement under which the dispute in question was to be settled otherwise than by proceedings in the courts of that country; and

(b) those proceedings were not brought in that court by, or with the agreement of, the person against whom the judgment was given; and

(c) that person did not counter claim in the proceedings or otherwise submit to the jurisdiction of that court.

(2)   Subsection (1) does not apply where the agreement referred to in paragraph (a) of the subsection was illegal, void or unenforceable or was incapable of being performed for reasons not attributable to the fault of the party bringing the proceedings in which the judgment was given.

(3)   In determining whether a judgment given by a court of an overseas country should be recognised or enforced in the United Kingdom, a court in the United Kingdom shall not be bound by any decision of the overseas court relating to any of the matters mentioned in subsection (1) or (2).

(4)   Nothing in subsection (1) shall affect the recognition or enforcement in the United Kingdom of—

(a) a judgment which is required to be recognised or enforced there under the 1968 Convention or the Lugano Convention or the Regulation . . .

Panel 15.3 State (sovereign) immunity
Civil Jurisdiction and Judgments Act 1982 (as amended), section 31

Section 31 Overseas judgments given against states, etc.

(1)   A judgment given by a court of an overseas country against a state other than the United Kingdom or the state to which that court belongs shall be recognised and enforced in the United Kingdom if, and only if—

(a) it would be so recognised and enforced if it had not been given against a state; and

(b) that court would have had jurisdiction in the matter if it had applied rules corresponding to those applicable to such matters in the United Kingdom in accordance with sections 2 to 11 of the State Immunity Act 1978.

(2)   References in subsection (1) to a judgment given against a state include references to judgments of any of the following descriptions given in relation to a state—

(a) judgments against the government, or a department of the government, of the state but not (except as mentioned in paragraph (c)) judgments against an entity which is distinct from the executive organs of government;

(b) judgments against the sovereign or head of state in his public capacity;

(c) judgments against any such separate entity as is mentioned in paragraph (a) given in proceedings relating to anything done by it in the exercise of the sovereign authority of the state . . . [remainder omitted]

● Under a common-law rule, it will not be recognized if it concerned real rights in immovable property situated in another country.[36]

§ 3.5   Conclusions

It will be seen from the above discussion that there is still a gap between the jurisdiction English courts claim for themselves and the jurisdiction they are willing

---

36 *Duke* v. *Andler* [1932] SCR 734; [1932] 4 DLR 529 (Supreme Court of Canada); *Re Trepca Mines* [1960] 1 WLR 1273 at p. 1277. For the 1933 Act, see section 4(3)(a). There is a similar exception with regard to intellectual property: see Chapter 12, § 1.2, above.

to accord to the courts of foreign countries. As we shall see in later chapters, in Canada and the United States this gap is largely, if not completely, closed.

Further reading

Briggs, 'Which Foreign Judgments Should We Recognise Today?' (1987) 36 ICLQ 240
  'Crossing the River by Feeling the Stones: Rethinking the Law on Foreign Judgments'
    (2004) 8 *Singapore Year Book of International Law* 1
Oppong, 'Mere Presence and International Competence in Private International Law'
    (2007) 3 *Journal of Private International Law* 321
Pitel, 'A Modern Approach to Enforcing Foreign Judgments' [2004] LMCLQ 288

CHAPTER 16

English law: defences

Even if the foreign court had jurisdiction in English eyes, and even if the foreign judgment is final and conclusive and for a sum of money, it will still not be recognized or enforced if the judgment-debtor can establish one of a number of defences open to him. The most important are:

- the judgment was obtained by fraud;[1]
- the foreign proceedings were contrary to natural justice (due process or fair procedure);[2]
- recognition of the judgment would be contrary to public policy;[3]
- recognition of the judgment would be contrary to human rights as laid down in the European Convention on Human Rights (given direct effect in the United Kingdom by the Human Rights Act 1998);
- the judgment was for a tax or penalty, or was based on some other public law;[4] or
- the judgment conflicts with another judgment.

§ 1 Fraud

Under English law, a foreign judgment will not be recognized if it was obtained by fraud. The onus of raising and proving fraud is on the judgment-debtor.[5] Fraud may be committed either by the judgment-creditor or by the court. Accepting a bribe would be an example of the latter, though that would also constitute an infringement of natural justice. It is of course extremely difficult to prove.

Fraud by a party would include lying to the court. If the judgment-debtor can prove this, the judgment will not be recognized. What is unusual about the English rule is that it is not necessary for the judgment-debtor to produce any new evidence. He can simply put forward the same evidence that was produced to, and rejected by, the foreign court. This rule, which is of long standing,[6] was reaffirmed by the House of Lords in 1992 in our next case.

---

1 For the 1920 Act, see section 9(2)(d); for the 1933 Act, see section 4(1)(a)(iv).
2 Natural justice is not expressly mentioned in either of the two Acts, but it would almost certainly come under the rubric of 'public policy'.
3 For the 1920 Act, see section 9(2)(f); for the 1933 Act, see section 4(1)(a)(v).
4 This is not expressly mentioned in either of the Acts, but it would almost certainly come under the rubric of 'public policy'.
5 An unjustified allegation of fraud may be struck out by the court as an abuse of process: *Owens Bank Ltd v. Etoile Commerciale SA* [1995] 1 WLR 44 (PC).
6 See *Abouloff v. Oppenheimer & Co.* (1882) 10 QBD 295 (CA).

England
Owens Bank v. *Bracco*
House of Lords
[1992] AC 443; [1992] 2 WLR 621; [1992] 2 All ER 193

Background

In this case, a bank incorporated in the Caribbean island State of St Vincent and the Grenadines claimed that it was owed money by a company belonging to an Italian, Mr Bracco, under a loan made in 1979 at a hotel in Geneva, Switzerland. The bank claimed that the money (nine million Swiss francs) had been handed over in cash to Mr Bracco by one of the bank's employees, Mr Nano, also an Italian. A document, signed by Bracco, was produced to prove this. The document contained a choice-of-court agreement conferring jurisdiction on the courts of St Vincent.

In proceedings brought by the bank in St Vincent, Bracco argued that the claim was fraudulent. He said that the bank had taken another document signed by him, cut off the text and written in the 'contract' above his signature. This defence was rejected by the St Vincent court, which gave judgment for the bank. When proceedings were brought (under the Administration of Justice Act 1920) to enforce the judgment in England, Bracco raised the same defence, a defence expressly permitted by section 9(2)(d) of the 1920 Act.[7] However, he was unable to produce any evidence that was not put before, and rejected by, the court in St Vincent.

Lord Bridge of Harwich

[After discussing various preliminary matters, Lord Bridge continued:]

It is not in dispute that if the loan documents were indeed forgeries and the account given by Nano in his evidence in the court in St. Vincent of the transaction on 31 January 1979 at the Hôtel du Rhône in Geneva was a fabrication, the St. Vincent judgment was obtained by fraud. But it is submitted for the bank that the language of section 9(2)(d) [of the Administration of Justice Act 1922] must be construed as qualified by the common law rule that the unsuccessful party who has been sued to judgment is not permitted to challenge that judgment on the ground that it was obtained by fraud unless he is able to prove that fraud by fresh evidence which was not available to him and could not have been discovered with reasonable diligence before the judgment was delivered. Here, it is said, there is no such fresh evidence. This is the rule to be applied in an action brought to set aside an English judgment on the ground that it was obtained by fraud. The rule rests on the principle that there must be finality in litigation which would be defeated if it were open to the unsuccessful party in one action to bring a second action to relitigate the issue determined against him simply on the ground that the opposing party had obtained judgment in the first action by perjured evidence. Your Lordships were taken, in the course of argument, through the many authorities

---

7 Section 9(2)(d) of the 1920 Act and section 4(1)(a)(iv) of the 1933 Act both say that a judgment will not be recognized if it was 'obtained by fraud'.

in which this salutary English rule has been developed and applied and which demonstrate the stringency of the criterion which the fresh evidence must satisfy if it is to be admissible to impeach a judgment on the ground of fraud. I do not find it necessary to examine these authorities. The rule they establish is unquestionable and the principle on which they rest is clear. The question at issue in this appeal is whether a defendant who is seeking to resist the enforcement against him of a foreign judgment, either by an action on the foreign judgment at common law or under the statutory machinery for the enforcement of foreign judgments, is placed in the same position as if he were a plaintiff in an action seeking to set aside the judgment of an English court on the ground that it was obtained by fraud and can therefore only rely upon evidence which satisfies the English rule.

A foreign judgment given by a court of competent jurisdiction over the defendant is treated by the common law as imposing a legal obligation on the judgment-debtor which will be enforced in an action on the judgment by an English court in which the defendant will not be permitted to reopen issues of either fact or law which have been decided against him by the foreign court. But this is subject to the special defence that the foreign judgment was obtained by fraud. The starting point in considering the scope of that defence is the decision of the Court of Appeal in *Abouloff* v. *Oppenheimer & Co.* (1882) 10 QBD 295. The plaintiff had obtained judgment against the defendant in a Russian court, the District Court of Tiflis, for the return of certain goods or payment of their value, which was affirmed on appeal by the High Court of Tiflis. She sought to enforce the judgment by action in England. To this action the defendants pleaded that the judgment had been obtained by the fraud of the plaintiff and her husband by falsely representing to the courts in Russia that the goods in question were not in their possession when in fact they were. On demurrer to this plea the Court of Appeal, affirming the Queen's Bench Division, held that the defence pleaded was good. The judgments are particularly instructive in the context of the present appeal in so far as they address and reject the very argument which your Lordships are now invited by the bank to affirm.

[Lord Bridge then discussed *Abouloff* v. *Oppenheimer & Co.* and *Vadala* v. *Lawes* (1890) 25 QBD 310. He continued:]

These decisions have been criticised by academic writers and have not been followed by the Canadian courts: see Dicey & Morris, *The Conflict of Laws*, 11th ed. (1987), vol. 1, p. 469, n. 66. But they have been followed and applied by the Court of Appeal . . . and must stand as establishing the relevant English law unless and until overruled by your Lordships' House.

[Counsel for the bank] submits that the time has come when they should be overruled either as having been wrongly decided in the first place or, alternatively, even if the original decisions could have been justified 100 years ago, on the ground that they rest on a principle which is unacceptable today and out of accord with the approach of the courts to other issues arising in the field of private international law.

I appreciate the force of this submission and, if the issue were governed only by the common law, I would think it necessary to examine in detail both the relevant authorities prior to *Abouloff* v. *Oppenheimer & Co.*, 10 QBD 295 and the elaborate arguments skilfully deployed by [counsel for the bank] in support of his general thesis. But that is not the position. As I have pointed out, enforcement in the United Kingdom of the judgments of courts in the Commonwealth is governed by section 9 of the Act of 1920 which is here directly in issue. The enforcement in the United Kingdom of the judgments of courts in countries with which this country has concluded reciprocal enforcement arrangements is governed by the Foreign Judgments (Reciprocal Enforcement) Act 1933. That is not here directly in issue, but it provides by section 4(1)(a)(iv) that registration of a judgment, which will have been effected *ex parte* under section 2, is to be set aside if the registering court is satisfied 'that the judgment was obtained by fraud' and thus appears to raise an issue of construction which it would, I think, be difficult to differentiate from that raised here by section 9(2)(d) of the Act of 1920. Subject to possible penalties in costs, it is still open to a foreign judgment-creditor to resort to a common law action to enforce his foreign judgment, but such resort is now only necessary in the case of judgments delivered in countries to which, in the absence of reciprocal enforcement arrangements, the Act of 1933 has not been extended. In these circumstances it seems to me clear that before considering the possibility of overruling *Abouloff* v. *Oppenheimer & Co.* and *Vadala* v. *Lawes*, 25 QBD 310 it is necessary first to determine the scope of the fraud defence available to a judgment-debtor resisting statutory enforcement in reliance on section 9(2)(d) of the Act of 1920.

The Act of 1920 was preceded by the report in 1919 of a committee chaired by Lord Sumner, Report of the Committee Appointed by the Lord Chancellor to Consider the Conduct of Legal Proceedings between Parties in this Country and Parties Abroad and the Enforcement of Judgments and Awards (1919) (Cmd. 251). One proposal with respect to reciprocal enforcement within the British Empire which was considered by the Sumner Committee was the adoption of a draft Bill, which had been circulated in 1916 to overseas governments within the Empire, and which followed the lines of the Judgments Extension Act 1868 (31 & 32 Vict. c. 54). The Act of 1868 made the judgments of superior courts in England, Scotland and Ireland reciprocally registrable on satisfying purely formal requirements, whereupon they became enforceable as if they were judgments of the courts in which they were registered. The Sumner Report points out that the adoption of this principle of strict reciprocity would give to all judgments of courts within the Empire an equal status and currency in all parts of the Empire and that some overseas governments had commented adversely on this principle. The committee accepted the criticism and recommended a much more cautious approach, the reasons for which the report explains in detail. This caution leads to the specific recommendations in paragraph 35 (a) and (b) which were in due course directly implemented by section 9(1) and (2)(a) to (e) of the Act of 1920.

Even without reference to the Sumner Report section 9(2)(d) would have to be construed with reference to the common law as understood in 1920. But the context in which the recommendations which came to be embodied in section 9(2) were made leaves no room for doubt. If the Sumner Committee had embraced the strict reciprocity principle of the Act of 1868 and recommended giving to Commonwealth judgments the full status and currency of United Kingdom judgments, this would still have left such judgments open to challenge on the ground that they had been obtained by fraud in so far as the fraud could be established within the strict limits of the English rule. Having rejected that principle, the committee's recommendation that it should be one of the express bars to the enforcement of a Commonwealth judgment that it had been obtained by fraud can only have been intended to apply the much wider rule which the court had applied to foreign judgments in *Abouloff* v. *Oppenheimer & Co.*, 10 QBD 295 and *Vadala* v. *Lawes*, 25 QBD 310 and section 9(2)(d) must be construed accordingly.

Confronted with this difficulty [counsel for the bank] submitted that section 9(2)(d) should nevertheless be held to do no more than embody a common law principle which was still capable of development and adaptation. The fact that Parliament had given legislative expression to the principle should not be allowed to arrest that process or to freeze the principle immutably in the form which the common law gave it in 1920. More specifically he submitted that the difference in the basis on which the court will allow a judgment to be challenged on the ground that it was obtained by fraud as between a plaintiff seeking to set aside an English judgment on the one hand and a defendant resisting enforcement of a foreign judgment on the other hand is a matter of procedure, not of substantive law, and that accordingly nothing in section 9(2)(d) need inhibit the House from adapting and modernising the procedure applicable to the enforcement of judgments under section 9 by confining the judgment-debtor's attack on the foreign judgment within the strict limits of the English rule.

I cannot accept this submission. The difference in question is not, in my opinion, one of procedure but of substantive law and is of fundamental importance. An English judgment, subject to any available appellate procedures, is final and conclusive between the parties as to the issues which it decides. It is in order to preserve this finality that any attempt to reopen litigation, once concluded, even on the ground that judgment was obtained by fraud, has to be confined within such very restrictive limits. In the decisions in *Abouloff* v. *Oppenheimer & Co.* and *Vadala* v. *Lawes* the common law courts declined to accord the same finality to foreign judgments, but preferred to give primacy to the principle that fraud unravels everything. In the Judgments Extension Act 1868 Parliament provided for full reciprocal enforceability as between the judgments of the superior courts in the different jurisdictions within the United Kingdom, with the effect that a judgment given in one jurisdiction and registered in another would enjoy the same finality as a judgment given in that jurisdiction, with no obstacle placed in the way of registration. By contrast, the judgment-creditor seeking registration under the Act of 1920 must first surmount the obstacles which section 9(2) places in his way and section 9(2)(d), construed, as I think it must be, as an adoption of the common law approach to foreign judgments, specifically denies finality to the judgment if it can be shown to have been obtained by fraud.

I recognise that, as a matter of policy, there may be a very strong case to be made in the 1990s in favour of according to overseas judgments the same finality as the courts accord to English judgments. But enforcement of overseas judgments is now primarily governed by the statutory codes of 1920 and 1933. Since these cannot be altered except by further legislation, it seems to me out of the question to alter the common law rule by overruling *Abouloff* v. *Oppenheimer & Co.* and *Vadala* v. *Lawes*. To do so would produce the absurd result that an overseas judgment-creditor, denied statutory enforcement on the ground that he had obtained his judgment by fraud, could succeed in a common law action to enforce his judgment because the evidence on which the judgment-debtor relied did not satisfy the English rule. Accordingly the whole field is effectively governed by statute[1] and, if the law is now in need of reform, it is for the legislature, not the judiciary, to effect it.

I would dismiss the bank's appeal with costs.

1 *Editor's note*: if by this Lord Bridge meant that the recognition of judgments from all countries is now governed by statute, he was mistaken. Judgments from many countries – for example, Japan, the United States and Russia – may be recognized and enforced only under the common law. However, there is no doubt that it would be undesirable to have a different rule under the common law from that under the statutes.

The other members of the court agreed. **Result**: the appeal was dismissed.

Comment

As acknowledged by Lord Bridge, in some countries a defence of fraud may be raised only if new evidence is produced that was not available to the defendant at the time of the foreign trial.[8] This is the rule for setting aside an English judgment, and it is said that one should not discriminate between local judgments and foreign judgments. However, there is *reason* to discriminate: the standard of justice in the United Kingdom is generally high; in some foreign countries it is low. The problem is particularly acute where, as in the *Owens Bank* case, the foreign court's jurisdiction rests on a choice-of-court agreement which is itself alleged to be fraudulent. Indeed, the fraudulent party might have chosen a particular court precisely *because* he thought it would be unsympathetic to allegations of fraud.[9] In the *Owens Bank* case, Bracco could not dispute the jurisdiction of the St Vincent court (on the ground that the choice-of-court clause was fraudulent) because he submitted to it by defending the case on the merits. So a defence of fraud going to the merits was his only chance. It was not his fault that no new evidence was available. Moreover, there were grounds for doubting the correctness of the St Vincent judgment: an Italian court subsequently convicted Nano of fraud for his part in the affair and sentenced him to six years' imprisonment.[10]

Fraud was not Bracco's only defence in the *Owens Bank* case. The bank had previously instituted proceedings in Italy to enforce the St Vincent judgment and Bracco had raised the fraud issue in those proceedings as well. Those proceedings

8 For Canada, see now *Beals* v. *Saldanha* [2003] 3 SCR 416 at paragraphs 43 *et seq.* (Supreme Court of Canada). Under the Brussels I Regulation, there is no provision that fraud may be raised to bar recognition even if there *is* new evidence, this despite the fact that judicial corruption is not unknown in some Member States: see Chapter 14, § 11, above.

9 There was no evidence that this was so in the *Owens Bank* case.

10 At the time of the House of Lords' judgment, an appeal was pending from this judgment.

were pending when the English proceedings were commenced. Bracco's second defence was that the English proceedings had to be dismissed or stayed under the *lis pendens* rule in the Brussels Convention[11] because the Italian courts were seised first. The House of Lords referred this matter to the European Court.

European Community
Owens Bank Ltd* v. *Fulvio Bracco and Bracco Industria Chimica SpA
Court of Justice of the European Communities
Case C-129/92, [1994] ECR I-117; [1994] 2 WLR 759

Judgment

15. Fulvio Bracco and Bracco SpA maintain that [proceedings under the 1920 Act for the registration of a foreign judgment] involve civil and commercial matters as defined in Article 1 of the Convention and that consequently they fall within the scope of the Convention.

16. That view cannot be accepted.

17. First, it follows from the wording of Articles 26 and 31 of the Convention, which must be read in conjunction with its Article 25, that the procedures envisaged by Title III of the Convention, concerning recognition and enforcement, apply only in the case of decisions given by the courts of a Contracting State.

18. Articles 26 and 31 refer only to 'a judgment given in a Contracting State' whilst Article 25 provides that, for the purposes of the Convention, 'judgment' means any judgment given by a court or tribunal of a Contracting State, whatever the judgment may be called.

19. Next, as regards the rules on jurisdiction contained in Title II of the Convention, the Convention is, according to its preamble, intended to implement provisions in Article 220 of the EEC Treaty by which the Member States of the Community undertook to simplify formalities governing the reciprocal recognition and enforcement of judgments of courts or tribunals.

20. Moreover, according to its preamble, one of the objectives of the Convention is to strengthen in the Community the legal protection of persons therein established.

21. The experts' report drawn up at the time when the Convention was drafted (Official Journal 1979 C 59, p. 1, in particular at p. 15), states in this regard that

> 'the purpose of the Convention is . . . by establishing common rules of jurisdiction, to achieve . . . in the field which it was required to cover, a genuine legal systematization which will ensure the greatest possible degree of legal certainty. To this end, the rules of jurisdiction codified in Title II determine which State' s courts are most appropriate to assume jurisdiction, taking into account all relevant matters . . .'.

---

11 Articles 21 and 22 of the Convention (Articles 27–30 of the Brussels I Regulation), discussed in Chapter 10, § 1, above.

22. To that end, Title II of the Convention establishes certain rules of jurisdiction which, after laying down the principle that persons domiciled in a Contracting State are to be sued in the courts of that State, go on to determine restrictively the cases in which that principle is not to apply.

23. So it is clear that Title II of the Convention lays down no rules determining the forum for proceedings for the recognition and enforcement of judgments given in non-contracting States.

24. Contrary to the arguments advanced by Fulvio Bracco and Bracco SpA, Article 16(5), which provides that in proceedings concerned with the enforcement of judgments the courts of the Contracting State in which the judgment has been or is to be enforced are to have exclusive jurisdiction, must indeed be read in conjunction with Article 25, which, it will be recalled, applies only to judgments given by a court or tribunal of a Contracting State.

25. The conclusion must therefore be that the Convention does not apply to proceedings for the enforcement of judgments given in civil and commercial matters in non-contracting States.

26. Fulvio Bracco and Bracco SpA argue that a distinction should be made between an order for enforcement *simpliciter* and a decision of a court of a Contracting State on an issue arising in proceedings to enforce a judgment given in a non-contracting State, such as the question whether the judgment in question was obtained by fraud. Decisions of the second type are, they argue, independent of the enforcement proceedings and should be recognized in the other Contracting States in accordance with Article 26 of the Convention.

27. According to the defendants, that interpretation follows from the principles and objectives of the EEC Treaty and of the Convention, as identified by the Court. It is therefore necessary, in the interests of the proper administration of justice, to prevent parallel proceedings before the courts of different Contracting States and the conflicting decisions which might result from them, and, similarly, to preclude as far as possible a situation where a Contracting State refuses to recognize a decision of another Contracting State on the ground that it is irreconcilable with a decision given between the same parties in the State in which recognition is sought . . .

28. That interpretation cannot be accepted.

29. First, the essential purpose of a decision given by a court of a Contracting State on an issue arising in proceedings for the enforcement of a judgment given in a non-contracting State, even where that issue is tried *inter partes*, is to determine whether, under the law of the State in which recognition is sought or, as the case may be, under the rules of any agreement applicable to that State' s relations with non-contracting States, there exists any ground for refusing recognition and enforcement of the judgment in question. That decision is not severable from the question of recognition and enforcement.

30. Secondly, according to Articles 27 and 28 of the Convention, read in conjunction with Article 34, the question whether any such ground exists in the case of judgments given in another Contracting State falls to be determined in the proceedings in which recognition and enforcement of those judgments are sought.

31. There is no reason to consider that the position is any different where the same question arises in proceedings concerning the recognition and enforcement of judgments given in non-contracting States.

32. On the contrary, the principle of legal certainty, which is one of the objectives of the Convention . . . militates against making the distinction advocated by Fulvio Bracco and Bracco SpA.

33. The rules of procedure governing the recognition and enforcement of judgments given in a non-contracting State differ according to the Contracting State in which recognition and enforcement are sought.

34. Lastly, it is clear from the judgment in [the *Marc Rich* case][1] that if, by virtue of its subject-matter, a dispute falls outside the scope of the Convention, the existence of a preliminary issue which the court must resolve in order to determine the dispute cannot, whatever that issue may be, justify application of the Convention.

. . .

37. The answer to the first and second questions must therefore be that the Convention, in particular Articles 21, 22 and 23, does not apply to proceedings, or issues arising in proceedings, in Contracting States concerning the recognition and enforcement of judgments given in civil and commercial matters in non-contracting States.

1 Set out in Chapter 10, § 5, above.

Result: the Italian proceedings did not prevent the English proceedings from continuing.

Comment

The European Court's judgment establishes that proceedings to enforce a judgment from a non-member State are outside the scope of the Convention (now the Regulation). This has two consequences: not only does it mean that the *lis pendens* doctrine in the Regulation does not apply; it also means that a judgment in such proceedings is not enforceable in another Member State under the Regulation. Thus, if Owens Bank had obtained a judgment in Italy for the enforcement of the St Vincent judgment, the Italian judgment would not have been binding under the Convention in England. This is logical because, as the European Court pointed out, the enforcement of non-member State judgments depends on the national law of the State in which the enforcement proceedings are brought. The conditions for enforcement in Italy are different from those in England. So there is no reason why England should be required to recognize a non-member State judgment just because Italy decides to do so.

The judgment of the European Court on the second issue raised by Bracco highlights an important principle of the Regulation. It seems that, in deciding whether proceedings are within the scope of the Regulation, one has to look at the final ruling sought in the case, not at any preliminary issue. In the *Owens Bank* case, the final ruling sought by the claimant was that the judgment from St Vincent should be recognized. This was outside the scope of the Convention; so the doctrine of *lis pendens* could not apply to it. This being so, it automatically followed, in the opinion of the European Court, that any preliminary issue, such as whether the judgment had been obtained by fraud, was also outside the scope of the Convention. The same approach was followed in the *Marc Rich* case. The English proceedings in that case were for the appointment of an arbitrator and were, for that reason, outside the scope of the Convention. This meant that the *lis pendens* doctrine laid down in the Convention could not apply to them, even though they involved a preliminary issue – the validity of the arbitration agreement – which, if it had arisen in different circumstances, might have been within its scope.

§ 2   Public policy, natural justice and human rights

Public policy, natural justice and human rights all provide grounds on which the recognition of a foreign judgment may be refused. The English doctrine of public policy is similar to that applicable under EC law (discussed in Chapter 14, § 5, above). Natural justice is concerned with procedural fairness in the foreign trial ('due process' in US terminology). An infringement of natural justice in the foreign proceedings would almost certainly also make the foreign judgment unenforceable for reasons of public policy; so there is a considerable overlap here, even though public policy has substantive aspects as well.

Article 6 of the European Convention on Human Rights guarantees the right to a fair trial in civil and criminal proceedings. This, therefore, covers most (if not all) of the ground covered by natural justice. We saw in Chapter 14, § 5, above, that, in *Krombach* v. *Bamberski*,[12] the European Court (EC) held that a Member State was entitled under the Brussels Convention to refuse recognition to a foreign judgment on public-policy grounds, if the foreign trial did not meet the requirements of the European Convention.

In *Krombach* v. *Bamberski*, the European Court merely said that the courts of a Member State are *entitled* to refuse recognition on these grounds. In *Pellegrini* v. *Italy*,[13] the European Court of Human Rights had to decide whether the European Convention *required* courts of Contracting States to do so. Mrs Pellegrini was an Italian whose husband brought proceedings against her to annul their marriage.

---

12 Case C-7/98, [2000] ECR I-1935.
13 Judgment of 20 July 2001 (available on www.echr.coe.int).

The proceedings were brought in an ecclesiastical court of the Catholic Church, which the European Court of Human Rights characterized as a court of the Vatican, a State (the Holy See) which is not a party to the European Convention. The proceedings did not satisfy the requirements of Article 6, since Mrs Pellegrini was not given a proper opportunity to defend herself. The ecclesiastical court pronounced a decree of nullity, a ruling upheld by the Rota in Rome. Mr Pellegrini asked the Italian courts to recognize the decree. Mrs Pellegrini objected, arguing that the proceedings by which it had been obtained infringed her rights under Article 6 of the European Convention on Human Rights; nevertheless, the Italian courts recognized it.

She then brought proceedings against Italy before the European Court of Human Rights. The court held that, before recognizing the decree, the Italian courts should have satisfied themselves that the proceedings 'fulfilled the guarantees of Article 6', a review that is required whenever a decision made by the courts of a non-contracting State is sought to be recognized in the courts of a Contracting State.[14] Because the Italian courts had not conducted such a review, Italy was held to have violated the Convention.

The same question subsequently came before the English courts in *United States* v. *Montgomery (No. 2)*.[15] The *Montgomery* case concerned the registration and enforcement in England of a confiscation order (for over US$7 million) made by a federal district court in the United States. The order related to shares which had been owned by Mr Barnette, an American who had been convicted of defrauding the US Government over laundry contracts for servicemen in Germany. The shares, which were in a Panamanian company, were said to represent the proceeds of his crimes. Before he was convicted, Mr Barnette had transferred most of the shares to Mrs Montgomery, his then wife. However, the district court held that this did not prevent their confiscation, since the order was retrospective to the date on which the last of Mr Barnette's crimes had been committed.

Mrs Montgomery left the United States and came to live in England. In proceedings in America to enforce the confiscation order, the district court made an order for discovery against her, but she did not comply with it. She did not contest the confiscation order in the district court, but sought to appeal against it to the US Court of Appeals. The Court of Appeals dismissed her appeal under the 'fugitive disentitlement doctrine'. Although Mrs Montgomery had not been accused of any crime, she was regarded as a 'fugitive' because she had not obeyed the discovery order. The Court of Appeals said that it would be wrong to allow her to benefit from an order in her favour if an order against her could not be enforced. As will be remembered from the discussion in Chapter 14, § 5, above, this would have constituted an infringement of Article 6 ECHR if the Convention had been applicable in the United States.

The United States then brought proceedings to enforce the confiscation order in England. Since the order was of a quasi-criminal nature, it was almost

14 Paragraph 40 of the judgment.
15 [2004] 1 WLR 2241; [2004] 4 All ER 289 (HL).

certainly unenforceable under the common law. Provision for the enforcement of such orders was, however, made by the Criminal Justice Act 1988, section 97 of which provided (at the time in question) for the registration of external confiscation orders made in a 'designated country'. The United States was such a country. The order was duly registered by the High Court and Mrs Montgomery appealed to the Court of Appeal, which dismissed her appeal. She then appealed to the House of Lords, relying on the *Pellegrini* decision. She argued that a court of a State to which the ECHR applies is guilty of a breach of Article 6 if it enforces a judgment made in a non-contracting State if that judgment would have infringed Article 6 if the Convention had applied to the State in question. The House of Lords, however, rejected her appeal. It said that the rule laid down in the *Pellegrini* case applies only to the recognition of decrees of ecclesiastical courts in Italy, a ruling that finds no support in the words of the judgment in *Pellegrini*.[16] It will be interesting to see whether, if Mrs Montgomery takes her case to the European Court of Human Rights, the *Pellegrini* case is followed.[17]

§ 3   Taxes, penalties and other rules of public law

There is a long-standing rule that foreign judgments will not be recognized if they are for taxes or penalties. Not only will the English courts refuse to enforce a foreign tax law;[18] they will also refuse to enforce a foreign judgment based on such a law.[19] Although the rule is equally clear with regard to penalties, it is less clear what is meant by 'penalty' for this purpose. Our next case deals with this question.

Ontario
Huntington* v. *Attrill
Privy Council (on appeal from the Supreme Court of Appeal for Ontario)
[1893] AC 150

Background

A New York statute provided that, if a director of a company signed a certificate that was false in any material respect, he would be personally liable for the debts of the company. The defendant had been a director of a New York company and had signed such a certificate. The claimant was owed a debt by the company and he sued the defendant in a New York court to recover the debt. He claimed that the defendant was personally liable under the statute. This claim was upheld by the New York court, which gave judgment for the claimant. When the claimant sought to enforce this judgment in Ontario, the defendant argued that it was for

---

16 Briggs, 'Foreign Judgments and Human Rights' (2005) 121 LQR 185; Fawcett, 'The Impact of Article 6(1) of the ECHR on Private International Law' (2007) 57 ICLQ 1 at pp. 35–6 ('Getting it Wrong').
17 The *Pellegrini* case was only a decision of a Chamber; any new case would almost certainly go to a Grand Chamber.
18 *Government of India* v. *Taylor* [1955] AC 491.
19 For Canada, see *United States* v. *Harden* [1963] SCR 366; (1963) 41 DLR (2d) 721 (Supreme Court of Canada); for the United States, see *The Queen in Right of British Columbia* v. *Gilbertson*, 597 F 2d 1161 (9th Cir. 1979).

a penalty and was, therefore, unenforceable in Ontario. The trial court upheld this plea. The Supreme Court of Appeal for Ontario was equally divided; so the judgment of the trial court was upheld. The case then came before the Privy Council in London.[20]

Lord Watson

Their Lordships cannot assent to the proposition that, in considering whether the present action was penal in such sense as to oust their jurisdiction, the courts of Ontario were bound to pay absolute deference to any interpretation which might have been put upon the statute of 1875 in the State of New York. They had to construe and apply an international rule, which is a matter of law entirely within the cognizance of the foreign court whose jurisdiction is invoked. Judicial decisions in the State where the cause of action arose are not precedents which must be followed, although the reasoning upon which they are founded must always receive careful consideration, and may be conclusive. The court appealed to must determine for itself, in the first place, the substance of the right sought to be enforced; and, in the second place, whether its enforcement would, either directly or indirectly, involve the execution of the penal law of another State. Were any other principle to guide its decision, a court might find itself in the position of giving effect in one case and denying effect in another, to suits of the same character, in consequence of the causes of action having arisen in different countries; or in the predicament of being constrained to give effect to laws which were, in its own judgment, strictly penal.

The general law upon this point has been correctly stated by Mr Justice Story in his *Conflict of Laws*,[1] and by other text writers; but their Lordships do not think it necessary to quote from these authorities in explanation of the reasons which have induced courts of justice to decline jurisdiction in suits somewhat loosely described as penal, when these have their origin in a foreign country. The rule has its foundation in the well-recognised principle that crimes, including in that term all breaches of public law punishable by pecuniary mulct or otherwise, at the instance of the State Government, or of some one representing the public, are local in this sense, that they are only cognizable and punishable in the country where they were committed. Accordingly no proceeding, even in the shape of a civil suit, which has for its object the enforcement by the State, whether directly or indirectly, of punishment imposed for such breaches by the *lex fori*, ought to be admitted in the courts of any other country.

Their Lordships have already indicated that, in their opinion, the phrase 'penal actions', which is so frequently used to designate that class of actions which, by the law of nations, are exclusively assigned to their domestic forum, does not afford an accurate definition. In its ordinary acceptation, the word 'penal' may

---

1 *Editor's note*: originally published in 1834, Joseph Story, *Commentaries on the Conflict of Laws*, was for many years the leading textbook on conflict of laws in the United States and indeed in the whole common-law world. In 1811, Story became a judge on the US Supreme Court, and in 1829 he became a professor at Harvard Law School.

20 Judgments of the Privy Council, though strictly speaking precedents only for the country from which the appeal came, are in practice also regarded as authorities in English law (and the law of other Commonwealth countries).

embrace penalties for infractions of general law which do not constitute offences against the State; it may for many legal purposes be applied with perfect propriety to penalties created by contract; and it therefore, when taken by itself, fails to mark that distinction between civil rights and criminal wrongs which is the very essence of the international rule. The phrase was used by . . . and also by Chief Justice Marshall,[2] who, in *The Antelope*,[3] thus stated the rule with no less brevity than force: 'The courts of no country execute the penal laws of another.' Read in the light of the context, the language used by these eminent lawyers is quite intelligible, because they were dealing with the consequences of violations of public law and order, which were unmistakably of a criminal complexion. But the expressions 'penal' and 'penalty', when employed without any qualification, express or implied, are calculated to mislead, because they are capable of being construed so as to extend the rule to all proceedings for the recovery of penalties, whether exigible by the State in the interest of the community, or by private persons in their own interest.

The Supreme Court of the United States had occasion to consider the international rule in *Wisconsin* v. *the Pelican Insurance Company*.[4] By the statute law of the State of Wisconsin, a pecuniary penalty was imposed upon corporations carrying on business under it who failed to comply with one of its enactments. The penalty was recoverable by the commissioner of insurance, an official entrusted with the administration of the Act in the public interest, one half of it being payable into the State Treasury, and the other to the commissioner, who was to defray the costs of prosecution. It was held that the penalty could not be enforced by the Federal Court, or the judiciary of any other State. In delivering the judgment of the bench, Mr. Justice Gray, after referring to the text books, and the dictum by Chief Justice Marshall already cited, went on to say:

> 'The rule that the courts of no country execute the law of another applies not only to prosecutions and sentences for crimes and misdemeanors, *but to all suits in favour of the State* for the recovery of pecuniary penalties for any violation of statutes for the protection of its revenue or other municipal laws, and to all judgments for such penalties.'

Their Lordships do not hesitate to accept that exposition of the law, which, in their opinion, discloses the proper test for ascertaining whether an action is penal within the meaning of the rule. A proceeding, in order to come within the scope of the rule, must be in the nature of a suit in favour of the State whose law has been infringed. All the provisions of municipal statutes for the regulation of trade and trading companies are presumably enacted in the interest and for the benefit of the community at large; and persons who violate these provisions are, in a certain sense, offenders against the State law, as well as against individuals who may be injured by their misconduct. But foreign tribunals do not regard these violations of statute law as offences against the State, unless their vindication rests with the State itself, or with the community which it represents. Penalties may be attached to them, but that circumstance will not bring them within the rule, except in cases

---

2 *Editor's note*: Marshall was Chief Justice of the US Supreme Court.
3 (1825) 10 Wheaton 123; 23 US 66 (US Supreme Court).
4 (1888) 127 US 265.

where these penalties are recoverable at the instance of the State, or of an official duly authorized to prosecute on its behalf, or of a member of the public in the character of a common informer.[5] An action by the latter is regarded as an *actio popularis* pursued, not in his individual interest, but in the interest of the whole community.

The New York statute of 1875 provides for the organization and regulation of corporations formed for the purpose of carrying on all kinds of lawful business with the exception of certain branches therein specified. It confers rights and privileges upon persons who choose to form a trading association, and to become incorporated under its provisions, with full or with limited liability; and, in either case, it varies and limits the rights and remedies which, under the common law, would have been available to creditors of the association, as against its individual members. On the other hand, for the protection of those members of the public who may deal with the corporation, the Act imposes upon its directors and officers various stringent obligations, the plain object of which is to make known, from time to time, to all concerned, the true condition of its finances. Thus they are required (sect. 18) to publish an annual report stating the amount of capital, the proportion actually paid in, the amount and nature of existing assets and debts, the names of the shareholders and the dividends, if any, declared since last report; and (sect. 37) to certify the amount of capital stock paid in within thirty days after payment of the last instalment. In both cases the consequence of the report or certificate being false in any material representation, is that every director or officer who vouched its accuracy becomes, under sect. 21, liable personally for all the debts of the corporation contracted during his period of office.

The provisions of sect. 21 are in striking contrast to the enactments of sect. 34, which inflicts a penalty of $100 upon every director or officer of a corporation with limited liability, who authorises or permits the omission of the word 'limited' from its seal, official publications, or business documents. In that case, the penalty is recoverable 'in the name of the people of the State of New York by the district attorney of the county in which the principal office of such corporation is located, and the amounts recovered shall be paid over to the proper authorities for the support of the poor of such county.' It does not admit of doubt that an action by the district attorney would be a suit in favour of the State, and that neither the penalty, nor the decree of a New York Court for its amount, could be enforced in a foreign country.

In one aspect of them, the provisions of sect. 21 are penal in the wider sense in which the term is used. They impose heavy liabilities upon directors, in respect of failure to observe statutory regulations for the protection of persons who have become or may become creditors of the corporation. But, in so far as they concern creditors, these provisions are in their nature protective and remedial. To use the language of Mr. Justice Osler, they give 'a civil remedy only to creditors whose rights the conduct of the company's officers may have been calculated to injure, and which is not enforceable by the State or the public.' In the opinion of their

---

5 *Editor's note*: a common informer is someone who claims a penalty even though he has no personal interest in the matter.

> Lordships, these enactments are simply conditions upon which the Legislature permits associations to trade with corporate privileges, and constitute an implied term of every contract between the corporation and its creditors.

Result: the appeal was allowed, and the New York judgment enforced.

Comment

It would seem to follow from the definition of 'penalty' given in this case that a judgment for punitive damages[21] is in principle enforceable in England, though there is no clear authority on the point.[22] In at least some civil-law countries, such judgments are not enforceable.[23]

A rather different question arose in our next case.

England
United States of America v. Inkley
Court of Appeal
[1989] 2 QB 255; [1988] 3 WLR 304; [1988] 3 All ER 344

Background

Mr Inkley, a British citizen, had been arrested in the United States on a criminal charge arising out of alleged fraudulent activities on his part (selling non-existent oil wells). He obtained his release by signing a bail bond under which he undertook to pay a sum of money if he failed to appear for trial. The bail bond contained a choice-of-court agreement in favour of an American court. He returned to England and did not appear for trial. The US Government brought proceedings against him in the specified court under the bail bond. He did not defend the proceedings, and a default judgment was given against him. The US Government then brought proceedings to enforce the judgment in England. The Master held that the judgment could not be enforced. The US appealed to the High Court, which reversed this decision. Inkley then appealed to the Court of Appeal.

Purchas LJ

[After referring to the authorities, including *Huntington v. Attrill*]

From these authorities the following propositions seem to emerge which are relevant to the present appeal: (1) the consideration of whether the claim sought to be enforced in the English courts is one which involves the assertion of foreign sovereignty, whether it be penal, revenue or other public law, is to be determined according to the criteria of English law; (2) that regard will be had to the attitude

---

21 These are damages awarded to the victim, over and above what is required to compensate him, in order to punish the wrong-doer and to deter him from doing the same thing in future. Such damages are common in the United States; they are rare, but not unknown, in England.
22 See *SA Consortium General Textiles v. Sun and Sand Agencies Ltd* [1978] QB 279 at pp. 299–300, *per* Lord Denning MR (*obiter*) (CA); Dicey, Morris and Collins, pp. 476 and 526; Cheshire, North and Fawcett, pp. 557–8. On the other hand, judgments for multiple damages – for example, treble damages under the US Sherman Act – are not enforceable in England: section 5 of the Protection of Trading Interests Act 1980 (discussed in Chapter 34, § 4.5, below).
23 For Germany, see Case IX ZR 149/91 [1994] ILPr 602 (German Federal Supreme Court).

adopted by the courts in the foreign jurisdiction which will always receive serious attention and may on occasions be decisive; (3) that the category of the right of action, i.e. whether public or private, will depend on the party in whose favour it is created, on the purpose of the law or enactment in the foreign state on which it is based and on the general context of the case as a whole; (4) that the fact that the right, statutory or otherwise, is penal in nature will not deprive a person, who asserts a personal claim depending thereon, from having recourse to the courts of this country; on the other hand, by whatever description it may be known if the purpose of the action is the enforcement of a sanction, power or right at the instance of the state in its sovereign capacity, it will not be entertained; (5) that the fact that in the foreign jurisdiction recourse may be had in a civil forum to enforce the right will not necessarily affect the true nature of the right being enforced in this country.

Applying the above criteria to the facts of this case we have come firmly to the conclusion that the general context and background against which the appearance bond was executed was criminal or penal. The power to require the execution of the bond arose from section 3146 *et seq.* of the United States Code Annotated for Crimes and Criminal Procedure. The circumstances in which it came into existence were clearly criminal in nature and breaches of the conditions incorporated in it could give rise to further criminal process. Finally, the whole purpose of the bond was to ensure, so far as it was possible, the presence of the executor of the bond to meet justice at the hands of the state in a criminal prosecution. The fact that the obligations under the bond were the subject matter of a declaratory judgment in a civil court does not affect, in our judgment, the basic characteristic of the right which that judgment itself enforced, namely the right of the state as the administrator of public law and justice to ensure the due observance of the criminal law or the exaction of pecuniary penalties if that course was frustrated. Notwithstanding its civil clothing, the purpose of the action initiated by the writ issued in this case was the due execution by the United States of America of a public law process aimed to ensure the attendance of persons accused of crime before the criminal courts.

Result: the appeal was allowed (US judgment not enforced)

Comment

This case shows that a foreign judgment will be refused enforcement not only if it is for a tax or penalty, but also if it is based on some other public law. The bail-bond agreement, though in the form of a private-law contract, was intended to ensure that the accused stood trial in the United States. It was thus part of the criminal process, and would not be enforced in England.[24]

The idea behind the English rule that a foreign judgment for taxes, penalties or other rules of public law will not be enforced is the same as that behind the rule of EC law that, to be enforceable under the Brussels I Regulation,

---

24 For a different attitude towards the enforcement of bail bonds, see *National Surety Co.* v. *Larsen* [1929] 4 DLR 918 (British Columbia Court of Appeal).

judgments must be in respect of a civil or commercial matter (see Chapter 3, § 9, above). However, under EC law, the rule concerns the subject-matter scope of the Regulation, while under English law it is a defence to the enforcement of a foreign judgment. The policy considerations are, however, the same and many of the arguments discussed in Chapter 3, § 9, are equally relevant here.

§ 4 Conflicting judgments

Under EC law, a foreign judgment is not recognized if it is inconsistent with a local judgment or with an earlier foreign judgment that is subject to recognition in the State of the forum.[25] English law is almost certainly the same, though clear authority appears to be available only for the latter part of the rule.[26]

§ 5 Res judicata and issue estoppel

Normally, a foreign judgment is recognized in order to enforce it. However, recognition is sometimes an end in itself. The most obvious example is where the foreign court gives judgment for the defendant: if the claimant sues the same defendant on the same cause of action in England, the defendant may ask the court to recognize the foreign judgment as a defence. The court will normally do this. Since the claimant himself chose the foreign court, he is regarded as having submitted to its jurisdiction with regard to the claim; so he cannot argue in the English proceedings that it lacked jurisdiction. As a result, there are only a limited number of defences (for example, fraud or public policy) that he may raise. Unless he can raise such a defence successfully, the foreign judgment will be recognized and the new action will fail.

In this respect, the Brussels I Regulation is no different from the common law. The doctrine of *res judicata* applies and – in the absence of a very small number of defences (for example, public policy) – the foreign judgment must be recognized.[27] However, in at least some civil-law countries, the obligation to recognize a foreign judgment applies only to the final order, not to any preliminary ruling given by the foreign court, even if it was a necessary step in the chain of reasoning that led to the final order. If this approach is followed with regard to the Regulation, a gap will be opened up between the Regulation and English common law, since, under the doctrine of issue estoppel, such preliminary rulings can also be binding on the party against whom they were made.

It is not easy to explain estoppel in a few words, though the core idea is that a person should not be able to say one thing one moment and something different

---

25 See Chapter 14, § 6, above.
26 In *Showlag* v. *Mansour* [1995] 1 AC 431; [1994] 2 WLR 615; [1994] 2 All ER 129 (PC). This case held that, if the conflicting judgments are both foreign, the earlier will prevail. This is subject to an exception if the party in favour of whom the earlier judgment was given is estopped from relying on it. On estoppel, see § 5, below.
27 No special procedure is required: Article 33(1) of the Regulation.

the next, depending on what suits him. If he makes an assertion on one occasion, he is estopped (prevented) from denying it on a later occasion. This core idea has, however, been expanded and now includes what is called estoppel *per rem judicatam*: if something has been settled through judicial proceedings – if it has become *res judicata* – a party cannot challenge it on a later occasion.

This applies both to a judicial determination in England and to one in a foreign court. Thus, it we take the example given above of a claimant suing a defendant unsuccessfully in a foreign country and then bringing the same claim again in England, an English court might say that it is *recognizing* the foreign judgment or it might say that it is applying *cause-of-action estoppel* (a sub-category of estoppel *per rem judicatam*). Both amount to the same thing. Thus far, the common law and the civil law are the same, though they may use different terminology.

However, estoppel *per rem judicatam* can also apply more widely. Under the doctrine of issue estoppel[28] (another sub-category of estoppel *per rem judicatam*), a determination by an English or foreign court of a preliminary issue can also create an estoppel. An example will make this clear. Assume that the claimant sues the defendant in England for infringement of a particular UK patent. The English court gives judgment for the defendant on the ground that the patent is invalid. If the claimant then sues the defendant again for a different infringement of the same patent, the defendant can raise a defence of issue estoppel. Even though the cause of action is different (there is a new act of infringement) the preliminary issue (the validity of the patent) is the same.

A foreign judgment can also give rise to issue estoppel.[29] This can apply even if issue estoppel is not recognized under the law of the foreign court.[30] This is because estoppel is regarded in England as part of the law of evidence: it is governed by the *lex fori*.[31] However, it must be applied in a manner consistent with good sense. An estoppel should not be regarded as arising in circumstances in which this could cause injustice, something which might happen if the rules of procedure in the foreign court are not taken into account.

The leading case is *The Sennar (No. 2)*.

England
The Sennar (No. 2)
House of Lords
[1985] 1 WLR 490; [1985] 2 All ER 104

Background

The case arose out of a shipment of groundnuts (peanuts) from Port Sudan, Sudan, to Rotterdam, Netherlands. The shippers were a Sudanese company, Malik, and the shipowners were a Sudanese company, Sudan Shipping Line Ltd. The bills of lading were dated 30 August 1973. Clause 27 gave exclusive jurisdiction to the courts of the Sudan; there was also a Sudanese choice-of-law

---

28 In the United States, known as 'issue preclusion' or 'collateral estoppel'.
29 *The Sennar (No. 2)* [1985] 1 WLR 490 (HL).
30 In *The Sennar (No. 2)*, the judgment was given by a Dutch court.
31 *Carl Zeiss Stiftung* v. *Rayner and Keeler Ltd* [1967] AC 853 at p. 919, *per* Lord Reid.

clause. Malik sold the goods to Pagco, a Swiss company, which sold them to GfG, a German company.[32] GfG sold them to European Grain and Shipping Ltd, an English company. All three contracts contained a clause that half the goods had to be shipped in July or August 1973. In part-performance of these contracts, Malik presented the bills of lading to Pagco. Pagco accepted them and presented them to GfG, which likewise accepted them and presented them to European Grain and Shipping.

In September 1973, the price of Sudanese groundnuts fell sharply. It also became known that the goods on board the *Sennar* had in fact been shipped in September 1973. The date on the bills of lading was fraudulent. In these circumstances, European Grain and Shipping claimed rescission of their contract with GfG. GfG gave them back their money and claimed rescission from Pagco. Unfortunately, Pagco was now insolvent; so GfG had to bear the loss. GfG then sued the shipping company, Sudan Shipping, in a Dutch court. They obtained jurisdiction by arresting a sister ship of the *Sennar* in Rotterdam. Their action was brought in tort: they claimed that Sudan Shipping had caused them loss by entering a false date on the bills of lading. The Dutch courts, however, held that GfG's only claim was in contract – by accepting the bills of lading, they were entitled to benefit from, and were bound by, their terms – and that their claim was subject to the Sudanese choice-of-court clause. So the Dutch courts had no jurisdiction.

DSV, successors in title to GfG, then arrested another sister ship of the *Sennar* in an English port. This gave the English courts jurisdiction *in rem*. The shipowners, Sudan Shipping, obtained the release of the ship by giving security and agreeing to accept the jurisdiction of the English courts. This gave the English courts jurisdiction *in personam* over Sudan Shipping. DSV's claim (for the falsification of the bills of lading) was in tort. Sudan Shipping, however, argued that the claim was subject to the Sudanese jurisdiction clause. They argued that the Dutch judgment estopped the German company from challenging this. They asked for a stay of the proceedings. The Court of Appeal granted a stay and the Germans (referred to in the judgment as 'the dealers') appealed to the House of Lords.

Lord Diplock

In English law when a plaintiff, who, basing his claim on a particular set of facts, has already sued the defendant to final judgment in a foreign court of competent jurisdiction and lost, then seeks to enforce a cause of action in an English court against the same defendant based on the same set of facts, the defendant's remedy against such double jeopardy is provided by the doctrine of issue estoppel.

It is far too late, at this stage of the development of the doctrine, to question that issue estoppel can be created by the judgment of a foreign court if that court is recognised in English private international law as being a court of competent

---

32 The claimants, DSV, another German company, were successors in title to GfG.

jurisdiction. Issue estoppel operates regardless of whether or not an English court would regard the reasoning of the foreign judgment as open to criticism. Although in the instant case some 15 days were taken up by oral argument in the courts below, together with voluminous citation of authorities, nevertheless the facts appear to me to present a case to which the now well-established doctrine of issue estoppel resulting from a foreign judgment incontestably applies.

To make available an issue estoppel to a defendant to an action brought against him in an English court upon a cause of action to which the plaintiff alleges a particular set of facts give rise, the defendant must be able to show: (1) that the same set of facts has previously been relied upon as constituting a cause of action in proceedings brought by that plaintiff against that defendant in a foreign court of competent jurisdiction; and (2) that a final judgment has been given by that foreign court in those proceedings.

It is often said that the final judgment of the foreign court must be 'on the merits.' The moral overtones which this expression tends to conjure up may make it misleading. What it means in the context of judgments delivered by courts of justice is that the court has held that it has jurisdiction to adjudicate upon an issue raised in the cause of action to which the particular set of facts give rise; and that its judgment on that cause of action is one that cannot be varied, re-opened or set aside by the court that delivered it or any other court of co-ordinate jurisdiction although it may be subject to appeal to a court of higher jurisdiction.

My Lords, misdated bills of lading are regrettably not unknown in the commodity markets in which prices are liable to large and rapid changes. What takes the instant case out of the general run of cases where there has been a string of contracts of sale between dealers in the market in the form of GAFTA 100 and it is discovered after the documents have been accepted that a false date of shipment has been inserted in the bill of lading, is that a buyer lower in the string returns the documents to his immediate seller and recovers from him the price that he had paid and so on up the string. The shipowner who signed the misdated bill of lading (usually at the request of the shipper) is not normally brought into the proceedings between the parties to the string at all. It was only because the appellants' (whom I refer to hereafter as 'the dealers') immediate seller, Pagco, became insolvent that they decided to bring proceedings against the respondents ('the shipowners') for damages for fraudulent misrepresentation contained in the bill of lading and consisting of the statement that the Sudanese groundnut expellers covered by the bill of lading No 7 were received on board the *Sennar* on 30 August 1973.

The jurisdiction of the Dutch courts was invoked by the dealers by their arrest at Rotterdam of a sister ship of the *Sennar*. The particular set of facts relied upon by the dealers as constituting a cause of action against the shipowners in the Dutch proceedings was identical with the facts upon which the dealers sought to rely in the English proceedings which the Court of Appeal has ordered to be stayed.

At the hearing of the appeal from that stay it was repeatedly urged upon Your Lordships that all that the judgment of the Dutch Court of Appeal had done was no more than to hold that it had no jurisdiction over the dealers' claim against the shipowners and so did not fall into the category of a judgment on the merits. But this is to confuse issue estoppel with cause of action estoppel.

I ventured in the course of the hearing to summarise in a single sentence what the Dutch Court of Appeal had decided by its judgment of 21 March 1980: upon the particular set of facts on which the dealers relied in the Dutch action their only claim against the shipowners is for breach of the contract of carriage which, as a result of the Sudanese jurisdiction clause that it contains, is enforceable in the courts of the Sudan and nowhere else.

In my view that constitutes a final judgment 'on the merits' (as I have interpreted that term) upon two issues: the first is that the dealers have no claim against the shipowners for their wrongful act of inserting a false date upon the bill of lading, other than a claim for breach of the contract of carriage; the second is that the effect of the jurisdiction clause in the contract of carriage is to make any remedy for breach of that contract enforceable only in a Sudanese court unless the shipowners elect otherwise.

Result: DSV's action was stayed.

Comment

Although the Dutch courts held that they had no jurisdiction to decide the substantive claim against Sudan Shipping, they *did* have jurisdiction to decide whether or not they had jurisdiction to decide that claim. This latter question required them to decide whether the substantive claim was subject to the choice-of-court clause. They held that it was. This ruling was binding on the German company: issue estoppel precluded them from disputing it in the English courts. The German company could not claim that the Dutch courts had no jurisdiction over them: they had *chosen* to bring their claim in the Netherlands.

Two further examples of issue estoppel will be given. The first is based on *House of Spring Gardens Ltd* v. *Waite*.[33] The essential facts were as follows. The claimant sued the defendant in Ireland and was successful. Subsequently, the defendant brought a new action in Ireland to have the first judgment set aside on the ground that it was obtained by fraud. This new action was unsuccessful: it was held that the first action had not been obtained by fraud. The claimant then sought to enforce the first judgment in England. The defendant raised the defence of fraud. However, the English courts held that he was estopped from doing so: the ruling in the second judgment that the first judgment had not been obtained by fraud gave rise to an estoppel that was binding on the defendant. Since there was no allegation that the second judgment had been obtained by fraud, it could not be challenged in England.

The second example concerns *Marc Rich and Co.* v. *Società Italiana Impianti*[34] (set out in Chapter 10, § 5, above).[35] It will be remembered that Marc Rich and Impianti had concluded a contract for the sale of oil. Marc Rich claimed that the oil was

---

33 [1991] 1 QB 241; [1990] 3 WLR 347; [1990] 2 All ER 990 (CA).
34 Case C-190/89, [1991] ECR I-3855.
35 See also Chapter 14, § 10, above.

contaminated. It also claimed that the contract contained an arbitration clause, providing for arbitration in London. It called on Impianti to take the dispute to arbitration. Impianti instead brought proceedings before a court in Genoa, Italy, for a declaration of non-liability. Marc Rich argued that the Italian court had no jurisdiction because the dispute was subject to arbitration. This preliminary issue went to the *Corte Suprema di Cassazione*, the highest civil court in Italy, for decision.

While this was happening, Marc Rich tried to get the arbitration under way. Impianti refused to co-operate by appointing its arbitrator. Marc Rich then applied to the English court to appoint an arbitrator on Impianti's behalf. Impianti argued that these proceedings were blocked by the *lis pendens* doctrine under the Brussels Convention, because the matter was already pending before the Genoa court. The English court referred the matter to the European Court, which decided (after a delay of over two years) that the English proceedings were outside the subject-matter scope of the Convention; so the *lis pendens* doctrine in the Convention did not apply to them. It was at this point that we left the case.

However, while the European Court was deliberating, matters had been moving forward in Italy. The *Corte Suprema di Cassazione* held that the arbitration agreement was invalid. The case then went back to the Genoa court for the substance of the claim to be decided. At this point, Marc Rich, having lost on the jurisdictional point, could have walked away from the proceedings. However, it decided (understandably enough) to defend on the merits. These proceedings were still continuing when the application for the appointment of an arbitrator came back before the English court.[36] That court decided that, under English law, Marc Rich's decision to defend the substantive proceedings on the merits constituted a submission to the jurisdiction of the Italian courts. This applied retrospectively to the earlier proceedings in the case; consequently, the interlocutory decision of the *Corte Suprema di Cassazione* on the preliminary issue of the validity of the arbitration agreement gave rise to an issue estoppel binding Marc Rich. As a result, it could no longer claim in the English proceedings that there was a valid arbitration agreement. So its claim that the English court should appoint an arbitrator fell away. The Italians, therefore, won in the end. If the European Court had decided the matter more quickly, the outcome might have been different. This shows that judicial delay can affect the rights of parties. Asking for a reference to the European Court was, therefore, a clever move by Impianti. Even though Impianti lost that particular round of the dispute, the resultant delay enabled it to win in the end.

§ 5.1   *English law or EC law?*

It will have been noticed that the English court decided the issue-estoppel point entirely on the basis of the common law. It is doubtful whether there was any obligation under EC law to give effect to the decision of the *Corte Suprema di Cassazione* that the arbitration agreement was invalid.[37] On the other hand, there

---

36 *Marc Rich & Co. AG v. Società Italiana Impianti pA (No. 2)* [1992] 1 Lloyd's Rep 624 (CA).
37 At the time of the English proceedings, the Italian courts had given no ruling on the substance of the claim in the case.

seems to be no rule of EC law that *precludes* the courts of a Member State from giving effect to the decision of a court of another Member State even when not required to do so under the Regulation. Since estoppel is a matter of evidence, it is proper that the law of the forum should decide when it applies.

§ 5.2   *Judgment for the claimant*

What happens if the claimant is successful in the foreign proceedings: can he sue again in England on the original cause of action? The rule under the common law was that he could do so, provided that the foreign judgment had not been satisfied. If it was satisfied (if the defendant paid the amount awarded), that extinguished the claim; but, if it was not satisfied, the claimant could choose whether to sue on the judgment in England or to sue on the original claim. He might choose the latter, if he thought that an English court would award more generous damages.

This has now been changed by section 34 of the Civil Jurisdiction and Judgments Act 1982 (Panel 16.1), which provides that a foreign judgment in favour of the claimant is a bar to further proceedings by him on the same cause of action, unless the foreign judgment is not enforceable in England. Even if the foreign judgment is not satisfied, therefore, the claimant cannot sue on the original cause of action.[38]

> **Panel 16.1 Foreign judgments as a bar to new proceedings**
> **Civil Jurisdiction and Judgments Act 1982 (as amended), section 34**
>
> **Section 34 Certain judgments a bar to further proceedings on the same cause of action**
>
> No proceedings may be brought by a person in England and Wales or Northern Ireland on a cause of action in respect of which a judgment has been given in his favour in proceedings between the same parties, or their privies, in a court in another part of the United Kingdom or in a court of an overseas country, unless that judgment is not enforceable or entitled to recognition in England and Wales or, as the case may be, in Northern Ireland.

Further reading

Barnett (Peter), *Res Judicata, Estoppel and Foreign Judgments*, Oxford University Press, Oxford, 2001

Barnett, 'The Prevention of Abusive Cross-Border Re-Litigation' (2002) 51 ICLQ 943

Briggs, 'Crossing the River by Feeling the Stones: Rethinking the Law on Foreign Judgments' (2004) 8 *Singapore Yearbook of International Law* 1

Campbell, 'Res Judicata and Decisions of Foreign Tribunals' (1994) 16 *Sydney Law Review* 311

Casad, 'Issue Preclusion and Foreign Country Judgments: Whose Law?' (1984) 70 *Iowa Law Review* 53

Collier, 'Fraud Still Unravels Foreign Judgments' [1992] CLJ 441

Fawcett, 'The Impact of Article 6(1) of the ECHR on Private International Law' (2007) 57 ICLQ 1

Garnett, 'Fraud and Foreign Judgments: The Defence that Refuses to Die' (2002) 1 *Journal of International Commercial Law* 161

Rogerson, 'Issue Estoppel and Abuse of Process in Foreign Judgments' [1998] CJQ 91

---

38 On the operation of this provision, see *Republic of India* v. *India Steamship Co. Ltd (No. 2)* [1998] AC 878 (HL).

CHAPTER 17

The Canadian conflicts (judgments) revolution

Canada is a federation made up of a number of provinces. All except Quebec apply the common law. For conflict-of-laws purposes, each province is a separate country, and the recognition and enforcement of foreign judgments, including judgments from another province, are governed by provincial law. Until 1990, the rules of jurisdiction applied for this purpose were the same as in England. In 1990, however, the position was radically altered by the judgment of the Supreme Court of Canada in our next case.

§ 1 Jurisdiction of the foreign court

Canada
Morguard Investments Ltd* v. *De Savoye
Supreme Court of Canada
[1990] 3 SCR 1077; (1990) 76 DLR (4th) 256; [1991] 2 WWR 217; (1990) 52 BCLR (2d) 160

Background

De Savoye was liable to Morguard for a debt under a mortgage of land in Alberta. He had originally resided in Alberta, but later moved to British Columbia. He defaulted on the mortgage and Morguard sued him in Alberta. The court took jurisdiction under provincial rules permitting service of the writ outside Alberta. De Savoye received the writ but did not defend, and a default judgment was given against him. Morguard sold the land, but the money raised was insufficient to cover the outstanding debt; so it brought enforcement proceedings in British Columbia for the balance. Under the English rules, the judgment would not have been enforced because the Alberta courts would not be regarded as having had jurisdiction.[1] However, the Supreme Court of Canada thought the time had come for a new approach.

La Forest J, giving the judgment of the court:

The issue

No one denies the Alberta court's jurisdiction to entertain the actions and enforce them there if it can. It would be surprising if they did. They concern transactions

---

1 The mortgage agreement did not contain a choice-of-court clause and De Savoye did not otherwise submit to the jurisdiction of the Alberta court.

entered into in Alberta by individuals who were resident in Alberta at the time of the transactions and involve land situate in that province. Though the defendant appellant was outside Alberta at the time the actions were brought and judgment given, the Alberta rules for service outside the jurisdiction permitted him to be served in British Columbia. These rules are similar to those in other provinces, and specifically British Columbia. The validity of such rules does not appear to have been subjected to much questioning, a matter to which I shall, however, return.

The issue, then, as already mentioned, is simply whether a personal judgment validly given in Alberta against an absent defendant may be enforced in British Columbia where he now resides.

[La Forest J then discussed the development of the law in England and in Canada. He continued:]

Analysis

The common law regarding the recognition and enforcement of foreign judgments is firmly anchored in the principle of territoriality as interpreted and applied by the English courts in the 19th century . . . This principle reflects the fact, one of the basic tenets of international law, that sovereign states have exclusive jurisdiction in their own territory. As a concomitant to this, states are hesitant to exercise jurisdiction over matters that may take place in the territory of other states. Jurisdiction being territorial, it follows that a state's law has no binding effect outside its jurisdiction. Great Britain, and specifically its courts, applied that doctrine more rigorously than other states . . . The English approach, we saw, was unthinkingly adopted by the courts of this country, even in relation to judgments given in sister-provinces.

Modern states, however, cannot live in splendid isolation and do give effect to judgments given in other countries in certain circumstances. Thus a judgment *in rem*, such as a decree of divorce granted by the courts of one state to persons domiciled there, will be recognized by the courts of other states. In certain circumstances, as well, our courts will enforce personal judgments given in other states. Thus . . . our courts will enforce an action for breach of contract given by the courts of another country if the defendant was present there at the time of the action or has agreed to the foreign court's exercise of jurisdiction. This, it was thought, was in conformity with the requirements of comity, the informing principle of private international law, which has been stated to be the deference and respect due by other states to the actions of a state legitimately taken within its territory. Since the state where the judgment was given had power over the litigants, the judgments of its courts should be respected.

But a state was under no obligation to enforce judgments it deemed to fall outside the jurisdiction of the foreign court. In particular, the English courts refused to enforce judgments on contracts, wherever made, unless the defendant was within the jurisdiction of the foreign court at the time of the action or had submitted to its jurisdiction. And this was so, we saw, even of actions that could most appropriately be tried in the foreign jurisdiction, such as a case like the present where the personal obligation undertaken in the foreign country was in respect of property located there. Even in the 19th century, this approach gave difficulty, a difficulty in my view resulting from a misapprehension of the real nature of the idea of comity, an idea based not simply on respect for the dictates of a foreign sovereign, but on the convenience, nay necessity, in a world where legal authority is divided among sovereign states, of adopting a doctrine of this kind.

For my part, I much prefer the more complete formulation of the idea of comity adopted by the Supreme Court of the Unites States in *Hilton* v. *Guyot*, 159 US 113 (1895), at pp. 163–64, in a passage cited by Estey J in *Spencer* v. *The Queen* [1985] 2 SCR 278, at p. 283, as follows:

> 'Comity' in the legal sense, is neither a matter of absolute obligation, on the one hand, nor of mere courtesy and good will, upon the other. But it is the recognition which one nation allows within its territory to the legislative, executive or judicial acts of another nation, having due regard both to international duty and convenience, and to the rights of its own citizens or of other persons who are under the protection of its laws . . .

As Dickson J in *Zingre* v. *The Queen* [1981] 2 SCR 392, at p. 400, citing Marshall CJ in *The Schooner Exchange* v. *M'Faddon*, 11 US (7 Cranch) 116 (1812), stated, 'common interest impels sovereigns to mutual intercourse' between sovereign states. In a word, the rules of private international law are grounded in the need in modern times to facilitate the flow of wealth, skills and people across state lines in a fair and orderly manner. Von Mehren and Trautman have observed in 'Recognition of Foreign Adjudications: A Survey and A Suggested Approach' (1968), 81 *Harv. L Rev.* 1601, at p. 1603: 'The ultimate justification for according some degree of recognition is that if in our highly complex and interrelated world each community exhausted every possibility of insisting on its parochial interests, injustice would result and the normal patterns of life would be disrupted.'

. . .

[After saying that the content of comity must be adjusted in the light of a changing world order, La Forest J continued:]

The approach adopted by the English courts in the 19th century may well have seemed suitable to Great Britain's situation at the time. One can understand the difficulty in which a defendant in England would find himself in defending an action initiated in a far corner of the world in the then state of travel and communications. The approach, of course, demands that one forget the difficulties of the plaintiff in bringing an action against a defendant who has moved to a distant land. However, this may not have been perceived as too serious a difficulty by English courts at a time when it was predominantly Englishmen who carried on enterprises in far away lands. As well, there was an exaggerated concern about the quality of justice that might be meted out to British residents abroad . . .

The world has changed since the above rules were developed in 19th century England. Modern means of travel and communications have made many of these 19th century concerns appear parochial. The business community operates in a world economy and we correctly speak of a world community even in the face of decentralized political and legal power. Accommodating the flow of wealth, skills and people across state lines has now become imperative. Under these circumstances, our approach to the recognition and enforcement of foreign judgments would appear ripe for reappraisal. Certainly, other countries, notably the United States and members of the European Economic Community, have adopted more generous rules for the recognition and enforcement of foreign judgments to the general advantage of litigants.

However that may be, there is really no comparison between the interprovincial relationships of today and those obtaining between foreign countries in the 19th century. Indeed, in my view, there never was and the courts made a serious error in transposing the rules developed for the enforcement of foreign judgments to the enforcement of judgments from sister-provinces. The considerations underlying the rules of comity apply with much greater force between the units of a federal state, and I do not think it much matters whether one calls these rules of comity or simply relies directly on the reasons of justice, necessity and convenience to which I have already adverted. Whatever nomenclature is used, our courts have not hesitated to co-operate with courts of other provinces where necessary to meet the ends of justice . . .

In any event, the English rules seem to me to fly in the face of the obvious intention of the Constitution to create a single country. This presupposes a basic goal of stability and unity where many aspects of life are not confined to one jurisdiction. A common citizenship ensured the mobility of Canadians across provincial lines . . . In particular, significant steps were taken to foster economic integration. One of the central features of the constitutional arrangements incorporated in the Constitution Act 1867 was the creation of a common market. Barriers to interprovincial trade were removed by s. 121. Generally trade and commerce between the provinces was seen to be a matter of concern to the country as a whole . . .

These arrangements themselves speak to the strong need for the enforcement throughout the country of judgments given in one province. But that is not all. The Canadian judicial structure is so arranged that any concerns about differential quality of justice among the provinces can have no real foundation. All superior court judges – who also have superintending control over other provincial courts and tribunals – are appointed and paid by the federal authorities. And all are subject to final review by the Supreme Court of Canada, which can determine when the courts of one province have appropriately exercised jurisdiction in an action and the circumstances under which the courts of another province should recognize such judgments. Any danger resulting from unfair procedure is further avoided by sub-constitutional factors, such as for example the fact that Canadian lawyers adhere to the same code of ethics throughout Canada. In fact, since *Black* v. *Law Society of Alberta* [[1989] 1 SCR 591] we have seen a proliferation of interprovincial law firms.

These various constitutional and sub-constitutional arrangements and practices make unnecessary a 'full faith and credit' clause such as exists in other federations, such as the United States and Australia. The existence of these clauses, however, does indicate that a regime of mutual recognition of judgments across the country is inherent in a federation. Indeed, the European Economic Community has determined that such a feature flows naturally from a common market, even without political integration. To that end its members have entered into the 1968 Convention on Jurisdiction and Enforcement of Judgments in Civil and Commercial Matters.

The integrating character of our constitutional arrangements as they apply to interprovincial mobility is such that some writers have suggested that a 'full faith and credit' clause must be read into the Constitution and that the federal Parliament is, under the 'Peace, Order and Good Government' clause, empowered to legislate respecting the recognition and enforcement of judgments throughout Canada . . . The present case was not, however, argued on that basis, and I need not go that far. For present purposes, it is sufficient to say that, in my view, the application of the underlying principles of comity and private international law must be adapted to the situations where they are applied, and that in a federation this implies a fuller and more generous acceptance of the judgments of the courts of other constituent units of the federation. In short, the rules of comity or private international law as they apply between the provinces must be shaped to conform to the federal structure of the Constitution.

This Court has, in other areas of the law having extraterritorial implications, recognized the need for adapting the law to the exigencies of a federation.

[La Forest J then discussed *Aetna Financial Services* v. *Feigelman*, [1985] 1 SCR 2, in which the Supreme Court of Canada held that the principles developed by the English courts regarding Mareva injunctions (freeze orders) in international cases were not appropriate for inter-provincial cases in Canada. He continued:]

A similar approach should, in my view, be adopted in relation to the recognition and enforcement of judgments within Canada. As I see it, the courts in one province should give full faith and credit, to use the language of the United States Constitution, to the judgments given by a court in another province or a territory, so long as that court has properly, or appropriately, exercised jurisdiction in the action. I referred earlier to the principles of order and fairness that should obtain in this area of the law. Both order and justice militate in favour of the security of transactions. It seems anarchic and unfair that a person should be able to avoid legal obligations arising in one province simply by moving to another province. Why should a plaintiff be compelled to begin an action in the province where the defendant now resides, whatever the inconvenience and costs this may bring, and whatever degree of connection the relevant transaction may have with another province? And why should the availability of local enforcement be the decisive element in the plaintiff's choice of forum?

These concerns, however, must be weighed against fairness to the defendant. I noted earlier that the taking of jurisdiction by a court in one province and its recognition in another must be viewed as correlatives, and I added that recognition in other provinces should be dependent on the fact that the court giving judgment 'properly' or 'appropriately' exercised jurisdiction. It may meet the demands of order and fairness to recognize a judgment given in a jurisdiction that had the greatest or at least significant contacts with the subject-matter of the action. But it hardly accords with principles of order and fairness to permit a person to sue another in any jurisdiction, without regard to the contacts that jurisdiction may have to the defendant or the subject-matter of the suit . . . Thus, fairness to the defendant requires that the judgment be issued by a court acting through fair process and with properly restrained jurisdiction.

As discussed, fair process is not an issue within the Canadian federation. The question that remains, then, is when has a court exercised its jurisdiction appropriately for the purposes of recognition by a court in another province? This poses no difficulty where the court has acted on the basis of some ground traditionally accepted by courts as permitting the recognition and enforcement of foreign judgments – in the case of judgments *in personam* where the defendant was within the jurisdiction at the time of the action or when he submitted to its judgment whether by agreement or attornment. In the first case, the court had jurisdiction over the person, and in the second case by virtue of the agreement. No injustice results.

The difficulty, of course, arises where, as here, the defendant was outside the jurisdiction of that court and he was served *ex juris*. To what extent may a court of a province properly exercise jurisdiction over a defendant in another province? The rules for service *ex juris* in all the provinces are broad, in some provinces, Nova Scotia and Prince Edward Island, very broad indeed. It is clear, however, that if the courts of one province are to be expected to give effect to judgments given in another province, there must be some limits to the exercise of jurisdiction against persons outside the province.

It will be obvious from the manner in which I approach the problem that I do not see the 'reciprocity approach' as providing an answer to the difficulty regarding *in personam* judgments given in other provinces, whatever utility it may have on the international plane . . .[1]

[La Forest J then discussed *Moran* v. *Pyle National (Canada) Ltd.*, a case set out above in Chapter 11, § 1.2. This case was not concerned with recognition of judgments but with jurisdiction in tort. However, he drew an important conclusion from this case:]

. . . I should observe that if this Court thinks it inherently reasonable for a court to exercise jurisdiction under circumstances like those described, it would be odd indeed if it did not also consider it reasonable for the courts of another province to recognize and enforce that court's judgment . . . If, as I stated, it is reasonable to support the exercise of jurisdiction in one province, it would seem equally reasonable that the judgment be recognized in other provinces. This is supported by the statement of Dickson J in *Zingre*, cited *supra*, that comity is based on the common interest of both the jurisdiction giving judgment and the recognizing jurisdiction. Indeed, it is in the interest of the whole country, an interest recognized in the Constitution itself.

---

1 *Editor's note*: the 'reciprocity approach' here means that a court should accord to other courts the same jurisdiction as it claims for itself. The British Columbia Court of Appeal had applied this principle in the *Morguard* case: it had held that it should recognize an Alberta judgment if the Alberta court took jurisdiction in circumstances in which, if the facts were transposed to British Columbia, the courts of British Columbia would have taken jurisdiction.

. . .

Turning to the present case, it is difficult to imagine a more reasonable place for the action for the deficiencies to take place than Alberta. As noted earlier, the properties were situate in Alberta, and the contracts were entered into there by parties then both resident in the province. Moreover, deficiency actions follow upon foreclosure proceedings, which should obviously take place in Alberta, and the action for the deficiencies cries out for consolidation with the foreclosure proceedings . . . A more 'real and substantial' connection between the damages suffered and the jurisdiction can scarcely be imagined. In my view, the Alberta court had jurisdiction, and its judgment should be recognized and be enforceable in British Columbia.

I am aware, of course, that the possibility of being sued outside the province of his residence may pose a problem for a defendant. But that can occur in relation to actions *in rem* now. In any event, this consideration must be weighed against the fact that the plaintiff under the English rules may often find himself subjected to the inconvenience of having to pursue his debtor to another province, however just, efficient or convenient it may be to pursue an action where the contract took place or the damage occurred. It seems to me that the approach of permitting suit where there is a real and substantial connection with the action provides a reasonable balance between the rights of the parties. It affords some protection against being pursued in jurisdictions having little or no connection with the transaction or the parties. In a world where even the most familiar things we buy and sell originate or are manufactured elsewhere, and where people are constantly moving from province to province, it is simply anachronistic to uphold a 'power theory' or a single *situs* for torts or contracts for the proper exercise of jurisdiction.

[La Forest J then considered whether the Canadian Constitution imposed limits on the power of courts to take jurisdiction over defendants in another province. He concluded:]

I must confess to finding this approach attractive, but as I noted earlier, the case was not argued in constitutional terms and it is unnecessary to pronounce definitively on the issue . . .

There are as well other discretionary techniques that have been used by courts for refusing to grant jurisdiction to plaintiffs whose contact with the jurisdiction is tenuous or where entertaining the proceedings would create injustice, notably the doctrine of *forum non conveniens* and the power of a court to prevent an abuse of its process . . .

There may also be remedies available to the recognizing court that may afford redress to the defendant in certain cases such as fraud or conflict with the law or public policy of the recognizing jurisdiction. Here, too, there may be room for the operation of s. 7 of the *Charter*.[2] None of these questions, however, are relevant to the facts of the present case and I have not given them consideration.

---

2 *Editor's note*: the Canadian Charter of Rights and Freedoms is a constitutionally protected charter of human rights. Article 7 is similar to the Due Process clause of the US Constitution. It reads: 'Everyone has the right to life, liberty and security of the person and the right not to be deprived thereof except in accordance with the principles of fundamental justice.' La Forest J had previously said that Article 7 might constitute a basis for a constitutionally mandated limit to jurisdiction, but he did not give a final ruling on the matter.

[La Forest J then dealt with the fact that reciprocal-enforcement legislation in British Columbia, which was applicable in the case, was based on the English principles of judgment recognition. He held that this did not affect the matter, since the legislation in question expressly said that it did not deprive a judgment-creditor of the right to enforce a judgment at common law.]

Result: appeal dismissed (Alberta judgment recognized).

Comment

This case lays down the rule that, for judgment-recognition purposes, a foreign court is to be regarded as having had jurisdiction if there is 'a real and substantial connection' with that court. It was not made clear what it is that must have a real and substantial connection with the territory of the court of origin: the judgment suggests that it is primarily the cause of action or claim,[2] but it has subsequently been settled that it may be either the cause of action (claim) or the defendant.[3]

It seems that the traditional rules of jurisdiction continue to apply; so that the new test will be of importance only where the defendant was served outside the territory of the forum.[4]

Although there were hints that there may be a constitutional element to the new rule, the court did not base it on that ground.[5] So it must be derived from a reinterpretation of the common law. The Supreme Court of Canada can do this because, unlike the Supreme Court of the United States, it can give judgments on the common law, even if the matter is within provincial jurisdiction.[6]

The basic argument in the judgment is that principles suitable for international application in nineteenth-century England are not suitable for inter-provincial application in modern Canada. There is no doubt that this is true: it would make sense, for the reasons given in the judgment, to have virtually automatic recognition and enforcement of judgments between different provinces. However, despite the fact that the *Morguard* case was expressly argued in inter-provincial terms and the judgment was expressly limited to such cases, the principle of the case has subsequently been extended to international cases.[7]

Here, the vagueness of the 'real and substantial connection' test can cause problems. The judgment gives almost no guidance on when the test will be satisfied. The result is that a Canadian defendant is in a difficult position

---

2 See (1990) 76 DLR (4th) 256 at p. 277, where it is said that the connection must be with the 'damages', and p. 278, where it is said, first, that it must be with 'the action' and, subsequently, with 'the transaction or the parties'.
3 *Beals* v. *Saldanha* (below) at paragraph 23.
4 See (1990) 76 DLR (4th) 256 at p. 274.
5 See *ibid.*, p. 272.
6 Although the court spoke in general terms of the recognition of judgments between different provinces, there is no specific mention of Quebec, the one civil-law province. One assumes that it will be fitted into the system in some way.
7 See *Beals* v. *Saldanha* (below).

when he is sued in a foreign country. He can almost never be sure whether the foreign court will be regarded as having jurisdiction in Canadian eyes; so he always has to defend. If he does defend, however, it will not matter whether the foreign court had jurisdiction or not: the judgment will be recognized in Canada under the 'submission' rule.[8] This means that, in practice, foreign judgments will always be recognized in Canada (at least as far as jurisdiction is concerned) unless there is no significant connection at all with the foreign court. In a world in which many courts are biased or corrupt, this might be regarded as going too far.

The subsequent decision of the Supreme Court of Canada in *Beals* v. *Saldanha*[9] is an example of the application of the *Morguard* principle at the international level. In this case, a number of Ontario residents were sued in Florida in a dispute over land they had sold to the plaintiffs for US$8,000. They did not defend, and a default judgment was given against them for US$210,000 compensatory damages plus US$50,000 punitive damages; post-judgment interest was set at 12 per cent per annum. Under Florida law, they could have applied to have the judgment set aside, or appealed against it. They took no action because an Ontario lawyer advised them that the judgment would not be enforced in Ontario. Since this happened a year after the decision of the Supreme Court of Canada in *Morguard*,[10] it is surprising they were given this advice. Perhaps the lawyer thought that the *Morguard* rule did not apply to judgments from outside Canada, something which, as we have seen, was justified by the terms of the judgment.[11]

Enforcement proceedings were brought in Ontario in 1993. By the time the case was heard in 1998, the damages had grown to C$800,000. The proceedings were dismissed on the ground that the judgment was obtained by fraud. This was reversed by the Ontario Court of Appeal, and the case then went to the Supreme Court of Canada. The Supreme Court of Canada confirmed that the 'real and substantial connection' test applies to judgments from outside Canada.[12] Since the test was clearly satisfied in the case, the only defences that could be raised were fraud and public policy.[13] They were dismissed;[14] so the defendants had to pay.[15] Many commentators thought that this was unfair.[16]

---

8 It was made clear in *Beals* v. *Saldanha* (below) that the 'submission' rule continues to apply under the new regime: see paragraph 34 of the *Beals* judgment.

9 [2003] 3 SCR 416 (Supreme Court of Canada).

10 The Supreme Court of Canada gave its judgment in *Morguard* on 20 December 1990; the defendants in the *Beals* case were informed of the Florida judgment in late December 1991.

11 However, it was widely thought at the time that the judgment might be extended to judgments from outside Canada. In *Beals*, the Supreme Court of Canada characterized the legal advice given to the defendants as 'negligent', presumably because the lawyer should have anticipated that the judgment would be extended. Whether this was reasonable is a matter on which opinions will differ.

12 However, this is subject to any relevant provincial legislation: paragraph 28 of the judgment.

13 The court said that the defences available are natural justice, public policy, fraud and *forum non conveniens*: paragraph 35 (see also paragraphs 39 *et seq.*). The defence of *forum non conveniens* does not apply in England.

14 It was argued that the amount of the award was grossly excessive and that its recognition would, therefore, be contrary to public policy. This was rejected by the majority: see paragraph 73.

15 It is possible that they could sue the lawyer who advised them not to appeal in Florida.

16 See, for example, Briggs, 'Crossing the River by Feeling the Stones: Rethinking the Law on Foreign Judgments' (2004) 8 *Singapore Yearbook of International Law* 1 at pp. 12 *et seq.*

§ 2   Enforcement of non-money judgments

As we saw in Chapter 15, § 1, above, English courts are not willing to enforce non-money judgments, such as injunctions and decrees for specific performance. In Canada, this principle was challenged in *Pro Swing Inc.* v. *Elta Golf Inc.*[17]

Canada
Pro Swing Inc.* v. *Elta Golf Inc.
Supreme Court of Canada
[2006] 2 SCR 612; (2006) 273 DLR (4th) 663

Background

Pro Swing, an American company, manufactured and sold custom-made golf clubs. Elta Golf, a company resident in Ontario, sold golf clubs on the Internet. Pro Swing sued Elta Golf in Ohio for infringement of its US trade marks. Elta Golf settled the case by giving various undertakings, which were incorporated into a consent judgment. It then broke the undertakings. Pro Swing brought further proceedings, and the Ohio court made a contempt order. In addition to awarding money damages, the Ohio court issued various injunctions – for example, that Elta Golf should surrender all infringing clubs in its possession, that it should give Pro Swing the names and addresses of the suppliers and purchasers of the infringing goods, and that it should account for all profits made from their sale. When Pro Swing tried to enforce these orders in Ontario, Elta Golf objected on the grounds that the orders were not final, that they were not money judgments, and that the contempt order was quasi-criminal.

The trial court enforced the consent decree and parts of the contempt order, which to some extent duplicated the consent decree. The Court of Appeal stated that it was inclined to agree that the time was ripe for a re-examination of the rules governing the enforcement of foreign non-monetary judgments;[18] nevertheless, it held that the orders were not sufficiently certain in their terms to be enforced. Pro Swing appealed to the Supreme Court of Canada.

The seven-judge panel in the Supreme Court of Canada split four–three. The majority were in favour of a change in the law but unwilling to make it in that particular case. The minority (McLachlin CJ, Bastarache and Charron JJ) were in favour of restoring the judgment of the trial court. The issues which concerned the majority were, first, that a radical widening of the kinds of judgments subject to enforcement might require a rethinking of the defences available;[19] secondly, that the contempt order had a criminal element that, as a matter of principle,

---

17 [2006] 2 SCR 612; (2006) 273 DLR (4th) 663 (Supreme Court of Canada).
18 (2004) 71 OR (3d) 566, at paragraph 9.
19 The court quoted Briggs, 'Crossing the River by Feeling the Stones: Rethinking the Law on Foreign Judgments' (2004) 8 *Singapore Yearbook of International Law* 1 at p. 22: 'It cannot be right to make radical changes to [jurisdiction] while supposing that this has no impact on the [defences] . . . [I]ncremental, intuitive, coherent, development is what common law does best, and is how the common law conflict of laws works best.'

precluded its enforcement in Canada;[20] thirdly, that the policing of such orders could be burdensome on the judiciary in Canada;[21] and, finally, that it would be difficult for the Canadian courts to interpret the precise meaning and scope of the American orders because of their lack of familiarity with American law.

The flavour of the judgment is conveyed by the following short extracts, taken from the beginning and end.

Deschamps J (delivering her judgment and that of LeBel, Fish and Abella JJ):

1.   Modern-day commercial transactions require prompt reactions and effective remedies. The advent of the Internet has heightened the need for appropriate tools. On the one hand, frontiers remain relevant to national identity and jurisdiction, but on the other hand, the globalization of commerce and mobility of both people and assets make them less so. The law and the justice system are servants of society, not the reverse. The Court has been asked to change the common law. The case for adapting the common law rule that prevents the enforcement of foreign non-money judgments is compelling. But such changes must be made cautiously. Although I recognize the need for a new rule, it is my view that this case is not the right one for implementing it.

     . . .

G. Summary

62. In summary, the orders are problematic from many points of view. The contempt order is quasi-criminal in nature and the intended territorial scope of the injunctive relief in the consent order is uncertain. Moreover, it is unclear that recognition and enforcement of the judgment is the appropriate tool amongst the various judicial assistance mechanisms or that the matter is an appropriate one for lending judicial assistance in the form requested. Additional concerns relating to the potential violation of privacy rights should also be addressed.

63. The list of problems is long, too long to use the courts' equitable jurisdiction to accommodate Pro Swing . . . To refuse to enforce the orders is an appropriate exercise of equitable discretion and amounts to allowing the Ohio court to continue the proceedings with the judicial assistance of the Ontario courts, but to a lesser extent than has been requested.

VII. Conclusion

64. Private international law is developing in response to modern realities. The real and substantial connection test and the enforcement of equitable relief granted in foreign countries are but two examples of its evolution. The Internet puts additional pressure on the courts to reach out to the same

---

20 The minority considered that the contempt order could be enforced because it was for civil contempt, not criminal contempt, but the majority took the view that, in Canada, all forms of contempt were regarded as having at least a quasi-criminal nature.
21 The majority considered that a better way for Pro Swing to obtain the names and addresses would have been by means of letters rogatory addressed to the Canadian court (discussed in Chapter 21, below),

> extent as the Web. At the same time, courts must be cautious to preserve their nation's values and protect its people. The time is ripe to change the common law rule against the enforcement of foreign non-monetary judgments, but, owing to problems with the orders the appellant seeks to have enforced, the Court cannot accede to its request.

Result: the appeal was dismissed (US judgment not enforced)

§ 3 Conclusions

The adoption in *Morguard* of a flexible test for foreign-court jurisdiction puts Canadian law on a different footing, not only from English law, but also from that of Continental Europe. As we shall see in the next chapter, however, a similar approach has been applied in at least some states in the United States. Whether the resulting uncertainty is justified will remain a matter of debate: a more generous approach to the recognition of foreign judgments is admirable, but this should be done through clear rules so that defendants know where they stand.

The Supreme Court's willingness to move towards the enforcement of non-money judgments, on the other hand, brings Canada closer to the EC system where, as we saw in Chapter 14, § 2, above, non-money judgments such as injunctions and orders for specific performance are also covered. The problems raised in *Pro Swing* will, therefore, have to be tackled by the English courts in this context, even if they do not expand the common law.

Further reading

Black, 'Canada and the US Contemplate Changes to Foreign-Judgment Enforcement'
    (2007) 3 *Journal of Private International Law* 1
Briggs, 'Crossing the River by Feeling the Stones: Rethinking the Law on Foreign
    Judgments' (2004) 8 *Singapore Yearbook of International Law* 1
Pitel, 'A Modern Approach to Enforcing Foreign Judgments' [2004] LMCLQ 288
    'Enforcement of Foreign Non-Money Judgments in Canada (and Beyond)' (2007) 3
    Journal of Private International Law 241

CHAPTER 18

US law: some highlights

This chapter does not give full coverage of US law on the recognition and enforcement of judgments: it merely picks out certain highlights that will be of interest to lawyers in other countries.

§ 1 Reciprocity

In 1895, the Supreme Court of the United States decided *Hilton* v. *Guyot*,[1] a case on the recognition of a French judgment. Although it applied general common-law principles, it held that reciprocity was a requirement. At the time, American judgments could be reviewed on the merits in France (*révision au fond*); so the Supreme Court said that French judgments would not be given conclusive effect in the United States.

In *Hilton*, the federal courts had jurisdiction on diversity grounds. Some forty years after it was decided, the Supreme Court held that federal courts sitting in diversity must apply the law, including the conflict of laws, of the state in which they are sitting.[2] Since *Hilton*, most federal courts have held that, in the absence of a federal statute, a treaty or some other basis – for example, Admiralty – for federal jurisdiction, recognition of foreign-country judgments is a matter for state law.[3] Most state courts have taken the view that *Hilton* is not binding on them.[4] Reciprocity has been generally rejected by both state and federal courts.[5]

§ 2 Uniform legislation

In 1962, the National Conference of Commissioners of Uniform State Laws adopted the Uniform Foreign Money-Judgments Recognition Act.[6] The National Conference is a body of state-appointed officials who promote uniform laws among the

---

1 159 US 113; 16 S Ct 139; 40 L Ed 95.
2 *Erie Railroad Co.* v. *Tomkins*, 304 US 64; 58 S Ct 817; 82 L Ed 1188 (1938); *Klaxon Co.* v. *Stentor Electric Mfg Co.*, 313 US 487; 61 S Ct 1020; 85 L Ed 1477 (1941).
3 See, for example, *British Midland Airways Ltd* v. *International Travel Inc.*, 497 F 2d 869 (9th Cir. 1974).
4 See, for example, *Johnston* v. *Compagnie Générale Transatlantique*, 242 NY 381; 152 NE 121 (1926).
5 See *Johnston* v. *Compagnie Générale Transatlantique*, 242 NY 381; 152 NE 121 (1926); *Falcon Manufacturing (Scarborough) Ltd* v. *Ames*, 53 Misc 2d 332; 278 NYS 2d 684 (Civ. Ct NY 1967); *Somportex Ltd* v. *Philadelphia Chewing Gum Corporation*, 453 F 2d 435 (3rd Cir. 1971); cert. denied 405 US 1017; 92 S Ct 1294; 31 L Ed 2d 479 (1972); *Toronto-Dominion Bank* v. *Hall*, 367 F Supp 1009 (ED Ark., 1973); *Bank of Montreal* v. *Kough*, 612 F 2d 467 (9th Cir. 1980); *Chabert* v. *Bacquie*, 694 So 2d 805 (Fla Ct App. 1997).
6 For the text, see the website of the National Conference, www.nccusl.org.

states.[7] Their decisions are not binding on the states, which are free to decide whether or not to accept their recommendations. Uniform legislation has to be enacted by the state legislatures just like any other law. Moreover, the states often make small alterations when they adopt a text: uniform Acts are not always entirely uniform. Thus, while the Uniform Act does not require reciprocity and this has been accepted by most states, a few have added a reciprocity requirement.[8] More than half the states, including the most important ones,[9] have adopted the Act.

In 2005, the National Conference adopted an updated version of the Act, called the Uniform Foreign-Country Money Judgments Recognition Act.[10] This did not involve any major policy changes, but was simply a tidying up of the 1962 Act.[11] At the time of writing, it has already been adopted by five states[12] and it will probably be adopted by others by the time this book is published. The appendix to this chapter sets out the corresponding provisions of the two UK Acts and the two US Acts.

The Acts were based on the 1933 British Act and are similar to it in many ways. However, there is one important difference: while the 1933 Act applies only to judgments from countries specified in an Order in Council, the US Acts apply to judgments from all foreign countries.[13] The latter are therefore much more significant than the 1933 Act.

The rules for determining the jurisdiction of a foreign court are laid down in section 5 of the Uniform Acts (the 2005 version is set out in Panel 18.1[14]). The most

---

Panel 18.1 Foreign-court jurisdiction
Uniform Foreign-Country Money Judgments Recognition Act, section 5

Section 5 Personal jurisdiction

(a)   A foreign-country judgment may not be refused recognition for lack of personal jurisdiction if:

(1) the defendant was served with process personally in the foreign country;

(2) the defendant voluntarily appeared in the proceeding, other than for the purpose of protecting property seized or threatened with seizure in the proceeding or of contesting the jurisdiction of the court over the defendant;

(3) the defendant, before the commencement of the proceeding, had agreed to submit to the jurisdiction of the foreign court with respect to the subject matter involved;

(4) the defendant was domiciled in the foreign country when the proceeding was instituted or was a corporation or other form of business organization that had its principal place of business in, or was organized under the laws of, the foreign country;

(5) the defendant had a business office in the foreign country and the proceeding in the foreign court involved a [cause of action] [claim for relief] arising out of business done by the defendant through that office in the foreign country; or

(6) the defendant operated a motor vehicle or airplane in the foreign country and the proceeding involved a [cause of action] [claim for relief] arising out of that operation.

(b)   The list of bases for personal jurisdiction in subsection (a) is not exclusive. The courts of this state may recognize bases of personal jurisdiction other than those listed in subsection (a) as sufficient to support a foreign-country judgment.

---

7 Their website is www.nccusl.org.

8 For example, Texas and Colorado.

9 For example, California, Florida, Illinois, Michigan, New York, Ohio, Pennsylvania and Texas.

10 For the text, see the website of the National Conference, www.nccusl.org.

11 One change worth mentioning is that it expressly restricts the fraud exception to 'fraud that deprived the losing party of an adequate opportunity to present its case' (§ 4(c)(2)). The 1962 Act referred simply to 'fraud', without being more specific.

12 California, Colorado, Idaho, Michigan and Nevada.

13 It does not entirely replace the common law, however, because it permits foreign judgments to be recognized on other grounds: see 1962 Act, § 7; 2005 Act, § 11.

14 The differences between it and the 1962 Act are only minor.

important differences compared with the 1933 UK Act are, first, that the Uniform Acts accept one specific instance of 'cause-of-action' jurisdiction, namely, actions arising out of the operation of a motor vehicle or aircraft;[15] and, secondly, that other bases of jurisdiction may be recognized.[16] This latter provision has been used by courts in some states to accept *any* ground of jurisdiction consistent with the 'minimum-contacts' doctrine of the US Constitution. Our next case is an example.

United States (California)
Bank of Montreal v. *Kough*
US Court of Appeals for the Ninth Circuit
612 F 2d 467 (1980)

Background

Kough, a California resident, was a minority shareholder in a British Columbia corporation. The corporation borrowed money from the Bank of Montreal, a Canadian bank, and Kough guaranteed the loan. The contract of guarantee was executed in British Columbia. When the corporation defaulted, the bank sued Kough on the guarantee in British Columbia. The writ was served on him at his home in California. He did not appear, and a default judgment was given against him. The bank sought to enforce it in California.

Bartels, District Judge:[1]

Recognition and enforcement of the British Columbia judgment in this case depends upon the proper construction of the Uniform Foreign Money Judgments Recognition Act[17] (the 'Uniform Act' or the 'Act'), adopted by California as California Code of Civil Procedure ('CCP') §§ 1713 *et seq.* According to the provisions of that Act, unless one of the grounds for non-recognition listed in § 1713.4 is present, a foreign judgment which is final where rendered is conclusive between the parties to the extent that it grants a recovery of a sum of money, and is enforceable in the same manner as the judgment of a sister state, if that judgment is entitled to full faith and credit. One of the grounds for non-recognition listed in § 1713.4, and the only one in issue here, is the lack of personal jurisdiction over the defendant in the foreign forum. But subsection (a) of § 1713.5 lists six bases of personal jurisdiction over the defendant which will suffice for purposes of recognition of the foreign judgment in California. None of these provisions specifically addresses the situation in this case, in which personal jurisdiction over the defendant in the foreign forum was premised upon what we refer to as long-arm jurisdiction principles. A catch-all provision is provided, however, in subsection (b) of § 1713.5, which reads: 'The courts of this state may recognize *other* bases of jurisdiction.' (Emphasis supplied.)[18] It was on this latter provision that the district court relied in extending recognition to the foreign judgment against Kough, thus deciding an issue that had not heretofore been presented to a California court.

1 Sitting by designation.

---

15 See 1962 Act, § 5(a)(6); 2005 Act, § 5(a)(6).
16 See 1962 Act, § 5(b); 2005 Act, § 5(b).
17 *Editor's note*: this was the 1962 Uniform Act.
18 *Editor's note*: this was the California version of § 5(b) of the 1962 Uniform Act.

The district court held that, in the absence of any of the other grounds for non-recognition listed in § 1713.4, the British Columbia judgment would be recognized pursuant to the 'other bases of jurisdiction' category set forth in § 1713.5(b) as long as American due process standards were not offended by the Canadian court's assertion of personal jurisdiction over Kough. The issues raised on this appeal, therefore, are: first, whether the British Columbia court's assertion of jurisdiction over Kough was in fact consistent with due process; and second, whether compliance with American due process standards is the only criterion in this case for recognition of the foreign judgment under the 'other bases of jurisdiction' category of § 1713.5(b).

Due process

The Supreme Court has repeatedly recognized that a constitutionally valid judgment which is entitled to full faith and credit in sister states may be entered by a state court as long as there is 'a sufficient connection between the defendant and the forum state as to make it fair to require defense of the action in the forum', and provided that the defendant has received 'reasonable notice' of the proceedings against him . . .

This appeal involves the recognition by California of the judgment of a Canadian province, not that of a sister state, but the language of § 1713.5(b), authorizing recognition of foreign judgments predicated upon 'other bases of jurisdiction', seems to us intended to leave the door open for the recognition by California courts of foreign judgments rendered in accordance with American principles of jurisdictional due process.[2]

With respect to both minimum contacts with the forum state and adequate notice, those principles were satisfied in this case. Kough did have substantial contacts with British Columbia not only by means of the execution and breach of the guarantee there, but also by prior negotiations there involving the guarantee and by other promissory notes to the Bank previously executed. Since Kough was served at his California residence, no question can be seriously raised as to the adequacy of the personal service . . .

We find no merit in Kough's contention that the district court should have conducted an evidentiary hearing on the nature of his contacts with British Columbia before ruling that the provincial court had personal jurisdiction over him, because the facts are undisputed, and his real objection is to the application of the law to those facts.

2 'In codifying what bases for assumption of personal jurisdiction will be recognized, which is an area of the law still in evolution, the Act adopts the policy of listing bases accepted generally today and preserving for the courts the right to recognize still other bases . . .'. 13 Uniform Laws Annotated 269 (1975) (Commissioner's Prefatory Note). In asserting jurisdiction over Kough, the British Columbia court apparently relied on Order XI, Rule 1(e), of its Supreme Court Rules, which provides: '1. Service out of the jurisdiction of a writ of summons or notice of a writ of summons may be allowed by the Court or a Judge whenever: . . . (e) The action is in respect of a breach committed within the jurisdiction of a *contract wherever made*, even though such breach was preceded or accompanied by a breach out of the jurisdiction which rendered impossible the performance which ought to have been performed within the jurisdiction' (emphasis supplied). If the British Columbia judgment had been obtained after jurisdiction over Kough was secured on the basis of the mere breach of a 'contract wherever made', without more, it might be founded upon too tenuous a contact, by American standards of due process. However, we need not reach this issue because Kough did have substantial contacts with the province.

Reciprocity

Kough also invokes the doctrine of reciprocity to defeat the recognition of the Canadian judgment. He predicates this argument upon his contention that British Columbia would refuse to recognize a default judgment rendered against one of its citizens in the United States under similar circumstances . . .

The difficulty with appellant's argument is that the section of the Uniform Act specifically dealing with the circumstances where recognition should or may be denied . . . makes no mention of reciprocity, and we find nothing in the Act which authorizes us to read such a prerequisite into the statutory scheme by implication.

Indeed, Professor Willis Reese of Columbia Law School and Professor Kurt Nadelmann of Harvard Law School, the draftsmen of the Uniform Act . . . consciously rejected reciprocity as a factor to be considered in recognition of foreign money judgments, apparently on the ground that the due process concepts embodied in the Act were an adequate safeguard for the rights of citizens sued on judgments obtained abroad. Transcript, 'Proceedings in Committee of the Whole, Uniform Recognition of Foreign-Money Judgments Act', August 5, 1961, at 8–9.[3]

The parties have not cited, and our research has not disclosed any California cases citing reciprocity as a criterion for the recognition of foreign judgments. But it is to be noted that in diversity cases, as to a matter of local law that has not been decided by the highest state court, the opinion of the district judge, as a member of the state bar, will be given great weight . . . and will not be overruled unless 'clearly wrong. 'The district judge found no basis in the Act for barring recognition of the Canadian judgment for lack of reciprocity, and we agree.

. . .

The decision of the district court is in all respects AFFIRMED.

3 Professor Kurt Nadelmann of Harvard Law School, in introducing the Uniform Foreign Money Judgments Recognition Act to the Uniform Law Commissioners, contrasted it with a British statute dealing with recognition of foreign judgments: 'The British Act does not include a due process requirement. Our draft does. I think it would seem obvious that no legislation should be enacted without a due process requirement. The British Act does not contain it because the British Act has a reciprocity clause. The British tried to pick their own partners and they just won't . . . certify the existence of reciprocity if they do not like their partner. These are different approaches, different possibilities. The two draftsmen believe that our draft is sounder.'

Result: the Canadian judgment was enforced.

Comment

Together with Canada, the states where this rule applies must in this respect be the most internationalist in the world.

Two other features of the Uniform Acts are, first, that they do not apply if the foreign court was a *forum non conveniens*;[19] and, secondly, that they do not apply unless the country of origin had a judicial system providing impartial tribunals.[20] The former rule is found in Canada, but not in England. The latter rule could prevent the recognition of judgments from countries that the US Government regards as politically objectionable. Thus, the system of justice in Iran was held

19 See 1962 Act, § 4(b)(6); 2005 Act, § 5(b)(6).
20 See 1962 Act, § 4(a)(1); 2005 Act, § 4(b)(1).

acceptable before the Revolution,[21] but unacceptable after it.[22] Moreover, US courts have also refused, on grounds of *forum non conveniens*, to allow actions to be brought in American courts against the family of the former Shah with regard to claims arising from their activities in Iran before the Revolution.[23] Put together, these policies have made the Pahlavi family virtually judgment-proof in the case of such claims.

Appendix: foreign-judgment recognition legislation (UK and US)

Major heads of jurisdiction of the foreign court

	UK 1920	UK 1933	US 1962	US 2005
Individual defendant: service within the foreign country	–	–	5(a)(1)	5(a)(1)
Individual defendant: residence/domicile	9(2)(b)	4(2)(a)(iv)	5(a)(4)	5(a)(4)
Company: principal place of business	9(2)(b)[27]	4(2)(a)(iv)	5(a)(4)	5(a)(4)
Company: incorporation	–	–	5(a)(4)	5(a)(4)
Place of business: proceedings arise out of it	9(2)(b)[28]	4(2)(a)(v)	5(a)(5)	5(a)(5)
Voluntary appearance: contest on merits	9(2)(b)	4(2)(a)(i)	5(a)(2)	5(a)(2)
Choice-of-court agreement	9(2)(b)	4(2)(a)(iii)	5(a)(3)	5(a)(3)

Other requirements and defences

	UK 1920	UK 1933	US 1962	US 2005
Final and conclusive	–	1(2)(a)[29]	2	3(a)(2)
Only money-judgments enforced	12(1)	1(2)(b)[30]	1(2), 3	3(a)(1)
Sufficient notice of proceedings	9(2)(c)	4(1)(a)(iii)	4(b)(1)	4(c)(1)
Fraud	9(2)(d)	4(1)(a)(iv)	4(b)(2)	4(c)(2)
Public policy	9(2)(f)	4(1)(a)(v)	4(b)(3)	4(c)(3)
Contrary to choice-of-court or arbitration agreement	CJJA[31] 32	CJJA[32] 32	4(b)(5)	4(c)(5)
Tax or penalty	–	1(2)(b)[33]	1(2)	3(b)(1), 3(b)(2)
Conflicting judgment	–	4(1)(b)	4(b)(4)	4(c)(4)

---

21 *Cooley* v. *Weinberger*, 518 F 2d 1151 (10th Cir. 1975).
22 *Bank Melli Iran* v. *Pahlavi*, 58 F 3d 1406 (9th Cir. 1995).
23 See *Islamic Republic of Iran* v. *Pahlavi*, 62 NY 2d 474; 478 NYS 2d 597 (Court of Appeals, NY, 1984).
27 Under the 1920 Act, any place of business is sufficient: it does not have to be the principal place of business.
28 Under the 1920 Act, carrying on business applies even if the cause of action did not arise out of the business in question.
29 As amended.
30 As amended.
31 Civil Jurisdiction and Judgments Act 1982.
32 Civil Jurisdiction and Judgments Act 1982.
33 As amended.

Further reading

Casad, 'Issue Preclusion and Foreign Country Judgments: Whose Law?' (1984) 70 *Iowa Law Review* 53

Juenger, 'The Recognition of Money Judgments' (1988) 36 *American Journal of Comparative Law* 1

Reese, 'The Status in This Country of Judgments Rendered Abroad' (1950) 50 *Columbia Law Review* 783

Smit, 'International Res Judicata and Collateral Estoppel' (1962) 9 *UCLA Law Review* 44

Von Mehren (Arthur), 'Recognition and Enforcement of Foreign Judgments' (1981) 167 *Recueil des Cours* 9

  'Recognition and Enforcement of Sister State Judgments: Reflections on General Theory and Current Practice in the EEC and the US' (1981) 81 *Columbia Law Review* 1044

Von Mehren (Arthur) and Trautman, 'Recognition of Foreign Adjudications: A Survey and a Suggested Approach' (1968) 81 *Harvard Law Review* 601

Von Mehren (Robert) and Patterson, 'Recognition and Enforcement of Foreign-Country Judgments in the United States' (1974) 6 *Law and Policy in International Business* 37

PART IV
PROCEDURE

CHAPTER 19

Freezing assets

§ 1 Introduction

If you decide to sue an internationally based defendant, an immediate problem arises: how can you stop him taking his property out of the country and thus making it impossible to satisfy the judgment? The answer is to obtain a court order freezing his assets. This has to be done *ex parte*, before service of the claim form; otherwise, he will have time to defeat the order. Such orders have been obtainable in most countries for many years. In England, they were not possible until 1975.[1] In that year, however, the Court of Appeal allowed asset-freezing orders under section 45 of the Supreme Court of Judicature (Consolidation) Act 1925. This occurred in two cases, *Nippon Yusen Kaisha* v. *Karageorgis*[2] and *Mareva Compania Naviera SA* v. *International Bulkcarriers SA*.[3] The orders were originally called '*Mareva* injunctions', after the name of the second of these two cases. Today, they are known as 'freezing orders' in England,[4] though they are still called '*Mareva* injunctions' in Commonwealth countries.

Originally, the order could be granted only if the defendant was out of the country, but this rule was first modified, and then dropped, by the courts. This was confirmed by section 37(3) of the Supreme Court Act 1981 (Panel 19.1), which also makes clear that the order not only prohibits the removal of assets from the jurisdiction, but also forbids dealing with them within the jurisdiction in any way that prevents the creditor from satisfying the judgment.[5]

It is important to understand the nature of an English freezing order. In some countries, you attach specific assets and obtain an order that operates *in rem* with regard to them. This is not how an English freezing order

> **Panel 19.1 Power to grant injunctions**
> **Supreme Court Act 1981, section 37**
>
> **Section 37**
> (1) The High Court may by order (whether interlocutory or final) grant an injunction or appoint a receiver in all cases in which it appears to the court to be just and convenient to do so.
> (2) Any such order may be made either unconditionally or on such terms and conditions as the court thinks just.
> (3) The power of the High Court under subsection (1) to grant an interlocutory injunction restraining a party to any proceedings from removing from the jurisdiction of the High Court, or otherwise dealing with, assets located within that jurisdiction shall be exercisable in cases where that party is, as well as in cases where he is not, domiciled, resident or present within that jurisdiction . . .

---

1 See *Lister & Co.* v. *Stubbs* (1890) LR 45 Ch D 1 (CA), where it was held that, in general, the court has no power to make a defendant give security before judgment.
2 [1975] 1 WLR 1093.
3 [1980] 1 All ER 213; [1975] 2 Lloyd's Rep 509.
4 The change took place in 1999 when the CPR came into force.
5 *Z Ltd* v. *A-Z* [1982] 2 WLR 288 at p. 571, *per* Lord Denning (CA).

works. It operates *in personam*[6] and requires the person against whom it is made not to deal with his assets so as to defeat judgment-creditors. The person who obtains the order gets no special rights over the defendant's assets: he has no priority over other creditors.[7]

As we shall see, a third party who knowingly assists in the breach of a freezing order is guilty of contempt, even if the order has not yet been served on the defendant and the latter is unaware of it. This is not because the order is binding on the third party, but because he is interfering in the administration of justice by causing the court's order to be thwarted. On the other hand, a third party – or the defendant himself – is not guilty of contempt if he has no knowledge of the order.

Since the order is directed against the person concerned, not against the property, its enforcement involves taking proceedings for contempt of court against the person who has breached it. The normal penalties for contempt of court are a fine, sequestration of assets and imprisonment. These are effective only if the defendant is within the jurisdiction or he has assets there. Another penalty that has often been applied is that, if the person concerned is a party to proceedings before the court, he will be precluded from defending the case (if he is the defendant) or bringing it (if he is the claimant). However, this latter remedy might be a violation of his human rights as laid down by Article 6 of the European Convention on Human Rights.[8]

§ 2   Procedure

The procedure was explained by Lord Denning with characteristic lucidity in our next case.

England
Third Chandris Shipping Corporation* v. *Unimarine SA
Court of Appeal
[1979] 3 WLR 122

Lord Denning MR

The law

It is just four years ago now since we introduced here the procedure known as *Mareva* injunctions. All the other legal systems of the world have a similar procedure. It is called in the civil law *saisie conservatoire*. It has been welcomed in

---

6 The statement by Lord Denning in *Z Ltd* v. *A–Z* (above) that they operate *in rem* is now regarded as incorrect: in *Attorney General* v. *Times Newspapers Ltd* [1992] 1 AC 191 at p. 215 Lord Ackner said that this statement was made *per incuriam*; see also *Cretanor Maritime Co. Ltd* v. *Irish Marine Management Ltd* [1978] 1 WLR 966 at pp. 976–7, *per* Buckley LJ (CA).
7 Consequently, a freezing order will normally be varied to permit a defendant to pay debts incurred in the ordinary course of business.
8 On this, see Chapter 14, § 5, above. See also *Gambazzi* v. *Daimler Chrysler Canada*, Case C-394/07 (ECJ) (not decided at the time of writing).

the City of London and has proved extremely beneficial. It enables a creditor in a proper case to stop his debtor from parting with his assets pending trial.

. . .

In the *Siskina* case [1979] AC 210 the House [of Lords] placed this restriction upon the procedure. It applies only in the case of an 'interlocutory order.' In order to obtain a *Mareva* injunction there has to be in existence a substantive cause of action on which the plaintiff is suing or about to sue in the High Court in England or is enforcing or about to enforce by arbitration in England . . . [1]

The guidelines

Much as I am in favour of the *Mareva* injunction, it must not be stretched too far lest it be endangered. In endeavouring to set out some guidelines, I have had recourse to the practice of many other countries which have been put before us. They have been most helpful. These are the points which those who apply for it should bear in mind:

(i) The plaintiff should make full and frank disclosure of all matters in his knowledge which are material for the judge to know . . .

(ii) The plaintiff should give particulars of his claim against the defendant, stating the ground of his claim and the amount thereof, and fairly stating the points made against it by the defendant.

(iii) The plaintiff should give some grounds for believing that the defendant has assets here . . . [2] In most cases the plaintiff will not know the extent of the assets. He will only have indications of them. The existence of a bank account in England is enough, whether it is in overdraft or not.

(iv) The plaintiff should give some grounds for believing that there is a risk of the assets being removed before the judgment or award is satisfied. The mere fact that the defendant is abroad is not by itself sufficient. No one would wish any reputable foreign company to be plagued with a *Mareva* injunction simply because it has agreed to London arbitration. But there are some foreign companies whose structure invites comment. We often see in this court a corporation which is registered in a country where the company law is so loose that nothing is known about it – where it does no work and has no officers and no assets. Nothing can be found out about the membership, or its control, or its assets, or the charges on them. Judgment cannot be enforced against it. There is no reciprocal enforcement of judgments. It is nothing more than a name grasped from the air, as elusive as the Cheshire Cat. In such cases the very fact of incorporation there gives some ground for believing there is a risk that, if judgment or an award is obtained, it may go unsatisfied. Such registration of such companies may carry many advantages to the individuals who control them, but

---

1 *Editor's note*: today, it is also possible to obtain an order if the proceedings are pending, or about to be brought, in a foreign country: see § 4, below.
2 *Editor's note*: this requirement is no longer necessary in all cases. With the advent of the worldwide freezing order (discussed in § 5, below) it has become possible to obtain an order even if the defendant has no assets in the jurisdiction.

they may suffer the disadvantage of having a *Mareva* injunction granted against them. The giving of security for a debt is a small price to pay for the convenience of such a registration. Security would certainly be required in New York. So also it may be in London. Other grounds may be shown for believing there is a risk. But some such should be shown.

(v)   The plaintiff must, of course, give an undertaking in damages – in case he fails in his claim or the injunction turns out to be unjustified. In a suitable case this should be supported by a bond or security: and the injunction only granted on it being given, or undertaken to be given.

In setting out those guidelines, I hope we shall do nothing to reduce the efficacy of the present practice. In it speed is of the essence. *Ex parte* is of the essence. If there is delay, or if advance warning is given, the assets may well be removed before the injunction can bite . . .

§ 3   Third parties

The position of third parties is explained by Lord Denning in our next case.

England
Z Ltd v. *A-Z*
Court of Appeal
[1982] 2 WLR 288

Lord Denning MR

Hitherto the cases and the statutes have been concerned primarily with the injunction against the defendant. Now we have to consider the position of the banks or other innocent third parties who hold the assets.

The nature of the problem

To show the nature of the problem I will take the type of case which first came before the courts. A shipowner is owed £10,000 by a foreign company. He knows that that company has an account at a London bank. He is fearful that the foreign company will remove its money and not pay him. He issues a writ against the foreign company claiming the money, but he cannot serve it because it is out of the jurisdiction and it will take a long time. He goes to the court and gets a *Mareva* injunction against the foreign company restraining it from disposing of its assets. He notifies the bank. The bank, on receiving that notification, freezes the foreign company's bank account. It remains frozen until the foreign company pays up – or the action is tried.

What is the justification of the bank for freezing the bank account? The bank is not a party to the action. No order has been made by the court upon the bank . . . No authority was given by the customer for his account to be frozen. What right has the bank to freeze it? On what principle is the bank justified in freezing their customer's bank account?

A simple type of case

Take a case where the *Mareva* injunction is served on the defendant restraining him from disposing of his assets in his account at a named bank. The plaintiff notifies the bank of the injunction. But the defendant, then in breach of the injunction, draws a cheque in favour of a tradesman. The defendant is clearly guilty of a contempt of court. If the bank should honour the cheque, it would be guilty of aiding and abetting the contempt of the defendant . . .

A usual type of case

Next take a case – a very usual case – where the *Mareva* injunction is not served on the defendant at the outset. He may be out of the jurisdiction or away from home, or simply not available. So the plaintiff simply gives notice to the bank of the injunction. Sometimes the plaintiff deliberately delays serving the defendant: because the defendant, on being served himself, would whisk the money away before the bank had notice of it. In such cases the defendant, not having been served, is not guilty of a contempt himself. So the bank cannot be guilty of aiding and abetting.

What then is the principle? It seems to me to be this. As soon as the judge makes his order for a *Mareva* injunction restraining the defendant from disposing of his assets, the order takes effect at the very moment that it is pronounced . . . Even though the order has not then been drawn up – even though it has not then been served on the defendant – it has immediate effect on every asset of the defendant covered by the injunction. Every person who has knowledge of it must do what he reasonably can to preserve the asset. He must not assist in any way in the disposal of it. Otherwise he is guilty of a contempt of court.

Operation in rem

The reason is because a *Mareva* injunction is a method of attaching the asset itself. It operates *in rem* just as the arrest of a ship does . . . [1]

Arrest of a bank account

So also here, once a bank is given notice of a *Mareva* injunction affecting goods or money in its hands, it must not dispose of them itself, nor allow the defendant or anyone else to do so – except by the authority of the court. If the bank or any of its officers should knowingly assist in the disposal of them, it will be guilty of a contempt of court. For it is an act calculated to obstruct the course of justice . . .

The bank's defence

You may ask: Suppose the defendant sued the bank for dishonouring a cheque, what would be the answer of the bank? In my opinion the *Mareva* injunction makes it unlawful for the bank to honour the cheque . . . Alternatively, it can be said that the customer has only authorised the bank to do what it is lawful for the bank to do – and not that which is unlawful – so that any prior mandate from the

---

1 *Editor's note*: as pointed out above, it is now accepted that Lord Denning was wrong in saying that a *Mareva* injunction operates *in rem*: it operates only *in personam*.

customer is automatically annulled when the bank receives notice of the *Mareva* injunction . . .

The juristic principle

The juristic principle is therefore this: As soon as the bank is given notice of the *Mareva* injunction, it must freeze the defendant's bank account. It must not allow any drawings to be made on it, neither by cheques drawn before the injunction nor by those drawn after it. The reason is because, if it allowed any such drawings, it would be obstructing the course of justice – as prescribed by the court which granted the injunction – and it would be guilty of a contempt of court.

I have confined my observations to banks and bank accounts. But the same applies to any specific asset held by a bank for safe custody on behalf of the defendant. Be it jewellery, stamps, or anything else, and to any other person who holds any other asset of the defendant. If the asset is covered by the terms of the *Mareva* injunction, that other person must not hand it over to the defendant or do anything to enable him to dispose of it. He must hold it pending further order.

The injunction does not prevent payment under a letter of credit or under a bank guarantee . . . but it may apply to the proceeds as and when received by or for the defendant. It does not apply to a credit card. The bank must honour all credit cards issued to the defendant and used by him, except when they have been used fraudulently or wrongly. It can debit the amount against the customer's account.

The things which follow

Such being the juristic principle, some things necessarily follow in justice to the bank or other innocent third party who is given notice of the *Mareva* injunction or knows of it.

(1) Indemnity

In so far as the bank, or other innocent third party, is asked to take any action – or the circumstances require him to take any action – and he is put to expense on that account, he is entitled to be recouped by the plaintiff: and in so far as he is exposed to any liability, he is entitled to be indemnified by the plaintiff. This is because when the plaintiff gives notice of the injunction to the bank or innocent third party, he impliedly requests them to freeze the account or otherwise do whatever is necessary or reasonable to secure the observance of the injunction. This implied request gives rise to an implied promise to recoup any expense and to indemnify against any liability . . . In addition, in support of this implied promise, so as to ease the mind of the third party, the judge, when he grants the injunction, may require the plaintiff to give an undertaking in such terms as to secure that the bank or other innocent third party does not suffer in any way by having to assist and support the course of justice prescribed by the injunction . . .

(2) Precise notice

The bank, or other innocent third party, should be told, with as much certainty as possible, what he is to do or not to do. The plaintiff will, no doubt, obtain his *Mareva* injunction against the defendant in wide terms so as to prevent the defendant disposing, not only of any named asset, but also of any other asset he has within the jurisdiction. The plaintiff does this because he often does not know in advance exactly what assets the defendant has or where they are situate. But, when the plaintiff gives notice to the bank or other innocent third party, then he should identify the bank account by specifying the branch and heading of the account and any other asset of the defendant [with as much precision as is reasonably practicable] . . .

(3) Search

If the plaintiff cannot identify the bank account or other asset with precision, he may request the bank or other innocent third party to conduct a search so as to see whether he holds any asset of the defendant, provided that he undertakes to pay the costs of the search . . . He may, for example, ask the bank to search the accounts of its branches in inner London to see if the defendant has an account at any of them. The bank may not tell the plaintiff the result of the search, lest it breaks the confidence of the customer. But, if it finds that the defendant has an account, it will freeze it for its own protection: so that it will not be in contempt of court. We are told that in one case the Inland Revenue requested the bank to make a 'trawl' of all its branches to see if the defendant had account at any of them. The bank could not be expected to do this, except on the footing that all the expense was to be paid by the plaintiff.

(4) Tell the judge

In view of the impact of the *Mareva* injunction on banks and other innocent third parties, it is desirable that the judge should be told on the application the names of the banks and third parties to whom it is proposed to give notice: but it should not preclude the plaintiff from giving notice to others on further information being obtained.

(5) Maximum amount

When we first granted *Mareva* injunctions, we did not insert any maximum amount. But nowadays it has become usual to insert the maximum amount to be restrained. The maximum amount is the sum claimed by the plaintiff from the defendant. This is done in case it should be that the defendant has assets which exceed the amount of the plaintiff's claim. If such should be the case, it is not thought right to restrain him from dealing with the excess. That is all very well so far as the defendant is concerned, because he knows, or should know, the value of his assets. But it is completely unworkable so far as the bank or other innocent third party is concerned: because it does not know what other assets the defendant may have or their value.

What then is to be done? In some cases the best course may be to omit the maximum amount altogether: and to make the injunction comprehensive against all the assets of the defendant, as we used to do. This would cause the defendant little inconvenience. Because he could come along at once to the court and ask for the excess to be released – by disclosing the whereabouts of his assets and the extent of them. If he chooses not to do so, it would be because he knows there is no excess. If notice is given to a bank or other third party, they know that they must not deal with any of the assets of the defendant.

In other cases, however, it may still be desirable to insert a maximum amount in the general injunction as against the defendant himself. But, as this is unworkable against a bank, it would at the same time be desirable to add a special injunction restraining the defendant from disposing of any of the sums standing to the credit of the defendant in a specified bank account in excess of the maximum: or from disposing of any item deposited with the specified bank for safe custody. The reason being that every bank or other innocent third party should know exactly what it should or should not do.

(6) Normal living expenses

Likewise, if in any case it is thought desirable to allow the defendant to have the use of sums for 'normal living expenses', or such like, the injunction should specify the sums as figures: without saying what they are to be used for. The bank should not be required to inquire what use is to be made of them. A special account should be opened for such sums.

(7) Joint account

If it is thought that the defendant may have moneys in a joint account, with others, the injunction shall be framed in terms wide enough to cover the joint account – if the judge thinks it desirable for the protection of the plaintiff.

(8) Return day

When granting a *Mareva* injunction *ex parte*, the court may sometimes think it right only to grant it for a few days until the defendant and the bank or other innocent third party can be heard. The injunction is such a serious matter for all concerned that all of them should be given the earliest possible opportunity of being heard. The plaintiff will, of course, in his own interest, give notice to the bank or other innocent third parties at once – either by telephone or telex – and he must follow it up immediately by a written confirmation to be delivered by hand or earliest means. The notice should set out the terms of the injunction, and request that it be observed. The plaintiff should also serve the defendant straight away so that he can apply to discharge it if so advised . . . But in other cases where service on the defendant is not immediately practicable, for some reason or another, the return day could be later.

(9) Undertakings

The plaintiff who seeks a *Mareva* injunction should normally give an undertaking in damages to the defendant, and also an undertaking to a bank or other innocent third party to pay any expenses reasonably incurred by them. The judge may, or may not, require a bond or other security to support this undertaking: but this may not be insisted on when the plaintiff is legally-aided . . . But the undertakings only cover damages or expenses reasonably incurred. If the defendant or third party could have reduced it by taking reasonable steps, it is his duty to do so . . .

(10) Discovery

In order to make a *Mareva* injunction fully effective, it is very desirable that the defendant should be required in a proper case to make discovery. If he comes on the return day and says that he has ample assets to meet the claim, he ought to specify them. Otherwise his refusal to disclose them will go to show that he is really evading payment. There is ample power in the court to order discovery . . .

Similar judgments were given by Eveleigh and Kerr LJJ.

§ 4   Jurisdiction

In some countries, attaching assets of the defendant is a ground of jurisdiction for the substantive action. This is not the case in England. Neither the presence of assets, nor their attachment, gives the court jurisdiction. As Lord Denning made clear in the *Third Chandris* case, a freezing order is not a free-standing remedy: it can only be granted if the court has jurisdiction (on some other basis) in the substantive action or if the claim is going to arbitration.[9]

There is, however, an exception. If a foreign court has jurisdiction, and the action is pending (or about to be brought) there, it is now possible to apply for a freezing order in England in order to ensure that, if the claimant obtains judgment in the foreign court, that judgment can be satisfied if enforcement proceedings are brought in England.[10]

This is done under section 25 of the Civil Jurisdiction and Judgments Act 1982 (Panel 19.2), subsection (1) of which allows a freezing order to be granted in England when the substantive proceedings have been, or are to be, commenced in another Community or Lugano State.[11] Subsection (3) makes it possible for this provision to be extended to non-Community countries, and this was done by Order in Council in 1997.[12] The result is that English courts can now

Panel 19.2 Foreign judgments
Civil Jurisdiction and Judgments Act 1982 (as amended), section 25

Section 25

(1) The High Court in England and Wales or Northern Ireland shall have power to grant interim relief where—

(a) proceedings have been or are to be commenced in a Brussels or Lugano Contracting State or a Regulation State other than the United Kingdom or in a part of the United Kingdom other than that in which the High Court in question exercises jurisdiction; and

(b) they are or will be proceedings whose subject-matter is within the scope of the Regulation as determined by Article 1 of the Regulation (whether or not the Regulation has effect in relation to the proceedings).

(2) On an application for any interim relief under subsection (1) the court may refuse to grant that relief if, in the opinion of the court, the fact that the court has no jurisdiction apart from this section in relation to the subject-matter of the proceedings in question makes it inexpedient for the court to grant it.

(3) Her Majesty may by Order in Council extend the power to grant interim relief conferred by subsection (1) so as to make it exercisable in relation to proceedings of any of the following descriptions, namely—

(a) proceedings commenced or to be commenced otherwise than in a Brussels or Lugano Contracting State or Regulation State . . .

---

9 *The Siskina* [1979] AC 210. It is not necessary for the substantive action to be pending when the application for the order is made. Normally, the application is made first. However, jurisdiction in the substantive action must exist, and the claimant must intend to bring it as soon as possible.
10 This was not possible when *The Siskina* (above) was decided, since the Civil Jurisdiction and Judgments Act 1982 was not then in force.
11 See Article 31 of the Brussels I Regulation, discussed in § 8, below.
12 Civil Jurisdiction and Judgments Act 1982 (Interim Relief) Order 1997, SI 1997 No. 302.

grant a freezing order if the substantive proceedings are pending (or about to be brought) anywhere in the world. However, it is unlikely that they would do so if they considered that the foreign court had no jurisdiction (in English eyes) or if its judgment would not be enforced in England for some other reason.[13]

§ 5 Worldwide orders

Up to now, we have been assuming that the order has effect only within the territory of the forum. In 1990, however, English courts began to issue orders that also applied to conduct abroad: they prohibited the defendant from doing anything in England *or abroad* that would prevent the claimant from enforcing the judgment. This was first done in a case called *Babanaft International Co. SA* v. *Bassatne*.[14] These worldwide orders were created in response to ever more sophisticated frauds, and were granted even if the defendant had no assets in England. If freezing orders purported to create rights *in rem*, this extension would be open to serious objection; however, they operate only *in personam*. If the English court has jurisdiction over the defendant, there is no reason why it should not order him to do, or to refrain from doing, something outside England. If he breaches the order, he will be guilty of contempt of court. If he is out of the country and has no assets in England, it may be difficult to enforce the order, but that is another matter.

§ 5.1 *Worldwide orders in aid of foreign proceedings*

This extension raised a number of issues. One was whether worldwide orders should be made only where the substantive proceedings are in England or whether this extension could be combined with the extension brought about by section 25 of the Civil Jurisdiction and Judgments Act 1982 (§ 4, above), so that worldwide orders could be granted in support of foreign proceedings.

It might be argued that it should be left to the foreign court to grant such measures. It will be remembered that, in *Airbus Industrie* v. *Patel*,[15] the House of Lords refused to grant an antisuit injunction to restrain proceedings brought against a French company in the United States when England was not the natural forum for those proceedings.[16] Lord Goff, who gave the leading judgment, said that the English courts should not 'take it on themselves to act as policeman of the world'.[17] Should they act differently with regard to worldwide freezing orders? Is it relevant whether the foreign court had the power to grant such a measure but decided not to do so, or did not have the power and could

---

13 Section 25(2) of the 1982 Act gives it a discretion. Cf. *Motorola Credit Corporation* v. *Uzan (No. 2)* [2004] 1 WLR 113, paragraphs 130–3 (CA).
14 [1990] Ch 13.
15 [1999] 1 AC 119; [1998] 2 WLR 686; [1998] 2 All ER 257 (HL).
16 See Chapter 9, § 2.2, above.
17 [1999] 1 AC 119 at p. 121.

not have granted it even if it had wanted to do so? These questions are discussed in our next case.

England
Crédit Suisse Fides Trust SA* v. *Cuoghi
Court of Appeal
[1998] QB 818; [1997] 3 WLR 871

Background

Cuoghi was domiciled in England. Crédit Suisse Fides Trust (CSFT) began proceedings against him in Switzerland claiming that he was involved in the misappropriation by one of its employees, Mr Voellmin, of a sum of money. Criminal proceedings were also commenced in Switzerland against Cuoghi. CSFT then made an application in England under section 25 of the Civil Jurisdiction and Judgments Act 1982 (discussed in § 4, above) for a worldwide freezing order and a worldwide disclosure order[18] against Cuoghi, things that were not available under Swiss law. The judge granted the orders, but subjected them to restrictions designed to ensure that Mr Cuoghi was not forced to incriminate himself in the Swiss proceedings. Mr Cuoghi appealed on the ground that the orders were too wide, and CSFT appealed against the restrictions.

Millett LJ

The worldwide Mareva injunction

By granting a worldwide *Mareva* injunction in aid of substantive proceedings abroad, the judge combined two far-reaching jurisdictions of recent development and with international aspects. CSFT recognises that such an order should be made with caution. Mr Cuoghi submits that it should not be made at all save in very exceptional circumstances and that no such circumstances exist in the present case.

[Millett LJ then discussed the development of freezing orders and considered the matters outlined in § 4, above. He said that the English court should in principle be willing to grant appropriate interim relief in support of substantive proceedings taking place elsewhere, and that it should not be deterred from doing so by the fact that its role is only an ancillary one, unless the circumstances of the particular case make the grant of such relief inexpedient. He continued:]

Mr Cuoghi accepts: (1) CSFT has a good arguable case that Mr Cuoghi was an accomplice of Mr Voellmin and was implicated in the misappropriation of US $21.66m.; (2) CSFT has made a sufficient case for the grant of a domestic *Mareva* injunction against Mr Cuoghi together with an ancillary disclosure order limited to assets located in England and Wales; (3) the English court has jurisdiction to grant worldwide *Mareva* relief in support of the Swiss proceedings under section 25(1) of the Act of 1982; (4) if CSFT had chosen to bring the substantive proceedings in England instead of in Switzerland (as it could have done, since Mr Cuoghi is

---

18 To discover the whereabouts of his assets.

domiciled in England), then the English courts could and almost certainly would have granted worldwide *Mareva* relief.

Accordingly, the question resolves itself into this: does the fact that the substantive proceedings are taking place in Switzerland and not in England make it inexpedient to grant worldwide, as distinct from merely domestic, *Mareva* relief? The judge did not think so, and I agree with him.

Mr Cuoghi submits that it is primarily for the courts of the State where the assets are located to determine whether and if so what protective measures should be ordered. He accepts that their jurisdiction cannot be invoked until the whereabouts of the assets is known, but he says that it is for the court which is seised of the substantive proceedings to decide whether and to what extent a defendant should be ordered to disclose the whereabouts of his overseas assets. He points out that England is neither the State where the substantive proceedings are taking place nor the State where the assets affected by the disputed aspects of the *Mareva* injunction are located. He says that the Swiss courts have no power to order a non-resident to disclose the whereabouts of assets located outside Switzerland, and submits that we should not, by making orders with extraterritorial effect, seek to remedy defects in the laws of other countries.

I cannot accept the submission that it is inappropriate to exercise the jurisdiction conferred by section 25 to grant a worldwide *Mareva* injunction in support of proceedings pending in another country. As Lawrence Collins points out in *Essays in International Litigation and the Conflict of Laws* (1994), there is no reason in principle why an English injunction should not restrain a person properly before the court from disposing of assets abroad. The order operates *in personam*. It is

> 'not grounded upon any pretension to the exercise of judicial or administrative rights abroad, but on the circumstance of the person to whom the order is addressed being within the reach of the court:' see *Kerr on Injunctions*, 6th ed. (1927), p. 11.

It is, of course, the case that, statute and Convention apart, the jurisdiction of the English court does not depend on domicile but on service. Proceedings may be served on persons temporarily present within the jurisdiction, or with leave . . . on persons outside the jurisdiction. It is a strong thing to restrain a defendant who is not resident within the jurisdiction from disposing of assets outside the jurisdiction. But where the defendant is domiciled within the jurisdiction such an order cannot be regarded as exorbitant or as going beyond what is internationally acceptable. To treat it as such merely because the substantive proceedings are pending in another country would be contrary to the policy which informs both Article 24 [of the Lugano Convention][1] and section 25 [of the Civil Jurisdiction and Judgments Act].

Where a defendant and his assets are located outside the jurisdiction of the court seised of the substantive proceedings, it is in my opinion most appropriate that protective measures should be granted by those courts best able to make their orders effective. In relation to orders taking direct effect against the assets, this means the courts of the State where the assets are located; and in relation to

---

1 *Editor's note*: this is equivalent to Article 31 of the Brussels I Regulation.

orders *in personam*, including orders for disclosure, this means the courts of the State where the person enjoined resides.

I recognise that an ancillary jurisdiction ought to be exercised with caution, and that care should be taken not to make orders which conflict with those of the court seised of the substantive proceedings. But I do not accept that interim relief should be limited to that which would be available in the court trying the substantive dispute; or that by going further we would be seeking to remedy defects in the laws of other countries. The principle which underlies Article 24 is that each Contracting State should be willing to assist the courts of another Contracting State by providing such interim relief as would be available if its own courts were seised of the substantive proceedings . . . By going further than the Swiss courts would be prepared to go in relation to a defendant resident outside Switzerland, we would not be seeking to remedy any perceived deficiency in Swiss law, but rather to supplement the jurisdiction of the Swiss courts in accordance with Article 24 and principles which are internationally accepted.

In other areas of law, such as cross-border insolvency, commercial necessity has encouraged national courts to provide assistance to each other without waiting for such co-operation to be sanctioned by international convention. International fraud requires a similar response. It is becoming widely accepted that comity between the courts of different countries requires mutual respect for the territorial integrity of each other's jurisdiction, but that this should not inhibit a court in one jurisdiction from rendering whatever assistance it properly can to a court in another in respect of assets located or persons resident within the territory of the former.

In the present case it is the disclosure order which is the most valuable part of the relief granted by the judge. Without it CSFT would be unable to apply to the local courts for effective orders against assets abroad. Mr Cuoghi makes much of the fact that the order extends to assets in Switzerland, and submits that this is an unwarranted interference with the jurisdiction of the court trying the substantive dispute. The short answer to this is that the terms of the order will not allow it to be directly enforced in Switzerland without an order of the Swiss courts. We do not seek to force our co-operation on those who do not welcome it. Finally, Mr Cuoghi submits that it is established by authority that the English courts should make orders having extraterritorial effect in aid of substantive proceedings being carried on abroad only in 'very exceptional circumstances.' For this proposition he relies on an observation of Lord Donaldson of Lymington MR in *Rosseel NV* v. *Oriental Commercial Shipping (UK) Ltd* [1990] 1 WLR 1387, 1388–1389:

> Where this court is concerned to determine rights then it will, in an appropriate case, and certainly should, enforce its own judgment by exercising what would be described as a long arm jurisdiction. But, where it is merely being asked under a convention or an Act of Parliament to enforce in support of another jurisdiction, whether in arbitration or litigation, it seems to me that, save in an exceptional case, it should stop short of making orders which extend beyond its own territorial jurisdiction . . . apart from the very exceptional case, the proper attitude of the English courts . . . is to confine themselves to their own territorial area, save in cases in which they are the court or tribunal which determines the rights of the parties. So long as they are merely being used as enforcement agencies they should stick to their own last.

In that case the plaintiffs were seeking to enforce a New York arbitration award in England, and applied for a worldwide *Mareva* injunction pending satisfaction of the award. No application had been made to the New York court to enforce the award, perhaps because the relevant defendants were resident in England, though this fact does not appear from the report. Hirst J granted a domestic *Mareva* injunction, but refused worldwide relief, holding that the New York court was the appropriate court to grant such relief. His decision was upheld by this court. I find the decision surprising, given that the court was being asked to exercise its enforcement jurisdiction against defendants resident in England . . . I would not for my part accept that the English court was being asked to exercise a long-arm jurisdiction;[2] indeed, I think that an order of the New York court might well have qualified for this description.

The explanation, to my mind, is that no or no sufficient regard was paid to the fact that the defendants were resident in England. The case was regarded as comparable with *Republic of Haiti* v. *Duvalier* [1990] 1 QB 202, where worldwide *Mareva* relief was granted against non-resident defendants in support of substantive proceedings in France. The only connection with England was the presence here of solicitors who knew where the assets were located. That was an extreme case, which Professor Collins describes as perhaps going 'to the very edge of what is permissible': *Essays in International Litigation and the Conflict of Laws*, p. 207. The circumstances can be said to have been 'very exceptional', though to my mind the circumstance which justified the exercise of the jurisdiction was that otherwise no effective protection could be given to the plaintiffs anywhere.

. . .

It is in my judgment regrettable that a gloss has been placed on the words of section 25(2). The question for consideration is not whether the circumstances are exceptional or very exceptional, but whether it would be inexpedient to make the order. Where an application is made for *in personam* relief in ancillary proceedings, two considerations which are highly material are the place where the person sought to be enjoined is domiciled and the likely reaction of the court which is seised of the substantive dispute. Where a similar order has been applied for and has been refused by that court, it would generally be wrong for us to interfere. But where the other court lacks jurisdiction to make an effective order against a defendant because he is resident in England, it does not at all follow that it would find our order objectionable.

Mr Cuoghi is resident and domiciled in England. He carries on business here in a substantial way, and he is alleged to have committed acts in England which were part of the fraud. He is believed to have assets in other jurisdictions, but the Swiss court has no power to order him to disclose their whereabouts. Unless we make such an order, CSFT cannot apply to the courts where the assets are located for appropriate protective measures, and any final judgment obtained in Switzerland may be rendered ineffective. There is no danger of conflicting jurisdictions, and although the Swiss court cannot make an order against Mr Cuoghi because he

---

2 *Editor's note*: the court is here using 'long-arm jurisdiction' in a slightly pejorative sense, implying that it is exorbitant. However, it does not necessarily have this implication.

is not resident in Switzerland, there is no reason to believe that it would not welcome assistance from the courts of the country where he is resident. If CSFT ultimately obtains final judgment in Switzerland against Mr Cuoghi, we will be bound to give effect to it, and it will be our responsibility to execute it against an English domiciliary. It is beyond dispute that at that stage we will have all necessary powers to ascertain the whereabouts of Mr Cuoghi's assets both here and abroad. It cannot be said to be inexpedient to compel disclosure now so that appropriate steps can be taken to prevent Mr Cuoghi frustrating an eventual judgment of the Swiss court. It would be a very different matter if we were being asked to make a worldwide order against Mr Voellmin, but we are not.

In my judgment the judge's decision to grant worldwide ancillary *Mareva* relief is unassailable. I would dismiss Mr Cuoghi's appeal.

Lord Bingham of Cornhill CJ

[After stating that he agreed with Millett LJ, and discussing certain preliminary matters, said:]

It would be unwise to attempt to list all the considerations which might be held to make the grant of relief under section 25 inexpedient or expedient, whether on a municipal or a worldwide basis. But it would obviously weigh heavily, probably conclusively, against the grant of interim relief if such grant would obstruct or hamper the management of the case by the court seized of the substantive proceedings ('the primary court'), or give rise to a risk of conflicting, inconsistent or overlapping orders in other courts. It may weigh against the grant of relief by this court that the primary court could have granted such relief and has not done so, particularly if the primary court has been asked to grant such relief and declined. On the other hand, it may be thought to weigh in favour of granting such relief that a defendant is present in this country and so liable to effective enforcement of an order made *in personam*, always provided that by granting such relief this court does not tread on the toes of the primary court or any other court involved in the case. On any application under section 25 this court must recognise that its role is subordinate to and must be supportive of that of the primary court . . .

The lower court had limited the disclosure order so that it would not apply to any disclosure that might result in Mr Cuoghi incriminating himself in the Swiss criminal proceedings. The Court of Appeal accepted that this was correct. CSFT's appeal against this aspect of the order was also dismissed.

Our next case develops the law further.

> **England**
> *Motorola Credit Corporation v. Uzan (No. 2)*
> **Court of Appeal**
> **[2003] EWCA Civ 752; [2004] 1 WLR 113**

Background

There were four defendants in this case. The second was the father; the others were his children. The first defendant was a son. He had assets in England (a valuable London property, a Rolls Royce car and shares in a company), but was neither resident nor domiciled there. The second defendant (the father) had no assets in England and was not resident or domiciled there. The third defendant was another son. He had no assets in England and was not resident or domiciled there. The fourth defendant was a daughter. She had assets in England and had been resident there, but she seems to have left at the time of the judgment. The first three defendants lived in Turkey; all four were members of a rich and powerful Turkish family. *Forbes* magazine listed them as among the 500 richest persons in the world. One of their business interests was a Turkish telecommunications company called Telsim.

Motorola was a major American company in the telecommunications industry. It claimed that the defendants (and others) had defrauded it of more than US$1 billion. Motorola had brought proceedings in a federal district court in New York before Judge Rakoff in which it was claiming more than US$2 billion.[19] At the time of the English judgment, these proceedings were continuing. As far as can be ascertained, the facts of the case had no connection at all with England. Nevertheless, Motorola applied to the English courts under section 25 of the 1982 Act for worldwide freezing orders and ancillary worldwide asset-disclosure orders. These orders were granted. The defendants were required to attend court in London to disclose their assets. When they failed to do so, they were sentenced to imprisonment for contempt.[20] Since they were all in Turkey at the time, it is doubtful whether the sentences could be carried out.[21]

While these applications were being heard, the Turkish courts granted antisuit injunctions precluding Motorola from continuing the US proceedings or the ancillary English proceedings. Motorola responded by first trying to get the Turkish judge removed for bias. This was unsuccessful. It then asked the judge in the US proceedings (Judge Rakoff) to make an order requiring the defendants to have the Turkish injunction rescinded. Judge Rakoff made the order, but the Turkish courts granted a second antisuit injunction, this time at the request of some Telsim employees. Motorola appeared to have had no intention of obeying these orders.

The four defendants in the English proceedings then appealed to the Court of Appeal against the freezing orders and disclosure orders.[22] In his judgment, Potter LJ defined the issue as follows:

> The point of principle which lies at the heart of the appeals is whether a worldwide freezing order should be made under section 25 of the 1982 Act in support of an action in another jurisdiction in circumstances where the defendant in question is neither domiciled nor resident within the jurisdiction and there is no substantial connection between the relief sought and the territorial jurisdiction of the English court.

---

19 This included a claim for treble and punitive damages under the Racketeer Influenced and Corrupt Organizations Act, Title 18, United States Code, Chapter 96 (RICO).
20 Three were sentenced to fifteen months; the fourth defendant was given six months.
21 There was talk of extradition, but this seems unrealistic.
22 The appeal was actually directed against the order of David Steel J dated 22 July 2002 by which he refused to discharge the worldwide freezing orders.

There were certain subsidiary points, but this is the issue on which we will focus.

Potter LJ[1]

114. The issue in this case arises because, on the face of it, the only fetter placed upon the otherwise apparently unlimited powers which the court has as a result of the combination of section 37 of the Supreme Court Act 1981,[2] section 25 of the Civil Jurisdiction and Judgments Act 1982, and CPR rule 6.20 [now CPR 6.36 and Practice Direction 6 B, paragraph 3.1(5)][3] is its power to refuse to grant relief if its absence of jurisdiction apart from section 25 makes such grant 'inexpedient'. It is plain that, in relation to the grant of worldwide relief, the jurisdiction is based on assumed personal jurisdiction: as such it has the potential for extra-territorial effect in the case of non-residents with assets abroad. Thus it is likely that the jurisdiction will prove extremely popular with claimants anxious to obtain security against defendants in disputes yet to be decided where they cannot obtain it in the court of primary jurisdiction or the court of the defendant's residence or domicile, which courts are the natural fora in which to make such applications. There is thus an inherent likelihood of resort to the English jurisdiction as an 'international policeman', to use the phrase employed by Moore-Bick J, in cases of international fraud. We would do nothing to gainsay, and indeed would endorse, the observations of Millett LJ in *Cuoghi's* case [above] to the effect that international fraud requires courts, within the limits of comity, to render whatever assistance they properly can without the need for express provision by an international convention requiring it. However, even in the case of Article 24 of the Brussels Convention it has been made clear that

> . . . the granting of provisional or protective measures on the basis of Article 24 is conditional on, inter alia, the existence of a real connecting link between the subject matter of the measures sought and the territorial jurisdiction of the contracting state of the court before which those measures are sought [paragraph 40 of the judgment of the ECJ in the *Van Uden* case, set out in § 8.2, below].

> Further, in so far as 'police' action is concerned, policing is only practicable and therefore expedient if the court acting in that role has power to enforce its powers if disobeyed . . .

115. As the authorities show, there are five particular considerations which the court should bear in mind, when considering the question whether it is inexpedient to make an order. First, whether the making of the order will interfere with the management of the case in the primary court e. g. where the order is inconsistent with an order in the primary court or overlaps with it. That consideration does not arise in the present case. Second, whether

---

1 This was the judgment of the court.
2 Set out in Panel 19.1, above.
3 *Editor's note*: this permits a claim form to be served out of the jurisdiction with the permission of the court if a claim is made for an interim remedy under section 25(1) of the 1982 Act.

.it is the policy in the primary jurisdiction not itself to make worldwide freezing/disclosure orders. Third, whether there is a danger that the orders made will give rise to disharmony or confusion and/or risk of conflicting inconsistent or overlapping orders in other jurisdictions, in particular the courts of the state where the person enjoined resides or where the assets affected are located. If so, then respect for the territorial jurisdiction of that state should discourage the English court from using its unusually wide powers against a foreign defendant. Fourth, whether at the time the order is sought there is likely to be a potential conflict as to jurisdiction rendering it inappropriate and inexpedient to make a worldwide order. Fifth, whether, in a case where jurisdiction is resisted and disobedience to be expected, the court will be making an order which it cannot enforce.

116. Further, we accept the submission of [counsel for the first, second and third defendants] that in such cases the position of each defendant falls to be considered separately. There was no evidence before the judge, nor is there now, that the four defendants owned or held assets jointly. In so far as the claimant relies on the fact that the defendants all own shares in many of the same Turkish companies, it is not suggested that any is other than the individual owner of his or her own shareholding and it is accepted that the prospects of enforcement on those shareholdings are remote. Further, the fourth defendant's admitted residence and the first defendant's valuable house and assets within the jurisdiction, while subject to the powers of enforcement of the court in their own cases, do not render it any more likely that orders against the second and third defendants will be effective or any the more acceptable from the point of view of the US or Turkish courts. We therefore propose to consider the position of the second and third defendants (identical as between themselves), before turning to the position of the first and fourth defendants.

117. In the light of our observations we turn briefly to the points made by [counsel for the first, second and third defendants] . . .

118. First, we do not consider that the judge was wrong to say that in *Cuoghi's* case . . . Millett LJ had rejected the notion that the court's power to grant section 25 relief ancillary to a claim in a foreign court was circumscribed by the availability of similar relief in that court. It is plain that he did reject it . . . While the context in which Millett LJ did so was that of a Convention case, his remarks were not limited to such cases. We accept, however, that the court in *Cuoghi's* case stressed the subordinate nature of the English court's role under section 25 and emphasised that those courts best able to make the orders effective were the courts of the defendant's residence or the place where his assets were located . . .

119. In this connection, [counsel for the first, second and third defendants] . . . argued that, now the position has been made clear [by the decision of the US Supreme Court in *Grupo Mexicano de Desarrollo*, set out in § 7, below], and given the absence of power in the New York court to grant *Mareva*-type relief in the general or worldwide form available in this country, refusal

was the appropriate course in this case. We do not think that follows. It seems to us that the position being contemplated by Millett LJ was one where the primary court has the jurisdiction to grant relief but would refuse to exercise it on the merits or for other substantial reasons ... and not the position where the foreign court simply lacks the jurisdiction (as now made clear to be the position in the US in the *Grupo Mexicano* case). In the latter event, the English court may judge it 'not inexpedient', and indeed is likely to regard it as desirable in cases of international fraud, to be supportive of the processes of the primary court.

120. Second, we agree that the judge should have attached, but did not attach, weight to the likelihood of conflict, disharmony and confusion developing between the Turkish courts and the English court if the latter made a worldwide freezing order which was likely to inhibit dealings in the shares or other assets of the second and third defendants in Turkey.

121. Third, we consider that this was a case where the principle stated in *Derby & Co Ltd* v. *Weldon (Nos 3 and 4)* [1990] Ch 65 [that a court should refrain from making an order in cases of this kind if there is reason to suppose it will be disobeyed and if, should that occur, there would be no real sanction] required consideration and application in the light of the absence of any connection between the second and third defendants and this jurisdiction.

122. Fourth, as we have already indicated at paragraph 116 above, we consider that the judge erred in his collective treatment of the defendants for the purpose of establishing a connection with the jurisdiction in relation to expediency.

123. Fifth, albeit the fraud alleged against the defendants was, if correct, fraud on a massive scale, we do not think it stands relevant comparison with *Duvalier's* case ... Finally, we also agree that no question of comity arose for consideration in *Duvalier's* case which rendered it inconsistent with the submissions made for the first three defendants.

124. In those circumstances, it is appropriate for us to revisit the exercise of the judge's discretion informed by developments since his decision.

125. In this connection, the court is no longer faced simply with the potential for conflict with the courts of the domicile of the second and third defendants in Turkey, but with a situation in which the Turkish court has granted antisuit injunctions against the claimant pursuing both the primary proceedings in the US and the ancillary proceedings here and the claimant is participating in those proceedings. It also appears that, at the suit of Telsim employees, an injunction has been granted to stay execution of such proceedings, prohibiting both the claimant and the defendants from taking part in those proceedings. Albeit Gross J found, and there is no reason to doubt, that the second and third defendants colluded in those proceedings, they well illustrate the wisdom of the principle that where there is reason in cases of this kind to suppose that the order made against a foreign

defendant will be disobeyed *and* that, if that should occur, no real sanction would exist, then the court should refrain from making an order. In the light of the defendant's behaviour in the US proceedings and the stance taken in their witness statements, there was every reason to suppose that the orders of the English court would be disobeyed and that, if that were so, then no real sanction would exist against the second and third defendants. While we well understand the concern of the judge to assist in a case of international fraud, it is above all, as it seems to us, this consideration which he overlooked and which, quite apart from considerations of comity, it is important to bear in mind in a case where the connection of the defendant with this country is tenuous or non-existent. In our view the circumstances before the judge did indeed render it inexpedient to grant the relief claimed against the second and third defendants when no sanction was available against them in the event of their disobedience.

126. In the case of the second and third defendants therefore we would allow their appeals against the order of David Steel J dated 22 July 2002 by which he refused to discharge the worldwide freezing orders against them.

127. Turning to the position of the fourth defendant and the first defendant, we see no reason to disturb the decision of the judge. The fourth defendant did not, nor could she, dispute the jurisdiction of the court to grant worldwide relief against her. She was resident and had substantial assets here . . .

128. So far as the first defendant is concerned, he did not dispute the jurisdiction of the English court to make the order originally made against him for domestic relief[4] in respect of his house and other assets here. His application for discharge of that order rested solely upon the ground that risk of dissipation had not been demonstrated (in respect of which no appeal is pursued). His objection to the grant of worldwide relief against him in respect of his foreign assets was couched in largely similar terms to those of the second defendant. There was thus reason to suppose in his case that relief in those terms might be disobeyed. However, his was not a case where the court would be devoid of means of enforcement if that were so, by reason of the existence within the jurisdiction of assets worth millions of pounds. The rationale of the principle stated in *Derby & Co Ltd* v. *Weldon (Nos 3 and 4)* [1990] Ch 65 was thus not available to assist the fourth defendant. In those circumstances, we are not prepared to interfere with the judge's exercise of discretion in an apparently serious case of international fraud.

4 *Editor's note*: 'domestic relief' means an order limited to assets in England.

Comment

The end result was that the worldwide freezing orders (and orders for imprisonment) were rescinded against the second and third defendants, but not against the first and fourth defendants. The fourth defendant was resident in England; so there were jurisdictional grounds for making the order against her. There were no such grounds for making the order against the first defendant. The reason the second and third defendants won their appeals, but the first defendant lost, was simply that there were no means of enforcing the orders against the former, but there were against the latter. It will be remembered that he owned a valuable London property and a Rolls Royce car. These could be taken from him to punish him for his contempt.

Some people will find all this disturbing. The case had no connection with England. There was no jurisdictional link between the first defendant and England other than his English assets. These might have justified a freezing order applicable within England, but they could not have justified an extraterritorial order. Section 25 of the 1982 Act was intended to ensure that, if a foreign judgment was enforced in England, there would be assets available. That justifies the assumption of jurisdiction to make a freezing order applicable against assets in England; it does not justify a worldwide order.[23]

It was said at the beginning of this book[24] that, for jurisdiction to exist, there must either be a link between the defendant and the territory of the forum, or between the claim and the forum, or the defendant must consent to jurisdiction. None of these justifications existed with regard to the first defendant. He was a Turkish businessman, resident in Turkey, who was involved in a dispute with an American company that had no connection with England. Nevertheless, he was ordered by the English court to come to England and disclose his worldwide assets. When he failed to obey, he was sentenced to fifteen months' imprisonment. It is not difficult to imagine the outcry that would occur in England if a Turkish court had done the same to an English businessman. The justification was supposed to be that fraud was involved, but there was no judgment to that effect in America, only some remarks by the US judge.

As far as is known, England is the only country in the world that applies its law extraterritorially in this way. Section 25 of the 1982 Act was originally based on what is now Article 31 of the Brussels I Regulation. As we shall see in § 8, below, the European Court allows this latter provision to be used only with regard to property within the territory of the forum: it cannot be used to grant extraterritorial orders. The position is similar in the United States (discussed in § 7, below). There is no common-law power to grant even domestic freezing orders, let alone worldwide ones. Although there are certain statutory powers, they do not appear to be used where the American court has no jurisdiction over the substantive proceedings.

The result of this is that savvy litigators in foreign proceedings come to England to obtain worldwide orders.[25] These can be used to put pressure on an opponent in a business dispute. The English courts are all too ready to oblige. *Mobil Cerro Negro Ltd* v. *Petroleos de Venezuela SA*[26] is an example. This case involved a dispute between two oil companies; one (Mobil) was part of the Exxon Mobil group and the other

---

23 Cf. Collins, 'The Territorial Reach of Mareva Injunctions' (1989) 105 LQR 262 at p. 281, where it is said: 'For an English court to enjoin a person *properly subject to its jurisdiction* from disposing of assets abroad cannot in this sense be regarded as exorbitant' (emphasis added). The author goes on to say that the grant of a worldwide order in *Republic of Haiti* v. *Duvalier* went to the very edge of what is permissible.
24 Chapter 2, § 5, above.
25 This has not escaped the notice of English judges: see the comments of Potter LJ in paragraph 114 of the *Motorola* case.
26 [2008] EWHC 532; [2008] 1 Lloyd's Rep 684. It is not known whether this case will go on appeal.

was a state-owned Venezuelan company. The dispute was subject to arbitration in New York. There was no connection with England; nevertheless, Mobil came to England to ask for a worldwide freezing order against the Venezuelan company in the sum of US$12 billion.[27] Unlike the *Motorola* case, there was no question of fraud; yet the order was granted. Admittedly, it was lifted shortly afterwards,[28] but the fact that it was granted at all was outrageous.

English lawyers and courts like to criticize other countries for claiming exorbitant jurisdiction and for applying their law extraterritorially. As we shall see in Part VI of this book, the US is a favourite target. In some areas, English courts are careful not to overstep the mark;[29] yet, in this instance, they go further than those of any other country. They seem to think they have the right to act as policemen of the world.

§ 5.2   *Worldwide orders and third parties*

The effect of worldwide orders on third parties, especially banks, is also a problem. This was considered in our next case.

England
Derby & Co. Ltd* v. *Weldon (Nos. 3 and 4)
Court of Appeal
[1989] 2 WLR 412

Lord Donaldson of Lymington MR

(2) The effect on third parties

Here there is a real problem. Court orders only bind those to whom they are addressed. However, it is a serious contempt of court, punishable as such, for anyone to interfere with or impede the administration of justice. This occurs if someone, knowing of the terms of the court order, assists in the breach of that order by the person to whom it is addressed. All this is common sense and works well so long as the 'aider and abettor' is wholly within the jurisdiction of the court or wholly outside it. If he is wholly within the jurisdiction of the court there is no problem whatsoever. If he is wholly outside the jurisdiction of the court, he is either not to be regarded as being in contempt or it would involve an excess of jurisdiction to seek to punish him for that contempt. Unfortunately, juridical persons, notably banks, operate across frontiers. A foreign bank may have a branch within the jurisdiction and so be subject to the English courts. An English bank may have branches abroad and be asked by a defendant to take action at such a branch which will constitute a breach by the defendant of the court's order. Is action by the foreign bank to be regarded as contempt, although it would not be so regarded but for the probably irrelevant fact that it happens to have an English branch? Is

---

27 Under section 44 of the Arbitration Act 1996.
28 It was granted *ex parte* on 24 January 2008 and lifted on 18 March 2008; so it remained in force for almost eight weeks.
29 See *Mackinnon* v. *Donaldson, Lufkin & Jenrette Securities Corporation* (set out in Chapter 20, § 2.1, below) and *Société Eram Shipping Co. Ltd* v. *Compagnie Internationale de Navigation* (set out in Chapter 30, § 2.1, below).

action by the foreign branch of an English bank to be regarded as contempt, when other banks in the area are free to comply with the defendant's instructions?

[This problem had been considered in *Babanaft International Co. SA* v. *Bassatne*,[1] and the solution adopted was to make the order subject to a proviso intended to protect third parties. This provision was known as the '*Babanaft* proviso'. The court in *Darby* v. *Weldon* made its order subject to an improved version. It read:]

> Provided that, in so far as this order purports to have any extraterritorial effect, no person shall be affected thereby or concerned with the terms thereof until it shall be declared enforceable or be enforced by a foreign court and then it shall only affect them to the extent of such declaration or enforcement unless they are:
>
> (a) a person to whom this order is addressed or an officer of or an agent appointed by a power of attorney of such a person or
> (b) persons who are subject to the jurisdiction of this court and
>   (i) have been given written notice of this order at their residence or place of business within the jurisdiction, and
>   (ii) are able to prevent acts or omissions outside the jurisdiction of this court which assist in the breach of the terms of this order.

1 [1990] Ch 13.

In short, this means that (except to the extent that it is enforced by a foreign court) the freezing order will apply extraterritorially only to the person to whom it is addressed (the defendant)[30] or to persons subject to the jurisdiction of the English court who are given written notice of the order and are able to prevent acts outside England which assist in its breach.

This version of the proviso has many advantages, but the words 'able to prevent' in paragraph (b)(ii) are ambiguous: do they mean 'factually able to prevent' or do they mean '*legally* able to prevent'? The question is important for a bank. It may in practice be able to prevent the customer withdrawing money, but, if the order is not recognized under the law of the place where the branch operates, this might constitute a breach of contract under that law.

This question arose in our next case.

England
Bank of China* v. *NBM LLC
Court of Appeal
[2002] 1 WLR 844

Background

The claimant in this case was the Bank of China. It had brought proceedings in New York against a number of defendants whom it accused of defrauding it. It then invoked section 25 of the Civil Jurisdiction and Judgments Act 1982 to obtain a worldwide freezing order from the English courts in support of the New York proceedings.[31] The order, which was subject to a proviso along the lines of that granted in *Derby* v. *Weldon* (above), was served on a third party, Union Bank of

30 If the defendant is a company, it applies also to its officers.
31 The New York courts could not grant such an order.

Switzerland (UBS), a Swiss bank with a branch in London, which appeared to have had a relationship with some of the defendants in the past. On the application of UBS, the trial court had amended the proviso to include the words 'nothing in this order shall, in respect of assets located outside England and Wales, prevent UBS AG or its subsidiaries from complying with . . . what it reasonably believes to be its obligations, contractual or otherwise under the laws and obligations of the country or State in which those assets are situated or under the proper law of any bank account in question'. These additional words, which clarify the meaning of paragraph (b)(ii) of the proviso in *Derby* v. *Weldon*, are sometimes called the '*Baltic* proviso' after the case in which they were first adopted.[32] The Bank of China was willing to accept this addition in so far as it referred to the criminal law of the country where the assets were situated, but it objected to extending it further to cover contractual and other obligations. It therefore appealed to the Court of Appeal.

Tuckey LJ

[After outlining the development of the law, said:]

17. The cases to which I have referred do, I think, establish two general propositions. Firstly the limit of the court's territorial jurisdiction and the principle of comity require that the effectiveness of freezing orders operating upon third parties holding assets abroad should normally derive only from their recognition and enforcement by the local courts. In this respect it is worth remembering that the English court's jurisdiction to grant freezing and disclosure orders is a good deal more extensive than in most other jurisdictions, notably the United States. Secondly, third parties amenable to the English jurisdiction should be given all reasonable protection.

18. It follows that any order of the English court which has the effect of requiring a third party to do or refrain from doing something abroad is exceptional. With this in mind, what does 'able to prevent' in the *Derby* v. *Weldon* proviso mean? It was not spelt out in that case and [counsel for the claimant] accepts that it does not require the third party to disobey the local criminal law or an order of the local court. Her submission is, however, that it does require the third party to breach its contractual obligations to its customer (its mandate) and that if it has to pay damages as a result, it is adequately protected by the terms of the standard form undertaking which the claimant gives which says:

> The applicant will pay the reasonable costs of anyone other than the respondent which have been incurred as a result of this order . . . and if the court later finds that this order has caused such person loss, and decides that such person should be compensated for that loss, the applicant will comply with any order the court may make.

[Counsel for the claimant] submits that if the bank was unwilling to breach its mandate it could apply to the local court for relief so that anything it did or did not do would not be in contempt of the English court.

---

32 *Baltic Shipping Co.* v. *Translink Shipping Ltd* [1995] 1 Lloyd's Rep 673.

19. This analysis, if nothing else, shows that the *Derby* v. *Weldon* proviso is unclear. A third party would be 'able' to disobey the local criminal law or an order of the local court, but it is rightly conceded that the proviso does not require it to do this. Should it be required to breach its contractual obligations? I do not think so. Those obligations could be enforced by order of the local court which the third party would have to obey. I see no logical justification for distinguishing between the third party's contractual and other legal obligations under the local law. The onus should be upon the claimant to obtain relief from the local court rather than upon the third party.

20. . . . I do not think the undertaking in damages provides sufficient protection for the claimant. Damage to reputation and regulatory consequences abroad could not be adequately compensated. The bank might also be forced into litigation abroad with a customer or a third party or be faced with arguments here as to whether any particular loss fell within the terms of the undertaking.

21. . . . [T]here have been problems with the *Derby* v. *Weldon* proviso and we were told by UBS that claimants usually agree to the *Baltic* proviso being added to the standard form so I do not think it can be assumed that the standard form has not given rise to problems in practice. The *Baltic* proviso does of course only require the third party to have a reasonable belief as to what its obligations are, but I think it is entitled to this degree of protection. As Clarke J pointed out in *Baltic Shipping Co.* v. *Translink Shipping Ltd* . . . if the court had to decide whether the third party was able to prevent a breach of the order this might involve a prolonged and contentious inquiry as to what the local law in fact was.

22. So, like the three experienced commercial judges who have previously had to consider this point, I conclude that the need to avoid unwarranted extraterritorial jurisdiction, the need to provide reasonable protection for third parties affected by freezing orders and the need to clarify the *Derby* v. *Weldon* proviso will usually entitle third parties to have the *Baltic* proviso added to the worldwide freezing order unless the court considers on the particular facts of the case that this is inappropriate. As third parties are not represented when the order is first made, I think the *Baltic* proviso should be included in the standard form.

23. I see no reason for not including the *Baltic* proviso in this case. The claimant deserves the best protection which this court can give, not least because it does not know where the defendant's assets, if any, are. On the other hand none of the defendants are domiciled or resident in this country and there is no evidence or suggestion that UBS have held any of their assets here.

§ 5.3 Conclusions

Although the English courts have tried to respect the interests of third parties, such as banks, their willingness to grant extraterritorial freezing orders against persons not domiciled in England (or otherwise significantly connected with it) in situations in which they do not have jurisdiction over the substantive proceedings needs reconsideration.

§ 6   Commonwealth countries

Mareva injunctions (as they are still called in Commonwealth countries) have been adopted by the courts in many Commonwealth countries,[33] but they do not appear to be applied extraterritorially.

§ 7   The United States

Our next case takes up the story in the United States.

United States
Grupo Mexicano de Desarrollo SA* v. *Alliance Bond Fund Inc.
Supreme Court
527 US 308; 119 S Ct 1961 (1999)

Background

It was argued in this case that the US courts should adopt the *Mareva* remedy that had been developed in England. The district court granted an injunction along these lines, which was affirmed by the Court of Appeals for the Second Circuit. There was then an appeal to the US Supreme Court.

Justice Scalia delivered the opinion of the Court

[After discussing the development of the remedy in England and various other matters, he said:]

IV

The parties and *amici*[1] discuss various arguments for and against creating the preliminary injunctive remedy at issue in this case. The United States[2] suggests that the factors supporting such a remedy include

> 'simplicity and uniformity of procedure; preservation of the court's ability to render a judgment that will prove enforceable; prevention of inequitable conduct on the part of defendants; avoiding disparities between defendants that have assets within the jurisdiction (which would be subject to pre-judgment attachment 'at law') and those that do not; avoiding the necessity for plaintiffs to locate a forum in which the defendant has substantial assets; and, in an age of easy global mobility of capital, preserving the attractiveness of the United States as a center for financial transactions.' Brief for United States as *Amicus Curiae* 16.

1 *Amici* = *amici curiae* (plural of *amicus curiae*), 'friends of the court', non-parties who intervene in the proceedings to put arguments that might be helpful to the court.
2 *Editor's note*: the US Government filed an *amicus* brief in favour of the remedy.

---

33 See the cases cited in Dicey, Morris and Collins, p. 208, nn. 7–9. In Canada, they are applied more restrictively, at least in the inter-provincial context: see *Aetna Financial Services Ltd* v. *Feigelman* [1985] 1 SCR 2 (Supreme Court of Canada).

But there are weighty considerations on the other side as well, the most significant of which is the historical principle that before judgment (or its equivalent) an unsecured creditor has no rights at law or in equity in the property of his debtor . . .

The requirement that the creditor obtain a prior judgment is a fundamental protection in debtor-creditor law – rendered all the more important in our federal system by the debtor's right to a jury trial on the legal claim. There are other factors which likewise give us pause . . . by adding, through judicial fiat, a new and powerful weapon to the creditor's arsenal, the new rule could radically alter the balance between debtor's and creditor's rights which has been developed over centuries through many laws – including those relating to bankruptcy, fraudulent conveyances, and preferences. Because any rational creditor would want to protect his investment, such a remedy might induce creditors to engage in a 'race to the courthouse' in cases involving insolvent or near-insolvent debtors, which might prove financially fatal to the struggling debtor . . .

. . .

We do not decide which side has the better of these arguments. We set them forth only to demonstrate that resolving them in this forum is incompatible with the democratic and self-deprecating judgment we have long since made . . . Even when sitting as a court in equity, we have no authority to craft a 'nuclear weapon' of the law like the one advocated here . . .

The debate concerning this formidable power over debtors should be conducted and resolved where such issues belong in our democracy: in the Congress.

Note

The above was supported by a majority in the Supreme Court but only a bare majority: four out of nine judges dissented from it.

Although there is no general, judge-made power in the United States similar to that in England and the Commonwealth, there are a number of particular powers which have been created by statute. Our next case concerns one of them, a federal tax lien.

United States
United States* v. *First National City Bank
Supreme Court
379 US 378; 85 S Ct 528; 13 L Ed 2d 365 (1965)

Background

Omar was a Uruguayan corporation, which allegedly owed income tax to the United States.[34] The First National City Bank was a New York bank that had a branch in Montevideo, Uruguay. Omar had an account at the branch in Montevideo. The US tax authorities served notice of a federal tax lien on the bank, and commenced proceedings against the bank and against Omar in a

---

34 It was not said in the judgment that Omar was resident or domiciled in the United States. It seems that it was not.

federal district court in New York. The US asked for foreclosure of the tax lien on all of Omar's property, including money in the Montevideo branch. It also asked for a temporary injunction prohibiting the bank from transferring any money out of the account. The district court was said to have jurisdiction *in personam* over Omar, though, at the time of the proceedings, Omar had not been served. The district court granted a temporary injunction freezing the account in Montevideo, though it said that it would modify it if the injunction was shown to be contrary to Uruguayan law. The Court of Appeals reversed, and an appeal went to the US Supreme Court.

Mr Justice Douglas delivered the opinion of the Court

If personal jurisdiction over Omar is acquired, the creditor (the United States) will be able to collect from respondent what the debtor (Omar) could collect. The opportunity to make that collection should not be lost *in limine* merely because the debtor (Omar) has not made the agreed-upon demand on respondent [the bank] at the time and place and in the manner provided in their contract.

Whether the Montevideo branch is a 'separate entity', as the Court of Appeals thought, is not germane to the present narrow issue. It is not a separate entity in the sense that it is insulated from respondent's managerial prerogatives. Respondent has actual, practical control over its branches; it is organized under a federal statute . . . which authorizes it 'To sue and be sued, complain and defend, in any court of law and equity, as fully as natural persons' – as one entity, not branch by branch. The branch bank's affairs are, therefore, as much within the reach of the *in personam* order entered by the District Court as are those of the home office. Once personal jurisdiction of a party is obtained, the District Court has authority to order it to 'freeze' property under its control, whether the property be within or without the United States . . .

That is not to say that a federal court in this country should treat all the affairs of a branch bank the same as it would those of the home office. For overseas transactions are often caught in a web of extraterritorial activities and foreign law beyond the ken of our federal courts or their competence. We have, however, no such involvement here, for there is no showing that the mere 'freezing' of the Montevideo accounts, pending service on Omar, would violate foreign law . . . or place respondent under any risk of double liability . . . The District Court reserved power to enter any protective order of that character . . . And if, as is argued in dissent, the litigation might in time be embarrassing to United States diplomacy, the District Court remains open to the Executive Branch, which, it must be remembered, is the moving party in the present proceeding.

The temporary injunction issued by the District Court seems to us to be eminently appropriate to prevent further dissipation of assets. If such relief were beyond the authority of the District Court, foreign taxpayers facing jeopardy assessments might either transfer assets abroad or dissipate those in foreign accounts under control of American institutions before personal service on the foreign taxpayer could be made. Such a scheme was underfoot here, the affidavits aver . . . We conclude that this temporary injunction is 'a reasonable measure to preserve the status quo' pending service of process on Omar and an adjudication of the merits.

Reversed.

Note

There were two dissenting opinions.

QUESTION

What do you think Omar's next move is likely to be? If it sued the bank in Uruguay, would the court accept the US judgment as a defence?

§ 8 The European Union

Article 31 of the Brussels I Regulation (Panel 19.3) permits the courts of a Member State to grant such provisional, including protective, measures as may be available under the law of the State in question, even if, under the Regulation, the courts of another Member State have jurisdiction as to the substance of the matter.

> **Panel 19.3 Provisional, including protective, measures**
> **Brussels I Regulation (Regulation 44/2001), Article 31**
>
> **Article 31**
> Application may be made to the courts of a Member State for such provisional, including protective, measures as may be available under the law of that State, even if, under this Regulation, the courts of another Member State have jurisdiction as to the substance of the matter.

Section 25 of the Civil Jurisdiction and Judgments Act 1982 was originally enacted to give effect to this provision (see § 4, above).

Although the text says 'provisional, including protective' measures, the European Court seems to require that the measure in question be *both* provisional *and* protective. In other words, it must be only temporary (not final) and it must be intended to preserve the situation pending a final judgment. Thus, the court has defined the measures in question as measures which are 'intended to preserve a factual or legal situation so as to safeguard rights the recognition of which is otherwise sought from the court having jurisdiction as to the substance of the case'.[35] Although it applies to other measures as well, this provision certainly covers freezing orders.

---

35 *Reichert and Kockler* v. *Dresdner Bank*, Case C-261/90, [1992] ECR I-2149, paragraph 32. The *Reichert* case concerned a German couple who owned land in France, which they gave to their son by notarial act. It seems that they were trying to keep the land out of the hands of the bank, to which they owed money. The bank brought a so-called *action paulienne* in France to have the transfer set aside. This is a procedure under which a creditor can have a transfer of property by his debtor set aside if the transfer was made in fraud of the creditor's rights. It was argued that the French court had jurisdiction under Article 24, but the European Court ruled that an *action paulienne* is much more than a provisional or protective measure as understood by Article 24.

§ 8.1   *Jurisdiction over the substance*

We first consider the position where the court granting the order has jurisdiction over the substance of the claim. This was (apparently) the situation in our next case; the court granting the order did not, therefore, need Article 24 of the Convention to obtain jurisdiction, but could its order be enforced in another Contracting State?

European Union
Denilauler* v. *Couchet Frères
Court of Justice of the European Communities
Case 125/79, [1980] ECR 1553

Background

The claimant in the original proceedings, Couchet Frères, was a French company. It had transported goods for a German undertaking, Denilauler. When the latter failed to pay, Couchet sued it in a French court. In the course of these proceedings, the French court issued an order authorizing Couchet to have Denilauler's account frozen at a bank in Germany.[36] The order was made *ex parte*. Couchet then asked the relevant German court to enforce the order, and to issue an attachment. At this time, Denilauler had not been informed of the order: this was crucial if he was not to be allowed to remove the money. The German court granted the order for enforcement, and the attachment was made. Denilauler, who was informed at this point, appealed, and the appeal court made a reference to the European Court. In essence, the question before the European court was whether an order such as that made by the French court could be enforced under the Convention.

Judgment

[After stating that the relevant provisions of the Convention were not designed to be applied to *ex parte* orders, and after considering the arguments of the Commission and the Italian Government that such orders should nevertheless be enforced (partly on the ground that the Convention did not expressly say they were excluded), the court said:]

13.   All the provisions of the Convention, both those contained in Title II on jurisdiction and those contained in Title III on recognition and enforcement, express the intention to ensure that, within the scope of the objectives of the Convention, proceedings leading to the delivery of judicial decisions take place in such a way that the rights of the defence are observed. It is because of the guarantees given to the defendant in the original proceedings that the Convention, in Title III, is very liberal in regard to recognition and enforcement. In the light of these considerations it is clear that the Convention is fundamentally concerned with judicial decisions which, before the recognition and enforcement of them are sought in a State other than the State of origin, have been, or have been capable of being, the subject in that State of origin

---

36 Judging by its name, it seems to have been a French bank with a branch in Germany.

and under various procedures, of an inquiry in adversary proceedings. It cannot therefore be deduced from the general scheme of the Convention that a formal expression of intention was needed in order to exclude judgments of the type in question from recognition and enforcement.

. . .

15. An analysis of the function attributed under the general scheme of the Convention to Article 24, which is specifically devoted to provisional and protective measures,[1] leads, moreover, to the conclusion that, where these types of measures are concerned, special rules were contemplated. Whilst it is true that procedures of the type in question authorizing provisional and protective measures may be found in the legal systems of all the Contracting States and may be regarded, where certain conditions are fulfilled, as not infringing the rights of the defence, it should however be emphasized that the granting of this type of measure requires particular care on the part of the court and detailed knowledge of the actual circumstances in which the measure is to take effect. Depending on each case and commercial practices in particular the court must be able to place a time-limit on its order or, as regards the nature of the assets or goods subject to the measures contemplated, require bank guarantees or nominate a sequestrator and generally make its authorization subject to all conditions guaranteeing the provisional or protective character of the measure ordered.

16. The courts of the place or, in any event, of the Contracting State, where the assets subject to the measures sought are located, are those best able to assess the circumstances which may lead to the grant or refusal of the measures sought or to the laying down of procedures and conditions which the plaintiff must observe in order to guarantee the provisional and protective character of the measures ordered. The Convention has taken account of these requirements by providing in Article 24 that application may be made to the courts of a Contracting State for such provisional, including protective, measures as may be available under the law of that State, even if, under the Convention, the courts of another Contracting State have jurisdiction as to the substance of the matter.

17. Article 24 does not preclude provisional or protective measures ordered in the State of origin pursuant to adversary proceedings – even though by default – from being the subject of recognition and an authorization for enforcement on the conditions laid down in Articles 25 to 49 of the Convention. On the other hand the conditions imposed by Title III of the Convention on the recognition and the enforcement of judicial decisions are not fulfilled in the case of provisional or protective measures which are ordered or authorized by a court without the party against whom they are directed having been summoned to appear and which are intended to be enforced without prior service on that party. It follows that this type of judicial decision is not covered by the simplified enforcement procedure

---

1 *Editor's note*: this is the same as Article 31 of the Regulation, set out in Panel 19.3, above.

> provided for by Title III of the Convention. However, as the Government of
> the United Kingdom has rightly observed, Article 24 provides a procedure
> for litigants which to a large extent removes the drawbacks of this situation.
> 18.   The reply to Questions 1 and 2 should therefore be that judicial decisions
>   authorizing provisional or protective measures, which are delivered without
>   the party against which they are directed having been summoned to appear
>   and which are intended to be enforced without prior service do not come
>   within the system of recognition and enforcement provided for by Title III of
>   the Convention.

Comment

Although the actual ruling in this case is that a freezing order is not enforceable
if it was *ex parte*, it also appears to hold that, where the court granting it had jurisdiction over the substance, it is enforceable if it was granted after the defendant
has been given the opportunity to put his case in *inter partes* proceedings.

§ 8.2   No jurisdiction over the substance

We now consider the situation where the court granting the order had no jurisdiction over the substance of the claim. Here it must rely on Article 31 (Article
24 of the Convention) to obtain jurisdiction.

> **European Union**
> ***Van Uden* v. *Deco Line***
> **Court of Justice of the European Communities**
> **Case C-391/95, [1998] ECR I-7091**

Background

The case concerned a shipping contract between a Dutch and a German firm. The
contract contained a clause providing for arbitration in the Netherlands. A dispute arose when the German firm allegedly failed to pay invoices, and the Dutch
firm commenced arbitration. In addition, it invoked Article 24 of the Convention
to ask the Dutch courts for an interim order for payment of the money allegedly
owed. It did this under the *kort geding* procedure of the Dutch courts. *Kort geding*
means 'summary proceedings'. Under it, an order (granted by the president of
the court) can be obtained, in a matter of weeks, after a hearing often lasting
less than a day. The order is interim in the sense that it can be overturned in an
action under the normal procedure; however, there is usually no obligation on
the claimant to bring such an action[37] and, if neither he nor the defendant does
so, the order will be definitive. In practice, the *kort geding* order is normally the
end of the matter. The fact that the order does not merely seek to preserve the
status quo but often grants the claimant the remedy he is seeking – for example,
damages or an injunction – has caused controversy in the past, since it blurs the

---

37 The court has power to order him to do so, but this power is rarely exercised.

distinction between interim measures and summary judgment, as understood in England.

In the case, the Dutch court before which the *kort geding* proceedings were brought awarded the Dutch firm a little less than half the disputed sum as an interim payment. The German firm argued that the court had no jurisdiction, but this was rejected. The court held that the proceedings concerned a provisional measure under Article 24 of the Brussels Convention, and that it was consequently entitled to take jurisdiction under Dutch law. The provision it chose was Article 126(3) of the Dutch Code of Civil Procedure, a provision giving jurisdiction to the courts of the *claimant's* domicile if the defendant is neither resident nor domiciled in the Netherlands.[38] This provision was expressly outlawed by the second paragraph of Article 3 of the Convention as regards cases where the defendant was domiciled in another Contracting State. In the *Van Uden* case, the defendant was domiciled in Germany; however, the court thought that Article 24 of the Convention created an exception.[39]

The case went on appeal and a reference was made to the European Court. There were two main issues: the first was whether Article 24 applied when the claim was subject to arbitration (paragraphs 23–34 of the judgment); the second concerned the circumstances in which Article 24 may be invoked (paragraphs 35–47).

Judgment

19. The first point to be made, as regards the jurisdiction of a court hearing an application for interim relief, is that it is accepted that a court having jurisdiction as to the substance of a case in accordance with Articles 2 and 5 to 18 of the Convention also has jurisdiction to order any provisional or protective measures which may prove necessary.

20. In addition, Article 24, in Section 9 of the Convention, adds a rule of jurisdiction falling outside the system set out in Articles 2 and 5 to 18, whereby a court may order provisional or protective measures even if it does not have jurisdiction as to the substance of the case. Under that provision, the measures available are those provided for by the law of the State of the court to which application is made.

. . .

23. However, in the present case, the contract signed between Van Uden and Deco-Line contains an arbitration clause.

[The court then summarized the arguments of the German and United Kingdom Governments (they considered that Article 24 did not apply) and those of Van Uden and the Commission (they considered that it did). It continued:]

---

38 There must in addition be certain minimum contacts with the Netherlands, but the court seemed to consider that this was merely a matter of ensuring that any resulting judgment could be enforced. It held that this requirement was satisfied on two grounds: first, because the defendant was engaged in international trade and would probably become entitled to payments in the Netherlands at some time in the future; and, secondly, because the judgment would be recognized in Germany (presumably under the Brussels Convention). When the case went on appeal, the appellate court (the *Gerechtshof te 's-Gravenhage*) held that there must actually be assets in the Netherlands at the time of the proceedings out of which the judgment can be satisfied: it is not enough that assets may exist in the future.
39 The European Court agreed: see paragraph 42 of the judgment.

28. It must first be borne in mind here that Article 24 of the Convention applies even if a court of another Contracting State has jurisdiction as to the substance of the case, provided that the subject-matter of the dispute falls within the scope *ratione materiae* of the Convention, which covers civil and commercial matters.

29. Thus the mere fact that proceedings have been, or may be, commenced on the substance of the case before a court of a Contracting State does not deprive a court of another Contracting State of its jurisdiction under Article 24 of the Convention.

30. However, Article 24 cannot be relied on to bring within the scope of the Convention provisional or protective measures relating to matters which are excluded from it . . .

31. Under Article 1, second paragraph, point 4, of the Convention, arbitration is excluded from its scope. By that provision, the Contracting Parties intended to exclude arbitration in its entirety, including proceedings brought before national courts [reference to the *Marc Rich* case, set out in Chapter 10, § 5, above].

32. The [Schlosser Report, at pp. 92–93] specifies that the Convention does not apply to judgments determining whether an arbitration agreement is valid or not or, because it is invalid, ordering the parties not to continue the arbitration proceedings, or to proceedings and decisions concerning applications for the revocation, amendment, recognition and enforcement of arbitration awards. Also excluded from the scope of the Convention are proceedings ancillary to arbitration proceedings, such as the appointment or dismissal of arbitrators, the fixing of the place of arbitration or the extension of the time-limit for making awards.

33. However, it must be noted in that regard that provisional measures are not in principle ancillary to arbitration proceedings but are ordered in parallel to such proceedings and are intended as measures of support. They concern not arbitration as such but the protection of a wide variety of rights. Their place in the scope of the Convention is thus determined not by their own nature but by the nature of the rights which they serve to protect . . .

34. It must therefore be concluded that where, as in the case in the main proceedings, the subject-matter of an application for provisional measures relates to a question falling within the scope *ratione materiae* of the Convention, the Convention is applicable and Article 24 thereof may confer jurisdiction on the court hearing that application even where proceedings have already been, or may be, commenced on the substance of the case and even where those proceedings are to be conducted before arbitrators.

[After summarizing the arguments put before the court on the applicability of Article 24, the court continued:]

37. In that regard, it must be remembered that the expression 'provisional, including protective, measures' within the meaning of Article 24 of the Convention is to be understood as referring to measures which, in matters within the scope of the Convention, are intended to preserve a factual or legal situation so as to safeguard rights the recognition of which is otherwise sought from the court having jurisdiction as to the substance of the case (*Reichert and Kockler . . .* paragraph 34).

38. The granting of this type of measure requires particular care on the part of the court in question and detailed knowledge of the actual circumstances in which the measures sought are to take effect. Depending on each case and commercial practices in particular, the court must be able to place a time-limit on its order or, as regards the nature of the assets or goods subject to the measures contemplated, require bank guarantees or nominate a sequestrator and generally make its authorisation subject to all conditions guaranteeing the provisional or protective character of the measure ordered [*Denilauler* v. *Couchet*, paragraph 15].

39. In that regard, the Court held at paragraph 16 of *Denilauler* that the courts of the place – or, in any event, of the Contracting State – where the assets subject to the measures sought are located are those best able to assess the circumstances which may lead to the grant or refusal of the measures sought or to the laying down of procedures and conditions which the plaintiff must observe in order to guarantee the provisional and protective character of the measures authorised.

40. It follows that the granting of provisional or protective measures on the basis of Article 24 is conditional on, *inter alia*, the existence of a real connecting link between the subject-matter of the measures sought and the territorial jurisdiction of the Contracting State of the court before which those measures are sought.

41. It further follows that a court ordering measures on the basis of Article 24 must take into consideration the need to impose conditions or stipulations such as to guarantee their provisional or protective character.

42. With regard more particularly to the fact that the national court has in this instance based its jurisdiction on one of the national provisions listed in the second paragraph of Article 3 of the Convention, it must be borne in mind that, in accordance with the first paragraph of that Article, persons domiciled in a Contracting State may be sued in the courts of another Contracting State only by virtue of the rules set out in Sections 2 to 6 of Title II, that is to say Articles 5 to 18, of the Convention. Consequently, the prohibition in Article 3 of reliance on rules of exorbitant jurisdiction does not apply to the special regime provided for by Article 24.

[The court then summarized the arguments put before the court with regard to the question whether an interim order requiring payment of a contractual consideration may be classified as a provisional measure within the meaning of Article 24 of the Convention. It continued:]

45. Here, it must be noted that it is not possible to rule out in advance, in
     a general and abstract manner, that interim payment of a contractual
     consideration, even in an amount corresponding to that sought as principal
     relief, may be necessary in order to ensure the practical effect of the
     decision on the substance of the case and may, in certain cases, appear
     justified with regard to the interests involved . . .
46. However, an order for interim payment of a sum of money is, by its very
     nature, such that it may pre-empt the decision on the substance of the
     case. If, moreover, the plaintiff were entitled to secure interim payment of a
     contractual consideration before the courts of the place where he is himself
     domiciled, where those courts have no jurisdiction over the substance of
     the case under Articles 2 to 18 of the Convention, and thereafter to have
     the order in question recognised and enforced in the defendant's State, the
     rules of jurisdiction laid down by the Convention could be circumvented.
47. Consequently, interim payment of a contractual consideration does not
     constitute a provisional measure within the meaning of Article 24 unless,
     first, repayment to the defendant of the sum awarded is guaranteed if the
     plaintiff is unsuccessful as regards the substance of his claim and, second,
     the measure sought relates only to specific assets of the defendant located
     or to be located within the confines of the territorial jurisdiction of the court
     to which application is made.

Comment

The most important ruling in this case is that made in paragraph 47: an
interim-payment order is covered by Article 24 only if it relates to specific
assets of the defendant located or to be located within the territory of the
court to which application is made; so there can be no question of enforcing
such an order in another Member State. The position regarding other measures granted under Article 24 is less clear. All the court said was that there
must be a real connecting link between the subject-matter of the measures
sought and the territory of the forum. This remains to be clarified in later
cases.

The requirement that repayment to the defendant of the sum awarded is
guaranteed if the claimant is unsuccessful as regards the substance of his claim
is also important. However, it is not entirely clear how this will work since,
under the Dutch procedure, there appears to be no obligation on the claimant
to commence substantive proceedings. If he does not do so, the only way the
defendant can protect himself is to commence proceedings for a declaration of
non-liability. But where would he do this? The courts of his own country would
have jurisdiction in proceedings brought *against* him by the claimant, but not
(presumably) in proceedings brought *by* him for a declaration of non-liability. If
he had to go to the claimant's country, the effect of the application under Article
24 (now Article 31) would be to confer jurisdiction on the courts of the claimant's
country. This would undermine the jurisdictional system of the Convention/
Regulation.

The problem could be solved if the judgment in *Van Uden* were interpreted to mean that a court cannot invoke Article 31 (Article 24 of the Convention) to grant a provisional-payment order unless there is an obligation on the claimant to commence proceedings on the substance before a court with jurisdiction under the Convention. However, it is not clear that the judgment means this.

European Union
Mietz* v. *Intership Yachting Sneek
Court of Justice of the European Communities
Case C-99/96, [1999] ECR I-2277

Background

Mietz, who was domiciled in Germany, signed a contract with a Dutch firm, Intership, under which he agreed to buy a yacht for DM250,000. The money was payable in five instalments, but the yacht, which was to be built to his order by Intership, was not to be delivered to him until he had paid all of the instalments. Mietz defaulted and Intership brought *kort geding* proceedings in the Netherlands. The Dutch court awarded it DM143,750 plus interest and it then applied to a German court to enforce the judgment. The relevant *Landgericht* (German court of first instance) did so, and Mietz appealed. The *Bundesgerichtshof* (the German Supreme Court) made a reference to the European Court.

We know from the judgment in the *Van Uden* case that, if the Dutch court's jurisdiction was based solely on Article 24 of the Convention, the judgment should have been restricted to assets in the Netherlands (which appeared to be non-existent) and there should have been a guarantee of repayment; but *Van Uden* had not been decided when the proceedings took place.[40] Even if it had been, the German courts would have been faced with a problem, since one of the basic principles of the Convention is that, subject to certain exceptions, a court asked to recognize a judgment under the Convention is not entitled to ask itself whether the court which granted it had jurisdiction.[41] Consequently, even if the *Van Uden* case had been decided before the enforcement proceedings were brought before the German courts, it might have been thought that the German courts could not question the jurisdiction of the Dutch courts.

Judgment

46. Article 24 of the Convention expressly provides that a court has jurisdiction under its national law to grant an application for such measures, even if does not have jurisdiction as to the substance of the matter. That jurisdiction must be exercised within the limits set out in Article 24 of the Convention with regard, in particular, to the granting of measures ordering interim payment, limits which do not apply where the court has jurisdiction as to the substance of the matter . . .

---

40 *Van Uden* was decided in 1998. The judgment of the Dutch court and that of the *Landgericht* in *Intership Yachting* were both given in 1993; the *Bundesgerichtshof* made its reference in *Intership Yachting* in 1996. The European Court did not give judgment until 1999, over three years later. The *kort geding* procedure may be speedy, but the procedure for referring a question to the European Court is not.
41 Article 28, third paragraph, of the Convention.

47. However, it is important to ensure that enforcement, in the State where it is sought, of provisional or protective measures allegedly founded on the jurisdiction laid down in Article 24 of the Convention, but which go beyond the limits of that jurisdiction, does not result in circumvention of the rules on jurisdiction as to the substance set out in Articles 2 and 5 to 18 of the Convention . . .

48. Next, it should be noted that although, in the main proceedings, the court of origin ordered only one measure – namely interim payment – it may happen, in other situations, that the court of origin orders several measures, some of which are to be classified as provisional or protective measures within the meaning of Article 24 of the Convention, while others go beyond the limits provided for in that provision.

49. The question which arises for the court to which application for enforcement is made therefore relates not to the jurisdiction, as such, of the court of origin, but rather to the extent to which it is possible to seek enforcement of a judgment delivered in the exercise of the jurisdiction recognised by Article 24. That jurisdiction constitutes, within the context of the Convention, a special regime . . .

50. Finally, it must be stressed that this is not a case where the court of origin has expressly based its jurisdiction to order interim payment by reference to its jurisdiction under the Convention to deal with the substance of the matter, nor a case where such jurisdiction is evident from the actual terms of its judgment, as would in particular be the case if the judgment showed that the defendant was domiciled in the Contracting State of the court of origin and none of the types of exclusive jurisdiction set out in Article 16 of the Convention was applicable.

51. In such circumstances, only the provisions of Article 27 and, if appropriate, the first paragraph of Article 28 of the Convention would be capable of preventing recognition and enforcement of the judgment of the court of origin.

52. Contrary, however, to the submissions of the United Kingdom Government and the Commission, the fact that the defendant appears before the court dealing with interim measures in the context of fast procedures intended to grant provisional or protective measures in case of urgency and which do not prejudice the examination of the substance cannot, by itself, suffice to confer on that court, by virtue of Article 18 of the Convention, unlimited jurisdiction to order any provisional or protective measure which the court might consider appropriate if it had jurisdiction under the Convention as to the substance of the matter.

53. Unlike the circumstances outlined above, the Netherlands judgment, for the enforcement of which an order is sought in the main proceedings, has the following characteristics:
   – it was delivered at the end of proceedings which were not, by their very nature, proceedings as to substance, but summary proceedings for the granting of interim measures;

- the defendant was not domiciled in the Contracting State of the court of origin and it does not appear from the Netherlands judgment that, for other reasons, that court had jurisdiction under the Convention as to the substance of the matter;
- it does not contain any statement of reasons designed to establish the jurisdiction of the court of origin as to the substance of the matter

and

- it is limited to ordering the payment of a contractual consideration, without, on the one hand, repayment to the defendant of the sum awarded being guaranteed if the plaintiff is unsuccessful as regards the substance of his claim or, on the other, the measure sought relating only to specific assets of the defendant located or to be located within the confines of the territorial jurisdiction of the court to which application is made.

54. It follows from the reply to the fourth question [not set out here] that, if the court of origin had expressly indicated in its judgment that it had based its jurisdiction on its national law in conjunction with Article 24 of the Convention, the court to which application for enforcement was made would have had to conclude that the measure ordered – namely unconditional interim payment – was not a provisional or protective measure within the meaning of that Article and was therefore not capable of being the subject of an enforcement order under Title III of the Convention.

55. So, where the court of origin is silent as to the basis of its jurisdiction, the need to ensure that the Convention rules are not circumvented (see, in this respect, paragraph 47 of this judgment) requires that its judgment be construed as meaning that that court founded its jurisdiction to order provisional measures on its national law governing interim measures and not on any jurisdiction as to substance derived from the Convention.

56. It follows that, in a case having the characteristics set out in paragraph 53 of the present judgment, the court to which application for enforcement was made should conclude that the measure ordered is not a provisional measure within the meaning of Article 24 and for that reason cannot be the subject of an enforcement order under Title III of the Convention.

Comment

This case could be regarded as adding a further exception to the rule that the jurisdiction of the original court cannot be questioned in recognition proceedings, though the European Court claimed that it did not involve the jurisdiction 'as such' of the original court.[42] Since Article 24 allows a court to avoid the jurisdictional restrictions imposed by Article 3 of the Convention, such a power is necessary; nevertheless, it shows that the general principle of non-reviewability of jurisdiction is less absolute than might have been thought.

---

42 Paragraph 49 of the judgment.

In the *Mietz* case, the Dutch court had not expressly said that it was acting under Article 24, nor did it expressly say that it was assuming jurisdiction on the basis of Article 126(3) of the Dutch Code of Civil Procedure. In view of this, the German courts were really called upon to perform two operations: first, they had to determine whether the Dutch court had jurisdiction, if at all, only under Article 24; and, secondly, they had to determine whether the order granted was a provisional and protective measure in terms of Article 24. In these circumstances, it is hard to see how the jurisdiction 'as such' of the Dutch court was not in issue.

The problem in the *Mietz* case arose because of genuine doubt as to the scope of Article 24 and the extent to which *kort geding* proceedings could come within it, doubt that was not resolved until the European Court gave judgment in *Van Uden*. The judgment of the Dutch court in *Mietz* was given in good faith. However, it turned out to go beyond what is permitted by the Convention. Mietz could of course have appealed to the *Hoge Raad* (the Dutch Supreme Court) and asked for a reference to the European Court. This is what the German company did in *Van Uden*. However, it may be unrealistic to expect defendants to do this in every case. They may not be able to afford the cost. They may not think about it. So the European Court was right to allow the German courts to decide the matter for themselves. It was also right to reject the argument put forward by the United Kingdom (which intervened in the case) that, because Mietz had entered an appearance before the Dutch court, this gave it jurisdiction under Article 18.[43]

§ 8.3   Enforcing a judgment from another Member State

Our last question concerns the position where a court is asked to grant a freezing order when proceedings are brought to enforce a judgment from another Member State. Here Article 47 of the Regulation (Panel 19.4) is relevant. This permits an English court to grant a freezing order that applies within England and Wales; but does it permit a worldwide order? This question arose in our next case.

Panel 19.4 Provisional measures in enforcement proceedings
Brussels I Regulation (Regulation 44/2001), Article 47

Article 47

1. When a judgment must be recognised in accordance with this Regulation, nothing shall prevent the applicant from availing himself of provisional, including protective, measures in accordance with the law of the Member State requested without a declaration of enforceability under Article 41 being required.
2. The declaration of enforceability shall carry with it the power to proceed to any protective measures.
3. During the time specified for an appeal pursuant to Article 43(5) against the declaration of enforceability and until any such appeal has been determined, no measures of enforcement may be taken other than protective measures against the property of the party against whom enforcement is sought.

England
Banco Nacional de Comercio Exterior SNC v. Empresa de Tele-comunicaciones de Cuba SA
Court of Appeal
[2007] EWCA Civ 662; [2008] 1 WLR 1936; [2007] 2 All ER (Comm) 1093; [2007] 2 Lloyd's Rep 484

Background

This case concerned a dispute between two Latin American companies. Banco Nacional de Comercio Exterior (BNC) had obtained a judgment from a court

---

43 Paragraph 52 of the judgment.

in Turin against Empresa de Telecomunicaciones de Cuba (ETC). It brought enforcement proceedings under the Regulation in England. Relying on Article 47, it obtained a domestic freezing order. However, it wanted a worldwide order. The trial court granted it, and ETC appealed.

Tuckey LJ gave the judgment of the court

19. Before the judge BNC submitted that Article 47 (1) gave the court jurisdiction to grant the worldwide order. ETC submitted that the only purpose of registration was to enforce the judgment against ETC's assets in England. It followed that there was no basis for granting worldwide relief since this would extend to assets which would not be the subject of enforcement within the jurisdiction. In support of its submissions ETC relied on Article 31 and the decision of the ECJ in [*Van Uden*] to the effect that the granting of provisional or protective measures under that Article was conditional on the existence of a real connecting link between the relief sought and the territorial jurisdiction of the State of the court applied to.

20. The judge rejected these submissions. He contrasted Chapters II and III of the Regulations and after citing Article 47 (1) and (2) said:

> 29. Accordingly, Article 47 provides an unrestricted and discrete code for the granting of provisional or protective measures in the context of enforcement. I detect no basis for restricting the measures to the freezing of domestic assets and/or for limiting the disclosure to domestic assets.
>
> 30. The limitations on such measures in Article 31, exemplified by the *Van Uden* case, afford no analogy with the situation post judgment as the recitals to the Regulation demonstrate. This is all the more so where, as here, the court exercising substantive jurisdiction had no power to grant anything other than a domestic freezing order.

It is not clear which of the recitals the judge is referring to. He was right however to say that neither the Turin court or indeed any of the other courts in which enforcement proceedings have been taken had the power to grant worldwide relief.

21. Before us BNC supported the judge's construction of Article 47 but also sought to put its case on jurisdiction in an alternative way. To that end they relied on section 25 (1) of the Civil Jurisdiction and Judgments Act 1982 which as amended gives the English court jurisdiction to grant interim relief where proceedings have been started in a state to which the Regulation applies. But section 25 (2) says that the court:

> may refuse to grant that relief if, in the opinion of the court, the fact that the court has no jurisdiction apart from this section in relation to the subject matter of the proceedings in question makes it inexpedient for the court to grant it.
>
> . . .

24. We will start with the Article 47 point. [Counsel] for BNC reminded us that Article 47 (1) did not appear in the Brussels Convention. Article 39 [of the Convention] had only contained the provisions which are now Articles 47 (2) and (3), which [counsel for BNC] accepts apply only to domestic relief. But he says those provisions are concerned with enforcement; Article 47 (1) is not.

It applies once a judgment has to be recognised. If so the applicant is able to avail himself of any protective measures available in the state concerned. The English court has the power to grant worldwide freezing orders under section 37 Supreme Court Act 1981 and this free-standing provision enables it to do so even if the judgment has not been registered. Recognition not registration is the basis for jurisdiction.

25. We do not accept these submissions. All parts of Article 47 are directed at enforcement. Article 47 (1) is simply dealing with the position before a declaration of enforceability/registration has taken place. All it is saying is that if the applicant is able to show that he has a judgment which must be recognised he is not prevented from availing himself of protective measures before the formalities which lead to registration have been completed. Such measures might well be necessary the moment judgment has been given in another member state or at least before the formalities required for registration, which include translation, have been completed. Each of the provisions of Article 47 deals with the time at which things can or cannot be done. Thus Article 47 (1) deals with the time before registration; (2) with the time after registration; and (3) with the time after registration where there is an appeal pending.

26. If [counsel for BNC's] submission was correct the addition of Article 47 (1) to the Regulation would have added significantly to the earlier provisions contained in Article 39 of the Brussels Convention. We therefore asked to see any *travaux préparatoires* or other material which cast light on what the Council intended by the addition of this new provision. The Regulation recites that, among other things, the Council had regard to the opinion of the Economic and Social Committee (OJC 117–26/4/2000). Paragraph 2.1.4.2 of this document says:

> For provisional and protective measures, the regulation stipulates that a foreign decision which has not yet been declared enforceable in the state addressed, nevertheless does establish the existence of a credit claim warranting provisional and protective measures (according to the legislation of the state addressed). Such a measure will protect the interests of the creditor pending the enforcement decision.

We think this statement entirely supports our construction of Article 47 (1). A similar statement appears in 4.1.2.2 of this document. Nothing in the document or any of the other material which we were shown supports [counsel for BNC's] construction.

27. So we turn to consider section 25 of the 1982 Act as the basis for the court's jurisdiction to make the worldwide freezing order. Article 31 (formerly Article 24 of the Brussels Convention) enables an applicant to avail himself of this provision in a case to which the Regulation applies. These provisions have been the subject of a number of decisions of this court and the European Court to which we were referred. The applicable principles are well known and we do not need to rehearse them at any length in this judgment.

[The court then set out an extract from the judgment of Millett LJ in *Credit Suisse Fides Trust SA* v. *Cuoghi* (above) and paragraphs 37–40 of the judgment in *Van Uden* (above); it continued:]

29. Applying these principles to the facts of this case we think there can be no doubt that it would be inexpedient to grant BNC a worldwide freezing order. ETC is not resident here. Any assets here are protected by the domestic order. The worldwide order is only directed at assets outside the jurisdiction. There is therefore no connecting link at all between the subject matter of the measure sought and the territorial jurisdiction of this court. It is not suggested that the worldwide order should be made in order to assist the Italian court or any of the other courts of the Member States which have been involved in enforcement proceedings.

30. These reasons alone would justify refusing worldwide relief but there are additional reasons for doing so which we take from paragraph 115 of *Motorola v. Uzan* [set out in § 5.1, above] where this court identified a number of particular considerations to be borne in mind when considering the question of inexpediency. It is not the policy of the Italian court to grant worldwide freezing orders. Given the multiplicity of enforcement proceedings in other member states there is a danger that an English worldwide freezing order would give rise to disharmony or confusion and/or risk conflicting, inconsistent or overlapping orders in other jurisdictions.

31. For these reasons we do not think this court had jurisdiction to make a worldwide freezing order in this case and we would allow ETC's appeal and discharge the order first made by David Steel J on 23 October 2006. When we say jurisdiction we do not mean jurisdiction in the strict sense but the obligation to disclaim or decline jurisdiction as a matter of principle having regard to the restrictions and limitations imposed by a combination of the provisions of the 1982 Act, the Regulation and judicial precedent.

Comment

Though the conclusion reached in this case was surely right, it could have been reached more easily. Having rejected Article 47(1) as a foundation for a worldwide order, the court turned to Article 31, which, it thought, could allow the application of section 25 of the 1982 Act. However, as we have seen, the European Court held in *Van Uden* that Article 31 only authorizes measures relating to 'specific assets of the defendant located or to be located within the confines of the territorial jurisdiction of the court to which application is made'. So it cannot be used to allow worldwide measures.

§ 8.4 When does the Regulation apply?

It will be apparent from the cases we have been considering in this chapter that the Brussels I Regulation only permits domestic freezing orders (orders applying only to property within the territory of the forum). English law, however, provides for worldwide (extraterritorial) orders. The question then arises: when is an English court bound by the restrictions of the Regulation[44] and when is it free to make extraterritorial orders?

---

44 The discussion that follows is couched in terms of the Regulation, but similar considerations would apply to the Lugano Convention.

In discussing this question, it is important to remember that freezing orders are often ancillary measures. If the English court is seised of a substantive claim over which it has jurisdiction under the Regulation, and if the freezing order is ancillary to that claim, the freezing order will not constitute a separate claim for jurisdictional purposes.[45] No separate ground of jurisdiction will be needed; so it will not be necessary for the court to have resort to Article 31.[46] If, on the other hand, there are no substantive proceedings before the English court and the freezing order stands on its own, it will constitute a separate claim for the purposes of the Regulation. This would be the case with regard to orders under section 25 of the 1982 Act.

With these thoughts in mind, we can consider the issues.

§ 8.4.1 Subject-matter scope.
Clearly, the Regulation applies only to proceedings falling within its subject-matter scope; so its restrictions do not apply to proceedings dealing with other matters. However, if the subject-matter would otherwise fall within its scope, Article 31 still applies even if the dispute is subject to arbitration. This was decided in the *Van Uden* case.

§ 8.4.2 Judgment in another Member State.
Article 47 applies where a judgment has been given in another Member State that is subject to recognition under the Regulation. Here, the domicile of the defendant (judgment-debtor) is irrelevant, and it does not matter whether the Member State of origin had jurisdiction under the Regulation or under its national law: in both cases, its judgment must be recognized in other Member States. As we have seen, Article 47 does not permit worldwide freezing orders.[47]

§ 8.4.3 No judgment in another Member State.
Where there is no judgment from the courts of another Member State, Article 31 permits provisional measures to be granted under the law of the forum 'even if, under this Regulation, the courts of another Member State have jurisdiction as to the substance of the matter'. This seems to envisage two situations. The first is where the courts of another Member State are already seised of the case; the second is where they are not seised, but the English court would otherwise be precluded from hearing the case.

§ 8.4.4 A court of another Member State is seised first.
If proceedings involving the same cause of action and between the same parties are already pending before the courts of another Member State, Article 27 (*lis pendens*) requires the English courts to decline jurisdiction. Article 31 creates an exception to this, but, except to the extent that Article 31 applies, Article 27 would preclude the grant of a freezing order in aid of the foreign proceedings under section 25 of the 1982 Act. This is because the freezing order, being in aid of the foreign claim, would 'involve the same cause of action' in terms of Article 27. Since it is not ancillary

---

45 See *Masri* v. *Consolidated Contractors International* [2008] EWCA Civ 625, especially at paragraphs 31, 35, 41 and 59 (CA). This case concerned an antisuit injunction, but the principle is the same.
46 *Van Uden*, paragraph 19 of the judgment.
47 *Banco Nacional de Comercio Exterior SNC* v. *Empresa de Telecomunicaciones de Cuba SA*, § 8.3, above.

to English proceedings on the substance, it would constitute separate 'proceedings' for the purposes of Article 27.

The result is that, if the English courts want to grant a freezing order in aid of proceedings in another Member State, they are subject to the restrictions laid down by Article 31: any order granted must be limited to specific assets of the defendant located or to be located within England. Worldwide orders cannot be made. Since Article 27 applies irrespective of the domicile of the defendant,[48] it applies even if the court first seised bases its jurisdiction on its national law.

§ 8.4.5 No other Member State court is seised.

Here we assume that there are no proceedings before the courts of another Member State, but the English court wants to grant a freezing order in aid of proceedings before the courts of a third State – for example, New York. Since Article 27 would not apply – it applies only when the other proceedings are pending in the courts of a Member State – the English court would be free to grant any remedy permitted under English law, unless some other provision of the Regulation precluded it from doing so.

The provision most likely to be relevant is Article 3(1), which provides that persons domiciled in a Member State may be sued in another Member State only by virtue of the rules set out in Sections 2 to 7 of Chapter II of the Regulation.[49] Therefore, if the defendant is domiciled in another Member State and none of those rules gives it jurisdiction, the English court cannot grant a freezing order except under Article 31.

Assume, for example, that proceedings are pending in New York and the defendant in those proceedings is domiciled in Germany. The claimant comes to England and asks the English court to grant a worldwide freezing order under section 25 of the 1982 Act. Since such an order would not be ancillary to any proceedings before the English court which it has jurisdiction to hear under the Regulation, it would constitute a separate claim, which can be entertained only if jurisdiction exists under the Regulation. Unless some other provision was applicable, Article 31 would constitute the only ground of jurisdiction. In this situation too, the English court would be unable to grant a worldwide order.

It is true that the freezing order could be regarded as ancillary to proceedings in England to enforce the New York judgment (once it is given). This might justify the grant of a domestic freezing order, but would not justify an extraterritorial one. The latter cannot be regarded as ancillary to proceedings to enforce the New York judgment. It would be strange if Community law permitted an English court to grant a more far-reaching order against a Community domiciliary to enforce a non-Community judgment than to enforce a Community judgment.

§ 8.4.6 Conclusions.

The result is that an English court is precluded from granting an extraterritorial freezing order under section 25 of the 1982 Act in cases within the subject-matter scope of the Brussels I Regulation where:

---

48 *Overseas Union Insurance* v. *New Hampshire Insurance*, Case C-351/89, [1991] ECR I-3317.
49 Articles 22 (exclusive jurisdiction) and 23 (choice-of-court agreements) could also deprive the English courts of jurisdiction. They apply irrespective of domicile, but are unlikely to be relevant in practice.

- a court in another Member State has granted a judgment which must be recognized under the Regulation and the freezing order is in support of that judgment;
- the substantive proceedings are pending in the courts of another Member State and the freezing order is in support of those proceedings; or
- the order is in support of proceedings in the courts of a non-member State, but the jurisdictional provisions of the Regulation apply and the English courts have no jurisdiction under them.

Further reading

Aird, 'The Scottish Arrestment and the English Freezing Order' (2002) 51 ICLQ 155

Capper, 'Worldwide Mareva Injunctions' (1991) 54 MLR 329

Collins (Lawrence), *Essays in International Litigation and the Conflict of Laws* (Clarendon Press, Oxford, 1994), pp. 1 *et seq.* (this is a reprint of Sir Lawrence Collins' Hague Academy Lectures, originally published in (1992-III) *Recueil des Cours* 9)

'The Territorial Reach of Mareva Injunctions' (1989) 105 LQR 262

Devonshire, 'Mareva Injunctions and Third Parties: Exposing the Subtext' (1999) 62 MLR 539

'Freezing Orders, Disappearing Assets and the Problem of Enjoining Non-Parties' (2002) 118 LQR 124

Dicey, Morris and Collins, *The Conflict of Laws* (Sweet & Maxwell, London, 14th edn, 2006), pp. 207–23

Kennett (Wendy), *The Enforcement of Judgments in Europe* (Oxford University Press, Oxford, 2000), Chapter 5

Maher and Rodger, 'Provisional and Protective Remedies: The British Experience of the Brussels Convention' (1999) 48 ICLQ 302

McLachlan, 'Transnational Applications of Mareva Injunctions and Anton Piller Orders' (1987) 36 ICLQ 669

Obtaining evidence abroad: forum procedures

In international litigation, you often need to obtain evidence situated in a foreign country. There are basically two ways to do this: you can rely on the powers and procedures of the court hearing the case, or you can seek the assistance of the foreign court. In this chapter, we consider the first of these; in the next chapter, we will consider the second.

§ 1 Evidence from parties to the proceedings

§ 1.1 England

Under English law, parties to legal proceedings are obliged to disclose relevant documents to the other party before the trial. This applies to documents that are, or have been, in their control. The other party must be allowed to inspect them and be given a copy if he so requests. This procedure, which is laid down in CPR 31, is known as 'disclosure of documents'. It was previously called 'discovery of documents', its name in most other common-law systems.

Documents are not excluded from disclosure just because they are in a foreign country. However, a businessman with something to hide might put documents in the hands of a subsidiary or third party in the foreign country. He might choose a country under the law of which disclosure of business secrets is illegal. Whether this puts the documents beyond the reach of the English courts depends in part on the interpretation given to the word 'control' in the CPR, a word defined in CPR 31.8 (Panel 20.1).

These issues arose in our next case. At the time of the case, the relevant rule of court was contained in Order 24 of the Rules of the Supreme Court, the forerunner of the CPR. The terms of this rule are set out in the judgment. It uses the word 'power', rather than 'control', but these words really mean the same thing. The definition given in CPR 31.8 did not exist at the time.

> **Panel 20.1 Disclosure and inspection of documents**
> **Civil Procedure Rules, Rule 31.8**
>
> **Rule 31.8 Duty of disclosure limited to documents which are or have been in party's control**
>
> (1) A party's duty to disclose documents is limited to documents which are or have been in his control.
> (2) For this purpose a party has or has had a document in his control if—
> (a) it is or was in his physical possession;
> (b) he has or has had a right to possession of it; or
> (c) he has or has had a right to inspect or take copies of it.

England
Lonrho Ltd v. *Shell Petroleum Co. Ltd*
House of Lords
[1980] 1 WLR 627

Background

In 1965, the white minority Government of Rhodesia (now Zimbabwe), a country that was then a British colony, declared itself independent.[1] The British Government responded by adopting legislation which made it illegal to import oil into Rhodesia (sanctions). The British Government confidently asserted that this would soon bring the Rhodesians to heel. This did not happen, however, since the oil companies made secret arrangements to ship oil through South Africa, then also a white-minority regime.

Lonrho was a company that owned an oil pipeline, running from the Mozambique port of Beira to Rhodesia. As a result of the sanctions, no oil flowed through this pipeline, and Lonrho lost a great deal of money. It claimed that Shell and BP were responsible, since, by illegally violating the sanctions, they were prolonging Rhodesian independence, which in turn prolonged the period during which the pipeline was not operating.

Lonrho's claim against the oil companies went to arbitration. In order to substantiate its arguments, Lonrho wanted to obtain documents in the hands of oil companies in South Africa and Rhodesia which were indirectly controlled by Shell and BP. The latter refused to hand over the documents. It would have been an offence under the law of South Africa and Rhodesia for the documents to be disclosed without government permission, since both countries imposed criminal penalties on anyone revealing the secrets of the 'sanctions-busting' operations.

One of the questions before the House of Lords was whether Shell and BP were obliged to produce the documents.

Lord Diplock

The relevant rule of the Supreme Court dealing with the discovery that is sought . . . is Ord. 24, r. 3, which empowers the court to make an order upon any party to a cause or matter to make and serve on any other party a list of the documents 'which are or have been in his possession, custody or power relating to any matter in question in the cause or matter . . .' The documents of which discovery is sought are documents which, although they do relate to matters in question in the arbitration, are not and never have been in the possession or custody of Shell or BP. They are and always have been in the sole possession and custody of the subsidiary companies of the groups which operated in Southern Africa and . . . are resident in South Africa or Rhodesia and, for the most part, also incorporated there. Lonrho's contention . . . is that because of the company structure of the groups these documents are in the 'power' of either Shell or BP severally or Shell and BP jointly.

My Lords, neither Shell nor BP is a direct shareholder in any of the relevant subsidiary companies. In some Shell is a shareholder at one remove and BP at two

---

1 This was done to avoid African rule.

removes though a company, the Consolidated Petroleum Co. Ltd ('Consolidated'), in which Shell holds 50 per cent. of the share capital and BP, through a wholly-owned subsidiary, Britannic Estates Ltd, holds the remaining 50 per cent. Some of the operating companies in Southern Africa are wholly-owned subsidiaries of Consolidated; Shell Mozambique Ltd is one of these. In others the shares are held by subsidiaries of Consolidated and in yet others the shares are held not through Consolidated at all but as to 50 per cent. by another wholly-owned subsidiary of Shell and as to the remaining 50 per cent. by another wholly-owned subsidiary of BP.

. . .

The articles of association of all the subsidiaries vest the management of the company in its board of directors. It is the board that has control of the company's documents on its behalf; the shareholders as such have no legal right to inspect or to take copies of them. If requested to allow inspection of the company's documents, whether by a shareholder or by a third party, it is the duty of the board to consider whether to accede to the request would be in the best interests of the company. These are not exclusively those of its shareholders but may include those of its creditors. Needless to say, if the local law of the country in which the company is resident forbids disclosure, the company through its board must comply with that local law.

Such is the case with the subsidiaries that are resident in South Africa or Rhodesia. In each of those countries it would have been a criminal offence for the board of a subsidiary to disclose the company's documents to Shell or BP unless they could obtain a ministerial licence permitting them to do so. Shell and BP did in fact inquire of the boards of the subsidiary companies resident in South Africa and Rhodesia whether they were willing to disclose their companies' documents of which Lonrho seeks discovery in the subsidiaries appeal. The boards refused upon the grounds that it would constitute a criminal offence to do so and that, in any event, it would not be in the best interests of the company.

My Lords, in the circumstances it seems to me to be quite unarguable that the documents of subsidiaries resident in South Africa or Rhodesia are or have ever been in the 'power' of Shell or BP within the meaning of RSC, Ord. 24. Nevertheless your Lordships were pressed with the contention that there were a series of steps open to Shell and BP which, if taken, might have the result of giving them a legal right to inspect and take copies of documents belonging to those subsidiaries . . . The suggested steps would be for Shell and BP, as holders between them of all the shares in Consolidated, to procure the board of Consolidated to exercise that company's power to alter the articles of association of each of those companies of which Consolidated is itself the sole shareholder, so as to entitle the shareholders to inspect and take copies of the documents of any of the subsidiaries or sub-subsidiaries of Consolidated. Any copies taken by Consolidated would be the property of that company; so a similar alteration at least would be needed in the articles of association of Consolidated itself; nor is it clear how the board of Consolidated could be procured to act as suggested in relation to its subsidiaries if it did not consider that it was in the best interest of Consolidated to do so. Clearly, however, no alteration in the articles of association of the operating subsidiaries could overcome the obstacle of the prohibition upon disclosure of the documents imposed by the local law. So, it is said, Shell and BP ought to procure Consolidated to procure the operating subsidiaries to apply for a ministerial licence permitting the disclosure. It is Lonrho's contention that until all this has been done and the licence has actually been refused, neither Shell nor BP will be in a position to say that the documents in the possession of the operating subsidiaries are not in Shell and BP's own power.

My Lords, this argument only requires to be stated to be rejected. Your Lordships are not concerned with any other consequences of the relationship between parent and subsidiary companies than those which affect the duty of a parent company of a multi-national group, whose company structure is that of the Shell or BP groups, to give discovery of documents under RSC, Ord. 24; and this, as I have pointed out, depends upon the true construction of the word 'power' in the phrase 'the documents which are or have been in his possession, custody or power.'

The phrase, as the Court of Appeal pointed out, looks to the present and the past, not to the future. As a first stage in discovery, which is the stage with which the subsidiaries appeal is concerned, it requires a party to provide a list, identifying documents relating to any matter in question in the cause or matter in which discovery is ordered. Identification of documents requires that they must be or have at one time been available to be looked at by the person upon whom the duty lies to provide the list. Such is the case when they are or have been in the possession or custody of that person; and in the context of the phrase 'possession, custody or power' the expression 'power' must, in my view, mean a presently enforceable legal right to obtain from whoever actually holds the document inspection of it without the need to obtain the consent of anyone else. Provided that the right is presently enforceable, the fact that for physical reasons it may not be possible for the person entitled to it to obtain immediate inspection would not prevent the document from being within his power; but in the absence of a presently enforceable right there is, in my view, nothing in Order 24 to compel a party to a cause or matter to take steps that will enable him to acquire one in the future.

. . .

In dismissing the subsidiaries appeal on its own special facts, I expressly decline any invitation to roam any further into the general law of discovery. In particular, I say nothing about one-man companies in which a natural person and/or his nominees are the sole share-holders and directors. It may be that, depending upon their own particular facts, different considerations may apply to these.

Comment

The effect of this judgment is that, even if disclosure had been legal under the foreign law, Shell and BP would still not have been required to hand over the documents. The changes to the relevant procedural rule do not seem to have altered the position in this regard. The negative approach of the House of Lords in this case may have been influenced by political considerations: at the time, there was considerable popular support in Britain for the white-minority regime in Rhodesia. Some people even believed that the British Government, while officially trying to end Rhodesian independence, was secretly colluding with the oil companies to ensure that the sanctions were ineffective. For this reason, the House of Lords may have been reluctant to take a strong line against the oil companies. As we shall see in our next case, US courts take a less formalistic approach to the question of when a company has power/control over evidence.

In the *Lonrho* case, it seems to have been accepted that illegality under the law of the country where the documents were located would have been a complete excuse for their non-production. Later cases have taken a different view. Two cases involved the question whether the French 'blocking statute' (Article 1 *bis* of Law 80-538) excuses production of documents by French parties to English proceedings.

Blocking statutes were originally passed by a number of countries (including the United Kingdom) to prevent the United States from applying its law extraterritorially, especially in antitrust cases. They are discussed in Chapter 34, below.[2] The French legislation made it a criminal offence for anyone to disclose commercial documents or information for use in foreign proceedings, unless the disclosure was made under a convention between France and the other country.

In two cases before the High Court in England in the 1990s, French defendants claimed that they could not disclose documents located in France because they would be exposed to criminal prosecution if they did so.[3] In a way, this was a rather specious argument since it seems that the French law was not normally enforced. However, the cases did raise an issue of principle: should a foreign party to English litigation be excused from granting disclosure on the ground that this would be a criminal offence under the law of his country?

English and American courts do not take kindly to such arguments. As a distinguished English judge has said, 'If you join the game, you must play according to the local rules.'[4] Everywhere in the world, procedure is governed by the *lex fori*, the law of the country where the court is situated. If the case is before an English court, English procedure must apply. A party cannot expect to have special privileges just because he is foreign. The other party is entitled to expect disclosure from foreign parties according to the English rules. Foreign law cannot dictate to English courts what procedure they must apply. For these reasons, the English courts usually order disclosure.[5]

However, English law must be applied flexibly in order to ensure that justice is done. If the risk of prosecution is genuine, the foreign party will refuse to comply. In such a case, the English court would have to consider what action to take. Automatically precluding the defaulting party from taking any further part

---

2 The British blocking statute, the Protection of Trading Interests Act 1980, is outlined in Chapter 34, § 4, below.
3 *Partenreederei M/S Heidberg* v. *Grosvenor Grain & Feed Co. (No. 1)* [1993] 2 Lloyd's Rep 324; *Morris* v. *Banque Arabe et Internationale d'Investissement* [2001] ILPr 37; *The Times*, 23 December 1999. See also *Arab Monetary Fund* v. *Hashim* [1989] 1 WLR 565; *Brannigan* v. *Davison* [1997] AC 238 (PC).
4 *Per* Hoffmann J in *Mackinnon* v. *Donaldson Lufkin & Jenrette Securities* [1986] Ch 482 at pp. 494–5 (set out in § 2.1, below).
5 They generally say that they have a discretion in the matter, but that discretion is usually exercised in favour of disclosure.

in the proceedings would be unjustified, unless this is the only way to protect the rights of the other party. As we shall see in our next case, the US Supreme Court has taken this view. Moreover, automatic debarment by an English court might be an infringement of Article 6 of the European Convention on Human Rights.[6] However, other remedies are possible – for example, the burden of proof could be shifted to the defaulting party with regard to questions of fact that might have been elucidated if disclosure had been granted. Adverse findings of fact may even be made. A nuanced approach along these lines would uphold the rights of the other party without being unfair to the defaulting party.

§ 1.2   United States

Rule 34 of the Federal Rules of Civil Procedure (the federal equivalent of the English CPR) requires disclosure of documents in a party's 'possession, custody or control'. The application of this rule came before the Supreme Court of the United States in our next case, decided more than twenty years before *Lonrho* v. *Shell*.

> **United States**
> *Société Internationale* **v. Rogers**
> **Supreme Court**
> **357 US 197; 78 S Ct 1087; 2 L Ed 2d 1255 (1958)**

Background

During World War II, the US Government seized assets in the United States that were believed to be under the control of IG Farben, a German company. They included stock in a company called General Aniline. After the war, Société Internationale, a Swiss company also known as IG Chemie or Interhandel (referred to in the judgment as the 'petitioner'), brought proceedings to recover the assets. It claimed that they did not belong to the German company but to it. The US Government maintained that, even if the assets were in the formal ownership of Société Internationale, they were really under the control of the German company. In order to prove its case, the US Government demanded that Société Internationale produce documents, including the banking records of another company, Sturzenegger. The US Government claimed that Société Internationale and Sturzenegger were 'substantially identical', something denied by Société Internationale. Société Internationale also argued that disclosure of the banking records would violate Swiss banking-secrecy laws and would expose it to criminal penalties, including imprisonment. The Swiss Government (federal attorney) then 'confiscated' the banking records on the ground that their disclosure would be illegal. This 'confiscation' left the records in Sturzenegger's possession but forbade their disclosure. The district court (trial court) referred the matter to the Master, who reported that there was no evidence that Société Internationale had acted in bad faith or had colluded with the Swiss Government in blocking disclosure of the documents. Despite this, the district court found that the documents

---

6 See Chapter 14, § 5, above.

were in Société Internationale's control and ordered their production. A large number of documents were then produced; however, others were not. As a result, the district court dismissed the petition for failure to comply with the discovery order.[7] The case went on appeal to the Supreme Court.

Judgment

We consider first petitioner's contention that the District Court erred in issuing the production order because the requirement of Rule 34, that a party ordered to produce documents must be in 'control' of them, was not here satisfied. Without intimating any view upon the merits of the litigation, we accept as amply supported by the evidence the findings of the two courts below that, apart from the effect of Swiss law, the Sturzenegger documents are within petitioner's control. The question then becomes: Do the interdictions of Swiss law bar a conclusion that petitioner had 'control' of these documents within the meaning of Rule 34?

We approach this question in light of the findings below that the Swiss penal laws did in fact limit petitioner's ability to satisfy the production order because of the criminal sanctions to which those producing the records would have been exposed. Still we do not view this situation as fully analogous to one where documents required by a production order have ceased to exist or have been taken into the actual possession of a third person not controlled by the party ordered to produce, and without that party's complicity. The 'confiscation' of these records by the Swiss authorities adds nothing to the dimensions of the problem under consideration, for possession of the records stayed where it was and the possibility of criminal prosecution for disclosure was of course present before the confiscation order was issued.

In its broader scope, the problem before us requires consideration of the policies underlying the Trading with the Enemy Act. If petitioner can prove its record title to General Aniline stock, it certainly is open to the Government to show that petitioner itself is the captive of interests whose direct ownership would bar recovery. This possibility of enemy taint of nationals of neutral powers, particularly of holding companies with intricate financial structures, which asserted rights to American assets was of deep concern to the Congress when it broadened the Trading with the Enemy Act in 1941 '. . . to reach enemy interests which masqueraded under those innocent fronts.'

In view of these considerations, to hold broadly that petitioner's failure to produce the Sturzenegger records because of fear of punishment under the laws of its sovereign precludes a court from finding that petitioner had 'control' over them, and thereby from ordering their production, would undermine congressional policies made explicit in the 1941 amendments, and invite efforts to place ownership of American assets in persons or firms whose sovereign assures secrecy of records. The District Court here concluded that the Sturzenegger records might have a vital influence upon this litigation insofar as they shed light upon petitioner's confused background. Petitioner is in a most advantageous position to plead with

---

7 Further offers were made by Société Internationale, but these were rejected as insufficient by the district court.

> its own sovereign for relaxation of penal laws or for adoption of plans which will at the least achieve a significant measure of compliance with the production order, and indeed to that end it has already made significant progress. United States courts should be free to require claimants of seized assets who face legal obstacles under the laws of their own countries to make all such efforts to the maximum of their ability where the requested records promise to bear out or dispel any doubt the Government may introduce as to true ownership of the assets.
>
> We do not say that this ruling would apply to every situation where a party is restricted by law from producing documents over which it is otherwise shown to have control. Rule 34 is sufficiently flexible to be adapted to the exigencies of particular litigation. The propriety of the use to which it is put depends upon the circumstances of a given case, and we hold only that accommodation of the Rule in this instance to the policies underlying the Trading with the Enemy Act justified the action of the District Court in issuing this production order.

Note

Although the Supreme Court held that the discovery orders were justified, it went on to rule that, in view of the finding that Société Internationale had acted in good faith, dismissal of the proceedings was too severe a sanction for non-compliance. It was contrary to the Due Process Clause of the US Constitution (Fifth Amendment) to dismiss the claim without a hearing on the merits, though the courts would be justified, where appropriate, in making adverse inferences of fact against Société Internationale where production of the documents might have helped the government to prove its case.

Result: the appeal was allowed and the case remanded for further proceedings.

Comment

This case seems to be the origin of the US doctrine that illegality under the foreign law does not preclude disclosure, but that such illegality is to be taken into account when the question arises of imposing a penalty for failure to comply.

§ 2   Evidence from third parties

We now deal with disclosure from third parties. In this situation, the position is a little different, since one can hardly tell them, 'If you join the game, you must play according to the local rules.' After all, they do not want to join the game.

§ 2.1   England

In England, disclosure from third parties is possible only in special cases. One such case is under the rule in *Norwich Pharmacal*. This originated in a case called *Norwich Pharmacal Co.* v. *Customs and Excise Commissioners*.[8] Norwich Pharmacal discovered that a chemical compound was being imported into the United Kingdom

---

8 [1974] AC 133; [1973] 3 WLR 164.

in violation of its patent rights. It wanted to sue the importer, but did not know who it was. The Commissioners of Customs and Excise (British Customs) knew the name of the importer but refused to reveal it. They considered that they were under no duty to do so. Norwich Pharmacal sued them in order to obtain discovery (disclosure). The House of Lords held that this was possible. The rule laid down was that if, through no fault of his own, a person gets mixed up in the tortious acts of others so as to facilitate their wrongdoing, he comes under a duty to assist the person who has been wronged by giving him full information and disclosing the identity of the wrongdoers. In this situation, an innocent third party, who is not himself liable, may nevertheless be required to disclose information to the claimant. Since this occurs before the action is brought – the claimant cannot bring the action until he knows whom to sue – it is rather different from normal disclosure.

Our next case shows how this rule has been applied in international cases.

England
Bankers Trust Co. v. Shapira
Court of Appeal
[1980] 1 WLR 1274

Background

Two men, Mr Shapira and Mr Frei, fraudulently induced Bankers Trust in New York to pay them US$1 million. Some of the money was paid into the London branch of a Swiss bank, the Discount Bank. Bankers Trust responded by bringing proceedings in England against Shapira (then in jail in Switzerland), Frei (thought to be in Liechtenstein) and the Discount Bank. Neither Shapira nor Frei was served. The Discount Bank was served, even though it was not liable to Bankers Trust: the purpose of the action was to discover what happened to the money after it was deposited with the Discount Bank. The trial judge held that the order for disclosure would not be made until the first two defendants were served. Bankers Trust appealed.

Lord Denning MR

[After referring to the rule in *Norwich Pharmacal* and stating that the Discount Bank was in no way liable, he said:]

This new jurisdiction must, of course, be carefully exercised. It is a strong thing to order a bank to disclose the state of its customer's account and the documents and correspondence relating to it. It should only be done when there is a good ground for thinking the money in the bank is the plaintiff's money – as, for instance, when the customer has got the money by fraud or other wrongdoing – and paid it into his account at the bank. The plaintiff who has been defrauded has a right in equity to follow the money. He is entitled, in Lord Atkins' words, to lift the latch of the banker's door . . . The customer, who has *prima facie* been guilty of fraud, cannot bolt the door against him. Owing to his fraud, he is disentitled from relying on the confidential relationship between him and the bank . . . If the plaintiff's equity is to be of any avail, he must be given access to the bank's books and documents – for that is the only way of tracing the money or of knowing what has happened to it . . . So the court, in order to give effect to equity, will be prepared in a proper case to make an order on the bank for their discovery. The plaintiff must of course give an undertaking in damages to the bank and must pay all and any expenses to which the bank is put in making the discovery: and the documents, once seen, must be used solely for the purpose of following and tracing the money: and not for any other purpose. With these safeguards, I think the new jurisdiction – already exercised in the three unreported cases – should be affirmed by this court.

Applying this principle, I think the court should go to the aid of the Bankers Trust Co. It should help them follow the money which is clearly theirs: to follow it to the hands in which it is: and to find out what has become of it since it was put into the Discount Bank (Overseas) Ltd.

If the courts were to wait until these two men were served, goodness knows how many weeks might elapse. Meanwhile, if some of it has got into the hands of third persons, they may dispose of it elsewhere. It seems to me that the fact that these two men have not been served does not deprive the court of its power to make such an order. These two men have gone out of the jurisdiction in circumstances in which it is clear that the court should do all it can to help the innocent people to find out where their money has gone.

In those circumstances – while expressing our indebtedness to both counsel – I would allow the appeal and make the order as asked in the notice of appeal.

Waller LJ and Dunn LJ agreed.

Comment

In this case, the records were in England. Our next case shows what happens when they are abroad.

Power to obtain disclosure from banks is also given by section 7 of the Bankers' Books Evidence Act 1879. This provides that, on the application of a party to legal proceedings, a court may permit that party to inspect, and take copies of, any entries in a banker's books for the purposes of those proceedings. This provision featured in our next case.

England
Mackinnon* v. *Donaldson, Lufkin & Jenrette Securities Corporation
High Court (Chancery Division)
[1986] Ch 482; [1986] 2 WLR 453

Background

In this case, the claimant, Mr Mackinnon, said that he had been swindled out of US$250,000 by two other gentlemen, Mr Shepherd and Mr Lanciault. The latter had told Mackinnon that they could procure a loan of US$360 million to buy property in Hong Kong. They had asked for a fee of US$250,000 to be paid into the account of a Bahamian company, International Advisory Services (IAS), at a New York branch of an American bank, Citibank. The money was paid, but the loan was not forthcoming. It was all a fraud. Mackinnon wanted to get his money back. So he sued Shepherd and Lanciault in England. IAS was named as a defendant and would normally have been obliged to disclose documents regarding the whereabouts of the money. However, IAS had ceased to exist: it had been struck off the Bahamian register of companies on the ground that it had no assets or liabilities and was no longer operating. So Mackinnon could not obtain the information he needed from IAS. Instead, he tried to get it from Citibank, which was not a party to the proceedings. Citibank had a branch in London. A subpoena was served on its London branch under the Bankers' Books Evidence Act 1879, requiring it to provide details of IAS's account.

As Hoffmann J pointed out, the information could also have been obtained by seeking the assistance of the New York courts. Either the English court could have issued letters of request (discussed in Chapter 21, § 1, below) addressed to the appropriate New York court, or Mackinnon could have gone directly to the New York courts (see Chapter 21, § 3, below). However, it seems that Mackinnon's lawyers thought that that would take too long. So they applied to the English court. The Master made the order requested. Two days later, Mackinnon also caused subpoenas *ad testificandum* and *duces tecum* to be issued. By this means too, Citibank was required to provide details of IAS's account in New York. The order and subpoenas were served on Citibank at its London branch. Citibank moved to discharge the order and to set aside the subpoenas. It claimed that the order exceeded the international jurisdiction of the English court and infringed the sovereignty of the United States. As we shall see in Chapter 34, this is the sort of claim that the British Government and the English courts were often making at the time with regard to orders made by American courts having effect in England.

Hoffmann J

The argument in support of the subpoena and order by [counsel] for the plaintiff is simple. Citibank carries on business in London. It has complied with the provisions of section 691 of the Companies Act 1985 by registering, *inter alia*, the names and addresses of persons resident within the jurisdiction authorised to accept service of process on the bank's behalf. It has applied for and obtained the privileges of recognition as a bank by the Bank of England under the Banking Act 1979. Citibank has therefore submitted itself to the jurisdiction of the English court. It follows that it can be required to comply with a subpoena in the same way as an English company. Unless there is some good reason for non-production, for example, that production would be unlawful by the law of the place where the documents are kept, the fact that the documents in question happen to be out of the jurisdiction is no reason for discharging the subpoena.

I think that this argument confuses personal jurisdiction, i.e., who can be brought before the court, with subject matter jurisdiction, i.e., to what extent the court can claim to regulate the conduct of those persons. It does not follow from the fact that a person is within the jurisdiction and liable to be served with process that there is no territorial limit to the matters upon which the court may properly apply its own rules or the things which it can order such a person to do. As Dr. Mann observed in a leading article, 'The Doctrine of Jurisdiction in International Law', (1964) 111 *Recueil des cours* 146:

> 'The mere fact that a state's judicial or administrative agencies are internationally entitled to subject a person to their personal or 'curial' jurisdiction does not by any means permit them to regulate by their orders such person's conduct abroad. This they may do only if the state of the forum also has substantive jurisdiction to regulate conduct in the manner defined in the order. In other words, for the purpose of justifying, even in the territory of the forum, the international validity of an order, not only its making, but also its content must be authorised by substantive rules of legislative jurisdiction.'

See also by the same author 'The Doctrine of International Jurisdiction Revisited after Twenty Years', (1984) 196 *Recueil des cours* 9, 19.

The content of the subpoena and order is to require the production by a non-party of documents outside the jurisdiction concerning business which it has transacted outside the jurisdiction. In principle and on authority it seems to me that the court should not, save in exceptional circumstances, impose such a requirement upon a foreigner, and, in particular, upon a foreign bank. The principle is that a state should refrain from demanding obedience to its sovereign authority by foreigners in respect of their conduct outside the jurisdiction. It is perhaps ironic that the most frequent insistence upon this principle by Her Majesty's Government has been as a result of its violation by the courts and government agencies of the United States. In particular, Her Majesty's Government has on several occasions objected to the application by United States courts and agencies of the United States antitrust laws to British companies in respect of their conduct outside the United States. It has also objected to demands made upon such companies for the production of documents situated outside the United States and concerned with transactions taking place abroad . . .

[Hoffmann J referred to *In re Westinghouse Electric Corporation Uranium Contract Litigation* (Chapter 34, § 2, below) and *X AG* v. *A Bank* (§ 3, below). He then continued:]

Conversely, it seems to me that the subpoena and order in this case, taking effect in New York, are an infringement of the sovereignty of the United States. The need to exercise the court's jurisdiction with due regard to the sovereignty of others is particularly important in the case of banks. Banks are in a special position because their documents are concerned not only with their own business but with that of their customers. They will owe their customers a duty of confidence regulated by the law of the country where the account is kept. That duty is in some countries reinforced by criminal sanctions and sometimes by 'blocking statutes' which specifically forbid the bank to provide information for the purpose of foreign legal proceedings: compare section 2 of our Protection of Trading Interests Act 1980. If every country where a bank happened to carry on business asserted a right to require that bank to produce documents relating to accounts kept in any other such country, banks would be in the unhappy position of being forced to submit to whichever sovereign was able to apply the greatest pressure.

I have stated the principle as being a self-imposed limitation upon a state's sovereign authority and I must clarify this concept by distinguishing certain other cases relied on by [counsel for the plaintiffs]. First, I am not concerned with the enforcement of private rights arising out of matters properly subject to the jurisdiction of the court. For example, a foreigner may have agreed by a contract over which the court has jurisdiction to perform various acts abroad. There can be no objection in principle to the enforcement of those rights by injunction or specific performance, even though this requires the performance of acts abroad ... But a subpoena does not involve the enforcement of a private right. It is an exercise of sovereign authority to require citizens and foreigners within the jurisdiction to assist in the administration of justice.

Secondly, I am not concerned with the discovery required by RSC, Ord. 24 from ordinary parties to English litigation who happen to be foreigners. If you join the game you must play according to the local rules. This applies not only to plaintiffs but also to defendants who give notice of intention to defend ... Of course, a party may be excused from having to produce a document on the grounds that this would violate the law of the place where the document is kept ... But, in principle, there is no reason why he should not have to produce all discoverable documents wherever they are.

...

International law generally recognises the right of a state to regulate the conduct of its own nationals even outside its jurisdiction, provided that this does not involve disobedience to the local law. But banks, as I have already said, are in a special position. The nature of banking business is such that if an English court invokes its jurisdiction even over an English bank in respect of an account at a branch abroad, there is a strong likelihood of conflict with the bank's duties to its customer under the local law. It is therefore not surprising that any bank, whether English or foreign, should as a general rule be entitled to the protection of an order of the foreign court before it is required to disclose documents kept at a branch or head office abroad.

... In this case there are, as I have mentioned, two methods by which the documents could be obtained without infringing United States sovereignty and without depriving Citibank of the protection of a New York order. [Counsel for the bank] submits that as between states which are party to the Hague Convention or similar bilateral treaties, evidence should ordinarily be obtained only by the methods prescribed or permitted in the convention ...

[Hoffmann J then considered the authorities and concluded that an order in respect of documents held at a bank's foreign branch or head office should not be made save in very exceptional circumstances.]

Before turning to the question of whether such exceptional circumstances exist in this case, I must address another argument advanced by [counsel for the plaintiffs]. On the particular facts of this case, he says, the order and subpoena seeking information about the IAS account should be equated to ordinary discovery against a defendant. It follows that in accordance with the general rules of discovery, production should be ordered unless there are grounds on which it should be excused. The basis of this submission is that under the rule in [*Norwich Pharmacal*] as extended by the Court of Appeal in [*Bankers Trust* v. *Shapira*], the plaintiff would be entitled to join Citibank as a defendant and demand discovery of the documents in question in order to be able to trace the proceeds of his US $250,000. [Counsel for the bank] agreed that for the purpose of deciding this point I should deal with the matter as if there was a motion before me to join Citibank as a defendant and require production of the documents by way of *Bankers Trust Co.* discovery.

[After discussing the *Bankers Trust* and *Norwich Pharmacal* cases, Hoffmann J continued:]

It seems to me that for the purposes of the jurisdictional rules now under consideration, the *Norwich Pharmacal* case is much more akin to the subpoena directed to a witness than the discovery required of an ordinary defendant. It is a general duty imposed upon persons who become 'mixed up' in tortious acts to produce evidence and documents *before trial* comparable with the general duty upon all persons who have relevant knowledge or documents to give evidence *at the trial*. It is, therefore, also an exercise of sovereign authority and not merely a condition of being allowed to take part as plaintiff or defendant in an English trial. In the United States there is a general right to discovery from third parties but the fact that this process is characterised as discovery does not alter its nature for the purposes of international jurisdiction . . .

In *Bankers Trust Co.* v. *Shapira* the order was made against an English bank in respect of an account maintained in London. The question of international jurisdiction was not considered. However, in one of the cases cited by the Court of Appeal, *London and County Securities Ltd. (In Liquidation)* v. *Caplan* (unreported), 26 May 1978, Templeman J. had ordered an English bank to procure from its foreign banking subsidiaries documents relating to accounts connected with the defendant in order to trace assets which he was said to have embezzled.[1] Templeman J. described the relief which he was granting as 'onerous and . . . to be granted only in the most exceptional circumstances.' The exceptional circumstances were that the case was one of crime and fraud where 'unless effective relief is granted, justice may well become impossible because the evidence and the fruits of crime and fraud may disappear.' The foreign subsidiary banks were indemnified against liability in damages under the local law by the cross-undertaking in damages and the infringement of sovereignty was excused by a commercial equivalent of hot pursuit.

In my judgment, the authorities on *Bankers Trust Co.* v. *Shapira* . . . discovery against a bank are consistent with what seems to me to be correct in principle,

---

1 *Editor's note*: the part of Lord Denning's judgment in which this case is discussed was omitted when the case was set out above.

namely, that its international jurisdictional limits are the same as those of a subpoena *duces tecum* or an order under the Bankers' Books Evidence Act 1879.

I therefore come finally to the question of whether this can be regarded as an exceptional case justifying the making of an exorbitant order.

[Hoffmann J examined the circumstances of the proceedings and concluded that they did not justify doing so. He therefore decided to discharge the order and subpoena.]

Result: the order and subpoenas were discharged.

Comment

This case shows that, where third parties are involved, English courts are generally reluctant to order the production of documents in a foreign country.

QUESTION

Would the result have been different if, instead of using the Bankers' Books Evidence Act 1879, the claimant had made Citibank a party, as in *Bankers Trust Co.* v. *Shapira*?

The concept of 'subject-matter jurisdiction', introduced by Hoffmann J at the beginning of his judgment, is an important one. It is normally referred to as 'extra-territoriality' or 'jurisdiction to prescribe'.[9] It will be considered in Chapter 32, below. However, even though he used the word 'jurisdiction', Hoffmann J accepted that he had the *power* to order disclosure: he simply exercised his discretion against making the order.

It is worth noting that disclosure of the documents would not have been a criminal offence under New York law. Two other banks in the case, Chase Manhattan and Bank of America, had in fact complied with similar orders without complaint. Under New York law (as under English law), a bank is liable to the customer for breach of contract if it discloses details of his account without being authorized to do so. However, since in this case the customer (IAS) had ceased to exist, it is hard to see what harm the bank would have suffered.

Our next case concerns another innovatory pre-trial remedy developed by the English courts at the same time as *Mareva* injunctions. What was originally called an *Anton Piller* order (now, a search order) is an order issued in civil proceedings allowing a party to litigation (existing or contemplated) to search the premises of a named person in order to obtain evidence for the proceedings. The party conducting the search is not allowed to enter the premises against the will of the occupier. However, the order requires the person to whom it is addressed

---

9 The term 'subject-matter jurisdiction' is usually used to mean something different, namely, whether a court has jurisdiction to hear a dispute with regard to a particular subject-matter (see Chapter 2, § 1, above). In the United States, it is used to refer to the question whether a federal court, as distinct from a state court in the same state, has jurisdiction: see Chapter 7, § 1.1, above.

to admit the person in whose favour it is made. Failure to do so would constitute contempt of court. The procedure is often used in intellectual-property-infringement cases.

England
Altertext Inc. v. Advanced Data Communications Ltd
High Court (Chancery Division)
[1985] 1 WLR 457

Background

The first defendant, Advanced Data Communications, was a British company. The other defendants were associated with it. The first five were located in England, but the sixth operated in Belgium. Advanced Data Communications had agreed with Altertext, an American company, to market the latter's software in Europe. Subsequently, Altertext came to believe that the defendants were misusing its secret information. It brought legal proceedings in England for injunctions and various other remedies. Before serving the claim form, it applied for *Anton Piller* orders (search orders) to search the defendants' premises. These were granted with regard to the five English defendants. The question before the court was whether an order should be granted to allow the search of the sixth defendant's premises in Belgium. This could not have been done if the order had purported to operate *in rem*. However, *Anton Piller* orders operate only *in personam*: they require the defendant to permit the claimant to carry out the search. Was this possible where the premises were outside the jurisdiction?

Scott J

The plaintiff's omission to serve the writ or give any notice to the defendants of the proceedings follows the usual practice where *Anton Piller* orders are to be sought. On the plaintiff's evidence the whole point of the *Anton Piller* order would otherwise have been lost. The plaintiff proposed that the writ, notice of motion and affidavit evidence should be served on the defendants, together with the *Anton Piller* order itself which would then immediately be executed.

In the case of English defendants, service presents no legal difficulty. The writ and other documents can be served in England. But where service abroad is necessary, leave of the court, under RSC, Order 11, must first be obtained and the case brought within one or other of the paragraphs of rule 1(1) of that order. Since the sixth defendant is a Belgian company with no place of business in England, service on the sixth defendant required leave under Order 11. Accordingly, the plaintiff applied for such leave and relied on paragraph (j) of Order 11, rule 1(1) as covering the case. Paragraph (j) enables leave to be given:

> if the action begun by writ being properly brought against a person duly served within the jurisdiction, a person out of the jurisdiction is a necessary or proper party thereto.

That paragraph only applies if some defendant has been duly served within the jurisdiction. In the present case, no one had yet been served. But, if the facts are otherwise appropriate for leave to be given under paragraph (j), I do not see why, in a case such as the present, leave should not be given but expressed to be conditional upon service first being duly effected upon some proper defendant within the jurisdiction.

The plaintiff's evidence satisfied me, if the allegations in the affidavits are correct, that the sixth defendant represented one of the means whereby the two principal individual defendants combined to misuse the copyright material and the secret information of the plaintiff and one of the means whereby the first defendant committed breaches of the agreement under which that material and information was put at its disposal. I was, therefore, satisfied that this was, or would be, after service on an English defendant had been effected, a proper case for leave to be given for service abroad on the sixth defendant. Accordingly, I gave leave conditional upon service first being duly effected on the first defendant. But the conclusion that the requisite leave under Order 11 should be granted does not dispose, to my mind, of the difficulty of granting an *Anton Piller* order against the sixth defendant intended to be executed against that company's premises in Belgium before any service of process has been effected on that defendant.

There are difficulties both of jurisdiction and of discretion. I will deal first with jurisdiction. The High Court has a territorial jurisdiction. It has jurisdiction to make orders in respect of goods or land within the jurisdiction, or against premises subject to jurisdiction. It frequently exercises such Jurisdiction *ex parte* and before service of process on the relevant defendant. It often, upon appropriate undertakings being given for the issue of a writ, exercises such jurisdiction before any action has actually been commenced. In these cases the question whether the desired *ex parte* order should or should not be made is generally one of discretion, not of jurisdiction.

But a foreign defendant is, *prima facie*, not subject to the jurisdiction of the court. Such a defendant may become subject to the jurisdiction of the court if service of process can be effected on the defendant in England, or if the defendant submits to the jurisdiction – as, for instance, by instructing solicitors to accept service – or if the court assumes jurisdiction by authorising service under Order 11. But until service has been effected the foreign defendant does not become subject to the jurisdiction of the court. The remedy of a foreign defendant against whom an order under RSC, Order 11 for service abroad has been made is to apply to set aside that order. It is well established that such an application is not a submission to the jurisdiction. If the application succeeds, and the order is set aside, the court is, in effect, declining to assume jurisdiction over that foreign defendant.

But an *Anton Piller* order is a mandatory order intended for immediate execution. The effect of execution of an *Anton Piller* order cannot, in practice, wholly be reversed by the setting aside of that order or, in the case of foreign defendants, by the setting aside of the leave given under Order 11. The foreign premises will have been entered into, the documents in those premises will have been copied or taken away by the plaintiff's solicitors. The documents taken away are likely to have been taken out of the jurisdiction of the foreign country and brought into this country. They can all be returned, but the plaintiff and his solicitors will already have seen their contents. And all this will have happened at a time when the propriety of the assumption by the court or jurisdiction has not been tested at any *inter partes* hearing.

In *Cook Industries Inc.* v. *Galliher* [1979] Ch 439 an order was made by Templeman J against a foreign defendant requiring the foreign defendant to permit the plaintiff to enter his flat in Paris and to take an inventory of the furniture in the flat. But the foreign defendant had already been properly served in England, had entered an appearance and, indeed, was represented by counsel at the hearing before Templeman J. The question was raised before Templeman J whether the English court had jurisdiction to entertain the action at all, involving, as it did, title to a flat in Paris and to the furniture in that flat. Templeman J held that the court did have jurisdiction since the plaintiff's claim was based upon an equity and sought *in personam* relief against the defendants. But there is nothing in the judgment of Templeman J to indicate whether he would have felt able to make the interlocutory order he did if the plaintiff's application had been made before service of the proceedings on the foreign defendant.

. . .

An *Anton Piller* order is an *in personam* order. It is an order which it is within the power of the court to make in an action in which the court has jurisdiction. It ought not, however, in my view, to be made except against a party over whom the court does have jurisdiction. If the order is sought *ex parte* before service of the writ and against a foreign defendant in respect of foreign premises, an essential requirement must be that the case is one in which leave under Order 11 for service outside the jurisdiction ought to be given. Otherwise the court has no jurisdiction over that defendant. But since the initial application is *ex parte* and since the foreign defendant may seek to have the leave under Order 11 set aside, the assumption by the court of jurisdiction is, in a sense, provisional only. In my view, where an *Anton Piller* order against a foreign defendant has to be accompanied by leave under Order 11 for service abroad, the *Anton Piller* order ought not to be executed until the foreign defendant has been given the opportunity to apply to set aside the Order 11 leave. The assumption by the court of jurisdiction over foreign defendants is, under Order 11, strictly controlled. It would be wrong, in my view, for the court to assume jurisdiction over a foreign defendant on an *ex parte* application, and then require a mandatory order of an *Anton Piller* character to be executed by the foreign defendant before he has had an opportunity to challenge the court's assumption of jurisdiction over him.

Accordingly, I indicated to [counsel for the claimant] that, having granted leave for service on the sixth defendant outside the jurisdiction, I was prepared to grant an *Anton Piller* order against that defendant in respect of its premises in Belgium but with a proviso that execution of the *Anton Piller* order was to be suspended for a short period sufficient to enable the sixth defendant to apply to set aside the Order 11 leave. [Counsel for the claimant] took the view that that proviso would render the *Anton Piller* order valueless against the sixth defendant and pressed his application for that order without any such proviso. For the reasons I have given I declined to make it. I indicated to [counsel for the claimant] that I doubted my jurisdiction to do so. On reflection I am not sure that, strictly, the point is one of jurisdiction. The court has, I think, jurisdiction arising out of the leave given under Order 11 and the service abroad of the writ pursuant to that leave. As I have said, the plaintiff's intention was to serve the writ and the *Anton Piller* order together. The point is rather, I think, one of discretion. The court is not, in my view, justified in acting upon an assumed jurisdiction in order to make against a foreign defendant in respect of foreign premises a mandatory order required to be executed before the foreign defendant has had a chance of contesting the jurisdiction.

It does not follow that persons in the position of the plaintiff are without alternative remedy. [Counsel for the claimant] accepted that it might have been possible for effective concurrent proceedings to have been commenced in Belgium for the purpose of obtaining or preserving any relevant evidence situated in the sixth defendant's Belgian premises. But *Anton Piller* orders to be executed in respect of foreign premises ought not to be granted, in my view, except against defendants over whom the courts have unquestionable jurisdiction . . .

Comment

The person against whom the order was requested in this case (the sixth defendant) was not exactly a 'defendant' at the time of the proceedings, since it had not yet been served. What the court was saying was that, until it was served and thereby became a party to the proceedings, it should be treated more like a third party for the purpose of making the order.

§ 2.2 The United States

In the United States (unlike England), discovery against third parties is routine. Our next case shows its operation in a rather special situation – where no legal proceedings had yet begun.

> **United States (Florida)**
> *In re Grand Jury Proceedings Bank of Nova Scotia*
> **US Court of Appeals for the Eleventh Circuit**
> **740 F 2d 817 (1984)**

Background

In the United States, a grand jury operates before criminal proceedings have begun.[10] Its purpose is to consider whether an indictment should be issued. In the case we are about to consider, a federal grand jury in Florida was investigating possible drug dealing. For this purpose, the US Government wanted to obtain banking records held by the Bank of Nova Scotia in the Cayman Islands, the Bahamas and Antigua. The Bank of Nova Scotia was a Canadian bank, which also had branches in the United States, including Florida. A subpoena *duces tecum* was issued by the grand jury. The bank responded by arguing that disclosure of the records would expose it to criminal penalties under the bank-secrecy laws of

---

10 Grand juries have been abolished in England.

the Cayman Islands. Although it produced some documents, it failed to produce others. So the district court imposed a fine of US$25,000 per day until it did so. The bank appealed.

Fay, Circuit Judge

A. Lack of Good Faith

The Bank of Nova Scotia was served with a subpoena from the grand jury on March 4, 1983. The Bank produced no documents at its March appearance before the grand jury and instead moved to quash the subpoena. The district court gave the Bank two months to search for the documents and ordered production by May 31, 1983. Instead of trying to comply with the district court's order during this time the Bank spent most of its time corresponding through counsel with the Assistant United States Attorney handling the case . . .

The district court correctly concluded that the Bank failed to exercise good faith in its efforts to comply with the subpoena . . . Nothing was substantially done by the Bank until the $25,000 per day fine imposed by the district court started to accumulate.

The documents actually produced at different times virtually speak for themselves in showing lack of good faith. On October 20, 1983, seven months after the grand jury subpoena had been served, the only document produced by the Bank was a Xerox copy of a draft drawn to Paula Brady for $163,892.33. The Assistant United States Attorney advised Bank's counsel that there were many more documents in existence which were responsive to the subpoena. Nevertheless, the Bank blithely ignored these warnings and on November 14, 1983, tendered copies of the documents relating to that one transaction as the only records in the Bahamian branches called for by the subpoena. The prosecutor once more warned the Bank that he considered the production inadequate. The Bank insisted that they had diligently searched all ten branches in the Bahamas and had produced all documents. On November 17, 1983, the Bank turned over all of its records from the Cayman Islands. The IRS agent working on the case once more warned Bank's counsel that there were many more documents sought by the subpoena which the Bank had not produced.

Having chosen to ignore all warnings until the fine had started to accumulate, the Bank belatedly became concerned and ordered Mr. Nicol, in late November, 1983, to go to the Bahamas and insure that an effective search had been carried out. Nicol's search began in obvious places which had been previously ignored or overlooked. As a result of his efforts numerous additional documents were discovered at two of the Bank's Bahamian branches. Nine months after the original service of the subpoena, on December 5, 1983, the Bank produced photocopies of voluminous records from 1979. While examining the original documents from the December fifth turnover Mr. Nicol discovered that there were other documents which obviously still were missing. He requested another search of the box of records and obtained the missing documents. These documents were produced on January 25, 1984.

The flurry of activity undertaken by the Bank to discover documents after the trial court entered its order of contempt cannot save the Bank from the consequences of its previous extensive pattern of delay . . . It is clear that the Bank had ample time to search its records and fully comply with the grand jury subpoena at least between April 27, 1983, when the trial court first ordered compliance, and November 14, 1983, when the fines began accumulating . . .

B. Balancing Competing Interests

The Bank also asserts that compliance with the United States grand jury subpoena would require it to violate the Cayman Islands secrecy laws. It therefore contends that it would be appropriate for the United States to moderate the exercise of its judicial enforcement powers in this case since the conflicting laws impose inconsistent obligations on the Bank. The district court, balancing the several factors enumerated in Section 40 of the Restatement (Second) of Foreign Relations Law of the United States (1965), properly concluded that enforcement of the subpoena was proper.

Section 40 provides:

> Limitations on Exercise of Enforcement Jurisdiction
> Where two states have jurisdiction to prescribe and enforce rules of law and the rules they may prescribe require inconsistent conduct upon the part of a person, each state is required by international law to consider, in good faith, moderating the exercise of its enforcement jurisdiction, in the light of such factors as:
> (a) vital national interests of each of the states,
> (b) the extent and the nature of the hardship that inconsistent enforcement actions would impose upon the person,
> (c) the extent to which the required conduct is to take place in the territory of the other state,
> (d) the nationality of the person, and
> (e) the extent to which enforcement by action of either state can reasonably be expected to achieve compliance with the rule prescribed by that state.

Restatement (Second) of Foreign Relations Law of the United States (1965).[1]

The first Restatement factor is the relative interest of the states involved. In this case, the United States seeks to obtain information concerning the money transactions of individuals who are the target of a narcotics investigation. Stemming the narcotics trade has long been a concern of paramount importance to our nation. Congress has steadily enlarged the means available for the detection, prosecution and punishment of those who violate the narcotics laws of this country . . . Illegal narcotics trade generates enormous amounts of cash. Tracing the flow of these dollars is indispensable to this nation's efforts to stop the narcotics trade . . .

The Cayman Islands, on the other hand, sees preservation of bank secrecy as vital to the expansion of the Island's principal industry – banking and off-shore finance. Yet the law does not operate as a blanket guarantee of privacy and has many exceptions. As the Court of Appeal in Jamaica has stated:

---

1 *Editor's note*: in the current version of the *Restatement*, these principles are formulated a little differently: see *Restatement of the Law Third: Foreign Relations Law of the United States*, §§ 403 and 431 (volume 1, pp. 244 and 321).

It would therefore appear that the policy of the legislature is that the Confidentiality Laws of the Cayman Islands should not be used as a blanket device to encourage or foster criminal activities . . . [T]here is nothing in the statute to suggest that it is the public policy of the Cayman Islands to permit a person to launder the proceeds of crime in the Cayman Islands, secure from detection and punishment.

In re Confidential Relationships (Preservation) Law, United States v. *Carver*, (Jamaica Ct App. 1982) (Joint Brief of the United Kingdom and the Cayman Islands, Appendix L.) Furthermore, even if the Cayman Islands had an absolute right to privacy, this right could not fully apply to American citizens. The interest of American citizens in the privacy of their bank records is substantially reduced when balanced against the interests of their own government engaged in a criminal investigation since they are required to report those transactions to the United States pursuant to [US legislation] . . .

We agree with the district court that the Bank suffered no hardship as a result of inconsistent enforcement actions. The Bank and the *amici* argue that it is unfair to require the Bank to be put in the position of having to choose between the conflicting commands of foreign sovereigns. Yet such occasions will arise and a bank indeed will have to choose. As we stated in *In re Grand Jury Proceedings United States* v. *Field*, 532 F 2d 404, 410 (5th Cir.); cert. denied, 429 US 940, 97 S Ct 354, 50 L Ed. 2d 309 (1976):

> In a world where commercial transactions are international in scope, conflicts are inevitable. Courts and legislatures should take every reasonable precaution to avoid placing individuals in the situation [the Bank] finds [it]self. Yet, this court simply cannot acquiesce in the proposition that United States criminal investigations must be thwarted whenever there is conflict with the interest of other states.

Consideration of the other factors set forth by the Restatement does not alter our conclusion that the district court properly enforced the subpoena and imposed contempt sanctions. The disclosure to the grand jury would take place in the United States. The foreign origin of the subpoenaed documents should not be a decisive factor. The nationality of the Bank is Canadian, but its presence is pervasive in the United States. The Bank has voluntarily elected to do business in numerous foreign host countries and has accepted the incidental risk of occasional inconsistent governmental actions. It cannot expect to avail itself of the benefits of doing business here without accepting the concomitant obligations. As the Second Circuit noted years ago, 'If the Bank cannot, as it were, serve two masters and comply with the lawful requirements both of the United States and Panama, perhaps it should surrender to one sovereign or the other the privileges received therefrom.' *First National City Bank of New York* v. *Internal Revenue Service*, 271 F 2d 616, 620 (2nd Cir. 1959); cert. denied, 361 US 948, 80 S Ct. 402, 4 L Ed. 2d 381 (1960).

Enforcement of the subpoena is consistent with the grand jury's goals of investigating criminal matters. It is also entirely consistent with the Cayman policy against the use of its business secrecy law 'to encourage or foster criminal activities.' *In the Matter of*

Proceedings Pending in the United States District Court for the District of Columbia between United States of America and Ray R. Carver, et al., (Ct of Appeal, Jamaica 1982) quoted in Joint Brief of the United Kingdom and the Cayman Islands at 26–27. We conclude that enforcement of the subpoena and the sanctions imposed in this case are proper under the balancing approach of Section 40.

. . .

We have previously recognized that international friction is provoked by enforcement of subpoenas such as the one in this case . . . But under our tripartite form of government federal courts remain open to the legislative and executive branches for assistance if matters such as this prove to have international repercussions . . . The grand jury is a centuries-old, common law institution which is vital to our system of government. It has both the right and the duty to inquire into the existence of possible criminal conduct . . . Indispensable to the exercise of its power is the authority to require the production of evidence . . . The district judge in this case was extremely patient. He gave the Bank ample chances to comply with the subpoena. But the Bank was just sloppy in its search. The remedy for violation of the district court's order is civil contempt. The imposition of a coercive fine is not improper . . . and will be reversed only for an abuse of discretion . . . The order of contempt and the fine in this case did not constitute an abuse of the district court's discretion.

AFFIRMED

Comment

This case shows that, in the United States, even a third party will have to produce documents located in a foreign country, despite the fact that their disclosure would be a criminal offence under the foreign law. However, there is no doubt that the lack of good faith on the part of the bank was a significant factor in the refusal to set aside the fine.

In the *Bank of Nova Scotia* case, the court applied a balancing test, which weighed up the competing interests of the United States and the Cayman Islands. It held that the balance favoured the interests of the United States. Two years after that case was decided, Hoffmann J commented on this approach in *Mackinnon* v. *Donaldson, Lufkin & Jenrette Securities Corporation* (§ 2.1, above):[11]

> I think that it would be wrong to undertake a process of weighing the interests of this country in the administration of justice and the interests of litigants before its courts against those of the United States . . . [T]his is an exercise which has frequently been undertaken by the courts of the United States. It is extremely difficult to perform in a way which carries conviction outside the forum. Distinguished American commentators as well as foreign observers have not failed to notice that the balance invariably comes down in favour of the interests of the United States. It is equally hard for a court in this country, with a duty to administer justice here, to put objectively into the scales the interests of a foreign country in the integrity of its sovereignty over persons or transactions within its jurisdiction.

11 [1986] 2 WLR 453 at pp. 464–5. This passage was omitted when the case was set out above.

QUESTION

QUESTION

Is it right to say to a bank operating in States that impose inconsistent obligations that it must choose which to obey and cease operations in the one it decides not to obey?

§ 3   Foreign proceedings

Up to now, we have been looking at the problem from the point of view of the court where the proceedings are taking place. Now we shift the focus and consider the position of the courts of the country in which the evidence is situated. Our next case shows how English courts react when a foreign court tries to obtain evidence situated in the English branch of a foreign bank.

England
***X AG* v. *A Bank* (also known as *X, Y and Z* v. *B*)**
High Court (Queen's Bench Division (Commercial Court))
[1983] 2 All ER 464; [1983] 2 Lloyd's Rep 535

Background

The identity of the three claimants in this case had been kept hidden by the court. They were known simply as X, Y and Z. Two were incorporated in Switzerland and one in Panama. The defendant was a New York bank with a London branch. Temporary injunctions had previously been granted against the bank preventing it from complying with subpoenas issued by a federal district court in New York requiring it to produce documents relating to the three claimants that were in the possession of the London branch. The question before the court was whether the injunctions should be continued.

The X company was incorporated in Switzerland and had offices in some thirty countries around the world. The Y company, a subsidiary of the X company, was also incorporated in Switzerland; it had a major branch in New York. The Z company, which was associated with the X company, was incorporated in Panama, but had its head office in Switzerland. X and Z carried on business wholly outside the United States; Y, on the other hand, had major American operations. The companies were being investigated for possible federal tax evasions before a grand jury in New York.

In the US proceedings, a subpoena was served on the Y company, as a result of which it produced some 75,000 documents. Subsequently, a subpoena was served on the X company: it refused to comply (on the ground that it was not subject to US jurisdiction) and applied to have the subpoena quashed. The US court refused to quash it; the company was subsequently held to be in contempt. The US Government's next move was to serve a subpoena on the bank. The bank appears to have told the companies about this, and they obtained temporary injunctions from the English court precluding the bank from complying.

Leggatt J

The predicament in which the bank in consequence finds itself is obvious. The subpoena is binding on it. United States law obliges the bank to comply with it. It involves the relevant documents – when I say 'relevant' I mean relevant in the sense of being those documents which are identified in the subpoena – being produced to the Court and there is by way of endorsement of the subpoena an express order of the Court also binding upon the bank. On the other hand, there are now current in this country injunctions prohibiting the bank from obeying that subpoena, being a subpoena supported by the order of a competent Court of the United States.

There is no dispute that the bank is subject to a duty of confidentiality. Apparently the nature of the duty is no different in New York from the duty to which it is regarded as subject in London. For convenience, I would describe the duty as arising from an implied term of the contract governing the relationship of banker and customer and as being that, subject to certain qualifications which it may be material to consider, a banker shall not without the consent of the customer disclose to any other person any document or other information obtained by the banker in the course of that relationship.

There is no dispute that disclosure of the documents to the grand jury would constitute or create a breach of that duty. It would be so, as it appears from the evidence, not merely in the technical sense of the grand jury itself constituting a third person to whom disclosure of confidential documents would constitute a breach of that confidentiality, but also in the far wider and more material sense that, as it would appear, there is in practice no secrecy in relation to matters entrusted to grand juries . . .

The other matter which is not in dispute is the nature and the extent of the harm which the plaintiffs would suffer were such breach of confidentiality to occur in this case. The damage which the X company would sustain is described as immediate, irreparable and incalculable, and similar descriptions are given to that which would be suffered by the other plaintiffs in like circumstances . . .

[The court then discussed the harm that the companies would suffer and considered what would happen to the bank if it did not obey the subpoena.]

[A] substantial affidavit has been sworn on behalf of the plaintiffs by Professor Lowenfeld, Professor of Law at the Law School of New York University. He is a person of the greatest academic distinction and one of the leading authorities in the particular field of law with which this case is concerned. He is, indeed, an associate reporter of the American Law Institute's current revision of the Restatement of the Foreign Relations Law of the United States. His principal responsibility in that capacity is for Part IV of the Restatement, concerning jurisdiction and judgments, and including in particular the sections concerning resolution of conflicting exercises of jurisdiction, which are the subject of the present dispute.

The professor says that he believes it highly unlikely that a United States bank or its officers would be held in contempt for conduct in compliance with the order of a British Court in the circumstances stated, that is, an injunction restraining the transfer or disclosure of records kept in London in respect of a bank account maintained by a non-American corporation at the bank's London branch. He declares himself quite certain—

> . . . that no United States court has ever held a bank or other party in contempt in such circumstances . . . [1]

assuming, as he does, that there is no suggestion of wrongdoing by the bank either in transferring overseas records ordinarily kept in New York or in any way assisting the depositor in a scheme of concealment or non-disclosure.

After reciting the basic rule in the event of conflict between commands of the Courts of different jurisdictions, which apparently is that no one is to be put in the position of fearing punishment irrespective of whether he does or does not do an act, the Professor cites authority for that proposition.

The authorities include one which it behoves me to mention and that is *British Nylon Spinners Ltd* v. *Imperial Chemical Industries Ltd*, [1953] Ch 19. That case is of general importance in this matter for the comments of Sir Raymond Evershed MR, at p. 27, where he says that—

> . . . the courts of this country will, in the natural course, pay great respect and attention to the superior courts of the United States of America; but I conceive that it is none the less the proper province of these courts, when their jurisdiction is invoked, not to refrain from exercising that jurisdiction if they think that it is their duty so to do for the protection of rights which are peculiarly subject to the protection of the English courts. In so saying, I do not conceive that I am offending in any way against the principles of comity . . .

Looking at that case, it is convenient also to mention the comment on p. 28 of Lord Justice Denning:

> . . . The writ of the United States does not run in this country, and if due regard is had to the comity of nations, it will not seek to run here.

There is, as would appear from the professor's affidavit, a doctrine in the United States, or at any rate in New York, known as the doctrine of foreign government compulsion, which depends, as he explains, on a prohibition in one state conflicting with a command in another . . .

. . .

The professor . . . summarizes the matter by reference to his current draft of paragraph 420 of the *Restatement of Foreign Relations Law*, which deals specifically with requests for disclosure and foreign government compulsion. Subparagraph (2) of that section reads, so far as is material:

> (a) the person to whom the order is directed may be required by the court to make a good faith effort to secure permission from the foreign authorities to make the information available; (b) the court may not ordinarily impose the sanction of

---

1 *Editor's note*: a year later, the Bank of Nova Scotia was held in contempt in similar circumstances (see § 2.2 above). No doubt, it will be said that the bank had not acted in good faith in that case; nevertheless, the actions of the banks in the two cases do not seem to have been so very different.

contempt, dismissal, or default on the party that has failed to comply with the order for production, except in cases of deliberate concealment or removal of information or of failure to make a good faith effort in accordance with paragraph (a).[2]

It has been explained that the Restatement is intended to be declaratory of existing law in the United States.

In those circumstances, the professor summarizes his conclusion by saying that an injunction by a foreign Court having jurisdiction over the branch where the documents are located—

> . . . would, I believe, come within the foreign compulsion defence, provided (a) the bank at all times acted in good faith as defined; and (b) disobedience of the injunction would subject the branch and its officers to serious sanction.

I accept that conclusion. It represents, in my judgment, an accurate summary of the law of New York so far as applicable, from which it follows that the bank, having properly pursued its good faith efforts to relieve itself from the consequences of an injunction in this country, ought not to be held liable for contempt in any proceedings brought to that end in New York.

[After discussing the arguments of other parties at some length, and pointing out that the applications were interlocutory (to continue the injunctions until trial), Leggatt J continued:]

I can summarize in a sentence the balance of convenience as I see it. On the one hand, there is involved in the continuation of the injunction impeding the exercise by the United States Court in London of powers which, by English standards, would be regarded as excessive, without in so doing causing detriment to the bank: on the other hand, the refusal of the injunctions, or the continuation of them, would cause potentially very considerable commercial harm to the plaintiffs, that cannot be disputed, by suffering the bank to act for its own purposes in breach of the duty of confidentiality admittedly owed to its customers.

That represents the balance of convenience, against the background that indisputably there is a serious issue to be tried. Damages would not constitute an adequate remedy for the plaintiffs. I am not satisfied that the bank will suffer any detriment, even allowing for the probability that any contempt proceedings that might be brought will be dealt with before the trial of the actions. In those circumstances, it appears to me that the balance of convenience clearly favours the plaintiffs.

. . .

I would not leave these applications without remarking that I do not see this as a matter of conflict between jurisdictions. I can fully understand that the United States District Court would wish to see where the line is in practice drawn by the Courts of this country; but, having been firmly drawn where it has, I find it hard to believe that the bank is in any danger of being held to be in contempt, since the

---

2 For the final version of this provision, see *Restatement of the Law Third: Foreign Relations Law of the United States*, § 442 (Volume 1, pp. 348–9).

adequacy of the excuse that it makes for non-production of the documents sought is now obvious indeed. Any sanction imposed now on the bank would look like pressure on this Court, whereas, as it seems to me, it is for the New York Court to relieve against the dilemma, in which it turns out to have placed its own national, by refraining from holding it in contempt if contempt proceedings are issued.

For those reasons, I shall continue the injunctions now running against the defendants.

§ 4   Conclusions

Although the word 'jurisdiction' is used from time to time, it is clear in all these cases that the matter is not really one of jurisdiction but of policy and discretion. That having been said, however, it is apparent that English courts are unwilling – except in rare and special circumstances – to order persons who are not parties to disclose evidence located outside the jurisdiction. American courts, on the other hand, do so on a routine basis, though they take the foreign law into account when deciding what penalties to impose for non-compliance. This difference may reflect the different approaches of the two legal systems to pre-trial disclosure; it may also show the more confident – some might say, more overbearing – attitude of the dominant world power.

Further reading

Dockray and Laddie, 'Piller Problems' (1990) 106 LQR 601
Morse, 'Obtaining Evidence Abroad: English and American Comparisons', in Plender (R.)
    (ed.), *Legal History and Comparative Law: Essays in Honour of Albert Kiralfy* (Frank Cass,
    London, 1990)

CHAPTER 21

Obtaining evidence abroad: international co-operation

§ 1 Introduction

The normal method of obtaining the assistance of a foreign court is through letters of request, also known as letters rogatory.[1] English and American courts, like other common-law courts, will respond to such requests, even if there is no convention obliging them to do so; in other countries, however, such a convention may be a pre-condition. Many conventions exist; most are bilateral, but some are multilateral. By far the most important is the Hague Convention of 18 March 1970 on the Taking of Evidence Abroad in Civil or Commercial Matters.[2] It is in force in over forty States, including the United Kingdom, the United States, China, Russia, India and most European countries.

The Convention may be used to obtain both documentary and oral evidence. As its name indicates (and as is specified in Article 1), it applies only in 'civil or commercial matters', a phrase to which we shall return. It may be used only to obtain evidence to be put before a court in judicial proceedings:[3] it cannot be used to obtain evidence for an investigation; nor may it be used to obtain documents that will not themselves constitute evidence, even if they lead to other documents that will constitute evidence. The proceedings do not have to have commenced at the time of the request, but they must at least be contemplated.

The court needing the evidence sends a letter of request to the designated 'Central Authority' of the State in which the evidence is located. The latter will pass the letter to the appropriate authority (normally a court) for execution. A hearing is arranged at which the parties and their representatives may be present. In the case of oral evidence, the witness is examined and his testimony is put in writing and sent back to the court that issued the request.

The letter of request is executed according to the procedure of the executing State. However, the court executing it will follow a request from the original court that a special method or procedure be followed, 'unless this is incompatible with the internal law of the State of execution or is impossible of performance by reason of its internal practice and procedure or by reason of practical difficulties'.[4] Witnesses may be compelled to give evidence and persons in possession of

---

1 The word 'rogatory' comes from the Latin *rogare*, to ask or request.
2 Text available on www.hcch.net/index_en.php?act=conventions.text&cid=82/.
3 Article 1.
4 Article 9. The court of origin may request that the evidence be videotaped. For a case in which an English court acceded to such a request from an American court, see *J. Barber & Sons* v. *Lloyd's Underwriters* [1986] 3 WLR 515. Evidence given in a foreign court for use in an English court may be transmitted by

documents may be compelled to produce them. The same measures of compulsion will be applied as in the case of proceedings under the local law.[5]

A person may refuse to give evidence if he is permitted to do so either under the law of the State of execution or under that of the State of origin, provided, in the latter case, that the privilege has been specified in the letter of request or has been confirmed (at the instance of the requested authority) by the requesting authority.[6]

The State addressed may refuse to execute a letter of request if it considers that its sovereignty or security would be prejudiced thereby.[7] Execution may not, however, be refused solely on the ground that, under its internal law, the State of execution claims exclusive jurisdiction over the subject-matter of the action, or that its internal law would not admit a right of action on it.[8]

Under Article 23, a Contracting State may declare that it will not execute letters of request issued 'for the purpose of obtaining pre-trial discovery of documents as known in Common Law countries'. This provision is generally regarded as intended to exclude wide-ranging pre-trial disclosure requests from US courts. Declarations under it have been made by the great majority of Contracting States, including the United Kingdom and other Commonwealth countries, such as Australia and India, as well as many European, Asian and Latin-American countries.[9] No declaration has been made by the United States.

In its declaration under Article 23, the United Kingdom stated that it understood the exclusion to cover any letter of request which requires a person:

(a)   to state what documents relevant to the proceedings to which the letter of request relates are, or have been, in his possession, custody or power; or

(b)   to produce any documents other than particular documents specified in the letter of request as being documents appearing to the requested court to be, or to be likely to be, in his possession, custody or power.

The terms of this declaration are reproduced in section 2(4) of the Evidence (Proceedings in Other Jurisdictions) Act 1975, discussed in § 2, below. It also constitutes the origin of the rule precluding 'fishing expeditions', a topic that will be explored in § 2.1, below.

In Europe, there is an EC Regulation which covers much the same ground as the Hague Convention.[10] Many provisions of the latter – for example, refusal to provide evidence[11] – are reproduced in the Regulation. The Regulation replaces the Convention where both the State of origin and the State of execution are Members of the EU.[12]

Footnote 4 (*cont.*)

television link: *Garcin* v. *Amerindo Investment Advisors Ltd* [1991] 1 WLR 1140. For the question whether a foreign claimant may give evidence before an English court by video link-up because he fears arrest and extradition to a third country if he comes to England, see *Polanski* v. *Condé Nast Publications Ltd* [2005] UKHL 10; [2005] 1 WLR 637; [2005] 1 All ER 945 (HL).

5 Article 10.
6 Article 11.
7 Article 12.
8 *Ibid.*
9 For full details, see www.hcch.net/index_en.php?act=conventions.statusprint&cid=82/.
10 Regulation 1206/2001, OJ 2001 L 174 p. 1.
11 Compare Article 11 of the Convention with Article 14(1) of the Regulation.
12 Article 21(1) of the Regulation.

§ 2   England

The relevant legislation in the United Kingdom is the Evidence (Proceedings in Other Jurisdictions) Act 1975. This Act is the most recent in a long line of statutes, stretching back to 1856. It was adopted to enable the United Kingdom to ratify the Hague Convention, but this was not its only purpose, since it can be used to assist foreign courts under bilateral conventions or even if there is no convention at all. Sections 1–4 apply to evidence in civil proceedings; section 5 applies to evidence in criminal proceedings; and section 6 applies to evidence for international proceedings. These latter two kinds of proceedings are outside the scope of the Hague Convention.

Sections 1–4 apply only to obtaining evidence for the purposes of civil proceedings[13] which have been commenced or are contemplated.[14] The rules on privilege are the same as in the Convention.[15] As already mentioned, the terms of the UK declaration on pre-trial disclosure are reproduced in section 2(4) of the Act.

§ 2.1   'Fishing expeditions'

When a fisherman casts a line, he does not normally know what fish – if any – are lurking beneath the surface: he just hopes something is there. This analogy is used by English courts to refer to the tactic adopted by some lawyers in pre-trial disclosure proceedings: they do not know if the person against whom disclosure is sought has any relevant documents; so they ask for disclosure in wide and general terms in the hope that something useful will turn up. This is called a 'fishing expedition' or simply 'fishing'. Section 2(4) of the Act was intended to outlaw it in the United Kingdom. Our next case shows how it is interpreted.

England
In re Asbestos Insurance Coverage Cases
House of Lords
[1985] 1 WLR 331; [1985] 1 All ER 716

Background

This case concerned letters of request from a California court which requested production of broad categories of documents in connection with asbestos litigation.

Lord Fraser of Tullybelton

The meaning of the expression 'particular documents specified in the order' in subsection (4)(b) [of section 2 of the Evidence (Procedure in Other Jurisdictions) Act 1975] was considered by several of the noble and learned lords who took part in the [*Westinghouse* case, set out below in Chapter 34, § 2]. They were all emphatic that the expression should be given a strict construction. Having regard to the

---

13 Defined in section 9(1) as 'proceedings in any civil or commercial matter'.
14 Section 1(b).
15 Compare Article 11 of the Convention with section 3 of the Act.

purpose of subsection (4) which, as I have already mentioned, is to preclude pre-trial discovery, it is to be construed so as not to permit mere 'fishing' expeditions.

[After quoting Lord Wilberforce and Lord Diplock in the *Westinghouse* case, the latter using the phrase 'individual documents separately described', Lord Fraser continued:]

I do not think that by the words 'separately described' Lord Diplock intended to rule out a compendious description of several documents provided that the exact document in each case is clearly indicated. If I may borrow (and slightly amplify) the apt illustration given by Slade LJ in the present case, an order for production of the respondents' 'monthly bank statements for the year 1984 relating to his current account' with a named bank would satisfy the requirements of the paragraph, provided that the evidence showed that regular monthly statements had been sent to the respondent during the year and were likely to be still in his possession. But a general request for 'all the respondent's bank statements for 1984' would in my view refer to a class of documents and would not be admissible.

The second test of particular documents is that they must be actual documents, about which there is evidence which has satisfied the judge that they exist, or at least that they did exist, and that they are likely to be in the respondent's possession. Actual documents are to be contrasted with conjectural documents, which may or may not exist.

. . .

In the *Westinghouse* case, at p. 611, Lord Wilberforce was willing to extend 'particular documents specified' to include replies to letters 'where replies must have been sent.' I would go that far with him, but I would not extend the expression to documents which may or may not exist.

Comment

The purpose of the 'anti-disclosure' rule is to protect people in the United Kingdom from burdensome disclosure requests. This case shows that it is vigorously enforced.

§ 2.2   Civil or commercial matters

Since both the Convention and the Act refer to 'civil or commercial matters', it is important to know what this means.

England
In Re State of Norway's Application
House of Lords
[1990] 1 AC 723; [1989] 2 WLR 458; [1989] 1 All ER 745

Background

This concerned a request by a court in Sandefjord, Norway, for evidence from two individuals in England for use in a tax case. After receiving the request, the Master made an order under section 2 of the 1975 Act. The two potential witnesses appealed on the ground (among others) that the Norwegian case did not concern 'civil proceedings', as required by section 1 of the Act, and the Court of Appeal held (in 'Norway 1')[16] that the test was whether the proceedings were civil under the law of the requesting State. It decided that they were. The Norwegian court then made a second request and an order was again made under the Act. The potential witnesses again appealed. This time, the Court of Appeal (differently constituted) held (in 'Norway 2')[17] that an international definition (based on the civil law) should be given to the concept. It decided that the proceedings were not civil or commercial under this test. An appeal was taken to the House of Lords. The excerpt below is concerned only with the 'civil or commercial' point.

Lord Goff of Chieveley

Jurisdiction

The submissions of the witnesses on this point are, in summary, as follows. It was submitted that the main purpose of the Act of 1975 was to give effect to the 1970 Hague Convention. The words 'civil or commercial matters' in section 9(1) of the Act reflect the same words in article 1 of the Convention, and should be given the same meaning. Furthermore, the distinction drawn between 'civil' and 'commercial' matters is inconsistent with the English procedural classification, in which civil matters embrace all matters which are not criminal, and in particular include commercial matters. This suggests that the words 'civil or commercial matters' in section 9(1) of the Act should, like the same words in the English text of article 1 of the Convention, be regarded as derived from the words '*matiére civile ou commerciale*' in the French text of article 1. In France, as in other civil law countries, civil matters are categorised as a matter of substance and are regarded as limited to private law matters, excluding public law matters and in particular fiscal matters. This approach was commended as 'internationalist;' and it was suggested that it would achieve uniformity in the construction of article 1 of the Convention, and a consistent construction of section 9(1) of the Act which is derived from it. In *Norway 1* this approach was rejected . . . However it found favour with the majority of the Court of Appeal in *Norway 2*, who felt free to depart from the conclusion reached upon it by the Court of Appeal in *Norway 1*.

Your Lordships are here concerned with the construction of certain words used in an Act of Parliament (the Act of 1975) which is primarily concerned with conferring jurisdiction on courts in the United Kingdom (in England, the High Court) to obtain evidence pursuant to a request from a court or tribunal outside the jurisdiction of the court (whether elsewhere in the United Kingdom or abroad). The Act of 1975 is not the first legislation to be found in the statute book conferring jurisdiction of this kind; and the expression 'civil or commercial matter' is to be found in the earliest Act of Parliament concerned with this subject, the Foreign Tribunals Evidence Act 1856. The question has therefore arisen whether it is legitimate to have recourse to the earlier legislation for the purpose of construing the Act of 1975.

---

16 [1989] 1 All ER 661 (CA).
17 [1989] 1 All ER 701 (CA).

... When it is said that the Act of 1975 was passed with, in part, the purpose of giving effect to the 1970 Hague Convention, this is no doubt true; and where words in the Act are derived directly from the Convention, it may well be right that reference to previous Acts of Parliament in aid of construction would not be appropriate. This is particularly so where, under the Act, the jurisdiction of the courts in this country is enlarged to accommodate the Convention; though I have to say that only minor provisions were required for this purpose. But it is not to be forgotten that the Act of 1975 was not only passed to ensure that our domestic law accommodated the 1970 Hague Convention and so to enable its ratification by the United Kingdom. It was also passed to embrace within one Act of Parliament the relevant powers of superior courts in the United Kingdom, previously contained in a number of Acts of Parliament; and the Act of 1975 confers powers which apply in relation to other jurisdictions within the United Kingdom and, like its predecessors, enables courts in the United Kingdom to assist courts in other jurisdictions throughout the world, whether in convention countries (including not only the 1970 Hague Convention but other conventions to which this country is party) or in non-convention countries (of which there are still a large number). In these circumstances, in considering the scope of the jurisdiction conferred by the Act of 1975, it is, in my opinion, both legitimate and appropriate to have regard to the legislative history of the Act.

I turn therefore to the earlier legislation. As I have already indicated, the first Act of Parliament concerned with the obtaining of evidence for the assistance of foreign courts and tribunals is the Foreign Tribunals Evidence Act 1856 ... The origins of this Act are obscure; all that we know is that the Act has no direct treaty base.

[After quoting section 1 of the Act, Lord Goff continued:]

Here we find the first mention in an Act of Parliament, at least in this context, of the expression 'civil or commercial matter.' It is plain that here the word 'matter' is used as referring to the relevant proceedings; because in section 1 the 'matter' is required (consistently with the long title and section 2 of the Act) to be pending before the foreign court or tribunal. This reinforces the natural inference that, in section 1 of the Act, the expression 'civil matter' is being given no restricted meaning, and would be understood in this country as referring to civil, as opposed to criminal, proceedings. It is true that this gives no weight to the words 'or commercial' so far as the law of this country is concerned: but it is not surprising to find these words added in relation to a jurisdiction which will be invoked by courts or tribunals in foreign countries, many of which differentiate between civil and commercial matters.

[After referring to various other statutes, Lord Goff continued:]

These provisions remained in force for many years, until the repeal of all ... by the Act of 1975. They were so repealed because, as is evident from the long title of the Act of 1975, one important purpose of the Act was to make new provision, in one statute, for the jurisdiction of superior courts in the United Kingdom in relation to obtaining evidence for the assistance of courts or tribunals in other jurisdictions, whether elsewhere in the United Kingdom, or in the few surviving

British dominions (which include the important commercial centre of Hong Kong), or in other countries (whether or not members of the Commonwealth) . . .

Such is the legislative history. I turn to the conventions. It appears from the evidence before your Lordships' House that the first international conventions concerned with obtaining evidence for the assistance of courts or tribunals in foreign jurisdictions consist of a series of 23 bilateral conventions entered into between the United Kingdom and various foreign countries.

[Lord Goff then considered the various conventions and stated that in each, the Convention is stated (in the English text) to apply 'in civil or commercial matters', a phrase translated, in the conventions with France and Belgium, as '*en matière civile ou commerciale.*' He concluded:]

In all the circumstances, however, I do not regard it as a legitimate inference that the English expression 'civil or commercial matters' in these conventions is a translation from the French '*matière civile ou commerciale*', especially bearing in mind that the expression 'any civil or commercial matter' was also to be found in the United Kingdom statute conferring the then relevant jurisdiction on our courts, which had been on the statute book for nearly 70 years before the Convention of 1922 with France. Doubtless all states which were parties to these conventions interpreted the expression, as used in their own languages, in their own ways. Even so, as appears from preparatory documents relating to the 1970 Hague Convention, no difficulty was experienced in practice in the operation of these conventions. Each provided that any such difficulties as might arise should be settled through the diplomatic channel. Indeed, the jurisdiction of national courts, as in this country, is no doubt established by domestic legislation, which may well be (in Norway, as in this country) of wider application, on its face not expressly related to (though no doubt framed to accommodate) any convention to which the country is party.

. . .

It is against this background that I turn to consider the Act of 1975, and in particular the expression 'civil proceedings' in section 1(b) of the Act, as defined in section 9(1), viz. '"civil proceedings", in relation to the requesting court, means proceedings in any civil or commercial matter.'

[After mentioning a slight difference in terminology between the Acts of 1856 and 1975, Lord Goff continued:]

. . . [T]he argument advanced on behalf of the witnesses would involve a profound departure from the established legal practice of conferring a very broad jurisdiction upon the courts in the United Kingdom to enable them to provide assistance for courts in other jurisdictions by obtaining evidence for them. There is no hint in the statute itself that any such departure was intended; indeed the long title to the Act makes no reference at all to the 1970 Hague Convention. I wish to dwell for a moment on the consequences if the witnesses' contention were to be accepted, and the expression 'proceedings in any civil or commercial matter' in section 9(1) were to be given a restricted construction, derived from the French text of article 1 of the Convention, limited by reference to a civil law meaning to be derived from the words in the French text.

I first refer to the fact that the jurisdiction under the Act can be invoked to obtain evidence for the assistance of a court or tribunal in another jurisdiction in the United Kingdom. No doubt, within the United Kingdom, it is normal for a court desiring to obtain evidence from another jurisdiction in the United Kingdom now to take advantage (where necessary) of the extended power of subpoena embodied in section 4 of the Act of 1975. But it may not always be possible to obtain evidence in this way, for example where a witness is ill and so unable to comply with a subpoena; and the simple fact remains that the jurisdiction under the Act is not restricted to obtaining evidence in aid of foreign jurisdictions. It is surely improbable that Parliament should, in these circumstances, have legislated that the jurisdiction should be restricted to proceedings in a civil or commercial matter in a sense understood in civil law countries.

Next, for over a century since 1859, courts or tribunals in British dominions, most of them now independent members of the Commonwealth, have been able to take advantage of an unrestricted jurisdiction in all actions, suits or proceedings. It would be strange indeed if, in relation to these countries, the jurisdiction should now be limited with reference to the law of civil law countries, not only in relation to the remaining Crown colonies, but also in relation to members of the Commonwealth whose courts continued after independence to enjoy an unrestricted jurisdiction. All (or very nearly all) of these countries are, as I have said, members of the common law legal family, to whom the restricted meaning of 'civil or commercial matters', deriving as it does from a different system of law, is unknown.

Furthermore the Act of 1975 confers, as I have said, a jurisdiction exercisable (like the old jurisdiction under the Act of 1856) in order to assist courts or tribunals in all countries, whether or not parties to the 1970 Hague Convention. It is understandable that that Convention should have prompted the passage of the Act of 1975; but it is very difficult to see why Parliament should, for the first time, have here restricted this universal jurisdiction with reference to the French text of the Convention, and most unlikely that it should have done so *sub silentio*, i.e. without making it express that this was indeed the legislative purpose.

Lastly the Act provides, consistently with the law as it has stood for over 100 years (since section 24 of the Act of 1870), for courts in the United Kingdom to have jurisdiction to assist courts in other countries by obtaining evidence in criminal proceedings. This power has nothing to do with private law at all; and it would be surprising if Parliament was expressly to perpetuate the power in relation to criminal proceedings, which are *par excellence* proceedings brought by the foreign state itself, and at the same time be held, by reference to section 9(1), to have restricted the meaning of the words 'civil or commercial matter' by excluding from them what are recognised (in varying forms) as public law cases by the law of certain states. Indeed, the argument for the witnesses leads to the remarkable conclusion that, if penal proceedings in the requesting court are categorised as criminal proceedings, the English court can assist under section 5; but if they are not criminal proceedings, the English court has no jurisdiction to assist.

But the matter does not stop there. Your Lordships' House has, like the courts below, been provided with a most helpful selection of comparative law material. Study of this material reveals that it is very difficult to attribute any uniform meaning to *'matière civile ou commerciale'* or 'civil or commercial matter' in civil law countries. There appears to be little doubt that, in most if not all civil law countries, an important distinction is drawn between private law and public law, and that public law matters are generally excluded from civil or commercial matters. But the identification of public law matters differs from country to country, sometimes in minor respects, sometimes in major respects. I . . . have derived great assistance from the substantial account, given by Professor Charles Szladits of the Columbia Law School, of the distinction between public law and private law in the civil law system, contained in volume 2 of the *International Encyclopedia of Comparative Law*. Volume 2, entitled 'The Legal Systems of the World: Their Comparison and Unification', is under the chief editorship of Professor René David: Professor Szladits' account forms part of chapter 2 of the volume, entitled 'Structure and the Divisions of the Law.' In his *Introduction*, Professor Szladits states, at paragraph 25:

'The fundamental division between private law and public law is considered a basic distinction, the *summa divisio*, in all legal systems belonging to the civil law family of laws. The scope of this division, however, differs considerably within the different legal systems, and consequently the theoretical analysis and the reasons, as well as the practical effects, of these divisions also differ. From the point of view of comparative law, the description of divisions of law and its explanation is a bewildering and difficult task because of their kaleidoscopic nature. Although the same categories can be found – more or less – in all the legal systems of the civil law, the disparity of premises on which they have been established points rather to historical accident and practical convenience than to any all-embracing logical or structural basis.'

Later, in paragraph 31, he states:

'The dual division of law into public law and private law has been accepted in all the civil law systems. This uniformity disappears, however, when we consider the scope of the division, namely, what branches of law are subsumed under the one or the other.'

He then proceeds in this section (and in the following section, concerned with specific traits of public law) to illustrate by detailed reference the divergences of approach in the various civil law systems, considering that it is in the French and German legal systems that the didactic classification of law differs most. It is not necessary for me to go into detail, but I wish to quote from Professor Szladits on this distinction, at paragraph 57:

'The distinction between public law and private law "seems to many Continental European lawyers to be fundamental, necessary and, on the whole, evident. Institutional works, student manuals and treatises contain discussions of the dichotomy, often in confidently dogmatic terms that put to rest incipient doubts." This is an excellent summary of the situation generally prevailing in the civil law systems. Yet this division is far from "necessary" and far from 'evident.' The criteria of distinction are established neither in theory nor in the practice of courts; and, in view of the ever increasing interpenetration of public law and private law the dichotomy appears to be in process of dissolution, which may indicate that it is not even so 'fundamental' as it has been hitherto thought to be. Yet in spite of these doubts and contradictions, the dichotomy is firmly rooted in the thinking of the civilian lawyer.'

In these circumstances, it is scarcely surprising to find, in Preliminary Document No. 3 of August 1968 relating to what became the 1970 Hague Convention (Report of the Special Commission established by M. Amram) the statement:

'The opening phrase of article 1 immediately precipitated a spirited debate on the scope of the Convention. There was no disagreement that the Convention should be limited to "civil and commercial matters" but there was debate on the definition of a "civil and commercial matter".'

However, having ascertained that previous conventions in which this phrase was used (including the bilateral conventions to which the United Kingdom was party) had worked effectively without any need for specific definition of the phrase, and having regard to the historic policy of the Hague Conference to include neither a definition nor a rule of conflicts to resolve a dispute between the states on such an issue, it was decided that article 1 should follow the historic pattern without any definition of 'civil or commercial matters.'

In these circumstances, it must in any event be very difficult to identify, by reference to civil law systems, any 'internationally acceptable definition' of the expression 'civil or commercial matters.' Even if it were appropriate to define the expression in the Act of 1975 with reference to the text of the 1970 Hague Convention, no internationally acceptable definition could be derived from that source. This reinforces my opinion that Parliament did not intend, by any such means, to make the profound change, now adumbrated by the witnesses, in the jurisdiction of the courts of the United Kingdom.

. . .

For these reasons . . . I have come to the conclusion that the words 'civil or commercial matters' in the Act of 1975 cannot be construed with reference to any internationally acceptable meaning. There remains therefore the question how they should be construed; and to answer that necessary to consider by reference to which system of law this question should be answered.

[Lord Goff then considered what the right approach should be. He concluded that, since an internationally acceptable interpretation was impossible, a request should be regarded as covered by the 1975 Act if the proceedings concerned a civil or commercial matter under the law of both the requesting country (Norway) and the requested country (England). He decided, after considering the expert evidence before the court, that the proceedings before the court did concern a civil matter under Norwegian law.[1] He then turned to consider the position under English law:]

I have no doubt that, under English law, the words in section 9(1) should be given their ordinary meaning, so that proceedings in any civil matter should include all

---

[1] It seems that, under Norwegian law, civil matters covered everything other than criminal matters; they therefore included tax.

proceedings other than criminal proceedings, and proceedings in any commercial matter should be treated as falling within proceedings in civil matters. On this simple approach, I do not see why the expression should be read as excluding proceedings in a fiscal matter; so that the High Court can have jurisdiction in respect of such a matter under the Act of 1975.

In his case note on *Norway 1* in (1986) 102 LQR 505, 509, Dr F A Mann stated that: 'it can be asserted with confidence that very few states (if any) will ever regard a tax claim as a civil or commercial matter.' I myself have little doubt that this is broadly true in the case of most civil law countries, with their classification of law into public law matters (including fiscal matters) and private law matters (with which alone civil and commercial matters are concerned); though this does not appear to be true of the law of Norway, having regard to the evidence of Professor Fleischer and the terms of the relevant parts of the Norwegian Law Courts Act. But, so far as common law countries are concerned, the matter is, on the material before your Lordships' House, completely unresolved. The American Restatement of Foreign Relations Law indicates (see paragraph 471, comment (f) and paragraph 473, comment (c)) that the practice in the United States is to consider any proceeding which is not criminal as coming within the provisions of the Hague Convention, and that letters of request may be used in administrative proceedings, including proceedings concerning fiscal matters. This view appears to be consistent with the Report of the United States Delegation to the Special Commission on the Operation of the 1970 Hague Convention, dated June 1978, in which it is stated that the United Kingdom delegates concurred with the United States' interpretation of the Convention and stated that the United Kingdom Central Authority followed the same practice as the United States. There appears however to be no decision of any court in the United States on the point: nor has any relevant decision from any other common law country been drawn to the attention of your Lordships' House.

[Lord Goff then considered whether the rule that English courts will not enforce foreign tax obligations was relevant to the proceedings. He decided that it was not. The English court was not being asked to enforce Norwegian tax law, but only to assist the Norwegian court in its task of enforcing it.]

Appeal allowed: the evidence should be obtained.

QUESTION

Which do you think is more 'internationalist' – a uniform interpretation based on the civil law that has the effect of making it more difficult for English courts to assist foreign courts, or an interpretation based on the law of the two countries involved that makes it easier to do so?

Comment

This case shows that different results ensue depending on the method of interpretation adopted. It also shows that a little comparative-law learning is a dangerous thing: the comparative method is not always appropriate when interpreting a British statute, even if that statute is based – in part – on an international convention.

§ 3   The United States

The United States is also a party to the Hague Convention. However, its legislation (28 USC § 1782(a), set out in Panel 21.1) is even wider than that of the United Kingdom. Its most notable feature is that the request does not have to come from the foreign court: a party to foreign proceedings may go directly to a federal district court with a request for assistance.

The provision has the following additional features:

- it is not limited to civil or commercial matters;
- it covers criminal proceedings;
- no convention is necessary;
- it also applies to proceedings before international tribunals;
- there is no provision precluding pre-trial discovery.

The first four of these points also apply to the UK Act. The last one does not.

In *Intel Corporation* v. *Advanced Micro Devices*,[18] the US Supreme Court held that the provision could be invoked by a complainant (not, strictly speaking, a party) to competition proceedings before the EC Commission (not, strictly speaking, a court). The Supreme Court also held that assistance was not ruled out just because the document would not be discoverable under the foreign law.

Panel 21.1 Assistance to foreign and international tribunals 28 USC § 1782(a)

§ 1782(a)

The district court of the district in which a person resides or is found may order him to give his testimony or statement or to produce a document or other thing for use in a proceeding in a foreign or international tribunal, including criminal investigations conducted before formal accusation. The order may be made pursuant to a letter rogatory issued, or request made, by a foreign or international tribunal or upon the application of any interested person and may direct that the testimony or statement be given, or the document or other thing be produced, before a person appointed by the court. By virtue of his appointment, the person appointed has power to administer any necessary oath and take the testimony or statement. The order may prescribe the practice and procedure, which may be in whole or part the practice and procedure of the foreign country or the international tribunal, for taking the testimony or statement or producing the document or other thing. To the extent that the order does not prescribe otherwise, the testimony or statement shall be taken, and the document or other thing produced, in accordance with the Federal Rules of Civil Procedure.

A person may not be compelled to give his testimony or statement or to produce a document or other thing in violation of any legally applicable privilege.

---

§ 4   England: initiative by a party

We have seen that US law permits a federal district court to grant judicial assistance, even if the request comes from a party. Should an English court object if a

---

18 542 US 241; 124 S Ct 2466; 159 L Ed 2d 355 (US Supreme Court, 2004).

party to proceedings before it takes the initiative in this way? The question arose in our next case.

England
South Carolina Insurance Co. v. Assurantie Maatschappij 'de Zeven Provincien' NV
House of Lords
[1987] AC 24; [1986] 3 WLR 398; [1986] 3 All ER 487

Background

In this case, defendants before the English courts (referred to in the judgment as the 're-re-insurers') needed documents in the hands of third parties in the United States to establish their defence. The claimant, South Carolina Insurance, used its influence with the third parties to induce them not to disclose the documents. The defendants then made an application to a federal district court in the United States for an order to force them to disclose the documents. South Carolina Insurance objected: it maintained that a party should not be allowed to do this without the approval of the English court. Hobhouse J agreed: he granted an injunction prohibiting the defendants from taking any further steps in the US application. This injunction was upheld by the Court of Appeal. The defendants appealed to the House of Lords.

Lord Brandon of Oakbrook

The first matter to which attention needs to be drawn is the existence of an essential difference between the civil procedures of the High Court in England on the one hand, and of courts of the United States on the other, with regard to what may be compendiously described as pre-trial discovery. Under the civil procedure of the High Court in England, pre-trial discovery may take two forms. The first form, which is far and away the more common, is by way of disclosure and inspection of relevant documents under RSC, Order 24. The second form, which is comparatively rare, is by way of the asking and answering on oath of interrogatories under RSC, Order 26. Such discovery is, however subject to two important limitations, one relating to its scope and the other to the stage of an action at which it normally takes place. So far as the scope of discovery is concerned, it is limited to the disclosure and inspection of documents in the possession or power of the parties to the action, or to the asking and answering on oath of interrogatories as between such parties. So far as the stage of an action at which discovery normally takes place is concerned, it is the general rule that the two forms of discovery to which I have referred do not take place until the formal pleadings by both sides have been completed and the issues in disputes thereby fully and clearly defined. In this connection, however, it is right to say that the court has power to order either form of discovery at any stage of an action, including a stage earlier than the completion of pleadings; but such power is rarely exercised and then only on special grounds, for instance when discovery is needed in order that justice may be done in interlocutory proceedings.

Because of the first limitation to which I have referred, there is no way in which a party to an action in the High Court in England can compel pre-trial discovery as against a person who is not a party to such action, either by way of the disclosure and inspection of documents in his possession or power, or by way of giving oral or written testimony.[1] I would, however, stress the word 'compel' which I have used in the preceding sentence, for there is nothing to prevent a person who is not a party to an action from voluntarily giving to one or other or both parties to it either disclosure and inspection of documents in his possession or oral or written testimony.

The procedure of the High Court in England, while not enabling parties to an action to compel pre-trial discovery as against a person who is not a party to such action, nevertheless affords ample means by which such a person, provided that he is within the jurisdiction of the court, can be compelled either to give oral testimony, or to produce documents in his possession or power, at the trial of the action itself. Under RSC, Order 38, Part II, such a person may be compelled to give oral testimony at the trial by the issue and service on him of a subpoena *ad testificandum*, or to produce documents in his power or possession (so long as they are adequately described and defined) by the issue and service on him of a subpoena *duces tecum*. The issue of such subpoenas is in the first instance a ministerial rather than a judicial act, and a party may therefore issue subpoenas of either kind as he thinks fit; the court, however, has power to set aside any subpoena on proper grounds, for instance, irregularity of form, irrelevance, oppressiveness or abuse of the process.

The procedure of the High Court in England includes a further power of the court, conferred on it by RSC, Order 38, rule 13, to order any person to attend any proceedings in a cause or matter and produce any document to be specified or described in the order, the production of which appears to the court to be necessary for the purpose of that proceeding. It has, however, long been established that this rule is not intended to be used, and cannot properly be used, to enable a party to an action to obtain pre-trial disclosure and inspection of documents in the possession or power of a person who is not a party to such action. It is a rule of limited application, involving the production of a document or documents to the court itself rather than to either of the parties to an action.

My Lords, the civil procedure of courts in the United States differs essentially from that in the High Court in England in that under it parties to an action can compel, as against persons who are not parties to it, a full measure of pre-trial discovery, including both the disclosure and production for inspection and copying of documents, and also the giving of oral or written testimony. This power of compulsion can be, and regularly is, used at an early stage of an action.

The second matter to which attention needs to be drawn is that 28 United States Code, section 1782, as appears from its terms which I set out earlier, expressly provides that an order made under it may prescribe the practice and procedure, which may be in whole or in part the practice and procedure of the foreign country

---

1 *Editor's note*: as we saw in Chapter 20, above, there are actually some exceptions.

or the international tribunal, for taking the testimony or statement or producing the document or other thing; and that, to the extent that the order does not prescribe otherwise, the testimony or statement shall be taken, and the document or other thing produced, in accordance with the Federal Rules of [Civil] Procedure.

[Lord Brandon then considered US case-law on the question whether material could be obtained under 28 USC § 1782 if it was not discoverable under the foreign law. (This was a matter of controversy in the United States at the time, though, as we have seen, it has now been settled that it can.)[2] He concluded that this was not a question which the House of Lords could decide for itself.

He next considered the power of the courts to grant injunctions. He said this could be done only if a party can show (1) that the other party has invaded, or is threatening to invade, a legal or equitable right of his; or (2) that he is behaving, or threatening to behave, in a manner which is unconscionable. He considered the first possibility and concluded that it did not apply. He continued:]

Has South Carolina shown that the re-re-insurers, by beginning and intending to prosecute their application to the United States district court, have acted in a manner which is unconscionable? It is difficult, and would probably be unwise, to seek to define the expression 'unconscionable conduct' in anything like an exhaustive manner. In my opinion, however, it includes, at any rate, conduct which is oppressive or vexatious or which interferes with the due process of the court.

Although neither Hobhouse J at first instance, nor Griffiths LJ in the Court of Appeal, stated in terms that they thought it right to grant injunctions on the ground that the conduct of the re-re-insurers in making their application to the United States district court was unconscionable, it seems to me to be implicit in their reasons that they regarded it as being so. Hobhouse J based his decision expressly on the need for the court to retain control of its own process, with the necessary implication that the re-re-insurers' conduct was an interference with such control and therefore an interference with the due process of the court. Griffiths LJ based his decision on three grounds: first (like Hobhouse J), that the court must retain control of its own process; secondly, that the civil procedure of United States courts is significantly different from that of English courts, and the parties, by submitting to the jurisdiction of an English court, must be taken to have accepted its procedure; and, thirdly, that unrestricted access to foreign procedural remedies was liable to produce hardship in the form of increased costs and inconvenience. I shall consider each of these grounds in turn.

I consider, first, the ground that the re-re-insurers' conduct was an interference with the court's control of its own process. It is not clear to me why this should be so. Under the civil procedure of the High Court the court does not, in general, exercise any control over the manner in which a party obtains the evidence which he needs to support his case. The court may give him help, certainly . . . Subject, however, to the help of the court in these various ways, the basic principle underlying the preparation and presentation of a party's case in the High Court

2 *Intel Corporation v. Advanced Micro Devices*, 542 US 241; 124 S Ct 2466; 159 L Ed 2d 355 (US Supreme Court, 2004), discussed in § 3, above.

in England is that it is for that party to obtain and present the evidence which he needs by his own means, provided always that such means are lawful in the country in which they are used. It was not in dispute that, if [the third parties in the US who held the evidence], uninfluenced by the control exercised over them by South Carolina on the advice of the latter's English solicitors, had freely and voluntarily allowed the re-re-insurers to inspect, and where necessary to copy, all the documents referred to in the latter's application, it could not possibly have been said that there had been any interference with the English court's control of its own process. That being so, I cannot see why, since the federal law of the United States authorises an application of the kind made by the re-re-insurers in this case, the making of such application, which may or may not succeed in whole or in part, should be regarded as being such an interference either. I cannot, therefore, agree with the first ground of decision relied on by the Court of Appeal.

I consider, secondly, the ground that the procedure of United States courts is significantly different from that of English courts, and the parties, by submitting to the jurisdiction of an English court, must be taken to have accepted its procedure . . . I cannot see that the re-re-insurers, by seeking to exercise a right potentially available to them under the federal law of the United States, have in any way departed from, or interfered with, the procedure of the English court. All they have done is what any party preparing his case in the High Court here is entitled to do, namely to try to obtain in a foreign country, by means lawful in that country, documentary evidence which they believe that they need in order to prepare and present their case. It was said that the re-re-insurers could have applied to the High Court . . . for letters of request to issue to the proper judicial authorities in the United States. But 28 United States Code, section 1782, allows an application to be made either indirectly by the foreign court concerned or directly by an interested party, and I can see no good reason why the re-re-insurers should not have chosen whichever of these two alternatives they preferred. It is, I think, of the utmost importance to appreciate that the reason why English procedure does not permit pre-trial discovery of documents against persons who are not parties to an action is for the protection of those third parties, and not for the protection of either of the persons who are parties to the action. I cannot, therefore, agree with the second ground of decision relied on by the Court of Appeal.

[Lord Brandon then considered whether the injunction was justified on the ground that the re-re-insurers' action resulted in increased costs and inconvenience. He held that it did not. He concluded:]

My Lords, the result of the views which I have expressed is that there was, in my opinion, no such interference with the procedure of the English High Court by the re-re-insurers as would amount to unconscionable conduct on their part, and so justify, in accordance with the basic principles which I stated earlier, the exercise of the court's power to grant injunctions against them. It follows that I would allow the appeal and set aside the orders of Hobhouse J . . . and of the Court of Appeal . . .

Result: the injunctions were set aside.

§ 5   The Hague Convention: a blocking device?

The Hague Convention provides a mechanism to make it easier to obtain evidence abroad. In our next case, however, it was argued that it could also serve the opposite purpose: it could constitute a means of preventing a court from using its own procedures to obtain the production of documents by a party to proceedings before it. If this had been correct, the common-law countries would have very much regretted having signed it.

> **United States**
> *Société Nationale Industrielle Aérospatiale v. United States District*
>   *Court for the Southern District of Iowa*
> **US Supreme Court**
> **482 US 522; 107 S Ct 2542; 96 L Ed 2d 461 (1987)**

Background

The petitioner in this case, Société Nationale Industrielle Aérospatiale (SNIAS), was a French state-owned aircraft-manufacturer. It did extensive business in the United States and was clearly subject to the jurisdiction of the US courts. One of its aircraft crashed in Iowa, and the victims sued it in a federal court in Iowa, claiming that the aircraft was defective. SNIAS did not challenge the jurisdiction of the court; however, although it complied with initial requests for pre-trial discovery, it refused to comply with further requests. It claimed that the Hague Convention constituted the exclusive and mandatory means for obtaining documents and information located in the territory of a foreign sovereign. The French Government supported this in an *amicus* brief. SNIAS also pointed out that, under the French blocking statute,[19] it was a criminal offence to disclose information for use in foreign proceedings except under the terms of an international agreement.

SNIAS therefore filed a motion for a protective order precluding discovery except under the Convention. This was refused by the magistrate. An appeal, by way of *mandamus*, was rejected by the Court of Appeals for the Eighth Circuit. The case then went on certiorari to the US Supreme Court.

Stevens J delivered the opinion of the court

In arguing their entitlement to a protective order, petitioners correctly assert that both the discovery rules set forth in the Federal Rules of Civil Procedure and the Hague Convention are the law of the United States . . . [1] This observation, however, does not dispose of the question before us; we must analyze the interaction between these two bodies of federal law. Initially, we note that at least four different interpretations of the relationship between the federal discovery rules and the Hague Convention are possible. Two of these interpretations assume

1 *Editor's note*: in the United States, self-executing treaties are directly applicable federal law.

19 See Chapter 20, § 1.1, above.

that the Hague Convention by its terms dictates the extent to which it supplants normal discovery rules. First, the Hague Convention might be read as requiring its use to the exclusion of any other discovery procedures whenever evidence located abroad is sought for use in an American court. Second, the Hague Convention might be interpreted to require first, but not exclusive, use of its procedures. Two other interpretations assume that international comity, rather than the obligations created by the treaty, should guide judicial resort to the Hague Convention. Third, then, the Convention might be viewed as establishing a supplemental set of discovery procedures, strictly optional under treaty law, to which concerns of comity nevertheless require first resort by American courts in all cases. Fourth, the treaty may be viewed as an undertaking among sovereigns to facilitate discovery to which an American court should resort when it deems that course of action appropriate, after considering the situations of the parties before it as well as the interests of the concerned foreign state.

In interpreting an international treaty, we are mindful that it is 'in the nature of a contract between nations' to which '[g]eneral rules of construction apply.' We therefore begin 'with the text of the treaty and the context in which the written words are used.' The treaty's history, '"the negotiations, and the practical construction adopted by the parties"' may also be relevant . . .

We reject the first two of the possible interpretations as inconsistent with the language and negotiating history of the Hague Convention. The Preamble of the Convention specifies its purpose 'to facilitate the transmission and execution of Letters of Request' and to 'improve mutual judicial co-operation in civil or commercial matters.' The Preamble does not speak in mandatory terms which would purport to describe the procedures for all permissible transnational discovery and exclude all other existing practices. The text of the Evidence Convention itself does not modify the law of any contracting state, require any contracting State to use the Convention procedures, either in requesting evidence or in responding to such requests, or compel any contracting state to change its own evidence-gathering procedures.

The Convention contains three chapters. Chapter I, entitled 'Letters of Requests', and Chapter II, entitled 'Taking of Evidence by Diplomatic Officers, Consular Agents and Commissioners', both use permissive rather than mandatory language. Thus, Article 1 provides that a judicial authority in one contracting state 'may' forward a letter of request to the competent authority in another contracting state for the purpose of obtaining evidence. Similarly, Articles 15, 16, and 17 provide that diplomatic officers, consular agents, and commissioners 'may . . . without compulsion', take evidence under certain conditions. The absence of any command that a contracting state must use Convention procedures when they are not needed is conspicuous.

Two of the Articles in Chapter III, entitled 'General Clauses', buttress our conclusion that the Convention was intended as a permissive supplement, not a pre-emptive replacement, for other means of obtaining evidence located abroad. Article 23 expressly authorizes a contracting state to declare that it will not execute any letter of request in aid of pre-trial discovery of documents in a common law country.

Surely, if the Convention had been intended to replace completely the broad discovery powers that the common law courts in the United States previously exercised over foreign litigants subject to their jurisdiction, it would have been most anomalous for the common law contracting parties to agree to Article 23, which enables a contracting party to revoke its consent to the treaty's procedures for pre-trial discovery. In the absence of explicit textual support, we are unable to accept the hypothesis that the common law contracting States abjured recourse to all pre-existing discovery procedures at the same time that they accepted the possibility that a contracting party could unilaterally abrogate even the Convention's procedures. Moreover, Article 27 plainly states that the Convention does not prevent a contracting State from using more liberal methods of rendering evidence than those authorized by the Convention. Thus, the text of the Evidence Convention, as well as the history of its proposal and ratification by the United States, unambiguously supports the conclusion that it was intended to establish optional procedures that would facilitate the taking of evidence abroad . . .

An interpretation of the Hague Convention as the exclusive means for obtaining evidence located abroad would effectively subject every American court hearing a case involving a national of a contracting State to the internal laws of that State. Interrogatories and document requests are staples of international commercial litigation, no less than of other suits, yet a rule of exclusivity would subordinate the court's supervision of even the most routine of these pre-trial proceedings to the actions or, equally, to the inactions of foreign judicial authorities. As the Court of Appeals for the Fifth Circuit observed in *In re Anschuetz & Co., GmbH*, 754 F 2d 602, 612 (1985); cert. pending, No. 85-98:

> 'It seems patently obvious that if the Convention were interpreted as pre-empting interrogatories and document requests, the Convention would really be much more than an agreement on taking evidence abroad. Instead, the Convention would amount to a major regulation of the overall conduct of litigation between nationals of different signatory states, raising a significant possibility of very serious interference with the jurisdiction of United States courts.
>
> . . .
>
> 'While it is conceivable that the United States could enter into a treaty giving other signatories control over litigation instituted and pursued in American courts, a treaty intended to bring about such a curtailment of the rights given to all litigants by the federal rules would surely state its intention clearly and precisely identify crucial terms.'

The Hague Convention, however, contains no such plain statement of a pre-emptive intent. We conclude accordingly that the Hague Convention did not deprive the District Court of the jurisdiction it otherwise possessed to order a foreign national party before it to produce evidence physically located within a signatory nation.[2]

---

2 The opposite conclusion of exclusivity would create three unacceptable asymmetries. First, within any lawsuit between a national of the United States and a national of another contracting party, the foreign party could obtain discovery under the Federal Rules of Civil Procedure, while the domestic party would be required to resort first to the procedures of the Hague Convention . . . Second, a rule of exclusivity would enable a company which is a citizen of another contracting state to compete with a domestic company on uneven terms, since the foreign company would be subject to less extensive discovery procedures in the event that both companies were sued in an American court. Petitioners made a voluntary decision to market their products in the United States. They are entitled to compete on equal terms with other companies

IV

While the Hague Convention does not divest the District Court of jurisdiction to order discovery under the Federal Rules of Civil Procedure, the optional character of the Convention procedures sheds light on one aspect of the Court of Appeals' opinion that we consider erroneous. That court concluded that the Convention simply 'does not apply' to discovery sought from a foreign litigant that is subject to the jurisdiction of an American court . . . Plaintiffs argue that this conclusion is supported by two considerations. First, the Federal Rules of Civil Procedure provide ample means for obtaining discovery from parties who are subject to the court's jurisdiction, while before the Convention was ratified it was often extremely difficult, if not impossible, to obtain evidence from nonparty witnesses abroad. Plaintiffs contend that it is appropriate to construe the Convention as applying only in the area in which improvement was badly needed. Second, when a litigant is subject to the jurisdiction of the District Court, arguably the evidence it is required to produce is not 'abroad' within the meaning of the Convention, even though it is in fact located in a foreign country at the time of the discovery request and even though it will have to be gathered or otherwise prepared abroad . . .

Nevertheless, the text of the Convention draws no distinction between evidence obtained from third parties and that obtained from the litigants themselves; nor does it purport to draw any sharp line between evidence that is 'abroad' and evidence that is within the control of a party subject to the jurisdiction of the requesting court. Thus, it appears clear to us that the optional Convention procedures are available whenever they will facilitate the gathering of evidence by the means authorized in the Convention. Although these procedures are not mandatory, the Hague Convention does 'apply' to the production of evidence in a litigant's possession in the sense that it is one method of seeking evidence that a court may elect to employ . . .

V

Petitioners contend that even if the Hague Convention's procedures are not mandatory, this Court should adopt a rule requiring that American litigants first resort to those procedures before initiating any discovery pursuant to the normal methods of the Federal Rules of Civil Procedure . . . The Court of Appeals rejected this argument because it was convinced that an American court's order ultimately requiring discovery that a foreign court had refused under Convention procedures would constitute 'the greatest insult' to the sovereignty of that tribunal . . . We disagree with the Court of Appeals' view. It is well known that the scope of American discovery is often significantly broader than is permitted in other

Footnote 2 (*cont.*)
operating in this market. But since the District Court unquestionably has personal jurisdiction over petitioners, they are subject to the same legal constraints, including the burdens associated with American judicial procedures, as their American competitors. A general rule according foreign nationals a preferred position in pre-trial proceedings in our courts would conflict with the principle of equal opportunity that governs the market they elected to enter. Third, since a rule of first use of the Hague Convention would apply to cases in which a foreign party is a national of a contracting state, but not to cases in which a foreign party is a national of any other foreign state, the rule would confer an unwarranted advantage on some domestic litigants over others similarly situated.

jurisdictions, and we are satisfied that foreign tribunals will recognize that the final decision on the evidence to be used in litigation conducted in American courts must be made by those courts. We therefore do not believe that an American court should refuse to make use of Convention procedures because of a concern that it may ultimately find it necessary to order the production of evidence that a foreign tribunal permitted a party to withhold.

Nevertheless, we cannot accept petitioners' invitation to announce a new rule of law that would require first resort to Convention procedures whenever discovery is sought from a foreign litigant. Assuming, without deciding, that we have the lawmaking power to do so, we are convinced that such a general rule would be unwise. In many situations the Letter of Request procedure authorized by the Convention would be unduly time consuming and expensive, as well as less certain to produce needed evidence than direct use of the Federal Rules. A rule of first resort in all cases would therefore be inconsistent with the overriding interest in the 'just, speedy, and inexpensive determination' of litigation in our courts . . .

. . .

American courts, in supervising pre-trial proceedings, should exercise special vigilance to protect foreign litigants from the danger that unnecessary, or unduly burdensome, discovery may place them in a disadvantageous position. Judicial supervision of discovery should always seek to minimize its costs and inconvenience and to prevent improper uses of discovery requests. When it is necessary to seek evidence abroad, however, the district court must supervise pre-trial proceedings particularly closely to prevent discovery abuses. For example, the additional cost of transportation of documents or witnesses to or from foreign locations may increase the danger that discovery may be sought for the improper purpose of motivating settlement, rather than finding relevant and probative evidence. Objections to 'abusive' discovery that foreign litigants advance should therefore receive the most careful consideration. In addition, we have long recognized the demands of comity in suits involving foreign states, either as parties or as sovereigns with a coordinate interest in the litigation . . . American courts should therefore take care to demonstrate due respect for any special problem confronted by the foreign litigant on account of its nationality or the location of its operations, and for any sovereign interest expressed by a foreign state. We do not articulate specific rules to guide this delicate task of adjudication.

VI

In the case before us, the Magistrate and the Court of Appeals correctly refused to grant the broad protective order that petitioners requested. The Court of Appeals erred, however, in stating that the Evidence Convention does not apply to the pending discovery demands. This holding may be read as indicating that the Convention procedures are not even an option that is open to the District Court. It must be recalled, however, that the Convention's specification of duties in executing states creates corresponding rights in requesting states; holding that the Convention does not apply in this situation would deprive domestic litigants of access to evidence through treaty procedures to which the contracting states have assented. Moreover, such a rule would deny the foreign litigant a full and fair opportunity to demonstrate appropriate reasons for employing Convention procedures in the first instance, for some aspects of the discovery process.

Accordingly, the judgment of the Court of Appeals is vacated, and the case is remanded for further proceedings consistent with this opinion.

It is so ordered.

Comment

If the petitioners' view had been accepted, it would have meant that significant parts of civil procedure in American courts would have been governed by foreign law whenever a foreigner was a party. This would have created an impossible situation.

§ 6   Conclusions

Attitudes towards the questions considered in this chapter will vary depending on the system of procedural law with which one is familiar. In many civil-law countries, it is virtually impossible to obtain documents or other evidence before trial. Lawyers from such countries may believe that a party should be able to prepare his case without expecting assistance from his opponent or from third parties. Such lawyers may feel hostile to the principle of pre-trial disclosure. They might concede that common-law countries, especially the United States, are entitled to apply their own system to their own people, but they might feel that, where the evidence is located in another country, the law of that country should decide whether it should be produced. If this were accepted, however, it would completely undermine the common-law system of procedure. It would mean that an American party would have to produce documents according to the American system, but his foreign opponent would not. This would be like a football match in which different rules applied to the two sides. It is hardly surprising that US courts have rejected it.

England takes a middle way. Pre-trial disclosure by a party is governed by the law of the forum; disclosure by a third party, on the other hand, is regarded as predominantly a matter for the law of the country in which that party resides. If that law provides a mechanism for compelling production of the evidence, a party may take advantage of it; if not, he cannot. In the latter case, the Hague Convention – with all its limitations – may constitute the sole means of obtaining the evidence.

Further reading

Collins, 'Opportunities for and Obstacles to Obtaining Evidence in England for Use in Litigation in the United States' (1979) 13 *International Lawyer* 27

'The Hague Evidence Convention and Discovery: A Serious Misunderstanding' (1986) 35 ICLQ 765

Kennett, 'The Production of Evidence within the European Community' (1993) 56 MLR 342

Lipstein, 'The Evidence (Proceedings in Other Jurisdictions) Act 1975: An Interpretation' (1990) 39 ICLQ 120

McClean (David), *International Judicial Assistance* (Oxford University Press, Oxford, 2002)

Morse, 'Obtaining Evidence Abroad: English and American Comparisons', in Plender (R.) (ed.), *Legal History and Comparative Law: Essays in Honour of Albert Kiralfy* (Frank Cass, London, 1990)

Stahr, 'Discovery under 28 USC § 1728 for Foreign and International Proceedings' (1990) 30 *Virginia Journal of International Law* 597

Sutherland, 'The Use of the Letter of Request (or Letter Rogatory) for the Purpose of Obtaining Evidence for Proceedings in England or Abroad' (1982) 31 ICLQ 784

PART V
CHOICE OF LAW

CHAPTER 22

Introduction to choice of law

§ 1 Why apply foreign law?

Why should a court apply foreign law? It might be imagined that everything could be satisfactorily decided under its own law. A moment's thought, however, reveals that there are at least some situations in which foreign law has to be applied. Take the case of two people, a man and a woman, who have lived all their lives in country X. They are citizens of that country and are domiciled there. They marry there, taking care to ensure that they comply with the requirements of the local law. If, many years later, they go to country Y on a visit, it would be monstrous if their marriage was not recognized because they had not complied with the formalities laid down by the law of country Y.

Marriage is a status, but it is not only in this case that foreign law has to be applied. Think of a testator who makes his will according to what appears to be the only relevant law. It would again be monstrous if a foreign country refused to recognize the will because it did not comply with its own law. Or take the case of a person who ensures that his actions are lawful under what appears to be the only relevant law. Would it be right if a court in another country held that he had committed a tort because what he did would have been a tort under its law?

One can generalize from these examples by saying that, if a person tailors his actions to comply with what appears to be the relevant law, a foreign court ought not to upset his expectations by refusing to apply that law. One can in fact go further and say that a court ought to be willing to apply foreign law whenever this is necessary to uphold the reasonable expectations of the parties, even if there is no evidence that either of them made a special effort to comply with that law.

Upholding expectations is one of the main policy objectives of choice of law. However, it is not the only one. There might also be public purposes that require foreign law to be applied. For example, it would be wrong for an English court to uphold a contract that requires one party to go to a foreign country and do something there that would be a criminal offence under the local law. Respect for the interests of the foreign State should preclude such a result.

Considerations such as these constitute the beginnings of choice-of-law theory. From these beginnings, a substantial edifice has been constructed. Today, almost the whole of private law has been subjected to choice-of-law analysis, and almost every issue has its own special choice-of-law rule to determine when foreign law applies and when forum law applies. It might even be said that – in theory – a court should begin its consideration of every case by determining what the applicable law is.

Until World War II, all Western legal systems (and many non-Western ones as well) applied the same general system, what might be called traditional choice-of-law theory. Subsequently, there was something of a revolution in the United States, and American courts began to apply different theories, at least in some cases. In Europe, however, the traditional approach is still followed, though possibly with less dogmatism. This means that, in this area, the divide is not so much between the common law and the civil law – though significant differences do exist – but rather between Europe (including England) and the United States.

We will first look at the main features of the traditional system and then turn to the American theories.

§ 2   Traditional choice-of-law theory

§ 2.1   The methodology of categorization

We start with the methodology of traditional choice of law. It is a methodology based on categorization. Exactly *what* is categorized has never been entirely settled. Some would say it is legal issues or relationships; others that it is laws or legal rules. However, whichever way one looks at it, the fundamental process is still the same: classification.

When faced with a choice-of-law problem, you start with a category – for example, laws dealing with immovable property or issues concerning immovable property – and then decide whether the particular law or issue at hand fits into that category. If it does, you then derive a *connecting factor* that goes with the category – in the case of immovable property, it is the place where the land is situated – and that tells you what law is applicable. Three typical connecting factors are:

- the *situs* of land;
- the domicile, habitual residence or nationality of a person;[1] and
- the place where a tort is committed.

Traditional methodology may be represented diagrammatically as shown in Figure 22.1. This structure gives the appearance of a logical mechanism capable of delivering certainty in solving choice-of-law cases. As we shall see, however, this is not the case.

Figure 22.1 Traditional choice-of-law methodology

---

1 Domicile, nationality and (habitual) residence are all ways of connecting a person with a country. A generalized term for the law of a country with which a person is thus connected is 'personal law'.

A word should be said about each of these three elements:

- As regards the first element, the difficult question is how to decide whether a given rule or issue should be regarded as fitting into a particular category. This process is known as 'characterization' or 'classification'.[2]
- As regards the second element, there is often a problem in deciding how a connecting factor should be applied. How, for example, does one decide where a person is domiciled? What is the *situs* (location) of an intangible right, such as that given by a letter of credit? This process is known as 'determination of the connecting factor'.
- As regards the third element, once one knows what legal system is to be applied, how does one discover what that law is (problem of the ascertainment of foreign law)? Moreover, what is one to do if one discovers that, under the relevant foreign choice-of-law rule, the law of that country is not applicable? Should one ignore this, or should one apply the law that is applicable under the foreign choice-of-law rule (problem of *renvoi*)? Finally, if the foreign law is regarded as unfair or if it produces results that are regarded as unacceptable, should it be applied all the same (problem of 'public policy')?

These various matters will be considered further below.

§ 2.2 Substance and procedure

It will be noticed that all the examples given so far concern the application of foreign *substantive* law. This is because choice of law applies only to substantive law, never to procedural law. Questions of procedure are always decided by the law of the court hearing the case: it would be too complicated and difficult to do otherwise. Exactly what constitutes procedure is sometimes controversial, but, besides the rules for bringing an action and holding a hearing, it also covers evidence and remedies.[3]

§ 2.3 Some basic ideas

Ever since the beginnings of European choice-of-law theory, certain basic ideas have persisted. We mention three. The first is that matters of a personal nature concerning an individual should be governed by the system of law most closely connected with the individual concerned (usually called the personal law). The second is that matters closely connected with an item of property should be governed by the law of the place where the property is situated (*lex situs*). The third is that the legal effects of transactions or events should be governed by the law of the place where the transaction or event occurs (*lex loci actus*).

---

2 In French, it is known as '*qualification*', but 'qualification' is incorrect in English, since the English word 'qualification' does not (today) mean 'determination of the qualities of something'.
3 Public law (including administrative law and criminal law) is another area in which choice of law does not apply: the law of the forum is always applicable.

§ 2.3.1 The personal law: individuals. Today, it is generally accepted that the personal law should play a major role in personal matters. In English law, it determines, for example, capacity to marry and succession to movable property; in other countries, it plays a similar role. However, there is a marked divergence of views among the legal systems of the world as to how the personal law should be determined. Originally, all were agreed (at least in the West) that domicile should be the test. In the nineteenth century, however, some European countries adopted nationality as the criterion. This was a result of theories of nationalism that were prevalent at the time. The common-law countries retained domicile; so a split opened up. Moreover, domicile in England became rigid and unresponsive,[4] while in the United States, it retained much of its old flexibility; so the concept was not uniform even in the common-law world.

Today, on the international level, an attempt is being made to re-create the original unity through the use of habitual residence as the criterion.[5] This is deliberately not defined; so the courts can mould the law to the requirements of justice in the individual case. On the European Community level, this concept plays an important role in both the Rome I Regulation,[6] which deals with choice of law regarding contracts,[7] and the Rome II Regulation,[8] which deals with choice of law regarding torts and certain other matters.[9] It has the merit of being more flexible, and better suited to determining the country to which a person belongs, than either domicile or nationality. For this reason, it will probably grow in importance in the future.

§ 2.3.2 The personal law: companies. For a company, or other corporation, the personal law decides whether the company has been validly created; what its constitution is; what the powers are of its organs, officers and shareholders; whether it has been merged with another company; and whether it has been dissolved. Again, there is a split between different legal systems. This was discussed when we were considering jurisdiction (Chapter 3, § 6.4, above), where we saw that the common-law countries and some civil-law countries – for example, Japan and the Netherlands – apply the law of the country in which, or under the law of which, the company was incorporated (*lex incorporationis*); most civil-law countries, on the other hand, look to the law of the corporate seat (in French, the *siège social*). This can be determined in different ways. According to one view, one looks at the official headquarters of the company, as determined by its constitution. This concept, which is similar to the English idea of the registered office,

---

4 Under the English common law, an immigrant to England can retain his original domicile, even if he has lived many years in England, provided he has the intention of going home even if it is only at some vaguely defined moment in the future, or on the occurrence of some uncertain future event: see *Ramsay* v. *Liverpool Royal Infirmary* [1930] AC 588.

5 This is the concept normally applied in the international conventions adopted by the Hague Conference on Private International Law, though the Convention on Choice of Court Agreements 2005 uses residence.

6 Regulation 593/2008: see Articles 4, 5, 6, 7, 10 and 11.

7 See Chapters 24 and following.

8 Regulation 864/2007: see Articles 4(2), 5(1)(a), 10(2), 11(2) and 12(2)(b).

9 See Chapter 23.

is called the *siège statutaire*.[10] However, some jurists regard this as artificial; they think that the personal law of a company should be the law of the country in which its central administration is *in fact* situated (*siège réel*).

Although it may not be so easy for an outsider to determine as the law of the country of incorporation or the *siège statutaire*, it has the great merit of pointing to the country with which the company has the closest connection. This is important because business people sometimes incorporate their companies in 'corporate havens' like Panama or Liechtenstein. These may be chosen because their law minimizes the rights of creditors and shareholders. If the law of the country of incorporation or of the *siège statutaire* is applied, an inappropriate system of law may determine important issues. Nevertheless, the common-law countries continue to apply the law of the *lex incorporationis* for most purposes. Our next case (from the US) is an example.

Delaware
McDermott Inc.* v. *Lewis
Supreme Court of Delaware
531 A 2d 206 (1987)

Background

Delaware could be regarded as the 'Panama' of the United States: it is a small state that has deliberately set out to make itself the most desirable place in the United States in which to incorporate a company. The resulting business, especially for Delaware attorneys and accountants, has benefited the state's economy. McDermott Inc., a company with its headquarters in New Orleans, Louisiana, had originally been incorporated in Delaware, a state with which it appeared to have had no connection. Then it came up with a better idea: if it incorporated in Panama, it could gain important tax advantages. So a new company, McDermott International, was set up in Panama, and shareholders in McDermott Delaware were invited to exchange their shares for shares in McDermott International. Most did. The result was that 92 per cent of McDermott Delaware's shares were owned by McDermott International. Approximately 10 per cent of the latter's shares were owned by McDermott Delaware.

The plaintiffs (Lewis and others) challenged this reorganization. In particular, they claimed that McDermott Delaware could not vote the shares it held in McDermott International. This was because Delaware, like most or all other US states (including Louisiana), did not permit a subsidiary to vote any shares it held in its parent company. In Panama, on the other hand, this was permitted (except in circumstances not relevant to the case). What law applied? The lower court held that it was Delaware or Louisiana law; so the Delaware company could not vote the shares. The company appealed.

---

10 This is usually translated as the 'statutory seat'; however, this can be misleading because it is not determined by statute (legislation) but by the *statut* (constitution) of the company.

Moore J

Internal corporate affairs involve those matters which are peculiar to the relationships among or between the corporation and its current officers, directors, and shareholders . . .

The internal affairs doctrine requires that the law of the state of incorporation should determine issues relating to internal corporate affairs . . . Under Delaware conflict of laws principles and the United States Constitution, there are appropriate circumstances which mandate application of this doctrine.

A.

Delaware's well established conflict of laws principles require that the laws of the jurisdiction of incorporation – here the Republic of Panama – govern this dispute involving McDermott International's voting rights . . .

The traditional conflicts rule developed by courts has been that internal corporate relationships are governed by the laws of the forum of incorporation . . . As early as 1933, the Supreme Court of the United States noted:

> It has long been settled doctrine that a court – state or federal – sitting in one state will, as a general rule, decline to interfere with, or control by injunction or otherwise, the management of the internal affairs of a corporation organized under the laws of another state but will leave controversies as to such matters to the courts of the state of the domicile . . .

Rogers v. *Guaranty Trust Co of New York*, 288 US 123, 130; 53 S Ct 295, 297; 77 L Ed. 652 (1933) . . .

However, in *Western Air Lines, Inc.* v. *Sobieski*, Cal. App., 191 Cal. App. 2d 399; 12 Cal. Rptr 719 (1961), a California court upheld an order of the California Commissioner of Corporations directing a Delaware corporation having major contacts with California to follow the cumulative voting requirements imposed by California law. After the *Western Air* decision, commentators noted that the case signaled the alleged start of a 'conflicts revolution.' *See* Kozyris, 'Corporate Wars and Choice of Law', 1985 Duke L J 1 (hereinafter 'Kozyris') . . . The 'new' conflicts theory weighs the interests and policies of the forum state in determining whether the law of the forum – *lex fori* – should be applied . . . Thus, the *Western Air Lines* case 'was to be the harbinger of a new conflicts approach in corporate law that would limit or perhaps discard the *lex incorporationis*.' Kozyris, *supra* at 17.

A review of cases over the last twenty-six years, however, finds that in all but a few, the law of the state of incorporation was applied without any discussion . . .

The policy underlying the internal affairs doctrine is an important one, and we decline to erode the principle:

> Under the prevailing conflicts practice, neither courts nor legislatures have maximized the imposition of local corporate policy on foreign corporations but have consistently applied the law of the state of incorporation to the entire gamut of internal corporate affairs. In many cases, this is a wise, practical, and equitable choice. It serves the vital need for a single, constant and equal law to avoid the fragmentation of continuing, interdependent internal relationships. The *lex incorporationis*, unlike the *lex loci*

delicti, is not a rule based merely on the *priori* concept of territoriality and on the desirability of avoiding forum-shopping. It validates the autonomy of the parties in a subject where the underlying policy of the law is enabling. It facilitates planning and enhances predictability. In fields like torts, where the typical dispute involves two persons and a single or simple one-shot issue and where the common substantive policy is to spread the loss through compensation and insurance, the preference for forum law and the emphasis on the state interest in forum residents which are the common denominators of the new conflicts methodologies do not necessarily lead to unacceptable choices. By contrast, applying local internal affairs law to a foreign corporation just because it is amenable to process in the forum or because it has some local shareholders or some other local contact is apt to produce inequalities, intolerable confusion, and uncertainty, and intrude into the domain of other states that have a superior claim to regulate the same subject matter . . .

Kozyris, *supra* at 98.

B.

Given the significance of these considerations, application of the internal affairs doctrine is not merely a principle of conflicts law. It is also one of serious constitutional proportions – under due process, the commerce clause and the full faith and credit clause – so that the law of one state governs the relationships of a corporation to its stockholders, directors and officers in matters of internal corporate governance. The alternatives present almost intolerable consequences to the corporate enterprise and its managers. With the existence of multistate and multinational organizations, directors and officers have a significant right, under the fourteenth amendment's due process clause, to know what law will be applied to their actions. Stockholders also have a right to know by what standards of accountability they may hold those managing the corporation's business and affairs. That is particularly so here, given the significant fact that in the McDermott Group reorganization, and after full disclosure, 89.59 per cent of the total outstanding common shares of McDermott Delaware were tendered in the exchange offer . . . Thus, by an overwhelming choice those stockholders received shares in International, and thereby selected the laws of Panama to govern *inter se* the corporate relations between themselves, International, its directors, officers and agents . . . Such issues have been the subject of litigation and scholarly discussions for decades. However, an attitude has developed in some quarters which exalts local interests over more fundamental doctrines. We approach such teachings with reservations.

. . .

In conclusion, the trial court erred as a matter of law in ignoring the uncontroverted Panamanian law, and in applying Delaware and/or Louisiana law to the internal affairs of International contrary to established Delaware law and important constitutional principles. Accordingly the judgment of the Court of Chancery is REVERSED.

Comment

In view of Delaware's own position as a 'corporate haven', it is hardly surprising that its Supreme Court should apply the *lex incorporationis*, since in most cases this doctrine will favour Delaware. As mentioned in the judgment, there are also decisions of the US Supreme Court which suggest that constitutional considerations are relevant.

However, the judgment shows the drawbacks of the theory. The reason for the Delaware rule prohibiting a subsidiary from voting any shares it has in its parent is that, if allowed, this could enable the management, which would normally control the subsidiary, to obtain a stranglehold over the parent company. This concern was apparently shared by other US states. Panama, on the other hand, appeared to take a different view. It might be argued that, as the issue concerned the corporate governance of the parent, Delaware had no interest. This was true. However, Louisiana, as the state in which the central management was located, *did* have an interest. The Delaware court should have applied Louisiana law, which happened to be the same as Delaware law.

In Europe, the two approaches are more evenly balanced, since important countries support the *siège réel* theory. However, there is a 'constitutional' element in Europe in well. In a series of cases, the European Court of Justice has held that a Member State of the EC cannot use the *siège réel* theory to prevent a company incorporated in one Member State from doing business in another.[11]

The first case was *Centros*.[12] Two Danes wanted to incorporate a company to do business in Denmark. Under Danish law, all companies had to have a minimum capital of DKr200,000 (approximately £17,000). In order to avoid this requirement, they incorporated the company in the United Kingdom, where there were no minimum capital requirements. They then applied to the Danish Registrar of Companies to register a branch in Denmark. This was refused on the ground that, since the company did no business in the United Kingdom, the Danish 'branch' would in fact be the main establishment. The European Court, however, held that this refusal was contrary to EC law, since it was an impediment to freedom of establishment, a fundamental right under EC law.

This approach was continued in *Überseering*.[13] The company was incorporated in the Netherlands and originally had its central management there. Subsequently, all its shares were acquired by German nationals. When it sought to bring legal proceedings in Germany, the German courts, applying the *siège réel* theory, said that its central management had been transferred to Germany; consequently, German law determined whether it existed as a legal person. Since it had not been incorporated in Germany, it had no legal personality under German law; so it could not bring legal proceedings unless it first reincorporated in Germany. This too was held to contravene EC law.

These cases apply only to companies incorporated in an EC Member State. Where this is the case, however, they impose limits on the application of the *siège réel* theory. They do not, however, rule it out entirely. In particular, they do not prevent the application of the law of the country of the *siège réel* where this

---

11 For a succinct account, see Barnard (Catherine), *The Substantive Law of the EC* (Oxford University Press, Oxford, 2004), pp. 320–4.
12 Case C-212/97, [1999] ECR I-1459.
13 Case C-208/00, [2002] ECR I-9919.

would not prevent the company from doing business in another Member State. In the context of contract and torts, the EU Commission seems to favour the *siège réel* theory: in both the Rome I and Rome II Regulations, the personal law of a company is the law of the country of its habitual residence, defined as the place of its central administration.[14]

§ 2.3.3 The lex situs. The application of the law of the country where property is located has a great deal to recommend it in the case of tangible (corporeal) property, especially when it is immovable (land): not only is its location obvious to third parties but the courts of the *situs* are often the only ones able to enforce legal rights concerning it. However, when applied to intangible property – for example, contractual debts, bank accounts, bonds, stocks and shares – it creates problems. Since intangible property has no natural location, an artificial location must be ascribed to it. If this is done, all the advantages of applying the *lex situs* – predictability and ease of ascertainment – are lost. These issues will constitute a major theme in Chapters 28 and following.

§ 2.3.4 The lex loci actus. The application of the law of the place where an act, event or transaction occurs also has the advantage that the applicable law is easily ascertainable by third parties. For this reason, it plays a major role with regard to torts.[15] However, it can be fortuitous; so it is usually subject to exceptions, or combined with other rules. Its application in the area of torts is considered in Chapter 23, below. It used to be important for contracts, but today it plays only a minor role.

§ 2.4 *Methodological problems and escape devices*

It was said above that classical choice-of-law methodology, the methodology of categorization, gives rises to technical problems. Characterization, *renvoi* and the 'incidental question'[16] are the best-known examples. These can be solved fairly easily if one adopts a common-sense approach. Unfortunately, many conflicts writers – and even some courts – have not done this. The writers have tried to adopt a totally logical approach that foresees all possible problems and solves them in advance.[17] In real life, there are too many variables for this to

---

14 For Rome I, see Article 19(1); for Rome II, see Article 23(1).

15 For Rome II, see Article 4(1).

16 The problem of the incidental question arises when the question before the court has to be decided by a foreign system of law, but under that law the answer depends on another question (the 'incidental question'). According to some theorists, the 'incidental question' should be decided by the choice-of-law rules, not of the forum, but of the legal system the law of which decides the original question. The following is an example. Assume that the question before the court is whether the marriage between H and W is valid. Assume that, under the choice-of-law rules of the forum, the validity of this marriage has to be decided by the law of, say, Bulgaria. Assume further that the validity of this marriage depends on whether an earlier marriage between H and another woman is valid. Then, according to the theory, one should apply Bulgarian choice-of-law rules to decide the validity of the earlier marriage. The difficulties and complications that ensue can be immense. One possible result is that the second marriage is held valid, even though, in the eyes of the forum, the first marriage is also valid. The husband would then be validly married to two wives, each marriage purporting to be monogamous.

17 They also seem anxious to produce a value-free system that could be accepted by all the States in the world, another example of the attempt to produce international uniformity: see Chapter 1, § 4, above.

be possible. Moreover, the resulting theories are too abstract and complicated for practical use. The theories can also be interpreted in different ways; so they can be manipulated to produce almost any result. To this extent, they can be regarded as escape devices, which enable the court to avoid the normal effect of the choice-of-law rule it is applying. The theory of public policy has never been anything but an escape device.

We will now give brief consideration to these matters. As this is not intended as a theoretical study, they will not detain us long.

§ 2.4.1 Characterization.

We saw above that classical choice-of-law methodology is based on categorization. It operates on the basis of categories such as procedure, form, succession, contract, etc. Sometimes it may not be clear which the appropriate one is. If, for example, there is a rule of law that the marriage of a testator revokes a will made previously, is this rule to be characterized as falling under the law of marriage or the law of wills? How should a court decide this? Theorists have created a choice-of-law problem within a choice-of-law problem by asking what law should be applied to characterize a particular issue or rule.

Some theorists have answered this question by saying that each rule should be characterized by the legal system to which it belongs.[18] The results that can ensue are well illustrated by the infamous decision of the German *Reichsgericht* (Supreme Court) of 1882.[19] In this case, an action was brought in a German court on promissory notes issued in Tennessee and governed by the law of that state. The limitation period[20] had expired under both Tennessee law and German law; so one might have thought that the action was bound to fail. The *Reichsgericht*, however, held that it could succeed. It reached this conclusion by characterizing the Tennessee limitation rule by Tennessee law and the German limitation rule by German law. Under Tennessee law, the Tennessee rule was regarded as procedural because it was concerned with remedies; under German law, the German rule was regarded as substantive, because it took away the right. Since foreign procedural law can never be applied, the Tennessee rule could not be applied by the German court. However, since the substance of the claim was governed by the law of Tennessee, the German rule could not be applied either. So the claimant won the case. One cannot help wondering whether the judges who decided this case felt proud of what they had done. Did they feel that their fidelity to theory, even when carried to such lengths, was meritorious?[21]

A better approach, it is suggested, is to give up theorizing, and to decide each case as it comes along in the way that produces the best results. If the correct characterization is obvious, there is no problem. One just applies that characterization. If it is not obvious – if there are two or more possibilities that seem plausible – one should adopt the one that best gives effect to the policies of the law. As was explained above, choice-of-law rules have a purpose. So do rules of

---

18 See, for example, Wolff (Martin), *Private International Law* (Clarendon Press, Oxford, 2nd edn, 1950), p. 154.
19 *Entscheidungen des Reichsgerichts*, vol. VII, p. 21.
20 The period within which proceedings must be brought.
21 This decision has not been followed in later cases in Germany.

substantive law. One should solve the characterization problem with this in mind.[22]

For example, the reason why, under English law, the marriage of a testator revokes his or her will is that it is assumed that the will was not made with marriage in mind;[23] so, by holding the will revoked, English law tries to give effect to the presumed intention of the testator. The best way of achieving this internationally is to apply the law that the testator most likely had in mind at the time of marriage, perhaps the law of his or her domicile. There are various ways in which this might be achieved. The best might be to treat the matter as neither marriage law nor succession law but as falling into a special category with its own choice-of-law rule.

§ 2.4.2 Renvoi. Assume that a case comes before an English court. The English choice-of-law rule says that French law applies. However, the French choice-of-law rule says that English law applies. Should the English court ignore the French choice-of-law rule and apply French law, or should it 'accept the *renvoi*' and apply English law? This is a problem about which a great deal has been written. The only advantage of applying *renvoi* in a situation such as this is that it permits a court to escape from the obligation to apply foreign law. This, of course, is true only if the foreign choice-of-law rule refers *back* to the law of the forum, and not *on* to the law of a third country. However, in most of the cases in which the matter has arisen for decision, this has been the situation. Hence the name *renvoi*, French for 'sending back'. The application of *renvoi* in this situation can, therefore, be regarded as an escape device: it allows the court to escape from the difficulties of applying foreign law.

However, there is a further problem. If the English court is going to apply the French choice-of-law rule, why should it stop there? Why not also apply the French theory of *renvoi*? Why not ask what a French court would do if its choice-of-law rule refers to the law of England but the English choice-of-law rule refers back to France? Would it accept the *renvoi*? If it would, should not the English court end up by applying French law after all?

This second approach is sometimes called 'total *renvoi*',[24] to distinguish it from 'partial *renvoi*'[25] (the application of the foreign choice-of-law rule but not the foreign theory of *renvoi*). In the example given above, it produces the same result as not applying *renvoi* at all. However, it does this only if the foreign court itself applies (partial) *renvoi*. If it does not, total *renvoi* would reach the same result as partial *renvoi*.[26]

---

22 Courts often do this, but they rarely admit to doing it.

23 If it was, the rule will not apply.

24 Also known as the 'foreign court theory'.

25 Also called 'simple *renvoi*'.

26 In the situation set out above, if England and France both reject *renvoi*, each would apply the other's law. If both apply partial *renvoi*, each would apply its own law. If England applied total *renvoi* and France applied no *renvoi*, both would end up applying English law. If England applied total *renvoi* and France applied partial *renvoi*, both would end up applying French law. In the rare cases in which English courts apply *renvoi* (succession and family law), it seems to be total *renvoi* that they apply. See Dicey, Morris and Collins, Chapter 4.

We can now see that things are getting very complicated. At this point, it is legitimate to ask what it is all for. It was said above that the only possible purpose of partial *renvoi* is to avoid having to apply foreign law. What is the purpose of total *renvoi*? The only purpose served by it is to ensure that the forum will end up applying the same law as the foreign court would. However, total *renvoi* achieves this only if the foreign court does not itself apply total *renvoi*. If it does, the result is deadlock – hardly a recommendation for the theory.

Luckily for us, *renvoi* is rarely applied by common-law courts in the areas covered by this study; nor is it applied by the Rome I or Rome II Regulations.[27] So we need not consider it further at this point.[28]

§ 2.4.3 **Public policy.** Public policy (*ordre public* in French) is the escape device *par excellence*. It allows the court to avoid applying foreign law whenever the substantive content of the foreign rule is sufficiently objectionable. Unlike normal choice-of-law rules, therefore, it is not concerned with *connections* between the foreign system and the facts of the case: it depends simply on what the foreign rule *is*.[29] It usually applies either when the foreign rule is regarded as unacceptable on grounds of morality and justice – for example, if it is contrary to human rights[30] – or when it would prejudice some important policy of the forum.[31]

In common-law countries, public policy can be used not only to avoid the application of foreign law (negative application of public policy), but also to insist on the application of forum law (or even foreign law)[32] when it would not otherwise be applicable (positive application of public policy). Here, the effect of declaring a rule to be based on public policy is similar to that of declaring that it is mandatory in terms of the Rome I Regulation.[33]

§ 3   Choice-of-law rules in international instruments

Somewhat different considerations apply where choice-of-law rules are laid down in international instruments – for example, Hague conventions or EC regulations. However, most of these instruments are noteworthy for avoiding doctrinal complications. Where possible, they solve characterization problems in advance by specifying how particular issues are to be characterized, and they almost always state that *renvoi* is excluded.[34] Moreover, if its approach to the Brussels Convention is any guide, one can expect the European Court to avoid

---

27 Article 20 of the Rome I Regulation and Article 24 of the Rome II Regulation.
28 But see *Neilson* v. *Overseas Projects Corporation of Victoria Ltd*, discussed in Chapter 23, § 3, below.
29 Nevertheless, connections may still play some role, since the court may require a higher level of unacceptability where all the connections are with the foreign country.
30 A foreign rule invalidating a marriage on racial grounds would be an example.
31 A foreign rule permitting the evasion of an export embargo imposed by the State of the forum would be an example.
32 See *Regazzoni* v. *Sethia* [1958] AC 301; [1957] 3 WLR 752; [1957] 3 All ER 286 (HL), discussed in Chapter 25, § 4.1.1, below.
33 See Chapter 25, § 3.5, below.
34 See, for example, Article 20 of the Rome I Regulation and Article 24 of the Rome II Regulation.

applying national law to characterize issues under EC choice-of-law measures. It is more likely to adopt an autonomous ('European') characterization.

§ 4 American theories

After World War II, there was a move in the United States to abolish the old system of conflict of laws (the methodology of categorization) and start anew. This is sometimes called the American 'conflicts revolution'.

§ 4.1 Interest analysis

Interest analysis is the most important idea to come out of the American 'conflicts revolution', and the writer most closely associated with it is Brainerd Currie. In a seminal article published in 1958,[35] he took *Millikin* v. *Pratt*,[36] a case decided in 1878, and used it as an example for the analysis of legal policies. In this case, Mrs Pratt, a married woman domiciled and resident in Massachusetts, agreed with a supplier, who was resident in Maine, that she would stand surety for her husband, who was buying goods on credit from the supplier. Mr Pratt defaulted, and the supplier sued Mrs Pratt in Massachusetts. Under Massachusetts law, as it stood at the time, a married woman could not bind herself as surety; under Maine law, she could.

Was the suretyship agreement valid? The Massachusetts court held that this depended on the place where the contract was made. It ruled that this was Maine: it treated the document executed by Mrs Pratt in Massachusetts as an offer, which was accepted in Maine when the goods were shipped. The *lex loci contractus* was, therefore, Maine and the contract was valid.

Currie begins his analysis of the case by postulating that, shortly before the relevant events occurred, the Massachusetts legislature had considered, and rejected, a Bill to change the law so as to allow married women to stand surety.[37] He also postulated that the legislature did so expressly on the ground that they regarded married women as especially susceptible to entering into improvident contracts. In other words, the reason for retaining the rule – and Currie (writing in the late 1950s) regarded this as the only rationale 'even remotely intelligible in modern times' – was to protect married women from their own rashness.

Now, given this, how should the Massachusetts rule be applied to transactions with ramifications extending beyond the state? Currie first says – and this is obviously right – that, when a legislature considers the law, it normally does so only in domestic terms. Thus, when it was considering the hypothetical Bill postulated above, it almost certainly addressed its mind only to Massachusetts

---

35 'Married Women's Contracts: A Study in Conflict-of-Laws Method' (1958) *University of Chicago Law Review* 227.
36 (1878) 125 Mass 374.
37 This is not what actually occurred. Massachusetts law was in fact changed, after Mrs Pratt's contract but before the case was decided, to permit married women to enter into such contracts.

problems, and had no intention of legislating for situations having no connection with the state.

This disposes of the wholly foreign transaction, but does not help with regard to mixed cases, cases concerned partly with Massachusetts and partly with another state. Currie then says that, if one were to ask a typical member of the Massachusetts General Assembly (state legislature) exactly what scope was intended for the Massachusetts law, he would probably say that he had not thought about it and that this was a matter for conflict of laws. Again, this is a thoroughly realistic assumption, which would probably be equally true for the average European legislator.[38]

Having drawn a blank in this direction, Currie then feels justified in considering the matter for himself. 'Left thus to our own devices', he says, 'we may inquire what policy can reasonably be attributed to the legislature, and how it can best be effectuated by the courts in their handling of mixed cases.' This passage is important because it clearly shows that, in the normal case, the determination of legislative policy – the cornerstone of interest analysis – depends on the assumptions of the writer or court concerned with the case. Currie honestly accepts that a policy is *attributed* to the legislature: one cannot usually be sure what the actual policy was.

Applying this method to the case, Currie concludes that Massachusetts, in common with all other American states, believed in the security of commercial transactions, but it also believed that married women required protection. It had, therefore, subordinated its policy of upholding contracts to that of protecting married women. Hence the refusal to change the law. Maine, of course, had reached the opposite conclusion.

Now Currie reaches the crux of his argument. He asks the question: *which* married women did Massachusetts wish to protect? The answer he gives is: Massachusetts married women. This answer is the essence of his argument, since it indicates how the international application of Massachusetts law should be delimited. It is therefore useful to pause at this point and consider why this should be. Is Currie saying that Massachusetts has no interest in protecting women from other states? In a sense he is, though he does not deal with the point. In one sense, of course, he is quite right: from a purely selfish point of view – one might perhaps say, a short-sightedly selfish point of view – Massachusetts has no interest in protecting Maine women. However, this analysis leaves him open to the criticism that he excludes the possibility of a state wishing to help persons from other states.

There are in fact many cases in which countries *do* apply their laws and policies to foreigners. For example, England, like the United States (today), believes in freedom and is opposed to slavery. There can be no doubt that both countries carry their opposition to slavery beyond the confines of their own borders: after Britain abolished the slave trade in 1807, and slavery itself in 1833, it sent its

---

38 As Currie himself points out, however, there are some statutes which expressly state what their international scope is.

navy to patrol the Atlantic to prevent other countries from transporting slaves.[39] To take a more modern example, assume that Massachusetts enacts legislation to protect consumers. Would it be reasonable to say that Massachusetts had no interest in protecting out-of-state consumers, so that its legislation would not be applied to a Maine consumer who did some shopping in Massachusetts? One reason why it might wish to apply it would be to encourage shoppers from other states to buy goods in Massachusetts.

Currie was well aware of all this. In fact, his article makes clear that his analysis is predicated on the assumption that the contractual incapacity of married women was regarded at the time – as indeed it was – as something about which there could be different opinions. It seems, therefore, that what Currie is saying is that, where the policy embodied in a law for the protection of a given class of individuals is, according to opinion prevailing in the country which enacted it, one about which reasonable people may differ, it should be assumed that the country in question intended the law to apply only to its own people.

Once one accepts this, the rest is easy. Currie points out that Massachusetts is also concerned with upholding contracts, even though it considers that protecting Massachusetts women is more important. It follows from this that a Massachusetts court should apply the Massachusetts law on married women when the woman lives in Massachusetts – irrespective of whether the creditor lives in Massachusetts or elsewhere – but should not apply it when the woman lives outside Massachusetts. If, for example, the woman lives in Maine and the creditor in Massachusetts, there would be no point in applying Massachusetts law to defeat the contract: this would run counter to Massachusetts' policy of upholding contracts – a policy which would here benefit a Massachusetts creditor – without prejudicing the policy of protecting Massachusetts women. After all, there is no reason to protect Maine women to a greater extent than Maine itself would.

Currie concludes from this analysis that the Massachusetts law on married women's contracts should be applied by a Massachusetts court whenever the woman lives in Massachusetts, but not otherwise: the place where the contract is made is of no significance. The decision reached by the Massachusetts court in the actual case was, therefore, wrong: they should have held in favour of Mrs Pratt.

So far we have been considering the matter from the point of view of Massachusetts. What about the policy of Maine law? Since it had abolished the incapacity of married women, it is apparent that Maine regarded the security of contracts as more important than the protection of married women, if indeed it regarded married women as being in need of protection at all. Clearly, Maine had an interest in applying its law whenever the creditor lived in Maine. Thus, on the facts of *Millikin* v. *Pratt*, there was a clash of policies: Massachusetts wanted to protect Mrs Pratt, a Massachusetts woman, and Maine wanted to

---

39 See *Buron* v. *Denman* (1848) 2 Exch 167.

protect Millikin, a Maine creditor. Currie recognizes this. He states – and here he differs from many other American writers – that courts are not entitled to weigh up competing policies to decide which should prevail. Where each state has a genuine interest in the application of its law, the courts of each state must apply their own law: a Massachusetts court must protect Massachusetts women and a Maine court must uphold the rights of Maine creditors.[40] According to Currie, no other solution is possible in the case of a 'true conflict' – that is, where each state has an interest in the application of its own law. The result, therefore, depends on where the action is brought, something which traditionalists have always tried to avoid.

It should be pointed out, however, that, in the converse case of a Massachusetts creditor and a Maine woman, there is no genuine conflict of interests. Here, Massachusetts has no interest in the protection of the woman, and both states would be happy to see the contract enforced. This is what Currie calls a 'false conflict', a concept of great importance in his analysis. Where there is a false conflict, all states can adopt the same solution: their interests can be reconciled.

The idea of a false conflict has turned out to be one of the most fruitful to come out of the new approach. It offers a rational solution to a good many cases. In the case of a true conflict, however, Currie's solution is less happy, and later writers have advocated various methods of weighing up the interests at stake,[41] though there is little agreement as to how this should be done.

How should one assess Currie's theory? Its strength is that it tries to find rational solutions in place of the mechanical approach of the traditionalists. Its weaknesses are several. First, it requires the court to decide what the policy of the law is: this may be difficult in some cases. Secondly, it involves the limitation of a state's concern in a way which works only if the policy is not so strong that the state would want to apply it in every case, as in the example of slavery discussed above. Moreover, if the policy is very weak – if the state itself has doubts about it – it might, as Currie himself points out, apply it only in wholly domestic situations. Determination of the strength of a policy can also be difficult. Thirdly, the method (as applied by Currie) has no solution for a true conflict. Currie argues that there *is* no solution. Finally, it could be argued that Currie puts too much emphasis on the interest of states and too little on that of the parties.

Currie himself advocated the abandonment of traditional choice-of-law rules and their replacement by interest analysis. This has never been wholly accepted in America and has not been accepted at all in the rest of the world. In the case of mandatory rules (discussed in Chapter 25, below), however, interest analysis

---

40 It is this which distinguishes Currie's theory from a traditional choice-of-law rule – for example, a rule that the contractual capacity of a married woman is governed by the law of the state in which she resides: under such a rule, a Maine court would apply Massachusetts law whenever the woman lived in that state; under Currie's theory, it would not.

41 Under Baxter's 'comparative impairment' approach, for example, the court must decide which state's domestic policies would be less impaired if its law was not applied: would Massachusetts' policy of protecting married women suffer less than Maine's policy of upholding contracts? See Baxter, 'Choice of Law and the Federal System' (1963) 16 *Stanford Law Review* 1 at pp. 18–19. For another approach, see Cavers (David F.), *The Choice-of-Law Process* (University of Michigan Press, Ann Arbor, MI, 1965).

is much more attractive, since the objections mentioned above apply with much less force: by definition, mandatory rules are the fruit of specific policies, and those policies are regarded as being of such importance that they override the interests of the parties.

§ 4.2 The primacy of forum law

Albert Ehrenzweig proposed a different approach.[42] He decried the idea that forum law and foreign law should be treated as equal. In his view, the application of forum law is the norm; the application of foreign law is an exception. So foreign law should be applied only where there is a good reason for doing so.

He said that courts only pretend to follow traditional conflicts theory. Though cloaked in the garb of traditional methodology, their judgments are actually based on something quite different, what he called 'true rules'. These are the rules actually applied by courts, rather than the rules they purport to apply. To discover them, one must look at the results of cases, not the reasoning. They alone justify departure from the basic rule of applying forum law.

His ideas have much to commend them. His emphasis on the primacy of the *lex fori* is a useful corrective to the more extreme 'universalist' approaches;[43] while his idea of 'true rules' finds justification in the fact that courts manipulate choice-of-law methodology to produce the result they want.

§ 4.3 The 'better-law' theory

According to this theory, when other considerations are inapplicable or evenly balanced, the court should choose whichever of the two competing rules is intrinsically better.[44] This idea has something in common with public policy, in that it focuses on the substantive content of a rule; however, it is comparative, rather than absolute, in its evaluation. It has been adopted in some American states,[45] where, in personal-injury tort cases involving insurance companies, it has led to the application of the law that is more favourable to the victim.[46] In this respect, it is similar to the result-oriented choice-of-law rules sometimes found in Europe – for example, those designed to uphold the formal validity of wills.[47]

---

42 Ehrenzweig (Albert), *A Treatise on the Conflict of Laws* (West Publishing Co., St Paul, MN, 1962). For a shorter version of his views, see Ehrenzweig (Albert), *Conflicts in a Nutshell* (West Publishing Co., St Paul, MN, 1965). See also Ehrenzweig, 'The Lex Fori – Basic Rule in the Conflict of Laws' (1960) 58 *Michigan Law Review* 637.
43 By this is meant approaches that seek to formulate choice-of-law rules that could command universal acceptance.
44 Leflar, 'Choice-Influencing Considerations in Conflicts Law' (1966) 41 *New York University Law Review* 267; Leflar, 'Conflicts Law: More on Choice-Influencing Considerations' (1966) 54 *California Law Review* 1584.
45 See, for example, *Milkovich v. Saari*, set out in Chapter 23, § 5, below.
46 Symeonides (Symeon C.), Perdue (Wendy Collins) and von Mehren (Arthur T.), *Conflict of Laws: American, Comparative, International* (West Publishing Co., St Paul, MN, 1998), pp. 164–9.
47 Hague Convention of 5 October 1961 on the Conflict of Laws Relating to the Form of Testamentary Dispositions. Article 1 of this provides that a will is valid as to form if it complies with any of five systems of law. In other words, the applicable law as to the formal validity of a will is any reasonably connected system of law under which it is valid.

§ 5   Proof of foreign law

If foreign law is to be applied, how is the court to discover what it is? This is no easy matter: the judge will not have studied it; it may be written in a foreign language; and legal materials may be unobtainable in the country of the forum. In these circumstances, different countries adopt different approaches, though they mostly fall into one or other of two categories, or some combination of them or compromise between them.[48] The first approach is to treat foreign law in much the same way as forum law: it may be more difficult to ascertain, but it is still the court's job to ascertain it. Germany is the most notable exponent of this view. The other possibility is to regard the ascertainment of foreign law as essentially a different task from the ascertainment of forum law. In theory, it is regarded as fact, not law: it must be pleaded and proved by the party wishing to rely on it. England follows this approach.

These two approaches appear radically different. It might even be thought that countries following the first display a true internationalist spirit and show proper respect for foreign law, while those following the second are parochial and patronizing. However, what actually happens in English courts shows that this distinction is false and misleading, at least in present-day conditions. A typical example is given below, where part of the judgment in the *Anton Durbeck* case is set out. It will be seen that the judge in that case treats foreign law with the same respect as English law, and exercises the same care in ascertaining it.

The main differences between the two approaches are, first, that, under the English approach, the party wishing to invoke foreign law must plead it. This puts the other party on notice that foreign law might be relevant: he must then try to discover what it is, usually by contacting a lawyer in the country concerned. If neither party pleads foreign law, the court will normally apply English law, even if, under the relevant English choice-of-law rule, foreign law is applicable.[49]

Under the other approach, foreign law is applied by the court of its own motion, even if it is not pleaded by either party. This approach is regarded by some as more 'correct'. Under the English approach, however, if either party has anything to gain from the application of foreign law, he will plead it; so, if neither party pleads it, it is probably because it is not realistically possible to discover what it is, or because it is the same as English law. In either case, there is no point in going to the trouble and expense of trying to ascertain it. The interests of justice are best served by applying English law.[50]

The second difference between the two approaches is that, under the English

---

48 For a general survey, see Hartley, 'Pleading and Proof of Foreign Law: The Major European Systems Compared' (1996) 45 ICLQ 271.

49 There are some exceptions to this: see Hartley, 'Pleading and Proof of Foreign Law: The Major European Systems Compared' (1996) 45 ICLQ 271 at pp. 285–9.

50 There are exceptions to this, especially where the application of foreign law is required to protect the public interest or the interest of some foreign State. For further discussion, see Hartley, 'Pleading and Proof of Foreign Law: The Major European Systems Compared' (1996) 45 ICLQ 271.

approach, the party relying on foreign law must prove it.[51] This means he must put evidence before the court to establish what the foreign rule is. Normally, a person who is qualified as an expert in the foreign system must draw up a report on the foreign law which can be put in as evidence. Often he will give oral evidence as well, in which case he will be subject to cross-examination by the other side.

Where expert witnesses are called, they are normally called by one or other of the parties.[52] An expert is not obliged to give evidence; so the party calling him must pay him a fee. This is usually substantial. The expert will probably be a practising lawyer, professor or judge from the foreign country, and it would not be worth his while to research the law and travel to a foreign country unless he was well paid. However, a party is not going to part with a large sum of money to pay a witness who gives evidence contrary to his interests. Why should he? So the solicitor will explain to the expert what his client hopes the foreign rule will turn out to be, and will ask him if he is able to give evidence to this effect. If he is not able to give this assurance, the solicitor will approach another expert. The result is that expert witnesses almost always give evidence favourable to the party who engaged them. In many ways, they are more like advocates of that party's claim than impartial witnesses.[53]

If one party calls an expert on the foreign law, the other will almost certainly do so as well – at least, if the foreign law admits of any doubt. If it does not, the other party may concede that the foreign law is against him and base his case on other arguments. If this happens, the parties may put an agreed statement of foreign law before the court. No witnesses will then have to be called.

Assuming that the point of foreign law is contested, and that each party calls his own witness, each party will try to destroy the credibility of the other's witness through cross-examination. This may take the form of putting contrary precedents and other authorities to him. Sometimes, it may even be possible to find a passage in one of the witnesses own writings that says the opposite of what he is saying in court. This can be devastating. He may reply that he has changed his mind since then, but the court will be sceptical.

At the end of the day, the court will have to decide which view it prefers. It will do this by considering the evidence before it. The experts will cite authority (legislative provisions, case law and scholarly writing) to support their contentions, and these can be put before the court, translated if necessary. The court will consider them to decide whether they support one view or the other. It will then give its ruling.

This approach is not very different from the German approach or indeed from

---

51 If he fails to do this (and if the parties do not agree on what the foreign law is), the court will apply English law (again there are exceptions).

52 The court has the power under CPR 35.7 to direct that the evidence is to be given by a single expert. However, it never seems to exercise this power with regard to foreign law, probably because it is thought fairer for each party to appoint his own expert and for the court to decide between them. The parties could themselves appoint a joint expert, but this too does not seem to happen, possibly because a party will not want to pay the expert's fee unless he is confident that his evidence will be favourable.

53 This is not supposed to be the position. The expert's first duty is supposed to be towards the court, and he is supposed to state truthfully what he honestly believes to be the position: CPR 35.3.

the ascertainment by an English court of English law. In either case, the parties will put their arguments before the court, citing appropriate authorities, and the court will have to decide which is right. In either case, therefore, the court decides on the basis of the arguments put before it and the authorities cited. In essence, the process is the same, though in the case of foreign law the court will be more cautious in relying on its own knowledge and expertise.[54]

Our next case is a typical example of the English method: it was not chosen because there is anything special about it.

England
Anton Durbeck v. *Den Norske Bank*
High Court (Queen's Bench Division (Commercial Court))
[2005] EWHC 2497 (Comm); [2006] 1 Lloyd's Rep 93

Background

This is the case we looked at in Chapter 4, § 1.3.2, above, when we were considering jurisdiction under Article 5(5) of the Brussels I Regulation.[55] It will be remembered that the London branch of a Norwegian bank had lent money to the owner of a Cyprus-registered ship, and had obtained a mortgage over the ship as security. The borrower defaulted and the bank arrested the ship as it was going through the Panama Canal. It was subsequently sold at an auction to allow the bank (in part) to recover the loan.

When it was arrested, the ship was carrying a cargo of bananas belonging to Anton Durbeck, a German company that had chartered the ship to carry them from Ecuador through the Panama Canal to Germany. Since there was no market for the bananas in Panama and it was not feasible to ship them elsewhere, they were allowed to perish. This caused loss to Durbeck. Normally, it could have claimed against the ship owner under the bill of lading, and obtained compensation from the ship's insurers, but the insurance had been cancelled through non-payment of premiums. So Durbeck sued the bank.

The judgment considered in Chapter 4 concerned the question whether the English courts had jurisdiction under Article 5(5).[56] The Court of Appeal held that they did. The next question was whether the bank was liable. This was decided in subsequent proceedings before Christopher Clarke J. The first issue was the applicable law. Was it the law of Cyprus, the country of registration of the ship, or that of Panama, the country where the arrest took place?[57] The court held that the relevant law was that of Panama. The court then had to determine what the law of Panama was.

---

54 However, it will be more likely to do so if the foreign law is that of an English-speaking, common-law jurisdiction (for example, Australia) than that of a country with radically different traditions, like Japan.
55 In the *Anton Durbeck* case, the defendant was a Norwegian bank; so the relevant provision was actually Article 5(5) of the Lugano Convention, but this is exactly the same as Article 5(5) of the Brussels I Regulation.
56 This was Article 5(5) of the Lugano Convention. It is exactly the same as Article 5(5) of the Brussels I Regulation.
57 It was agreed by both parties that Cypriot law was the same as English law; so the court could decide the law of Cyprus by deciding what the position was under English law. This is an example of the establishment of foreign law by agreement between the parties.

Christopher Clarke J

[After stating that both parties agreed that, as between the mortgagor (the owner of the ship) and the mortgagee (the bank), the arrest and sale of the ship were lawful, Christopher Clarke J said the question was whether the bank could nevertheless incur liability towards a third party, such as Anton Durbeck. He outlined two potentially relevant provisions of the Panamanian Civil Code, the general tort provision (Article 1644), which grounds liability on fault or negligence, and Article 217 of the Panamanian Judicial Code, under which liability can result if a procedural right is exercised with 'temerity' or in bad faith.[1] He then turned to the expert evidence:]

The expert evidence

35. I have read and heard the evidence of Dr Jorge Fabrega, who was called by the claimant and Dr Eligio Salas, who was called by the defendant. They are both distinguished Panamanian lawyers. Dr Fabrega has been a practising lawyer in Panama since 1955 and is currently a partner in the law firm Moreno y Fabrega. He is a former alternate Justice of the Court of Appeal (First Judicial District) and a current alternate Justice of the Supreme Court of Panama and has been such since 1970. Dr Salas was from 1996 to 2001 a Supreme Court Justice and is currently in private practice. Their task (and mine) is rendered more difficult by two matters. First, Panama, like many civil law countries, does not have a doctrine of precedent similar to ours. But the Panamanian courts have adopted the approach that three Supreme Court decisions constitute a 'probable doctrine', which should be followed in comparable or analogous circumstances. Even then it sometimes happens that the continuum of development of the law is broken. In that case a judgment would have to be given explaining the reason for the change. Second, neither expert was aware of a case in which damages had been awarded in favour of someone in the position of the claimant, i.e. an innocent third party who suffered loss from an arrest that was valid as between ship and arrestor, nor one in which they had been refused.

36. Dr Fabrega's view was that, although article 185 of the Maritime Procedural Code was not directly applicable, it established that there could be liability for effecting an arrest which arose from error, and that, by analogy with it, the standard set in article 217 of the Panamanian Judicial Code should be set more liberally when dealing with damage done to innocent third parties in maritime cases. Article 31 of the Code provides that:

   Any circumstances not contemplated in the proceedings, or doubts in the interpretation of this law, shall be decided applying analogy, procuring in each case respect for the rights of defence, and principles of procedural law.

   He accepted that it was very unlikely that a debtor who was adversely affected by an arrest brought by a legitimate creditor could sue for damages in reliance

---

1 In Spanish, 'con sus actuaciones procesales temerarias o de mala fe'. The meaning of the Spanish word *temeridad* (the noun from *temerarias*), translated as 'temerity', was one of the principal issues in the case.

on article 217. But it would not be impossible if, say, a creditor were to sequester the operations of a plainly solvent company instead of seeking to arrest a cash account. He expressed the opinion, based on the Court of Appeal case to which I refer below . . . that a Panamanian court could find that the bank was liable if it could without injury to itself have refrained from exercising its rights or could have exercised them in a manner that did not injure a third party.

37.   Dr Salas's opinion may be summarised as follows:

    (i) Article 1644, which is the general provision for delictual liability in the Civil Code, is inapplicable. The complaint here is that the claimant has suffered damage as a result of a procedural act. That is dealt with by article 217 of the Panamanian Judicial Code. Article 217 applies to claims by both defendants and third parties.

    (ii) In order to succeed under 217 there must be evident bad faith and an intention to do harm. This was supported by Supreme Court decisions and textbook writings including Dr Fabrega's own.

    (iii) If, but only if, that was shown it was possible to fall within article 217 even if a legitimate right was exercised.

38.   In my judgment Panamanian law gives a bill of lading holder, whose cargo is damaged or lost on account of a valid arrest of the carrying vessel a right to sue if the arrest, albeit legitimate as between the arrestor and the ship, was carried out in bad faith or with the deliberate intention of harming the bill of lading holder. The fact that an arrest would be likely to cause or, at any rate, risk causing damage to cargo is not sufficient. I reach that conclusion for a number of reasons.

39.   First, article 217 is expressed disjunctively and, although the distinction between 'bad faith' and 'temerity' may be difficult to draw, the two concepts are not identical. Second, article 217 is dealing with at least two situations: a claim by a successful defendant to an action against the unsuccessful claimant, and a claim by a third party who has been injured by legal action that has been successfully taken against another and, *qua* him, legitimately. In the former case the decisions of the Supreme Court, to which I refer below, indicate that a very high test has been adopted and there is, to my mind, no reason why the test should be lower in the latter.

[Christopher Clarke J then considered the relevant Supreme Court decisions (which were not directly in point) and continued:]

43.   These decisions appear to me to amount to a probable doctrine as to the ambit of article 217, and, even if they do not, I find in them a helpful guide as to the approach of the Panamanian Supreme Court . . .

44.   Third, neither the Panamanian Supreme Court nor the Panamanian Court of Appeal has adopted the test suggested by Dr Fabrega in evidence that light negligence ('*culpa leve*') suffices . . .

45.   Fourth, such a conclusion appears to me consistent with principle. In the present case the bank availed itself of its legal right to arrest the vessel. That arrest has never been set aside; nor has it been suggested that there were grounds to do so. The circumstances in which someone who invokes

against X a procedural remedy given to him by the law which causes damage to Y ought to be limited. The cargo owner is not thereby without legal remedy since he will have a remedy against the other party to the bill of lading contract. In most cases, but not this one, that other party will be insured.

46. Fifth, such a conclusion is consistent with Dr Fabrega's own book . . . The conclusion is also consistent with his definition of 'temeridad' in a legal dictionary that he published (for students) in 2004 with others as 'conscious of lacking a right', although he cites other dictionaries which give it a lesser meaning such as recklessly, rashly, inconsiderately or imprudently. These include the respected *Diccionario Jurídico Espasa* which defines 'temeridad' as 'failing to take the care and diligence which the least careful, attentive or diligent person may be required to take'.

47. The law of England cannot determine the law of Panama. It is, however, noticeable that the test which I hold applicable under the law of Panama is close to that which applies in England in cases of wrongful arrest or malicious prosecution.

48. In the light of the matters to which I have referred I do not accept that article 217 should be given a broader interpretation so as to impose liability in the case of an arrest which affects third parties if there is negligence . . .

49. I have reached my conclusion on the basis of the relevant statutory material, the rulings of the Panamanian Courts and text book authority. I should add, however, that I derived greater assistance from the evidence of Dr Salas than that of Dr Fabrega.

[Christopher Clarke J then referred to certain points in Dr Fabrega's report which seemed incorrect. After further discussion of the facts, he concluded as follows:]

Conclusion
Panamanian law

77. Bad faith is not alleged. Nor, in my judgment, do the facts begin to support an inference that the bank intended to harm the claimant or even that it was recklessly indifferent to whether it did so or not. It was entitled to look to its own interests and to take advantage of the security to which it was lawfully entitled, even if that prejudiced the claimant, to which it owed no duty of care. In those circumstances the claimant has no claim against the bank under Panamanian law.

78. Nor do I regard this as a case where the bank could have abstained from arresting the vessel without harm to itself. To allow her to sail without P & I cover[2] would have exposed the bank to the risk that she might be arrested and detained for e.g. cargo, collision, pollution or crew claims with no means of releasing her, unless security was provided by the bank. It may

---

2 *Editor's note*: 'P & I cover' (protection and indemnity cover) is insurance.

be that the mortgage would, in most cases, rank in advance of any claim by the arresting party, but in some jurisdictions that would not be so in respect of some claims. In addition there was potential harm to the bank's reputation if, having arrested the vessel it then allowed it to sail without P & I cover of any kind.

[Christopher Clarke J then considered the position under English law and decided that the bank would not be liable under that law either. He concluded:]

80.   Thus, in my judgment, whichever law applies, the claim fails.

Result: judgment for the bank

Comment

This judgment shows that, in actual fact, English courts treat foreign law as law, not fact. It is hard to imagine how they could do otherwise. However, the fact that the judge, though he has a good understanding of general legal principles, has no particular knowledge of the foreign law necessarily imposes limits on the methods that can be adopted to ascertain it.

We end this section with an extract from an article on comparative law.

Pleading and Proof of Foreign Law: The Major European Systems Compared[1]

It might be thought that a comparative analysis should begin with the division between those systems that regard foreign law as fact and those that regard it as law. Though it may appear fundamental, this distinction is actually of limited importance, since few countries in either camp accept the full consequences of their official position. Even if a country regards foreign law as law, it will not necessarily treat it on a par with forum law: it is law, but law of a special kind. Countries in the foreign-law-as-fact camp, on the other hand, may regard foreign law as 'fact of a peculiar kind',[2] not to be treated in the same way as normal fact. The result is that there is often little difference in practice between the attitudes of the two camps to particular issues.

Appeals[3] furnish an example. In most countries, it is more difficult to appeal on a point of fact than on a point of law. In the case of the highest court, appeals on a point of fact may be impossible. The distinction between fact and law might, therefore, be thought important for the purpose of determining whether a right of appeal exists on a point of foreign law. However, a country that treats foreign law as law will not necessarily allow appeals on points of foreign law to the highest court. Germany is an example.[4] On the other hand, there is at least one country in the foreign-law-as-fact camp – England – where foreign law is treated almost

---

1 By Trevor C. Hartley, published in (1996) 45 ICLQ 271. The extract appears on p. 272. The text has been rearranged and slightly modified.
2 This is the position in England: see *Parkasho* v. *Singh* [1968] P 223 at p. 250.
3 The word 'appeals' is used here in a broad sense to include such remedies as *Revision* in German law and *cassation* in French law.
4 German law distinguishes between two kinds of appeal: *Berufung*, an appeal to an intermediate court of appeal (an *Oberlandesgericht*), and *Revision*, an appeal to the highest civil court, the *Bundesgerichtshof*. The former may be on questions of either law or fact, but the latter may be only on questions of federal German law. As a result, an appeal on a point of foreign law may be made only to an intermediate court of appeal, not (subject to very limited exceptions) to the *Bundesgerichtshof*.

the same as forum law for the purpose of appeals. Appellate courts in England are reluctant to interfere with findings of fact made by the trial judge; however, they are much more willing to reverse a finding of foreign law than of a 'normal' fact.[5]

Moreover, the House of Lords has entertained at least one appeal that turned entirely on a point of foreign law.[6] The law was that of New Zealand. It is true that, at the time, the Privy Council was the final court of appeal for New Zealand, but the House of Lords is not the Privy Council, even if the composition of the two bodies is largely identical.

Jury trials are another example. If foreign law is fact, it ought to fall within the province of the jury. This was originally the case in England, but the position has been changed by statute: questions of foreign law are now decided by the judge, not the jury.[7]

5 *Parkasho* v. *Singh* [1968] P 223 at p. 250; approved in *Dalmia Dairy Industries Ltd* v. *National Bank of Pakistan* [1978] 2 Lloyd's Rep 223 at p. 286 (CA); *Bumper Corporation* v. *Comr of Police of Metropolis* [1991] 1 WLR 1362 at p. 1370 (CA); *MCC Proceeds* v. *Bishopsgate* [1999] CLC 417 (CA); *Morgan Grenfell* v. *SACE* [2001] EWCA Civ 1932 (CA); *King* v. *Brandywine Reinsurance Co.* [2005] EWCA Civ 235; [2005] 1 Lloyd's Rep 655 (CA).
6 *Attorney General of New Zealand* v. *Ortiz* [1984] AC 1.
7 This was originally brought about by the Administration of Justice Act 1920, section 15. For the High Court, see now the Supreme Court Act 1981, section 69(5); for county courts, see the County Courts Act 1984, section 68. For criminal cases, see *R.* v. *Hammer* [1923] 2 KB 786.

§ 6   Conclusions

In this chapter, we have outlined the general considerations that apply in all areas of choice of law. We have discussed some of the theories that provide the foundations for the law. In the United States, these theories are sometimes applied directly to decide cases. Examples will be given in the next chapter. In Europe, on the other hand, they constitute the background against which a court or the legislature creates a new choice-of-law rule.

We have also seen that the traditional choice-of-law mechanism gives rise to structural problems like characterization or *renvoi*. We shall see in the chapters that follow that these devices are sometimes used deliberately to avoid the result that would normally follow from the choice-of-law rule. This prompts the thought that it might be better to have more flexible choice-of-law rules, so that such escape mechanisms are unnecessary.

Finally, whenever foreign law is applied, the court is faced with the task of discovering what it is. If the issue in question is not squarely addressed by legislation and has never come before the foreign courts – as was the situation in the *Anton Durbeck* case – the English court is in effect *creating* the foreign rule, even if it does so according to the methods and logic of the foreign system.

Moreover, though it is often said that the English court should strive to reach the decision that the highest court in the foreign country would have reached, there are some cases in which this was plainly not achieved. *Szechter* v. *Szechter*[58] is an example. In that case, a young woman in poor health had been imprisoned in Poland for anti-government activities during the Communist period. A friend,

58 [1971] P 286; [1971] 2 WLR 170; [1970] 3 All ER 905.

Dr Szechter, was apparently able to leave the country. It seemed that the young woman would be released from prison and allowed to emigrate if she married Dr Szechter. They did this and she was released. After the couple arrived in England, they wanted their marriage annulled, since it had been no more than a subterfuge to get her out of prison. The English court held that Polish law was applicable and found (following the evidence of an expert) that, under Polish law, the marriage was invalid for duress.

It is impossible to believe, however, that a court in Communist Poland would have held that a lawfully imposed sentence of imprisonment could constitute duress so that it would invalidate a marriage contracted to obtain the release of the convicted person. One cannot say, therefore, that the English court reached – or was even trying to reach – the result that would have been reached by a Polish court. Rather, it was trying to reach the result it thought right, and was using foreign law as a tool for this purpose.

In other cases, courts apply foreign law only after excising those parts of it that they do not like, something that is permissible under the doctrine of public policy. In yet other cases, they use the doctrine of *renvoi* to end up applying their own law, even though it is uncertain that the foreign court would have done the same.[59] For these reasons, it is sometimes said that a court never applies foreign law as such: it merely applies a rule of its own law modelled, to a greater or lesser extent, on the foreign law. There is a great deal of truth in this statement.

In the chapters that follow, we shall consider choice of law in specific areas of the law. We start with torts, an area in which many of these considerations are of special importance.

Further reading

Choice-of-law theory

Baxter, 'Choice of Law and the Federal System' (1963) 16 *Stanford Law Review* 1

Cavers (David F.), *The Choice-of-Law Process* (University of Michigan Press, Ann Arbor, MI, 1965)

Currie, 'Married Women's Contracts: A Study in Conflict-of-Laws Method' (1958) *University of Chicago Law Review* 227

Ehrenzweig, 'The Lex Fori – Basic Rule in the Conflict of Laws' (1960) 58 *Michigan Law Review* 637

Gamillscheg, 'Rules of Public Order in Private International Labour Law', Hague Academy of International Law, General Course on Private International Law (1983), Volume III, *Collected Courses* (Martinus Nijhoff Publishers, The Hague, Boston and London, 1984)

Leflar, 'Choice-Influencing Considerations in Conflicts Law' (1966) 41 *New York University Law Review* 267

'Conflicts Law: More on Choice-Influencing Considerations' (1966) 54 *California Law Review* 1584

Symeonides, 'The American Revolution and the European Evolution in Choice of Law: Reciprocal Lessons' (2008) 82 *Tulane Law Review* 1741

---

59 This can occur where the court applies the foreign choice-of-law rule without considering the foreign approach to *renvoi*.

Company law

Barnard (Catherine), *The Substantive Law of the EC* (Oxford University Press, Oxford, 2004), pp. 320–4

Drury, 'Migrating Companies' (1999) 24 *European Law Review* 354

Kaplan, 'Foreign Corporations and Local Corporate Policy' (1968) *Vanderbilt Law Review* 433

Kozyris, 'Corporate Wars and Choice of Law' [1985] *Duke Law Journal* 1

Rammeloo (Stephen), *Corporations in Private International Law* (Oxford University Press, Oxford, 2001)

Reese and Kaufman, 'The Law Governing Corporate Affairs: Choice of Law and the Impact of Full Faith and Credit' (1958) 58 *Columbia Law Review* 1118

Roth, 'From Centros to Überseering: Free Movement of Companies, Private International Law, and Community Law' (2003) 52 ICLQ 177

Siems, 'Convergence, Competition, Centros and Conflict of Laws: European Company Law in the 21st Century' (2002) 27 *European Law Review* 47

Proof and application of foreign law

Dolinger, 'Application, Proof, and Interpretation of Foreign Law: A Comparative Study in Private International Law' (1995) 12 *Arizona Journal of International and Comparative Law* 225

Fentiman (Richard), *Foreign Law in English Courts: Pleading, Proof, and Choice of Law* (Clarendon Press, Oxford, 1998)

'Law, Foreign Law and Facts' (2006) 59 CLP 391

Geeroms (Sophie), *Foreign Law in Civil Litigation* (Oxford University Press, Oxford, 2004)

Hartley, 'Pleading and Proof of Foreign Law: The Major European Systems Compared' (1996) 45 ICLQ 271

CHAPTER 23

Torts

§ 1   England: historical development

Choice of law for torts has had a long and interesting history in England, a history that illustrates many of the issues and problems in choice of law. We start by looking at some key cases.

England
The Halley
Privy Council
(1868) LR 2 PC 193

Background

A British ship had collided with a Norwegian ship in Belgian waters. At the time of the collision, the British ship was under the control of a pilot. Under Belgian law, the British ship was obliged to take the pilot on board and give him control of the ship. Nevertheless, under Belgian law, the owner of the British ship was responsible for the consequences of the pilot's negligence. Under English law, on the other hand, a shipowner was not responsible for the negligence of a compulsory pilot. The owner of the Norwegian ship brought an action *in rem* against the British ship in England. The Court of Admiralty held that the action could be founded on Belgian law. The defendant (the British ship owner) appealed to the Privy Council.

> **Lord Justice Selwyn**
>
> [T]he liability of the Appellants, and the right of the Respondents to recover damages from them, as the owners of the Halley, if such liability or right exists in the present case, must be the creature of the Belgian law; and the question is, whether an English Court of Justice is bound to apply and enforce that law in a case, when, according to its own principles, no wrong has been committed by the Defendants, and no right of action against them exists.
>
> The Counsel for the Respondents, when challenged to produce any instance in which such a course had been taken by any English Court of Justice, admitted his inability to do so, and the absence of any such precedent is the more important, since the right of all persons, whether British subjects or aliens, to sue in the English Courts for damages in respect of torts committed in Foreign countries has long since been established; and . . . there seems to be no reason why aliens

should not sue in England for personal injuries done to them by other aliens abroad, when such injuries are actionable both by the law of England and also by that of the country where they are committed, and the impression which had prevailed to the contrary seems to be erroneous.

. . .

It is true that in many cases the Courts of England inquire into and act upon the law of Foreign countries, as in the case of a contract entered into in a Foreign country, where, by express reference, or by necessary implication, the Foreign law is incorporated with the contract, and proof and consideration of the Foreign law therefore become necessary to the construction of the contract itself. And as in the case of a collision on an ordinary road in a Foreign country, where the rule of the road in force at the place of collision may be a necessary ingredient in the determination of the question by whose fault or negligence the alleged tort was committed. But in these and similar cases the English Court admits the proof of the Foreign law as part of the circumstances attending the execution of the contract, or as one of the facts upon which the existence of the tort, or the right to damages, may depend, and it then applies and enforces its own law so far as it is applicable to the case thus established; but it is, in their Lordships' opinion, alike contrary to principle and to authority to hold, that an English Court of Justice will enforce a Foreign Municipal law, and will give a remedy in the shape of damages in respect of an act which, according to its own principles, imposes no liability on the person from whom the damages are claimed . . .

Result: the British defendant was not liable

Comment

In this case, the Privy Council seemed reluctant to pay any attention to foreign law except as providing some sort of background to the claim. It was certainly unwilling to allow it to serve as the foundation for a claim in tort when the defendant's act was not a tort under English law.

QUESTION

If you think this decision was wrong, how would you formulate the argument on the basis of which you would criticize it?

England
Phillips* v. *Eyre
Court of Exchequer Chamber
(1870) LR 6 QB 1

Background

Eyre had been the Governor of the British colony of Jamaica. He had suppressed a rebellion with great brutality. One of the victims sued him in tort in England.

What he had done may have been a tort under English law, but it was not under Jamaican law. The reason was that Governor Eyre had taken the precaution of passing an Act of Indemnity in Jamaica,[1] legislation that retrospectively declared lawful everything that had been done to suppress the rebellion. Phillips nevertheless argued that, if the act was a tort under English law, he could recover damages.

Willes J

The last objection to the plea of the colonial Act was of a more technical character;[1] that assuming the colonial Act to be valid in Jamaica and a defence there, it could not have the extra-territorial effect of taking away the right of action in an English court. This objection is founded upon a misconception of the true character of a civil or legal obligation and the corresponding right of action. The obligation is the principle to which a right of action in whatever court is only an accessory, and such accessory, according to the maxim of law, follows the principle, and must stand or fall therewith . . . A right of action, whether it arise from contract governed by the law of the place or wrong, is equally the creature of the law of the place and subordinate thereto. The terms of the contract or the character of the subject-matter may shew that the parties intended their bargain to be governed by some other law; but, *prima facie*, it falls under the law of the place where it was made. And in like manner the civil liability arising out of a wrong derives its birth from the law of the place, and its character is determined by that law. Therefore, an act committed abroad, if valid and unquestionable by the law of the place, cannot, so far as civil liability is concerned, be drawn in question elsewhere unless by force of some distinct exceptional legislation, superadding a liability other than and besides that incident to the act itself. In this respect no sound distinction can be suggested between the civil liability in respect of a contract governed by the law of the place and a wrong.

. . . As a general rule, in order to found a suit in England for a wrong alleged to have been committed abroad, two conditions must be fulfilled. First, the wrong must be of such a character that it would have been actionable if committed in England; therefore, in *The Halley*, the Judicial Committee pronounced against a suit in the Admiralty founded upon a liability by the law of Belgium for collision caused by the act of a pilot whom the shipowner was compelled by that law to employ, and for whom, therefore, as not being his agent, he was not responsible by English law. Secondly, the act must not have been justifiable by the law of the place where it was done . . .

1 *Editor's note*: the other objections concerned the legality or constitutionality of the Act of Indemnity.

Result: Governor Eyre was not liable.

Comment

It would clearly be wrong to hold a person liable in tort for something that was lawful under the law of the place where it was done; so, once it was established

1 It was assented to by the Crown.

that the Act of Indemnity was constitutionally valid, the court had to hold for Governor Eyre. The result was the famous 'double-actionability' rule, a rule that was applied in English law for almost a century. It is usually expressed as follows:

As a general rule, in order to found a suit in England for a wrong alleged to have been committed abroad, two conditions must be fulfilled:

- first, the wrong must be of such a character that it would have been actionable if committed in England;
- secondly, the act must not have been justifiable by the law of the place where it was done.

The following points should be noted:

- The formulation of the rule is preceded by the words 'as a general rule', thus indicating that there may be exceptions (it was almost a hundred years before effect was given to this possibility).
- The rule applies only when the tort is committed abroad: when it is committed in England, only English law applies.
- While the first limb of the rule requires that the act must be 'actionable' under English law, the second limb requires only that it should not be 'justifiable' under the law of the place where it was committed. This difference of terminology has given rise to considerable debate. Although it is understandable in the context of the case – the Act of Indemnity had indeed 'justified' Governor Eyre's otherwise-illegal acts – it could be argued that it constitutes a lesser requirement than that under the first limb. This point arose in our next case.

England
Machado v. *Fontes*
Court of Appeal
[1897] 2 QB 231

Background

In this case, the alleged tort took place in Brazil. It took the form of a libel in a publication in the Portuguese language. The claimant sued in England. One of the defences was that, under Brazilian law, a libel, while a criminal offence, was not a tort.

Lopes LJ

[After referring to the defendant's plea that libel was not a tort under the law of Brazil, said:]

Now the principle applicable in the present case appears to me to be this: where the words have been published outside the jurisdiction, then, in order to maintain an action here on the ground of a tort committed outside the jurisdiction, the act complained of must be wrongful – I use the word 'wrongful' deliberately – both by the law of this country, and also by the law of the country where it was committed; and the first thing we have to consider is whether those conditions are complied with.

[Lopes LJ referred to *Phillips* v. *Eyre* and another case, and continued:]

Both those cases seem to me to go this length: that, in order to constitute a good defence to an action brought in this country in respect of an act done in a foreign country, the act relied on must be one which is innocent in the country where it was committed. In the present case there can be no doubt that the action lies, for it complies with both of the requirements which are laid down by Willes J. The act was committed abroad, and was actionable here, and not justifiable by the law of the place where it was committed. Both those conditions are complied with; and, therefore, the publication in Brazil is actionable here.

It then follows, directly the right of action is established in this country, that the ordinary incidents of that action and the appropriate remedies ensue. Therefore, in this case, in my opinion, damages would flow from the wrong committed just as they would in any action brought in respect of a libel published in this country . . .

Rigby LJ

Willes J, in *Phillips* v. *Eyre*, was laying down a rule which he expressed without the slightest modification, and without the slightest doubt as to its correctness; and when you consider the care with which the learned judge prepared the propositions that he was about to enunciate, I cannot doubt that the change from 'actionable' in the first branch of the rule to 'justifiable' in the second branch of it was deliberate. The first requisite is that the wrong must be of such a character that it would be actionable in England. It was long ago settled that an action will lie by a plaintiff here against a defendant here, upon a transaction in a place outside this country. But though such action may be brought here, it does not follow that it will succeed here, for, when it is committed in a foreign country, it may turn out to be a perfectly innocent act according to the law of that country; and if the act is shewn by the law of that country to be an innocent act, we pay such respect to the law of other countries that we will not allow an action to be brought upon it here. The innocency of the act in the foreign country is an answer to the action. That is what is meant when it is said that the act must be 'justifiable' by the law of the place where it was done.

It is not really a matter of any importance what the nature of the remedy for a wrong in a foreign country may be. The remedy must be according to the law of the country which entertains the action . . .

Comment

This case establishes that 'not justifiable' requires only that the act should be in some sense unlawful: it is not necessary that it should give rise to civil liability; criminal liability would be sufficient. This has been subject to considerable criticism; nevertheless, it has a certain logic. If foreign law is applicable only to protect a defendant who acted in reliance on it, it should not matter what form the illegality takes.

The law laid down in these three cases continued to apply in England until 1969, when the House of Lords decided *Chaplin* v. *Boys* [2] (set out in § 4, below). In this case, a majority in the House of Lords overruled *Machado* v. *Fontes* and held that the act must give rise to civil actionability under the foreign law: criminal liability is not sufficient. The House of Lords also held that the 'double-actionability' rule is subject to an exception: in certain circumstances, English law alone may be applied. In a subsequent decision, it was held by the Privy Council on appeal from Hong Kong that, in exceptional circumstances, the foreign law alone may be applied.[3] These two exceptions made the rule more flexible.

The 'double-actionability' rule was finally abolished by the Private International Law (Miscellaneous Provisions) Act 1995, which established the general rule that the applicable law is the law of the place where the tort was committed, though this too was subject to exceptions.[4] This was not quite the end of the 'double-actionability' rule, however, since the British press launched a successful campaign when the Bill was going through Parliament to retain the rule in defamation cases. Their concern was that, if the foreign law alone were applicable, a true, but defamatory, article about a foreign dictator might give rise to liability in England if, under the foreign law, the truth of the statement was no defence.

It is not necessary to consider the Act because it has now been replaced by the EC Rome II Regulation, which applies from 11 January 2009.[5] This will be discussed below. However, when the Regulation was going through the European Parliament, European media interests, led by the British press, launched a campaign to have defamation excluded from it. This, too, was successful.[6] The result is that the 'double-actionability' rule still applies to defamation in England. It is considered further in § 7, below.

§ 2 The Rome II Regulation: general rule

In this section, we will consider the rule applying to torts in general. (There are special rules for certain specific torts: see § 6, below.)

§ 2.1 The country in which the damage occurs

The general rule laid down by the Regulation in Article 4(1) is that the applicable law is that of the country in which the damage occurs (Panel 23.1). The rule refers to the place where the damage occurs, rather than the place where

---

2 [1971] AC 356; [1969] 3 WLR 322; [1969] 2 All ER 1085.
3 *Red Sea Insurance Co. Ltd* v. *Bouygues SA* [1995] 1 AC 190.
4 On this, see Morse, 'Torts in Private International Law: A New Statutory Framework' (1996) 45 ICLQ 888.
5 It applies to events giving rise to damage which occurs after its entry into force: Article 31. Here 'entry into force' seems to mean 19 August 2007: see Dicey, Morris and Collins, *First Supplement to the Fourteenth Edition* (Sweet & Maxwell, London, 2007) (hereinafter, 'Dicey, Morris and Collins, *First Supplement*'), paragraph S 35-168. If correct, this means that the Regulation applies to proceedings brought on or after 11 January 2009 if the event giving rise to the damage occurred on or after 19 August 2007. See SI 2008 No. 2986.
6 The question will be reviewed by the Commission in a report to be submitted by the end of 2008: Article 30(2).

Panel 23.1 Torts: the general rule
Rome II Regulation (Regulation 864/2007), Article 4

Article 4 General rule

1. Unless otherwise provided for in this Regulation, the law applicable to a non-contractual obligation arising out of a tort/delict shall be the law of the country in which the damage occurs irrespective of the country in which the event giving rise to the damage occurred and irrespective of the country or countries in which the indirect consequences of that event occur.
2. However, where the person claimed to be liable and the person sustaining damage both have their habitual residence in the same country at the time when the damage occurs, the law of that country shall apply.
3. Where it is clear from all the circumstances of the case that the tort/delict is manifestly more closely connected with a country other than that indicated in paragraphs 1 or 2, the law of that other country shall apply. A manifestly closer connection with another country might be based in particular on a preexisting relationship between the parties, such as a contract, that is closely connected with the tort/delict in question.

the tort occurs, to cover the situation where the wrongful act of the defendant takes place in one country and the damage occurs in another. As we saw in Chapter 4, § 1.2, above, this has caused problems with regard to jurisdiction. The words 'irrespective of the country in which the event giving rise to the damage occurred' are intended to ensure that the law of the country where the wrongful act of the defendant took place will not apply, while the words 'irrespective of the country or countries in which the indirect consequences of that event occur' are intended to ensure that the rule in *Dumez* v. *Hessische Landesbank* and *Marinari* v. *Lloyds Bank* (Chapter 4, § 1.2, above) remains applicable. No attempt has been made to clarify the ambiguities in these cases.

§ 2.2   Common habitual residence

Article 4(1) is subject to an exception laid down in Article 4(2): if the tortfeasor and victim have their habitual residence in the same country, the law of that country will be the governing law. The most important situation in which this will apply is where there is a pre-existing relationship between the parties. An example is where two friends (or members of a family) living in England drive to Spain in a car owned by one of them. They have an accident in Spain in which the passenger is injured. In this situation, there are strong arguments for applying English law.

Article 4(2) also applies where there is no pre-existing relationship – for example, if an Englishman drives to Spain, has an accident there, and discovers, to his surprise, that the driver of the other car is also English: here, too, the applicable law will be English law. This solution is less clearly right, but it is probably better on balance than applying the law of the place where the accident occurs.

§ 2.2.1 Rules of the road. In both these examples, English law cannot be applied with regard to the rules of the road. Here, Spanish law should apply, even if both parties are English. This is made clear by Article 17 (Panel 23.2), which provides that rules of safety and conduct in force at the time and place of the accident must be taken into account, in so far as appropriate, in order to assess the conduct of the defendant.

Panel 23.2 Rules of safety and conduct
Rome II Regulation (Regulation 864/2007), Article 17

Article 17

In assessing the conduct of the person claimed to be liable, account shall be taken, as a matter of fact and in so far as is appropriate, of the rules of safety and conduct which were in force at the place and time of the event giving rise to the liability.

§ 2.2.2 Multi-party cases. In a multi-party case, different laws could be applied to different parties. Assume, for example, that an Englishman and his wife go to Spain on holiday and rent a car there. While the English husband is driving, they are involved in an accident with a car driven by a Spanish driver. Both the Spaniard and the English wife sue the English driver. Here, the claim by the Spaniard would be governed by Spanish law, while the claim by the wife would be governed by English law.

§ 2.2.3 Meaning of 'country'. Where a State consists of two or more territorial units, each with its own law of tort, each is regarded as a separate country for the purpose of the Regulation. This is laid down in Article 25 (Panel 23.3), which also provides that Member States are not required to apply the Regulation to conflicts solely between such units.[7] This means that England and Scotland are separate countries for the purpose of the Regulation. Consequently, if an Englishman[8] takes his Scottish girlfriend[9] in his car on a trip to Spain and an accident occurs there, the applicable law if she sues him will be Spanish law (unless there is some reason to apply the third paragraph of Article 4).[10]

Panel 23.3 States with more than one legal system Rome II Regulation (Regulation 864/2007), Article 25
Article 25 1. Where a State comprises several territorial units, each of which has its own rules of law in respect of non-contractual obligations, each territorial unit shall be considered as a country for the purposes of identifying the law applicable under this Regulation. 2. A Member State within which different territorial units have their own rules of law in respect of non-contractual obligations shall not be required to apply this Regulation to conflicts solely between the laws of such units

The definition of 'country' in Article 25(1) gives rise to difficulty. A territorial unit is a separate country if it has 'its own rules of law in respect of non-contractual obligations'. 'Non-contractual obligations' is wider than 'tort', since it includes unjust enrichment, *negotiorum gestio* and *culpa in contrahendo*.[11] It is not clear what happens if the unit in question has its own rules on some of these matters but not others. The best solution would be to consider whether the particular question in issue is subject to different rules, but the wording of the Regulation provides no support for this view.

On almost any basis, Scotland and England are different countries for the purposes of the Regulation.[12] So are the different US states.[13] On the other hand, German *Länder* and Swiss cantons are not: both Germany and Switzerland have civil codes which apply nationally and cover the law of non-contractual obligations. Australia, however, presents difficulties. Most aspects of the law of tort

---

7 The United Kingdom has decided to apply the Regulation between its constituent countries – for example, between England and Scotland: SI 2008 No. 2986, reg. 6; and SI 2008 No. 404, reg. 4 (Scotland).
8 Having his habitual residence in England.
9 Having her habitual residence in Scotland.
10 This would not be affected by any decision (under the second paragraph of Article 25) as to whether or not the Regulation will apply as between England and Scotland.
11 See Articles 10–13 of the Regulation.
12 England and Wales are not: they constitute one 'country' for the purposes of the Regulation, even though politically and culturally they are different countries.
13 The common law in each state is a separate legal system. The US Supreme Court has no jurisdiction to interpret it. Subject to minor exceptions, there is no federal common law: *Erie Railroad Company* v. *Thompkins*, 304 US 674; 58 S Ct 817; 82 L Ed 1188 (1938).

(and probably other non-contractual obligations) are governed by the common law. Although each state is a separate jurisdiction, with its own legislature, judiciary and executive, there is one system of common law for the whole of Australia.[14] The High Court of Australia, a court with jurisdiction over the whole of Australia, can resolve any differences in the common law that may develop in different states. On the other hand, certain peripheral matters, like limitation periods, are subject to state legislation and, therefore, potentially different in different states.[15]

The following example illustrates the problem. Two Australian friends, habitually resident in different states,[16] come to Europe on holiday. They rent a car in Spain. An accident occurs there and the passenger is injured. If Australian law were applied, all issues in the case would be governed by the common law. Spanish law, on the other hand, would lead to a different result. It would be absurd to apply Spanish law just because the two parties are habitually resident in different Australian states.[17]

In view of this problem, it is unfortunate that the Regulation does not contain a provision stating that, if the parties are resident in different countries but the law of those countries is the same as regards the point in issue, they will be treated as if they were resident in the same country. The Louisiana Civil Code has such a provision.[18]

§ 2.2.4 Meaning of 'habitual residence'. Article 23 (Panel 23.4) provides a partial definition of habitual residence. Article 23(1) states that the habitual residence of a company is the place of its central administration. However, it goes on to say that, if the event giving rise to the damage, or the damage itself, takes place in the course of the operation of a branch, the company's habitual residence is to be regarded as the place where the branch is located.

There is no definition of the habitual residence of an individual (natural person), but the second paragraph of Article 23 provides that, where an individual acts in the course of his business, his principal place of business is to be treated as his habitual residence.

Panel 23.4 Habitual residence
Rome II Regulation (Regulation 864/2007), Article 23

Article 23

1. For the purposes of this Regulation, the habitual residence of companies and other bodies, corporate or unincorporated, shall be the place of central administration.

   Where the event giving rise to the damage occurs, or the damage arises, in the course of operation of a branch, agency or any other establishment, the place where the branch, agency or any other establishment is located shall be treated as the place of habitual residence.

2. For the purposes of this Regulation, the habitual residence of a natural person acting in the course of his or her business activity shall be his or her principal place of business.

---

14 *Lange* v. *Australian Broadcasting Corporation* (1997) 189 CLR 520 at p. 563.
15 The position appears to be the same in the common-law provinces of Canada, but Quebec is clearly a separate country.
16 They attended the same university.
17 The same problem of definition arises under the third paragraph of Article 4, though it might be possible to use it to apply the law of one particular state.
18 Article 3544(1).

§ 2.3 Flexibility

The third paragraph of Article 4 provides much-needed flexibility by stating that, where it is clear from all the circumstances that the tort is manifestly more closely connected with a country other than that indicated in paragraphs 1 or 2, the law of that other country applies. A defect, however, is that the tort as a whole must be more closely connected. It is not enough for a particular *issue* to be more closely connected – for example, whether a wife can sue her husband in tort, or whether the victim's claim against the tortfeasor passes to the victim's estate on his death. So, if paragraph 3 is applied, *all* aspects of the tort must be governed by some other system of law. As we shall see below, American law is more carefully crafted than this.

Paragraph 3 states that a manifestly closer connection might be based on a pre-existing relationship between the parties.[19] If such a relationship exists, the parties will often have their habitual residence in the same country, in which case paragraph 2 would apply. Where this is not the case, paragraph 3 would be applicable. An example of such a relationship is a contract between the parties.

§ 3 Pre-existing relationship

In this section, we are going to take a particular situation and consider the legal problems that arise. The situation is that where a pre-existing relationship exists between the claimant and the defendant. The most common example is where two persons are travelling in the same car when an accident occurs. Their relationship is based in one country, but the accident takes place in another. They may set out from country X, where they both have their home, and cross into country Y, where the accident occurs. If the passenger would have had a right to sue the driver (and claim compensation from his insurer) under the law of their home country, he should not be deprived of that right because of the chance fact that the accident occurred after they had crossed into country Y.

In the past, this situation resulted in considerable litigation in North America because many jurisdictions had 'guest statutes'. These were laws that applied to non-paying passengers in motor vehicles. They usually barred any action by the 'guest' against the driver for personal injury or wrongful death, unless gross negligence was proved. Ostensibly, they were to protect the driver from suit by an 'ungrateful' guest; in reality, they were passed at the behest of insurance companies in order to limit their liability to compensate the 'guest'. The insurance companies argued that the 'guest' would often be a friend of the driver or a member of his family; so the driver might have an incentive to exaggerate his negligence to allow the 'guest' to recover. Their effect was usually to deprive the passenger of any compensation. For this reason, they were regarded as unjust

---

19 The words 'in particular' are EC jargon indicating that this is not intended to exclude other possibilities.

by many people. They were prevalent in the 1950s and 1960s, but now seem to have been phased out.

Canada
McLean v. *Pettigrew*
Supreme Court of Canada
[1945] SCR 62; [1945] 2 DLR 65

Both the parties to this case lived in the province of Quebec, Canada. The plaintiff accepted the defendant's offer of a lift to Ottawa. While they were going through the province of Ontario, the car crashed, seriously injuring the plaintiff. The defendant was driving at the time and, in the opinion of the court, the accident was due to his negligence. He was charged in Ontario with the offence of driving without due care and attention, but was acquitted. The plaintiff then sued him in Quebec. If the accident had occurred in Quebec, he would undoubtedly have been liable. However, a 'guest statute' was in force in Ontario and this would have barred the plaintiff's claim under the law of that province.

The Supreme Court of Canada, affirming the judgments of the Quebec courts, held that the plaintiff could recover. It applied the rule in *Machado* v. *Fontes*, under which it was sufficient if the defendant's conduct constituted a criminal offence under the law of the place where the accident occurred, even if it did not give rise to civil liability. The Supreme Court of Canada ruled that the Quebec courts were not bound by the acquittal in the Ontario criminal proceedings, and were entitled to make up their own minds as to whether or not the defendant was guilty of a criminal offence under Ontario law.

This decision has been subject to criticism for manipulating the law to obtain the desired result, and has now been overruled.[20] However, it succeeded in producing a just result. Under Article 4(2) of the Rome II Regulation, the applicable law would have been that of Quebec. It would not have been necessary to consider the law of Ontario, except with regard to the rules of the road. Under present-day Canadian law, on the other hand, the applicable law would have been that of Ontario, and the action would have failed.[21] This shows the superiority of the EC rule.

Scotland
M'Elroy v. *M'Allister*
Court of Session (Inner House)
1949 SC 110; 1949 SLT 139

In this case, the pursuer (Scottish terminology for 'claimant') was Mrs Annie M'Elroy, widow of Mr Joseph M'Elroy. The couple lived in Glasgow, Scotland. Mr M'Elroy worked for a company in Glasgow. As part of his employment, he went in a truck driven by Mr M'Allister, who also lived in Glasgow. The truck crossed

---

20 *Tolofson* v. *Jensen* [1994] 3 SCR 1022; (1994) 120 DLR (4th) 289 (Supreme Court of Canada).
21 *Ibid*. This case lays down the rule that the law of the place of the tort applies. In inter-provincial cases, there are no exceptions.

into England and was involved in a collision. Mr M'Elroy was severely injured and died shortly afterwards. His widow claimed that the accident was the fault of Mr M'Allister and brought legal proceedings against him in a Scottish court.

If the accident had taken place in Scotland, and if negligence had been proved, Mrs M'Elroy would have been able to claim a *solatium* (damages for emotional distress) and also compensation for financial loss. The result would have been a substantial sum of money.

If all the facts had taken place in England, and if the action had been brought there, she could – if she proved negligence – obtain damages under two heads. Under the Fatal Accidents Acts 1864 to 1908, she could have obtained compensation for the financial support she could have expected from her husband. However, there was a short limitation period under this statute – the action had to be brought within twelve months of the accident – and her action was outside this time limit. Under another statute, the Law Reform (Miscellaneous Provisions) Act 1934, the right of action which her husband had against Mr M'Allister would have passed to his estate and inured to the benefit of his widow.[22]

The case came on appeal before a special seven-judge court. They held that Mrs M'Elroy could get nothing, except a small sum for funeral expenses. Their reasons were as follows. They interpreted the rule in *Phillips* v. *Eyre* as requiring civil liability under both systems, thus rejecting the English case of *Machado* v. *Fontes*. Moreover, they held that civil liability must exist under both systems of law as regards *each head* of liability. Because English law gave no right to a *solatium*, she could not claim that in Scotland. Because she brought the Scottish action more than twelve months after the accident, she had no right under English law to obtain compensation for financial loss. Therefore, she could not claim for financial loss under Scottish law.[23] Finally, she could not claim as executrix of her deceased husband's estate because, under Scottish law, such a claim does not pass to the estate. Consequently, the double-actionability rule was not satisfied with regard to any claim, except funeral expenses.

It is hard to fault the reasoning in each step of the argument. Yet the result was monstrous. Why should the widow be unable to claim just because the accident took place on the wrong side of the border, when she would have received substantial damages in either country if all the facts had taken place in that country?

Of the seven judges, only one dissented. Lord Keith[24] pointed out that the rule in *Phillips* v. *Eyre* merely required that the act of the defender (defendant) should not be justifiable under the law of the place where it was committed: even if the time limit under the Fatal Accidents Acts had expired, one could hardly say that causing a fatal accident was *justifiable* under English law.

It might be thought that the problem was the double-barrelled choice-of-law rule applied by the court. This was partly the court's own choice, since they could have interpreted 'not justifiable' as meaning something less than civil

---

22 This rule was abolished in 1982 by the Administration of Justice Act, section 1.
23 The court refused to characterize the English period of limitation as procedural: they said it was substantive, and therefore applicable in a Scottish court. Today, this characterization is expressly laid down by Article 15(h) of the Regulation.
24 Lord Keith went on to a distinguished legal career in the House of Lords.

liability, as was done in the English case of *Machado* v. *Fontes*. The only alternative at the time would have been to apply (only) the law of the place where the tort occurred. This was the rule accepted in most countries. However, it would have raised a second characterization problem. How should one characterize the English rule that a right of action in negligence survives the death of the victim? Is this part of the law of tort or part of the law of succession?[25] If it was the latter, Mrs M'Elroy would still have lost the case, since succession to Mr M'Elroy's estate was governed by the law of Scotland, his domicile at death.[26]

Under the Rome II Regulation,[27] Scottish law alone would have applied.[28] Again this shows the merit of Article 4.

New York
Babcock v. *Jackson*
New York Court of Appeals
12 NY 2d 473; 240 NYS 2d 743; 191 NE 2d 279 (1963)

Background

This was another 'guest statute' case. The facts were similar to those in *McLean* v. *Pettigrew*, except that the parties lived in New York, not Quebec. Miss Babcock was a guest in a car driven by her friends, Mr and Mrs Jackson. They all lived in New York. They went on a trip to Ontario and the crash occurred in Ontario while Mr Jackson was driving. Miss Babcock was badly injured. She sued Mr Jackson in New York. Ontario had a guest statute; New York did not. The 'double-actionability' rule was not followed in the United States. American courts normally applied the law of the place where the tort occurred (referred to in the case as the 'traditional rule'). The lower court applied this rule and found for the defendant. Miss Babcock appealed.

Fuld J

Realization of the unjust and anomalous results which may ensue from application of the traditional rule in tort cases has also prompted judicial search for a more satisfactory alternative in that area . . .

. . .

The 'center of gravity' or 'grouping of contacts' doctrine adopted by this court in conflicts cases involving contracts impresses us as likewise affording the appropriate approach for accommodating the competing interests in tort cases with multi-State contacts. Justice, fairness and 'the best practical result' may

---

25 Article 15(e) of the Rome II Regulation specifies that this question is decided by the law governing the tort.

26 See the California decision of *Grant* v. *McAuliffe*, 41 Cal 2d 859; 264 P 2d 944 (Supreme Court of California, 1953), in which a California court applied California law to decide this question, even though the accident took place in Arizona. In that case, however, the right of action passed to the victim's estate under California law but not under Arizona law; so the effect of characterizing it as falling under the law of succession was to allow recovery.

27 Assuming that it applied as between England and Scotland: see Article 25(2) of the Regulation (discussed above).

28 This would have been true irrespective of where the proceedings were brought. An English court would also have applied Scottish law.

best be achieved by giving controlling effect to the law of the jurisdiction which, because of its relationship or contact with the occurrence or the parties, has the greatest concern with the specific issue raised in the litigation. The merit of such a rule is that 'it gives to the place "having the most interest in the problem" paramount control over the legal issues arising out of a particular factual context' and thereby allows the forum to apply 'the policy of the jurisdiction "most intimately concerned with the outcome of [the] particular litigation."'

. . .

Comparison of the relative 'contacts' and 'interests' of New York and Ontario in this litigation, *vis-à-vis* the issue here presented, makes it clear that the concern of New York is unquestionably the greater and more direct and that the interest of Ontario is at best minimal. The present action involves injuries sustained by a New York guest as the result of the negligence of a New York host in the operation of an automobile, garaged, licensed and undoubtedly insured in New York, in the course of a week-end journey which began and was to end there. In sharp contrast, Ontario's sole relationship with the occurrence is the purely adventitious circumstance that the accident occurred there.

New York's policy of requiring a tort-feasor to compensate his guest for injuries caused by his negligence cannot be doubted – as attested by the fact that the Legislature of this State has repeatedly refused to enact a statute denying or limiting recovery in such cases . . . – and our courts have neither reason nor warrant for departing from that policy simply because the accident, solely affecting New York residents and arising out of the operation of a New York based automobile, happened beyond its borders. *Per contra*, Ontario has no conceivable interest in denying a remedy to a New York guest against his New York host for injuries suffered in Ontario by reason of conduct which was tortious under Ontario law. The object of Ontario's guest statute, it has been said, is 'to prevent the fraudulent assertion of claims by passengers, in collusion with the drivers, against insurance companies' and, quite obviously, the fraudulent claims intended to be prevented by the statute are those asserted against Ontario defendants and their insurance carriers, not New York defendants and their insurance carriers. Whether New York defendants are imposed upon or their insurers defrauded by a New York plaintiff is scarcely a valid legislative concern of Ontario simply because the accident occurred there, any more so than if the accident had happened in some other jurisdiction.

It is hardly necessary to say that Ontario's interest is quite different from what it would have been had the issue related to the manner in which the defendant had been driving his car at the time of the accident. Where the defendant's exercise of due care in the operation of his automobile is in issue, the jurisdiction in which the allegedly wrongful conduct occurred will usually have a predominant, if not exclusive, concern. In such a case, it is appropriate to look to the law of the place of the tort so as to give effect to that jurisdiction's interest in regulating conduct within its borders, and it would be almost unthinkable to seek the applicable rule in the law of some other place.[1]

---

1 *Editor's note*: compare Article 17 of the Regulation (Panel 23.2), where the same solution is adopted.

The issue here, however, is not whether the defendant offended against a rule of the road prescribed by Ontario for motorists generally or whether he violated some standard of conduct imposed by that jurisdiction, but rather whether the plaintiff, because she was a guest in the defendant's automobile, is barred from recovering damages for a wrong concededly committed. As to that issue, it is New York, the place where the parties resided, where their guest-host relationship arose and where the trip began and was to end, rather than Ontario, the place of the fortuitous occurrence of the accident, which has the dominant contacts and the superior claim for application of its law. Although the rightness or wrongness of defendant's conduct may depend upon the law of the particular jurisdiction through which the automobile passes, the rights and liabilities of the parties which stem from their guest-host relationship should remain constant and not vary and shift as the automobile proceeds from place to place. Indeed, such a result, we note, accords with 'the interests of the host in procuring liability insurance adequate under the applicable law, and the interests of his insurer in reasonable calculability of the premium.' (Ehrenzweig, 'Guest Statutes in the Conflict of Laws' 69 Yale LJ 595, 603.)

. . .

In conclusion, then, there is no reason why all issues arising out of a tort claim must be resolved by reference to the law of the same jurisdiction. Where the issue involves standards of conduct, it is more than likely that it is the law of the place of the tort which will be controlling but the disposition of other issues must turn, as does the issue of the standard of conduct itself, on the law of the jurisdiction which has the strongest interest in the resolution of the particular issue presented.

Result: the appeal was allowed; the Ontario 'guest statute' was not applicable.

Comment

This case applied a mixture of two approaches – grouping of contacts (closest connection) and interest analysis – in order to reach a good result. The former approach is also applicable under the Regulation, though only in exceptional circumstances: see Article 4(3) (Panel 23.1, above). We will consider interest analysis further below.

Australia
Neilson* v. *Overseas Projects Corporation of Victoria Ltd
High Court of Australia
[2005] HCA 54; (2005) 223 CLR 331; (2005) 221 ALR 213[29]

The plaintiff in this case was Mrs Neilson, a resident of Western Australia. Her husband was sent by his Australian employer, OPC, to work temporarily in Wuhan, China, and Mrs Neilson went with him. OPC provided accommodation for the couple. Mrs Neilson fell down the stairs in the flat provided and injured

---

29 For comments, see Mortensen, '"Troublesome and Obscure": The Renewal of Renvoi in Australia' (2006) 2 *Journal of Private International Law* 1; Mills, 'Renvoi and the Proof of Foreign Law in Australia' [2006] CLJ 37.

herself. She subsequently sued OPC in a court in Western Australia. In a previous case, *Regie Nationale des Usines Renault SA* v. *Zhang*,[30] the High Court of Australia (the highest court in Australia) had ruled that claims in tort are governed by the law of the place where the tort occurs. There are no exceptions to this rule. As applied to the *Neilson* case, this seemed to require the application of the law of China. However, under Chinese law a claim of this kind had to be brought within one year of the accident, and Mrs Neilson's claim was not within this time limit.

It would seem that she was bound to lose. However, the Chinese choice-of-law rule for torts was less inflexible than the Australian rule. Although it applied the law of the place of the tort as the primary rule, it contained an exception, worded in rather unclear terms, which could suggest that, where the parties had the same nationality or the same domicile, the court could apply that law instead.[31] On this basis, the trial court held that applying Chinese law actually meant applying Australian law (both parties being Australian nationals), since this is what a Chinese court would (or might) do. The court was thus able to avoid the Chinese limitation period and find for Mrs Neilson. This was an application of the *renvoi* doctrine, discussed in Chapter 22, § 2.3.2, above. The judgment was reversed on appeal by the Full Court of the Supreme Court of Western Australia. Mrs Neilson appealed to the High Court of Australia.

The High Court allowed the appeal and restored the judgment of the trial court. Different judges gave different reasons, but the following points had majority support. First, the High Court affirmed its ruling in *Zhang* that there can be no exceptions to the strict application of the law of the place of the tort. Secondly, a majority held (on dubious grounds) that a Chinese court would have applied Australian law. Thirdly, a majority held that *renvoi* should be applied and that the particular brand of *renvoi* to be applied was the theory of 'total *renvoi*' (see Chapter 22, § 2.4.2, above).[32] In other words, the Australian court had to apply both the Chinese choice-of-law rule and the Chinese theory of *renvoi* (if any). It had to decide the case by the same system of substantive law as would be applied by a Chinese court. This, it held, was Australian law; so Mrs Neilson won the case.

Though the result was right, the means used had little to recommend them. The cause of the problem was Australia's inflexible choice-of-law rule. The High Court said that this was necessary in order to attain certainty. However, once it saw what this would lead to, it used the discredited theory of *renvoi* to provide an escape route. The result was to produce greater uncertainty than would have followed from a flexible choice-of-law rule like that in the Rome II Regulation. To understand the Chinese choice-of-law rule was hard enough – it is doubtful whether, on the extremely limited evidence available, the court got it right[33] – but it is even more doubtful whether the court had any real ground for thinking

---

30 (2002) 210 CLR 491.
31 The Chinese law said 'the court may also apply . . .', thus suggesting that the court had a discretion.
32 Of the seven judges hearing the case, six favoured some form of *renvoi* and five favoured 'total' *renvoi*.
33 Some of the judges admitted this but decided the case on the ground that, in the absence of proof to the contrary, foreign law is presumed to be the same as Australian law.

it knew whether or not the Chinese court would apply *renvoi*. A further problem is that, if Chinese law had applied *renvoi* and if it too had applied 'total' *renvoi*, there would have been no solution: the Australian court would want to do whatever the Chinese courts would do, but the Chinese courts would want to do whatever the Australian courts would do.

The main ground on which the court sought to justify the application of *renvoi* was that it would lead to the same result as a Chinese court would have reached if it had decided the case.[34] Since the case was not being, and would never be, decided in a Chinese court, it is hard to see the importance of this. The High Court tried to justify its position by saying that it would discourage 'forum-shopping', by which is meant a plaintiff's bringing his action in the court likely to produce the most favourable result for him. However, the *forum non conveniens* doctrine, applicable in Australia, would ensure that the case would not go ahead in Australia if Australia was a clearly inappropriate forum. Given this, it is hard to see the objection to 'forum-shopping'. In any event, on the facts of the case, Australia was clearly the natural forum. In fact, it was the only forum that one could ever imagine the case being brought in. The cultural, financial, linguistic and practical difficulties of suing in China would have been immense.

Moreover, it was naive in the extreme to suggest that *renvoi* would ensure that the result would be the same as that in a Chinese court. In a Chinese court, the lawyers would have been different and they would probably have been funded in a different way. The rules of procedure and evidence would have been different. If the evidence on Australian law available to the Chinese court had been as sketchy as the evidence on Chinese law available to the Australian court, they would almost certainly have applied a very different version of Australian 'law' from an Australian court. Moreover, concepts like negligence and reasonableness would have been interpreted in a completely different way. The chances of the same result ensuing would have been almost zero.

How would this case have been decided under the Rome II Regulation? Since *renvoi* is expressly excluded,[35] the solution adopted by the High Court of Australia would not have been followed. Under the first paragraph of Article 4 of the Regulation, the law of China would have been applied. This would have included the limitation period under Chinese law.[36] Would the second paragraph have been applicable? The plaintiff, Mrs Neilson, was habitually resident in Western Australia. The defendant, OPC, had its central administration in another Australian state, Victoria. It is not clear whether it had a branch in Western Australia and, if it did, whether the event giving rise to the damage, or the damage itself, occurred in the course of operation of that branch.[37] If, as seems likely, the plaintiff and defendant were habitually resident in different Australian states, the next question is whether each state counts as a separate

---

34 This is an example of the continuing influence of the once-prevalent theory that achieving uniformity of result is the most important objective of conflict of laws. It was criticized in Chapter 1, § 4, above.
35 Article 24.
36 Article 15(h) states that limitation periods are to be characterized as pertaining to tort law.
37 On this, see Article 23(1) of the Regulation, set out in Panel 23.4, above.

country for the purposes of Article 4.[38] This was considered in § 2.2.3, above. It is not clear what the answer is. If they are separate countries, the Regulation would lead to the unsatisfactory result of applying Chinese law.[39] The only possibility of avoiding this would be to apply the third paragraph of Article 4 and to find that the country with the closest connection was Western Australia.

§ 4 Common origin

We now consider the situation where the parties come from the same country but have no pre-existing relationship. Here, the right answer is less obvious.

> **New York**
> *Dym* v. *Gordon*
> **New York Court of Appeals**
> **16 NY 2d 120; 209 NE 2d 792; 262 NYS 2d 463 (1965)**

Background

Ms Dym and Mr Gordon were both New Yorkers. Although they had known each other in New York, they went independently to Colorado to attend summer school. The accident occurred when Ms Dym was a passenger in Mr Gordon's car on a short trip within Colorado, and involved a car driven by a Kansas resident. Colorado had a 'guest statute'; New York did not. Ms Dym sued Mr Gordon in New York for injuries received in the accident. The lower court, following *Babcock* v. *Jackson*, held New York law applicable. The Appellate Division reversed this judgment, and the case then came to the Court of Appeals.

Burke J

Following our approach in *Babcock*, it is necessary first to isolate the issue, next to identify the policies embraced in the laws in conflict, and finally to examine the contacts of the respective jurisdictions to ascertain which has a superior connection with the occurrence and thus would have a superior interest in having its policy or law applied. The issue here is simply whether in an automobile host-guest relationship a negligent driver should be liable to his injured passenger. The New York law finds nothing in the host-guest relationship which warrants a digression from the usual negligence rule of ordinary care. In Colorado, however, this relationship is treated specially and, while ordinary negligence is usually enough for recovery in that state, injuries arising out of this relationship are compensable only if they result from 'willful and wanton' conduct. Contrary to the narrow view advanced by plaintiff, the policy underlying Colorado's law is threefold: the protection of Colorado drivers and their insurance carriers against fraudulent claims, the prevention of suits by 'ungrateful guests', and the priority of

---

38 The question in issue in the case, limitation of actions, was governed by state statutes, but the action was brought within the time period laid down by the statutes in both Western Australia and Victoria.
39 This result cannot be avoided by characterizing limitation of actions as procedural: the Regulation expressly provides that it is part of the law of tort (Article 15(h)).

injured parties in other cars in the assets of the negligent defendant. Examining Colorado's interest in light of its public policy we find that over and above the usual interest which Colorado may bring to bear on all conduct occurring within its boundaries, Colorado has an interest in seeing that the negligent defendant's assets are not dissipated in order that the persons in the car of the blameless driver will not have their right to recovery diminished by the present suit.

Finally we come to the question of which state has the more significant contacts with the case such that its interest should be upheld. In this regard, the factual distinctions between this case and *Babcock* do have considerable influence. *Babcock* did not involve a collision between two cars; thus only New Yorkers were involved and it was unnecessary for us to consider the interests of Ontario in the rights of those in a car of a non-negligent driver. In *Babcock* we pointed out that the host-guest relationship was seated in New York and that the place of the accident was 'entirely fortuitous'. In this case the parties were dwelling in Colorado when the relationship was formed and the accident arose out of Colorado based activity; therefore, the fact that the accident occurred in Colorado could in no sense be termed fortuitous. Thus it is that in this case, where Colorado has such significant contacts with the *relationship itself* and the *basis of its formation*, the application of its law and underlying policy are clearly warranted.

Of compelling importance in this case is the fact that here the parties had come to rest in the State of Colorado and had thus chosen to live their daily lives under the protective arm of Colorado law. Having accepted the benefits of that law for such a prolonged period, it is spurious to maintain that Colorado has no interest in a relationship which was formed there. In *Babcock* the New Yorkers at all times were *in transitu* and we were impressed with the fundamental unfairness of subjecting them to a law which they in no sense had adopted.

Fuld J (dissenting)[1]

[After stating that the rule laid down in *Babcock* was that the law to be applied to resolve a particular issue in a tort case with multi-jurisdictional contacts is 'the law of the jurisdiction which, because of its relationship or contact with the occurrence or the parties, has the greatest concern' with the matter in issue and 'the strongest interest' in its resolution, he continued:]

The rule thus announced is not, and does not profess to be, a talisman of legal certainty, nor does it of itself provide a formulary means for resolving conflicts problems. What it does provide is a method, a conceptual framework, for the disposition of tort cases having contacts with more than one jurisdiction. Although the majority in this case reaffirms *Babcock's* abandonment of the prior inflexible rule of *lex loci delicti*, its decision, nevertheless, in essence, reflects the adoption of an equally mechanical and arbitrary rule that, in litigation involving a special relationship, controlling effect must be given to the law of the jurisdiction in which the relationship originated, notwithstanding that that jurisdiction may not have the slightest concern with the specific issue raised or that some other state's

---

1 *Editor's note*: it will be remembered that Fuld J gave the judgment of the court in *Babcock* v. *Jackson*.

relationship or contact with the occurrence or the parties may be such as to give it the predominant interest in the resolution of that issue.

...

Nothing turns on the circumstance that in this case the guest-host relationship was formed in the foreign jurisdiction. It seems indisputably clear that a jurisdiction may be said to be 'concerned' with a specific issue, if that term is to have any meaningful content, only when its governmental interests and policies enter into the making of a particular decision. Accordingly, the decisive consideration, in the present case, is that Colorado's guest statute, paralleling Ontario's, has as its prime objective the protection of Colorado driver-defendants and their insurance carriers against fraudulent claims and lawsuits ... Manifestly, that policy of Colorado can in no way be served by applying its statute to an action, such as the present, which is brought in New York and involves not residents of Colorado or their insurance carriers but only New Yorkers and a New York based and insured vehicle. The mere fact that the guest-host relationship between the New York parties originated in Colorado has, in truth, as little relevance to the policy underlying that state's guest statute and, by that token, as little bearing on that statute's applicability as did the fact, in *Babcock*, of the occurrence of the accident in Ontario in relation to the similar policy embodied in its guest statute. Under the circumstances of the present case, then, Colorado, to paraphrase what we wrote in *Babcock*, 'has no conceivable interest in denying a remedy to a New York guest against his New York host for injuries suffered in [Colorado] by reason of conduct which was tortious under [Colorado] law'.

Nor is the majority's position advanced by its further suggestion ... that the Colorado statute also reflects (1) an antipathy on the part of Colorado to suits by 'ungrateful' guests ... and (2) a policy to assure 'the priority of injured parties in other cars in the assets of the negligent defendant.' Indeed, as regards the latter asserted policy, there does not appear to be any Colorado pronouncement even to intimate that the Colorado Legislature was motivated by any such objective. In any event, though, Colorado would be legitimately concerned with the application of these alleged policies only in relation to matters within its legislative competence, such as the burdens of the Colorado courts, the regulation of the affairs and relationships of Colorado citizens or the protection of Colorado claimants or insurers ... Whether such considerations might be of significance in particular circumstances not here present, they certainly have no relevance in the context of this suit between New York domiciliaries in a New York court, in which no burden is being imposed on the Colorado courts and no citizen of Colorado appears to be in any way interested. The majority's emphasis on the involvement of another vehicle in the accident ... is thus misplaced since the other automobile was driven by a resident from Kansas and was apparently licensed in that state.

New York, on the other hand, just as in *Babcock*, as the permanent residence of the plaintiff and the defendant and the place to which they returned to live shortly after the accident, has a predominant interest in vindicating its own policy of requiring negligent driving hosts to compensate their injured guests. It is apparent that the consequences resulting from an uncompensated injury generally affect the community in which the injured party resides, in this case, New York. If a plaintiff who returns to live here after sustaining injuries in another state requires additional medical treatment, as is usually the case, or is unable to meet his normal economic commitments and becomes a public charge, it is the people of New York – whose services will go uncompensated and whose tax dollars will be charged in the form of welfare payments – who will feel the repercussions of such eventualities and not the distant and unconcerned residents of the state of injury, where a guest-host relationship between the New York parties may have been formed . . . There is thus no question but that Colorado's 'contacts', though quantitatively greater than those of Ontario in *Babcock*, are still not 'significant' as respects the specific issue presented and that the 'contacts' of New York in relation to that issue are decidedly superior.

Result: Colorado law (and its 'guest statute') was applicable.

QUESTIONS

1 Which analysis do you prefer: that of the majority or that of Fuld J?
2 What would the result have been if the Rome II Regulation had applied?

England
Chaplin* v. *Boys
House of Lords
[1971] AC 356; [1969] 3 WLR 322; [1969] 2 All ER 1085

Background

The parties were both British subjects resident in England. They were both in the British Army and were temporarily stationed in Malta. There was no pre-existing relationship between them, unless being in the British Army could be regarded as a relationship. The parties were in separate vehicles when the accident occurred: the claimant was a passenger on a motor scooter which collided with a car negligently driven by the defendant. Liability existed under both English and Maltese law. However, there was a difference regarding the heads of damage: under English law damages could be claimed for pain and suffering; under Maltese law they could not. The result was that, under Maltese law, the claimant could recover only £53, while, under English law, he could recover £2,303.

The trial court awarded the claimant the higher sum, relying on *Machado* v. *Fontes*. This was affirmed by the Court of Appeal, though different judges gave different reasons. The case then came before the House of Lords. It again affirmed, though again different judges gave different reasons. There was, however, a majority in favour of overruling *Machado* v. *Fontes*: the rule was laid down that *civil* liability must exist both under the foreign law and under English law. This meant that some other ground had to be found to reach the desired result. The reasoning of Lord Wilberforce has probably been most influential in subsequent cases.

Lord Wilberforce

Given the general rule, as stated above, as one which will normally apply to foreign torts, I think that the necessary flexibility can be obtained from that principle which represents at least a common denominator of the United States decisions, namely, through segregation of the relevant issue and consideration whether, in relation to that issue, the relevant foreign rule ought, as a matter of policy . . . to be applied. For this purpose it is necessary to identify the policy of the rule, to inquire to what situations, with what contacts, it was intended to apply; whether not to apply it, in the circumstances of the instant case, would serve any interest which the rule was devised to meet. This technique appears well adapted to meet cases where the *lex delicti* either limits or excludes damages for personal injury: it appears even necessary and inevitable. No purely mechanical rule can properly do justice to the great variety of cases where persons come together in a foreign jurisdiction for different purposes with different pre-existing relationships, from the background of different legal systems. It will not be invoked in every case or even, probably, in many cases. The general rule must apply unless clear and satisfying grounds are shown why it should be departed from and what solution, derived from what other rule, should be preferred. If one lesson emerges from the United States decisions it is that case to case decisions do not add up to a system of justice. Even within these limits this procedure may in some instances require a more searching analysis than is needed under the general rule. But unless this is done, or at least possible, we must come back to a system which is purely and simply mechanical.

I find in this approach the solution to the present case. The tort here was committed in Malta; it is actionable in this country. But the law of Malta denies recovery of damages for pain and suffering. *Prima facie* English law should do the same: if the parties were both Maltese residents it ought surely to do so; if the defendant were a Maltese resident the same result might follow. But in a case such as the present, where neither party is a Maltese resident or citizen, further inquiry is needed rather than an automatic application of the rule. The issue, whether this head of damage should be allowed, requires to be segregated from the rest of the case, negligence or otherwise, related to the parties involved and their circumstances, and tested in relation to the policy of the local rule and of its application to these parties so circumstanced.

So segregated, the issue is whether one British subject, resident in the United Kingdom, should be prevented from recovering in accordance with English law, against another British subject, similarly situated, damages for pain and suffering which he cannot recover under the rule of the *lex delicti*. This issue must be stated, and examined, regardless of whether the injured person has or has not also a recoverable claim under a different heading (e.g., for expenses actually incurred) under that law. This Maltese law cannot simply be rejected on grounds of public policy or some general conception of justice. For it is one thing to say or presume that domestic rule is a just rule, but quite another, in a case where a foreign element is involved, to reject a foreign rule on any such general ground. The foreign rule must be evaluated in its application.

The rule limiting damages is the creation of the law of Malta, a place where both plaintiff and defendant were temporarily stationed. Nothing suggests that the Maltese state has any interest in applying this rule to persons resident outside it, or in denying the application of the English rule to these parties. No argument has been suggested why an English court, if free to do so, should renounce its own rule. That rule ought, in my opinion, to apply.

Comment

The result would have been the same under the Rome II Regulation.

§ 5   US law: interest analysis and the 'better law' theory

So far, we have been looking at cases in which the claimant was denied recovery by the law of the place where the tort occurred, but could obtain it under some other law. What happens in the reverse situation? Under a rule-based system, such as the Rome II Regulation, the result would be the same. The position is, however, different if we apply interest analysis or the 'better law' theory. This is the approach usually followed by American courts.

> **Minnesota**
> ***Milkovich* v. *Saari***
> **Supreme Court of Minnesota**
> **295 Minn 155; 203 NW 2d 408 (1973)**

Background

The plaintiff and both defendants were residents of Ontario. They drove to Duluth, Minnesota, to do some shopping and attend a play. The car belonged to the first defendant, Ms Saari. After they crossed the border, the second defendant, Ms Rudd, took over the driving. The car crashed in Minnesota about forty miles south of the border, and the plaintiff was injured. The car was garaged, registered and insured in Ontario. Ontario had a 'guest statute'; Minnesota did not. The action was brought in Minnesota.

Todd J

[After discussing the authorities and stating that Minnesota courts had adopted the 'better law' approach, he said:]

The compelling factors in this case are the advancement of the forum's governmental interests and the application of the better law. While there may be more deterrent effect in our common-law rule of liability as opposed to the guest statute requirement of gross negligence, the main governmental interest involved in that of any 'justice-administering state.' Leflar, 'Conflicts Law: More on Choice-Influencing

Considerations' 54 Calif. L Rev. 1584, 1594. In that posture, we are concerned that our courts not be called upon to determine issues under rules which, however, accepted they may be in other states, are inconsistent with our own concept of fairness and equity. We might also note that persons injured in automobile accidents occurring within our borders can reasonably be expected to require treatment in our medical facilities, both public and private. In the instant case, plaintiff incurred medical bills in a Duluth hospital which have already been paid, but we are loath to place weight on the individual case for fear it might offer even minor incentives to 'hospital shop' or to create litigation-directed pressures on the payment of debts to medical facilities. Suffice it to say that we recognize that medical costs are likely to be incurred with a consequent governmental interest that injured persons not be denied recovery on the basis of doctrines foreign to Minnesota.

In our search for the better rule, we are firmly convinced of the superiority of the common-law rule of liability to that of the Ontario guest statute. We can find little reason for the strict limitation of a host's liability to his guest beyond the fear of collusive suits and the vague disapproval of a guest 'biting the hand that feeds him.' Neither rationale is persuasive. We are convinced the judicial system can uncover collusive suits without such overinclusive rules, and we do not find any discomfort in the prospect of a guest suing his host for injuries suffered through the host's simple negligence.

Accordingly, we hold that Minnesota law should be applied to this lawsuit.

Comment

If the 'better law' approach is adopted, two matters must be clarified. First, what are the criteria to decide which law is better? In Minnesota, it seems to be that, in personal-injury cases in which the defendant is insured, the 'better law' is the law most favourable to the plaintiff. The second question is: from among which legal systems can the court choose? Is the choice limited to the law of the place of the accident and the law of the common domicile or habitual residence of the parties? If these two issues can be satisfactorily resolved, the 'better law' approach has much to recommend it.

In the EU, it has been adopted in a modified form in several provisions. For example, under Article 7 of the Rome II Regulation (Panel 23.5), which deals with environmental damage, the claimant can choose either the law of the country where the damage occurred or the law of the country in which the event occurred which gave rise to the damage. Here 'better law' means the law more favourable to the claimant, and the choice is between the two laws mentioned above. Thus, if pollutants are put into the River Rhine in France and cause environmental damage in the Netherlands, the claimant can choose to have the case decided under either French law or Dutch law.

Another example is found in Article

Panel 23.5 Environmental damage
Rome II Regulation (Regulation 864/2007), Article 7

Article 7

The law applicable to a non-contractual obligation arising out of environmental damage or damage sustained by persons or property as a result of such damage shall be the law determined pursuant to Article 4(1), unless the person seeking compensation for damage chooses to base his or her claim on the law of the country in which the event giving rise to the damage occurred.

18 of the Regulation, under which a direct action is possible against the tortfeasor's insurer if this is permitted by either the law governing the tort or that governing the insurance policy.

In our last two cases, we change the focus and look at a different situation. Several American states have a rule that, if a bar, tavern or other such establishment serves alcoholic drinks to a customer who is already clearly drunk, the owner of the bar is liable in tort to anyone injured by the customer while he is in an inebriated condition. Our next two cases are concerned with the situation in which the bar is in one state and the injury occurs in another.

District of Columbia
Rong Yao Zhou* v. *Jennifer Mall Restaurant Inc.
District of Columbia Court of Appeals
534 A 2d 1268 (1987)

Background

The plaintiff and his wife were seriously injured when they were hit by a car in Chevy Chase, Maryland. The car was driven by a man called Joray, who was drunk. He was returning from a restaurant in Washington, DC, owned by the defendant. In the restaurant, he had unlawfully been served with alcoholic liquor even though he was already obviously intoxicated. It was in this state that he left the restaurant, got into the car and drove away. The accident happened shortly afterwards. In these circumstances, the victim had a claim in tort against the restaurant owner under DC law.[40] Under Maryland law, he did not. The action was brought against the restaurant owner in the District of Columbia.

Newman, Associate Judge

[After saying that the District of Columbia followed the governmental-interests approach, he continued:]

In applying governmental interests analysis to the facts of this case, we consider the interests, respectively, of Maryland and the District of Columbia. From the ruling of Maryland's highest court . . . we understand that state to adhere to a policy of protecting negligent bar owners from civil liability, although they remain subject to the criminal penalties that attach for serving a person who is 'visibly under the influence'. By contrast, a District of Columbia rule that would make tavern keepers answerable in tort, as well as under the criminal sanctions of D C Code § 25–121(b) (1981), would signify interests of this jurisdiction in compensating victims for resulting injuries, as well as in deterring harmful conduct.

The apparent clash of policies between Maryland and the District of Columbia presents a 'false conflict' in the context of this case. A 'false conflict' occurs when the policy of one state would be advanced by application of its law, while that of the other state would not be advanced by application of its law. In such a situation, the law of the interested jurisdiction prevails . . . Here, Maryland's

---

40 A number of US states have such a rule, which may be either judge-made or statutory.

interest in protecting tavern owners from tort liability is not implicated where the negligent restaurant is situated in the District of Columbia and the unlawful conduct occurred therein. Hence we apply the law of the interested jurisdiction, the District of Columbia.[1]

1 The only interest of Maryland that is implicated in this litigation, an interest in protecting public safety which we infer from its statutory prohibition on serving persons under the influence, is consistent with rather than in conflict with applying a District of Columbia rule of civil liability.

Result: DC law applies.

It is in situations like this that the EC rule is shown up as crude and unsophisticated. Under the general rule in Article 4(1), the law of the place where the damage occurs will be applied, irrespective of where the restaurant or tavern is located, unless it happens that the parties are all habitually resident in the same country. The third paragraph of Article 4 might provide a means of escape, but only if the tort as a whole – rather than the particular issue before the court – was more closely connected with the country in which the bar was situated. However, interest analysis provides a much more satisfactory means of determining the applicable law than a simple weighing up of contacts.

The *Rong* case suggests that the crucial fact in the United States is the location of the restaurant or tavern. Our next case shows that this is not necessarily so.

California
Bernhard v. *Harrah's Club*
Supreme Court of California
16 Cal 3d 313; 546 P 2d 719; 128 Cal Rptr 215 (1976)

Background

The defendant was a Nevada corporation. It operated a gambling establishment in Nevada that sold alcoholic liquor. It advertised extensively in California. The plaintiff was a Californian resident who was injured when a car coming in the opposite direction along a California highway crossed the centreline and collided head-on with his motorcycle. The car was driven by a California resident called Fern Myers. He and his brother, Philip, were returning from a night out at an establishment in Nevada owned by the defendants. They had gone there as a result of the defendant's advertisements. They had been served with alcoholic liquor when they were already obviously drunk. It was in this state that they left the establishment and drove away. After crossing into California, their car hit the plaintiff. They were still drunk at the time of the accident. Under California law, the defendant, Harrah's Club, was liable to compensate the victim; under Nevada law, it was not. The plaintiff brought the action in California.

Sullivan J

Although California and Nevada, the two 'involved states' have different laws governing the issue presented in the case at bench, we encounter a problem in selecting the applicable rule of law only if both states have an interest in having their respective laws applied . . .

Defendant contends that Nevada has a definite interest in having its rule of decision applied in this case in order to protect its resident tavern keepers like defendant from being subjected to a civil liability which Nevada has not imposed either by legislative enactment or decisional law . . . Accordingly defendant argues that the Nevada rule of decision is the appropriate one for the forum to apply.

Plaintiff on the other hand points out that California also has an interest in applying its own rule of decision to the case at bench. California imposes on tavern keepers civil liability to third parties injured by persons to whom the tavern keeper has sold alcoholic beverages when they are obviously intoxicated 'for the purpose of protecting members of the general public from injuries to person and damage to property resulting from the excessive use of intoxicating liquor.' California, it is urged, has a special interest in affording this protection to all California residents injured in California.

Thus, since the case at bench involves a California resident (plaintiff) injured in this state by intoxicated drivers and a Nevada resident tavern keeper (defendant) which served alcoholic beverages to them in Nevada, it is clear that each state has an interest in the application of its respective law of liability and nonliability. It goes without saying that these interests conflict. Therefore . . . in the instant case for the first time since applying a governmental interest analysis as a choice of law doctrine . . . we are confronted with a 'true' conflicts case. We must therefore determine the appropriate rule of decision in a controversy where each of the states involved has a legitimate but conflicting interest in applying its own law in respect to the civil liability of tavern keepers.

The search for the proper resolution of a true conflicts case, while proceeding within orthodox parameters of governmental interest analysis, has generated much scholarly examination and discussion. The father of the governmental interest approach, Professor Brainerd Currie, originally took the position that in a true conflicts situation the law of the forum should always be applied . . . However, upon further reflection, Currie suggested that when under the governmental interest approach a preliminary analysis reveals an apparent conflict of interest upon the forum's assertion of its own rule of decision, the forum should re-examine its policy to determine if a more restrained interpretation of it is more appropriate. '[T]o assert a conflict between the interests of the forum and the foreign state is a serious matter; the mere fact that a suggested broad conception of a local interest will create conflict with that of a foreign state is a sound reason why the conception should be re-examined, with a view to a more moderate and restrained interpretation both of the policy and of the circumstances in which it must be applied to effectuate the forum's legitimate purpose . . .' (Currie, *The Disinterested Third State* (1963) 28 Law & Contemp. Prob., pp. 754, 757.) This process of re-examination requires identification of a 'real interest as opposed to a hypothetical interest' on the part of the forum (Sedler, *Value of Principled Preferences*, 49 Texas L Rev. 224) and can be approached under principles of 'comparative impairment.' (Baxter, *Choice of Law and the Federal System* . . . 16 Stan. L Rev. 1–22 . . .)

Once this preliminary analysis has identified a true conflict of the governmental interests involved as applied to the parties under the particular circumstances of the case, the 'comparative impairment' approach to the resolution of such conflict seeks to determine which state's interest would be more impaired if its policy were subordinated to the policy of the other state. This analysis proceeds on the principle that true conflicts should be resolved by applying the law of the state whose interest would be the more impaired if its law were not applied. Exponents of this process of analysis emphasize that it is very different from a weighing process. The court does not '"weigh" the conflicting governmental interests in the sense of determining which conflicting law manifested the "better" or the "worthier" social policy on the specific issue. An attempted balancing of conflicting state policies in that sense . . . is difficult to justify in the context of a federal system in which, within constitutional limits, states are empowered to mold their policies as they wish . . . [The process] can accurately be described as . . . accommodation of conflicting state policies, as a problem of allocating domains of law-making power in multi-state contexts – limitations on the reach of state policies – as distinguished from evaluating the wisdom of those policies . . . [E]mphasis is placed on the appropriate scope of conflicting state policies rather than on the "quality" of those policies . . .' (Horowitz, *The Law of Choice of Law in California – A Restatement* . . . 21 UCLA L Rev. 719, 753 . . .) However, the true function of this methodology can probably be appreciated only casuistically in its application to an endless variety of choice of law problems . . .

. . .

Mindful of the above principles governing our choice of law, we proceed to re-examine the California policy underlying the imposition of civil liability upon tavern keepers. At its broadest limits this policy would afford protection to all persons injured in California by intoxicated persons who have been sold or furnished alcoholic beverages while intoxicated regardless of where such beverages were sold or furnished. Such a broad policy would naturally embrace situations where the intoxicated actor had been provided with liquor by out-of-state tavern keepers. Although the State of Nevada does not impose such *civil* liability on its tavern keepers, nevertheless they are subject to *criminal* penalties under a statute making it unlawful to sell or give intoxicating liquor to any person who is drunk or known to be an habitual drunkard . . .

We need not, and accordingly do not here determine the outer limits to which California's policy should be extended, for it appears clear to us that it must encompass defendant, who as alleged in the complaint, 'advertis[es] for and otherwise solicit[s] in California the business of California residents at defendant Harrah's Club Nevada drinking and gambling establishments, knowing and expecting said California residents, in response to said advertising and solicitation, to use the public highways of the State of California in going and coming from defendant Harrah's Club Nevada drinking and gambling establishments.' Defendant by the course of its chosen commercial practice has put itself at the heart of California's regulatory interest, namely to prevent tavern keepers from selling alcoholic beverages to obviously intoxicated persons who are likely to act in California in the intoxicated state. It seems clear that California cannot reasonably effectuate its policy if it does not extend its regulation to include out-of-state tavern keepers such as defendant who regularly and purposely sell intoxicating beverages to California residents in places and under conditions in which it is reasonably certain these residents will return to California and act therein while still in an intoxicated state. California's interest would be very significantly impaired if its policy were not applied to defendant.

Since the act of selling alcoholic beverages to obviously intoxicated persons is already proscribed in Nevada, the application of California's rule of civil liability would not impose an entirely new duty requiring the ability to distinguish between California residents and other patrons. Rather the imposition of such liability involves an increased economic exposure, which, at least for businesses which actively solicit extensive California patronage, is a foreseeable and coverable business expense. Moreover, Nevada's interest in protecting its tavern keepers from civil liability of a boundless and unrestricted nature will not be significantly impaired when as in the instant case liability is imposed only on those tavern keepers who actively solicit California business.

Therefore, upon re-examining the policy underlying California's rule of decision and giving such policy a more restrained interpretation for the purpose of this case pursuant to the principles of the law of choice of law discussed above, we conclude that California has an important and abiding interest in applying its rule of decision to the case at bench, that the policy of this state would be more significantly impaired if such rule were not applied and that the trial court erred in not applying California law.

. . .

The judgment is reversed and the cause is remanded to the trial court with directions to overrule the demurrer and to allow defendant a reasonable time within which to answer.

Comment

In this case, the applicable law under the Rome II Regulation would have been that of California, the place where the damage occurred. However, the Regulation gives no scope for the subtle analysis of interests used by the California court to reach its result.

§ 6   The Rome II Regulation: special rules

The rule in Article 4 is subject to exceptions that apply in five special situations:

- products liability (Article 5);
- unfair competition and acts restricting free competition (Article 6);
- environmental damage (Article 7);[41]
- infringement of intellectual property rights (Article 8); and
- industrial action (Article 9).

We shall consider only two of these.

---

41 Set out in Panel 23.5, above.

§ 6.1 Products liability

Choice of law in products-liability cases is determined by Article 5 of the Regulation. This is set out in Panel 23.6.

§ 6.1.1 Structure. Article 5(1) is in the form of a 'cascade': it lays down a number of possibilities, but each possibility (other than the first) applies only if the preceding ones are inapplicable. The first possibility – the primary rule – appears to be Article 4(2), since the reference to this comes first. If that is inapplicable, the next possibility is sub-paragraph (a) of Article 5(1); if that is inapplicable, the next possibility is sub-paragraph (b), then sub-paragraph (c).

The last sentence of Article 5(1), which will henceforth be referred to as the 'however' clause, qualifies the rules in sub-paragraphs (a), (b) and (c), but not, it seems, Article 4(2).[42] Article 5(2) qualifies the rules in sub-paragraphs (a), (b) and (c); it also qualifies the rule in Article 4(2) either in its own right or because it is repeated in identical terms in Article 4(3).

§ 6.1.2 Primary rule. The primary rule is contained in Article 4(2). This was discussed in § 2.2, above. It applies where both parties have their habitual residence in the same country at the time of the tort.

§ 6.1.3 Second-ranking rule. The second-ranking rule is that contained in sub-paragraph (a) of Article 5(1). Under this, the governing law is the law of the country of the victim's habitual residence – provided that the product was marketed in that country. This proviso is repeated in sub-paragraphs (b) and (c). Its meaning will be discussed below.

§ 6.1.4 Third-ranking rule. The third-ranking rule is that contained in sub-paragraph (b). Under this, the governing law is the law of the country in which the product was acquired – provided that the product was marketed in that country. 'Acquired' presumably means purchased or otherwise obtained – for example, by gift.

Panel 23.6 Products liability
Rome II Regulation (Regulation 864/2007), Article 5

Article 5

1. Without prejudice to Article 4(2), the law applicable to a non-contractual obligation arising out of damage caused by a product shall be:
   (a) the law of the country in which the person sustaining the damage had his or her habitual residence when the damage occurred, if the product was marketed in that country; or, failing that,
   (b) the law of the country in which the product was acquired, if the product was marketed in that country; or, failing that,
   (c) the law of the country in which the damage occurred, if the product was marketed in that country.
   However, the law applicable shall be the law of the country in which the person claimed to be liable is habitually resident if he or she could not reasonably foresee the marketing of the product, or a product of the same type, in the country the law of which is applicable under (a), (b) or (c).
2. Where it is clear from all the circumstances of the case that the tort/delict is manifestly more closely connected with a country other than that indicated in paragraph 1, the law of that other country shall apply. A manifestly closer connection with another country might be based in particular on a pre-existing relationship between the parties, such as a contract, that is closely connected with the tort/delict in question.

---

42 Since the 'however' clause refers to the law of the producer's habitual residence, it would lead to the same result as Article 4(2); so it does not matter whether it qualifies Article 4(2) or not.

§ 6.1.5 Fourth-ranking rule. The fourth-ranking rule is that contained in sub-paragraph (c). Under this, the governing law is the law of the country in which the damage occurred. This is the same as the general rule in Article 4(1). It is again subject to the condition that the product has been marketed in that country.

§ 6.1.6 Product marketed. Sub-paragraphs (a), (b) and (c) are all subject to the 'product marketed' proviso. This raises two questions: the meaning of 'product' and the meaning of 'marketed'.

The first question is whether 'product' refers to the particular item or good that actually caused the damage or whether it also covers other goods of the same type. For example, if the harm was caused by contamination in a can of beer, must it be proved that the particular can that was contaminated was marketed in the country in question, or is it enough that other cans of the same kind were marketed there? As a matter of plain English[43] and common sense, the latter should be the answer. If the manufacturer sells the identical product in the country in question, it should not make any difference if the particular can was purchased by the claimant in another country while he was on holiday there. However, the fact that the 'however' clause refers to marketing of the product, 'or a product of the same type', suggests that the common-sense answer is not the correct one. If the proviso to sub-paragraphs (a), (b) and (c) was intended to cover products of the same type, those additional words would have been repeated there too.

The next question is the meaning of 'marketed'. This cannot mean the same as 'acquired', since the latter is used in sub-paragraph (b) to mean something different. On the other hand, the product does not have to be marketed by the defendant, since the 'however' clause indicates that the product might be marketed without the knowledge of the defendant. It is suggested that marketing requires the organized, mass selling of a standardized product. This need not be by the defendant or with his consent.

§ 6.1.7 No rule applicable. What happens if none of the rules laid down in Article 5(1) is applicable? The 'however' clause does not establish an independent rule, since it is clearly geared to sub-paragraphs (a), (b) and (c): it cannot apply if none of those sub-paragraphs is applicable. The same applies to the rule in Article 5(2): this cannot apply unless one of the provisions of Article 5(1) applies.

In view of this, there are only three possibilities. The first is that no claim can be made. This would constitute a denial of justice and would be contrary to Article 6(1) of the European Convention on Human Rights; so it must be rejected. The second possibility is that national conflict of laws applies. However, it is unlikely that this was intended. The third possibility is that the general rule in Article 4 applies.[44] This must be the correct solution.

---

43 It is thought that the same is true of French.
44 Since we would not have reached the situation we are considering if the second paragraph of Article 4 had been applicable, we are really concerned only with the first and third paragraphs.

Though correct, this has strange consequences. Assume that the first three rules are inapplicable and that one has to consider the rule in sub-paragraph (c). This requires the application of the law of the country in which the damage occurred, provided that the product was marketed in that country. If the product was not marketed in that country, you fall back on the general rule and apply the law of the country in which the damage occurred even if the product was not marketed there.[45] In other words, the 'marketed' proviso is meaningless. However, if the product *was* marketed there, but this could not have been foreseen by the defendant, you then apply the 'however' clause, which leads to the law of the country of the defendant's habitual residence. There is no logic in this.

These rules are extremely complicated, but in practice the answer will usually be fairly obvious. The following examples show how the rules will apply.

Example 1: Assume that a beer manufacturer in Germany markets its product in England through a branch. The claimant, who lives in England, buys it in England and consumes it there. The beer is contaminated and he suffers illness as a result. Here, English law would apply under the rule in Article 4(2). The German company's habitual residence would be regarded as being in England, since the beer would have been marketed through the English branch (Article 23). It would make no difference if the claimant had taken the beer to France on holiday and consumed it there.

Example 2: A German beer manufacturer markets its product in England through an independent distributor. The claimant, who lives in England, buys it in England and consumes it there. The beer is contaminated and he suffers illness as a result. Article 4(2) would not apply here, because the defendant would not be habitually resident in England. However, English law would still apply under Article 5(1)(a), since the claimant would be habitually resident in England and the product would have been marketed there. The 'however' clause would not apply. Again, it would make no difference if the beer were consumed in another country.

Example 3: A French resident comes to England to support his side in a rugby match. While in England, he buys beer manufactured by a German company. One can of the beer is not consumed in England. He takes it back to France and consumes it there. That can is contaminated and he suffers illness as a result. In this situation, Article 4(2) would not apply: the claimant would be habitually resident in France but not the defendant.[46] If 'product' in the proviso to sub-paragraph (a) means the particular can of beer that caused the problem, it would not have been marketed in France; so sub-paragraph (a) would not apply. However, since the product was acquired in England, sub-paragraph (b) would apply. The governing law would be English law (unless the defendant could not

---

45 This is subject to the escape clause in Article 4(3).

46 The defendant would be habitually resident in either Germany (central administration) or England (if there is a branch there) but not in France. This would be true even if it had a branch in France: a company is not habitually resident where it has a branch unless the event giving rise to the damage, or the damage itself, arises in the course of operation of the branch (Article 23(1)). If the contaminated can was bought in England, the existence of a branch in France would be irrelevant.

foresee that the product would be marketed in England).[47] It is unlikely that Article 5(2) would apply: the tort is not manifestly more closely connected with France.

Example 4: The defendant is a Korean car manufacturer. It markets its cars throughout the EC. One car is sold to X in France. X sells it in France to Y, who is habitually resident in Belgium. Y takes it to Belgium and is injured in an accident there. He sues the manufacturer in Belgium. Here, Article 4(2) will not apply because the defendant would not be habitually resident in Belgium for the purpose of the case.[48] Sub-paragraph (a) will not apply because the product (the particular vehicle in question) was not marketed in Belgium. However, sub-paragraph (b) will apply. The car was acquired by Y in France and the car was marketed there. French law will govern.

Example 5: The facts are as in the previous example, except that X took the car to Belgium and sold it there to Y. In this example, none of the provisions of Article 5(1) would apply. Article 4(2) would not apply because the company would not be habitually resident in Belgium for the purpose of the case and none of the sub-paragraphs would apply because the particular vehicle in question was not marketed in Belgium. If what was said above was correct, one would then fall back on the general rule in Article 4(1) and apply Belgian law because the damage occurred in Belgium. Article 4(3) would not apply because it could not be said that the tort is manifestly more closely connected with France or any other country.

§ 6.1.8 Conclusions. As will be appreciated, Article 5 is complex. This complexity is due to the fact that consumers' and producers' lobbies are both powerful in the EC, and both fought hard for their respective interests. Whether a simpler, but more flexible, rule would have been better is a matter on which opinions may differ.

§ 6.2   Intellectual property

Panel 23.7 Infringement of intellectual property rights
Rome II Regulation (Regulation 864/2007), Article 8

Article 8

1. The law applicable to a non-contractual obligation arising from an infringement of an intellectual property right shall be the law of the country for which protection is claimed.
2. In the case of a non-contractual obligation arising from an infringement of a unitary Community intellectual property right, the law applicable shall, for any question that is not governed by the relevant Community instrument, be the law of the country in which the act of infringement was committed.
3. The law applicable under this Article may not be derogated from by an agreement pursuant to Article 14.

The law applicable to the infringement of an intellectual-property right is the law of the country for which protection is claimed. This will be the law of the country in which the right is registered or, if unregistered, the law under which the right was granted or arose. This is laid down in Article 8 of the Regulation (Panel 23.7), which

---

[47] If this was the case, German law would apply.
[48] It would make no difference if it has a branch in Belgium, since the vehicle in question would not have been sold through that branch: see note 46, above.

also deals with the infringement of unitary intellectual-property rights arising under EC law.

§ 7 Defamation

Article 1(2)(g) excludes from the scope of the Regulation 'non-contractual obligations arising out of violations of privacy and rights relating to personality, including defamation'. Since the British legislation – the Private International Law (Miscellaneous Provisions) Act 1995 – did not apply to defamation[49] (see § 1, above), the English common law still applies to defamation in England.

The common law was discussed in § 1, above. It will be remembered that *Machado* v. *Fontes* was overruled by the House of Lords in *Chaplin* v. *Boys*;[50] so it must now be shown that the defendant's act would be actionable as a tort under English law and that the defendant incurred civil liability under the law of the country where the tort was committed. This is subject to the exceptions laid down in *Chaplin* v. *Boys* and in *Red Sea Insurance Co. Ltd* v. *Bouygues SA*.[51] The result is that, as regards publication in England (it must be remembered that, under English law, each sale is a separate 'publication'), English law alone will apply; as regards publication abroad, the 'double-actionability' test must be satisfied. In either case, if there is a defence under English law – for example, that the statement is true – judgment will be given for the defendant.

§ 8 Choice of law by agreement

Under Article 14, the parties are, in certain circumstances, permitted to choose the applicable law by agreement (Panel 23.8). Normally, this is possible only after the tort has been committed (paragraph 1), but, where all the parties are pursuing a commercial activity, it is possible beforehand,

> **Panel 23.8 Freedom of choice**
> **Rome II Regulation (Regulation 864/2007), Article 14**
>
> **Article 14**
> 1. The parties may agree to submit non-contractual obligations to the law of their choice:
>   (a) by an agreement entered into after the event giving rise to the damage occurred; or
>   (b) where all the parties are pursuing a commercial activity, also by an agreement freely negotiated before the event giving rise to the damage occurred.
>   The choice shall be expressed or demonstrated with reasonable certainty by the circumstances of the case and shall not prejudice the rights of third parties.
> 2. Where all the elements relevant to the situation at the time when the event giving rise to the damage occurs are located in a country other than the country whose law has been chosen, the choice of the parties shall not prejudice the application of provisions of the law of that other country which cannot be derogated from by agreement.
> 3. Where all the elements relevant to the situation at the time when the event giving rise to the damage occurs are located in one or more of the Member States, the parties' choice of the law applicable other than that of a Member State shall not prejudice the application of provisions of Community law, where appropriate as implemented in the Member State of the forum, which cannot be derogated from by agreement.

---

49 Sections 9(3), 10 and 13. Defamation is defined for this purpose in section 13(2). Since the area excluded from the Regulation is wider than that excluded from the Act, certain matters – for example, violations of privacy – will continue to be covered by the Act.
50 [1971] AC 356; [1969] 3 WLR 322; [1969] 2 All ER 1085.
51 [1995] 1 AC 190 (PC).

provided the agreement is freely negotiated. This is unlikely to apply very often – parties do not normally foresee that a tort will be committed – but one could imagine that, if the parties have a continuing business relationship – for example, a joint venture – they might conclude such an agreement.

The requirement at the end of paragraph 1 (that the choice must be 'expressed or demonstrated with reasonable certainty by the circumstances of the case') is based on Article 3(1) of the Rome Convention, now to be replaced by the Rome I Regulation, discussed in the chapters that follow.[52] Paragraphs 2 and 3 of Article 14 are similar to paragraphs 3 and 4 of Article 3 of the Rome I Regulation (discussed in Chapter 25, § 3.1, below).

Panel 23.9 Subject-matter scope of the Rome II Regulation
Rome II Regulation (Regulation 864/2007), Article 1

Article 1 Scope

1. This Regulation shall apply, in situations involving a conflict of laws, to non-contractual obligations in civil and commercial matters. It shall not apply, in particular, to revenue, customs or administrative matters or to the liability of the State for acts and omissions in the exercise of State authority (acta iure imperii).
2. The following shall be excluded from the scope of this Regulation:
   (a) non-contractual obligations arising out of family relationships and relationships deemed by the law applicable to such relationships to have comparable effects including maintenance obligations;
   (b) non-contractual obligations arising out of matrimonial property regimes, property regimes of relationships deemed by the law applicable to such relationships to have comparable effects to marriage, and wills and succession;
   (c) non-contractual obligations arising under bills of exchange, cheques and promissory notes and other negotiable instruments to the extent that the obligations under such other negotiable instruments arise out of their negotiable character;
   (d) non-contractual obligations arising out of the law of companies and other bodies corporate or unincorporated regarding matters such as the creation, by registration or otherwise, legal capacity, internal organisation or winding-up of companies and other bodies corporate or unincorporated, the personal liability of officers and members as such for the obligations of the company or body and the personal liability of auditors to a company or to its members in the statutory audits of accounting documents;
   (e) non-contractual obligations arising out of the relations between the settlors, trustees and beneficiaries of a trust created voluntarily;
   (f) non-contractual obligations arising out of nuclear damage;
   (g) non-contractual obligations arising out of violations of privacy and rights relating to personality, including defamation.
3. This Regulation shall not apply to evidence and procedure, without prejudice to Articles 21 and 22.

Appendix: subject-matter scope of the Regulation

The subject-matter scope of the Regulation is laid down in Article 1, set out in Panel 23.9.

---

52 The equivalent provision in the Rome I Regulation is also Article 3(1).

Further reading

Baxter, 'Choice of Law and the Federal System' (1963) 16 *Stanford Law Review* 1

Carruthers, 'Substance and Procedure in the Conflict of Laws: A Continuing Debate in Relation to Damages' (2004) 53 ICLQ 691

Cavers, 'The Proper Law of Producers' Liability' (1977) 26 ICLQ 703

Currie, 'The Disinterested Third State' (1963) 28 *Law and Contemporary Problems* 754

Dicey, Morris and Collins, *First Supplement to the Fourteenth Edition* (Sweet & Maxwell, London, 2007), pp. 183–224 (by C. G. J. Morse)

Dickinson (Andrew), *The Rome II Regulation: A Commentary* (Oxford University Press, Oxford, 2008)

Dornis, 'Contribution and Indemnification among Joint Tortfeasors in Multi-State Conflict Cases: A Study of Doctrine and the Current Law in the US and under the Rome II Regulation' (2008) 4 *Journal of Private International Law* 237

Ehrenzweig, 'Guest Statutes in the Conflict of Laws – Towards a Theory of Enterprise Liability under "Foreseeable and Insurable Laws"' (1960) 69 *Yale Law Journal* 595

Gray, 'Loss Distribution Issues in Multinational Tort Claims: Giving Substance to Substance' (2008) 4 *Journal of Private International Law* 279

Graziano, 'The Law Applicable to Product Liability: The Present State of the Law in Europe and Current Proposals for Reform' (2005) 54 ICLQ 475

Horowitz, 'The Law of Choice of Law in California – A Restatement' (1974) 21 *UCLA Law Review* 719

Morse (C.G.J.), *Torts in Private International Law* (North-Holland Publishing Co., Amsterdam, 1978)

'Rights Relating to Personality, Freedom of the Press and Private International Law: Some Common Law Comments' (2005) 58 CLP 133

Mortensen, 'Homing Devices in Choice of Tort Law: Australian, British and Canadian Approaches' (2006) 55 ICLQ 839

Plender (Richard) and Wilderspin (Michael), *The European Private International Law of Obligations* (Sweet & Maxwell, London, publication expected in 2009)

Symeonides, 'Resolving Punitive-Damages Conflicts' (2003) 5 *Yearbook of Private International Law* 1

'Rome II and Tort Conflicts: A Missed Opportunity' (2008) 56 *American Journal of Comparative Law* 173

CHAPTER 24

Contracts: the principle of party autonomy

§ 1 Introduction

Freedom of contract is an important legal principle. Giving effect to it involves determining whether the parties reached agreement, and what it was they agreed to. It also involves filling in the gaps in their agreement and deciding what to do if they fail to carry it out. In all these matters, the policy of the law should be to give effect to what the parties intended or would have intended if they had considered the matter. As far as choice of law is concerned, this policy involves determining the system of law that they might reasonably have expected to apply. The purpose of choice-of-law rules in this area should be to identify this system.

There is, however, another aspect of the law of contract. In some situations, the law is not concerned with discovering what the parties intended (or might have intended). Its purpose is to override their intention: it prohibits them from agreeing to certain terms or imposes certain terms on them. This is done either to protect the weaker party or to give effect to some governmental policy. Consumer-protection rules are an example of the former; export embargoes adopted for foreign-policy reasons are an example of the latter. These are sometimes called mandatory rules. Where they are in issue, it makes no sense to select the applicable law on the basis of the intention, actual or presumed, of the parties: their intention is not relevant. Rather, one should consider whether it is reasonable for the system of law in question to impose itself on the contract against the will of the parties.

This chapter is concerned with the first of these two aspects of contract law, the area where freedom of contract is the guiding principle. It may in some ways be regarded as the primary aspect, since, if no contract exists, there can be no question of mandatory rules. The second aspect will be considered in the next chapter.

§ 2 The theory of the proper law

What system of law should apply to determine the issues described above as following from the principle of freedom of contract? In the past, attempts were made to find a simple, easy-to-apply formula. The first solution was to choose the law of the place where the contract was made (*lex loci contractus*). This was simple. However, it was not always easy to apply. If the parties meet face to face to conclude the contract, there is no problem; but, if they are in different countries, it is not obvious where the contract is made. For example, assume that X in England writes to Y in Germany to make him an offer. Y receives the letter and accepts the offer in another letter, posted in Germany. Is the contract made in England, where X receives the acceptance, or in Germany, where it is posted? Though many legal systems have developed rules to answer this question, they are artificial: there is no obvious answer.[1] Moreover, the place of making the contract may be a matter of chance: the parties may happen to be in the same city for different reasons, and agree to meet there.

A later solution was to apply the law of the place of performance (*lex loci solutionis*). This was thought to provide a more substantial connection. However, the contract may be performed in different places – for example, the seller in a contract of sale may agree to deliver the goods in Mexico, and the buyer may agree to make payment in New York. What law should apply?

In the nineteenth century, English courts decided that the parties to a contract should be entitled to choose the governing law for themselves.[2] This was the beginning of the doctrine of the 'proper law'. The proper law was the system of law that applied in general to a contract: it governed the 'freedom-of-contract' aspects of a contract. If the parties agreed on what it was to be, and expressed that agreement in the contract, the law thus chosen was the proper law.

In England, it has never been necessary for there to any connection with the chosen law. The parties have always been completely free in their choice. This was established in *Vita Food Products Inc.* v. *Unus Shipping Co. Ltd*,[3] a case decided by the Privy Council on appeal from Nova Scotia.[4] It concerned a contract to carry goods from Newfoundland to New York on a ship owned by a Nova Scotia corporation. The bills of lading, issued in Newfoundland, contained a choice-of-law clause in favour of English law. There was no apparent connection with England. Nevertheless, the Privy Council held that the choice of law was valid.

What if there was no express choice? In such a case, the courts looked for an implied choice. However, 'implied choice' can mean different things. On the one hand, it can mean that both of the parties thought about the matter, they both thought the answer was so obvious that it was not necessary to state it, and they had the same view as to what the answer was. However, 'implied choice' can also mean something different. It can simply mean that a reasonable person would have thought that a particular system of law was obviously applicable. In

---

1 The English rule is that, where the parties communicate by instantaneous (or near-instantaneous) means of communication (for example, telephone, fax or e-mail), the contract is made where the offeror receives the acceptance (England, in the example). Where, on the other hand, it is by non-instantaneous means of communication (for example, by post), it is where the letter of acceptance is mailed. In the example, this would be Germany. See *Entores* v. *Miles Far Eastern Corporation* [1955] 2 QB 327 (CA).

2 For some earlier cases which might be regarded as taking the first hesitant steps in this direction, see *Gienar* v. *Meyer* (1796) 2 Hy Bl 603 (126 ER 728), a case mainly on choice of court, and *Robinson* v. *Bland* (1760) Black W 257 at p. 259 (96 ER 141 at pp. 141–2).

3 [1939] AC 277 (PC).

4 Nova Scotia is a province of Canada. At that time, the Privy Council (which sits in London) heard appeals from Canada. Most of the members of the Privy Council in its judicial capacity were Law Lords (judges from the House of Lords in its judicial capacity), though sometimes senior Commonwealth judges also sat. Appeals to the Privy Council from Canada have now been abolished. Today, the Supreme Court of Canada is the highest court in Canada.

the latter case, the parties might not have thought about the matter at all. The difference between these two approaches is that the former is subjective, while the latter is objective. In the former, the test is what the parties actually thought; in the latter, it is what is reasonable. In practice, of course, the two approaches may often lead to the same conclusion.

In some cases, the English courts seem to have applied the objective test to ascertain the choice of the parties, or at least not to have distinguished clearly between it and the subjective test. *The Assunzione*[5] is one example. This concerned the law applicable to a charterparty entered into between Italian shipowners and French charterers for a voyage from France to Italy. Birkett LJ began his judgment by saying:[6]

> The principle upon which that kind of question has to be determined is really not in doubt; it has been laid down in a long line of cases. If the intention of the parties is not expressed in the contract itself, the court must ascertain as best it can what is the implied or the presumed intention to be gathered from the whole of the facts.

He concluded, however, by saying:[7]

> I have been confronted from the very beginning of this case with a sense of unreality. If parties do express in their contract the law by which they desire the contract to be governed, well and good; but if, as in this case (and I rather gather in the majority of cases), no thought whatever is given to it, and it is said to a court, 'You have to discover and ascertain, if possible, what it would have been if these people had really considered it', then this situation arises, [counsel for the charterers] saying with great force: 'I cannot conceive [the charterers] ever agreeing to Italian law under any circumstances', and [counsel for the shipowners] saying with equal force: 'I cannot conceive [the shipowners] ever accepting French law'. One side urges French law, the other Italian law; but, of course, no one has said expressly which is to apply, and this court has therefore to examine the facts of the case and to consider what inference or presumption arises from those facts, and then, regarding the parties as just and reasonable people, to say after that full consideration what is the reasonable inference to be drawn and what was the probable intention of the parties.

In this passage, Birkett LJ seems to acknowledge that the concept of presumed intention is not really apt to describe what the court is doing in such a situation. It is really applying a wholly objective test.

This was recognized in a later case, *Coast Lines Ltd* v. *Hudig & Veder Chartering NV*,[8] which also concerned a charterparty, this time between English shipowners and Dutch charterers. In his judgment, Lord Denning MR said:[9]

> In order to determine the proper law of the contract . . . we have to ask ourselves: What is the system of law with which the transaction has the closest and most real connection? This is not dependent on the intentions of the parties. They never thought about it. They had no intentions upon it.

---

5 [1954] P 150 (CA).
6 At p. 180.
7 At pp. 185–6.
8 [1972] 2 QB 34 (CA). For an earlier case, see *Bonython* v. *Commonwealth of Australia* [1951] AC 201 at p. 219 (PC).
9 At p. 44.

Megaw LJ said:[10]

> What is the proper law of the contract? In this charterparty the parties did not express their actual intention as to the proper law. No inference can be drawn from any one or more of the express terms of the contract as to the *actual* common intention of the parties. Hence the question to be answered is: what is the system of law with which the transaction has its closest and most real connection?

And Stephenson LJ said:[11]

> What is the proper law of this contract? English or Dutch? This question cannot be answered by ascertaining the actual intention of the parties. If they had applied their minds to it the English shipowners would probably have answered 'English' and the Dutch charterers 'Dutch'. If they had been asked to agree on the application of the other's law to the charterparty each would probably have refused and there would have been no contract; but there is a contract . . . The parties have not expressed their actual choice of the proper law to govern this contract. So the court has to infer the intention, which they have not expressed and one of them would probably disclaim, from the terms and the nature of the contract and from the relevant contemporary circumstances; or, if that is impossible, to ascertain the country and system of law with which the contract and transaction have the closest and most real connection.

As a result of this shift, it became clear that there was a three-step approach. The first step was to determine whether there was an express choice of law. If there was, that applied. If there was no express choice, the court had to consider whether there was an implied choice. If there was, that determined the proper law. However, the concept of an implied choice was now restricted to cases in which the court believed that the parties had genuinely considered the matter. If there was no implied choice under this more limited concept, the court would apply the objective test of the closest and most real connection.

The difference between the second step (implied choice) and the third step (objective test) was important when the grounds for believing that the parties intended a particular system of law to apply were based on the terms of the contract, rather than on external factors. This is illustrated by *Amin Rasheed Shipping Corporation* v. *Kuwait Insurance Co.*,[12] discussed in § 4.5, below. The case concerned a contract of marine insurance between a Kuwaiti insurance company and a shipping company incorporated in Liberia with its head office in Dubai. The basic facts surrounding the contract indicated little contact with England, certainly not enough to say that the closest and most substantial connection was with England. However, at the time in question, Kuwait had no law of marine insurance; moreover, the contract, which was written in English, used obsolete language that had little meaning in modern English. However, the relevant words and phrases were all found in the Lloyd's SG policy, as scheduled to the Marine Insurance Act 1906, a British statute. Thus, the contract could be interpreted only on the basis of English law. It was for this reason that the House of Lords held that English law was the proper law. The parties must have intended it to govern.

10 At p. 46.
11 At p. 50.
12 [1984] AC 50 (HL).

The courts used to apply a number of presumptions to determine the objective proper law. Once the proper-law theory had become well established, however, these presumptions largely fell away: they tended to get in the way of the search for the closest connection. However, in the case of certain specific contracts, they continued to have some effect. For example, a contract concerning rights *in rem* in land was presumed to be governed by the law of the place where the land was situated (*lex situs*) and a contract for the carriage of goods by sea was presumed to be governed by the law of the flag of the ship carrying the goods. Outside these rather specific instances, however, presumptions were rejected by the English courts.

The theory of the proper law in many ways constituted a significant advance, since, if used with skill, it permitted a court to apply the system of law most likely to accord with the parties' reasonable expectations. However, there was a price to pay: its very flexibility could lead to uncertainty. This is illustrated by *Whitworth Street Estates Ltd* v. *Miller*,[13] a case concerning a building (construction) contract between the English owner of property in Scotland and the Scottish builder. The contract contained no express choice of law. There was an arbitration clause, and the actual point at issue was the law governing the procedure of the arbitration. The arbitration took place in Scotland, and their lordships were unanimous in saying that it was governed by Scots law. However, they also considered the law governing the contract. Here, they were divided. Two judges said it was Scots law and three said it was English law. The two judges favouring Scots law[14] did so on the basis of the objective test: they considered that there was no implied choice of law and that the closest and most real connection was with Scotland. Of the three judges favouring English law, two considered that there was an implied choice in favour of English law.[15] The remaining judge (Lord Guest) said that the parties had not indicated any intention to be bound by English law; he nevertheless held that the applicable law was English law, apparently on the basis of the objective test.

One of the judges who considered that there was an implied choice of English law,[16] said that, if the case had been decided on the basis of the objective test, the closest and most real connection was with Scotland. Thus, three judges thought that there was no implied choice and that the objective test should be applied. Moreover, three judges considered that, if the objective test were applied, the closest and most real connection was with Scotland. Nevertheless, the majority held that the proper law was that of England. This difference of opinion among Britain's most respected judges highlights the level of uncertainty inherent in the doctrine.

The common law no longer applies in England. It was almost entirely replaced, first by the Rome Convention, and now by the Rome I Regulation.[17] However, it continues to apply in the Commonwealth – for example, in Canada

---

13 [1970] AC 583 (HL).
14 Lord Reid and Lord Wilberforce.
15 Viscount Dilhorne and Lord Hodson. The contract was based on a form, drafted in terms of English law, recommended by the Royal Institute of British Architects. It was adopted because the architect was English.
16 Viscount Dilhorne.
17 Regulation 593/2008. The common law may still apply in some of the special cases in which the Rome I Regulation does not apply: see Article 1.

and Australia. Similar principles apply in the United States, though there are differences of detail.[18] Moreover, the three-step approach outlined above has been adopted by the Rome Convention and now by the Rome I Regulation; so it continues to apply in England as well.

§3   The Rome Convention

The Rome Convention[19] was negotiated after the United Kingdom had become a Member of the European Community; so its provisions represent something of a compromise between the approaches of the common law and the civil law. It remained in force for a number of years, but will be abrogated when the Rome I Regulation becomes applicable.[20] It will not be discussed here. However, most of its principles have been taken over by the Regulation. When the latter is discussed, the main differences between it and the Convention will be explained. It should, however, be mentioned that there was an official report on the Convention, the Giuliano–Lagarde Report,[21] which provided valuable guidance on the interpretation of the Convention and, today, on those provisions of the Regulation that are derived from it.

§4   The Rome I Regulation

The Rome I Regulation[22] was negotiated in the course of 2007, and formally adopted on 17 June 2008. It came into force on the twentieth day following its publication in the *Official Journal of the European Union*,[23] and applies to contracts concluded after 17 December 2009.[24] Contracts concluded prior to that date will still be governed by the Convention.

§4.1   *Subject-matter scope*

The subject-matter scope of the Regulation is set out in Article 1 (Panel 24.1). Article 1 contains a positive definition and exceptions. The former makes clear that it is limited to contractual obligations (thus excluding torts and other non-contractual obligations such as unjust enrichment) in civil and commercial matters (thus excluding public law).

---

18 Some American lawyers think that the parties should not have a completely free choice of the applicable law: see Uniform Commercial Code, section 1-105(1) (the parties may choose the law of a state only if the transaction 'bears a reasonable relation' to that state), but see the New York General Obligations Law, Title 14, § 5-1401, in which this restriction is rejected in most cases; see also the American Law Institute, *Restatement of the Law Second: Conflict of Laws*, § 187(1); compare *ibid.*, § 187(2). As regards the applicable law in the absence of a choice, the *Restatement* lists the contacts to be taken into account: see § 188.
19 The Convention on the Law Applicable to Contractual Obligations 1980.
20 Article 24 of the Regulation.
21 Giuliano and Lagarde, 'Report on the Convention on the Law Applicable to Contractual Obligations', OJ 1980 L 282.
22 Regulation 593/2008, OJ 2008 L 177, p. 6.
23 It was published in the *Official Journal of the European Union* dated 4 July 2008.
24 Article 28.

Panel 24.1 Subject-matter scope of the Rome I Regulation
Rome I Regulation (Regulation 593/2008), Article 1

Article 1 Material scope

1. This Regulation shall apply, in situations involving a conflict of laws, to contractual obligations in civil and commercial matters.
   It shall not apply, in particular, to revenue, customs or administrative matters.
2. This Regulation shall not apply to:
   (a) questions involving the status or legal capacity of natural persons, without prejudice to Article 13;
   (b) obligations arising out of family relationships and relationships deemed by the law applicable to such relationships to have comparable effects, including maintenance obligations;
   (c) obligations arising out of matrimonial property regimes, property regimes of relationships deemed by the law applicable to such relationships to have comparable effects to marriage, and wills and succession;
   (d) obligations arising under bills of exchange, cheques and promissory notes and other negotiable instruments to the extent that the obligations under such other negotiable instruments arise out of their negotiable character;
   (e) arbitration agreements and agreements on the choice of court;
   (f) questions governed by the law of companies and other bodies corporate or unincorporated such as the creation, by registration or otherwise, legal capacity, internal organisation or winding up of companies and other bodies corporate or unincorporated and the personal liability of officers and members as such for the obligations of the company or body;
   (g) the question whether an agent is able to bind a principal, or an organ to bind a company or body corporate or unincorporated, in relation to a third party;
   (h) the constitution of trusts and the relationship between settlors, trustees and beneficiaries;
   (i) evidence and procedure, without prejudice to Article 18;
   (j) obligations arising out of dealings prior to the conclusion of a contract;
   (k) insurance contracts arising out of operations carried out by organisations other than undertakings referred to in Article 2 of Directive 2002/83/EC of the European Parliament and of the Council of 5 November 2002 concerning life assurance[1] the object of which is to provide benefits for employed or self-employed persons belonging to an undertaking or group of undertakings, or a trade or group of trades, in the event of death or survival or of discontinuance or curtailment of activity, or of sickness related to work or accidents at work.

1 OJ L 345, 19.12.2002, p. 1. Directive as last amended by Directive 2007/44/EC.

The exceptions are largely self-explanatory. For our purposes, the most important are:

- obligations under bills of exchange, cheques and promissory notes;
- obligations under other negotiable instruments to the extent that those obligations arise out of their negotiable character;
- arbitration and choice-of-court agreements;
- company law – for example, the creation, legal capacity, internal organization and winding up of companies and the personal liability of their officers and members for the obligations of the company;
- whether an agent is able to bind a principal; and
- obligations arising out of dealings before the conclusion of a contract.

These will be considered further in the appropriate place.

§ 4.2   *International scope*

Like the Rome II Regulation (discussed in the previous chapter), but unlike the Brussels I Regulation (considered in Part II of this book), the Rome I Regulation does not apply only to conflicts between the legal systems of the European Union. A choice between the laws of Mexico and Peru falls just as much within its scope as one between the laws of France and Germany. This is expressly laid down in Article 2, which provides that: 'Any law specified by this Regulation shall be applied whether or not it is the law of a Member State.'

However, it does not, as a matter of Community law, apply to conflicts between the laws of different units within a Member State. This is laid down by Article 22(2), set out in Panel 24.2. Thus, there is no Community obligation on the United Kingdom to apply it between England and Scotland, but it will be so applied as a matter of United Kingdom law.[25]

Panel 24.2　States with more than one legal system
Rome I Regulation (Regulation 593/2008), Article 22

Article 22

1. Where a State comprises several territorial units, each of which has its own rules of law in respect of contractual obligations, each territorial unit shall be considered as a country for the purposes of identifying the law applicable under this Regulation.
2. A Member State where different territorial units have their own rules of law in respect of contractual obligations shall not be required to apply this Regulation to conflicts solely between the laws of such units.

---

§ 4.3 Meaning of 'country'

Article 22(1) (set out in Panel 24.2, above) defines 'country' for the purposes of the Regulation. This definition is identical to that in Article 25(1) of the Rome II Regulation, except that 'contractual' replaces 'non-contractual'. The problems raised by this definition were discussed in Chapter 23, § 2.2.3, above. It need only be repeated here that England (including Wales) and Scotland are separate countries for this purpose.

§ 4.4 Express choice

§ 4.4.1 Freedom of choice. The right of the parties to choose the applicable law is recognized by Article 3(1), set out in Panel 24.3. There is no requirement that the law chosen should have any connection with the parties or the contract. The choice is completely free.[26]

§ 4.4.2 Non-state law. The original Commission proposal permitted the parties to choose a system of 'law' that was not in force in any country – for example, a code drawn up by some international body, but never adopted. This was rejected by the Member States.

Panel 24.3　Express and implied choice of law
Rome I Regulation (Regulation 593/2008), Article 3

Article 3 Freedom of choice

1. A contract shall be governed by the law chosen by the parties. The choice shall be made expressly or clearly demonstrated by the terms of the contract or the circumstances of the case.
   By their choice the parties can select the law applicable to the whole or a part only of the contract.
2. The parties may at any time agree to subject the contract to a law other than that which previously governed it, whether as a result of an earlier choice under this Article or of other provisions of this Regulation. Any change in the law to be applied that is made after the conclusion of the contract shall not prejudice its formal validity under Article 11 or adversely affect the rights of third parties.

---

[25] The Regulations will be entitled the Law Applicable to Contractual Obligations (England and Wales and Northern Ireland) Regulations 2009. Separate regulations will apply in Scotland.
[26] For exceptions, see Article 5(2) (carriage of passengers), discussed in § 4.6.7, below, and Article 7(3) (insurance).

So the law chosen must be in force in some country in the world. However, there is nothing to prevent the parties incorporating such a code (or, indeed, any other set of rules) into their contract by reference.[27] Where a set of rules is incorporated by reference into a contract, it is as if those rules were set out in the contract. They then take effect as terms of the contract. There is an important difference between this and choice of law. It is the latter that gives legal force to the former.[28]

§ 4.5   Implied choice

Under Article 3(1) (Panel 24.3, above), the choice must be made expressly or 'clearly demonstrated by the terms of the contract or the circumstances of the case'.[29] Thus, an implied choice is possible, but such a choice must nevertheless be real in the sense explained in § 2, above. This was made clear in the Giuliano–Lagarde Report.[30]

Our next case illustrates this. It was decided under the common law, but it applies the same principle.

England
Amin Rasheed Shipping Corporation* v. *Kuwait Insurance Co.
House of Lords
[1984] AC 50

Background

The case concerned a contract of marine insurance between a Kuwaiti insurance company and Amin Rasheed Shipping Corporation, a shipping company incorporated in Liberia with its head office in Dubai. Amin Rasheed insured its ships though the London office of an English company that was a member of the Amin Rasheed group. Insurance was effected through London brokers. Premiums were paid through the brokers in London. Policies were issued in Kuwait and sent to London to be passed on to the English company. Claims, though expressed in the policies to be payable in Kuwait, were in practice settled in London.

The case arose when the *Al Wahab*, a ship belonging to Amin Rasheed, was seized by the Saudi authorities. Amin Rasheed claimed under the policy, but the insurance company was unwilling to pay: they said that the ship was engaged in smuggling. Amin Rasheed wanted to sue the insurance company in England. To obtain jurisdiction, it argued that the applicable law was English law.[31] The

---

27 Recital 13 in the Preamble.
28 The law applied under a choice-of-law clause is that law as it exists from time to time. Relevant changes after the contract is made are applied. Where, on the other hand, a set of rules is incorporated by reference, subsequent changes are not taken into account – except perhaps where the contract expressly so provides.
29 Under the English text of the Convention, it had to be 'demonstrated with reasonable certainty by the terms of the contract or the circumstances of the case'. In the French text, the word 'reasonable' was omitted: 'Ce choix droit être exprès ou demonstré de façon certaine des dispositions du contrat ou des circonstances de la cause.' It seems that this discrepancy was deliberate: the negotiators agreed on the two texts as part of the compromise that brought a successful conclusion to the negotiations.
30 Paragraph 3, p. 17.
31 This is a ground of jurisdiction under the traditional English rules: see Chapter 5, § 4.2.3, above.

trial judge rejected this: he held that it was the law of Kuwait. Amin Rasheed's appeal was dismissed by the Court of Appeal. The case then came before the House of Lords.

Lord Diplock

[A]lthough the policy contains no express provision choosing English law as the proper law of the contract, nevertheless its provisions taken as a whole, in my opinion, by necessary implication point ineluctably to the conclusion that the intention of the parties was that their mutual rights and obligations under it should be determined in accordance with the English law of marine insurance.

. . .

The crucial surrounding circumstance . . . is that it was common ground between the expert witnesses on Kuwaiti law that at the time the policy was entered into there was no indigenous law of marine insurance in Kuwait. Kuwait is a country in which the practice since 1961, when it began to develop as a thriving financial and commercial centre, has been to follow the example of the civil law countries and to embody the law dealing with commercial matters, at any rate, in written codes. In Kuwait there had been in existence since 1961 a Commercial Code dealing generally with commercial contracts but not specifically with contracts of marine insurance. The contract of marine insurance is highly idiosyncratic; it involves juristic concepts that are peculiar to itself such as sue and labour, subrogation, abandonment and constructive total loss; to give but a few examples. The general law of contract is able to throw but little light upon the rights and obligations under a policy of marine insurance in the multifarious contingencies that may occur while the contract is in force. The lacuna in the Kuwaiti commercial law has since been filled in 1980 by the promulgation for the first time of a code of marine insurance law. This code does not simply adopt the English law of marine insurance; there are significant differences. However, it did not come into operation until August 15, 1980, and it is without retrospective effect. It does not therefore apply to the policy which was entered into at a time before there was any indigenous law of marine insurance in Kuwait.

. . .

Turning now to the terms of the policy itself, the adoption of the obsolete language of the Lloyd's SG policy as scheduled to the Marine Insurance Act 1906 makes it impossible to discover what are the legal incidents of the mutual rights and obligations accepted by the insurers and the assured as having been brought into existence by the contract, unless recourse is had not only to the rules for construction of the policy contained in the first schedule, but also to many of the substantive provisions of the Act which is (accurately) described in its long title as: 'An Act to codify the law relating to marine insurance.' To give some examples: the policy is a valued policy; the legal consequences of this in various circumstances are prescribed by sections 27, 32, 67 and 68. The policy contained two type-written insertions 'Warranted Lloyd's class to be maintained throughout the policy period' and 'Warranted trading in Arabian Gulf waters only'; the legal consequences of the use of these expressions in a policy of insurance is laid down in sections 33 to 35. On the other hand, the printed words include the so-called memorandum: 'NB The ship and freight are warranted free from average under three pounds per cent. unless general, or the ship be stranded, sunk or burnt', where 'warranted' is used in a different sense; to ascertain the legal effect of the expression in this context recourse must be had to sections 64 to 66 and 76. The legal effect of the sue and labour clause included in the policy is laid down in section 78. These are but a few examples of the more esoteric provisions of the policy of which the legal effect is undiscoverable except by reference to the Marine Insurance Act 1906; but the whole of the provisions of the statute are directed to determining what are the mutual rights and obligations of parties to a contract of marine insurance, whether the clauses of the contract are in the obsolete language of the Lloyd's SG policy (which, with the FC & S clause added, is referred to in the Institute War and Strikes Clauses Hull-Time, as 'the Standard Form of English Marine Policy'), or whether they are in the up-to-date language of the Institute War and Strike Clauses that were attached to the policy. Except by reference to the English statute and to the judicial exegesis of the code that it enacts it is not possible to interpret the policy or to determine what those mutual legal rights and obligations are. So, applying, as one must in deciding the jurisdiction point, English rules of conflict of laws, the proper law of the contract embodied in the policy is English law.

How then did it come about that two such experienced commercial judges as Robert Goff LJ and Bingham J came to the conclusion that the contract embodied in the policy was not governed by English law? There was evidence, and even in the absence of evidence your Lordships could I think take judicial notice of the fact, that the Standard Form of English Marine Policy together with the appropriate Institute Clauses attached, was widely used on insurance markets in many countries of the world, other than those countries of the Commonwealth that have enacted or inherited statutes of their own in the same terms as the Marine Insurance Act 1906. The widespread use of the form in countries that have not inherited or adopted the English common law led both Bingham J and Robert Goff LJ to conclude that the Standard Form of English Marine Policy and the Institute Clauses had become internationalised; the 'lingua franca' and the 'common currency' of international insurance were the metaphors that Bingham J used to describe it; while Robert Goff LJ [1983] 1 WLR 228, 249, identified what he described as the basic fallacy in the argument of counsel for the assured as being:

> 'that, although the historical origin of the policy may be English and although English law and practice may provide a useful source of persuasive authority on the construction of the policy wherever it may be used, nevertheless the use of a form which has become an international form of contract provides of itself little connection with English law for the purpose of ascertaining the proper law of the contract.'

My Lords, contracts are incapable of existing in a legal vacuum. They are mere pieces of paper devoid of all legal effect unless they were made by reference to some system of private law which defines the obligations assumed by the parties to the contract by their use of particular forms of words and prescribes the remedies enforceable in a court of justice for failure to perform any of those obligations; and this must be so however widespread geographically the use of a contract employing a particular form of words to express the obligations assumed by the parties may be. To speak of English law and practice providing a useful source of *persuasive* authority on the construction of the policy wherever it may be used, begs the whole question: why is recourse to English law needed at all? The necessity to do so is common ground between the experts on Kuwaiti law on either side; it is because in the absence of an indigenous law of marine insurance in Kuwait English law was the only system of private law by reference to which it was possible for a Kuwaiti court to give a sensible and precise meaning to the language that the parties had chosen to use in the policy. As the authorities that I have cited earlier show, under English conflict rules, which are those your Lordships must apply in determining the jurisdiction point, that makes English law the proper law of the contract.

Result: Amin Rasheed thus won on the choice-of-law point; however, the House of Lords still dismissed the appeal: they held that the English courts should not take jurisdiction on *forum-non-conveniens* grounds.[32]

Comment

It is likely that the authors of the Giuliano–Lagarde Report had this case in mind when, in the passage[33] quoted in the *Oldendorff* case (below), they said that the use of a standard form of contract, such as a Lloyd's policy of marine insurance, could indicate an implied choice of law.

According to Recital 12 in the Preamble to the Regulation, 'An agreement of the parties to confer on one or more courts or tribunals of a Member State exclusive jurisdiction to determine disputes under the contract should be one of the factors to be taken into account in determining whether a choice of law has been clearly demonstrated.' English courts have long taken the view that a choice-of-court agreement is an important pointer to an implied choice of law. If a particular court is to have jurisdiction, it would make sense for that court to apply its own law, the only system with which it is really familiar. So such a clause could indicate an implied choice of law, but it is not conclusive: it is just one factor to be taken into account.

The Recital does not mention arbitration clauses. In our next case, the court had to decide whether they too could constitute an indication of an implied choice of law. The case was decided under the Rome Convention, which is the same as the Regulation, except that it says (in the English text) that the choice must be demonstrated with 'reasonable' certainty, a word omitted in the French text of the Convention and in the Regulation.

---

32 On the doctrine of *forum non conveniens*, see Chapter 9, § 2.1, above.
33 Page 17, paragraph 3.

England
Oldendorff v. *Libera Corporation*
High Court (Queen's Bench Division (Commercial Court))
[1996] 1 Lloyd's Rep 380

Background

This case concerned a contract between a German partnership and a Japanese corporation for the ten-year time-charter by the Germans of two ships to be built in Japan. The German charterers had an option to purchase the ships. The contract (charterparty) was in a well-known English-language form and contained standard clauses with well-known meanings in English law. It contained no express choice of law, but there was an agreement providing for arbitration in London.

Clarke J

[After referring to Article 3 of the Convention, said:]

The question is therefore whether the choice of English law is demonstrated with reasonable certainty by the terms of the contract or the circumstances of the case.

The plaintiffs [the German partnership] say that it is. Their case may be summarised as follows. The agreed form of charter-party incorporated a London arbitration clause, providing for disputes to be resolved by arbitrators conversant with shipping matters. The inference in all the circumstances is, they say, that the parties intended English law to govern . . . [The court then quoted from the Giuliano–Lagarde Report]:[1]

> The choice of law by the parties will often be express but the Convention recognizes the possibility that the Court may, in the light of all the facts, find that the parties have made a real choice of law although this is not expressly stated in the contract. For example, the contract may be in a standard form which is known to be governed by a particular system of law even though there is no express statement to this effect, such as a Lloyd's policy of marine insurance. In other cases a previous course of dealing between the parties under contracts containing an express choice of law may leave the court in no doubt that the contract in question is to be governed by the law previously chosen where the choice of law clause has been omitted in circumstances which do not indicate a deliberate change of policy by the parties. In some cases the choice of a particular forum may show in no uncertain manner that the parties intend the contract to be governed by the law of that forum, but this must always be subject to the other terms of the contract and all the circumstances of the case. Similarly references in a contract to specific Articles of the French Civil Code may leave the court in no doubt that the parties have deliberately chosen French law, although there is no expressly stated choice of law. Other matters that may impel the court to the conclusion that a real choice of law has been made might include an express choice of law in related transactions between the same parties, or the choice of a place where disputes are to be settled by arbitration in circumstances indicating that the arbitrator should apply the law of that place.

1 Page 17, paragraph 4.

This Article does not permit the court to infer a choice of law that the parties might have made where they had no clear intention of making a choice. Such a situation is governed by Article 4.

. . .

The plaintiffs add these considerations. Charter-parties normally have provisions for the resolution of disputes. Where parties reside and carry on business in countries which have different systems of law it is not uncommon for parties to agree a forum which is as between them 'neutral'. Having agreed a neutral forum it is highly unlikely that they would expect that tribunal to apply other than a 'neutral' law. Moreover, having agreed a particular forum it is unlikely that the parties would agree that that forum would apply a law which was foreign to it, especially a law which was the law of the country of one of the parties but not of the other.

On the facts of the instant case the plaintiffs say as follows. London is a neutral forum. It would make no sense for them to have agreed either Japanese law or German law. Moreover, having agreed arbitration in London by arbitrators conversant with shipping matters, it is equally unlikely that the parties intended not to make any choice of law. The obvious inference is that the parties intended that the arbitrators would apply English maritime law. That is especially so having regard to the fact that the parties chose an amended NYPE form of charter-party and an amended Norwegian Saleform, both of which are well known English language contracts which have been subject to settled and widely known interpretation under English law. There is no evidence that either of them has been the subject of interpretation under either German or Japanese law.

The dealings between the parties as set out above show that they were conducting their negotiations by reference to English rather than Japanese or German law. They used expressions with established meanings in English maritime law. So for example the expression 'subject to details' has a well settled meaning in English law . . .

. . .

[T]he party relying upon Article 3 must demonstrate with reasonable certainty that the parties have chosen a particular law as the governing or applicable law. I accept the submission that, as the Giuliano-Lagarde report says, it must be a real choice which the parties had a clear intention to make . . .

. . .

Before turning to the question whether the parties chose English law in the instant case, it is appropriate to give some consideration to the significance (if any) of an arbitration clause in this connection, both at common law and under the Convention.

. . .

[Clarke J then considered the common-law English authorities and referred to Dicey & Morris (12th edn, 1993), which, after stating that whether an implied choice of law can be inferred from an arbitration clause will depend on the circumstances, says (at pp. 1226–1227):]

> [S]econdly, an arbitration clause which clearly demonstrates that the arbitration will take place in a particular country and that the arbitrators will be of that nationality or carrying on business in that country will permit an inference that the parties intended that the law of that country should be applied; thus an arbitration clause providing for arbitration in London by English maritime arbitrators, or by London brokers, or by a local association or exchange may be regarded as an implied choice of law; thirdly, the indication of an implied choice of law will be much weaker where the arbitration clause, although it specifies a place of arbitration, does not provide for a method of identifying the arbitrators except through an appointment by an international arbitral body such as the International Chamber of Commerce.

That approach seems to me to be correct . . .

[O]n all the facts of this case, when set in the context of the terms of the contract as a whole and of the circumstances of the case, the arbitration clause here is in my judgment a strong indication of the parties' intention to choose English law as the applicable law as well as the curial law . . . In short, having agreed English arbitration for the determination in London of disputes arising out of a well known English language form of charter-party which contains standard clauses with well known meanings in English law, it is in my judgment to be inferred that the parties intended that law to apply. Having agreed a 'neutral' forum the reasonable inference is that they intended that forum to apply a 'neutral' law, namely English law and not either German or Japanese law.

. . .

Result: English law applies.

Comment

It is hard to fault this reasoning. Businessmen, and even lawyers who are not specialists in conflict of laws, rarely distinguish between a choice of court and a choice of law. They assume that a court will apply its own law. The same is true of an arbitration clause. For this reason, it is proper to regard an arbitration or choice-of-court clause as an indication of the parties' intention. It is not decisive, but may lead a court to a particular conclusion if other factors suggest that there was a tacit – though real – choice of law.

§ 4.6 *Applicable law in the absence of choice*

The rules for determining the applicable law in the absence of choice are laid down in Article 4 of the Regulation. Before analysing this, however, we will first look at the corresponding provision of the Convention in order to see what the negotiators were trying to achieve when they were drafting the Regulation.

§ 4.6.1 Structure and general principles. Article 4 of the Rome Convention tried to achieve a balance between certainty and flexibility. It did this by first establishing a general principle (laid down in paragraph 1) that, if there was no express or implied choice of law, the contract would be governed by the law of the country with which it was most closely connected. It then tried to provide more predictability by laying down a presumption (in paragraph 2) as to what that law was. This was based on the theory of 'characteristic performance', a doctrine invented by the Swiss Federal Court. Under it, a contract is presumed to be most closely connected with the country of the party who is to effect the characteristic performance.[34]

The characteristic-performance doctrine, which also underlies several provisions of the Regulation, is based on the idea that, in most types of contract, one party undertakes to do no more than pay money. Since this is common to most kinds of contract, it is disregarded. The characteristic performance must, therefore, be that of the other party. In a contract of sale, for example, the characteristic performer is the seller; in a contract for the provision of services, it is the provider of the service; in a banking contract, it is the banker; in an insurance contract, it is the insurer; in a contract of employment, it is the employee. The idea is that the contract is likely to be more closely connected with that party than with the other party; so, in the absence of some indication to the contrary, it should be governed by that party's law.

The Convention contained provisions to determine what the characteristic performer's law was. In a commercial case, it was the law of the country in which the characteristic performer had its principal place of business; however, where, under the terms of the contract, the performance was to be effected through a place of business other than the principal place of business, it was the law of the country where that other place of business was situated.

Two things should be noted at this point. First, the doctrine does not refer to the law of the country in which the characteristic performance is to be *carried out*, but to the law of the country in which the party who is to carry out that performance is established. Thus, if an English company agrees to sell goods to a French company and delivery is to take place in France, the applicable law is the law of England, not that of France. However, the rule concerning branch offices ('a place of business other than the principal place of business') was a step towards the place of performance.

The second point is that some contracts do not have a characteristic performance. A contract of barter is one example. If company X agrees to give company Y crude oil in return for aircraft, one cannot say that either party is the characteristic performer. This was recognized by the Convention, which stated (in paragraph 5) that the presumption in paragraph 2 would not apply if the characteristic performance could not be determined. After all, it was only a presumption.

However, the Convention did not want to move too far from the closest-connection principle. So, it provided (also in paragraph 5) that the presumption was to be disregarded if it appeared from the circumstances as a whole that the

---

34 This presumption did not apply to contracts the subject-matter of which was a right in immovable property or a right to use immovable property (Article 4(3)); contracts for the carriage of goods (Article 4(4)); certain consumer contracts (Article 5); or individual contracts of employment (Article 6).

contract was more closely connected with another country. This 'escape clause' gave the court the flexibility to apply the law that a reasonable person would have expected to apply in those cases in which the characteristic-performance doctrine did not produce an acceptable result.

The result was that the principle was that of the closest connection; there was a presumption based on the characteristic-performance doctrine; but it was made clear that this was not to be followed if in fact the contract was more closely connected with another country. However, the precise balance between the general test and the presumption became a matter of controversy. Many Continental courts applied the presumption almost as if it were the rule; English courts, on the other hand, frequently departed from it.

It seems that the EC Commission favoured the Continental approach. Certainty was, in its eyes, more important than upholding the expectations of the parties. So, in its original proposal for the Regulation, the structure of Article 4 was changed. The principle of the closest connection was replaced (in paragraph 1) by a set of rules largely based on the characteristic-performance doctrine as applied to particular kinds of contract. Thus, for example, paragraph 1(a) provided that contracts of sale were to be governed by the law of the country of the seller's habitual residence and paragraph 1(b) stated that contracts for the provision of services were to be governed by the law of the country of the service provider's habitual residence. Under paragraph 2, the characteristic-performance doctrine was to be applied directly to contracts not specifically covered in paragraph 1. Only where there was no characteristic performance, was resort permitted to the closest-connection principle. There was no escape clause allowing the court to disregard these rules in exceptional cases.

This proposal was felt by the United Kingdom (and others) to be too inflexible. After extensive debate, it was agreed to reinstate the escape clause. The final result is set out in Panel 24.4.

It will be seen that the closest-connection principle no longer applies as such. It has been replaced by a set of eight specific rules applicable to different kinds of contract. Four of these rules[35] are based on the characteristic-performance doctrine.

The second paragraph deals with two situations in which the first paragraph cannot provide a solution. The first is where the contract is not one of the specific types listed in that paragraph; the second is where the contract contains elements of two or more of those types. In both cases, the applicable law is that of the country in which the characteristic performer has its habitual residence. Here the characteristic-performance doctrine is applied directly.[36]

---

[35] Sub-paragraphs (a), (b), (e) and (f). The concept of 'sale of goods' in sub-paragraph (a) and 'provision of services' in sub-paragraph (b) are to have the same meaning as in Article 5(1)(b) of the Brussels I Regulation: see Recital 17 in the Preamble to the Rome I Regulation.

[36] According to Recital 19 in the Preamble to the Regulation, in the case of a contract consisting of a bundle of rights and obligations capable of being categorized as falling within more than one of the specified types of contract, the characteristic performance of the contract should be determined having regard to its centre of gravity.

Panel 24.4 Applicable law in the absence of choice
Rome I Regulation (Regulation 593/2008), Article 4

Article 4

1. To the extent that the law applicable to the contract has not been chosen in accordance with Article 3 and without prejudice to Articles 5 to 8, the law governing the contract shall be determined as follows:

   (a) a contract for the sale of goods shall be governed by the law of the country where the seller has his habitual residence;

   (b) a contract for the provision of services shall be governed by the law of the country where the service provider has his habitual residence;

   (c) a contract relating to a right *in rem* in immovable property or to a tenancy of immovable property shall be governed by the law of the country where the property is situated;

   (d) notwithstanding point (c), a tenancy of immovable property concluded for temporary private use for a period of no more than six consecutive months shall be governed by the law of the country where the landlord has his habitual residence, provided that the tenant is a natural person and has his habitual residence in the same country;

   (e) a franchise contract shall be governed by the law of the country where the franchisee has his habitual residence;

   (f) a distribution contract shall be governed by the law of the country where the distributor has his habitual residence;

   (g) a contract for the sale of goods by auction shall be governed by the law of the country where the auction takes place, if such a place can be determined;

   (h) a contract concluded within a multilateral system which brings together or facilitates the bringing together of multiple third-party buying and selling interests in financial instruments, as defined by Article 4(1), point (17) of Directive 2004/39/EC, in accordance with non-discretionary rules and governed by a single law, shall be governed by that law.

2. Where the contract is not covered by paragraph 1 or where the elements of the contract would be covered by more than one of points (a) to (h) of paragraph 1, the contract shall be governed by the law of the country where the party who is required to effect the performance of the contract which is characteristic of the contract has his habitual residence.

3. Where it is clear from all the circumstances of the case that the contract is manifestly more closely connected with a country other than that indicated in paragraphs 1 or 2, the law of that other country shall apply.

4. Where the law applicable cannot be determined pursuant to paragraphs 1 or 2, the contract shall be governed by the law of the country with which it is most closely connected.

The third paragraph contains the 'escape clause'.[37] This allows the court to disregard the rules in the previous paragraphs where the contract is 'manifestly' more closely connected with another country.[38] Apart from this word, it is the same (in this respect) as the escape clause in Article 4(5) of the Convention.

The fourth paragraph deals with cases in which the applicable law cannot be determined under paragraphs 1 and 2. It also applies the closest-connection principle.[39]

This Article was the result of much discussion and debate, discussion in which the United Kingdom played a major role. In the opinion of many, it achieves a fair balance between the conflicting concerns of certainty and appropriateness.

§ 4.6.2 Meaning of 'habitual residence'. Several of the rules in Article 4 apply the law of the habitual residence of a particular party. Thus, habitual residence now forms the test for determining the law of the party who carries out the

---

37 The phrase 'escape clause' is used in Recital 20 in the Preamble to the Regulation.

38 Such escape clauses are to be found in other provisions of the Regulation: see Articles 5(3), 7(2) (last sentence) and 8(4). In the last of these, the word 'manifestly' does not appear.

39 The word 'manifestly' does not apply here.

Panel 24.5 Meaning of 'habitual residence' Rome I Regulation (Regulation 593/2008), Article 19
Article 19
1. For the purposes of this Regulation, the habitual residence of companies and other bodies, corporate or unincorporated, shall be the place of central administration. The habitual residence of a natural person acting in the course of his business activity shall be his principal place of business.
2. Where the contract is concluded in the course of operation of a branch, agency or any other establishment, or if, under the contract, performance is the responsibility of such an establishment, the place where the branch, agency or any other establishment is located shall be treated as the place of habitual residence.
3. When determining the habitual residence the relevant point of time shall be the time of the conclusion of the contract.

characteristic performance. 'Habitual residence' is defined in Article 19, set out in Panel 24.5. For a company, it is the place of its central administration. This is another departure from the Convention, where for a company acting in the course business (as most companies do) it was the principal place of business.[40] This is in accord with what seems to be a general policy under which the personal law of a company is deemed to be the law of the country where it has its central administration.[41] In the case of a natural person (individual), on the other hand, the test of the principal place of business is retained where he is acting in the course of business.

The Convention had a special rule that, where, under the terms of the contract, the performance was to be effected through a place of business other than the principal place of business, the law of the country in which that other place of business was situated was to apply. This rule is retained (and broadened) under the Regulation. The phrase 'place of business other than the principal place of business' is replaced by 'branch, agency or any other establishment', a phrase taken from Article 5(5) of the Brussels Regulation (see Chapter 4, § 1.3, above). Now, however, this exception applies not only where, under the terms of the contract, performance is to be carried out through the subsidiary establishment, but also where the contract is concluded in the course of the operation of that establishment.

§ 4.6.3 Linked contracts. In modern business, projects are frequently carried out by means of a set of linked contracts. Serious problems are caused if these linked contracts are governed by different laws. One result might be that some are valid and others invalid: this could mean that the contract imposing obligations on a party was valid while the contract giving that party rights was invalid. This problem is acknowledged in Recital 20 in the Preamble to the Regulation, where it is stated that, when the escape clause is applied, account should be taken, *inter alia*, of whether the contract in question has a very close relationship with another contract or contracts.[42] This appears to be an invitation to apply the escape clause where necessary in such a situation.

Our next case provides an example. The case was decided under the Convention, where (as we have seen) the provisions are slightly different; nevertheless, the problem of linked contracts raises the same issues.

---

40 For the difference between these two concepts, see Chapter 3, § 6.4, above.
41 See *ibid*.
42 See also Recital 21.

England
Bank of Baroda v. *Vysya Bank*
High Court (Queen's Bench Division (Commercial Court))
[1994] 2 Lloyd's Rep 87

Background

The case concerned obligations under a letter of credit payable in London. The underlying contract (for the sale of goods) was between an Irish company, acting through its London office (the seller), and an Indian company (the buyer). The buyer had contracted with an Indian bank called Vysya Bank to issue the letter of credit. Vysya had no branch in London; so it contracted with another Indian bank, the Bank of Baroda, for the latter to confirm the letter of credit. It did so, thus concluding a contract with the seller to pay in London.

One of the features of a letter of credit is that, though there is in essence one commercial transaction, there are a number of autonomous contracts between different parties. In the *Baroda* case, the court considered four contracts. None of them contained an express choice of law. They were:

- the contract between the buyer and the issuing bank (Vysya);
- the contract between the issuing bank and the confirming bank (Baroda);
- the contract between the confirming bank and the seller; and
- the contract between the issuing bank and the seller.

Baroda (the confirming bank) had paid the seller in London and sought reimbursement from Vysya. The latter refused to pay because the buyer had obtained an injunction against it in the Indian courts.

Baroda then sued Vysya in England. The latter had no office there, but Baroda argued that the English courts had jurisdiction because the contract between it and Vysya was governed by English law.[43] It was for this purpose (at least in the first instance) that the English court had to determine the applicable law.

Mance J

It was common ground before me . . . that the proper law of the present contract, however it was made, must be determined in accordance with the Convention . . .

[Mance J then considered Article 4 of the Convention and concluded that, under Article 4(2), the characteristic-performance doctrine applied. He continued:]

It raises the question: what is 'the performance which is characteristic of the contract' made between Vysya and Bank of Baroda? Bank of Baroda says that the answer is the addition of its confirmation to the credit and the honouring of the liability accepted thereby. Vysya says that this fails to distinguish the contract between Vysya and Bank of Baroda from the contract between Bank of Baroda as confirming banker and Granada as beneficiary. In Vysya's submission the performance which is characteristic of the contract between Vysya and

---

43 Under Order 11, Rule 1(1)(d)(iii), of the Rules of the Supreme Court, this gave the English courts jurisdiction in cases not governed by the Brussels Convention. See now Rule 6.18(5)(c) of the Civil Procedure Rules.

Bank of Baroda is the former's obligation to pay the latter upon presentation of conforming documents.

There are several different contractual relationships which can be identified in a situation such as the present. Leaving aside the underlying sale contract, there are contracts between (i) the buyer and the issuing bank, (ii) the issuing bank and the confirming bank, (iii) the confirming bank and the seller and (iv) the issuing bank and the seller. The last two relationships co-exist, giving a beneficiary two banks which he may hold responsible for payment. As the Uniform Customs[1] put it in Article 10(b):

> When an issuing bank authorizes or requests another bank to confirm its irrevocable credit and the latter has added its confirmation, such confirmation constitutes a definite undertaking of such bank (the confirming bank), in addition to that of the issuing bank, provided that the stipulated documents are presented and that the terms and conditions of the credit are complied with . . .

Article 11(d) provides:

> By nominating a bank other than itself, or by allowing for negotiation by any bank, or by authorizing or requesting a bank to add its confirmation, the issuing bank authorizes such bank to pay, accept or negotiate, as the case may be, against documents which appear on their face to be in accordance with the terms and conditions of the credit, and undertakes to reimburse such bank in accordance with the provisions of these Articles.

As between issuing bank and confirming bank the relationship is one of agency, although as against the beneficiary the confirming bank commits itself as principal . . . That the relationship is one of agency is also shown by the language used in the instant case . . .

[After discussing the facts and saying that both parties agreed that the confirmation was the object or focus of the contract, he continued:]

[The accounts of both parties] confirm the appropriateness of the general conclusion, at which I would anyway arrive, that under a contract between an issuing bank and a confirming bank the performance which is characteristic of the contract is the adding of its confirmation by the latter and its honouring of the obligations accepted thereby in relation to the beneficiary.[2] The liability on the part of the issuing bank to reimburse or indemnify the confirming bank is consequential on the character of the contract; it does not itself characterize the contract.

The fact that reimbursement was to be claimed and made in New York is doubly insignificant, being probably a mere matter of convenience because this was a dollar credit and in any event unrelated to any country whose law could conceivably govern . . .

---

1 *Editor's note*: the Uniform Customs and Practice for Documentary Credits are published by the International Chamber of Commerce. For their precise legal status, see Roy Goode, *Commercial Law* (Penguin Books, London, 3rd edn, 2004), pp. 968 *et seq.*
2 *Editor's note*: under the Regulation, the contract would almost certainly be characterized as one for the provision of services under Article 4(1)(b). The question would then arise who the provider of the service was. Mance J's analysis of characteristic performance is equally applicable to answer this question.

[After referring to the Giuliano-Lagarde Report, Mance J continued:]

It follows in the present case, looking at the position of Bank of Baroda in relation to the confirmation given to Granada, that the performance characteristic of Bank of Baroda's contract with Vysya, however made, was the addition and honouring of its confirmation of the credit in favour of Granada. That performance was to be effected through Bank of Baroda's City of London office, viz 'a place of business other than [its] principal place of business' and so by the express terms of Article 4(2) the presumption is that English law governs the contract between Vysya and Bank of Baroda. For reasons which will further appear below, any wider examination of the circumstances under Article 4(5) simply confirms the application of English law.

So far I have focused on the contract between Vysya and Bank of Baroda which is the contract immediately in issue. It is relevant to consider the matter more widely, as the arguments before me did, and in this context to consider the proper laws of other contracts involved in the present situation. Whether one looks at Article 4(2) or at Article 4(5) of the Rome Convention, the contract of confirmation between Bank of Baroda's City of London branch as confirming bank and Granada as beneficiary was clearly governed by English law . . . A suggestion that English law did not, as between beneficiary and confirming bank, govern a credit confirmed through the London branch of a foreign bank for payment in London would be wholly uncommercial.

Vysya submits however that, although Granada's contract as beneficiary with Bank of Baroda as the confirming bank is subject to English law, Granada's parallel contract with Vysya as the issuing bank falls as a result of the Rome Convention (and contrary to the previous common law position) to be regarded as subject to Indian law. It submits that the contract between the buyer and Vysya in India must also be subject to Indian law. In its submission different legal systems govern different contracts involved in the present situation and there is no particular incongruity in holding that the contract between the two Indian banks is subject to Indian law.

. . .

A point of importance is involved in the submission that the contract between Granada as beneficiary and Vysya as issuing bank is subject to Indian law. That would mean that, by force of [the Rome Convention], one and the same credit is here governed by two different laws, and that the applicable law varies according to the bank against which the beneficiary decides to enforce the credit. If the beneficiary enforces the credit against the Bank of Baroda, English law applies, and presumably (whatever the governing law of the contract between confirming and issuing banks) Bank of Baroda can then claim reimbursement from Vysya in respect of liabilities which it has incurred subject to English law. However if the beneficiary chooses to pursue the issuing bank direct, Indian law applies. Counsel for Vysya contemplated this with equanimity as a necessary result of the [Rome Convention], but I do not. In my judgment it would involve precisely [a] wholly undesirable multiplicity of potentially conflicting laws . . .

As between the beneficiary and Vysya, the position under Article 4(2) is that there is a presumption that Indian law applies. This presumption applies, although the performance which is characteristic of the contract is the issue of the letter of credit in London which was to be and was effected in London through National Westminster, initially at least as advising bank, with Bank of Baroda later adding its confirmation. Although such performance was to take place in London, Article 4(2) refers one back, *prima facie*, to India as the place of Vysya's central administration.[3]

In my judgment this is a situation where it would be quite wrong to stop at Article 4(2). The basic principle is that the governing law is that of the country with which the contract is most closely connected (Article 4(1)). Art. 4(2) is, as stated in Professors Giuliano and Lagarde's report, intended to give 'specific form and objectivity' to that concept. In the present case the application of Article 4(2) would lead to an irregular and subjective position where the governing law of a letter of credit would vary according to whether one was looking at the position of the confirming or the issuing bank. It is of great importance to both beneficiaries and banks concerned in the issue and operation of international letters of credit that there should be clarity and simplicity in such matters. Article 4(5) provides the answer. The Rome Convention was not intended to confuse legal relationships or to disrupt normal expectations in the way which is implicit in Vysya's submissions. Under Article 4(5) the presumptions in Article 4(2), (3) and (4) are to be

> ... disregarded if it appears from the circumstances as a whole that the contract is more closely connected with another country.

I accept that the presumptions are to be applied unless there is valid reason, looking at the circumstances as a whole, not to do so ...

The present situation provides in my judgment a classic demonstration of the need for and appropriateness of Article 4(5). I conclude that English law applies to the contract between Vysya and Granada.

...

I therefore conclude that the letter of credit was governed by English law as between the beneficiary and each of the banks. On this basis, it would be wholly anomalous if English law were not also to govern the contract between Vysya and Bank of Baroda and in my opinion it does. As between Bank of Baroda and Vysya the application of the presumption arising under Article 4(2) accords with good sense and sound policy and there is therefore no reason to depart from it.

3 *Editor's note*: this is a slip by the judge: since Vysya was acting in the course of business, he should have said that India was Vysya's principal place of business.

QUESTION

Is there any reason to believe that this case would be decided differently under the Regulation?

---

§ 4.6.4 **The escape clause.** The escape clause in paragraph 3 permits the court to disregard the rules in paragraphs 1 and 2 if the contract is manifestly more closely connected with a country other than that indicated by those paragraphs. We next look at two cases in which, under the less strict test in the Convention (the word 'manifestly' being omitted), the court held that recourse to the escape clause was justified.

England
Definitely Maybe Ltd* v. *Lieberberg GmbH
High Court (Queen's Bench Division)
[2001] 1 WLR 1745

Background

The claimant, Definitely Maybe, was an English company. It had agreed with Lieberberg, a German company, that it would arrange for a pop group, Oasis, to perform in Germany. The pop group did so, but without one of its members. As a result, Lieberberg refused to pay the full amount stipulated in the contract. Definitely Maybe sued it in England. It argued that the English courts had jurisdiction under Article 5(1) of the Brussels Convention, since England was the place of performance of the obligation in question – the obligation to pay.[44] This raised a problem. The place of payment was not specified in the contract. In such circumstances, English law would regard it as being in England, where the creditor had its headquarters, while German law would consider that it was in Germany, the debtor's domicile. Thus the place of payment – and therefore the jurisdiction of the court – depended on the applicable law. The English court had jurisdiction only if English law was applicable.

The Master had held that the case should be heard in Germany. The claimant appealed to the High Court. There was little doubt that, under the presumption in paragraph 2, the applicable law was that of England. Definitely Maybe was the characteristic performer and, as it had no place of business in Germany, the governing law was that of the country in which its principal place of business was situated. This was England.

Morison J

7.   The real issue between the parties centres on the relationship between these two paragraphs of Article 4. Whilst paragraph (2) looks to the location of the principal performer, paragraph (5) looks more widely to a connection between the contract and a country. If there is a divergence between the location of the principal performer and the place of substantial or characteristic performance, what then? On the one hand, were the presumption to be displaced whenever such divergence existed, the presumption would be of little weight or value. Paragraph (2) must have

44 Under the Brussels Regulation, the position would have been different: the revised version of Article 5(1) provides that, in the case of a contract for the provision of services, the courts having jurisdiction are those for the place where, under the contract, the services were provided or should have been provided. This would have been Germany. The German courts would thus have had jurisdiction under Article 5(1), even if the action was for payment and the payment was to be made in a different country.

been inserted to provide a 'normal' rule which is simple to apply. Giving wide effect to paragraph (5) will render the presumption of no value and represent a return to the English common law test of ascertaining the proper law, which places much less weight on the location of the performer and much more on the place of performance, and the presumed intention of the parties.

8. Rather than seeking to find an answer to this issue, I turn to those factors which are said to show a closer connection between the contract and Germany than with England. The contract provided for Oasis to perform live in Germany; that was the place of the characteristic or substantial performance of the contract. The defendants were obliged to make arrangements in Germany to enable the performances to take place (for example, marketing and promotion) and to provide facilities such as security and bits of equipment. Thus, the contract required performance of contractual obligations in Germany by both parties. For what it is worth, the defendant company is German and payment was to be made in Deutschmarks and subject to deduction for German tax. Apart from the location of the claimants and the group, and the place of payment, there is no other connection between England and the contract. The centre of gravity of the dispute is, I think, Germany. Therefore, if the test were simply that laid down in paragraph (5), namely, to say with which country was the contract most closely connected, I would have said Germany, rather than England.

9. But I return to the issue of the relationship between paragraphs (2) and (5) of Article 4 and the legal effect of the presumption. There are, I think, two schools of thought. The first is to say that the presumption in paragraph (2), which is expressly made subject to paragraph (5), is weak and will more readily be displaced where the place of performance differs from the place of business of the performer. The second, adopts a narrower view of the 'exception' to the presumption in paragraph (5) and gives firm dominance to the presumption.

10. In relation to the first approach, the editors of *Dicey & Morris, The Conflict of Laws*, 13th edn (2000), vol. 2, paragraphs 32–124, state that 'the presumption may most easily be rebutted in those cases where the place of performance differs from the place of business of the party whose performance is characteristic of the contract'. That is this case. In *Crédit Lyonnais* v. *New Hampshire Insurance Co.* [1997] 2 Lloyd's Rep 1, 5, the Court of Appeal noted that Article 4(5) 'formally, makes the presumption very weak'.

11. In support of the more restricted view, the claimants rely upon a Dutch case, *Société Nouvelle des Papéteries de l'Aa SA* v. *BV Machinefabriek BOA* 1992 Nederlandse Jurisprudentie No 750, noted in 'Some Dutch Judicial Reflections on the Rome Convention, Article 4(5)' [1996] LMCLQ 18, where the court gave a most restrictive interpretation to paragraph (5). It appears that the Supreme Court in Holland concluded that

'this exception to the main rule of section 2 has to be applied restrictively, to the effect that the main rule should be disregarded only if, in the special circumstances of the case, the place of business of the party who is to effect the characteristic performance has no real significance as a connecting factor' (see [1996] LMCLQ 18, 20).

12. The problem is caused, I think, by the fact that the factor which identifies the governing law in paragraph (2) (namely the location of the principal performer) may well not play an important part in determining the closest connection between country and contract. Thus, the presumption to which it gives rise is likely to be capable of being rebutted in most cases, and as such the presumption may be worthless. Yet, if paragraph (2) has the dominance suggested by the Dutch court, the presumption becomes a rule of law to which paragraph (5) must be treated as an exception, and that is not the language of the convention.

13. In well presented and interesting submissions counsel concentrated on this problem. [Counsel] for the claimants adopted the Dutch position although he said that he did not need to go that far. He submitted that the court was required to give full effect to the presumption and to the thinking behind it. The scheme of Article 4 was to provide a simple and easily applied test. If, as was said in an obiter remark, the presumption was weak, then parties would not know where they stood and the Convention would not work as it was intended. He said that there were many cases where paragraph (5) might apply; for example, those cases where there was a link between one contract and another. Thus, he accepted as an archetype, the case where the court accepted that the rights of the beneficiary against the confirming bank were governed by the same law as his rights against the issuing bank. Or, he said, a case of a guarantee being construed as being subject to the same governing law as that which applied to the contract between debtor and creditor. For the defendant, it was submitted that the Dutch case was wrong in law, in that it added words which were not in Article 4 and that I should not follow it. He submitted that it was not necessary to adopt any extreme position in relation to Article 4. The presumption would do its work in the majority of cases, but where there was a divergence between the place of business of the principal performer and the place of performance it was right that the presumption should be displaced if the factors showed a closer connection with the place of performance. But if the factors were evenly balanced, then the place of business of the principal performer would be decisive. In that way, the presumption had some meaning, yet it was rebuttable where appropriate.

14. I must confess that I have not found this an easy case to decide. To some extent the court must recognise, I think, a natural tendency to wish to maintain the old, well developed common law position where factors were weighed and attempts were made to ascertain the true intention of the parties. Intention does not appear to exist as a factor any more,

save in an Article 3 context. Although Article 18 of the Rome Convention encourages a uniform interpretation of the Convention, that is less easy to achieve than to say. The importance attached to the location of the principal performer stems from Swiss law. The provisions of Article 4 have been the subject of much criticism by academics; it is rightly pointed out that the Giuliano-Lagarde Report on the Convention (1980) (OJ C282, p. 1) (to which reference may be made) does not provide much useful guidance as to the interpretation of Article 4 although the authors accept that judges have been left with a measure of discretion or judgment. It may be that the Convention represents a compromise between different positions adopted by different countries during the negotiation of its terms.

15.   It seems to me not to be helpful to characterise Article 4 by asking whether there is a one, two or three stage test. Nor am I attracted to the notion that the words of the Article should be twisted so as to accord with what is thought to be the intention of the draftsman. With an international Convention of this sort, I prefer to stay with the words and apply them as best as possible. On that basis, it seems to me that the presumption in Article 4(2) 'shall be disregarded' (not rebutted) if it appears from the circumstances as a whole that the contract is more closely connected with Germany rather than England. I accept that it is for the defendant to show that the presumption should be disregarded, by establishing factors which point to Germany. I accept that this will be more readily achievable where the place of performance is different from the place of the performer's business. But, in carrying out what must be regarded as a comparative exercise, due weight must be given to the factor identified in Article 4(2).

16.   Here, the defendants have established to my satisfaction that, overall, the contract between the parties has a closer connection with Germany than with England. Even recognising the Convention's emphasis on England as the place of the performer's business, having regard to the place of performance by both parties and the other factors referred to above, Germany has more attachment to or connection with the contract than England. Aside from any other consideration, the centre of gravity of the dispute is Germany, which will provide the more convenient forum for deciding to what extent Oasis without Noel Gallagher was worth anything, and, if so, how much.

17.   Thus, in the result, I endorse the decision of Master Foster and dismiss the appeal.

QUESTION

Would this case be decided differently under the Rome I Regulation?

England
Kenburn Waste Management Ltd v. *Bergmann*
Court of Appeal
[2002] EWCA Civ 98; [2002] ILPr 33

Background

This was another case on jurisdiction. Mr Bergmann was domiciled in Germany. He held the United Kingdom patent for a certain kind of waste-disposal machine. Kenburn, a British company, sold a different kind of waste-disposal machine. Bergmann thought that this latter machine infringed his patent. He wrote to one of Kenburn's customers threatening a patent-infringement action. Kenburn responded by warning Bergmann that it would sue him under section 70 of the Patents Act 1977, a British statute that allows a person in Kenburn's situation to obtain a declaration that the threat of a patent-infringement action is unjustifiable, an injunction against its continuance and damages for any loss suffered. Bergmann then wrote a letter to Kenburn which the latter regarded as an undertaking not to repeat the threats to any of its customers in England. As a result, the action under section 70 was not brought. Subsequently, Bergmann made further threats to a different customer. Kenburn responded by bringing an action in England for breach of the undertaking which it claimed existed.

Bergmann challenged the jurisdiction of the court. Kenburn said that the court had jurisdiction under Article 5(1) of the Brussels Convention, since the obligation in question – the obligation not to make threats – was to be performed in England. The lower court accepted this. It held that the contract not to make threats was governed by English law, though it seems that the position would have been the same under German law. Bergmann appealed.

The Court of Appeal considered whether the lower court was right in concluding that the applicable law was that of England. Since the characteristic obligation was the obligation not to make threats, the characteristic performer was Mr Bergmann. His principal place of business was in Germany. So, under the presumption, the applicable law was that of Germany. However, the characteristic obligation was to be performed in England. Moreover, the contract (assuming it existed) had been concluded to compromise a threatened action in the English courts under an English statute. The lower court considered that these facts were sufficient to rebut the presumption and establish that the closest connection was with England. The Court of Appeal agreed. So the applicable law was that of England. To hold that it was that of Germany would have meant that a contract to compromise an action to be brought in England under an English statute concerning the infringement in England of a United Kingdom patent would have been governed by German law. This would have been unjustifiable.

Examples based on the *Definitely Maybe* and *Kenburn* cases were used by the United Kingdom in the negotiations on the Rome I Regulation as part of its campaign to have the escape clause reinstated in the Regulation. It is not known whether the other Member States found these examples convincing, but these are both cases in which it is at least arguable that the escape clause should be applied under the Regulation as well.

§ 4.6.5 Exceptions. The rules laid down in Article 4 of the Regulation do not apply to certain kinds of contracts. These are:

- contracts for the carriage of goods (Article 5(1));
- contracts for the carriage of passengers (Article 5(2));
- consumer contracts (Article 6);
- insurance contracts (Article 7); and
- individual employment contracts (Article 8).

At this point, we will consider only the first two.[45]

§ 4.6.6 Carriage of goods. Article 5(1) is set out in Panel 24.6. It is partly based on the characteristic-performance doctrine. The carrier is the characteristic performer; so the applicable law should be that of the country of its habitual residence. However, Article 5(2) adopts this solution only if some other factor provides an additional link with that country. The possible links are:

- the place of receipt (of the goods);
- the place of delivery (of the goods); or
- the habitual residence of the consignor.

If one of these links is not present, the law of the country of the agreed place of delivery is applicable. This latter requirement leads to the law of the *place of performance* of the characteristic obligation.[46]

§ 4.6.7 Carriage of passengers. Contracts for the carriage of passengers – for example, by air, road or sea – are governed by Article 5(2), set out in Panel 24.7. This is not based on the characteristic-performance doctrine (under which the law of the habitual residence of the carrier would govern), since contracts for the carriage of passengers are usually con-

---

Panel 24.6 Carriage of goods
Rome I Regulation (Regulation 593/2008), Preamble (Recital 22) and Article 5(1)

Preamble

22 As regards the interpretation of contracts of carriage of goods, no change in substance is intended with respect to Article 4(4), third sentence, of the 1980 Convention on the law applicable to contractual obligations.[1] Consequently, single-voyage charter parties and other contracts the main purpose of which is the carriage of goods should be treated as contracts for the carriage of goods. For the purposes of this Regulation, the term 'consignor' should refer to any person who enters into a contract of carriage with the carrier and the term 'the carrier' should refer to the party to the contract who undertakes to carry the goods, whether or not he performs the carriage himself.

Article 5(1)

1. To the extent that the law applicable to a contract for the carriage of goods has not been chosen in accordance with Article 3, the law applicable to such contracts shall be the law of the country of the habitual residence of the carrier, provided that the place of receipt or the place of delivery or the habitual residence of the consignor is also situated in that country. If those requirements are not met, the law of the country where the place of delivery as agreed by the parties is situated shall apply.

1 OJ C 334, 30.12.2005, p. 1.

---

45 Consumer and employment contracts are discussed in Chapter 26, § 4 (employment) and § 5 (consumers), below.
46 Additional provisions on the interpretation of Article 5(1) are to be found in Recital 22 in the Preamble to the Regulation (set out in Panel 24.6).

sumer contracts. (As we will see in the next chapter, the policy of the Regulation, like that of the Convention, is to give special protection to consumers on the ground that they are in an economically weak position.) For this reason, the primary rule is that the law of the passenger's habitual residence applies. However, there must again be an additional link: either the place of departure or the place of destination must also be situated in that country. This will be so in most cases, though sea cruises may be an exception unless the flight to the port of embarkation is part of the cruise package. Where the additional link does not exist, the applicable law is that of the carrier's habitual residence. At this point, the characteristic-performance doctrine comes into play again.

> **Panel 24.7 Carriage of passengers**
> **Rome I Regulation (Regulation 593/2008), Article 5(2)**
>
> **Article 5(2)**
> 2. To the extent that the law applicable to a contract for the carriage of passengers has not been chosen by the parties in accordance with the second subparagraph, the law applicable shall be the law of the country where the passenger has his habitual residence, provided that either the place of departure or the place of destination is situated in that country. If these requirements are not met, the law of the place where the carrier has his habitual residence shall apply. The parties may choose as the law applicable to the contract for the carriage of passengers in accordance with Article 3 only the law of the country where:
>   (a) the passenger has his habitual residence; or
>   (b) the carrier has his habitual residence; or
>   (c) the carrier has his place of central administration; or
>   (d) the place of departure is situated; or
>   (e) the place of destination is situated.
> 3. Where it is clear from all the circumstances of the case that the contract, in the absence of a choice of law, is manifestly more closely connected with a country other than that indicated in paragraphs 1 or 2, the law of that other country shall apply.

Two interesting features of this provision are, first, that there is an escape clause along the lines of that considered in § 4.6.4, above; and, secondly, that the power of the parties to choose the applicable law is limited to the law of five specified countries. This is probably done to prevent the carrier from choosing the law of a totally unconnected country simply because it is unfavourable to the passenger.

§ 4.7   *The problem of consent*

We must now deal with a basic problem in choice-of-law theory regarding contracts: if the applicable law depends on the parties' choice, how do you decide whether that choice is itself valid? Assume, for example, that the parties conclude a contract in circumstances in which one party would not, by any relevant legal system, be regarded as having consented. Perhaps his 'consent' was subject to duress or vitiated by misrepresentation. Could it not be said that the choice-of-law clause was itself invalid so that it could not determine the applicable law for the contract as a whole?

This view is rejected by the Regulation, which provides in Article 10(1) (Panel 24.8) that the existence and validity of a contract are governed by the law that would be applicable to it if it were valid. However, this could give rise to injustice since the other

> **Panel 24.8 Consent and material validity**
> **Rome I Regulation (Regulation 593/2008), Article 10**
>
> **Article 10**
> 1. The existence and validity of a contract, or of any term of a contract, shall be determined by the law which would govern it under this Regulation if the contract or term were valid.
> 2. Nevertheless, a party may rely upon the law of the country in which he has his habitual residence to establish that he did not consent if it appears from the circumstances that it would not be reasonable to determine the effect of his conduct in accordance with the law specified in paragraph 1.

party might deliberately insert into the contract a choice-of-law clause in favour of the law of a country under which it was valid, even though that country had no connection to the parties or the 'contract', and even though, under the law of all countries connected to the parties or the 'contract', there was no consent. To avoid this, Article 10(2) (also Panel 24.8) allows the party in question to rely on the law of the country of his habitual residence to establish that he did not consent, if this would be reasonable in the circumstances.

The following example shows how this would work. Assume that there is one country in the world, country X, where a person is regarded as having consented to a contract if he has received an offer and does not reject it within a specified period of time. A fraudster habitually resident in England e-mails a victim habitually resident in Germany and makes him an offer. The offer contains a choice-of-law clause specifying the law of country X. It ends with the words, 'If I have not heard from you within seven days, you will be deemed to have assented.' The victim does not reply. Seven days later, the fraudster claims that a contract has been concluded. This would have been the case if Article 10(1) alone existed; however, thanks to Article 10(2), the victim can invoke German law to establish that there is no contract.

§ 4.8   Capacity

A similar theoretical problem exists with regard to capacity. If a party has no capacity to conclude a contract under the law that would otherwise apply, can he give himself capacity by agreeing to a choice-of-law clause in favour of the law of a country under which he would have capacity? Here, the Regulation takes a somewhat different position. It does not claim that the capacity of a party is governed by the law that would apply to the contract if it were valid. This is because Article 1(2)(a) states that the Regulation does not apply to the status and legal capacity of natural persons (human beings). The matter is, therefore, left to national law. However, Article 1(2)(a) says that it is without prejudice to Article 13. The latter (set out in Panel 24.9) contains provisions intended to restrict the right of a party to invoke his incapacity under a foreign law if this would be unfair to the other party.

Panel 24.9 Incapacity
Rome I Regulation (Regulation 593/2008), Article 13

Article 13
In a contract concluded between persons who are in the same country, a natural person who would have capacity under the law of that country may invoke his incapacity resulting from the law of another country, only if the other party to the contract was aware of that incapacity at the time of the conclusion of the contract or was not aware thereof as a result of negligence.

It is not entirely clear what the choice-of-law rule for capacity is under English common law,[47] and it is hard to imagine a situation in which Article 13 would be applied by an English court. In some civil-law countries, capacity is governed by the law of the person's nationality. Assume that, under the law of Ruritania (an imaginary country), no

---

47 Dicey, Morris and Collins suggests that a person has capacity to contract if he has it under either the law of the country with which the contract is most closely connected or under the law of his domicile and residence: Rule 209(1), p. 1621. However, the use of the word '*semble*' in the Rule indicates that authority is lacking.

one has capacity to contract until he is twenty-five. A Ruritanian citizen aged twenty-four goes to an EU Member State under the law of which contractual capacity begins at eighteen and under the conflict of laws of which capacity is governed by the law of the nationality. The Ruritanian concludes a contract with a local person, who has no way of knowing that he is dealing with a Ruritanian. In these circumstances, Article 13 would prevent the Ruritanian from invoking his incapacity under Ruritanian law to avoid his obligations under the contract.

§ 4.9   Other provisions

Certain other provisions should be mentioned briefly. Article 11 (Panel 24.10) has rules on the formal validity of contracts and Article 12 (also in Panel 24.10) has rules on the scope of the applicable law. Article 20 provides that *renvoi* is inapplicable unless provided otherwise in the Regulation.[48] *Renvoi* is discussed in Chapter 22, § 2.3.2, above.

Panel 24.10 Other provisions
Rome I Regulation (Regulation 593/2008), Articles 11 and 12

Article 11 Formal validity

1. A contract concluded between persons who or whose agents are in the same country at the time of conclusion is formally valid if it satisfies the formal requirements of the law which governs it in substance under this Regulation or of the law of the country where it is concluded.
2. A contract concluded between persons who or whose agents are in different countries at the time of conclusion is formally valid if it satisfies the formal requirements of the law which governs it in substance under this Regulation, or of the law of either of the countries where either of the parties or their agent is present at the time of conclusion, or of the law of the country where either of the parties had his habitual residence at that time.
3. A unilateral act intended to have legal effect relating to an existing or contemplated contract is formally valid if it satisfies the formal requirements of the law which governs or would govern the contract in substance under this Regulation or of the law of the country where the act was done or the law of the country where the person who effected it had his habitual residence at that time.
4. Paragraphs 1, 2 and 3 shall not apply to contracts that fall within the scope of Article 6. The form of such contracts shall be governed by the law of the country where the consumer has his habitual residence.
5. Notwithstanding paragraphs 1 to 4, a contract the subject matter of which is a right *in rem* in immovable property or a tenancy of immovable property shall be subject to the requirements of form of the law of the country where the property is situated if by that law those requirements are imposed irrespective of the country where the contract is concluded and irrespective of the law governing the contract, and which cannot be derogated from by agreement.

Article 12 Scope of the applicable law

1. The law applicable to a contract by virtue of this Regulation shall govern in particular:
   (a) interpretation;
   (b) performance;
   (c) within the limits of the powers conferred on the court by its procedural law, the consequences of the total or partial breach of obligations, including the assessment of damages in so far as it is governed by rules of law;
   (d) the various ways of extinguishing obligations, and prescription and limitation of actions;
   (e) the consequences of nullity of the contract.
2. In relation to the manner of performance and the steps to be taken in the event of defective performance, regard shall be had to the law of the country in which performance takes place.

---

48 The words 'unless provided otherwise in the Regulation' are apparently a reference to Article 7(3) (second indent), a provision relating to insurance, which might be regarded as implying some form of *renvoi*. This reads: 'Where . . . the Member States referred to grant greater freedom of choice of the law applicable to the insurance contract, the parties may take advantage of that freedom.'

Further reading

Atrill, 'Choice of Law in Contract: The Missing Pieces of the Article 4 Jigsaw?' (2004) 53
    ICLQ 549

Blom, 'Choice of Law Methods in the Private International Law of Contract' (1978) 16
    Canadian Yearbook of International Law 230; (1979) 17 *Canadian Yearbook of International
    Law* 206; and (1980) 18 *Canadian Yearbook of International Law* 161

Briggs (Adrian), *Agreements on Jurisdiction and Choice of Law* (Oxford University Press,
    Oxford, 2008)

Hill, 'Choice of Law in Contract under the Rome Convention: The Approach of the UK
    Courts' (2004) 53 ICLQ 325

Kaye (Peter), *The New Private International Law of Contract of the European Community:
    Implementation of the EEC's Contractual Obligations Convention in England and Wales under
    the Contracts (Applicable Law) Act 1990* (Dartmouth Publishing Co., Aldershot, 1993)

Morse, 'Contracts (Applicable Law) Act 1990', in *Current Law Statutes Annotated* 1990,
    Volume III (Sweet & Maxwell, London, 1991)
    'Letters of Credit and the Rome Convention' [1994] *Lloyd's Maritime and Commercial Law
    Quarterly* 560

Nygh (Peter E), *Autonomy in International Contracts* (Clarendon Press, Oxford; Oxford
    University Press, New York, 1999)

Plender (Richard) and Wilderspin (Michael), *The European Private International Law of
    Obligations* (Sweet & Maxwell, London, publication expected in 2009)

CHAPTER 25

Contracts: legal policy and choice of law

§ 1   Introduction

In the previous chapter, we said that the basic principle of contract law is to give effect to the intention of the parties. There is, however, another principle. In certain circumstances, the law rejects what the parties agreed on, or it insists that the contract should be subject to terms they did not agree on. This is because the law pursues policy aims, and it pursues these aims (in many cases) even against the will of the parties. The policies can have many objectives: political (for example, sanctions against a foreign country); economic (exchange controls); cultural (prohibiting the export of works of art) and social (anti-discrimination legislation). In many cases, the justification for imposing legal rules on the parties is that the interests of society outweigh those of the individual; in others, it is simply the desire to help parties regarded as being in a weak bargaining position (for example, consumers). In all situations, however, the result is the same: what the parties agreed on is overridden by the law.

If freedom of contract is restricted in the domestic context in order to achieve these objectives, it would be surprising if the same did not apply in the international context. The freedom of the parties to choose the applicable law should not permit them to evade legal policies regarded as overriding. However, different considerations might apply in the international context, so that some rules that cannot be derogated from in the domestic context may be subject to derogation in the international context.

In this chapter, we consider some of the more general aspects of this question. Further aspects will be discussed in Chapters 26 and 27.

§ 2   Terminology

The concept of legal rules that cannot be derogated from by agreement is widely accepted in choice-of-law instruments. For example, the American *Restatement of the Law Second: Conflict of Laws* distinguishes between an issue 'which the parties could have resolved by an explicit provision in their agreement directed to that issue' and an issue which they could not have so resolved.[1]

In the Rome I Regulation, the concept appears in no fewer than five provi-

---

1 See § 187.

sions – Articles 3(3), 3(4), 6(2), 8(1) and 11(5). There have, however, been changes in terminology. In the Convention, the phrase 'mandatory rules' was used to designate such provisions. In the Regulation, the concept remains the same,[2] but the phrase is no longer used for this purpose. It is now used only to refer to a different concept, 'overriding mandatory provisions'. These are a sub-category of the first concept, and are defined in Article 9(1) (set out in Panel 25.1). It is expressly stated in Recital 37 in the Preamble to the Regulation that this latter concept must be distinguished from 'provisions which cannot be derogated from by agreement' and must be construed more restrictively.

In order to facilitate discussion, provisions which cannot be derogated from by agreement will henceforth be referred to as 'non-derogable' provisions to distinguish them from overriding mandatory provisions as defined in Article 9(1). The latter are also provisions that cannot be derogated from by agreement, but are distinguished by the fact that this is so irrespective of the law applicable to the contract (and possibly in other ways as well).

Panel 25.1 Overriding mandatory provisions
Rome I Regulation (Regulation 593/2008), Article 9(1)

Article 9(1)

1. Overriding mandatory provisions are provisions the respect for which is regarded as crucial by a country for safeguarding its public interests, such as its political, social or economic organisation, to such an extent that they are applicable to any situation falling within their scope, irrespective of the law otherwise applicable to the contract under this Regulation.

---

§ 3   The Rome I Regulation

The scheme of the Regulation is as follows. Under Article 3, paragraphs 3 and 4, non-derogable provisions override a choice of law in the case of a purely domestic contract (a contract with no international element). This is a general rule that applies to all types of contract. The rule is wide as regards subject-matter, but narrow as regards the circumstances of its application.

Then there are rules dealing with three specific types of contract – consumer contracts (Article 6), individual employment contracts (Article 8) and contracts concerning immovable property (Article 11(5)). In these three cases, certain non-derogable provisions override a choice of law in a wider range of circumstances. These provisions are restricted as regards subject-matter, but wide as regards the circumstances of their application.

Finally, Article 9 makes it possible for overriding mandatory provisions (defined above) to override a choice of law even in the case of an international contract. This rule is wide both as regards the types of contracts covered (subject-matter) and as regards the circumstances of its application, but it is limited to a sub-category of non-derogable provisions. Moreover, in the case of foreign law, it does no more than *permit* the application of such provisions: the court is not obliged to apply them.

---

2 See Recital 15 in the Preamble to the Regulation.

§ 3.1 Purely domestic contracts

The general rules on non-derogable provisions are contained in paragraphs 3 and 4 of Article 3. These are set out in Panel 25.2. Paragraph 3 provides that, when all the elements 'relevant to the situation at the time of the choice' other than a choice of law or a choice of jurisdiction[3] are located in a country other than that of the chosen law, a choice of law will not prevent the application of non-derogable provisions of that country.

Panel 25.2 Non-derogable provisions
Rome I Regulation (Regulation 593/2008), Article 3

Article 3

3. Where all other elements relevant to the situation at the time of the choice are located in a country other than a country whose law has been chosen, the choice of the parties shall not prejudice the application of provisions of the law of that country which cannot be derogated from by agreement.
4. Where all other elements relevant to the situation at the time of the choice are located in one or more Member States, the parties' choice of applicable law other than that of a Member State shall not prejudice the application of provisions of Community law, where appropriate, as implemented in the Member State of the forum, which cannot be derogated from by agreement.

This rule is derived from Article 3(3) of the Convention. Though the wording has been changed, it was not intended to change the meaning.[4] Article 3(3) of the Convention was apparently the result of a compromise. Some delegations wanted the Convention to provide that the parties could not make a valid choice of law in the case of a purely domestic contract; other delegations, notably that of the United Kingdom, were opposed to this limitation on the parties' freedom of choice. The compromise was to allow a free choice, but to exclude non-derogable provisions from its operation.[5]

The Regulation does not clarify what elements are to be regarded as 'relevant to the situation' for the purpose of Article 3(3). The domicile and residence of the parties and the place or places of performance would clearly be relevant; on the other hand, some connections would be of such minor importance that they would be disregarded. The determination of what elements are relevant is for the national court.[6]

Article 3(3) applies only where all relevant elements (other than a choice of law or a choice of court) are connected with a single country.[7] In some ways, this is quite restrictive. Article 3(3) will not apply if all such elements are connected with either one or other of two countries, even if the non-derogable provision is the same in both of them. However, if the non-derogable provision is part of, or based on, EU law, Article 3(4) comes into play. This provision, which was not found in the Convention, applies the same rule with regard to EU law even if the relevant elements are located in two or more countries, provided all those

---

3 Article 3(3) does not refer to choice-of-court clauses, but Recital 15 in the Preamble to the Regulation makes clear that such a clause does not make any difference to the application of the rule in Article 3(3).
4 Recital 15 in the Preamble to the Regulation.
5 Giuliano and Lagarde, 'Report on the Convention on the Law Applicable to Contractual Obligations', OJ 1980 L 282, p. 18.
6 Philip, 'Mandatory Rules, Public Law (Political Rules) and Choice of Law in the EEC Convention on the Law Applicable to Contractual Obligations', in North (P.M.) (ed.), *Contract Conflicts* (North-Holland Publishing Company, Amsterdam, 1982), p. 81 at p. 95.
7 The text of the Regulation is somewhat ambiguous on this point, but the Convention was absolutely clear: 'where all the other elements relevant to the situation at the time of the choice are connected with one country only'. Since Recital 15 in the Preamble to the Regulation states that no change of substance was intended in this provision, one is entitled to look to the Convention to interpret the Regulation. The wording to Recital 15 ('all other elements relevant to the situation are located in a country other than the country whose law has been chosen') also makes this clear.

countries are Member States. It makes sense to treat the EU as a single unit where the non-derogable provision in question is a rule of Community law – for example, a regulation – or is based on a rule of Community law – for example, a Member State law implementing a Community directive.

An example of the latter is the Commercial Agents Directive,[8] which lays down non-derogable provisions intended to protect commercial agents. The Directive has been implemented by national legislation. Such national legislation would be covered by Article 3(4). Since there may be small differences in the legislation adopted in different Member States, Article 3(4) specifies that it is the legislation of the forum that applies.

§ 3.2 Consumer contracts

Article 6 (Panel 25.3) contains special rules on consumer contracts. A consumer contract is a contract between a consumer and a professional (non-consumer).

Panel 25.3 Consumer contracts
Rome I Regulation (Regulation 593/2008), Article 6

Article 6

1. Without prejudice to Articles 5 and 7, a contract concluded by a natural person for a purpose which can be regarded as being outside his trade or profession ('the consumer') with another person acting in the exercise of his trade or profession ('the professional') shall be governed by the law of the country where the consumer has his habitual residence, provided that the professional:
    (a) pursues his commercial or professional activities in the country where the consumer has his habitual residence, or
    (b) by any means, directs such activities to that country or to several countries including that country, and the contract falls within the scope of such activities.
2. Notwithstanding paragraph 1, the parties may choose the law applicable to a contract which fulfils the requirements of paragraph 1, in accordance with Article 3. Such a choice may not, however, have the result of depriving the consumer of the protection afforded to him by such provisions that cannot be derogated from by contract by virtue of the law which, in the absence of choice, would have been applicable on the basis of paragraph 1.
3. If the requirements in points (a) or (b) of paragraph 1 are not fulfilled, the law applicable to a contract between a consumer and a professional shall be determined pursuant to Articles 3 and 4.
4. Paragraphs 1 and 2 shall not apply to:
    (a) a contract for the supply of services where the services are to be supplied to the consumer exclusively in a country other than that in which he has his habitual residence;
    (b) a contract of carriage other than a contract relating to package travel within the meaning of Council Directive 90/314/EEC of 13 June 1990 on package travel, package holidays and package tours;[1]
    (c) a contract relating to a right *in rem* in immovable property or a tenancy of immovable property other than a contract relating to the right to use immovable properties on a timeshare basis within the meaning of Directive 94/47/EC;
    (d) rights and obligations which constitute a financial instrument and rights and obligations constituting the terms and conditions governing the issuance or offer to the public and public take-over bids of transferable securities, and the subscription and redemption of units in collective investment undertakings in so far as these activities do not constitute provision of a financial service;
    (e) a contract concluded within the type of system falling within the scope of Article 4(1)(h).

1 OJ L 158, 23.6.1990, p. 59.

---

8 Directive 86/653, OJ 1986 L 352, p. 17.

A 'consumer' is a person acting for a purpose outside his trade or profession; a professional is someone acting in the exercise of his trade or profession.

The general idea is that the law of the country of the consumer's habitual residence should apply, provided that the professional in some way 'targeted' the consumer's country and the contract was concluded within the framework of that targeting.[9] The concept of 'targeting' has begun to be used in the context of choice of law and jurisdiction, especially in connection with the Internet. It is not an easy concept to define, but sub-paragraphs (a) and (b) of Article 6(1) provide that the law of the country of the consumer's habitual residence will apply (a) if the professional pursues his activities there or (b) if he directs his activities there (or to several countries including that country).

If one of these conditions is fulfilled, the law of the country of the consumer's habitual residence is the applicable law in the absence of a choice of law. To this extent, Article 6 applies instead of Article 4. In addition, the non-derogable consumer-protection provisions of that law will apply even if there *is* a choice of law. Here, the choice of law is overridden.

These rules are subject to a number of exceptions. First of all, Article 6 is subject to Article 5, which means that the law applicable in the absence of choice to contracts for the carriage of goods and passengers is determined by the rules in Article 5,[10] not those in Article 6(1). Article 6 is also subject to Article 7 (insurance contracts). So the law applicable to insurance contracts in the absence of choice is determined by the rules in Article 7, not those in Article 6(1). Nevertheless, the rules in Article 6 on non-derogable consumer-protection provisions still apply to contracts for carriage and insurance.

In addition, *neither* set of rules[11] applies to:

- contracts for the supply of services where the services are to be supplied to the consumer exclusively in a country other than that in which he has his habitual residence;
- contracts of carriage other than for package travel;[12]
- contracts relating to immovable property other than time-share contracts; and
- contracts relating to various financial matters.

It should finally be said that there are a number of Recitals relevant to Article 6. These are set out in Panel 25.4.

§ 3.3 *Individual employment contracts*

Individual employment contracts are governed by Article 8 (Panel 25.5). This follows a similar pattern. Paragraphs 2–4 specify the law applicable in the

---

9 Recitals 24 and 25 in the Preamble to the Regulation.
10 See Chapter 24, §§ 4.6.6 and 4.6.7, above.
11 That is, neither the rules in Article 6 on the applicable law in the absence of choice nor those on non-derogable consumer-protection provisions.
12 In the case of package travel (as defined in Directive 90/314), the rules in Article 6 on non-derogable consumer-protection provisions apply, but not those on the law applicable in the absence of choice.

Panel 25.4 Consumer contracts: Rome I Regulation (Regulation 593/2008), Recitals 23–32

Recitals 23–32

(23) As regards contracts concluded with parties regarded as being weaker, those parties should be protected by conflict-of-law rules that are more favourable to their interests than the general rules.

(24) With more specific reference to consumer contracts, the conflict-of-law rule should make it possible to cut the cost of settling disputes concerning what are commonly relatively small claims and to take account of the development of distance-selling techniques. Consistency with Regulation (EC) No 44/2001 requires both that there be a reference to the concept of directed activity as a condition for applying the consumer protection rule and that the concept be interpreted harmoniously in Regulation (EC) No 44/2001 and this Regulation, bearing in mind that a joint declaration by the Council and the Commission on Article 15 of Regulation (EC) No 44/2001 states that 'for Article 15(1)(c) to be applicable it is not sufficient for an undertaking to target its activities at the Member State of the consumer's residence, or at a number of Member States including that Member State; a contract must also be concluded within the framework of its activities'. The declaration also states that 'the mere fact that an Internet site is accessible is not sufficient for Article 15 to be applicable, although a factor will be that this Internet site solicits the conclusion of distance contracts and that a contract has actually been concluded at a distance, by whatever means. In this respect, the language or currency which a website uses does not constitute a relevant factor.'.

(25) Consumers should be protected by such rules of the country of their habitual residence that cannot be derogated from by agreement, provided that the consumer contract has been concluded as a result of the professional pursuing his commercial or professional activities in that particular country. The same protection should be guaranteed if the professional, while not pursuing his commercial or professional activities in the country where the consumer has his habitual residence, directs his activities by any means to that country or to several countries, including that country, and the contract is concluded as a result of such activities.

(26) For the purposes of this Regulation, financial services such as investment services and activities and ancillary services provided by a professional to a consumer, as referred to in sections A and B of Annex I to Directive 2004/39/EC, and contracts for the sale of units in collective investment undertakings, whether or not covered by Council Directive 85/611/EEC of 20 December 1985 on the coordination of laws, regulations and administrative provisions relating to undertakings for collective investment in transferable securities (UCITS),[1] should be subject to Article 6 of this Regulation. Consequently, when a reference is made to terms and conditions governing the issuance or offer to the public of transferable securities or to the subscription and redemption of units in collective investment undertakings, that reference should include all aspects binding the issuer or the offeror to the consumer, but should not include those aspects involving the provision of financial services.

(27) Various exceptions should be made to the general conflict-of-law rule for consumer contracts. Under one such exception the general rule should not apply to contracts relating to rights *in rem* in immovable property or tenancies of such property unless the contract relates to the right to use immovable property on a timeshare basis within the meaning of Directive 94/47/EC of the European Parliament and of the Council of 26 October 1994 on the protection of purchasers in respect of certain aspects of contracts relating to the purchase of the right to use immovable properties on a timeshare basis.[2]

(28) It is important to ensure that rights and obligations which constitute a financial instrument are not covered by the general rule applicable to consumer contracts, as that could lead to different laws being applicable to each of the instruments issued, therefore changing their nature and preventing their fungible trading and offering. Likewise, whenever such instruments are issued or offered, the contractual relationship established between the issuer or the offeror and the consumer should not necessarily be subject to the mandatory application of the law of the country of habitual residence of the consumer, as there is a need to ensure uniformity in the terms and conditions of an issuance or an offer. The same rationale should apply with regard to the multilateral systems covered by Article 4(1)(h), in respect of which it should be ensured that the law of the country of habitual residence of the consumer will not interfere with the rules applicable to contracts concluded within those systems or with the operator of such systems.

---

1 OJ L 375, 31.12.1985, p. 3. Directive as last amended by Directive 2008/18/EC of the European Parliament and of the Council (OJ L 76, 19.3.2008, p. 42).

2 OJ L 280, 29.10.1994, p. 83.

Panel 25.4 (continued)

(29) For the purposes of this Regulation, references to rights and obligations constituting the terms and conditions governing the issuance, offers to the public or public take-over bids of transferable securities and references to the subscription and redemption of units in collective investment undertakings should include the terms governing, *inter alia*, the allocation of securities or units, rights in the event of over-subscription, withdrawal rights and similar matters in the context of the offer as well as those matters referred to in Articles 10, 11, 12 and 13, thus ensuring that all relevant contractual aspects of an offer binding the issuer or the offeror to the consumer are governed by a single law.

(30) For the purposes of this Regulation, financial instruments and transferable securities are those instruments referred to in Article 4 of Directive 2004/39/EC.

(31) Nothing in this Regulation should prejudice the operation of a formal arrangement designated as a system under Article 2(a) of Directive 98/26/EC of the European Parliament and of the Council of 19 May 1998 on settlement finality in payment and securities settlement systems.[3]

(32) Owing to the particular nature of contracts of carriage and insurance contracts, specific provisions should ensure an adequate level of protection of passengers and policy holders. Therefore, Article 6 should not apply in the context of those particular contracts.

3 OJ L 166, 11.6.1998, p. 45.

---

absence of choice, while paragraph 1 says that, though the parties may choose another law, such a choice will not prevent the application of the non-derogable employee-protection provisions of the law that would have been applicable in the absence of choice.

The rule laid down in paragraph 2 must be applied if it can be applied, unless resort is had to the escape clause. The rule in paragraph 3 may be applied only if that in paragraph 2 cannot be applied.[13] The escape clause is along standard lines; however, it does not contain the word 'manifestly'. These provisions are partly based on those in Article 19(2) of the Brussels I Regulation, discussed in Chapter 4, § 4.1, above. The new wording in Article 8(2) of the Rome I Regulation seems to have been intended to ensure that the ruling in *Mulox* v. *Geels*[14] applies here as well.

The following example will illustrate the position. Assume that an English company employs a man

Panel 25.5 Individual employment contracts Rome I Regulation (Regulation 593/2008), Article 8

Article 8

1. An individual employment contract shall be governed by the law chosen by the parties in accordance with Article 3. Such a choice of law may not, however, have the result of depriving the employee of the protection afforded to him by such provisions that cannot be derogated from by contract under the law that, in the absence of choice, would have been applicable pursuant to paragraphs 2, 3 and 4.

2. To the extent that the law applicable to the individual employment contract has not been chosen by the parties, the contract shall be governed by the law of the country in which or, failing that, from which the employee habitually carries out his work in performance of the contract. The country where the work is habitually carried out shall not be deemed to have changed if he is temporarily employed in another country.

3. Where the law applicable cannot be determined pursuant to paragraph 2, the contract shall be governed by the law of the country where the place of business through which he was engaged is situated.

4. Where it appears from the circumstances as a whole that the contract is more closely connected with a country other than that indicated in paragraphs 2 or 3, the law of that other country shall apply.

---

13 In *Mulox* v. *Geels*, Case C-125/92, [1993] ECR I-4075, Advocate General Jacobs said, with reference to the revised version of Article 5(1) of the Brussels Convention, that a determined effort should be made to identify the place where the employee habitually carries out his work, so that the courts of that country would have jurisdiction, rather than those of the country in which the place of business is located through which the employee was engaged. He regarded this latter provision as unsatisfactory. The same reasoning could be applied both to Article 19(2) of the Brussels I Regulation and to Article 8 of the Rome I Regulation. If this is accepted, Article 8(2) of the latter should be applied wherever possible in preference to Article 8(3).
14 Above.

habitually resident in France as its sales representative in Germany, Benelux and Scandinavia. His office is in France, where his wife answers the phone and deals with e-mails. He spends most of the week on the road in his sales territory. Since he does not habitually carry out his work *in* any one country, but does habitually carry it out *from* his base in France, the applicable law in the absence of choice will be that of France. The courts of France will also have jurisdiction to hear an employment-law claim by him against his employer.[15]

If the parties had chosen English law to govern the contract, this choice, though valid, would not deprive the employee of the protection of the non-derogable rules of French law. It would seem that he could also invoke the employee-protection rules of English law, unless they were incompatible with those of French law. So he might enjoy double protection.

§ 3.4 *Contracts concerning immovable property*

Article 11(5) (set out in Chapter 24, Panel 24.10, above) provides that, in the case of a contract concerning a right *in rem* in immovable property or a tenancy of immovable property, the non-derogable requirements of form of the law of the country where the property is situated will apply, irrespective of the law otherwise applicable.

§ 3.5 *Overriding mandatory provisions*

The rules on overriding mandatory provisions are laid down in Article 9 (Panel 25.6). Their most striking feature is the sharp distinction drawn between overriding mandatory provisions of the forum and overriding mandatory provisions of foreign law. This is because courts are obliged to respect overriding mandatory provisions of their own legal system, but are less willing to do so with regard to those of foreign systems of law.

The first paragraph of Article 9 defines the concept of an overriding mandatory provision (already discussed, in § 2, above). The second paragraph deals with overriding mandatory provisions of the forum: it states that nothing in the Regulation will restrict their application. The third paragraph deals with overriding mandatory provisions of foreign law: it *permits*, but does not *require*, the application of the overriding mandatory provisions of the country of performance, if those provisions render that

Panel 25.6 Overriding mandatory provisions
Rome I Regulation (Regulation 593/2008), Article 9

Article 9

1. Overriding mandatory provisions are provisions the respect for which is regarded as crucial by a country for safeguarding its public interests, such as its political, social or economic organisation, to such an extent that they are applicable to any situation falling within their scope, irrespective of the law otherwise applicable to the contract under this Regulation.
2. Nothing in this Regulation shall restrict the application of the overriding mandatory provisions of the law of the forum.
3. Effect may be given to the overriding mandatory provisions of the law of the country where the obligations arising out of the contract have to be or have been performed, in so far as those overriding mandatory provisions render the performance of the contract unlawful. In considering whether to give effect to those provisions, regard shall be had to their nature and purpose and to the consequences of their application or non-application

---

15 Under Article 19(2)(a) of the Brussels I Regulation: see *Mulox v. Geels*, Case C-125/92, [1993] ECR I-4075.

performance unlawful. In other words, the overriding mandatory provisions of a third country (not the country of the forum and not that of the applicable law) are applicable only if the contract is to be performed, in whole or in part, in that country, and the acts to be performed in that country are unlawful under the law of that country. The only doubt is what 'unlawful' means: must the performance constitute a criminal offence, or is it sufficient if it is contrary to public policy? One assumes that it would not be enough if the obligation were merely unenforceable.

This is a controversial rule and was subject to protracted negotiation. The background is as follows. The equivalent provision in the Rome Convention was Article 7(1) (Panel 25.7), which laid down a much wider rule. It was not restricted to overriding mandatory provisions of the place of performance, but applied to the overriding mandatory provisions of any country with which the situation had a 'close connection'; moreover, it was not restricted to provisions that rendered the performance of the contract unlawful, but could apply to *any* overriding mandatory provisions. This was

> **Panel 25.7 Overriding mandatory provisions of foreign law**
> **Rome Convention, Article 7**
>
> **Article 7**
> 1. When applying under this Convention the law of a country, effect may be given to the mandatory rules of the law of another country with which the situation has a close connection, if and in so far as, under the law of the latter country, those rules must be applied whatever the law applicable to the contract. In considering whether to give effect to these mandatory rules, regard shall be had to their nature and purpose and to the consequences of their application or non-application.

too much for some countries – especially the United Kingdom – and it was agreed that Contracting States could opt out of it.[16] Several, including the United Kingdom and Germany, did so. There is no opt-out for the new provision; so it had to be made more restrictive. It is thought by many lawyers in the United Kingdom that it goes no further than the English common law.

§ 3.5.1 **Overriding mandatory provisions of the forum.** Article 9(2) gives unrestricted effect to overriding mandatory provisions of the forum. To come within the scope of Article 9(2), the provision must fall within the definition in paragraph 1. It must be regarded as crucial by the country of the forum for safeguarding its public interests and it must be applicable irrespective of the law otherwise applicable to the contract. It is for the law of each country to decide for itself what provisions fall within this definition. Although the provision in question must be applicable irrespective of the law otherwise applicable to the contract, it is not necessary that this should be expressly laid down by legislation; otherwise, no rule of common law could fall within the definition.

Article 9(2) is very similar to Article 7(2) of the Convention (set out in Panel 25.8). In the Convention, the word

> **Panel 25.8 Overriding mandatory provisions of the forum**
> **Rome Convention, Article 7**
>
> **Article 7**
> 2. Nothing in this Convention shall restrict the application of the rules of the law of the forum in a situation where they are mandatory irrespective of the law otherwise applicable to the contract.

---

16 By entering a reservation under Article 22(1)(a).

'mandatory' means 'non-derogable'.[17] So it covered any provision of forum law that was non-derogable irrespective of the law otherwise applicable to the contract. The only difference from the Regulation is the absence of the requirement that the provision must be regarded as crucial by the country for safeguarding its public interests. However, it could be said that the provision would not be non-derogable irrespective of the law otherwise applicable to the contract, unless this were the case.

Our first case concerns a provision adopted by the United Kingdom in order to implement a Community directive, the Commercial Agents Directive.[18] If the case had arisen today, Article 3(4) of the Regulation (discussed in § 3.1, above) would not have been applicable because a significant element – the domicile and residence of one of the parties – was located outside the Community; so the relevant provision would have been Article 9(2).

European Community
Ingmar GB Ltd* v. *Eaton Leonard Technologies Inc.
Court of Justice of the European Communities
Case C-381/98, [2000] ECR I-9305

Background

Ingmar was a British company. Eaton Leonard was a Californian company. In 1989, Eaton Leonard appointed Ingmar as its agent in the United Kingdom and Ireland. The contract contained a choice-of-law clause specifying the law of California. The contractual relationship between the parties ended in 1995, and Ingmar brought proceedings against Eaton Leonard for compensation under the Commercial Agents (Council Directive) Regulations 1993 (the United Kingdom legislation implementing the Commercial Agents Directive). The Directive and the Regulations gave an agent the right to claim compensation on the termination of the agency, even if there was no provision for this in the contract. The Directive and Regulations expressly said that the right to compensation was non-derogable, but did not say that this was so irrespective of the law otherwise applicable.

Eaton Leonard argued that the Regulations were inapplicable because the contract was governed by California law. Ingmar said that the relevant provisions should override the choice of law. Since the contract was concluded before the Rome Convention entered into force in the United Kingdom, the Convention did not apply to it.[19] However, the common-law rules on the application of non-derogable rules of English law were the same as those in Article 7(2) of the Convention. The English court, therefore, made a reference to the European Court asking it whether the relevant provisions of the Directive, as implemented in the Member States, were applicable in the circumstances of the case – in other words, whether they were non-derogable irrespective of the law otherwise applicable.

---

17 Article 3(3) of the Convention.
18 Council Directive 86/653/EEC, OJ 1986 L 382, p. 17.
19 See Article 17 of the Convention.

Judgment

14. By its question, the national court seeks to ascertain, essentially, whether Articles 17 and 18 of the Directive, which guarantee certain rights to commercial agents after termination of agency contracts, must be applied where the commercial agent carried on his activity in a Member State although the principal is established in a non-member country and a clause of the contract stipulates that the contract is to be governed by the law of that country.

15. The parties to the main proceedings, the United Kingdom and German Governments and the Commission agree that the freedom of contracting parties to choose the system of law by which they wish their contractual relations to be governed is a basic tenet of private international law and that that freedom is removed only by rules that are mandatory.[1]

16. However, their submissions differ as to the conditions which a legal rule must satisfy in order to be classified as a mandatory rule for the purposes of private international law.

17. Eaton contends that such mandatory rules can arise only in extremely limited circumstances and that, in the present case, there is no reason to apply the Directive, which is intended to harmonise the domestic laws of the Member States, to parties established outside the European Union.

18. Ingmar, the United Kingdom Government and the Commission submit that the question of the territorial scope of the Directive is a question of Community law. In their submission, the objectives pursued by the Directive require that its provisions be applied to all commercial agents established in a Member State, irrespective of the nationality or the place of establishment of their principal.

19. According to the German Government, in the absence of any express provision in the Directive as regards its territorial scope, it is for the court of a Member State seised of a dispute concerning a commercial agent's entitlement to indemnity or compensation to examine the question whether the applicable national rules are to be regarded as mandatory rules for the purposes of private international law.

20. In that respect, it should be borne in mind, first, that the Directive is designed to protect commercial agents . . .

21. The purpose of Articles 17 to 19 of the Directive, in particular, is to protect the commercial agent after termination of the contract. The regime established by the Directive for that purpose is mandatory in nature. Article 17 requires Member States to put in place a mechanism for providing reparation to the commercial agent after termination of the contract. Admittedly, that Article allows the Member States to choose between indemnification and compensation for damage. However, Articles 17 and 18 prescribe a precise framework within which the Member States may

---

1 *Editor's note*: following the usage of the Convention, the court is using 'mandatory' to mean 'non-derogable'.

22.   exercise their discretion as to the choice of methods for calculating the indemnity or compensation to be granted.

22.   The mandatory nature of those Articles is confirmed by the fact that, under Article 19 of the Directive, the parties may not derogate from them to the detriment of the commercial agent before the contract expires. It is also borne out by the fact that, with regard to the United Kingdom, Article 22 of the Directive provides for the immediate application of the national provisions implementing the Directive to contracts in operation.

23.   Second, it should be borne in mind that, as is apparent from the second recital in the preamble to the Directive, the harmonising measures laid down by the Directive are intended, *inter alia*, to eliminate restrictions on the carrying-on of the activities of commercial agents, to make the conditions of competition within the Community uniform and to increase the security of commercial transactions . . .

24.   The purpose of the regime established in Articles 17 to 19 of the Directive is thus to protect, for all commercial agents, freedom of establishment and the operation of undistorted competition in the internal market. Those provisions must therefore be observed throughout the Community if those Treaty objectives are to be attained.

25.   It must therefore be held that it is essential for the Community legal order that a principal established in a non-member country, whose commercial agent carries on his activity within the Community, cannot evade those provisions by the simple expedient of a choice-of-law clause. The purpose served by the provisions in question requires that they be applied where the situation is closely connected with the Community, in particular where the commercial agent carries on his activity in the territory of a Member State, irrespective of the law by which the parties intended the contract to be governed.

26.   In the light of those considerations, the answer to the question must be that Articles 17 and 18 of the Directive, which guarantee certain rights to commercial agents after termination of agency contracts, must be applied where the commercial agent carried on his activity in a Member State although the principal is established in a non-member country and a clause of the contract stipulates that the contract is to be governed by the law of that country.

Comment

It is hard to believe that this case would not be decided the same way under the Regulation. If correct, this shows that it is not necessary for the non-derogable provision to state expressly that it is non-derogable irrespective of the system of law otherwise applicable.[20]

---

20 After the European Court's judgment, the case went back to the English courts. For the judgment of the English court awarding compensation to the agent, see *Ingmar GB Ltd* v. *Eaton Leonard Inc.* [2001] CLC 1825 (QBD).

§ 3.5.2 Overriding mandatory provisions of foreign law. The provisions of Article 9(3) of the Regulation have already been discussed. There do not seem to have been any cases on either it or the equivalent provision of the Convention (Article 7(1)). However, there is considerable case law under the common law, and this will now be considered.

§ 4 Foreign illegality under English common law

In this section, we are concerned with the effect on a contract of illegality under foreign law other than the proper (applicable) law. We deal with the position under English common law. In a purely domestic context, a contract is invalid if the performance it requires is illegal.[21] What happens where the performance is to be carried out in a foreign country and it is illegal under the law of that country?

§ 4.1 Initial illegality

We begin by considering the position where the contract was illegal at all material times (initial illegality); then (in § 4.2, below) we will look at the position where it was legal when it was concluded but subsequently became illegal (supervening illegality).

§ 4.1.1 Contracts to commit a crime. The first situation to discuss is where the contract requires one party to do something in a foreign country which is a crime under the law of that country.

> **England**
> ***Foster* v. *Driscoll***
> **Court of Appeal**
> **[1929] 1 KB 470**

Background

This case concerned an agreement under which a group of people in Britain formed a partnership for the purpose of smuggling whisky into the United States during Prohibition, something that was a criminal offence under US law. Various sums of money were contributed, and it was planned to buy whisky in Scotland which would clear British customs in the normal way and would then be transferred to the smugglers' boat at some point outside the United Kingdom. The plan was never put into operation and the smugglers fell out among themselves. Legal proceedings resulted, and the question before the Court of Appeal

---

21 The question of illegality under English common law is extremely complex: for a discussion, see the relevant chapters in Beatson (J.), *Anson's Law of Contract* (Oxford University Press, Oxford, 28th edn, 2002); Furmston (Michael), *Cheshire, Fifoot and Furmston's Law of Contract* (Oxford University Press, Oxford, 15th edn, 2007); and Peel (Edwin), *Treitel's The Law of Contract* (Sweet & Maxwell, London, 12th edn, 2007).

was whether the contract was unenforceable under English law because it was illegal. A majority held that it was.[22]

Lawrence LJ

On principle however I am clearly of opinion that a partnership formed for the main purpose of deriving profit from the commission of a criminal offence in a foreign and friendly country is illegal, even though the parties have not succeeded in carrying out their enterprise, and no such criminal offence has in fact been committed; and none the less so because the parties may have contemplated that if they could not successfully arrange to commit the offence themselves they would instigate or aid and abet some other person to commit it. The ground upon which I rest my judgment that such a partnership is illegal is that its recognition by our Courts would furnish a just cause for complaint by the United States Government against our Government (of which the partners are subjects), and would be contrary to our obligation of international comity as now understood and recognized, and therefore would offend against our notions of public morality.

Comment

This case establishes that a contract to commit a criminal offence in a foreign country is (in at least some cases) illegal under English common law. The question of the applicable law did not arise in *Foster* v. *Driscoll* – it was accepted on all sides that English law applied – but it cannot be doubted that the result would have been the same if the parties had chosen a foreign system of law to govern the contract, even if, under that law, the contract had been valid.

Though there can be no doubt that the result would be the same today, it is not so easy to say how the case should be fitted into the structure of the Regulation. At the time of the decision, an English lawyer would have said that the court was applying a rule of *English* law, a rule he would have characterized as a rule of public policy,[23] but which today would be regarded (under the terminology of the Regulation) as an overriding mandatory rule of the forum. This is the rule that a contract will be unenforceable under English law if it requires a party to do something in a foreign country that is a criminal offence under the law of that country. As stated by Lawrence LJ, the rationale of the rule is that enforcement of the contract would be contrary to international comity since it would infringe the sovereignty of a foreign State. On this basis, the relevant provision of the Regulation would be Article 9(2).

Looked at through modern eyes, however, it would seem that the appropriate provision is Article 9(3), a provision which permits the application of foreign law in just such a situation as this. The comity argument is simply the ground on which the English court would decide to exercise the power conferred by Article 9(3), a provision which, it should be remembered, does not require the

---

22 Scrutton LJ dissented on the ground that the parties had a back-up plan to land the whisky lawfully in Canada or some other suitable place and there sell it to some third party who would smuggle it into the United States. The majority, however, held that the fact that the parties had this possibility in mind did not affect the matter.
23 This is an example of the positive application of the public-policy doctrine: see Chapter 22, § 2.4.3, above.

application of foreign law, but merely permits it. For this reason, it is suggested that, if the case were to arise today, it should be decided under Article 9(3).

England
Regazzoni* v. *K. C. Sethia (1944) Ltd
House of Lords
[1958] AC 301; [1957] 3 WLR 752; [1957] 3 All ER 286

Background

An English company (Sethia Ltd) agreed to sell to a Swiss resident (Regazzoni) a quantity of jute to be delivered in Italy. On the surface, there was nothing in the contract that was illegal by English law (the governing law) or Italian law (the *lex loci solutionis*). The contract contained no statement as to the origin of the jute, but both parties knew that it could be obtained from only one source – India. The ultimate destination was also not stated, but both parties knew that the buyer intended to re-export it to South Africa. The significance of this was that at the time India operated an embargo against South Africa: it was illegal under Indian law to export jute from India if the ultimate destination was South Africa. The seller failed to deliver the goods and the buyer sued in England for breach of contract.

Viscount Simonds

[After stating that the only question before the House of Lords was whether the respondents (the English company, Sethia Ltd) were justified in repudiating the contract, he continued:]

Their broad proposition is that whether or not the proper law of the contract is English law, an English court will not enforce a contract, or award damages for its breach, if its performance will involve the doing of an act in a foreign and friendly State which violates the law of that State. For this they cite the authority of the well-known case of *Foster* v. *Driscoll* [above] and much of the debate in this House has been whether that case was rightly decided, and if so, whether it is distinguishable from the present case. The appellant contends that it was not rightly decided, and further invokes a familiar principle which he states in these wide but questionable terms, 'An English court will not have regard to a foreign law of a penal, revenue, or political character', and claims that the Indian law here in question is of such a character.

My Lords, in the consideration of this matter I deem it of the utmost importance to bear in mind that we are not here concerned with a suit by a foreign State to enforce its laws . . . but with a very different question, *viz.*, whether in a suit between private persons the court will enforce a contract which involves the doing in a foreign country of an act which is illegal by, and violates, the law of that country. When I say 'foreign country' I mean a foreign and friendly country and will not repeat the phrase.

In the statement of the question I call particular attention to the words 'the doing in a foreign country', for it may well be that different considerations will arise and a different conclusion will be reached if the law of the contract is English and the contract can be wholly performed in England, or at least in some other country than that whose law makes the act illegal . . . There are points at which the two questions appear to touch each other, and sometimes the one proposition has been treated as an exception on the other. But there is, I think, a fundamental difference. It can hardly be regarded as a matter of comity that the courts of this country will not entertain a suit by a foreign State to enforce its revenue laws. It is, on the other hand, nothing else than comity which has influenced our courts to refuse as a matter of public policy to enforce, or to award damages for the breach of, a contract which involves the violation of foreign law on foreign soil, and it is the limits of this principle that we have to examine. If the principle is, as I think it clearly is, based on public policy, your Lordships will not hesitate, while disclaiming any intention to create any new head of public policy, to apply an old principle to new circumstances.

It will be observed that I have said that the appellant's contention is that the English courts will not pay regard to the penal, revenue, or political laws of a foreign State, not merely that they will not enforce such laws at the suit of a foreign State. If he is right, then *Foster* v. *Driscoll* [above] was wrongly decided and nothing stands in the way of the success of this appeal except the counter argument that the Indian law with which we are concerned does not fall within this category.

But before examining the cases in which the question has been the enforcement of a contract involving the violation of a foreign law, it is perhaps desirable to refer to the analogous cases in which contracts involving the violation of English law have been considered. I say 'analogous cases' because here, too, public policy is involved. Whether the illegality be robbery on Hounslow Heath or smuggling goods into England contrary to our law . . . or the hiring of a brougham[1] to a prostitute for the purpose of her trade, a party cannot recover in a court of justice on a contract so tainted . . .

Just as public policy avoids contracts which offend against our own law, so it will avoid at least some contracts which violate the laws of a foreign State, and it will do so because public policy demands that deference to international comity. The question is what contracts? 'It occurred to me at the trial that it was contrary to the law of nations', said Best CJ in *De Wütz* v. *Hendricks*[2] 'for persons in England to enter into engagements to raise money to support the subjects of a Government in amity with our own, in hostilities against their Government, and that no right of action could arise out of such a transaction.'

More than a hundred years later in *De Beéche* v. *South American Stores (Gath & Chaves) Ltd*[3] it was said in this House: 'It cannot be controverted that the law of this country will not compel the fulfilment of an obligation whose performance involves the doing in a foreign country of something which the supervenient[4] law of that country has rendered it illegal to do.'

---

1 *Editor's note*: a brougham is a kind of carriage.
2 (1824) 2 Bing 314 at pp. 315–16.
3 [1935] AC 148.
4 *Editor's note*: 'supervenient illegality' is illegality which exists at the time of performance but not at the time when the contract was made.

I make two observations upon this citation; first, the case is *a fortiori* if the illegality is not supervenient but, as in the case under appeal, existent and known at the time of the contract; secondly – and I say this in deference to an argument that was vigorously addressed to us – it would, as Scrutton LJ said in *Luther* v. *Sagor*[5] [set out below in Chapter 28], 'be a serious breach of international comity, if a State is recognized as a sovereign independent State, to postulate that its legislation is contrary to essential principles of justice and morality.' Your Lordships were in effect invited to say that the relevant Indian legislation was of such a character. I can only say that there could be no possible justification for such a view, however hardly the Act may bear on the Union of South Africa.

[Viscount Simonds then considered various cases in which an exception was made to the principle. He continued:]

It is sufficient, however, for the purposes of the present appeal to say that, whether or not an exception must still be made in regard to the breach of a revenue law in deference to old authority, there is no ground for making an exception in regard to any other law. I should myself have said – and this is, I think, the only point upon which I do not agree with the Court of Appeal – that the present case was precisely covered by the decision in *Ralli Brothers* [set out in § 4.2, below]. For when the fact is found that the very thing which the parties intended to do was to export the jute bags from India in order that they might go via Genoa to the Union of South Africa, it appears to me irrelevant that upon the face of the documents that wrongful intention was not disclosed. But, whether this is so or not, it is clearly covered by *Foster* v. *Driscoll*, a decision the correctness of which is not to be doubted . . . So, here, it has been conclusively found that the common intention of the parties was to violate the law of India, and it is of no consequence that the documents did not disclose their intention. I ought not to part from the case without noting that Sankey LJ observed that the cases relating to the breach of a revenue law were not germane to the issue. Nor are they germane to this appeal. Whether they are still to be regarded as a binding authority is a question that must await determination.

The appeal should, in my opinion, be dismissed with costs.

Lord Reid

To my mind, the question whether this contract is enforceable by English courts is not, properly speaking, a question of international law. The real question is one of public policy in English law: but in considering this question we must have in mind the background of international law and international relationships often referred to as the comity of nations. This is not a case of a contract being made in good faith but one party thereafter finding that he cannot perform his part of the contract without committing a breach of foreign law in the territory of the foreign country. If this contract is held to be unenforceable, it should, in my opinion, be because from the beginning the contract was tainted so that the courts of this country will not assist either party to enforce it.

5 [1921] 3 KB 532 at pp. 558–9.

I do not wish to express any opinion about a case where parties agree to deal with goods which they both know have already been smuggled out of a foreign country, or about a case where the seller knows that the buyer intends to use the goods for an illegal purpose or to smuggle them into a foreign country. Such cases may raise difficult questions. The crucial fact in this case appears to me to be that both parties knew that the contract could not be performed without the respondents procuring a breach of the law of India within the territory of that country.

On that question I do not get very much assistance from the older cases. Most of them do not deal with that point and, further, it must, I think, be borne in mind that they date from a time when international relationships were somewhat different and when theories of political economy now outmoded were generally accepted. Many dealt with revenue laws or penal laws, which have always been regarded as being in a special position, and I do not wish on this occasion to say more than that probably some re-examination of some of these cases may in future be necessary . . .

. . .

Finally, it was argued that, even if there be a general rule that our courts will take notice of foreign laws so that agreements to break them are unenforceable, that rule must be subject to exceptions and this Indian law is one of which we ought not to take notice. It may be that there are exceptions. I can imagine a foreign law involving persecution of such a character that we would regard an agreement to break it as meritorious. But this Indian law is very far removed from anything of that kind. It was argued that this prohibition of exports to South Africa was a hostile act against a Commonwealth country with which we have close relations, that such a prohibition is contrary to international usage, and that we cannot recognize it without taking sides in the dispute between India and South Africa.

My Lords, it is quite impossible for a court in this country to set itself up as a judge of the rights and wrongs of a controversy between two friendly countries. We cannot judge the motives or the justifications of governments of other countries in these matters and, if we tried to do so, the consequences might seriously prejudice international relations. By recognizing this Indian law so that an agreement which involves a breach of that law within Indian territory is unenforceable we express no opinion whatever, either favourable or adverse, as to the policy which caused its enactment. In my judgment this appeal should be dismissed.

Lord Keith of Avonholme

In the present case I see no escape from the view that to recognize the contract between the appellant and the respondent as an enforceable contract would give a just cause for complaint by the Government of India and should be regarded as contrary to conceptions of international comity. On grounds of public policy, therefore, this is a contract which our courts ought not to recognize. It is said that the Indian legislation is discriminatory legislation against a country which is a member of the Commonwealth and with which this country is on friendly terms.

But that, in my opinion, is irrelevant. The English courts cannot be called on to adjudicate upon political issues between India and South Africa. The Indian law is not a law repugnant to English conceptions of what may be regarded as within the ordinary field of legislation or administrative order even in this country. It is the illegality under the foreign law that is to be considered and not the effect of the foreign law on another country.

Result: the appeal was dismissed, and the contract not enforced.

Comment

This case differs from *Foster* v. *Driscoll* in that the illegality was more remote. In *Foster* v. *Driscoll*, the whole purpose of the agreement was to smuggle whisky into the United States (though the parties had a fallback plan to sell it in Canada if this was not possible); in *Regazzoni* v. *Sethia*, on the other hand, the agreement was perfectly legal on the surface: it made no mention of India, simply requiring delivery in Italy. According to the terms of the contract, the jute could have been obtained anywhere. India came into the picture only because both parties knew that the jute would come from there.

It could also be argued that the contract might not actually have required a criminal offence to be committed in India. The English company would probably have bought the jute, and arranged for its shipment, by issuing instructions from England. Depending on how one regarded the matter, it could be argued that it would not have acted in India. The persons in India who would have arranged for the shipment might not have been aware of its ultimate destination; consequently, they might have lacked the *mens rea* that was presumably necessary for a criminal offence under Indian law. The House of Lords apparently regarded all this as irrelevant.[24] This shows that the English courts take a realistic, purposive view of these matters and do not allow themselves to be deflected by narrow legal technicalities.

Again, there can be no doubt that the result would have been the same if the parties had chosen a system of law other than English law – perhaps South African law – as the governing law. It would have made no difference if the contract had been valid under that law. This is because, under English law as it stood at the time, the rule was based on (international) public policy. Today, the same result could be attained under Article 9(3) of the Regulation. This, it is suggested, is the appropriate provision.

§ 4.1.2 Foreign public policy. The cases considered so far have been ones in which the performance of the contract would have been a criminal offence under the law of the country in which it was to have been carried out. Our next case concerns the situation in which it is merely contrary to the public policy of that country.

---

24 See [1958] AC 301 at pp. 317 (Viscount Simonds) and 326 (Lord Keith of Avonholm). These passages were not included in the extracts set out above.

England
Lemenda Trading Co. Ltd v. African Middle East Petroleum Co. Ltd
High Court (Queen's Bench Division)
[1988] 2 WLR 735

Background

This case concerned two contracts. The first, which will be called the 'lobbying contract', was between Lemenda, a company incorporated in the Bahamas, and African Middle East Petroleum, a company registered in London. The latter was anxious to secure renewal of the second contract, an oil-supply contract with a state-owned oil company in Qatar. In the lobbying contract, it was agreed that the principal shareholder in Lemenda, a Saudi Arabian called Mr Yassin, would use his influence to help African Middle East Petroleum to obtain renewal of the oil-supply contract. It was agreed that if, as a result of his efforts, African Middle East Petroleum obtained renewal of the contract, it would pay Lemenda a commission. It did obtain renewal of the contract, but it did not pay the commission. Lemenda sued it in England. Both parties accepted that the lobbying contract was governed by English law.

Phillips J

[After considering the law of Qatar, under which a lobbying contract of the kind in issue was contrary to public policy, but not contrary to an actual rule of law, Phillips J said:]

There is a clear distinction between acts which infringe public policy and acts which violate provisions of law. I have been referred to no decided case that supports the proposition that the English courts should, as a matter of comity, refuse to enforce an English law contract on the sole ground that performance would be contrary to the public policy of the country of performance. The public policy of Qatar cannot, of itself, constitute any bar to the enforcement of the agreement in this case. It may, however, be a relevant factor when considering whether the court ought to refuse to enforce the agreement in this case under principles of English public policy.

[Phillips J then considered English law and concluded:]

Had the agreement related to the procurement of a contract from a British Government department or a state-owned industry, I am in no doubt that it would have been unenforceable by reason of English public policy. Is this a policy a bar to enforcement having regard to the fact that performance of the relevant obligation was to take place not in England but in Qatar? This is no easy question.

. . .

The practice of exacting payment for the use of personal influence, particularly when the person to be influenced is likely to be unaware of the pecuniary motive involved, is unattractive whatever the context. Yet it is questionable whether the moral principles involved are so weighty as to lead an English court to refuse to enforce an agreement regardless of the country of performance and regardless of the attitude of that country to such a practice. The later English decisions [on the consequences of such agreements in England] were influenced, at least in part, by the effect of the practice in question upon good government in England. It is at this stage that, in my judgment, it becomes relevant to consider the law of Qatar . . . In the present case Qatar, the country in which the agreement was to be performed and with which, in my view, the agreement had the closest connection, has the same public policy as that which prevails in England. Because of that policy, the courts of Qatar would not enforce the agreement.

In my judgment, the English courts should not enforce an English law contract which falls to be performed abroad where: (i) it relates to an adventure which is contrary to a head of English public policy which is founded on general principles of morality, and (ii) the same public policy applies to the country of performance so that the agreement would not be enforceable under the law of that country.

In such a situation international comity combines with English domestic public policy to militate against enforcement.

For these reasons the court will not entertain this action and the claim must be dismissed.[1]

---

1 Phillips J went on to consider what the position would have been if the lobbying contract had been enforceable. He concluded that the claimants would still have lost because it was not proved that the renewal of the oil-supply contract had been the result of their efforts.

Result: the contract was not enforced.

Comment

In this case, the proper (applicable) law was English law, and the contract would have been invalid (on grounds of public policy) if it had involved lobbying British ministers or officials. It is clear from the judgment, however, that Phillips J did not consider that this was enough in itself to establish that the contract was invalid. In a part of the judgment not reproduced above, he drew a distinction between those heads of English public policy that apply irrespective of the place of performance and those that apply only if performance is to take place in England. In modern terminology, the former might be called rules of international public policy and the latter rules of domestic public policy. It seems clear that the rule in question fell within the latter category;[25] otherwise, there would have been no need to consider the law of Qatar. It was the *combined* effect of English and Qatar public policy that made the contract invalid.

§ 4.1.3 Wider forms of illegality.

We now consider the position where the relationship between the contract and the illegality is more remote.

---

25 The use in the judgment of the phrase 'a head of English public policy which is founded on general principles of morality' rather muddies the waters, since it might be thought that a head of public policy founded on such principles would be a matter of international public policy. However, it is clear from other passages in the judgment that this was not the case.

England
Euro-Diam Ltd* v. *Bathurst
Court of Appeal
[1990] QB 1; [1988] 2 WLR 517; [1988] 2 All ER 23; [1988] 1 Lloyd's Rep 228

Background

Euro-Diam were English diamond merchants. They sold a consignment of diamonds to a German buyer, and the managing director of Euro-Diam (a certain Mr Laub) provided an invoice that understated the value of the diamonds. This was done at the request of an intermediary. Mr Laub must have realized that the reason he had been asked to do this was to allow the German buyers to defraud the German tax authorities. The diamonds were stolen when they were still at Euro-Diam's risk. Euro-Diam had insured them with the defendant (Bathurst) at their true value and paid the correct premium. The insurance contract was governed by English law. The insurer refused to pay and, when sued by Euro-Diam, raised the *ex turpi causa* defence.[26] The question before the court was whether the false invoice rendered the insurance contract illegal so that the defence applied.

Kerr LJ

[After discussing the English authorities, Kerr J said:]

The *ex turpi causa* defence ultimately rests on a principle of public policy that the courts will not assist a plaintiff who has been guilty of illegal (or immoral) conduct of which the courts should take notice. It applies if in all the circumstances it would be an affront to the public conscience to grant the plaintiff the relief which he seeks because the court would thereby appear to assist or encourage the plaintiff in his illegal conduct or to encourage others in similar acts . . .

[After pointing out that the insurers were entirely innocent and the contract of insurance was wholly unaffected by any illegality, Kerr LJ concluded that the '*ex turpi causa*' defence failed. He gave his reasons as follows:]

Mr Laub's issue of the understated invoice was undoubtedly reprehensible. He realised that it would probably be used to deceive the German customs, and his action was criminal under the laws of the Federal Republic. But he did not issue the invoice for his own or the plaintiffs' purposes, but at the request of [the intermediary] . . . The understated invoice also involved no deception of the insurers, since the true value of the diamonds was recorded in the plaintiffs' register and the correct premium was paid. In these circumstances there could in my view be no question of any affront to the public conscience . . .

. . .

[The plaintiffs] derived no tangible benefit from the understated invoice . . . the possible goodwill advantage to the plaintiffs of having acceded to [the

---

[26] This is the defence, recognized by most systems of law, that an action cannot be based on an illegal or immoral foundation.

intermediary's] request is so shadowy that it is not surprising that the judge made no mention of it at all. Although I felt bound to accept [the submission of counsel for Bathurst] that the potential benefit of the understated invoice was not exclusively on the side of [the German buyers], the impact of this aspect is virtually negligible.

. . .

For all these reasons I am in full agreement with the judge [in the court below] that the *ex turpi causa* defence fails. In these circumstances we found it unnecessary to hear [counsel for Euro-Diam] on another aspect raised by way of cross-appeal, although the judge also dealt with this. This concerned the question whether, if the plaintiffs were to fail on the matters already discussed, they could nevertheless succeed because Mr Laub's issue of the understated invoice did not constitute any breach of English law but only of German law, and of a German revenue law at that. The judge [in the court below] rejected this . . . Although we have heard no argument on the point I have no doubt that his conclusion was right. It would be extraordinary if our law were to countenance an agreement involving the commission of a criminal offence in a friendly foreign country with impunity by holding that on that ground the agreement is not to be regarded as contrary to public policy. [*Regazzoni* v. *Sethia*, above] is a sufficient answer to this contention, which appears to fly in the face of all principles of comity, and as regards the point that Mr Laub's action constituted an offence under a foreign revenue law . . . while our courts do not enforce such laws, they will obviously not assist in their breach.

. . .

Accordingly, I share the judge's views entirely and would dismiss this appeal.

[Russell LJ and Sir Denys Buckley agreed]

Comment

This case was outside the principle laid down in *Regazzoni* v. *Sethia*, since the contract before the court (the insurance contract) did not require either party to do anything illegal. The issue was simply whether the illegality which had taken place in the context of the contract of sale affected the validity of the insurance contract. Most of the judgment was taken up with a lengthy discussion of the effect of illegality in a purely domestic context. This depends on how close the relationship is between the claim and the illegality. In the *Euro-Diam* case, the court held that the link between the false invoice and the insurance was too remote for the *ex turpi causa* defence to apply. If the relationship had been more direct, however, the insurance contract would almost certainly have been unenforceable. Assume, for example, that a person exports a work of art from a foreign country contrary to the law of that country. He insures it against loss and it is in fact lost. On these facts, it is hard to imagine that an English court would allow the exporter to claim under the insurance contract, since this would have allowed him to enjoy the fruits of his illegal activity.

What is particularly interesting in the *Euro-Diam* case is that (in the last paragraph set out above) the court rejected out of hand the suggestion that defrauding foreign tax authorities was any less serious than defrauding British tax authorities. Thus, the case would have been decided in exactly the same way if the false invoice had been used to deceive the British tax authorities.

Since the insurance contract in the *Euro-Diam* case was governed by English law, there would be no need to resort to Article 9 if the case were decided under the Regulation. The question would simply be whether the contract was valid under the applicable law. If the applicable law had been that of another country, the court would have applied that law. If the insurance contract had been invalid under that law, the claim would have failed. If it had been valid, however, the question might still have arisen whether some rule of English (international) public policy would have applied. If it had, the court could resort to Article 9(2) in order to invalidate the contract. Article 9(3) would have been inapplicable because the insurance contract did not require anything illegal to be done in Germany.

§ 4.1.4 Arbitration. We have seen that English courts will not enforce a contract that requires the commission of a crime in a foreign country. The question now to be considered is whether parties can use an arbitration agreement in order to insulate their contract from English public policy. If there had been an arbitration clause in the contract in *Foster* v. *Driscoll* or in *Regazzoni* v. *Sethia*, and if the arbitrator had seen fit to ignore the foreign illegality, could the claimants in those cases have obtained an award of damages? This is the question which arose in our next case.

England
Soleimany* v. *Soleimany
Court of Appeal
[1999] QB 785; [1998] 3 WLR 811; [1999] 3 All ER 847

Background

This was a dispute between father and son. Both were Iranian Jews. The father left Iran and came to England. The son remained in Iran. Together they operated a scheme for the illegal export of carpets from Iran. Subsequently, the son came to England and demanded his share of the profits. The father refused. The parties agreed to take their dispute to the London *Beth Din*, a Jewish court which applied Jewish law. The *Beth Din* has no official standing as a court in England: English law regards it simply as an arbitral tribunal. The arbitrator recognized that the contract was illegal under Iranian law and this was expressly stated in the award, but it seems that this did not affect the matter under Jewish law. As a result, the son was awarded more than £500,000. The father refused to pay and the son brought proceedings in the English courts to enforce the award.

Waller LJ

Is it apparent from *the award itself* what type of contract the arbitrator was dealing with? We pose the question in this way because it seems to us important to emphasise that we are dealing with a case where it is apparent from the face of the award that . . . the arbitrator was dealing with what he termed an illicit enterprise under which it was the joint intention that carpets would be smuggled out of Iran illegally . . .

It must follow that Dayan Berkovits was right in the affidavit he has sworn for the purposes of these proceedings that the arbitrator did not take the same view as an English court would have taken, but considered the illegality to be of no relevance 'since he was applying Jewish law, under which any purported illegality would have no effect on the rights of the parties.'

What attitude would the English court take if a foreign court had decided as a matter of fact that there was a contract entered into with the object of committing an illegal act in a foreign and friendly State, but by the law of the foreign court, either illegality of that sort had no effect on the rights of the parties, or the foreign court was empowered to award compensation, and had awarded compensation? . . .

[Waller LJ then mentioned that the courts of some countries might take a more 'relaxed' approach to foreign illegality than English courts. He pointed out, however, that a foreign judgment may be refused recognition in England on the ground of public policy. After considering the circumstances in which this might be done, he continued:]

However, it would seem to us that if what the foreign court did was to recognise by its judgment that a contract had been entered into with the object of committing an illegal act in a State which England recognised as a foreign and friendly State, and to enforce the rights of the parties under it, then there would be no room for recognising the more relaxed approach of a different jurisdiction. That, as it would seem to us, is the very type of judgment which the English court would not recognise on the grounds of public policy.

We stress that we are dealing with a judgment which *finds as a fact* that it was the common intention to commit an illegal act, but enforces the contract. Different considerations may apply where there is a finding by the foreign court to the contrary or simply no such finding, and one party now seeks such a finding from the enforcing court. Thus our conclusion would be that if the award were a judgment of a foreign court, the English court would not enforce it.

[Waller LJ then considered whether the position was any different in the case of an arbitration award. After some discussion, he concluded:]

Even if we were wrong in the view already expressed that an arbitration agreement between robbers (for example) to arbitrate their disputes would itself be void, it is in our view inconceivable that an English court would enforce an award made on a joint venture agreement between bank robbers, any more than it would enforce an agreement between highwaymen . . . Where public policy is involved, the interposition of an arbitration award does not isolate the successful party's claim from the illegality which gave rise to it . . .

The reason, in our judgment, is plain enough. The court declines to enforce an illegal contract . . . not for the sake of the defendant, nor (if it comes to the point) for the sake of the plaintiff. The court is in our view concerned to preserve the integrity of its process, and to see that it is not abused. The parties cannot override that concern by private agreement. They cannot by procuring an arbitration conceal that they, or rather one of them, is seeking to enforce an illegal contract. Public policy will not allow it . . .

The difficulty arises when arbitrators have entered upon the topic of illegality, and have held that there was none. Or perhaps they have made a non-speaking award, and have not been asked to give reasons. In such a case there is a tension between the public interest that the awards of arbitrators should be respected, so that there be an end to lawsuits, and the public interest that illegal contracts should not be enforced. We do not propound a definitive solution to this problem, for it does not arise in the present case. So far from finding that the underlying contract was not illegal, the Dayan [arbitrator] in the Beth Din found that it was.

It may, however, also be in the public interest that this court should express some view on a point which has been fully argued and which is likely to arise again. In our view, an enforcement judge, if there is *prima facie* evidence from one side that the award is based on an illegal contract, should inquire further to some extent. Is there evidence on the other side to the contrary? Has the arbitrator expressly found that the underlying contract was not illegal? Or is it a fair inference that he did reach that conclusion? Is there anything to suggest that the arbitrator was incompetent to conduct such an inquiry? May there have been collusion or bad faith, so as to procure an award despite illegality? Arbitrations are, after all, conducted in a wide variety of situations; not just before high-powered tribunals in international trade but in many other circumstances. We do not for one moment suggest that the judge should conduct a full-scale trial of those matters in the first instance. That would create the mischief which the arbitration was designed to avoid. The judge has to decide whether it is proper to give full faith and credit to the arbitrator's award. Only if he decides at the preliminary stage that he should not take that course does he need to embark on a more elaborate inquiry into the issue of illegality.

. . .

We should make it clear that we have been considering only initial illegality, present when the underlying contract was made. Nothing that we have said touches on supervening illegality . . .

Finally, under this head, we should state explicitly what may already have been apparent: when considering illegality of the underlying contract, we do not confine ourselves to English law. An English court will not enforce a contract governed by English law, or to be performed in England, which is illegal by English domestic law. Nor will it enforce a contract governed by the law of a foreign and friendly State, or which requires performance in such a country, if performance is illegal by the law of that country. That is well established as appears from the citations earlier in this judgment. This rule applies as much to the enforcement of an arbitration award as to the direct enforcement of a contract in legal proceedings.

Result: the appeal was allowed; the award was not enforced.

Comment

As was made clear in the judgment, there is a tension between the policy of respecting the sovereignty of foreign States and that of respecting the decisions of arbitrators. This case shows that, where the award recognizes the illegality and nevertheless awards damages, the court may refuse to enforce it. Where, on the other hand, the arbitrator finds that there is no illegality, the court will be unlikely to refuse recognition simply because it would take a different view.[27]

§ 4.2 Supervening illegality

Up to now, we have been assuming that the contract was illegal all along. Now, we consider the position where it was legal when concluded but became illegal when it was to be performed.

> **England**
> ***Ralli Brothers* v. *Compania Naviera Sota y Aznar***
> **Court of Appeal**
> **[1920] 2 KB 287**

Background

This case arose out of a contract between a Spanish shipowner and an English charterer to ship jute from India to Spain. Under the contract, which was governed by English law, half the freight (money payable for transporting the goods) was payable in England when the ship left India and half was payable in Spain when it arrived. When entered into, the contract was lawful by all relevant systems of law. The ship duly left India with its cargo and the English company paid half the freight in England. Before it reached its destination, however, Spain adopted price-control legislation that imposed a limit on the freight. This legislation was in force when the second instalment became due. As payment was to be made in Spain, and as the maximum permitted was less than the contractual amount, payment in full would have been illegal under Spanish law and penalties could have been imposed on anyone infringing it. The English company offered to pay the maximum permitted by Spanish law, but refused to pay more. The Spanish company brought legal proceedings in England: it argued that, since the governing law of the contract was English law, the Spanish legislation could not justify the English company's failure to pay the full amount.

Lord Sterndale MR

It was illegal in Spain to pay or receive more freight for imported jute than 875 pesetas a ton, and therefore the performance of the contract was illegal by the law of the place of its performance. In my opinion the law is correctly stated by Professor Dicey in his work on the *Conflict of Laws*, 2nd ed., at p. 553, where he says:

> A contract . . . is, in general, invalid in so far as . . . the performance of it is unlawful by the law of the country where the contract is to be performed . . .

---

27 *Westacre Investments Inc.* v. *Jugoimport-SPDR Ltd* [2000] QB 288; [1999] 3 WLR 811; [1999] 3 All ER 864 (CA).

. . .

I think on principle and on authority that the charterers are not bound to perform that part of the contract, that is, the payment of freight above the maximum allowed by Spanish law, which has become illegal by the law of the place of its performance.

Warrington LJ

Professor Dicey at p. 553 of the 2nd ed. of his *Conflict of Laws* makes the following statement accepted by both parties in the present case as an accurate statement of the law:

> A Contract (whether lawful by its proper law or not) is, in general, invalid in so far as (1.) the performance of it is unlawful by the law of the country where the contract is to be performed . . .

It must be remembered that not only is it illegal in Spain for the Spanish [cargo] receivers to pay more than the legal rate of freight but it is unlawful for the [ship] owners who are also Spaniards to receive it. I think it must be held that it was an implied condition of the obligation of the charterers that the contemplated payment by Spaniards to Spaniards in Spain should not be illegal by the law of that country.

Had the performance of the contract so far as it was to be performed in England become illegal by English law performance would, in my opinion, have been excused, and on the ground that the contract was subject to an implied condition that its performance should not be illegal . . .

Scrutton LJ

In my opinion the law is correctly stated by Professor Dicey in *Conflict of Laws*, 2nd ed., p. 553, where he says:

> A contract . . . is, in general, invalid in so far as . . . the performance of it is unlawful by the law of the country where the contract is to be performed . . .

If I am asked whether the true intent of the parties is that one has undertaken to do an act though it is illegal by the law of the place in which the act is to be done, and though that law is the law of his own country; or whether their true intent was that the doing of that act is subject to the implied condition that it shall be legal for him to do the act in the place where it has to be done, I have no hesitation in choosing the second alternative. 'I will do it provided I can legally do so' seems to me infinitely preferable to and more likely than 'I will do it, though it is illegal.'

Result: the appeal was dismissed; the charterer was not obliged to pay more than the sum permitted by Spanish law.

Comment

All the judges accepted the view of Professor Dicey that questions of legality are decided by the law of the country in which performance is to take place; however, two of the judges also considered that there is a rule of English domestic law under which there is an implied term in all contracts that performance is to be effected only if it is legal under the law of the country where it is to take place, a principle that is today regarded as falling under the doctrine of frustration, rather than that of illegality. The first rationale can no longer apply as such, since the Rome I Regulation contains no such principle. However, Article 9(3) does permit the application in such circumstances of the law of the country in which performance is to take place; so an English court could still reach the same result, if it so chose, by resorting to Article 9(3). The second rationale would also allow it to do this, though this would be possible only if the applicable law was that of England.

It seems from this case that the rule in *Regazzoni* v. *Sethia* also applies in cases of supervening illegality, though there may be exceptions. In both situations, Article 9(3) will allow the English court to reach the appropriate result.

§ 4.3 Conclusions

The cases discussed above were all decided before the Rome I Regulation came into effect. However, in view of Article 9(3), they could all be decided exactly the same way today. For this reason, they are still relevant: they indicate when an English court will make use of the power conferred by Article 9 to take account of foreign illegality.

§ 5 Foreign illegality under US law

The application of non-derogable provisions of foreign law is dealt with in the *Restatement of the Law Second: Conflict of Laws*. Though not binding, the rules in the *Restatements* are often followed by American courts. The question whether a court may depart from the law chosen by the parties is covered in § 187(2), set out in Panel 25.9. This states that, in the case of an issue 'which the parties could not have resolved by an explicit provision in their agreement directed to that issue', in other words, a non-derogable provision, the chosen law will be applied unless either (a) the chosen state has no substantial relationship to the parties or the transaction and there is no other reasonable basis for the parties' choice, or (b) the application of the law of the chosen state would be contrary to a fundamental policy of a state which has a materially greater interest than the chosen state in the determination of the particular issue and which would be the state of the applicable law in the absence of an effective choice of law by the parties.

> **Panel 25.9 Restatement of the Law Second Conflict of Laws, § 187(2)**
>
> **§ 187(2)**
>
> 2 The law of the state chosen by the parties to govern their contractual rights and duties will be applied, even if the particular issue is one which the parties could not have resolved by an explicit provision in their agreement directed to that issue, unless either
>   (a) the chosen state has no substantial relationship to the parties or the transaction and there is no other reasonable basis for the parties' choice, or
>   (b) application of the law of the chosen state would be contrary to a fundamental policy of a state which has a materially greater interest than the chosen state in the determination of the particular issue and which, under the rule of § 188, would be the state of the applicable law in the absence of an effective choice of law by the parties.

The most important difference between this provision and that in Article 9(3) of the Rome I Regulation is that it applies with regard to any non-derogable provisions: it is not necessary that the performance of the contract should be unlawful under the foreign law.

In order to see how the provision in § 187(2) works, let us assume that the parties choose the law of State X to govern their contract, but it is argued before the court that a non-derogable provision of State Y should nevertheless be applied. It will be seen that § 187(2) provides two possible routes for doing this. Under route (a) it must be shown that there was no reasonable basis for the choice of the law of State X.[28] This will be hard to do in practice because there will usually be *some* reasonable basis for the parties' choice. Consequently, route (b) will normally be the one followed.

If we follow route (b), we find that three conditions must be fulfilled. The first is that the facts must be such that a fundamental policy of State Y would be jeopardized if its non-derogable provision were not applied. This involves determining whether State Y has a genuine interest in the application of its rule in the circumstances of the case, a determination that calls for interest analysis.[29]

If this condition is satisfied, it must next be established that State Y has a materially greater interest than State X in the determination of the question before the court. If State X has no real interest – in other words, if there is a false conflict – this will be easy to decide. If both states have a genuine interest – if there is a true conflict – their interests will have to be balanced.

The final condition is that the facts must be such that the law of State Y would have been the applicable law in the absence of a valid choice. Under § 188, this is determined by a process of evaluating contacts. It differs from the process under the Rome I Regulation in that it is determined specifically with regard to the issue before the court: the applicable law is chosen on the basis of the most significant relationship, *with respect to that issue*, of the transaction and the parties. Moreover, under the last sentence of § 188(2), the contacts 'are to be evaluated according to their relative importance with respect to the particular issue'.

Not all American states apply this provision of the *Restatement*. Those that do not will most likely apply pure interest analysis. They would analyse the interests of the two states in the application of their law and, where there is a true conflict, try to balance those interests. They would probably not consider what law would have been applied in the absence of a choice. This might make a difference in some cases.

Our next case shows how these principles apply in a situation similar to those considered in § 4, above.

---

28 If this is established, the law of State X will not be applied. However, in order to obtain the application of the law of State Y, it will be necessary to show that its law would be applicable, with regard to the issue in question, under § 188, which sets out the rules for determining the governing law in the absence of an effective choice by the parties.
29 See Chapter 22, § 4.1, above.

United States (New York)
Triad Financial Establishment v. *Tumpane Company*
United States District Court, Northern District of New York
611 F Supp 157 (1985)

Background

Triad was a Liechtenstein entity owned by a Saudi Arabian, Mr Khashoggi. Tumpane was an American company, which wanted to obtain a military contract with the Government of Saudi Arabia. In 1971, it concluded a lobbying contract with Triad, under which the latter was entitled to a commission if the lobbying was successful. The lobbying contract contained a forum-selection clause in favour of New York, a clause which the American court read as a choice-of-law clause in favour of New York law. Tumpane obtained the military contract. Triad demanded its commission, but Tumpane refused to pay, since a Saudi decree had been passed in 1975 prohibiting lobbying agreements, with retroactive effect. In 1985, Triad sued Tumpane in New York for the commission.

Judgment

As noted previously, the Marketing Agreement between the parties contains a forum selection clause designating New York as the jurisdiction that would govern the interpretation of the contracts. New York courts will normally honor the parties' choice of forum provided the forum selected has a substantial relationship to the parties or the transaction and the application of the forum's law would not be contrary to a fundamental policy of a state with a materially greater interest than the forum state . . .[1]

Tumco contends that Saudi Arabia has a far greater interest in this litigation than New York does and, consequently, Saudi law should apply notwithstanding the forum selection clause. Triad contends that Saudi Arabia has no interest in this controversy and accordingly, this court should honor the parties' choice of forum.

In determining what law should apply, this court must weigh the relative interests of the states involved to determine which state has the greatest interest at stake in this litigation. The court must also consider which forum has the most significant relationship with the parties and transaction.

Plaintiff Triad is a Liechtenstein entity. Defendant Tumco is incorporated in New York with its main office in Vancouver, Washington. At the height of the Peace Hawk program Tumco had only two employees in New York compared with 3750 in Saudi Arabia, 500 in Montana, 250 in California, 200 in Spain, and 100 in Washington. None of the relevant agreements were negotiated, executed, or performed in New York. It appears that New York's only significant contact with this litigation is via the forum selection clause contained in the Marketing Agreement.

In contrast, Saudi Arabia has a significant connection to this litigation and a compelling interest in the application of the law. Although Triad is a Liechtenstein

---

1 The parties agree that New York's policy with regard to this issue is based on the Restatement (Second) of Conflict of Laws, § 187 . . . Tumco contends that this case falls squarely within § 187(2)(b).

entity, it has characterized itself as a 'Saudi sales agent.' Its reputation as an effective marketing agent is based almost entirely on Mr. Khashoggi's purported influence in Saudi Arabia. In addition, the Northrop-Tumco contracts, which are predicates to the Triad-Tumco contracts, were negotiated primarily in Saudi Arabia and call for performance entirely in Saudi Arabia. Moreover, Saudi Arabia has a compelling interest in having its law applied to this controversy. The Kingdom of Saudi Arabia prohibits the payment of agent's fees on contracts for arms and related services. The Saudi prohibition was formally expressed in Decree No. 1275 which was issued on September 17, 1975. The Decree prohibits the payment of any agent's fees in connection with the sale of armaments or related equipment:

1. No firm holding a contract with the Saudi Government for the supply of arms or equipment required by the Saudi Government may pay any sum as a commission to any intermediary, sales agent, representative, or broker. This prohibition shall apply regardless of the nationality of the firm or the nationality of the intermediary, sales agent, representative, or broker. It shall apply also whether the contract was concluded directly between the Saudi Government and the firm or through a third-party state. No recognition is accorded to any commission agreement previously concluded by any of such firm with any party, and such agreement shall have no validity vis-à-vis the Saudi Government.

2. If among the foreign firms mentioned in paragraph 1 above there are any that are obligated by commission agreements that they have made, they are to stop payment of the commissions due after having been warned by this decision . . .

The Saudis enacted Decree No. 1275 in an attempt to root out corruption and bribery in military contracts. To allow a forum selection clause to circumvent this strong Saudi policy would render Decree No. 1275 meaningless. In contrast, New York has no policy at stake in this litigation New York has little or no interest in upholding Triad's claim for fees. In view of the significant connection to Saudi Arabia, the fundamental Saudi policy against agent's fees in military contracts, and the negligible relation between this case and New York, the court finds that Saudi Arabian law should apply . . .

Under the concept of [*dépeçage*],[2] Saudi law will only be applied after September 17, 1975 as the Saudi interest in this action did not arise until Decree No. 1275 was issued. There is no reason to displace the parties' choice of forum prior to the issuance of the Decree . . .

2 *Editor's note:* *dépeçage* is a French term meaning 'cutting up'. In conflict-of-laws terminology, it means applying different legal systems to govern different parts of a contract.

Comment

It is not expressly stated in the judgment that the lobbying contract involved the commission of a criminal offence in Saudi Arabia, since this is not required to be established under US doctrines.

Our next case shows more clearly that the rule in the *Restatement* is not limited to cases of illegality.

United States (New York)
Business Incentives Co.* v. *Sony Corporation of America
United States District Court, Southern District of New York
397 F Supp 63 (1975)

Background

Business Incentives was a small New Jersey corporation. Sony was a large New York corporation. They concluded a contract under which Business Incentives would interest business concerns located in the New York metropolitan area in the purchase of Sony products as prizes in their employee incentive programmes. Thus, Business Incentives served as an independent salesman for Sony goods. The contract allowed either party to terminate it on fifteen days' notice.

Two years later, having successfully built up the 'territory' of New York, the plaintiff was told by Sony to restrict its operations to the less lucrative 'territory' of New Jersey. The plaintiff was advised that, unless it agreed to this change, Sony would exercise its rights under the termination clause. Accordingly, on 1 September 1967, the parties entered into an agreement which modified and superseded the 1965 contract, by limiting the plaintiff's 'territory' to New Jersey. On 22 March 1972, this second agreement was modified, again at Sony's insistence, by a downward revision of the commission rate schedule. Subsequently, by letter dated 2 November 1973, Sony elected, in accordance with the termination clause, to terminate the agreement.

Business Incentives then sued Sony in a Federal Court in New York for damages, claiming that the termination of the contract was unlawful. It relied on a New Jersey statute and on New Jersey common law.

Judgment

Preliminarily, we must decide which law applies – that of New York or that of New Jersey. The problem arises because although the Tenth Paragraph of the parties' Agreement specifically provides that the Agreement 'shall be governed by the laws of the State of New York', plaintiff's second category of Counts . . . seeks relief under a New Jersey statute. And the first category of Counts . . . can be construed as claiming relief in a common law area where New Jersey has expressed a strong public policy. With respect to the statutory claim, if we should determine that the Act in question does indeed govern the parties' relationship, there is no doubt that plaintiff would have a claim for damages for Sony's reduction of the commission rate and its termination of the Agreement without just cause.

In general, courts will ordinarily honor contractual choice of law provisions, as long as the state selected has sufficient contacts with the transaction in question and the application of that state's law would not be contrary to any fundamental policy of a state which has a materially greater interest than the chosen state in the determination of the particular issue at bar, and which would be the state of the applicable law in the absence of an effective choice of law by the parties. [Reference to § 187 of the Restatement.] Despite the provision in the parties' Agreement that New York law would apply, it appears that, under the above test, New Jersey law should govern instead. The only contacts with New York are that defendant is a New York corporation and the original 1965 contract provided for performance in the New York metropolitan area. New Jersey, on the other hand, would seem to have a materially greater interest in the application of its law by virtue of the fact that plaintiff is a New Jersey corporation, that the performance of the contract now in issue (executed in 1967 and modified in 1972) contemplated performance exclusively in New Jersey, and, most importantly, that New Jersey has a strong public policy – enunciated both by its courts and its legislature – in favor of protecting the relatively powerless consumer or small businessman from more powerful commercial giants, such as automobile manufacturers, oil companies, and, presumably, electronics manufacturers . . . In light of the foregoing, there is no doubt but that New Jersey law should apply, despite the parties' agreement to the contrary.[1]

1 In the end, the court found that the plaintiff failed on most counts.

Comment

In this case, it was not suggested that performance of the contract was unlawful under the law of New Jersey. The New Jersey provisions were simply concerned with protecting the weaker party. This shows that § 187(2) is significantly wider than Article 9(2) of the Rome I Regulation.

Further reading

See the general works cited in the previous chapter

CHAPTER 26

Contracts: regulating business, protecting employees and helping consumers

In this chapter, we continue our discussion of situations in which the law imposes provisions irrespective of the intention of the parties. We now focus on particular policies. Under the Regulation, three specifically defined policies are given special treatment. These concern employees, consumers and insurance. In a broad sense, all three could be regarded as aspects of business regulation. In countries outside Europe – and this chapter will be mainly concerned with such countries – the categories are more fluid. The basic issue, however, is the same: when should non-derogable provisions of law be applied if they are not part of the proper (applicable) law?

Before we consider different policy areas, however, we must first look at some theoretical issues.

§ 1 Legal principles

In the common-law world, there is nothing exactly similar to Article 9 of the Rome I Regulation. In the United States, § 187(2) of the *Restatement* contains the rules concerning the application of non-derogable provisions of a legal system other than that chosen by the parties. These were discussed in Chapter 25, § 5, above. They apply to both forum provisions and foreign provisions.

In the United Kingdom and the Commonwealth, there is no equivalent to this. However, non-derogable provisions of the forum, if contained in a statute, may be applied under the doctrine of an 'overriding statute';[1] if they constitute a rule of common law, they may be applied under the doctrine of public policy.[2]

The doctrine of overriding statutes is based on the fact that (apart from Community law) conflict of laws, which is almost entirely based on the common law, is not entrenched or otherwise given a special status. Conflicts rules can be set aside by a statute, just like any other rule of common law (or of an earlier statute). Consequently, if a statute provides – expressly or by implication – that it is to override the normal choice-of-law rules, it will do so.

---

1 For a general discussion, see Dicey, Morris and Collins, pp. 18 *et seq*. Much of the original thinking was done by J. H. C. Morris. See, for example, Morris, 'The Scope of the Carriage of Goods by Sea Act 1971' (1979) 95 LQR 59. Morris's ideas were challenged by F. A. Mann (see (1979) 95 LQR 346) but were upheld by the courts: *The Hollandia (The Morviken)* [1982] QB 872; [1982] 2 WLR 556; [1982] 1 All ER 1076 (CA), especially *per* Lord Denning MR [1982] QB 872 at pp. 880–4. This case went on appeal to the House of Lords but no further challenges were made to Morris' approach: [1983] AC 565; [1982] 3 WLR 1111; [1982] 3 All ER 1141.
2 This is an example of the positive application of the public-policy doctrine: see Chapter 22, § 2.4.3, above.

There can be no disputing the constitutional correctness of this doctrine. The only problem is the interpretation of the statute. If it does not expressly say when it is to apply in an international context, how is one to decide whether it is intended to do so in a particular case? Here, British and Commonwealth courts tend to apply something similar to American interest analysis, though they do not normally call it by that name. They ask what the purpose of the statute is – what policies it seeks to promote – and they determine its international scope on that basis. Common-law rules based on public policy are treated in a similar way. We saw examples in the previous chapter. The result is that, in the case of non-derogable rules of forum law, the position in the United Kingdom and the Commonwealth is not so very dissimilar from that in the United States.

The position *is* different in the case of foreign law. Non-derogable rules of foreign law cannot be applied (if not part of the proper law) unless they come within the rule in *Regazzoni* v. *Sethia* or are applicable by reason of some other rule of English public policy. These doctrines were explained in the last chapter. Here there is a clear difference between the law in the United States, on the one hand, and that in the United Kingdom and the Commonwealth, on the other.

We can now consider the cases in various policy areas. We start with the regulation of professional activities, taking estate agents as an example.

§ 2   Estate agents

The profession known in England as that of estate agent and in the United States as that of real estate broker or realtor is subject to regulation in many countries. This is done in the interests of buyers and sellers of land, as well as in the interests of other estate agents[3] and of the public at large. The legislation usually lays down rules designed to ensure the integrity of the profession, and it may provide that estate agents who infringe the rules have no legal claim to the commission which forms their main source of remuneration. Our cases will show how this legislation applies in an international situation.

> **Australia**
> ***Freehold Land Investments Ltd v. Queensland Estates Pty Ltd***
> **High Court of Australia**
> **(1970) 123 CLR 418; (1970) 44 ALJR 329**

Background

The estate agent was a company, Golden Acres, which was incorporated in Hong Kong and carried on business there. It was registered as an estate agent in Hong Kong. The seller of the land was a developer, Queensland Estates, a company incorporated in Queensland, Australia. The land was also in Queensland. The seller approached the estate agent in Hong Kong, apparently hoping to attract buyers from that territory. The contract between the seller and the estate agent,

---

3 Disreputable estate agents damage the profession generally.

which was actually made in Queensland, contained a clause stating that it was deemed to have been made in Hong Kong. This could be regarded as a choice-of-law clause in favour of Hong Kong law.

The estate agent succeeded in finding a number of buyers (some of whom were from Hong Kong) but, when it claimed the commission agreed in the contract, the seller refused to pay. It gave two grounds: first, that the estate agent was not licensed in Queensland; and, secondly, that the rate of commission was above that specified in regulations adopted under the relevant Queensland legislation, the Auctioneers, Real Estate Agents, Debt Collectors and Motor Dealers Acts 1922 to 1961. This legislation required estate agents to be licensed, and provided that unlicensed estate agents had no legal right to their fees. It also provided that commission above that laid down in regulations under the legislation could not in any event be claimed. If the legislation applied, the estate agent had no right to its commission. The estate agent claimed that the legislation was not applicable, since the governing law was that of Hong Kong.

The case came before a Queensland court.[4] The court held that the choice-of-law clause was invalid and ineffective, since it was not *bona fide*. Public policy seems to have been an additional ground. This decision was based on *Vita Food Products* v. *Unus Shipping*,[5] in which it was held that a choice-of-law clause is valid and effective provided it is *bona fide* and not contrary to public policy.

In applying this rule to the case before it, the Queensland court reasoned as follows: in the absence of a valid choice of law, the governing law would be that of Queensland; it would be contrary to the public interest if the application of legislation that would otherwise apply could be circumvented by the 'simple device' of choosing the law of another country; the attempted selection of Hong Kong law was for no other purpose than to avoid the application of the legislation; therefore, the choice of law was not *bona fide*. The result was that the choice-of-law clause was invalid and the law governing the contract as a whole was that of Queensland. The legislation applied and the estate agent lost its claim.

The case went on appeal to the High Court of Australia (the highest court in Australia).

Menzies J

The Act clearly enough is not concerned with what is done outside Queensland, even if it be done in accordance with a contract the proper law of which is the law of Queensland. On the other hand, whatever may be the proper law of an agency contract, the Act applies to a person who acts as, or carries on the business of, a real estate agent in Queensland and a Queensland court would give effect to it. It is not, therefore, possible to support the conclusion which his Honour [the judge in the Queensland court] reached on the ground upon which his Honour based it.

The critical question is rather, did the claimant, in doing what it did pursuant to its agency contract with the owner, act as, or carry on the business of, a real estate

---

4 *Golden Acres* v. *Queensland Estates* [1969] St R Qd 378 (Queensland).
5 [1937] AC 227 (PC).

agent in Queensland? The circumstances here are such that unless the claimant acted as a real estate agent in Queensland in the transaction with which we are concerned it did not carry on business as a real estate agent in Queensland, so that the question can be narrowed down to whether or not, in the course of the negotiation of the sale from Queensland Estates Pty. Ltd. to Golden Acres Ltd., it acted as a real estate agent in Queensland.

Walsh J

The Parliament of Queensland could have legislated validly for the control of agents who engaged, either in Queensland or elsewhere, in selling or buying or otherwise dealing with land or other property situated within the State of Queensland. It might have selected the locality of the property rather than the locality of the activities of the agents as providing a sufficient territorial connexion between the legislation and the State of Queensland. However the Act does not contain any express statement by which its general words are confined by some territorial limitation . . . However I am of opinion that it is right to suppose that the relevant provisions of the Act . . . should be construed so as to apply only to persons who in Queensland act as real estate agents or carry on the business of a real estate agent.

All the judges agreed that the Act should be applied on the basis set out above. A majority agreed that Golden Acres acted as an estate agent in Queensland. The appeal was dismissed: the commission was not recoverable.

Comment

This case is a good example of the application of the doctrine of an overriding statute. Even though the proper law was that of Hong Kong – the High Court rejected the Queensland court's argument that the choice of law was invalid – the statute could still override that choice of law if this is what the legislature intended. The problem was simply one of determining its intended international scope: was it intended to apply whenever the land was in Queensland or when the estate agent acted in Queensland? The High Court decided that the latter was the correct interpretation.

United States (District of Columbia)
Dorothy K. Winston & Co. v. Town Heights Development Inc.
United States District Court, District of Columbia
376 F Supp 1214 (1974)

Background

This case is the opposite of the previous case, since the action was brought in the estate agent's state, rather than in that in which the land was situated. Dorothy Winston was an estate agent registered in the District of Columbia; Town Heights was a property development company in Florida. The land was in Florida. It seems that the developer's agent went to the District of Columbia and approached the estate agent there. In her attempts to find a buyer, the estate agent did not specifically target Florida, but sought buyers in various states in the eastern United States. In the end, the buyer came from Florida, but the court found that this was purely fortuitous.

The developers refused to pay the estate agent's fee on the ground that she was not registered in Florida. Under Florida legislation, an unregistered estate agent could not sue for his fee. The developers argued that the Florida statute was applicable because the land was situated there.

June L Green, District Judge

The third of defendant's motions concerns choice of law. It is defendant's position that the case law of the District of Columbia directs this Court to apply the substantive law of Florida, which would clearly result in a dismissal of this action. It is undisputed that [the Florida statute] precludes recovery of a real estate sales commission for the sale of Florida land unless the real estate broker is duly registered and licensed by the State of Florida. The plaintiffs are not now, and were not during the period in question, registered real estate brokers in the State of Florida.

Defendant's conclusion that Florida law must be applied is reached by the following process: First, defendant argues that the conflict of laws standard applicable in the District of Columbia is 'interest analysis', which requires a sorting out of the different 'significant contacts with this controversy' which each jurisdiction has 'in an attempt to determine the relationship of each jurisdiction to the controversy, and to evaluate the interest of each in the application of its own rule of law.'

. . .

The Court finds that Florida's law is intended to protect the Florida land purchasing community from disreputable real estate dealers, primarily local dealers. If the plaintiffs sought out the defendant in Florida and actively proposed business deals in Florida, then Florida's registration law should be given extra-territorial effect in a suit filed in the District of Columbia. But in this case, the plaintiffs were approached by defendant's agent in DC and the contract was formed in DC to be performed in DC, Florida and other Eastern states. In this fact situation, DC's interest in insuring performance of this contract would be unduly hampered by the application of Florida law while not significantly advancing Florida's public policy. Whereas, if DC law is applied, performance can be insured with only a minimal compromise of Florida's interest.

DC law will thus govern this case and defendant's motion to the contrary is denied.

Comment

This case shows interest analysis applied to determine the scope of foreign law. The phrase 'Florida land purchasing community' presumably refers to Florida residents who purchase land, rather than to persons (from any state) who purchase land in Florida. Florida had no interest in the application of its law if the estate agent was not targeting Florida buyers. The fact that the Florida seller came to the estate agent in DC was not strictly relevant to Florida's interest in the application of its law, but it was relevant to DC's interest in the application of its law. If persons from another state come to DC to do business with local persons, they cannot take restrictive provisions of their law with them.

These cases both show how the international reach of a statute can be discovered by an analysis of its purpose. There have been several similar cases in Canada. However, though the right result was reached, the reasoning in them was unsatisfactory.[6]

PROBLEM

Two estate agents, both licensed in Ontario, work in Toronto. The company they work for is retained to lease space in a building in Calgary, Alberta. They agree that any commission earned will be shared between them. The contract states that it is governed by the law of Ontario. At first, they commute between Toronto and Calgary, but the defendant later moves to Calgary and becomes licensed there. The plaintiff, who never becomes licensed in Alberta, remains in Toronto and eventually ceases working actively in Calgary. For this reason, the defendant refuses to give him any share in the commission. The plaintiff sues him in Alberta. Alberta has a statute precluding an unlicensed estate agent from claiming commission for real estate activities. How should the court decide?[7] How should the court decide under the Rome I Regulation?

§ 3   Lawyers

The legal profession is also subject to regulation. The reasons for this are similar to those applicable to estate agents. Our next case shows how such legislation applies in an inter-state context.

United States (New Jersey)
Newcomb* v. *Daniels, Saltz, Mongeluzzi & Barrett Ltd
United States District Court for the District of New Jersey
847 F Supp 1244 (1994); affirmed 67 F 3d 292 (3rd Cir. 1995); cert. denied 516 US 1117; 116 S Ct 921; 133 L Ed 2d 850 (US Supreme Court, 1996)

Background

Newcomb, a resident of New Jersey, had been injured in an industrial accident in that state. The defendants were a law firm which represented him in proceedings

---

6 *Block Bros Realty* v. *Mollard* (1981) 122 DLR (3d) 323 (British Columbia Court of Appeal); *Ross* v. *McMullen* (1971) 21 DLR (3d) 228 (Alberta); *Gillespie Management Corporation* v. *Terrace Properties* (1989) 62 DLR (4th) 221; (1989) 39 BCLR (2d) 337 (British Columbia Court of Appeal).
7 This case is based on *Ross* v. *McMullen* (1971) 21 DLR (3d) 228, but the facts have been changed by stating that the contract has an express choice of law in favour of the law of Ontario.

to obtain compensation. Mongeluzzi, a partner in the firm who was an attorney in both New Jersey and Pennsylvania, had originally approached Mr and Mrs Newcomb at their home in New Jersey. Some time later, an agreement was signed in New Jersey under which the law firm would conduct the case in return for a contingent fee of 40 per cent. Such a fee was legal under Pennsylvania law, but was illegal in New Jersey under rules designed to prevent excessive fees.[8] Legal proceedings were commenced in Pennsylvania and the action was settled for US$1 million. Mr and Mrs Newcomb, however, refused to give the law firm 40 per cent of this. They found new lawyers and brought suit in New Jersey claiming that the fee agreement was invalid under New Jersey law.

Gerry, Chief Judge

The issue of which state's law should apply is the major point of contention in this case. The defendant contends that Pennsylvania law, which would permit the 40 per cent fee arrangement, applies. The plaintiffs contend that New Jersey law, which would limit the fee to a significantly lower percentage, applies. In a diversity action, the court's choice of law is governed by the law of the state where the court sits . . . Thus, New Jersey choice of law rules apply in this case.

The defendant firm points out that New Jersey choice of law rules generally favor the enforcement of an express choice of law by the parties to a contract, and urges that such an express choice of law exists here. Although the defendant acknowledges that the contract at issue never explicitly mentions Pennsylvania law, the defendant argues that the 40 per cent fee arrangement suggests that the parties intended Pennsylvania law to apply because such a provision would be valid only under Pennsylvania law. The defendant further argues that Mr Mongeluzzi's discussions with the Newcombs prior to the signing of the contract, wherein he advised the Newcombs of the differences between Pennsylvania and New Jersey contingent fee law further support the contention that the 40 per cent provision expresses the parties' intention to have Pennsylvania law apply.

Based on the defendant's argument, we acknowledge that at least one genuine issue of fact relevant to the issue of whether the parties made an effective choice of law remains. However, for the reasons set forth below, we conclude that any fact relevant to this issue is immaterial to the resolution of the case, because even if we were to assume that the parties made an explicit choice of Pennsylvania law in this contract, this court could not enforce such a choice.

Under New Jersey law, if the parties to a contract agree that a particular state's law will govern their rights and duties under the contract, the courts will generally honor the agreement, unless . . . [the court then set out § 187(b) of the Restatement.] . . . The present facts present a situation calling for the application of § 187(b).

In order to override the choice of law of the parties to the contract under the considerations of § 187(b), a court must find: (1) that the application of Pennsylvania law would be contrary to a fundamental policy of New Jersey;

---

8 The maximum permitted was 33 per cent on the first US$250,000; 25 per cent on the next US$250,000 and 20 per cent on the next US$500,000. This would have worked out at a little over half the agreed fee.

(2) that New Jersey has a materially greater interest than Pennsylvania in the determination of the particular question at issue; and (3) that under the general choice of law considerations of § 188 of the Restatement (Second) of Conflict of Laws, New Jersey law would apply.

. . .

The facts of the present situation compel reasoning similar to that employed in [a New Jersey precedent]. First, we find that under the present circumstances, the choice of another state's law would violate New Jersey public policy. New Jersey has a strong interest in regulating the economic relationship between New Jersey attorneys and their clients in tort cases . . . New Jersey's contingent fee rules are designed to protect clients negotiating fee arrangements from the greater knowledge and bargaining power of their attorneys . . . One New Jersey court has noted that when the contingent fee rule was promulgated, the Director of the Administrative Office of the Courts issued a notice to the bar emphasizing this policy:

> The Supreme Court considers that [the limits set forth in R 1:21–7(c)] apply to any Contingent Fee arrangement in a tort matter entered into by a New Jersey attorney, without regard to the Court in which an action may subsequently be filed, and to any participation by a New Jersey attorney in a Contingent Fee arrangement entered into outside the State of New Jersey with respect to litigation in this State. This is not intended to deny the authority of the Federal Courts to apply a different standard to implement some other Federal policy.
> Notice to the Bar, 95 NJLJ 341 (1972) . . .

As indicated in this notice, the policy embodied in the fee limitation rule extends to the present facts. Here, a New Jersey attorney entered into a contingent fee arrangement in New Jersey in connection with a cause of action for which the attorney subsequently filed a claim in another state. In fact, the present facts provide even more support for the application of New Jersey public policy than the situation described in the notice: the subject of the underlying dispute was an accident that took place in New Jersey.

Judicial enforcement of a choice of law provision such as the one at issue here would permit attorneys to circumvent the strong public policy of the State of New Jersey in protecting its citizens . . . [I]t would permit attorneys to wipe away the protective effects of the New Jersey contingent fee limitations 'with the sweep of a pen.'

Applying the second prong of the § 187(b) analysis . . . we find that New Jersey has a greater interest in applying its law to the particular circumstances than does Pennsylvania. Although Pennsylvania has an interest equal to New Jersey's in protecting its citizens from the overreaching of attorneys in contingent fee cases, Pennsylvania's interest does not apply where the client involved is a New Jersey citizen injured in New Jersey who negotiated his contingent fee contract in New Jersey with a New Jersey-licensed attorney . . . [W]e assume that the other state with an interest here would apply its own law in converse circumstances: we assume that Pennsylvania would apply its own contingent fee law to a case where the Pennsylvania client who was injured in Pennsylvania negotiated his contingent fee contract in Pennsylvania with a Pennsylvania-licensed attorney. Thus, we conclude that New Jersey has a materially greater interest than Pennsylvania in the determination of the issues here.

The third § 187(b) consideration requires us to consider whether New Jersey has a more 'significant relationship', as defined by § 188, to the contract or transaction than Pennsylvania does . . . [After setting out § 188(1). the court continued:]

We conclude that New Jersey law would apply under these factors.

In following § 188's directive that we evaluate the various contacts enumerated 'according to their relative importance with respect to the particular issue', we find that some of the § 188 factors weigh more heavily than others in the context of this case. The goal of the contingent fee limitations in achieving client protection counsels in favor of assigning greater weight to the place of contract, the place of negotiation and the domicile of the clients, rather than the place of performance. The former factors focus on the clients' location and their reasonable expectations when entering into an attorney's fee agreement.

Given these considerations, we find that New Jersey holds a greater interest in having its state's law applied than does Pennsylvania. The clients to be protected here, the plaintiffs, lived in New Jersey. The negotiations took place in their New Jersey home. Furthermore, the attorney who contacted the plaintiffs, Mr Mongeluzzi, is a member of the New Jersey bar. The only factor weighing in favor of the application of Pennsylvania law in this case is that the performance was to take place in Pennsylvania. This factor being less important in this particular consideration, and all the other more important factors weighing in favor of the application of New Jersey law, we conclude that New Jersey law would apply under the 'most significant relationship' test of § 188.

In sum . . . we find that the contravention of the strong New Jersey public policy protecting clients in attorney contingent fee contracts by the choice of Pennsylvania law under the circumstances demonstrated here should not and would not be countenanced by a court of this state. Further, we find that New Jersey holds a more significant interest in having its law applied in such circumstances. Finally, in applying general choice of law principles, we find that New Jersey has the more significant relationship to the contract in this case. We accordingly hold that we would refuse to enforce the agreement in this case if there was one, and that New Jersey law applies here.

Comment

Since the purpose of the New Jersey rules was to protect clients, it was reasonable to look to the residence of the clients and the place where they were approached by the attorney. The same result would be reached under Article 6 of the Rome I Regulation.

In the common law, there used to be a rule prohibiting a lawyer from taking a case on the basis of a contingent fee, that is, a fee payable only if the proceedings are successful. Originally, this constituted the crime (and tort) of champerty, now abolished in England. The rationale for prohibiting contingent fees was that, if the lawyer has a stake in the outcome of the case, he might be tempted to act dishonestly.

This is the background to *Grell* v. *Levy*,[9] a case decided in 1864, at a time when contingent fees were still unlawful in England. Grell, a national and resident of France, was owed a debt by someone in England. He agreed with Levy, an English attorney,[10] that, if Levy would recover the debt for him, Levy could keep half of it as his fee. The agreement was made in France and was written in French. Levy recovered the debt (the action against the debtor was settled) and gave half the proceeds to Grell. The latter, however, claimed the whole debt, arguing that the agreement with Levy was illegal under English law. Levy argued that it was governed by French law. The court rejected this argument: it was irrelevant that it was valid in France, since Levy was an English attorney practising in England. He was therefore obliged to hand over the rest of the money (minus his costs).

This decision was plainly right under the law as it stood at the time, and the same result has been reached in Canada.[11] The purpose of the rule was to ensure the integrity of judicial proceedings and to prevent the corruption of the legal profession; so the rule had to be applied if the proceedings took take place in the territory of the forum or the lawyer practised there.

§ 4   Employees

We now consider provisions for the protection of employees. Two problems have been selected: clauses in a contract of employment exempting the employer from liability for injury to the employee and clauses under which the employee agrees not to compete with the employer if he leaves his employ.

§ 4.1   Exemption clauses

In many legal systems, an employer is liable to compensate an employee if the latter is injured in the course of his work. A clause in the contract of employment exempting the employer from such liability is normally invalid. This is the case in the United Kingdom, where a statute (applicable to both England and Scotland), the Law Reform (Personal Injuries) Act 1948, section 1(3), states that such clauses are invalid. It provides:

---

9 (1864) 10 CB (NS) 73 (143 ER 1052).
10 In England at that time, an attorney was a lawyer practising before the courts of common law and a solicitor was a practitioner before the courts of equity; both would instruct barristers to appear in court. Today in England, the persons formerly known as attorneys and those formerly known as solicitors are both called solicitors. Barristers are still a separate profession. In the United States, on the other hand, all these professions have been merged into one and the persons practising it are normally called attorneys. See Garner (Bryan A.), *A Dictionary of Modern Legal Usage* (2nd edn, 1995), p. 90.
11 *MacMahon* v. *Taugher* (1914) 32 OLR 494; 20 DLR 521 (CA); *Waters* v. *Campbell* (1914) 17 DLR 79 (Alberta CA).

Any provision contained in a contract of service[12] or apprenticeship, or in an agreement collateral thereto (including a contract or agreement entered into before the commencement of this Act), shall be void in so far as it would have the effect of excluding or limiting any liability of the employer in respect of personal injuries caused to the person employed or apprenticed by the negligence of persons in common employment with him.

When will this apply in an international context?

England
Sayers* v. *International Drilling Co. NV
Court of Appeal
[1971] 1 WLR 1176

Background

This case concerned a contract of employment on an oil rig in Nigerian waters. The employer was a Dutch company and the employee was English. The contract was in the English language, was signed in England and provided for payment of the employee's salary to be made in British currency in England. It gave the employee certain rights to compensation in the event of injury but, beyond this, excluded any liability on the part of the employer. This clause was void under the Law Reform (Personal Injuries) Act 1948, section 1(3). Although there was a similar provision under Dutch law, this applied – it seems – only if the employment took place within the Netherlands. Where it took place outside the Netherlands, the exclusionary clause was valid. The employee was injured on the oil rig in Nigeria and he sued the employer in tort in England. The employer raised the exemption clause as a defence.

On a trial of a preliminary issue, the lower court held that the proper law of the contract was that of the Netherlands. An interlocutory appeal on this point was taken to the Court of Appeal.

Lord Denning MR

[After setting out the terms of section 1(3) of the 1948 statute, said:]

The Dutch company, however, seek to avoid that English statute. They say that Mr Sayers' contract of service was not governed by English law, but by Dutch law. It appears that Dutch law has a somewhat similar provision in Article 1638X of the Netherlands Civil Code. It says that:

> Any condition whereby these obligations of the employer are excluded or restricted is void.

But the Dutch company say that that Dutch Article only applies to a contract which is entirely a Dutch contract. It, they say, does not apply to an international contract such as the one signed by Mr Sayers. They say that according to Dutch law the exclusion clause in this contract would be valid.

---

12 This means a contract of employment.

In view of this controversy, the master ordered a preliminary issue to be tried. The issue shortly is whether the Dutch company can rely on the exemption clause as an answer to the action.

The issue raises an important question of private international law. On the one hand, the claim by the plaintiff is a claim founded on tort. In considering that claim, we must apply the proper law of tort, that is, the law of the country with which the parties and the acts done have the most significant connection . . .[1]

On the other hand, the defence by the defendants is a defence based on contract. In considering that defence we must apply the proper law of the contract, that is, the system of law with which the contract has its closest and most real connection . . .

But it is obvious that we cannot apply two systems of law, one for the claim in tort, and the other for the defence in contract. We must apply one system of law by which to decide both claim and defence. To decide it I would ask this question: What is the proper law by which to determine the issues in this case? And I would answer it by saying: it is the system of law with which the issues have the closest connection.

So far as the claim in tort is concerned, the accident took place in the territorial waters of *Nigeria*. But it took place on an oil drilling rig owned and controlled by a *Dutch* company and manned by employees of that company. The Nigerians had nothing to do with the rig. So Nigeria is out. The injured man was *English*, but his fellow employees (who were negligent) may have been English or American or of some other nationality. The only common bond between them was that they were employed by the Dutch company. So Dutch is in. If I were asked to decide the proper law of the *tort* (apart from contract) I should have said it was *Dutch* law.

So far as the defence in contract is concerned, the contract with Mr Sayers was negotiated and *made* in England. It was for the services of Mr Sayers, an *Englishman*, asking him to go overseas for a spell of work. It was in the *English* language. His salary was to be paid in the *English* currency, sterling. He was insured under the *English* national insurance scheme. He was to come back on leave to his home in *England*. True it is that the employers were Dutch (who employed personnel of all nationalities), but the contract was administered in London. The records were kept in London, Texas and Holland. If I were asked to decide the proper law of the contract (apart from the tort) I should be inclined to say that it was English.

But seeing that the action is founded on tort and the proper law of the tort is Dutch, I would say that, as between the two systems, English or Dutch, the issue of liability should be determined by Dutch law. In any case, there is a provision in clause 8 of the contract which turns the scale against English law. It runs thus:

> As the company is a Netherlands corporation, and as my employment contract hereby applied for will be wholly performable overseas and outside of United Kingdom, the company does not subscribe to or carry workmen's compensation

---

1 *Editor's note*: as explained in the 'Comment' below, this was an incorrect statement of English law.

> insurance under the laws of United Kingdom. Accordingly, I realize that I shall not
> be covered by virtue of my proposed employment with the company by workmen's
> compensation insurance or benefits under the law of United Kingdom . . . I am
> satisfied with the provisions and benefits of the said Compensation Program.

Seeing that English law is in terms excluded, I think that the issue of liability has its closest connection with Dutch law: and should be determined by Dutch law. According to that law this exemption clause is valid and effective to bar Mr Sayers' claim in tort. His claim must be limited to the benefits in the Dutch company's Compensation Program.

I am confirmed in this view by the very fair answers given by Mr Sayers to the judge. Bean J asked him:

> 'You realised in signing the contract you were accepting the company's scheme
> for compensation in the event of injury as opposed to what you might have been
> entitled to by way of compensation under English law?' Mr Sayers answered: 'Having
> signed it, I would have to.' The judge asked him: 'Can you help me as to what you
> thought at the time of signing?' Mr Sayers answered: 'It says that if you are injured
> and the company is at fault you would be looked after, you place your faith in the
> company.'

Seeing that Mr Sayers put his faith in the company, I trust that the company will play fair by him and grant him just compensation for his injuries.

I agree with the judge that the matter is governed by Dutch law and is not to be determined by the English law. I would dismiss the appeal accordingly.

Salmon LJ

I agree that this appeal should be dismissed.

The action is for damages for negligence. The defendants by their defence deny negligence and allege contributory negligence. They take the preliminary point, however, that the proper law of the contract of employment is Dutch law, that in Dutch law this contract is what is known as an international contract, and that accordingly clause 8 of the contract, which excludes the plaintiff's right to recover damages otherwise than under what is called the Compensation Program, is a complete answer to the claim for damages for negligence. The plaintiff contends that the contract of employment is governed by English law and that accordingly the exclusion clause is rendered nugatory by section 1(3) of the Law Reform (Personal Injuries) Act 1948. The master left all the issues other than negligence and contributory negligence to be decided as a preliminary point. The judge who tried that preliminary point decided it and all the issues it comprised in the defendants' favour. It is plain that under Dutch law in the ordinary way any term of a contract of employment which excludes the master's liability for negligence is of no effect. However, according to the evidence called before the judge, there is in Dutch law a distinction between an ordinary contract and what is called an international contract of employment. As far as an international contract is concerned the clause excluding the master's liability for negligence is effective. There was no explanation in the evidence of the Dutch lawyer as to what constitutes an international contract; nor any authority cited as to the effect of such a contract. However, there was no cross-examination and no evidence called on the part of the plaintiff on this issue. The judge accordingly had no alternative other than to accept as he did the evidence of the Dutch lawyer. Therefore the only point which then remained was as to what system of law governs the contract. Accordingly, if the defendants are correct in their contention that the proper law of the contract is Dutch law, having regard to the view of the Dutch law which on the evidence was necessarily accepted by the judge, this action is dead.

It follows that the only point on this appeal is: was the judge right in coming to the conclusion that the proper law of the contract of employment is Dutch law? I confess that I do not find this at all an easy point . . . My difficulty in this case is that I can find very little clue in the contract as to what the parties intended, and very little indication that the contract has a very real or close connection with any particular system of law. I agree, however, with Lord Denning MR, that on the whole the conclusion at which the judge arrived ought not to be disturbed.

One thing about which everyone was agreed was that whatever system of law ought to be applied to this contract, it should not be the Nigerian system of law. The work under the contract was being carried out in the territorial waters of Nigeria. The contract itself, however, stated that although the work was expected to be done in Nigeria, the company had the right to change the venue of the work; in other words, under this contract the plaintiff could have been ordered to work in any part of the world other than the United Kingdom. So Nigerian law is out, and that leaves us with a choice of English or Dutch law. There are, as Lord Denning MR has said, a number of factors supporting the view that perhaps English law was intended to be the law governing the contract. The contract was made with an Englishman in England; it is in the English language and payment under it is to be made in sterling. I do not, however, think that in this case those factors have very much significance. Looking at the contract itself, one finds that it is entered into on a printed form of contract drawn up by the Dutch company for the purpose of engaging European personnel. The printed form leaves a blank for the country of origin of the servant to be engaged under the contract. He may be of any European nationality. It is apparent, I think, that although this contract is in the English language and refers to payment in sterling, it is using a language and a currency of convenience for the purpose of dealing with a multiplicity of nationals. Moreover, as [counsel for International Drilling] points out without any disrespect, this contract, having regard to its phraseology and spelling, could be described as being in the American rather than in the English language, and therefore the fact that it is written in what may be English has even less significance than it would ordinarily have, and it never has very much. Anyone reading the contract would see that it had been drafted by an American and everyone concerned in this case knew that the parent of the defendant company was a United States company; but no one could have supposed that the law applicable to the contract was intended to be American law. The ordinary intelligent prospective servant reading through this contract would, I think, recognise – as indeed Mr Sayers did – that the form of contract could well be used for engaging an Italian, a Spaniard, a Greek and an Englishman or any other European. It could not be supposed that if, for example, an Italian were to be engaged in Italy under this form of contract he would expect the contract to be governed by English or even Italian law any more than would the Dutch company. The plaintiff entering into this form of contract in England must, I think, have recognised that when he went out to Nigeria or to whatever other part of the world he might be sent, he could well find himself working on a rig with an Italian, a Greek and a Spaniard. He could not have believed that his contractual rights would be governed by a different law from that of his fellow employees, still less that there would be five different laws governing the contractual rights of, say, five different employees. If it were so, it would be awkward for the employers, awkward for their employees, and difficult to give the contracts ordinary business efficacy. Therefore, in spite of the fact that the contract is in the English language, payment in sterling, and the nationality of the plaintiff is English, I cannot accept the argument that this contract is governed by English law.

. . .

If English and Nigerian law are to be excluded, this leaves only Dutch law as the law which governs the contract. I think that since the Dutch employers were engaging people of various nationalities in different parts of the world to work abroad together it certainly gives the greatest business efficacy to such contracts to presume that the parties must have intended to adhere to the law of Holland, or, put in a different way, that that system of law has the closest and most real connection with the contract.

Another pointer which I think indicates Dutch law is that under that system of law it is permissible, in this type of contract, to exclude the employer's ordinary liability in negligence and to substitute for it the rights under what is called the Compensation Program. This is a pointer (although its importance must not be exaggerated) which suggests that the parties may well have intended the contract to be governed by a system of law under which it would be valid rather than invalid, namely, Dutch law rather than English law.

On the whole, therefore, although not without doubt, I have come to the conclusion that the proper law of this contract is Dutch law and that accordingly this appeal should be dismissed.

Stamp LJ agreed that the proper law was Netherlands law. His reasons were similar to those given by Salmon LJ. **Result:** the interlocutory appeal was dismissed: the trial judge was correct in holding that the law of the Netherlands was the proper law of the contract.

Comment

It must be borne in mind that this was an interlocutory appeal. It was not an appeal against a final judgment by the trial court – this had not yet been given – but simply against one ruling by the trial court: that the contract of employment was governed by Dutch law. This was all that the Court of Appeal had to decide. On this basis, the ruling, by Salmon and Stamp LJJ, that the contract of employment was governed by Dutch law was not unreasonable. What is not acceptable is the conclusion – which Lord Denning reached by a different route – that this disposed of the employee's claim.[13]

The mistake of the majority (Salmon and Stamp LJJ) was the assumption that the case was entirely a matter of contract, despite the fact that the claim was brought in tort. Lord Denning accepted that the claim was in tort, but his solution was open to criticism on two counts. First, his statement that the choice-of-law rule for torts was the proper law of the tort was simply wrong. As will be remembered from the discussion in Chapter 23, the leading case at the time was *Chaplin* v. *Boys*.[14] When this case came before the Court of Appeal, Lord Denning put forward his theory of the proper law of the tort. The case then went on appeal to the House of Lords. Although the members of the House of Lords were not in agreement as to the correct rule, they clearly rejected this theory. So Lord Denning ought not to have said in *Sayers* that the proper-law theory applied to torts. Secondly, there was no justification for applying a combined proper law of the contract-plus-tort.

How should the case have been decided, assuming that it was procedurally possible for the court to decide the whole case in one judgment? Since, under English law, a claimant in a situation like this is entitled to frame his action in either contract or tort,[15] and since the claimant in this case had chosen to frame it in tort, the court should have started off by deciding what the applicable law for the tort was. Under the law as it stood at the time (*Chaplin* v. *Boys*), the claimant had to show that he would have had a cause of action in tort if the tort had been committed in England and, in addition, that there was civil liability under the law of the country where the tort was committed. This 'double-actionability' rule was subject to an exception, but it is doubtful whether that exception would have been applicable in *Sayers*, since one cannot say that the tort was clearly more closely connected with either England or the Netherlands. So the case was probably governed by the general rule.[16]

The correct way of dealing with the exemption clause would have been, first, to see whether the law governing the tort permitted the claim to be excluded by a contractual provision.[17] If the answer was negative, that should have been the end of the matter as far as the exemption clause was concerned. If it was positive, then – and only then – should the court have looked at the proper law of the contract.[18]

---

13 The case was subject to strong criticism when it was decided: Smith, 'International Employment Contracts – Contracting Out' (1972) 21 ICLQ 164; and Collins, 'Exemption Clauses, Employment Contracts and the Conflict of Laws' (1972) 21 ICLQ 320. This criticism has continued: North, 'Contract as a Tort Defence in the Conflict of Laws' (1977) 26 ICLQ 914 at pp. 923–7; Morse (C. G. J), *Torts in Private International Law* (North-Holland Publishing Co., Amsterdam, 1978), pp. 192–4.
14 [1971] AC 356; [1969] 3 WLR 322; [1969] 2 All ER 1085 (HL) (discussed in Chapter 23, § 4, above).
15 In some legal systems, the position is different.
16 If the case were decided under the Rome II Regulation, the law of the country where the accident took place (Nigeria) would be applicable: Article 4(1). It is doubtful whether the escape clause in Article 4(3) would apply, since the pre-existing (contractual) relationship between the parties was not clearly based on either English or Dutch law; so one could not say that the tort was *manifestly* more closely connected with a country other than Nigeria.
17 Under Article 15(b) of the Rome II Regulation, the law applicable to the tort governs 'the grounds for exemption from liability'.
18 Dicey, Morris and Collins, pp. 1918–19.

Applying this approach to the facts of the case, we must first consider whether the law governing the tort permitted claims in tort to be excluded by contract. Under the 'double-actionability' rule, this would have to be decided twice, first under English law and then under Nigerian law.[19] Under English law, the answer was clear: section 1(3) of the Act said that exemption clauses could not deprive the claimant of his right to sue in tort.[20] Then one would have to look to Nigerian law to see what it said. In the case, the court was not able to do this because neither party pleaded or proved Nigerian law. However, if the claim had been properly argued, this would have been done. If Nigerian law had been the same as English law, the exemption clause would have had no effect, no matter what Dutch law said.

The failure of the English courts to adopt this approach was mainly due to the way in which it was argued by the claimant. The result was unfortunate. There can be no doubt that, if the employee had worked (and the accident had taken place) in either England or the Netherlands, the exemption clause would have been void.[21] The only ground for reaching a different result when the employee worked (and the accident occurred) in a third country was that the law of that country should apply. However, the court expressly disclaimed any reliance on the law of Nigeria: it said it was irrelevant. So there was no justification for making the employee worse off, because he was in an international situation, than he would have been if all the facts had been located in one country only.

Lord Denning, a judge renowned for his sense of justice, seems to have been unhappy at the outcome. Hence his rather pathetic statement that he trusted the company would play fair by the worker and grant him just compensation. It is hard to imagine that the company would have paid any attention to this.[22] Altogether, this was an unfortunate decision.

In our next case, decided in Scotland, the facts were similar, except for one important difference: the accident occurred in the United Kingdom.

Scotland
Brodin v. *A/R Seljan*
Court of Session (Outer House)
1973 SC 213

Background

The pursuer (claimant) was a seaman. He was a Norwegian citizen, but was domiciled in Scotland. He had signed a contract with a Norwegian shipping company to work on one of their ships. The accident took place in a Scottish port and the seaman sued the employer for damages in Scotland.[23] The employer claimed that the contract of employment was governed by Norwegian law, under which any

---

19 Under the Rome II Regulation, it would only have to be decided once.
20 Our next case, *Brodin* v. *Seljan*, establishes this. This assumes that the tort took place in England, an assumption that must be made under the first prong of the 'double-actionability' rule.
21 For England, see our next case, *Brodin* v. *Seljan*.
22 According to the law report, he had been paid only 'small sums' by the company.
23 The employee subsequently died and his widow continued the action.

liability in tort on the part of the employer was excluded. As mentioned above, section 1(3) of the Law Reform (Personal Injuries) Act 1948 applied in Scotland as well as England.

Lord Kissen

The essence of the argument for the pursuer was that the delict,[1] which is the basis of the pursuer's action, occurred in Scotland, that therefore the law which governs the rights of the parties in this action is Scots law, that said section 1(3) of the said Act of 1948 accordingly applies and that the defence, based on Norwegian law, is irrelevant. The submission was, in other words, that the *lex loci delicti*, which in this case is also the *lex fori*, was paramount. The essence of the argument for the first defenders was that the law which governed the rights of the parties in this reparation action was the proper law of the said contract of service, under which the deceased was employed at the material time, that this was Norwegian law, and that said section 1(3) could not apply in these circumstances. The fact that the said accident occurred in Scotland had, it was said, no bearing on the rights of the parties. The submission was, in other words, that the *lex loci contractus* was paramount.

. . .

I propose to consider, firstly, the submissions which were made on behalf of the first defenders. Not only is this approach more convenient but it is also consistent with my view that, in the particular circumstances of this case, the onus is on the first defenders to prove that said section 1(3) does not apply in this case because of Norwegian Law . . .

[Lord Kissen then referred to the *Sayers* case, and continued:] The vital difference from the present case is that the accident occurred when the plaintiff was employed on the defendants' oil rig off the Nigerian coast and in the territorial waters of Nigeria. The Court of Appeal decided that said section 1(3) did not apply and could not be invoked by the plaintiff. The ground of the decision by Lord Denning MR was that the proper law of the tort was Dutch, and that, as the claim was founded on tort, the issue of liability should be decided by Dutch Law, despite the fact that, according to him, the proper law of the contract of employment was English. On the other hand, the ground of the decision by both Salmon LJ and Stamp LJ was that the proper law of the contract of employment was Dutch and that accordingly the rights of the plaintiff were governed by Dutch Law.

I do not think that this case can assist the first defenders. The facts were different in that, in the present case, the accident occurred in Scotland where section 1(3) of the said Act of 1948 is part of the law relating to delicts. Another difference is that the terms of employment were such that the pursuer in the present case would be employed, at times, in ports in England where said section 1(3) is also part of the law relating to torts . . . Apart altogether from this, I have some difficulty in finding any consistent principle from the differing grounds for that decision. The first defenders' counsel founded strongly on the majority grounds but they cannot,

1 *Editor's note*: 'delict' is the Scots word for 'tort'.

in my opinion, apply to the completely different circumstances here. It might be possible to argue, from Lord Denning's opinion, that the 'law of the tort' in this case was Scots law in that the acts done have most connection with Scotland where the accident occurred and where the deceased was domiciled. I think, however, as I have said, that this case is of no assistance. I add that I was referred by pursuer's counsel to strong criticisms of this decision in two articles in Volume 21 of the International and Comparative Law Quarterly at pp. 164 and 335.[2]

The principle governing the decision in *Sayers, supra* was, it was maintained by the first defenders' counsel, in line with a general principle which supported their argument. This general principle of statutory construction was that there was a presumption against the application of a statute 'extra-territorially', that 'extra-territorially' included the operation of a contract which was governed by foreign law and that said section 1(3) could not therefore apply to the contract of employment which was governed by Norwegian law . . .

[After referring to *English* v. *Donnelly*, set out below in § 5, Lord Kissen continued:] The terms of said section 1(3) of the said Act of 1948 are as mandatory and as peremptory as [the statutory provision in issue in *English* v. *Donnelly*]. An object of the contract on which the first defenders found in this case is the 'contracting out' of a peremptory statutory provision of the *lex fori* and the *lex loci delicti*. There is, furthermore, no limitation stated and the application must be to persons and conduct in, among other places, Scotland. Whatever the law chosen by the parties to govern a contract or whatever the law of a contract may be, that law must, I think, yield to an Act of Parliament which has provided otherwise. The provision is, in other words, unenforceable in Scotland, whatever its effect elsewhere.

2 *Editor's note*: 335 seems to be a misprint for 320.

Result: section 1(3) was applicable: the contract of employment could not exclude the seaman's right of action in tort.

Comment

In this case, the law governing the tort was unquestionably Scottish law. So section 1(3) of the Act was, as the judge said, applicable as part of the law of the tort (*lex loci delicti*). However, since it was a non-derogable provision, it was applicable to the contract even if the contract was governed by Norwegian law. Under the terminology of the time, it was an overriding statute; under the terminology of the Rome I Regulation, it was an overriding mandatory provision of the law of the forum, in terms of Article 9(2). Article 8 would also have been relevant, though the case does not provide sufficient facts to make clear how it would have applied.

§ 4.2   Agreements not to compete

When an employee works for an employer, the contract of employment sometimes provides that the employee cannot compete with the employer in the same line of business for a specified period after ceasing to work for him. In some legal systems, such a clause is invalid because it limits the employee's right to work and because it would have a bad effect on the economy. However, the employer might have a legitimate interest in ensuring that the employee does not use the employer's business secrets to set up a rival business. For this reason, some legal systems permit such clauses, provided they are no wider than necessary to protect the employer's legitimate interests. These differences could give rise to choice-of-law problems.

Georgia
Nasco Inc. v. *Gimbert*
Supreme Court of Georgia
239 Ga 675; 238 SE 2d 368 (1977)

Background

The employer was a Tennessee corporation and the employee was resident in Georgia. The work was performed in Georgia. The employee agreed that, for a period of two years, he would not compete with the employer, nor would he solicit business from the employer's customers or disclose the employer's business secrets. The contract contained a choice-of-law clause in favour of Tennessee law. The employee stopped working for the employer and allegedly violated these restrictive covenants. The employer sued in Georgia. The trial court ruled that Georgia law was applicable and held for the employee. The employer appealed.

Hill, Justice

Although the plaintiff and the defendant had agreed that the contract would be construed pursuant to the law of Tennessee, the trial court applied the law of Georgia. We find no error. The law of the jurisdiction chosen by parties to a contract to govern their contractual rights will not be applied by Georgia courts where application of the chosen law would contravene the policy of, or would be prejudicial to the interests of, this state . . . Covenants against disclosure, like covenants against competition, affect the interests of this state, namely the flow of information needed for competition among businesses, and hence their validity is determined by the public policy of this state . . .

Comment

In European terms, one could say that Georgia law was applied as an overriding mandatory provision of the forum. A European court, applying the Rome I Regulation, could approach the case on this basis, or it might resort to Article 8. The problem with the latter is that Article 8(1) allows the court to override the parties' choice of law only with regard to provisions for the protection of the employee. While the Georgia provisions were partly for the protection of the employee, they also had other objectives – for example, free competition.

United States (Georgia)
Nordson Corporation v. *Plasschaert*
US Court of Appeals for the Eleventh Circuit
674 F 2d 1371 (1982)

Background

The employer was an Ohio corporation and the employee was of Dutch origin, though he had worked in various countries in Europe. He later moved to Georgia and there entered into an agreement not to reveal the employer's confidential information or to work in the same line of business for two years after leaving Nordson's employ. The contract contained a choice-of-law clause in favour of Ohio law. The employee subsequently left the company and was intending to go into the same line of business in Europe. The company sued him in a federal court in Georgia for an injunction to stop this. Under Georgia law, the non-competition agreement would have been unenforceable because it contained no territorial limit; under Ohio law it would have been enforceable to the extent of the employer's legitimate interest.

Godbold, Chief Judge

Plasschaert asserts that despite the provision for governance by Ohio law the district court sitting in Georgia must as a matter of Georgia public policy apply Georgia law. As a federal court in a diversity case we must follow Georgia conflict of laws rules . . . Absent the choice of law provision in the agreement Georgia courts would not enforce this covenant not to compete . . . Even when the contract provides for a choice of law under which the covenant would be enforceable, Georgia may elect not to enforce it . . .

Though our analysis is somewhat different from that of the district court, we consider essentially the same factors that it examined, and we agree with the district judge that under the facts of this case a Georgia court would honor the parties' choice of law and apply Ohio law.

Like the Georgia Supreme Court in *Gimbert* [above], we look to the Restatement (Second) of Conflict of Laws § 187(2) (1971) to see if Georgia will honor the state law chosen by the parties . . . [After setting out § 187(2), he continued:] Therefore, Georgia will honor the choice of law provision unless there was no reasonable basis for the parties' choice or unless the provision is 'contrary to a fundamental policy of a state which has a materially greater interest than the chosen state.' Since Nordson is an Ohio corporation headquartered in Ohio, there is a reasonable basis for choosing Ohio law. The provision, however, is contrary to the fundamental Georgia policy against restraints of competition [reference to Georgia legislation]. Thus the controlling determination is whether Georgia has a materially greater interest than Ohio in this issue.[1] We hold that it does not.

1 Not only must Georgia have a materially greater interest than Ohio in the controversy but also Georgia courts must choose Georgia as the state of applicable law if there is no effective choice of law by the parties. At least three European countries – Belgium, the Netherlands, and Germany – as well as Georgia and Ohio, have an interest in this controversy. We assume without deciding that Georgia courts would have applied Georgia law if the parties had not stipulated that Ohio law would govern. The remaining issue, whether Georgia has a materially greater interest in this controversy than Ohio, controls our decision.

If the parties have not chosen the law of a state to govern their contract, a court deciding which state law applies must consider contacts with the relevant states, the parties' expectations, the policies of the individual states, and the basic policy underlying the field of law . . . If the parties have chosen an applicable law the court must balance these same factors, and the interests of another state must be materially greater than those of the chosen state to override the parties' choice of law. Each case must be analyzed on its own facts. There are no simple directives in a case as close as this one, where there are Georgia cases involving fundamental Georgia policy that apply Georgia law despite the parties' choice of law and other Georgia cases that apply a foreign law even though the parties did not choose a specific state law . . .

The facts favor honoring the parties' choice of law. Nordson is an international corporation. Plasschaert worked for Nordson in the Netherlands, in Belgium, and in Georgia. Although Plasschaert signed the agreement in Georgia, his signing there, like the bringing of this suit there, was more 'an accident of time and geography than through any reason giving rise to a substantial state interest in the litigation.' [Reference to the trial court judgment.] He had just arrived from Belgium. Most of the negotiations and preparation for the transfer were conducted while Plasschaert was still in Belgium. The agreement implies that Plasschaert might be transferred to different territories during his employment, and it states explicitly that Plasschaert would not compete in any territory in which he worked for Nordson during any part of the two-year period immediately preceding his termination. Thus, the place of performance of the covenant not to compete is Western Europe as well as Georgia. Moreover, both parties are primarily concerned with the agreement's effect in Western Europe because, although Plasschaert worked in Georgia for most of the last two years of his employment, he was already setting up his European business when he quit Nordson. Finally, Plasschaert's domicile, residence, and citizenship are more rooted in Western Europe than in Georgia. Plasschaert's contacts, therefore, are at least as closely related to Western Europe, particularly Belgium, as to Georgia.

Georgia emerges from this analysis as the state where Plasschaert and Nordson carried out a substantial part of the contract performance, but in the sequence of events leading up to the signing of the agreement and the relationship between Nordson and Plasschaert after Plasschaert resigned, Georgia interests are all but nonexistent. Neither party expected Plasschaert to spend his career in Georgia, and he was expected to move as needed in the company's business. If Plasschaert had remained with Nordson, Ohio would have had continuing contacts regardless of where he worked. When the employment relationship ended Plasschaert almost immediately returned to Belgium to live in Brussels, the same city he left to come to Georgia.

Because each state (Georgia, Ohio, Belgium, and the Netherlands) has an interest in this dispute and because the employment relationship touched each of these states and to a large extent transcended political borders, no state has a 'materially greater interest' in the controversy than any other state. Therefore, each state, including Georgia, should defer to the parties' choice of law if that choice has a reasonable basis, and this one does. Moreover, Georgia has even less of an interest in the controversy than its contacts suggest since the injunction would apply mainly to Plasschaert's activities in Western Europe, not in Georgia.

Despite the dispersed contacts in this case a Georgia court still might refuse to enforce the provision under Ohio law if it finds it '*particularly* distasteful' to do so ... The terms of this restriction are reasonable, however. Georgia's concern is that the restraint might cause undue injury to the employee or unreasonable injury to the public in general ... The provision in paragraph 4c of the agreement for continued compensation equal to three fourths of Plasschaert's pay, especially as adjusted upwardly by the trial judge as permitted under Ohio law ... alleviates any concern a court may have about his personal well being. Injury to the Georgia public is minimal, if any, since Plasschaert intended to compete mainly in Europe. Moreover, both Georgia and Ohio favor the freedom of parties to contract, both states acknowledge an employer's right to safeguard his confidential information, and both recognize that in protecting its legitimate interests the employer must burden the employee as little as possible ... Thus, a Georgia court would not find it 'particularly distasteful' to enforce the agreement.

...

AFFIRMED.

Comment

This is a sophisticated example of interest analysis. However, the judgment could be criticized for focusing exclusively on Georgia and not considering the law of other countries. If Plasschaert was intending to work in Belgium, Belgian law had the greatest interest in deciding whether he should be precluded from doing so by reason of the agreement he had signed. The court's failure to consider Belgian law was probably due to the fact that it was not invoked by either of the parties.

How would this case be decided under the Rome I Regulation? If it approached it under Article 9, a court in Europe could adopt a similar analysis. If we assume that Georgia was an EC country, a Georgia court could adopt interest analysis to determine whether the forum rule was mandatory in terms of Article 9(2) when the employee wanted to work in another country.[24] A similar analysis could be carried out to determine whether the overriding mandatory provisions of a foreign country should be applied.

If a court in an EC country chose to approach the case under Article 8 of the Regulation, it would be faced with several problems. First, the relevant Georgia law had other objectives besides the protection of the employee. Secondly, Article 8 does not permit the balancing of interests. Thirdly, Article 8 would require the court to look to the contract between Plasschaert and Nordson and consider:

- the place where the work *under that contract* was habitually carried out;
- the place where the business through which he was engaged *for that contract* was situated; or
- the country with which *that contract* was most closely connected.

---

24 This would involve the definition in Article 9(1), which requires the court to decide whether the case concerns a situation falling within the scope of the provision.

The problem is that the country where his *new* activities would take place was much more relevant. The law of that country – Belgium, on the facts of the case – should decide whether he should be precluded from working because of the agreement he had signed. Article 8 does not permit this. If the agreement not to compete was enforceable under Belgian law, it would be wrong to strike it down on the basis of Georgia law. For these reasons, Article 8 does not seem well suited to a case such as this.

United States
Barnes Group Inc. v. C&C Products Inc.
US Court of Appeals for the Fourth Circuit
716 F 2d 1023; 38 Fed R Serv 2d 433 (1983)

Background

In this case, the action was between two employers. Six salesmen, who had originally worked for Bowman, a division of Barnes Group, as independent contractors, not employees, moved over to C&C Products, a firm in the same line of business. The salesmen's contract with Bowman contained a non-competition clause under which they agreed that, for two years after leaving Bowman, they would not sell similar products to any customer with whom they had dealt during their last two years with Bowman. Barnes Group (Bowman) was an Ohio corporation and the contract contained a choice-of-law clause in favour of Ohio law.

When the six salesmen moved to C&C in violation of the agreements not to compete, Barnes Group sued C&C in tort for interference with its contracts with the salesmen.[25] Three of the salesmen worked and resided in Alabama; and one each in Maryland, Louisiana and South Carolina.

The action was brought in a federal court in Ohio, but was transferred to South Carolina. Under US law, the latter court had to apply the same choice-of-law rules that would have been applied by an Ohio court. The district court found for Barnes Group and the defendant appealed to the US Court of Appeals for the Fourth Circuit.

James Dickson Phillips, Circuit Judge[1]

This case presents two difficult and interrelated choice-of-law questions that we find were resolved erroneously, at least in part, by the district court. We address first the question of the law that properly should govern a threshold determination of whether the restrictive covenants at issue are enforceable between the parties, and then turn to consider the law that should govern questions of tort liability for interference with the contracts found enforceable.

A

As the parties concede, a necessary element of the tort of intentional interference with contract is that the contract at issue be valid and enforceable as between

1 Giving the opinion of the majority.

---

25 Under the common law, interference with a contract can be a tort.

the parties to it . . . In this case particularly, C&C's liability for tortious interference hinges almost entirely upon whether the Bowman restrictive covenants are enforceable, because the facts clearly establish all other elements of the tort.

On appeal, C&C's principal assignment of error is that the trial court erred, as a matter of law, in applying Ohio law to determine the enforceability of the restrictive covenants with which C&C allegedly interfered. The district court's application of Ohio law was based entirely upon the stipulation in the standard Bowman contract that it 'shall be construed in accordance with' Ohio law. The first potentially dispositive question on appeal therefore is whether, as a matter of law, the contractual choice-of-law provision is controlling.

[T]he district court was bound, as are we, to apply here the prevailing law of the transferor forum, the District Court for the Northern District of Ohio, which in turn would apply Ohio choice-of-law principles in this diversity action . . .

Seeking the applicable Ohio choice-of-law rule, we have looked first to the possibility that there might be directly controlling Ohio precedent for the specific rule of decision. Finding none, we have turned, therefore, to general choice-of-law doctrine and principles, as currently applied by the Ohio courts, for guidance to the applicable rule. That inquiry has persuaded us that the Ohio courts currently apply contemporary choice-of-law doctrine based upon interest analysis, the most significant relationship, and the Restatement (Second) of Conflicts . . . We therefore look to that general body of doctrine as a guide to the specific rule of decision that Ohio would presumably apply to the choice-of-law issues before us here.

A basic principle under contemporary choice-of-law doctrine is that parties cannot by contract override public policy limitations on contractual power applicable in a state with materially greater interests in the transaction than the state whose law is contractually chosen. See Restatement (Second) of Conflicts § 187(2)(b) (1971). While contemporary doctrine recognizes a sphere of party autonomy within which contractual choice-of-law provisions will be given effect, it also limits the extent to which deft draftsmanship will be allowed to bypass legislative judgments as to basic enforceability or validity. This is implicit in the Restatement (Second) of Conflicts § 187(2)(b), which provides that a contractual choice-of-law clause will not be given effect on matters such as 'capacity, formalities and substantial validity', id. comment d, when 'application of the law of the chosen state would be contrary to a fundamental policy of a state which has a materially greater interest than the chosen state in the determination of the particular issue and which . . . would be the state of the applicable law in the absence of an effective choice of law by the parties.' We believe Ohio would apply this choice-of-law rule here as part of its contemporary choice-of-law doctrine . . .

Applying the Restatement (Second) § 187 formulation, we think it clear that, absent the contractual choice-of-law provision, Ohio conflicts principles would mandate application here of the substantive laws of Alabama, Louisiana, Maryland, and South Carolina – where the six salesmen whose contracts are at issue work and reside – to determine the basic enforceability of these restrictive covenants between the contracting parties. The local jurisdictions involved here have interests at two levels in applying their own law on the enforceability of restrictive covenants: to protect employee-residents from contractually abrogating their ability to earn a livelihood, and to control the degree of free competition in the local economy. These interests in regulating business relationships within the states outweigh any generalized interest Ohio might have in applying its own law to protect the interstate contracts of its domiciliary . . . and compel the conclusion that, under Ohio choice-of-law rules, the laws of these other jurisdictions would control if there were no contractual stipulation of Ohio law . . . [2]

The remaining and most vexing element of the Restatement (Second) formulation, in determining whether to adhere to the contractual choice-of-law provision, concerns whether application of Ohio law would be 'contrary to a fundamental policy' of any or all of the jurisdictions involved, all of which undoubtedly have a 'materially greater interest' than does Ohio in whether these covenants are enforceable [reference to *Nordson Corporation* v. *Plasschaert*, above]. It is apparent that there can be no clear-cut delineation of those policies that are sufficiently 'fundamental', within the meaning of § 187(2)(b), to warrant overriding a contractual stipulation of controlling law. See Restatement (Second) of Conflicts § 187 comment g. Nonetheless, a few general landmarks offer some structure for this inquiry. First, not every situation where contractually chosen law diverges merely in degree from that of the state whose law would otherwise apply impinges upon the fundamental policy of that state . . . This is seen most clearly in regard to usury statutes, where the parties' choice of law has been held to validate interest rates that would be usurious and unenforceable in the jurisdiction whose law would prevail absent the contractual stipulation of controlling law . . . At the other extreme, it seems apparent that where the law chosen by the parties would make enforceable a contract flatly unenforceable in the state whose law would otherwise apply, to honor the choice-of-law provision would trench upon that state's 'fundamental policy'

The district court's application of Ohio law to determine the enforceability of the restrictive covenants at issue presents both ends of this spectrum. Under Ohio law, covenants not to compete are enforceable if reasonable . . . a test similar to that applied under the laws of South Carolina . . . Maryland . . . and Louisiana . . . These latter jurisdictions differ from Ohio, if at all, only in degree concerning the enforceability of covenants not to compete; hence the district court properly applied Ohio law to the covenants of the Maryland, South Carolina, and Louisiana salesmen, as stipulated by the parties, because it is not 'contrary to a fundamental policy' of those states.

---

[2] Professor Brainerd Currie's original formulation of interest analysis rejected the proposition that a court could or should weigh the competing interests of two jurisdictions in resolving a true conflict of law such as that presented here. See Currie, 'Notes on Methods and Objectives in the Conflict of Laws' (1959) Duke LJ 171, 176–8; see also Sedler, 'The Governmental Interest Approach to Choice of Law: An Analysis and a Reformulation' (1977) 25 UCLA L Rev 181, 227 (arguing that the forum should apply its own law when faced with a true conflict of law in which it has a real interest). But the commentators and courts – including Ohio, which we follow here . . . – have almost uniformly embraced a weighing of conflicting government interests. See J. Martin, *Conflict of Laws: Cases and Materials* (1978), pp. 234–36; Note, 'Comparative Impairment Reformed: Rethinking State Interests in the Conflict of Laws' (1982) 95 Harvard L Rev 1079, 1083 n. 19. This process of weighing government interests might more appropriately be considered under a theory of 'comparative impairment'. See *ibid.*, at pp. 1087–99.

Under Alabama law, however, covenants not to compete, whether or not reasonable, are void as against public policy and cannot be enforced . . . To honor the contractual choice of law would make enforceable a contract flatly unenforceable in Alabama, surely impinging upon 'fundamental policy' of Alabama. It was error, therefore, for the district court to apply Ohio law to determine the enforceability of the Alabama salesmen's covenants not to compete.

B

After determining the enforceability of the covenants not to compete, the district court applied Ohio law to determine the contours of the cause of action for tortious interference with contract, because in its view Ohio was the *lex loci delicti*. Without addressing whether the court's conclusion concerning the place of injury was correct, we think it plain that Ohio has abandoned *lex loci delicti* as the choice-of-law rule in torts cases in favor of the contemporary approach based upon interest analysis . . . And it is equally plain, applying this approach, that the local jurisdictions involved here – Alabama, Louisiana, South Carolina, and Maryland – have far greater interests than does Ohio in applying their law on tortious interference with contracts involving their residents that were to be performed solely within their boundaries . . .

Although the district court thus erred in applying Ohio law, for the most part this error was harmless because both South Carolina . . . and Maryland . . . as does Ohio . . . recognize a classic common law cause of action for tortious interference with contract.

In contrast, however, no cause of action for tortious interference with contract exists under Louisiana law . . . Accordingly, the court's error in applying Ohio law to the alleged interference with the personal service contracts being performed in Louisiana was prejudicial and requires correction.

C

Our conclusions on the choice-of-law issues presented by this appeal can be summarized briefly. The district court properly honored the contractual choice-of-law provision in applying Ohio law to assess the enforceability of the restrictive covenants involving the Maryland, South Carolina, and Louisiana salesmen. But Alabama law, which holds such covenants unenforceable, should have been applied to the contracts of the three Alabama salesmen, and the court committed reversible error in not doing so. The district court committed reversible error as well in applying Ohio law to the claim for tortious interference with respect to the contract of the Louisiana salesman. We therefore affirm the district court's determinations that C&C tortiously interfered with the contracts of the Maryland and South Carolina salesmen, but reverse its determinations that C&C tortiously interfered with the contracts of the Alabama and Louisiana salesmen . . .

Comment

How would this case have been decided under the Rome I Regulation? Article 8 would not have applied, because the contracts with the salesmen were not contracts of employment: the salesmen were independent operators. The choice of law would, therefore, have been enforced, unless the court could have applied Article 9(3). It will be remembered that the American court declared the agreements not to compete invalid in the case of the Alabama salesmen because of Alabama's strong policy against such agreements. However, it is doubtful whether Alabama law made the performance of these agreements unlawful, as required by Article 9(3). It seems they were simply unenforceable. If so, Article 9(3) would not apply. Under the Rome I Regulation, therefore, the restrictive covenants would have been upheld in the case of all the salesmen.[26]

As far as the tortious aspect of the case was concerned, the Rome II Regulation would have been the relevant measure. Under Article 4,[27] the claim against the Louisiana salesman would probably be governed by Louisiana law, since this was the place where the damage occurred.[28] So, on this aspect of the case, the result would have been the same.

§ 5   Consumers

Consumer protection is an important policy in many countries. Since consumers are in a weak bargaining position, the law often gives them non-derogable rights to ensure that they are fairly treated. This policy in domestic law is reflected in conflict of laws. The relevant provisions of the Rome I Regulation were discussed in Chapter 25, § 3.2, above. Here we consider a Scottish case decided many years before the Regulation (or the Convention) came into existence.

Scotland
English* v. *Donnelly
Court of Session (First Division)
1958 SC 494

Background

This case concerned a hire-purchase (credit sale) agreement for a motor car. The parties to the agreement were the purchaser, who was resident in Scotland, and the finance company, the Twentieth Century Banking Corporation Ltd, which was English. The purchaser signed the agreement in Scotland and it was then sent to England where the finance company signed it. Subsequently, the purchaser defaulted on his payments. The finance company terminated the agreement and obtained indemnification from the seller, to whom it had assigned its rights under the agreement. The seller then sued the purchaser in Scotland, demanding the return of the vehicle and payment of money owing under the agreement.

The purchaser invoked a provision in a Scottish statute, the Hire Purchase and

---

26 If the forum had been Alabama, however, Article 9(2) would have applied with regard to the Alabama salesman and the restrictive covenant would have been struck down.
27 Even if one regarded what C&C did as an act of unfair competition, Article 6 would not have applied because the interests of only one competitor (Barnes Group) would have been affected: Article 6(2).
28 The indirect consequences might have occurred in Ohio, where Barnes Group might have suffered financial loss, but, under Article 4(1), this would have been irrelevant.

Small Debt (Scotland) Act 1954, under which a hire-purchase agreement was not binding on the purchaser unless a written copy was delivered to him within fourteen days from the date on which he signed it, something that had not been done. The hire-purchase agreement, however, contained a choice-of-law clause in favour of English law and the seller argued that the Scottish Act was therefore inapplicable. The lower court (the Sheriff) rejected this argument and held for the purchaser.

Lord President (Clyde)

In the first place it appears to me to be clear, in the light of the express statutory provision in section 1 [of the Act],[1] that Parliament intended that parties should not be able to contract out of the Act, if it applied; and this seems to me to be confirmed by the provisions of section 9 of the Act whereby 'any contract or agreement by virtue of which any right conferred by this Act on the hirer, purchaser, cautioner or guarantor under a contract to which this Act applies, is taken away or limited shall to that extent be void.' Accordingly, if the contract in question is one to which the Act applies, the fact that parties have agreed to invoke the law of England will not displace the obligations imposed in regard to the contract by the Scottish Act.

In the second place, therefore, I must consider whether the Scottish Act applies or not. It is quite true that in general under private international law it can be said that the validity of a contract is governed by the proper law of the contract, namely, by the law which the parties intend or may fairly be presumed to have intended to invoke . . . But that general rule is displaced where an Act of Parliament has expressly provided otherwise, and has applied certain conditions as necessary for the validity of the contract. The situation might have been different if the statutory provisions had not been mandatory . . .

In the present case, however, the statutory provision contained in the Scottish Act of 1932 (as amended in 1954) is mandatory. The object of section 2 of the Scottish Act is to lay down certain conditions precedent for valid hire purchase contracts, designed to ensure that persons who hire goods under them are properly certiorated of the conditions contained in the agreements into which they are entering. The Act is a piece of social legislation designed for the protection of certain persons, *i.e.*, members of the public who hire articles through companies such as the Twentieth Century Banking Corporation Limited. It is not intended to benefit or to protect these companies. The way the protection operates is the avoidance of the contract of hire if certain statutory safeguards in the hirer's interest are not satisfied. Hence it follows that the test for the applicability of the Act, which under section 11 extends only to Scotland, is whether or not the contract was entered into in Scotland (see section 1), irrespective of where that contract is ultimately completed or is to be executed. The first defender in the present case undoubtedly entered into this contract in Scotland, and it necessarily follows that the Scottish Act therefore applies. If so, the general rules of private international law applicable to contracts are superseded by this express statutory provision . . .

1 *Editor's note*: section 1 provided: 'This Act shall apply to any contract entered into after the passing of this Act, notwithstanding anything contained in such contract . . .'

In these circumstances, in my opinion, the Sheriff arrived at the correct conclusion and the appeal should accordingly be refused.

Lord Carmont

I agree.

Lord Sorn

The defence here arises under section 2 of the Scottish Act of 1932 which lays down certain conditions for the validity of hire purchase contracts. These conditions amount to the imposing of what might be described as prerequisites for a valid contract. What the section plainly sets out to do is to give a protection to the hirer at the time when he is committing himself to a contract and at the time his signature is obtained – whether that signature be the actual completion of the contract or only a step in that direction. The Act is made to apply to Scotland, and the natural meaning to take out of section 2 is that the protection is intended to be given to the hirer who signs a contract of this kind in Scotland. The question is: have we been shown any reason for not extending the protection of section 2 towards the defender in this case? The argument has been that clause 13 [the choice-of-law clause in the contract] imports the law of England as the law which the parties chose to govern the contract, and no doubt this has the result of making the law of England the proper law of the contract. But, in my opinion, that does not have the effect at all of displacing section 2 of the Act, and I say this particularly because of the words to be found in section 1 which are as follows: 'This Act shall apply to any contract entered into after the passing of this Act, notwithstanding anything contained in such contract . . .' To hold that clause 13 had the effect of superseding section 2 would, it seems to me, be to ignore these words and to ignore the manifest purpose of the Act which was to give to persons entering into hire purchase contracts in Scotland a measure of protection against those persons with whom they are dealing. This just means that, if financiers from the other side of the Border wish to do valid business with hirers in Scotland, they must do so with due regard to the Scottish Act, and that they cannot get round the Act by putting in a clause to the effect that some other law is to apply to the contract.

Result: the contract was not enforced.

Comment

This case is an excellent example of the application of the theory of an overriding statute. It is also worth noting that the basis on which the statute was held applicable – that the consumer had, in Scotland, taken all the steps necessary on his part for the conclusion of the contract – was one of the criteria subsequently adopted by the Rome Convention[29] for the applicability of its consumer-protection provisions.[30]

Under the normal rules, the contract would have been regarded as made in England, since this is where it was signed by the last party to sign it. The court,

---

29 Article 5(2), first indent.
30 Article 6(1) of the Rome I Regulation is in wider terms, but would undoubtedly cover the case.

however, realized that this would have made it too easy for suppliers to manipulate the rules in order to evade the Act.

This decision may be compared to an Australian case, which followed the same general approach to mandatory rules, but took a different view on this final point. This is *Kay's Leasing Corporation* v. *Fletcher*,[31] in which the facts were similar. The supplier, Kay's Leasing, was a Victoria company which sold a tractor to the purchasers, who were resident in New South Wales. The purchasers signed the documents in New South Wales and they were then sent to Victoria, where they were signed by the supplier. There was hire-purchase legislation in both states and the court held that the place of contracting, rather than the proper law, determined the applicability of the legislation. However, it applied the *locus contractus* in the technical sense, rather than looking to where the purchaser signed; it therefore held that the Victoria statute applied. This is less satisfactory than the approach in *English* v. *Donnelly*.[32]

Further reading

See the general works in the Further reading to Chapter 24.

Dicey, Morris and Collins, *The Conflict of Laws* (Sweet and Maxwell, London, 14th edn, 2006), pp. 18 *et seq*

Ehrenzweig, 'Adhesion Contracts in the Conflict of Laws' (1953) 53 *Columbia Law Review* 1072

'The Real Estate Broker and the Conflict of Laws' (1959) 59 *Columbia Law Review* 303

Morris, 'The Scope of the Carriage of Goods by Sea Act 1971' (1979) 95 LQR 59

Morse, 'Consumer Contracts, Employment Contracts and the Rome Convention' (1992) 41 ICLQ 1

North, 'Contract as a Tort Defence in the Conflict of Laws' (1977) 26 ICLQ 914

Smith and Cromack, 'International Employment Contracts: The Applicable Law' (1993) 22 *Industrial Law Journal* 1

---

31 (1964) 116 CLR 124 (High Court of Australia).
32 Although *English* v. *Donnelly* had been decided some four years previously, it seems that it was not cited before the court.

CHAPTER 27

Foreign currency

In this chapter, we look at the problems caused by the fact that there are different currencies in the world and that rates of exchange fluctuate. We first consider the effect of exchange controls.

§ 1   Exchange controls

More prevalent in the past than they are today, exchange controls are intended to protect foreign-exchange reserves. They normally apply to residents or nationals of the State in question. Although they vary from country to country, they usually make it a criminal offence to make payments in foreign currency anywhere in the world without permission from the relevant national authority; they also require persons who obtain foreign currency to remit it to the country concerned and sell it to the national bank for the national currency. They often prohibit other things as well.

As will be apparent, exchange controls can have a serious effect on international business. They are often invoked by debtors as an excuse for non-payment. What is particularly galling for the creditor is that a person from a foreign country receives goods or services and then says that he cannot pay because the exchange-control regulations of his country forbid it. This can seem like a way of getting something for nothing, since the debtor presumably knew the requirements of his law, while the creditor may have been ignorant of them. What is the law to do?

One of the features of the law in this area is that there is a marked contrast between the attitude of courts towards the exchange-control regulations of their own country and those of other countries. As might be expected, courts usually enforce the exchange-control regulations of the forum according to their terms and refuse to uphold contracts that violate them.

§ 1.1   Exchange controls of the forum

Our first case concerns British exchange controls. These were introduced in the United Kingdom during World War II and retained (in a less severe form) for a considerable period thereafter.[1] They have now been abolished.

---

1 They were lifted in 1979.

England
Boissevain v. *Weil*
House of Lords
[1950] AC 327

Background

This case concerned two people who were resident in Monaco during World War II. One was British and one Dutch. The British subject, Mrs Weil, was Jewish. She needed money to prevent her son from being sent to Germany. She borrowed it from the Dutchman, Mr Boissevain. The loan was in French francs, which were legal tender in Monaco, and it was agreed that she would repay it after the war in pounds sterling at an agreed exchange rate. She gave him cheques drawn on an English bank for the sum in question.

When the war was over, she failed to repay the money and it turned out that she had no account at the bank on which the cheques were drawn. Boissevain sued her in England. Her defence was that the loans were contrary to British exchange-control regulations in force at the time. As will be seen from the judgment, these regulations were extremely wide in scope.

Lord Radcliffe

My Lords, the action out of which the present appeal arises represents the appellant's endeavour to obtain from the courts of this country a judgment against the respondent for the sum of £6,000. I think that this endeavour must fail because I am satisfied that the respondent [Mrs Weil] broke the law of this country and committed an offence when she borrowed these sums in francs from the appellant [Mr Boissevain]. If that is so, he can get no relief in respect of that transaction from an English court, and it would afford no material assistance to him if I were to express my sympathy with him in the predicament in which he is placed or my distaste for the attitude which the respondent appears to have taken up against her benefactor. But before I come to the legal issues involved it is necessary to say something of the course of the proceedings in the courts below . . .

[Lord Radcliffe discussed the way the procedure of the case developed and said that since Mr Boissevain had not pleaded unjust enrichment in the beginning, he could not raise it at this stage as an alternative to the contractual claim.[1] He also said that the United Kingdom exchange-control regulations prohibited the borrowing of foreign currency. He then continued:]

Now, that this operation was a borrowing of foreign currency within the meaning of the regulation seems to me inescapable. 'Foreign currency' is defined by reg. 10 as meaning any currency other than sterling, unless the context otherwise requires; and here there is nothing in the context that permits, let alone requires, another meaning. Any person subject to the regulation who receives notes of a currency other than sterling on an undertaking to repay what he receives

1 *Editor's note*: there also appear to have been reasons why the claim would have failed even if, procedurally, it could have been made.

borrows foreign currency. What else can one say of it? One may speculate whether the makers of this regulation may have had in mind some more limited and specialized meaning for the words, when they spoke here of borrowing and lending currency; but in truth there is no material upon which to feed the speculation and your Lordships are bound to treat these words as meaning no less than what they so plainly say. The range of what they prohibit, so understood, is indeed exceedingly wide, and it is this very width that lends plausibility to the suggestion that there must be implied some qualification either of the class of persons affected or of the kind of transaction that is brought under control. Two instances have been used in argument to illustrate what is said to be the inacceptable absurdity of reading the regulation according to its literal meaning. There is the case of the escaping prisoner of war who borrows some money in the country through which he passes, promising to make it good if he can make good his escape. And there is the case of the British subject resident in a foreign country who raises some every-day loan from a friend or, perhaps, his banker there against his promise to repay in the same currency. Can it be thought that such harmless transactions were intended to be made criminal offences by this regulation?

For my part, I think that the escaping prisoner of war can be left out of consideration. His would have been a wholly exceptional case and would have been so treated: it would be quite unreasonable to base any particular construction of this general regulation on its circumstances. The British subject resident abroad presents more difficulty and does legitimately raise the query whether it can be right to interpret the regulation as governing his merely local transactions. But I think that it must be so interpreted . . .

There is only one further matter that I wish to notice before I conclude. Fully as I agree with the Court of Appeal's view that reg. 2 prohibited this borrowing and therefore renders the appellant's claim for repayment unmaintainable, I do not find it possible to base my view either on the circumstance that this transaction was an exchange of francs for sterling, or on the fact, if it be a fact, that the proper law of this contract was the law of England. Indeed, it seems to me an unmaintainable proposition that if a British subject who is within the ban carries out such a transaction in foreign currency as the regulation describes, he commits or does not commit an offence according to whether the proper law of the transaction is English or foreign. These Defence Regulations were concerned with prohibiting certain acts, under the sanction of severe penalties and their interpretation cannot be assisted by considering in what circumstances the rules of private international law would uphold or reject contracts arising from those acts. I think that both the sterling element and the proper law factor are really irrelevant . . .

Comment

This case shows the injustice that can be caused by exchange controls. It also shows that, when the forum's own exchange controls are in issue, questions of choice of law are irrelevant: forum exchange controls are enforced as overriding legislation, whatever the proper law may be. Under the Rome I Regulation, they would be enforced under Article 9(2) as overriding mandatory provisions of the law of the forum.

§ 1.2 Foreign exchange controls

The picture is different when foreign exchange-control regulations are in issue. The situation here has been profoundly altered by the International Monetary Fund Agreement. We first consider the position before this was adopted.

§ 1.2.1 General principles.

Our next case shows how the general principles of English conflict of laws apply in this area.

England
Kleinwort, Sons and Company v. Ungarische Baumwolle Industrie
Court of Appeal
[1939] 2 KB 678

Background

In this case, a Hungarian company entered into a contract with an English bank under which the former was obliged to pay a sum of money in British currency in England. When the contract was concluded, it was lawful by all relevant systems of law. Before the time for payment arrived, however, Hungary introduced exchange-control legislation under which it would have been illegal for the Hungarian company to make the payment. It defaulted, and the English bank sued it in England. The Hungarian company raised the Hungarian legislation as a defence.

Mackinnon LJ

[The defendant claims] that, if a contract is made to do something in London which becomes illegal by the law of one of the parties in his own country, the English Courts will not enforce it. For that proposition two authorities were relied on: *Ralli Brothers* v. *Compania Naviera Sota y Aznar* [set out in Chapter 25, § 4.2] [and another case]. But it is obvious, directly one looks at those cases, that they are dealing with a totally different set of facts. This is an English contract to do something in England. In those cases the contract was to do something in a foreign country, and, when the law of that foreign country had made it illegal to do that act in that foreign country, it was held that the English Courts would not compel its performance or make the man who had failed to perform it liable in damages. The whole principle is stated by Scrutton LJ [in the *Compania Naviera* case]:

> I should prefer to state the ground of my decision more broadly and to rest it on the ground that where a contract requires an act to be done in a foreign country, it is, in the absence of very special circumstances, an implied term of the continuing validity of such a provision that the act to be done in the foreign country shall not be illegal by the law of that country.

That proposition seems to have no application whatever to the facts of this case. This is no contract to do anything in Budapest or elsewhere in Hungary, but a contract to do something in London . . .

> The principle is stated with characteristic lucidity and precision in that great work, Dicey on *Conflict of Laws*. Rule 160, 5th ed., p. 647, states:
>
>> The material or essential validity of a contract is (subject to the Exceptions hereinafter mentioned) governed by the proper law of the contract.
>
> The proper law of this contract is English law.
>
> The third Exception, p. 657, states:
>
>> A contract (whether lawful by its proper law or not) is, in general, invalid in so far as (1.) the performance of it is unlawful by the law of the country where the contract is to be performed (*lex loci solutionis*).
>
> Here it is said that to pay this money in London is unlawful by the law of Hungary. If this contract had been to pay money in Budapest, no doubt that principle would have applied, and the law of Hungary would have been the *lex loci solutionis*, but the payment of the money was to be made in England, and the law of England is the *lex loci solutionis*. Therefore the exception where the performance is unlawful by the law of the country where the contract is to be performed does not arise, and the defendants can base no defence on that principle.
>
> The attempted extension of the principle would obviously lead to preposterous results. Suppose the Kingdom or Legislature of Ruritania passed a law that no Ruritanian subject should pay a hotel bill which he had incurred in England. When the Ruritanian subject was sued in the county court by the hotel proprietor the county court judge, if that principle were correct, would have to give judgment for the defendant. That seems to me obviously absurd and I do not think that I need discuss the matter any further.
>
> . . . I think that this appeal fails and must be dismissed, with costs.

Comment

This case shows that, in the absence of special provisions, English courts will allow foreign exchange controls to be invoked as a defence to an action in contract only if either they form part of the governing law of the contract or if payment is to take place in the foreign country. In this latter event, the case would be covered by the rule in *Regazzoni* v. *Sethia* or *Ralli Bros*. Under the Rome I Regulation, the normal rules would apply where the contract was illegal under the applicable law and Article 9(3) could be used where it was illegal under the law of the country of performance.

§ 1.2.2 The IMF Agreement. As World War II was nearing its end, the leading nations of the world met in Bretton Woods, New Hampshire, in an attempt to resolve the financial problems that had inflamed international relations before the war. What they came up with was the International Monetary Fund Agreement 1945. Article VIII(2)(b) of the Agreement provides:

> Exchange contracts which involve the currency of any member and which are contrary to the exchange-control regulations of any member maintained or imposed consistently with this agreement shall be unenforceable in the territories of any member.

This provision, which is part of the law of many countries,[2] provides a new ground for refusing to enforce contracts contrary to foreign exchange-control regulations.

Article VIII(2)(b) raises a number of issues. First, it applies only in the case of an exchange contract. The meaning of this phrase will be considered below. Secondly, it applies only if the contract involves the currency of a member of the IMF. Almost all countries of the world are members. Thirdly, the contract must be contrary to the exchange-control regulations of a member which are maintained or imposed consistently with the IMF Agreement. Where this question arises in legal proceedings, the legal department of the IMF is usually willing to give an opinion on it. Though not binding, such an opinion has considerable weight.

In our next case, the Court of Appeal had to decide what constitutes an exchange contract.

England
Wilson, Smithett & Cope Ltd v. *Terruzzi*
Court of Appeal
[1976] QB 703; [1976] 2 WLR 418; [1976] 1 All ER 818; [1976] 1 Lloyd's Rep 509

Background

Wilson, Smithett & Cope was a firm of dealers on the London Metal Exchange. Terruzzi was an Italian who had an account with the firm. When one of his deals resulted in a heavy loss, he refused to pay on the ground that the transaction was contrary to Italian exchange-control regulations. Since the governing law was English and the place of payment was England, this would have constituted no defence under the traditional principles. However, he invoked Article VIII(2)(b).

Lord Denning MR

[After referring to Article VIII(2)(b), he continued:]

Signor Terruzzi, the defendant, lives in Milan. He is a dealer in metals, trading under the name Terruzzi Metalli. But he is also, it seems, a gambler in differences. He speculates on the rise or fall in the price of zinc, copper and so forth. He speculated in 1973 on the London Metal Exchange. He did so in plain breach of the Italian laws of exchange control. These provide that residents in Italy are not to come under obligations to non-residents save with ministerial authority. Signor Terruzzi never obtained permission.

In making his speculations, Signor Terruzzi established an account with London dealers, Wilson, Smithett & Cope Ltd, the plaintiffs . . . Sometimes Signor Terruzzi was a 'bull.' That is, he thought that the price was likely to rise in the near future. So he bought metal from the London dealers at a low price for delivery three

---

2 It has legal force in the United Kingdom under the Bretton Woods Agreements Order in Council 1946, SR&O 1946 No. 36, Article 3, made under the Bretton Woods Agreements Act 1945. The relevant parts of the Act were repealed by the International Monetary Fund Act 1979, but section 6(2) of the Schedule to the latter Act preserves the Order in Council.

months ahead: not meaning ever to take delivery of it, but intending to sell it back to the London dealers at a higher price before the delivery date; thus showing him a profit in his account with the London dealers. At other times he was a 'bear.' That is, he thought that the price was likely to fall in the near future. So he sold metal 'short' (which he had not got) to the London dealers at a high price for delivery three months ahead; not meaning ever to deliver it, but intending to buy back from the London dealers a like quantity at a lower price before the delivery date; thus showing him a profit in his account with the London dealers . . .

The critical months here were October and November 1973. The price of zinc was very high . . . Signor Terruzzi thought that the price was much too high and that it was likely to fall soon. So he made a series of contracts with the London dealers whereby he sold to them 1,200 tons of zinc for delivery in the next three months. He sold 'short', that is, he had then no zinc to meet his obligations. Unfortunately for Signor Terruzzi, his forecast was wrong . . . [T]he price did not fall. It rose steeply.

. . .

Now for the Bretton Woods Agreement. Bretton Woods is a small town in New Hampshire, USA, but it has a place in history. During the Second World War, even in the midst of raging hostilities, there was a conference there attended by the members of the United Nations. The object was to organise their monetary systems so as to meet the post-war problems. At this conference the United Kingdom was represented by the distinguished economist Lord Keynes, and by the legal adviser to the Foreign Office, Sir Eric Beckett. In July 1944 Articles of Agreement were drawn up and signed.

[After setting out Article VIII(2)(b), he continued:]

That provision is part of the law of England, but it has given rise to much controversy, particularly as to the meaning of the words 'exchange contracts'. There are two rival views. First, the view of Professor Nussbaum set out in 59 *Yale Law Journal* (1949), pp. 426–427. He said that an 'exchange contract' is exclusively concerned with the handling of 'international media of payment' as such. Therefore, contracts involving securities or merchandise cannot be considered as exchange contracts except when they are monetary transactions in disguise. This view is in accord with the meaning given by Lord Radcliffe in *In re United Railways of Havana and Regla Warehouses Ltd* [1961] AC 1007, 1059: 'a true exchange contract', he said, 'is a contract to exchange the currency of one country for the currency of another.'

Second, the view of Dr F A Mann set out in the *British Year Book of International Law* (1949), p. 279; and in *The Legal Aspect of Money*, Mann, 3rd ed. (1971). He suggests at p. 441 that '"exchange contracts" are contracts which in any way affect a country's exchange resources', a phrase which I accepted without question in *Sharif* v. *Azad* [1967] 1 QB 605, 613–614, in the belief that, coming from such a source, it must be right. Dr. Mann recognises that his view makes the word 'exchange' redundant and thus seems 'counter to established principles of interpretation.' But he contends that it is in better harmony with the purpose of the agreement.

Dr Mann suggests (p. 439) that the lawyers did not take much part in drafting the agreement of Bretton Woods. In this he is mistaken. I trust that I may be forgiven a digression if I borrow from the argument of [counsel for the plaintiffs], and recite part of the speech which Lord Keynes made at the final Act of the Conference, as recorded by Sir Roy Harrod in *The Life of John Maynard Keynes*, at p. 690:

> And for my own part, I should like to pay a particular tribute to our lawyers. All the more so because I have to confess that, generally speaking, I do not like lawyers. I have been known to complain that, to judge from results in this lawyer-ridden land, the Mayflower, when she sailed from Plymouth, must have been entirely filled with lawyers. When I first visited Mr. Morgenthau in Washington some three years ago accompanied only by my secretary, the boys in your Treasury curiously inquired of him – where is your lawyer? When it was explained that I had none – 'Who then does your thinking for you?' was the rejoinder . . . only too often [our] lawyers have had to do our thinking for us . . .

So the lawyers did play a large part . . .

[After discussing the problems that speculating in foreign currency can cause, Lord Denning continued:]

The mischief being thus exposed, it seems to me that the participants at Bretton Woods inserted Article VIII(2)(b) so as to stop it. They determined to make exchange contracts of that kind – for the exchange of currencies – unenforceable in the territories of any member. I do not know of any similar mischief in regard to other contracts, that is, contracts for the sale or purchase of merchandise or commodities. Businessmen have to encounter fluctuations in the price of goods, but this is altogether different from the fluctuations in exchange rates. So far from there being any mischief, it seems to me that it is in the interest of international trade that there should be no restriction on contracts for the sale and purchase of merchandise and commodities: and that they should be enforceable in the territories of the members.

The Bretton Woods Agreement itself makes provision to that end. Thus Article I(ii) says that one of the purposes of the International Monetary Fund is 'To facilitate the expansion and balanced growth of international trade.' Article VI(3), and Article VIII(2)(a), coupled with Article XIX(i) says that no member is to impose restrictions on 'payments due in connection with foreign trade, other current business, including services, and normal short term banking and credit facilities.'

In conformity with those provisions, I would hold that the Bretton Woods Agreement should not do anything to hinder legitimate contracts for the sale or purchase of merchandise or commodities. The words 'exchange contracts' in Article VIII(2)(b) refer only to contracts to exchange the currency of one country for the currency of another. The words 'which involve the currency of any member' fit in well with this meaning: but it is difficult to give them any sensible meaning in regard to other contracts. They show that the section is only dealing with the currencies of members of the fund, and not with the currencies of non-members. The reference to regulations 'maintained or imposed consistently with this agreement', covers such regulations as those of Italy here.

It is no doubt possible for men of business to seek to avoid Article VIII(2)(b) by various artifices. But I hope that the courts will be able to look at the substance of the contracts and not at the form. If the contracts are not legitimate contracts for the sale or purchase of merchandise or commodities, but are instead what Professor Nussbaum calls 'monetary transactions in disguise', 59 *Yale Law Journal*, p. 427, as a means of manipulating currencies, they would be caught by section 2(b).

. . . In my opinion the contracts here were legitimate contracts for the sale and purchase of metals. They were not 'exchange contracts.' The London dealers are entitled to enforce them in this country. I would dismiss the appeal, accordingly.

Result: the appeal was dismissed and the contract enforced.

Comment

As will be appreciated, this interpretation of 'exchange contract' considerably narrows the scope of Article VIII(2)(b). Although it has received support in the United States,[3] it has been attacked by Sir Joseph Gold, the former General Counsel and Director of the Legal Department of the IMF.[4] However, it has great merit from the practical point of view since it stops a person who has been provided with goods or services from using the IMF Agreement as a means of avoiding payment.

> **England**
> *Sing Batra* **v.** *Ebrahim*
> **Court of Appeal**
> *The Times*, **3 May 1977**

Dr Sing Batra was resident in England. He wanted to send some money to India and he did it through Ebrahim, a London moneychanger. The deal was simple: Sing Batra gave pounds sterling to Ebrahim in England and the latter promised to deposit rupees in Sing Batra's daughter's bank account in India. The exchange rate was very favourable to Sing Batra. No doubt Ebrahim intended to find someone in India who wished to get money out of India contrary to Indian exchange-control regulations, and he could then reverse the procedure, ensuring that the rate of exchange gave him a profit overall.

On this occasion, however, Ebrahim failed to honour his agreement. Sing Batra sued him in England. The court held for Ebrahim on the ground that the transaction was contrary to Indian exchange-control regulations. Since it was an exchange contract – Sing Batra was giving pounds in England in exchange for rupees in India – it was covered by Article VIII(2)(b). So Sing Batra lost his money.

In the *Terruzzi* case, Lord Denning referred to the problem of 'monetary transactions in disguise'. Our next case is one in which this problem actually arose.

---

3 See the cases cited in Dicey, Morris and Collins, p. 2011, n. 60.
4 Gold, 'Exchange Contracts, Exchange Control and the IMF Articles of Agreement: Some Animadversions on Wilson, Smithett and Cope Ltd v. Terruzzi' (1984) 33 ICLQ 777.

England
United City Merchants v. Royal Bank of Canada
House of Lords
[1983] AC 168; [1982] 2 WLR 1039; [1982] 2 All ER 720

Background

This case concerned a complex transaction which involved a number of issues. For our purposes, the relevant facts may be stated as follows. A British company agreed to sell goods to a Peruvian company. The price was in dollars and payment was to be made in England. At the request of the Peruvian company, the English company agreed to invoice them for double the agreed price and to deposit the difference in the Miami bank account of an associate of the Peruvian company. This was clearly intended to allow the Peruvian company to evade Peruvian exchange controls, since it could use the false invoice to obtain permission from the Peruvian authorities to buy twice the amount of dollars needed to pay for the goods.

An advance payment was made and the British company duly deposited half in the Miami bank. When the goods arrived in Peru, however, the Peruvian company refused to accept them. Legal proceedings were brought in England by the sellers and the company to whom they had assigned the debt. The trial judge held for the defendants (the Peruvian buyers) on the ground that the entire contract was unenforceable under Article VIII(2)(b). On appeal, the Court of Appeal held that Article VIII(2)(b) did not apply to the part of the contract that was not a monetary transaction in disguise, but dismissed the appeal on other grounds (the documentary credit point). The claimants appealed. The House of Lords decided the documentary credit point in favour of the claimants/appellants (this part of the judgment is not reproduced). It then had to decide what effect Article VIII(2)(b) had on the contract.

Lord Diplock

[After dealing with the documentary credit point, said:]

The Bretton Woods point arises out of the agreement between the buyers and the seller collateral to the contract of sale of the goods between the same parties that out of the payments in US dollars received by the sellers under the documentary credit in respect of each instalment of the invoice price of the goods, they would transmit to the account of the buyers in America one half of the US dollars received.

[After referring to Article VIII(2)(b), he continued:]

My Lords, I accept as correct the narrow interpretation that was placed upon the expression 'exchange contracts' in this provision of the Bretton Woods Agreement by the Court of Appeal in *Wilson, Smithett & Cope Ltd* v. *Terruzzi* [above]. It is confined to contracts to exchange the currency of one country for the currency of another; it does not include contracts entered into in connection with sales of goods which require the conversion by the buyer of one currency into another in order to enable him to pay the purchase price. As was said by Lord Denning MR in his judgment in the *Terruzzi* case at p. 714, the court in considering the application of the provision should look at the substance of the contracts and not at the form. It should not enforce a contract that is a mere 'monetary transaction in disguise.'

I also accept as accurate what was said by Lord Denning MR in a subsequent case, as to the effect that should be given by English courts to the word 'unenforceable.' The case, *Batra* v. *Ebrahim* [summarized above], is unreported, but the relevant passage from Lord Denning's judgment is helpfully cited by Ackner LJ in his own judgment in the instant case: [1982] QB 208, 241F–242B. If in the course of the hearing of an action the court becomes aware that the contract on which a party is suing is one that this country has accepted an international obligation to treat as unenforceable, the court must take the point itself, even though the defendant has not pleaded it, and must refuse to lend its aid to enforce the contract. But this does not have the effect of making an exchange contract that is contrary to the exchange control regulations of a member state other than the United Kingdom into a contract that is 'illegal' under English law or render acts undertaken in this country in performance of such a contract unlawful. Like a contract of guarantee of which there is no note or memorandum in writing it is unenforceable by the courts and nothing more.

[The judge at first instance in the present case], professing to follow the guidance given in the *Terruzzi* case . . . rejected out of hand what he described as a 'rather remarkable submission' that the sellers could recover that half of the invoice price which represented the true sale price of the goods, even if they could not recover that other half of the invoice price which they would receive as trustees for the buyers on trust to transmit it to the buyer's American company in Florida. He held that it was impossible to sever the contract constituted by the documentary credit; it was either enforceable in full or not at all.

In refusing to treat the sellers' claim under the documentary credit for that part of the invoice price that they were to retain for themselves as the sale price of the goods in a different way from that in which he treated their claim to that part of the invoice price which they would receive as trustees for the buyers, I agree with all three members of the Court of Appeal the learned judge fell into error.

I avoid speaking of 'severability', for this expression is appropriate where the task upon which the court is engaged is construing the language that the parties have used in a written contract. The question whether and to what extent a contract is unenforceable under the Bretton Woods Agreements Order in Council 1946 because it is a monetary transaction in disguise is *not* a question of construction of the contract, but a question of the substance of the transaction to which enforcement of the contract will give effect. If the matter were to be determined simply as a question of construction, the contract between the sellers and the confirming bank constituted by the documentary credit fell altogether outside the Bretton Woods Agreement; it was not a contract to exchange one currency for another currency but a contract to pay currency for documents which included documents of title to goods. On the contrary, the task on which the court is engaged is to penetrate any disguise presented by the actual words the parties have used, to identify any monetary transaction (in the narrow sense of that expression as used in the *Terruzzi* case . . .) which those words were intended to conceal and to refuse to enforce the contract to the extent that to do so would give effect to the monetary transaction.

In the instant case there is no difficulty in identifying the monetary transaction that was sought to be concealed by the actual words used in the documentary credit and in the underlying contract of sale. It was to exchange Peruvian currency provided by the buyers in Peru for US $331,043 to be made available to them in Florida; and to do this was contrary to the exchange control regulations of Peru. Payment under the documentary credit by the confirming bank to the sellers of that half of the invoice price (viz. $331,043) that the sellers would receive as trustees for the buyers on trust to remit it to the account of the buyer's American company in Florida, was an essential part of that monetary transaction and therefore unenforceable; but payment of the other half of the invoice price and of the freight was not; the sellers would receive that part of the payment under the documentary credit on their own behalf and retain it as the genuine purchase price of goods sold by them to the buyers. I agree with the Court of Appeal that there is nothing in the Bretton Woods Agreements Order in Council 1946 that prevents the payment under the documentary credit being enforceable to this extent.

As regards the first instalment of 20 per cent. of the invoice price, this was paid by the confirming bank in full. No enforcement by the court of this payment is needed by the buyers. The confirming bank, if it had known at the time of the monetary transaction by the buyers that was involved, could have successfully resisted payment of one half of that instalment; but even if it was in possession of such knowledge there was nothing in English law to prevent it from voluntarily paying that half too. As regards the third instalment of 10 per cent. of the invoice price, that never fell due within the period of the credit. What is in issue in this appeal is the second instalment of 70 per cent. of the invoice price and 100 per cent. of the freight which, as I have held under the documentary credit point, fell due upon the re-presentation of the documents on December 22, 1976. In my opinion the sellers are entitled to judgment for that part of the second instalment which was not a monetary transaction in disguise; that is to say: 35 per cent. of the invoice price and 100 per cent. of the freight, amounting in all to US $262,807.49, with interest thereon from December 22, 1976.

§1.3 Conclusions

In this area, the country imposing the exchange controls has an interest in their enforcement, but other countries have an interest in ensuring that sellers receive payment for the goods they deliver. The law developed by the English courts in this area attempts to balance these interests. Such an attempt is possible only if the court adopts a functional approach.

§ 2   Claims in foreign currency

§ 2.1   *The 'breach-date' rule*

Contracts are often based on foreign currency – for example, the price of goods or the currency in which a loan is expressed; and the most appropriate measure of loss in a tort claim may also be in foreign currency. This means that a claim in legal proceedings will sometimes be most naturally expressed in foreign currency. In the past, however, a procedural rule prevented English or American courts from giving judgment in foreign currency; so the court had to make a conversion into the currency of the forum. If the currencies in question were fluctuating, at what date should the conversion be made?

The answer common-law courts came up with was the so-called 'breach-date rule' (also called the 'breach-*day* rule'). It is important not to misunderstand this phrase. The rule was that the conversion should be made at the rate of exchange prevailing on the date when the cause of action arose. In the case of a claim for breach of contract, this would be the date of the breach. Hence the name. However, the phrase 'breach-date rule' was also used for other claims. Thus, if the claim was in tort, it would be the date on which the tort was committed.

We illustrate this rule with two American cases. It so happens that both concern foreign judgments. However, it must not be thought that the breach-date rule is applicable only where the claim is on a foreign judgment. As explained in the previous paragraph, it can happen in a wide range of circumstances.

What is the 'breach date' for a claim based on a foreign judgment? Since the judgment creates a new cause of action, which replaces the original claim, the 'breach date' is different from that of the original cause of action. It is the date of the foreign judgment. Our next case applies this rule and illustrates some of the problems that can arise.

> **United States (New York)**
> **Competex v. LaBow**
> **US Court of Appeals for the Second Circuit**
> **783 F 2d 333 (1986)**

Background

LaBow, a New Yorker, lost a substantial sum of money through speculation in copper on the London Metal Exchange. His broker, Competex, a Swiss corporation, satisfied these debts. Competex sued LaBow for breach of contract in England, and obtained a default judgment for £187,929.82.

Competex then brought a diversity action in a federal court in New York to enforce the English judgment. The trial judge held that the English judgment was entitled to recognition and enforcement. Because determination of the date on which to convert a foreign currency debt into dollars is a substantive question, he applied New York law.[5] At the time, this was the breach-date rule (referred to in the judgment as the 'breach-day' rule). Since Competex's claim was based on the English judgment rather than on the underlying contract, the trial judge applied the conversion rate prevailing on the date of the English judgment: £1 = $2.20. He entered judgment for US$583,201.78. The pound depreciated substantially relative to the dollar between the dates of the English and American judgments. On the date of the American judgment, the conversion rate was: £1 = $1.50. The pound continued to depreciate. LaBow then paid the English judgment, with interest, in pounds. He claimed he had thereby satisfied the American judgment. This was rejected by the district court, which held that the American judgment could be satisfied only by paying the dollar amount specified in it. The district court credited LaBow's payment against the American judgment at the conversion rate prevailing on the date of payment: £1 = $1.20. This left a balance owing on the American judgment of approximately $236,000. LaBow appealed against this ruling.

Jon O. Newman, Circuit Judge

[After discussing the merits and demerits of the breach-date rule, said:]

If we were free to choose a conversion rule, we would select either the judgment-day or the payment-day rule. However, as noted, we are not free to do so because the conversion question is one of New York law . . . Our task is to predict what satisfaction of judgment rule New York would apply.

. . . [W]e believe that New York's choice of the breach-day conversion rule clearly implies that New York would require satisfaction of a New York enforcing judgment by payment of the dollar amount specified in that judgment and would not consider an enforcing judgment satisfied by payment of the amount of the underlying judgment in foreign currency. The breach-day rule protects the judgment-creditor against fluctuation in currency values to the point of allowing him to speculate without risk. It would be anomalous to suggest that New York would allow its creditor's preference rule to be undercut by giving the judgment-debtor the opportunity to satisfy his New York judgment by paying the underlying judgment in depreciated pounds. Therefore, [the district court judge] was correct in holding that Competex's American judgment could be satisfied only in dollars. As a corollary, any pounds paid must be credited in dollars at the rate prevailing on the date the pounds were paid.

LaBow contends that our holding is contrary to the principle that a judgment-debtor can prevent entry of an enforcing judgment by satisfying the original judgment . . . However, once an enforcing judgment is entered, a new obligation in dollars is created, and jurisdictions that follow the breach-day or the judgment-day rule view this enforcing judgment as primary. Where that judgment is regarded as primary, the opportunity to prevent its *entry* by paying in pounds does not imply the right to *satisfy* it by paying in pounds . . .

Result: the order of the district court was affirmed.

---

5 A federal court sitting in diversity (as to which, see Chapter 7, § 1.1, above) applies federal procedural law but state substantive law.

QUESTION

In what circumstances could LaBow have satisfied all claims against him by paying in pounds the sum for which the English judgment was given?

United States (New York)
Indag SA v. *Irridelco Corporation*
Federal District Court for the Southern District of New York
658 F Supp 763 (1987)

Background

This was an action to enforce a judgment in favour of Indag. The judgment was given by the Cantonal Court of Vaud, Switzerland, on 12 June 1985 and was affirmed by the Federal Court of Switzerland on 25 November 1985. Indag brought enforcement proceedings in New York.

Leisure, District Judge

The primary issue in dispute concerns the selection of the appropriate date for conversion of the Swiss currency debt into dollars. This is a 'substantive question' on which the Court is 'compelled to apply New York law.' [Reference to the *Competex* case]. New York uses the breach-day conversion rule, entitling a plaintiff to recover an amount in dollars which reflects the exchange rate between dollars and the relevant foreign currency at the time of breach, plus statutory interest . . . The parties accept the relevance of the breach-day rule, but differ in its application to this case.

[After discussing various other issues, Judge Leisure continued:]

The last remaining issue involves a determination of the date on which the Swiss judgment debt 'became due.' Defendants argue that the date of the award of damages by the Cantonal Court of Vaud is controlling . . . Plaintiffs contend that the damage award was not enforceable during the pendency of defendants' appeal . . . and thus argue that the judgment debt first became due when the Federal Court of Switzerland affirmed the award . . .

[The New York provision], which provides for recognition of foreign country money judgments, applies to any such judgment 'which is final, conclusive and enforceable where rendered even though an appeal therefrom is pending or it is subject to appeal.'[1] . . . Accordingly, the Court concludes that a New York court enforcing plaintiffs' Swiss judgment would select June 12, 1985, for application of the breach-day rule, even though the judgment rendered on that date was subsequently appealed by defendants.

---

1 *Editor's note*: this is *New York Civil Practice Law and Rules* 5302, New York's enactment of the Uniform Foreign Money-Judgments Recognition Act, discussed in Chapter 18, § 2, above.

QUESTION

What would the position be if the trial court had given judgment for the defendant, but the claimant had appealed and the appeal court had given judgment for him?

§ 2.2 Judgment in foreign currency

Although the breach-date rule has had a long history in England, it was finally abandoned (for at least some claims) in 1976. This occurred in our next case, a decision which is also of interest for the light it throws on the English doctrine of precedent (*stare decisis*).

England
Miliangos* v. *George Frank (Textiles) Ltd
House of Lords
[1976] AC 443; [1975] 3 WLR 758; [1975] 3 All ER 801; [1976] 1 Lloyd's Rep 201

Background

Miliangos (the respondent in the appeal) was Swiss. George Frank (Textiles) Ltd (the appellant) was British. George Frank had agreed to buy polyester yarn from Miliangos. The proper law of the contract was Swiss and the agreed price was in Swiss francs. The goods were delivered but the British company never paid. Miliangos sued in England. Originally, he claimed for a sum in pounds converted at the rate of exchange prevailing on the date of the breach of the contract. However, he subsequently amended his claim to ask for the agreed sum in Swiss francs. Since the pound had fallen against the Swiss franc, this was more advantageous.

The breach-date rule had originally been laid down in a case called *In re United Railways of Havana and Regla Warehouses Ltd*,[6] a judgment of the House of Lords. Under the English rules of precedent, lower courts are bound by judgments of the House of Lords. Miliangos had originally claimed in pounds because he assumed that the breach-date rule was still good law. However, before the case came on for trial, the Court of Appeal rejected the breach-date rule in *Schorsch Meier GmbH* v. *Hennin*.[7] Since the Court of Appeal was bound by the *United Railways of Havana* case, it ought not to have done this; however, it tried to distinguish the *United Railways* case. It was in response to this development that Miliangos amended his claim.

All this put the trial judge in the *Miliangos* case in a difficult position. Faced with two conflicting precedents, he decided to follow the *United Railways* case.

---

6 [1961] AC 1007.
7 [1975] QB 416 (CA).

Miliangos appealed. The Court of Appeal allowed the appeal, following *Schorsch Meier*. The case then came before the House of Lords.

Prior to 1966, the House of Lords had itself been bound by its own decisions: the only way in which a decision of the House of Lords could be overruled was by legislation. In 1966, however, the House of Lords made a declaration that in future it would not be bound by its previous decisions;[8] so, when the *Miliangos* case came before it, it was able to depart from the *United Railways* case.

Lord Wilberforce

[After reciting the facts set out above and remarking that 'some distortion of the judicial process has been brought about', continued:]

It has to be reaffirmed that the only judicial means by which decisions of this House can be reviewed is by this House itself, under the declaration of 1966. Whether it can or should do so is a difficult enough question, which I shall now examine.

My Lords, although the 'breach date rule' has a long history, possibly, but, I think, not clearly, extending back to the Year Books, consideration of it at the present time as regards foreign money debts must start from the [*United Railways of Havana* case].

[After a detailed consideration of the judgments in that case, Lord Wilberforce continued:]

My Lords, I have quoted extensively from these opinions, not only because they embody the standing authority on the question now at issue, but also in order to make clear what, I think, appears from all of them to be the basic presupposition. This is that procedurally an action cannot be brought here for recovery or payment of a sum expressed in foreign currency, and that, in effect, it can only be brought for a sum expressed in sterling, recoverable by way of damages. I now have to ask, what is the position at the present time? Have any fresh considerations of any substance emerged which should induce your Lordships to follow a different rule? I will endeavour to state those which appear to me to be significant.

1.   The courts have evolved a procedure under which orders can be made for payment of foreign currency debts in the foreign currency. The Court of Appeal has given its approval to the form:

> It is adjudged . . . that the defendant do pay to the plaintiff [the sum in foreign currency] or the sterling equivalent at the time of payment . . .

I can find no reason in principle why such orders cannot be made. The courts have generally power to order delivery *in specie*[1] whenever, in their opinion, damages are an inadequate remedy. In cases such as the present, indeed, one of the arguments against making orders for payment of foreign currency *in specie* has been that damages are an adequate remedy . . . But if, in the circumstances

---

1 *Editor's note*: 'delivery *in specie*' means delivery in kind: giving a particular commodity or object, rather than paying money.

8 Practice Statement (Judicial Precedent) [1966] 1 WLR 1234.

of today, damages are not an adequate remedy, as they clearly may not be if the breach date rule is applied in times of floating currencies, this argument, in any case nothing more than an appeal to discretion, loses its force. The jurisdiction is clear, on general principle: how the courts' discretion is to be exercised depends on the circumstances. I return to this later. Further, I can find nothing in the Rules of the Supreme Court[2] which prevents such orders being made . . . I shall return to this subject later with particular reference to the question of the date of conversion. At the present stage what is relevant is that orders in this form are jurisdictionally legitimate and procedurally workable.

2.   The situation as regards currency stability has substantially changed even since 1961. Instead of the main world currencies being fixed and fairly stable in value, subject to the risk of periodic re- or devaluations, many of them are now 'floating', i.e., they have no fixed exchange value even from day to day. This is true of sterling. This means that, instead of a situation in which changes of relative value occurred between the 'breach date' and the date of judgment or payment being the exception, so that a rule which did not provide for this case could be generally fair, this situation is now the rule. So the search for a formula to deal with it becomes urgent in the interest of justice. This leads to the next point.

[After referring to developments in the law of arbitration, where awards were beginning to be made in foreign currency, and to the law of Admiralty, where similar developments had been taking place, and considering whether EC law was relevant, Lord Wilberforce continued:]

My Lords, before attempting the task of deciding where, in the end, this House should stand as regards the [*United Railways of Havana*] rule there are some other general observations I think should be made.

First, I do not for myself think it doubtful that, in a case such as the present, justice demands that the creditor should not suffer from fluctuations in the value of sterling. His contract has nothing to do with sterling: he has bargained for his own currency and only his own currency. The substance of the debtor's obligations depends upon the proper law of the contract (here Swiss law): and though English law (*lex fori*) prevails as regards procedural matters, it must surely be wrong in principle to allow procedure to affect, detrimentally, the substance of the creditor's rights. Courts are bound by their own procedural law and must obey it, if imperative, though to do so may seem unjust. But if means exist for giving effect to the substance of a foreign obligation, conformably with the rules of private international law, procedure should not unnecessarily stand in the way.

There is, unfortunately, as Lord Radcliffe pointed out in the *Havana Railways* case, a good deal of confusion in English cases as to what the creditor's rights are. Appeal has been made to the principle of nominalism,[3] so as to say that the creditor must take the pound sterling as he finds it . . . The creditor has no concern

---

2 *Editor's note*: the Rules of the Supreme Court were the forerunner to the CPR.
3 *Editor's note*: nominalism is the principle that, if an obligation is expressed in a given currency, it may be satisfied by payment of the nominal amount of the debt in the currency in question, even if that currency is worth much less in real terms.

with pounds sterling: for him what matters is that a Swiss franc for good or ill should remain a Swiss franc . . . Another argument is that the 'breach date' makes for certainty whereas to choose a later date makes the claim depend on currency fluctuations. But this is only a partial truth. The only certainty achieved is certainty in the sterling amount – but that is not in point since sterling does not enter into the bargain. The relevant certainty which the rule ought to achieve is that which gives the creditor neither more nor less than he bargained for. He bargained for 415,522.45 Swiss francs; whatever this means in (unstipulated) foreign currencies, whichever way the exchange into those currencies may go, he should get 415,522.45 Swiss francs or as nearly as can be brought about. That such a solution, if practicable, is just, and adherence to the 'breach date' in such a case unjust in the circumstances of today, adds greatly to the strength of the argument for revising the rule or, putting it more technically, it adds strength to the case for awarding delivery *in specie* rather than giving damages.

Secondly, and I must deal with this point more briefly than historically it deserves, objections based on authority against making an order *in specie* for the payment or delivery of foreign money, are not, on examination, found to rest on any solid principle or indeed on more than the court's discretion.

[After considering the authorities, Lord Wilberforce continued:]

These considerations and the circumstances I have set forth, when related to the arguments which moved their Lordships in the *Havana Railways* case . . . lead me to the conclusion that, if these circumstances had been shown to exist in 1961, some at least of their Lordships, assuming always that the interests of justice in the particular case so required, would have been led, as one of them very notably has been led,[4] to take a different view.

This brings me to the declaration made by this House in 1966. Under it, the House affirmed its power to depart from a previous decision when it appears right to do so, recognising that too rigid adherence to precedent might lead to injustice in a particular case and unduly restrict the proper development of the law. My Lords, on the assumption that to depart from the *Havana Railways* case would not involve undue practical difficulties, that a new and more satisfactory rule is capable of being stated, I am of opinion that the present case falls within the terms of the declaration. To change the rule would, for the reasons already explained, avoid injustice in the present case. To change it would enable the law to keep in step with commercial needs and with the majority of other countries facing similar problems . . .

I return then to the two preconditions.

1.   Can a better rule be stated? I would make it clear that, for myself, I would confine my approval at the present time of a change in the breach-date rule to claims such as those with which we are here concerned, i.e., to foreign money

---

4 *Editor's note*: this was a reference to Lord Denning, who was one of the judges in the *United Railways* case; he subsequently moved to the Court of Appeal (as Master of the Rolls) and sat on the *Schorsch Meier* case and the *Miliangos* case. In the *United Railways* case, he supported the breach-date rule, but changed his mind in the *Schorsch Meier* case.

obligations, *sc.* obligations of a money character to pay foreign currency arising under a contract whose proper law is that of a foreign country and where the money of account and payment is that of that country, or possibly of some other country but not of the United Kingdom.

I do not think that we are called upon, or would be entitled in this case, to review the whole field of the law regarding foreign currency obligations: that is not the method by which changes in the law by judicial decision are made. In my opinion it should be open for future discussion whether the rule applying to money obligations, which can be a simple rule, should apply as regards claims for damages for breach of contract or for tort . . .

As regards foreign money obligations (defined above), it is first necessary to establish the form of the claim to be made. In my opinion acceptance of the argument already made requires that the claim must be specifically for the foreign currency – as in this case for a sum stated in Swiss francs. To this may be added the alternative 'or the sterling equivalent at the date of . . .' (see below). As regards the conversion date to be inserted in the claim or in the judgment of the court, the choice, as pointed out in the *Havana Railways* case . . . is between (i) the date of action brought, (ii) the date of judgment, (iii) the date of payment. Each has its advantages, and it is to be noticed that the Court of Appeal in *Schorsch Meier* and in the present case chose the date of payment meaning, as I understand it, the date when the court authorises enforcement of the judgment in terms of sterling. The date of payment is taken in the convention annexed to the Carriage of Goods by Road Act 1965 (Article 27(2)). This date gets nearest to securing to the creditor exactly what he bargained for. The date of action brought, though favoured by Lord Reid and Lord Radcliffe in the *Havana Railways* case, seems to me to place the creditor too severely at the mercy of the debtor's obstructive defences (*cf.* this case) or the law's delay . . . The date of judgment is shown to be a workable date in practice by its inclusion in the Carriage by Air Act 1961 which gave effect to the Hague Convention of 1965 varying, on this very point, the Warsaw Convention of 1929, but, in some cases particularly where there is an appeal, may again impose on the creditor a considerable currency risk. So I would favour the payment date, in the sense I have mentioned. In the case of a company in liquidation, the corresponding date for conversion would be the date when the creditor's claim in terms of sterling is admitted by the liquidator . . .

2. A rule in the form suggested above would not, in my opinion, give rise to any serious procedural difficulty. Suggestions were made at the Bar that as regards such matters as set-off, counterclaim, payment into court, it would be difficult or impossible to apply. I would say as to these matters that I see no reason why this should be so: it would be inappropriate to discuss them here in detail and unnecessary since the Court of Appeal has assessed the procedural implications and has not been impressed with any difficulty . . .

My Lords, in conclusion I would say that, difficult as this whole matter undoubtedly is, if once a clear conclusion is reached as to what the law ought now to be, declaration of it by this House is appropriate. The law on this topic is judge-made: it has been built up over the years from case to case. It is entirely within this House's duty, in the course of administering justice, to give the law a new direction in a particular case where, on principle and in reason, it appears right to do so. I cannot accept the suggestion that because a rule is long established only legislation can change it – that may be so when the rule is so deeply entrenched that it has infected the whole legal system, or the choice of a new rule involves more far-reaching research than courts can carry out . . . Indeed, from some experience in the matter, I am led to doubt whether legislative reform, at least prompt and comprehensive reform, in this field of foreign currency obligation, is practicable. Questions as to the recovery of debts or of damages depend so much upon individual mixtures of facts and merits as to make them more suitable for progressive solutions in the courts. I think that we have an opportunity to reach such a solution here. I would accordingly depart from the *Havana Railways* case and dismiss this appeal.

Result: the appeal was dismissed, and the breach-date rule not applied.

As Lord Diplock said, the *Miliangos* case abolished the breach-date rule only where the debt was expressed in foreign currency. He left other situations to be decided subsequently. In our next cases (two cases were decided in one judgment), the House of Lords had to determine what would happen in the case of an action for damages in tort and, in the second case, for breach of contract.

England
Owners of the Eleftherotria* v. *Owners of the Despina R
***Services Europe Atlantique Sud (SEAS)* v. *Stockholms Rederiaktiebolag Svea*[9]**
House of Lords
[1979] AC 685; [1978] 3 WLR 804; [1979] 1 All ER 421; [1979] 1 Lloyd's Rep 1

Lord Wilberforce

My Lords, in the *Miliangos* case [above], this House decided that a plaintiff suing for a debt payable in Swiss francs under a contract governed by Swiss law could claim and recover judgment in this country in Swiss francs. Whether the same, or a similar, rule could be applied to cases where (i) a plaintiff sues for damages in tort, or (ii) a plaintiff sues for damages for breach of contract, were questions expressly left open for later decision . . . Now these questions are directly raised in the present appeals . . .

Owners of MV Eleftherotria v. Owners of MV Despina R

These are two Greek vessels which collided in April 1974 off Shanghai. On July 7, 1976, a settlement was arrived at under which it was agreed that the appellants should pay to the respondents 85 per cent. of the loss and damage caused to the respondents by the collision. This is therefore a tort case based upon negligence.

After the collision *Eleftherotria* was taken to Shanghai where temporary repairs were carried out. She then went to Yokohama for permanent repairs, but it turned

---

9 These two cases (the *Despina R* and *SEAS*) were decided together.

out that these could not be carried out for some time. She was therefore ordered to Los Angeles, California, USA, for permanent repairs. Expenses were incurred under various headings . . . in foreign currencies, namely, renmimbi yuan ('RMB'), Japanese yen, US dollars, and as to a small amount in sterling. The owners of the ship are a Liberian company with head office in Piraeus (Greece). She was managed by managing agents with their principal place of business in the State of New York, USA. The bank account used for all payments in and out on behalf of the respondents in respect of the ship was a US dollar account in New York – so all the expenses incurred in the foreign currencies other than US dollars were met by transferring US dollars from this account. The expenses incurred in US dollars were met directly by payment in that currency from New York.

The judge ordered that the following questions be tried separately, namely: (a) whether, where the plaintiffs have suffered damage or sustained loss in a currency other than sterling, they are entitled to recover damages in respect of such damage or loss expressed in such other currency, (b) if, in such a case, the plaintiffs are only entitled to recover damages expressed in sterling, at what date the conversion into sterling should be made. Under question (a) there are two alternatives. The first is to take the currency in which the expense or loss was immediately sustained. This I shall call 'the expenditure currency.' The second is to take the currency in which the loss was effectively felt or borne by the plaintiff, having regard to the currency in which he generally operates or with which he has the closest connection – this I shall call 'the plaintiff's currency.' These two solutions have to be considered side by side with the third possible solution, namely, the sterling solution, taken at the date when the loss occurred . . . or at some other date.

[After considering the authorities, Lord Wilberforce continued:]

My Lords, I do not think that there can now be any doubt that, given the ability of an English court (and of arbitrators sitting in this country) to give judgment or to make an award in a foreign currency, to give a judgment in the currency in which the loss was sustained produces a juster result than one which fixes the plaintiff with a sum in sterling taken at the date of the breach or of the loss. I need not expand upon this because the point has been clearly made both in [the *Miliangos* case], and in cases which have followed it, as well as in commentators who, prior to *Miliangos*, advocated abandonment of the breach-date-sterling rule. To fix such a plaintiff with sterling commits him to the risk of changes in the value of a currency with which he has no connection: to award him a sum in the currency of the expenditure or loss, or that in which he bears the expenditure or loss, gives him exactly what he has lost and commits him only to the risk of changes in the value of that currency, or those currencies, which are either his currency or those which he has chosen to use.

I shall consider the objections against the use of that currency or those currencies, but first it is necessary to decide between the expenditure currency and the plaintiff's currency – a matter which gave the judges below some difficulty . . .

My Lords, in my opinion, this question can be solved by applying the normal principles, which govern the assessment of damages in cases of tort (I shall deal with contract cases in the second appeal). These are the principles of *restitutio in integrum* and that of the reasonable foreseeability of the damage sustained. It appears to me that a plaintiff, who normally conducts his business through a particular currency, and who, when other currencies are immediately involved, uses his own currency to obtain those currencies, can reasonably say that the loss he sustains is to be measured not by the immediate currencies in which the loss first emerges but by the amount of his own currency, which in the normal course of operation, he uses to obtain those currencies. This is the currency in which his loss is felt, and is the currency which it is reasonably foreseeable he will have to spend.

There are some objections to this, but I think they can be answered. First, it is said that to use the method of finding the loss in the plaintiff's currency would involve the court or arbitrators in complicated inquiries. I am not convinced of this. The plaintiff has to prove his loss: if he wishes to present his claim in his own currency, the burden is on him to show to the satisfaction of the tribunal that his operations are conducted in that currency and that in fact it was his currency that was used, in a normal manner, to meet the expenditure for which he claims or that his loss can only be appropriately measured in that currency (this would apply in the case of a total loss of a vessel which cannot be dealt with by the 'expenditure' method). The same answer can be given to the objection that some companies, particularly large multi-national companies, maintain accounts and operate in several currencies. Here again it is for the plaintiff to satisfy the court or arbitrators that the use of the particular currency was in the course of normal operations of that company and was reasonably foreseeable. Then it is said that this method produces inequality between plaintiffs. Two claimants who suffer a similar loss may come out with different sums according to the currency in which they trade. But if the losses of both plaintiffs are suffered at the same time, the amounts awarded to each of them should be equivalent even if awarded in different currencies: if at different times, this might justify difference in treatment. If it happened that the currencies of the two plaintiffs relatively changed in value before the date of judgment, that would be a risk which each plaintiff would have to accept. Each would still receive, for himself, compensation for *his* loss.

Finally it is said (and this argument would apply equally if the expenditure currency were taken) that uncertainty will take the place of certainty under the present rule. Undoubtedly the present (sterling-breach-date) rule produces certainty – but it is often simpler to produce an unjust rule than a just one. The question is whether, in order to produce a just, or juster, rule, too high a price has to be paid in terms of certainty.

I do not think so. I do not see any reason why legal advisers, or insurers, should not be able, from their knowledge of the circumstances, to assess the extent of probable liability. The most difficult step is to assess the quantum of each head of damage. Once this is done, it should not be difficult, on the basis of information which the plaintiff must provide, to agree or disagree with his claim for the relevant currency. I wish to make it clear that I would not approve of a hard and fast rule that in all cases where a plaintiff suffers a loss or damage in a foreign currency the right currency to take for the purpose of his claim is 'the plaintiff's currency.' I should refer to the definition I have used of this expression and emphasise that it does not suggest the use of a personal currency attached, like nationality, to a plaintiff, but a currency which he is able to show is that in which he normally conducts trading operations. Use of this currency for assessment of damage may and probably will be appropriate in cases of international commerce. But even in that field, and still more outside it, cases may arise in which a plaintiff will not be able to show that in the normal course of events he would use, and be expected to use, the currency, or one of several currencies, in which he normally conducts his operations (the burden being on him to show this) and consequently the conclusion will be that the loss is felt in the currency in which it immediately arose. To say that this produces a measure of uncertainty may be true, but this is an uncertainty which arises in the nature of things from the variety of human experience. To resolve it is part of the normal process of adjudication. To attempt to confine this within a rigid formula would be likely to produce injustices which the courts and arbitrators would have to put themselves to much trouble to avoid.

. . .

In my opinion the Court of Appeal reached a right conclusion on this case and I would dismiss the appeal.

Services Europe Atlantique Sud (SEAS) of Paris v. Stockholms Rederiaktiebolag Svea of Stockholm

This case arises out of a charterparty under which the appellants chartered the *Folias* to the respondents for a round voyage from the Mediterranean to the East Coast, South America. The hire was expressed to be payable in US dollars, but there was a provision that in any general average adjustment disbursements in foreign currencies were to be exchanged in a European convertible currency or in sterling or in dollars (US). The appellants are Swedish shipowners, the respondents are a French company which operates shipping services. The proper law of the contract was English law.

In July 1971 the respondents shipped a cargo of onions at Valencia (Spain) for carriage to Brazilian ports. They issued bills of lading in their own name. There was a failure of the vessel's refrigeration as a result of which the cargo was found to be damaged on discharge. The cargo receivers claimed against the respondents and, with the concurrence of the appellants as to quantum, this claim was settled in August 1972 by a payment in Brazilian currency of cruzeiros 456,250. In addition, the respondents incurred legal and other expenses.

The respondents discharged the receivers' claim by purchasing the necessary amount of cruzeiros with French francs. The arbitrators found that French francs were the currency in which the respondents accounted and that it was reasonable to contemplate that, being a French corporation and having their place of business in Paris, they would have to use French francs to purchase other currencies to meet cargo claims.

The respondents then claimed against the appellants for the French francs which they had expended and for the amount of their expenses. In the alternative they claimed the equivalent in US dollars, that being said to be the currency of the contract (*viz.* the charterparty). The basis of their claim was for damages for breach of the contract of affreightment.

The claim was referred to arbitration in London, and the arbitrators held that they had jurisdiction to make an award in a foreign currency . . . They awarded the sum claimed in French francs for the reason that this seemed to them to be the most appropriate and just result. On the hearing of the special case, Robert Goff J set aside the arbitrators' award and held that damages should have been awarded in Brazilian cruzeiros. This judgment was in turn reversed by the Court of Appeal which restored the award of the arbitrators.

My Lords, the effect of the decision of this House in [the *Miliangos* case, above] is that, in contractual as in other cases a judgment (in which for convenience I include an award) can be given in a currency other than sterling. Whether it should be, and, in a case where there is more than one eligible currency, in which currency, must depend on general principles of the law of contract and on rules of conflict of laws. The former require application, as nearly as possible, of the principle of *restitutio in integrum*, regard being had to what was in the reasonable contemplation of the parties. The latter involve ascertainment of the proper law of the contract, and application of that law. If the proper law is English, the first step must be to see whether, expressly or by implication, the contract provides an answer to the currency question. This may lead to selection of the 'currency of the contract.' If from the terms of the contract it appears that the parties have accepted a currency as the currency of account and payment in respect of all transactions arising under the contract, then it would be proper to give a judgment for damages in that currency . . .

But there may be cases in which, although obligations under the contract are to be met in a specified currency, or currencies, the right conclusion may be that there is no intention shown that damages for breach of the contract should be given in that currency or currencies . . . In the present case the fact that US dollars have been named as the currency in which payments in respect of hire and other contractual payments are to be made, provides no necessary or indeed plausible reason why damages for breach of the contract should be paid in that currency. The terms of other contracts may lead to a similar conclusion.

If then the contract fails to provide a decisive interpretation, the damage should be calculated in the currency in which the loss was felt by the plaintiff or 'which most truly expresses his loss.' This is not limited to that in which it first and immediately arose. In ascertaining which this currency is, the court must ask what is the currency, payment in which will as nearly as possible compensate the plaintiff in accordance with the principle of restitution, and whether the parties must be taken reasonably to have had this in contemplation. It would be impossible to devise a simple rule, other than the general principles I have mentioned, to cover cases on the sale of goods, on contracts of employment, on international carriage by sea or air: in any of these types of contract the terms of the individual agreement will be important.

My Lords, it is obvious that this analysis, involving as it does a reversion to the ordinary law governing damages for breach of contract, necessitates a departure from older cases decided upon the 'breach-date-sterling' rule . . .

[After commenting on some of the older cases, Lord Wilberforce continued:]

The present case is concerned with a charterparty for carriage by sea, the parties to which are Swedish and French. It was in the contemplation of the parties that delivery of the goods carried might be made in any of a number of countries with a currency different from that of either of the parties. Loss might be suffered, through non-delivery or incomplete delivery, or delivery of damaged or unsuitable goods, in any of those countries, and if any such loss were to fall upon the charterer, he in turn might have a claim against the shipowners. Although the proper law of the contract was accepted to be English by virtue of a London arbitration clause, neither of the parties to the contract, nor the contract itself, nor the claim which arose against the charterers, nor that by his charterers against the owners, had any connection with sterling, so that *prima facie* this would be a case for giving judgment in a foreign currency. This is not disputed in the present appeal, and the only question is which is the appropriate currency in which to measure the loss.

Prima facie, there is much to be said in favour of measuring the loss in cruzeiros: the argument for this was powerfully stated by Robert Goff J. The initial liability of the charterers was measured in that currency by the difference between the value of sound goods arrived at the port of discharge and the damaged value at that port. To require or admit a further conversion can be said to introduce an unnecessary complication brought about by an act of the charterers' choice. I am unable in the end to accept this argument. The essential question is what was the loss suffered by the respondents. I do not find this to be identical with that suffered by the cargo receivers: the charterers' claim against the owners is not one for indemnity in respect of expenditure sustained but is one for damages for breach of contract . . .

I think it must follow from this that their loss, which they claim as damages, was the discharge of the receivers' claim, together with the legal and other expenses they incurred. They discharged all these by providing francs – until they provided the francs to meet the receivers' claim they suffered no loss. Then secondly was this loss the kind of loss which, under the contract, they were entitled to recover against the owners? The answer to this is provided by the arbitrators' finding that it was reasonable to contemplate that the charterers, being a French corporation and having their place of business in Paris, would have to use French francs to purchase other currencies to settle cargo claims arising under the bills of lading. So in my opinion the charterers' recoverable loss was, according to normal principle, the sum of French francs which they paid.

My Lords, there may be many variants of situations . . . in which a loss arises immediately in the form of expenditure or indebtedness in one currency, but is ultimately felt in another, which other may be the normal trading currency of the plaintiff. In my opinion a decision in what currency the loss was borne or felt can be expressed as equivalent to finding which currency sum appropriately or justly reflects the recoverable loss. This is essentially a matter for arbitrators to determine. A rule that arbitrators may make their award in the currency best suited to achieve an appropriate and just result should be a flexible rule in which account must be taken of the circumstances in which the loss arose, in which the loss was converted into a money sum and in which it was felt by the plaintiff. In some cases the 'immediate loss' currency may be appropriate, in others the currency in which it was borne by the plaintiff. There will be still others in which the appropriate currency is the currency of the contract. Awards of arbitrators based upon their appreciation of the circumstances in which the foreign currency came to be provided should not be set aside for, as such, they involve no error of law.

The arbitrators' decision in the present case was both within the permissible area of decision, and further was in my opinion right.

I agree with the Court of Appeal that the award ought not to have been set aside and with the judgments in that court. I would dismiss the appeal.

These two decisions set the course of the law in England. However, there were still some problems. Our next case illustrates one of them.

England
Attorney General of Ghana v. *Texaco Overseas Tankships Ltd*
House of Lords
[1994] 1 Lloyd's Rep 473

Background

The claimant (appellant) was a Ghanaian state-owned company, represented by the Attorney General of Ghana. The respondent was the owner of a tanker, the *Texaco Melbourne*. The Ghanaian company (referred to in the judgment as 'the department') had owned some oil, which was in the Ghanaian port of Tema. It wanted the oil shipped to another Ghanaian port, Takoradi. It contracted with the respondent to do this. The oil never arrived. Though this was not due to any misconduct on the part of the shipowners, it was agreed that they were liable for breach of contract.

The only question was the currency in which damages should be measured. The Ghanaian company operated at all times only in the Ghanaian currency, cedis. Ghanaian exchange-control regulations precluded them from holding any other currency. The Ghanaian company's loss was the value of the oil in Takoradi at the time when it should have been delivered. It was assumed that this should be calculated on the basis of how much it would have cost them to obtain a replacement cargo from the nearest available market (Italy) and ship it to Takoradi. They would have had to buy the oil in US dollars and the total cost would have been US$2,886,187.10. To obtain this money, they would have spent 7,937,014 cedis.

On the basis of the previous case, this would have seemed the appropriate sum, and this is what the shipowners proposed to pay. However, the Ghanaian cedi had fallen catastrophically and, at the date of the trial, 7,937,014 cedis were worth only US$31,046. The Ghanaians, therefore, claimed that their loss should be calculated in US dollars: they wanted US$2,886,187.10. The trial judge awarded them this latter sum, but the Court of Appeal reversed the judgment. The case then came before the House of Lords.

Lord Goff

Although the difference in terms of dollars between the two alternative awards is very striking, it is important not to be mesmerised by it. We have at all times to bear in mind that fluctuations in the relevant currency between the date of breach and the date of judgment are not taken into account. The award of damages is assessed as at the date of breach and, the appropriate currency (usually sterling) in which that award is to be made as at that date is identified. Delay between the date of breach and the date of judgment is compensated for by an award of interest (as indeed is delay in the satisfaction of the judgment). But, as I have said, no account is taken of fluctuations in the relevant currency as against other currencies between the date of breach and the date of judgment. So, if that currency appreciates as against other currencies, no compensating reduction is made in the amount of the award; nor is any compensating increase made if the currency depreciates. Indeed, it would in any event not be easy to select and identify another particular currency against which any such appreciation or depreciation is to be measured. Of course, in ordinary circumstances, any such fluctuation is unlikely to be very great, and so will not attract any particular attention. In the present case, an unusual set of circumstances may prompt the desire to respond to a perceived need to protect the department from the impact of the depreciation of the Ghanaian cedi against other currencies. These circumstances are (1) a delay of nearly nine years between the date of breach and the date of judgment; (2) an extraordinary depreciation during that period in the value of the cedi, as against other currencies; and (3) the identification of a particular currency, the US dollar, against which that depreciation might be measured, to show that, if an award is made in cedis, the value of the award in terms of dollars is, at the date of judgment, worth less than one per cent. of the value of an award in US dollars as at the date of breach. But to pay too much regard to this startling result can be most misleading, because it can lead to the conclusion that, contrary to the law, account *should* be taken of the fluctuation in the value of the relevant currency between the date of breach and the date of judgment. The proper approach is to identify, in accordance with established principle, the appropriate currency in which the award of damages is to be made, and to award an appropriate sum by way of damages in that currency, and also of interest in that currency to compensate for the delay between the date of breach and the date of judgment.

. . .

It is at this point that I have to consider the argument advanced on behalf of the department . . . [Counsel] for the department recognized that, in cases of non-delivery of goods under a contract of carriage, the plaintiff's damages are assessed by reference to the market value of the goods at the time and place at which they ought to have been delivered. Even so, he submitted, the 'principle of mitigation' requires that the plaintiff will be deemed to be obliged to go out into the nearest available market and purchase replacement goods at the earliest available opportunity, and will not be able to recover by way of damages more than the price he would have to pay for those replacement goods. Here the nearest available market for replacement goods was Italy, where replacement oil would have had to be paid for in US dollars. Accordingly, to make *restitutio in integrum* to the department in respect of the damages it had suffered by reason of non-delivery of its cargo, those damages should be assessed in US dollars.

I feel bound to say at once that, assuming that this argument is *prima facie* well-founded, nevertheless there is a short answer to it on the facts of the present case. Here it is plain on the findings of fact that, if the department had indeed bought such a replacement cargo in Italy under a contract under which the price was payable in US dollars, nevertheless in order to obtain those dollars the department, which carried on its business in Ghanaian cedis, would have had to expend cedis in order to acquire the US dollars from the Bank of Ghana. This being so, I find it impossible to distinguish this situation from that in [*The Folias*, above] in which your Lordships' House held that the currency in which the French charterers felt their loss was not Brazilian cruzeiros, the currency in which they discharged their liability to the receivers, but French francs, the currency in which they carried on their business, and with which they purchased the necessary cruzeiros. Let it be assumed that, in the present case, the Ghanaian cedi had over the relevant period appreciated in value as against the US dollar, I feel confident that any argument by the shipowners that the damages payable by them to the department should be assessed in US dollars rather than in Ghanaian cedis would have been rejected on this ground.

[After considering, and rejecting, other arguments advanced on behalf of the Ghanaians, Lord Goff concluded:]

There has been no challenge to the amount of the sum in cedis awarded by the Court of Appeal. For the reasons I have given, I would dismiss the appeal with costs.

Comment

Under the breach-date rule, the sum of 7,937,014 cedis or US$2,886,187.10 would have been converted into pounds at the exchange rate prevailing at the date on which the oil should have been delivered;[10] judgment would have been given for this sum. The result would have been much closer to the value at the date of the judgment of the dollar amount than to that of the cedi amount.

In some legal systems, it might have been possible for the Ghanaians to demand that the shipowners deliver the relevant quantity of oil to them (specific performance) or give them the present value of that oil; but this was not possible under English law.

---

10 It would not have mattered whether the sum in cedis or in dollars was taken: at this date, they were worth the same.

§ 2.3 Developments in New York

In 1987, legislation in the state of New York brought about a change in the New York rule. Under the new rule, the sum in foreign currency is converted to US dollars at the rate prevailing when the American judgment is entered: see Panel 27.1. This is very close to the English rule.

§ 3 Currency-exchange loss

Panel 27.1 Computation of judgments and accounts
New York Judiciary Law, § 27

§ 27

a Except as provided in subdivision (b) of this section, judgments and accounts must be computed in dollars and cents. In all judgments or decrees rendered by any court for any debt, damages or costs, in all executions issued thereupon, and in all accounts arising from proceedings in courts the amount shall be computed, as near as may be, in dollars and cents, rejecting lesser fractions; and no judgment, or other proceeding, shall be considered erroneous for such omissions.

b In any case in which the cause of action is based upon an obligation denominated in a currency other than currency of the United States, a court shall render or enter a judgment or decree in the foreign currency of the underlying obligation. Such judgment or decree shall be converted into currency of the United States at the rate of exchange prevailing on the date of entry of the judgment or decree.

Our final topic in this chapter is compensation for currency-exchange loss. Assume that the contract requires payment in dollars and the debtor pays in dollars. However, he pays late. The creditor intended to convert the sum paid into his own currency and did in fact do this. However, the dollar fell as against his own currency between the date on which payment should have been made and the date on which it was made. As a result, the creditor obtained less money in his own currency as a result of the late payment. Can he claim compensation for this loss if it was reasonably foreseeable that he would make the currency conversion? This is a different question from that considered in the previous section. It arose in our next case.

England
Ozalid Group (Export) Ltd* v. *African Continental Bank Ltd
High Court (Queen's Bench Division (Commercial Court))
[1979] 2 Lloyd's Rep 231

Background

In payment for goods exported to Nigeria, the African Continental Bank was under an obligation to pay Ozalid, a British company, the sum of US$125,939.22 in London on 5 October 1977. The payment was in fact made on 12 December 1977. Under UK exchange-control regulations in force at the time, Ozalid was obliged to convert any foreign currency received by it to pounds. The bank knew, or ought to have known, that this was the case. When it received the money,

Ozalid converted it. However, because the dollar had fallen since 5 October, it obtained fewer pounds than it would have obtained if payment had been made on time. It claimed the difference as damages.

Donaldson J

Notwithstanding that in the present case the price of the goods was agreed to be paid in US dollars, it is clear that the plaintiffs' loss was incurred in sterling and that this was foreseeable by the defendants. In the light of the foreign exchange regulations of this country, the value of foreign currency to an English company engaged in the export trade must be the amount of sterling which that currency will buy. It is nothing to the point that the plaintiffs took the risk of changes in the sterling value of the US dollar between the date of the contract and the due date for payment. The risk was still a sterling risk, but it was their risk and not that of the defendants. The plaintiffs undertook it for that period, but for no longer. If there had been no payment by the defendants at any time, the plaintiffs would have been entitled to sue for £71,656.32, being the sterling equivalent of US $125,939.22 on Oct. 5, 1977, when payment should have been made.

Does it make any difference that the defendants have paid the plaintiffs the full US dollar sum before the writ was issued or, to put it in another way, at what rate of exchange should those dollars be converted into pounds sterling?

. . .

Once it is proved that the plaintiffs' true loss is to be measured in sterling, any payment on account made in a different currency falls to be credited against that sterling loss at the rate of exchange ruling at the date of that payment.

It follows that the plaintiffs are entitled to judgment for £71,656.32 being the sterling loss suffered by them when the defendants defaulted on Oct. 5, 1977, less £68,669.15 being the sterling benefit received by them when the defendants paid them the sum of US $125,939.22 on Dec. 12 . . .

Note

In *President of India* v. *Lips Maritime Corporation*,[11] Lord Brandon made clear that claims for currency-exchange losses as damages for breach of contract are subject to the normal rules for damages for breach of contract.[12]

Further reading

Anderson, 'Exchange Losses in Contract' (1987) *Law Society Gazette* 2264
Becker, 'The Currency of Judgment' (1977) 25 *American Journal of Comparative Law* 152
Gold, 'Exchange Contracts, Exchange Control and the IMF Articles of Agreement: Some Animadversions on Wilson, Smithett and Cope Ltd v. Terruzzi' (1984) 33 ICLQ 777
　'The Restatement of Foreign Relations Law of the United States (Revised) and International Monetary Law' (1988) 22 *International Lawyer* 3

11 [1988] AC 395; [1987] 3 WLR 572; [1987] 3 All ER 110; [1987] 2 Lloyd's Rep 311 (HL).
12 [1988] AC at p. 424.

New York City Bar Association, 'Foreign Currency Judgments: 1985 Report of the
    Committee on Foreign and Comparative Law' (1986) 18 *International Law and Politics*
    791
Williams, 'Extraterritorial Enforcement of Exchange Control Regulations under the
    International Monetary Fund Agreement' (1975) 15 *Virginia Journal of International Law*
    319
Zamora, 'Recognition of Foreign Exchange Controls in International Creditors' Rights
    Cases: The State of the Art' (1987) 21 *International Lawyer* 1055

CHAPTER 28

Property: tangible movables

§ 1   Introduction

Our next theme is property. We saw in Chapter 22, § 2.3.3, above, that the view is widely held that property matters are governed by the *lex situs*, the law of the country where the property is situated. However, it was suggested that, while this works well in the case of tangible property, it is unsatisfactory when applied to intangible rights, such as contractual debts, bank accounts, shares, bonds, certificates of deposit, letters of credit and other financial instruments. We will therefore separate these two kinds of property: this chapter will deal with tangible property and the next with intangible rights.

Tangible property may be either movable (goods) or immovable (land). The application of the *lex situs* to land is so obvious that almost nothing needs to be said about it: all property rights (rights *in rem*) in land are governed by the law of the country in which the land is located. Many countries, including England, also apply this rule to succession. The result is that the deceased's property may be split up into a number of different estates. If, for example, he dies domiciled in England, leaving a flat in France and a villa in Spain, he will be treated by an English court as having three estates: his movable property, wherever situated, would constitute one estate, governed by English law (the law of his domicile); the French immovables would be a second estate, governed by French law (the *lex situs*); and the Spanish immovables would constitute a third estate, governed by Spanish law (also as the *lex situs*).[1] This could lead to considerable difficulties, especially in the case of intestacy;[2] so the modern tendency is to apply the same law (usually the law of the deceased's habitual residence) to the whole estate. It is likely that, at some time in the future, the EC will adopt legislation along these lines.[3]

Movable property is more problematic, since it may be moved from one country to another. The basic rule – the *lex situs* rule – is that the question whether property rights are acquired in goods depends on the law of the place

---

1 An English court would not actually apply the *lex situs* as such to the foreign immovables, but would apply whatever law a court in the country of the *situs* would apply (the theory of total *renvoi*: see Chapter 22, § 2.4.2, above). If the foreign court did not itself follow the *lex situs*, this could be another system of law, even English law.

2 If, as might be the case, the beneficiaries of the three estates are different, it becomes important to decide out of which estate the debts should be paid. There is no easy answer to this question. Another difficulty is that, if a certain beneficiary (for example, the surviving spouse) is entitled to a lump sum from the estate on an intestacy, he or she might get this three times over if all three estates have the same rule.

3 Whether the UK will opt into such legislation remains to be seen.

where the goods are situated at the time of the act or event as a result of which it is claimed that the rights are acquired. Thus, if X, in London, sends hides to Y in Quebec to be tanned and returned, and Y, without X's knowledge or consent, pledges them in Quebec with Z as security for a loan, the question whether Z's rights in the hides prevail over those of X will depend on the law of Quebec, the country in which the hides were situated at the time of the alleged pledge.[4]

This rule seems reasonable if the owner chooses to send his goods to a foreign country, but what if they were taken there without his consent? This question arose in our next case.

§ 2 Stolen property

England
Winkworth* v. *Christie Manson and Woods Ltd
High Court (Chancery Division)
[1980] 2 WLR 937

Background

Some works of art were stolen from Winkworth in England. The thief apparently took them to Italy where they were bought (allegedly in good faith) by the second defendant, Dr Paolo Dal Pozzo D'Annone, who sent them back to England to be sold by the English art dealers, Christies. When they came to England, Winkworth claimed them. Under English law, stolen goods remained the property of the owner, even if resold (except if resold 'in market overt',[5] which had not occurred). Dr D'Annone, however, said that, as he had bought them in Italy, Italian law should apply. It seems that, under Italian law, a *bona fide* purchaser could acquire title to stolen goods.[6] The English court had to decide what law applied.

Slade J

It is common ground that at the time of the theft the plaintiff was the owner of the goods, and that they were in his lawful possession. It is also common ground that he neither knew of nor consented to their removal to Italy or any subsequent dealing with or movements of them up to the time when the undertakings were given by Christie's. There is no suggestion in the agreed facts or on the pleadings that any person not a party to these proceedings ever acquired a title to the goods which would have destroyed the plaintiff's immediate right to possession of them.

---

4 *City Bank* v. *Barrow* (1880) 5 App Cas 664 (HL).
5 Under English law as it stood at the time, a person who bought goods in good faith in a legally constituted market ('market overt') could obtain good title to them even if they were stolen. This rule was abolished by the Sale of Goods (Amendment) Act 1994.
6 According to Dr D'Annone, a purchaser of movables acquired a good title under Italian law, notwithstanding any defect in the seller's title or in that of prior transferors, provided that (1) the purchaser was in good faith at the time of delivery; (2) the documentation was appropriate for a transaction of the type in question; and (3) the purchaser was not aware of any unlawful origin of the goods at the time when he acquired them.

It is therefore plain that, on any footing, at least until the sale in Italy, nothing had occurred which destroyed such right.

On the other hand, if the effect of the subsequent sale in Italy was to confer on the second defendant [Dr D'Annone] a title to ownership of the goods, which is valid even against the plaintiff and is of such a nature that it must now be recognised by the English court, it would necessarily follow that, in the events which have happened, the plaintiff has lost and the second defendant has acquired, the immediate right to possession of them.

In the circumstances, a crucial issue in the present case must be: was the effect of the sale in Italy to confer on the second defendant a title to ownership of the goods which is valid even against the plaintiff? And the question of law now before the court resolves itself to the question whether this issue falls to be determined in accordance with English domestic law or Italian domestic law . . .

The grounds upon which [counsel for the second defendant] submitted the crucial issue falls to be determined in accordance with Italian law are essentially very simple. There is, he submits, a general rule of private international law that the validity of a transfer of movable property and its effect on the proprietary rights of any persons claiming to be interested therein are governed by the law of the country where the property is situated at the time of the transfer ('*lex situs*').

[Slade J then analysed the relevant authorities, especially the leading case on the *lex situs* rule, *Cammell* v. *Sewell*.[1] It was agreed by both sides that there were a number of exceptions to the *lex situs* rule – for example, where the goods are in transit and their location is not known, or where public policy applies. Counsel for the claimant argued, however, that there was a further exception, which he formulated as follows:]

[W]here movables have been stolen from country A or otherwise unlawfully taken from the owner in country A and are then removed from country A without the owner's knowledge or consent and are then dealt with in country B without his knowledge or consent and are then returned voluntarily to country A, the law of country A should be applied to determine whether the original owner is or is not still the owner of the movables.

[Counsel for the claimant] accepted that there is no English authority which directly supports this proposition, but submitted that there is likewise no authority which shows it to be incorrect. Three particular considerations, he suggested, support the conclusion that as a matter of public policy, regardless of the content of the particular law of country B, the court should apply the law of country A, rather than that of country B, in the circumstances which he postulated. First, if at the time of the court hearing, the goods are situated in country A rather than country B, there can be no objection on the grounds of ineffectiveness to the court in country A applying its own law. Secondly, he pointed out, in the circumstances postulated, there has been no voluntary act on the part of the original owner, which has led to the connection of the goods with the legal system of country B.

---

1 (1858) 3 H & N 617; on appeal (1860) 5 H & N 728 (Exchequer Chamber).

Thirdly . . . the concept of security of titles is an important one and country A is justified in making an exception to the general principle of *Cammell* v. *Sewell*, for the purpose of securing a prior title recognised by its own system of law.

As to the first of these three considerations, the presence of the goods in country A at the time of the trial certainly removes one potential practical obstacle, which might otherwise deter the court in that country from applying its own law; no court likes to make an order which will probably be unenforceable in practice. In my judgment, however, it affords no further positive support at all to [counsel for the claimant's] proposition. There have been many cases, for example, *Cammell* v. *Sewell* itself . . . in which the court of country A has declined to apply the law of that country, despite the presence of the goods in question in that country at the time of the trial.

As to the second of these considerations . . . it appears that in the United States of America the courts of at least a number of states regard the knowledge of an owner that his chattel has been removed into another state as being relevant to the question whether the law of that other state should be applied for the purpose of determining whether his title has been divested.[2] I was referred to Beale's *Treatise on the Conflict of Laws* (1935), vol. 1, pp. 298, 299. There it was submitted that the great weight of authority in the United States of America supported the view that:

> . . . the law of a state into which chattels have been surreptitiously removed without the knowledge of an owner and against his will does not apply its law to divest the title of the absent owner . . . Such little authority as there is, therefore, is to the effect that a state has no jurisdiction over the title of an absent owner in a chattel which has been brought into the state without any act of his sufficient to submit his interest in the chattel to the jurisdiction of the state.

I was however also referred to a learned monograph by P A Lalive, *The Transfer of Chattels in the Conflict of Laws* (1955), see particularly at pp. 175–184, and an article by Dr J H C Morris, 'The Transfer of Chattels in the Conflict of Laws', in *The British Year Book of International Law* 1945, p. 232, see particularly, at pp. 240–241, in which the theories advanced in this context by Mr Beale have been subjected to searching criticism. [Counsel for the claimant] did not go so far as to adopt any of Mr Beale's wide propositions for the purpose of his argument. He suggested however, that the broad considerations of policy, which have influenced many American states in protecting the title of an owner who has not consented to his goods being removed to another state, are relevant for this court, in determining whether it should formulate the new exception to the rule in *Cammell* v. *Sewell* which he invites me to apply . . .

Despite this second consideration advanced . . . in support of the suggested exception to the principle of *Cammell* v. *Sewell*, there have been a number of English cases, for example, *Cammell* v. *Sewell* itself . . . in which the court of country A has applied the law of country B to determine the ownership of goods,

---

2 *Editor's note*: it is doubtful whether US law is in fact any different from English law: see *Restatement of the Law Second: Conflict of Laws*, § 245.

even though there has been no kind of voluntary act on the part of the original owner, which has led to the connection of the goods with the legal system of country B . . . I find it impossible to derive from the English cases any principle that the absence of such voluntary act should preclude or even deter the court of country A from applying the law of country B in accordance with the principle of *Cammell* v. *Sewell*. For all these reasons I do not think that the absence of any such voluntary act or the fact of an original unlawful removal constitutes an affirmative reason why I should adopt the suggested exception to that principle. At best it removes one additional obstacle which might have confronted the plaintiff, if he had expressly or implicitly agreed to the goods going to the foreign country or knew that they were going there . . .

I turn now to the remaining consideration urged on me by [counsel for the claimant], namely that, on the facts of his hypothetical case, country A is justified in making an exception to the general principle of *Cammell* v. *Sewell* for the purpose of securing a title recognised by its own system of law. This, I think, is by far his strongest point. In principle, any court must surely regard, with some initial sympathy, the position of a blameless person, such as the plaintiff in the present case, who, if attention is paid solely to the law of the country of that court, has at all material times had and retained good title to the goods which are the subject of his claim.

On the other hand, there are other equally powerful – I think more powerful – counter-balancing considerations. Security of title is as important to an innocent purchaser as it is to an innocent owner whose goods have been stolen from him. Commercial convenience may be said imperatively to demand that proprietary rights to movables shall generally be determined by the *lex situs* under the rules of private international law. Were the position otherwise, it would not suffice for the protection of a purchaser of any valuable movables to ascertain that he was acquiring title to them under the law of the country where the goods were situated at the time of the purchase; he would have to try to effect further investigations as to the past title, with a view to ensuring, so far as possible, that there was no person who might successfully claim a title to the movables by reference to some other system of law; and in many cases even such further investigations could result in no certainty that his title was secure. In these circumstances, there are, in my view, very strong grounds of business convenience for applying the principle of *Cammell* v. *Sewell* even in a case such as the present. I think . . . that most undesirable uncertainty in the commercial world would result if the choice of the system regulating the validity of a disposition of chattels were to depend not only on the situation of the goods at the time of the disposition, but also on the additional factors suggested on behalf of the plaintiff.

It must be accepted that exclusive reference to the *lex situs* must cause hardship to a previous owner in some cases, particularly if his goods have been moved to and sold in a foreign country without his knowledge or consent. Crompton J, however, in the passage already quoted,[3] from 5 H & N 728, 744–745, in the majority judgment in *Cammell* v. *Sewell*, expressly recognised that the English law

---

3 *Editor's note*: this part of the judgment was not set out above.

> as to stolen goods acquired by a purchaser under sale in market overt might seem harsh to a former foreign owner, but expressed the view that it made no difference that such owner did not intend them to be sent to the country where they were sold. The English court, I do not doubt, would ordinarily expect a foreign court to apply the principle of *Cammell* v. *Sewell* and recognise the title of a person who has acquired a title to goods under English law, by virtue of a purchase in England in market overt at a time when they were situated in England, and this will be the case even though such foreign court on an exclusive application of its own law, would have regarded a previous owner, from whom the goods had been stolen, as having a better title. If this would be the attitude of the English court, it could not, in my judgment, solely on the pretext of a newly formulated exception to the rule in *Cammell* v. *Sewell* either logically or reasonably, refuse to recognise the title to goods of a person who has acquired a title to them under Italian law by virtue of a purchase in Italy at a time when they were situated in Italy, and it makes no difference that the English court, on an exclusive application of its own law, would have regarded the previous owner, from whom the goods had been stolen in England, as having a better title to them.

Result: Italian law had to be applied to determine whether Dr D'Annone had obtained a good title as a result of the sale to him in Italy.

QUESTION

Do you agree that Italian law should have been applied?

The illegal art trade (trade in stolen or illegally exported works of art, or cultural artefacts) is said to be the second greatest worldwide criminal activity after the drug trade.[7] Many people feel that the law should not assist this trade by giving title to dealers who acquire works in dubious circumstances. Today, there are various checks and searches that art dealers can, and should, make before acquiring an item. Failure to do so could be regarded as casting doubt on their good faith. Our next case shows how legal and factual elements were used by one American court to ensure that a work of art was restored to its rightful owner.

Autocephalous Greek-Orthodox Church of Cyprus v. *Goldberg*[8] concerned four sixth-century mosaics stolen from a Greek-Orthodox church in northern Cyprus during the Turkish occupation. The thief smuggled them to Germany, where they were kept for a period of time. They were then sold to an American art dealer, Peg Goldberg, who took delivery of them in the free-port area of Geneva airport. The free-port area is a part of the airport where goods in transit can be stored on a temporary

---

[7] Drum, 'DeWeerth v. Baldinger: Making New York a Haven for Stolen Art?' (1989) 64 *NYU Law Review* 909 at p. 909. Estimates of the value of this trade range between US$10 billion and US$40 billion: *ibid*. For a full discussion of the legal aspects of the international art trade, see Siehr, 'International Art Trade and the Law' (1993) 243 *Recueil des Cours* 9.

[8] 717 F Supp 1374 (Federal District Court for the Southern District of Indiana, 1989); affirmed 917 F 2d 278 (7th Cir. 1990).

basis without having to clear Swiss customs. The mosaics had been flown in from Germany, and were flown out to the US as soon as the sale was complete. When Peg Goldberg tried to resell them to a museum in the US (for a vastly inflated price), the museum contacted the Cypriot authorities, and the Autocephalous Greek-Orthodox Church of Cyprus, the original owner, claimed them.

Peg Goldberg relied on Swiss law, under which a good-faith purchaser could (if certain requirements were satisfied) obtain title to stolen property. The court, however, found for the Church. There were three separate routes by which it reached this conclusion. First, it applied interest analysis, under which it concluded that Indiana, the state in which Peg Goldberg had her art gallery, had a greater interest than Switzerland. Under Indiana law, a *bona fide* purchaser did not obtain title to stolen goods. Secondly, it concluded (after hearing expert evidence) that a Swiss court would not have applied Swiss law to the mosaics, because they were only passing through Switzerland in transit; a Swiss court, it was said, would apply the law of the country of destination, Indiana. Thirdly, even if Swiss law did apply, Peg Goldberg had not acquired the mosaics in good faith. She should have checked the origin of the mosaics and, if she had, she would quickly have discovered that they were stolen.

The American courts involved in the case clearly wanted to reach this result, and their 'result-oriented' approach (Peg Goldberg would probably have used a different word) contrasts with the coldly neutral approach of the English court in *Winkworth* v. *Christie*. However, it must not be forgotten that all the Court of Appeal decided in the *Winkworth* case was that Italian law applied. The question of the buyer's good faith was left over for later determination.[9]

Our next case also concerned goods in transit, though in rather different circumstances.

§ 3   Tax claims

England
Brokaw* v. *Seatrain UK Ltd
Court of Appeal
[1971] 2 QB 476; [1971] 2 WLR 791; [1971] 2 All ER 98; [1971] 1 Lloyd's
   Rep 337

Background

Mr and Mrs Shaheen were US citizens, who lived in the United States. They wanted to send a consignment of furniture and household effects to their son-in-law in England. The goods were loaded on board a US ship, the Transoregon, which was registered in the US and flew the US flag. It was owned by Seatrain Lines, a US company. When the ship was on the high seas, a notice of levy was

---

9 For a case in which a foreign government used a somewhat different way of asserting its interest in an illegally exported work of art, see *Spain* v. *Christie's* [1986] 1 WLR 1120; [1986] 3 All ER 28 (Ch D). Here, the English court seemed more willing to consider the wider issues.

served on the shipowners in the US on behalf of the US Treasury. The US claimed that Mr and Mrs Shaheen owed money for back taxes, and under US law the effect of the notice of levy was to confer a lien (a property interest) on the US as security for the taxes. When the ship docked in England, the US claimed possession of the goods. Mr Brokaw (the son-in-law) also claimed them. The English court had to decide who was entitled to them.

Lord Denning

The United States Government say that these goods were in the possession of the shipowners, who were 'legally obligated under American law to surrender the goods' to the United States Government: that they were encumbered by a federal tax lien and were in the possession of the United States Government who had a possessory interest in them: and that the Government were, therefore, in the constructive possession of the goods.

It is well established in English law that our courts will not give their aid to enforce, directly or indirectly, the revenue law of another country . . . The United States Government submit that that rule only applies to actions in the courts of law by which a foreign government is seeking to collect taxes, and that it does not apply to this procedure by notice of levy, which does not have recourse to the courts. I cannot accept this submission. If this notice of levy had been effective to reduce the goods into the possession of the United States Government, it would, I think, have been enforced by these courts, because we would then be enforcing an actual possessory title. There would be no need for the United States Government to have recourse to their revenue law . . .

If the United States Government had taken these goods into their actual possession, say in a warehouse in Baltimore, or may be by attornment of the master to an officer of the United States Government, that might have been sufficient to enable them to claim the goods. But there is nothing of that kind here. The United States Government simply rely on this notice of levy given to the shipowners, and that is not, in my view, sufficient to reduce the goods into their possession.

Apart from this point, it appears to me that the United States Government are seeking the aid of these courts. They come as claimants in these interpleader proceedings. By so doing they are seeking the aid of our courts to collect tax. It is not a direct enforcement (as it would be by action for tax in a court of law), but it is certainly indirect enforcement by seizure of goods. It comes within the prohibition of our law whereby we do not enforce directly or indirectly the revenue law of another country. If the position were reversed, I do not think that the United States courts would enforce our revenue laws. For no country enforces the revenue laws of another.

I think the United States Government has no valid claim in England to these goods, and I would dismiss the appeal.

Comment

Some people think that a ship is a piece of floating territory of the State of the flag that it flies. This is incorrect. For certain limited purposes, the law of the

State of the flag may be applied to it, but it is not part of the territory of that State. If it is not in the territorial waters of a State, its *situs* is not in any State. When the notice of levy was served on the shipowners, the Transoregon was on the high seas. The *situs* was no longer the US. There was no *lex situs*. So the *lex situs* rule could not apply in the normal way. It is in fact recognized that the *lex situs* rule does not apply when the goods are in transit and their *situs* is fortuitous or not known. What law should apply in such circumstances is unclear. In the *Autocephalous Greek-Orthodox Church of Cyprus* case it was said that a Swiss court would apply the law of the country of destination. Whether an English court would adopt this view is not known. In any event, the *Brokaw* case cannot be regarded as conflicting with the *lex situs* rule. As Lord Denning said, the position would have been different if the US had obtained a property right over the goods while they were still on US soil.

§ 4   Nationalization: England and its colonies

We now come to a topic of some importance and difficulty: the effect on property of legislative or executive acts by a foreign government. Governments seize goods for various reasons: they may be pursuing a socialist policy of nationalization; they may be persecuting a racial minority; they may be taking the property of enemy aliens in time of war; they may be taking property on the ground that it is the fruit of crime or was used to commit a crime; or they may be taking it to enforce a tax obligation, as was the case in *Brokaw* v. *Seatrain*. As we saw, the court in that case accepted that the *lex situs* rule applies. In our next case, the court was faced with issues that were more politically controversial.

England
Luther Co. v. Sagor & Co.
Court of Appeal
[1921] 3 KB 532

Background

Luther was a Russian company that operated there before the Revolution. After the Revolution, some plywood owned by it in Russia was nationalized by the Soviet Government. The Soviets took possession of it in Russia, and sold it to an American company, Sagor & Co. It was shipped to England, where it was claimed by Luther. When the action was originally brought, the United Kingdom did not recognize the Soviet regime as the lawful government of Russia; so the trial court gave judgment for Luther. However, by the time the appeal was heard, the Soviet Government was recognized and this recognition was regarded as retrospective to cover the period during which the plywood was seized.

Bankes LJ

It is necessary now to deal with the point made by the respondents [Luther], that the decree of confiscation of June, 1918, even if made by the Government which is now recognized by His Majesty's Government as the *de facto* Government of Russia, is in its nature so immoral, and so contrary to the principles of justice as recognized by this country, that the Courts of this country ought not to pay any attention to it. This is a bold proposition. The question before the Court is not one in which the assistance of the Court is asked to enforce the law of some foreign country to which legitimate objection might be taken . . . The question before the Court is as to the title to goods lying in a foreign country which a subject of that country, being the owner of them by the law of that country, has sold under an f.o.b. contract for export to this country. The Court is asked to ignore the law of the foreign country under which the vendor acquired his title, and to lend its assistance to prevent the purchaser dealing with the goods. I do not think that any authority can be produced to support the contention. Authority appears to negative it . . .

Warrington LJ

It is well settled that the validity of the acts of an independent sovereign government in relation to property and persons within its jurisdiction cannot be questioned in the Courts of this country: 'Every sovereign state is bound to respect the independence of every other sovereign state, and the Courts of one country will not sit in judgment on the acts of the Government of another done within its own territory': *per* Clarke J. delivering the judgment of the Supreme Court of the United States of America in *Oetjen* v. *Central Leather Co.*[1] The existence of this principle of law is implicit in the speeches of both Lord Macnaghten and Lord Shaw in *Lecouturier* v. *Rey*,[2] and is not disputed by counsel for the respondents in the present case.

Some reliance was placed by the respondents upon the principle . . . that the Courts of this country will not enforce a contract invalid by our law as being in contravention of some essential principle of justice or morality, notwithstanding that by the law of the country where it was made no such objection could be raised to it. In my opinion this principle has no application. The appellants are not seeking to enforce such a contract. They are resisting an endeavour on the part of the respondents to induce the Court to ignore and override legislative and executive acts of the Government of Russia and its agents affecting the title to property in that country; it is that which, in my opinion, we are not at liberty to do . . .

Scrutton LJ

It remains to consider the argument that the English Courts should refuse to recognize the Soviet legislation and titles derived under it as confiscatory and unjust. This was based on the general principle stated by Mr Dicey in his work on the *Conflict of Laws*[3] that 'English Courts will not enforce a right otherwise duly acquired under the law of a foreign country . . . (B) where the enforcement

---

1 246 US 297 at 303; 38 S Ct 309 (US Supreme Court, 1918). *Editor's note*: this was itself a quotation from *Underhill* v. *Hernandez*, 168 US 250 at p. 252; 18 S Ct 83 at p. 84; 42 L Ed 456. The full quotation is to be found in *Banco Nacional de Cuba* v. *Sabbatino*, set out at the end of this chapter.
2 [1910] AC 262.
3 2nd edn (1908), p. 33.

of such right is inconsistent with the policy of English law, or with the moral rules upheld by English law, or with the maintenance of English political institutions.'But it appears a serious breach of international comity, if a state is recognized as a sovereign independent state, to postulate that its legislation is 'contrary to essential principles of justice and morality.' Such an allegation might well with a susceptible foreign government become a *casus belli*; and should in my view be the action of the Sovereign through his ministers, and not of the judges in reference to a state which their Sovereign has recognized ... Individuals must contribute to the welfare of the state, and at present British citizens who may contribute to the state more than half their income in income tax and super tax, and a large proportion of their capital in death duties, can hardly declare a foreign state immoral which considers (though we may think wrongly) that to vest individual property in the state as representing all the citizens is the best form of proprietary right. I do not feel able to come to the conclusion that the legislation of a state recognized by my Sovereign as an independent sovereign state is so contrary to moral principle that the judges ought not to recognize it. The responsibility for recognition or non-recognition with the consequences of each rests on the political advisers of the Sovereign and not on the judges.

Appeal allowed.

Result: the Soviet nationalization was recognized.

Comment

After the Russian Revolution, many countries applied the *lex situs* rule with regard to the nationalization of property: if the property was within Soviet territory, it was recognized; if it was not, it was not recognized, even if the owner was a Soviet citizen.

Our next case shows that some courts have applied a different rule where strong national interests were involved.

> **Aden**
> ***Anglo-Iranian Oil Co. Ltd* v. *Jaffrate (The Rose Mary)***
> **Supreme Court of Aden**
> **[1953] 1 WLR 246**

Background

This case concerned Iran. Unlike most Asian countries, Iran was never a formal colony of any Western country. However, for a significant part of the twentieth century, it was a client state of first the United Kingdom and then the United States.[10] After the Russian Revolution, British troops invaded Russia from Iran. In 1921, an Iranian army officer, Reza Khan, seized power with British support and,

---

10 During the earlier part of the twentieth century, Russia enjoyed considerable influence in the northern part of the country.

in 1925, deposed the previous dynasty.[11] He subsequently became Shah. This was the origin of the Pahlavi dynasty.[12]

When Germany invaded Russia in 1941, Britain wanted to send supplies to Russia through Iran. Reza Shah (as he was then known) opposed this; so he was deposed by British and Soviet troops. He was replaced by his twenty-two-year-old son, Muhammad Reza Shah Pahlavi, who ruled Iran as Shah from 1941 until the Iranian Revolution of 1979.

In 1933, during the reign of Reza Shah, Iran granted a British company, the Anglo-Iranian Oil Company (later BP), a major oil concession on extremely favourable terms.[13] The concession was to run for sixty years and granted the company the exclusive right to extract oil from a wide area. In 1951, a man called Dr Mossadeq became Iran's first democratically elected prime minister. He decided to nationalize Iran's oil, and a law to this effect was passed by the Iranian Parliament. When negotiations with Anglo-Iranian over compensation broke down, Anglo-Iranian organized a worldwide boycott of Iranian oil. However, some oil was sold to an Italian company, EPIM, and a small part of this was resold to a Swiss company, Bubenberg AG. The latter chartered a tanker called the *Rose Mary* to transport the oil from Iran to Italy. As the tanker sailed away from the Persian Gulf, it was constantly circled by British bombers. It put into port in Aden, then a British colony, where the oil was claimed by Anglo-Iranian. The court had to decide who owned it – Bubenberg or Anglo-Iranian. This in turn depended on whether the expropriation of the oil would be recognized in Aden.

Campbell J

[After dealing with the question of jurisdiction, said:]

The second main issue is whether or not the plaintiffs have proved that this cargo of oil is their property. They say that their title to it is by virtue of a concession granted to them by the Persian Government as the result of an agreement entered into in 1933, and which was due to expire in 1993. By Article 21 of the agreement it was laid down that the concession should not be annulled by the Government and the terms therein contained should not be altered either by general or special legislation in the future, or by administrative measures, or any other acts whatever of the executive authorities.

On May 1, 1951, an Oil Nationalization Law was put into effect by the Persian Government. Although there is evidence that there was in existence another oil concession in Persia which had not produced any oil, it is not disputed that the law was passed to nationalize the plaintiff company only.

The plaintiffs contended that this Oil Nationalization Law was contrary to international law as being expropriation without compensation, and was really only confiscation, and that, as this court was bound to administer international law where it was appropriate, it should refuse to recognize any act which was contrary

---

11 This was the Qajar dynasty, which had held power since the late eighteenth century.
12 For a study of Iran, written shortly before the Revolution, see Halliday (Fred), *Iran: Dictatorship and Development* (Penguin Books, Harmondsworth, 1979).
13 At the time, Anglo-Iranian was mainly owned by the British Government.

to international law. It must be decided, therefore, whether this expropriation was with or without compensation.

[Campbell J then considered the question of compensation and held that the provisions of the Oil Nationalization Law concerning compensation were completely unsatisfactory. He then continued:]

That the courts in England will do nothing to invalidate an act of confiscation by a sovereign State of the property of its nationals is not disputed by the plaintiffs ... What has to be decided is whether the reverse is true when the property confiscated is that of a non-national.

The plaintiffs' contention can be based on two grounds: first, that no State can be expected to give effect within its territorial jurisdiction to a foreign law that is contrary to its own public policy or essential principles of morality; and secondly, that a foreign law that is contrary to international law or in flagrant violation of international comity need not be regarded.

International law is the settled practice of nations ... This settled practice can be ascertained from decided cases and from the writings of jurists, and to these I now turn.

[Campbell J then considered various authorities, both British and foreign. The last of these was *Luther* v. *Sagor*, above. After quoting from the judgment of Scrutton LJ, he continued:]

The court was considering the effect of the conduct of a sovereign State in regard to its subjects. If Scrutton LJ had been specifically considering such conduct in regard to aliens, a far wider question of international law, I feel no confidence that he would have expressed the same opinion. His remarks were a good deal wider than necessary for the decision of the case. On the whole I think that the relevance to this case of a great part of the judgment in [*Luther* v. *Sagor*] is more apparent than real, and that the case is in no way decisive here.

. . .

For the reasons set out above, I am satisfied that, following international law as incorporated in the domestic law of Aden, this court must refuse validity to the Persian Oil Nationalization Law in so far as it relates to nationalized property of the plaintiffs which may come within its territorial jurisdiction. I find the oil in dispute to be still the property of the plaintiffs.

Result: Anglo-Iranian was entitled to the oil.

Comment

The decision in this case was overtaken by events. The British Government decided that litigation was not the best solution; instead, they opted for a coup. The agent MI6 chose to carry out the operation was a man called Christopher Montague ('Monty') Woodhouse, a Greek scholar who had conducted guerrilla operations against the Germans in Greece during World War II.[14] The British

---

14 Robert Fisk interviewed Woodhouse on the Iranian coup in 1997, not long before the latter's death. See Fisk (Robert), *The Great War for Civilization: The Conquest of the Middle East* (Fourth Estate, London, 2005), pp. 112 *et seq.*

worked in conjunction with the US. The CIA man was Kermit Roosevelt, a grandson of former US president, Theodore Roosevelt. Arms and money were flown into Iran, and Mossadeq was overthrown in August 1953.[15] He was put in jail and later died under house arrest. The Shah returned to power, and ruled as a dictator with the help of his secret police service, SAVAK. A deal was struck with Anglo-Iranian: it was agreed that the oil would remain formally under state ownership, but that the oil companies – Anglo-Iranian was forced to allow other companies, mainly American, to participate[16] – would control production and sales.[17]

Britain's decision to overthrow Iran's democratically elected government shows that its attachment to international law was highly selective: it invoked international law when it suited its purpose – the United Kingdom had brought proceedings against Iran in the International Court of Justice – but ignored it when it did not.

Though the decision in the *Anglo-Iranian* case was (unusually) reported in the *Weekly Law Reports*, the Aden Supreme Court was not an English court and its decisions were not precedents in England. Its ruling that a foreign expropriation will not be recognized if it is against international law was controversial. Many people took the view that remedies under international law should be pursued on the international plane, and that violation of international law should not in itself affect the operation of the *lex situs* rule, even if the property was owned by a foreign citizen.[18]

Our next case is one example. This case is considered in detail in the next chapter. Here, we simply set out the part of the judgment dealing with the *Anglo-Iranian* case.

England
Re Helbert Wagg & Co. Ltd
High Court (Chancery Division)
[1956] Ch 323; [1956] 2 WLR 183; [1956] 1 All ER 129

Upjohn J

[After referring to the *Anglo-Iranian* case, said:]

I do not challenge the correctness of the decision in the *Rose Mary* case upon the facts of that case, but Campbell J came to the conclusion that the authorities both of this and other countries justified the formulation of a more general principle,

---

15 For the details, see Kinzer, *All the Shah's Men: An American Coup and the Roots of Middle East Terror* (John Wiley & Sons Inc., Hoboken, NJ, 2008). The ground had been prepared by a campaign of personal vilification against Mossadeq: he was attacked on account of the colour of his face (said to be yellow) and his nose (said to be runny): see Fisk, *The Great War for Civilization: The Conquest of the Middle East* (Fourth Estate, London, 2005), pp. 115–16.
16 Anglo-Iranian (BP) retained a 40 per cent interest; American companies got another 40 per cent, and the remainder went to Shell and others: see Halliday, *Iran: Dictatorship and Development* (Penguin Books, Harmondsworth, 1979), pp. 140–2.
17 *Ibid.*
18 See, for example, the passage from the judgment of the US Supreme Court in *Oetjen* v. *Central Leather Co.* quoted by Warrington LJ in *Luther* v. *Sagor* (above). It could also be argued that the concession agreement did not give Anglo-Iranian ownership of oil in the ground until it was extracted by them. If this was correct, oil extracted by the Iranian Government never was Anglo-Iranian's property: see *Nelson Bunker Hunt* v. *Coastal States Gas Producing Company*, below.

namely: (1) all legislation that expropriates without compensation is contrary to international law; and (2) that such law is incorporated in the domestic law of Aden and accordingly such legislation will not be recognized as valid in the courts of Aden. Unless the law of England takes a different view of international law from the law of Aden, the judge's conclusions can only be correct if his interpretation of [*Luther* v. *Sagor*] and *Princess Paley Olga* v. *Weisz*[1] is correct. Those cases, both in the Court of Appeal, were concerned with the effect of Russian legislation introduced shortly after the Russian Revolution of 1917 which in fact expropriated certain types of private property situate in Russia without any compensation. They established the principle that this court will not inquire into the legality of acts done by a foreign government in respect of property situate in its own territory. Campbell J considered that principle to be valid only where the property confiscated belongs (as in both those cases) to subjects of the confiscating State. However, all three judgments in *Luther* v. *Sagor* laid down the principle in perfectly general terms and it was in no way limited, at any rate in express terms, to a recognition of the validity of such legislation in relation only to nationals of the confiscating State.

[Upjohn J then considered the authorities, and concluded:]

With all respect to Campbell J, I think that *Luther* v. *Sagor* and *Princess Paley Olga* v. *Weisz*[2] laid down principles of general application not limited to nationals of the confiscating State. In my judgment the true limits of the principle that the courts of this country will afford recognition to legislation of foreign States in so far as it affects title to movables in that State at the time of the legislation . . . rests in considerations of international law, or in the scarcely less difficult considerations of public policy as understood in these courts. Ultimately I believe the latter is the governing consideration. But, whatever be the true view, the authorities I have reviewed do show that these courts have not on either ground recognized any principle that confiscation without adequate compensation is *per se* a ground for refusing recognition to foreign legislation.

1 [1929] 1 KB 718; 45 TLR 365.
2 Supra.

§ 5   Nationalization: United States

We now consider the leading US case on the matter.

United States
Banco Nacional de Cuba* v. *Sabbatino
United States Supreme Court
376 US 398; 84 S Ct 923; 11 L Ed 2d 804 (1964)

Background

After the Revolution, Cuba nationalized some sugar in Cuba that had belonged to a Cuban company (CAV) owned mainly by American shareholders. The provisions for compensation seemed rather limited. The question before the Supreme

Court was whether the expropriation should be recognized. It was argued that the expropriation was contrary to international law and, for this reason, should not be recognized. The lower courts accepted this. The case then came before the US Supreme Court.

Harlan J

The classic American statement of the act of state doctrine . . . is found in *Underhill* v. *Hernandez*, 168 US 250, p. 252; 18 S Ct 83, p. 84; 42 L Ed. 456 (1897), where Chief Justice Fuller said for a unanimous Court:

> Every sovereign state is bound to respect the independence of every other sovereign state, and the courts of one country will not sit in judgment on the acts of the government of another, done within its own territory. Redress of grievances by reason of such acts must be obtained through the means open to be availed of by sovereign powers as between themselves.

Following this precept the Court in that case refused to inquire into acts of Hernandez, a revolutionary Venezuelan military commander whose government had been later recognized by the United States, which were made the basis of a damage action in this country by Underhill, an American citizen, who claimed that he had been unlawfully assaulted, coerced, and detained in Venezuela by Hernandez.

None of this Court's subsequent cases in which the act of state doctrine was directly or peripherally involved manifest any retreat from Underhill . . . On the contrary in two of these cases, *Oetjen*[1] and *Ricaud*,[2] the doctrine as announced in *Underhill* was reaffirmed in unequivocal terms.

Oetjen involved a seizure of hides from a Mexican citizen as a military levy by General Villa, acting for the forces of General Carranza, whose government was recognized by this country subsequent to the trial but prior to decision by this Court. The hides were sold to a Texas corporation which shipped them to the United States and assigned them to defendant. As assignee of the original owner, plaintiff replevied[3] the hides . . . In affirming a judgment for defendant, the Court . . . described the designation of the sovereign as a political question to be determined by the legislative and executive departments rather than the judicial department, invoked the established rule that such recognition operates retroactively to validate past acts, and found the basic tenet of *Underhill* to be applicable to the case before it.

> The principle that the conduct of one independent government cannot be successfully questioned in the courts of another is as applicable to a case involving the title to property brought within the custody of a court, such as we have here, as it was held to be to the cases cited, in which claims for damages were based upon acts done in a foreign country, for it rests at last upon the highest considerations of international comity and expediency. To permit the validity of the acts of one

1 *Oetjen* v. *Central Leather Co.*, 246 US 297; 38 S Ct 309; 62 L Ed 726.
2 *Ricaud* v. *American Metal Co.*, 246 US 304; 38 S Ct 312; 62 L Ed 733.
3 *Editor's note*: replevin is a legal procedure by which the owner of goods can recover them from another person. This word is no longer used in English law.

sovereign state to be re-examined and perhaps condemned by the courts of another would very certainly 'imperil the amicable relations between governments and vex the peace of nations.'[4]

In *Ricaud* the facts were similar – another general of the Carranza forces seized lead bullion as a military levy – except that the property taken belonged to an American citizen. The Court found *Underhill, American Banana*,[5] and *Oetjen* controlling. Commenting on the nature of the principle established by those cases, the opinion stated that the rule

> does not deprive the courts of jurisdiction once acquired over a case. It requires only that when it is made to appear that the foreign government has acted in a given way on the subject-matter of the litigation, the details of such action or the merit of the result cannot be questioned but must be accepted by our courts as a rule for their decision. To accept a ruling authority and to decide accordingly is not a surrender or abandonment of jurisdiction but is an exercise of it. It results that the title to the property in this case must be determined by the result of the action taken by the military authorities of Mexico . . . [6]

To the same effect is the language of Mr Justice Cardozo in the *Shapleigh* case,[7] where, in commenting on the validity of a Mexican land expropriation, he said (299 US at 471, 57 S Ct at 262, 81 L Ed. 355): 'The question is not here whether the proceeding was so conducted as to be a wrong to our nationals under the doctrines of international law, though valid under the law of the *situs* of the land. For wrongs of that order the remedy to be followed is along the channels of diplomacy.'

[After discussing, and rejecting, various arguments that might have made the act of state doctrine inapplicable, Harlan J continued:]

The outcome of this case, therefore, turns upon whether any of the contentions urged by respondents against the application of the act of state doctrine in the premises is acceptable: (1) that the doctrine does not apply to acts of state which violate international law, as is claimed to be the case here; (2) that the doctrine is inapplicable unless the Executive specifically interposes it in a particular case; and (3) that, in any event, the doctrine may not be invoked by a foreign government plaintiff in our courts.

V.

Preliminarily, we discuss the foundations on which we deem the act of state doctrine to rest, and more particularly the question of whether state or federal law governs its application in a federal diversity case.[8]

---

4 *Oetjen* v. *Central Leather Co.*, 246 US 297 at pp. 303–4; 38 S Ct 309 at p. 311; 62 L Ed 726.
5 *American Banana Co.* v. *United Fruit Co.*, 213 US 347; 29 S Ct 511; 53 L Ed 826 (set out in Chapter 33, § 2, below).
6 *Ricaud* v. *American Metal Co.*, 246 US 304 at p. 309; 38 S Ct 312 at p. 314.
7 *Shapleigh* v. *Mier*, 299 US 468; 57 S Ct 261; 81 L Ed 355.
8 *Editor's note*: for the meaning of diversity jurisdiction, see Chapter 7, § 1.1, above. When federal courts exercise jurisdiction on diversity grounds, non-procedural matters are usually governed by state law. The act of state doctrine is an exception.

That international law does not require application of the doctrine is evidenced by the practice of nations . . . If international law does not prescribe use of the doctrine, neither does it forbid application of the rule even if it is claimed that the act of state in question violated international law. The traditional view of international law is that it establishes substantive principles for determining whether one country has wronged another. Because of its peculiar nation-to-nation character the usual method for an individual to seek relief is to exhaust local remedies and then repair to the executive authorities of his own state to persuade them to champion his claim in diplomacy or before an international tribunal . . . Although it is, of course, true that United States courts apply international law as a part of our own in appropriate circumstances . . . the public law of nations can hardly dictate to a country which is in theory wronged how to treat that wrong within its domestic borders.

[After stating that the text of the Constitution did not require the act of state doctrine, Harlan J continued:]

The act of state doctrine does, however, have 'constitutional' underpinnings. It arises out of the basic relationships between branches of government in a system of separation of powers. It concerns the competency of dissimilar institutions to make and implement particular kinds of decisions in the area of international relations. The doctrine as formulated in past decisions expresses the strong sense of the Judicial Branch that its engagement in the task of passing on the validity of foreign acts of state may hinder rather than further this country's pursuit of goals both for itself and for the community of nations as a whole in the international sphere. Many commentators disagree with this view; they have striven by means of distinguishing and limiting past decisions and by advancing various considerations of policy to stimulate a narrowing of the apparent scope of the rule. Whatever considerations are thought to predominate, it is plain that the problems involved are uniquely federal in nature. If federal authority, in this instance this Court, orders the field of judicial competence in this area for the federal courts, and the state courts are left free to formulate their own rules, the purposes behind the doctrine could be as effectively undermined as if there had been no federal pronouncement on the subject.

. . .

[A]n issue concerned with a basic choice regarding the competence and function of the Judiciary and the National Executive in ordering our relationships with other members of the international community must be treated exclusively as an aspect of federal law . . .

VI.

If the act of state doctrine is a principle of decision binding on federal and state courts alike but compelled by neither international law nor the Constitution, its continuing vitality depends on its capacity to reflect the proper distribution of functions between the judicial and political branches of the Government on matters bearing upon foreign affairs. It should be apparent that the greater the degree of codification or consensus concerning a particular area of international law, the more appropriate it is for the judiciary to render decisions regarding it, since the courts can then focus on the application of an agreed principle to circumstances of fact rather than on the sensitive task of establishing a principle not inconsistent with the national interest or with international justice . . . Therefore, rather than laying down or reaffirming an inflexible and all-encompassing rule in this case, we decide only that the (Judicial Branch) will not examine the validity of a taking of property within its own territory by a foreign sovereign government, extant and recognized by this country at the time of suit, in the absence of a treaty or other unambiguous agreement regarding controlling legal principles, even if the complaint alleges that the taking violates customary international law.

[One of the recognized exceptions to the act of state doctrine is the 'Bernstein exception', named after two closely related cases in which it was first formulated, *Bernstein* v. *Van Heyghen Frères SA*;[9] and *Bernstein* v. *NV Nederlandsche-Amerikaansche Stoomvaart-Maatschappij*.[10] Under this, the act of state doctrine will not be applied if the US Government clearly states that it does not object to the court's examination of the validity of the foreign State's act. No such statement had been made in the *Sabbatino* case, but it was argued that the rule should be changed so that the doctrine would not apply unless there was a statement by the Executive that it *did* object. This argument was rejected by Harland J. He concluded:]

However offensive to the public policy of this country and its constituent States an expropriation of this kind may be, we conclude that both the national interest and progress toward the goal of establishing the rule of law among nations are best served by maintaining intact the act of state doctrine in this realm of its application.

[Harlan J then considered whether it made a difference that Cuba was a party to the case. He held that it did not.]

The judgment of the Court of Appeals is reversed and the case is remanded to the District Court for proceedings consistent with this opinion. It is so ordered.

Judgment of Court of Appeals reversed and case remanded to the District Court.

9 163 F 2d 246 (2nd Cir. 1947); cert. denied 332 US 772; 92 L Ed 357; 68 S Ct 88.
10 173 F 2d 71 (2nd Cir. 1949), amended 210 F 2d 375 (2nd Cir. 1954).

Comment

After this judgment was given, Congress adopted the Hickenlooper Amendment to the Foreign Assistance Act of 1964, 22 USC § 2370(e)(2), set out in Panel 28.1. This was intended to reverse in part the judgment in the *Sabbatino* case: it provides that the act of state doctrine will not apply where the taking of property was contrary to international law, unless the President decides that the doctrine should be applied in a given case and a statement to this effect is put before the court. This could be regarded as an extension of the *Bernstein* exception, under which the doctrine would not apply if the Executive puts before the court a statement that the doctrine should not apply. The position now is that the doctrine does not apply (subject to the other provisions of the Amendment) unless the President positively asserts that it *should* apply.

The scope of the Hickenlooper amendment is unclear. It was apparently passed contrary to the wishes of the US Government, and it has been narrowly construed by the courts.[19] Our next case shows how it has been interpreted in Texas.

Texas
Nelson Bunker Hunt* v. *Coastal States Gas Producing Company
Supreme Court of Texas
583 SW 2d 322 (1979); cert. denied 444 US 992; 100 S Ct 523; 62 L Ed 2d 421 (1979); rehearing denied 444 US 1103; 100 S Ct 1071; 62 L Ed 2d 790 (1980)

> **Panel 28.1 Hickenlooper Amendment**
> **Foreign Assistance Act 1964, 22 USC § 2370(e)(2)**
>
> **§ 2370(e)(2)**
>
> Notwithstanding any other provision of law, no court in the United States shall decline on the ground of the federal act of state doctrine to make a determination on the merits giving effect to the principles of international law in a case in which a claim of title or other right to property is asserted by any party including a foreign state (or a party claiming through such state) based upon (or traced through) a confiscation or other taking after January 1, 1959, by an act of that state in violation of the principles of international law, including the principles of compensation and the other standards set out in this subsection: Provided, That this subparagraph shall not be applicable (1) in any case in which an act of a foreign state is not contrary to international law or with respect to a claim of title or other right to property acquired pursuant to an irrevocable letter of credit of not more than 180 days duration issued in good faith prior to the time of the confiscation or other taking, or (2) in any case with respect to which the President determines that application of the act of state doctrine is required in that particular case by the foreign policy interests of the United States and a suggestion to this effect is filed on his behalf in that case with the court.

Background

This case concerned three Texans, Nelson Bunker Hunt, Herbert Hunt and Lamar Hunt (collectively referred to as 'Hunt'). They were suing two Texas companies, Coastal States Gas Producing Company and Coastal States Marketing Inc. ('Coastal States'). In 1957, Libya had granted Hunt a concession which gave him the right, for fifty years, to explore, drill and extract oil in an area now identified as the Sarir field. Oil was produced from the field. In 1969, Colonel Mu'ammar al-Qadhafi (also written 'Gadaffi', 'Gaddafi', etc.) assumed power in Libya, and in 1973 Libya nationalized all Hunt's rights in the oil concession and assigned them to a Libyan state-owned company called AGECO. Compensation was to be decided by a committee appointed by the Government of Libya. Hunt then tried to organize a boycott of oil from the Sarir field by threatening to sue anyone buying it. However, Coastal States bought some oil and resold it in Italy. Coastal States remitted the profits to the United States. Hunt then sued it in a state court in Texas for conversion of the oil.

Barrow J

Hunt's claim against Coastal States is necessarily based upon the assertion that Libya's expropriation was invalid so that Coastal States acquired no title from AGECO. The critical question involved in Hunt's appeal is the applicability of the Act of State Doctrine and more precisely, whether Hunt's suit comes within the exception to the doctrine created by the Hickenlooper Amendment, 22 USC s.

---

19 *Nelson Bunker Hunt* v. *Coastal States Gas Producing Company*, below.

2370(e)(2). The lower courts have held that the doctrine bars inquiry by a Texas court into the validity of acts done by a foreign sovereign.

The Act of State Doctrine is a judicially created doctrine of restraint. The landmark case of *Banco Nacional de Cuba* v. *Sabbatino* . . . reaffirmed the doctrine as originally articulated in *Underhill* v. *Hernandez* . . .

In *Hunt* v. *Mobil Oil Corporation*, 550 F 2d 68 (2nd Cir. 1977), Cert. denied, 434 US 984, 98 S Ct 608, 54 L Ed. 2d 477, the Act of State Doctrine was held to bar Hunt's inquiry into the validity of Libya's nationalization of Hunt's concession. In holding that the trial court properly dismissed Hunt's claim against seven major oil producers in the Persian Gulf area for damages under the anti-trust statute, the circuit court said:

> We conclude that the political act complained of here was clearly within the act of state doctrine and that since the disputed pleadings inevitably call for a judgment on the sovereign acts of Libya the claim is non-justiciable.

This final judgment against Hunt in that case controls his present suit for conversion unless it comes within the exception to the Act of State Doctrine created by the Hickenlooper Amendment . . .

The Hickenlooper Amendment was enacted by Congress in 1964 shortly after the *Sabbatino* holding and in obvious reaction to it . . .

It must be recognized at the outset that this exception which was adopted over the objections of the Executive Department of the United States has been narrowly construed by our courts . . .

The statute enumerates three requirements which must exist in order to avoid the Act of State Doctrine under the Hickenlooper Amendment. 1. Expropriated property must come within the territorial jurisdiction of the United States. 2. The act of the expropriating nation must be in violation of international law. 3. The asserted claim must be a claim of title or other right to property . . . The court of civil appeals concluded, without consideration of the first two requirements, that the Hickenlooper Amendment is not applicable to this case because Hunt acquired only a contract right by the agreement with Libya. We agree with this conclusion and therefore limit our consideration to the third requirement stated above.

Since Libya is both the place of the contract's execution and performance as well as the location of the subject matter, Libyan substantive law governs the interpretation and construction of the rights conferred to Hunt by the Concession Agreement.

[Barrow J then considered the terms of the concession agreement and concluded that it only gave Hunt a contractual right. Ownership of oil in the ground remained with Libya; it passed to Hunt when extracted. He continued:]

The Hickenlooper Amendment by its express terms applies only to a claim of title or other right to property. This construction was made abundantly clear in 1965 when Congress added the words 'to property' following the phrase 'claim of title or other right.' Thus this exception to the Act of State Doctrine has no application here where only a contractual right was expropriated from Hunt . . . We have been cited to no case, and have discovered no case, holding to the contrary.

The trial court and the court of civil appeals did not err in concluding that the Act of State Doctrine bars judicial inquiry into the validity of Libya's actions.

Result: Hunt loses his claim.[20]

Comment

According to this case, application of the Hickenlooper Amendment depends on the distinction between contract and property, a distinction considered in some detail in the next chapter. The facts in the case are similar to those in the *Anglo-Iranian* case, except that the oil was not seized in the territory of the forum. However, on the court's analysis, it would have made no difference if a cargo of oil sold to the defendants had been seized in Texas: since the oil never belonged to Hunt, he could have no claim to it.[21]

§ 6 Conclusions

It will be seen from the authorities set out in this chapter that the effect of international law in this area is highly controversial. As far as England is concerned, the better view is probably that violation of international law is not in itself a ground for refusing to recognize a foreign expropriation under the *lex situs* rule. However, such an expropriation will not be recognized if it is contrary to English public policy, and international law is a factor to be taken into account when deciding this question. Although it is hard to say when recognition will be refused on public-policy grounds, most people would probably agree that an expropriation should not be recognized if it is part of a policy of victimizing a racial minority. This issue arose in our next case.

> **England**
> ***Oppenheimer* v. *Cattermole***
> **House of Lords**
> **[1976] AC 249; [1975] 2 WLR 347; [1975] 1 All ER 538**

Background

This was a tax case. The taxpayer, a Jew of German origin, was liable to United Kingdom tax unless he had German nationality during a specified period. He had been born in Germany and had originally been a German citizen. In 1939, he left Germany and came to England, where he had lived ever since. In 1941, a German

---

20 Steakley J and two other judges dissented. For a decision by the highest court in New York, the New York Court of Appeals, also adopting a restrictive interpretation of the Hickenlooper Amendment, see *French v. Banco Nacional de Cuba*, set out in Chapter 31, § 4, below.
21 The argument that oil in the ground never belonged to Anglo-Iranian was not considered by the court in the *Anglo-Iranian* case.

decree provided, 'A Jew loses his German citizenship if . . . at the date of entry into force of this regulation, he has his usual place of abode abroad'. The decree also provided for the confiscation of his property. One of the issues canvassed before the court was whether this decree should be recognized by the British courts. In the end, the decision did not depend on this, since it was established that, under Article 116(2) of the German *Grundgesetz* (Constitution) of 1949, the decree of 1941 was null and void *ab initio* in German law. This did not, however, mean that the taxpayer was a German national: under Article 116(2), he did not regain[22] German nationality unless either (a) he was resident in Germany (in which case, he automatically became a German citizen unless he expressly said he did not want to do so) or (b) he expressly asked for German citizenship (in which case, his request was automatically granted).[23] Since neither of these rules applied to the taxpayer in the case, he did not have German nationality at the relevant time.

Our interest in the case is confined to the issue – which in the end turned out to be irrelevant – whether British courts should refuse recognition to the 1941 decree. Of the five judges hearing the case, three[24] took the view that the decree should not be recognized; two dissented.[25] We give extracts from the judgments of two members of the majority.

Lord Cross of Chelsea

A judge should, of course, be very slow to refuse to give effect to the legislation of a foreign state in any sphere in which, according to accepted principles of international law, the foreign state has jurisdiction . . . But what we are concerned with here is legislation which takes away without compensation from a section of the citizen body singled out on racial grounds all their property on which the state passing the legislation can lay its hands and, in addition, deprives them of their citizenship. To my mind a law of this sort constitutes so grave an infringement of human rights that the courts of this country ought to refuse to recognise it as a law at all.[1]

Lord Salmon

The comity of nations normally requires our courts to recognise the jurisdiction of a foreign state over all its own nationals and all assets situated within its own territories. Ordinarily, if our courts were to refuse to recognise legislation by a sovereign state relating to assets situated within its own territories or to the status of its own nationals on the ground that the legislation was utterly immoral and unjust, this could obviously embarrass the Crown in its relations with a sovereign state whose independence it recognised and with whom it had and hoped to maintain normal friendly relations.

[Lord Salmon then discussed *Luther* v. *Sagor* and set out the passage from the judgment of Scrutton LJ in which the latter said it would be a serious breach of

---

1 Lord Hodson agreed with this view.

22 Though the matter is far from clear, it seems that the taxpayer lost his German nationality under Article 116(2) of the *Grundgesetz*, though Article 116(2) also provided the means by which he could regain it.
23 The purpose of these rules was to ensure that German citizenship was not forced on those who did not want it.
24 Lord Hodson, Lord Cross of Chelsea and Lord Salmon.
25 Lord Hailsham of St Marylebone and Lord Pearson.

international comity to refuse to recognize foreign legislation on the ground that it was contrary to justice and morality.]

The alleged immorality of the Soviet Republic's 1918 decree was different in kind from the Nazi decree of 1941. The latter was without parallel. But, even more importantly, England and Russia were not at war in 1918 whilst England was at war with Germany in 1941 – a war which . . . was presented in its later stages as a crusade against the barbarities of the Nazi regime of which the 1941 decree is a typical example. I do not understand how, in these circumstances, it could be regarded as embarrassing to our government in its relationship with any other sovereign state or contrary to international comity or to any legal principles hitherto enunciated for our courts to decide that the 1941 decree was so great an offence against human rights that they would have nothing to do with it.

Comment

It will be seen that Lord Cross and Lord Salmon give slightly different reasons for their opinion that the 1941 decree should not be recognized. Lord Cross's view is based on human rights and some fundamental concepts as to the nature of law; Lord Salmon, while also referring to human rights, is more concerned with not embarrassing the Executive, the reason normally given by US courts for applying the act of state doctrine. Nevertheless, these statements suggest that courts in England will not apply the *lex situs* rule where the relevant legislation involves racial persecution.

It should finally be said that most of the cases we have considered concern the situation where the foreign State had taken possession of the property within its territory before it was sent to another country. Where the original owner retains possession all along and himself takes the property to another country, different considerations arise. In this situation, it might be said that the question is not one of recognition but one of enforcement of the foreign law.[26] This would probably not be granted if the foreign law was penal or for taxes, and possibly in other circumstances as well. *Brokaw* v. *Seatrain* may be partly explained on this ground.

Further reading

Carruthers (Janeen M.), *The Transfer of Property in the Conflict of Laws* (Oxford University Press, Oxford, 2005)

Dicey, Morris and Collins, *The Conflict of Laws* (Sweet and Maxwell, London, 14th edn, 2006), Chapters 24 and 25

Fawcett (James J.), Harris (Jonathan M.) and Bridge (Michael), *International Sale of Goods in the Conflict of Laws* (Oxford University Press, Oxford, 2005)

Restatement of the Law Third: Foreign Relations Law of the United States, §§ 442 and 443 (pp. 366–89)

---

26 Dicey, Morris and Collins, pp. 1211–12, paragraph 25-012.

CHAPTER 29

Contractual rights and property interests – I

§ 1   Introduction

In this and the following chapters, we consider intangible property. This may be created by contract – for example, a debt, bond, certificate of deposit, or bank account – or it may be non-contractual in origin – for example, an intellectual-property right. In this area, contractual rights and property interests are hard to distinguish; so we deal with both. Indeed, many of the cases we will consider are primarily concerned with drawing this distinction. This chapter and Chapter 30 will be limited to the law of England and the Commonwealth; Chapter 31 deals with US law.

While it is generally accepted that contractual rights are governed by the law applicable to the contract (determined in accordance with the rules discussed in Chapters 24–27), there is a tendency to apply the *lex situs* rule to property interests. Hence the importance of distinguishing the two. If the issue is held to concern a property interest, a second question arises: what is the *situs* of the property in question?

§ 2   Situs

The principle applied is that of effectiveness: it is said that the applicable law must be the law of the country that can most effectively deal with the matter. For this reason, the general rule in the case of a debt is that the applicable law – the *lex situs* – is the law of the country in which the debtor resides.[1] What if he resides in two countries, as may often be the case where the debtor is a multinational corporation? In this situation, though in this situation only, the place of payment is relevant: if, in the ordinary course of business, the debt would be paid in one of the countries in which the debtor is resident, the *situs* is in that country. This rule is important in the case of bank accounts, which are regarded as situate in the country of the branch at which they are held.

It is unclear what the position would be if the debtor had two or more residences and payment would take place in a country in which he was not

---

1 It is possible that this rule will have to be modified in cases in which jurisdiction is determined by the Brussels I Regulation (or the Lugano Convention), since these instruments use domicile as the main criterion; see Dicey, Morris and Collins, pp. 1120–1.

resident. However, if he has only one residence, the *situs* is in that country, even if payment is to take place in another.

As we shall see, these rules are subject to exceptions. In any event, they do not apply to other kinds of intangible property. An intellectual-property right, for example, has its *situs* in the country under the law of which it was created. In the case of a registered right, this would be the country of registration.[2]

§ 3 The distinction between contract and property

When does a claim relate to contract and when does it relate to property? A clear statement of principle on this question is hard to find in the English cases; nevertheless, it seems that, where the issue relates to the rights of the original parties to the contract, it is to be regarded as pertaining to contract. Where, on the other hand, a third party enters the picture and claims that he is entitled to rights, the issue is more likely to be regarded as one of property.

We will now consider the leading cases. These will be grouped according to subject-matter.

§ 4 Contractual debts and bonds

Our first case concerns a simple contractual debt.

England
Re Helbert Wagg & Co. Ltd
High Court (Chancery Division)
[1956] Ch 323; [1956] 2 WLR 183; [1956] 1 All ER 129

Background

In 1924, an English company ('the claimant') agreed to lend a German company ('the company') a sum of money denominated in sterling, secured by mortgages on land in Germany. Payment of interest and capital was to take place in London, but the contract provided that it would be construed by the law of Germany.

Germany subsequently underwent an economic crisis and currency collapse. To resolve the crisis, it passed the Moratorium Law of 30 June 1933. This provided that a *Konversionskasse* (conversion fund) for foreign debts would be established. Debts payable in foreign currency would be converted into Reichsmarks and paid into the *Konversionskasse*: if this was done, the debtor's liability to the creditor would be discharged.

The company duly paid Reichsmarks into the *Konversionskasse* at the appropriate rate of exchange, and continued to do so after the outbreak of war between Britain and Germany. By 1945, it had paid the full equivalent in Reichsmarks

---

2 For a general discussion of the *situs* of property, see Dicey, Morris and Collins, pp. 1117–29.

of the whole loan plus interest. The question whether this extinguished the debt arose in litigation between the claimant and the Administrator of German Enemy Property under the Distribution of German Enemy Property Act 1949 and orders made under it.[3]

It was argued by the claimant that the *situs* of the debt was England (because it was payable there) and that the German legislation should not, therefore, be applied. Alternatively, it was argued that the German legislation was confiscatory and, following the *Anglo-Iranian Oil Company* case, that it should not be applied to deprive a person who was not a German citizen of property rights. Counsel for the Administrator of German Enemy Property opposed these arguments on the basis that the matter was contractual, governed by German law.

> **Upjohn J**
>
> The first question that I must determine is whether the applicability of the Moratorium Law is to be tested by reference to the local situation of the debt [the *situs*] or by the proper law of the contract. I am concerned with the effect of a law passed in 1933 upon a series of debts which, although accrued, only became payable on or after September 3, 1939.
>
> In my judgment, the question whether a liability to pay a debt payable on a future date has become modified or annulled by legislation must depend upon the question whether such legislation affects the contractual obligation, for the matter still rests in contract . . . The power of legislation to affect a contract by modifying or annulling some term thereof is a question of discharge of the contract which, in general, is governed by the proper law . . .
>
> [Upjohn J then considered the law applicable to the contract and concluded that it was German law. He rejected the argument that the parties intended that German law as it stood in 1924 should govern their relationship, without having regard to subsequent changes. He continued:]
>
> For the reasons I have already given, I do not think that the *situs* of the debt is the relevant consideration, but as the matter has been very fully argued before me and I have been referred to an unreported decision of the Court of Appeal of over 20 years' standing, which is much in point, I think I ought to express my views thereon.
>
> The general rule is clear that the debt is locally situate where the debtor resides, in this case Germany. [Counsel for the claimant], however, submits that that rule is altered by the terms of the contract between the parties, and he relies upon the statement to be found in the sixth edition of Dicey's *Conflict of Laws*, p. 304: 'If the place of payment of a debt be stipulated it will be there situate, the general rule notwithstanding.' He also relies on a statement of the law by Eve J in *In re Russo-Asiatic Bank*,[1] where he said this: 'although as a general rule the location of simple contract debts is the place in which the debtor is to be found, that rule, in my opinion, does not apply here, where the obligation is in terms to pay in sterling

1 [1934] Ch 720 at p. 738.

3 This allowed persons owed debts by Germans to claim against German enemy property in England.

in London.' It is to be noted that in that case the debtor resided both in Russia and in England, and in those circumstances it was a perfectly accurate statement of the law, whatever interpretation is to be placed on the judgments in the Court of Appeal in *New York Life Insurance Co.* v. *Public Trustee*,[2] to which I now turn.

In that case all the three members of the court pointed out that, strictly, a debt can only be sued upon in the place where it is payable, and although no doubt in a proper case the creditor may have a right to sue the debtor in another place, such right is to sue not for debt but for breach of contract for the failure to pay the debt in the due place of payment; the conclusion would seem to follow that the debt is situate where the debt is payable.

On the other hand, [counsel for the administrator] submits that when properly understood, the Court of Appeal decided that the place of payment becomes relevant to the question of *situs* only when it is established that the debtor has two or more residences, and certainly some passages in the judgments of the judges who formed the court support that view. In my judgment, in this court the matter is concluded by the unreported case in the Court of Appeal already referred to, namely, *Deutsche Bank und Disconto Gesellschaft* v. *Banque des Marchands de Moscou*.[3] A transcript of the judgments has been made available to me. I have sent for the pleadings in that case, and it is clear that the plaintiffs were assignees of a bank (the Deutsche Bank), whose principal office was in Berlin, but who had a branch in England. The defendant, a Russian bank with no branch in England, was indebted to the London branch of the Deutsche Bank on current account and, therefore, in accordance with the general rule of banking law the debt was payable in London. It is clear that there was no express term of any contract making the debt payable in London. The point now under discussion was not dealt with by Scrutton LJ, but Greer LJ formulated a number of propositions, among them these: '(4) On January 10, 1920, the Treaty of Peace Order in Council came into operation whereby enemy choses in action[4] having a *situs* in this country became vested in the Custodian, afterwards called the Administrator, of German property. (5) At this time the bank had no residence in this country, but the debt was payable in this country. (6) The debt in question, therefore, did not pass to the administrator, residence of the debtor being an essential element in deciding the *situs* of the debt.'

Later on he said: 'With regard to the propositions numbered (4), (5) and (6). At the date when the Treaty of Peace Order in Council came into operation, namely, January 10, 1920, the defendants had no place of business in, and were therefore not resident in, the United Kingdom, and I think it is established by the decision in this court in *New York Life Insurance Co.* v. *Public Trustee*[5] that the debt had no *situs* in this country. I regard that case as establishing that it is an essential element in determining the *situs* of a debt due to a foreign corporation that at the material date the corporation should have a residence within the jurisdiction in which the debt is payable.'

2 [1924] 2 Ch 101.
3 Cited in [1954] 1 WLR 1108; reported on a point of practice (1931–1932) 107 LJKB 386.
4 *Editor's note*: 'choses in action' are intangible property such as debts.
5 [1924] 2 Ch 101.

Romer LJ, after discussing the *New York Life Insurance Company's* case, said this: 'As the debt in question was, in terms of the contract creating it, payable in this country, and in addition was recoverable here, its locality was held to be English. In the present case the debt is payable in this country, but the defendant bank was not residing here on January 10, 1920. It was in May of the same year, but that will not help the plaintiffs. The debt was also recoverable here on January 10, 1920, had the plaintiffs been successful in obtaining leave to serve the defendant bank out of the jurisdiction. But I know of no authority for the proposition that a simple contract debt is situate in this country at a time when the debtor is not resident here, namely, because he can be sued by putting into operation the provisions of Order XI.'[6]

It is true that in that case the decision of the court was ultimately of no effect upon this point for it was found upon further evidence that the defendant bank had no existence at the relevant time, but it is clear that the majority of the court intended to lay down finally their views upon the law '*de bene esse*' in the words of Greer LJ in case upon further inquiry the bank was found to be in existence. Therefore I do not think I can treat the observations of Greer LJ and Romer LJ as *obiter dicta*, and the case is binding upon me if applicable to the present circumstances. It seems to me that the only distinction that can be drawn between that case and this is that in this case the debt is payable in London by the terms of the contract and not by virtue of the general law applicable thereto and that circumstance is indeed strongly relied upon by the claimants. In my judgment, however, that forms no proper ground of distinction, for the law must be the same whether the debt is payable in a particular place by virtue of the express terms of the contract or by general law applicable thereto. Nor can I accept the argument that, as on one construction of section 8 of the Act[7] there is no appeal from my decision, I am at liberty to disregard a well-settled canon of procedural law, that decisions of the Court of Appeal are binding on this court. Accordingly, in my opinion, the locality of the debt in this case is Germany, the only place where the debtor resides.

[The second point put forward by counsel for the claimant – that the German Moratorium Law should not be applied if the *situs* was outside Germany] does not arise on the view I have formed, and I turn to his third main point, namely, that the 1933 Moratorium Law is confiscatory and will not be recognized as affecting the contractual rights of the parties even where the debt is situate in Germany and the proper law is German, save only in cases where German nationals are concerned.

I start with the elementary proposition that it is part of the law of England, and of most nations, that in general every civilized State must be recognized as having power to legislate in respect of movables situate within that State and in respect of contracts governed by the law of that State, and that such legislation must be recognized by other States as valid and effectual to alter title to such movables

---

6 *Editor's note*: Order XI of the Rules of the Supreme Court was the forerunner of the CPR provisions on service out of the jurisdiction (discussed in Chapter 5, § 4, above).

7 *Editor's note*: this was the Distribution of German Enemy Property Act 1949, the Act under which the proceedings were brought.

and to sustain, modify or dissolve such contracts. The substantial question I have to determine is what limit is to be imposed upon that proposition when the effect of such legislation comes to be debated in the courts of other States . . .

To this general principle of recognition in foreign courts of territorial validity of legislation there are undoubted limitations or exceptions as the following examples show: (1) No State will enforce the fiscal laws, however proper, of another State, nor penal statutes, using that phrase in the strict sense of meaning statutes imposing penalties recoverable by the State for infringement of some law . . . (2) English law will not recognize the validity of foreign legislation intended to discriminate against nationals of this country in time of war by legislation which purports to confiscate wholly or in part movable property situated in the foreign State . . .

(3) English courts will not recognize the validity of foreign legislation aimed at confiscating the property of particular individuals or classes of individuals: *Banco de Vizcaya* v. *Don Alfonso de Borbon y Austria*,[8] which treated the Spanish laws purporting to expropriate the ex-King of Spain's property as examples of penal legislation; and see *Anglo-Iranian Oil Co.* v. *Jaffrate (The Rose Mary)* [set out in the previous chapter], where Campbell J, sitting in the Supreme Court of Aden, held certain laws of the State of Persia which he found to be passed to nationalize the plaintiff company only without compensation were confiscatory and ineffectual to pass title.

[Upjohn J then considered the Anglo-Iranian case. This part of the judgment was set out in the previous chapter. He concluding by saying that, in his opinion, the principle laid down in *Luther* v. *Sagor* and *Princess Paley Olga* v. *Weisz* was not limited to nationals of the confiscating State. He then continued:]

In my judgment the true limits of the principle that the courts of this country will afford recognition to legislation of foreign States in so far as it affects title to movables in that State at the time of the legislation or contracts governed by the law of that State rests in considerations of international law, or in the scarcely less difficult considerations of public policy as understood in these courts. Ultimately I believe the latter is the governing consideration. But, whatever be the true view, the authorities I have reviewed do show that these courts have not on either ground recognized any principle that confiscation without adequate compensation is *per se* a ground for refusing recognition to foreign legislation. That view is further supported by the authorities on exchange control legislation which I must now consider.

It cannot be doubted that legislation intended to protect the economy of the nation and the general welfare of its inhabitants regardless of their nationality by various measures of foreign exchange control or by altering the value of its currency, is recognized by foreign courts although its effect is usually partially confiscatory. Probably there is no civilized country in the world which has not at some stage in its history altered its currency or restricted the rights of its inhabitants to purchase the currency of another country. Most countries, including

8 [1935] 1 KB 140.

the United Kingdom, are restricting those rights at this very moment.[9] In individual cases the result of such legislation is in fact to confiscate in some degree private rights of property but the right of the State to do so has never been challenged.

[After considering the authorities, Upjohn J concluded:]

In my judgment these courts must recognize the right of every foreign State to protect its economy by measures of foreign exchange control and by altering the value of its currency. Effect must be given to those measures where the law of the foreign State is the proper law of the contract or where the movable is situate within the territorial jurisdiction of the State. That, however, is subject to the qualifications that this court is entitled to be satisfied that the foreign law is a genuine foreign exchange law, that is, a law passed with the genuine intention of protecting its economy in times of national stress and for that purpose regulating (*inter alia*) the rights of foreign creditors, and is not a law passed ostensibly with that object, but in reality with some object not in accordance with the usage of nations. The title and expressed purpose of such legislation are not conclusive upon the point. For example, in *Frankfurther* v. *W L Exner Ltd*[10] a law was passed under the Hitler regime in Austria with the apparently innocent object of providing for receivers in certain cases, but with the real object of confiscating the property of Jews and others. Romer J expressed the view that this court is entitled to inquire what manner of legislation it really was, and for that purpose to see what was done under it . . .

Further, while every State is in the best position to know what measures of control are best suited to its particular needs, and must be allowed much latitude in its choice of control weapons, there are limits in the recognition to be afforded to such legislation; and this court must be entitled to consider whether, looking at all the circumstances, the law is so far-reaching in its scope and effect as really to offend against considerations of public policy of this country.

[Upjohn then considered the Moratorium Law is detail, and concluded that it was foreign-exchange-control legislation which had to be recognized in Britain as effective to modify contractual obligations where the proper law was German. After considering, and rejecting, various other arguments, he concluded that the claimant's appeal failed.]

---

9 *Editor's note*: exchange controls were still in force in the United Kingdom at the time of the case.
10 [1947] Ch 629.

Result: the German legislation applied: the debt was extinguished.

Comment

This case is an important authority both on the distinction between contract and property, and on the *situs* of intangible rights. On the former point, the case is in accord with the principle set out at the beginning of this chapter (§ 3, above) that legislation is to be regarded as contractual if all it does is to change the rights of the parties to the contract between themselves, without conferring rights on a third party. On the facts of the case, of course, the result would have been the same if the claim had been regarded as a property right, since the residence of the debtor, and hence the *situs*, would have been in Germany.

England
National Bank of Greece and Athens v. Metliss
House of Lords
[1958] AC 509; [1957] 3 WLR 1056; [1957] 3 All ER 608

Background

In 1927, a Greek bank, the National Mortgage Bank of Greece, issued mortgage bonds in British currency, repayable in 1957. The bonds contained a provision that they were governed by English law. They were guaranteed by another Greek bank, the National Bank of Greece. In 1941, when the Germans and Italians occupied Greece, payment of interest ceased, and, in 1949, Greek legislation (the moratorium law) provided that no further payments would be made under the bonds. Subsequently, a Greek law of 27 February 1953 (Act 2292) provided for the amalgamation of the National Bank of Greece and a third Greek bank, the Bank of Athens: the new bank was called the National Bank of Greece and Athens. The Greek law provided that the new bank was the universal successor to all the assets and liabilities of the old banks. A bondholder, Metliss, brought action in England against the new bank, claiming that it was liable under the guarantee. He claimed the interest due under the bonds from 1941 to 1955. He admitted that, if he had sued in Greece, the moratorium law would have provided a defence. He could not have sued the old bank in England because it had no place of business there. The new bank, however, did business in England and was therefore subject to the jurisdiction of the English courts. The lower courts found for Metliss, and the bank appealed.

Viscount Simonds

My Lords, your Lordships will see at once how important and novel a question is raised in this appeal. For I am not aware of any case, nor has the industry of counsel discovered one, in which in the courts of this country a plaintiff has, without a plea of novation or statutory assignment, recovered a sum due under a contract from one who was not a party to that contract. It will be necessary to examine closely the circumstances which in the opinion of Sellers J and the Court of Appeal support the claim.

A further question, not of general importance, is also raised whether, if the appellants are suable in this action, they can claim the benefit of a moratorium decreed by Greek law which would undoubtedly avail them if they were sued in Greece.

[Viscount Simonds stated the facts relating to the first question and continued:]

It must also be added that it has not been, and could not be, alleged that there has been a novation of the original contract between the respondent and the appellants. The respondent rests his claim against the appellants on Greek law and specifically on the decree of February 27, 1953, and on nothing else.

I have so far said nothing about the second point that arises in this case, *viz.*: how far the appellants can avail themselves of the Greek moratorium laws to which I will refer later, even if they are otherwise liable on the bonds. I propose to defer any discussion of this point until I have dealt with the main question.

To the respondent's claim the appellants object in brief that they were not parties to the original bonds and therefore are not liable in respect of them, that the proper law of the bonds was English law, and no foreign decree can operate to modify the terms thereof or to substitute one company for another as a party thereto and (stating the same proposition in other words) that English law does not recognize a succession imposed by a foreign law to an obligation arising under a contract governed by English law. Each one of these propositions is challenged by the respondent so far as it relates to the present claim except that it is now conceded, as was held by the trial judge, that the proper law of the contract is English.

My Lords, it must be apparent that, if the appellants are right, a strange situation is revealed. Here is a company whose status is recognized by the courts of this country because it is incorporated by the law of its domicile. By that law it is invested with duties, powers, assets, liabilities. It admits that, if sued in Greece, it would be liable on the bonds here in question, subject always to the benefit of any moratorium. It comes to this country, carries on its business, and assumes unchallenged possession of the assets of the dissolved company. It is the strange climax of this narrative that it then disclaims a liability to which that dissolved company was undoubtedly subject. I do not think that an English court of justice should readily give effect to such a pretension, and I will in the first place examine such authority as was cited by counsel for the appellants in support of his propositions.

[After considering the authorities cited by the appellants, Viscount Simonds continued:]

No other authority, I think, was cited in support of the appellants' contention. The question is rather one of principle and analogy, though analogies are dangerous and principles difficult to state with precision. The analogy, which has found some favour with the courts below and is not without its use, is in the conception of universal succession. That is a conception of the Roman law which found its way into many systems of law including, as my noble and learned friend Lord Keith of Avonholm has pointed out, the law of Scotland. It may be assumed that the Greek legislature using the words 'universal successor' in the relevant Act was looking to the familiar principle under which the heir was the universal successor of his testator and regarded as *eadem persona cum defuncto*,[1] and was asserting the identity of the new company with the old. But I do not care to rest my opinion upon a conception which is at the least artificial. The fact is that the new company is a new juristic entity which was not a party to any contract with the respondent, and I do not think that, when a competent legislature has created a corporation and vested in it all the powers, assets and liabilities of an old corporation, which is then dissolved, anything is added by a further reference to universal succession, unless indeed it can be said that such a reference makes the path seem more familiar and therefore easier.

In the same way it is easier to recognize the validity and efficacy of such a transfer if one recalls the many examples of statutory amalgamation of undertakings in

---

1 *Editor's note*: this is Latin for 'the same person as the deceased'.

this country, and, no doubt, in other countries. It might be said that it has become a commonplace feature of commerce and industry in the modern State that such amalgamations should take place, and that it has become a matter of comity to recognize them except in so far as they are in conflict with the positive law of the country where it is sought to give effect to them.

But, my Lords, in the end and in the absence of authority binding this House, the question is simply: What does justice demand in such a case as this? I believe that justice will be done if your Lordships think it right not only to recognize the fact that the new company exists by the law of its being but to recognize also what it is by the same law. It is conceded that its status must be recognized. That is a convenient word to use. But what does it include or exclude? If a corporation exists for no other purpose than to assume the assets, liabilities and powers of another company, what sense is there in our recognizing its existence if we do not also recognize the purposes of its existence and give effect to them accordingly. If, for reasons of comity, we recognize the new company as a juristic entity, neither the Greek Government, the creator, nor the new company, its creature, can complain that we too clothe it with all the attributes with which it has been invested. Thus and thus alone, as it appears, justice will be done. It may not be inappropriate that, in dealing with this Greek company, I have used language which may to some of your Lordships be reminiscent of the words of a Greek philosopher of more than 2,000 years ago.

I conclude, therefore, that the appellants fail in their first contention that they are not liable upon the bonds which were guaranteed by the old company. If I have to base my opinion on any principle, I would venture to say it was the principle of rational justice. I turn now to the second question, whether, being sued in this country, the appellants can claim the benefit of the moratorium imposed by successive Greek laws.

[Viscount Simonds stated the facts relating to the moratorium and continued:]

My Lords, I think that in the consideration of this question some confusion has arisen out of the evidence of the experts on Greek law who were called on either side. They could, of course, give evidence as to the meaning and effect in Greek law of the statutes to which I have referred and say what, in their opinion, the result would be if the appellants were sued upon the bonds in a Greek court. But they could not give evidence upon the question which our courts, and ultimately your Lordships, have to decide, whether and to what extent in an action here the moratorium laws will be regarded as capable of affecting the obligations under the bonds which are admittedly governed by English law.

I have read and re-read the evidence and the statutes to which they relate, and am unable to extract anything from it except what may be said to be obvious, that the new company succeeded to (*inter alia*) the liabilities of the old company, including the liability on these bonds, but that, if the bondholder sued in a Greek court, he would be met by the moratorium and his action would fail. I can find no firm evidence that upon a true construction of the amalgamation decree the new company was to be in a better position than the old in regard to foreign contracts. On the contrary, there was repeated affirmation of the proposition that the new company was to be in just the same position as the old, having truly the advantage of any law of which the old company had the benefit but having nothing more. I ask, then, what would have been the position of the old company if sued here upon these bonds, and am absolved from any further examination of the question by the concession freely and, I think, rightly made by the appellants that the old company could not have relied on the moratorium. Clearly the obligations in English law (the proper law of the contract) could not be affected by a Greek law which purported to vary its terms. I would, for this purpose, regard a law imposing a moratorium as in the same category as a law creating a new period of limitation. In this respect it is interesting to note that the appellants, though it did not become necessary for them to rely on it, in fact pleaded the English Statute of Limitations as a partial answer to the claim. But, whether the law of the foreign country imposes a moratorium or a period of limitation, it cannot avail a defendant sued in the courts of this country. For these reasons I think that the contentions of the appellants on the second point also fail . . .

The appeal should, in my opinion, be dismissed with costs.

Appeal dismissed: the National Bank of Greece and Athens had to honour the bonds.

Comment

On the amalgamation point, it will be remembered from the discussion in Chapter 22, § 2.3.2, above, that, in the common-law world, the personal law of a company – the law which controls its status – is the law of the country in which it was incorporated. In the *Metliss* case, this was Greek law.

The *Metliss* case is a good example of the theory of characterization or classification, discussed in Chapter 22, § 2.4.1, above. Under this, the applicable law depends on how the issue is classified, and can be different for different issues. Thus, questions concerning the status of a company are governed by the law of the country in which the company was incorporated; issues of contract, on the other hand, are governed by the law applicable to the contract. The court's implicit ruling that the moratorium law was a matter of contract was clearly in accord with the theory outlined at the beginning of this chapter, since the moratorium law did not confer rights on new parties but simply modified the rights and obligations of the original parties.

England
Adams* v. *National Bank of Greece
House of Lords
[1961] AC 255; [1960] 3 WLR 8; [1960] 2 All ER 421

Background

This case follows on from *National Bank of Greece and Athens* v. *Metliss*. Four days after judgment was given at first instance in that case, the Greek Government passed a new law (Act 3504) amending the law of 27 February 1953 (Act 2292) under which the banks were amalgamated. The amended law said that the new bank would be universal successor to all the rights and obligations of the old banks, except obligations, whether as principal or guarantor, under bonds payable in foreign currency. After this new law had been passed, the National Bank of Greece and Athens, which subsequently changed its name to the National Bank of Greece, refused to make payments under the bonds. Adams was a bondholder, who then sued the bank in the English courts. He won at first instance but lost in the Court of Appeal on the ground that the new law absolved the bank from liability. He appealed to the House of Lords.

Viscount Simonds

My Lords, these consolidated appeals are a sequel to the case of the *National Bank of Greece and Athens SA* v. *Metliss*, which was recently heard in the House. The bank, which was the appellant in that case, has changed its name to the National Bank of Greece SA, and is respondent to these appeals.

[Viscount Simonds stated the facts, and continued:]

My Lords, the argument before your Lordships ranged far and wide. That was not surprising, for neither side could claim to find precise authority for their contentions. Recourse was therefore had to analogies which were not always helpful. But I think that at least the contentions can be simply stated. The respondent bank say that at the dates when writs were issued against them (or at the dates when causes of action against them accrued) their juristic personality was created by the two Acts 2292 and 3504, not, they insist, by Act 2292 alone; therefore, in the words of Morris LJ, who delivered the judgment of the Court of Appeal, 'those who need recourse to Greek law must take it as they find it. If they assert that Greek law can endow, they must recognise that Greek law can disendow. If they aver that Greek law can create, they must accept that Greek law can change. If they need to have the foundation of Greek law upon which to build a claim, they can hardly say that Greek law as it used to be suits them far better than Greek law as it is.' The respondent bank could not wish to have their case stated more cogently.

But, say the appellants, this is to approach the question in the wrong way. At all material times the old bank and, after Act 2292 came into force, the new bank were under an obligation to the bondholders to pay the interest and principal of the bonds as they became due. The obligation of the old bank became the obligation of the new bank as its universal successor and was recognised as such by the English court. The proper law of the obligation, whether of the old bank or the new, was English law, and according to the well established principle of private international law as administered in our courts, the obligation could not be altered or discharged to the detriment of the English creditor by a decree of the Greek Government. It was, they said, immaterial that the Greek court might pay regard to the new law.

This, then, is the problem, and I hope I have stated fairly the rival contentions. It is, I think, obvious that that of the respondent bank rests on the assertion, which was reiterated with no lack of vigour, that the new bank did not come into any contractual relation with the bondholders and that, therefore, the principle of international law to which I have referred could have no application. It was said that in the *Metliss* case the English courts affirmed the liability of the respondent bank under Act 2292 because it recognised the status of the new bank as the 'universal successor' of the old bank: this was a question of status and, if the status was changed by Greek law, then the obligations originally imposed by Act 2292 would change also. The status (so the argument proceeded) was in fact changed by Act 3504 which purported to absolve the new bank from its former obligations: therefore the new bank was no longer liable.

My Lords, this argument is, in my opinion, unsound. It is no doubt true that in the *Metliss* case the decisive reason for holding the respondent bank liable to the bondholders was that, its status being recognised as universal successor to the old bank, it would be illogical to ignore such an essential incident of its creation as its liability for the old bank's obligations. But what does that mean but that the contractual relation which had existed between the bondholders and the old company now existed between them and the new company? The new company stood, it was said, in the shoes of the old, a metaphorical expression, no doubt, and to be distrusted accordingly, but vividly expressive of the consequences of universal succession. In the *Metliss* case their Lordships were not concerned with the question whether the legal relation between the parties ensuing from Act 2292 was contractual or something else for which I find no apt word. But, if I say that from that moment the new bank was bound by the old bank's obligations to the bondholders, and was at the same time entitled to all the defences which the old bank would have had by English law to their claims, I describe a relation which is indistinguishable from that which arises out of contract. There is nothing in the speeches of their Lordships in the *Metliss* case which suggests a contrary view.

This being the position from February 27, 1953, to July 16, 1956, I am at a loss to understand how any Act or law of the Greek Government after that date could affect the position. Greek law was the law of the respondent bank's being: it might therefore have been dissolved by Greek decree: but it would, nonetheless, have been subject to be wound up in the courts of this country and would have met the same claims, dead as alive. However, it was not dissolved, but by Act 3504 was declared not to be subject to certain liabilities of the old bank, and, moreover, retrospectively declared never to have been so liable. I think that it was admitted, at any rate I am clear that it could not be denied, that, if the obligation of the new bank under Act 2292 was contractual, no alteration of it by Greek law would be effective in our court. It is upon the reiteration of the blessed word 'status' that the respondents rely. The obligation rested on status: the status was altered: the obligation disappeared – in fact was never there. My Lords, I doubt whether anything is to be gained by debating whether Act 3504 should be described as an Act affecting status or an Act discharging contracts. Give it what label you will, its effect is that it purports to relieve the respondent bank of a liability theretofore enforceable against it, and, for my part, I should not hesitate to say that the principle of private international law in regard to discharge or alteration of a contract is applicable whatever device of nomenclature is used, if the effect of the challenged decree is the discharge or alteration of contractual rights.

My Lords, I must notice at this point what appears to be a conspicuous fallacy of the respondents' argument. It assumes that the relation between the parties commenced when the cause of action accrued, and that at that moment the appellants, having recourse to Greek law, must take it as it is in the whole, that is Act 2292 as amended by Act 3504. But this is a wrong assumption. From the moment that Act 2292 became operative the respondent bank was under an obligation to the bondholders, inchoate perhaps, but inescapable, when according to its terms it became enforceable. It was to that Act alone that the bondholders were entitled and bound to look. It is true enough that their right and duty arose because the English court recognised the new bank as having the status of universal successor of the old bank – a thing, I parenthetically observe, it surely would not have done if the Act had purported to vest assets but not liabilities – but it is not crucial or, strictly speaking, relevant to ask how or why such recognition was given or how or why the obligation arose. The fact, and the only material fact, was that it did arise, and, having arisen, it was not to be displaced by Greek law.

. . .

In my opinion this appeal should be allowed and the judgment of Diplock J restored. The respondents must pay the costs here and below.

Appeal allowed: the National Bank of Greece must honour the bonds.

Comment

This judgment too involves issues of characterization (classification). The original amalgamation law (Act 2292) was applied because it was characterized as concerning the status of two companies. This characterization led to the application of Greek law as the law of the country of incorporation. The new law (Act 3504) purported to be concerned with status as well. But was this really the case? We saw in Chapter 22, § 2.4.1, above, that there has been considerable debate in scholarly circles as to what law should decide questions of characterization. Although some writers have taken the view that a legal rule should be characterized by the legal system to which it belongs, the generally accepted view is that, in so far as this is a matter to be decided by any law, it should be decided by the *lex fori* (the law of the court hearing the case). On this basis, the English courts were not bound to adopt the characterization given to Act 3504 by Greek law. They could consider the matter for themselves. As Lord Simonds said, the effect of Act 3504 was to discharge the new bank, the Bank of Greece, from liability under the contract: whatever 'device or nomenclature' was used, its real nature was contractual. This, it is suggested, is the best way to regard the matter.

What would have happened if the original amalgamation law had provided that the successor bank would take all the assets of the old banks but not all the liabilities? Lord Denning dealt with the question:[4]

---

4 See also the passage in the judgment of Lord Simonds (set out above) in which he said: 'the English court recognised the new bank as having the status of universal successor of the old bank – a thing, I parenthetically observe, it surely would not have done if the Act had purported to vest assets but not liabilities. . . .'

English law may refuse to accept the amalgamation and wind up the former companies as though they had not been destroyed: or it may accept the amalgamation subject to the condition that, if the new amalgamated company takes possession of the assets, it must be responsible for the liabilities: for that is of the very essence of the process of amalgamation.

This view is surely right: if the so-called amalgamation law had not provided that the successor bank took over the liabilities, as well as the assets, of the original banks, it would not have been a true amalgamation law.

§ 5   Bank accounts

Our next topic is bank accounts.

England
Libyan Arab Foreign Bank* v. *Bankers Trust Co.
High Court (Queen's Bench Division (Commercial Court))
[1989] QB 728; [1989] 3 WLR 314; [1989] 3 All ER 252; [1988] 1 Lloyd's
   Rep 259

Background

The Libyan Arab Foreign Bank (the 'Libyan bank') was a state-owned Libyan bank. It had a banking agreement with a US bank, Bankers Trust, under which it had two accounts, one at Bankers Trust's London branch and one at its New York branch. Both were dollar accounts. The London account was a 'call account'. Interest was payable on it. The New York account was a 'demand account'. Interest was not payable. The London account had been opened in 1973, and, for some years, it was the only account the Libyan bank had with Bankers Trust. In 1980, the two banks entered into a managed account agreement, under which it was agreed that the Libyan bank's banking transactions would all go through New York. The New York account was opened. The Libyan bank was required to keep a 'peg balance' of US$500,000 in it. Since the account did not pay interest, this interest-free loan constituted profit for Bankers Trust. Every day, transfers were made between the two accounts: if the New York account fell below US$500,000, money was transferred into it in multiples of US$100,000; if it rose above US$500,000, the process would be reversed.[5]

   Then, politics intruded on the scene. In an attempt to make Libya back down in a political dispute, the United States decided to seize its assets. This decision was put into effect by means of an executive order signed by President Reagan 'blocking' all assets of the Libyan Government in the United States or within the control of 'US persons' outside the United States. The order was signed at 4.10

---

5 In April 1984, Bankers Trust secretly introduced changes in the procedure so as to reduce the Libyan bank's interest earnings. They hoped the latter would not notice. Eventually they did, and in November 1985 changes were made in the agreement which gave Bankers Trust what they wanted for the future. This eventually resulted in damages being awarded against Bankers Trust: see the following footnote.

pm New York time on 8 January 1986. It had the force of law and came into effect immediately. It applied to money in banks (of any nationality) in the US, and money in US banks in foreign countries. Bankers Trust immediately froze both accounts. At the relevant time, the London account stood at US$131,506,389.93; the New York account stood at US$251,129,084.53.

The Libyan bank brought proceedings in London. Various claims were made. First, it asserted that Bankers Trust had no right to freeze the London account: US law did not apply in England. Under this head, it claimed the amount standing in the London branch when the executive order came into force, approximately US$131 million. Secondly, it alleged that Bankers Trust had deliberately held up transfers to London so that there was far more money than there should have been in the New York account. If this money had been transferred to London as it should have been, the American sanctions could not have applied to it. Various other claims were made as well.

The English court had to decide whether these claims were justified.

Staughton J

[Staughton J first considered the claim for approximately $131 million relating to the money frozen in the London account. Here, two arguments were put forward on behalf of Bankers Trust. One was that the London account was governed by New York law; so the executive order applied as part of the law governing the banking contract. The other was that, even if English law applied, it was nevertheless impossible for Bankers Trust to give the Libyans their money without doing something in New York that was illegal by US law. After setting out these contentions, Staughton J continued:]

There is no dispute as to the general principles involved. Performance of a contract is excused if (i) it has become illegal by the proper law of the contract, or (ii) it necessarily involves doing an act which is unlawful by the law of the place where the act has to be done. I need cite no authority for that proposition . . . since it is well established and was not challenged. Equally it was not suggested that New York law is relevant because it is the national law of Bankers Trust, or because payment in London would expose Bankers Trust to sanctions under the United States legislation, save that [counsel for Bankers Trust] desires to keep the point open in case this dispute reaches the House of Lords.

There may, however, be a difficulty in ascertaining when performance of the contract 'necessarily involves' doing an illegal act in another country. In *Toprak Mahsulleri Ofisi* v. *Finagrain Compagnie Commerciale Agricole et Financiere SA* [1979] 2 Lloyd's Rep 98, Turkish buyers of wheat undertook to open a letter of credit 'with and confirmed by a first class United States or West European bank.' The buyers were unable to obtain exchange control permission from the Turkish Ministry of Finance to open a letter of credit, and maintained that it was impossible for them to open a letter of credit without exporting money from Turkey. It was held that this was no answer to a claim for damages for nonperformance of the contract. Lord Denning MR said, at p. 114:

In this particular case the place of performance was not Turkey. Illegality by the law of Turkey is no answer whatever to this claim. The letter of credit had to be a confirmed letter of credit, confirmed by a first-class West European or US bank. The sellers were not concerned with the machinery by which the Turkish state enterprise provided that letter of credit at all. The place of performance was not Turkey.

This case is really governed by the later case of *Kleinwort, Sons & Co.* v. *Ungarische Baumwolle Industrie* [set out above in Chapter 27, § 1.2.1] where bills of exchange were to be given and cover was to be provided in London, but at the same time there was a letter saying, 'We have to get permission from Hungary.' It was said that because of the illegality by Hungarian law in obtaining it, that would be an answer to the case. But Branson J and the Court of Appeal held that the proper law of the contract was English law; and, since the contract was to be performed in England, it was enforceable in the English courts even though its performance might involve a breach by the defendants of the law of Hungary.

That case has been quoted in all the authorities as now settling the law . . . The only way that [counsel for the Turkish state enterprise] could seek to escape from that principle was by saying – 'Although there was no term, express or implied, in the contract that anything had to be done in Turkey as a term of the contract, nevertheless it was contemplated by both parties. It was contemplated by both parties that the Turkish buyers would have to go through the whole sequence in Turkey of getting exchange control permission, and all other like things: and, if the contemplated method of performance became illegal, that would be an answer. Equally, if it became impossible, that would be a frustration.'

I am afraid that those arguments do not carry the day. It seems to me in this contract, where the letter of credit had to be a confirmed letter of credit – confirmed by a West European or US bank – the sellers are not in the least concerned as to the method by which the Turkish buyers are to provide that letter of credit. Any troubles or difficulties in Turkey are extraneous to the matter and do not afford any defence to an English contract . . .

From that case I conclude that it is immaterial whether one party has to equip himself for performance by an illegal act in another country. What matters is whether performance itself necessarily involves such an act. The Turkish buyers might have had money anywhere in the world which they could use to open a letter of credit with a United States or West European bank. In fact it would seem that they only had money in Turkey, or at any rate needed to comply with Turkish exchange control regulations if they were to use any money they may have had outside Turkey. But that was no defence, as money or a permit was only needed to equip themselves for performance, and not for performance itself.

[Counsel for Bankers Trust] took the same route as [counsel for the Turkish state enterprise] did in the *Toprak* case. He argued that the court could look at the method of performance which the parties had contemplated, and relied on *Regazzoni* v. *Sethia* [Chapter 25, § 4.1.1, above].

[Staughton J summarized the case, and continued:]

I am relieved from the task of distinguishing between the *Toprak* principle and *Regazzoni's* case by a most helpful analysis of Robert Goff J in the *Toprak* case itself at first instance which I gratefully adopt. He there held [1979] 2 Lloyd's Rep 98, 107 that there were two related but distinct principles. The principle of

Regazzoni's case was derived from the judgment of Sankey LJ in *Foster* v. *Driscoll* [set out in Chapter 25, § 4.1.1, above] at pp. 521–522:

> An English contract should and will be held invalid on account of illegality if the real object and intention of the parties necessitates them joining in an endeavour to perform in a foreign and friendly country some act which is illegal by the law of such country notwithstanding that there may be, in a certain event, alternative modes or places of performing which permit the contract to be performed legally.

Even if that principle can be applied to supervening illegality as opposed to illegality *ab initio* (a point which I would regard as open to question), it does not apply in this case. At no stage was it the real object and intention of the Libyan Bank that any illegal act should be performed in New York. That was not suggested in argument or in the course of the evidence. This case accordingly raises only the other principle, that performance is excused if it necessarily involves doing an act which is unlawful by the law of the place where the act has to be done.

Some difficulty may still be encountered in the application of that principle. For example, if payment in dollar bills in London was required by the contract, it would very probably have been necessary for Bankers Trust to obtain such a large quantity from the Federal Reserve Bank of New York, and ship it to England. That, [counsel for Bankers Trust] accepts, would not have been an act which performance necessarily involved; it would merely have been an act by Bankers Trust to equip themselves for performance, as in the *Toprak* case. By contrast, if the contract required Bankers Trust to hand over a banker's draft to the Libyan Bank in London, [counsel for Bankers Trust] argues that an illegal act in New York would necessarily be involved, since it is very likely that the obligation represented by the draft would ultimately be honoured in New York. I must return to this problem later.

(b) The proper law of the contract

As a general rule the contract between a bank and its customer is governed by the law of the place where the account is kept, in the absence of agreement to the contrary. Again there was no challenge to that as a general rule; the fact that no appellate decision was cited to support it may mean that it is generally accepted . . .

[Staughton J considered how this principle applied to the banking arrangements in the case, and concluded that, though there may have been two contracts, one governed by English law and one governed by New York law, his preferred view was that there was only one contract, partly governed by English law (as regards the English account) and partly by New York law (as regards the New York account). He then continued:]

There is high authority that branches of banks should be treated as separate from the head office . . .

That notion, of course, has its limits. A judgment lawfully obtained in respect of the obligation of a branch would be enforceable in England against the assets of the head office. (That may not always be the case in America.) As with the theory that the premises of a diplomatic mission do not form part of the territory of the receiving state, I would say that it is *true for some purposes* that a branch office of a bank is treated as a separate entity from the head office.

This reasoning would support [the argument on behalf of the Libyan bank] that there were two separate contracts, in respect of the London account and the New York account. It also lends some support to the conclusion that if, as in my preferred solution, there was only one contract, it was governed in part by English law and in part by New York law. I hold that the rights and obligations of the parties in respect of the London account were governed by English law.

[The result of this ruling was that the executive orders could not apply to the London account as part of the law governing the contract. Staughton J then had to deal with the alternative argument on behalf of Bankers Trust. This was that giving the Libyan bank its money would necessarily involve doing something in New York that was illegal under US law. To decide whether this was so, he had to consider the different methods of payment that might be used. Ten possible methods were considered, the last two being payment in cash in dollar bills in London and payment in cash in sterling in London.]

(ix) Cash – dollar bills

I am told that the largest notes in circulation are now for US $100, those for US $500 having been withdrawn. Hence there would be formidable counting and security operations involved in paying US $131m. by dollar bills. Bankers Trust would not have anything like that amount in their vault in London. Nor, on balance, do I consider that they would be likely to be able to obtain such an amount in Europe. It could be obtained from a Federal Reserve Bank and sent to London by aeroplane, although several different shipments would be made to reduce the risk. The operation would take some time – up to seven days.

. . .

(x) Cash – sterling

There would be no difficulty for Bankers Trust in obtaining sterling notes from the Bank of England equivalent in value to US $131m., although, once again, there would be counting and security problems. Bankers Trust would have to reimburse the Bank of England, or the correspondent through whom it obtained the notes, and this would probably be done by a transfer of dollars in New York. But, again, it was not argued that such a transfer would infringe New York law.

[Those means of transfer were irrelevant as long as the managed account arrangement continued in force, since it was a term of that arrangement that all the Libyan Bank's transactions would pass through New York. However, Staughton J held that the Libyan bank was entitled to terminate that agreement on reasonable notice, and had done so in either April or July 1986. Various other arguments were put forward as to why payment could not be made in cash in London, including implied terms and usages, but Staughton J rejected them all.

He then gave further consideration to the various possible methods of payment. There was some objection with regard to most of them. After considering the others, he returned to the options of paying in cash.]

(ix) Cash – dollar bills

[After some discussion, Staughton J concluded:]

[I]n my view every obligation in monetary terms is to be fulfilled, either by the delivery of cash, or by some other operation which the creditor demands and which the debtor is either obliged to, or is content to, perform. There may be a term agreed that the customer is not entitled to demand cash; but I have rejected the argument that there was any subsisting express term, or any implied term, to that effect. [Counsel for Bankers Trust] argued that an obligation to pay on demand leaves very little time for performance, and that US $131m. could not be expected to be obtainable in that interval. The answer is that either a somewhat longer period must be allowed to obtain so large a sum, or that Bankers Trust would be in breach because, like any other banker they choose, for their own purposes, not to have it readily available in London.

Demand was in fact made for cash in this case, and it was not complied with. It has not been argued that the delivery of such a sum in cash in London would involve any illegal action in New York. Accordingly I would hold Bankers Trust liable on that ground.

(x) Cash – sterling

[Staughton J next considered the possibility of paying in cash in sterling in London. According to Dicey & Morris, *The Conflict of Laws*, 11th ed., Rule 210 (p. 1453), an obligation to pay foreign currency in England may be discharged (at the debtor's choice) by payment either in the foreign currency or in sterling. If the latter option is chosen, conversion is at the rate of exchange prevailing on the day of payment. Staughton J considered whether this rule had been abrogated by the *Miliangos* case, set out above in Chapter 27, § 2.2. After an analysis of the authorities, he concluded that it had not. Although such an option may be excluded by agreement, Staughton J found that there was no such agreement subsisting between the parties. Consequently, there were two methods of payment that would not require the doing in the United States of something illegal by US law. So the second defence fell away: the first claim was justified. The Libyan bank was awarded some $131 million for this.

Staughton J then considered the claim for breach of contract resulting from the fact that Bankers Trust had wrongfully failed to transfer money from the New York account to the London account. He held that this claim was justified: on balance, the sum of some $161 million was wrongfully withheld in New York. So Bankers Trust had to pay the Libyan bank $131 million plus $161 million.][1]

1 They also had to pay damages for the loss of interest between April 1984 and November 1985. This had nothing to do with the US executive order. See the previous footnote.

Result: judgment for the Libyan bank.

Comment

At the beginning of his judgment, Staughton J pointed out that, while the US had imposed sanctions against Libya, the United Kingdom had not. The judgment shows that he was determined to ensure that the US sanctions did not apply in Britain.

From the conflict-of-laws point of view, it is noteworthy that there was no suggestion that the matter involved property interests. Since the technical requirement of the US order was simply that Bankers Trust was not to pay Libya their money – there was no requirement that the money be paid to the US Government – the matter was one of contract in terms of the theory set out at the beginning of this chapter. From the Libyan bank's point of view, on the other hand, it made very little difference whether their money was held by Bankers Trust or by the US Government: the practical effect as far as they were concerned was the same.

In the case of a bank account, it actually makes little difference whether the matter is regarded as contract or property, since the applicable law of the contract will be that of the country in which the account is held, and the *situs* of the account will also be in that country.

It should finally be noted that it was not considered whether the US action was contrary to international law as a confiscation without compensation.

§ 6   Letters of credit

The applicable law for letters of credit was discussed in Chapter 24, § 4.6.3, above, where the case of *Bank of Baroda* v. *Vysya Bank* was set out. There, it was held that the law of the place of payment applies. Our next case is an earlier decision – decided before the Rome Convention came into force – but it is of interest because the question of *situs* is raised.

> **England**
> ***Power Curber International Ltd* v. *National Bank of Kuwait***
> **Court of Appeal**
> **[1981] 1 WLR 1233; [1981] 3 All ER 607; [1981] 2 Lloyd's Rep 394**

Background

Power Curber, an American company, exported goods to Kuwait. The goods were to be paid for by an irrevocable letter of credit issued by a Kuwaiti bank, the National Bank of Kuwait, to a US bank, the Bank of America. Payment was to be made in North Carolina, through another American bank, the North Carolina Bank. The goods were shipped, and 25 per cent of the price was paid. Subsequently, the buyers obtained an order of provisional attachment from a Kuwaiti court against the remaining sums payable under the letter of credit. This had the effect of preventing the National Bank of Kuwait from making any further payments. Power Curber began proceedings against the National Bank of Kuwait in North Carolina, but discontinued them. Instead, it sued it in

England, where it had a branch. The English courts had to decide whether the Kuwaiti order constituted a defence. The trial court (Parker J) granted summary judgment in favour of Power Curber. The case then came before the Court of Appeal.

Lord Denning MR

On the face of it, the National Bank of Kuwait are in default. They promised to pay the sums due under the letter of credit at maturity. They have not paid those sums.

[Counsel for the bank] submits, however, that the 'provisional attachment' gives the bank an arguable defence. He says that the proper law of the contract was Kuwaiti law and that, by that law, the payment of the sums was unlawful. Alternatively, he says that the *lex situs* of the debt was Kuwait: and it is that law which governs the effect of the attachment. If the attachment was lawful by Kuwaiti law, he says that all other countries should give effect to it.

I cannot accept [these] submissions. The proper law of the contract is to be found by asking: With what law has the contract its closest and most real connection? In my opinion it was the law of North Carolina where payment was to be made (on behalf of the issuing bank) against presentation of documents . . .

Nor can I agree that the *lex situs* of the debt was Kuwait. It was in North Carolina. A debt under a letter of credit is different from ordinary debts. They may be situate where the debtor is resident. But a debt under a letter of credit is situate in the place where it is in fact payable against documents. I would hold therefore that Parker J was right in giving summary judgment against the National Bank of Kuwait for the sums due.

Griffiths LJ

The bank submit that the judge should give leave to defend because payment of the sums due under the letter of credit is unlawful according to the proper law of the contract. This submission depends upon the proper law of the letter of credit being Kuwaiti law. In my view the proper law of the letter of credit was the law of the state of North Carolina. Under the letter of credit the bank accepted the obligation of paying or arranging the payment of the sums due in American dollars against presentation of documents at the sellers' bank in North Carolina. The bank could not have discharged its obligation by offering payment in Kuwait. Furthermore the bank undertook to reimburse the advising bank if they paid on their behalf in dollars in America . . .

Secondly, it was submitted that payment was unlawful according to the *lex situs* of the debt which it is said is Kuwait. But this is a debt that is owed in American dollars in North Carolina; I do not regard the fact that the bank that owes the debt has a residence in Kuwait as any reason for regarding Kuwait as the *lex situs* of the debt. The *lex situs* of the debt is North Carolina, and this ground for giving leave to defend cannot be supported . . .

Waterhouse J

[After saying that he agreed with the other two judges with regard to the proper law, he continued:]

The more difficult issue for me has been that relating to the *lex situs* of the debt.

A debt is generally to be looked upon as situate in the country where it is properly recoverable or can be enforced and it is noteworthy that the sellers here submitted voluntarily to the dismissal of their earlier proceedings against the bank in North Carolina. We have been told that they did so because of doubts about the jurisdiction of the North Carolina court, which was alleged in the pleadings to be based on the transaction of business by the bank there, acting by itself or through another named bank as its agent. As for the question of residence, the bank has been silent about any residence that it may have within the United States of America. In the absence of any previous binding authority, I have not been persuaded that this debt due under an unconfirmed letter of credit can be regarded as situate in North Carolina merely because there was provision for payment at a branch of a bank used by the sellers in [North Carolina]: and I do not regard the analogy of a bill of exchange or a security transferable by delivery as helpful.

Nevertheless, Parker J was right, in my judgment, to refuse the bank leave to defend because the Kuwaiti provisional order of attachment did not affect the existence of the debt. Counsel for the bank has submitted that the effect of that order was to alter the debt from one due to the sellers to a debt due to the court or held to the order of the court awaiting a decision as to whom it should be paid. I agree with Parker J that this submission is based upon a single sentence in an affidavit and that it does not bear that weight. There is no acceptable evidence that, according to the law of Kuwait, the debt has ceased to be due to the sellers. There is no ground, therefore, for granting leave to defend and counsel for the bank has not sought to argue that a stay of proceedings is justified if leave to defend was properly refused.

Parker J had stayed execution of the judgment until further notice; this stay was lifted by the Court of Appeal. Result: the Bank of Kuwait must pay immediately.

Comment

The ruling on the applicable law is in accord with the *Bank of Baroda* case (discussed in Chapter 24, § 4.6.3, above). The ruling on the *situs* of the obligation is (as the court accepted) contrary to the ordinary rule, and is generally regarded as an exception applicable only to letters of credit. The court seemed to feel that this was required by commercial needs: in a part of the judgment not reproduced above, Lord Denning stressed the commercial importance of ensuring that letters of credit are honoured according to their terms. However, the fact that the court was willing to lay down an exception without much analysis suggests that it regarded the concept as somewhat artificial. The case thus shows that *situs* is not always based on the principle of effectiveness: even if the courts of North Carolina had had jurisdiction over the Bank of Kuwait, there was no way in which they could have enforced their judgment. That was why Power Curber came to London, where the Bank of Kuwait had a branch.

It is noteworthy that none of the three judges was willing to say whether the case involved contract or property. By holding that the *situs* was North Carolina, the court was able to avoid deciding this question. In terms of the theory set out at the beginning of this chapter, it would seem to involve property. The contract in issue was between the Bank of Kuwait and Power Curber. The Kuwaiti order of provisional attachment had been obtained by the buyer of the goods; so it could be said that a new party was involved. Moreover, the order of provisional attachment was presumably the prelude to something akin to garnishee proceedings, and, as we shall see in Chapter 30, § 2.1, below, the latest word from the House of Lords (2003) is that the *lex situs* applies to such proceedings.[6]

§ 7 Voluntary assignments: the Rome I Regulation

Article 14 of the Rome I Regulation, set out in Panel 29.1, deals with the applicable law for voluntary assignment and contractual subrogation.[7] It does not apply to involuntary assignments such as a governmental expropriation of a debt or the attachment of a debt to satisfy a judgment against the person to whom the debt is owed.

§ 7.1 The structure of Article 14

It will be seen that Article 14 has two substantive paragraphs[8] – paragraph 1 and paragraph 2 – that deal with different aspects of assignment. Paragraph 1 deals with the mutual rights and obligations of the assignor and assignee under the contract of assignment. These issues, which are governed by the law that applies to the contract under which the right is assigned, will henceforth be referred to as 'paragraph-1 issues'.

Paragraph 2 deals with the legal position of the debtor. It covers:

> **Panel 29.1 Voluntary assignment and contractual subrogation**
> **Rome I Regulation (Regulation 593/2008), Article 14**
>
> **Article 14**
>
> 1. The relationship between assignor and assignee under a voluntary assignment or contractual subrogation of a claim against another person ('the debtor') shall be governed by the law that applies to the contract between the assignor and assignee under this Regulation.
> 2. The law governing the assigned or subrogated claim shall determine its assignability, the relationship between the assignee and the debtor, the conditions under which the assignment or subrogation can be invoked against the debtor and whether the debtor's obligations have been discharged.
> 3. The concept of assignment in this Article includes outright transfers of claims, transfers of claims by way of security and pledges or other security rights over claims.

---

6 *Société Eram Shipping Co. Ltd* v. *Compagnie Internationale de Navigation* [2004] 1 AC 260; [2003] 3 WLR 21; [2003] 3 All ER 465; [2003] 2 Lloyd's Rep 405; [2003] UKHL 30 (See Chapter 30, § 2.1, below).
7 A subrogation is like an assignment in that one party (the subrogee) replaces another (the subrogor) as the creditor of a claim against a third party (the debtor). The best-known example is where an insurer agrees to indemnify the insured for damage to property and it is agreed that, if the insurer satisfies a claim, the insurer will be subrogated to the insured's rights in tort (if any) against the person who damaged his property. Subrogation comes in two forms: subrogation by virtue of a contract (contractual subrogation) and subrogation by operation of law. Article 14 applies only to contractual subrogation.
8 The present paragraph 3 does no more than provide a definition.

- the assignability of the claim;
- the relationship between the assignee and the debtor;
- the conditions under which the assignment or subrogation can be invoked against the debtor; and
- whether the debtor's obligations have been discharged.

These questions will henceforth be referred to as 'paragraph-2 issues'. According to Article 14, they are governed by the law governing the assigned claim.

In the negotiations leading up to the adoption of the Rome I Regulation, it was intended to have a third substantive paragraph. Unfortunately, there was not sufficient time to reach full agreement on this; so it was omitted from the final text. However, Article 27(2) contains a review clause, under which the Commission is obliged to submit a report on the issues that would have been covered. According to Article 27(2), these are as follows:

- the effectiveness of an assignment or subrogation of a claim against third parties; and
- the priority of the assigned or subrogated claim over a right of another person.

Henceforth, these will be referred to as 'paragraph-3 issues'. They are concerned with the position of 'third parties', by which is meant persons other than the assignor, the assignee and the debtor. It is reasonable to assume that these issues are not covered by the present text of Article 14; they must still be governed by Member State choice-of-law rules.

According to Article 27(2), the Commission's report must (if appropriate) be accompanied by a proposal to amend the Regulation. The form this might take will be considered in § 7.4, below.

§ 7.2 *The problem of characterization (classification)*

This threefold division, necessary though it is, gives rise to a problem of characterization (classification): how do you decide when a case is governed by paragraph 1, paragraph 2 or what might become paragraph 3? This determines not only whether Member State law or EC law applies but, if the latter is applicable, which paragraph of Article 14 governs the case. The problem of characterization was discussed in Chapter 22, § 2.4.1, above. However, in this context, the position is slightly different, since EC law is involved. This means that the European Court will have the final say, and it will almost certainly hold that the issues cannot be characterized on the basis of national law: a uniform, Community-law solution will have to be found. At present, one can only speculate as to what this will be.

The problem of characterization arose in our next case, a case decided when the Rome Convention was in force. Article 12 of the Rome Convention was substantially the same as Article 14 of the Regulation. At the time of the case, the European Court had no jurisdiction to interpret the Convention; so the final decision still rested with Member State courts. Paragraph-3 issues were (as now) governed by Member State law. In England, the *lex situs* would have been applicable.

England
Raiffeisen Zentralbank Österreich* v. *Five Star Trading
Court of Appeal
[2001] EWCA Civ 68; [2001] QB 825; [2001] 2 WLR 1344; [2001] 3 All ER
**   257; [2001] 1 Lloyd's Rep 597**

Background

Five Star Trading was a Dubai company that owned the vessel *Mount I*. It insured the ship with a group of French insurers. The insurance policy, which included coverage for collision liability, was expressly governed by English law. Five Star borrowed money from Raiffeisen Zentralbank Österreich (RZB), an Austrian bank with a branch in London. As part of the loan agreement, Five Star granted RZB a mortgage over the *Mount I*.[9] It also assigned its rights under the insurance policy to RZB. The assignment was governed by English law.[10]

Subsequently, on 26 September 1997, the *Mount I* collided with a ship called the *ICL Vikraman*, which sank with serious loss of life. The cargo on the *Vikraman* was also lost. The owners of the *Vikraman* had the *Mount I* arrested in Malaysia. She was sold by order of court. Proceedings *in rem* were brought in Malaysia by the owners of the *Vikraman* and of its cargo (the latter being Taiwanese companies) against the *Mount I*. The claim was in tort.

The cargo owners then brought proceedings in a court in France (where the insurers were domiciled) to attach the insurance policies. They obtained a provisional order of attachment (*saisie conservatoire*) from the French court. It seems that, if they were successful in their collision claim in Malaysia, their plan was to take the proceeds of the sale of the *Mount I* in Malaysia and, if that was not enough, to claim that the insurers were obliged to indemnify Five Star for its liability in Malaysia but that the money payable to Five Star was a potential asset out of which they could satisfy their claim against Five Star. It seems that, under the law of Malaysia, the cargo owners' claim for the collision outranked RZB's claim under the mortgage. If they could also get priority over the insurance proceeds, they would get paid in full before RZB obtained anything at all.

The provisional orders were obtained in France between 9 October and 6 November 1997. However, two days earlier, on 7 October 1997, the assignment of the insurance was notified to the insurers by fax. This was a valid notification under English law, but not under French law, which did not accept notification by fax for this purpose. Under French law, the assignment had to be notified to the debtors (the insurers) by a bailiff. If this was not done, the assignment did not bind the debtors, unless they accepted it by *acte authentique*,[11] which had not occurred.

---

9 The mortgage was governed by the law of St Vincent and the Grenadines.
10 The deed of assignment also contained a choice-of-court agreement in favour of the courts of England.
11 This is a formal document, usually authenticated by a notary.

RZB responded to the attachments by bringing proceedings in England against Five Star and the insurers, claiming a declaration that the assignment of the insurance policy was valid, and that the proceeds under the policy had to be paid to it and not to Five Star. It subsequently added the owners of the *Vikraman* and its cargo as parties to the proceedings. All the parties accepted the jurisdiction of the English court.

The question before the court was the validity of the assignment. Since both the insurance policy itself, and its assignment, were governed by English law, it seems fairly clear that, as between Five Star, RZB and the insurers, the applicable law was English. This followed from Article 12 of the Convention. It did not matter whether the rights of the parties were characterized as paragraph-1 issues or paragraph-2 issues: on the facts of the case, both were governed by English law.

Did it make a difference that the owners of the *Vikraman* and its cargo were also parties? Did this raise paragraph-3 issues, and therefore take the matter outside the Rome Convention? Put differently, one could ask whether the issue should be characterized as contractual or proprietary. If it was the latter, it would not be governed by the Convention, and (under English law) the *lex situs* would apply. This would have been the law of France, the country of residence of the debtors (the insurers). As we have seen, under French law, the assignment was invalid.

The cargo owners argued that they were 'third parties' and that their rights raised paragraph-3 issues, governed by the *lex situs*. In the case, the parties – and the court – did not use the terminology set out above; they spoke of 'contractual issues' (what we have called 'paragraph-1 issues' and 'paragraph-2 issues') and 'proprietary issues' (what we have called 'paragraph-3 issues'). But the meaning was the same.

In the trial court, the judge decided that the issues were contractual, governed by Article 12 of the Convention, and not proprietary, governed by the *lex situs*. The cargo owners appealed.

Mance LJ

The issue(s)

19. I turn to the opposing analyses of the issue. In RZB's submission, the issue is whether the insurance contract, and/or the right to claim unliquidated damages from insurers for failure to pay under it, was effectively and validly assigned by Five Star to RZB. This, in its submission, is a contractual issue. The judge was therefore right in his general approach. The cargo owners, in contrast, maintain that the relevant issue concerns the validity against 'third parties' of an assignment of an intangible right of claim against insurers. In support of their analysis, the cargo owners submit that the dispute is essentially between RZB as purported assignee and the cargo owners, who attached the insurance claim and have no other nexus, let alone contractual, with anyone. So viewed, the dispute in their submission raises an essentially proprietary issue, to be resolved by the *lex situs* of the

attached debt, that is by French law. Under French law, they submit, their attachment prevails over RZB's assignment in the absence of any bailiff's notification or debtor's acceptance by *acte authentique*.

20. These opposing analyses both assume that the factual complex raises only one issue and, in their differing identification of that issue, emphasise different aspects of the facts. In my judgment a more nuanced analysis is required. This can be demonstrated by a chronological approach. Prior to 9 October 1997 there was no attachment or competing claim to any insurance moneys at all. On 7 October 1997 notice of assignment was given by fax by the sub-brokers to the insurers. From 7 to 9 October 1997 the only persons with any conceivable right to claim or receive sums payable under the insurance were Five Star and/ or RZB. The first issue for consideration raised by the parties' opposing cases is whether, in the light of the assignment and notice and apart from any attachment, the right or title to such claim and sums as against the insurers was and is in RZB or Five Star (or both). This is an issue concerning the effect on insurers' liability under the contract of insurance of Five Star's voluntary assignment to RZB (coupled with RZB's notice of such assignment to insurers).

21. If, consequent on such assignment and notice, RZB acquired no right or title to any insurance claim arising, the matter ends there. But, even if RZB had such right and title from 7 to 9 October 1997, it is possible to conceive of a second issue, arising from 9 October 1997. That is whether the cargo owners' attachments of any insurance claim in France override such right and title, or, putting the point the other way around, whether the cargo owners as attachers are bound to recognise the transfer of Five Star's right or title to RZB. This second issue (if it arises at all – see below) concerns the effect (involuntary as regards all three contracting parties) of the preventive attachments obtained by third parties (the cargo owners) in the French courts.

[Mance LJ first dealt with the issue of characterization (classification), on which he concluded:]

32. The cargo owners emphasise that the Rome Convention is concerned with the law applicable to contractual obligations. The . . . 'Giuliano-Lagarde Report' states in its commentary on Article 1 (scope of the Convention), at p. 10:

> First, since the Convention is concerned only with the law applicable to contractual obligations, property rights and intellectual property are not covered by these provisions. An Article in the original preliminary draft had expressly so provided. However, the group considered that such a provision would be superfluous in the present text, especially as this would have involved the need to recapitulate the differences existing between the various legal systems of the member states of the Community.

33. National courts must clearly strive to take a single, international or 'autonomous' view of the concept of contractual obligations that is not

blinkered by conceptions – such as perhaps consideration or even privity – that may be peculiar to their own countries. Further – and perhaps particularly so when the search is for an autonomous international view – the man-made concepts of contractual obligations and proprietary rights are neither so clear nor so inflexible that they may not receive shape from the subject matter and wording of the Convention itself.

Application of principles to present case

34. Approaching the present issue on this basis, I confess to an initial impression that the case fits readily into a contractual, and less readily into a proprietary, slot. The dominant theme influencing the modern international view of contract is party autonomy. Parties are free to determine with whom they contract and on what terms. They are free to cancel or novate their contracts and make new contracts with third parties. A simple issue whether a contractual claim exists or has arisen in these situations cannot be regarded as an issue about property, however much an acknowledged contractual right may be identified as property in certain other contexts. An issue whether a contract has been novated appears to me essentially contractual. Under a contract which, from its outset, purports to confer on a third party a right of action, an issue whether the third party may enforce that right appears to me again essentially contractual. An issue whether, following an assignment, the obligor must pay the assignee rather than the assignor falls readily under the same contractual umbrella.

35. The cargo owners seek to redescribe the issue as being whether the title to the right of suit or cause of action which formerly vested in the assignor was vested in or was now owned by the assignee. In this way they seek to give the issue a proprietary aspect. However, it is unclear why it is necessary to talk of 'title to the right', or to focus on its transfer from assignor to assignee, rather than upon the simple question: who was in the circumstances entitled to claim as against the debtor? The artificiality seems to me to be underlined at the next stage of the argument, which seeks to refer any dispute about title to sue to the place where the 'property' consisting of such title is 'situated' (see below).

36. [Counsel for the cargo owners] relies upon various factors as supporting a categorisation of the issue as involving property rights. He argues that there should be a single rule for all types of property, tangible and intangible. The rationale of the characterisation of issues as proprietary, and of the rule of English law referring such issues to the *lex situs*, is that control of property is exercisable at the place it is sited. In the case of intangible property, English law has, for various purposes (e. g. inheritance), traditionally allocated to it a *situs* at the place of the debtor's residence. This is on the basis that the debtor is there directly subject to the coercive power of the courts to enforce the obligation. The location of a right of action in this or any way is, however, evidently artificial . . .

37. Modern conditions underline the artificiality of selecting supposed control at the debtor's residence as an appropriate basis for characterisation or choice of the relevant law to determine questions regarding the validity or effect as against the debtor of an assignment. Jurisdiction may be grounded on consent and various other bases apart from residence. Obligations are commonly enforced today not against the person, but against assets. Debtors often trade or hold some or even all of their assets overseas. Proceedings are as a result often begun and enforced against debtors in countries other than that of their residence, as in this case. The move towards single legal markets, like those involving countries party to the Brussels and Lugano Conventions, makes judgments readily exportable between countries . . . To my mind, the 'control' or coercive power over a debt which may be exercised by the courts of a debtors' residence is not a persuasive reason either for treating a debt as property in the present context or for looking to the law of the place of the debtor's residence to determine the effect of an assignment as between the assignee and the debtor.

38. Advocates of a proprietary view themselves acknowledge that the application of the *lex situs* cannot provide a satisfactory solution in all cases. Thus, they accept that in cases of global assignments, for example under factoring or discounting arrangements, it may well not be appropriate to adopt a rule which would make the validity of assignment depend upon consideration of the residence of each debtor and *lex situs* of each debt assigned: see Roy Goode, *Commercial Law* (2nd edn, 1995), p. 1128[1] . . . and Mark Moshinsky 'The Assignment of Debts in the Conflict of Laws' (1992) 108 LQR 591, 613. Professor Goode and Mr Moshinsky both favour the law of the assignor's residence as the applicable law in such cases. In the present case it happens that all the co-insurers were French resident companies. But this is by no means typical in international insurance business. Under a typical co-insurance involving insurers from different countries, the *lex situs* rule could require the separate consideration of each of a large number of different laws of the *situs*, with a view to determining separately, as regards each insurer's proportionate share, the validity of a purported assignment of insurance proceeds. That would undermine the general intention, evident in the present case in the leading underwriter provisions, that there should be a homogeneous treatment of insurance underwriting and claims, despite the ultimate limitation of each insurer's financial liability to its own proportionate share.

39. [Counsel for the cargo owners] submits that a proprietary analysis is appropriate, because any assignment diminishes the assignor's assets to the potential detriment of its creditors, and that the *lex situs* ought to determine the validity of any such assignment. This argument may have force in relation to physical assets in the apparent ownership of an assignor in his country of residence. But it also demonstrates why it is not

---

1 *Editor's note*: see now Goode (Roy), *Commercial Law* (Penguin, Harmondsworth, 3rd edn, 2004), pp. 1107–11.

necessarily appropriate to attempt an analogy between physical assets and intangible rights. Whether a person has acquired or retains contractual rights is a matter about which creditors are, especially in modern business conditions, often unlikely to know anything.

40.   [Counsel for the cargo owners] argues that the application of the *lex situs* in cases of voluntary assignment would be consistent with its application in cases of involuntary assignment . . . But consensual and non-consensual situations are, in their nature, quite different and it is neither surprising nor even inconvenient if the differences lead to the application of different laws.

41.   [Counsel for the cargo owners] next submits that any potential assignee or a third party can without difficulty consider the *lex situs* in order to assess the validity of any assignment. The submission assumes knowledge about the original contract and the assignment. Assuming such knowledge, the same submission can be made in favour of either the proper law of the obligation assigned or, indeed, the proper law of the assignor's place of business.

      . . .

43.   In my view, there is a short answer to both characterisation and resolution of the present issue as between the insurers, Five Star and RZB. It is that Article 12(2) of the Rome Convention manifests the clear intention to embrace the issue and to state the appropriate law by which it must be determined. Article 12(1) regulates the position of the assignor and assignee as between themselves. Under Article 12(2), the contract giving rise to the obligation governs not merely its assignability, but also 'the relationship between the assignee and the debtor' and 'the conditions under which the assignment can be invoked against the debtor', as well as 'any question whether the debtor's obligations have been discharged'. On its face, Article 12(2) treats as matters within its scope, and expressly provides for, issues both as to whether the debtor owes moneys to and must pay the assignee (their 'relationship') and under what 'conditions', e.g. as regards the giving of notice.

44.   [Counsel for the cargo owners] submits that this is to read Article 12(2) too comprehensively. In his submission, the 'relationship' between debtor and assignee merely refers to their relationship under the contract, *provided* there has been an effective passing of property; the reference to 'conditions' under which the assignment can be invoked merely refers to any *contractual* conditions, which must be satisfied before any assignment will be recognised; it says nothing again about the general requirement that there should have been an effective *passing of property*; and that requirement must be further satisfied in each case by reference to the *lex situs* of the relevant property.

45.   To my mind, however, these submissions by [counsel for the cargo owners] postulate a most unlikely thought process on the part of the draftsmen

of the Convention, and a misleadingly drafted Article. Article 12(1) concentrates on its face on the contractual relationship between assignor and assignee. In contrast, there is no hint in Article 12(2) of any intention to distinguish between contractual and proprietary aspects of assignment. The wording appears to embrace all aspects of assignment. If the draftsmen had conceived that the basic issue, whether and under what conditions an assignee acquires the right to sue the obligor, could involve reference to a quite different law to either of the two mentioned in Article 12(1) and (2), one would have expected them to say so, if only to avoid confusion. Further, on [the case put forward by counsel for the cargo owners], it is unclear why the draftsmen troubled to refer so explicitly in Article 12(2) to the relationship of the parties and the conditions under which the assignment could be invoked against the debtor. It seems self-evident that an assignee could not succeed to any other relationship with the debtor than that established by the contract assigned, and that he could not avoid any conditions prescribed by that contract . . .

47.   The Giuliano-Lagarde Report . . . states bluntly under Article 12:

> 'The words "conditions under which the assignment can be invoked" cover the conditions of transferability of the assignment as well as the procedures required to give effect to the assignment in relation to the debtor.'

48.   That, in my judgment, is a compelling indication that (whatever might be the domestic legal position in any particular country) the Rome Convention now views the relevant issue – that is, what steps, by way of notice or otherwise, require to be taken in relation to the debtor for the assignment to take effect as between the assignee and debtor – not as involving any 'property right', but as involving – simply – a contractual issue to be determined by the law governing the obligation assigned.

     . . .

57.   I therefore conclude that Article 12 of the Rome Convention applies and that the effect, as between insurers, Five Star and RZB, of Five Star's assignment to RZB falls to be determined by reference to English law.

[Mance LJ then considered whether the assignment, which (he held) included collision liability claims, was valid under English law. It was not valid under section 50 of the Marine Insurance Act 1906 or under section 136(1) of the Law of Property Act 1925; however, it was valid in equity. As between the assignor and assignee (Five Star and RZB) it took effect immediately. As regards the debtor (the insurers), it took effect – subject to notice – from the moment that the expectancy under the policy developed into an actuality. This occurred when the collision took place on 26 September 1997. Consequently, once the insurers were notified on 7 October 1997, they were bound by the assignment: from that date, they were obliged to pay RZB, rather than Five Star. Mance LJ said that appropriate declarations would be granted.]

Charles J and Aldous J agreed.

Comment

In this case, the action was for a declaration. Although the exact terms were not given, this would presumably be to the effect that, as between the insurers, Five Star and RZB, the assignment by Five Star to RZB took effect on 7 October 1997.

Mance LJ did not say what the position of the cargo owners was. However, Five Star lost its interest in the insurance on 7 October 1997. The provisional attachments took place on 9 October 1997 and on subsequent dates. They were the first step in a procedure under which the cargo owners were planning to satisfy the Malaysian judgment they were hoping to obtain against Five Star. The French courts had to decide the validity and effect of the provisional attachments. However, since the insurance claims no longer belonged to Five Star when the provisional attachments took place, it would be odd if the French courts were to hold that they could nevertheless be attached. You cannot normally satisfy a debt against one person by taking the property of another.

However, though the insurers were obliged to pay the insurance money to RZB and would extinguish their obligations under the insurance contract by doing so, the cargo owners might nevertheless sue RZB and claim that it should hand over to them what the insurers had paid it. If they did so, the cargo owners would argue that the English judgment did not apply between them and RZB, since it only said that, *as between Five Star, the insurers and RZB*, the assignment was valid. The cargo owners could then claim that the effect of the assignment should be reconsidered by the French court, applying whatever law was appropriate under French choice-of-law rules. It is not known whether this would be English law (because the insurance policy and the assignment were both governed by English law) or French law (because the *lex situs* of the policy was French law). It need hardly be said that this would have been very awkward for RZB, which probably thought that, once it had won the English case, that would be the end of the matter.

It is not known what happened in the end; nevertheless, these considerations require us to return to Article 14 and consider in more detail the relationship between the different paragraphs of that Article.

§ 7.3   When will each paragraph of Article 14 apply?

The third paragraph of Article 14 will apply only if a 'third party' (actually a fourth party) enters the picture. This is most likely to occur if there are two voluntary assignments – to different assignees. Let us assume that A is the creditor and that he has a claim against B (the debtor). A assigns this claim first to one assignee (C-1) and then to another (C-2). If either, or both, of the assignees approaches B demanding payment, the question whom he must pay is a paragraph-2 issue: the law governing the claim assigned will decide this question. Presumably, one assignee will get paid; the other will not. Let us assume that C-1 is entitled to payment.

C-2 will not be able to do anything more as regards B. He might then turn to

A. If he claims a remedy from A – perhaps rescission, perhaps damages – the law governing the contract of assignment between the two of them will apply: this would be a paragraph-1 issue.

Let us assume that C-2 gets no satisfaction from A. Perhaps the latter is bankrupt. The only remaining possibility is for him to sue C-1. The issue would now be one of priority of rights. Here we are in paragraph-3 territory. The law applicable under paragraph 3 would decide which assignment has priority. If under that law – unlike the law governing the claim assigned – the assignment to the C-2 has priority over that to C-1, the latter would have to hand over the payment to the former.

We must now consider what law should apply to paragraph-3 issues.

§ 7.4 What law should apply under paragraph 3?

It will be seen from the analysis above that it would cause needless complications for a different law to apply to paragraph-3 issues compared with paragraph-2 issues. Unless there is a good reason for a different law, paragraph-3 issues should be governed by the same law as applies to paragraph-2 issues (the law governing the claim assigned).

Are there any reasons for applying a different law? It is clear that the applicable law should be neutral as between the two assignees. For this reason, it would be wrong to apply the law governing the contract of assignment: there will be two such contracts and they might be governed by different laws. It is also desirable that the law should be readily ascertainable by the two assignees, but this requirement is satisfied if we apply the law governing the claim assigned. In principle, therefore, this law should apply under paragraph 3.

The particular advantage of this proposal is that it benefits assignees. An assignee will have to consider the law governing the claim assigned in any event, since this law will govern his right to claim payment from the debtor. If paragraph-3 issues are governed by a different system of law, he would also have to look to that law; otherwise, what he obtained from the debtor could be taken from him by a competing assignee. If both sets of issues are governed by the same law, it will make life simpler for both assignees.

There is, however, a problem in the case of factoring and related activities. Factoring is the operation under which one person (the factor/assignee) buys the claims (accounts receivable) of another person (the assignor), usually someone engaged in business. This is done at a discount, the discount being the factor's commission. There are various different kinds of factoring – depending, for example, on whether the factor assumes the risk of bad debts – but the advantage to the assignor is that he obtains payment right away for accounts that may be payable only at some future date. For this, he is willing to accept less than the full value of the claims.

The problem with applying the law of the claim assigned is that a factor buys claims in bulk: he would typically buy all the assignor's accounts receivable at a given date. It would be burdensome for the factor to ascertain the applicable law for each of those claims. For this reason, some writers have proposed that the law of the assignor's habitual residence should be applied in this situation.[12] This would mean that a single system of law would govern all the claims assigned.

In the negotiations leading up to the Rome I Regulation, the United Kingdom proposed that in principle paragraph-3 issues should be governed by the law applicable to the claim assigned. However, it accepted that an exception should be made for factoring; it should be governed by the law of the habitual residence of the assignor. This required a definition of factoring, something that was not without its difficulties.[13] It was also agreed, as a compromise with those who wanted the law of the assignor's habitual residence to apply more widely, that, where the assignor is a natural person (not a company) acting outside the course of his business or profession, the law of his habitual residence also governs.[14] The United Kingdom insisted, however, that, where there was a conflict between two assignments – one governed by the law of the claim assigned and one by the law of the assignor's habitual residence – the former law should decide which prevailed.[15] The final text, on which agreement was almost reached, is set out in Panel 29.2. This will probably form the basis for negotiations on a possible amendment to Article 14.

Panel 29.2 Proposed amendment to Article 14 of the Rome I Regulation

Article 14

1. . . .
2. . . .
3. In the case of—
   (a) a bulk assignment of debts made by way of a business activity undertaken by the assignee ('the financier'), which purchases debts owed to the assignor ('the client') arising from the supply of goods or services by the client to third parties, for the sole purpose of recovering and collecting those debts and in circumstances where the financier invoices the client in respect of a commission or fee; or[1]
   (b) an assignment by a natural person acting outside the course of his business or profession, unless the assignment concerns a claim which has arisen through the holding of a bank account or financial instrument;[2]
   the question of the effectiveness of the assignment or subrogation against third parties and priority of the assigned or subrogated claims over a right of another person shall be governed by the law of the country where the assignor or the author of the subrogation has his habitual residence. For the purposes of this paragraph and notwithstanding Article 18(1), the habitual residence of a company or other body, incorporate or unincorporated, shall be its place of business or, if it has a place of business in more than one country, the place of its central administration . . .

1 A recital should make it clear that 'factoring', 'quasi-factoring' and 'invoice discounting' are contemplated here. Furthermore, it is essential to retain the reference to the payment of a commission or fee in the text if securitisation is to be excluded from this paragraph.
2 A recital should make it clear that the Rome I Regulation applies not only to claims under commercial law, but also to civil law claims, such as the claims for which the formalities in Article 1690 of the French Code Civil were provided. The relevant assignments are usually restricted to a single claim, for example the assignment to a lender (as a guarantee or as a transfer of property) of a rent claim. For these assignments, it may be that the law of the assignor is the appropriate law. However, the recital should also make it clear that the law of the assignor's residence is clearly not appropriate for retail bank accounts or the holding of transferable securities (and interests therein) by retail investors, since the possibility that the individual may change his location would cause unacceptable levels of certainty for the bank or financial markets participant by whom the debt or claim is owed.

---

12 See paragraph 38 of the judgment in *Raiffeisen*, where this point is made.
13 See Article 14(3)(a) of the proposed amendment to Article 14 (Panel 29.2, below).
14 See Article 14(3)(b) of the proposed amendment to Article 14 (Panel 29.2, below).
15 See Article 14(5) of the proposed amendment to Article 14 (Panel 29.2, below).

Panel 29.2 (continued)

4. In other cases, the question of the effectiveness of the assignment or subrogation against third parties and priority of the assigned or subrogated claim over a right of another person shall be governed by the law of the country designated by paragraph 2.
5. If conflicting rights to a claim result from different assignments some of which fall under paragraph 3 and some of which fall under paragraph 4 (and each of the rights is effective against third parties under the governing law identified in the relevant paragraph), the question of priority is governed by paragraph 3.
6. The concept of assignment in this Article includes outright transfers of claims, transfers of claims by way of security as well as the creation of a pledge or other security right.

§ 7.5   The lex situs

In the Rome I negotiations, no one suggested that the *lex situs* should have any role to play in Article 14. So the *lex situs* will probably disappear from the picture, once Article 14 is amended,[16] as far as assignments covered by Article 14 are concerned. However, this will not affect its position with regard to involuntary assignments or matters outside the scope of Article 14.[17] In the next chapter, we will consider some of these matters.

Further reading

Carruthers (Janeen M.), *The Transfer of Property in the Conflict of Laws* (Oxford University Press, Oxford, 2005)

Dicey, Morris and Collins, *The Conflict of Laws* (Sweet and Maxwell, London, 14th edn, 2006), pp. 1116–25

Goode (Roy), *Commercial Law* (Penguin, Harmondsworth, 3rd edn, 2004), pp. 1107–11

Kieninger, 'General Principles on the Law Applicable to the Assignment of Receivables in Europe', in Basedow (Jürgen), Baum (Harald) and Nishitani (Yoko), *Japanese and European Private International Law in Comparative Perspective* (Mohr Siebeck, Tübingen, 2008), p. 153

Moshinsky, 'The Assignment of Debts in the Conflict of Laws' (1992) 108 LQR 591

Rogerson, 'The Situs of Debts on the Conflict of Laws – Illogical, Unnecessary and Misleading' [1990] CLJ 441

---

16 Even under the present law, the *Raiffeisen* case suggests that it will not have a significant role in the case of voluntary assignments of contractual debts.
17 Even with regard to voluntary assignments, the scope of Article 14 is rather uncertain. It is not clear whether it applies, for example, to shares (which are not regarded as contractual in many legal systems) or intellectual property.

CHAPTER 30

Contractual rights and property interests – II

In the previous chapter, we considered various kinds of contractual debts. In this chapter, we take the matter further by considering more complicated questions – shares in a company, and the procedure for debt enforcement now known as a third-party debt order.

§ 1   Shares

Under English law, the rights of a shareholder against the company are regarded as being based on contract.[1] This is not, however, the position in many other legal systems. If a shareholder deals with his shares – whether by transferring them outright or by pledging them as security for a debt – his rights against the other party under the contract of sale or pledge are governed by the law applicable to that contract. However, as soon as other parties enter the picture, the *lex situs* becomes important. Deciding what the *situs* of a share is can give rise to problems.

§ 1.1   The common law

We first consider the position under the common law; then we will see whether the Rome I Regulation affects the matter.

Canada
Braun* v. *Custodian
Exchequer Court of Canada
[1944] 3 DLR 412; affirmed [1944] SCR 339; [1944] 4 DLR 209 (Supreme Court of Canada)[2]

Background

In 1919, Braun, a naturalized US citizen, went to Germany and bought shares in the Canadian Pacific Railway Company, a company incorporated in Canada by a special Act of the Canadian Parliament. The previous owners of the shares were German nationals. Canada had confiscated the property of enemy aliens during World War I and Canadian legislation, the Consolidated Orders respecting Trading with the Enemy 1916, provided that no transfer by or on behalf of an

---

1 Companies Act 1985, section 14; Companies Act 2006, section 33.
2 The judgment of the Exchequer Court, rather than that of the Supreme Court, is given because the latter affirms the former without much discussion.

enemy alien of any securities would confer any rights on the transferee. A vesting order made by a Canadian court provided that the shares in question vested in the Custodian. However, it was argued on behalf of Braun that, as Canadian Pacific maintained a share register in New York and the shares in question were transferable only on that register, the *situs* of the shares was outside Canada; so they were not subject to confiscation by Canada.

At the time of the case, Braun had died and the question before the court was whether Braun's estate or the Custodian owned the shares.

Thorson J

22. It is contended on behalf of the claimant [Braun's estate] that this vesting order was a nullity so far as the shares in question are concerned on the grounds already stated, namely, that the *situs* of the shares was in New York because transfers were registrable only there, that the shares were, therefore, not property in Canada and that, consequently, no Canadian court could validly deal with them.

23. The strength of this contention must be examined and the authorities dealing with the question of the *situs* of shares must be considered. Before this question is dealt with it is necessary to consider the kind of securities that are involved. The transfers on the back of the share certificates were all endorsed in blank by the registered owners and were part of a group of certificates issued by the Company to be traded in on the stock exchanges in Germany and other European countries as bearer securities.

   . . .

   A share certificate by itself is merely evidence of ownership of the share, but when the transfer on the back of it has been endorsed in blank by the registered owner the document is something more than mere evidence of ownership for it has become a valuable and marketable document in itself because of the right of the holder of it to fill in his own name as transferee and become the registered owner of the share, but it should be noted that this peculiar quality in the nature of negotiability or currency which the document possesses is derived from the endorsement of the transfer in blank and not from the certificate itself. The certificate even with the transfer endorsed in blank is, however, not the same thing as the share. Ownership of the share certificate implies a *jus ad rem*, a right to the thing, that is, a right to obtain the property of the share, whereas ownership of the share denotes a *jus in re*, a right in the thing itself, that is, the property of the share itself. The distinction is as between the property itself and the right to obtain the property. It follows, I think, as a matter of course, that the rights of the holder of such a certificate and transfer endorsed in blank may exist in one place, whereas the share itself may be property in another. In so far as the right to obtain a particular property is in itself property which has value and is marketable as such, a share certificate with a transfer endorsed in blank is property in that sense, but it is not the same property as the property of the share itself. The fallacy of the claimant's contention as to *situs* of the shares now in dispute results largely from failure to observe the distinction between the share certificate and the share . . .

24. In considering decisions as to the *situs* of shares it is necessary to observe certain cautions. A share is intangible property, a chose in action, a relationship between the shareholder and the company involving rights and duties. In that sense, shares have no fixed and certain physical locality such as land or a chattel would have, but for certain purposes a *situs* must be found for them . . .

[Thorson J then considered the cases on the *situs* of shares for succession-duty purposes.[1] These cases establish that, for succession-duty purposes, shares are situate where they can be 'effectively dealt with as between the shareholder and the company.'[2] This is regarded as being where the share register is kept on which the shares may be transferred. If they may be transferred on two or more registers, and if the transfers on the back have been endorsed in blank, the situs is where the certificates are located, at least if they are located in the country in which one of the registers is situated. Thorson J then continued:]

30. It is apparent that, in fixing the *situs* of shares, the courts have not adopted a uniform standard for all purposes. Decisions on the subject must be applied with great care and always with due regard to the purpose for which the *situs* was fixed.

31. The Court is not now concerned with the *situs* of the shares for taxation purposes . . . In the present case, the Court must ascertain the *situs* of the shares for the purpose of determining the dispute as to their ownership between the claimant and the respondent. For this purpose . . . the test is not where the shares can be effectively dealt with 'as between the shareholder and the company', but rather, where the dispute as to their ownership can be effectively dealt with; that is, where can the shares be effectively dealt with 'by the court' in the sense that it can enforce its judgment as to their ownership and the answer is that the court can effectively deal with the shares where it has jurisdiction over the company which issued them, in accordance with the law of the domicile of the company[3] under which it was created and to which it is subject.

[After discussing further authorities, he concluded:]

37. It is, I think, a sound rule of law that the *situs* of shares of a company for the purpose of determining a dispute as to their ownership is in the territory of incorporation of the company, for that is where the court has jurisdiction over the company in accordance with the law of its domicile and power to order a rectification of its register, where such rectification may be necessary, and to enforce such order by a personal decree against it. It is at such place that the shares can be effectively dealt with by the court.

38. The Canadian Pacific Railway Company was incorporated in Canada under the law of Canada and is governed by it and, under such law, is subject to

1 *Attorney General* v. *Higgins* (1857) 2 H & N 339; *Brassard* v. *Smith* [1925] AC 371 (PC); *Rex* v. *Williams* [1942] AC 541 (PC).
2 *Rex* v. *Williams* [1942] AC 541 at p. 558 (PC).
3 *Editor's note*: in the common-law countries, the domicile of a company is the country of incorporation: see Chapter 22, § 2.3.2, above.

the jurisdiction of the Canadian courts. The *situs* of the shares in dispute for the purposes of the present case is, therefore, in Canada and they constitute property in Canada ...

39.   The result is that under the Consolidated Orders respecting Trading with the Enemy, 1916, Braun had no rights in the shares at all and the Custodian had a valid title to them.

Comment

This case establishes that shares may have a different *situs* for different purposes. For purposes of succession duty, the *situs* is where the relevant share register is kept; for purposes of expropriation, it is where the company is incorporated, even if the shares in question are transferable only on a register kept in another country.

England
Macmillan Inc.* v. *Bishopsgate Investment Trust plc (No. 3)
Court of Appeal
[1996] 1 WLR 387; [1996] 1 All ER 585

Background

The case concerned shares in Berlitz, a company incorporated in New York. The shares belonged to, and had previously stood in the name of, Macmillan Inc., a company incorporated in Delaware. Macmillan was a wholly owned subsidiary of an English company, Maxwell Communications, a company controlled by Robert Maxwell, who subsequently died in mysterious circumstances when he disappeared from his luxury yacht somewhere in the Atlantic. Before he died, the shares had been transferred into the name of Bishopsgate Investment Trust, a British company, to be held by it as trustee for Macmillan. Subsequently, certain of the share certificates in Berlitz were, without the knowledge or consent of Macmillan, deposited in England with various other companies and used as security for loans for the benefit of companies owned by Maxwell. After Maxwell's death, the borrowers defaulted and a dispute arose regarding the shares: did Macmillan's interest prevail over that of the lenders? The claimants were Macmillan; the defendants were Bishopsgate and various banks and other lenders. Macmillan said it was the equitable owner. The lenders said they were transferees for value in good faith without notice of Macmillan's interest. The main issue was what law applied: was it the law of New York, the place of incorporation of Berlitz, the company in which the shares were held, or was it the law of England, the place where the loans were concluded? The trial court held that the applicable law was that of New York. It held for the defendants. There was an appeal, initially limited to the question of choice of law.

Staughton LJ

I conclude that an issue as to who has title to shares in a company should be decided by the law of the place where the shares are situated (*lex situs*). In the ordinary way, unless they are negotiable instruments by English law, and in this case, that is the law of the place where the company is incorporated. There may be cases where it is arguably the law of the place where the share register is kept, but that problem does not arise today. The reference is to the domestic law of the place in question; at one time there was an argument for *renvoi*, but mercifully (or sadly, as the case may be) that has been abandoned.[1]

Auld LJ

. . . In my view, there is authority and much to be said for treating issues of priority of ownership of shares in a corporation according to the *lex situs* of those shares. That will normally be the country where the register is kept, usually but not always the country of incorporation.

. . .

I, therefore, conclude that the shares are in the same position as chattels and that the dispute as to priority of ownership of them should be determined by the law of New York as the *lex situs*.

Aldous LJ

. . .

For myself, I am of the view that the authorities indicate, rather than decide, that the appropriate law to apply when deciding whether one party has a better title to shares is the *lex situs*, that being the law of incorporation.

[After referring to *Braun* v. *Custodian* and various other authorities, Aldous LJ concluded:]

As a matter of principle I believe the appropriate law to decide questions of title to property, such as shares, is the *lex situs*, which is the same as the law of incorporation. No doubt contractual rights and obligations relating to such property fall to be determined by the proper law of the contract. However, it is not possible to decide whether a person is entitled to be included upon the register of the company as a shareholder without recourse to the company's documents of incorporation as interpreted according to the law of the place of incorporation. If that be right, then it is appropriate for the same law to govern issues to title including issues as to priority, thus avoiding recourse to different systems of law to essentially a single question. Further, it is to the courts of that place which a person is likely to have to turn to enforce his rights.

The conclusion that the appropriate law is the law of incorporation is, I believe, also consistent with the general rule relating to moveables and land. In both cases the courts look to the law of the place where the moveable or land is situated. Further, the conclusion that it is the law of incorporation which should be used to decide questions of title, including questions as to priority of title, does, I believe, lead to certainty as opposed to applying the *lex loci actus* which can raise doubt as to what is the relevant transaction to be considered and where it takes place. That is particularly so in modern times with the explosion of communication

---

1 *Editor's note*: on *renvoi*, see Chapter 22, § 2.4.2, above.

technology. The conclusion is, I also believe, consistent with the trend of authority both in this country and abroad . . .

Result: New York law applies.

Comment

In this case, Auld LJ took the view that the *situs* of a share was where the register was kept on which the share was transferable; Aldous LJ seemed to regard the register as irrelevant – he cited *Braun* v. *Custodian* with approval; and Staughton LJ left the matter open. Since the register was kept in the country of incorporation, the point was not relevant to the decision. If we accept the theory of effectiveness, the country of incorporation should constitute the *situs*, since the courts of that country have the greatest power over the company.

Another issue – also not relevant for the decision – concerned share certificates that are negotiable instruments. Both Staughton LJ and Auld LJ, following textbook authority,[3] said that the *situs* of the shares in such a case is the country in which the certificates are located at the relevant time; moreover, they considered that the *lex situs* of the certificates also decides whether they are negotiable.[4] However, this view appears to confuse ownership of the certificates with ownership of the shares. A share is intangible property that entitles the holder to certain rights against the company. The nature of these rights is determined by the law of the country in which the company is incorporated, the personal law of the company.[5] This latter law must, in the last analysis, decide who is entitled to these rights.

At one time, governments wishing to nationalize property expropriated the assets of companies incorporated in their territory. The company itself would then be an empty shell and might be wound up. The drawback of this procedure was that there was no way they could get their hands on the assets located in other countries. But what if the company is kept in existence and just its shares are nationalized? Our next case concerns this possibility.

England
Williams & Humbert Ltd v. *W&H Trade Marks (Jersey) Ltd*
House of Lords
[1986] AC 368; [1986] 2 WLR 24; [1986] 1 All ER 129

Background

In this case, the Spanish Government wanted to nationalize a Spanish-incorporated company, Rumasa SA. Instead of taking its assets, it expropriated its shares. This was done under a Spanish law dated 29 June 1983. Compensation

---

3 Dicey and Morris, 12th edn, 1993, p. 1420. This passage is in a chapter dealing with negotiable instruments, not with shares. For the latter, see *ibid.*, pp. 931–2, where it is concluded: 'The consequence is that, although shares may in certain cases be regarded as situate in some place other than that of the incorporation of the company, this attributed *situs* applies only by virtue of the law of the place of incorporation and may at any time be overridden or revoked by the latter.' This passage also occurs in the current edition; see Dicey, Morris and Collins, p. 1127.
4 See [1996] 1 WLR at pp. 400 (Staughton LJ) and 411–12 (Auld LJ).
5 See Chapter 22, § 2.3.2, above.

was paid. Rumasa owned all the shares in an English-incorporated company, Williams & Humbert; so, when the Spanish Government gained control of Rumasa, they also gained control of Williams & Humbert, which produced a well-known brand of sherry under the 'Dry Sack' trademark. The essential question before the English courts was whether they would recognize this state of affairs.[6] It was argued that the effect of doing so would be to allow a foreign government to expropriate property – for example, UK trademarks – situated in England. Since they could not do this directly, it was argued that they should not be able to do it indirectly.

Lord Templeman

[After referring to the defendants' pleading that the plaintiffs were 'not entitled to the relief sought or any relief by reason of the fact that the proceedings represent an attempt to enforce a foreign law which is penal or which otherwise ought not to be enforced by this court and further, or alternatively, that it would be contrary to public policy to grant the relief sought or any relief', he continued:]

This pleading could be justified if English law abhorred the compulsory acquisition legislation of every other country, or if international law abhorred the compulsory acquisition legislation of all countries. But in fact compulsory acquisition is universally recognised and practised. As early as 1789 the Declaration of the Rights of Man, more recently repeated in the French Constitutions of 1946 and 1958, provided that no one should be deprived of property 'except in case of evident public necessity legally ascertained and on condition of just indemnity.' In the United States the Fifth Amendment to the Constitution of 1791 provided that private property should not 'be taken for public use, without just compensation.' In modern times written constitutions recognise compulsory acquisition in the public interest subject to the payment of compensation; see, for example, the 1949 Basic Law of the German Federal Republic, the 1949 Constitution of India, the 1969 South American Convention on Human Rights, and the written constitutions of the African states which achieved independence from colonial rule. The United Nations and European Conventions recognise compulsory acquisition in the public interest and in accordance with domestic law and international law. In the United Kingdom, the courts are bound to accept and enforce any compulsory acquisition authorised by the United Kingdom parliament and to recognise compulsory acquisitions by other governments subject only to limitations for the safeguarding of human rights.

There is undoubtedly a domestic and international rule which prevents one sovereign state from changing title to property so long as that property is situate in another state. If the British government purported to acquire compulsorily

---

6 The actual facts of the case were complicated. One aspect of it concerned another company, W&H Trademarks, to which Williams & Humbert had transferred its trademarks before the nationalization. This had been done by the original owners of Rumasa to prevent the trademarks – especially its 'Dry Sack' trademark – falling into the hands of the Spanish Government. The new management of Williams & Humbert wanted to get the trademarks back. When they brought proceedings before the English courts for this purpose, W&H Trademarks, which was still controlled by the original owners of Rumasa, claimed that the new management was not entitled to act in the name of Williams & Humbert. This raised the question whether the effect of the nationalization on Williams & Humbert would be recognized in England.

the railway lines from London to Newhaven and the railway lines from Dieppe to Paris, the ownership of the railway lines situate in England would vest in the British government but the ownership of the railway lines in France would remain undisturbed. But this territorial limitation on compulsory acquisition is not relevant to the acquisition of shares in a company incorporated in the acquiring state. If the British government compulsorily acquired all the shares in a company incorporated in England which owned a railway line between Dieppe and Paris, the ownership of that railway line would remain vested in the company, subject to any exercise by a French government of power compulsorily to acquire the railway line. In the present case, the Spanish government acquired all the shares in Rumasa . . . Ownership of the shares in Williams & Humbert was and remained vested in Rumasa. Ownership of any right of action to recover the Dry Sack trade mark and to recover damages was and remained vested in Williams and Humbert . . .

There is another international rule whereby one state will not enforce the revenue and penal laws of another state. This rule with regard to revenue laws may in the future be modified by international convention or by the laws of the European Economic Community in order to prevent fraudulent practices which damage all states and benefit no state. But at present the international rule with regard to the non-enforcement of revenue and penal laws is absolute.

It is, in my view, doubtful whether the Spanish law dated 29 June 1983 can properly be described as a penal law for present purposes, but in any event the plaintiffs . . . are not seeking to enforce the Spanish law . . . Nourse J, [the trial judge] . . . succinctly observed that the object of the Spanish law of 29 June 1983

> was to acquire direct ownership and control of Rumasa and the two banks and indirect ownership and control of Williams and Humbert. That object has been duly achieved by perfection of the state's title in Spain. Accordingly, on a simple but compelling view of the matter there is nothing left to enforce.

I agree. An attempt was made to argue that the [action constituted an attempt] by the Spanish government indirectly to enforce the law dated 29 June 1983 by recovering the Dry Sack trade mark of Williams and Humbert . . . for the benefit of the Spanish government. This heretical submission flies in the face of the principle established in *Salomon* v. *A Salomon & Co. Ltd* [1897] AC 22 and re-affirmed in E B M Co. Ltd v. Dominion Bank [1937] 3 All ER 555, 564–565 where Lord Russell of Killowen said that it was:

> of supreme importance that the distinction should be clearly marked, observed and maintained between an incorporated company's legal entity and its actions, assets, rights and liabilities on the one hand and the individual shareholders and their actions assets, rights and liabilities on the other hand.

If the appellants are correct and the trade marks action and the banks' action are attempts indirectly to enforce the Spanish law to which the English courts will not lend their aid, then the practical effect of the Spanish law was to release from liability outside Spain every tortfeasor guilty of inflicting a civil wrong on any company comprised in the Rumasa group and every contracting party who defaulted in his obligations towards any company comprised in the Rumasa group . . . The alleged effect of the Spanish law outside Spain is admitted to apply (if at all) not only in favour of every former shareholder and director but in favour of all persons who incurred liability to the Rumasa group of companies . . . If English sherry clients owe Williams and Humbert £2 million for sherry purchased before 30 June 1983, then that sherry can now be consumed free of charge. A submission which produces such anarchic results and which releases all wrongdoers from liability must be fallacious . . .

[Lord Templeman then referred to the authorities, including *Luther* v. *Sagor*, and continued:]

These authorities illustrate the principle that an English court will recognise the compulsory acquisition law of a foreign state and will recognise the change of title to property which has come under the control of the foreign state and will recognise the consequences of that change of title. The English court will decline to consider the merits of compulsory acquisition. In their pleadings the appellants seek to attack the motives of the Spanish legislators, to allege oppression on the part of the Spanish government and to question the good faith of the Spanish administration in connection with the enactment, terms and implementation of the law of the 29 June 1983. No English judge could properly entertain such an attack launched on a friendly state which will shortly become a fellow member of the European Economic Community.

[Counsel for the original owners sought to rely on cases in which attempts to nationalize property outside the foreign state were rebuffed by the English courts; he also referred to a case concerning persecution of Jews by the Nazis. After referring to these cases, Lord Templeman continued:]

[T]he present case does not involve enforcement of a foreign law which offends principles of human rights or the enforcement of a title to property conferred by Spanish law to property situate in England . . .

An English court, by English law and international law must recognise that Spanish law and accept its consequences. The consequences are that the management of the three Spanish companies and of their Spanish, English and other subsidiaries have passed to representatives of the Spanish government . . .

My Lords, on principle and authority the appellants' attempt to persuade an English court to ignore the effect and consequences of the Spanish law dated 29 June 1983 is misconceived . . .

Result: the appeal was dismissed: the Spanish Government's right to take control of Williams & Humbert was recognized.

Comment

The questions discussed in the previous chapter (compensation, etc.) did not arise in this case. Subject to those questions, it is clear that a government can gain control of foreign property owned by a company incorporated within its territory by expropriating the shares in that company. It can also expropriate assets owned by a foreign company located within its territory. All this is made clear by Lord Templeman's example concerning the railway running from London to Newhaven (both in England) and from Dieppe to Paris (both in France).

§ 1.2   The Rome I Regulation

Although the Rome I Regulation undoubtedly applies to the rights of the buyer and seller under a contract for the sale of shares, it is doubtful whether Article 14 (or any other provision) applies to the property aspects of a share transfer.[7]

If the share is a negotiable instrument, it falls outside the scope of the Regulation to the extent that the obligation in question arises out of its negotiable character. This follows from Article 1(2)(d) of the Regulation, set out in Panel 30.1. Even if the share is not negotiable, it seems that the rights of the shareholder against the company are excluded by Article 1(2)(f) (also in Panel 30.1). In fact, the language of Article 14 is not apt for dealing with shares: it would require the company to be the 'debtor' and the shareholder to be the 'creditor'.

In the *Bishopsgate* case, the Court of Appeal did not seem to think that Article 12 of the Rome Convention (the equivalent of Article 14 of the Rome I Regulation) was applicable.[8] It did not explain why, but it probably thought that shares were outside its scope, or at least outside the scope of paragraph 2, the provision that would presumably have been relevant if the Convention had been applicable.

So it seems – at least as things stand at present – that the common law still governs the property aspects of share transfers.

> **Panel 30.1 Material scope (company shares)**
> **Rome I Regulation (Regulation 593/2008), Article 1**
>
> **Article 1**
> 2. This Regulation shall not apply to:
>   ...
>   (d) obligations arising under bills of exchange, cheques and promissory notes and other negotiable instruments to the extent that the obligations under such other negotiable instruments arise out of their negotiable character;
>   (f) questions governed by the law of companies and other bodies corporate or unincorporated such as the creation, by registration or otherwise, legal capacity, internal organisation or winding up of companies and other bodies corporate or unincorporated and the personal liability of officers and members as such for the obligations of the company or body . . .

§ 2   Third-party debt orders and garnishment

We now consider a range of procedures, known by different names in different countries, by which debts (including bank accounts) may be taken by a judgment-creditor in order to satisfy the judgment. The situation we are considering is one in which A has a claim under a judgment against B, and B has a claim against C. One way in which A can satisfy the judgment is to

---

7 In any event, involuntary assignments are – as we saw in Chapter 29, § 7, above – excluded, since Article 14 applies only to voluntary assignments.
8 According to Staughton LJ ([1996] 1 WLR at p. 402), it was not argued that Article 12 applied; Auld LJ said (*ibid.*, pp. 410–11) that Article 12 (and the Rule in Dicey and Morris based on it) was not a suitable route for selecting the applicable law in the case.

obtain what in England is now called a 'third-party debt order'.[9] In the past, it was called a 'garnishee order', and it is still called this in other common-law countries. Under it, A can require C to pay him what C owed to B up to the amount that B owed to A. This sum is then deducted from the debt owed by C to B. In an international context, the problem with this procedure is that it may be possible for B to sue C in a foreign country. If the foreign courts do not recognize that the effect of C's paying A is to relieve C of his debt to B, C will end up having to pay twice.

There are two steps in the procedure. The first is for the judgment-creditor (A, in the above terminology) to obtain an interim order (previously called an order *nisi*) in without-notice proceedings (*ex parte* proceedings). The interim order is served on the third party (C, previously called the garnishee)[10] and on the judgment-debtor (B). Both have the right to put their case to the court as to why the order should not be made final (absolute). If they do not do so, or if the court is not convinced by their arguments, a final order (order absolute) is made.

We first consider these matters purely on the basis of English law; we will then see whether EC law affects the matter.

§ 2.1 *English law*

At one time, in England, it was considered that such an order could not be obtained unless the *situs* of the debt from C to B was in England. The authority usually cited was *Richardson* v. *Richardson*,[11] a case in which the English courts had granted a divorce to the wife and had awarded her costs. She wanted to satisfy the order for costs by obtaining a garnishee order against a bank, the National Bank of India, a company which, despite its name, was incorporated in England and had its headquarters in London. The bank accounts in question were in East Africa.[12] Could the English courts garnish them? Hill J held that they could not. He first pointed out that a bank is, in the first instance, liable to pay an account holder only in the place where the account is kept. It is only if a demand is made there and payment is refused that the bank is liable to be sued in other countries. He then said:

> The debt must be properly recoverable within the jurisdiction. In principle, attachment of debts is a form of execution, and the general power of execution extends only to property within the jurisdiction of the Court which orders it. A debt is not property within the jurisdiction if it cannot be recovered here.

The advantage of this rule – apart from any question of comity and respect for the sovereignty of other countries – is that, if it is followed, the foreign courts are more likely to recognize that the English attachment extinguishes the debt, thus ensuring that C, the garnishee (third party), does not have to pay twice.

---

9 CPR Part 72.
10 As soon as this happens, the debt is frozen: the third party (C) is not allowed to pay the debt to B (or to anyone else) until the court has made a final decision.
11 *Richardson* v. *Richardson* [1927] P 228.
12 There was also a small sum of money in an account in London. There was no dispute concerning this.

In *SCF Finance* v. *Masri (No. 3)*,[13] however, the Court of Appeal cast doubt on the principle. It seems that they thought it sufficient if the garnishee (C) was within the jurisdiction; they did not consider that the *debt* had to be within the jurisdiction,[14] though they admitted that this would be relevant to the exercise of the court's discretion. However, since they held that the debt *was* within the jurisdiction, the question was not really relevant.

Our next case shows the problems that can arise.

England
Deutsche Schachtbau- und Tiefbohrgesellschaft mbH v. Ras
   Al-Khaimah National Oil Co
House of Lords
[1990] 1 AC 295; [1988] 3 WLR 230; [1988] 2 All ER 833; [1988] 2 Lloyd's
   Rep 293

Background

Deutsche Schachtbau- und Tiefbohrgesellschaft mbH (DST) was a German oil-drilling company. Ras Al-Khaimah National Oil Co. ('Rakoil') was an oil company owned by the Government of Ras Al-Khaimah, an emirate on the Persian Gulf.[15] DST and Rakoil had entered into a contract, which contained an arbitration clause. A dispute arose and DST commenced arbitration proceedings.[16] Rakoil responded by obtaining a judgment from the courts of Ras Al-Khaimah declaring the arbitration clause null and void.[17] DST did not accept this and continued with the arbitration, which eventually resulted in an award in its favour. This award was registered in England, which meant that, in English law, it had the same effect as an English judgment. It was not, however, recognized in Ras Al-Khaimah. Since Rakoil had no assets in England at the time, the award could not be enforced.

Subsequently, a British company, Shell International Petroleum Co. Ltd ('Sitco'), became indebted to Rakoil for US$4.8 million, a sum that was smaller than that owed by Rakoil to DST under the award. DST moved to garnish[18] this sum. Since Sitco ('C', the garnishee) was resident in England, the *situs* of the debt was in England. However, the Government of Ras Al-Khaimah brought proceedings in the Civil Court in Ras Al-Khaimah, and obtained an order requiring Sitco to pay the money to the State of Ras Al-Khaimah. It claimed that Rakoil was acting as agent for the Government when it dealt with Sitco.[19] Moreover, a ship on charter to one of Sitco's sister companies, which happened to be in Ras Al-Khaimah at the time, was arrested as security for the debt. In view of these developments, Sitco was in danger of having to pay twice, once to DST and once

---

13 [1987] 1 QB 1028; [1987] 2 WLR 81; [1987] 1 All ER 194 (CA).
14 They said this because the relevant rule then, as now, merely requires the third party (the garnishee, C) to be within the jurisdiction: it does not expressly say that the debt must be within the jurisdiction.
15 It is one of the United Arab Emirates.
16 The arbitration was in Switzerland.
17 This was not recognized in England.
18 At the time, this was still the appropriate term.
19 The English courts did not accept this: they considered that the money was owed to Rakoil as principal.

to the Government of Ras Al-Khaimah. Was this a ground for not going through with the English garnishment?[20]

Lord Goff

[After considering various other issues, Lord Goff continued:]

I turn next to the matter which I, like the Court of Appeal, consider to be the principal issue in the case, which is whether, having regard to the risk of execution upon their assets pursuant to the judgment of the Civil Court against Sitco, or alternatively, the commercial pressure to which Sitco is being subjected, it is appropriate to make a garnishee order absolute. However I can say at once that . . . I consider that, as a general rule, commercial pressure cannot of itself be enough to render it inequitable to make an order absolute . . . It is therefore upon the effect of the judgment of the Civil Court against Sitco that I have to concentrate.

For this purpose, it is necessary to identify the applicable principles. I turn therefore to the authorities for guidance. In considering the authorities it is, I think, important to bear in mind that the question at issue is whether it would be inequitable in the circumstances to make a garnishee order absolute, and that it is generally considered inequitable so to do if the garnishee would, in the circumstances, be compelled to pay the relevant debt twice over. So we can see, in the cases, the question being posed whether there was any real or substantial risk that the garnishee, having paid the judgment-creditor under a garnishee order absolute in this country, would be required to pay the amount over again in proceedings in a foreign country . . .

[After considering the authorities, Lord Goff concluded that they led to the conclusion that the English courts should act on the basis of an assumption as to how the foreign court will proceed. He continued:]

Furthermore, the cases have established the criteria which must be fulfilled before the English judgment is regarded as one to which foreign courts of justice may be expected to give effect. These appear to be threefold. (1) The underlying judgment entered by the English court in favour of the judgment-creditor against the judgment-debtor has been entered by a court which is, by generally accepted principles of international law, a court of competent jurisdiction. (2) The *situs* of the attached debt, owing by the garnishee to the judgment-debtor, is England. (3) Payment of the attached debt by the garnishee pursuant to the garnishee order absolute has the effect of discharging that debt. Of these three criteria, there can really be no difficulty about the third, because that is the effect of the English legislation, now embodied in RSC, Ord. 49. The litigation has therefore been concerned with the first two criteria . . .

So much is, I think, established law. But the question arises whether cases of this kind are to be solved by exclusive reference to this assumption. The point may arise in two ways. First, let it be supposed that one or other of the two criteria is not fulfilled, i.e. that the English court is not, by accepted principles of

---

20 The trial court (Hobhouse J) had decided to make the order absolute (final), and the Court of Appeal had dismissed Rakoil's appeal. The matter then came before the House of Lords.

international law, competent with regard to the underlying judgment against the judgment-debtor, or alternatively that the *situs* of the attached debt is not England. Will the English court in such circumstances automatically decline to make the garnishee order absolute, on the ground that there is a real risk that a foreign court may, despite payment by the garnishee pursuant to such a garnishee order absolute, nevertheless enforce the attached debt against the garnishee overseas? Second, let it be supposed that both criteria are fulfilled. Will an English court, in such circumstances, make a garnishee order absolute in accordance with the assumption, and exclude as irrelevant and inadmissible any evidence that a foreign court will nevertheless not recognise payment under the English order as effective to discharge the attached debt?

I have mentioned that there are these two questions, for the sake of completeness; but I doubt whether the answer to the first question has much bearing on the answer to the second question with which your Lordships' House is here concerned . . .

Here we are concerned with the situation where both criteria are fulfilled. Will the English court, in such circumstances, automatically assume that any relevant foreign court will recognise payment under the English garnishee order as effective to discharge the attached debt? Or will it admit, and if appropriate act upon, evidence that a relevant foreign court will not do so? Having considered this question with care, I doubt whether it is susceptible of a logical answer. Powerful arguments of policy can be advanced in favour of either solution – the one favouring the interests of the garnishor in levying lawful execution upon the property of the judgment-debtor, and the other favouring the interests of the garnishee. On the one hand, it can be said that the garnishee must ordinarily have to bear the consequences of any commercial pressure which may be inflicted upon him by a powerful judgment-debtor, which may have serious financial consequences for him; it is not unreasonable, it may be argued, that he should likewise bear the consequences of action by some foreign court, invoked by the judgment-debtor, which departs from the accepted norms of private international law. On the other hand, it can be said that the principle which is here being applied is that a garnishee order absolute should not be made where it is inequitable to do so, and further that it is accepted in the authorities that it is inequitable so to do where the payment by the garnishee under the order absolute will not necessarily discharge his liability under the attached debt, there being a real risk that he may be held liable in some foreign court to pay a second time. To deprive the garnishee of the benefit of this equity merely because the court which may hold him liable a second time is not acting in accordance with accepted principles of international law would not be right, especially bearing in mind that the garnishee is a wholly innocent party who has been dragged into somebody else's dispute, and that the judgment-creditor has the opportunity of seeking elsewhere for assets of the judgment-debtor which he may seize in satisfaction of the judgment debt.

Faced with such nicely balanced arguments, the guidance of authority is especially helpful. Now it is true that the question has not arisen in earlier cases in the stark form which it has taken in the present case; and it is also true that the judgments in the cases (perhaps for that very reason) do not appear to speak with a united voice on the point. But, having read and re-read them, I have come to the conclusion that they favour the second solution which I have mentioned, i.e. that which favours the garnishee and so does not require an automatic application of the assumption. I say this for, in particular, two reasons. First, the test has been authoritatively stated as being whether there is a real (or substantial) risk that the garnishee will be compelled to pay the attached debt twice over . . . A test so stated is essentially one of fact, not susceptible of being satisfied by a conclusive assumption of law. Second, there are instances in the cases of judges considering factual evidence as bearing on the question whether there is such a real risk . . . The propositions which I derive from the authorities are these. First, if it appears that there is a real risk that the garnishee will be compelled by some other court to pay the attached debt a second time, it will generally be inequitable to expose him to that risk by making the garnishee order absolute. But, second, in the absence of evidence establishing such a real risk, the assumption I have referred to will be applied . . .

. . .

It follows that, in the present case, the crucial question is whether it appears that there is a real risk that the appellants, Sitco, may, if the garnishee order is made absolute, be required to pay the debt twice over. This was the question which the judge identified in his judgment as being the crucial question which he had to decide.

Here it is asserted by Sitco that there is indeed a real risk that they will be required, by execution upon their assets pursuant to the judgment of the Civil Court, to pay the debt a second time. We are not, of course, here concerned with the question of risk whether a judgment may be entered by a foreign court requiring the debt to be paid; that has already been done . . . The relevant risk which has to be evaluated is therefore the risk of execution upon the assets of Sitco pursuant to the judgment of the Civil Court.

. . .

[Lord Goff then considered various other matters, including the contention that because the jurisdiction exercised by the Civil Court in Ras Al-Khaimah was contrary to what the English courts regarded as accepted principles of private international law, no account should be taken of its order requiring Sitco to pay. On this he said:]

It is not to be forgotten that there are many countries in the world which exercise what are, in the eyes of international law, an exorbitant jurisdiction; indeed, in some cases the jurisdiction exercised by the courts of this country can be so regarded. But I cannot accept that the mere fact that the exercise of jurisdiction by the foreign court is regarded as exorbitant, or even as very exorbitant, can *of itself* affect the exercise of the English court's discretion to make a garnishee order absolute . . .

In the present case, DST made the forthright allegation that the judgment of the Civil Court was not merely an exorbitant exercise of jurisdiction, or erroneous in point of law: they asserted that it was a sham, in the sense that the court was acting not in accordance with the law as understood in the State, but as a tool of the executive of the State. I wish to state that, had those facts been established, they would have raised a difficult question whether such an exercise of power by a court could, on the facts of the case, properly be regarded as an order by a court of law at all, but should rather be regarded as an act of executive power by the State and so should be categorised with commercial pressure and as such be irrelevant to the making of a garnishee order absolute. I wish also to state that, in cases such as the present, the courts of this country must not shrink from the task of making the necessary assessment of the situation, reluctant though they will be to do so. I have therefore considered the evidence in the present case with great care. But, having done so, I have come to the conclusion, especially having regard to the rival affidavits placed before the courts below as to the law applicable in the State, that this allegation advanced by DST fails on the evidence.

. . .

On this basis, I ask myself whether Sitco has established that there was a real risk . . . Looking at the matter as a whole, and bearing in mind that it is enough that Sitco establishes a real risk, I am satisfied that Sitco has discharged the burden upon it to establish the existence of such a risk.

For these reasons, I would allow the appeal of Sitco against the order of the Court of Appeal making the garnishee order absolute.

[Lord Oliver gave judgment to the same effect. Lord Keith and Lord Brandon agreed with both Lord Oliver and Lord Goff. Lord Templeman dissented.]

Result: the appeal was allowed; the garnishee order was not made absolute.

Comment

The question posed by Lord Goff, which he considered the crux of the matter, was whether the court should consider merely whether the foreign court *ought* – under 'accepted norms of private international law' – to recognize the English order, or whether it should also consider whether in fact the foreign court *would* recognize it. Posed in these terms, there are powerful arguments, accepted by Lord Templeman in his dissenting judgment, in favour of the first alternative. However, this statement of the issues is based on a false premise. Accepted norms of private international law dealing with the question do not exist.[21] Even if they did, there is no reason to believe that they would accord with Lord Goff's three principles, which seem to have been derived exclusively from the English cases.

As far as is known, there is no case in which the English courts have ever recognized a foreign order of this kind. One case in which the matter was considered was the *Power Curber* case, set out in Chapter 29, § 6, above.[22] Here, it will

---

21 Between 1996 and 2001, the Hague Conference on Private International Law attempted to draw up an internationally acceptable convention in the areas of jurisdiction and the recognition of judgments. It failed. The question of recognizing third-party debt orders was never even discussed.

22 Another case in which the issue arose was *Rossano* v. *Manufacturers' Life Insurance Co.* [1963] 2 QB 352. There, the English court refused to recognize the attachment, partly because the original judgment (between 'A' and 'B') was for taxes and partly because it considered that the *situs* of the debt was not in the country where the order was made. It is possible that the third party (C) had to pay twice in this case.

be remembered, a Kuwaiti bank, the National Bank of Kuwait, owed a debt under a letter of credit to an American seller, Power Curber. The buyer had a claim against Power Curber, and he attached the debt in proceedings before a Kuwaiti court. This was presumably a preliminary to seeking the Kuwaiti equivalent to a third-party debt order. The question before the English court was whether the Kuwaiti order excused the bank from paying.

The Court of Appeal said it did not. According to principles accepted in England prior to the case, the *situs* of the debt was in Kuwait, the country in which the debtor (the bank) had its residence. However, the Court of Appeal did a neat about-turn and invented a new rule to determine the *situs* of letters of credit: it said that the *situs* was in North Carolina, a territory in which the debtor had no residence. This produced the answer the court wanted, but no consideration was given to 'accepted norms of private international law' when it laid down the new rule.

If English courts change the rules to reach the result they want – however convenient this may be in a domestic context – they can hardly expect foreign courts to act differently. Given the absence of any internationally accepted rules in this context, it is hard to see on what basis an English court could decide whether a foreign court ought to recognize an English order. Unless it can be shown that the foreign court is a mere tool of the government – something that Lord Goff refused to accept in the *DST* case – there is no alternative but to consider how in fact the foreign court will act.

Our next case is the most recent authority in the area.[23]

England
Société Eram Shipping Co. Ltd* v. *Compagnie Internationale de Navigation
House of Lords
[2003] UKHL 30; [2004] 1 AC 260; [2003] 3 WLR 21; [2003] 3 All ER 465; [2003] 2 Lloyd's Rep 405

Background

Société Eram (referred to in the judgment as the 'judgment-creditor') was a Romanian shipping company. It obtained a judgment from a French court against a Hong Kong Company (Société Oceanlink) and a Hong Kong-resident individual, Mr Yoon Sei Wha (both referred to in the judgment as 'the judgment-debtors'). It was unable to satisfy the judgment in France; so it came to England and had the judgment recognized under the Brussels Convention. It then had the same effect as an English judgment. It next had to find some assets of the judgment-debtors in England. It discovered that they had an account in Hong Kong with the Hong Kong and Shanghai Banking Corporation, a bank incorporated in Hong Kong (the 'third party'). The bank had a branch in England; so it was subject

---

23 See also *Kuwait Oil Tanker Co. SAK* v. *Qabazard* [2003] UKHL 31; [2004] 1 AC 300; [2003] 3 WLR 14; [2003] 3 All ER 501, a case decided by the House of Lords on the same day and in which the same principles were laid down.

to the jurisdiction of the English courts. Could the judgment-creditor satisfy the judgment by obtaining a third-party debt order against the bank in the English courts with regard to the Hong Kong bank account?

The trial judge (Tomlinson J) ruled against making the order, first, on the ground that it would not be recognized in Hong Kong, so that the bank would have to pay twice; and, secondly, on the ground that it was wrong to exercise jurisdiction over a foreigner with regard to conduct outside the territorial jurisdiction of the court. The judgment-debtor appealed to the Court of Appeal, which reversed this judgment. The case then came before the House of Lords.

Lord Bingham of Cornhill

24. To resolve the issues arising between the judgment-creditor and the third party in this appeal it is in my opinion necessary to return to very basic first principles. A garnishee or third party debt order is a proprietary remedy which operates by way of attachment against the property of the judgment-debtor. The property of the judgment-debtor so attached is the chose in action represented by the debt of the third party or garnishee to the judgment-debtor. On the making of the interim or *nisi* order that chose in action is (as it has been variously put) bound, frozen, attached or charged in the hands of the third party or garnishee. Subject to any monetary limit which may be specified in the order, the third party is not entitled to deal with that chose in action by making payment to the judgment-debtor or any other party at his request. When a final or absolute order is made the third party or garnishee is obliged (subject to any specified monetary limit) to make payment to the judgment-creditor and not to the judgment-debtor, but the debt of the third party to the judgment-debtor is discharged *pro tanto*.

[After referring to the fact that the discharge of the third party from making payment to the debtor has always been an integral part of the procedure, Lord Bingham continued:]

26. It is not in my opinion open to the court to make an order in a case, such as the present, where it is clear or appears that the making of the order will not discharge the debt of the third party or garnishee to the judgment-debtor according to the law which governs that debt. In practical terms it does not matter very much whether the House rules that the court has no jurisdiction to make an order in such a case or that the court has a discretion which should always be exercised against the making of an order in such a case. But the former seems to me the preferable analysis, since I would not accept that the court has power to make an order which, if made, would lack what has been legislatively stipulated to be a necessary consequence of such an order. I find myself in close agreement with the opinion of Hill J in *Richardson* v. *Richardson* [1927] P 228, subject only to the qualification (of little or no practical importance) that an order may be made relating to a chose in action sited abroad if it appears that by the law applicable in that *situs* the English order would be recognised as discharging *pro tanto* the

liability of the third party to the judgment-debtor. If (contrary to my opinion) the English court had jurisdiction to make an order in a case such as the present, the objections to its exercising a discretion to do so would be very strong on grounds of principle, comity and convenience: it is contrary in principle to compel a bank to pay out money owed by a customer if its liability to its customer is not reduced to the same extent; it is inconsistent with the comity owed to the Hong Kong court to purport to interfere with assets subject to its local jurisdiction; and the judgment-creditor has a straightforward and readily available means of enforcing its judgment against the assets of the judgment-debtors in Hong Kong.

27. It is of course true, as the judgment-creditor argued and as was accepted in *SCF Finance Co Ltd* v. *Masri (No 3)* [1987] QB 1028, 1044, that the legislation has from the beginning stipulated that the third party or garnishee should be within the jurisdiction but not that the debt to be attached should be within the jurisdiction. This seems to me a point of very little weight. The language used in 1854 has, until very recently, been reproduced with remarkably little change, and I think it rather unlikely that Parliament in 1854 was directing its mind to garnishees served within the jurisdiction but owing debts to the judgment-debtor abroad. Since no order attaching a foreign chose in action has been made in any reported case, there can have been no pressing need for the Rules Committee to clarify any suggested ambiguity in the rules.

[After discussing further issues, Lord Bingham concluded that the order should be set aside.]

Lord Hoffmann

[After discussing the authorities, Lord Hoffmann continued:]

54. My Lords, so far I have been considering the matter, as almost all the authorities have done, as one of fairness and equity between the parties. But there is another dimension. The execution of a judgment is an exercise of sovereign authority. It is a seizure by the state of an asset of the judgment-debtor to satisfy the creditor's claim. And it is a general principle of international law that one sovereign state should not trespass upon the authority of another, by attempting to seize assets situated within the jurisdiction of the foreign state or compelling its citizens to do acts within its boundaries.

55. In the modern world, banking is perhaps the strongest illustration of the importance of mutual respect for national sovereignties. There are nearly 500 foreign banks in London, to say nothing of British banks with branches overseas. Banking is a highly regulated activity and each head office or branch has to comply with the laws of the jurisdiction in which it operates. If the courts of one country in which a bank operates exercise no restraint about using their sovereign powers of compulsion in relation to accounts maintained with that bank at branches in other countries, conflict and chaos is likely to follow.

56.   There is already a hint of this in Willes J's example of the foreign banker (*cuius pecunia est alter sanguis*)[1] who was entitled to say *civis Romanus* (or wherever) *sum* and not be mulcted by foreign attachment in the City of London on account of an alleged debt owing at his foreign place of business. But sensitivity to foreign sovereignty appears most clearly in the rules which have been developed for that younger offspring of foreign attachment, the *Mareva* injunction or freezing order. Unlike the case of its elder sibling, there is no question of a freezing order putting a bank in the position of having to pay twice. Nevertheless, unless carefully limited, a freezing order applying to foreign banking debts can put the bank in the position of having to choose between being in contempt of an English court and having to dishonour its obligations under a law which does not regard the English order as a valid excuse.

[Lord Hoffmann then mentioned *Babanaft International Co. SA* v. *Bassatne*, referred to Chapter 19, § 5, above. This was the case in which the '*Babanaft*' proviso was laid down, a rule limiting the effect of worldwide *Mareva* injunctions. He continued:]

59.   The conclusion I draw from this survey of principle and authority is that there are strong reasons of principle for not making a third party debt order in respect of a foreign debt. I agree with my noble and learned friend, Lord Millett, that the application of such principles is not at all the same as the exercise of a discretion. To that extent, the references to a discretion in cases like *SCF Finance Co. Ltd* v. *Masri (No 3)* . . . are misleading. On the other hand, a principle is not the same as a statutory rule restricting the jurisdiction. It may have to give way to some other overriding principle. But I find it hard to think what such a principle might be. Until this case there was no reported instance in which the normal principle had not been applied.

1 *Editor's note*: this is Latin; loosely translated, it means: 'who regards his money as another kind of blood'.

Comment

In this case, the *situs* rule was reinstated, though its basis is now said to rest in part on considerations of comity, or respect for the sovereignty of other countries, considerations that we have already seen applied with regard to freezing orders (Chapter 19) and orders for the production of evidence from third parties (Chapter 20). They will be considered further in Part VI of this book with regard to the question of extraterritoriality.

§ 2.2   EC law

The Rome I Regulation does not affect these matters, since Article 14 applies only to voluntary assignments. A third-party debt order is not a voluntary assignment. The position regarding the Brussels I Regulation is more complex. As a result of the *Société Eram* case, the English courts will not make third-party debt orders with regard to debts the *situs* of which is in another EC country. But what if the courts of such a country make an order with regard to a debt the *situs* of which is in England?

Let us assume that A obtains a judgment in France against B, and that A then obtains the French equivalent of a third-party debt order with regard to B's account in England with the C bank. Would the English courts have to regard this as extinguishing C's liability to B in England? It is hard to believe that the French courts (or those of any other EC Member State) would make an order in such circumstances, but, if they did, and if B and C were parties to the proceedings and were bound by the order, it seems that the English courts would have to recognize it, unless Article 22(5) could be invoked. This provision states that, in proceedings concerned with the enforcement of a judgment, the courts of the Member State in which the judgment is enforced have exclusive jurisdiction. It could perhaps be argued that, since a third-party debt order is a means of enforcing a judgment, it cannot be made with regard to a debt situated in another Member State since it would necessarily have to be enforced in that Member State.

§ 3   Conclusions

The situations considered in this chapter are ones in which the *situs* plays a role. In part, the reason for this is to obtain a reasonable division of jurisdiction between the courts of different countries. However, there is still considerable uncertainty as to how exactly the *situs* is determined, and, until internationally acceptable rules on the matter are found, problems will continue to arise.

Further reading

Carruthers (Janeen M.), *The Transfer of Property in the Conflict of Laws* (Oxford University Press, Oxford, 2005)

Dicey, Morris and Collins, *The Conflict of Laws* (Sweet and Maxwell, London, 14th edn, 2006), pp. 1125–32 and 1197–202

Kennett (Wendy), *The Enforcement of Judgments in Europe* (Oxford University Press, Oxford, 2000), Chapter 8

Ooi (Maisie), *Shares and Other Securities in the Conflict of Laws* (Oxford University Press, Oxford, 2003)

CHAPTER 31

Contractual rights and property interests – III

So far, we have been considering the law of England and the Commonwealth. In this chapter, we turn to the United States. In the beginning, US courts adopted the same approach as English courts.

§ 1   Original approach

United States (New York)
Republic of Iraq* v. *First National City Bank
US Court of Appeals for the Second Circuit
353 F 2d 47 (1965)[1]

Background

In 1968, a revolution took place in Iraq, which resulted in the abolition of the monarchy and the establishment of a republic. The United States recognized the new regime. The erstwhile king, Faisal II, was killed in the course of the revolution. Subsequently, the new government adopted legislation (Ordinance No. 23) confiscating all the property of his dynasty. The late king had had a deposit account in New York with a New York trust company, Irving Trust; he had also owned shares in a Canadian investment trust which were in a custody account with Irving Trust. The question before the court was whether the confiscation would be recognized with regard to these items of property. The district court held that it would not. The Republic of Iraq appealed.

Friendly, Circuit Judge

The principal questions raised in this appeal are the proper definition of the act of state doctrine and its application to foreign confiscation decrees purporting to affect property within the United States. Although difficulty is sometimes encountered in drawing the line between an 'act of state' and more conventional foreign decrees or statutes claimed to be entitled to respect by the forum, the Ordinance involved in this case is nowhere near the boundary. A confiscation decree, which is precisely what Ordinance No. 23 purported to be, is the very archetype of an act of state . . .

The Supreme Court has declared that a question concerning the effect of an act of state 'must be treated exclusively as an aspect of federal law.' [Reference

---

1 Cert. denied 382 US 1027; 86 S Ct 648; 15 L Ed 2d 540.

to the *Sabbatino* case, set out in Chapter 28, § 5, above]. We deem that ruling to be applicable here even though, as we conclude below, this is not a case in which the courts of the forum are bound to respect the act of the foreign state. Like the traditional application of the act of state doctrine to preclude judgment with respect to another government's acts concerning property within its own territory at the time ... the exercise of discretion whether or not to respect a foreign act of state affecting property in the United States is closely tied to our foreign affairs, with consequent need for nationwide uniformity. It is fundamental to our constitutional scheme that in dealing with other nations the country must speak with a united voice ... It would be baffling if a foreign act of state intended to affect property in the United States were ignored on one side of the Hudson but respected on the other; any such diversity between states would needlessly complicate the handling of the foreign relations of the United States. The required uniformity can be secured only by recognizing the expansive reach of the principle, announced by Mr Justice Harlan in *Sabbatino*, that all questions relating to an act of state are questions of federal law, to be determined ultimately, if need be, by the Supreme Court of the United States.

Under the traditional application of the act of state doctrine, the principle of judicial refusal of examination applies only to a taking by a foreign sovereign of property within its own territory ... when property confiscated is within the United States at the time of the attempted confiscation, our courts will give effect to acts of state 'only if they are consistent with the policy and law of the United States.' Restatement [of Foreign Relations Law of the United States (Proposed Official Draft), 1962] § 46.

In this case, neither the bank account nor the shares in the Canadian investment trust can realistically be considered as being within Iraq simply because King Faisal resided and was physically present there at the time of his death; in the absence of any showing that Irving Trust had an office in Iraq or would be in any way answerable to its courts, we need not consider whether the conclusion would differ if it did ... So far as appears on this record, only a court in the United States could compel the bank to pay the balance in the account or to deliver the certificates it held in custody. The property here at issue thus was within the United States. Although the nationality of King Faisal provided a jurisdictional basis for the Republic of Iraq to prescribe a rule relating to his property outside Iraq, Restatement [of Foreign Relations Law of the United States (Proposed Official Draft), 1962] § 30(1)(b), this simply gives the confiscation decree a claim to consideration by the forum which, in the absence of such jurisdiction, it would not possess – not a basis for insisting on the absolute respect which, subject to the qualifications of *Sabbatino* ... the decree would enjoy as to property within Iraq at the time.

Extra-territorial enforcement of the Iraqi ordinance as to property within the United States at the date of its promulgation turns on whether the decree is consistent with our policy and laws. We perceive no basis for thinking it to be. Confiscation of the assets of a corporation has been said to be 'contrary to our public policy and shocking to our sense of justice', *Vladikavkazsky Ry Co.* v. *New York Trust*

Co. 263 NY 369, 378; 189 NE 456, 460; 91 ALR 1426 (1934) . . . Confiscation of the assets of an individual is no less so, even if he wears a crown . . . Our Constitution sets itself against confiscations such as that decreed by Ordinance No. 23 not only by the general guarantees of due process in the Fifth and Fourteenth Amendments but by the specific prohibitions of bills of attainder in Article I . . . It is true that since these provisions are addressed to action by the United States or a state, they might not prevent a court of the United States from giving effect to a confiscatory act of a foreign state with respect to property in the United States. But at least they show that, from its earliest days under the Constitution, this nation has had scant liking for legislative proscription of members of a defeated faction, although – or perhaps because – many states, in their dealings with property of the loyalists immediately after the Revolution, had practiced exactly that . . . Foreigners entrusting their property to custodians in this country are entitled to expect this historic policy to be followed save when the weightiest reasons call for a departure.

. . .

Affirmed.

Comment

We saw in the *Sabbatino* case (set out in Chapter 28, § 5, above) that the question whether a foreign confiscatory decree will be recognized in the United States is a matter of federal law. This is true whether or not the property is located within the foreign State at the relevant time. If it is so located, it will be recognized (subject to the exceptions discussed in Chapter 28, § 5, above); if it is not, it will not be recognized unless it is consistent with US policy and laws. English law is slightly different: in England, a foreign confiscatory decree will never be recognized with regard to property located in England at the time of the decree. There is nothing equivalent to the US rule, a kind of reverse public policy exception.[2] However, this difference is more apparent than real, since such a confiscation is almost never recognized in the US either.

United States
United Bank Ltd* v. *Cosmic International Inc.
US Court of Appeals for the Second Circuit
542 F 2d 868 (1976)

Background

This case concerned Pakistan. Originally, the territory of Pakistan consisted of two parts – one to the west of India and one to the east. In 1971, there was a revolution in East Pakistan: it broke away and became the independent Republic of Bangladesh. The territory of Pakistan was then reduced to the western part. On 28 February 1972, the Government of Bangladesh issued a decree expropriating all Pakistani-owned property. It seems that no compensation was paid.

---

2 *Peer International Corporation* v. *Termidor Music Publishers Ltd (No. 1)* [2003] EWCA Civ 1156; [2004] Ch 212; [2004] 2 WLR 849 (CA). See, further, Dicey, Morris and Collins, pp. 1206–8.

Cosmic International was an American corporation. Before the Revolution, it had bought jute in East Pakistan. It admitted that it owed the money. The question was: to whom should it be paid? The jute mills (in East Pakistan) that had sold the jute to Cosmic were owned by (West) Pakistani companies whose East Pakistani interests had been expropriated by the Bangladeshi decree. The claims had apparently been assigned to two Pakistani banks, United Bank and National Bank, who were the plaintiffs in the case. They demanded the money. These claims were contested by the Government of Bangladesh, which argued that it was entitled to the money by virtue of the decree of expropriation. The district court held in favour of the two Pakistani banks. The Government of Bangladesh appealed.

Coffrin, District Judge

[After discussing the act of state doctrine, Coffrin J said that since the *situs* of the debts was in the United States at the time of the expropriation, the act of state doctrine did not apply. Expropriation without compensation was contrary to US policy; so the expropriation would not be recognized. He then continued:]

The Bangladesh plaintiffs, however, maintain that the act of state doctrine should govern this controversy because the decrees in question, while admittedly confiscatory, were not of an extraterritorial nature. Three arguments are offered in support of the position that these debts had their *situs* within Bangladesh: (1) Cosmic's creditors are said to be located there; (2) the Bangladesh courts are alleged to have jurisdiction over the debtor; and (3) the Cosmic debt secured the indebtedness of the jute mills to the banks, and since these latter debts were located in Bangladesh at the time of the seizure, Cosmic's obligation passed as an incident of that taking. All of these contentions are plainly lacking in merit.

The first proposition advanced by the Bangladesh plaintiffs was directly refuted by this Court in *Menendez* v. *Saks and Company* 485 F 2d. 1355 (2nd Cir. 1973). There it was indicated that '(f)or purposes of the act of state doctrine, a debt is not "located" within a foreign state unless the state has the power to enforce or collect it.' [at p. 1364]. On this basis, the *Menendez* opinion proceeded to distinguish two Supreme Court decisions which treated the debt as situated in the creditor's domicile for tax and escheat purposes:

> Those cases, however, had nothing to do with the power to enforce payment of a debt, which was the basis of our decision in *Republic of Iraq* [above] and which generally depends on jurisdiction over the person of the debtor . . . Rather the Supreme Court's concern in those cases was to establish principles of comity which would avoid the odious possibility of double taxation or double liability. In both cases the Court recognized the difficulty of applying to intangible obligations, which 'have no actual territorial *situs*', the general rule permitting states to tax or escheat only that property found within its territory and concluded that for such purposes intangible obligations would be 'treated' as if localized at the creditor's domicile. The policy which underlay the Court's *situs* determination for purposes of enforcing tax or escheat claims has no relevancy or application to claims based upon a foreign government's purported confiscation.

Id., at 1365. [After referring to the *Tabacalera* case (set out in § 2, below), Judge Coffrin continued:] In the absence of any new arguments which would compel a different approach in this case, we decline to modify the conclusions reached by the *Menendez* Court in this regard.

Next, the Bangladesh plaintiffs argue that if *situs* cannot be fixed in Bangladesh on the basis of a 'creditor's domicile' theory, this result is nevertheless mandated on jurisdictional grounds. In support of this position they rely principally on the following dictum from the *Menendez* opinion:

> In the absence of any showing that the importers or their agents were present in Cuba or subject to the jurisdiction of Cuban courts at the time of the intervention, we are persuaded by the reasoning of *Republic of Iraq* that no legal effect should be accorded to Cuba's purported confiscation of the importers' debts to the owners.

Menendez v. *Saks and Company, supra*, 485 F 2d at 1365. The district court, however, quite properly indicated that isolated statements such as the one quoted above were not 'intended to overturn a rule firmly embedded in American jurisprudence . . . Significantly, the Bangladesh plaintiffs have not called our attention to any cases which actually applied jurisdictional considerations in fixing *situs* at a place other than the debtor's domicile. Moreover, since jurisdictional determinations would inevitably require American courts to engage in complex interpretations of foreign statutory and case law pertaining to jurisdiction, resolving *situs* questions on such a basis would deprive the act of state doctrine of certainty and predictability . . . An even more fundamental reason for declining to adopt this approach is that the act of state doctrine would thereby be given needless scope. Where an act of state has not 'come to complete fruition within the dominion of . . . (a foreign) government', *Tabacalera Severiano Jorge, SA* v. *Standard Cigar Co.*, 392 F 2d at 715–16, no *fait accompli* has occurred which would otherwise effectively prevent an American court from reviewing the act's validity. More importantly, in the absence of such a *fait accompli*, there is less likelihood that any ensuing judicial review would jeopardize this country's foreign relations . . .

. . .

The Bangladesh plaintiffs' final argument is that, even if the *situs* of these debts is in New York, the seizures in question were consistent with established American standards which permit confiscatory taking in wartime situations. Admittedly, there is considerable case law which would support the principle that '(t)here is no constitutional prohibition against confiscation of enemy properties.' Indeed, the Trading with the Enemy Act, 50 USC App. §§ 1 *et seq.*, which gives the President of the United States authority to employ confiscatory measures, has long been considered to be an exercise of Congressional war-making power under the Constitution . . . However, neither this legislation nor any of the cases we have reviewed suggest even remotely that confiscatory seizures of an extraterritorial nature can ever be *consistent* with American public policy.

It would hardly be 'consistent' with American public policy to create a special exception for extraterritorial seizures committed in wartime. Aside from the antagonistic effect which such an exception would inevitably have on our foreign relations with previously friendly nations, this Court has already recognized that citizens of friendly sovereigns have a legitimate expectation that their property interests in the United States will receive the benefit of any protection our law affords . . . Since the circumstances of this case do not warrant departing from this policy, the district court's holding with regard to the act of state doctrine is affirmed in all respects.

Result: the two (West) Pakistani banks get the money.

United States
Vishipco Line* v. *Chase Manhattan Bank
US Court of Appeals for the Second Circuit
660 F 2d 854 (1981)

Background

Chase Manhattan was a New York bank. It had a branch (not separately incorporated) in Saigon. The plaintiffs, who were Vietnamese, had accounts there. The accounts were denominated in piastres, the currency of South Vietnam in the days when the country was divided into two States, North and South Vietnam. At noon on 24 April 1975, when it was clear that Saigon was about to fall to the (North) Vietnamese army, the staff of the bank closed the office, gave the keys and records to the French embassy, and went back to the United States. The plaintiffs also went to the United States, where they demanded their money from Chase: they wanted dollars in New York. Chase refused. The plaintiffs sued, but the district court held for Chase. The plaintiffs appealed.

Mansfield, Circuit Judge

[One of the arguments put forward by Chase as to why it was not obliged to pay the plaintiffs was that the accounts in question had been seized by the new Vietnamese Government. On this, Judge Mansfield said:]

[U]pon Chase's departure from Vietnam the deposits no longer had their *situs* in Vietnam at the time of the confiscation decree. As we have said in the past, '(f)or purposes of the act of state doctrine, a debt is not "located" within a foreign state unless that state has the power to enforce or collect it.' *Menendez* v. *Saks and Co.*, 485 F 2d 1355, 1364 (2nd Cir. 1973), rev'd on other grounds *sub nom. Alfred Dunhill of London, Inc.* v. *Republic of Cuba*, 425 US 682, 96 S Ct 2201, 48 L Ed. 2d 815 (1976) . . . the power to enforce payment of a debt depends on jurisdiction over the debtor. Since Chase had abandoned its Saigon branch at the time of the Vietnamese decree, and since it had no separate corporate identity in Vietnam which would remain in existence after its departure, the Vietnamese decree could not have had any effect on its debt to the corporate plaintiffs. As one qualified commentator has observed:

> The *situs* of a bank's debt on a deposit is considered to be at the branch where the deposit is carried, but if the branch is closed . . . the depositor has a claim

> against the home office; thus, the *situs* of the debt represented by the deposit would spring back and cling to the home office. If the *situs* of the debt ceased to be within the territorial jurisdiction of [the confiscating state] from the time the branch was closed, then at the time the confiscatory decree was promulgated, [the confiscating state would] no longer [have] sufficient jurisdiction over it to affect it . . . [U]nder the act of state doctrine, the courts of the United States are not bound to give effect to foreign acts of state as to property outside the acting state's territorial jurisdiction.

Heininger, 'Liability of US Banks for Deposits Placed in Their Foreign Branches' 11 Law & Pol. Int'l Bus. 903, 975 (1979) (footnotes omitted) ('Heininger').

[Chase also argued that if the plaintiffs were entitled to their money, currency conversion should take place at the date of judgment, by which time the South Vietnamese piastre was worthless, it having been abolished by the new Government of Vietnam. However, the court held that a federal court sitting in diversity had to follow state law on this point. At the time in question, New York state applied the breach-date rule (see Chapter 27, § 2.1), under which conversion from piastres to dollars had to take place at the rate prevailing at the date of the breach. Except for one plaintiff who owned a certificate of deposit maturing at a later date, the breach date was 24 April 1975, the date when Chase pulled out of Vietnam.]

Therefore, plaintiffs are entitled to recover an amount in dollars which reflects the exchange rate between dollars and South Vietnamese piastres at the time of breach, plus statutory interest.

Comment

In these three cases, the American courts take the same approach as the English courts. All three concern governmental expropriations, which English courts would consider governed by the *lex situs*. It is true that the American courts reach the *lex situs* by a slightly different route, going via the act of state doctrine, rather than directly (they say that a court cannot inquire into the validity of the expropriation – and therefore must regard it as valid – if the property is situated within the foreign state); nevertheless the result is the same. It is also true that they consider that the *situs* of a debt is the *domicile* of the debtor, rather than his residence; however, the American concept of domicile is much closer to residence than to the English common-law concept of domicile.

§ 2   New approaches

In the 1980s, however, the courts began to adopt a variety of approaches that often differed quite sharply from English law. We give two examples, the *Allied Bank* case (like the cases previously set out, a decision of the Second Circuit) and the *Callejo* case (Fifth Circuit). Since the first of these is partly based on an earlier decision of the Fifth Circuit, the *Tabacalera* case, we first set out an extract from the judgment in that case.

United States
Tabacalera Severiano Jorge SA v. *Standard Cigar*
US Court of Appeals for the Fifth Circuit
392 F 2d 706 (1968)[3]

Background

In this case, an American company, Standard Cigar, owed money to a Cuban company, Tabacalera Severiano Jorge, for tobacco it had purchased from Tabacalera. Tabacalera assigned this claim to its sole shareholder, Jorge. The Fifth Circuit held that the measures taken by the Cuban Government did not amount to confiscation of the claim; so the question of *situs* was actually irrelevant. Nevertheless, it had the following to say on the matter.

Tuttle, Circuit Judge

The underlying thought expressed in all of the cases touching on the Act of State Doctrine is a common-sense one. It is that when a foreign government performs an act of state which is an accomplished fact, that is when it has the parties and the *res* before it and acts in such a manner as to change the relationship between the parties touching the *res*, it would be an affront to such foreign government for courts of the United States to hold that such act was a nullity. Furthermore, it is plain that the decisions took into consideration the realization that in most situations there was nothing the United States courts could do about it in any event.

In the case before us, it cannot be doubted that whatever may be the ordinary concept of the *situs* of a debt, the government of Cuba was not physically in a position to perform a *fait accompli* in the nature of the acquisition by the Cuban government . . . of the money owed to Tabacalera by Standard Cigar Company. It was simply not within the power of Cuba to accomplish this result. To this extent, we think it clear that whatever efforts were made by the Cuban government dealing with Tabacalera, these acts are to be recognized under the Act of State Doctrine only insofar as they were able to come to complete fruition within the dominion of the Cuban government . . .

The Supreme Court has fully recognized in its decisions over the years that the *situs* of intangible personal property is a shifting concept . . .

Here, we do not have a case in which affected third parties are litigating over the accomplished fact of 'takeover' of an asset in Cuba. We are dealing rather with a change in the form of the asset from an account receivable into cash, which can be accomplished only in the courts of the United States. In attempting to fashion a rule fixing the *situs* of an indebtedness for the very limited purpose of deciding whether it is 'property within (Cuba's) own territory', we find no compelling requirement that we accept the fiction that the *situs* is irrevocably at the domicile of the creditor, a fiction sometimes used for other commercial purposes. For the purpose of our inquiry we find this debt was not property in Cuba.

We now consider the two later cases.

---

3 Cert. denied 393 US 924; 89 S Ct 255; 21 L Ed 2d 260.

United States (New York)
Allied Bank International v. Banco Credito Agricola de Cartago
US Court of Appeals for the Second Circuit
757 F 2d 516 (1985)[4]

Background

Three State-owned Costa Rican banks had issued promissory notes to a syndicate of US banks for which Allied Bank was the agent. The notes were denominated in US dollars and payable in New York. Subsequently, Costa Rica underwent an economic crisis, which made it impossible for it to meet all its foreign-currency obligations. In an attempt to deal with the situation, the Costa Rican Government issued directives (legislation) under which Costa Rican entities were not permitted to pay foreign-currency debts without the approval of the Central Bank.[5] Since this was not forthcoming, the banks were unable to honour the promissory notes.

Allied brought suit on behalf of the syndicate banks in a federal district court in New York. It applied for summary judgment, which the district court refused to grant. Costa Rica's foreign debt was then renegotiated through the IMF in an attempt to deal fairly with all the creditors. The renegotiation was accepted by thirty-eight of the banks in the syndicate, but rejected by one, Fidelity Union Trust Company of New Jersey. Allied appealed on behalf of this one bank. The Court of Appeals for the Second Circuit dismissed the appeal on the ground that the Costa Rican legislation was consistent with US law and policy. Allied applied for a rehearing. The Justice Department then came in as *amicus curiae* and said that, while the US supported the rescheduling of the debts, it considered that the Costa Rican legislation did not absolve the banks from the legal obligation to pay.

Meskill, Circuit Judge (on rehearing)

[After referring to the act of state doctrine, Judge Meskill continued:]

The extraterritorial limitation, an inevitable conjunct of the foreign policy concerns underlying the doctrine, dictates that our decision herein depends on the *situs* of the property at the time of the purported taking.[1] The property, of course, is Allied's right to receive repayment from the Costa Rican banks in accordance with the agreements. The act of state doctrine is applicable to this dispute only if, when the decrees were promulgated, the *situs* of the debts was in Costa Rica. Because we conclude that the *situs* of the property was in the United States, the doctrine is not applicable.

As the Fifth Circuit explained in *Tabacalera*, the concept of the *situs* of a debt for act of state purposes differs from the ordinary concept. It depends in large part on whether the purported taking can be said to have 'come to complete fruition within the dominion of the [foreign] government.' In this case, Costa Rica could not wholly extinguish the Costa Rican banks' obligation to timely pay United States dollars to Allied in New York. Thus the *situs* of the debt was not Costa Rica.

1 It seems clear that, if the decrees are given effect and Allied's right to receive payment in accordance with the agreements is thereby extinguished, a 'taking' has occurred.

4 Cert. dismissed 473 US 934; 106 S Ct 30; 87 L Ed 2d 706.
5 As will be apparent to the reader by now, this is standard practice for dealing with such situations.

The same result obtains under ordinary *situs* analysis. The Costa Rican banks conceded jurisdiction in New York and they agreed to pay the debt in New York City in United States dollars. Allied, the designated syndicate agent, is located in the United States, specifically in New York; some of the negotiations between the parties took place in the United States. The United States has an interest in maintaining New York's status as one of the foremost commercial centers in the world. Further, New York is the international clearing center for United States dollars. In addition to other international activities, United States banks lend billions of dollars to foreign debtors each year. The United States has an interest in ensuring that creditors entitled to payment in the United States in United States dollars under contracts subject to the jurisdiction of United States courts may assume that, except under the most extraordinary circumstances, their rights will be determined in accordance with recognized principles of contract law.

In contrast, while Costa Rica has a legitimate concern in overseeing the debt situation of state-owned banks and in maintaining a stable economy, its interest in the contracts at issue is essentially limited to the extent to which it can unilaterally alter the payment terms. Costa Rica's potential jurisdiction over the debt is not sufficient to locate the debt there for the purposes of act of state doctrine analysis. [Reference to the *Cosmic International* case, set out in § 1, above.]

Thus, under either analysis, our result is the same: the *situs* of the debt was in the United States, not in Costa Rica . . . The act of state doctrine is, therefore, inapplicable.

IV

Acts of foreign governments purporting to have extraterritorial effect – and consequently, by definition, falling outside the scope of the act of state doctrine – should be recognized by the courts only if they are consistent with the law and policy of the United States . . . Thus, we have come full circle to reassess whether we should give effect to the Costa Rican directives. We now conclude that we should not.

[After examining the objections to the Costa Rican directives, Judge Meskill continued:]

The Costa Rican directives are inconsistent with the law and policy of the United States. We refuse, therefore, to hold that the directives excuse the obligations of the Costa Rican banks. The appellees' inability to pay United States dollars relates only to the potential enforceability of the judgment; it does not determine whether judgment should enter . . .

V

The parties agreed below that no questions of material fact remained as to Allied's motion for summary judgment. The act of state doctrine was the only defense raised by the Costa Rican banks to Allied's motion and the only ground for the district court's denial of that motion. Moreover, the doctrine was the sole basis for the district court's dismissal of the action. We hold today that the act of state doctrine is not applicable to this litigation. Therefore, the district court's rulings cannot stand.

We vacate our previous decision, reverse the district court's denial of Allied's motion for summary judgment and its dismissal of the action and direct the district court to enter judgment for Allied.

Comment

Basing itself on the *Tabacalera* decision, the court states that *situs* comes in two varieties – *situs* for act of state purposes and 'ordinary' *situs*.[6] It deals first with the former. This, it says, depends on whether the purported taking came to 'complete fruition' within the dominion of the foreign government. No explanation is given as to what this entails, but the court takes it for granted that the test was not satisfied.[7] In our next case, however, we shall see that, on similar facts involving Mexican exchange-control regulations (*Callejo* v. *Bancomer*), the Fifth Circuit held that the *Tabacalera* test *was* satisfied.

It then turns to an 'ordinary' *situs* analysis. What we are given here is a typical choice-of-law analysis: weighing up of contacts and balancing of interests. Neither is thorough. As regards contacts, we are told simply that Allied was located in the US and some of the negotiations took place there; the defendants' location is not mentioned, nor is it revealed where the other negotiations took place.

The interest analysis is even less convincing. We are told that the US has an interest in maintaining New York as one of the world's leading financial centres (something that might be jeopardized if US courts allowed debtors to avoid payment). Costa Rica's interest in maintaining a stable economy, on the other hand, can be taken into account only to the extent to which Costa Rica 'can unilaterally alter the payment terms'. As the Costa Rican directives had already done this, the statement must mean that Costa Rica's interest could be taken into account only to the extent to which US courts would recognize the Costa Rican directives. Since this was the precise question before the court, the argument was circular.[8]

When reading this part of the judgment, one cannot help thinking of Lord Hoffmann's statement that, when American courts decide cases by weighing up the interests of the United States against those of foreign countries, 'the balance invariably comes down in favour of the interests of the United States'.[9] Perhaps this is why Brainerd Currie said that, where there is a true conflict of governmental interests, those of the forum must always prevail.[10]

---

6 The *Tabacalera* case made clear that there is no such thing as 'ordinary' *situs*. *Situs* has different meanings for different purposes: see the quotation from *Tabacalera* set out below in the judgment in *Callejo* ('The *situs* may be in one place for *ad valorem* tax purposes ...').

7 If this refers to the practical enforceability of the Costa Rican legislation, the position is hard to evaluate. Since it is unclear whether the Costa Rican banks had assets in the US (the judgment suggests they did not), any US judgment ordering the banks to pay might be unenforceable. In any event, it is hard to see how the legal position can depend on issues of this kind, which are often impossible for a court to determine.

8 On the question whether the Costa Rican legislation could be enforced in practice, see the previous footnote.

9 The full passage is set out in Chapter 20, § 2.2, above, in the 'Comment' to the *Bank of Nova Scotia* case.

10 See Chapter 22, § 4.1, above.

How would an English court have decided the case? Since the Costa Rican directives did not transfer the claims to another person but merely altered the rights of the parties to the original contracts, it would have regarded it as contractual. If the Rome I Regulation applied, the relevant provision would be Article 4, since there appears to have been no express or implied choice of law. Application of Article 4 to the facts of the case would be no easy matter, since it is not clear whether either party was providing a service to the other, or, if paragraph 2 is applicable, which party effected the characteristic performance. There is little doubt, however, that an English court would apply New York law if it was able to find a way of doing so. So it would probably reach the same result by a different route.

United States
Callejo v. *Bancomer*
US Court of Appeals for the Fifth Circuit
764 F 2d 1101 (1985)

Background

Bancomer was a Mexican bank, which had a branch in Nuevo Laredo, Mexico. Mr and Mrs Callejo were US citizens resident in Texas. They owned certificates of deposit, denominated in US dollars, issued by the branch of Bancomer in Nuevo Laredo.[11] In August 1982, Mexico was facing a severe monetary crisis. To deal with it, the Mexican Government adopted exchange-control regulations, which required Mexican banks to pay principal and interest on dollar-denominated certificates of deposit in pesos rather than dollars, at a specified rate of exchange. Subsequently, the Mexican Government nationalized all privately owned Mexican banks, including Bancomer. Bancomer then notified the Callejos that they would pay the principal and interest on their certificates of deposit in pesos at the specified rate of exchange. Since this was substantially below the market rate, the Callejos brought legal proceedings against Bancomer in the United States.[12] Bancomer pleaded sovereign immunity and act of state. The district court dismissed the proceedings on the ground of sovereign immunity. The Callejos appealed.

Goldberg, Circuit Judge

[After ruling that the proceedings were not barred by sovereign immunity, Judge Goldberg proceeded to deal with the defence of act of state. The Callejos put forward three grounds for claiming that the act of state doctrine did not apply: (1) Mexico's promulgation of the exchange control regulations was a commercial act, not an act of state; (2) the 'treaty exception' to the act of state doctrine applied, since the exchange control regulations violated Mexico's obligations under the Articles of Agreement of the International Monetary Fund; and (3) the *situs* of the certificates of deposit was Texas rather than Mexico. After dismissing the first two

---

11 It seems that they bought the CDs by depositing money with Bancomer's account in a Texas bank on the US side of the border, in Laredo, Texas.
12 The case was originally brought in a state court, but was removed to a federal court by Bancomer.

arguments (he said that the adoption of exchange control regulations was not a commercial act, and that the regulations did not violate the IMF Agreement), Judge Goldberg considered the *situs* of the CDs.]

C. The *Situs* of the Deposits

The final argument advanced by the Callejos for not applying the act of state doctrine is that the *situs* of their CDs was Texas rather than Mexico. The Callejos argue that under traditional choice-of-law rules pegging the choice of law to the *situs* of the property, Texas law should govern the certificates. Application of the act of state doctrine, they contend, would improperly give extraterritorial effect to the Mexican decrees.

. . .

On a previous occasion, we noted that '[t]he *situs* of intangible property is about as intangible a concept as is known to the law.' *Tabacalera* 392 F 2d at 714. 'The *situs* may be in one place for *ad valorem* tax purposes . . . it may be in another place for venue purposes, i.e., garnishment . . . it may be in more than one place for tax purposes in certain circumstances . . . it may be in still a different place when the need for establishing its true *situs* is to determine whether an overriding national concern, like the application of the Act of State Doctrine is involved.' *Id*. at 714–715. In determining the *situs* of an obligation, we take as our guide the general policies of the act of state doctrine rather than narrow rules developed in other contexts . . .

[Judge Goldberg then turned to the Fifth Circuit's judgment in *Tabacalera*. After discussing it in some detail, he then said:]

. . . we do not find it helpful here. In *Tabacalera*, the foreign government was attempting to collect a debt rather than attempting to avoid paying it; the question was whether the foreign decrees applied to an obligation owed by an American debtor. Here, in contrast, the situation is reversed: the foreign national is the debtor and the American national the creditor. If we simply applied the *Tabacalera* test, the *situs* of the certificates would clearly be Mexico, since Mexico can enforce the collection of debts owed by Bancomer, a Mexican domiciliary . . . In that event, the act of state doctrine would apply whenever a foreign state seized debts owed by its banks, no matter how many ties the debts had to this country.

We do not think that *Tabacalera* intended such results. The power to collect a debt is for the benefit of the creditor, not the debtor; the fact that a debt can be enforced by the creditor in one forum should not be the basis of depriving him of his ability to enforce the debt in a different forum. Otherwise, the sword of the creditor would become a shield for the debtor. Since we do not believe that debts owed by foreign banks to American nationals are always sitused in the foreign country – and consequently do not believe that the act of state doctrine always applies to such debts – we do not apply the *Tabacalera* test here . . .

Instead, for debts owed by foreign banks to American nationals, the proper test for determining *situs* is where the incidents of the debt, as a whole, place it.

One relevant factor is the place where the deposit is carried, but this is not the only factor. In addition, we must examine the place of payment, the intent of the parties (if any) regarding the applicable law, and the involvement of the American banking system in the transaction.[1] Together, these factors help us to determine the extent of the foreign government's interest in the debt. They therefore help to answer the ultimate question in the act of state context: Are the ties of the debt to the foreign country sufficiently close that we will antagonize the foreign government by not recognizing its acts? . . .

Here, the incidents of the certificates of deposit clearly place them in Mexico. The certificates of deposit were issued by Bancomer's Nuevo Laredo branch, where the Callejos' deposits were carried, and called for payment in Mexico. This grouping of contacts, when viewed through the gloss of the policies underlying the act of state doctrine, places the debt in Mexico and calls for the application of Mexican law.

. . .

Given Mexico's interest in these certificates of deposit, which were issued by a Mexican bank and payable in Mexico, disregarding Mexico's exchange regulations would be a serious affront. We decline to take this course. Instead, we apply the act of state doctrine and affirm the dismissal of the suit.

. . .

The judgment of the district court dismissing the present case is AFFIRMED.

1 These factors have been used on a number of occasions to determine the *situs* of debts owed by foreign banks. In *Garcia*, for example, the court located in the United States a certificate of deposit issued by Chase Manhattan's Cuban branch, on the ground that the certificate was guaranteed by Chase's New York office and could be repaid by presentation at any Chase branch. 735 F 2d at 650. Similarly, in *Libra Bank*, the court determined that the *situs* of a loan to a Costa Rican bank was the United States, since the loan agreement provided that New York law would govern, the Costa Rican bank consented to the jurisdiction of American courts, the place of payment was Chase Manhattan's New York branch, and the Costa Rican bank had substantial assets in the United States. 570 F Supp at 881–882. As the court noted, 'The Costa Rican decrees attempted to alter the legal relations between the parties with respect to the debt by extinguishing the legal right to repayment, the only property in question, whose *situs* was in New York.' *Ibid.* at 882; see also *Allied Bank*, 757 F 2d at 521 (*situs* of promissory notes issued by Costa Rican banks to syndicate of 39 creditor banks was New York, where notes payable, negotiations held, and syndicate agent located); *Weston Banking Corporation* v. *Turkiye Garanti Bankasi*, 57 NY 2d 315; 456 NYS 2d 684; 442 NE 2d 1195 (1982) (*situs* of promissory note issued by Turkish bank to Panamanian bank was United States, since note designated New York as proper jurisdiction for the resolution of disputes and as place of payment); *Restatement (Revised) of Foreign Relations Law of the United States*, at § 469 reporters' note 4; cf. *Dunn* v. *Bank of Nova Scotia*, 374 F 2d 876, 877–78 (5th Cir. 1967) (*situs* of deposit at place of deposit, unless alternative place of payment designated).

Comment

An English court would have regarded this case as presenting contractual issues and would almost certainly reach the same conclusion, assuming the Rome I Regulation permitted it to do so.

It is interesting to note that, in *Callejo*, the court said that it did not find the *Tabacalera* test helpful. However, a couple of months earlier, the Second Circuit had applied the *Tabacalera* test to reach a similar result in a case based on the same Mexican exchange-control regulations. We give a short extract from its judgment.

United States
Braka v. *Bancomer*
US Court of Appeals for the Second Circuit
762 F 2d 222 (1985)

Background

Braka and the other plaintiffs were resident in the United States. Before the Mexican exchange controls were imposed, they had bought certificates of deposit from Bancomer, the same Mexican bank as in the *Callejo* case. After the exchange controls were adopted, the plaintiffs sued Bancomer in a federal court in New York.

Meskill, Circuit Judge

In reviewing the district court's conclusion on the applicability of the act of state doctrine, we must first determine the *situs* of the property that was taken by the Mexican exchange controls. As we noted in *Allied*, 'the concept of the *situs* of a debt for act of state purposes differs from the ordinary concept.' The test we adopted in *Allied* was whether the purported taking was 'able to come to complete fruition within the dominion of the [Mexican] government.' [*Tabacalera*] Here, unlike *Allied*, it is clear that Mexico's actions meet this test.

. . .

The CDs named Mexico City as the place of deposit and of payment of interest and principal. Although some of the CDs were dollar-denominated, Bancomer never agreed to pay them in any location other than Mexico. The fact that plaintiffs' deposits were occasionally accepted and transmitted to Mexico by Bancomer's New York agency does not alter the *situs* of Bancomer's obligation. It is clear that the accomplishment of interbank transfers, which was the extent of the New York agency's participation, does not change the contractually mandated *situs* of plaintiffs' property. The CDs were located in Mexico and were therefore subject to the effects of the exchange control regulations. The Mexican government 'ha[d] the parties and the *res* before it and act[ed] in such a manner as to change the relationship between the parties touching the *res*.' *Tabacalera*, 392 F 2d at 715. To intervene to contradict the result of the exchange controls would be an impermissible intrusion into the governmental activities of a foreign sovereign.

§ 3   Situs under US law

The cases set out above demonstrate that the American courts have moved from the position that the *situs* of a debt is the domicile of the debtor to something akin to a grouping-of-contacts test, in which the domicile of the debtor is only one factor, other factors being the place of payment, the place of deposit, the applicable law, the applicable currency and whether the parties have concluded a forum-selection agreement.[13] As already mentioned, this is similar to the approach adopted by English courts in order to determine the closest connection of a contract for the purpose of choice of law.

The cases set out in this section were decided in the 1980s. They were part of a flood of litigation resulting from the financial crisis that swept Latin America in that decade. Other cases were the consequence of the Cuban Revolution, more than two decades earlier. Since then, the flood of cases has abated, but not entirely ceased. There have been no new developments: the same approaches are adopted and the same ambiguities persist.[14]

§ 4 The Hickenlooper Amendment

We finally consider the effect of the Hickenlooper Amendment on cases of the kind we have been discussing.

New York
French v. Banco Nacional de Cuba
Court of Appeals of New York
23 NY 2d 46; 295 NYS 2d 433 (1968)

Background

The case concerned a man called Ritter, an American citizen who had previously lived in Cuba. Before the Cuban Revolution, he had invested money in a farm in Cuba. Under the system prevailing at the time, he could have obtained a certificate entitling him to be given US dollars for Cuban pesos if he decided to sell up in Cuba. The certificates, called 'certificates of tax exemption', were issued by a Cuban Government body called 'the Currency Stabilization Fund'. In June 1959, six months after the Revolution, Ritter acquired eight such certificates, aggregating US$150,000. In July 1959, however, a Cuban decree withdrew the right to obtain dollars. The reason was that Cuba was running dangerously low on foreign exchange.

Ritter, who subsequently came to the US, assigned his rights under the certificates to the plaintiff in the case, Hazel French. She brought proceedings in a New York state court against the Cuban National Bank. The trial court (the Supreme Court)[15] gave judgment for the plaintiff, and this was affirmed on appeal by the Appellate Division of the Supreme Court. The case then came on a final appeal before the New York Court of Appeals. The Cubans raised the defence of act of state. The main issue in the appeal was whether this was barred by the Hickenlooper Amendment.

---

13 For further details, see footnote 14 above (originally, footnote 31 in the *Callejo* judgment).
14 See Born (Gary B.) and Rutledge (Peter B.), *International Civil Litigation in United States Courts: Commentary and Materials* (Wolters Kluwer, Austin, Boston, Chicago, New York, the Netherlands, 4th edn, 2007), Chapter 9, pp. 789–91, where developments are brought up to date and inconsistent decisions noted.
15 In New York, the trial-level court is called the Supreme Court; the highest court is the New York Court of Appeals.

Fuld, Chief Justice

[After setting out the terms of the Amendment, as to which see Chapter 28, Panel 28.1, Chief Justice Fuld continued:]

It is plain enough upon the face of the statute – and abundantly clear from its legislative history – that Congress was not attempting to assure a remedy in American courts for every kind of monetary loss resulting from actions, even unjust actions, of foreign governments. The law is restricted, manifestly, to the kind of problem exemplified by the *Sabbatino* case itself, a claim of title or other right to specific property which had been expropriated abroad. (See Henkin, Act of State Today: Recollections in Tranquillity, 6 Colum. J. of Transnatl. L. 175, 185, 186.)

The basic terms of the statute – to come directly to its wording – simply cannot be made to fit the present case. The amendment applies only if there is a 'claim of title or other right to property' and that claim is 'based upon (or traced through) a confiscation or other taking' of such property.

Ritter's loss is due not to a taking of property but, rather, to the breach of a promise upon which he had relied. What had happened – and undoubtedly to Ritter's financial loss – was that the Cuban law which governed the contract had been changed by the adoption of a government regulation which 'suspended', perhaps permanently, the conversion of pesos into dollars. In the strictest sense, and within the terms of the statute we are construing, just as no one has 'taken' the pesos from Ritter, so no one has 'taken' the contract from him; it is still his or his assignee's to enforce, or attempt to enforce, as the present action bears witness. No other party claims to be possessed of the contract rights that Ritter had acquired. It is not as though the Cuban Government had assumed title to a contract right or other chose in action that had belonged to Ritter and had then sought to enforce it against the obligor. Indeed, as will shortly appear . . . even if a true, outright confiscation of this kind had occurred – that is, an actual divesting of ownership of a contract right – it would still be outside the compass of the Hickenlooper Amendment.

If there could be any doubt that the amendment is inapplicable to claims for breach of contract, that doubt is dispelled by reference to the legislative history, both of the original enactment in 1964 and the change in wording adopted in 1965.

Throughout the committee hearings and proceedings in Congress, the supporters of the bill and those who commented upon it were quite explicit about the intended purpose of the proposal. That purpose was simply to permit an adjudication 'on the merits', despite the holding in *Sabbatino*, in those cases in which a party asserts 'a claim of title or other right' to property which has been confiscated or taken and such property becomes the subject of a lawsuit in the United States. Indeed, Senator Hickenlooper himself expressly declared, at one point, that the purpose of his proposal was to require our American courts to apply international law 'whenever expropriated property comes within the territorial jurisdiction of the United States', noting that, unless his proposal was accepted and the *Sabbatino* decision overruled, this country might become 'an international "thieves market"' (110 Cong. Rec. 19548).

The words 'confiscation' and 'taking', the debates and committee hearings established, were used synonymously with 'expropriation' and 'nationalization.' Nothing in the lengthy record of the congressional proceedings suggests that the amendment was designed to cover claims of breach of contracts by a foreign government such as the one in this case. Nor was there any intimation that Congress had in view the highly complex problems of exchange control regulations, repudiation of debts or depreciation of currency. Conspicuously absent from the hearings was the kind of expert testimony on international monetary problems which surely would have been sought if the Congress had been addressing itself to problems of that nature.

Further proof of the limited scope intended for the exemption from the act of state doctrine is found in the Senate's refusal to enact Senator Hickenlooper's original, broadly worded, draft of the amendment which would have made the act of state doctrine inapplicable to any case 'in which an act of a foreign state occurring after January 1, 1959 is alleged to be contrary to international law'. The statute, as actually adopted in 1964, contained the far more restrictive wording which we have already discussed.

In point of fact, to eliminate any possibility that the original language, adopted in 1964, might be construed to cover or encompass ordinary contract rights, or anything other than specific and identifiable and 'traceable' property, Congress amended the statute in 1965. In its original form, the amendment referred to cases in which 'a claim of title or other right is asserted . . . based upon (or traced through) a confiscation or other taking.' By the 1965 modification, the words, 'to property', were inserted after the words 'other right', so that the clarified provision now reads, as already noted, 'a claim of title or other right to property'. As the Senate Report explains, the words were inserted 'to make it clear that the law does not prevent banks, insurance companies and other financial institutions from using the act of state as a defense to multiple liability upon any contract, deposit or insurance policy in any case where such liability [*sic*] has been taken over or expropriated by a foreign state.' Thus, not even contract rights which are taken over and are sought to be enforced in this country are covered by the Hickenlooper Amendment, much less claims for breach of a contract in a suit between the original parties to the agreement.

We may not ignore, or leave unexplained . . . the fact that, when Congress, in 1965, wished to assure the preservation of the act of state defense for the benefit of American insurance companies and banks who were sued on contract claims, it chose to do so not by adding a carefully limited exception, but – as noted in the text above – by inserting the words, 'to property', after the words, 'claim of title or other right' The use of these unqualified words can only signify that Congress decided to eliminate all contract claims from the statute rather than attempt the more subtle task of distinguishing between contract cases in which the act of state defense might be asserted and those in which it might not . . .

From all that has been said, it is apparent that the Hickenlooper Amendment has no application to the present case. The present lawsuit does not involve the assertion of a claim of title to property and, just as clearly, the Cuban Government's action did not involve a confiscation or taking of property. Certainly, it is not a case in which title or other right to a specific *res* (or its proceeds) confiscated by a foreign government is disputed on a claim either asserted by the original owner and defended by the government or asserted by the government and defended by the original owner.

It follows that the Hickenlooper Amendment is not applicable, that the act of state doctrine is decisive and that the defendant must prevail. This being so, it is not necessary to reach the further question whether the action of the Cuban Government offended principles of international law. Since, however, our dissenting brethren have concluded that such action did constitute a taking of property to which a claim of title or other right is asserted and have gone on to urge that it violated international law, we treat that question – of international law – briefly.

This is not an era, surely, in which there is anything novel or internationally reprehensible about even the most stringent regulation of national currencies and the flow of foreign exchange. Such practices have been followed, as the exigencies of international economics have required – and despite resulting losses to individuals – by capitalist countries and communist countries alike, by the United States and its allies as well as by those with whom our country has had profound differences. They are practices which are not even of recent origin but which have been recognized as a normal measure of government for hundreds of years, if not, indeed, as long as currency has been used as the medium of international exchange . . .

In short, the control of national currency and of foreign exchange is an essential governmental function . . .

In the case before us – whatever other economic measures the Cuban Government may have taken (and they are not reflected by evidence in the record) – there is no question that the actions complained of were aimed at protecting Cuba's scarce 'foreign exchange resources.' The testimony of the defendant's president that these actions were essential to prevent the wiping out of Cuba's foreign currency reserves is uncontradicted. Accordingly, that country's refusal to exchange Ritter's pesos for dollars, though it may be deplored, may not be characterized as so unreasonable or unjust as to outrage current international standards of governmental conduct. Even if the present case, then, involved 'a claim of title or other right to property' within the meaning of the Hickenlooper Amendment, the amendment would not permit us to disregard the act of state doctrine since the Cuban action did not violate international law.

In sum, then, it is our conclusion that the actions complained of constituted an act of state; that, under the rule announced in *Sabbatino*, we are required to give effect to that act of state; and that, since the record before us establishes that there was no taking of property to which a claim of title or other right is asserted, the Hickenlooper Amendment does not apply to require us to disregard the act of state doctrine. Consequently, the plaintiff or her assignor may seek a remedy in this country only through diplomatic efforts by the United States and arrangements established by Congress for the protection of the interests of all American claimants against Cuba.

The order of the Appellate Division should be reversed, with costs, and the complaint dismissed.

Order reversed

[Chief Justice Fuld's judgment was supported by three other judges; a further three dissented; so the appeal was allowed by a four–three majority.]

Comment

This case establishes that, in New York, the Hickenlooper Amendment is not interpreted as covering contractual rights of the kind in issue in exchange-control cases; indeed, it appears to be applicable only to tangible property.[16] This is in accord with the narrow interpretation usually given to it by American courts.[17]

It seems that the State Department was opposed to the Hickenlooper Amendment. The business community was generally in favour, but banks and insurance companies were against it. The reason the financial institutions were opposed was that they were afraid that, without the protection of the act of state doctrine, they might be forced to pay twice in some situations. The following example illustrates the problem.

An American bank opens a branch in Ruritania, an imaginary country. A Ruritanian resident deposits money with the bank. Subsequently, the Government of Ruritania confiscates all such deposits: the bank is forced to pay to the Government what it owed to the depositor. The depositor then flees to the US, where he demands his money.

Without legislation along the lines of the Hickenlooper Amendment, the bank would be protected by the act of state doctrine, since the *situs* of the debt would be Ruritania. However, if the Hickenlooper Amendment applied to the case, the bank might find that the US courts would say that the confiscation was contrary to international law and would not be recognized in the United States. The bank would then have to pay twice. To avoid this, the Hickenlooper Amendment was deliberately worded so as not to apply to the confiscation of contractual rights (intangibles), as distinct from the confiscation of tangible property.

---

16 For the position in Texas, see *Nelson Bunker Hunt* v. *Coastal States Gas Producing Company*, set out in Chapter 28, § 5, above. Since this is a question of federal law, the US Supreme Court would have the final say. So far, it has not ruled on the matter.

17 For further details, see Born (Gary B.) and Rutledge (Peter B.), *International Civil Litigation in United States Courts: Commentary and Materials* (Wolters Kluwer, Austin, Boston, Chicago, New York, the Netherlands, 4th edn, 2007), pp. 805–6, especially notes 96 and 97.

§ 5 Conclusions

We have already seen that, in considering the effect of governmental acts, there is a sharp distinction between the cases where such acts affect tangible property – in particular, goods – and the cases where they affect intangible property. The following comments are concerned solely with the latter.

§ 5.1 England and the US compared

Intangible property may be created by contract – for example, a contractual debt – or it may arise in other ways. Intellectual property and a claim in tort are examples. We are concerned with the former. The difficulty here is that the claim may have a contractual aspect and a property aspect. Since this can give rise to confusion, it is important to distinguish between (a) tangible property; (b) the property aspects of a contractual claim (a form of intangible property); and (c) the contractual aspects of a contractual claim. English courts regard categories (a) and (b) as governed by the *lex situs* and category (c) as governed by the law applicable to the contract.

The distinction between (b) and (c) under English law has never been clearly articulated, but it seems to be as follows: cases in which the rights of one party are taken from that party and given to another party are generally regarded as property cases; where, on the other hand, the parties remain the same but their rights are changed – for example, where an obligation to pay dollars is converted into an obligation to pay pesos – the English courts consider that only contractual issues are involved.

American courts do not normally draw a distinction between (b) and (c). Instead, they draw a distinction between acts of state – a concept that has never been clearly defined[18] – and commercial acts. The former are covered by the act of state doctrine, and benefit from presumptive validity, but only if they take place within the territory of the foreign State. Exchange controls and similar governmental acts affecting contractual rights are regarded as acts of state. In contrast to the English position, American courts consider that the *lex situs* is applicable to these cases as well. However, the current American test for *situs* in the case of rights created by a contract is similar to the English test for determining the law applicable to a contract.

The result is that, in cases that English courts would regard as falling under category (c) – for example, exchange-control cases – English courts (at least, until now)[19] reach much the same result as American courts, though they do so by different means. However, in cases that English courts regard as falling under category (b), the outcome can be different: in England, the residence of

---

18 It seems to refer to the kinds of things that only governments can do, as distinct from the kinds of things that both governments and private citizens can do, but it may be more complicated than this. See *Restatement of the Law Third: Foreign Relations Law of the United States*, Comment to § 443, especially paragraph (i), p. 372.
19 One cannot predict what effect the new Rome I Regulation will have.

the debtor is the crucial factor; in America, the same grouping-of-contacts test is applied.

§ 5.2 Should English law be changed?

Should English courts abandon the distinction between category (b) and category (c) and apply the law governing the contract in both cases? In some cases, this would make no difference. Bank accounts are an example. The *situs* of a bank account is the country in which the relevant branch is situated. It makes no difference where the head office is, or where the account holder is resident. The law applicable to the contract between the account holder and the bank will also be the law of that country. So, in the case of a bank account, it makes no difference whether a contractual approach or a property approach is followed.

In other cases, it will make a difference. Assume, for example, that B, who is at all times resident solely in Ruritania, owes a sum of money to A, who is resident in England. The debt is denominated in British currency and is payable in London. The contract under which it arose is governed by English law. If the Government of Ruritania adopts legislation under which foreign-currency obligations of Ruritanian residents are converted into obligations to pay Ruritanian currency in Ruritania, an English court would hold that the issues were purely contractual (category (c)). Since the contract was governed by English law, the Ruritanian legislation would be inapplicable.[20]

If, on the other hand, the Ruritanian Government adopts legislation under which the debt must be paid to it, rather than to A (confiscation), an English court would say that property issues were involved (category (b)). Recognition of the confiscation would depend on the *situs* of the debt. This would in turn be decided by the residence of the debtor. Since B is resident (only) in Ruritania, the confiscation would be recognized, unless it was contrary to public policy.[21] So, in this scenario, it *would* make a difference which approach is followed.

The argument for abandoning the distinction between category (b) and category (c) and applying the same approach in both cases is that the consequences for the creditor are the same: he loses his money, or, at least, he loses some of it. However, if we look at the matter from the point of view of the debtor, the position is different. In the first case, he pays less (or no) money; in the second case, he pays the same money but to a different person. The reason this difference is important is that, if the foreign legislation is refused recognition in the second case, there is a danger that the debtor may have to pay twice. In the example above, the Government of Ruritania could probably force the debtor (B) to pay the debt to it; so, if the English courts order him to pay it to A – and if they can

---

20 An American court would reach the same result by a different route: it would say that the Ruritanian legislation was an act of state but that, since the *situs* of the debt was outside Ruritanian territory, the American court was not precluded from judging the validity and effect of the legislation by applying American conflict-of-laws principles. Unless it was in accord with American law and policy (which would almost never be the case), the Ruritanian legislation would not be applied.

21 An American court, on the other hand, would treat this case in the same way as the previous one: it would say that the confiscation was an act of state, but that the *situs* was outside Ruritania. It would not recognize it.

enforce that order – he will have to pay the debt to two persons, the original creditor (A) and the Government of Ruritania.

This could be important with regard to insurance. Assume that an English insurance company had a branch in Ruritania. It writes life insurance for Ruritanian residents. The policies are payable in Ruritania (perhaps in pounds, euros or dollars). The applicable law is stated to be English. If Ruritania passes legislation that simply changes the terms of the contract – for example, it provides that payment will be in Ruritanian currency – the insurance company will not be able to benefit from it. This is not unreasonable.

If, on the other hand, the Ruritanian Government confiscates the policy, so that the proceeds have to be paid to it rather than to the policy holder, the matter will – as things stand at present – be characterized as affecting property and the law of the *situs* will apply. This will be Ruritanian law: the English company would be resident in Ruritania through its branch, since performance is to take place there. So the Ruritanian law would be applicable. Since the presence of the branch would in practice enable the Ruritanian Government to force the company to pay the proceeds to it, any other solution would mean that the company would have to pay twice.[22] So, in this scenario, the existing rule produces the better result.

We have considered only two scenarios, but there are many others. It is not possible to draw definite conclusions from such a limited number of examples, but enough has been said to show that any change in the law would have to be considered carefully. What appears logical at first sight may be found on closer examination to have serious defects.

Further reading

Born (Gary B.) and Rutledge (Peter B.), *International Civil Litigation in United States Courts: Commentary and Materials* (Wolters Kluwer, Austin, Boston, Chicago, New York, the Netherlands, 4th edn, 2007), Chapter 9, especially pp. 789–91

Carruthers (Janeen M.), *The Transfer of Property in the Conflict of Laws* (Oxford University Press, Oxford, 2005)

Gruson, 'The Act of State Doctrine in Contracts Cases as a Conflict-of-Laws Rule' [1998] *University of Illinois Law Review* 519

Heininger, 'Liability of US Banks for Deposits Placed in Their Foreign Branches' (1979) 11 *Law and Policy in International Business* 903

Lowenfeld, 'In Search of the Intangible: A Comment on Shaffer v. Heitner' (1978) 53 *NYU Law Review* 1102

Note, 'The Act of State Doctrine: Resolving Debt Situs Confusion' (1986) 86 *Columbia Law Review* 594

Restatement of the Law Third: Foreign Relations Law of the United States, Volume 1, pp. 366–89, especially pp. 375–7 (Reporter's Note 4)

---

22 It is not clear how an American court would decide this case. One assumes that it would manipulate the law to ensure that the company did not have to pay twice.

PART VI
EXTRATERRITORIALITY

CHAPTER 32

Introduction to extraterritoriality

§ 1   What is extraterritoriality?

In this Part of the book, we consider whether there are any limits on the activities of States in the area of private international law. These limits may be imposed by international law or by comity. Comity, it will be remembered, is the obligation of respect that States ought to display towards each other. In particular, it implies a duty to respect the sovereignty of other States. Acts which infringe these limits are often said to be extraterritorial. It will be remembered from the earlier parts of this book that, in some cases, the English courts have refused to make an order on the grounds that to do so would trespass on the sovereignty of another country.[1]

The word 'jurisdiction' is used in this context, but here 'jurisdiction' means something different from what it meant in Part II of this book. According to the *Restatement of the Law Third: Foreign Relations Law of the United States*, § 401, the limitations imposed on States under international law are concerned with three kinds of jurisdiction. These are:

(a)   jurisdiction to prescribe (sometimes called 'legislative jurisdiction');[2]
(b)   jurisdiction to adjudicate (sometimes called 'judicial jurisdiction'); and
(c)   jurisdiction to enforce ('executive jurisdiction').

As used in this context, 'prescribing' by a State means making its law applicable to the activities, relations or status of persons, or the interests of persons in things; 'adjudication' means subjecting persons or things to the process of its courts or administrative tribunals; and 'enforcing' means inducing or compelling compliance or punishing non-compliance with its laws or regulations.

The relationship between these concepts will be made clearer by an example. Assume that the United Kingdom decided to exceed generally recognized limits on its jurisdiction to prescribe by passing an Act of Parliament saying that it was an offence to smoke in the streets of Paris. This would be of little practical significance if it could not be enforced, something that would involve jurisdiction to enforce and jurisdiction to adjudicate. If British agents went to Paris and kidnapped smokers and brought them to England, there would be an infringement

---

1 See, for example, *Mackinnon* v. *Donaldson, Lufkin & Jenrette Securities Corporation*, set out in Chapter 20, § 2.1, above, and *Société Eram Shipping Co. Ltd* v. *Compagnie Internationale de Navigation*, set out in Chapter 30, § 2.1, above.
2 The phrase 'subject-matter jurisdiction' is sometimes used for jurisdiction to prescribe, but this causes confusion since it is usually used to mean something different.

of generally accepted norms regarding jurisdiction to enforce. If they were put on trial in England, there would probably also be an infringement of generally accepted norms of jurisdiction to adjudicate.

Though linked, these three kinds of jurisdiction are nevertheless distinct concepts. Passing the law is different from sending in the agents to kidnap offenders; and both these are different from putting offenders on trial. Moreover, it would be possible to enforce the law without infringing generally recognized jurisdictional limits. For example, the British authorities might receive information from British tourists regarding acts of smoking in Paris. This could be filed away and used for a prosecution if the miscreant ever came to England as an unsuspecting tourist. There would then be no violation of generally accepted norms of jurisdiction to enforce. Moreover, if prosecutions were brought only if a British citizen was in the vicinity and was forced to breathe some of the smoke, it could be argued that there was no infringement of generally accepted norms of jurisdiction to adjudicate, since the passive nationality principle could be invoked.[3]

In this Part of the book, we will not discuss jurisdiction to adjudicate. Internationally accepted norms seem rather thin on the ground – at least, as far as commercial cases are concerned – but, where they were relevant, they were considered in Part II. The most contentious area is jurisdiction to prescribe. This will constitute the main topic of this Part. However, we will start off by taking a brief look at jurisdiction to enforce.

§ 2 Jurisdiction to enforce

The most obvious limit on jurisdiction to enforce is territoriality. States are permitted to undertake executive action, including police action, within their own territories but not within the territories of other States. This, at least, is the theory. Our next case shows what happens in practice.

United States
United States* v. *Alvarez-Machain
US Supreme Court
504 US 655; 112 S Ct 2188; 119 L Ed 2d 441 (1992)

Background

This case concerned the US Drug Enforcement Administration (DEA), a body that operates under the Justice Department. It was established by President Nixon in 1973 to fight 'an all-out global war on the drug menace'. Today, it has over 5,000 special agents and a budget of over US$2 billion. It has eighty-seven foreign offices in sixty-three countries.

Mexico is a major field of operations. In 1985, a DEA agent called Enrique

---

3 Some States (but not the United Kingdom) consider that their courts have adjudicatory jurisdiction if the victim was one of their citizens.

Camarena Salazar was kidnapped by drug dealers outside the US Consulate in the Mexican city of Guadalajara. Subsequently, his body was found: it seems that he had been tortured and then killed. A Mexican, Dr Humberto Alvarez Machain, was alleged to have played a part in his murder. Alvarez Machain practised as a medical doctor in Guadalajara. It was claimed by the DEA that, when their agent was being tortured by the drug dealers, Alvarez Machain was in attendance: his job was to ensure that he did not die before he had been fully interrogated.

The DEA wanted to put Alvarez Machain on trial in the US. When informal negotiations with the Mexican authorities broke down, it was decided to kidnap him. The arrangements were made by a DEA informant called Garate. He recruited a gang of Mexicans for the purpose. Some were serving police officers, some were former police officers and some were civilians.[4] The operation was cleared at a high level in Washington.[5]

On 2 April 1990, at about 7.45 pm, Dr Alvarez Machain was in his consulting rooms, having just treated a patient. Suddenly, five or six armed men burst in. He was seized and taken to a house in Guadalajara. Subsequently, he was flown in a light aircraft to El Paso, Texas. When the plane landed, he was pushed into the hands of the DEA men waiting to receive him. He was charged before a federal district court with various offences under federal law, including the kidnapping of a federal agent[6] and felony-murder.[7] The district court held that his abduction (against which the Government of Mexico had lodged an official protest) was a violation of the extradition treaty with Mexico: it ordered that he be released and allowed to return to Mexico.[8] The US appealed, but the appeal was dismissed by the Ninth Circuit.[9] The case then came before the US Supreme Court.[10]

Chief Justice Rehnquist

Although we have never before addressed the precise issue raised in the present case, we have previously considered proceedings in claimed violation of an extradition treaty and proceedings against a defendant brought before a court by means of a forcible abduction . . .

In *Ker* v. *Illinois*, 119 US 436; 7 S Ct 225; 30 L Ed. 421 (1886) . . . we addressed the issue of a defendant brought before the court by way of a forcible abduction. Frederick Ker had been tried and convicted in an Illinois court for larceny; his presence before the court was procured by means of forcible abduction from Peru. A messenger was sent to Lima with the proper warrant to demand Ker by virtue of

---

4 They were offered US$50,000 plus expenses, though it is possible that only part of this was actually paid. After the kidnapping, some of the gang were allowed to live in America with their families. Those that remained in Mexico were arrested.

5 Evidence was given that the Deputy Director of the DEA gave his approval.

6 Contrary to 18 USC § 1201(a)(5).

7 Contrary to 18 USC § 1111(a). It was argued by Alvarez Machain that this and the other statutes under which he was charged did not have extraterritorial application, but this was rejected by the district court. Further possible issues of extraterritoriality were not considered.

8 *United States* v. *Rafael Caro-Quintero*, 745 F Supp 599 (1990).

9 *United States* v. *Humberto Alvarez-Machain*, 946 F 2d 1466 (9th Cir. 1991).

10 For earlier proceedings before the US Supreme Court arising out of the same incident, see *United States* v. *Verdugo-Urquidez*, 494 US 259; 110 S Ct 1056; 108 L Ed 2d 222 (US Supreme Court).

the extradition treaty between Peru and the United States. The messenger, however, disdained reliance on the treaty processes, and instead forcibly kidnaped Ker and brought him to the United States. We . . . rejected Ker's argument that he had a right under the extradition treaty to be returned to this country only in accordance with its terms. We rejected Ker's due process argument more broadly, holding in line with 'the highest authorities' that 'such forcible abduction is no sufficient reason why the party should not answer when brought within the jurisdiction of the court which has the right to try him for such an offence, and presents no valid objection to his trial in such court.' *Ker, supra*, at 444, 7 S Ct, at 229.

The only differences between *Ker* and the present case are that *Ker* was decided on the premise that there was no governmental involvement in the abduction, 119 US, at 443, 7 S Ct, at 229; and Peru, from which Ker was abducted, did not object to his prosecution. Respondent finds these differences to be dispositive . . . Therefore, our first inquiry must be whether the abduction of respondent from Mexico violated the Extradition Treaty between the United States and Mexico. If we conclude that the Treaty does not prohibit respondent's abduction, the rule in *Ker* applies, and the court need not inquire as to how respondent came before it.

In construing a treaty, as in construing a statute, we first look to its terms to determine its meaning. The Treaty says nothing about the obligations of the United States and Mexico to refrain from forcible abductions of people from the territory of the other nation, or the consequences under the Treaty if such an abduction occurs . . .

. . .

The history of negotiation and practice under the Treaty also fails to show that abductions outside of the Treaty constitute a violation of the Treaty. As the Solicitor General notes, the Mexican Government was made aware, as early as 1906, of the *Ker* doctrine, and the United States' position that it applied to forcible abductions made outside of the terms of the United States-Mexico Extradition Treaty. Nonetheless, the current version of the Treaty, signed in 1978, does not attempt to establish a rule that would in any way curtail the effect of *Ker*. Moreover, although language which would grant individuals exactly the right sought by respondent had been considered and drafted as early as 1935 by a prominent group of legal scholars sponsored by the faculty of Harvard Law School, no such clause appears in the current Treaty.

. . .

Thus, the language of the Treaty, in the context of its history, does not support the proposition that the Treaty prohibits abductions outside of its terms. The remaining question, therefore, is whether the Treaty should be interpreted so as to include an implied term prohibiting prosecution where the defendant's presence is obtained by means other than those established by the Treaty . . .

Respondent contends that the Treaty must be interpreted against the backdrop of customary international law, and that international abductions are 'so clearly prohibited in international law' that there was no reason to include such a clause in the Treaty itself . . . The international censure of international abductions is further evidenced, according to respondent, by the United Nations Charter and the Charter of the Organization of American States . . . Respondent does not argue that these sources of international law provide an independent basis for the right respondent asserts not to be tried in the United States, but rather that they should inform the interpretation of the Treaty terms.

The Court of Appeals deemed it essential, in order for the individual defendant to assert a right under the Treaty, that the affected foreign government had registered a protest. Respondent agrees that the right exercised by the individual is derivative of the nation's right under the Treaty, since nations are authorized, notwithstanding the terms of an extradition treaty, to voluntarily render an individual to the other country on terms completely outside of those provided in the treaty. The formal protest, therefore, ensures that the 'offended' nation actually objects to the abduction and has not in some way voluntarily rendered the individual for prosecution. Thus the Extradition Treaty only prohibits gaining the defendant's presence by means other than those set forth in the Treaty when the nation from which the defendant was abducted objects.

This argument seems to us inconsistent with the remainder of respondent's argument. The Extradition Treaty has the force of law, and if, as respondent asserts, it is self-executing, it would appear that a court must enforce it on behalf of an individual regardless of the offensiveness of the practice of one nation to the other nation . . .

More fundamentally, the difficulty with the support respondent garners from international law is that none of it relates to the practice of nations in relation to extradition treaties . . . Respondent would have us find that the Treaty acts as a prohibition against a violation of the general principle of international law that one government may not 'exercise its police power in the territory of another state.' There are many actions which could be taken by a nation that would violate this principle, including waging war, but it cannot seriously be contended that an invasion of the United States by Mexico would violate the terms of the Extradition Treaty between the two nations.

In sum, to infer from this Treaty and its terms that it prohibits all means of gaining the presence of an individual outside of its terms goes beyond established precedent and practice . . . The general principles cited by respondent simply fail to persuade us that we should imply in the United States–Mexico Extradition Treaty a term prohibiting international abductions.

Respondent and his *amici* may be correct that respondent's abduction was 'shocking', and that it may be in violation of general international law principles. Mexico has protested the abduction of respondent through diplomatic notes . . . and the decision of whether respondent should be returned to Mexico, as a matter outside of the Treaty, is a matter for the Executive Branch. We conclude, however, that respondent's abduction was not in violation of the Extradition Treaty between the United States and Mexico, and therefore the rule of *Ker* v. *Illinois* is fully applicable to this case. The fact of respondent's forcible abduction does not therefore prohibit his trial in a court in the United States for violations of the criminal laws of the United States.

So ordered.

Comment

Although the main focus of the judgment was on whether the kidnapping infringed the extradition treaty, the reasoning of the court was premised on the assumption that a violation of general international law would not constitute a bar to prosecution. Indeed, a subsequent attempt by Dr Alvarez Machain to challenge the indictment on this ground was rejected by the Ninth Circuit, partly for this reason.[11] This judgment shows, therefore, that, in at least some cases, US courts are not willing to take effective action to ensure that the US Government keeps within the limits laid down by international law with regard to enforcement jurisdiction.[12]

In a forceful dissent, Stevens J, joined by Blackmun and O'Connor JJ, argued that the case before the court differed from earlier cases in that the kidnapping had been carried out on the orders of the US Government. Reference was made to what is often regarded as the leading authority on international law, *Oppenheim's International Law*,[13] for the statement:

> It is . . . a breach of International Law for a State to send its agents to the territory of another State to apprehend persons accused of having committed a crime.

Stevens J also cited a South African case, decided during the days of apartheid, in which agents of the South African Government had kidnapped a dissident from a neighbouring State.[14] Basing itself partly on a decision of the Second Circuit that refused to follow *Ker* v. *Illinois*,[15] the South African court held that the kidnapping was contrary to international law and therefore contrary to South African law. It ruled that the South African courts had no jurisdiction to try the defendant.[16]

The judgment of the US Supreme Court provoked a strong protest from the Mexican Government. President Bush promised that there would be no more kidnappings, but he refused to hand Dr Alvarez Machain back. He was put on trial. However, it turned out that there was no evidence that he had been involved in the crime of which he was accused. Perhaps the Americans had kidnapped the wrong man. The district court ordered his release, and he returned to Mexico.[17]

---

11 *United States* v. *Humberto Alvarez-Machain*, 971 F 2d 310 (1992).
12 A few months prior to the kidnapping, the US Department of Justice had issued a legal opinion to the effect that, as a matter of US constitutional law, the President was not bound by international law when authorizing foreign operations by the FBI. See Lowe, 'Self-Evident and Inalienable Rights Stop at the US Frontier' [1991] CLJ 16 at pp. 18–19.
13 Volume 1, p. 295 and n. 1 (8th edn, 1955, by Lauterpacht).
14 *State* v. *Ebrahim*, 1991 (2) SA 553 (Supreme Court of South Africa (Appellate Division)).
15 *United States* v. *Toscanino*, 500 F 2d 267 (9th Cir. 1974).
16 For a subsequent English judgment to similar effect, see *R.* v. *Horseferry Road Magistrates' Court, ex parte Bennett* [1994] 1 AC 42; [1993] 3 WLR 90 (HL).
17 *The Independent*, 15 December 1992. See also *The Independent*, 18 December 1992. After his return to Mexico, Alvarez Machain brought proceedings in the US to obtain compensation for his ordeal, but the US Supreme Court ruled against him: *Sosa* v. *Alvarez-Machain*, 542 US 692; 124 S Ct 2739; 159 L Ed 2d 718 (2004).

Further reading

American Law Institute, *Restatement of the Law Third: Foreign Relations Law of the United States* (American Law Institute Publishers, St Paul, MN, 1986), pp. 230–339

Born (Gary B.) and Rutledge (Peter B.), *International Civil Litigation in United States Courts: Commentary and Materials* (Wolters Kluwer, Austin, Boston, Chicago, New York, the Netherlands, 4th edn, 2007), pp. 561–2

Lowenfeld (Andreas F.), *Conflict of Laws: Federal, State and International Perspectives* (LexisNexis, Newark, NJ, and San Francisco, CA, 2nd edn, 2002), pp. 869–71

CHAPTER 33

Extraterritorial application of US antitrust law

§ 1   Introduction

In this chapter, we will discuss the international reach of US antitrust law, that is to say, the extent to which American courts have held that US antitrust law applies extraterritorially. Antitrust law, an area on the border between public and private law, has been chosen because it has given rise to particular friction between the US and the international community. In the next chapter, we will discuss the reaction of other countries to what they perceive as the excessively wide reach of US law.

Antitrust law (called 'competition law' in Europe) was an American innovation. The Sherman Act,[1] adopted in 1890, prohibits monopolies and conspiracies in restraint of trade. It applies only to inter-state and international commerce.[2] It is supplemented by other statutes, including the Clayton Act (1914),[3] which creates further offences – for example, discrimination in price, services or facilities. US antitrust law has both a criminal and a civil aspect: in criminal proceedings, the accused may be fined or imprisoned; in civil proceedings, private parties may bring actions in tort for treble damages.[4] Injunctions may also be obtained.

Originally regarded with suspicion in Europe, antitrust/competition law is today recognized as an essential feature of an advanced economy. Similar legislation has been adopted in many European countries; it is also important in EC law. We will consider the international reach of EC competition law in Chapter 35.

§ 2   Act of state and choice of law

Our first case concerns American banana companies in Panama. Prior to 1903, Panama was part of Colombia. When Colombia refused to ratify a treaty with the US concerning what was to become the Panama Canal, America instigated

---

1 15 USC §§ 1–7.
2 Its application to US exports was modified by the Foreign Trade Antitrust Improvements Act of 1982 (15 USC § 6a).
3 15 USC §§ 12–27, 29 USC §§ 52–53.
4 These are calculated by first assessing the damages required to compensate the plaintiff for the loss caused by the illegal activities, and then multiplying the resulting sum by three. The additional, punitive element is justified as a way of discouraging illegal acts.

a rebellion which resulted in Panama declaring itself independent. The US navy ensured that Colombia did not use force to put the rebellion down.[5] Panama then gave America the treaty it wanted.[6] Since then, the US has maintained a large measure of control over Panama.[7]

While this political drama was being acted out, a commercial battle was being fought in the same territory between two American companies.

United States
American Banana Company v. *United Fruit Company*
US Supreme Court
213 US 347; 29 S Ct 511; 53 L Ed 826 (1909)

Background

United Fruit was a well-known American company that subsequently became United Brands and is now Chiquita Brands. It had an established position in the banana industry in several Latin American countries including Panama. American Banana was another American company that operated in the same field.

In 1903, shortly before Panama was detached from Colombia, a man called McConnell started a banana plantation in Panama and began building a railway to get his produce to the coast.[8] United Fruit had organized a cartel of banana producers in Panama, which controlled production and prices. McConnell was told that he must either join or get out. He refused to join. At United Fruit's instigation, Panama took a decision to let Costa Rica administer the territory through which the railway would run. After Panama declared itself independent, McConnell sold out to American Banana, which then tried to operate the plantation. In July 1904, Costa Rican troops,[9] acting at the behest of United Fruit, occupied American Banana's plantation. Since that date, they had prevented American Banana from producing bananas. American Banana turned to the US Government. In view of its position in the area, the US could have solved the problem, but it refused to act – allegedly because of United Fruit's influence.

---

5 At the time, the only way for Colombian troops to get to Panama was by sea.

6 To some extent, the Monroe Doctrine has given formal recognition to America's habit of intervening in Latin American countries. Proclaimed as part of President Monroe's State-of-the-Union Address in 1823, it was originally designed to prevent the European Powers from helping Spain regain its Latin American colonies. In time, however, it came to be used as a 'justification' for US hegemony over Latin American countries, especially those close at hand. In 1904, President Theodore Roosevelt declared that the Doctrine might force the United States, 'however reluctantly', to exercise an 'international police power' in the area. The following years saw many occasions on which the US invaded and occupied neighbouring States – for example, Cuba (1906–9 and 1912), Nicaragua (1912–25 and 1926–33); Haiti (1915–34) and the Dominican Republic (1916–24). Invasions have continued in more recent times – for example, the Dominican Republic (1965), Grenada (1983) and Panama (1989).

7 There have been short periods when things got out of hand. From 1983 to 1989, Manuel Noriega, one-time head of military intelligence, ruled Panama. He was a paid CIA agent; so the situation should have been ideal for the US. Unfortunately, Noriega got the idea into his head that he no longer needed America. He ceased to co-operate and went into the drug business. He had to be removed. When other methods failed, US troops invaded. Noriega was captured and taken to America for trial on charges of drug-dealing and money-laundering. He was given a lengthy prison sentence.

8 The facts set out in this paragraph are as claimed by American Banana in its complaint in the case. They had not been proved. However, because it was asserted by the defendant that American Banana's complaint disclosed no cause of action, the court had to decide the case on the basis that they were true.

9 This was in the days when Costa Rica still had an army. It was subsequently abolished.

American Banana then went to a US court and brought a tort action against United Fruit for treble damages under the Sherman Act. The lower court dismissed the complaint (which alleged the facts set out above) as not disclosing any cause of action. The judgment was affirmed by the Court of Appeals; the case then came before the US Supreme Court.

Holmes J

[After stating that in certain special cases, such as piracy, countries apply their laws extraterritorially, Holmes J continued:]

But the general and almost universal rule is that the character of an act as lawful or unlawful must be determined wholly by the law of the country where the act is done . . . For another jurisdiction, if it should happen to lay hold of the actor, to treat him according to its own notions rather than those of the place where he did the acts, not only would be unjust, but would be an interference with the authority of another sovereign, contrary to the comity of nations, which the other state concerned justly might resent. [References to *Phillips* v. *Eyre*, set out in Chapter 23, § 1 and Dicey, *Conflict of Laws* (2nd edn).]

Law is a statement of the circumstances, in which the public force will be brought to bear upon men through the courts. But the word commonly is confined to such prophecies or threats when addressed to persons living within the power of the courts. A threat that depends upon the choice of the party affected to bring himself within that power hardly would be called law in the ordinary sense. We do not speak of blockade running by neutrals as unlawful. And the usages of speech correspond to the limit of the attempts of the lawmaker, except in extraordinary cases. It is true that domestic corporations remain always within the power of the domestic law; but, in the present case, at least, there is no ground for distinguishing between corporations and men.

The foregoing considerations would lead, in case of doubt, to a construction of any statute as intended to be confined in its operation and effect to the territorial limits over which the lawmaker has general and legitimate power . . . Words having universal scope, such as 'every contract in restraint of trade', 'every person who shall monopolize', etc., will be taken, as a matter of course, to mean only everyone subject to such legislation, not all that the legislator subsequently may be able to catch. In the case of the present statute, the improbability of the United States attempting to make acts done in Panama or Costa Rica criminal is obvious, yet the law begins by making criminal the acts for which it gives a right to sue. We think it entirely plain that what the defendant did in Panama or Costa Rica is not within the scope of the statute so far as the present suit is concerned. Other objections of a serious nature are urged, but need not be discussed.

For again, not only were the acts of the defendant in Panama or Costa Rica not within the Sherman Act, but they were not torts by the law of the place, and therefore were not torts at all, however contrary to the ethical and economic postulates of that statute. The substance of the complaint is that, the plantation being within the *de facto* jurisdiction of Costa Rica, that state took and keeps possession of it by virtue of its sovereign power. But a seizure by a state is not a thing that can be complained of elsewhere in the courts. *Underhill* v. *Hernandez*, 168 U. S. 250, 42 L. ed. 456, 18 Sup. Ct. Rep. 83.[1] The fact, if it be one, that *de jure* the estate is in Panama, does not matter in the least; sovereignty is pure fact. The fact has been recognized by the United States, and, by the implications of the bill, is assented to by Panama.

The fundamental reason why persuading a sovereign power to do this or that cannot be a tort is not that the sovereign cannot be joined as a defendant or because it must be assumed to be acting lawfully . . . The fundamental reason is that it is a contradiction in terms to say that, within its jurisdiction, it is unlawful to persuade a sovereign power to bring about a result that it declares by its conduct to be desirable and proper. It does not, and foreign courts cannot, admit that the influences were improper or the results bad. It makes the persuasion lawful by its own act. The very meaning of sovereignty is that the decree of the sovereign makes law . . . In the case of private persons, it consistently may assert the freedom of the immediate parties to an injury and yet declare that certain persuasions addressed to them are wrong . . .

. . .

The acts of the soldiers and officials of Costa Rica are not alleged to have been without the consent of the government, and must be taken to have been done by its order. It ratified them, at all events, and adopted and keeps the possession taken by them . . . The injuries to the plantation and supplies seem to have been the direct effect of the acts of the Costa Rican government, which is holding them under an adverse claim of right. The claim for them must fall with the claim for being deprived of the use and profits of the place . . . Giving to this complaint every reasonable latitude of interpretation we are of opinion that it alleges no case under the act of Congress, and discloses nothing that we can suppose to have been a tort where it was done. A conspiracy in this country to do acts in another jurisdiction does not draw to itself those acts and make them unlawful, if they are permitted by the local law.

Further reasons might be given why this complaint should not be upheld, but we have said enough to dispose of it and to indicate our general point of view.

Judgment affirmed.

1 *Editor's note*: this is one of the classic early cases on the act of state doctrine.

Comment

This case shows the difficulties that arise when private companies obtain the services of a nominally independent State to further their own aims. To a significant extent, the decision of the court was based on the idea that the sovereignty of Costa Rica and Panama had to be respected. To apply US law to acts done in those countries would, the court said, be an interference with the authority of another sovereign and contrary to the comity of nations. However, these words have a hollow ring when set against the political background of the time.

The actual situation was that two American businesses, operating in the lawless territory of a 'banana republic', were competing with each other. One had obtained the services of the local army for use against the other. The latter appealed to a US court, which had to decide whether US law was applicable. In this context, local sovereignty hardly came into the picture: the issue was whether American companies should be free from US laws, and the policies contained in them, simply because they conducted their activities outside US territory.

The court, however, played the game of taking sovereignty seriously. Although the phrase 'act of state' is not used in the judgment – it appears to have come into use only at a later date – the reference to *Underhill* v. *Hernandez*, decided by the US Supreme Court in 1897, makes clear that this is what the court had in mind. In *Underhill*, the Supreme Court had applied the doctrine – again without using the phrase – to rule that US courts could not question executive action taken against an American by a Venezuelan military commander in Venezuela during a civil war in that country.[10]

The second basis for the judgment was the classic choice-of-law rule that a tort is governed by the law of the place where it is committed, a rule that was applied in its negative aspect – that an act is not actionable as a tort if it is justifiable under the *lex loci* – by the English courts in *Phillips* v. *Eyre* (set out in Chapter 23, § 1, above), a case cited by Holmes J. The court thus used choice-of-law principles as a ground for construing the Sherman Act so as not to apply outside US territory.[11] The result was that no extraterritorial effect was given to the Act.

§ 3   About turn!

The next case shows a change of course, though one that purported to respect the earlier decision.

United States
United States* v. *Sisal Sales Corporation
US Supreme Court
274 US 268; 47 S Ct 592; 71 L Ed 1042 (1927)

Background

This case concerned sisal, a fibre made from a Mexican plant. Binder twine, used by American farmers for harvesting grain crops, was made from it. Adequate quantities of sisal could be obtained only from the Mexican state of Yucatán. The

---

10 It could be argued that the doctrine did not apply if Costa Rica was acting outside its territory. However, the Government of Panama appeared to have consented to what it did; so it could be said to have acted under the authority of Panama.
11 This rigid territorialism in choice-of-law analysis is no longer in favour. Under Article 6(1) of the Rome II Regulation, for example: 'The law applicable to a non-contractual obligation arising out of an act of unfair competition shall be the law of the country where competitive relations or the collective interests of consumers are, or are likely to be, affected.' Since the bananas were apparently exported to the US and marketed there, this might well make US law applicable.

defendants (appellees) included three American banks, two American companies that dealt in sisal (one being the Sisal Corporation) and a Mexican company (Comisión Exportadora de Yucatán) that bought sisal from the producers. It was alleged that the defendants combined to create a monopoly. The Mexican company (Comisión Exportadora de Yucatán) became the sole purchaser of sisal from the producers in Mexico, and the Sisal Corporation became the sole importer into the US. This enabled the defendants to raise prices and make considerable profits. They seem to have enjoyed the support of the legislatures of Mexico and Yucatán, which passed legislation to help them; other buyers were forced out by discriminatory legislation.

The US Government (Attorney General) brought proceedings in a US court for an injunction to break up the cartel. The trial court held that *American Banana* was controlling and dismissed the suit. An appeal was taken to the US Supreme Court.

McReynolds J

The circumstances of the present controversy are radically different from those presented in *American Banana Co*. v. *United Fruit Co* . . . and the doctrine there approved is not controlling here . . .

[After outlining the facts of *American Banana*, McReynolds J continued:]

Here we have a contract, combination, and conspiracy entered into by parties within the United States and made effective by acts done therein. The fundamental object was control of both importation and sale of sisal and complete monopoly of both internal and external trade and commerce therein. The United States complain of a violation of their laws within their own territory by parties subject to their jurisdiction, not merely of something done by another government at the instigation of private parties. True, the conspirators were aided by discriminating legislation, but by their own deliberate acts, here and elsewhere, they brought about forbidden results within the United States. They are within the jurisdiction of our courts and may be punished for offenses against our laws.

. . .

The decree of the court below must be reversed.

Comment

The Supreme Court said that this case was radically different from *American Banana*. However, both cases concerned attempts to establish a monopoly regarding the export of a foreign product into the United States. The difference was supposed to be that in *Sisal Sales* the conspiracy was entered into in the US. However, in *American Banana*, Holmes J said: 'A conspiracy in this country to do acts in another jurisdiction does not draw to itself those acts and make them unlawful, if they are permitted by the local law.' The case represents a clear change of direction, though the court was not able to put forward a coherent rationale for the new policy.

This occurred in our next case.

§ 4   The effects doctrine

United States
United States* v. *Aluminum Company of America
US Court of Appeals for the Second Circuit
148 F 2d 416 (1945)

Background

The US Government brought proceedings under the Sherman Act against the Aluminum Company of America ('Alcoa') and Aluminum Limited ('Limited'). Alcoa was a Pennsylvania corporation; Limited was a Canadian corporation, which had been incorporated in 1928 to take over the assets of Alcoa outside the United States. In exchange, Limited issued its shares to Alcoa's shareholders. By 1931, the two companies had no officers in common, but two American families (the Davis and Mellon families) and the officers of Alcoa owned just under half of the shares in each company. In 1931, Limited entered into an agreement with Swiss, German, French and British corporations to limit production. This was done through a Swiss-incorporated company called Alliance. It was replaced by a new agreement in 1936.

The district court held for the defendants, and the United States appealed. The case came before the US Supreme Court, but the latter referred the case to the Second Circuit because it lacked a quorum of justices qualified to hear it. The Second Circuit held that Alcoa was not party to any unlawful agreement. That left Limited. The American courts had judicial jurisdiction over it because it had an important administrative office (perhaps its actual headquarters) in New York.

Learned Hand J

Did either the agreement of 1931 or that of 1936 violate § 1 of the Act? The answer does not depend upon whether we shall recognize as a source of liability a liability imposed by another state. On the contrary we are concerned only with whether Congress chose to attach liability to the conduct outside the United States of persons not in allegiance to it. That being so, the only question open is whether Congress intended to impose the liability, and whether our own Constitution permitted it to do so: as a court of the United States, we cannot look beyond our own law. Nevertheless, it is quite true that we are not to read general words, such as those in this Act, without regard to the limitations customarily observed by nations upon the exercise of their powers; limitations which generally correspond to those fixed by the 'Conflict of Laws.' We should not impute to Congress an intent to punish all whom its courts can catch, for conduct which has no consequences within the United States. [*American Banana* and other cases cited.] On the other hand, it is settled law – as 'Limited' itself agrees – that any state may impose liabilities, even upon persons not within its allegiance, for conduct outside its borders that has consequences within its borders which the state reprehends; and these liabilities other states will ordinarily recognize . . . It may be argued that this Act extends further. Two situations are possible. There may be agreements made beyond our borders not intended to affect imports, which do affect them, or which affect exports. Almost any limitation of the supply of goods in Europe, for example, or in South America, may have repercussions in the United States if there is trade between the two. Yet when one considers the international complications likely to arise from an effort in this country to treat such agreements as unlawful, it is safe to assume that Congress certainly did not intend the Act to cover them. Such agreements may on the other hand intend to include imports into the United States, and yet it may appear that they had no effect upon them. That situation might be thought to fall within the doctrine that intent may be a substitute for performance in the case of a contract made within the United States; or it might be thought to fall within the doctrine that a statute should not be interpreted to cover acts abroad which have no consequence here. We shall not choose between these alternatives; but for argument we shall assume that the Act does not cover agreements, even though intended to affect imports or exports, unless its performance is shown actually to have had some effect upon them. Where both conditions are satisfied, the situation certainly falls within such decisions as [various cases cited, including *Sisal Sales*] . . . It is true that in those cases the persons held liable had sent agents into the United States to perform part of the agreement; but an agent is merely an animate means of executing his principal's purposes, and, for the purposes of this case, he does not differ from an inanimate means; besides, only human agents can import and sell ingot.

Both agreements would clearly have been unlawful, had they been made within the United States; and it follows from what we have just said that both were unlawful, though made abroad, if they were intended to affect imports and did affect them.

[After an analysis of the facts, Judge Learned Hand continued:]

We shall dispose of the matter therefore upon the assumption that, although the shareholders intended to restrict imports, it does not appear whether in fact they did so. Upon our hypothesis the plaintiff would therefore fail, if it carried the burden of proof upon this issue as upon others. We think, however, that, after the intent to affect imports was proved, the burden of proof shifted to 'Limited.'

For these reasons we think that the agreement of 1936 violated § 1 of the Act.

Result: the judgment of the lower court was reversed and the case remanded. It was subsequently ordered that the link between Alcoa and Limited be dissolved.

Comment

In this case, the court says that the only questions were whether Congress intended to impose liability on Limited in the circumstances of the case, and whether the Constitution allowed it to do so. However, it admitted that, in interpreting the general words of the Act, regard should be had to 'the limitations customarily observed by nations upon the exercise of their powers.' Nevertheless, despite the fact that it admitted that these limitations generally correspond to those fixed by conflict of laws, the judgment contains no choice-of-law analysis. It is not suggested that the question whether an act is unlawful must be decided by the law of the place where it is done. Instead, the court adopts what has come to be known as the 'effects doctrine'. As formulated in this case, this says that an act done outside the United States by a foreign company may nevertheless come within the scope of the Act if two conditions are fulfilled: the act must be intended to affect US trade and it must in fact have such an effect. If both conditions are fulfilled, the Sherman Act can apply.

Although Judge Learned Hand seemed to think that this was generally accepted, the effects doctrine was subject to criticism abroad.[12] Later cases tried to find a compromise. We give an example.

§ 5   A balancing exercise

United States
Timberlane Lumber Co. v. Bank of America I
US Court of Appeals for the Ninth Circuit
549 F 2d 597 (1976)

Background

Timberlane Lumber Company was an Oregon partnership in the timber business. It wanted a source of supply for its US operations, and decided that Honduras was the answer. It set up two Honduran corporations, Danli and Maya, both of which were owned by the Timberlane partners. The court referred to Timberlane, Danli and Maya collectively as 'Timberlane'. Bank of America (the 'bank') was a well-known US bank. Timberlane alleged that Bank of America and various co-conspirators tried to drive it out of business in Honduras. Acting through a front man, the bank used a security interest it held in Timberlane's Honduran plant to obtain a court order called an 'embargo'. This was designed to preserve the asset, but Timberlane claimed that it was in fact used to disrupt its operations. A judicial officer called an 'interventor' was appointed by the court. He was allegedly on the payroll of the bank. He brought in troops who crippled Timberlane's activities. The bank also caused Timberlane's local manager to be falsely arrested and imprisoned. Timberlane claimed some US$5 million damages. It said that the claim was covered by US antitrust law because the defendants' activities had a direct effect on exports to the US.

The district court held for the defendants on the grounds of act of state and lack of subject-matter jurisdiction. Timberlane appealed.

---

12 The effects doctrine is generally accepted when applied to direct physical effects – for example, firing a bullet on one side of the frontier that kills someone on the other – but economic effects are regarded as a different matter.

Choy, Circuit Judge

[Judge Choy first considered the act of state doctrine. He took the view that it was not applicable because the acts in question did not constitute acts of state. Basing himself on *The Restatement (Second) of Foreign Relations Law of the United States* § 41 (1965), he said that an act of state is 'an act of a foreign state by which that state has exercised its jurisdiction to give effect to its public interests.' The allegedly sovereign acts of Honduras, he said, consisted of judicial proceedings initiated by one of the alleged co-conspirators, not by the Honduran Government itself. There was no indication that the actions of the Honduran court and authorities reflected a sovereign decision that Timberlane's efforts should be crippled or that trade with the United States should be restrained. He, therefore, held that the act of state doctrine did not apply. He then turned to the second ground of decision:]

Extraterritorial Reach of the United States Antitrust Laws

There is no doubt that American antitrust laws extend over some conduct in other nations. There was language in the first Supreme Court case in point [*American Banana*] casting doubt on the extension of the Sherman Act to acts outside United States territory. But subsequent cases have limited American Banana to its particular facts, and the Sherman Act – and with it other antitrust laws – has been applied to extraterritorial conduct . . . [Various cases, including *Sisal Sales* and *Alcoa* cited.] The Act may encompass the foreign activities of aliens as well as American citizens. *Alcoa* . . .

That American law covers some conduct beyond this nation's borders does not mean that it embraces all, however. Extraterritorial application is understandably a matter of concern for the other countries involved. Those nations have sometimes resented and protested, as excessive intrusions into their own spheres, broad assertions of authority by American courts . . . Our courts have recognized this concern and have, at times, responded to it, even if not always enough to satisfy all the foreign critics . . . In any event, it is evident that at some point the interests of the United States are too weak and the foreign harmony incentive for restraint too strong to justify an extraterritorial assertion of jurisdiction.

What that point is or how it is determined is not defined by international law . . . Nor does the Sherman Act limit itself. In the domestic field the Sherman Act extends to the full reach of the commerce power . . . To define it somewhat more modestly in the foreign commerce area courts have generally, and logically, fallen back on a narrower construction of congressional intent, such as expressed in Judge Learned Hand's oft-cited opinion in *Alcoa* . . .

[Judge Choy then quoted the passage from *Alcoa* set out above, beginning 'The only question open is whether Congress intended to impose . . .' He continued:]

It is the effect on American foreign commerce which is usually cited to support extraterritorial jurisdiction. *Alcoa* set the course, when Judge Hand declared . . .

[The passage set out above beginning 'it is settled law' was then quoted. Judge Choy continued:]

Despite its description as 'settled law', *Alcoa's* assertion has been roundly disputed by many foreign commentators as being in conflict with international law, comity, and good judgment. Nonetheless, American courts have firmly concluded that there is some extraterritorial jurisdiction under the Sherman Act.

Even among American courts and commentators, however, there is no consensus on how far the jurisdiction should extend. The district court here concluded that a 'direct and substantial effect' on United States foreign commerce was a prerequisite, without stating whether other factors were relevant or considered . . .

. . .

The effects test by itself is incomplete because it fails to consider other nations' interests. Nor does it expressly take into account the full nature of the relationship between the actors and this country. Whether the alleged offender is an American citizen, for instance, may make a big difference; applying American laws to American citizens raises fewer problems than application to foreigners . . .

American courts have, in fact, often displayed a regard for comity and the prerogatives of other nations and considered their interests as well as other parts of the factual circumstances, even when professing to apply an effects test.

. . .

A tripartite analysis seems to be indicated. As acknowledged above, the antitrust laws require in the first instance that there be *some* effect – actual or intended – on American foreign commerce before the federal courts may legitimately exercise subject matter jurisdiction under those statutes. Second, a greater showing of burden or restraint may be necessary to demonstrate that the effect is sufficiently large to present a cognizable injury to the plaintiffs and, therefore, a civil *violation* of the antitrust laws . . . Third, there is the additional question which is unique to the international setting of whether the interests of, and links to, the United States – including the magnitude of the effect on American foreign commerce – are sufficiently strong, *vis-à-vis* those of other nations, to justify an assertion of extraterritorial authority.

It is this final issue which is both obscured by undue reliance on the 'substantiality' test and complicated to resolve. An effect on United States commerce, although necessary to the exercise of jurisdiction under the antitrust laws, is alone not a sufficient basis on which to determine whether American authority *should* be asserted in a given case as a matter of international comity and fairness. In some cases, the application of the direct and substantial test in the international context might open the door too widely by sanctioning jurisdiction over an action when these considerations would indicate dismissal. At other times, it may fail in the other direction, dismissing a case for which comity and fairness do not require forbearance, thus closing the jurisdictional door too tightly – for the Sherman Act does reach some restraints which do not have both a direct and substantial effect on the foreign commerce of the United States. A more comprehensive inquiry is necessary. We believe that the field of conflict of laws presents the proper approach, as was suggested, if not specifically employed, in *Alcoa* in expressing the basic limitation on application of American laws . . .

[Judge Choy then set out the passage in *Alcoa* referring to 'conflict of laws.' After further discussion, he continued:]

What we prefer is an evaluation and balancing of the relevant considerations in each case . . .

The elements to be weighed include the degree of conflict with foreign law or policy, the nationality or allegiance of the parties and the locations or principal places of businesses or corporations, the extent to which enforcement by either state can be expected to achieve compliance, the relative significance of effects on the United States as compared with those elsewhere, the extent to which there is explicit purpose to harm or affect American commerce, the foreseeability of such effect, and the relative importance to the violations charged of conduct within the United States as compared with conduct abroad. A court evaluating these factors should identify the potential degree of conflict if American authority is asserted. A difference in law or policy is one likely sore spot, though one which may not always be present. Nationality is another; though foreign governments may have some concern for the treatment of American citizens and business residing there, they primarily care about their own nationals. Having assessed the conflict, the court should then determine whether in the face of it the contacts and interests of the United States are sufficient to support the exercise of extraterritorial jurisdiction.

We conclude, then, that the problem should be approached in three parts: Does the alleged restraint affect, or was it intended to affect, the foreign commerce of the United States? Is it of such a type and magnitude so as to be cognizable as a violation of the Sherman Act? As a matter of international comity and fairness, should the extraterritorial jurisdiction of the United States be asserted to cover it? The district court's judgment found only that the restraint involved in the instant suit did not produce a direct and substantial effect on American foreign commerce. That holding does not satisfy any of these inquiries.

The Sherman Act is not limited to trade restraints which have both a direct and substantial effect on our foreign commerce. Timberlane has alleged that the complained of activities were intended to, and did, affect the export of lumber from Honduras to the United States – the flow of United States foreign commerce, and as such they are within the jurisdiction of the federal courts under the Sherman Act. Moreover, the magnitude of the effect alleged would appear to be sufficient to state a claim.

The comity question is more complicated. From Timberlane's complaint it is evident that there are grounds for concern as to at least a few of the defendants, for some are identified as foreign citizens . . . Moreover, it is clear that most of the activity took place in Honduras, though the conspiracy may have been directed from San Francisco,[1] and that the most direct economic effect was probably on Honduras. However, there has been no indication of any conflict with the law or policy of the Honduran government, nor any comprehensive analysis of the

---

1 *Editor's note*: San Francisco was the headquarters of Bank of America.

relative connections and interests of Honduras and the United States. Under these circumstances, the dismissal by the district court cannot be sustained on jurisdictional grounds.

We, therefore, vacate the dismissal and remand the Timberlane action.

Vacated and remanded.

United States
Timberlane Lumber Co. v. Bank of America II
US Court of Appeals for the Ninth Circuit
749 F 2d 1378 (1984)

Background

After the judgment set out above, the case went back to the district court for further consideration. It applied the test laid down by the Ninth Circuit, but still dismissed the case. Timberlane appealed again.

Sneed, Circuit Judge

The district court applied *Timberlane's* analysis and, on the basis of its third part, concluded that jurisdiction should not be exercised in this case. Although we agree with the district court's conclusion regarding each part of the *Timberlane I* test, we do not expressly approve all of its analysis. Therefore, we discuss each part of the inquiry as set forth in *Timberlane I*.

1. 'Does the alleged restraint affect, or was it intended to affect, the foreign commerce of the United States?'

The first part of *Timberlane I's* analysis requires 'that there be *some* effect – actual or intended – on American foreign commerce before the federal courts may legitimately exercise subject matter jurisdiction under [the antitrust] statutes.'(emphasis in original). On appeal, Bank of America does not deny that Timberlane has met this requirement . . .

2. 'Is it of such a type and magnitude so as to be cognizable as a violation of the Sherman Act?'

Under the second part of *Timberlane I's* analysis, 'a greater showing of burden or restraint may be necessary to demonstrate that the effect is sufficiently large to present a cognizable injury to the plaintiffs and, therefore, a civil *violation* of the antitrust laws.'(emphasis in original). Courts and commentators, however, have had difficulty identifying the nature and extent of proof required to satisfy this part of the inquiry . . . The only issue under the second part of the inquiry is whether the magnitude of the effect identified in the first part of the test rises to the level of a civil antitrust violation, i.e., conduct that has a direct and substantial anticompetitive effect . . .

In this case Timberlane alleges that Bank of America conspired with its Honduran subsidiaries to prevent Timberlane from milling lumber in Honduras and exporting it to the United States. Our review of the complaint reveals that Timberlane has alleged an injury that would state a claim under the antitrust laws against Bank of America. Thus, it satisfies the second part of the analysis.

3. 'As a matter of international comity and fairness, should the extraterritorial jurisdiction of the United States be asserted to cover it?'

Under the third part of *Timberlane I's* analysis, the district court must determine 'whether the interests of, and links to, the United States – including the magnitude of the effect on American foreign commerce – are sufficiently strong, *vis-à-vis* those of other nations, to justify an assertion of extraterritorial authority.' This determination requires that a district court consider seven factors. The district court here found that the undisputed facts required that jurisdiction not be exercised in this case. We agree. To support our conclusion each factor will be examined.

a. 'The degree of conflict with foreign law or policy'

We must determine whether the extraterritorial enforcement of United States antitrust laws creates an actual or potential conflict with the laws and policies of other nations. Timberlane argues that no conflict exists between United States and Honduran law. We disagree. The application of United States antitrust law in this case creates a potential conflict with the Honduran government's effort to foster a particular type of business climate.

Although Honduras does not have antitrust laws as such, it does have definite policies concerning the character of its commercial climate. To promote economic development and efficiency within its relatively undeveloped economy, the Honduran Constitution and Commercial Code guarantee freedom of action. The Code specifically condemns any laws prohibiting agreements (even among competitors) to restrict or divide commercial activity. Under Honduran law, competitors may agree to allocate geographic or market territories, to restrict price or output, to cut off the source of raw materials, or to limit credit financing to obtain enterprises as long as the contracting parties are not *de facto* monopolists . . . It appears that Honduran law intimately regulates private commercial activity in that country. Honduran law also promotes agreements that improve the competitive position of domestic industries in world markets by promoting efficiency and economies of scale.

On balance, we believe that the enforcement of United States antitrust laws in this case would lead to a significant conflict with Honduran law and policy. This conflict, unless outweighed by other factors in the comity analysis, is itself a sufficient reason to decline the exercise of jurisdiction over this dispute.

b. 'The nationality or allegiance of the parties and the locations of principal places of business of corporations'

Next we should consider the citizenship of the parties and witnesses involved in the alleged illegal conduct. In this case, with only one exception, all of the named parties are United States citizens or nationals. But it is also true that '[a]ll of the crucial percipient witnesses to the incidents were either Honduran citizens or residents.' We believe, therefore, that the citizenship of the parties weighs slightly in favor of the exercise of jurisdiction.

c. 'The extent to which enforcement by either state can be expected to achieve compliance'

The weighing of this factor yields no clear answer. Of course, any judgment against Bank of America could easily be enforced in a United States court. Whether such a judgment could be enforced as easily in Honduras is less certain. We believe that the enforcement factor tips slightly in favor of the assertion of jurisdiction in this case.

d. 'The relative significance of effects on the United States as compared with those elsewhere'

A more definitive answer emerges when we compare the effect of the alleged illegal conduct on the foreign commerce of the United States with its effect abroad. The insignificance of the effect on the foreign commerce of the United States when compared with the substantial effect in Honduras suggests federal jurisdiction should not be exercised.

[The court then set out figures to prove this point.]

The actual effect of Timberlane's potential operations on United States foreign commerce is, therefore, insubstantial . . . In comparison, the effects of its activity on the considerably smaller Honduran lumber markets would have been much greater. The bank's actions also affect several other aspects of the Honduran economy such as the number of jobs, the amount of foreign exchange and taxes, and the internal competitive market. We believe that the relative significance of effects in this case weighs strongly against the exercise of jurisdiction.

e. 'The extent to which there is explicit purpose to harm or affect American commerce'

We should also consider whether the defendant's actions were intended to harm or affect the commerce of the United States. Our review of the record reveals that Bank of America's acts were directed primarily towards securing a greater return on its investment. Its actions were consistent with Honduran customs and practices. Timberlane has not demonstrated that Bank of America had any particular interest in affecting United States commerce.

f. 'The foreseeability of such effect'

A court should also consider whether, at the time of the alleged illegal behavior, the defendant should have foreseen an effect on the foreign commerce of the United States. Aside from the fact that American commerce has not been substantially affected, Timberlane has not shown that Bank of America should have foreseen the consequences of its actions. Bank of America simply enforced its mortgage in an attempt to recoup its investment. The effects of this action were merely part of the inevitable consequences that flow from attempting to salvage something from a failing business enterprise. We do not believe that a reasonable investor would have foreseen the minimal effect that has occurred here. This weighs against the exercise of jurisdiction.

g. 'The relative importance to the violations charged of conduct within the United States as compared with conduct abroad'

Finally, a court should consider the location of the alleged illegal conduct in order to assess the appropriateness of the exercise of extraterritorial jurisdiction. In this case both parties agree that virtually all of the illegal activity occurred in Honduras. This factor clearly weighs against the exercise of jurisdiction.

h. Resolving the Seven Factor Test

It follows that all but two of the factors in *Timberlane I*'s comity analysis indicate that we should refuse to exercise jurisdiction over this antitrust case. The potential for conflict with Honduran economic policy and commercial law is great. The effect on the foreign commerce of the United States is minimal. The evidence of intent to harm American commerce is altogether lacking. The foreseeability of the anticompetitive consequences of the allegedly illegal actions is slight. Most of the conduct that must be examined occurred abroad. The factors that favor jurisdiction are the citizenship of the parties and, to a slight extent, the enforcement effectiveness of United States law. We do not believe that this is enough to justify the exercise of federal jurisdiction over this case.

. . .

Affirmed.

QUESTIONS

1 Do you think the balancing test was correctly applied in *Timberlane II*?

2 Of the cases you have read so far, which one has the best approach?[13]

§ 6 The new hard line

United States
Hartford Fire Insurance Co. v. California
US Supreme Court
509 US 764; 113 S Ct 2891; 125 L Ed 2d 612 (1993)

Background

The case concerned insurance and reinsurance. Reinsurance is insurance taken out by ordinary insurance companies (primary insurers) to cover the risk of unusually large claims that might otherwise bankrupt them. There were various parties (the plaintiffs were a number of US states and individuals; the defendants

---

13 For another case in which a balancing test was applied, see *Mannington Mills* v. *Congoleum Corporation*, 595 F 2d 1287 (3rd Cir. 1979).

included primary insurers in the US and reinsurers based in London) and various issues. Two petitions were before the Supreme Court. One, brought by the US defendants, concerned purely domestic issues; the other, brought by the foreign defendants, raised the question whether US antitrust law could or should be applied to regulate the conduct of foreign reinsurance companies operating on the London market.

We shall concern ourselves solely with this latter question. Here, the allegation was that the London reinsurers agreed among themselves that they would not offer reinsurance for certain kinds of primary policies (commercial general liability insurance containing certain terms). Since London was the main market in the world for reinsurance and since the primary insurers could not offer insurance without reinsurance, this, it was said, effectively denied these kinds of primary insurance to people in America. It was claimed by the plaintiffs that this constituted a violation of the Sherman Act.

The defendants argued that, as the London reinsurance market was subject to comprehensive regulation by United Kingdom law and that what they had done was lawful in England, it would be contrary to comity for US courts to apply the Sherman Act. The United Kingdom Government intervened in the proceedings to support this view.

The district court dismissed the actions. The plaintiffs appealed and the Ninth Circuit reversed the judgment. The defendants appealed to the US Supreme Court. On the issue we are considering, the Supreme Court split five–four. We first give the majority judgment.

Souter J (majority opinion)

At the outset, we note that the District Court undoubtedly had jurisdiction of these Sherman Act claims, as the London reinsurers apparently concede . . . Although the proposition was perhaps not always free from doubt, [reference to *American Banana*], it is well established by now that the Sherman Act applies to foreign conduct that was meant to produce and did in fact produce some substantial effect in the United States . . . Such is the conduct alleged here: that the London reinsurers engaged in unlawful conspiracies to affect the market for insurance in the United States and that their conduct in fact produced substantial effect.

According to the London reinsurers, the District Court should have declined to exercise such jurisdiction under the principle of international comity. The Court of Appeals agreed that courts should look to that principle in deciding whether to exercise jurisdiction under the Sherman Act . . . This availed the London reinsurers nothing, however. To be sure, the Court of Appeals believed that 'application of [American] antitrust laws to the London reinsurance market "would lead to significant conflict with English law and policy"', and that '[s]uch a conflict, unless outweighed by other factors, would by itself be reason to decline exercise of jurisdiction.' But other factors, in the court's view, including the London reinsurers' express purpose to affect United States commerce and the substantial nature of the effect produced, outweighed the supposed conflict and required the exercise of jurisdiction in this case.

... We need not decide [whether a court with Sherman Act jurisdiction should ever decline to exercise such jurisdiction on grounds of international comity], for even assuming that in a proper case a court may decline to exercise Sherman Act jurisdiction over foreign conduct (or, as Justice Scalia would put it, may conclude by the employment of comity analysis in the first instance that there is no jurisdiction), international comity would not counsel against exercising jurisdiction in the circumstances alleged here.

The only substantial question in this litigation is whether 'there is in fact a true conflict between domestic and foreign law'[1] ... The London reinsurers contend that applying the Act to their conduct would conflict significantly with British law, and the British Government, appearing before us as *amicus curiae*, concurs ... They assert that Parliament has established a comprehensive regulatory regime over the London reinsurance market and that the conduct alleged here was perfectly consistent with British law and policy. But this is not to state a conflict. '[T]he fact that conduct is lawful in the state in which it took place will not, of itself, bar application of the United States antitrust laws', even where the foreign state has a strong policy to permit or encourage such conduct. *Restatement (Third) Foreign Relations Law* § 415, Comment *j* ... No conflict exists, for these purposes, 'where a person subject to regulation by two states can comply with the laws of both.' *Restatement (Third) Foreign Relations Law* § 403, Comment e. Since the London reinsurers do not argue that British law requires them to act in some fashion prohibited by the law of the United States ... or claim that their compliance with the laws of both countries is otherwise impossible, we see no conflict with British law ... We have no need in this litigation to address other considerations that might inform a decision to refrain from the exercise of jurisdiction on grounds of international comity.

Scalia J (dissenting opinion)

Petitioners in No. 91-1128,[2] various British corporations and other British subjects, argue that certain of the claims against them constitute an inappropriate extraterritorial application of the Sherman Act. It is important to distinguish two distinct questions raised by this petition: whether the District Court had jurisdiction, and whether the Sherman Act reaches the extraterritorial conduct alleged here. On the first question, I believe that the District Court had subject-matter jurisdiction over the Sherman Act claims against all the defendants (personal jurisdiction is not contested) ...

The second question – the extraterritorial reach of the Sherman Act – has nothing to do with the jurisdiction of the courts. It is a question of substantive law turning on whether, in enacting the Sherman Act, Congress asserted regulatory power over the challenged conduct ... If a plaintiff fails to prevail on this issue, the court does not dismiss the claim for want of subject-matter jurisdiction – want of power

---

1 *Editor's note*: this is a reference to the doctrine of foreign sovereign compulsion (also called foreign state compulsion), under which one State should not require a person to do something in another State that is prohibited by the law of that State: see *Restatement of the Law Third: Foreign Relations Law of the United States*, § 441.
2 *Editor's note*: this was the petition raising the international issues.

to adjudicate; rather, it decides the claim, ruling on the merits that the plaintiff has failed to state a cause of action under the relevant statute . . .

There is, however, a type of 'jurisdiction' relevant to determining the extraterritorial reach of a statute; it is known as 'legislative jurisdiction' or 'jurisdiction to prescribe', 1 *Restatement (Third) of Foreign Relations Law of the United States* 235 (1987) (hereinafter *Restatement (Third)*). This refers to 'the authority of a state to make its law applicable to persons or activities', and is quite a separate matter from 'jurisdiction to adjudicate', see *id.*, at 231. There is no doubt, of course, that Congress possesses legislative jurisdiction over the acts alleged in this complaint: Congress has broad power under Article I, § 8, cl. 3 [of the US Constitution], '[t]o regulate Commerce with foreign Nations', and this Court has repeatedly upheld its power to make laws applicable to persons or activities beyond our territorial boundaries where United States interests are affected . . . But the question in this litigation is whether, and to what extent, Congress *has* exercised that undoubted legislative jurisdiction in enacting the Sherman Act.

Two canons of statutory construction are relevant in this inquiry. The first is the 'long-standing principle of American law "that legislation of Congress, unless a contrary intent appears, is meant to apply only within the territorial jurisdiction of the United States."' We have, however, found the presumption to be overcome with respect to our antitrust laws; it is now well established that the Sherman Act applies extraterritorially . . .

But if the presumption against extraterritoriality has been overcome or is otherwise inapplicable, a second canon of statutory construction becomes relevant: '[A]n act of congress ought never to be construed to violate the law of nations if any other possible construction remains.' *Murray* v. *The Charming Betsy*, 2 Cranch 64, 118, 2 L Ed. 208 (1804) (Marshall, CJ). This canon is 'wholly independent' of the presumption against extraterritoriality . . . It is relevant to determining the substantive reach of a statute because 'the law of nations', or customary international law, includes limitations on a nation's exercise of its jurisdiction to prescribe. See *Restatement (Third)* §§ 401–416. Though it clearly has constitutional authority to do so, Congress is generally presumed not to have exceeded those customary international-law limits on jurisdiction to prescribe.

Consistent with that presumption, this and other courts have frequently recognized that, even where the presumption against extraterritoriality does not apply, statutes should not be interpreted to regulate foreign persons or conduct if that regulation would conflict with principles of international law . . .

[After referring to cases in which the extraterritorial reach of US law was limited on the ground of comity, Justice Scalia continued:]

The 'comity' they refer to is not the comity of courts, whereby judges decline to exercise jurisdiction over matters more appropriately adjudged elsewhere,[3] but rather what might be termed 'prescriptive comity': the respect sovereign nations afford each other by limiting the reach of their laws. That comity is exercised by

---

3 *Editor's note*: this appears to be a reference to the doctrine of *forum non conveniens*.

legislatures when they enact laws, and courts assume it has been exercised when they come to interpreting the scope of laws their legislatures have enacted. It is a traditional component of choice-of-law theory . . . Comity in this sense includes the choice-of-law principles that, 'in the absence of contrary congressional direction', are assumed to be incorporated into our substantive laws having extraterritorial reach . . . Considering comity in this way is just part of determining whether the Sherman Act prohibits the conduct at issue.

In sum, the practice of using international law to limit the extraterritorial reach of statutes is firmly established in our jurisprudence. In proceeding to apply that practice to the present cases, I shall rely on the *Restatement (Third)* for the relevant principles of international law. Its standards appear fairly supported in the decisions of this Court construing international choice-of-law principles . . . and in the decisions of other federal courts [reference to *Timberlane*]. Whether the Restatement precisely reflects international law in every detail matters little here, as I believe this litigation would be resolved the same way under virtually any conceivable test that takes account of foreign regulatory interests.

Under the Restatement, a nation having some 'basis' for jurisdiction to prescribe law should nonetheless refrain from exercising that jurisdiction 'with respect to a person or activity having connections with another state when the exercise of such jurisdiction is unreasonable.' *Restatement (Third)* § 403(1). The 'reasonableness' inquiry turns on a number of factors including, but not limited to: 'the extent to which the activity takes place within the territory [of the regulating state]', *id.*, § 403(2)(a); 'the connections, such as nationality, residence, or economic activity, between the regulating state and the person principally responsible for the activity to be regulated', *id.*, § 403(2)(b); 'the character of the activity to be regulated, the importance of regulation to the regulating state, the extent to which other states regulate such activities, and the degree to which the desirability of such regulation is generally accepted', *id.*, § 403(2)(c); 'the extent to which another state may have an interest in regulating the activity', *id.*, § 403(2)(g); and 'the likelihood of conflict with regulation by another state', *id.*, § 403(2)(h). Rarely would these factors point more clearly against application of United States law. The activity relevant to the counts at issue here took place primarily in the United Kingdom, and the defendants in these counts are British corporations and British subjects having their principal place of business or residence outside the United States. Great Britain has established a comprehensive regulatory scheme governing the London reinsurance markets, and clearly has a heavy 'interest in regulating the activity', *id.*, § 403(2)(g) . . . Considering these factors, I think it unimaginable that an assertion of legislative jurisdiction by the United States would be considered reasonable, and therefore it is inappropriate to assume, in the absence of statutory indication to the contrary, that Congress has made such an assertion.

It is evident from what I have said that the Court's comity analysis, which proceeds as though the issue is whether the courts should 'decline to exercise . . . jurisdiction' rather than whether the Sherman Act covers this conduct, is simply misdirected . . . In any event, if one erroneously chooses, as the Court does, to make adjudicative jurisdiction (or, more precisely, abstention) the vehicle for taking account of the needs of prescriptive comity, the Court still gets it wrong. It concludes that no 'true conflict' counseling nonapplication of United States law (or rather, as it thinks, United States judicial jurisdiction) exists unless compliance with United States law would constitute a *violation* of another country's law . . . That breathtakingly broad proposition . . . will bring the Sherman Act and other laws into sharp and unnecessary conflict with the legitimate interests of other countries – particularly our closest trading partners.

In the sense in which the term ['conflict'] . . . is generally understood in the field of conflicts of laws, there is clearly a conflict in this case. The petitioners here . . . were not compelled by any foreign law to take their allegedly wrongful actions, but that no more precludes a conflict-of-laws analysis here than it did [in other cases in which a conflict-of-laws analysis was adopted in order to limit the scope of US legislation][4] . . . Where applicable foreign and domestic law provide different substantive rules of decision to govern the parties' dispute, a conflict-of-laws analysis is necessary . . .

[After further criticisms of the majority approach, Scalia J concluded;]

I would reverse the judgment of the Court of Appeals on this issue, and remand to the District Court with instructions to dismiss for failure to state a claim on the three counts at issue in No. 91-1128.

4 *Editor's note*: the case specifically cited in this passage was *Lauritzen v. Larsen*, 345 US 571; 73 S Ct 921; 97 L Ed 1254 (US Supreme Court, 1953); but, in earlier passages, other Supreme Court decisions, such as *Romero* v. *International Terminal Operating Co.*, 358 US 354, 359; 79 S Ct 468, 473; 3 L Ed 2d 368 (US Supreme Court, 1959), were also cited.

Result: application of the Sherman Act to the London reinsurers is not precluded by considerations of comity.

QUESTION

Which judgment do you prefer: that of the majority or that of Scalia J?

Comment

A major difference between the majority and the minority concerns the question of what constitutes a 'conflict' or a 'true conflict'. The majority takes the view, based on the foreign sovereign-compulsion doctrine, that a true conflict exists only if English law prohibits what US law requires. However, in normal choice-of-law analysis – for example, in the theories of Brainerd Currie and other supporters of interest analysis[14] – a true conflict can exist equally well where one system of law *permits* what another forbids. This is the view normally applied in conflict-of-laws cases – for example, those on torts in Chapter 23, above.

However, the form of choice-of-law analysis put forward by Scalia J is very different from the rigidly territorial conceptualism to be found in *American*

14 See Chapter 22, § 4.1, above.

Banana. It is not suggested that foreign law should decide whether or not an act performed in a foreign country is illegal. Scalia's balancing test attempts to do something that Currie said could not be done: to balance the interests of the foreign country against those of the forum.

The most recent Supreme Court decision, *Hoffmann-LaRoche Ltd* v. *Empagran SA*,[15] concerned a slightly different issue, but its approach seems closer in spirit to that of Scalia J than that of the majority in *Hartford.* So the conflict continues between those who support a hard line that only considers American interests and those who favour some sort of compromise.

QUESTION

How would you formulate the rule to be applied in cases of the kind we have been considering?

Further reading

Born (Gary B.) and Rutledge (Peter B.), *International Civil Litigation in United States Courts: Commentary and Materials* (Wolters Kluwer, Austin, Boston, Chicago, New York, the Netherlands, 4th edn, 2007), Chapter 8

Lowe (A. V.), *Extraterritorial Jurisdiction: An Annotated Collection of Legal Materials* (Grotius Publications, Cambridge, 1983)

Robertson and Demetriou, '"But that was in another country . . .": The Extra-territorial Application of the US Antitrust Laws in the US Supreme Court' (1994) 43 ICLQ 417

Rosenthal (Douglas E.) and Knighton (William E.), *National Laws and International Commerce* (Royal Institute of International Affairs: Chatham House Papers, No. 17; Routledge & Kegan Paul, London, Boston and Henley, 1982)

Roth, 'Reasonable Extraterritoriality: Correcting the "Balance of Interests"' (1992) 41 ICLQ 245

Sornarajah, 'The Extraterritorial Enforcement of US Antitrust Laws' (1982) 31 ICLQ 127

Westbrook, 'Extraterritoriality, Conflict of Laws, and the Regulation of Transnational Business' (1990) 25 *Texas International Law Journal* 71

---

15 542 US 155; 124 S Ct 2359; 159 L Ed 2d 226 (US Supreme Court, 2004).

CHAPTER 34

The international response

§ 1 Patents

Patents are rights granted by the State, which confer a monopoly on the right-holder. They are regarded as being an attribute of sovereignty and are often thought to be within the exclusive jurisdiction of the State conferring them. So it is hardly surprising that foreign interference is resented.

> **England**
> ***British Nylon Spinners* v. *ICI***
> **Court of Appeal**
> **[1953] Ch 19; [1952] 2 All ER 780**

Background

ICI (Imperial Chemical Industries) was a major British company; Du Pont was a major American company. In 1946, they entered into a market-sharing agreement under which most of the world was divided up between them. They swapped patents to give effect to the agreement. The US Government subsequently brought proceedings against them before Judge Sylvester Ryan in a federal district court in the United States.[1] The claim was that the market-sharing agreement violated the Sherman Act.

The English proceedings concerned nylon, a synthetic fibre invented by Du Pont and patented by it in both the US and the UK. As part of the market-sharing agreement, Du Pont assigned the relevant UK patents to ICI. In 1947, ICI agreed to grant an irrevocable and exclusive licence to British Nylon Spinners (BNS), a British company 50 per cent owned by ICI, and 50 per cent owned by another British company, Courtaulds. At the time, BNS knew about the antitrust aspects of the matter and it seems that the arrangement was partly entered into in order to avoid the consequences of the American proceedings.

In May 1952, Judge Ryan gave final judgment in the American proceedings. He held that Du Pont and ICI had violated the Sherman Act. Jurisdiction to prescribe existed under the effects doctrine laid down in the *Alcoa* case (discussed in Chapter 33, § 4, above): the agreement was intended to affect imports into the US and did affect them. He made various orders designed to terminate the operation of the market-sharing agreement. One of these was an order requiring ICI to reconvey the UK nylon patents to Du Pont.

---

1 *United States* v. *Imperial Chemical Industries*, 100 F Supp 504 (SDNY, 1951); 105 F Supp 215 (SDNY, 1952).

BNS (which was not a party to the US action) then brought proceedings against ICI in England in which it asked for an order that ICI make a formal grant of the licences; it also wanted an injunction requiring ICI not to part with its patent rights in obedience to the US judgment. An interlocutory (interim) injunction was given in favour of BNS. ICI appealed.

Evershed MR

This is an interlocutory matter, and, therefore, it is inappropriate for the court to say more about the case, or the merits of the case, than is necessary to make clear the grounds of the conclusion which it reaches. It is plain that there is here a question of the comity which subsists between civilized nations. In other words, it involves the extent to which the courts of one country will pay regard and give effect to the decisions and orders of the courts of another country. I certainly should be the last to indicate any lack of respect for any decision of the district courts of the United States. But I think that in this case there is raised a somewhat serious question, whether the order, in the form that it takes, does not assert an extraterritorial jurisdiction which the courts of this country cannot recognize, notwithstanding any such comity. Applied conversely, I conceive that the American courts would likewise be slow (to say the least) to recognize an assertion on the part of the British courts of jurisdiction extending (in effect) to the business affairs of persons and corporations in the United States.

Having said that much, I must make one reference to a passage in the second of the opinions which his Honour delivered, dated May, 1952. It is plain that the judge considered this matter most carefully, and indeed, as Upjohn J pointed out, expressed his own doubts whether, in giving effect, as he felt it his duty to do, to the implications of the Sherman Act, he might not be going beyond the normally recognized limits of territorial jurisdiction. He said:

> It is not an intrusion on the authority of a foreign sovereign for this court to direct that steps be taken to remove the harmful effects on the trade of the United States.

If by that passage the judge intended to say (as it seems to me that he did) that it was not an intrusion on the authority of a foreign sovereign to make directions addressed to that foreign sovereign or to its courts or to nationals of that foreign Power effective to remove (as he said) 'harmful effects on the trade of the United States', I am bound to say that, as at present advised, I find myself unable to agree with it.

Questions affecting the trade of one country may well be matters proper to be considered by the government of another country. Tariffs are sometimes imposed by one country which obviously affect the trade of another country, and the imposition of such tariffs is a matter for the government of the particular country which imposes them. And if that observation of the judge were conversely applied to directions designed to remove harmful effects on the trade, say, of Great Britain or British nationals in America, I should myself be surprised to find that it was accepted as not being an intrusion on the rights and sovereign authority of the United States.

On the other hand, there is no doubt that it is competent for the court of
a particular country, in a suit between persons who are either nationals or
subjects of that country or are otherwise subject to its jurisdiction, to make
orders *in personam* against one such party – directing it, for example, to do
something or to refrain from doing something in another country affecting the
other party to the action. As a general proposition, that would not be open to
doubt. But the plaintiffs in this case [BNS] (unlike Imperial Chemical Industries)
are neither subjects nor nationals of the United States, nor were they parties
to the proceedings before his Honour, nor are they otherwise subject to his
jurisdiction.[1]

What the precise relationship, commercially or otherwise, is between the plaintiffs
and the defendants we have not at this stage of the proceedings considered at
all, and I proceed on the assumption (and I am not to be taken as hinting that the
contrary is the fact) that the plaintiffs are an independent trade corporation and
entitled to be treated as independent of Imperial Chemical Industries Ld. Being
so independent, they have beyond question, according to the laws of England,
certain rights, certain choses in action, by virtue of the contract of 1947, which the
courts of this country, in pursuance of the laws which the courts of this country
claim to be entitled to administer, will in this country protect and enforce. Broadly,
the right which they have may be described as their right under the contract,
being an English contract made between English nationals and to be performed
in England, to have it performed and, if necessary, to have an order made by the
courts of this country for its specific performance. That is a right – it might be
said, a species of property, seeing particularly that it is related to patents – which
is English in character and is subject to the jurisdiction of the English courts; and
it seems to me that the plaintiffs have at least established a *prima facie* case for
saying that it is not competent for the courts of the United States or of any other
country to interfere with those rights or to make orders, observance of which by
our courts would require that our courts should not exercise the jurisdiction which
they have and which it is their duty to exercise in regard to those rights.

But I think that the matter goes somewhat further. The subject-matter of the
contract of December, 1946, is a number of English and Commonwealth patents.
An English patent is a species of English property of the nature of a chose in
action and peculiar in character. By English law it confers certain monopoly rights,
exercisable in England, on its proprietor. A person who has an enforceable right to
a licence under an English patent appears therefore to have at least some kind of
proprietary interest which it is the duty of our courts to protect. And, certainly so
far as the English patents are concerned, it seems to me, with all deference to his
Honour's judgment, to be an assertion of an extraterritorial jurisdiction which we
do not recognize for the American courts to make orders which would destroy or
qualify those statutory rights belonging to an English national who is not subject to
the jurisdiction of the American courts.

. . .

---

1 *Editor's note*: the main ICI company was not a national of the US, but it was a party to the US
proceedings.

> I think it undesirable that I should say more, except to reaffirm the proposition that the courts of this country will, in the natural course, pay great respect and attention to the superior courts of the United States of America; but I conceive that it is none the less the proper province of these courts, when their jurisdiction is invoked, not to refrain from exercising that jurisdiction if they think that it is their duty so to do for the protection of rights which are peculiarly subject to the protection of the English courts. In so saying, I do not conceive that I am offending in any way against the principles of comity which apply between the two countries; and, like Upjohn J, I take some comfort from the doubts which Judge Sylvester Ryan himself entertained about the extent to which this order might, if carried to its logical conclusion, go.

Result: the appeal was dismissed: the interlocutory injunctions stood.

Note

The case subsequently came for a final decision before Danckwerts J.[2] In a judgment that was deferential but firm, he refused to give effect to the US order.[3] He granted a decree of specific performance requiring ICI to execute the exclusive licences; he also granted an injunction restraining ICI from doing anything to the contrary until the licences had been registered in the appropriate registry. One assumes that ICI was secretly glad to lose the case, since the English judgment would provide a justification for not obeying the US order.

§ 2   Obtaining evidence

One of the most common ways in which foreign courts show their disapproval of the extraterritorial application of US law is to refuse to assist US courts in obtaining evidence for use in proceedings in which this occurs. Our next case is an example.

Since this case is one of several concerning the post-war uranium cartel, something should be said by way of background. During, and immediately after, World War II, the main use for uranium was military. Subsequently, a market developed for it as a fuel for nuclear power stations. The American engineering company, Westinghouse, was one of the main manufacturers, supplying nuclear reactors to power companies in the US. As part of the deal, it often concluded long-term contracts to supply uranium at a fixed price. It thought it was safe to do this because the price of uranium was low at the time.

The low price of uranium was partly due to the fact that the US Government was selling off part of its military stockpile on the international market. Uranium was mined both in the US and in other countries. In order to help the US producers, Congress passed legislation that had the effect of excluding

---

2 *British Nylon Spinners* v. *ICI* [1955] Ch 37; [1954] 3 WLR 505; [1954] 3 All ER 88 (Ch D).
3 ICI argued that the case was covered by the principle in *Foster* v. *Driscoll* (set out in Chapter 25, § 4.1.1, above), but this was rejected. Since BNS was not asking ICI to do anything in the US, the principle was clearly inapplicable.

foreign uranium from the US market,[4] a move that the Government of Canada considered contrary to GATT. Since America was the major market, this had a devastating effect on the foreign producers, which included companies from Canada, Australia, Britain and other countries. To protect their position, they created a cartel. This was supported by at least some of their governments, and seems to have been organized in part by the Government of Canada. Under the cartel,[5] which was backed by legislation in Canada, uranium could not be sold for export below a stated price.[6] In time, the market price of uranium rose. The US then began to phase out the restrictions on foreign uranium, and the cartel was wound up.

The increase in the price of uranium had a serious impact on Westinghouse, since it was obliged to supply uranium to the power companies at an uneconomic price. It defaulted on the contracts and was sued by the power companies in proceedings brought in Richmond, Virginia. The damages claimed were large. Westinghouse raised various defences, one of which was that it was unable to carry out its contracts because of the cartel. It said that the setting up of the cartel was contrary to US antitrust law. The foreign uranium companies were not involved in these proceedings.

Westinghouse also brought proceedings against the uranium producers in Illinois, in which it claimed treble damages under the Sherman Act. In addition, the US Government began grand jury proceedings in Washington DC with a view to bringing criminal charges under the Sherman Act against the uranium producers. The British Government took the view that both the Illinois proceedings and the grand jury proceedings involved the extraterritorial application of US law in a way that prejudiced British sovereignty.

England
Westinghouse Electric Corporation Uranium Contract Litigation (Rio Tinto Zinc v. Westinghouse)
House of Lords
[1978] AC 547; [1978] 2 WLR 81; [1978] 1 All ER 434

Background

One of the companies sued by Westinghouse in Illinois was the British company, Rio Tinto Zinc (RTZ). Westinghouse claimed that it was a participant in the cartel. Westinghouse obtained letters rogatory from the court hearing the proceedings in Richmond. These were addressed to the English courts and requested their assistance in obtaining oral evidence from various individuals, and documentary evidence from RTZ and its associate companies. This evidence was requested for use in the Richmond proceedings, but RTZ thought it might also be used in the other proceedings.

In 1976, the High Court Master in England made an order under the Evidence

---

4 This did not stop US producers from selling outside the US.
5 The cartel expressly excluded exports to the US, but – for the reasons explained above – this was not, at the time, of practical importance.
6 The minimum prices were almost always below US prices.

(Proceedings in Other Jurisdictions) Act 1975[7] giving effect to the letters roga-tory. RTZ and most of the individual witnesses appealed, and the case eventually came before the House of Lords. Various arguments were advanced for not giving effect to the letters rogatory, including the argument about 'fishing expeditions' discussed in Chapter 21, § 2.1, above.

The individual (non-corporate) witnesses argued that, if they were forced to testify, their evidence might be used against them if they were prosecuted under the Sherman Act in the United States; so they claimed privilege against self-incrimination under the Fifth Amendment to the US Constitution.[8] A special hearing was held in the US embassy in London before the US judge hearing the Richmond proceedings, Judge Merhige. He ruled (on 14 June 1977) that the wit-nesses were entitled to the privilege; consequently, they did not have to give evidence.

The US Attorney General then intervened to grant them immunity from pros-ecution. The effect of this under US law[9] was that they could no longer claim the privilege and could, therefore, be compelled to give evidence. However, any evidence they gave could not be used in criminal proceedings against them. Judge Merhige then made an order (on 18 July 1977) that they had to give the evidence. The US Attorney General specifically said that he had granted them immunity because their evidence was needed for the grand jury proceedings in Washington: although the individual witnesses had immunity, criminal pro-ceedings could still be brought against the companies.

Many issues were discussed in the judgments. We consider only the extra-territoriality point.

Lord Wilberforce

[Lord Wilberforce first considered the position of RTZ and its subsidiaries. He held that they were entitled to claim privilege against self-incrimination under English law because the evidence requested might expose them to proceedings under EC competition law. He next turned to the individual defendants. He pointed out that the US Attorney General had expressly said that their evidence was to be put before the grand jury in Washington and could be used in criminal proceedings against the companies, even though it had been requested for use in the civil proceedings in Richmond. This gave rise to various problems. After discussing two other matters, he continued:]

Thirdly, the evidence is sought for the purpose of an anti-trust investigation into the activities of companies not subject to the jurisdiction of the United States. I think that in such circumstances the courts would properly, in accordance with accepted principle, refuse to give effect to the request on the grounds that the procedure of the Act of 1975 was being used for a purpose for which it was never intended and that the attempt to extend the grand jury investigation

---

7 This Act is discussed in Chapter 21, § 2, above.
8 Under section 3(1)(b) of the 1975 Act, a person cannot be compelled to give evidence before the English court if he could not be compelled to give it before a court in the State making the request.
9 18 USC §§ 6002–6003.

extra-territorially into the activities of the RTZ companies was an infringement of United Kingdom sovereignty – see *British Nylon Spinners Ltd.* v. *Imperial Chemical Industries Ltd . . .* But in the present case, there has been an intervention by HM Attorney General on behalf of the Government of the United Kingdom. In this intervention the Attorney General brought to the notice of your Lordships the following matters.

1.   Her Majesty's Government considers that the wide investigatory procedures under the United States anti-trust legislation against persons outside the United States who are not United States citizens constitute an infringement of the proper jurisdiction and sovereignty of the United Kingdom.

2.   That the grand jury have issued a subpoena to Westinghouse requiring that company to produce to the grand jury documents and testimony obtained in discovery in the Virginia proceedings. Therefore evidence given in pursuance of the letters rogatory will be available to the United States Government for use against a United Kingdom company and United Kingdom nationals in relation to activities occurring outside United States territory in anti-trust proceedings of a penal character.

3.   That the intervention of the United States Government followed by the grant of the order and immunity of July 18, 1977, shows that the execution of the letters rogatory is being sought for the purposes of the exercise by United States courts of extra-territorial jurisdiction in penal matters which in the view of Her Majesty's Government is prejudicial to the sovereignty of the United Kingdom.

My Lords, I think that there is no doubt that, in deciding whether to give effect to letters rogatory, the courts are entitled to have regard to any possible prejudice to the sovereignty of the United Kingdom – that is expressly provided for in Article 12(b) of the Hague Convention. Equally, that in a matter affecting the sovereignty of the United Kingdom, the courts are entitled to take account of the declared policy of Her Majesty's Government is in my opinion beyond doubt. Indeed, this follows as the counterpart of the action which the United States Government has taken. For, as the order of July 18, 1977,[1] and the letter of July 12, 1977,[2] make plain, the order compelling testimony and granting immunity is made in extraordinary circumstances relating to the public interest of the United States. That the making of the order is a matter of government policy, and not related to the civil proceedings in Richmond, is confirmed beyond doubt by the statement made before Judge Merhige on June 16, 1977, and repeated in the letter of the Attorney General of the United States of July 12, 1977, that there is a firm policy against seeking orders under sections 6002–6003[3] in private litigation. It appears that the present is the only case in which such an order has been made. (One other instance cited is not comparable.) But if public interest enters into this matter on one side, so it must be taken account of on the other: and as the views of the executive in the United

1 *Editor's note*: this was the US court order requiring the witnesses to give the evidence.
2 *Editor's note*: this contained the US Attorney General's decision to grant immunity from prosecution.
3 *Editor's note*: these are the provisions of US law permitting immunity to be granted so that a witness can be compelled to testify.

States of America impel the making of the order, so must the views of the executive in the United Kingdom be considered when it is a question of implementing the order here. It is axiomatic that in anti-trust matters the policy of one state may be to defend what it is the policy of another state to attack.

The intervention of Her Majesty's Attorney General establishes that quite apart from the present case, over a number of years and in a number of cases, the policy of Her Majesty's Government has been against recognition of United States investigatory jurisdiction extraterritorially against United Kingdom companies. The courts should in such matters speak with the same voice as the executive . . . they have, as I have stated, no difficulty in doing so.

For these reasons, I am of opinion that recognition should not be given to the order of July 18, 1977, granting immunity to the individual witnesses, that the matter should be treated as governed by the ruling – properly given in the civil proceedings in question – of June 14, 1977, that the witnesses were entitled to privilege under the Fifth Amendment.

. . .

I would allow the appeals of the RTZ companies and of the individual appellants and order that the order giving effect to the letters rogatory be discharged. I would dismiss the appeals of Westinghouse . . .

Result: the appeals by RTZ were allowed. Most of the other judges reached this conclusion on different grounds, though the sovereignty issue played a part.

After this case was decided, legislation was passed to allow the UK Government to block requests for evidence that it considered prejudicial to UK sovereignty. This was section 4 of the Protection of Trading Interests Act 1980, set out in Panel 34.1. As a result, the procedure under the 1975 Act can no longer be used in cases of this kind.

We now consider a case in which similar issues arose in Canada.

Ontario
Westinghouse Electric Corporation v. Duquesne Light Co.
Ontario High Court
(1977) 16 OR (2d) 273; 78 DLR (3d) 3

Background

The facts in this case were similar to those in the English *Westinghouse* case. The evidence was requested for use in the Richmond proceedings, but it was clear that it would also be used in Illinois and Washington. With one exception, the witnesses were all associated with one or other of the Canadian defendants in the Illinois

Panel 34.1 Obtaining evidence
Protection of Trading Interests Act 1980, section 4

Section 4 Restriction of Evidence (Proceedings in Other Jurisdictions) Act 1975

A court in the United Kingdom shall not make an order under section 2 of the Evidence (Proceedings in Other Jurisdictions) Act 1975 for giving effect to a request issued by or on behalf of a court or tribunal of an overseas country if it is shown that the request infringes the jurisdiction of the United Kingdom or is otherwise prejudicial to the sovereignty of the United Kingdom; and a certificate signed by or on behalf of the Secretary of State to the effect that it infringes that jurisdiction or is so prejudicial shall be conclusive evidence of that fact.

proceedings. The exception was a Canadian Government Minister, the Deputy Minister of Energy, Mines and Resources. The Canadian Attorney General intervened in the case in the same way as the English one.

The requests were rejected. As in the English case, there were various reasons for this, including blocking legislation adopted by the Government of Canada.[10] However, the sovereignty issue was a major factor, as is shown by the following extract.

Judgment

36. In my judgment, there are aspects to the present case which bear upon the Court's exercise of its discretion and militate against honouring these letters rogatory.

37. The most important of these is public policy. This case constitutes a rare occasion, certainly in relations with the United States, in which, in my opinion, legal assistance should be denied on the ground that to grant it would be to run counter to a public policy of this country. The policy I refer to has been clearly and forcefully expressed; it relates specifically to the evidence and documents in issue. By affidavit and public statement a Minister of the Crown has made it plain that the Government of Canada has, as a matter of public policy, taken the position that the information and documents sought should not be disclosed. Crown privilege has been asserted on the basis, *inter alia*, that the documents relate to the marketing of uranium which constituted 'an essential part of the policy' of the Government and in the public interest should not be produced or discovered; Security Regulations have been promulgated with the approval of the Governor in Council that prohibit the production of the documents or the disclosure of their contents; the Minister has indicated that the matter must be regarded as an issue of sovereignty. In these circumstances the Court, in my view, should take judicial cognizance of the stated public policy in exercising its discretionary power . . . and should not force the disclosure of information if to do so would, on the authority of the Government, be harmful to the public interest. To decline to lend a foreign Court assistance through the use of domestic judicial machinery in such circumstances is not to act in breach of the doctrine of comity but in accord with it.

38. Nor should the Court exercise its discretionary power to enforce letters rogatory of a foreign Court when one of the purposes of those letters rogatory is, as the argument was put to me, to procure evidence that 'the activities of the Federal Government and/or its representatives, relative to the cartel, constitute the commission of and/or the counselling of an offence under . . . the laws of the *lex fori*'.[1] It is inappropriate, in my opinion, to invoke the doctrine of comity of nations in an effort to search out testimony and documents designed to permit a foreign tribunal to

1 *Editor's note*: here *lex fori* refers to US law.

10 The Uranium Information Security Regulations, PC 1976-23268; SOR/76-644, 21 September 1976. These seem to have been adopted expressly for use in the uranium cases. Their validity was challenged by Westinghouse, but they were upheld by the court. Similar blocking legislation was adopted in Australia: see the Foreign Procedures (Prohibition of Certain Evidence) Act 1976.

> determine whether actions taken by or on behalf of the Government of Canada were contrary or inconsistent with the laws of a foreign country. It should not be necessary to add that Canada is a fully sovereign nation and not accountable to the tribunals of a foreign State. Similarly, in this very special factual situation, letters rogatory should not, in my opinion, be enforced against officers of Canadian corporations whose actions during the pertinent period had received the stamp of approval of the Canadian Government. The refusal of judicial assistance for these reasons does not disappoint comity.

Result: the letters rogatory were rejected.

§ 3   Meanwhile, back in the USA . . .

United States
In re Westinghouse Electric Corporation Uranium Contracts Litigation
Court of Appeals for the Tenth Circuit
563 F 2d 992 (1977)

Background

One of the companies involved in the Canadian *Westinghouse* case was Rio Algom. It was actually incorporated in Delaware, USA, but it headquarters were in Canada. In the Canadian case, Westinghouse had tried to gain access to its business records in Canada and to obtain evidence from its president, Mr Albino, who lived in Canada. After this failed, Westinghouse tried another tack. Rio Algom operated a uranium mine in Utah, USA; so Westinghouse went to the federal district court for Utah and asked it to issue discovery orders requiring Rio Algom and Mr Albino to produce the evidence that was located in Canada. Both refused, since this would have infringed the Canadian blocking legislation.[11] If Albino had revealed the Canadian evidence, he could have been sent to jail for five years. Despite this, the district court judged them in contempt and imposed a fine of US$10,000 per day on the company until such time as it complied. The company then made a formal request to the Canadian Government for permission to disclose the evidence, but permission was refused. This did not satisfy the district court, which considered them to be in bad faith. They appealed to the Tenth Circuit.

McWilliams, Circuit Judge

[The court held that a balancing exercise should be conducted.[1] After considering whether Rio Algom and its president, Mr Albino, were in bad faith and deciding (contrary to the district court) that they were not, Judge McWilliams continued:]

1 The court followed the decision of the US Supreme Court in *Société Internationale v. Rogers*, set out in Chapter 20, § 1.2, above.

11 The Uranium Information Security Regulations, PC 1976-23268; SOR/76-644, 21 September 1976. This was the same legislation in issue in the Canadian *Westinghouse* case.

We proceed now to a consideration of other relevant factors, namely the interests of Canada and the United States which place Rio Algom under contradictory demands. The records which Westinghouse seeks to examine are physically located in Canada. Such being the case, it would not seem unreasonable that the Canadian Government should have something to say about how those records will be made available to interested outsiders. That Canada has a legitimate 'national interest' in this matter is perhaps best illustrated by reading the opinion of the Ontario Supreme Court, wherein it declined to enforce the letters rogatory which Westinghouse caused to be issued. The Ontario Supreme Court determined that the nondisclosure regulations were in furtherance of a national interest in controlling and supervising atomic energy. The reader of this opinion is directed to the opinion of the Ontario Supreme Court which more fully sets forth the position of the Canadian Government.

The United States admittedly has a 'national interest' of its own. In the instant case the United States has an interest in making certain that any litigant in its courts is afforded adequate discovery to the end that he may fully present his claim, or defense, as the case may be. Such is an understandable and legitimate interest. In this regard, however, we do note that Westinghouse's defense in the Virginia litigation does not stand or fall on the present discovery order. Westinghouse has deposed the officers of various other uranium companies, and the present discovery, though admittedly of potential significance, is still in a sense cumulative. We are not here concerned with any grand jury investigation, or the enforcement, as such, of antitrust laws.

A 'balancing' of all of these various factors leads us to conclude that the trial court's order of contempt and the sanctions imposed in connection therewith are, on the basis of the present record, not justified.

. . .

We recognize that Rio Algom is a Delaware corporation doing business in Utah and hence enjoys the benefits and privileges afforded by the United States. The argument that because of such, Rio Algom is somehow ungrateful when it fails to obey the discovery orders of the local courts and that it is only proper that it be compelled to comply therewith is perhaps superficially appealing. However, this is but one side of the argument. The fact still remains that although Rio Algom is a domestic corporation doing business in Utah, the business records which Westinghouse seeks to examine are physically located in Canada. Canada has a legitimate interest in the disclosure of these documents and the district court erred in failing to consider such interest. There is nothing to indicate that the district court conducted any balancing of interests. On the contrary, the district court's reasoning was that the law of the forum would prevail, regardless of the particular facts of the case. Such approach is not in accord with *Societe*.[2]

Judgment reversed and the district court's order holding Rio Algom in contempt and imposing sanctions in connection therewith is hereby vacated.[3]

2 *Editor's note*: this is *Société Internationale* v. *Rogers* (see previous footnote).
3 One of the three judges dissented.

Comment

Here the US court tried to be conciliatory. In our next case, the position was somewhat different.

United States
In re Uranium Antitrust Litigation
Court of Appeals for the Seventh Circuit
617 F 2d 1248 (1980)

Background

This was the Illinois action, mentioned in § 2, above, in which Westinghouse was suing twenty-nine foreign and US producers for treble damages under the Sherman Act. Nine of the foreign producers did not appear, and the district court granted default judgments against them. Several of the defaulting defendants, especially RTZ, held assets in the US through wholly owned subsidiaries. At the request of Westinghouse, the court granted injunctions preventing these defendants from removing their assets from the US. It seems that, as soon as RTZ heard about this, it instructed its employees to remove as much money as possible from American banks. Various means were used to get money out of the country.

Interlocutory appeals were brought against these injunctions and other matters. The Governments of Australia, Canada, South Africa and the United Kingdom intervened as *amici curiae*, since companies from these countries were involved in the proceedings.[12] They argued that the district court lacked jurisdiction over the foreign defendants because it had not conducted a balancing exercise as required by *Timberlane I* (set out in Chapter 33, § 5, above) and another case laying down a similar requirement, *Mannington Mills* v. *Congoleum Corporation*.[13]

The court first considered the jurisdictional issues. It divided these into two: (1) did the district court have jurisdiction; and (2) if so, should it be exercised?

William J. Campbell, Senior District Judge

In its complaint Westinghouse alleges that twenty domestic and nine foreign corporations conspired to fix the price of uranium in the world market. The alleged meetings at which Westinghouse claims prices were agreed upon took place in France, Australia, South Africa, Illinois, the Canary Islands and England. At the present state of this litigation, there has been no opportunity for fact-finding. We must therefore accept all properly pleaded allegations as true for purposes of determining jurisdiction. Accordingly, the picture which emerges is one of concerted conduct both abroad and within the United States intended to affect the uranium market in this country. While the governments of the foreign participants in this alleged conspiracy are actively and admittedly sympathetic to the economic determinism of the defaulters, there is no claim that the alleged conduct of the defaulters is mandated by those governments. We therefore

---

12 Two British companies were involved, RTZ and one if its subsidiaries.
13 595 F 2d 1287 (3rd Cir. 1979).

conclude that Westinghouse's allegations against the defaulters do fall within the jurisdictional ambit of the Sherman Act, as defined in *Alcoa*.

The *amici*, in particular the United Kingdom, contend that *Alcoa* is 'no longer to be accepted by United States Courts as "settled law"', in light of the recent opinions of the United States Courts of Appeals in [*Timberlane I* (set out in Chapter 33, § 6) and *Mannington Mills*] . . .

The United Kingdom relies primarily on the comment in *Timberlane* that 'The effects test by itself is incomplete because it fails to consider other nations' interests.' This *amicus curiae* contends the critical discussion of the *Alcoa* effects test has undermined its continuing viability as the standard of extraterritorial jurisdiction of the Sherman Act. We do not read *Timberlane* so broadly. The 'jurisdictional rule of reason' espoused in *Timberlane* is that while an effect on American commerce is the necessary ingredient for extraterritorial jurisdiction, considerations of comity and fairness require a further determination as to 'whether American authority should be asserted in a given case.' The clear thrust of the *Timberlane* Court is that once a district judge has determined that he has jurisdiction, he should consider additional factors to determine whether the exercise of that jurisdiction is appropriate.

We conclude that nothing in *Timberlane* is inconsistent with our determination that Westinghouse's allegations of concerted conduct by foreign and domestic corporations are sufficient to confer jurisdiction on the District Court, under *Alcoa*. We turn now to the question of whether jurisdiction should be exercised in the present case.

In this case, unlike the situation in *Timberlane* and *Mannington Mills*, there has been a determination by the District Court as to whether jurisdiction should be exercised. In the order of January 3, 1979, and the order of September 17, 1979, the District Judge considered the unique circumstance presented in this case, and determined, in the exercise of his discretion, to proceed. Our task is to decide whether he abused his discretion in reaching that conclusion. We find that he did not.

In granting the requested default judgment, the District Court considered three factors: the complexity of the present multi-national and multi-party action; the seriousness of the charges asserted; and the recalcitrant attitude of the defaulters. The District Judge concluded that those factors all weighed heavily in favor of proceeding to judgment and damages.

The *amici* suggest that the District Court abused its discretion by not considering the factors set out in *Mannington Mills* in reaching this determination. While the considerations recommended in that case certainly provide an adequate framework for such a determination, we can hardly call the failure to employ those precise factors an abuse of discretion. First, the *Mannington Mills* factors are not the law of this Circuit.[1] Second, even assuming their adoption by this Court, the circumstances here are distinct from those found in *Timberlane* and *Mannington Mills*. In those

---

1 *Editor's note*: the court in this case was the Seventh Circuit, while *Mannington Mills* was a decision of the Ninth Circuit.

cases the defendants appeared and contested the jurisdiction of the District Court. In the present case, the defaulters have contumaciously refused to come into court and present evidence as to why the District Court should not exercise its jurisdiction. They have chosen instead to present their entire case through surrogates. Wholly owned subsidiaries of several defaulters have challenged the appropriateness of the injunctions, and shockingly to us, the governments of the defaulters have subserviently presented for them their case against the exercise of jurisdiction. If this Court were to remand the matter for further consideration of the jurisdictional question, the District Court would be placed in the impossible position of having to make specific findings with the defaulters refusing to appear and participate in discovery. We find little value in such an exercise.

We conclude that given the posture of this case, and the circumstances before the District Court, the Judge did not abuse his discretion in proceeding to exercise his jurisdiction. We therefore decline to remand the case to the District Court as requested by the *amici curiae*.

Comment

This case shows that direct pleas by foreign governments for restraint on the ground of extraterritoriality are not necessarily accepted.

§ 4 The Protection of Trading Interests Act 1980

The Protection of Trading Interests Act 1980 was adopted in response to what the United Kingdom regarded as the extraterritorial application of US law, especially US antitrust law. The uranium litigation was probably the catalyst. Similar statutes were adopted by many other countries; they are known generically as 'blocking' statutes. What follows is a short outline of the UK Act.

§ 4.1 General

The Act contains elaborate requirements designed to limit its application to situations in which foreign assertions of jurisdiction infringe British sovereignty. In addition, most of its provisions operate only if triggered by a government order. This is to ensure that it will not operate too widely. Many Continental statutes are different. For example, the French 'blocking' statute can apply in ordinary commercial litigation without any government order being necessary. We saw an example in Chapter 20, § 1.1, above.

§ 4.2 Overseas measures

Section 1 of the Act is concerned with measures under the law of an overseas country for regulating or controlling international trade. This could cover an injunction given by a foreign court, or a government order not to export goods to a specified country as part of an embargo. The Secretary of State has to adopt an order specifying the measures in question and applying section 1 to them. If he does so, he can issue directions requiring business persons to inform him of any such measures that are applied to them; he can also forbid compliance. Examples include the order in the *Laker Airways* case (§ 5, below) and that in the Siberian pipeline case (§ 6, below).

§ 4.3 Obtaining evidence

Sections 2 and 4 are concerned with preventing evidence from being provided for use in foreign proceedings that infringe British sovereignty. It will be remembered from the discussion in Part IV of this book that there are basically two ways in which a court can obtain evidence from a foreign country: one is for the court itself to order the person concerned to produce the evidence; the other is to request the help of a court in the foreign country. Section 2 is aimed at the first of these: it allows the Secretary of State to prohibit compliance with an order by a foreign court, tribunal or authority to produce commercial documents or information. Section 4 is aimed at the second possibility: it allows the Secretary of State to prevent the Evidence (Proceedings in Other Jurisdictions) Act 1975 from being used in these circumstances. It was discussed in § 2, above, where the text of section 4 was set out in Panel 34.1.

§ 4.4 Criminal penalties

Section 3 lays down criminal penalties for breaches of sections 1 or 2: a fine can be imposed on offenders. There is no upper limit on the fine.

§ 4.5 Foreign judgments

Section 5 precludes the enforcement of foreign judgments that are based on the extraterritorial application of foreign law. The text is set out in Panel 34.2. It applies principally to two kinds of judgments: those for multiple damages – for example, treble damages under the Sherman Act – and those based on a provision of foreign antitrust law specified by the Secretary of State in an order. This might also be the Sherman Act.

Panel 34.2 Enforcing judgments
Protection of Trading Interests Act 1980, section 5

Section 5 Restriction on enforcement of certain overseas judgments

(1)   A judgment to which this section applies shall not be registered under Part II of the Administration of Justice Act 1920 or Part I of the Foreign Judgments (Reciprocal Enforcement) Act 1933 and no court in the United Kingdom shall entertain proceedings at common law for the recovery of any sum payable under such a judgment.

(2)   This section applies to any judgment given by a court of an overseas country, being–
   (a) a judgment for multiple damages within the meaning of subsection (3) below;
   (b) a judgment based on a provision or rule of law specified or described in an order under subsection (4) below and given after the coming into force of the order; or

Panel 34.2 (continued)

(c) a judgment on a claim for contribution in respect of damages awarded by a judgment falling within paragraph (a) or (b) above.

(3) In subsection (2)(a) above a judgment for multiple damages means a judgment for an amount arrived at by doubling, trebling or otherwise multiplying a sum assessed as compensation for the loss or damage sustained by the person in whose favour the judgment is given.

(4) The Secretary of State may for the purposes of subsection (2)(b) above make an order in respect of any provision or rule of law which appears to him to be concerned with the prohibition or regulation of agreements, arrangements or practices designed to restrain, distort or restrict competition in the carrying on of business of any description or to be otherwise concerned with the promotion of such competition as aforesaid.

(5) The power of the Secretary of State to make orders under subsection (4) above shall be exercisable by statutory instrument subject to annulment in pursuance of a resolution of either House of Parliament.

(6) Subsection (2)(a) above applies to a judgment given before the date of the passing of this Act as well as to a judgment given on or after that date but this section does not affect any judgment which has been registered before that date under the provisions mentioned in subsection (1) above or in respect of which such proceedings as are there mentioned have been finally determined before that date.

The difference between the two is that, under the first, laid down in subsection 2(a), the judgment will be blocked only if multiple damages are actually awarded.[14] If they are, however, the whole judgment – including the non-punitive element – will be denied recognition.[15] Treble damages are awarded under the Sherman Act only if the plaintiff asks for them. If he claims only compensatory damages, subsection 2(a) would not apply. However, if the Sherman Act were specified in an order, even such a judgment would be denied recognition.

§ 4.6 'Claw-back'

Section 6 applies only to the punitive element in a multiple-damages award. It is designed to operate where a defendant has been forced to pay multiple damages as a result of a foreign judgment obtained at the suit of a private party; it allows him to bring proceedings in the United Kingdom against that party to reclaim the punitive element. It is subject to severe restrictions and, as far as is known, has never been used.

Section 7 makes it possible for a party who has obtained a 'claw-back' judgment under a similar provision in a foreign country – for example, Australia or Canada – to have the 'claw-back' judgment enforced in the United Kingdom. It, too, appears never to have been used.

§ 4.7 Conclusions

The passing of the Protection of Trading Interests Act shows how seriously the UK Government was concerned by what it regarded as the threat posed to British trading interests by the extraterritorial application of US legislation. This concern was felt by other countries; they too adopted 'blocking' statutes. Those on

---

14 Subsection 2(a) is one of the few provisions of the Act that does not have to be triggered by an order.
15 Dicey, Morris and Collins, paragraph 14-255, p. 683. It is possible that the punitive element would be denied recognition under the common law, though this is uncertain: see Chapter 16, § 3, above.

the Continent were rather different, but those in Canada[16] and Australia[17] were very similar to that in the UK.

§ 5   The Laker Airways case

The *Laker Airways* case was probably the first instance in which the Act was applied. Laker Airways was one of the original economy airlines. It began in England, flying out of Gatwick Airport to the United States, mainly New York. At the time in question, the airline industry was largely cartelized, and fares were fixed at a level that allowed even the most inefficient airline to make a profit.[18] Laker refused to join the cartel, and offered fares a long way below what the other airlines charged. He said he could still make a profit because his operation was so much more efficient.

For a time all went well and Laker took a significant market share. Then the other airlines struck back. They offered a huge reduction in their fares. Laker lost passengers and – after it failed to reschedule the debt it owed for the purchase of aircraft – went into liquidation. The other airlines immediately raised their fares to the previous level and carried on as before.

Then came a nasty shock: Laker Airways (in liquidation) brought antitrust proceedings in the United States against the other airlines. Some were British, some Continental and some American. It claimed that they had engaged in predatory pricing (illegal under US law) and had pressured McDonnell Douglas, the company that supplied Laker's aircraft, not to reschedule the debt he owed them. McDonnell Douglas was also joined as a defendant.

Two British airlines, British Airways and British Caledonian, responded by bringing proceedings in England for an antisuit injunction to preclude Laker from continuing the US proceedings. They argued that the proceedings sought the extraterritorial application of US antitrust law. An interim injunction was granted. Laker immediately went to the US court hearing the antitrust proceedings, the federal district court for the District of Columbia,[19] and obtained an injunction against the other defendants, precluding them from bringing proceedings in England to obtain an antisuit injunction against it (Laker).[20] This is what is sometimes called a counter-antisuit injunction. It meant that defendants other than British Airways and British Caledonian could not obtain antisuit injunctions in England.[21]

In England, the court had to decide whether to make permanent the injunc-

---

16 Foreign Extraterritorial Measures Act 1984 (RSC 1985, c. F-29). The legislation in issue in *Westinghouse Electric Corporation* v. *Duquesne Light Co.* (above), the Uranium Information Security Regulations, PC 1976-23268; SOR/76-644, was a forerunner of this.

17 Foreign Proceedings (Excess of Jurisdiction) Act 1984.

18 This was done through IATA (the International Air Transport Association).

19 Washington DC.

20 The various US proceedings were: *Laker Airways* v. *Sabena, Belgian World Airlines*, 731 F 2d 909 (DC Cir. 1984); *Laker Airways* v. *Pan American World Airways*, 596 F Supp 202 (DDC 1984); *Laker Airways* v. *Pan American World Airways*, 577 F Supp 348 (DDC 1983); *Laker Airways* v. *Pan American World Airways*, 568 F Supp 811 (DDC 1983); *Laker Airways* v. *Pan American World Airways*, 559 F Supp 1124 (DDC 1983) affirmed 731 F 2d 909 (DC Cir. 1984).

21 The English injunction precluded Laker from obtaining counter-antisuit injunctions against these two defendants.

tions it had granted. It decided not to do so: it did not consider that the US proceedings constituted an invasion of UK sovereignty.[22] However, it continued the injunctions on a temporary basis to allow for an appeal. The Secretary of State then made an order[23] under the Protection of Trading Interests Act and issued a direction prohibiting any British airline flying to the United States from giving the US authorities any documents or information relating to the case.[24] This was presumably intended to prevent Laker from proving its case.

When the case came before the Court of Appeal, it reversed the lower court's judgment.[25] It said the injunction should be made permanent on the ground that the Secretary of State's direction would make the US proceedings unfair: British Airways and British Caledonian would not be able to produce the evidence needed to defend themselves. This was a strange argument since one assumes that the order was intended to help them.

The case then came before the House of Lords.[26] They reversed the Court of Appeal and held that the injunctions should be set aside. They said that US law was not being applied extraterritorially because the airlines were flying aircraft into US territory. The argument based on the Secretary of State's direction under the Protection of Trading Interests Act was rejected because, if the British defendants thought that they were prejudiced by it, they could ask the Secretary to State to allow them to disclose the evidence they wanted to put before the US court. Permission would probably be granted, since the Secretary of State was 'on their side'.

This meant that the US case could go ahead. It was soon settled. The damages paid to Laker were much less than what had been claimed. This seems to have been because the Laker trial team was hoping to obtain evidence from an investigation by the US Department of Justice. When this was dropped (apparently on orders from President Reagan after a request from Mrs Thatcher, then British Prime Minister), Laker's position was significantly weakened.

This case is an example of the English courts refusing to 'speak with the same voice as the executive'. It is said that the British Government was put out by the judgment; however, this was not a case in which the Americans could be accused of unjustified extraterritoriality.

§ 6   The Soviet gas pipeline

Another occasion on which the British Government applied the Protection of Trading Interests Act was in connection with the Siberian gas pipeline in 1982. The US wanted to hit the Soviet Union as part of a political dispute. An embargo

---

22 *British Airways Board* v. *Laker Airways* [1984] QB 142,
23 The order was made under sections 1 and 2(1) of the Act.
24 This direction was made under section 2 of the Act. There was also a direction under section 1(3) prohibiting any UK airline flying to the US from complying with any order under US antitrust law made in the case.
25 *British Airways Board* v. *Laker Airways* [1984] QB 169 (CA).
26 *British Airways Board* v. *Laker Airways* [1985] AC 58 (HL).

on grain sales was ruled out for fear of offending US farmers. Instead, it was decided to block sales of equipment needed for the pipeline, then under construction, that was to bring Siberian gas to Western Europe. The embargo not only prohibited exports (by anyone) from the US, but it also applied to exports from third countries (such as Britain) if the exporting company was a subsidiary of an American company, if the product contained an American-manufactured component (even if exported prior to the embargo) or if the product was partly based on US technology – for example, processes for which the patent was owned by an American (even if the relevant licence had been granted prior to the embargo). Four British companies, which had manufactured equipment for the pipeline, were affected by the embargo.

The British Government took the view that this was an 'unacceptable extension of American extraterritorial jurisdiction in a way repugnant to international law'.[27] An order was made under section 1(1) of the Protection of Trading Interests Act, designating the relevant provisions of US law.[28] Directions were then issued to the four companies forbidding them from complying with the embargo.

The companies were then subject to contradictory orders. US law prohibited them from shipping the goods; UK law required them to do so. Penalties could be imposed for failure to obey each of the orders. The companies decided to obey UK law. The goods were shipped. It seems that the US did not penalize them.

§ 7   The Helms–Burton Act

While a country has jurisdiction to adopt measures curtailing trade between it and a foreign country, it is not regarded as having jurisdiction to limit trade between two foreign countries. This at least is the general view. In 1996, however, the US tried to stop third countries trading with Cuba when it passed the Cuban Liberty and Democratic Solidarity (Libertad) Act, widely known as the Helms–Burton Act.[29] One of its provisions stated that, if anyone 'trafficked' in property expropriated from an American, the former owner could sue him in America for the full value of the property. The precise effect of this provision would depend on the way it was interpreted, but it would seem to apply if, for example, a Spanish company bought sugar from a Cuban company and imported it into Spain: if it could be shown that the sugar had been grown on land in Cuba once owned by an American company, the latter could sue the Spanish company in America for the value not just of the sugar, but of the land on which it was grown.[30] In certain circumstances, it could obtain three times the value of the land. This would make it impossible for any company with assets in the

---

27 Lord Cockfield, Secretary of State for Trade, speaking in the House of Lords on 2 August 1982, reported in *The Times*, 3 August 1982.
28 SI 1982 No. 885.
29 For an analysis, see Lowe, 'US Extraterritorial Jurisdiction: The Helms–Burton and D'Amato Acts' (1997) 46 ICLQ 378; Lowenfeld, 'Agora: The Cuban Liberty and Democratic Solidarity (Libertad) Act: Congress and Cuba' (1996) 90 AJIL 419.
30 Lowenfeld, 'Agora: The Cuban Liberty and Democratic Solidarity (Libertad) Act: Congress and Cuba' (1996) 90 AJIL 419 at pp. 425–6.

US to trade with Cuba, since it would be difficult to know whether anything it did would infringe the Act. Since it imposed US law on parties neither of whom was American for things done by them outside US territory, it was clearly extraterritorial.

For these reasons, the European Union objected, and the provision in question was temporarily suspended by President Clinton. The EU also considered that the provision was contrary to GATT;[31] so it prepared to bring proceedings against the United States under the WTO Dispute Settlement Understanding.[32] The US made clear that it would not participate, and would ignore any decision against it.[33] The EU could have insisted on the formation of a WTO panel and, if the US refused to accept the panel's decision, the EU could have sought authority to suspend the application of concessions or other obligations towards the US. It did not, however, do this; instead, it entered into negotiations with the US. In May 1998, a deal was struck: the EU would take steps to discourage investment in property confiscated contrary to international law and the US would permanently suspend the offending provision.[34]

§ 8   Conclusions

We have seen in this chapter how law imperceptibly merges into politics. The dividing-line is not always easy to see, especially when the courts decide to 'speak with the same voice as the executive'. Some of the actions taken by both courts and governments are said to be based on international law, though this may sometimes have been no more than a cloak for political interests. Nevertheless, there is no denying the fact that violations of generally recognized limits on jurisdiction to prescribe can produce strong reactions from other States. However, it is not easy to state precisely what these limits are.

Further reading

Demaret, 'L'extraterritorialité des lois et les relations transatlantiques: une question de droit ou de diplomatie?' (1985) 21 *Revue trimestrielle de droit européen* 1

31 For EU legislation intended to counter the effects of the Helms–Burton Act, see Regulation 227/96, OJ 1996 L 309, p. 1.
32 On 8 October 1996, the EU requested formation of a panel under the DSU: see WTO Doc. WT/DS38/2/Corr.1.
33 Article 21 of GATT provides that nothing in the agreement prevents any Contracting Party from 'taking any action which it considers necessary for the protection of its essential security interests . . . taken in time of war or other emergency in international relations'. It seems that the United States considered that this provision justified its action. It was not, however, prepared to allow the panel to decide the point. It took the view that the mere *assertion* by a party that the provision applied was enough to deprive the panel of jurisdiction. It need hardly be pointed out that, if accepted, this argument would totally destroy the WTO Dispute Settlement Understanding. Any party that thought it might lose a case could simply invoke Article 21 to put a stop to the proceedings. For further analysis, see Schloemann and Ohlhoff, '"Constitutionalization" and Dispute Settlement in the WTO: National Security as an Issue of Competence' (1999) 93 AJIL 424.
34 See Smis and Van der Borght, 'The EU–US Compromise of the Helms–Burton and D'Amato Acts' (1999) 93 AJIL 227.

Libow, 'Laker Antitrust Litigation: The Jurisdictional Rule of Reason Applied to Transnational Injunctive Relief' (1986) 71 *Cornell Law Review* 645

Lowe, 'US Extraterritorial Jurisdiction: The Helms–Burton and D'Amato Acts' (1997) 46 ICLQ 378

   'Blocking Extraterritorial Jurisdiction: The British Protection of Trading Interests Act, 1980' (1981) 75 AJIL 257

Lowenfeld, 'Agora: The Cuban Liberty and Democratic Solidarity (Libertad) Act: Congress and Cuba' (1996) 90 AJIL 419

Maier, 'Interest Balancing and Extraterritorial Jurisdiction' (1983) 31 *American Journal of Comparative Law* 579

   'Resolving Extraterritorial Conflicts, or "There and Back Again"' (1984) 25 *Virginia Journal of International Law* 7

Toms, 'The French Response to the Extraterritorial Application of United States Antitrust Laws' (1982) 16 *International Lawyer* 585

Wood and Carrera, 'The International Uranium Cartel' (1979) 14 *Texas International Law Journal* 59

CHAPTER 35

Extraterritorial application of EC competition law

§ 1 Introduction

Though invented in the United States, antitrust law (called 'competition law' in Europe) has come to be accepted in Europe as an essential component of a free market. For this reason, the EC Treaty has contained provisions on competition law right from the start. Originally, the basic provisions were Articles 85 and 86 in the EC Treaty; today they have been renumbered Articles 81 and 82. They are set out in Panel 35.1. It will be seen that these provisions prohibit agreements, etc. which 'may affect trade between Member States' and which have as their 'object or effect' the restriction of competition within the Common Market.

Panel 35.1 EC rules on competition
EC Treaty, Articles 81 and 82

Article 81

1. The following shall be prohibited as incompatible with the common market: all agreements between undertakings, decisions by associations of undertakings and concerted practices which may affect trade between Member States and which have as their object or effect the prevention, restriction or distortion of competition within the common market, and in particular those which:
   (a) directly or indirectly fix purchase or selling prices or any other trading conditions;
   (b) limit or control production, markets, technical development, or investment;
   (c) share markets or sources of supply;
   (d) apply dissimilar conditions to equivalent transactions with other trading parties, thereby placing them at a competitive disadvantage;
   (e) make the conclusion of contracts subject to acceptance by the other parties of supplementary obligations which, by their nature or according to commercial usage, have no connection with the subject of such contracts.
2. Any agreements or decisions prohibited pursuant to this article shall be automatically void.
3. The provisions of paragraph 1 may, however, be declared inapplicable in the case of:
   – any agreement or category of agreements between undertakings,
   – any decision or category of decisions by associations of undertakings,
   – any concerted practice or category of concerted practices,
   which contributes to improving the production or distribution of goods or to promoting technical or economic progress, while allowing consumers a fair share of the resulting benefit, and which does not:
   (a) impose on the undertakings concerned restrictions which are not indispensable to the attainment of these objectives;
   (b) afford such undertakings the possibility of eliminating competition in respect of a substantial part of the products in question.

Article 82

Any abuse by one or more undertakings of a dominant position within the common market or in a substantial part of it shall be prohibited as incompatible with the common market in so far as it may affect trade between Member States.
Such abuse may, in particular, consist in:
   (a) directly or indirectly imposing unfair purchase or selling prices or other unfair trading conditions;

Panel 35.1 (continued)

(b) limiting production, markets or technical development to the prejudice of consumers;

(c) applying dissimilar conditions to equivalent transactions with other trading parties, thereby placing them at a competitive disadvantage;

(d) making the conclusion of contracts subject to acceptance by the other parties of supplementary obligations which, by their nature or according to commercial usage, have no connection with the subject of such contracts.

The requirement that the prohibited act must affect trade between Member States was intended to constitute the boundary between Member State jurisdiction and Community jurisdiction: if the act had effects only within a particular Member State, and did not affect trade between Member States, it would be dealt with under Member State competition law (if any). Only if it crossed the threshold laid down in the Treaty and affected trade between Member States would it become a matter for Community law.

However, even though this was the original purpose of the requirement, it is easy to see that it could be regarded as also fulfilling another function: that of delimiting the international scope of Community law. Together with the 'object or effect' provision, it could, in fact, be regarded as incorporating the effects doctrine into Community law. As we shall see, this has indeed been the conclusion reached on some occasions.

The EC Commission has the task of enforcing Community competition law. It investigates possible infractions and, if it thinks that a company has violated the law, it brings proceedings. These proceedings are of a quasi-criminal nature, and may result in fines and orders in the nature of an injunction. They are brought, in the first instance, before the Commission itself; so the latter is both prosecutor and judge;[1] however, an appeal lies to the European Court.

§ 2   Dyestuffs

European Community
ICI v. *Commission*
Court of Justice of the European Communities
Case 48/69, [1972] ECR 619

Background

This case involved alleged price-fixing by a group of dyestuff manufacturers. When one of them increased prices, they all did, something which the Commission regarded as proving that they were operating on the basis of a concerted practice. This is expressly forbidden by Article 81, if the other requirements of that Article are met.

Some of the manufacturers were Community companies; some were established outside the Community. However, the latter all had Community subsidiaries, and it was the subsidiaries that put the price increases into effect.

---

1 The personnel carrying out the two functions are different.

Under Community law, a parent and subsidiary are regarded as constituting one unit for the purposes of competition law; so the foreign producers were all considered to be operating within the Common Market. The Commission was of course concerned only with the price increases within the Common Market.

We will deal solely with the extraterritoriality issue. Here, the foremost complainant was the British company, ICI, the same company that featured in the *British Nylon Spinners* case in the previous chapter. At the time in question, the United Kingdom had not yet joined the EC.

The Commission decision

[The Commission held that the infringements had been proved, and imposed fines on the companies concerned, though the sums of money were ludicrously small by modern standards. The paragraph in the Commission decision dealing with extraterritoriality read as follows:]

[28.] This decision is applicable to all the undertakings which took part in the concerted practices, whether they are established within or outside the Common Market. Under Article 85 (1) of the Treaty instituting the EEC, all agreements between undertakings, all decisions by associations of undertakings and all concerted practices which may affect trade between Member States and the object or effect of which is to prevent, restrict or distort competition within the Common Market shall be prohibited as incompatible with the Common Market. The competition rules of the Treaty are, consequently, applicable to all restrictions of competition which produce within the Common Market effects set out in Article 85 (1). There is therefore no need to examine whether the undertakings which are the cause of these restrictions of competition have their seat within or outside the Community.

Comment

This cannot be regarded as anything other than the effects doctrine, which the Commission seemed to regard as built into Article 85 (now Article 81).

The case then came before the European Court. However, at this point the Commission changed its position: it now argued that its decision (which it was defending before the court) could be justified on the basis of the territoriality principle; the effects doctrine was not needed, though it continued to rely on it as a backup argument.

In accordance with EC procedure, the Advocate General, Mr Mayras, first gave his Opinion.[2] Basing himself partly on US law (especially the *Alcoa* case, set out in Chapter 33, § 4, above), he championed the effects doctrine. Provided certain requirements were met, he said, it was in accord with international law. He considered that these requirements were met in the case before the court.

---

2 On the function of the advocate general, see Chapter 3, § 1, above.

His conclusion was that the Community had legislative jurisdiction under the effects doctrine.

We now come to the judgment.

Judgment

126. Since a concerted practice is involved, it is first necessary to ascertain whether the conduct of the applicant has had effects within the Common Market.

127. It appears from what has already been said that the increases at issue were put into effect within the Common Market and concerned competition between producers operating within it.

128. Therefore the actions for which the fine at issue has been imposed constitute practices carried on directly within the Common Market.

129. It follows from what has been said in considering the submission relating to the existence of concerted practices, that the applicant company decided on increases in the selling prices of its products to users in the Common Market, and that these increases were of a uniform nature in line with increases decided upon by the other producers involved.

130. By making use of its power to control its subsidiaries established in the Community, the applicant was able to ensure that its decision was implemented on that market.

131. The applicant objects that this conduct is to be imputed to its subsidiaries and not to itself.

132. The fact that a subsidiary has separate legal personality is not sufficient to exclude the possibility of imputing its conduct to the parent company.

133. Such may be the case in particular where the subsidiary, although having separate legal personality, does not decide independently upon its own conduct on the market, but carries out, in all material respects, the instructions given to it by the parent company.

134. Where a subsidiary does not enjoy real autonomy in determining its course of action in the market, the prohibitions set out in Article 85(1) may be considered inapplicable in the relationship between it and the parent company with which it forms one economic unit.

135. In view of the unity of the group thus formed, the actions of the subsidiaries may in certain circumstances be attributed to the parent company.

136. It is well-known that at the time the applicant held all or at any rate the majority of the shares in those subsidiaries.

137. The applicant was able to exercise decisive influence over the policy of the subsidiaries as regards selling prices in the Common Market and in fact used this power upon the occasion of the three price increases in question.

138. In effect the Telex messages relating to the 1964 increase, which the applicant sent to its subsidiaries in the Common Market, gave the addressees orders as to the prices which they were to charge and the

139. other conditions of sale which they were to apply in dealing with their customers.

139. In the absence of evidence to the contrary, it must be assumed that on the occasion of the increases of 1965 and 1967 the applicant acted in a similar fashion in its relations with its subsidiaries established in the Common Market.

140. In the circumstances the formal separation between these companies, resulting from their separate legal personality, cannot outweigh the unity of their conduct on the market for the purposes of applying the rules on competition.

141. It was in fact the applicant undertaking which brought the concerted practice into being within the Common Market.

142. The submission as to lack of jurisdiction raised by the applicant must therefore be declared to be unfounded.

Comment

The theory that a parent company and its subsidiary are to be treated as one entity for certain purposes, put forward by the European Court in paragraphs 131 *et seq.*, is also applied in the United States.[3] It enabled the European Court to hold that the defendant companies were acting within the Community, thus avoiding any element of extraterritoriality. It was then unnecessary to consider whether the effects doctrine was part of Community law.

§ 3 Wood pulp

European Community
Ahlström* v. *Commission
Court of Justice of the European Communities
Joined Cases 89, 104, 114, 116, 117 and 125 to 129/85, [1988] ECR 5193

Background

This case was similar. It concerned wood pulp, a product used to make paper. It comes from softwood, grown mainly in Scandinavia and North America. The defendants were forty-one producers of wood pulp and two of their trade associations. All had their registered offices outside the Community – in Canada, the United States, Sweden and Finland. (At the time in question, Sweden and Finland were not yet Member States.)

The Commission found that infringements of Article 85 (now Article 81) of the EC Treaty were established: concerted practices ('concertations') had taken place among the defendants for the purpose of co-ordinating prices within the Community, contrary to Article 85. The defendants were fined.

---

3 See, for example, *Taca International Airlines* v. *Rolls-Royce of England*, 204 NE 2d 329 (NY Court of Appeals); *Hargrave* v. *Fibreboard*, 710 F 2d 1154 (5th Cir. 1982).

Proceedings were brought before the European Court to set the Commission decision aside. The Advocate General, this time Mr Darmon, said that the effects doctrine was the appropriate criterion for legislative jurisdiction in this area. He concluded that, provided the effects were direct, substantial and foreseeable, the effects doctrine was not against public international law. Like Advocate General Mayras, he placed considerable reliance on US case law.

Judgment

Grounds

3.   In paragraph 79 of the contested decision the Commission set out the grounds which in its view justify the Community's jurisdiction to apply Article 85 of the Treaty to the concertation in question. It stated first that all the addressees of the decision [the defendants] were either exporting directly to purchasers within the Community or were doing business within the Community through branches, subsidiaries, agencies or other establishments in the Community . . . The Commission concluded that: 'The effect of the agreements and practices on prices announced and/or charged to customers and on resale of pulp within the EEC was therefore not only substantial but intended, and was the primary and direct result of the agreements and practices.'

.   .   .

6.   All the applicants which have made submissions regarding jurisdiction maintain first of all that by applying the competition rules of the Treaty to them the Commission has misconstrued the territorial scope of Article 85. They note that in [*ICI* v. *Commission*, set out above] the Court did not adopt the 'effects doctrine' but emphasized that the case involved conduct restricting competition within the common market because of the activities of subsidiaries which could be imputed to the parent companies. The applicants add that even if there is a basis in Community law for applying Article 85 to them, the action of applying the rule interpreted in that way would be contrary to public international law which precludes any claim by the Community to regulate conduct restricting competition adopted outside the territory of the Community merely by reason of the economic repercussions which that conduct produces within the Community.

7.   The applicants which are members of the KEA [the American producers' association] further submit that the application of Community competition rules to them is contrary to public international law in so far as it is in breach of the principle of non-interference. They maintain that in this case the application of Article 85 harmed the interest of the United States in promoting exports by United States undertakings as recognized in the Webb–Pomerene Act of 1918 under which export associations, like the KEA, are exempt from United States anti-trust laws.[1]

1 The Webb–Pomerene Act provides that US antitrust law does not apply to exports from the US.

8. Certain Canadian applicants also maintain that by imposing fines on them and making reduction of those fines conditional on the producers giving undertakings as to their future conduct the Commission has infringed Canada's sovereignty and thus breached the principle of international comity.

    . . .

(a) The individual undertakings

11. In so far as the submission concerning the infringement of Article 85 of the Treaty itself is concerned, it should be recalled that that provision prohibits all agreements between undertakings and concerted practices which may affect trade between Member States and which have as their object or effect the restriction of competition within the common market.

12. It should be noted that the main sources of supply of wood pulp are outside the Community, in Canada, the United States, Sweden and Finland and that the market therefore has global dimensions. Where wood pulp producers established in those countries sell directly to purchasers established in the Community and engage in price competition in order to win orders from those customers, that constitutes competition within the common market.

13. It follows that where those producers concert on the prices to be charged to their customers in the Community and put that concertation into effect by selling at prices which are actually coordinated, they are taking part in concertation which has the object and effect of restricting competition within the common market within the meaning of Article 85 of the Treaty.

14. Accordingly, it must be concluded that by applying the competition rules in the Treaty in the circumstances of this case to undertakings whose registered offices are situated outside the Community, the Commission has not made an incorrect assessment of the territorial scope of Article 85.

15. The applicants have submitted that the decision is incompatible with public international law on the grounds that the application of the competition rules in this case was founded exclusively on the economic repercussions within the common market of conduct restricting competition which was adopted outside the Community.

16. It should be observed that an infringement of Article 85, such as the conclusion of an agreement which has had the effect of restricting competition within the common market, consists of conduct made up of two elements, the formation of the agreement, decision or concerted practice and the implementation thereof. If the applicability of prohibitions laid down under competition law were made to depend on the place where the agreement, decision or concerted practice was formed, the result would obviously be to give undertakings an easy means of evading those prohibitions. The decisive factor is therefore the place where it is implemented.

17. The producers in this case implemented their pricing agreement within the common market. It is immaterial in that respect whether or not they had

recourse to subsidiaries, agents, sub-agents, or branches within the Community in order to make their contacts with purchasers within the Community.

18. Accordingly the Community's jurisdiction to apply its competition rules to such conduct is covered by the territoriality principle as universally recognized in public international law.

19. As regards the argument based on the infringement of the principle of non-interference, it should be pointed out that the applicants who are members of KEA have referred to a rule according to which where two States have jurisdiction to lay down and enforce rules and the effect of those rules is that a person finds himself subject to contradictory orders as to the conduct he must adopt, each State is obliged to exercise its jurisdiction with moderation. The applicants have concluded that by disregarding that rule in applying its competition rules the Community has infringed the principle of non-interference.

20. There is no need to enquire into the existence in international law of such a rule since it suffices to observe that the conditions for its application are in any event not satisfied. There is not, in this case, any contradiction between the conduct required by the United States and that required by the Community since the Webb–Pomerene Act merely exempts the conclusion of export cartels from the application of United States anti-trust laws but does not require such cartels to be concluded.

21. It should further be pointed out that the United States authorities raised no objections regarding any conflict of jurisdiction when consulted by the Commission pursuant to the OECD Council Recommendation of 25 October 1979 concerning cooperation between member countries on restrictive business practices affecting international trade (*Acts of the organization*, Vol. 19, p. 376).

22. As regards the argument relating to disregard of international comity, it suffices to observe that it amounts to calling in question the Community's jurisdiction to apply its competition rules to conduct such as that found to exist in this case and that, as such, that argument has already been rejected.

23. Accordingly it must be concluded that the Commission's decision is not contrary to Article 85 of the Treaty or to the rules of public international law relied on by the applicants.

(b) KEA

24. According to its Articles of Association, KEA is a non-profit-making association whose purpose is the promotion of the commercial interests of its members in the exportation of their products and it serves primarily as a clearing-house for its members for information regarding their export markets. KEA does not itself engage in manufacture, selling or distribution.

25. It should further be pointed out that within KEA a number of groups have been formed, including the Pulp Group, to cover the different sectors of the pulp and paper industry. Under Article I of the by-laws of KEA, undertakings

may only join KEA by becoming a member of one of those groups. Article 2 of the by-laws provides that the groups enjoy full independence in the management of their affairs.

26.   It should lastly be noted that according to a policy statement adopted by the Pulp Group, referred to in paragraph 32 of the contested decision, the members of the group may conclude price agreements at meetings which they hold from time to time provided that each member is informed in advance that prices will be discussed and that the meeting is quorate. The unanimous agreement of the members present is also binding on members who are absent when the decision is adopted.

27.   It is apparent from the foregoing that KEA's price recommendations cannot be distinguished from the pricing agreements concluded by undertakings which are members of the Pulp Group and that KEA has not played a separate role in the implementation of those agreements.

28.   In those circumstances the decision should be declared void in so far as it concerns KEA.

Result: the objections to the decision were rejected, except as regards KEA; with regard to KEA, the decision was annulled.

Comment

The court was again able to uphold the decision on the basis of the territoriality principle. Its argument that there was no contradiction with US law – because the Webb–Pomerene Act merely permits, but does not *require*, the conduct prohibited by EC law – is similar to that put forward by the majority of the US Supreme Court in the *Hartford Fire Insurance* case, set out in Chapter 33, § 6, above.

KEA was the only defendant that could not be said to have acted within the Community: jurisdiction over it could have been obtained only under the effects doctrine. So, by finding substantive grounds for annulling the decision with regard to it, the court was able to avoid ruling on whether the effects doctrine is part of Community law.

§ 4   Conclusions

The European Court's desire to avoid committing itself on the question of the effects doctrine may be explained by the fact that, on the one hand, it does not want to make it difficult for the EC to protest against what it regards as extraterritoriality on the part of the United States, while, on the other hand, it realizes that some sort of effects doctrine may be necessary for the proper operation of EC competition law. Despite this ambiguity, however, there can be no doubt that, overall, the international application of EC law is more restrained than that of US law.

Bibliography

Only general works are listed below. Specialized items are listed in the 'Further reading' section at the end of the appropriate chapter.

American Law Institute, *Restatement of the Law Second: Conflict of Laws* (American Law Institute Publishers, St Paul, MN, 1971)
    Restatement of the Law Third: The Foreign Relations Law of the United States (American Law Institute Publishers, St Paul, MN, 1986)
Baade, 'An Overview of Transnational Parallel Litigation: Recommended Strategies' (1981) 1 *Review of Litigation* 191
Born, Gary B., and Rutledge, Peter B., *International Civil Litigation in United States Courts: Commentary and Materials* (Wolters Kluwer, Austin, Boston, Chicago, New York, the Netherlands, 4th edn, 2007)
Briggs, Adrian, *Agreements on Jurisdiction and Choice of Law* (Oxford University Press, Oxford, 2008)
    The Conflict of Laws (Clarendon Law Series, Oxford, 2nd edn, 2008)
Castel, Jean G., *Canadian Conflict of Laws* (Butterworths, Toronto, 4th edn, 1997)
Cheshire, North and Fawcett, *Private International Law* (14th edn, Oxford University Press, Oxford, 2008, by James Fawcett and Janeen Carruthers) (cited as 'Cheshire, North and Fawcett')
Clarkson, C. M. V., and Hill, Jonathan, *The Conflict of Laws* (Oxford University Press, Oxford, 2006)
Collier, John G., *Conflict of Laws* (Cambridge University Press, Cambridge, 3rd edn, 2001)
Collins, Lawrence, *Essays in International Litigation and the Conflict of Laws* (Clarendon Press, Oxford, 1994)
Dicey, Morris and Collins, *The Conflict of Laws* (Sweet and Maxwell, London, 14th edn, 2006 by Sir Lawrence Collins with specialist editors) (cited as 'Dicey, Morris and Collins')
Ehrenzweig, Albert H., *A Treatise on the Conflict of Laws* (West Publishing Co., St Paul, MN, 1962)
    Conflicts in a Nutshell (West Publishing Co., St Paul, MN, 1965)
Fawcett, 'The Impact of Article 6(1) of the ECHR on Private International Law' (2007) 56 ICLQ 1
Fentiman, Richard, *International Commercial Litigation* (Oxford University Press, Oxford, to be published in 2009)
Gaudemet-Tallon, Hélène, *Compétence et exécution des jugements en Europe* (LGDJ, Paris, 3rd edn, 2002)
Giuliano, Mario, and Lagarde, Paul, 'Report on the Convention on the Law Applicable to Contractual Obligations', OJ 1980 L 282 (cited as the 'Giuliano–Lagarde Report')
Goode, Roy, *Commercial Law* (Penguin Books, London, 3rd edn, 2004)
Hill, Jonathan, *International Commercial Disputes in English Courts* (Hart Publishing, Oxford and Portland, OR, 2005)
James, Michael, *Litigation with a Foreign Aspect: A Practical Guide* (Oxford University Press, Oxford, 2009)

Jenard, P., 'Report on the Convention of 27 September 1968 on Jurisdiction and the
  Enforcement of Judgments in Civil and Commercial Matters', OJ 1979 C 59, p. 1 (cited
  as the 'Jenard Report')
Kaye, Peter, *Civil Jurisdiction and Enforcement of Foreign Judgments: The Application in England
  and Wales of the Brussels Convention of 1968 on Jurisdiction and Enforcement of Judgments
  in Civil and Commercial Matters under the Civil Jurisdiction and Judgments Act 1982*
  (Professional Books, Abingdon, 1987)
  *The New Private International Law of Contract of the European Community: Implementation
  of the EEC's Contractual Obligations Convention in England and Wales under the Contracts
  (Applicable Law) Act 1990* (Dartmouth Publishing Co., Aldershot, 1993)
Layton, Alexander, and Mercer, Hugh (eds.), *European Civil Practice* (Sweet and Maxwell,
  London, 2nd edn, 2004)
Leflar, Robert A., *American Conflicts Law* (Bobbs-Merrill, Indianapolis, 3rd edn, 1977)
Lowenfeld, Andreas F., *International Litigation and the Quest for Reasonableness: Essays in
  Private International Law* (Clarendon Press, Oxford, 1996)
  Conflict of Laws: Federal, State and International Perspectives (LexisNexis, Newark, NJ, and
  San Francisco, CA, 2nd edn, 2002)
Mann, Frederick A., *The Legal Aspect of Money: With Special Reference to Comparative Private
  and Public International Law* (Clarendon Press, Oxford, 5th edn, 1992)
North, Peter M., *Reform, But Not Revolution* (Hague Academy of International Law, General
  Course on Private International Law, 1990), Volume I, *Collected Courses* (Martinus
  Nijhoff Publishers, The Hague, Boston and London, 1990)
Plender, Richard, and Wilderspin, Michael, *The European Private International Law of
  Obligations* (Sweet & Maxwell, London, publication expected in 2009)
Pritchard, 'A Systematic Approach to Comparative Law: The Effect of Cost, Fee, and
  Financing Rules on the Development of Substantive Law' (1988) 17 *Journal of Legal
  Studies* 451
Schlosser, Peter, 'Report on the Convention of 9 October 1968' (Denmark, Ireland and UK
  Accession), OJ 1979 C 59, p. 71 (cited as the 'Schlosser Report')
Scoles, Eugene F., and Hay, Peter, *Conflict of Laws* (West Group Publishing Co., St Paul, MN,
  3rd edn, 2000)
Stone, Peter, *The Conflict of Laws* (Longman, London, 1995)
Sykes, Edward I., and Pryles, Michael C., *Australian Private International Law* (Law Book Co.,
  North Ryde, 3rd edn, 1991)
Symeonides, Symeon C., Perdue, Wendy Collins, and von Mehren, Arthur T., *Conflict of
  Laws: American, Comparative, International* (West, St Paul, MN, 1998)
Treitel, G. H., *The Law of Contract* (Sweet & Maxwell, London, 10th edn, 1999)
Von Mehren, Arthur T., *Theory and Practice of Adjudicatory Authority in Private International
  Law: A Comparative Study of the Doctrine, Policies and Practices of Common- and Civil-
  Law Systems* (Hague Academy of International Law, General Course on Private
  International Law, 1996), (2002) 295 *Collected Courses* (Martinus Nijhoff Publishers, The
  Hague, Boston and London, 2003) 1971
Weintraub, Russell J., *Commentary on the Conflict of Laws* (Foundation Press, New York, 4th
  edn, 2001)
Wolff, Martin, *Private International Law* (Clarendon Press, Oxford, 2nd edn, 1950)
Wood, Philip R., *Law and Practice of International Finance* (Sweet & Maxwell, London, 1980)

Index